Australia

a travel survival kit

Hugh Finlay
Jon Murray
Alan Tiller
Charlotte Hindle
Tony Wheeler
John Noble
Susan Forsyth

CASSOWARY.

Australia – a travel survival kit

6th edition

Published by
Lonely Planet Publications
Head Office: PO Box 617, Hawthorn, Vic 3122, Australia
Branches: PO Box 2001A, Berkeley, CA 94702, USA and London, UK

Printed by
Singapore National Printers Ltd, Singapore

Photographs by
Sonia Berto (SB)
David Curl (DC)
Berthold Daum (BD)
Richard I'Anson (RI'A)
Charlotte Hindle (CH)
Chris Lee Ack (CLA)
Richard Nebesky (RN)
Paul Steel (PS)
Peter Turner (PT)
Bernard Wertheim (BW)
Tony Wheeler (TW)
Jeff Williams (JW)
Tourism Tasmania (TT)
Aboriginal painting: Depiction of 'Langabun' Country Dreaming by Willie Gudabi of Ngukurr
Front cover: The Olgas (RI'A)
Back cover: Frilled lizard (DC)
Russell Falls, Mt Field National Park, Tasmania (PS)

First Published
February 1977

This Edition
August 1992

Although the authors and publisher have tried to make the information as accurate as possible, they accept no responsibility for any loss, injury or inconvenience sustained by any person using this book.

National Library of Australia Cataloguing in Publication Data

Tony Wheeler
    Australia: a travel survival kit.

    6th ed.
    Includes index.
    ISBN 0 86442 134 6.
    1. Australia – Description and travel – 1990 – Guidebooks. I. Title.
    (Series: Lonely Planet travel survival kit)

919.40463

text & maps © Lonely Planet 1992
photos © photographers as indicated 1992

Hugh Finlay

Hugh abandoned civil engineering in the mid-70s, and took off around Australia, working at everything from parking cars to prospecting for diamonds, before heading further afield. He joined Lonely Planet in 1985. He wrote *Jordan & Syria*, and co-authored *Morocco, Algeria & Tunisia* and *Kenya*, among others. He co-ordinated this edition of *Australia* and updated the chapters on Victoria, Queensland and the Northern Territory. Hugh, Linda and their daughter Ella live in country Victoria, Australia.

Jon Murray

After trying everything from syrup-mixing in a soft drink factory to buying Christmas tree lights for the army, Jon achieved a balance of long-distance cycling, travel in Asia and working for various publishing houses in Melbourne, climaxing in a stint at Lonely Planet as marketing manager. For this edition of *Australia*, he updated the chapters on New South Wales, the Australian Capital Territory, and South Australia. He has contributed to several other guides and co-authored *South Africa, Lesotho & Swaziland.*

Alan Tiller

After migrating to Australia from England via the £10 passage, Alan finished degrees in science, education and editing, and travelled extensively in Europe, the USA and Australia. In between he worked as a short-order chef, kazoo player, teacher and in all manner of publications jobs until he came to rest at Lonely Planet as an editor in 1989. For this edition Alan covered much of Western Australia.

Charlotte Hindle

Charlotte was born in Caerphilly, Wales, and studied History of Art at Leicester University. She au-paired in France, worked in a Swiss ski-resort, and sold theatre tickets in London before travelling to Australia. In 1988 she joined Lonely Planet and worked at head office in Melbourne for 3½ years. In August 1991 she returned to London to set up and run Lonely Planet's London office. For this edition Charlotte updated the chapter on Tasmania.

Tony Wheeler

Tony was born in England but spent most of his youth overseas. He returned to England to do a university degree in engineering, worked as an automotive design engineer, returned to university to complete an MBA, then dropped out on the Asian overland trail with his wife Maureen. They've been travelling, writing and publishing guidebooks ever since, having set up Lonely Planet Publications in the mid-70s. Travel for the Wheelers is now considerably enlivened by their daughter Tashi and their son Kieran.

John Noble & Susan Forsyth

Susan Forsyth and John Noble come from Melbourne (Oz) and Clitheroe (England) respectively. They met in 1986 in Sri Lanka, where John was leaving no stone unturned on LP's behalf and Susan was a volunteer English teacher. Since then they have worked on *Australia* and *Indonesia*, and John has co-authored *Mexico* and, rather late in the day, *USSR*. John, Susan and their daughter Isabella are now based in the Ribble valley, Yorkshire, England.

This Book

Australia – a travel survival kit was first written by Tony Wheeler in 1977 and has been through successive transformations since that time. Among the major contributors to past editions were Simon Hayman and Alan Samalgalski (third edition), Mark Lightbody and Lindy Cameron (fourth edition), and Susan Forsyth, John Noble, Richard Nebesky and Peter Turner (fifth edition).

From the Authors

Hugh would like to thank the following people and organisations for their assistance to him while researching this edition: Victorian Tourism Commission, Northern Territory Tourist Commission, Western Australian Tourist Commission, and in the Kimberley Bernie Whewell, Karl Plunkett and Neil McGilp.

Alan Tiller would like to thank the following people for their assistance with the Western Australia chapter: the ravishing Amy Swift and the debonair David Chapman for their help and hospitality; his right holiness the much maligned and respected Dr Mark Harvey Jr III for his omniscience regarding matters of science and life (!); Dianne Clark for being a wonderful person; David Tiller for help with the driving; Greg Alford for information on Perth; and Rob van Driesum for advice on the Gunbarrel Highway.

Charlotte would like to thank the Tasmanian Travel Centre in Melbourne for their friendly advice; her brother Richard who accompanied her on her trip to Tasmania; and Chris Bold.

Thanks to all the readers whose letters helped us with this update. Their names are listed at the back of the book.

From the Publisher

This edition was edited by Caroline Williamson, Miriam Cannell and James Lyon, with help from Tom Smallman and Alan Tiller. Simone Calderwood helped with the proofing. Valerie Tellini handled the maps, the design, the layout and the cover. Katrina O'Loughlin drew new illustrations. Sharon Wertheim produced the index. Thanks to the many Lonely Planet staff who contributed their expert knowledge of Melbourne restaurants and entertainment, to Tom Smallman for his support, and to Jeff Williams and James Lyon for their enthusiastic work on the language and ski sections.

Warning & Request

Things change – prices go up, schedules change, good places go bad and bad places go bankrupt – nothing stays the same. So if you find things better or worse, recently opened or long since closed, please write and tell us and help make the next edition better! Your letters will be used to help update future editions and, where possible, important changes will also be included as a Stop Press section in reprints.

All information is greatly appreciated and the best letters will receive a free copy of the next edition, or any other Lonely Planet book of your choice.

Contents

Map Legend

BOUNDARIES

— · — · — · — .... International Boundary
— · — · — .... Internal Boundary
++++++++++ ....National Park or Reserve
— — — — — .... The Equator
················· .... The Tropics

SYMBOLS

◉ NEW DELHI ....National Capital
● BOMBAY ....Provincial or State Capital
● Pune ....Major Town
● Barsi ....Minor Town
■ .... Places to Stay
▼ .... Places to Eat
≙ ....Post Office
✕ ....Airport
i ....Tourist Information
◒ .... Bus Station or Terminal
66 .... Highway Route Number
☪ ✝ ✝ ...... Mosque, Church, Cathedral
∴ ....Temple or Ruin
✚ ....Hospital
✳ .... Lookout
Å .... Camping Area
⊼ .... Picnic Area
⌂ .... Hut or Chalet
▲ .... Mountain or Hill
.... Railway Station
.... Road Bridge
.... Railway Bridge
............................Road Tunnel
.... Railway Tunnel
.... Escarpment or Cliff
.... Pass
.... Ancient or Historic Wall

ROUTES

————— ....Major Road or Highway
------------ .... Unsealed Major Road
————— .... Sealed Road
------------ ..... Unsealed Road or Track
————— .... City Street
++++++++++ ....Railway
●——————● .... Subway
················· .... Walking Track
------------ .... Ferry Route
+++++++++++ .... Cable Car or Chair Lift

HYDROGRAPHIC FEATURES

.... River or Creek
..............Intermittent Stream
........Lake, Intermittent Lake
.... Coast Line
..................................Spring
.... Waterfall
................................Swamp

.... Salt Lake or Reef

................................Glacier

OTHER FEATURES

Park, Garden or National Park

.... Built Up Area

... Market or Pedestrian Mall

.... Plaza or Town Square

............................Cemetery

Note: not all symbols displayed above appear in this book

Introduction

It may be cliched to say Australia is a big country, but there are few places on earth with as much variety as Australia has to offer. And not just variety in things to see – in things to do, places to eat, entertainment, activities and just general good times.

What to see and do while tripping around our island continent is an open-ended question. There are cities big and small, some of them amazingly beautiful. If you fly in over its magnificent harbour, for example, Sydney is a city which can simply take your breath away. To really get to grips with the country, however, you must get away from the cities. Australian society may be a basically urban one but, myth or not, it's in the outback where you really find Australia – the endless skies, the endless red dirt, the laconic Aussie characters. And when you've seen the outback that still leaves you mountains and coast, superb bushwalks and big surf, the Great Barrier Reef and the Northern Territory's 'top end'.

Best of all Australia can be far from the rough and ready country its image might indicate. In the big cities you'll find some of the prettiest Victorian architecture going; Australian restaurants serve up an astounding variety of national cuisines with the freshest ingredients you could ask for (it's all grown here) and it's no problem at all to fall

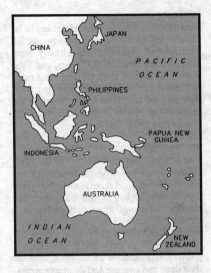

in love with Australian wines; plus Australia is still one of those lucky countries where you can walk down most streets at any time of day or night without worrying about your safety. It's not just exciting and invigorating, it's also very civilised. There's some fantastic travelling waiting for you around Australia: go for it.

Facts about the Country

Introduction

HISTORY

Australia was the last great landmass to be 'discovered' by the Europeans. However the continent of Australia had already been inhabited for about 40,000 years, and long before the British claimed it as their own, European explorers and traders had been dreaming of the riches to be found in the unknown, some said mythical, South Land – if only they could find it.

The Aborigines

It is believed that the ancestors of the Aborigines journeyed from Indonesia to the Australian mainland more than 40,000 years ago. Archaeological evidence suggests that the descendants of these first settlers colonised the whole of the continent within a few thousand years. They were among the earliest people in the world to manufacture polished edge-ground stone tools, cremate their dead and engrave and paint representations of themselves and the animals they hunted.

Aborigines were traditionally tribal people living in extended family groups. Wisdom and skills obtained over millennia enabled Aborigines to use their environment to the maximum. An intimate knowledge of the behaviour of animals and the correct time to harvest the many plants they utilised ensured that food shortages were rare. They never hunted an animal species or harvested a plant species to the point where it was threatened with extinction. Like other hunter-gatherer peoples of the world, the Aborigines were true ecologists.

Although Aborigines in northern Australia had been in regular contact with the farming peoples of Indonesia for at least 1000 years, the farming of crops and domestication of livestock held no appeal. The only major modification of the landscape practised by the Aborigines was the selective burning of undergrowth in forests and dead grass on the plains. This encouraged new growth, which in turn attracted game animals to the area, and prevented the build-up of combustible material in the forests, making hunting easier and reducing the possibility of major bush fires. Dingoes were domesticated to assist in the hunt and to guard the camp from intruders.

Similar technology – for example the boomerang and spear – was used throughout the continent, but techniques were adapted to the environment and the species being hunted. In the wetlands of northern Australia, fish traps hundreds of metres long made of bamboo and cord were built to catch fish at the end of the wet season. In the area now known as Victoria, permanent stone weirs many km long were used to trap migrating eels, while in the tablelands of Queensland finely woven nets were used to snare herds of wallabies and kangaroos. Dwellings ranged from the beehive stone houses of Victoria's windswept western district to elevated platforms constructed by the peoples of the humid, mosquito-infested tropics.

The simplicity of the Aborigines' technology is in contrast with the sophistication of their cultural life. Religion, history, law and art are integrated in complex ceremonies which depict the activities of the ancestral beings who created the landscape and its people, and prescribe codes of behaviour and responsibilities for looking after the land and all living things. Songs explain how the landscape contains these powerful creator ancestors, who can still exert either a benign or a malevolent influence. They also tell of the best places and the best times to hunt, where to find water in drought years, and specify kinship relations and correct marriage partners.

Ceremonies are still performed in many parts of Australia and the features of the landscape believed to be metamorphosed ancestral beings of the Dreamtime are commonly known as 'sacred sites'. Many such sites are believed to be dangerous and entry

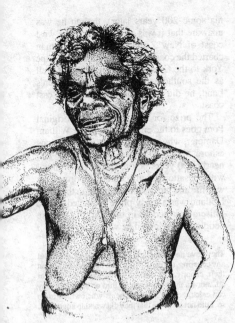

is prohibited under traditional Aboriginal law.

These restrictions may seem merely the result of superstition, but in many cases they have a pragmatic origin. One site in northern Australia was believed to cause sores to break out all over the body of anyone visiting the area. Subsequently, the area was found to have a dangerously high level of radiation from naturally occurring radon gas. In another instance, fishing from a certain reef was traditionally prohibited. This restriction was scoffed at by local Europeans until it was discovered that fish from this area had a high incidence of ciguatera, which renders fish poisonous if eaten by humans.

At the time of the settlement of Sydney Cove around 200 years ago, there were about 300,000 Aborigines in Australia and over 300 different languages. Many were as distinct from each other as English is from Chinese. Tasmania alone had five languages,

and tribes living on opposite sides of present-day Sydney Harbour spoke mutually unintelligible languages.

In a society based on family groups with an egalitarian political structure, a coordinated response to the European colonisers was not possible. When Governor Phillip raised the flag at Sydney Cove in 1788, the laws of England became the law governing all Aborigines in the Australian continent. All land in Australia was from that moment the property of the English Crown.

If the Aborigines had had a readily recognisable political system and had resisted colonisation by organised force of arms, then the English might have been forced to recognise a prior title to the land and therefore legitimise their colonisation by entering into a treaty with the Aboriginal land owners.

Without any legal right to the lands they once lived on, Aborigines throughout the country became dispossessed; some were driven from their country by force, and some succumbed to exotic diseases. Others voluntarily left their lands to travel to the fringes of settled areas to obtain new commodities such as steel and cloth, and experience hitherto unknown drugs such as tea, tobacco, alcohol and narcotics.

At a local level, individuals resisted the encroachment of settlers. Warriors including Pemulwy, Yagan, Dundalli, Pigeon and Nemarluk were, for a time, feared by the colonists in their areas. But although some settlements had to be abandoned, the effect of such resistance only temporarily postponed the inevitable.

By the early 1900s legislation designed to segregate and 'protect' Aboriginal people was passed in all states. The legislation imposed restrictions on Aborigines' right to own property, to seek employment, and even allowed the state to remove children from Aboriginal mothers if it was suspected that the father was non-Aboriginal. Many Aborigines are still bitter about having been separated from their families and forced to grow up apart from their people.

The process of social change was accelerated by WW II, and White Australians became increasingly aware of the inequity of their treatment of Aborigines. In 1967 Australians voted to give the Commonwealth government power to legislate for Aborigines in all states.

One of the major tasks facing the government is responding to Aborigines' request that a proportion of the land owned by their ancestors be returned. Aborigines in the Northern Territory have been granted title to large areas of marginal land, formerly designated as Aboriginal reserves. The granting of land rights in other states has been delayed because most land is privately owned, and would have to be bought by the government.

Aborigines form between 1% and 2% of the nation's population. Dozens of books have been written about them, yet they remain the least understood of Australia's ethnic minorities.

European Discovery & Exploration

Captain James Cook is popularly credited with Australia's discovery, but it was probably a Portuguese who first sighted the country, while credit for its earliest coastal exploration must go to a Dutchman.

Portuguese navigators had probably come within sight of the coast in the first half of the 16th century; and in 1606 the Spaniard Torres sailed through the strait between Cape York and New Guinea that still bears his name, though there's no record of his actually sighting the southern continent.

In the early 1600s Dutch sailors, in search of gold and spices, reached the west coast of Cape York and several other places on the west coast. What they found was a dry, harsh, unpleasant country, and they rapidly scuttled back to the kinder climes of Batavia in the Dutch East Indies (now Jakarta in Indonesia).

In 1642 the Dutch East India Company, in pursuit of fertile lands and riches of any sort, mounted an expedition to explore the land to the south. Abel Tasman made two voyages from Batavia in the 1640s during which he discovered the region he called Van Diemen's Land (which was renamed Tasma-

nia some 200 years later), though he was unaware that it was an island, and the west coast of New Zealand. Although Tasman charted the coast of New Holland from Cape York to the Great Australian Bight, as well as the southern reaches of Van Diemen's Land, he did not sight the continent's east coast.

The prize for being Australia's original Pom goes to the enterprising pirate William Dampier, who made the first investigations ashore about 40 years after Tasman and nearly 100 years before Cook. He returned with sensational, but accurate, reports of the wildlife and the general conclusion that New Holland was a lousy place inhabited by the 'miserablest people in the world'. Of these people and their land he wrote:

They have no houses, but lie in the open air, without any covering, the earth being their bed and the heaven their canopy...the earth affords them no food at all...nor (is there) any sort of bird or beast that they can catch, having no instruments wherewithal to do so. I did not perceive that they did worship anything...

Dampier's records of New Holland, from visits made to Shark Bay on the west coast in 1688 and 1698, influenced the European idea of a primitive and godless land and that perspective remained unchanged until Cook's more informed and better documented voyages of discoveries spawned romantic and erotic notions of the South Seas and the idealised view of the 'noble savage'.

This dismal continent was forgotten until 1768, when the British Admiralty instructed Captain James Cook to lead a scientific expedition to Tahiti, to observe the transit of the planet Venus, and then begin a search for the Great South Land. On board his ship *Endeavour* were also several scientists including an astronomer and a group of naturalists and artists led by Joseph Banks.

After circumnavigating both islands of New Zealand, Cook set sail in search of the Great South Land, planning to head west until he found the unexplored east coast of the land known as New Holland.

On 19 April 1770 the extreme south-eastern tip of the continent was sighted and named Point Hicks, and when the *Endeavour* was a navigable distance from shore Cook turned north to follow the coast and search for a suitable landfall. It was nine days before an opening in the cliffs was sighted and the ship and crew found sheltered anchorage in a harbour they named Botany Bay.

During their forays ashore the scientists recorded descriptions of plants, animals and birds, the likes of which had never been seen, and attempted to communicate with the few native inhabitants, who all but ignored these, the first White people to set foot on the east coast. Cook wrote of the Blacks: 'All they seemed to want was for us to be gone.'

After leaving Botany Bay Cook continued north, charting the coastline and noting that the fertile east coast was a different story from the inhospitable land the earlier explorers had seen to the south and west. When the *Endeavour* was badly damaged on a reef off north Queensland, Cook was forced to make a temporary settlement. It took six weeks to repair the ship, during which time Cook and the scientists investigated their surroundings further, this time making contact with the local Aborigines.

Unlike the unimpressed Dampier, Cook was quite taken with the indigenous people and wrote:

They may appear to some to be the most wretched people on earth but in reality they are far happier than we Europeans...They live in a tranquillity which is not disturbed by the inequality of condition...they seem to set no value upon anything we gave them, nor would they ever part with anything of their own...

After repairing the *Endeavour*, navigating the Great Barrier Reef and rounding Cape York, Cook again put ashore to raise the Union Jack, rename the continent New South Wales and claim it for the British in the name of King George III.

James Cook was resourceful, intelligent, and popularly regarded as one of the greatest and most humane explorers of all time. His incisive reports of his voyages make fascinating reading, even today. By the time he

was killed, in the Sandwich Islands (now Hawaii) in 1779, he had led two further expeditions to the South Pacific.

Convicts & Settlement
Following the American Revolution, Britain was no longer able to transport convicts to North America. With jails and prison hulks already overcrowded, it was essential that an alternative be found quickly. In 1779 Joseph Banks suggested New South Wales as a fine site for a colony of thieves and in 1786 Lord Sydney announced that the king had decided upon Botany Bay as a place for convicts under sentence of transportation. The fact that the continent was already inhabited was not considered significant.

Less than two years later, in January 1788, the First Fleet sailed into Botany Bay under the command of Captain Arthur Phillip, who was to be the colony's first governor. Phillip was immediately disappointed with the landscape and sent a small boat north to find a more suitable landfall. The crew soon returned with the news that in Port Jackson they had found the finest harbour in the world and a good sheltered cove.

The fleet, comprised of 11 ships carrying about 750 male and female convicts, 400 sailors, four companies of marines and enough livestock and supplies for two years, weighed anchor again and headed for Sydney Cove to begin settlement.

For the new arrivals New South Wales was a harsh and horrible place. The reasons for transportation were often minor and the sentences, of no less than seven years with hard labour, were tantamount to life sentences as there was little hope of returning home.

Although the colony of soldiers, sailors, pickpockets, prostitutes, sheep stealers and petty thieves managed to survive the first difficult years, the cruel power of the military guards made the settlement a prison hell.

At first, until farming could be developed, the settlers were dependent upon supplies from Europe and a late or, even worse, a wrecked supply ship would have been disastrous. The threat of starvation hung over the colony for at least 16 years.

The Second Fleet arrived in 1790 with more convicts and some supplies, and a year later, following the landing of the Third Fleet, the population increased to around 4000.

Convict cuffs and leg fetters

As crops began to yield, New South Wales became less dependent on Britain for food. There were still, however, huge social gulfs in the fledgling colony: officers and their families were in control and clinging desperately to a modicum of civilised British living; soldiers, free settlers and even emancipated convicts were beginning to eke out a living; yet the majority of the population were still in chains, regarded as the dregs of humanity and living in squalid conditions.

Little of the country was explored during those first years; few people ventured further than Sydney Cove, and though Governor Phillip had instructed that every attempt should be made to befriend the Blacks, this was not to be.

Phillip believed New South Wales would not progress if the colony continued to rely solely on the labour of convicts, who were already busy constructing government roads and buildings. He believed prosperity depended on attracting free settlers, to whom convicts could be assigned as labourers, and in the granting of land to officers, soldiers and worthy emancipists (convicts who had served their time).

This began to happen when Phillip returned to England and his second in command, Grose, took over. In a classic case of 'jobs for the boys', Grose tipped the balance of power further in favour of the military by granting land to officers of the New South Wales Corps.

With money, land and cheap labour suddenly at their disposal the officers became exploitative, making huge profits at the expense of the small farmers. To encourage convicts to work, the officers were given permission to pay them in rum. The officers quickly prospered and were soon able to buy whole shiploads of goods and resell them for many times their original value. New South Wales was becoming an important port on trade routes, and whaling and sealing were increasing.

The officers, meeting little resistance, continued to do virtually as they pleased, all the while getting richer and more arrogant. They – and in particular one John Macarthur – managed to upset, defy, out-manoeuvre and outlast three governors, including William Bligh of the *Bounty* mutiny fame.

Bligh actually faced a second mutiny when the officers rebelled and ordered his arrest. This rebellion was the final straw for the British government, which dispatched Lieutenant-Colonel Lachlan Macquarie with his own regiment and orders for the return to London of the New South Wales Corps.

John Macarthur, incidentally, was to have far-reaching effects on the colony's first staple industry. It was his understanding of the country's grazing potential that fostered his own profitable sheep breeding concerns and prompted his introduction of the merino in the belief that careful breeding could produce wool of exceptional quality. Though it was his vision, it was his wife, Elizabeth, who did most of the work – Macarthur remained in England for nearly a decade for his part in what became known as the Rum Rebellion.

Governor Macquarie, having broken the stranglehold of the New South Wales Corps officers, set about laying the groundwork for social reforms. He felt that the convicts who had served their time should be allowed rights as citizens, and began appointing emancipists to public positions.

While this meant the long-term future for convicts didn't appear quite so grim, by the end of Macquarie's term in 1821 New South Wales was still basically a convict society and there were often clashes between those who had never been imprisoned and those who had been freed.

During the 1830s and 1840s the number of free settlers to the colonies of New South Wales, Western Australia, Van Diemen's Land (present-day Tasmania) and Port Phillip (Victoria) was increasing, although it was the discovery of gold in the 1850s that was truly to change the face of the young country.

By the time transportation was abolished (to the eastern colonies in 1852 and to the west in 1868) more than 168,000 convicts had been shipped to Australia.

Colonial Expansion

Australia never enjoyed the systematic push westward that characterised the European settlement of America. Exploration and expansion basically took place for one of three reasons: to find suitable places of secondary punishment, like the barbaric penal settlements at Port Arthur in Van Diemen's Land; to create another colony in order to occupy land before anyone else arrived; or in later years because of the quest for gold.

By 1800 there were only two small settlements in Australia – at Sydney Cove and Norfolk Island. While unknown areas on world maps were becoming few and far between, most of Australia was still one big blank. It was even suspected that it might be two large, separate islands and it was hoped that there might be a vast sea in the centre.

In the ensuing 40 years a great period of discovery started as the vast inland was explored and settlements were established at Hobart, Brisbane, Perth, Adelaide and Melbourne. Some of the early explorers, particularly those who braved the hostile centre, suffered great hardship.

George Bass had charted the coast south of Sydney almost down to the present location of Melbourne during 1797-98, and in the following year, with Matthew Flinders, he

sailed around Van Diemen's Land, establishing that it was an island. Flinders went on in 1802 to sail right round Australia.

The first settlement in Van Diemen's Land, in 1803, was close to the present site of Hobart; by the 1820s Hobart Town rivalled Sydney in importance. The island was not named Tasmania, after its original European discoverer, until 1856 when, after the end of transportation, the inhabitants requested the name be changed to remove the stigma of what had been vicious penal colonies.

On the mainland, the Blue Mountains at first proved an impenetrable barrier, fencing in Sydney to the sea, but in 1813 a path was finally forced through and the western plains were reached by the explorers Blaxland, Wentworth and Lawson.

Port Phillip Bay in Victoria was originally considered as a site for the second settlement in Australia but was rejected in favour of Hobart, so it was not looked at again until 1835 when settlers from Tasmania, in search of more land, selected the present site of Melbourne. Perth was first settled in 1829, but as it was isolated from the rest of the country, growth there was very slow.

The first settlement in the Brisbane area was made by a party of convicts sent north from Sydney because the (by then) good citizens of that fair city were getting fed up with having all those crims about the place. By the time the Brisbane penal colony was abandoned in 1839, free settlers had arrived in force.

Adelaide, established in 1837, was initially an experiment in free-enterprise colonisation. It failed due to bad management and the British government had to take over from the bankrupt organisers and bail the settlement out of trouble.

In 1824 the explorers Hume and Hovell, starting from near present-day Canberra, made the first overland journey southwards, reaching the western shores of Port Phillip Bay. On the way they discovered a large river and named it after Hume, although it was later renamed the Murray by another great explorer, Charles Sturt. In 1829 it was Sturt who established how the Murrumbidgee and Darling River systems tied in with the Murray, and where the Murray met the sea. Up until that time there had been much speculation that many of the inland rivers might in fact drain a huge inland sea.

Twelve years later the colony's surveyor-general, Major Mitchell, wrote glowing reports of the beautiful and fertile country he had crossed in his expedition across the Murray River and as far south as Portland Bay. He dubbed the region (now called Victoria) Australia Felix, or 'Australia Fair'.

In 1840 Edward Eyre left Adelaide to try to reach the centre of Australia. He gave up at Mt Hopeless and then decided to attempt a crossing to Albany in Western Australia. The formidable task nearly proved too much as both food and water were virtually unobtainable and his companion, Baxter, was killed by two of their Aboriginal guides. Eyre struggled on, encountering a French whaling ship in Rossiter Bay, and reprovisioned managed to reach Albany. The road across the Nullarbor Plain from South Australia to Western Australia is named the Eyre Highway.

From 1844 to 1845 a German scientist by the name of Ludwig Leichhardt travelled through northern Queensland, skirting the Gulf of Carpentaria, to Port Essington, near modern-day Darwin. He turned back during an attempt in 1846 and 1847 to cross Australia from east to west, only to disappear on his second attempt; he was never seen again.

In 1848 Edmund Kennedy set out to travel by land up Cape York Peninsula while a ship, HMS *Rattlesnake*, explored the coast and islands. Starting from Rockingham Bay, south of Cairns, the expedition almost immediately struck trouble when their heavy supply carts could not be dragged through the swampy ground around Tully. The rugged land, harsh climate, lack of supplies, hostile Aborigines and missed supply drops, all took their toll and nine of the party of 13 died. Kennedy himself was speared to death in an attack by Aborigines when he was only 30 km from the end of the fearsome trek. His Aboriginal servant, Jacky Jacky, was the only expedition member to finally reach the supply ship.

Leaving Melbourne in 1860, the Burke & Wills expedition's attempt to cross the continent from south to north was destined to be one of the most tragic. Unlike earlier explorers, they tried to manage without Aboriginal guides. After reaching a depot at Cooper's Creek in Queensland they intended to make a dash north to the Gulf of Carpentaria with a party of four. Their camels proved far slower than anticipated in the swampy land close to the gulf and on their way back one of the party died of exhaustion.

Burke, Wills and the third survivor, King, eventually struggled back to Cooper's Creek, virtually at the end of their strength and nearly two months behind schedule, only to find the depot group had given up hope and left for Melbourne just hours earlier. They remained at Cooper's Creek, but missed a returning search party and never found the supplies that had been left for them. Burke and Wills finally starved to death, literally in the midst of plenty; their companion, King, was able to survive on food provided by local Aborigines until a rescue party arrived.

Departing from Adelaide in 1860, chasing a £2000 reward for the first south-north crossing, John Stuart reached the geographical centre of Australia, Central Mt Stuart, but shortly after was forced to turn back. A second attempt in 1861 got much closer to the Top End before he again had to return. Finally in 1862 he managed to reach the north coast near Darwin. The overland telegraph line, completed in 1872, and the modern Stuart Highway follow a similar route.

Gold, Stability & Growth

The discovery of gold in the 1850s brought about the most significant changes in the social and economic structure of Australia, particularly in Victoria, where most of the gold was found.

Earlier gold discoveries had been all but ignored, partly because they were only small finds and mining skills were still undeveloped, but mostly because the law stated that all gold discovered belonged to the government.

The discovery of large quantities near Bathurst in 1851, however, caused a rush of hopeful miners from Sydney and forced the government to abandon the law of ownership. Instead, it introduced a compulsory diggers' licence fee of 30 shillings a month, whether the miners found gold or not, to ensure the country earned some revenue from the incredible wealth that was being unearthed. Victorian businesspeople at the time, fearing their towns would soon be devoid of able-bodied men, offered a reward for the discovery of gold in their colony.

In 1851 one of the largest gold discoveries in history was made at Ballarat, followed by others at Bendigo and Mt Alexander (near Castlemaine), starting a rush of unprecedented magnitude.

While the first diggers at the gold fields that soon sprang up all over Victoria came from the other Australian colonies, it wasn't long before they were joined by thousands of migrants. The Irish and English, as well as Europeans and Americans, began arriving in droves, and within 12 months there were about 1800 hopeful diggers disembarking at Melbourne every week.

Similar discoveries in other colonies, in particular the Western Australian gold rush of the 1890s, further boosted populations and levels of economic activity.

The 19th-century history of Australia, however, had its shameful side. The Aborigines, who were looked upon as little more than animals, were ruthlessly pushed off their tribal lands as the White diggers and settlers continued to take up the land for mining and farming. In some places, Tasmania in particular, they were hunted and killed like vermin, while those that survived on the fringes of the new White society became a dispossessed and oppressed people.

The gold rushes also brought floods of diligent Chinese miners and market gardeners onto the Australian diggings, where violent White opposition led to a series of race riots and a morbid fear of Asian immigration which persisted well into this century.

Although few people actually made their fortunes on the gold fields, many stayed to settle the country, as farmers, workers and shopkeepers. At the same time the Industrial Revolution in England started to produce a strong demand for raw materials. With the agricultural and mineral resources of such a vast country, Australia's economic base became secure.

Besides the population and economic growth that followed the discovery of gold, the rush also contributed greatly to the development of a distinctive Australian folklore. The music brought by the English and Irish, for instance, was tuned in to life on the diggings, while poets, singers and writers began telling stories of the people, the roaring gold towns and the boisterous hotels, the squatters and their sheep and cattle stations, the swagmen, and the derring-do of the notorious bushrangers, many of whom became folk heroes.

The 20th Century

During the 1890s calls for the separate colonies to federate became increasingly strident. Supporters argued that it would improve the economy and the position of the workers by enabling the abolition of intercolonial tariffs and the protection of workers against competition from foreign labour.

Each colony was determined, however, that its interests should not be overshadowed by those of the other colonies. For this reason, the constitution that was finally adopted gave only very specific powers to the Commonwealth, leaving all residual powers with the states. It also gave each state equal representation in the upper house of parliament (the Senate) regardless of size or population. Today Tasmania, with a population of less than half a million, has as many senators in federal Parliament as New South Wales, with a population of more than 5½ million. As the upper house is able to reject legislation passed by the lower house, this legacy of Australia's colonial past has had a profound effect on its politics ever since, entrenching state divisions and ensuring that the smaller states have remained powerful forces in the government of the nation.

With federation, which came on 1 January 1901, Australia became a nation, but its loyalty and many of its legal and cultural ties to Britain remained. The mother country still expected to be able to rely on military support from its Commonwealth allies in any conflict, and Australia fought beside Britain in battles as far from Australia's shores as the Boer War in South Africa. This willingness to follow Western powers to war would be demonstrated time and again during the 20th century. Seemingly unquestioning loyalty to Britain and later the USA was only part of the reason. Xenophobia – born of isolation, an Asian location and a vulnerable economy – was also to blame.

The extent to which Australia regarded itself as a European outpost became evident with the passage of the Immigration Restriction Bill of 1901. The bill, known as the White Australia policy, was designed to prevent the immigration of Asians and Pacific Islanders. Prospective immigrants were required to pass a dictation test in a European language. The language in which the test was given could be as obscure a tongue as the authorities wished. The dictation test was not abolished until 1958.

The desire to protect the jobs and conditions of White Australian workers that had helped bring about the White Australia policy did, however, have some positive results. The labour movement had been a strong political force for many years, and by 1908 the principle of a basic wage sufficient to enable a male worker to support himself, a wife and three children had been established. By that time also, old age and invalid pensions were being paid.

When war broke out in Europe, Australian troops were again sent to fight thousands of km from home. The most infamous of the WW I battles in which Diggers took part, from Australia's perspective, was that intended to force a passage through the Dardanelles to Constantinople. Australian and New Zealand troops landed at Gallipoli only to be slaughtered by well-equipped and strategically positioned Turkish soldiers. Ever since, the sacrifices made by Australian soldiers have been commemorated on Anzac Day, the anniversary of the Gallipoli landing.

Interestingly, while Australians rallied to the aid of Britain during WW I, the majority of voters were only prepared to condone voluntary military service. Efforts to introduce conscription during the war led to bitter argument, both in Parliament and in the streets, and in referenda compulsory national service was rejected by a small margin.

Australia was hard hit by the Depression. In 1931 almost a third of breadwinners were unemployed and poverty was widespread. Swagmen became a familiar sight once more, as thousands of men took to the 'wallaby track' in search of work in the country. By 1932, however, Australia's economy was starting to recover, a result of rises in wool prices and a rapid revival of manufacturing.

In the years before WW II Australia became increasingly fearful of Japan. When war did break out, Australian troops fought beside the British in Europe, but after the Japanese bombed Pearl Harbor Australia's own national security finally began to take priority.

Singapore fell, the northern Australian towns of Darwin and Broome and the New Guinean town of Port Moresby were bombed, the Japanese advanced southward, and still Britain called for more Australian troops. This time the Australian Prime Minister, John Curtin, refused. Australian soldiers were needed to fight the Japanese advancing over the mountainous Kokoda Trail towards Port Moresby. In appalling conditions Australian soldiers confronted and defeated the Japanese at Milne Bay, east of Port Moresby, and began the long struggle to push them from the conquered Pacific territories.

Ultimately it was the USA, not Britain, that helped protect Australia from the Japanese, defeating them in the Battle of the Coral Sea. This event was to mark the beginning of a profound shift in Australia's allegiance away from Britain and towards the USA. Although Australia continued to support Britain in the war in Europe, its appreciation of its own vulnerability had been sharpened immeasurably by the Japanese advance.

One result of this was the post-war immigration programme, which offered assisted passage not only to the British but also to refugees from eastern Europe in the hope that the increase in population would strengthen Australia's economy and contribute to its ability to defend itself. 'Populate or Perish' became the catchphrase. Between 1947 and 1968 more than 800,000 non-British European migrants came to live in Australia. They have since made an enormous contribution to the country, enlivening its culture and broadening its vision.

As living conditions improved after the war Australia came to accept the American view that it was not so much Asia but *communism* in Asia that threatened the increasingly Americanised Australian way of life. Accordingly Australia followed the USA into the Korean War and joined it as a signatory to the treaties of ANZUS and the anti-communist Southeast Asia Treaty Organization (SEATO). Australia also provided aid to south-east Asian nations under the Colombo Plan, a scheme initiated by Australia but subscribed to by many other countries, including the USA, Britain, Canada and Japan.

In the light of Australia's willingness to join SEATO, it is not surprising that its conservative government applauded the USA's entry into the Vietnam War and, in 1965, committed troops to the struggle. Support for involvement was far from absolute, however. The leader of the Australian Labor Party, for example, believed the Vietnam conflict to be a civil war in which Australia had no part. Still more troubling for many young Australian men was the fact that conscription had been introduced during the previous year and those undertaking national service could now be sent overseas. By 1967 as many as 40% of Australians serving in Vietnam were conscripts.

The civil unrest aroused by conscription was one factor that contributed to the rise to power, in 1972, of the Australian Labor Party for the first time in more than 20 years. The Whitlam government withdrew Australian troops from Vietnam, abolished national service and higher-education fees, instituted a system of free and universally available health care, and supported land rights for Aborigines.

Labor, however, was hampered by a hostile Senate and talk of mismanagement. On 11 November 1975, the Governor General (the British monarch's representative in Australia) dismissed Parliament and installed a caretaker government led by the leader of the Opposition, Malcolm Fraser. Labor supporters were appalled. Such action was unprecedented in the history of the Commonwealth of Australia and the powers that the Governor General had been able to invoke had long been regarded by many as an anachronistic vestige of Australia's now remote British past, the office itself as that of an impotent figurehead.

Nevertheless, it was a conservative coalition of the Liberal and National Country parties that won the ensuing election. A Labor government was not returned until 1983, when a former trade union leader, Bob Hawke, led the party to victory. The current Labor government, pragmatic by comparison to the Whitlam government, has maintained close links with the union movement. In 1990 Hawke won a record third consecutive term in office, thanks in no small part to the lack of better alternatives offered by the Liberals. He was replaced as Prime Minister and Labor leader by Paul Keating, his long-time Treasurer, in late 1991.

In 1991 Australia found itself in recession again, mainly as a result of domestic economic policy but also because Australia is particularly hard hit when demand (and prices) for primary produce and minerals falls on the world markets. Unemployment was the highest it had been since the early 1930s, hundreds of farmers were being forced off the land because they couldn't keep afloat financially, there was a four-million-bale wool stockpile that no-one seemed to know how to shift, the building and manufacturing areas faced a huge slump and there was a general air of doom and gloom.

Despite the problems, most White and Asian Australians have a standard of living which is extremely high; it's a disgrace that the same can't be said for most of their Aboriginal counterparts. Many Aborigines still live in deplorable conditions, with outbreaks of preventable diseases and infant mortality running at an unacceptably high rate – higher even than in many Third World countries.

Land rights remain a contentious issue, but perhaps more controversial recently has been the increasing number of Aboriginal deaths in custody. Many Aborigines imprisoned for petty crimes such as drunkenness have been found dead in their cells, and the findings of an inquiry into the reasons for their deaths were inconclusive. Undeniably, social dislocation and White ignorance, intolerance and insensitivity have been contributing factors.

Socially, Australia is still coming to terms with its Asian environment. While it has accepted large numbers of Vietnamese and other Asian refugees during the past two decades, debate about its immigration policy surfaces periodically. It cannot be denied, however, that Asian immigration, together with immigration from other areas, has changed Australia, heightening its understanding of its neighbours and altering the aspect of its cities.

Perhaps Australia's most disturbing contemporary social failure has been its inability to improve significantly the situation of most of its Aborigines.

GEOGRAPHY

Australia is an island continent whose landscape – much of it uncompromisingly bleak and inhospitable – is the result of gradual changes wrought over millions of years. Although there is still seismic activity in the eastern and western highland areas, Australia is one of the most stable land masses, and for about 100 million years has been free of the mountain-building forces that have given rise to huge mountain ranges elsewhere.

From the east coast a narrow, fertile strip merges into the greatly eroded, almost continent-long Great Dividing Range. The mountains are mere reminders of the mighty range that once stood here. Only in the section straddling the New South Wales border with Victoria and in Tasmania are they high enough to have winter snow.

West of the range the country becomes increasingly flat, dry and inhospitable. The endless flatness is broken only by salt lakes, occasional mysterious protuberances like Ayers Rock (Uluru) and the Olgas, and some starkly beautiful mountains like the MacDonnell Ranges near Alice Springs. In places, the scant vegetation is sufficient to allow some grazing, so long as each animal has a seemingly enormous area of land. However, much of the Australian outback is a barren land of harsh, stone deserts and dry lakes with evocative names like Lake Disappointment.

The extreme north of Australia, the Top End, is a tropical area within the monsoon belt. Although the annual rainfall there looks adequate on paper, it comes in more or less one short, sharp burst. This has prevented the Top End from becoming seriously productive agriculturally.

The west of Australia consists mainly of a broad plateau. In the far west there is a mountain range and fertile coastal strip which heralds the Indian Ocean, but this is only to the south. In the north-central part of Western Australia, the dry country runs right to the sea.

Australia is the world's sixth largest country. Its area is 7,682,300 sq km, about the same size as the 48 mainland states of the USA and half as large again as Europe, excluding the former USSR. It is approximately 5% of the world's land surface. Lying between the Indian and Pacific oceans, Australia is about 4000 km from east to west and 3200 km from north to south, with a coastline 36,735 km long.

CLIMATE

Australian seasons are the antithesis of those in Europe and North America. It's hot in December and many Australians spend Christmas at the beach, while in July and August it's midwinter. Summer starts in December, autumn in March, winter in June and spring in September.

The climatic extremes aren't too severe in most parts of Australia. Even in Melbourne, the southernmost capital city on the mainland, it's a rare occasion when the mercury hits freezing point, although it's a different story in Canberra, the national capital. The poor Tasmanians, further to the south, have a good idea of what cold is.

As you head north the seasonal variations become fewer until, in the far north around Darwin, you are in the monsoon belt where there are just two seasons – hot and wet, and hot and dry. When the Wet hits Darwin, around November or December, it really does get wet. In the Snowy Mountains of southern New South Wales and the Alps of north-east Victoria there's a snow season with good skiing. The centre of the continent is arid – hot and dry during the day, but often bitterly cold at night.

Victoria and Tasmania are probably at their best at the height of summer, although spring and autumn are pretty good too. In the winter months of July and August, you might head south for the skiing but it's best to avoid Melbourne, which can be rather grey and miserable at this time.

By contrast, in the far north the best season is midwinter; Darwin is just right from July to August. In midsummer however it's often unbearably hot and humid; the sea is full of sea wasps (the deadly box jellyfish) and if there are cyclones about this is when they'll arrive. Similarly, in Alice Springs the midsummer temperatures can be far too high for comfort, while in midwinter the nights may be chilly but the days delightful.

A synopsis of average maximum and minimum temperatures and rainfall follows. Note that these are *average* maximums – even Melbourne gets a fair number of summer days hotter than 40°C (100°F). Temperatures in Australia are all expressed in degrees Celsius. As a rough rule of thumb, 20°C is about room temperature (70°F.)

Adelaide Maximum temperatures are from 25°C to 30°C from November to March; minimums can be below 10°C between June and September. Rainfall is heaviest, 50 to 70 mm per month, from May to September.

Alice Springs There are maximums of 30°C and above from October to April; minimums are 10°C and below from May to September. Rainfall is low all year round; from December to February there's an average of 30 mm of rain.

Brisbane Maximums are rarely below 20°C year round, peaking around 30° from November to February; rainfall is fairly heavy all year round, with more than 130 mm per month from December to March.

Canberra Maximums are in the mid to high 20s in the summer and minimums often close to freezing between May and October; rainfall is usually 40 to 70 mm a month, year round.

Cairns Maximums are about 25°C to 33°C year round, with minimums rarely below 20°C; rainfall is below 100 mm a month from May to October (lowest in July and August), but peaks from January to March at 400 to 450 mm.

Darwin Temperatures are even year round, with maximums from 30°C to 34°C and minimums from 20°C to 25°C; rainfall is minimal from May to September, but from December to March there's 250 to 400 mm a month.

Hobart Maximums top 20°C only from December to March, and from April to November minimums are usually below 10°C; rainfall is about 40 to 60 mm a month, year round.

Melbourne Maximums are 20°C and above from October to April, minimums 10°C and below from May to October; rainfall is even year round, at 50 to 60 mm almost every month.

Perth Maximums are around 30°C from December to March, but minimums are rarely below 10°C; rainfall is lightest from November to March (20 mm and below) and heaviest from May to August (120 to 200 mm).

Sydney Usually only in the middle of winter are minimums below 10°C; summer maximums are around 25°C from November to March; rainfall is in the 75 mm to 130 mm range year round.

FLORA & FAUNA
Native Plants

Despite vast tracts of dry and barren land, much of Australia is well vegetated. Forests cover 5%, or 410,000 sq km. Plants can be found even in the arid centre, though many of them grow and flower erratically. Human activities seriously threaten Australian flora but to date most species have survived.

Flowering gum

Origins Australia's distinctive vegetation began to take shape about 55 million years ago when Australia broke from the supercontinent of Gondwanaland, drifting away from Antarctica to warmer climes. At this time, Australia was completely covered by cool-climate rainforest, but due to its geographic isolation and the gradual drying of the continent, rainforests retreated, plants like eucalypts and wattles (acacias) took over and grasslands expanded. Eucalypts and wattles were able to adapt to warmer temperatures, the increased natural occurrence of fire and the later use of fire for hunting and other purposes by Aborigines. Now many species benefit from fire.

The arrival of Europeans 200 years ago saw the introduction of new flora, fauna and tools. Rainforests were logged, new crops and pasture grasses spread, hooved animals such as cows, sheep and goats damaged the soil, and watercourses were altered by dams. Irrigation, combined with excessive clearing of the land, gradually resulted in a serious increase in the salinity of the soil.

Distinctive Australian Plants The gum tree, or eucalypt, is ubiquitous in Australia except in the deepest rainforests and the most arid regions. Of the 700 species of the genus eucalyptus, 95% occur naturally in Australia, the rest in New Guinea, the Philippines and Indonesia.

Gum trees vary in form and height from the tall, straight hardwoods such as jarrah, karri, mountain ash and red river gum to the stunted, twisted snow gum with its colourful trunk striations. Other distinctive gums are the spotted variety of New South Wales's coast and the beautiful pink salmon gums of Katherine Gorge and elsewhere in the north. The gum tree features in Australian folklore, art and literature. Many varieties flower, the wood is prized and its oil is used for pharmaceuticals and perfumed products.

Fast-growing but short-lived wattles occur in many warm countries, but around 600 species are found in Australia, growing in a variety of conditions, from the arid inland to the rainforests of Tasmania. Many wattles have deep green leaves and bright yellow to orange flowers. Most species flower during late winter and spring. Then the country is ablaze with wattle and the reason for the choice of green and gold as our national colours is obvious. Wattle is Australia's floral emblem.

Wattle in flower

Many other species of Australian native plants flower but few are deciduous. Common natives include grevilleas, hakeas, banksias, waratahs, bottlebrushes (callistemons), paperbarks (melaleucas), teatrees, boronias, and bunya and hoop pines. An interesting book on the topic is *Field Guide to Native Plants of Australia* (Bay Books). You can see a wide range of Australian flora at the all-native National Botanic Gardens in Canberra. Brisbane's Mt Coot-tha Botanic Gardens features Australia's arid-zone plants.

Animals

Australia's most distinctive fauna are the marsupials and monotremes. Marsupials such as kangaroos and koalas give birth to partially developed young which they suckle in a pouch. Monotremes – platypuses and echidnas – lay eggs but also suckle their young on milk.

Since the arrival of Europeans in Australia 17 species of mammal have become extinct and 28 more are currently endangered. Many introduced non-native animals have been allowed to run wild and have caused a great deal of damage to native species and to Australian vegetation. Introduced animals include foxes, cats, pigs, goats, camels, donkeys, water buffalo, horses, starlings, blackbirds, cane toads and, best known of all, the notorious rabbit. Foxes and cats kill small native mammals and birds while rabbits denude vast areas of land, pigs carry disease and introduced birds take over the habitat of local species.

Kangaroos The extraordinary breeding cycle of the kangaroo is well adapted to Australia's harsh, often unpredictable environment.

The young kangaroo, or joey, just mm long at birth, claws its way unaided to the mother's pouch where it attaches itself to a nipple that expands inside its mouth. A day or two later the mother mates again, but the new embryo does not begin to develop until the first joey has left the pouch permanently.

At this point the mother produces two types of milk – one formula to feed the joey at heel, the other for the baby in her pouch. If environmental conditions are right, the mother will then mate again. If food or water is scarce, however, the breeding cycle will be interrupted until conditions improve.

Although kangaroos generally are not aggressive, males of the larger species, such as reds, can be dangerous when cornered. In the wild, boomers, as they are called, will grasp other males with their forearms, rear up on their muscular tails and pound their opponents with their hind feet, sometimes slashing them with their claws. Such behaviour can also be directed against dogs and, very rarely, people. It has also been said that kangaroos being pursued by dogs will sometimes hop into deep water and drown the dogs with their strong forearms.

There are now more kangaroos in Australia than there were when Europeans arrived, a result of the better availability of water and the creation of grasslands for sheep and cattle. Certain species, however, are threatened, as their particular environments are being destroyed. In all there are about 45 species.

About three million kangaroos are culled legally each year, but probably as many more are killed for sport or by those farmers who

Kangaroo

believe the cull is insufficient to protect their paddocks from overgrazing by the animals.

Large kangaroos can be a hazard to people driving through the outback – hitting a two-metre kangaroo at 110 km/h is no joke.

Possums There is an enormous range of possums in Australia – they seem to have been able to adapt to all sorts of conditions, including those of the city, where you'll find them in parks, sometimes tame enough to eat from your hand. Look for them at dusk. Some large species are found in suburban roofs and will eat cultivated plants and food scraps.

Certain possums are small and extremely timid, such as the tiny honey possum, which is able to extract nectar from blossoms with its tube-like snout. Others are gliders, able to jump from treetop to treetop by extending flaps of membrane between their legs.

Wombats Wombats are slow, solid, powerfully built marsupials with broad heads and short, stumpy legs. These fairly placid and easily tamed creatures are also legally killed by farmers, who object to the damage done to paddocks by wombats digging large burrows and tunnelling under fences.

Wombat

Koalas Koalas are distantly related to the wombat and are found along the eastern seaboard. Their cuddly appearance belies an irritable nature, and they will scratch and bite if sufficiently provoked.

Koalas initially carry their babies in pouches but later the larger young cling to their mothers' backs. They feed only on the leaves of certain types of eucalypt and are particularly sensitive to changes to their habitat. Today many koalas suffer from chlamydia, a sexually transmitted disease causing blindness and infertility.

Tasmanian Devils The carnivorous Tasmanian devil is as fierce as it looks. Although it lives in groups, it gives a very good impression of detesting every other devil in sight, including its own offspring.

It's an ugly little creature found only in Tasmania, where the locals will gleefully torment visitors with morbid tales of its hideous habits. Its ability to chew through bone as easily as if it were cork is at the heart of its fearsome reputation. In fact, it only eats small mammals and birds.

Tasmanian Tigers The Tasmanian tiger, like the Tasmanian devil, was a carnivorous marsupial. At one time both the tiger (*thylacine*) and the devil were threatened with extinction. Efforts to avert this disaster ensured the survival of the latter, but the larger, dog-like tiger was unable to recover its numbers. The last known specimen died in Hobart Zoo in 1936, although there is still much speculation as to whether tigers still exist. Regular 'sightings' are reported, and these are often the cause for much excitement in the press, but as yet none of these sightings has been confirmed.

Platypuses & Echidnas The platypus and the echidna are the only living representatives of the most primitive group of mammals, the monotremes. Both lay eggs, as reptiles do, but suckle their young on milk secreted directly through the skin from mammary glands.

The amphibious platypus has a duck-like bill, webbed feet and a beaver-like body. Males have a poisonous spur on their hind feet. Recent research has shown that the platypus is able to sense electric currents in the water and uses this ability to track its prey.

Echidnas are spiny anteaters that hide

from predators by digging vertically into the ground and covering themselves with dirt or rolling themselves into a ball and raising their sharp quills.

Dingoes Australia's native dog is the dingo, domesticated by the Aborigines and thought to have arrived with them 40,000 years ago. Dingoes now prey on rabbits and sometimes livestock, and are considered vermin by many farmers.

Birds

The Royal Australasian Ornithologists Union runs bird observatories in New South Wales, Victoria and West Australia, which provide accommodation and guides. Contact the RAOU (☎ (03) 370 1422) at 21 Gladstone St, Moonee Ponds, Victoria 3039.

Emus & Cassowaries The only bird larger than the emu is the African ostrich, also flightless. It's a shaggy-feathered, often curious bird. After the female lays the eggs the male hatches them and raises the young.

Cassowaries are smaller than emus and more colourful. They are found in the rainforests of north Queensland.

Parrots & Cockatoos There is an amazing variety of these birds throughout Australia. The noisy pink and grey galahs are amongst the most common, although the sulphur-crested cockatoos have to be the noisiest. Rosellas have one of the most brilliant colour schemes and in some parks they're not at all backward about taking a free feed from visitors.

Rainbow lorikeets are more extravagantly colourful than you can imagine until you've seen one. They're quite common from northern New South Wales up. Budgerigars are mainly found towards the Centre; they often fly in flocks numbering 10,000 or more.

Kookaburras A member of the kingfisher family, the kookaburra is heard as much as it is seen – you can't miss its loud, cackling cry. Kookaburras can become quite tame and pay regular visits to friendly households, but

only if the food is excellent. It's hard to impress a kookaburra with anything less than top-class steak.

Bower Birds The bower bird has a unique mating practice. The male builds a bower which he decorates with various coloured objects to attract females. In the wild, flowers or stones are used, but if artificial objects (clothes pegs, plastic pens, bottle tops – anything brightly coloured, but usually white, blue or green) are available, they'll certainly use them. The females are impressed by the males' neatly built bowers and attractively displayed treasures, but once they've mated all the hard work is left to her. He goes back to refurbishing the bower and attracting more females while she hops off to build a nest.

Snakes

Australian snakes are generally shy and try to avoid confrontations with humans. A few, however, are deadly. The most dangerous are the taipans and tiger snakes, although death adders, copperheads, brown snakes and red-bellied black snakes should also be avoided. Tiger snakes will actually attack. It's a good idea to stay right away from all snakes – and don't try stepping over them when they're asleep!

Crocodiles

There are two types of crocodile in Australia: the extremely dangerous saltwater crocodile, or saltie as it's known, and the less aggressive freshwater crocodile, or freshie.

Salties are not confined to salt water. They inhabit estuaries, and following floods may be found many km from the coast. They may even be found in permanent fresh water more than 100 km inland. It is important to be able to tell the difference between the saltie and its less dangerous relative, as both are prolific in northern Australia.

Freshies are smaller than salties – anything over four metres should be regarded as a saltie. Freshies are also more finely constructed and have much narrower snouts and smaller teeth. Salties, which can grow to

Saltwater crocodile

Freshwater crocodile

seven metres, will attack and kill humans. Freshies, though unlikely to seek human prey, have been known to bite, and children in particular should be kept away from them.

Spiders

Most Australian spiders bite. In particular, two spiders to keep away from are the redback, a relative of the American black widow, and the Sydney funnel-web. The latter is found only in Sydney, while the former is more widespread and has a legendary liking for toilet seats. Both are extremely poisonous and have been lethal. You should also beware of the white-tailed spider, commonly found in fields and gardens. It is about the size of the old 2c coin, with a distinct white spot on its grey-black back. Some people have extreme reactions to its bites and gangrene can result.

NATIONAL PARKS & RESERVES

Australia has more than 500 national parks –

non-urban protected wilderness areas of environmental or natural importance. Each state defines and runs its own national parks, but the principle is the same throughout Australia. National parks include rainforests, vast tracts of empty outback, strips of coastal dune land and long, rugged mountain ranges.

Public access is encouraged if safety and conservation regulations are observed. In all parks you're asked to do nothing to damage or alter the natural environment. Approach roads, campgrounds (often with toilets and showers), walking tracks and information centres are often provided for visitors.

Some national parks are so isolated, rugged or uninviting that you wouldn't want to do much except look unless you were an experienced, well-prepared bushwalker or climber. Other parks, however, are among Australia's major attractions and some of the most beautiful have been included on the World Heritage List (a United Nations list of natural or cultural places of world significance that would be an irreplaceable loss to the planet if they were altered).

Internationally, the World Heritage List includes the Taj Mahal, the Pyramids, the Grand Canyon and, currently, eight Australian areas: the Great Barrier Reef; most of Kakadu National Park in the Northern Territory; the Willandra Lakes region of far west New South Wales, where human bones about 40,000 years old have been found; the Lord Howe Island group off New South Wales; the Tasmanian wilderness heritage area (Lower Gordon Wild Rivers and Cradle Mountain – Lake St Clair national parks); the east coast temperate and subtropical rainforest parks (15 national parks and reserves, covering 1000 sq km in the eastern highlands of New South Wales); and the wet tropics area of far north Queensland, which is in the Daintree-Cape Tribulation area. Further areas – Shark Bay on the Western Australian coast, and Fraser Island off the Queensland coast – are currently nominated for listing and will almost certainly be added.

Before a site or area is accepted for the World Heritage List it has first to be proposed by its country then must pass a series of tests at the UN culminating, if it is successful, in acceptance by the UN World Heritage Committee which meets late each year. Any country proposing one of its sites or areas for the list must agree to protect the selected area, keeping it for the enjoyment of future generations even if to do so requires help from other countries.

While state governments have authority over their own national parks, the federal government is responsible for ensuring that Australia meets its international treaty obligations, and in any dispute arising from a related conflict between a state and the federal government, the latter can override the former.

In this way the federal government can force a state to protect an area with World Heritage listing, as it did when the Tasmanian government wanted, in the early 1980s, to dam the Gordon River in the south-west of the state and thereby flood much of the wild Franklin River.

For National Park authority addresses see the Information section of the Facts for the Visitor chapter.

State Forests

Another form of nature reserve you may discover is the state forest. These are owned by state governments and have fewer regulations than national parks. In theory, the state forests can be logged, but often they are primarily recreational areas with campgrounds, walking trails and signposted forest drives. Some permit horses and dogs.

GOVERNMENT

Australia is a federation of six states and two territories. Under the written constitution, the federal government, called the Commonwealth Government, is mainly responsible for the national economy and Reserve Bank, Customs and Excise, immigration, defence, foreign policy and the post office. The state governments are chiefly responsible for health, education, housing, transport and justice. There are both federal and state police forces.

Australia has a parliamentary system of government based on that of the UK, and the state and federal structures are broadly similar. In Federal Parliament, the lower house is the House of Representatives, the upper house the Senate. Queensland does not have an upper house: it was abolished in 1922. The party holding the greatest number of lower house seats forms the government. The Commonwealth government is run by a prime minister while the state governments are led by a premier.

Australia is a monarchy, but although Britain's king or queen is also Australia's, Australia is fully autonomous. The British sovereign is represented by a governor general and state governors, whose nominations for their posts by the respective governments are ratified by the monarch of the day.

Federal Parliament is based in Canberra, the capital of the nation. Like Washington DC in the USA, Canberra is in its own separate area of land, the Australian Capital

Territory (ACT), and is not under the rule of one of the states. Geographically, however, the ACT is completely surrounded by New South Wales. The state parliaments are in each state capital.

Governments are elected for a maximum of three years but elections can be (and often are) called earlier. Voting in Australian elections is compulsory for persons 18 years of age and over. Voting can be somewhat complicated as a preferential system is used whereby each candidate has to be listed in order of preference. This can result, for example, in Senate elections with 50 or more candidates to be ranked!

In Federal Parliament, the two main political groups are the Australian Labor Party (ALP) and the coalition between the Liberal Party and the National Party. These parties also dominate state politics but sometimes the Liberal and National Parties are not in coalition. The latter was once known as the National Country Party since it mainly represents country seats.

The only other political party of any real substance is the Australian Democrats, which has largely carried the flag for the ever-growing 'green' movement. In the current government the Democrats have quite a powerful position as they hold the balance of power in the upper house – so neither the government nor the opposition can have things completely their own way. Independent politicians with no affiliation to a particular party have also made it into the traditional political structure in recent times – in state elections in Tasmania five independents (the Green Independents) won seats and held the balance of power until 1992.

ECONOMY

Australia is a relatively affluent, industrialised nation but much of its wealth still comes from agriculture and mining. It has a small domestic market and a comparatively weak manufacturing sector. Nevertheless, a substantial proportion of the population is employed in manufacturing, and for much of Australia's history it has been argued that these indus-

tries need tariff protection from imports to ensure their survival.

Today, however, efforts are being made to increase Australia's international competitiveness. This has become more important as prices of traditional primary exports have become more volatile. The government has sought to restrain real wages with the assistance of the Australian Council of Trade Unions (ACTU), to make Australian products more competitive overseas and to promote employment within Australia.

This policy saw the creation of many new jobs, but the current recession has thrown many thousands back on to the dole queues – unemployment is around 10% – and the prospects for the immediate future look pretty grim.

Australia's greatest economic hope is tourism, with the numbers of visitors rising each year and projections for even greater numbers in the future.

The main economic challenge for Australians, as for everyone else, is to earn enough to pay for the standard of living to which they have become accustomed.

POPULATION & PEOPLE

Australia's population is about 17 million. The most populous states are New South Wales and Victoria, each with a capital city (Sydney and Melbourne) with a population of over three million. The population is concentrated along the east coast strip from Adelaide to Cairns and in the similar but smaller coastal region in Western Australia. The centre of the country is very sparsely populated. There are about 150,000 Aborigines, most heavily concentrated in central Australia and the far north.

Until WW II Australians were predominantly of British and Irish descent but that has changed dramatically since the war. First there was heavy migration from Europe creating major Greek and Italian populations but also adding Yugoslavs, Lebanese, Turks and other groups.

More recently Australia has had large influxes of Asians, particularly Vietnamese after the Vietnam war. In comparison to the country's population Australia probably took more Vietnamese refugees than any other Western nation. On the whole these 'new Australians' have been remarkably well accepted and 'multi-culturalism' is a popular concept in Australia.

If you come to Australia in search of a real Australian you will find one quite easily – they are not known to be a shy breed. He or she may be a Lebanese cafe owner, an English used-car salesperson, an Aboriginal artist, a Malaysian architect or a Greek greengrocer. And you will find them in pubs, on beaches, at barbecues, mustering yards and art galleries. And yes, you may meet a Mick (Crocodile) Dundee or two but he is strictly a country model – the real Paul Hogan was a Sydney Harbour Bridge painter, a job where after you finish at one end you just start again at the other.

LANGUAGE

Any visitor from abroad who thinks Australian (that's 'strine') is simply a weird variant of English/American will soon have a few surprises. For a start many Australians don't even speak Australian – they speak Italian, Lebanese, Turkish or Greek (Melbourne is said to be the third largest Greek city in the world). Then those who do speak the native tongue are liable to lose you in a strange collection of Australian words. Some have completely different meanings in Australia than they have in English-speaking countries north of the equator; some commonly used words have been shortened almost beyond recognition. Others derive from Aboriginal languages, or from the slang used by early convict settlers.

There is a slight regional variation in the Australian accent, while the difference between city and country speech is mainly a matter of speed. Some of the most famed Aussie words are hardly heard at all – 'mates' are more common than 'cobbers'. If you want to pass for a native try speaking slightly nasally, shortening any word of more than two syllables and then adding a vowel to the end of it, making anything you can into a diminutive (even the Hell's Angels can

become mere 'bikies') and peppering your speech with as many expletives as possible. The list that follows may help:

amber fluid – beer
am I ever – yes I really am
arvo – afternoon
ASIO – Australian Security & Intelligence Organisation – Aussie CIA
avagoyermug – traditional rallying call, especially at cricket matches
award wage – minimum pay rate

back o' Bourke – back of beyond, middle of nowhere
bail up – hold up, rob, earbash
bail out – leave
banana bender – resident of Queensland
barbie – barbecue (bbq)
barrack – cheer on team at sporting event, support (as in 'who do you barrack for?')
bathers – swimming costume (Victoria)
battler – hard trier, struggler
beaut, beauty, bewdie – great, fantastic
beg yours – I beg your pardon
bible basher – religious fanatic
bikies – motorcyclists
bikkies – biscuits
billabong – water hole in dried up riverbed, more correctly an ox-bow bend cut off in the dry season by receding waters
billy – tin container used to boil tea in the bush
bitumen road – surfaced road
black stump – where the 'back o' Bourke' begins
blowies – blow flies
bludger – lazy person, one who won't work
blue (ie have a blue) – to have an argument or fight
bluey – swag, or nickname for a red-haired person
bonzer – great, ripper (archaic)
boomer – very big, a particularly large male kangaroo
boomerang – a curved flat wooden instrument used by Aborigines for hunting
booze bus – police van used for random breath testing for alcohol
bottle shop – liquor shop

Buckley's – no chance at all
bug (Moreton Bay Bug) – a small yabbie
Bulamakanka – place even beyond the back o' Bourke, way beyond the black stump
bull dust – fine and sometimes deep dust on outback roads, also bullshit
bunyip – Australia's yeti or bigfoot
burl – have a try (as in 'give it a burl')
bush – country, anywhere away from the city
bush (ie *go bush*) – go back to the land
bushbash – to force your way through pathless bush
bushranger – Australia's equivalent of the outlaws of the American Wild West (some goodies, some baddies)
BYO – Bring Your Own (booze to a restaurant, meat to a barbecue etc)
BYOG – Bring Your Own Grog

caaarn! – come on, traditional rallying call, especially at football games, as in 'Caaarn the Blues!'
Captain Cook (ie *have a Captain Cook*) – look
cask – wine box (a great Australian invention)
Chiko roll – vile Australian junk food
chook – chicken
chuck a U-ey – do a U-turn
chunder – vomit, technicolour yawn, pavement pizza, curbside quiche, liquid laugh, drive the porcelain bus
cobber – mate (archaic)
cocky – small-scale farmer
come good – turn out all right
compo – compensation such as workers' compensation
cooee – Aboriginal bush greeting, signal that you are lost
cool change – sudden drop in temperature after heat wave
counter meal, countery – pub meal
cow cocky – small-scale dairy farmer
cozzie – swimming costume (New South Wales)
crook – ill, badly made, substandard
crow eater – resident of South Australia
cut lunch – sandwiches

dag, daggy – dirty lump of wool at back end of a sheep, also an affectionate or mildly abusive term for a socially inept person
daks – trousers
damper – bush loaf made from flour and water
dead horse – tomato sauce
deli – delicatessen, milk bar in South Australia
didgeridoo – tube-like musical instrument played by Aboriginal men
dill – idiot
dilly bag – small bag (from the Aboriginal word for basket)
dinkum, fair dinkum – honest, genuine
dinky-di – the real thing
divvy van – police divisional van
dob in – to tell on someone
donk – car or boat engine
don't come the raw prawn – don't try and fool me
drongo – worthless person
duco – car paint
dunny – outdoor lavatory
dunny budgies – blowies

earbash – talk nonstop
eastern states – the rest of Australia viewed from Western Australia
esky – large insulated box for keeping beer etc cold

fair go! – give us a break
fair crack of the whip! – fair go!
fairy floss – candyfloss
financial (ie *to be financial*) – to be OK for $$
fire plug – fire hydrant
FJ – most revered Holden car
flake – shark meat, used in fish & chips
floater – meat pie floating in pea soup – yuk
fossicking – hunting for gems or semi-precious stones

galah – noisy parrot, thus noisy idiot
garbo – person who collects your garbage
gibber – Aboriginal word for stony desert
give it away – give up
g'day – good day, traditional Australian greeting
good on yer – well done

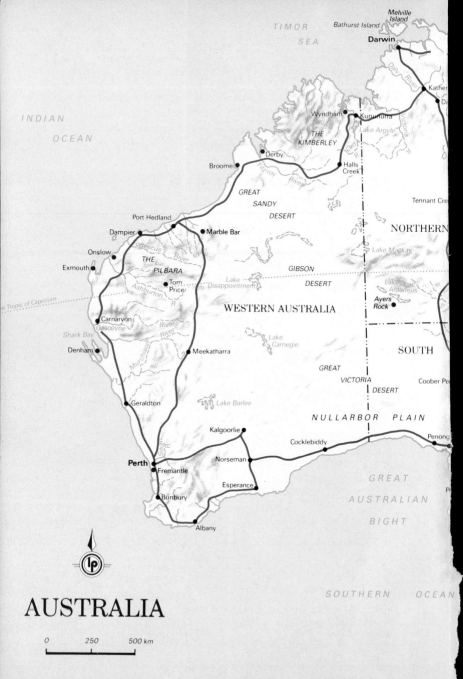

AUSTRALIA

0   250   500 km

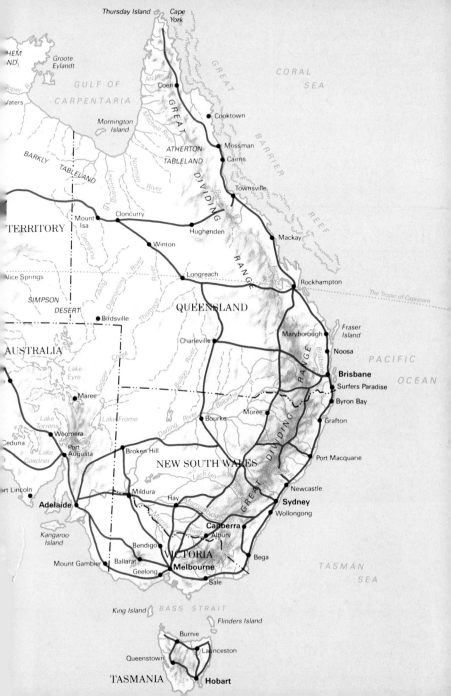

grazier – large-scale sheep or cattle farmer

grog – general term for beer, as in 'have a few grogs'

grouse – very good, unreal

hoon – idiot, hooligan, yahoo

how are yer – standard greeting, expected answer 'good, thanks, how are *you?*'

HQ – second most revered Australian car

hump – to carry, as in 'hump your bluey'

icy-pole – frozen lolly water or ice cream on a stick

jackaroo – young male trainee on farm

jillaroo – young female trainee on farm

journo – journalist

king hit – knockout blow, especially an unfair one

kiwi – New Zealander

knock – criticise, deride

knocker – one who knocks

Koori – Aborigine (mostly south of the Murray River)

lair – layabout, ruffian

lairising – acting like a lair

lamington – square of sponge cake covered in chocolate icing and coconut

larrikin – a bit like a lair

lay-by – put a deposit on an article so the shop will hold it for you

lollies – sweets, candy

lolly water – soft drink

lurk – a scheme

manchester – household linen

middy – 10 oz beer glass (New South Wales)

milk bar – corner shop

milko – milkman

mozzies – mosquitoes

never-never – remote country in the outback

new Australian – recent immigrant

no hoper – hopeless case, ne'er do well

northern summer – summer in the northern hemisphere

north island – mainland Australia, viewed from Tasmania

no worries, no wuckers – she'll be right, that's OK

nulla-nulla – wooden club used by Aborigines

ocker – an uncultivated or boorish Australian

off-sider – assistant or partner

O-S – overseas, as in 'he's gone O-S'

outback – remote part of the bush, back o' Bourke

OYO – own your own (flat or apartment)

Oz – Australia

pastoralist – large-scale grazier

pavlova – traditional Australian meringue and cream dessert, named after Anna Pavlova

perve – to gaze with lust

pineapple (rough end of) – stick (sharp end of)

piss – beer

pissed – drunk

pissed off – annoyed

piss turn – boozy party

pom – English person

pokies – poker machines, found in clubs, mainly in New South Wales

port – suitcase

postie – mailman

pot – 10 oz glass of beer (Victoria, Queensland)

push – gang of larrikins

Rafferty's rules – chaos, disorder

ratbag – friendly term of abuse

ratshit – lousy

rapt – delighted, enraptured

reckon! – you bet!, absolutely!

rego – registration, as in 'car rego'

ridgy-didge – original, genuine

ring, tingle (give someone a) – phone someone up

ripper – good (also 'little ripper')

road train – semi-trailer-trailer-trailer

root – have sexual intercourse

rooted – tired

ropable – very bad-tempered or angry

rubbish (ie to rubbish) – deride, tease

salvo – member of the Salvation Army

sandgroper – resident of Western Australia

scallops – potato cakes (Queensland), shell-fish (elsewhere)

school – group of drinkers

schooner – large beer glass (New South Wales, South Australia)

sealed road – surfaced road

sea wasp – deadly box jellyfish

see you in the soup – see you around

semi-trailer – articulated truck

session – lengthy period of heavy drinking

shellacking – comprehensive defeat

she'll be right – no worries

sherbet – beer

shoot through – leave in a hurry

shout – buy round of drinks (as in 'it's your shout')

sickie – day off work ill (or malingering)

smoke-o – tea break

snag – sausage

southern states – the rest of Australia, viewed from the Northern Territory

spunky – good looking, attractive (as in 'what a spunk')

squatter – pioneer farmer who occupied land as a tenant of the government

squattocracy – Australian 'old money' folk, who made it by being first on the scene and grabbing the land

station – large farm

stickybeak – nosy person

strides – daks

strine – Australian slang

stubby – small bottle of beer

sunbake – sunbathe (well, the sun's hot in Australia)

surfies – surfing fanatics

swag – gear, possessions

tall poppies – achievers (knockers like to cut them down)

Taswegian – resident of Tasmania

tea – evening meal

thingo – thing, whatchamacallit, hooza meebob, doo velacki, thingamejig

tinny – can of beer

togs – swimming costume (Queensland, Victoria)

too right! – absolutely!

Top End – northern part of the Northern Territory

trucky – lorry driver

true blue – dinkum

tucker – food

two-pot screamers – people unable to hold their drink

two-up – traditional heads/tails gambling game

uni – university

ute – utility, pickup truck

wag (ie to wag) – to skip school

walkabout – lengthy walk away from it all

wallaby track (on the) – to wander from place to place seeking work

weatherboard – wooden house

Wet (ie the Wet) – rainy season in the north

wharfie – docker

whinge – complain, moan

whingeing pom – the worst sort of pom

woolgrower – sheep farmer

wowser – spoilsport, puritan

wobbly – disturbing, unpredictable behaviour (as in throw a wobbly)

woomera – stick used by Aborigines for throwing spears

yabbie – small freshwater crayfish

yahoo – noisy, unruly person

yakka – work (from an Aboriginal language)

youse – plural of you

yobbo – uncouth, aggressive person

Facts for the Visitor

VISAS & EMBASSIES

Once upon a time, Australia was fairly free and easy about who was allowed to visit the country, particularly if you were from the UK or Canada. These days, only New Zealanders get any sort of preferential treatment and even they need at least a passport. Everybody else has to have a visa.

Australian Embassies

Australian consular offices overseas include:

Canada
Suite 710, 50 O'Connor St, Ottawa K1P 6L2 (☎ (613) 236 0841)
also in Toronto and Vancouver

China
15 Dongzhimenwai Dajie, San Li Tun, Beijing (☎ 532 2331)

Denmark
Kristianagade 21, 2100 Copenhagen (☎ 3126 2244)

Germany
Godesberger Allee 107, 5300 Bonn 2 (☎ (0228) 81030)
also in Frankfurt and Berlin

Greece
37 Dimitriou Soutsou St, Ambelokpi, Athens 11521 (☎ 644 7303)

Hong Kong
Harbour Centre, 24th floor, 25 Harbour Rd, Wanchai, Hong Kong Island (☎ (5) 73 1881)

India
Australian Compound, No 1/50-G Shantipath, Chanakyapuri, New Delhi 110021 (☎ 60 1336)
also in Bombay

Indonesia
Jalan Thamrin 15, Gambir, Jakarta (☎ 323109)
also in Denpasar

Ireland
Fitzwilton House, Wilton Terrace, Dublin 2 (☎ 76 1517)

Italy
Via Alessandria 215, Rome 00198 (☎ 832 721)
also in Milan

Japan
2-1-14 Mita, Minato-ku, Tokyo (☎ 5232 4111)
also in Osaka

Malaysia
6 Jalan Yap Kwan Seng, Kuala Lumpur 50450 (☎ 242 3122)

Netherlands
Camegielaan 12, 2517 KH The Hague (☎ (70) 310 8200)

New Zealand
72-78 Hobson St, Thorndon, Wellington (☎ 73 6411)
also in Auckland

Papua New Guinea
Independence Drive, Waigani, Port Moresby (☎ 25 9333)

Philippines
Bank of Philippine Islands Building, Paseo de Roxas, Makati, Manila (☎ 81 77911)

Singapore
25 Napier Rd, Singapore 10 (☎ 737 9311)

Sweden
Sergels Torg 12, Stockholm C (☎ 613 2900)

Switzerland
29 Alpenstrasse, Berne (☎ 43 0143)
also in Geneva

Thailand
37 South Sathorn Rd, Bangkok 10120 (☎ 2872680)

UK
Australia House, The Strand, London WC2B 4LA (☎ (071) 379 4334)
also in Edinburgh and Manchester

USA
1601 Massachusetts Ave NW, Washington DC, 20036 (☎ (202) 797 3000)
also in Los Angeles, Chicago, Honolulu, Houston, New York and San Francisco

Tourist Visas

Tourist visas are issued by Australian consular offices abroad; they are free and valid for a stay of *up to* six months. That is, you can say you want to stay for six months and if they like the look of you the immigration official can give you six months. If they don't you might end up with two weeks.

As well as the visa, visitors are also required to have an onward or return ticket and 'sufficient funds' – the latter is obviously open to interpretation. Like those of any country, Australian visas seem to cause their hassles, although the authorities do seem to be more uniform in their approach these days. Nevertheless, if you're kicking around Asia and take a fancy to dropping down to Oz for a spell, the travellers' grapevine will doubtless have handy hints about where the best place is to get a visa.

US citizens can now get visas from the Qantas offices in Los Angeles and San Francisco, if they are buying Qantas tickets.

Working Visas

Young visitors from certain countries – the UK, Ireland, Canada, Holland and Japan – may be eligible for a 'working holiday' visa. Young is fairly loosely interpreted as around 18 to 26, and working holiday means up to 12 months, but the emphasis is supposed to be on casual employment rather than a full-time job, so you are only supposed to work for three months. Officially this visa can only be applied for in your home country, but some travellers report that the rule can be bent.

See the section on Working later in this chapter for details of what sort of work is available and where.

Visa Extensions

Visa extensions are made through Department of Immigration offices in Australia and there's a $50 application fee. That's a fee simply for applying, and regardless of how long you want an extension for – *and* if they turn down your application they can still keep your 50 bucks! Some offices, like the one in Sydney, can be very thorough, requiring things like bank statements and interviews. Extending visas has always been a notoriously slow process and Australia's tourist boom has certainly not made it any easier. If you do end up overstaying your visa the fact that you did your damnedest to get the bureaucrats to extend it should stand in your favour.

Although Australia doesn't have any borders with other countries, it still manages to get plenty of illegal immigrants. The government is now clamping down, and illegal immigrants will probably not be able to negotiate permanent residence from within Australia; the foreign partners of Australian nationals usually have to go back to their own countries while applying to migrate. If you're trying to stay for longer in Australia

the book *Tourist to Permanent Resident in Australia* might be useful.

Foreign Embassies & Consulates in Australia

The principal diplomatic representations to Australia are in Canberra and you'll find a list of the addresses of relevant offices in the Canberra section. There are also representatives in various other major cities, particularly from countries with major connections with Australia like the USA, UK or New Zealand; or in cities with important connections, like Darwin which has an Indonesian consulate. Big cities like Sydney and Melbourne have nearly as many consular offices as Canberra. Look up addresses in the Yellow Pages phone book under 'Consulates & Legations'.

CUSTOMS

For visitors from abroad the usual sort of '200 cigarettes, one bottle of whisky' regulations apply to Australia, but there are two areas you should be very careful about. Number one is, of course, dope – Australian Customs have a positive mania about the stuff and can be extremely efficient when it comes to finding it. Unless you want to make first-hand investigations of conditions in Australian jails (not very good), don't bring any with you. This particularly applies if you are arriving from Indonesia or South-East Asia. You will be the object of suspicion, and people are often searched.

Problem two is animal and plant quarantine. The authorities are naturally keen to prevent weeds, pests or diseases getting into the country – Australia has so far managed to escape many of the agricultural pests prevalent in other parts of the world, and with all the sheep in Australia, that scruffy sheepskin jacket over your arm is not going to be popular. Fresh food is also unpopular, particularly meat, sausages, fruit, vegetables and flowers. You will be asked to declare all goods of animal or vegetable origin – wooden spoons, straw hats, the lot – and show them to an official. (There are also restrictions on taking fruit and vegetables between states.) If you've been anywhere near a farm recently, they may want to examine the shoes you were wearing at the time.

When it is time to leave there are duty-free stores at the international airports and their associated cities. Treat them with healthy suspicion. 'Duty-free' is one of the world's most overworked catchphrases, and it is often just an excuse to sell things at prices you can easily beat by a little shopping around. Discount film shops in big cities always have film at far cheaper prices than airport duty-free shops, for example. City duty-free shops are generally better value than the airport ones. However, there are some alcoholic bargains.

MONEY
Currency
Australia's currency is good, old-fashioned dollars and cents. When they changed over from pounds, shillings and pence there was consideration of calling the new unit the 'royal'; however, that foolish idea soon got the chop. There are coins for 5c, 10c, 20c, 50c, $1 and $2, and notes for $5, $10, $20, $50 and $100.

There are no notable restrictions on importing or exporting currency or travellers' cheques except that you may not take out more than A$5000 except with prior approval.

Exchange Rates
In recent years the Australian dollar has fluctuated quite markedly against the US dollar, although these days it seems to have stabilised.

C$1	=	A$1.15
DM 1	=	A$0.80
HK$10	=	A$1.70
NZ$1	=	A$0.70
UK£1	=	A$2.30
US$1	=	A$1.35
Y100	=	A$1.04

Changing Money
There is a variety of ways to carry your money around Australia with you. If your stay is limited then travellers' cheques are the most straightforward and they generally enjoy a better exchange rate than foreign cash in Australia.

Changing foreign currency or travellers' cheques is no problem at almost any bank. It's done quickly and efficiently and never

involves the sort of headaches and grand production that changing foreign currency in the USA always entails. American Express, Thomas Cook and other well-known international brands of travellers' cheques are all widely used in Australia. A passport will usually be adequate for identification; it would be sensible to carry a driver's licence, credit cards and a plane ticket in case of problems.

Commissions and fees for changing foreign currency travellers' cheques seem to vary from bank to bank and year to year. It's worth making a few phone calls to see which bank currently has the lowest charges. Some charge a flat fee for each transaction, while others take a percentage of the amount changed. The average fee to change a US$100 cheque is between A$2 and A$5. Australian dollar travellers' cheques can be exchanged immediately at the bank cashier's window without being converted from a foreign currency or incurring commissions, fees and exchange rate fluctuations.

Australian Bank Accounts

If you're planning to stay longer than just a month or so, it's worth considering other ways of handling money that give you more flexibility and are more economical. This applies equally to Australians setting off to travel around the country.

Passbook Account One of the neatest solutions is to open a bank account of some description. One option is a passbook savings account. All the banks operate these systems and with your passbook you can withdraw money from any branch of the bank in question in the country. There are limitations as to how much you can pull out in one hit but it's quite reasonable. This way, instead of paying to buy travellers' cheques, you actually get paid for having your money on deposit. The limitations are that you are limited to banking hours, and if there's no branch of that bank in the particular town you happen to be in, you're stuck.

If you open an interest-bearing account and there's any chance of its earning more

than $120 interest in a year, you should get your own tax file number (the form is available from post offices) and give it to the bank. Otherwise they may charge 48% tax on the interest.

Cashcard Account Most travellers these days tend to opt for an account where you get issued with a cash card, with which you can get cash from automatic banking machines now found all over Australia. You put your card in the machine and key in your pin number; you can then withdraw up to $400 a day from your account. Westpac, ANZ, National and Commonwealth bank branches are found nationwide, and in all but the most remote town there'll be at least one place where you can withdraw money from a hole in the wall. The advantages over a passbook account are obvious: you can withdraw money at any time of the day or night, and you can use your card in the machine of at least one other bank, although a small charge is often made if you utilise this service.

Many businesses, including most garages, are linked into the EFTPOS system (Electronic Funds Transfer at Point Of Sale), and at places with this facility you can use your bank cash card to pay for services or purchases direct, and sometimes withdraw cash as well. Bank cash cards and credit cards can also be used to make local, STD and international phone calls in special public telephones, found in most towns throughout the country.

To open an account at an Australian bank you have to produce two forms of identification. Documents such as a passport, birth certificate, driver's licence or credit card are all acceptable.

Credit Cards

Credit cards are widely accepted in Australia and are an alternative to carrying large numbers of travellers' cheques. The most common credit card, however, is the purely Australian Bankcard system. Visa, MasterCard, Diners Club and American Express are widely accepted. If you're planning to rent cars while travelling around

Australia, a credit card makes life much simpler; they're looked upon with much greater favour by rent-a-car agencies than nasty old cash.

Costs

Compared to the USA, Canada and European countries, Australia is cheaper in some ways and more expensive in others. Manufactured goods tend to be more expensive because they're either imported and have all the additional costs of transport and duties, or if they're locally manufactured they suffer from the extra costs entailed in making things in comparatively small quantities. Thus you pay more for clothes, cars and other manufactured items. On the other hand, food is both high in quality and low in cost.

In restaurants what you see is what you get – there are no service charges, and no sales or value-added taxes.

Tipping

In Australia tipping isn't a habit the way it is in the USA or Europe. It's only customary to tip in more expensive restaurants and only then if you want to. If the service has been especially good and you decide to leave a tip, 10% of the bill is the usual amount. Taxi drivers don't expect tips (of course, they don't hurl it back at you if you decide to leave the change). In contrast, just try getting out of a New York cab, or even a London one, without leaving your 10 to 15%. In fact Australian taxi drivers will often round fares down – if it comes to $8.10 you're quite likely to be told 'make it eight bucks, mate'.

TOURIST OFFICES

There are a number of information sources for visitors to Australia and, in common with a number of other tourist-conscious Western countries, you can easily drown yourself in brochures and booklets, maps and leaflets.

Local Tourist Offices

Within Australia, tourist information is handled by the various state and local offices. Each state and the ACT and Northern Territory have a tourist office of some form and you will find information about these centres in the various state sections. Apart from a main office in the capital cities, they often have regional offices in main tourist centres and also in other states. Tourist information in Victoria is handled by the Royal Automobile Club of Victoria (RACV) organisation in Melbourne.

As well as supplying brochures, price lists, maps and other information, the state offices will often book transport, tours and accommodation for you. Unfortunately, very few of the state tourist offices maintain information desks at the airports and, furthermore, the opening hours of the city offices are very much of the 9-to-5 weekdays and Saturday-morning-only variety. Addresses of the state tourist offices are:

Australian Capital Territory
Canberra Tourist Bureau, Jolimont Centre, Northbourne Ave, Canberra City, ACT 2601 (☎ (06) 254 6464)
New South Wales
Travel Centre of NSW, 19 Castlereagh St, Sydney, NSW 2000 (☎ (02) 231 4444)
Northern Territory
Northern Territory Government Tourist Bureau, 31 Smith St, Darwin, NT 0800 (☎ (089) 81 6611)
Queensland
Queensland Government Travel Centre, corner Adelaide and Edward Sts, Brisbane, Qld 4000 (☎ (07) 221 6111)
South Australia
South Australian Government Travel Centre, 18 King William St, Adelaide, SA 5000 (☎ (08) 212 1505)
Tasmania
Tasmanian Travel Centre, 80 Elizabeth St, Hobart, Tas 7000 (☎ (002) 30 0250)
Victoria
RACV Travel Centre, 230 Collins St, Melbourne, Vic 3000 (☎ (03) 650 1522)
Western Australia
Western Australian Tourist Centre, Forrest Place, Perth, WA 6000 (☎ (09) 483 1111)

A step down from the state tourist offices are the local or regional tourist offices. Almost every town in Australia seems to maintain a tourist office or centre of some type or other and in many cases these are really excellent, with much local information not readily available from the larger, state offices. This particularly applies where there is a strong local tourist trade.

Overseas Reps

The Australian Tourist Commission (ATC) is the government body intended to inform potential visitors about the country. There's a very definite split between promotion outside Australia and inside it. The ATC is strictly an external operator; they do minimal promotion within the country and have little contact with visitors to Australia. Within the country, tourist promotion is handled by state or local tourist offices.

ATC offices overseas have a useful free booklet that is a good introduction to the country, its geography, flora, fauna, states, transport, accommodation, food and so on. They also have a useful free map of the country. This literature is intended for distribution overseas only; if you want copies, get them before you come to Australia. Addresses of the ATC offices for literature requests are:

Australia
   Level 3, 80 William St, Woolloomooloo, Sydney, NSW 2011 (☎ (02) 360 1111)
Canada
   Suite 1730, 2 Bloor St West, Toronto, Ontario M4W 3E2 (☎ (416) 925 9575)
Germany
   Neue Mainzerstrasse 22, D6000 Frankfurt/Main 1 (☎ (069) 20 4006)
Hong Kong
   Suite 604-605, Sun Plaza, 28 Canton Rd, Tsimshatsui, Kowloon (☎ (3) 311 1555)
Japan
   8th floor, Sankaido Building, 9-13, Akasaka 1-chome, Minato-ku, Tokyo 107 (☎ (03) 582 2191)
   4th floor, Yuki Building, 3-3-9 Hiranomachi, Chuo-Ku, Osaka 541 (☎ (06) 229 3601)
New Zealand
   15th floor, Quay Towers, 29 Customs St West, Auckland 1 (☎ (09) 79 9594)
Singapore
   Suite 1703, United Square, 101 Thomson Rd, Singapore 1130 (☎ 255 4555)
UK
   Gemini House, 10-18 Putney Hill, London SW15 (☎ (071) 780 2227)
USA
   Suite 2130, 150 North Michigan Ave, Chicago,

IL 60601 (☎ (312) 781 5150)
   Suite 1200, 2121 Ave of the Stars, Los Angeles, CA 90067 (☎ (213) 552 1988)
   31st floor, 489 Fifth Ave, New York, NY 10017 (☎ (212) 687 6300)

USEFUL ORGANISATIONS
Automobile Associations

Australia has a national automobile association, the Australian Automobile Association, but this exists mainly as an umbrella organisation for the various state associations and to maintain international links. The day-to-day operations are all handled by the state organisations who provide an emergency breakdown service, literature, excellent maps and detailed guides to accommodation and camp sites.

The state organisations have reciprocal arrangements amongst the various states in Australia and with similar organisations overseas. So, if you're a member of the National Roads & Motorists Association (NRMA) in New South Wales, you can use RACV facilities in Victoria. Similarly, if you're a member of the AAA in the USA or the RAC or AA in the UK, you can use any of the state organisations' facilities. But bring proof of membership with you. More details about the state automobile organisations can be found in the relevant state sections. Some of the material they produce is of a very high standard. In particular there is a superb set of regional maps to Queensland produced by the Royal Automobile Club of Queensland (RACQ). The most useful state offices are:

New South Wales
   NRMA, 151 Clarence St, Sydney, NSW 2000 (☎ (02) 260 9222)
Northern Territory
   Automobile Association of the Northern Territory, 79-81 Smith St, Darwin, NT 0800 (☎ (089) 81 3837)
Queensland
   RACQ, 300 St Pauls Terrace, Fortitude Valley, Qld 4006 (☎ (07) 253 2406)
South Australia
   Royal Automobile Association of South Australia (RAA), 41 Hindmarsh Square, Adelaide, SA 5000 (☎ (08) 223 4555)

Tasmania
  Royal Automobile Club of Tasmania (RACT), corner Patrick and Murray Sts, Hobart, Tas 7000 (☎ (002) 38 2200)
Victoria
  RACV, 422 Little Collins St, Melbourne, Vic 3000 (☎ (03) 607 2137)
Western Australia
  Royal Automobile Club of Western Australia (RAC), 228 Adelaide Terrace, Perth, WA 6000 (☎ (09) 421 4444)

English Language Schools

If English isn't your first language and you've come to Australia to learn it, colleges specialising in teaching English include:

Australian College of English
  20th floor, Bondi Junction Plaza Building, 500 Oxford St, Bondi Junction, NSW 2022 (☎ (02) 389 0133)
Milner International College of English
  195 Adelaide Terrace, Perth, WA 6000 (☎ (09) 325 5444)
The International College of English
  226 Flinders Lane, Melbourne, Vic 3000 (☎ (03) 650 1700)

National Park Organisations

Australia has an extensive collection of national parks. In fact, the Royal National Park just outside Sydney is the second oldest national park in the world; only Yellowstone Park in the USA predates it.

The national park organisations in each state are state operated, not nationally run. They tend to be a little hidden away in their capital city locations, although if you search them out they often have excellent literature and maps on the parks. They are much more up-front in the actual parks where, in many cases, they have very good guides and leaflets to bushwalking, nature trails and other activities. The state offices are:

Australian Capital Territory
  Parks & Conservation, PO Box 158, Canberra, ACT 2601
  Australian National Parks & Wildlife Service, 3rd floor, Construction House, Turner, ACT 2601 (PO Box 636, Canberra City, ACT 2601)

New South Wales
  National Parks & Wildlife Service, 43 Bridge St, Hurstville, NSW 2220 (PO Box 1967, Hurstville, NSW 2220)
Northern Territory
  Conservation Commission of the Northern Territory, PO Box 1046, Alice Springs, NT 0800
  Australian National Parks & Wildlife Service, PO Box 1260, Darwin, NT 0800 (for Kakadu and Uluru National Parks)
Queensland
  National Parks & Wildlife Service, 160 Ann St, Brisbane, Qld 4000 (PO Box 155, North Quay, Qld 4002)
South Australia
  National Parks & Wildlife Service, Insurance Building, 55 Grenfell St, Adelaide, SA 5061 (GPO Box 667, Adelaide, SA 5001)
Tasmania
  Department of Parks, Wildlife & Heritage, 134 Macquarie St, Hobart, Tas 7000 (PO Box 44A, Hobart 7001)
Victoria
  Department of Conservation & Environment, 240 Victoria Parade, East Melbourne, Vic 3002 (PO Box 41)
Western Australia
  Department of Conservation & Land Management, 50 Hayman Rd, Como, Perth, WA 6152

Australian Conservation Foundation

The Australian Conservation Foundation (ACF) is the largest nongovernment organisation involved in conservation. Only nine to 10% of its income is from the government; the rest comes from memberships and subscriptions, and from donations (72%), which are mainly from individuals.

The ACF covers a wide range of issues, including the greenhouse effect and depletion of the ozone layer, the negative effects of logging, preservation of rainforests, the problems of land degradation, and protection of the Antarctic. They frequently work in conjunction with the Wilderness Society and other conservation groups.

With the growing focus on conservation issues and the increasing concern of the Australian public in regard to their environment, the conservation vote has now become increasingly important to all political parties.

Wilderness Society

The Tasmanian Wilderness Society was

formed by conservationists who had been unsuccessful in preventing the damming of Lake Pedder in south-west Tasmania but who were determined to prevent the destruction of the Franklin River. The Franklin River campaign was one of Australia's first major conservation confrontations and it caught the attention of the international media. In 1983, after the High Court decided against the damming of the Franklin, the group changed its name to the Wilderness Society because of their Australia-wide focus on wilderness issues.

The Wilderness Society is involved in issues concerning protection of the Australian wilderness, such as forest management and logging. Like the ACF, government funding is only a small percentage of their income, the rest coming from memberships, donations, the shops and merchandising. There are Wilderness Society Shops in all states (not in the Northern Territory) where you can buy books, T-shirts, posters, badges, etc.

Australian Trust for Conservation Volunteers

This nonpolitical, nonprofit group organises practical conservation projects (such as tree planting, track construction and flora & fauna surveys) for volunteers to take part in. Travellers are welcome and it's an excellent way to get involved with the conservation movement and, at the same time, visit some of the more interesting areas of the country. Past volunteers have found themselves working in places such as Tasmania, Kakadu and Fraser Island.

Most projects last for a week and all food, transport and accommodation is supplied in return for a small contribution to help cover costs. Most travellers who take part in ATCV join an Echidna Package, which lasts six weeks and includes six different projects. The cost is $460, and further weeks can be added for $63.

Contact the head office (☎ 008 032 501, toll-free) at PO Box 423, Ballarat, Vic 3350, or the state offices listed.

New South Wales
PO Box 198, Chatswood, NSW 2057 (☎ (02) 413 5502)
Northern Territory
PO Box 3520, Darwin, NT 0801 (☎ (089) 81 2848)
Queensland
PO Box 2673, Brisbane, Qld 4001 (☎ (07) 891 5778)
South Australia
PO Box 419, Campbell, South Australia 5074 (☎ (08) 365 1612)
Tasmania
PO Box 46, Kings Meadow, Tasmania 7249 (☎ (003) 41 5268)
Victoria
13 Duke St, South Caulfield, Vic 3162 (☎ (03) 532 8446)

National Trust

The National Trust is dedicated to preserving historic buildings in all parts of Australia. They actually own a number of buildings throughout the country which are open to the public. Many other buildings are 'classified' by the National Trust to ensure their preservation.

The National Trust also produces some excellent literature, including a fine series of walking-tour guides to many cities around the country, large and small. These guides are often available from local tourist offices or from National Trust offices and are usually free whether you're a member of the National Trust or not. Membership of the trust is well worth considering, however, because it entitles you to free entry to any National Trust property for your year of membership. If you're a dedicated visitor of old buildings this could soon pay for itself. Annual membership costs $39 for individuals, $55 for families and includes the monthly or quarterly magazine put out by the state organisation that you join. Addresses of the various National Trust state offices are:

Australian Capital Territory
6 Geills Court, Deakin, ACT 2600 (☎ (062) 81 0711)
New South Wales
Observatory Hill, Sydney, NSW 2000 (☎ (02) 258 0123)

Northern Territory
> 52 Temira Crescent, Myilly Point, Darwin, NT
> 0800 (☎ (089) 81 2848)

Queensland
> Old Government House, George St, Brisbane,
> Qld 4000 (☎ (07) 229 1788)

South Australia
> Ayers House, 288 North Terrace, Adelaide, SA
> 5000 (☎ (08) 223 1196)

Tasmania
> Franklin House, 413 Hobart Rd, Franklin
> Village, Tas 7249 (☎ (003) 446 233)

Victoria
> Tasma Terrace, Parliament Place, Melbourne,
> Vic 3002 (☎ (03) 654 4711)

Western Australia
> Old Observatory, 4 Havelock St, West Perth, WA
> 6005 (☎ (09) 321 6088)

Disabled Travellers

There is a number of organisations which can supply advice to disabled travellers, but many of them only operate within a single state. The national office of the Australian Council for Rehabilitation of the Disabled (PO Box 60, Curtin, ACT 2605, ☎ (062) 82 4333) produces information sheets for disabled travellers, including lists of state-level organisations, specialist travel agents, wheelchair and equipment hire and access guides. They can also sometimes help with specific queries. They would be grateful if enquirers could send at least the cost of postage.

BUSINESS HOURS & HOLIDAYS
Business Hours

Although Australians aren't great believers in long opening hours, they are a long way ahead of the Kiwis, thank you! Most shops close at 5 or 5.30 pm weekdays. In some states shops are open all day Saturday, but in other places they close at noon. In some places Sunday trading is starting to catch on. In most towns there are usually one or two late shopping nights each week, when the doors stay open until 9 or 9.30 pm. Usually it's Thursday and/or Friday night.

Banks are open from 9.30 am to 4 pm Monday to Thursday, and until 5 pm on Friday. Some large city branches are open 8 am to 6 pm Monday to Friday. Some are also open to 9 pm on Fridays. Of course there are some exceptions to Australia's unremarkable opening hours and all sorts of places stay open late and all weekend – particularly milk bars, delis and city bookshops.

Festivals, Holidays & Cultural Events

The Christmas holiday season is part of the long summer school vacation and the time you are most likely to find accommodation booked out and long queues. There are three other shorter school holiday periods during the year but they vary by a week or two from state to state, falling from mid-March to mid-April, late June to early July, and late September to early October.

Some of the most enjoyable Australian festivals are, naturally, the ones which are most typically Australian – like the surf lifesaving competitions on beaches all around the country during summer; or the outback race meetings, which draw together isolated townsfolk, the tiny communities from the huge stations and more than a few eccentric bush characters.

There are happenings and holidays in Australia all year round – the following is just a brief overview. Check the relevant state tourist authorities for dates and more details.

January
> *Sydney to Hobart Yacht Race* – Tas. The arrival (29 December to 2 January) in Hobart of the yachts competing in this annual New Year Race is celebrated with a Mardi Gras. The competitors in the *Melbourne to Hobart Yacht Race* arrive soon after.
> *Australia Day* – this national holiday, commemorating the arrival of the First Fleet, in 1788, is observed on the first Monday after 26 January.
> *Montsalvat Jazz Festival* – Vic. Australia's biggest jazz festival is held at the beautiful Montsalvat artists' colony at Eltham.

February
> *Royal Hobart Regatta* – Tas. This is the largest aquatic carnival in the southern hemisphere with boat races and other activities.
> *Sydney Gay Mardi Gras* – NSW. It's fun – there's a huge procession with extravagant costumes, and an incredible party along Oxford St.
> *Festival of Perth* – WA. This huge festival features local and international artists.

March

Adelaide Arts Festival – SA. Held on even-dated years, this is three weeks of music, theatre, opera, ballet, art exhibitions, light relief and plenty of parties.

Hunter Valley Vintage Festival – NSW. Wine enthusiasts flock to the Hunter Valley (north of Sydney) for wine tasting, and grape picking and treading contests.

Moomba – Melbourne. This week-long festival culminates in a huge street procession, usually on the Victorian Labour Day holiday. There's some doubt about the future of this one.

Port Fairy Folk Festival – Vic. Every Labour Day weekend the small coastal town of Port Fairy comes to life with music, dancing, workshops, storytelling, spontaneous entertainment and stalls. Australia's biggest folk music festival attracts all sorts of people and for three days the population swells from 2500 to over 10,000.

March to April

Sydney Royal Agricultural Show – NSW. Livestock contests and exhibits, ring events, sideshows and rodeos are features of this Easter show.

April

Anzac Day – This is a national public holiday, on 25 April, commemorating the landing of Anzac troops at Gallipoli in 1915. Memorial marches by the returned soldiers of both world wars and the veterans of Korea and Vietnam are held all over the country.

Melbourne Comedy Festival – Vic. The comedy capital of Australia puts on a terrific three week festival with local, out-of-town and international comedians, plays and other funny things.

Australian Motorcycle Grand Prix This round of the 500cc world championships is held in New South Wales.

May

Race Meetings – NT. There is a series of country race meetings at remote Northern Territory stations.

June

Queen's Birthday – a public holiday on the second Monday in June.

Melbourne Film Festival – Vic. This is Australia's longest-running international film event, presenting the best in contemporary world cinema.

July

NT Royal Shows Agricultural shows in Darwin, Katherine, Tennant Creek and Alice Springs.

August

Darwin Rodeo – NT. This includes international team events between Australia, the USA, Canada and New Zealand.

Darwin Beer Can Regatta – NT. Boat races for boats constructed entirely out of beer cans, of which there are plenty in the world's beer drinking capital.

Melbourne International Fringe Festival – Vic. Three weeks of theatre, dance, comedy, cabaret, writers' readings, exhibitions and other events help Melbourne celebrates the 'alternative' arts.

Sydney City to Surf – NSW. Australia's biggest foot race takes place with up to 25,000 competitors running the 14 km from Hyde Park to Bondi Beach.

Shinju Matsuri (Festival of the Pearl) – WA. Held in the old pearling port of Broome, this week-long festival is a great event and has Asiatic celebrations.

September

AFL Grand Final – Vic. Sporting attention turns to Melbourne with the Grand Final of Aussie rules football, when the MCG's 100,000 seats aren't enough to hold the spectators. It's the biggest sporting event in Australia.

Royal Melbourne Show – Vic. This attracts agricultural folk for the judging of livestock and produce, and lots of families for the sideshows.

Royal Perth Show – WA.

Western Australian Folk Festival – WA. Enjoy a weekend of music and dancing in Toodyay.

Tooheys 1000 – NSW. Motor racing enthusiasts flock to Bathurst for the annual 1000 km touring car race on the superb Mt Panorama circuit.

Melbourne International Festival – Vic. An annual festival offering the best of opera, theatre, dance and the visual arts from around Australia and the world.

Royal Adelaide Show – SA. One of the oldest royal shows in the country, with major agricultural and horticultural exhibits and entertainment.

October

Oktoberfests Traditional beerfests with food, plenty of beer and live entertainment for all ages are held all over the country including Darwin, Alice Springs and Melbourne.

Henley-on-Todd Regatta – NT. A series of races for leg-powered bottomless boats on the dry Todd River.

Royal Shows – Tas. The royal agricultural and horticultural shows of Hobart and Launceston are held this month.

November

Melbourne Cup – Vic. On the first Tuesday in November Australia's premier horse race is run at Flemington Race Course. It's a public holiday in Melbourne but the whole country shuts down for the three minutes or so when the race is on.

Australian Formula 1 Grand Prix – SA. This premier motor race takes place on a circuit around the streets and parklands of Adelaide. There are also festive events, concerts and street parties.

December to January

These are the busiest summer months with Christmas, school holidays, lots of beach activities, rock and jazz festivals, international sporting events including tennis and cricket, a whole host of outdoor activities and lots of parties.

Sydney to Hobart Yacht Race Sydney Harbour is a sight to behold on Boxing Day, 26 December, when boats of all shapes and sizes crowd its waters to farewell the yachts competing in this gruelling race. It's a fantastic sight as the yachts stream out of the harbour and head south. In Hobart there's a Mardi Gras to celebrate the finish of the race.

POST & TELECOMMUNICATIONS
Post

Australia's postal services are relatively efficient but not too cheap. It costs 45c to send a standard letter or postcard within Australia, while aerogrammes cost 60c.

Air-mail letters/postcards cost 70/65c to New Zealand, Singapore and Malaysia, 90/80c to Hong Kong and India, $1.10/85c to the USA and Canada, and $1.20/90c to Europe and the UK.

Post offices are open from 9 am to 5 pm Monday to Friday, but you can often get stamps from local post offices operated from newsagencies or from Australia Post shops, found in large cities, on Saturday mornings.

All post offices will hold mail for visitors and some city GPOs have very busy postes restantes. Cairns GPO poste restante, for example, can get quite hectic. You can also have mail sent to you at the American Express offices in big cities if you have an Amex card or carry Amex travellers' cheques.

Telephone

From the year dot the Australian phone system was wholly owned and run by the government, but these days the market has been marginally deregulated with room for a second player. It is still unclear what this will mean for the end user in terms of prices and level of service. Currently the system (still run by the government-owned Telecom) is really remarkably efficient and, equally important, easy to use. Local phone calls all cost 30c for an unlimited amount of time.

You can make local calls from gold or blue phones – often found in shops, hotels, bars, etc – and from Payphone booths.

It's also possible to make long-distance (STD – Subscriber Trunk Dialling) calls from virtually any public phone. Many public phones now accept the Telecom Phonecards, which are very convenient. The cards come in $2, $5 and $10 denominations, and are available from retail outlets such as newsagents and pharmacies, and these places display the phonecard logo. You keep using the card until the value has been used in calls. Otherwise, have plenty of 20c, 50c and $1 coins, and be prepared to feed them through at a fair old rate.

Many businesses and some government departments operate a toll-free service, so no matter where you are ringing from around the country it's only the cost of a local call, or free from a public phone. These numbers have the prefix 008, and we've listed them wherever possible throughout the book.

Some public phones are set up to take only bank cash cards or credit cards, and these too are convenient, although you need to keep an eye on how much the call is costing as it can quickly mount up. The minimum charge for a call on one of these phones is $1.20.

STD calls are cheaper at night. In ascending order of cost:

economy – from 6 pm Saturday to 8 am Monday; 10 pm to 8 am every night
night – from 6 to 10 pm Monday to Friday
day – from 8 am to 6 pm Monday to Saturday

From most STD phones you can also make ISD (International Subscriber Dialling) calls just like making STD calls. Dialling ISD you can get through to overseas numbers almost as quickly as you can locally and if your call is brief it needn't cost very much – 'Hi, I'll be on the flight to London next Tuesday' can cost no more than a postcard.

All you do is dial 0011 for overseas, the country code (44 for Britain, 1 for the USA or Canada, 64 for New Zealand), the city code (71 or 81 for London, 212 for New York, etc), and then the telephone number. And have a Phonecard or plenty of coins to hand. A call to the USA or Britain costs $1.60 a minute ($1.19 off peak), New Zealand is $1.30 a minute ($0.90 off peak). Off-peak times, if available, vary depending on the destination – see the front of the A-K phone book for more details. Saturdays are often the cheapest day to ring.

TIME

Australia is divided into three time zones: Western Time is plus eight hours from Greenwich Mean Time (Western Australia), Central Time is plus 9½ hours (Northern Territory, South Australia), and Eastern Time is plus 10 (Tasmania, Victoria, New South Wales, Queensland). When it's 12 noon in Western Australia it's 1.30 pm in the Northern Territory and South Australia and 2 pm in the rest of the country. During the summer things get slightly screwed up as daylight saving time (when clocks are put forward an hour) does not operate in Western Australia or Queensland.

ELECTRICITY

Voltage is 220-240 V and the plugs are three-pin, but not the same as British three-pin plugs. Users of electric shavers or hairdryers should note that, apart from in fancy hotels, it's difficult to find converters to take either US flat two-pin plugs or the European round two pin-plugs. Adapters for British plugs can be found in good hardware shops. You can easily bend the US plugs to a slight angle to make them fit.

WEIGHTS & MEASURES

Australia went metric in the early '70s. Petrol and milk are sold by the litre, apples and potatoes by the kg, distance is measured by the metre or km, and speed limits are in km per hour. But there's still a degree of confusion; it's hard to think of a six-foot person as being 183 cm.

For those who need help with metric there's a conversion table at the back of this book.

BOOKS

In almost any bookshop in the country you'll find a section devoted to Australiana with books on every Australian subject you care to mention. If you want a souvenir of Australia, a photographic record, try one of the numerous coffee-table books like *A Day in the Life of Australia*. There are many other Australian books which make good gifts: children's books with very Australian illustrations like Julie Vivar & Mem Fox's *Possum Magic* and Norman Lindsay's *The Magic Pudding* or cartoon books by some of Australia's excellent cartoonists. We've got a lot of bookshops and some of the better-

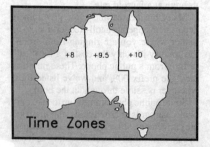

Time Zones

known ones are mentioned in the various city sections.

At the Wilderness Society Shops in each capital city and the Government Printing Offices in Sydney and Melbourne, you'll find a good range of wildlife posters, calendars and books.

Aborigines

The Australian Aborigines, by Kenneth Maddock, is a good cultural summary. The award-winning *Triumph of the Nomads*, by Geoffrey Blainey, chronicles the life of Australia's original inhabitants, and convincingly demolishes the myth that the Aboriginals were 'primitive' people trapped on a hostile continent. They were in fact extremely successful in adapting to and overcoming the difficulties presented by the climate and resources (or seeming lack of them) – the book's an excellent read.

For a sympathetic historical account of what's happened to the real Australians since Whites arrived read *Aboriginal Australians*, by Richard Broome. *A Change of Ownership*, by Mildred Kirk, covers similar ground to Broome's book, but does so more concisely, focusing on the land rights movement and its historical background.

The Other Side of the Frontier, by Henry Reynolds, uses historical records to give a vivid account of an Aboriginal view of the arrival and takeover of Australia by Europeans. His *With the White People* identifies the essential Aboriginal contributions to the survival of the early White settlers. *My Place*, Sally Morgan's prize-winning autobiography, traces her discovery of her Aboriginal heritage. *The Fringe Dwellers*, by Nene Gare, describes just what it's like to be an Aborigine growing up in a White-dominated society.

Ruby Langford's *Don't Take Your Love to Town* and Kath Walker's *My People* are also recommended reading for people interested in Aborigines' experience.

History

For a good introduction to Australian history, read *A Short History of Australia*, a most accessible and informative general history by the late Manning Clark, the much-loved Aussie historian, or *The Fatal Shore*, Robert Hughes's bestseller account of the convict era.

Finding Australia, by Russel Ward, traces the story of the early days from the first Aboriginal arrivals up to 1821. It's strong on Aborigines, women and the full story of foreign exploration, not just Captain Cook's role. There's lots of fascinating detail, including information about the appalling crooks who ran the early colony for long periods, and it's intended to be the first of a series.

The Exploration of Australia, by Michael Cannon, is coffee-table book in size, presentation and price, but it's a fascinating reference book about the gradual European uncovering of the continent.

Cooper's Creek, by Alan Moorehead, is a classic account of the ill-fated Burke & Wills expedition which dramatises the horrors and hardships faced by the early explorers.

The Fatal Impact, also by Moorehead, begins with the voyages of James Cook, regarded as one of the greatest and most humane explorers, and tells the tragic story of the European impact on Australia, Tahiti and Antarctica in the years that followed Captain Cook's great voyages of discovery. It details how good intentions and the economic imperatives of the time led to disaster, corruption and annihilation.

To get an idea of life on a Kimberley cattle station last century, *Kings in Grass Castles* and *Sore in the Saddle*, both by Dame Mary Durack, are well worth getting hold of.

Fiction

You don't need to worry about bringing a few good novels from home for your trip to Australia; there's plenty of excellent recent Australian literature including the novels and short stories of Helen Garner, Kate Grenville, Elizabeth Jolley, Thomas Kenneally, Peter Carey, Thea Astley, Tim Winton and Beverley Farmer.

Some Australian classics (these have also been made into films) include *The Getting of Wisdom* by Henry Handel Richardson, *Picnic at Hanging Rock* by Joan Lindsay, and *My Brilliant Career* by Miles Franklin. *For the Term of his Natural Life*, by Marcus Clarke, was one of the first books to be made into a film, in the late 19th century.

The works of Banjo Paterson *(The Man from Snowy River*, for example), Henry Lawson, Frank Hardy, Alan Marshall *(I Can Jump Puddles)* and Albert Facey *(A Fortunate Life)* make interesting reading. May Gibbs wrote *Snugglepot & Cuddlepie* – the story of two gumnut babies – one of the first bestselling Australian children's books.

The novels of the Nobel prizewinner Patrick White are difficult but rewarding – try *Voss*, the story of a 19th-century explorer and his lover left behind in the stifling social climate of middle-class Sydney.

Travel Accounts

Accounts of travels in Australia include the marvellous *Tracks*, by Robyn Davidson. It's the amazing story of a young woman who sets out alone to walk from Alice Springs to the Western Australia coast with her camels – proof that you can do anything if you try hard enough. It almost single-handedly inspired the current Australian interest in camel safaris!

Quite another sort of travel is Tony Horwitz's *One for the Road*, an often hilarious account of a high-speed hitchhiking trip around Australia (Oz through a windscreen). In contrast, *The Ribbon & the Ragged Square*, by Linda Christmas, is an intelligent, sober account of a nine-month investigatory trip round Oz by a *Guardian* journalist from England. There's lots of background and history as well as first-hand reporting and interviews.

In the Land of Oz recounts Howard Jacobson's circuit of the country. It's amusing at times, but through most of the book you're left wondering when the long-suffering Ros is finally going to thump the twerp!

The late Bruce Chatwin's book *The Songlines* tells of his experiences among central Australian Aborigines and makes more sense of the Dreamtime, sacred sites, sacred songs and the traditional Aboriginal way of life than 10 learned tomes put together. Along the way it also delves into the origins of humankind and throws in some pithy anecdotes about modern Australia.

Travel Guides

Burnum Burnum's Aboriginal Australia is subtitled 'a traveller's guide'. If you want to explore Australia from the Aboriginal point of view, this large and lavish hardback is the book for you.

For trips into the outback in your own car Brian Sheedy's *Outback on a Budget* includes lots of practical advice. There are a number of other books about vehicle preparation and driving in the outback.

Surfing Australia's East Coast by Aussie surf star Nat Young is a slim, cheap, comprehensive guide to the best breaks from Victoria to Fraser Island. He's also written the *Surfing & Sailboard Guide to Australia* which covers the whole country. Surfing enthusiasts can also look for the expensive coffee-table book *Atlas of Australian Surfing*, by Mark Warren.

If you want to really understand the Barrier Reef's natural history, look for *Australia's Great Barrier Reef*. It's colourful, expensive and nearly as big as the Barrier Reef itself. There's also a cheaper abbreviated paperback version. Lonely Planet's *Islands of Australia's Great Barrier Reef* book gives you all the practical info you'll need for making the most of the reef. *Australia's Wonderful Wildlife* (Australian Women's Weekly) is the shoestringer's equivalent of a coffee-table book – a cheap paperback with lots of great photos of the animals you didn't see, or those that didn't stay still when you pointed your camera at them.

Lonely Planet's *Bushwalking in Australia* describes 23 walks of different lengths and difficulty in various parts of the country, ranging from an easy two-day stroll along the coastline of the Royal National Park near Sydney, to a strenuous 10-day bushwalk on the exposed peaks of the Western Arthur Range in Tasmania.

There are state-by-state Reader's Digest guides to coasts and national parks, such as the *Coast of New South Wales*, and Gregory's guides to national parks, such as *National Parks of New South Wales* (a handy reference listing access, facilities, activities and so on for all parks).

MEDIA

Australia has a wide range of media although a few big companies (Rupert Murdoch's News Corporation and Kerry Packer's Consolidated Press being the best-known) own an awful lot of what there is to read and watch.

Newspapers & Magazines

Each major city tends to have at least one important daily, often backed up by a tabloid paper and also by evening papers. The *Sydney Morning Herald* and the Melbourne *Age* are two of the most important dailies. There's also the *Australian*, a Murdoch-owned paper and the country's only national daily.

Weekly newspapers and magazines include an Australian edition of *Time* and a combined edition of the Australian news magazine the *Bulletin* and *Newsweek*. The *Guardian Weekly* is widely available and good for international news.

Radio & TV

The national advertising-free TV and radio network is the ABC. In most places there are a couple of ABC radio stations and a host of commercial stations, both AM and FM, featuring the whole gamut of radio possibilities, from rock to talkback to 'beautiful music'.

In Sydney and Melbourne there are the ABC, three commercial TV stations and SBS, a government-sponsored multicultural TV station. Around the country the number of TV stations varies from place to place; there are regional TV stations but in some remote areas the ABC may be all you can receive.

FILM & PHOTOGRAPHY

If you come to Australia via Hong Kong or Singapore it's worth buying film there but otherwise Australian film prices are not too far out of line with those of the rest of the Western world. Including developing, 36-exposure Kodachrome 64 or Fujichrome 100 slide films cost from around $20, but with a little shopping around you can find it for around $15 – even less if you buy it in quantity.

There are plenty of camera shops in all the big cities and standards of camera service are high. Developing standards are also high, with many places offering one-hour developing of print film. Melbourne is the main centre for developing Kodachrome slide film in the South-East Asian region.

Photography is no problem, but in the outback you have to allow for the exceptional intensity of the light. Best results in the outback regions are obtained early in the morning and late in the afternoon. As the sun gets higher, colours appear washed out. You must also allow for the intensity of reflected light when taking shots on the Barrier Reef or at other coastal locations. In the outback, especially in the summer, allow for temperature extremes and do your best to keep film as cool as possible, particularly after exposure. Other film and camera hazards are dust in the outback and humidity in the tropical regions of the far north.

As in any country, politeness goes a long way when taking photographs; ask before taking pictures of people. Note that many Aborigines do not like to have their photographs taken, even from a distance.

HEALTH

So long as you have not visited an infected country in the past 14 days (aircraft refuelling stops do not count) no vaccinations are required for entry. Naturally, if you're going to be travelling around in outlandish places apart from Australia, a good collection of immunisations is highly advisable.

Medical care in Australia is first-class and only moderately expensive. A typical visit to the doctor costs around $35. Health insurance cover is available in Australia, but there is usually a waiting period after you sign up before any claims can be made. If you have an immediate health problem, contact the casualty section at the nearest public hospital.

Travel Insurance

Even if you normally carry health or hospitalisation insurance or live in a country where health care is provided by the government it's still a good idea to buy some inexpensive travellers' insurance that covers both health and loss of baggage.

Make sure the policy includes health care and medication in the countries you plan to visit and includes a flight home for you and anyone you're travelling with, should your condition warrant it.

Medical Kit

It's always a good idea to travel with a basic medical kit even when your destination is a country like Australia where most first aid supplies are readily available. Some of the items that should be included are: Band-Aids, a sterilised gauze bandage, elastoplast, cotton wool, a thermometer, tweezers, scissors, antibiotic cream and ointment, condoms (and other contraceptives if necessary), an antiseptic agent, burn cream, insect repellent and multivitamins. Calamine lotion, anti-histamine cream and old-fashioned Tiger Balm are all useful for insect bites.

Don't forget any medication you're already taking, and paracetamol or aspirin (for pain and fever).

Health Precautions

Travellers from the northern hemisphere need to be aware of the intensity of the sun in Australia. Those ultra-violet rays can have you burnt to a crisp even on an overcast day, so if in doubt wear protective cream, a wide-brimmed hat and a long-sleeved shirt with a collar. Australia has a high incidence of skin cancer, a fact directly connected to exposure to the sun. Be careful.

The contraceptive pill is available on prescription only, so a visit to a doctor is necessary. Doctors are listed in the Yellow Pages phone book or you can visit the outpatients section of a public hospital. Condoms are available from chemists, some all night stores such as 7-Eleven, and vending machines in the public toilets of hotels and universities.

EMERGENCY

For fire, police or ambulance, dial 000.

There is a telephone interpreter service available nationwide. Check the Community pages at the beginning of the White Pages phone book for the local number. Other telephone crisis services, such as Rape Crisis Centres, are also listed there.

DANGERS & ANNOYANCES
Animal Hazards

In Australia there are a few unique and sometimes dangerous creatures, although it's unlikely that you'll come across any of them, particularly if you stick to the cities. Here's a rundown just in case.

The best known danger in the Australian outback, and the one that captures visitors' imaginations, is snakes. Although there are many venomous snakes there are few that are aggressive, and unless you have the bad fortune to stand on one it's unlikely that you'll be bitten. Taipans and tiger snakes, however, will attack if alarmed. Sea snakes can also be dangerous.

To minimise your chances of being bitten always wear boots, socks and long trousers when walking through undergrowth where snakes may be present. Don't put your hands into holes and crevices, and be careful when collecting firewood.

Snake bites do not cause instantaneous death and antivenenes are usually available. Keep the victim calm and still, wrap the bitten limb tightly, as you would for a sprained ankle, and then attach a splint to immobilise it. Then seek medical help, if possible with the dead snake for identification. Don't attempt to catch the snake if there is even a remote possibility of being bitten again. Tourniquets and sucking out the poison are now comprehensively discredited.

We've got a couple of nasty spiders too, including the funnel-web, the redback and the white-tail, so it's best not to play with any spider. Funnel-web spiders are found in New South Wales and their bite is treated in the same way as snake bite. For redback bites apply ice and seek medical attention.

Among the splendid variety of biting insects the mosquito and march fly are the most common. The common bush tick (found in the forest and scrub country along the eastern coast of Australia) can be dangerous if left lodged in the skin, as the toxin the tick excretes can cause paralysis and sometimes death – check your body for lumps every night if you're walking in tick-infested areas. The tick should be removed by dousing it with stove fuel (shellite, methylated spirits and kerosene all work) and levering it out intact.

Leeches are common, and while they will suck your blood they are not dangerous and are easily removed by the application of salt or heat.

Up north the saltwater crocodile can be a real danger and has killed a number of people (travellers and locals). They are found in river estuaries and large rivers, sometimes a long way inland, so before diving into that inviting, cool water find out from the locals whether it's croc-free. (For more information see the Flora & Fauna section of the preceding chapter.)

In the sea, the box jellyfish, or sea wasp as it's known, occurs north of Great Keppel Island (see the Queensland chapter) during summer and can be fatal. It's responsible for more deaths than any other non-human creature in Australia (sharks, crocs and snakes included). The stinging tentacles spread several metres away from the sea wasp's body; by the time you see it you're likely to have been stung – and it's said you only get stung once in a lifetime! If someone is stung, they are likely to run out of the sea screaming and collapse on the beach, with weals on their body as though they've been whipped.

Box jellyfish

They may stop breathing. Douse the stings with vinegar (available on many beaches or from nearby houses), do not try to remove the tentacles from the skin, and treat as for snake bite. If there's a first-aider present, they may have to apply artificial respiration until the ambulance gets there. Above all, stay out of the sea when the sea wasps are around – the locals are ignoring that lovely water for an excellent reason.

The blue-ringed octopus and Barrier Reef cone shells can also be fatal so don't pick them up. If someone is stung, apply pressure bandage, monitor breathing carefully and conduct mouth-to-mouth resuscitation if breathing stops.

When reef walking you must always wear shoes to protect your feet against coral. In tropical waters there are stonefish – venomous fish that look like a flat piece of rock on the sea bed. Also, watch out for the scorpion fish which has venomous spines.

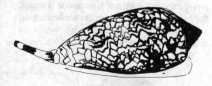

Cone shell

On the Road

Cows and kangaroos can be a real hazard to the driver. A collision with one will badly damage your car and probably kill the animal. Unfortunately, other drivers are even more dangerous and particularly those who drink. Australia has an appalling road toll, particularly in the countryside, so don't drink and drive and please take care. See the Getting Around chapter for more on driving hazards.

Bushfires & Blizzards

Bushfires happen every year in Australia. Don't be the mug who starts one. In hot, dry, windy weather, be extremely careful with any naked flame – no cigarette butts out of car windows, please. On a Total Fire Ban Day (listen to the radio or watch the billboards on country roads), it is forbidden even to use a camping stove in the open. The locals will not be amused if they catch you breaking this particular law.

If you're unfortunate enough to find yourself driving through a bushfire, stay inside your car and try to park off the road in an open space, away from trees, until the danger's past. Lie on the floor under the dashboard, covering yourself with a wool blanket if possible. The front of the fire should pass quickly, and you will be much safer than if you were out in the open.

Bushwalkers should take local advice before setting out. On a Total Fire Ban Day, don't go – delay your trip until the weather has changed. Chances are that it will be so unpleasantly hot and windy, you'll be better off anyway in an air-conditioned pub sipping a cool beer.

If you're out in the bush and you see smoke, even at a great distance, take it seriously. Go to the nearest open space, downhill if possible. A forested ridge is the most dangerous place to be. Bushfires move very quickly and change direction with the wind.

Having said all that, more bushwalkers die of cold than in bushfires! Even in summer, temperatures can drop below freezing at night in the mountains. The Tasmanian mountains can have blizzards at almost any time of year.

WORK

Officially, working in Australia on a regular tourist visa is completely *verboten*. If you have a 12-month 'working holiday' visa you can officially only work for three out of those 12 months, but there's little to stop you from doing more than that. Many travellers on tourist visas do surreptitiously find casual work, although it is becoming more difficult to do so. There are no social security cards, national insurance cards or the like in Australia *yet*, although it's getting harder to find work if you don't have a Tax File Number (see below).

With the current economic downturn in Australia, casual work has become increasingly difficult to find. Gone are the days when you could rock in to practically any town or city and find some sort of paid casual work. Many travellers who have budgeted on finding work are returning home early, simply because the work they hoped to find just isn't available. If you are coming to Australia with the intention of working, make sure you have enough funds to cover you for your stay, or have a contingency plan if the work is not forthcoming. Having said that, it *is* still possible to find short-term work, it's just that the opportunities are far fewer than in the past.

To receive wages in Australia you must be in possession of a Tax File Number. This applies even to casual work. Some people will employ you without a Tax File Number but you'll get taxed at 48%, as against 29% with a number. To apply for a number, pick up a form from a post office, or contact the Taxation Department in a capital city. You'll need to show your passport and a visa which entitles you to work. Unless you are a resident, you are not entitled to a tax refund. Fruit picking is one of the best known short-term job prospects – see the chart for what is being picked where and when. Travellers also sometimes find work at the resorts, particularly along the Barrier Reef. Getting a foot in the door is often difficult and the island resorts tend to work on the NBO (next boat out) principle, sacking excess staff as soon as times go slack, taking more on when school holidays roll around.

Other areas where travellers have traditionally found work include temporary secretarial or nursing, bar staff, fishing and prawn trawlers.

The Commonwealth Employment Service (CES) has over 300 offices around the country, and the staff usually have a good idea of what's available where.

The book *Work Your Way Around the World* by Susan Griffiths (Vacation Work, UK, or Writers Digest, USA) is a good information source on short-term jobs in many countries. The various backpackers' magazines, newspapers and hostels are good information sources – some local employers even advertise on their notice boards.

Fruit & Vegetable Picking Seasons The table here lists the main harvest times of the crops where casual employment is a possibility. Enquire at the local CES office.

New South Wales

Crop	Time	Region/s
Grapes	Feb-Mar	Griffith, Hunter Valley
Peaches	Feb-Mar	Griffith
Apples	Feb-Apr	Orange
Cherries	Nov-Jan	Orange
Oranges	Dec-Mar	Griffith
Bananas	year-round	North Coast

Queensland

Crop	Time	Region/s
Bananas	year-round	Innisfail
Grapes	Jan-Feb	Warwick
Pears	Feb-Mar	Warwick
Apples	Feb-Mar	Warwick
Various fruit & veg	May-Nov	Bowen
Asparagus	Aug-Dec	Warwick
Tomatoes	May-Nov	Bundaberg
Stone fruits	Dec	Warwick

South Australia

Crop	Time	Region/s
Dried fruits/peaches	Feb-Mar	Riverland
Wine grapes	Feb-Apr	Riverland, Barossa, Clare
Apples/pears	Feb-Apr	Adelaide Hills
Strawberries	Oct-Feb	Adelaide Hills
Apricots	Dec-Feb	Riverland

Tasmania

Crop	Time	Region/s
Apples/pears	Feb-May	Huon Valley, Tasman Pen.
Soft fruit	Dec-Jan	Huon Valley, Kingston, Derwent Valley

Victoria

Crop	Time	Region/s
Peaches	Jan-Mar	Shepparton
Grapes	Jan-Apr	Mildura
Tomatoes	Feb-Apr	Shepparton, Echuca
Strawberries	Oct-Apr	Echuca, Dandenongs
Cherries	Nov-Feb	Dandenongs

Western Australia

Crop	Time	Region/s
Grapes	Feb-Apr	Albany, Midland
Apples/pears	Mar-May	Manjimup
Melons, vegies	May-Oct	Kununurra

ACTIVITIES

Apart from the well-known spectator sports of football, cricket and tennis, there are plenty of activities that you can take part in while travelling round the country.

Australia has a flourishing skiing industry – a fact that takes a number of travellers by surprise – with snowfields that straddle New South Wales's border with Victoria. There's information on the Victorian snowfields in the Victorian Alps section of the Victoria chapter, and likewise for the Snowy Mountains in the New South Wales chapter. Tasmania's snowfields aren't as developed as those of Victoria and New South Wales, but if you do want to ski while in Tassie you can read all about it in the Activities section of the Tasmania chapter.

If skiing isn't your scene how about bushwalking? Not only is it cheap but you can do it anywhere. There are many fantastic walks in the various national parks around the country and information on how to get there is in Lonely Planet's *Bushwalking in Australia* as well as in the Activities sections of each state.

If you're interested in surfing you'll find great beaches and surf in most states. There's great scuba diving all around the coast but particularly along the Queensland Great Barrier Reef where there are also many dive schools. Many travellers come to Australia with the goal of getting a scuba certificate during their stay.

In Victoria you can go horse riding in the High Country and follow the route of the Snowy Mountains cattle people, whose lives were the subject of the film *The Man from Snowy River*, which in turn was based on the poem by Banjo Paterson. In northern Queensland you can ride horses through rainforests and along sand dunes and swim with them in the sea. You can find horses to hire just about anywhere in the country.

You can cycle all around Australia; for the athletic there are long, challenging routes and for the not so masochistic there are plenty of great day trips. In most states there are excellent roads and helpful bicycle societies with lots of maps and useful tips and advice. See the Getting Around chapter and individual state chapters for more advice.

For the more adventurous, camel riding has taken off in the Northern Territory. If you've done it in India or Egypt or you just fancy yourself as the explorer/outdoors type, then here's your chance. (You never know, next it might be croc riding!)

Windsurfing, paragliding, rafting and hang-gliding are among the many other sports enjoyed by Australians and available to travellers. For information on any of these or other activities see the relevant chapters or contact any of the state tourist bureaus.

ACCOMMODATION

Australia is very well equipped with youth hostels, backpackers' hostels and camp sites – the cheapest shelter you can find. Furthermore, there are plenty of motels around the country and in holiday regions like the Queensland coast intense competition tends to keep the prices down.

A typical town of a few thousand people will have a basic motel at around $35/45 for singles/doubles, an old town centre hotel with rooms (shared bathrooms) at say $25/30, and a caravan park – probably with tent sites for around $8 and on-site vans or cabins for $21 to $25 for two. If the town is on anything like a main road or is bigger, it'll probably have several of each. You'll rarely have much trouble finding *somewhere* to lay your head in Oz, even when there are no hostels, although some surprisingly small and seemingly insignificant towns have backpackers' hostels these days. If there's a group of you, the rates for three or four people in a room are always worth checking. Often there are larger 'family' rooms or units with two bedrooms.

There are a couple of give-away backpackers' newspapers available at hostels around the country, and these have fairly up-to-date listings of hostels, although they give neither prices nor details of each hostel.

For more comprehensive accommodation listings, the state automobile clubs produce directories listing hotels, motels, holiday flats, camp sites and even some backpackers' hostels, in almost every little town in the country. They're updated every year so the prices are generally fairly current. They're available from the clubs for a nominal charge if you're a member or a member of an affiliated club enjoying reciprocal rights. Alternatively, some state tourist offices (notably the Northern Territory and Western Australia) also put out frequently updated guides to local accommodation.

Camping & Caravanning

The camping story in Australia is partly excellent and partly rather annoying! The excellent side is that there is a great number of camp sites and you'll almost always find space available. If you want to get around Australia on the cheap then camping is the cheapest way of all, with nightly costs for two of around $8 to $15.

One of the drawbacks is that camp sites are often intended more for caravanners (house trailers for any North Americans out there) than for campers and the tent campers get little thought in these places. The New Zealanders could certainly show Australian camp site operators how it's done. Over there camp sites often have a kitchen and dining area where you can eat. If it's raining you're not stuck with huddling in your car or tent. The fact that in Australia most of the sites are called 'caravan parks' indicates who gets most attention.

In many Australian camp sites the top soil is scraped away to make the ground more suitable for caravans, so pitching a tent becomes very hard work.

Equally bad is that in most big cities sites are well away from the centre. This is not inconvenient in small towns, but in general if you're planning to camp around Australia you really need your own transport. Brisbane is the worst city in Australia in this respect because council regulations actually forbid tents within a 22-km radius of the centre. Although there are some sites in Brisbane within that radius, they're strictly for caravans – no campers allowed.

Still, it's not all gloom; in general Australian camp sites are well kept, conveniently located and excellent value. Many sites also have on-site vans which you can rent for the night. These give you the comfort of a caravan without the inconvenience of actually towing one of the damned things. On-site cabins are also widely available, and these are more like a small self-contained unit. They usually have one bedroom, or at least an area which can be screened off from the rest of the unit – just the thing if you have small kids. Cabins also have the advantage of having their own bathroom and toilet, although this is sometimes an optional extra. They are also much less cramped than a caravan, and the price difference is not always that great – say $25 to $30 for an on-site van, $30 to $40 for a cabin. In winter, if you're going to be using this sort of accommodation on a regular basis, it's worth investing in a small heater of some sort as many vans and cabins are unheated.

I've made trips around Australia using every sort of accommodation, from youth hostels to motels, but one of the most successful was a trip Maureen and I made on a motorcycle. We had a little tent strapped across the handlebars and managed to camp everywhere we went, from Canberra to Cooktown, Airlie Beach to Ayers Rock. On the few occasions when sitting in a tent listening to the rain beat down (one of those times being in Alice Springs, believe it or not!) was too oppressive, we managed to find an on-site van to shelter in.

– Tony Wheeler

Youth Hostels

Australia has a very active Youth Hostel Association (YHA) and you'll find hostels all over the country, with more official hostels and backpackers' hostels popping up all the time.

YHA hostels provide basic accommodation, usually in small dormitories or bunk rooms although more and more of them are providing twin rooms for couples. The nightly charges are rock bottom – usually between $8 and $15 a night.

With the increased competition from the proliferation of backpackers' hostels, many YHA hostels have done away with the old fetishes for curfews and doing chores, but still retain segregated dorms. Many even take non-YHA members, although there may be a small 'temporary membership' charge. To become a full YHA member in Australia costs $22 a year (there's also a $16 joining fee). You can join at a state office or at any youth hostel.

Youth hostels are part of an international organisation, the International Youth Hostel Federation (IYHF), so if you're already a member of the YHA in your own country, your membership entitles you to use the Australian hostels. Hostels are great places for meeting people and great travellers' centres, and in many busier hostels the visitors will outnumber the Australians. The annual *YHA Accommodation Guide* booklet, which is available from any YHA office in Australia and from some YHA offices overseas, lists all the YHA hostels around Australia with useful little maps showing how to find them. YHA members are eligible for discounts at various places and these facilities are also listed in the handbook.

You must have a regulation sheet sleeping bag or bed linen – for hygiene reasons a regular sleeping bag will not do. If you haven't got sheets they can be rented at many hostels (usually for $3), but it's cheaper, after a few nights' stay, to have your own. YHA offices and some larger hostels sell the official YHA sheet bag.

Most hostels have cooking facilities and some place where you can sit and talk. There are usually laundry facilities and often excellent notice boards. Many hostels have a maximum-stay period – because some hostels are permanently full it would hardly be fair for people to stay too long when others are being turned away.

The YHA defines its hostels as the simpler 'shelter' style and the larger 'standard' hostels. They range from tiny places to big modern buildings, with everything from historic convict buildings to a disused railway station in between. Most hostels have a manager who checks you in when you arrive, keeps the peace and assigns the chores. Because you have so much more contact with a hostel manager than the person in charge of other styles of accommodation he or she can really make or break the place. Good managers are often great characters and well worth getting to know.

Accommodation can usually be booked directly with the manager, through the YHA Central Reservations Bureau in Sydney (☎ (02) 267 3044) or with the state head office. The YHA handbook tells all.

The Australian head office is in Sydney, at the Australian Youth Hostels Association, 10 Hallett St, Camperdown, NSW 2050. If you can't get a YHA hostel booklist in your own country write to them but otherwise deal with the state offices:

New South Wales
    176 Day St, Sydney, NSW 2000 (☎ (02) 267 3044)
Northern Territory
    Darwin Hostel Complex, Beaton Rd via Hidden Valley Rd, Berrimah, NT 0828 (☎ (089) 84 3902)
Queensland
    154 Roma St, Brisbane, QLD 4000 (☎ (07) 236 1680)
South Australia
    38 Sturt St, Adelaide, SA 5000 (☎ (03) 231 5583)
Tasmania
    1st floor, 28 Criterion St, Hobart, Tas 7000 (☎ (002) 34 9617)
Victoria
    205 King St, Melbourne, Vic 3000 (☎ (03) 670 7991)
Western Australia
    65 Francis St, Northbridge, Perth, WA 6003 (☎ (09) 227 5122)

Not all of the approximately 130 hostels listed in the handbook are actually owned by the YHA. Some are 'associate hostels', which generally abide by hostel regulations but are owned by other organisations or individuals. You don't need to be a YHA member to stay at an associated hostel. Others are 'alternative accommodation' and do not totally fit the hostel blueprint. They might be motels which keep some hostel-style accommodation available for YHA members or camp sites with an on-site van or two kept aside, or even places just like hostels but where the operators don't want to abide by all the hostel regulations.

Backpackers' Hostels
In the last few years the number of backpackers' hostels has increased dramatically. This is partly a result of the recession in Australia; it seems that while tourist numbers are, in general, lower, the backpacker market continues to flourish. The standards of these hostels vary enormously. Some are rundown inner-city hotels where the owners have tried to fill empty rooms; unless renovations have been done, these

places are generally pretty gloomy and depressing. Others are former motels, so each unit, typically with four to six beds, will have fridge, TV and bathroom. When the climate allows, there's usually a pool too. The drawback with these places is that the communal areas and cooking facilities are often lacking, as motels were never originally designed for communal use. You may also find yourself sharing a room with someone who wants to watch TV all night – it happens!

Still other hostels are purpose built as backpackers' hostels; these are usually the best places in terms of facilities, although sometimes they are too big and lack any personalised service. As often as not the managers have backpackers running the places, and usually it's not too long before standards start to slip. Some of these places, particularly along the Queensland coast, actively promote themselves as 'party' hostels, so if you want a quiet time, they're often not the place to be. The best places are often the smaller, more intimate hostels where the owner is also the manager. These are usually the older hostels which were around long before the 'backpacker boom'.

With the proliferation of hostels has also come intense competition. Hop off a bus in any town on the Queensland coast and chances are there'll be at least three or four touts from the various hostels, all trying to lure you in. To this end many have introduced inducements, such as the first night free, and virtually all have courtesy buses. Even the YHA hostels have had to resort to this to stay in the race in some places.

Prices at backpackers' hostels are generally in line with YHA hostels, typically $10 to $12, although the $7 bed is still alive and well (in Cairns).

There are also a couple of organisations which you can join where, for a modest fee, you'll receive a discount card and a list of participating hostels. This is hardly a great inducement to join but you do also receive useful discounts on other services, such as Bus Australia and Greyhound passes, so they may be worth considering.

As with YHA hostels, the success of a hostel largely depends on the friendliness and willingness of the managers. One practice that many people find objectionable – in independent hostels only, since it never happens in YHAs – is the 'vetting' of Australians and sometimes New Zealanders, who may be asked to provide a passport or double ID which they may not carry. Virtually all city hostels ask everyone for some ID – usually a passport – but this can also be used as a way of keeping unwanted customers out.

Some places will actually only admit overseas backpackers. This happens mostly in cities and when it does it's because the hostel in question has had problems with some locals treating the place more as a doss house than a hostel – drinking too much, making too much noise, getting into fights and the like. Hostels which discourage or ban Aussies say it's only a rowdy minority that makes trouble, but they can't take the risk on who'll turn out bad. If you're an Aussie and encounter this kind of reception, the best you can do is persuade the desk people that you're genuinely travelling the country, and aren't just looking for a cheap place to crash for a while.

The Ys

In a number of places in Australia accommodation is provided by the YMCA or YWCA. There are variations from place to place – some are mainly intended for permanent accommodation, some are run like normal commercial guesthouses. They're generally excellent value and usually conveniently located. You don't have to be a YMCA or YWCA member to stay at them, although sometimes you get a discount if you are. Accommodation in the Ys is generally in fairly straightforward rooms, usually with shared bathroom facilities. Some Ys also have dormitory-style accommodation. Note, however, that not all YMCA or YWCA organisations around the country offer accommodation; it's mainly in the big cities.

Another organisation that sometimes offers accommodation is the CWA (Country

Women's Association), but this is mainly in the country and usually for women only.

Colleges

Although it is students who get first chance at these, nonstudents can also stay at many university colleges during the uni vacations. These places can be relatively cheap and comfortable and provide an opportunity for you to meet people. Costs are typically from about $15 for B&B for students, twice that if you're not a student.

This type of accommodation is usually available only during the summer vacations (from November to February). Additionally, it must almost always be booked ahead; you can't just turn up. Many of Australia's new universities are way out in the suburbs and are inconvenient to get to unless you have wheels.

Hotels

For the budget traveller, hotels in Australia are generally older places – new accommodation will usually be motels. To understand why Australia's hotels are the way they are requires delving into the history books a little. When the powers that be decided Australia's drinking should only be at the most inconvenient hours, they also decided that drinking places should also be hotels. So every place which in Britain would be a 'pub' in Australia was a 'hotel', but often in name only.

The original idea of forcing pubs to provide accommodation for weary travellers has long faded into history and this ludicrous law has been rolled back. Every place called a hotel does not necessarily have rooms to rent, although many still do. A 'private hotel', as opposed to a 'licensed hotel', really is a hotel and does not serve alcohol. A 'guesthouse' is much the same as a 'private hotel'.

New hotels being built today are mainly of the Hilton variety; smaller establishments will usually be motels. So, if you're staying in a hotel, it will normally mean an older place, often with rooms without private facilities. Unfortunately many older places are on the drab, grey and dreary side. You get a strong feeling that because they've got the rooms they try to turn a dollar on them, but without much enthusiasm. Others, fortunately, are colourful places with some real character. Although the word 'hotel' doesn't always mean they'll have rooms, the places that do have rooms usually make it pretty plain that they are available. If a hotel is listed in an accommodation directory you can be pretty sure it really will offer you a bed. If there's nothing that looks like a reception desk or counter, just ask in the bar.

You'll find hotels all around the town centres in smaller towns while in larger towns the hotels that offer accommodation are often to be found close to the railway stations. In some older towns, or in historic centres like the gold mining towns, the old hotels can be really magnificent. The rooms themselves may be pretty old-fashioned and unexciting, but the hotel facade and entrance area will often be quite extravagant. In the outback the old hotels are often places of real character. They are often the real 'town centre' and you'll meet all the local eccentrics there.

A bright word about hotels (guesthouses and private hotels, too) is that the breakfasts are usually excellent – big and 100% filling. A substantial breakfast is what this country was built on and if your hotel is still into serving a real breakfast you'll probably feel it could last you until breakfast comes around next morning. Generally, hotels will have rooms for around $20 to $30. When comparing prices, remember to check if it includes breakfast.

In airports and bus and railway stations, there are often information boards with direct-dial phones to book accommodation. These are generally for the more expensive hotels, but sometimes they offer discounts if you use the direct phone to book. The staff at bus stations are helpful when it comes to finding cheap and convenient places to stay.

Motels, Serviced Apartments & Holiday Flats

If you've got wheels and want a more

modern place with your own bathroom and other facilities, then you're moving in to the motel bracket. Motels cover the earth in Australia, just like in the USA, but they're usually located away from the city centres. Prices vary and with the motels, unlike hotels, singles are often not much cheaper than doubles. The reason is quite simple – in the old hotels many of the rooms really are singles, relics of the days when single men travelled the country looking for work. In motels, the rooms are almost always doubles. You'll sometimes find motel rooms for less than $30, and in most places will have no trouble finding something for $45 or less.

Holiday flats and serviced apartments are much the same thing and bear some relationship to motels. Basically holiday flats are found in holiday areas, serviced apartments in cities. A holiday flat is much like a motel room but usually has a kitchen or cooking facilities so you can fix your own food. Usually holiday flats are not serviced like motels – you don't get your bed made up every morning and the cups washed out. In some holiday flats you actually have to provide your own sheets and bedding but others are operated just like motel rooms with a kitchen. Most motels in Australia provide at least tea/coffee making facilities and a small fridge, but a holiday flat will also have cooking utensils, cutlery, crockery and so on.

Holiday flats are often rented on a weekly basis but even in these cases it's worth asking if daily rates are available. Paying for a week, even if you stay only for a few days, can still be cheaper than having those days at a higher daily rate. If there's more than just two of you, another advantage of holiday flats is that you can often find them with two or more bedrooms. A two-bedroom holiday flat is typically priced at about 1½ times the cost of a comparable single-bedroom unit.

In holiday areas like the Queensland coast, motels and holiday flats will often be virtually interchangeable terms – there's nothing really to distinguish one from the other. In big cities, on the other hand, the serviced apartments are often a little more obscure, although they may be advertised in the newspaper's classified ads.

Other Possibilities

That covers the usual conventional accommodation possibilities, but there are lots of less conventional ones. You don't have to camp in camp sites, for example. There are plenty of parks where you can camp for free, or (in Queensland at least) roadside shelters where short-term camping is permitted. Australia has lots of bush where nobody is going to complain about you putting up a tent – or even notice you.

In the cities if you want to stay longer the first place to look for a share flat or a room is the classified ad section of the daily newspaper. Wednesdays and Saturdays are the best days for these ads. Notice boards in universities, hostel offices certain popular bookshops and other contact centres are good places to look for flats/houses to share or rooms to rent.

Australia is a land of farms (sorry, stations) and one of the best ways to come to grips with Australian life is to spend a few days on a farm. Many farms offer accommodation where you can just sit back and watch how it's done, while others like to get you more actively involved in the day-to-day activities. This sort of accommodation has become increasingly popular in the last few years. With commodity prices falling daily, mountainous wool stockpiles and a general rural crisis, tourism offers the hope of at least some income for farmers, at a time when many are being forced off the land. The state tourist offices can advise you on what's available; prices are pretty reasonable.

Finally, how about life on a houseboat? – see the Murray River sections in Victoria and South Australia.

FOOD

The culinary delights can be one of the real highlights of Australia. Time was – like 25 years ago – when Australia's food (mighty steaks apart) had a reputation for being like England's, only worse. Well, perhaps not quite that bad, but getting on that way. Miracles happen and Australia's miracle was immigration. The Greeks, Yugoslavs, Italians, Lebanese and many others who flooded into Australia in the '50s and '60s brought, thank God, their food with them. More recent arrivals include the Vietnamese, whose communities are thriving in several cities.

So in Australia today you can have excellent Greek moussaka (and a bottle of retsina to wash it down), delicious Italian saltimbocca and pastas, or good, heavy German dumplings; you can perfume the air with garlic after stumbling out of a French bistro, or try all sorts of Middle Eastern and Arab treats. The Chinese have been sweet & souring since the gold-rush days, while more recently Indian, Thai and Malaysian restaurants have been all the rage. And for cheap eats, you can't beat some of the Vietnamese places.

Australian Food

Although there is no real Australian cuisine there is certainly some excellent Australian food to try. For a start there's the great Australian meat pie – every bit as sacred an institution as the hot dog is to a New Yorker. There are a few places that do a really good job on this classic dish, but the standard pie is an awful concoction of anonymous meat and dark gravy in a soggy pastry container. You'll have to try one though; the number consumed in Australia each year is phenomenal, and they're a real part of Australian culture.

Even more central to Australian eating habits is Vegemite. This strange, dark-coloured yeast spread is something only an Australian could love. Australians spread Vegemite on bread and become so addicted to it that anywhere in the world you find an Aussie, the jar of Vegemite is bound to be close at hand. Australian embassies the world over have the location of the nearest Vegemite retailer as one of their most-asked-for pieces of information.

The good news about Australian food is the fine ingredients. Nearly everything is grown right here in Australia so you're not eating food that has been shipped halfway around the world. Everybody knows about good Australian steaks ('This is cattle country, so eat beef you bastards', announce the farmers' bumper stickers), but there are lots of other things to try.

Australia has a superb range of seafood: fish like John Dory and the esteemed barramundi, or superb lobsters and other crustaceans like the engagingly named Moreton Bay bugs! Yabbies are freshwater crayfish and very good. Even vegetarians get a fair go in Australia; there are some excellent vegetarian restaurants and, once again, the vegetables are as fresh as you could ask for.

Where to Eat

If you want to feel right at home there are *McDonald's, Kentucky Frieds, Pizza Huts* and all the other familiar names looking no different than they do anywhere from New York to Amsterdam. There are also Chinese restaurants where the script is all in Chinese, little Lebanese places where you'd imagine the local PLO cell getting together for a meal, and every other national restaurant type you could imagine.

For real value for money there are a couple of dinky-di Australian eating places you should certainly try, though. For a start Australian delis are terrific and they'll put together a superb sandwich. Hunt out the authentic-looking ones in any big city and you'll get a sandwich any New York deli would have trouble matching, and I'm willing to bet it'll be half the price.

In the evening the best value is to be found in the pubs. Look for 'counter meals', so called because they used to be eaten at the bar counter. Some places still are just like that, while others are fancier, almost restaurant-like. Good counter meals are hard to beat for value for money, and although the food is usually of the simple steak-salad-chips variety, the quality is often excellent and prices are commendably low. The best counter meal places usually have serve-yourself salad tables where you can add as much salad, French bread and so on as you wish.

Counter meals are usually served as counter lunches or counter teas, the latter a hangover from the old northern English terminology where 'tea' meant the evening meal. One catch with pub meals is that they usually operate fairly strict hours. The evening meal time may be just 6 to 7.30 or 8 pm. Pubs doing counter meals often have a blackboard menu outside but some of the best places are quite anonymous – you simply have to know that this is the pub that does great food and furthermore that it's in the bar hidden away at the back. Counter meals vary enormously in price but in general the better class places with good serve-yourself salad tables will be in the $6 to $14 range for all the traditional dishes: steak, veal, chicken, and so on.

For rock-bottom prices the real shoe-stringers can also check out university and college cafeterias, the big department store cafeterias (Woolworths and Coles, for example), or even try sneaking into public service office cafeterias. Australians love their fish & chips just as much as the British and, just like in Britain, their quality can vary enormously – all the way from stodgy and horrible to really superb. Hamburger and fish & chip shops usually serve both these Aussie favourites. We've also got the full range of takeaway foods, from Italian to Mexican, Chinese to Lebanese.

DRINKS

In the nonalcoholic department Australians knock back Coke and flavoured milk like there's no tomorrow and also have some excellent mineral water brands. Coffee enthusiasts will be relieved to find good Italian cafes serving cappuccino and other coffees, often into the wee small hours and beyond. Beer and wine need their own explanations.

Beer

Australia's beer must be considered alongside the country's drinking habits.

The Six O'Clock Swill Way back in WW I the government of the day decided that all pubs should shut at 6 pm as a wartime austerity measure. Unfortunately when the war ended this wartime emergency move didn't. On one side the wowsers didn't want anybody to drink, and if Australia couldn't have prohibition like the USA, stopping drinking at 6 pm was at least a step in the right direction in their view. The other supporters of this terrible arrangement were, believe it or not, the breweries and pub owners. They discovered that shutting the pubs at 6 pm didn't really cut sales at all and it certainly cut costs. You didn't have to pay staff until late in the evening and you didn't have to worry about making your pub a pleasant place for a drink. People left work, rushed around to the pub and swallowed as much beer as they could before 6 pm. They definitely didn't have time to admire the decor.

This unhappy story didn't even end after WW II. In fact it carried right on into the '50s, before common sense finally came into play and the 'six o'clock swill' was consigned to history. Since that time the idea of the Australian pub as a bare and cheerless beer barn has gradually faded and there are now many pleasant pubs. More recently, drinking hours have been further relaxed and pubs can now open later in the evening and on Sundays.

Enough of the history, now for the beer. Australian beer will be fairly familiar to North Americans; it's similar to what's known as lager in the UK. It may taste like lemonade to the European real ale addict, but it packs quite a punch. It is invariably chilled before drinking.

Fosters is, of course, the best known international brand with a worldwide reputation. Each Australian state has its own beer brand and there'll be someone to sing the praises of each one: XXXX, pronounced fourex, and Powers (Queensland); Swan (Western Australia); Tooheys (New South Wales); and VB – Victoria Bitter (Victoria). Although most big-name beers are associated in particular with one state, they are available across the country. The smaller breweries generally seem to produce better beer – Cascade (Tasmania) and Coopers (South Australia) being two examples. Coopers also produce a stout which is popular among connoisseurs. A lot of Australians drink a mixture of stout and lemonade called portagaff.

Small 'boutique' brewers have also been making a comeback so you'll find one-off brands scattered around the country. Beers such as Redback, Dogbolter and Eumundi, while being more expensive than the big commercial brands, are definitely worth a try. For the homesick European, there are a few pubs in the major cities that brew their own bitter. Guinness is occasionally found on draught, usually in Irish pubs.

A word of warning to visitors: Australian beer has a higher alcohol content than British or American beers. Standard beer is generally around 4.9% alcohol, although most breweries now produce 'lite' beers, with an alcohol content of between 2% and 3.5%. Toohey's Blue – a new and tastier light beer – is sweeping the country as we go to press. And another warning: people who drive under the influence of alcohol lose their licences (unfortunately, drink-driving is a real problem in Australia). The maximum permissible blood alcohol concentration level for drivers in most parts of Australia is 0.05%.

All around Australia, beer, the containers it comes in, and the receptacles you drink it from are called by different names. Beer comes in stubbies, long necks, bottles, tinnies and twisties, depending on where you are. Ordering at the bar can be an intimidat-

ing business for the newly arrived traveller. A seven-oz beer is a glass (Victoria), a beer (Tasmania) or a seven (Queensland); a 10-oz beer is a pot (Victoria and Queensland), a middy (New South Wales and Western Australia) or a tenner (Queensland); while in New South Wales and Western Australia they also have the 15-oz schooner. In New South Wales, they're likely to ask if you want new or old, new being ordinary beer and old being stout. If in doubt, take local advice, which will readily be offered!

Beer Consumption Australians are not the world's greatest consumers of beer – that title goes to the Germans, who knock back nearly 150 litres per capita per year. But Darwin is reckoned to be the No 1 city for beer drinking. Its peak was the equivalent of 230 litres per man, woman and child in one year; with so much beer disappearing down Darwinites' throats, it's no surprise that they can run a boating regatta solely for boats made out of beer cans. When a party of Darwinites sailed to Singapore in the '70s in a beer-can boat, it was locally mooted that they inspired boatloads of Vietnamese refugees to take their chances in the opposite direction in real boats.

Australians are reckoned to be about the third biggest beer consumers in the world, about five to 10 litres behind the Germans, a litre or so less than the Belgians and neck and neck with the thirsty Czechs. The Poms are about 25 litres back in 10th place. Americans don't even rate. Australia's per capita beer consumption has, however, been on a steady decline for the past decade or so.

Wine
If you don't fancy Australian beer, then turn to wines. Australia has a great climate for wine producing and some superb wine areas. Best known are the Hunter Valley of New South Wales and the Barossa Valley of South Australia, but there are a great number of other wine-producing areas, each with its own enthusiastic promoters.

European wine experts now realise just how good Australian wines can be. So good in fact that the French have been getting rather miffed about the number of competitions they've been losing. Furthermore, Australia's wines are cheap and readily available. We pay less for our wine than the Californians do for theirs.

It takes a little while to become familiar

with Australian wineries and their styles but it's an effort worth making. All over Australia, but particularly in Melbourne, you'll find restaurants advertising that they're BYO. The initials stand for 'Bring Your Own' and it means that they're not licensed to serve alcohol but you are permitted to bring your own with you. This is a real boon to wine-loving but budget-minded travellers because you can bring your own bottle of wine from the local bottle shop or from that winery you visited last week and not pay any mark-up. In fact, most restaurants make only a small 'corkage' charge (typically 60c to $1 per person) if you bring your own, even though it's conceivable that without it they might sell you a bottle of mineral water or something.

An even more economical way of drinking Australian wine is to do it free at the wineries. In the wine-growing areas, most wineries have free tastings: you just zip straight in and say what you'd like to try. However, free wine tastings do not mean open slather drinking – the glasses are generally thimble-sized and it's expected that you will buy something if, for example, you taste every chardonnay that that vineyard has ever produced. Some wineries have decided that enough is enough and now have a small 'tasting fee' of a couple of dollars, refundable if you buy any wine.

ENTERTAINMENT
Cinema
The Australian film industry began as early as 1896, a year after the Lumière brothers opened the world's first cinema in Paris. Maurice Sestier, one of the Lumières' photographers, came to Australia and made the first films in the streets of Sydney and at Flemington Race Course during the Melbourne Cup.

Cinema historians regard an Australian film, *Soldiers of the Cross*, as the world's first 'real' movie. It was originally screened at the Melbourne Town Hall in 1901, cost £600 to make and was shown throughout America in 1902.

The next significant Australian film, *The*

Story of the Kelly Gang, was screened in 1907, and by 1911 the industry was flourishing. Low-budget films were being made in such quantities that they could be hired out or sold cheaply. Over 250 silent feature films were made before the 1930s when the *talkies* and Hollywood took over.

In the 1930s, film companies like Cinesound sprang up. Cinesound made 17 feature films between 1931 and 1940, many based on Australian history or literature. *Forty Thousand Horsemen*, directed by Cinesound's great film maker Charles Chauvel, was a highlight of this era of locally made and financed films which ended in 1959, the year of Chauvel's death.

Before the introduction of government subsidies during 1969 and 1970, the Australian film industry found it difficult to compete with US and British interests. The New Wave era of the 1970s, a renaissance of Australian cinema, produced films like *Picnic at Hanging Rock*, *Sunday Too Far Away*, *Caddie* and *The Devil's Playground*, which appealed to large local and international audiences. Since the '70s, Australian actors and directors like Mel Gibson, Judy Davis, Greta Scacchi, Paul Hogan, Bruce Beresford, Peter Weir, Gillian Armstrong and Fred Schepesi have gained international recognition. Films like *Gallipoli*, *The Year of Living Dangerously*, *Mad Max*, *Malcolm*, *Crocodile Dundee I* and *II*, *Proof*, *Holidays on the River Yarra* and *The Year My Voice Broke* have entertained and impressed audiences worldwide.

Spectator Sports
If you're an armchair – or wooden bench – sports fan Australia has plenty to offer. Australians play at least four types of football, each type being called 'football' by its aficionados. The season runs from about March to September.

Soccer is a bit of a poor cousin: it's widely played on an amateur basis but the national league is only semiprofessional and attracts a pathetically small following. It's slowly gaining popularity thanks in part to the success of the national team. At local level, there are ethnically based teams representing a wide range of national origins.

Rugby is the main game in New South Wales and Queensland, and it's rugby league, the 13-a-side working-class version, that attracts the crowds. The Winfield Cup competition produces the world's best rugby league – fast, fit and clever. Most of its teams are in Sydney but there are others in Canberra, Wollongong, Newcastle and Brisbane and on the Gold Coast. Rugby union, the 15-a-side game for amateurs, was less popular until Australia won the World Cup in 1991; it is now enjoying a revival!

Aussie rules is unique – only Gaelic football is anything like it. It's played by teams of 18 on an oval field with an oval ball that can be kicked, caught, hit with the hand or carried and bounced. You get six points for kicking the ball between two central posts (a goal) and one point for kicking it through side posts (a behind). A game lasts for four quarters of 25 minutes each. To take a 'mark' a player must catch a ball on the volley from a kick – in which case the player gets a free kick. A typical final score for one team is between 70 and 110.

Players cannot be sent off in the course of a game; disciplinary tribunals are held the following week. Consequently there are some spectacular brawls on field – while the crowds, in contrast, are noisy but remarkably peaceful (a pleasant surprise for visiting soccer fans).

Melbourne is the national (and world) centre for Australian Rules, and the Australian Football League (AFL) is the national competition. Ten of its 15 teams are from Melbourne; the others are from Geelong, Perth, Sydney, Adelaide and Brisbane. Adelaide is also a stronghold of Aussie Rules but it's nowhere near as big-time there as it is in Melbourne, where crowds regularly exceed 30,000 at top regular games and 70,000 at finals.

Australian rules is a great game to get to know. Fast, tactical, skilful, rough and athletic, it can produce gripping finishes when even after 100 minutes of play the outcome hangs on the very last kick. It also inspires fierce spectator loyalties and has made otherwise obscure Melbourne suburbs (Hawthorn, Essendon, Collingwood etc) national names.

The other (nonfootball) half of the year there's cricket. The Melbourne Cricket Ground (MCG) is the world's biggest, and international Test and one-day matches are played virtually every summer there and in Sydney, Adelaide, Perth and Brisbane. There is also an interstate competition (the Sheffield Shield) and numerous local grades.

Basketball too is growing in popularity as a spectator sport since the recent formation of a national league. And surfing competitions such as that held each year at Bells Beach, Victoria, are world class.

Australia loves a gamble, and hardly any town of even minor import is without a horse racing track or a Totalisator Agency Board (TAB) betting office. Melbourne and Adelaide must be amongst the only cities in the world to give a public holiday for horse races. The prestigious Melbourne Cup is held on the first Tuesday in November.

There's also yacht racing, some good tennis and golf. The Australian Formula 1 Grand Prix is held in Adelaide each November, and the Australian round of the World 500cc Motorcycle Grand Prix is held annually in April.

THINGS TO BUY

There are lots of things definitely not to buy – like plastic boomerangs, fake Aboriginal ashtrays and T-shirts, and all the other terrible souvenirs with which tacky souvenir shops in the big cities are stuffed. Most of them come from Taiwan or Korea anyway.

Top of the list for any real Australian purchase, however, would have to be Aboriginal art. It's an amazingly direct and down-to-earth art which has now gained international appreciation. If you're willing to put in a little effort you can see superb examples of the Aborigines' art in its original form, carved or painted on rocks and caves in many remote parts of Australia. Now (and really just in time) skilled Aboriginal artists are also working on their art in a more portable form. Nobody captures the essence of outback Australia better than the Aborigines, so if you want a real souvenir of Australia this is what to buy. Have a look at the spectacular Aboriginal artworks hanging in the big state art galleries before you make your choice. Prices of the best works are way out of reach for the average traveller, but among the cheaper artworks on sale are prints, baskets, small carvings, and some very beautiful screen-printed T-shirts produced by Aboriginal craft co-operatives – and a larger number of commercial rip-offs. It's worth shopping around and paying a few dollars more for the real thing.

Crafts such as pottery and jewellery are flourishing. Check out some of the many craft markets if you want to buy direct from the producer.

The big galleries produce a wide range of reproductions of Australian works of art at reasonable prices.

There are some interesting alternatives, like the sturdy farming gear worn by those bronzed Aussie blokes on outback stations – Akubra hats, Drizabone coats, R M Williams moleskin trousers, or boots and shirts, all made to last. Or there are all sorts of sheep-skin products, from car seat covers to ugg boots. A high-quality sheepskin to put in a child's pushchair – or to sit on yourself! – can cost as little as $50.

Surfing equipment is, of course, a major industry in Australia. You can find some terrific Australian books of the coffee-table variety and Australian children's books can be equally attractive.

The seeds of many of Australia's native plants are on sale all over the place. Try growing kangaroo paws back home, if your own country will allow them in.

For those last-minute gifts, drop into a deli. Australian wines are well known overseas; but why not try honey (leatherwood honey is one of a number of powerful local varieties), macadamia nuts (native to Queensland) or Bundaberg rum with its unusual sweet flavour. We have heard rumours of tinned witchetty grubs, honey ants and other bush tucker.

Australia's national gemstone is the opal, most common in South Australia. They're very beautiful but buy wisely; as with all precious and semiprecious stones, there are many tall tales and expert 'salespeople' around.

Getting There & Away

Basically getting to Australia means flying. Once upon a time the traditional transport between Europe and Australia was by ship, but those days are long gone. Infrequent and expensive cruise ships apart, there are no regular shipping services to Australia. It is, however, sometimes possible to hitch a ride on a yacht to or from Australia. See the Getting Around chapter for more details.

The basic problem with getting to Australia is that it's a long way from anywhere. Coming from Asia, Europe or North America there are lots of competing airlines and a wide variety of airfares, but there's no way you can avoid those great distances. Australia's current international popularity adds another problem – flights are often heavily booked. If you want to fly to Australia at a particularly popular time of year (the middle of summer, ie Christmas time, is notoriously difficult) or on a particularly popular route (like Hong Kong-Sydney or Singapore-Sydney) then plan well ahead.

Australia has a large number of international gateways. Sydney and Melbourne are the two busiest international airports with flights from everywhere. Perth also gets many flights from Asia and Europe and has direct flights to New Zealand and Africa. Other international airports include Hobart in Tasmania (New Zealand only), Adelaide, Port Hedland (Bali only), Darwin, Cairns and Brisbane. One place you can't arrive at directly from overseas is Canberra, the national capital.

Although Sydney is the busiest gateway it makes a lot of sense to avoid arriving or departing there. Sydney's airport is stretched way beyond its capacity and flights are frequently delayed on arrival and departure. Furthermore the Customs and Immigration facilities are cramped, crowded and too small for the current visitor flow so even after you've finally landed you may face further long delays. If you can organise your flights to avoid Sydney it's a wise idea but unfortunately many flights to or from other cities (Melbourne in particular) still go via Sydney. If you're planning to explore Australia seriously then starting at a quieter entry port like Cairns in far north Queensland or Perth in Western Australia can make a lot of sense.

Discount Tickets

Buying airline tickets these days is like shopping for a car, a stereo or a camera – five different travel agents will quote you five different prices. Rule number one if you're looking for a cheap ticket is to go to an agent, not directly to the airline. The airline can usually only quote you the absolutely straight-up-and-down, by-the-rule-book regular fare. An agent, on the other hand, can offer all sorts of special deals particularly on competitive routes.

Ideally an airline would like to fly all their flights with every seat in use and every passenger paying the highest fare possible. Fortunately life usually isn't like that and airlines would rather have a half-price passenger than an empty seat. When faced with the problem of too many seats, they will either let agents sell them at cut prices, or occasionally make one-off special offers on particular routes – watch the travel ads in the press.

Of course what's available and what it costs depends on what time of year it is, what route you're flying and who you're flying with. If you're flying on a popular route (like from Hong Kong) or one where the choice of flights is very limited (like from South America or from Africa) then the fare is likely to be higher or there may be nothing available but the official fare.

Similarly the dirt cheap fares are likely to be less conveniently scheduled, go by a less convenient route or with a less popular airline. Flying London/Sydney, for example, is most convenient with airlines like Qantas, British Airways, Thai International or Singapore Airlines. They have flights every day, they operate the same flight straight through to Australia and they're good, reliable, comfortable, safe airlines. At the other extreme you could fly from London to an Eastern European or Middle East city on one flight, switch to another flight from there to Asia, change to another airline from there to Australia. It takes longer, there are delays and changes of aircraft along the way, the airlines may not be so good and furthermore the connection only works once a week and that means leaving London at 1.30 on a Wednesday morning. The flip side is it's cheaper.

TO/FROM THE UK

The cheapest tickets in London are from the numerous 'bucket shops' (discount ticket agencies) which advertise in magazines and papers like *Time Out, City Limits, Southern Cross* and *TNT*. Pick up one or two of these publications and ring round a few bucket shops to find the best deal. The magazine *Business Traveller* also has a great deal of good advice on airfare bargains. Most bucket shops are trustworthy and reliable but the occasional sharp operator appears – *Time Out* and *Business Traveller* give some useful advice on precautions to take.

Trailfinders (☎ (071) 938 3366) at 46 Earls Court Rd, London W8 and STA Travel (☎ (071) 581 4132) at 74 Old Brompton Rd, London SW7 and 117 Euston Rd, London NW1 (☎ (071) 465 0484) are good, reliable agents for cheap tickets.

The cheapest London to Sydney or Melbourne bucket shop tickets are about £300 one-way or £550 return. Such prices are usually only available if you leave London in the low season – March to June. In September and mid-December fares go up about 30% while the rest of the year they're somewhere in between. Perth is usually about £20 cheaper than Sydney or Melbourne one-way, £30 to £50 cheaper return. Average fares are around £480 one-way and £860 return.

Many cheap tickets allow stopovers on the way to or from Australia. Rules regarding how many stopovers you can take, how long you can stay away, how far in advance you

have to decide your return date and so on, vary from time to time and ticket to ticket, but recently most return tickets have allowed you to stay away for any period between 14 days and one year, with stopovers permitted anywhere along your route. As usual with heavily discounted tickets the less you pay the less you get. Nice direct flights, leaving at convenient times and flying with popular airlines, are going to be more expensive than flying from London to Singapore or Bangkok with some Eastern European or Middle East airline and then changing to another airline for the last leg.

From Australia you can expect to pay around A$800 one-way, and A$1550 return to London and other European capitals, with stops in Asia on the way.

TO/FROM NORTH AMERICA

There are a variety of connections across the Pacific from Los Angeles, San Francisco and Vancouver to Australia including direct flights, flights via New Zealand, island-hopping routes or more circuitous Pacific rim routes via nations in Asia. Qantas, Air New Zealand, United and Continental all fly USA/Australia; Qantas, Air New Zealand and Canadian Airlines International fly Canada/Australia.

One advantage of flying Qantas or Air New Zealand rather than Continental or United is that on the US airlines, if your flight goes via Hawaii, the west coast to Hawaii sector is treated as a domestic flight. This means that you have to pay for drinks and headsets; goodies that are free on international sectors. Furthermore when coming in through Hawaii from Australasia it's not unknown for passengers who take a long time clearing Customs to be left behind by the US airline and have to take the next service!

To find good fares to Australia check the travel ads in the Sunday travel sections of papers like the *Los Angeles Times, San Francisco Chronicle-Examiner, New York Times* or *Toronto Globe & Mail*. The straightforward return excursion fare from the USA west coast is around US$1000 to US$1500 depending on the season but plenty of deals are available. You can typically get a one-way ticket from US$500 west coast or US$550 east coast, returns from US$800 west coast or US$900 east coast. At peak seasons – particularly the Australia summer/Christmas time – seats will be harder to get and the price will probably be higher. In the US good agents for discounted tickets are the two student travel operators, Council Travel and STA Travel, both of which have lots of offices around the country. Canadian west coast fares out of Vancouver will be similar to the US west coast. From Toronto fares go from around C$1500 return.

The French airline UTA have an interesting island-hopping route between the US west coast and Australia which includes the French colonies of New Caledonia and French Polynesia (Tahiti, etc). The UTA flight is often discounted and its multiple Pacific stopover possibilities makes it very popular with travellers. The UTA ticket typically costs about US$760 Los Angeles/Sydney one-way.

If Pacific island-hopping is your aim, several other airlines offer interesting opportunities. One is Hawaiian Airlines who fly Honolulu/Sydney via Pago Pago in American Samoa once a week. Qantas can give you Fiji or Tahiti along the way, Air New Zealand can offer both and the Cook Islands as well. See the Circle Pacific section for more details.

One-way/return fares available from Australia include: San Francisco A$750/1100, New York A$900/1460 and Vancouver $900/1449.

TO/FROM NEW ZEALAND

Air New Zealand and Qantas operate a network of trans-Tasman flights linking Auckland, Wellington and Christchurch in New Zealand with most major Australian gateway cities. You can fly directly between a lot of places in New Zealand and a lot of places in Australia.

Fares vary depending on which cities you fly between and when you do it but from New Zealand to Sydney you're looking at around NZ$540 one-way and NZ$699 return, to Melbourne NZ$605 one-way and NZ$799 return. There is a lot of competition on this route – with United, Continental and British Airways all flying it as well as Qantas and Air New Zealand, so there is bound to be some good discounting going on.

Cheap fares to New Zealand from Europe will usually be for flights via the USA. A straightforward London/Auckland one-way bucket shop ticket costs from £350, or you could make that London/Auckland/Sydney or Melbourne from £510. Coming via Australia you can continue right around on a Round-the-World (RTW) ticket which will cost from around £1000 for a ticket with a comprehensive choice of stopovers.

TO/FROM ASIA

Ticket discounting is widespread in Asia, particularly in Singapore, Hong Kong, Bangkok and Penang. There are a lot of fly-by-nights in the Asian ticketing scene so a little care is required. Also the Asian routes have been particularly caught up in the capacity shortages on flights to Australia. Flights between Hong Kong and Australia are notoriously heavily booked while flights to or from Bangkok and Singapore are often part of the longer Europe-Australia route so they are also sometimes very full. Plan ahead. For much more information on South-East Asian travel and on to Australia see Lonely Planet's *South-East Asia on a shoestring*.

Typical one-way fares to Australia from Asia include from Hong Kong for around HK$2750 (US$370) or from Singapore for around S$600 (US$300). These fares are to the east coast capitals. Brisbane, Perth or Darwin are sometimes a bit cheaper.

You can also pick up some interesting tickets in Asia to include Australia on the way across the Pacific. UTA were first in this market but Qantas and Air New Zealand are also offering discounted trans-Pacific tickets. On the UTA ticket you can stop over in Jakarta, Sydney, Noumea, Auckland and Tahiti.

From Australia some typical return fares

from the east coast include Singapore $865, Kuala Lumpur $869, Bangkok $695, Hong Kong $990 and Delhi $1325.

The cheapest way out of Australia is take one of the flights operating between Darwin and Kupang (Timor, Indonesia). Current one-way/return fares are $198/330. See the Darwin Getting There & Away section for full details.

TO/FROM AFRICA & SOUTH AMERICA

The flight possibilities from these continents are not so varied and you're much more likely to have to pay the full fare. There is only one direct flight between Africa and Australia and that is from Zimbabwe – the weekly Qantas Harare/Perth/Sydney route. A much cheaper alternative from East Africa is to fly from Nairobi to India or Pakistan and on to South-East Asia, then connect from there to Australia.

Two routes now operate between South America and Australia. The long-running Chile connection involves a Lan Chile flight Santiago/Easter Island/Tahiti from where you fly Qantas or another airline to Australia. Alternatively there is a route which skirts the Antarctic circle, flying Buenos Aires/Auckland/Sydney, operated by Aerolineas Argentinas in conjunction with Qantas.

ROUND-THE-WORLD TICKETS

Round-the-World tickets have become very popular in the last few years and many of these will take you through Australia. The airline RTW tickets are often real bargains and since Australia is pretty much at the other side of the world from Europe or North America it can work out no more expensive, or even cheaper, to keep going in the same direction right round the world rather than U-turn when you return.

The official airline RTW tickets are usually put together by a combination of two airlines, and permit you to fly anywhere you want on their route systems so long as you do not backtrack. Other restrictions are that you (usually) must book the first sector in advance and cancellation penalties then apply. There may be restrictions on how many stops you are permitted and usually the tickets are valid from 90 days up to a year. Typical prices for these South Pacific RTW tickets are from £760 to £1000 or US$2500 to US$3000.

An alternative type of RTW ticket is one put together by a travel agent using a combination of discounted tickets from a number of airlines. A UK agent like Trailfinders can put together interesting London-to-London RTW combinations including Australia for £1500 to £2000.

CIRCLE PACIFIC TICKETS

Circle Pacific fares are a similar idea to RTW tickets which use a combination of airlines to circle the Pacific – combining Australia, New Zealand, North America and Asia. Examples would be Continental-Thai International, Qantas-Northwest Orient, Canadian Airlines International-Cathay Pacific and so on. As with RTW tickets there are advance purchase restrictions and limits to how many stopovers you can take. Typically fares range between US$1200 and US$2000. A possible Circle Pacific route is Los Angeles/Hawaii/Auckland/Sydney/Singapore/Bangkok/Hong Kong/Tokyo/Los Angeles.

ARRIVING & DEPARTING
Arriving in Australia

Australia's dramatic increase in visitor arrivals has caused some severe bottlenecks at the entry points, particularly at Sydney where the airport is often operating at more than full capacity and delays on arrival or departure are frequent. Even when you're on the ground it can take ages to get through Immigration and Customs. One answer to this problem is to try not to arrive in Australia at Sydney. Sure, you'll have to go there sometime – but you can save yourself a lot of time and trouble by making Brisbane, Cairns, Melbourne or another gateway city your arrival point.

First-time travellers to Australia may be alarmed to find themselves being sprayed with insecticide by the airline stewards. It happens to everyone.

For information about how to get to the city from the airport when you first arrive in Australia check the To/From the Airport section under the relevant city. There is generally an airport bus service at the international airports and there are always taxis available.

Leaving Australia

When you finally go remember to keep $10 aside for the departure tax.

Warning

This chapter is particularly vulnerable to change – prices for international travel are volatile, routes are introduced and cancelled, schedules change, rules are amended, special deals come and go, borders open and close.

Airlines and governments seem to take a perverse pleasure in making price structures and regulations as complicated as possible and you should check directly with the airline or travel agent to make sure you understand how a fare (and ticket you may buy) works.

In addition, the travel industry is highly competitive and there are many lurks and perks. The upshot of this is that you should get opinions, quotes and advice from as many airlines and travel agents as possible before you part with your hard-earned cash. The details given in this chapter should be regarded only as pointers and cannot be any substitute for your own careful, up-to-date research.

Getting Around

AIR

Australia is so vast (and at times so empty) that unless your time is unlimited you will probably have to take to the air sometime. It has been calculated that something like 80% of long-distance trips by public transport are made by air.

The big news on the air travel front in Australia has been the deregulation of the domestic airline industry. For 40-odd years Australia had the 'two-airline policy'; just two airlines, Australian and Ansett, had a duopoly on domestic flights. With this cosy cohabitation the airlines could charge virtually what they liked, and operate virtually identical schedules. All this meant that for the traveller, domestic airline travel within Australia was expensive and the choices of flights limited, particularly on the low-volume routes.

With deregulation, which arrived in late 1990, came a new player on the scene, Compass Airlines. With just two wide-bodied aircraft it took on the two big operators, offering drastically reduced fares on the major runs. In just a short time it had captured a creditable 6% of the market – a huge achievement given the size of its fleet. Virtually overnight prices tumbled as the big airlines scrambled to keep up with their new fleet-footed opposition.

In December 1991, however, Compass went bust, and as we go to press its fate is still uncertain. If it does survive in any form, it may be a very different outfit. There are still quite a few bargain airfares on the domestic market, however, so shop around before you buy.

Note that all domestic flights in Australia are nonsmoking.

Cheap Fares

Random Discounting A major feature of the deregulated air travel industry seems to be random discounting. As the airlines try harder to fill planes, they are offering discounts of up to 70% on selected routes. Although this seems to apply mainly to the heavy volume routes, that's not always the case – at one stage Ansett were offering $100 seats from Alice Springs to Melbourne (normally $411), just for one flight.

To make the most of the discounted fares, you need to keep in touch with what's currently on offer, mainly because there are usually conditions attached to cheap fares – such as booking 14 or so days in advance, only flying on weekends, or between certain dates and so on. Also the number of seats available is usually fairly limited. The further ahead you can plan the better.

The places which this sort of discounting applies to are the main centres – Melbourne, Sydney, Brisbane, Cairns, Adelaide and Perth. For example, the full economy return fare from Melbourne to Perth is $1016; but the airlines are also currently offering special return flights for around $280.

Stand-by Stand-by fares are still the only discount offered on many routes. Basically they save you around 20% of the regular economy fare – Melbourne/Sydney, for example, is $229 one-way economy but only $175 stand-by (but specials of $80 one-way were on offer for much of 1991).

You have no guarantee of a seat when travelling stand-by. You buy your ticket at the airport, register at the stand-by desk and then wait for the flight to board. If at that time there is sufficient room for the stand-by passengers, on you go. If there's room for 10 additional passengers and 20 are on stand-by then the first 10 to have registered get on. If you miss the flight you can stand-by for the next one (you'll be that much further up the line if some stand-by passengers have got on) or you can try the other airline.

A catch with stand-by fares is that they only work on a sector basis. If you want to fly Melbourne/Perth and the flight goes via Adelaide you may have to stand-by on the

Melbourne/Adelaide sector and then for the Adelaide/Perth sector. Furthermore the fares will be a combination of the two sectors, not a reduction from the direct Melbourne/Perth fare. Fortunately there are a lot more direct flights these days.

If you intend to stand-by the most likely flights will be, of course, the ones at the most inconvenient times. Very early in the morning, late at night or in the middle of the day are your best bets. Many inter-capital flights in Australia are really commuter services – Mr/Ms Businessperson zipping up from Sydney to Brisbane for a day's dealings – so the flights that fit in with the 9 to 5 life are the most crowded. 'Up for the weekend' flights – leaving Friday evening, coming back Sunday afternoon – also tend to be crowded. At other times you've got a pretty good chance of getting aboard.

Other Possibilities If you're planning a return trip and you have 21 days up your sleeve then you can save 40% by travelling Apex. You have to book and pay for your tickets 21 days in advance and once you're inside that 21-day period you cannot alter your booking in either direction. If you cancel you lose 50% of the fare.

Excursion fares, called Excursion 45 by Australian Airlines and Flexi-Fares by Ansett, give a 45% reduction on a round-trip ticket, can only be booked between four and 14 days prior to travel and the maximum stay away is 21 days. You book a flight for a nominated day and contact the airline before 12 noon on the day prior to departure to be advised of which flight you will be on. Your travel arrangements need to be flexible.

University or other higher education students under the age of 26 can get a 25% discount off the regular economy fare. An airline tertiary concession card is required for Australian students. Overseas students can use their International Student Identity Card, a New Zealand student card or an overseas airline ticket issued at the 25% student reduction. The latter sounds a good bet!

All international travellers can get a 25% discount on internal flights to connect with their arriving or departing international flight – so if you're flying in to Sydney from Los Angeles but intend to go on to the Black Stump you get 25% off the Sydney/Black Stump flight.

Non-Australian travellers coming to Australia by any inbound international flight, or even by ship, can get 25% off all regular fares so long as you buy the tickets before you arrive or within 30 days of arriving and complete all travel within 60 days of arriving. Whew!

International visitors can also get a good deal on domestic flights with Qantas. Normally Qantas isn't allowed to carry domestic passengers but if you're a visitor to Australia with an international ticket you can fly Qantas at 50% of the standard economy fare. The catch is that these flights are often just the finishing or starting sectors of longer international flights and often operate at less convenient times. Also, although domestic passengers are spared a great deal of the international rigmarole the departure and arrival formalities still take rather longer than with a regular domestic flight.

There are also some worthwhile cheaper deals with regional airlines such as East-West or a number of Queensland operators. On some lesser routes these operators undercut the big two. Keep your eyes open for special deals at certain times of the year. When the Melbourne Cup horse race is on in early November and when the football Grand Final happens (also in Melbourne) at the end of September lots of extra flights are put on. These flights would normally be going in the opposite direction nearly empty so special fares are offered to people wanting to leave Melbourne when everybody else wants to go there. The Australian Grand Prix in Adelaide in late October or early November is a similar one-way-traffic event.

Air Passes

Ansett and Australian Airlines both have special round the country fares – Australian Airlines' is called an Explorer Airpass, Ansett's is a Kangaroo Airpass. Both have

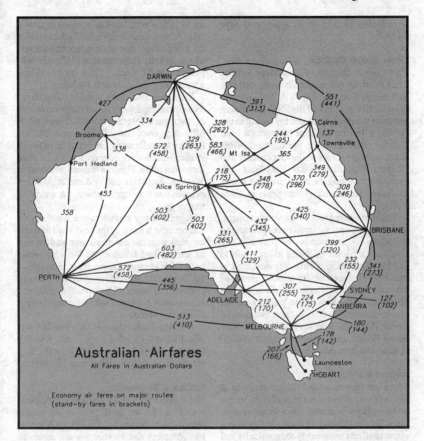

427

334

391
(313)

551
(441)

DARWIN

Broome

338

Port Hedland

572
(458)

329
(263)

328
(262)

583
(466) Mt Isa

244
(195)

Cairns

137

Townsville

365

349
(279)

453

218
(175)

Alice Springs

348
(278)

370
(296)

308
(246)

358

503
(402)

503
(402)

331
(265)

432
(345)

425
(340)

BRISBANE

603
(482)

411
(329)

399
(320)

232
(155)

341
(273)

PERTH

572
(458)

445
(356)

307
(255)

224
(175)

SYDNEY

127
(102)

ADELAIDE

212
(170)

CANBERRA

513
(410)

MELBOURNE

180
(144)

178
(142)

207
(166)

Launceston

HOBART

Australian Airfares

All Fares in Australian Dollars

Economy air fares on major routes
(stand—by fares in brackets)

two tickets available – 6000 km for $949 and
10,000 km for $1499. There are a number of
restrictions applied to these tickets, despite
which they can be a good deal if you want to
see a lot of country in a short period of time.
You do not need to start and finish at the same
place; you could start in Sydney and end in
Darwin for example.

Restrictions include a minimum travel
time (10 days) and a maximum (45 days). On
the 6000-km pass you must stop at least
twice but at most three times. On the 10,000-
km pass you must stop at least three times
but at most seven. One of the stops must be

at a non-capital-city destination and be for at
least four days. There are requirements about
changing reservations although generally
there is no charge unless the ticket needs to
be rewritten.

On a 6000-km airpass you could, for
example, fly Sydney/Alice Springs/Cairns/
Brisbane/Sydney. That gives you three stops
and two of them are in non-capital cities. The
regular fare for that circuit would be $1378,
so you save $429. A one-way route might be
Adelaide/Melbourne/Sydney/Alice Springs/
Perth. There are three stops of which one is
a non-capital city. Regular cost for that route

would also be $1378, so again you save
$429.

Other Airline Options

There are a number of secondary airlines
apart from the two major domestic carriers.
In Western Australia there's Ansett WA with
an extensive network of flights to the mining
towns of the north-west and to Darwin in the
Northern Territory. Ansett NT operate from
Darwin down to Alice Springs and Ayers
Rock and also across to the Queensland and
Western Australian coasts. East-West Air-
lines operate along the east coast, and across
to Ayers Rock and Alice Springs from
Sydney.

There are numerous other smaller operators. Sunstate operate services in Queensland
including out to a number of islands. They
also have a couple of routes in the south to
Mildura and Broken Hill. Skywest have a
number of services to remote parts of
Western Australia. Eastern Airlines operate
up and down the New South Wales coast and
also inland from Sydney as far as Bourke and
Cobar. Air NSW have services all over New
South Wales, up to Brisbane, down to Melbourne and in to Alice Springs.

Airport Transport

There are private or public bus services at
almost every major town in Australia. In one
or two places you may have to depend on
taxis but in general you can get between
airport and city reasonably economically and
conveniently by bus. Quite often a taxi
shared between three or more people can be
cheaper than the bus.

BUS

Bus travel is generally the cheapest way from
A to B, other than hitching of course, but the
main problem is to find the best deal.

There are only two truly *national* bus networks – Greyhound/Pioneer and Bus
Australia. Greyhound and Pioneer were once
separate companies, and although they still
operate their own buses, tickets on either
company are interchangeable. Bus Australia
is the cheaper of the two networks, with fares

up to 10% lower, but this is offset against a
smaller network of services. Students under
26 years of age can get a discount on some
routes, usually 10%; ditto for YHA and backpacker card holders. YHA travel offices
sometimes offer discounts on buses.

There are also many smaller bus companies operating locally or specialising in one
or two main intercity routes. These often
offer the best deals – Firefly costs $40 for
Sydney to Melbourne, for example. In South
Australia Stateliner operate around the state
including to the Flinders Ranges. Westrail in
Western Australia and V/Line in Victoria
operate bus services to places the trains no
longer go.

A great many travellers see Australia by
bus because it's one of the best ways to come
to grips with the country's size and variety
of terrain, and because the bus companies
have such comprehensive route networks –
far more comprehensive than the railway
system. The buses all look pretty similar and
are similarly equipped with air-conditioning,
toilets and videos.

In many places there is now one bus terminal shared by all the operators. Big city
terminals are generally well equipped – they
usually have toilets, showers and facilities.

Routes & Stopovers

The bus companies do not operate identical
routes and it's the small print on the tickets
which can make the big differences between
one company and another when it comes to
stopovers and other important considera-
tions. Always check the stopover deals if you
want to make stops en route to your final
destination, as you can save quite a few
dollars on supposedly similar fares.

Bus Passes

Set Period Version Bus Australia and Greyhound both have bus passes which offer
unlimited travel for a set period, but you
should think very carefully before getting
one. It *sounds* good but many travellers find
that the passes are too restrictive and that to
make proper use of them they have to travel
faster than they would wish. This particu-

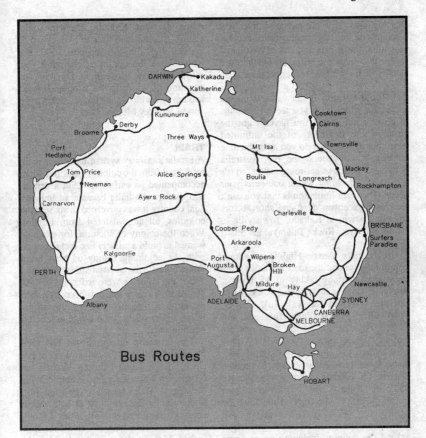

Bus Routes

larly seems to apply to people who buy their passes before they arrive in Australia. Often there are cheap deals making it attractive to buy a pass in advance. So think carefully about exactly which, if any, pass is best for you and whether you really can't wait till you get to Oz before laying out the cash.

Bus passes generally go from 15 to 90 days although there are some shorter seven or 10-day passes. The very short passes really don't make sense. If you started in Adelaide, travelled to Melbourne, spent four days there, travelled to Canberra, spent two days there, travelled to Sydney, spent four days

there and then travelled to Brisbane you'd have run through a 15-day pass (around $450) and only got around $175 of bus travel out of it. Even if you'd started in Perth, and only spent a couple of days in each place the sector fare would still have cost you only $335 on Greyhound, generally the most expensive bus line.

A 15-day pass typically costs about $450, a 21-day pass about $630, a 30-day pass $850, a 60-day pass $1250, and a 90-day pass $1700. Greyhound/Pioneer, with the most extensive route network and the most frequent services, is more expensive than

Bus Australia. Your bus pass also gives you discounts on local sightseeing tours, accommodation, rental cars and so on. Neither of the big two operate in Tasmania but there are usually tie ins with the local operators.

Set Route Version Better value is the set route pass, which gives you six or 12 months to cover a set route. You haven't got the go-anywhere flexibility of the unlimited travel bus pass but nor do you have the time constraints. Greyhound and Bus Australia both have numerous set-route passes, so it's a matter of deciding which one suits your needs. The main limitation is that you can't backtrack, except on 'dead-end' short sectors such as Darwin to Kakadu, Townsville to Cairns and Ayers Rock (Yulara) to the Stuart Highway.

Greyhound's 'Aussie Highlights' allows you to loop around the eastern half of Australia from Sydney taking in Melbourne, Adelaide, Coober Pedy, Ayers Rock, Alice Springs, Darwin (& Kakadu), Cairns, Townsville, Whitsundays, Brisbane and Surfers Paradise for A$584. Or there are one-way passes, such as the 'Go West' pass from Sydney to Cairns via Melbourne, Adelaide, Ayers Rock, Alice Springs, Katherine, Darwin (& Kakadu), and Townsville for $535; or 'Trans Aussie', which goes from Cairns to Perth via the Top End and down the centre, for $477. There's even an 'All Australian' pass which takes you right around the country, including up or down through the centre, for $916. I reckon that would be far better value than a 90-day bus pass since you'd be utterly wrecked trying to cover all that ground in a mere two or three months!

Distance Version The most recent variety of bus pass offers six to 12 months' travel to any combination of destinations, priced according to the distance you expect to travel: a minimum 2000 km from Greyhound/ Pioneer for $110 (1500 km for $85 from Bus Australia), plus $50 for every subsequent 1000 km. The trip from Sydney through Melbourne, Adelaide, Ayers Rock, Alice, Darwin, Kakadu, Darwin again, Cairns, Brisbane and back to Sydney would amount to 11,500 km and cost $600. You would have the option of changing your mind halfway through at Darwin and zooming off to Perth via Broome instead, leaving you with enough unused ticket to get you to Monkey Mia and back.

TRAIN

Australia's railway system has never really recovered from the colonial bungling which accompanied its early days over a century ago. Before Australia became an independent country it was governed as six separate colonies, all administered from London. When the colony of Victoria, for example, wanted to build a railway line it checked not with the adjoining colony of New South Wales but with the colonial office in London. When the colonies were federated in 1901 and Australia came into existence, by a sheer masterpiece of misplanning not one state had railway lines of the same gauge as a neighbouring state!

The immense misfortune of this inept planning has dogged the railway system ever since. The situation between Victoria and New South Wales is a typical example. When New South Wales started to lay a line from Sydney to Parramatta in 1850 their railway engineer convinced the authorities it should be built to wide gauge – five foot three inches. Victoria also started to build to this gauge in order to tie in with the New South Wales system if, at some time in the future, a Melbourne-Sydney rail link was completed. Unfortunately New South Wales then switched railway engineers and their new man was not enamoured of wide gauge. New South Wales railways accordingly switched to standard gauge – four foot eight inches – but Victoria decided their railway construction had gone too far to change.

Thus when the New South Wales and Victorian railway lines met in Albury in 1883 they, er, didn't meet. The Victorian railway tracks were seven inches wider apart than the New South Wales ones. For the next 79 years

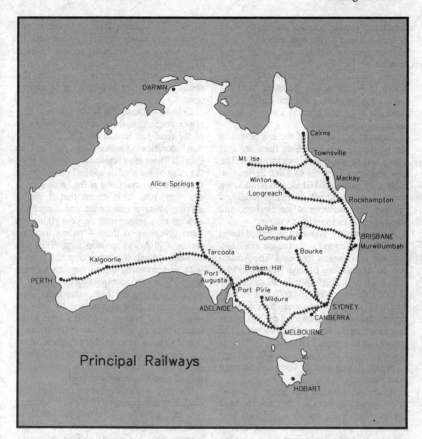

Principal Railways

a rail journey between Melbourne and Sydney involved getting up in the middle of the night at the border in order to change trains!

In 1962 a standard gauge line was opened between Albury and Melbourne and standard gauge lines have also been built between the New South Wales-Queensland border and Brisbane. In 1970 the standard gauge rail link was completed between Sydney and Perth and the famous, and very popular, Indian-Pacific run was brought into operation. There are also, however, narrow gauge railways in Australia. They came about

because they were believed to be cheaper. The old Ghan line between Adelaide and Alice Springs was only replaced by a new standard gauge line in 1980. Apart from different gauges there's also the problem of different operators. Basically the individual states run their own services, or a combination of them for interstate services. Railways of Australia is an association of the government-owned systems in Queensland, New South Wales, Victoria and Western Australia, and this body goes some way to co-ordinating the major services.

Rail travel in Australia today is basically

something you do because you really want to – not because it's cheaper, especially now with the reduced airfares, and certainly not because it's fast. Rail travel is generally the slowest way to get from anywhere to anywhere in Australia. On the other hand the trains are comfortable and you certainly see Australia at ground level in a way no other means of travel permits.

Australia is also one of the few places in the world today where new lines are still being laid or are under consideration. The new line from Tarcoola to Alice Springs, to replace the rickety old Ghan, was an amazing piece of work, and talk of finally building a railway line between Alice Springs and Darwin surfaces from time to time.

Austrail passes, allowing unlimited travel on all Australian rail systems, are available, but only for overseas residents. The Australian dollar costs are 14 days $415 ($690 1st class), 21 days $535 ($850), 30 days $650 ($1050), 60 days $930 ($1460) and 90 days $1070 ($1680). The economy pass does not cover meals and berth charges on trips where these are charged for as additional costs. The passes can be bought in Australia (as long as you don't live here) or in the UK through Compass Travel and in the USA through Tour Pacific.

Australian students can get a 50% discount on regular fares but they need to have a railways student concession card from their college or university. Caper fares are an advance purchase deal which gives a saving of up to 30% and on some major routes there are stand-by tickets. On interstate rail journeys you can usually break your journey at no extra cost provided you complete the trip within two months on a one-way ticket, or six months with a return ticket.

On some routes you can take your car with you by train.

For timetables and fares for the major interstate routes, contact the Railways of Australia, 85 Queen St, Melbourne (☎ (03) 608 0811).

CAR

Australia is a big, sprawling country with large cities where public transport is not always very comprehensive or convenient. Like America the car is the accepted means of getting from A to B and many visitors will consider getting wheels to explore the country – either by buying a car or renting one.

Driving in Australia holds few real surprises. Australians drive on the left-hand side of the road just like in the UK, Japan and most countries in south and east Asia and the Pacific. There are a few local variations from the rules of the road as applied elsewhere in the West. The main one is the 'give way to the right' rule. This means that if you're driving along a main road and somebody appears on a minor road on your right, you must give way to them – unless they are facing a give-way or stop sign. This rule caused so much confusion over the years – with cars zooming out of tiny tracks onto main highways and expecting everything to screech to a stop for them – that most intersections are now signposted to indicate which is the priority road. It's wise to be careful because while almost every intersection is signposted in southern capitals, when you get up to towns in the north of Queensland, stop signs are few and far between and the old give-way rules will apply.

The give-way ruling has a special and very confusing interpretation in Victoria where if two cars travelling in opposite directions both turn into the same street, the vehicle turning right has priority. This rule only applies in Victoria and causes no end of headaches and confusion for non-Victorian drivers.

There's another special hazard in Melbourne – trams. You can only overtake trams from the left lane and must stop behind them when they stop to pick up or drop off passengers. Be aware of trams – they weigh about as much as the *Queen Mary* and cannot swerve to avoid foolish drivers. In central Melbourne there are also a number of intersections where a special technique, mastered only by native Melbournians, must be employed when making right hand turns. You must wait until the light of the road you're turning into turns green, and then turn from the left-hand side of the road. Got that?

The general speed limit in built-up areas in Australia is 60 km/h and out on the open highway it's usually 100 or 110 km/h depending on where you are, although in the Northern Territory there is no speed limit outside of built-up areas. The police have radar speed traps and are very fond of using them in carefully hidden locations in order to raise easy revenue – don't exceed the speed limit in inviting areas where the boys and girls in blue may be waiting for you. On the other hand, when you get far from the cities and traffic is light, you'll see a lot of vehicles moving a lot faster than 100 km/h. An oncoming driver who flashes his/her lights at you may be giving you a friendly indication of a speed trap ahead.

Australia was one of the first countries in the world to make the wearing of seat belts compulsory. All new cars in Australia are required to have seat belts back and front and if your seat has a belt then you're required to wear it. You're liable to be fined if you don't. Small children must be belted into an approved safety seat.

Although overseas licences are acceptable in Australia for genuine overseas visitors, an International Driving Permit is even more acceptable.

On the Road

Australia is not crisscrossed by multi-lane highways. There simply is not enough traffic and the distances are too great to justify them. You'll certainly find stretches of divided road, particularly on busy roads like the Sydney-to-Melbourne Hume Highway or close to the state capital cities – the last stretch into Adelaide from Melbourne, the Pacific Highway from Sydney to Newcastle, the Surfers Paradise-Brisbane road, for example. Elsewhere Australian roads are only two-lane well-surfaced (though a long way from the billiard-table surfaces the poms are used to driving on) on all the main routes.

You don't have to get very far off the beaten track, however, to find yourself on dirt roads, and anybody who sets out to see the country in reasonable detail will have to expect to do some dirt-road travelling. If you really want to explore outlandish places, then you'd better plan on having four-wheel drive (4WD) and a winch. A few useful spare parts

Distances by road (km)

	Adelaide	Brisbane	Canberra	Darwin	Melbourne	Perth	Sydney
Adelaide		2130	1210	3215	745	2750	1430
Alice Springs	1690	3060	2755	1525	2435	3770	2930
Brisbane	2130		1295	3495	1735	4390	1030
Broome	4035	4320	5100	1965	4780	2415	4885
Cairns	2865	1840	3140	2795	3235	6015	2870
Canberra	1210	1295		4230	655	3815	305
Darwin	3215	3495	4230		3960	4345	4060
Melbourne	755	1735	655	3960		3495	895
Perth	2750	4390	3815	4345	3495		3990
Sydney	1430	1030	305	4060	895	3990	

These are the shortest distances by road; other routes may be considerably longer. For distances by coach, check the companies' leaflets.

are worth carrying if you're travelling on highways in the Northern Territory or the north of Western Australia. A broken fan belt can be a damn nuisance if the next service station is 200 km away.

Driving standards in Australia aren't exactly the highest in the world but to a large extent the appalling accident rate is due to the habit that suitably boozed country drivers have of flying off the road into the gum trees. Drive carefully, especially on the weekend evenings when the drinking-drivers are about. Note also that the police are doing their best to make drinking and driving a foolish practice, even if you don't hit something. Random breath tests and goodbye licence if you exceed '.05' are the order of the day.

Petrol is available from stations sporting the well-known international brand names. Prices vary from place to place and from price war to price war but generally it's in the 60c to 70c a litre range (say around $2.70 to $3.20 an imperial gallon). In the outback the price can soar and some outback service stations are not above exploiting their monopoly position. Distances between fill-ups can be long in the outback and in some remote areas deliveries can be haphazard – it's not unknown to finally arrive at that 'nearest station x hundred km' only to find there's no fuel until next week's delivery!

Between cities signposting on the main roads is generally quite OK, but around cities it's usually abysmal. You can spend a lot of time trying to find street-name signs, and as for indicating which way to go to leave the city – until recently you were halfway to Sydney from Melbourne before you saw the first sign telling you that you were travelling in the right direction.

Cows and kangaroos are two common hazards on country roads, and a collision is likely to kill the animal and seriously damage your vehicle. Kangaroos are most active around dawn and dusk, and they travel in groups. If you see one hopping across the road in front of you, slow right down – its friends are probably just behind it. Many Australians avoid travelling altogether between 5 pm and 8 am, because of the hazards posed by animals, despite the temptation of cooler temperatures.

Way Outback Travel

Although you can now drive all the way round Australia on Highway 1 or through the middle all the way from Adelaide in the south to Darwin in the north without ever leaving sealed road, that hasn't always been so. The Eyre Highway across the Nullarbor Desert in the south was only surfaced in the 1970s, the final stretch of Highway 1 in the Kimberley region of Western Australia was done in the mid-80s and the final section of the Stuart Highway from Port Augusta up to Alice Springs was finished in 1987.

If you really want to see outback Australia there are still lots of roads where the official recommendation is that you report to the police before you leave one end, and again when you arrive at the other. That way if you fail to turn up at the other end they can start the search parties. Nevertheless many of these tracks are now much better kept than in years past and you don't need 4WD or fancy expedition equipment to tackle them. You do need to be carefully prepared and to carry important spare parts, however. Backtracking 500 km to pick up some minor malfunctioning component or, much worse, to arrange a tow, is unlikely to be easy or cheap.

You will of course need to carry a fair amount of water in case of disaster – around 20 litres a person is sensible – stored in more than one container. Food is less important – the space might be better allocated to an extra spare tyre.

The state automobile associations can advise on preparation and supply maps and track notes. Most tracks have an ideal time of year – in the centre it's not wise to attempt the tough tracks during the heat of summer (November-March) when the dust can be severe, chances of mechanical trouble are much greater and water will be scarce and hence a breakdown more dangerous. Similarly in the north travelling in the wet season may be impossible due to flooding and mud.

Outback Tracks

If you do run into trouble in the back of beyond, stay with your car. It's easier to spot a car than a human being from the air, and you wouldn't be able to carry your 20 litres of water very far anyway.

Some of the favourite tracks include:

Birdsville Track Running 499 km from Marree in South Australia to Birdsville just across the border in Queensland, this is one of the best-known routes in Australia and these days is quite feasible in any well-prepared vehicle.

Strzelecki Track This track covers much the same territory, starting south of Marree at Lyndhurst and

going to Innamincka, 473 km north-east and close to the Queensland border. From there you can loop down to Tibooburra in New South Wales. The route has been much improved due to work on the Moomba gas fields. It was at Innamincka that the hapless early explorers Burke and Wills died.

Oodnadatta Track Parallel to the old Ghan railway line to Alice Springs, the Oodnadatta Track is now comprehensively bypassed with the new sealed Stuart Highway in operation. It's 465 km from Marree to Oodnadatta and another 202 km from there to the Stuart Highway at Marla. Any well-prepared vehicle should be able to manage this route.

Simpson Desert Crossing the Simpson Desert from

Birdsville to the Stuart Highway is becoming increasingly popular but this route is still a real test. Four-wheel drive is definitely required and you should be in a party of at least three or four vehicles equipped with long-range two-way radios. There are two routes generally followed, the French Track or the easier WAAA Line.

Warburton Road/Gunbarrel Highway This route runs west from Ayers Rock by the Aboriginal settlements of Docker River and Warburton to Laverton in Western Australia. From there you can drive down to Kalgoorlie and on to Perth. The route passes through Aboriginal reserves and permission to enter them should be obtained in advance if you want to leave the road. A well-prepared conventional vehicle can complete this route although ground clearance can be a problem and it is very remote. From the Yulara resort at Ayers Rock to Warburton is 567 km, and it's another 568 km from there to Laverton. It's then 361 km on sealed road to Kalgoorlie. For 300 km near the Giles Meteorological Station the Warburton Rd and the Gunbarrel Highway run on the same route. Taking the old Gunbarrel (to the north of the Warburton) all the way to Wiluna in Western Australia is a much rougher trip requiring 4WD. The Warburton Rd is now commonly referred to as the Gunbarrel – just to make life simple.

Tanami Track Turning off the Stuart Highway just north of Alice Springs the Tanami Track goes north-west across the Central Desert to Halls Creek in Western Australia. Conventional vehicles with sufficient ground clearance are OK but there are long sandy stretches.

Canning Stock Route This old stock trail runs south-west from Halls Creek to Wiluna in Western Australia. It crosses the Great Sandy Desert and Gibson Desert, and since the track has not been maintained for over 30 years it's a route to be taken seriously. Like the Simpson Desert crossing you should only travel in a well-equipped party and careful navigation is required.

Plenty Highway & Sandover Highways These two routes run east from the Stuart Highway, to the north of Alice Springs, to Mt Isa in Queensland. They're suitable for conventional vehicles.

Cape York The Peninsula Development Rd up to the top of Cape York, the furthest northerly point in Australia, is a popular route with a number of rivers to cross. It can only be attempted in the dry season when the water levels are lower. The original Cape York Rd along the old telegraph line definitely requires 4WD. Conventional vehicles can take the new 'Heathlands' road to the east beyond the Wenlock

River, that bypasses the most difficult sections, but the Wenlock River itself can be a formidable obstacle.

Gibb River Road This is the 'short cut' between Derby and Kununurra, and runs through the heart of the spectacular Kimberley in northern Western Australia. Although fairly badly corrugated in places, it can be easily negotiated by conventional vehicles in the dry season, and it's 720 km, compared with about 920 km via the bitumen Northern Highway.

Buying a Car

If you want to explore Australia by car and haven't got one or can't borrow one, then you've either got to buy one or rent one. Australian cars are not cheap – another product of the small population. Locally manufactured cars are made in small, uneconomic numbers and imported cars are heavily taxed so they won't undercut the local products. If you're buying a second-hand vehicle reliability is all important. Mechanical breakdowns way out in the outback can be very inconvenient – the nearest mechanic can be a hell of a long way down the road.

Shopping around for a used car involves much the same rules as anywhere in the Western world but with a few local variations. First of all, used car dealers in Australia are just like used car dealers from Los Angeles to London – they'd sell their mother into slavery if it turned a dollar. For any given car you'll probably get it cheaper by buying privately through newspaper small ads rather than through a car dealer. Buying through a dealer does give the advantage of some sort of guarantee, but a guarantee is not much use if you're buying a car in Sydney and intend setting off for Perth next week. Used-car guarantee requirements vary from state to state – check with the local automobile organisation.

There's much discussion amongst travellers about where is the best place to buy used cars. Popular theories exist that you can buy a car in Sydney or Melbourne, drive it to Darwin and sell it there for a profit. Or was it vice versa? It's quite possible that prices do vary but don't count on turning it to your advantage. See the section on buying cars in

Sydney for the situation at that popular starting/finishing point.

What is rather more certain is that the further you get from civilisation, the better it is to be in a Holden or a Ford. New cars can be a whole different ball game of course, but if you're in an older vehicle, something that's likely to have the odd hiccup from time to time, then life is much simpler if it's a car for which you can get spare parts anywhere from Bourke to Bulamakanka. When your fancy Japanese car goes kaput somewhere back of Bourke it's likely to be a two-week wait while the new bit arrives fresh from Fukuoka. On the other hand, when your rusty old Holden goes bang there's probably another old Holden sitting in the ditch with a perfectly good widget waiting to be removed. Every scrap yard in Australia is full of good ole Holdens.

Note that in Australia third-party personal injury insurance is always included in the vehicle registration cost. This ensures that every vehicle (as long as it's currently registered) carries at least minimum insurance. You're wise to extend that minimum to at least third-party property insurance as well – minor collisions with Rolls Royces can be surprisingly expensive.

When you come to buy or sell a car there are usually some local regulations to be complied with. In Victoria, for example, a car has to have a compulsory safety check (Road Worthiness Certificate – RWC) before it can be registered in the new owner's name – usually the seller will indicate if the car already has a RWC. In New South Wales, on the other hand, safety checks are compulsory every year when you come to renew the registration. Stamp duty has to be paid when you buy a car and, as this is based on the purchase price, it's not unknown for buyer and seller to agree privately to understate the price! It's much easier to sell a car in the same state that it's registered in, otherwise it has to be re-registered in the new state. It may be possible to sell a car without re-registering it, but you're likely to get a lower price.

Finally, make use of the automobile organisations – see the Facts for the Visitor chapter for more details about them. They can advise you on any local regulations you should be aware of, give general guidelines about buying a car and, most importantly, for a fee (around $50) will check over a used car and report on its condition before you agree to purchase it. They also offer car insurance to their members.

For the previous update of this book, we decided to buy a car, drive it round Australia and sell it again at the end. Apart from providing the transport we needed to get around it also meant we'd have an idea of what was involved in the buying and selling game. In the end, we did 30,000 km at a total cost of around $25 per day, including all costs except fuel. Rental costs at the time for a similar car (a late model Ford Falcon) would have been around twice that, plus fuel.

Renting a Car

If you've got the cash there are plenty of car rental companies ready and willing to put you behind the wheel. Competition in the Australian car rental business is pretty fierce so rates tend to be variable and lots of special deals pop up and disappear again. Whatever your mode of travel on the long stretches, it can be very useful to have a car for some local travel. Between a group it can even be reasonably economical. There are some places – like around Alice Springs – where if you haven't got your own wheels you really have to choose between a tour and a rented vehicle since there is no public transport and the distances are too great for walking or even bicycles.

The three major companies were Budget, Hertz and Avis with offices in almost every town that has more than one pub and a general store. Budget went into liquidation in 1992 but franchise holders continued to operate, and have taken over the airport desks. The second-string companies which are also represented almost everywhere in the country are Thrifty and National. Then there is a vast number of local firms or firms with outlets in a limited number of locations. You can take it as read that the big operators will generally have higher rates than the local firms but it ain't necessarily so, so don't jump to conclusions.

The big firms have a number of big advantages, however. First of all they're the ones at the airports – Avis, Budget, Hertz and, quite often, Thrifty, are represented at most airports. If you want to pick up a car or leave a car at the airport then they're the best ones to deal with. In some but not all airports other companies will also arrange to pick up or leave their cars there. It tends to depend on how convenient the airport is.

The second advantage of the big companies is if you want to do a one-way rental – pick up a car in Adelaide, leave it in Sydney. There are however, a variety of restrictions on these. Usually it's a minimum-hire period rather than repositioning charges. Only certain cars may be eligible for one-ways. Check the small print on one-way charges before deciding on one company rather than another. One-way rentals are generally not available into or out of the Northern Territory or Western Australia. Special rules may also apply to one-ways into or out of other 'remote areas'.

The major companies all offer unlimited km rates in the city, but in country and 'remote' areas it's a flat charge plus so many cents per km. On straightforward off-the-card city rentals they're all pretty much the same price. It's on special deals, odd rentals or longer periods that you find the differences. Weekend specials – usually three days for the price of two – are usually good value. If you just need a car for three days around Sydney make it the weekend rather than midweek. Budget offer 'stand-by' rates and you may see other special deals available. When picking up a car in Townsville once I saw a sign offering cars free, so long as you got them to Cairns within 24 hours!

Daily metropolitan rates are typically about $60 a day for a small car (Ford Laser, Toyota Corolla, Nissan Pulsar), about $75 a day for a medium car (Holden Camira, Toyota Camry, Nissan Pintara) or about $80 to $90 a day for a big car (Holden Commodore, Ford Falcon). Add another $12 a day for insurance. Typically country rates will be metropolitan plus $5 a day plus 30c a km beyond 200 km a day. Remote rates will be metropolitan plus $10 a day plus 30c a km beyond 100 km a day. It soon gets expensive!

There is a whole collection of other factors to bear in mind about this rent-a-car business. For a start, if you're going to want it for a week, a month or longer then they all have lower rates. If you're in Tasmania, where competition is very fierce, there are often lower rates, especially in the low season. If you're in the really remote outback (places like Darwin and Alice Springs are only vaguely remote) then the choice of cars is likely to be limited to the larger, more expensive ones. You usually must be at least 21 to hire from most firms.

OK, that's the big hire companies, what about all the rest of them? Well some of them are still pretty big in terms of numbers of shiny new cars. In Tasmania, for example, the car-hire business is really big since many people don't bring their cars with them. There's a plethora of hire companies and lots of competition. In many cases local companies are markedly cheaper than the big boys, but in others what looks like a cheaper rate can end up quite the opposite if you're not careful. Quick, what's cheaper: $40 a day, or $20 a day plus 15c a km in excess of 100 km – if you do 200 km? And if you do 300?

Don't forget the 'rent-a-wreck' companies. They specialise in renting older cars – at first they really were old, and a flat rate like '$10 a day and forget the insurance' was the usual story. Now many of them have a variety of rates, typically around $35 a day. If you just want to travel around the city, or not too far out, they can be worth considering.

Mokes In lots of popular holiday areas – like on the Gold Coast, around Cairns, on Magnetic Island, around Alice Springs, in Darwin – right at the bottom of the rent-a-car rates will be the ubiquitous Moke. To those not in the know, a Moke is a totally open vehicle looking rather like a miniature Jeep. They're based on the Mini so they're FWD (front-wheel drive) not 4WD (four-wheel drive) and they are not suitable for getting way off the beaten track. For general good fun in places with a sunny climate, however, they simply can't be beaten. No vehicle has more air-conditioning than a Moke, and as the stickers say 'Moking is not a wealth hazard' – they cover lots of km on a litre of petrol.

If you do hire a Moke there are a few points to watch. Don't have an accident in one, they offer little more protection than a motorcycle. There is absolutely no place to lock things up so don't leave your valuables inside, and the fuel tanks are equally accessible so if you're leaving it somewhere at night beware of petrol thieves – not that there are a great number in Australia, but it does happen.

4WDs Renting a 4WD (four-wheel drive) vehicle is within the budget range if a few people get together – often you can get a 4WD for around $90 a day plus fuel (plus a hefty deposit which you get back if you do no damage to it). Having 4WD enables you to get right off the beaten track and out to some of the great wilderness and outback places, to see some of the Australian natural wonders that most travellers don't see.

Renting Other Vehicles

There are lots of other vehicles you can rent apart from cars. In remote outback areas you can often rent 4WD vehicles. In many places you can rent campervans – they're particularly popular in Tasmania. Motorscooters are also available in a number of locations – they are popular on Magnetic Island and in Cairns for example – and you only need a car licence to ride one. Best of all, in many places you can rent bicycles.

MOTORCYCLE

Motorcycles are a very popular way of getting around. The climate is just about ideal for biking most of the year, and the many small trails from the road into the bush often lead to perfect spots to spend the night in the world's largest camping ground.

The long, open roads are really made for large-capacity machines above 750 cc,

which Australians prefer once they outgrow their 250 cc learner restrictions. But that doesn't stop enterprising individuals – many of them Japanese – from tackling the length and breadth of the continent on 250 cc trail bikes. Doing it on a small bike is not impossible, just tedious at times.

Rob van Driesum, former editor of *Australian Motorcycle News* and currently an editor with Lonely Planet, offers the following advice:

If you want to bring your own motorcycle into Australia you'll need a *carnet de passages*, and when you try to sell it you'll get less than the market price because of restrictive registration requirements (not so severe in Western and South Australia and in the Northern Territory). Shipping from just about anywhere costs a fair bit and you'd better have a good reason for doing so. Forget about hiring, unless you only want a 50cc moped to zip around the coastal tourist resorts in Western Australia or along the Queensland coast, where a car licence will do for this sort of thing.

But with a little bit of time up your sleeve, getting mobile on two wheels in Australia is quite feasible thanks to the chronically depressed motorcycle market. Australian newspapers and the lively local bike press have extensive classified advertisement sections where $2500 gets you something that will easily take you around the country if you know a bit about bikes. But you'll have to try and sell it again afterwards.

An easier option is a buy-back arrangement with a large motorcycle dealer in a major city (Elizabeth St near Franklin St in Melbourne is a good hunting ground). They're keen to do business, and basic negotiating skills allied with a wad of cash (say, $8000) should secure an excellent second-hand bike with a written guarantee that they'll buy it back in good condition minus $1500 after your four-month, round-Australia trip. Popular brands for this sort of thing are BMWs, large-capacity, shaft-driven Japanese bikes and possibly Harley-Davidsons (very popular in Australia). The percentage drop on a 600 cc trail bike (for, say, $3000) will be much greater, though the amount should be similar – if you can find a dealer willing to come to the party.

You'll need a rider's licence and a helmet. Some motorcyclists in New South Wales have special permission to ride without a helmet, ostensibly for medical reasons. A fuel range of 350 km will cover fuel stops up the centre and on highway No 1 around the continent. Beware of dehydration in the dry, hot air – force yourself to drink plenty of water, even if you don't feel thirsty. In Tasmania (a top bicycling and motorcycling destination) you should be prepared for rotten weather in winter, and rain any time of year.

The 'roo bars (outsize bumpers) on interstate trucks and many outback cars tell you never to ride at night, or in the early morning and evening. Marsupials are nocturnal, sleeping in the shade during the day and feeding at night, and road ditches provide luscious grass for them to eat. Cows and sheep also stray onto the roads at night. Be wise, enjoy the freedom that Australia offers, and head off into the bush at around 5 pm to set up camp. If you want to wash, many roadhouses offer showers free of charge or for a nominal fee. They're meant for truck drivers, but other people often use them too.

It's worth carrying some spares and tools even if you don't know how to use them, because someone else often does. If you do know, you'll probably have a fair idea of what to take. The basics include: a spare tyre tube (front wheel size, which will fit on the rear but usually not vice versa); puncture repair kit with levers and a pump (or tubeless tyre repair kit with two or three carbon dioxide cartridges); a spare tyre valve, and a valve cap that can unscrew same; the bike's standard tool kit for what it's worth (aftermarket items are better); spare throttle, clutch and brake cables; tie wire, cloth tape ('gaffer' tape) and nylon 'zip-ties'; a handful of bolts and nuts in the usual emergency sizes (M6 and M8), along with a few self-tapping screws; one or two fuses in your bike's ratings; a bar of soap for fixing tank leaks (knead to a putty with water and squeeze into the leak); and, most important of all, a workshop manual for your bike (even if you can't make sense of it, the local motorcycle mechanic can).

You'll never have enough elastic straps (octopus or 'ocky' straps) to tie down your gear. Make sure you carry water everywhere – at least two litres on major roads in central Australia, more off the beaten track. And finally, if something does go hopelessly wrong in the back of beyond, park your bike where it's clearly visible and observe the cardinal rule: DON'T LEAVE YOUR VEHICLE.

BICYCLE

Whether you're hiring a bike to ride around a city or wearing out your Bio-Ace chainwheels on a Melbourne-Darwin marathon, you'll find that Australia is a great place for cycling. There are bike tracks in most cities, and in the country you'll find thousands of km of good roads which carry so little traffic that the biggest hassle is waving back to the drivers. Especially appealing is that in many areas you'll ride a very long way without encountering a hill.

Bicycle helmets are compulsory wear in Victoria and Queensland, and other states are thinking about legislation.

It's possible to plan rides of any duration and through almost any terrain. A day or two cycling around South Australia's wineries is popular, or you could meander along beside the Murrumbidgee for weeks. Tasmania is very popular for touring, and mountain bikes would love Australia's deserts – or its mountains, for that matter.

And from his bike saddle Jon Murray, who updated the New South Wales and South Australia chapters for this edition, reports:

Cycling has always been popular here, and not only as a sport: some shearers would ride for huge distances between jobs, rather than use less reliable horses. It's rare to find a reasonably sized town that doesn't have a shop stocking at least basic bike parts.

If you're coming specifically to cycle it makes sense to bring your own bike. Check your airline for costs and the degree of dismantling/packing required. Within Australia you can load your bike onto a bus or train to skip the boring bits. Note that bus companies require you to dismantle your bike, and some don't guarantee that it will travel on the same bus as you. Trains are easier, but supervise the loading and if possible tie your bike upright, otherwise you may find that the guard had stacked crates of Holden spares on your fragile alloy wheels.

You can buy a good steel-framed touring bike here for about $400 (plus panniers). It may be possible to rent touring bikes and equipment from a few of the commercial touring organisations.

Much of eastern Australia seems to have been settled on the principle of not having more than a day's horse-ride between pubs, so it's possible to plan even ultra-long routes and still get a shower at the end of the day. Most people do carry camping equipment, but it's feasible to travel from town to town staying in hotels or on-site vans.

You can get by with standard road maps, but as you'll probably want to avoid both the highways and the low-grade unsealed roads, the Government series is best. The 1:250,000 scale is the most suitable but you'll need a lot of maps if you're covering much territory. The next scale up, 1:1,000,000 is adequate. They are available in capital cities and elsewhere.

Until you get fit you should be careful to eat enough to keep you going – remember that exercise is an appetite suppressant. It's surprisingly easy to be so depleted of energy that you end up camping under a gum tree just 10 km short of a shower and a steak.

No matter how fit you are, water is still vital. Dehydration is no joke and can be life-threatening. I rode my first 200-km-in-a-day on a bowl of cornflakes and a round of sandwiches, but the Queensland sun forced me to drink nearly five litres. Having been involved in a drinking contest with stockmen the night before may have had something to do with it, though.

It can get very hot in summer, and you should take things slowly until you're used to the heat. Cycling in 35°C-plus temperatures isn't too bad if you wear a hat and plenty of sunscreen, and drink *lots* of water. In the eastern states, be aware of the blistering 'hot northerlies', the prevailing winds that make a north-bound cyclist's life uncomfortable in summer. In April, when the south-east's clear autumn weather begins, the Southerly Trades prevail, and you can have (theoretically at least) tailwinds all the way to Darwin.

Of course, you don't have to follow the larger roads and visit towns. It's possible to fill your mountain bike's panniers with muesli, head out into the mulga, and not see anyone for weeks. Or ever again – outback travel is very risky if not properly planned. Water is the main problem in the 'dead heart', and you can't rely on it where there aren't settlements. That tank marked on your map may be dry or unbearably salty, and those station buildings probably blew away years ago. That little creek marked with a dotted blue line? Forget it – the only time it has water is when the country's flooded for hundreds of km.

Always check with locals if you're heading into remote areas, and notify the police if you're about to do something particularly adventurous. That said, you can't rely too much on local knowledge of road conditions – most people have no idea of what a heavily loaded touring bike needs. What they think of as a great road may be pedal-deep in sand or bull dust, and I've happily ridden along roads that were officially flooded out.

Information

In each state there are touring organisations which can help with information and put you in touch with touring clubs:

Australian Capital Territory
    Pedal Power ACT, PO Box 581, Canberra, ACT 2601 (☎ (06) 248 7995)
New South Wales
    Bicycle Institute of New South Wales, 82 Campbell St, Surry Hills 2010 (☎ (02) 212 5628)
Queensland
    Bicycle Institute of Queensland, The Web, 142 Agnew St, Norman Park 4101 (☎ (07) 899 2988)
South Australia
    Bicycle Institute of South Australia, 11 Church Rd, Mitcham 5062 (☎ (08) 271 5824)
Tasmania
    Pedal Power Tasmania, c/o Environment Centre, 102 Bathurst St, Hobart 7000 (☎ (002) 34 5566)
Victoria
    Bicycle Victoria, 29 Somerset Place, Melbourne 3000 (☎ (03) 670 9911)
Western Australia
    Cycle Touring Association, PO Box 174, Wembley 6014 (☎ (09) 349 2310)

There are many organised tours available of varying lengths, and if you get tired of talking to sheep as you ride along, it might be a good idea to include one or more tours in your itinerary. Most provide a support vehicle and take care of accommodation and cooking, so they can be a nice break from solo chores.

HITCHING

Travel by thumb may be frowned upon by the boys and girls in blue in some places but it can be a good way of getting around and it is certainly interesting. Sometimes it can even be fast, but it's usually foolish to try and set yourself deadlines when travelling this way – you need luck. Successful hitching depends on several factors, all of them just plain good sense.

The most important is your numbers – two people are really the ideal, any more make things very difficult. Ideally those two should comprise one male and one female – two guys hitching together can expect long waits. It is probably not advisable for women to hitch alone, or even in pairs. Queensland in particular is notorious for attacks on women travellers. Factor two is position – look for a place where vehicles will be going slowly and where they can stop easily. A junction or freeway slip road are good places if there is stopping room. Position goes beyond just where you stand. The ideal location is on the outskirts of a town – hitching from way out in the country is as hopeless as from the centre of a city. Take a bus out to the edge of town.

Factor three is appearance. The ideal appearance for hitching is a sort of genteel poverty – threadbare but clean. Looking too good can be as much of a bummer as looking too bad! Don't carry too much gear – if it looks like it's going to take half an hour to pack your bags aboard you'll be left on the roadside.

Factor four is knowing when to say no. Saying no to a car-load of drunks or your friendly rapist may be pretty obvious, but it can be time-saving to say no to a short ride that might take you from a good hitching point to a lousy one. Wait for the right, long ride to come along. On a long haul, it's pointless to start walking as it's not likely to increase the likelihood of you getting a lift and it's often an awfully long way to the next town.

Trucks are often the best lifts but they will only stop if they are going slowly and can get started easily again. Thus the ideal place is at the top of a hill where they have a downhill run. Truckies often say they are going to the next town and if they don't like you, will drop you anywhere. As they often pick up hitchers for company, the quickest way to create a bad impression is to jump in and fall asleep. It's also worth remembering that while you're in someone else's vehicle, you are their guest and should act accordingly – many drivers no longer pick up people because they have suffered from thoughtless hikers in the past. It's the hitcher's duty to provide entertainment!

Hitching in Australia is reasonably safe if you travel in pairs and take care with your rides. Of course people do get stuck in outlandish places but that is the name of the game. If you're visiting from abroad a nice prominent flag on your pack will help, and a sign announcing your destination can also be useful. Uni and hostel notice boards are good places to look for hitching partners. The main law against hitching is 'thou shalt not stand in the road' – so when you see the law coming, step back.

BOAT

Not really. Once upon a time there was quite a busy coastal shipping service but now it only applies to freight, and apart from specialised bulk carriers, even that is declining rapidly. The only regular shipping service is between Victoria and Tasmania

and unless you are taking a vehicle with you the very cheapest ticket on that often-choppy route is not all that much cheaper than the airfare. You can occasionally travel between Australian ports on a liner bound for somewhere but very few people do that.

On the other hand it *is* quite possible to make your way round the coast or even to other countries like NZ, PNG or Indonesia by hitching rides or crewing on yachts. Ask around at harbours, marinas or yacht or sailing clubs. Good places on the east coast include Coffs Harbour, Great Keppel Island, Airlie Beach/Whitsundays, Cairns – anywhere where boats call. Usually you have to chip in something like $10 a day for food.

A lot of boats move north to escape the winter, so April is a good time to look for a berth in the Sydney area.

TOURS

There are all sorts of tours around Australia including some interesting camping tours. Adventure tours include 4WD safaris in the Northern Territory and up into far north Queensland. Some of these go to places you simply couldn't get to on your own without large amounts of expensive equipment. You can also walk, ski, boat, raft, canoe, horseride, camel-ride or even fly.

YHA tours are good value – find out about them at YHA Travel offices in capital cities. In major centres like Sydney, Darwin and Cairns there are many tours aimed specially at backpackers – good prices, good destinations, good fun.

STUDENT TRAVEL

STA Travel is the main agent for student travellers in Australia. They have a network of travel offices around the country and apart from selling normal tickets also have special student discounts and tours. STA Travel don't only cater to students, they also act as normal travel agents to the public in general. The STA Travel head office is in Faraday St, Melbourne but there are a number of other offices around the various cities and at the universities. The main offices are:

Australian Capital Territory
Arts Centre, Australian National University, Canberra 2600 (☎ (06) 251 4688)

New South Wales
1A Lee St, Railway Square, Sydney 2000 (☎ (02) 519 9866)

Queensland
Northern Security Building, 40 Creek St, Brisbane 4000 (☎ (07) 221 9388)

South Australia
235 Rundle St, Adelaide 5000 (☎ (08) 223 2426)

Victoria
220 Faraday St, Carlton 3053 (☎ (03) 347 4711)

Western Australia
426 Hay St, Subiaco 6008 (☎ (09) 382 3977)

Australian Capital Territory

Area	2366 sq km
Population	274,000

When the separate colonies of Australia were federated in 1901 and became states, the decision to build a national capital was part of the constitution. The site was selected in 1908, diplomatically situated between arch rivals Sydney and Melbourne, and an international competition to design the capital was won by the American architect Walter Burley Griffin. In 1911 the Commonwealth government bought land for the Australian Capital Territory (ACT) and in 1913 decided to call the capital Canberra, believed to be an Aboriginal term for 'meeting place'.

Development of the site was slow and it was not until 1927 that parliament was first convened in the capital. From 1901 until then, Melbourne was the seat of the national government. The Depression virtually halted development and things really only got underway after WW II – in the '50s, '60s and '70s progress was incredibly rapid. Carefully planned satellite cities developed quickly at Belconnen and Woden. In 1960 the population topped 50,000, reaching 100,000 by 1967. Today the ACT has more than 270,000 people.

Canberra is unlike other large Australian cities: it's amazingly ordered and neat, and it is an inland city. Despite its reputation as a boring, soulless place to live, it has a fairly young population and there's a great deal to see and do. It also has a beautiful setting, surrounded by hills, and is no distance at all from good bushwalking and skiing country.

INFORMATION

The Canberra Tourist Bureau has its interstate offices at 14 Martin Place, Sydney, NSW 2000 (☎ (02) 233 3666) and 102 Elizabeth St, Melbourne, Vic 3000 (☎ (03) 654 5088).

ACTIVITIES
Bushwalking

Several of the parks and reserves in the south of the ACT have very good bushwalks. Tidbinbilla Fauna Reserve has marked trails. For other places see the Around Canberra section. Contact the Canberra Bushwalking Club through the Environment Centre (☎ (06) 247 3064), Kingsley St, Acton. Here you can buy *Above the Cotter* ($13.65), which details walks and drives in the area. Graeme Barrow's *Twenty-five Family Bushwalks In & Around Canberra* can be found in most city bookshops. There are also some good rock climbing areas.

Water Sports

Boating Boats, canoes, windsurfers and catamarans can be rented from Dobel Boat Hire (☎ (06) 249 6861) near the Acton Park Ferry Terminal on Lake Burley Griffin. They're open daily, with canoes at $10 an hour, windsurfers $14 and catamarans $20. Private power boats are not permitted on the lake. Canoeing in the Murrumbidgee River is also popular.

Swimming It's 150 km to the nearest surf beaches at Batemans Bay in New South Wales – there's a daily Murrays bus service.

Swimming pools around the city include the Olympic Pool on Allara St, Civic. There's river and lake swimming outside the city – see the Around Canberra section. Swimming in Lake Burley Griffin is not recommended.

Skiing

The New South Wales snowfields are within four hours' drive of Canberra. The Canberra Tourist Bureau can supply the latest news on conditions, as can the YMCA (☎ (06) 247 7606), which has lodges for members at Guthega and Thredbo. Some local garages, as well as the ski shops, hire equipment.

Cycling

Canberra has a great series of bicycle tracks – probably the best in Australia. A useful map and brochure is available from the tourist office. One popular track is a circuit of the lake; there are also peaceful stretches of bushland along some of the suburban routes. See the Getting Around section for bike rental information.

Canberra

Population 220,000

Don't let people in other states put you off visiting Canberra. Those who were dragged around the capital on school excursions probably remember it as a cold place full of nothing but buildings about which they had to write assignments, and for those who have done time in the Public Service, Canberra looms as the Mecca of all that bureaucratic lunacy. But for visitors without whip-cracking teachers or memories of pen-pushing, it's well worth seeing.

Some of the best architecture and exhibitions in Australia are here and the whole city is fascinating because it is totally planned and orderly, although if you don't have a car you'll appreciate that living here might not be such fun. If you do have wheels you'll enjoy some of the best urban driving conditions anywhere – but don't buy petrol on

Public Service paydays (alternate Thursdays), when the price mysteriously rises.

Canberra is a place of government with few local industries and it has that unique, stimulating atmosphere that's only to be found in national capitals. It is also acquiring the furnishings of a true centre of national life – like the exciting National Gallery, the new and splendid Parliament House and the excellent National Botanic Gardens. What's more, Canberra has quite a young population, including a lot of students, and entertainment is livelier than we're usually led to expect. Finally, this is the only city in Australia that's really *Australian* – as opposed to South Australian, Victorian, Western Australian or whatever.

Orientation

The city is arranged around the natural looking, but artificial, Lake Burley Griffin. On the north side is Canberra's city centre, known as Civic. Nearby are most of the short-term accommodation, the university, and a number of the neighbourhoods which are the basic unit of Canberra's urban structure. Each neighbourhood has its own centre with schools, shops and community services. They could be called satellite towns but they have very little local employment; they are more like dormitory suburbs from which people commute to work in other parts of the city. Most of the interesting government buildings are south of the lake.

The huge Vernon Circle is the centre point of the north side. Close to the circle are the tourist office, post office, airline and bus terminals, and the shops and restaurants of Civic; the oldest and most established shopping centre. Here, the mirror-image Sydney and Melbourne Buildings flank the beginning of Northbourne Ave, the main artery north of the lake. The main shopping and restaurant area is in the Sydney building and in the nearby pedestrian malls – Garema Place, City Walk and Petrie Plaza.

From Vernon Circle, Commonwealth Ave runs south over the Commonwealth Ave Bridge to Capital Circle, which surrounds the new Parliament House on Capital Hill.

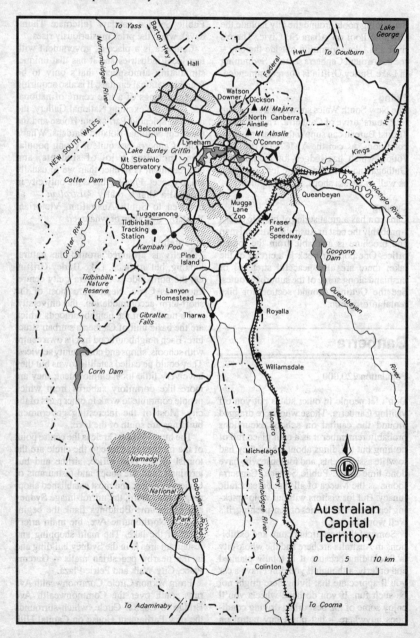

To Yass

Barton Hwy

Murrumbidgee River

To Goulburn

Lake George

Federal Hwy

Hall

Watson
Downer

Dickson

▲ Mt Majura

North Canberra

Ainslie

▲ Mt Ainslie

Belconnen

Lyneham

O'Connor

Kings Hwy

NEW SOUTH WALES

Lake Burley Griffin

Mt Stromlo
Observatory

Molonglo River

Cotter Dam

Queanbeyan

Cotter River

Mugga
Lane Zoo

Fraser
Park
Speedway

Googong
Dam

Tuggeranong

Tidbinbilla
Tracking
Station

Kambah Pool

Pine
Island

Queanbeyan River

Tidbinbilla
Nature
Reserve

Lanyon
Homestead

Royalla

Gibraltar
Falls

Tharwa

Williamsdale

Corin Dam

Namadgi

Murrumbidgee River

Monaro Hwy

National

Michelago

Park

Boboyan Road

Australian
Capital
Territory

0   5   10 km

Colinton

To Adaminaby

To Cooma

Capital Circle is the apex of Walter Burley Griffin's parliamentary triangle, formed by Commonwealth Ave, Kings Ave and the lake. Many of Canberra's important buildings are concentrated within this triangle, including the National Library, the High Court, the National Gallery and the old parliament house. South-east of Capital Hill is Manuka Circle, with another large shopping centre. Kings Ave also crosses the lake on the north-east side.

The biggest of the suburbs/satellite towns are Belconnen to the north-west and Woden to the south-west. Together with central Canberra they form the rough Y-shape the city planners first envisaged.

Information

Tourist Information The Canberra Tourist Bureau (☎ 245 6464) is in the Jolimont Centre, which is also the main long-distance bus station. It's open from 8.30 am to 5.15 pm Monday to Friday, from 8.30 am to 5 pm Saturday and from 8.30 am to 1.30 pm Sunday and holidays. The Jolimont Centre is on Northbourne Ave two blocks north of Vernon Circle, on the corner of Alinga St.

There's another information centre (with parking spaces) on Northbourne Ave, Dickson, about two km north of the Jolimont Centre. It's open from 9 am to 5 pm daily (7 pm in school holidays). The NRMA (☎ 243 8800) is at 92 Northbourne Ave. They have excellent maps of Canberra. The YHA has a useful walking tour leaflet.

Canberra's STD telephone area code is 06.

Post Have mail addressed to poste restante at the Canberra City Post Office on Alinga St, Civic.

Foreign Embassies With Canberra's slow development, embassies were also slow to show up, preferring to stay in the established cities, particularly Sydney and Melbourne, until the capital really existed. The British High Commission was the first diplomatic office to move here, arriving in 1936. It was followed in 1940 by the American Embassy. Today there are about 60 high commissions and embassies (Commonwealth countries have high commissions instead of embassies).

Enthusiasts of embassy spotting can pick up the tourist office's *Embassies in Canberra* folder or buy *Canberra's Embassies* by Graeme Barrow (Australian National University Press). A few of them are worth looking at, although many operate from rather nondescript suburban houses. Most are in Yarralumla, the area south of the lake and west and north of Parliament House. Here you'll also find Canberra's mosque, on the corner of Hunter St and Empire Circuit. Three times a year, on a Sunday in January, June and October, there's an embassies open day, when you can visit a number of them for about $5.

The US Embassy is a splendid facsimile of a mansion in the style of those in Williamsburg, Virginia, which in turn owe much to the English Georgian style. The Thai Embassy, with its pointed, orange-tiled roof, is in a style similar to that of temples in Bangkok. The Indonesian Embassy is no architectural jewel, but beside the dull embassy building there's a small display centre exhibiting Indonesia's colourful culture. It's open weekdays from 9.30 am to 12.30 pm and from 2 to 5 pm; if you're lucky you might catch a shadow puppet play put on for a visiting school group. The steps up to the centre are flanked by Balinese temple-guardian statues. Papua New Guinea's High Commission looks like a 'haus tambaran' spirit-house from the Sepik River region of PNG. There's a display room with colour photos and artefacts, open weekdays from 10 am to 12.30 pm and 2.30 to 4.30 pm.

Embassy and high commission addresses include:

Austria
  12 Talbot St, Forrest (☎ 295 1533)
Canada
  Commonwealth Ave, Yarralumla (☎ 273 3844)

Indonesia
    80 Darwin Ave, Yarralumla (☎ 273 3222)
Germany
    119 Empire Court, Yarralumla (☎ 270 1911)
Ireland
    20 Arkana St, Yarralumla (☎ 273 3022)
India
    3 Moonah Place, Yarralumla (☎ 273 3774)
Japan
    112 Empire Circuit, Yarralumla (☎ 273 3244)
Malaysia
    7 Perth Ave, Yarralumla (☎ 273 1543)
Netherlands
    120 Empire Circuit, Yarralumla (☎ 273 3111)
New Zealand
    Commonwealth Ave, Yarralumla (☎ 273 3611)
Norway
    17 Hunter St, on the corner of Fitzgerald St,
    Yarralumla (☎ 273 3444)
Papua New Guinea
    Forster Crescent, Yarralumla (☎ 273 3322)
Singapore
    Forster Crescent, Yarralumla (☎ 273 3944)
Sweden
    Turrana St, Yarralumla (☎ 273 3033)
Switzerland
    7 Melbourne Ave, Forrest (☎ 273 3977)
Thailand
    111 Empire Circuit, Yarralumla (☎ 273 1149)
UK
    Commonwealth Ave, Yarralumla (☎ 270 6666)
USA
    21 Moonah Place, Yarralumla (☎ 270 5000)

Bookshops There are many good bookshops; Dalton's, in the Capital Centre, near Barry Drive, is probably the best. There's an excellent second-hand bookshop in Lyneham shopping centre, near Tilley's bar. Canberra is well stocked with overseas information centres and libraries – good places to keep up with foreign magazines, papers and films.

Lookouts

There are fine views of the lake and the city from the surrounding hills. Immediately west of Civic, Black Mountain rises to 825 metres and is topped by the 195-metre Telecom Telecommunications Tower, complete with a revolving restaurant. The food is the revolving restaurant norm: expensive and inferior to the view. The view alone can be taken in for $2 from 9 am to 10 pm. There are splendid vistas from nearby lookouts and

from the approach road. Bus No 904 runs to the tower from the Jolimont Centre at noon and 1 pm, or you can walk up the mountain – quite a pleasant stroll apart from the mad traffic. There are good bushwalks round the back of the mountain too.

Other mountain lookouts, all with roads to them, are the 722-metre Red Hill, the 840-metre Mt Ainslie and the 665-metre Mt Pleasant. Mt Ainslie is close to the city on the north-east side and has particularly fine views across the city and out over the airport. From the top you'll also appreciate how green and full of parks Canberra is. The view is excellent at night. There are foot trails up Mt Ainslie from behind the War Memorial, and out behind Mt Ainslie to 888-metre Mt Majura four km away. You may see a kangaroo or two on the hike up.

Lake Burley Griffin

The lake was named after Canberra's designer, but was not finally created until the Molonglo River was dammed in 1963. The lake is not recommended for swimming, but you can go boating (beware of strong winds which can blow up suddenly from nowhere) or cycle around it. You can hire boats and bikes from beside the Acton Park Ferry Terminal, on the north side of the lake – see the Getting Around section and this chapter's Activities section.

There are a number of places of interest around the 35 km shore. The most visible is the **Captain Cook Memorial Water Jet** which flings a six-tonne column of water 140 metres into the air, and will give you a free shower if the wind is blowing from the right direction. (This is despite an automatic switch-off which is supposed to operate if the wind speed gets too high.) The jet, built in 1970 to commemorate the bicentenary of Captain Cook's visit to Australia, usually operates from 10 am to noon and 2 to 4 pm daily. At **Regatta Point**, nearby on the northern shore, is a skeleton globe, three metres in diameter, with Cook's three great voyages traced on it.

The **Canberra Planning Exhibition**, also at Regatta Point, is open daily from 9 am to

5 pm and has displays on the growth of the capital. Further round the lake, to the east, is **Blundell's Farmhouse** which dates from 1858, long before the selection of the area as the capital. The simple stone and slab cottage is a reminder of the area's early farming history. It's now maintained as a small museum and is open from 2 to 4 pm daily; entry is $1.50.

A little further around the lake, at the far end of Commonwealth Park which stretches east from the Commonwealth Ave Bridge, is the **Carillon**, on Aspen Island. The 53-bell tower was a gift from Britain in 1963, Canberra's 50th anniversary. The Carillon was completed in 1970, and the bells weigh from seven kg to six tonnes. There are recitals on Sunday at 2.45 pm, on Wednesday at 12.45 pm and on public holidays.

West of the bridge, still on the north side of the lake, are Acton and Black Mountain peninsulas. The south shore of the lake, along which the impressive National Gallery and High Court are situated, forms the base of the parliamentary triangle.

Parliament House

South of the lake, the four-legged flagmast on top of Capital Hill marks Parliament House, at the end of Commonwealth Ave. This, the most recent aspect of Walter Burley Griffin's vision to become a reality, sits at the apex of the parliamentary triangle. Opened by the Queen in 1988, it cost $1.1 billion, took eight years to build and replaces the 'temporary' old parliament house lower down the hill on King George Terrace, which served for 11 years longer than its intended 50-year life. The new Parliament was designed by the US-based Italian Romaldo Giurgola, who won a competition entered by more than 300 architects.

It's built into the top of the hill and the roof has been grassed over so that it resembles the original hilltop. Part of the building is subterranean, which has provoked jibes about MPs being buried in a 'sci-fi mausoleum', but the interior design and decoration is splendid. Seventy new art and craft works were commissioned from Australian artists

and a further 3000 bought for the building. A different combination of Australian timbers is used in each of its principal sections.

The main axis of the building runs northeast to south-west, in a direct line from the old parliament, the Australian War Memorial across the lake, and Mt Ainslie. On either side of this axis two high, granite-faced walls curve out from the centre to the corners of the site – on a plan they look like back-to-back boomerangs. The House of Representatives is to the east of these walls, the Senate to the west. They're linked to the centre by covered walkways.

Extensive areas of Parliament House are open to the public from 9 am to 5 pm every day. You enter through the white marble Great Verandah at the north-east end of the main axis, where Nelson Tjakamarra's *Meeting Place* mosaic, within the pool, represents a gathering of Aboriginal tribes. Inside, the grey-green marble columns of the foyer symbolise a forest, while marquetry panels on the walls depict Australian flora. From the 1st floor you look down on the Reception Hall, with its 20-metre-long Arthur Boyd tapestry. A public gallery above the Reception Hall has a 16-metre-long embroidery, worked on by 1000 people.

Beyond the Reception Hall you reach the gallery above the Members' Hall, the central 'crossroads' of the building, with the flagmast above it and passages to the debating chambers on each side. One of only four known originals of the Magna Carta is on display here. South of the Members' Hall are the committee rooms and ministers' offices. The public can view the committee rooms and attend some of their proceedings. Other visitor facilities include a cafeteria, a terrace with views over the city, and a small theatre telling the story of Australian democracy. You can also wander over the grassy top of the building. If you want to make sure of a place in the House of Representatives gallery, book by phone (☎ 277 4889) or write to the Principal Attendant, House of Representatives, Parliament House, Canberra. There are always some seats left unbooked,

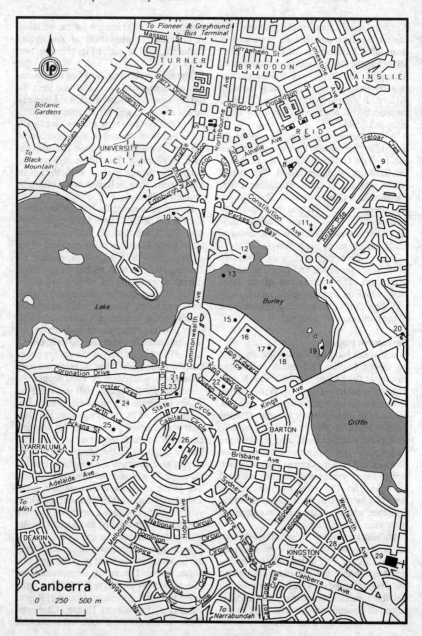

1	Academy of Science
2	University Students Union
3	GPO
4	Jolimont Centre
5	Gorman House
6	Acacia Motor Lodge
7	Ainslie Hotel
8	Narellan House
9	War Memorial
10	Ferry Terminal, Bike & Boat Hire
11	Church of St John The Baptist
12	Canberra Planning Exhibition
13	Captain Cook Water Jet
14	Blundell's Farmhouse
15	National Library
16	Australian Science & Technology Centre
17	High Court
18	National Gallery
19	Carillon
20	Australian-American Memorial
21	UK High Commission
22	Old Parliament House
23	PNG High Commission
24	Indonesian Embassy
25	US Embassy
26	Parliament House (on Capital Hill)
27	Thai Embassy
28	Victor Lodge
29	Central Station

but on sitting days you'd have to queue early to get one. Seats in the Senate gallery are almost always available.

On non-sitting days there are free guided tours every half hour; on sitting days there's a talk on the building in the Great Hall Gallery every half hour. For $3 you can hire a cassette and player for a self-guided tour.

Bus No 777 runs right into the underground carpark.

Old Parliament House

On King George Terrace, halfway between the new Parliament House and the lake, this building was the seat of government from 1927 to 1988. Its parliamentary days were ended in style: as the corridors of power echoed to the Defence Minister's favourite Rolling Stones records, the Prime Minister and Leader of the Opposition sang together

arm in arm, and bodies were seen dragging themselves away well after dawn the next morning – and that's just what got into print.

For the present, the building is not open to the public (a Constitutional Museum is planned) but there are fine views from its grounds.

Australian National Gallery

At the bottom of the parliamentary triangle, on Parkes Place, beside the High Court and Lake Burley Griffin, is the art gallery, opened in 1982. Works were bought back in the '70s when a 'truly fabulous' sum for Jackson Pollock's *Blue Poles* was paid. More gee-whizz purchases from time to time have kept the gallery in the public eye.

The Australian collection ranges from traditional Aboriginal art through to 20th-century works by Arthur Boyd, Sidney Nolan and Albert Tucker. Aboriginal works include bark paintings from Arnhem land, burial poles from the Tiwi people of Melville and Bathurst Islands off Darwin, printed fabrics by the women of Utopia and Ernabella in central Australia, and paintings from Yuendumu, also in central Australia. There are often temporary exhibitions from the Kimberley and other areas where Aboriginal art is flourishing.

In addition to works from the early decades of European settlement and the 19th-century romantics, there are examples of the early nationalistic statements of Charles Conder, Arthur Streeton and Tom Roberts. The collection is not confined to paintings: sculptures, prints, drawings, photographs, furniture, ceramics, fashion, textiles and silverware are all on display.

The Sculpture Garden is landscaped with Australian plants and has a variety of striking sculptures, some very large. The gallery is open from 10 am to 5 pm daily, and tours are given at 11.15 am, 1.15 and 2.15 pm. Admission is $3 (free if you have a student card). Free lectures are given on Tuesday, Wednesday and Thursday at 12.45 pm. On the last Thursday night of each month, there's a free session beginning with a guided tour, followed by informal discussion groups, a film and then a guest lecture. Phone the gallery for details (☎ 271 2502). There are two gallery restaurants.

High Court

The High Court building, by the lake next to the National Gallery, is open from 10 am to 4 pm most days of the year. Opened in 1980, its grandiose magnificence caused it to be dubbed 'Gar's Mahal', a reference to Sir Garfield Barwick, Chief Justice during the building's construction. To tell the truth, there is a touch of Indian Moghul palace about the ornamental watercourse burbling alongside the entrance path to this grand building.

Questacon – National Science & Technology Centre

This is a 'hands on' science museum in the snappy new white building between the High Court and the National Library. It's open daily from 10 am to 5 pm and entry is $5 (☎ 270 2800). There are 200 'devices' in the centre's five galleries and outdoor areas where you can use 'props' to get a feeling for a scientific concept, and then see its application to an everyday situation. It might be educational but it's also great fun.

National Library

Also on Parkes Place, beside the lake, is the National Library (☎ 262 1159), one of the most elegant buildings in Canberra. It has more than 4½ million books, and displays include rare books, paintings, early manuscripts and maps, a cannon from Cook's ship the *Endeavour*, a fine model of the ship itself and varying special exhibitions. The foyer is dominated by three huge tapestries. The library is open from 9 am to 9 pm Monday to Thursday, 9 am to 4.45 pm Friday and Saturday, and 1.30 to 4.45 pm on Sunday. There are guided tours (☎ 269 1699) and free films on Tuesday lunchtime and Thursday night – phone for programmes (☎ 262 1475).

Royal Australian Mint

The mint, on Denison St, Deakin, south of the lake, produces all Australia's coins.

Through plate glass windows (to keep you at arm's length from the readies) you can see the whole process, from raw materials to finished coins. There's a collection of rare coins in the foyer. The mint is open from 9 am to 4 pm Monday to Friday and 10 am to 3 pm on weekends and holidays. If you are considering visiting on a Friday ring first (☎ 283 3244), as workers have a rostered day off once a month. Bus Nos 230, 231 and 267 go there.

Australian War Memorial

The massive war memorial, north of the lake and at the foot of Mt Ainslie, looks directly along Anzac Parade to the old parliament house across the lake. The war memorial was conceived in 1925 and finally opened in 1941, not long after WW II broke out in the Pacific. It houses an amazing collection of pictures, dioramas, relics and exhibitions, including a fine collection of old aircraft. For anyone with a toy soldier interest, the miniature battle scenes are absorbing. The shrine is the focus of the memorial. It features a quite beautiful interior, some superb stained-glass windows and a dome made of six million Italian mosaic pieces. The memorial is open from 9 am to 4.45 pm daily except for Christmas Day and admission is free (☎ 243 4211). Bus Nos 302 and 303 run from the city.

Australian National University

The ANU's attractive grounds occupy most of the Acton area between Civic and the foot of Black Mountain. It's pleasant to wander around its colleges, lawns, fields, pathways, roads and lakes. The uni was founded in 1946. There's an information centre, on Balmain Crescent, open from 9 am to 5 pm Monday to Friday, with free maps and other information. The University Union on University Ave offers a variety of cheap eats and, sometimes, entertainment. On the corner of Kingsley St and Barry Drive is the Drill Hall Gallery, an offshoot of the National Gallery with changing exhibitions of contemporary art. It's open from noon to 5 pm Wednesday to Sunday. Admission is free.

National Film & Sound Archive

The archive is on McCoy Circuit, at the eastern edge of the university area, and is open from 9.30 am to 4 pm daily. Admission is free. Film and sound exhibitions from the archive's collections are shown. Over the road is the Australian Academy of Science (not open to the public), known locally as the Martian Embassy. It does indeed look like a misplaced flying saucer.

National Botanic Gardens

Yes, a botanic garden was part of Walter Burley Griffin's plan too – one dedicated to Australia's unique native flora. Like so much of Canberra it has taken a long time for his vision to become a reality – planting only started in 1950 and the gardens were officially opened in 1970. On the lower slopes of Black Mountain, behind the ANU, the beautiful 50-hectare gardens have several educational walks, including one amongst plants used by Aborigines.

A highlight is the rainforest area, achieved in this dry climate by a 'misting' system. The eucalypt lawn has 600 species of this ubiquitous Australian tree, while the mallee section displays the typical vegetation of South Australia and Victoria. The herbarium (collection of pressed and dried plant specimens used for research) and nursery are closed to the public, but if you're a botanist you may be able to talk your way in.

The gardens are reached from Clunies Ross St and are open from 9 am to 6 pm daily. There are guided tours at 10 am and 2 pm on Sunday. The information centre, open from 10 am to 4 pm daily, has an introductory video and there's a small theatre showing films about botany at 11 am and 2 pm. The Botanical Bookshop in the information centre has an excellent range of books, cards and posters. Near where the walks start and finish is a restaurant with good food, reasonable prices and a pleasant outdoor section.

National Museum of Australia

The site for the museum is on Lady Denman Drive, beside the north-west shore of Lake Burley Griffin. The museum has not been built yet – there doesn't seem to be a definite date when construction will start, but it's scheduled to be finished in 2001. Money is the problem. There's a visitors' centre on the site (☎ 256 1111), open from 10 am to 4 pm weekdays and from 1 to 4 pm weekends, showing items from the museum's collection. One item is the heart of Phar Lap, Australia's wonder racehorse of the 1930s, who died in suspicious circumstances in California. The rest of him is in the National Museum of Victoria in Melbourne.

Australian Institute of Sport

Founded in 1981 as part of an effort to improve Australia's performance at events like the Olympics, the AIS is on Leverrier Crescent, in the northern suburb of Bruce, not far from the YHA hostel. It provides training facilities for the country's top sportspeople. The tennis courts and swimming pool are open to visitors (☎ 252 1281). Guided tours of the institute ($1) are given daily at 2 pm (☎ 252 1444). Bus No 431 will take you there from the city centre.

National Aquarium

Near Scrivner Dam, the west end of the lake, the aquarium (☎ 287 1211) is impressive but expensive – $9.50 ($8.50 with a student card, less with a YHA card) – and there's no public transport nearby. As well as watching the fish you can catch your own trout. Fly-fishing gear is available for $5 an hour, and there are lessons for $5.

Other Buildings

You can do no more than drive by and peek in the gates of the prime minister's official Canberra residence, **The Lodge**, on Adelaide Ave, Deakin – Australia's 10 Downing St. The same is true of **Government House**, the residence of the governor general, which is on the south-west corner of Lake Burley Griffin, but there's a lookout beside Scrivener Dam at the end of the lake, giving a good view of the building. The governor general is the representative on earth – sorry, in Australia – of the British monarch, who is Australia's head of state.

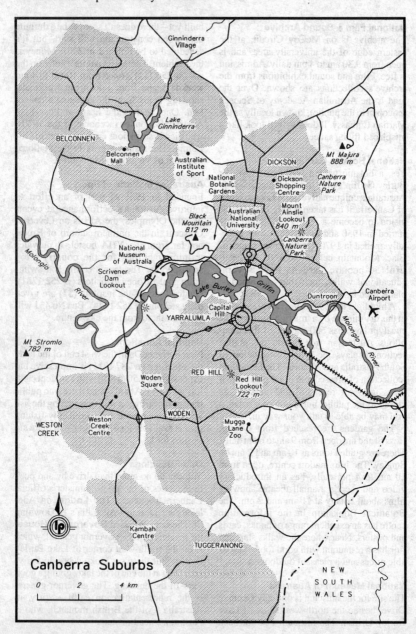

Canberra Suburbs

0   2   4 km

At the east end of Kings Ave the **Australian-American Memorial**, a 79-metre-high pillar topped by an eagle, is a memorial to American support of Australia during WW II.

The **Church of St John the Baptist**, in Reid, just east of Civic, was built between 1841 and 1845 and thus predates the capital. The stained-glass windows show pioneering families of the region. There is an adjoining schoolhouse with some early relics, open Wednesday from 10 am to noon, and weekends from 2 to 4 pm. The **Serbian Orthodox Church** in Forrest has its walls and ceiling painted with a series of biblical murals.

The **Royal Military College, Duntroon**, was once a homestead, and parts of it date from the 1830s. Tours of the grounds start at the sign in Starkey Park, Jubilee Ave, at 2.30 pm on weekdays (except public holidays), February to November.

Other Sights

The Canberra **Tradesmen's Union Club** in Badham St, Dickson, near Dickson Place, has what it claims to be 'the world's second-largest collection of unusual bicycles'. It's good for kids and there's a BMX track next door which hires out bikes. There's also a gym and squash courts. The club also runs the nearby **Downer Club**, off Antill St near Hawdon St. Here they aren't second-best – they claim the world's largest beer collection and there's also an observatory with an astronomer on duty. Admission to all this is free.

Organised Tours

The Tourist Bureau has information on the many city tours. Canberra Cruises (☎ 295 3544) has cruises on Lake Burley Griffin from $8. There is a variety of day trips to places like the Snowy Mountains, nature reserves, the satellite tracking station, sheep stations, horse studs and fossicking areas around the ACT. For $34 you can take a half-hour flight over Canberra, and given the grand scale of the planning it might be a good way to get a feel for the city. Phone for details (☎ 248 6766 or 249 7044).

Festivals

The Canberra Festival takes place over 10 days each March and celebrates the city's birthday with music, food, mardi gras, displays, an exciting raft race, a birdman rally (birdwomen welcome), and a big parade. Many of the events are held in Commonwealth Park, which is the site of a carnival. In September there's the Floriade, concentrating on flowers but with a lot of related events.

Places to Stay

Hostels 'The best YHA I've ever seen' is how one traveller described the *Canberra YHA Hostel* (☎ 248 9759). It's new, purpose-built and has good dorms, kitchens and a kiosk. Their free discount card gets sizeable reductions at many places around town, including about 30% off some bus fares to Sydney and a few other places. Nightly charges are $15, plus $3 if you need a sleeping sheet and there are some twin rooms with attached bathrooms for $19 a person. You can check in up until midnight if you give advance warning. The hostel is on Dryandra St, O'Connor, about six km north-west of Civic, on the edge of bushland near the Institute of Sport. Bus No 380 departs every half hour from the city centre for the Scrivener St stop on Miller St, O'Connor. From there, follow the signs. Driving, turn west off Northbourne Ave onto Macarthur Ave and after about two km turn right onto Dryandra. You can hire bicycles at the hostel.

On the other side of town in Manuka, a couple of km from Parliament House, the *Kingston Hotel* (☎ 295 0123) on the corner of Canberra Ave and Giles St offers bunk accommodation for $12 per person, plus $3 linen hire. There are no cooking facilities but counter meals are under $5 (extra for chips). The bars are open 24 hours.

Guesthouses & Private Hotels As you enter Canberra from the Hume Highway, there's a clutch of guesthouses on the left (east) side of Northbourne Ave, Downer, just south of where the Barton Highway from Yass and the Federal Highway from

Goulburn meet. All are plain and straight-forward but clean and quite comfortable. They're cheaper by the week. It's four km or so into town, but buses run along Northbourne Ave.

At No 524, The *Blue & White Lodge* (☎ 248 0498), which also runs the *Blue Sky* at No 528, has shared rooms for about $17 a person and singles between $26 and $30. Prices include cooked breakfast and all rooms have TV, but bathrooms are shared. *Chelsea Lodge* (☎ 248 0655), at No 526, is $30/40 a single/double including breakfast, or $40/50 with private bathroom. At the *Northbourne Lodge* (☎ 257 2599) at No 522 you can get a bed in a shared room for $18 or singles/doubles for $30/40, all with break-fast. Rooms have TV, and bathrooms are communal. They will pick you up from the bus station if you phone.

Within easy walking distance of the city centre is the *Gowrie Private Hotel* (☎ 249 6033), a couple of tower blocks at 210 Northbourne Ave, Braddon, on the corner of Ipima St. It's a former government hostel, still run by the government but now as a hotel, with no less than 570 rooms. Singles/doubles with common bathroom are $30/50 (much cheaper by the week) includ-ing a big breakfast. The rooms are plain and smallish but it's clean and well-heated.

The *Macquarie Private Hotel* (☎ 273 2325), south of the lake, at 18 National Circuit, Barton, on the corner of Bourke St, has 500 rooms and the same setup and prices as the Gowrie. There are other guest houses, but they're mostly not as conveniently situ-ated, or their prices are a lot higher.

Motels Most motels are quite expensive. You might do better than the prices listed here if you book at the tourist office, as they often have special rates. The *Acacia Motor Lodge* (☎ 249 6955), at 65 Ainslie Ave, is $60/65 including light breakfast, and it's only a half km from the centre of Civic. It has barbecues in the courtyard. Cheaper but not so central, the *Motel 7* (☎ 295 1111), on Jerrabomberra Rd (Cooma Rd), Nar-rabundah, is about eight km south-east of the

centre. It has most mod cons, a swimming pool and a restaurant, and costs $40/44 ($4 per extra person) for a small room.

There are a few more middle-range motels in Narrabundah, including *Crestwood Gardens* (☎ 295 0174), at 39 Jerrabomberra Ave, at $55/65; and *Sundown Village* (☎ 239 0333), at the corner of Jerrabomberra Ave and Narrabundah Lane, which is quite attrac-tive, with self-contained 'villas' costing $70 a double plus $10 for each extra person, and two-bedroom villas at $80 plus $10 per extra person.

Victor Lodge (☎ 295 7432), at 29 Dawes St, Kingston, half a km from the railway station and a couple of km south-east of Capital Hill, is a simple but decent place with shared facilities from $30/45 with breakfast or $25/40 without. Bunks in dorm rooms cost $15. Next door at No 27, the *Motel Monaro* (☎ 295 2111) has special offers, such as doubles from $50 or $60 with a full breakfast.

Some caravan parks also have motel-type accommodation: the *Canberra Lakes Carotel* (☎ 241 1377), just off the Federal Highway at Watson, six km north of the centre, has 'chalets' which sleep up to 12 people, with cooking facilities, TVs and bathrooms from $45 a double. Bedding is provided and there's a pool and a cafeteria. The *Red Cedars Accommodation Centre* (☎ 241 3222), on the corner of Stirling Ave and Aspinall St, Watson, has units with kitch-ens from $48/55 a single/double, with extra people charged $7 each. Again, there's a pool and TVs. The *South Side Motor Park* (☎ 280 6176), on Canberra Ave, Fyshwyck, about nine km south-east of the centre, charges $38/45 for non-air-con rooms with private facilities.

Colleges The Australian National Univer-sity, in Acton, near Civic, has a selection of residential places which may have empty rooms during the May, June, August or November to February uni vacations. Charges are around $20/30 for students/non-students, much less by the week. The uni campus is a very pleasant place to stay. Try

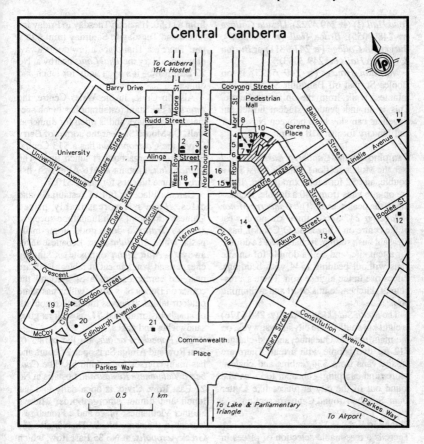

Central Canberra

1 Dalton's Bookshop
2 Canberra City Post Office
3 Tourist Office, Australian Airlines
   Office & Bus Station
   (Jolimont Centre)
4 Ansett Airlines
5 YWCA
6 Action Information Centre
   (Local Buses)
7 Mama's Trattoria
8 Pizzeria
9 Angus & Robertson
   Bookshop & Dorettes
10 Gus's
11 Gorman House & Clarry's
    Restaurant
12 Narellan House
13 Bushgear
14 Canberra Theatre Centre
15 Canberra Vietnamese Restaurant
16 Private Bin Nightclub
17 Honeydew Restaurant
18 Malaysian Restaurant
19 National Film & Sound Archive
20 Academy of Science
21 Lakeside International Hotel

Toad Hall (!) (☎ 249 4722), *Ursula College* (☎ 248 9055), *Bruce Hall* (☎ 249 2827), *Burgmann College* (☎ 247 9811) or *Burton & Garran Halls* (☎ 249 3083).

Narellan House (☎ 249 6125) is on Boolee St, just off Balumbir St, Reid, five minutes' walk from the Jolimont Centre. This is an independent student hostel but travellers can stay here between November and January for just $10 a night.

Camping At the *Canberra Lakes Carotel* (see the Motels section), tent sites cost $10 a double, and $2 for each extra person. There are on-site vans from $40 a double, increasing in the peak season. The *Canberra Motor Village* (☎ 247 5466), three km north-west of the centre on Kunzea St, O'Connor, has a pleasant bush setting. It charges $13 a double for a tent site, and $39 a double for on-site vans without bedding ($44 with bedding). Prices rise in the high season. There's a restaurant, kitchen, tennis court and swimming pool.

The *South Side Motor Park* (☎ 280 6176) is eight km south of the city in Fyshwyck, on the main road to Queanbeyan, and charges $12 for two people with a tent. There are on-site vans from $34, cabins and chalets. More rural camping – cheaper too – can be found out of the city at places like Cotter Dam. See the Around Canberra section.

Places to Eat
There is a reasonable selection of places in Civic and a few further away. *Waffles Restaurant* inside the *Private Bin* nightclub complex, at 50 Northbourne Ave, described eloquently by a local as a 'basic pig-out joint', offers food of the steak, pasta, burger, pizza variety at around $10 for a main meal, although there are daily $3 specials which include a free beer in *The Tavern*, also in the Private Bin complex. On the same side of the block there are Chinese and Indonesian restaurants and a waffle place, all of them medium priced. On the other side of Northbourne Ave the *Honeydew*, at No 55, is a 'gourmet wholemeal' place with main courses for lunch from $8 and for dinner

from $11.50. It's open Tuesday to Friday for lunch, and Tuesday to Saturday from 6 to 9 pm. There's a Thai place a few doors away, or you could try the *Thai Lotus* nearby at No 27 East Row – it's open daily for lunch and dinner.

Also in Civic, in the Wales Centre, the *Anarkali* Pakistani restaurant has lunch specials on weekdays and is open for dinner as well. On Moore St, near the corner of Barry Drive, the *Cosmopolitan* has a $13 Central European smorgasbord at lunch time. The *Chinese Inn*, upstairs at 116 Alinga St, has three-course lunches for under $10.

Garema Place is full of restaurants and cafes. *Happy's* is a reasonably priced Chinese restaurant with lunchtime specials. *Mama's Trattoria* does good home-made pasta, while *Ali Baba* does Lebanese takeaways – *Alaa Dean* opposite is slightly cheaper and you can eat at tables. Both are near the corner of Bunda St. Around the corner on Bunda St is *Gus's*, which has some outdoor tables. It serves meals like goulash or spaghetti for around $7, as well as good sandwiches and cakes.

The *Pancake Parlour*, on the corner of East Row and Alinga St, is open 24 hours and has main courses for around $8. The *Canberra Vietnamese Restaurant*, upstairs at No 21 East Row, Civic, is open daily and has lunch and dinner smorgasbords. There's another Vietnamese place and a French restaurant in the same block. There's also the Greek *Acropolis*, at No 35 East Row, which has main courses for around $8. It's open until 9 pm, but closed on Sunday.

At the south end of East Row, on the corner of London Circuit (known as Bailey's Corner), is the *Corner Coffee Shop*, a tiny place doling out what must be Canberra's best coffee. The *Malaysian Restaurant*, on the south side of the Melbourne Building, is very good; main courses are from about $8. The *Rasa Sayang*, also Malaysian, at No 43 Woolley St, Dickson, is quite good and reasonably priced.

Clarry's, in the Gorman House Arts Centre, on Ainslie Ave, Braddon, a few minutes' walk north-east of Civic, is a good vegetarian cafe open Tuesday to Saturday, with main courses at $5. It's particularly lively on Saturday when a market is held there.

Cheap food can be found at the ANU students union *Refectory* in the university. Late-night appetites are catered for by the *Tuckerbuses*, known as 'Dog Houses', that appear nightly at strategic spots. They're open till very late. *Dolly's*, on the corner of Marcus Clark St and Barry Drive, is the best of them. *Jimmy's*, on the corner of Mort and Bunda Sts, is another.

North of the centre and to the west of Northbourne Ave, good fish & chips are served up at the *Lyneham Fish Shop* in the Lyneham Shopping Centre. Also in Lyneham, at 96 Wattle St, is *Tilley's*, a cafe, bar and art gallery offering healthy food (if you don't count the great cakes). In the same shopping centre there's a good Thai restaurant.

South of the lake, not far from Capital Hill, is the Manuka Shopping Village, which services the diplomatic corps and the well-heeled bureaucrats from surrounding neighbourhoods. Amongst the pricey speciality shops you'll find the good and reasonably priced Turkish *Alanya*, on the 2nd floor of the Style Arcade (closed Sunday). The banquet is good value for three or more. Among the many other places are *Caph's*, for straightforward, good food; *My Mother's Favourites* for breakfast, muffins and coffee; and *Timmy's Kitchen*, a very popular Malaysian/Chinese place.

In O'Connor are two good Vietnamese restaurants, the *Vung Thao* and the *Vietnam*. There are some Chinese places in Dickson too – fairly convenient if you're staying in one of the guest houses at the top of Northbourne Ave.

Entertainment

Canberra is more lively than its reputation suggests. For one thing, liberal licensing laws allow hotels unlimited opening hours and there are some 24-hour bars, in contrast to the rest of Australia. The Thursday *Canberra Times* has full entertainment listings,

and the Radio 2CC has a 'what's on' slot at 4.30 and 5.30 pm on Thursday and Friday, and at 9.45 am on Saturday. If you're tired of Oz club culture, ring up one of the clubs catering to Australians of foreign descent, to see if visitors are welcome – see the Yellow Pages under 'Clubs, Social'.

The Canberra Theatre Centre, on Civic Square, has several theatres with a varied range of events from rock bands and drama to ballet, opera and classical concerts. Also check with the foreign cultural organisations like Maison de France and the Goethe Centre to find out what's on. Gorman House Arts Centre, on Ainslie Ave, Braddon, sometimes has theatre or dance performances or exhibitions. There's an interesting market held every Saturday from 10 am to 4 pm, with arts, crafts, books, etc. The Brickworks Market, held on weekends between 11 am and 5 pm, on Denman St in Yarralumna, has antiques, junk and everything in between.

Dancing & Drinking There's live music two or three nights a week during term at the ANU union and there's an excellent juke box in the bar too. Big touring acts often play the Refectory here.

The Old Canberra Inn has live music on most nights, and here you can sample the local Eaglehawk Bitter. The Ainslie Hotel, on Limestone Ave, Ainslie, has a piano/jazz bar and a popular, often crowded, beer garden. Tilley's often has live music, usually a cut above pub bands, on Friday, Saturday and Sunday nights. The Southern Cross Club, in Woden, sometimes has good jazz. One of the most relaxed and comfortable places is Dorettes, upstairs near Mama's Trattoria in Garema Place – a semi-Bohemian wine bar with live acoustic music, where you can have a drink or spend about $20 on dinner.

Other places that sometimes have live bands – often top line touring bands – include the central Canberra Workers' Club, on Childers St, which has a rock disco, and the Canberra Labor Club, on Chandler St, Belconnen. You can usually get cheap meals – and play the pokies – at these and similar clubs. The Rose & Crown in Brierly St, Weston, has bands on weekends, as does Platform 3, out in the Tuggeranong Market.

Better nightclubs and discos include Inner City, in Alinga St, and Pandora's, nearby on the corner of Alinga and Mort Sts. The Private Bin, on Northbourne Ave, Civic, is a big nightclub which is open late and you can get meals. The Circus, on Garema Place, plays alternative dance music until late. Rascals, on Petrie Plaza, is a cocktail bar and restaurant as well as a nightclub, and it's popular. Also in Civic, on the south side of the Sydney Building is Moose Heads, a bar and cafe with bands Thursday to Saturday. Club Asmara, at 128 Bunda St near Garema Place, is a fairly pricey African restaurant but if you turn up after 9 pm you can listen to the music (sometimes live) without ordering a meal, although there's a $4 cover charge on Friday and Saturday.

During the summer, the Monaro Folk Group hold a woolshed dance on the last Saturday of the month at the Woolshed, Yarralumla, near the governor general's place. It's a Canberra occasion.

Cinemas There are a number of cinemas around the Civic Square and London Circuit area. The Boulevard Twin Cinemas, on Akuna St, are collectively known as Electric Shadows and show repertory type films.

The National Library runs free films on Tuesday lunchtimes and Thursday evenings with good, varied programmes, but they're not well advertised – phone for details (☎ 262 1475). The National Gallery has concerts and films on Saturday and Sunday afternoons at around 2.30 pm. You have to be a member to get into the ANU film group's showings.

Getting There & Away
Air Canberra is not an international airport. Sydney is normally just half an hour away; the standard fare with the two major airlines is $127; Melbourne is about an hour's flight and costs $180. Direct flights to Adelaide cost $273 and to Brisbane it's $270. There

are always special offers around which may be lower than these fares.

Fares on Eastern, Hazelton and Ansett Express (which was Air NSW) are about the same as the regular flights, although they do fly much more often. They fly smaller planes which are slower but perhaps less impersonal than the big jets, and the lower altitude means you can see more. Other smaller airlines fly to NSW country destinations.

Australian Airlines (☎ 246 1811 or 13 1313 for bookings) is in the Jolimont Centre, Northbourne Ave; Ansett (☎ 13 1300) is at 4 Mort St.

Bus Murrays (☎ 295 3611), at the Jolimont Centre, is a smaller company that operates to Sydney three times daily for $24. They also run to destinations along the south coast, including Batemans Bay ($21), Bega ($21), Nowra ($37) and Wollongong ($32). There's a big discount on some services if you book through the YHA. Pioneer has the most frequent Sydney service ($24) including some direct from Sydney Airport ($28). It takes four to five hours. Greyhound/Pioneer and Bus Australia also cover the Canberra to Adelaide route (about $115) and Greyhound/Pioneer run between Canberra and Melbourne ($48).

Deanes/Pioneer Tours (☎ 299 3722) is a franchise with daily services to the New South Wales snowfields for about $32 (including park entry fees), and $18 to Cooma. The service is frequent in winter; less so at other times. They also travel three times a week to Bega ($25) on the coast.

Capital Coachlines, which can be booked through Pioneer, go to Bathurst ($33), Orange ($33) and Dubbo ($48) two to four times weekly. Other smaller bus lines include MIA (to Griffith, $43) and Hunts (to Orange and Bathurst). Sid Fogg (☎ toll-free 008 045 942) has a daily service to Newcastle, via Sydney and Gosford.

Most major bus lines have their booking offices and main stop at the Jolimont Centre. Pioneer (☎ 257 4555) and Greyhound (☎ 257 2659), however, share a terminal at the Canberra Rex Hotel, on the corner of

Northbourne Ave and Ipima Ave, a few blocks north of the centre. There's also a booking office in the Jolimont Centre. You can book SW Countrylink buses at the railway station (☎ 239 0133) or at the Jolimont Centre (☎ 257 1576).

Train The railway station (☎ 239 0111, 6 am to 6 pm daily) is south of Lake Burley Griffin, on Wentworth Ave, Kingston. You can make bookings for trains and connecting buses at the rail travel centre in the Jolimont Centre. To Sydney there are two or three trains daily. The trip costs $45 in 1st class and $32 in economy.

There is no direct train to Melbourne. The daily V/Line Canberra Link service involves a train between Melbourne and Wodonga and a connecting bus to Canberra. This costs $44 in economy and takes about 10 hours. From Melbourne you depart at noon Monday to Friday (much earlier at weekends); from Canberra you leave at 7 am Monday to Friday (later at weekends).

Car Rental Cheaper outfits include Rumbles (☎ 280 7444), at the corner of Kembla and Wollongong Sts, Fyshwick, which has interesting deals for Friday to Monday rentals, and Susan's Rent a Dent (☎ 257 5947), which charges from $33 per day including insurance and 100 km. Ring and they will pick you up from the Jolimont Centre.

Getting Around

To/From the Airport The airport is seven km from the city centre. Note all the government cars lined up outside waiting to pick up 'pollies' and public servants. Hertz, Budget, Avis and Thrifty have airport car rental desks. The taxi fare from Civic is around $8.50. The only airport bus service is ACT Mini Buses which charges $4.50 and picks up from the Jolimont Centre, various hotels and the YHA. You have to book (☎ 018 625 719 – this is a mobile phone and calls to it are charged at STD rates, so you don't get much time for your 30c).

Bus Around Canberra there are frequent services on Action buses. The main interchange is on the corner of Alinga St and East Row in Civic, across from the Jolimont Centre. The information kiosk here is open Monday to Friday from 7.15 am to 5.30 pm, Saturday from 6 am to 5.30 pm; and Sunday and holidays from 8.30 to 11.15 am and 2.15 to 6.30 pm. Phone for information from 6 am to 11.30 pm Monday to Saturday and from 8.30 am to 6.30 pm Sunday (☎ 251 6566). Timetables and a free map of the bus system are available. For $2 you can buy a detailed book.

The flat 'one route' fare is $1.40 and if you pay cash you must have the exact change. If you buy a book of 10 Fare Go tickets you'll pay about 30% less. A Bus Week ticket lets you go anywhere for a week and costs $15.60.

Some of the Action buses are known as sightseeing specials and for these you need a Sightseeing ticket ($4.60, or $9.20 if you're going further afield to places like Bungendore, Bywong or Tidbinbilla) which enable you to use all Action buses for the day. You get them from main bus interchanges or the tourist bureau – they're not sold on the bus. The bus information kiosk has pamphlets on these services: they include route No 904 which goes to the Botanic Gardens and the tower atop Black Mountain; No 905 to Parliament House, Regatta Point and several embassies in Yarralumla; and No 909 to Rehwinkel's Animal Park, Bywong Historic Village and Bungendore.

The Canberra Explorer runs a 25-km route with 19 stops at points of interest. You get a printed guide and can get on and off the bus wherever you like. It departs hourly from the Jolimont tourist bureau from 10.15 am to 4.15 pm daily, and the $9 ticket is sold on the bus or at the information kiosk. If you just want to make one circuit without getting off, you can use a $4.50 ticket.

Bicycle Canberra is a cyclist's paradise, with bike paths making it possible to ride around the city hardly touching a road. Get a copy of the invaluable *Canberra Cycleways* map from the tourist bureau. Mr Spokes Bike Hire

(☎ 257 1188), near the Acton Park Ferry Terminal, charges $4 an hour or $16 a day, with a $2 deposit. The rates are similar at Glebe Park, on Coranderrk St, a few blocks west of Vernon Circle. Another company is Dial a Bicycle (☎ 254 0550 or 018 626 956), which will deliver the bike. They hire by the day: $18 for one day, $50 for five days. The YHA also rents bikes.

Around Canberra

The ACT is 80 km from north to south and about 30 km wide. There's plenty of unspoiled bush just outside the urban area and a network of paved roads into it. Both the NRMA's *Canberra & District* map and the tourist bureau's *Canberra Sightseeing Guide with Tourist Drives* are helpful.

The plains and isolated hills of the ACT's north, where Canberra lies, rise to rugged ranges in the south and west of the territory. The Murrumbidgee River flows across the territory from south-east to north-west. Namadgi National Park in the south covers 40% of the ACT. You can pick up leaflets on walking trails, swimming spots and camping sites put out by the ACT Parks & Conservation Service at their shops. The most central (☎ 279 3128) is in the Office of City Management building on East Row in Civic.

Picnic & Walking Areas

There are picnic and barbecue spots in and around Canberra, many with gas barbecues. There are good swimming spots along the Murrumbidgee and Cotter rivers. **Black Mountain**, just west of the city, is a convenient place for picnics. Other riverside areas include **Uriarra Crossing**, 24 km north-west, on the Murrumbidgee near its meeting with the Molonglo River; **Casuarina Sands**, 19 km west, at the meeting of the Cotter and Murrumbidgee; **Kambah Pool** 21 km further upstream (south) on the Murrumbidgee; the **Cotter Dam**, 23 km, on the Cotter, which also has a camping site; **Pine Island** and **Point Hut Crossing**, on the

Murrumbidgee, upstream of Kambah Pool; and **Gibraltar Falls**, 48 km south-west, which also has a camping site.

There are good walking tracks along the Murrumbidgee from Kambah Pool to Pine Island (seven km), or to Casuarina Sands (about 21 km).

The spectacular **Ginninderra Falls** are at Parkwood, north-west of Canberra, and actually just across the New South Wales border. The area is open from 10 am to 5 pm daily and includes a fine nature trail, gorge scenery, canoeing and camping. There's a $2.50 admission charge.

The **Tidbinbilla Nature Reserve**, 40 km south-west of the city, in the hills beyond the Tidbinbilla tracking station, has bushwalking tracks, some leading to interesting rock formations. There's also an animal reserve. The reserve is open from 9 am to 6 pm; the animal enclosures from 11 am to 5 pm. South-west of here in the Corin Forest, there's a one-km-long metal 'bobsled' run; rides are $3, 40 km south-west of the city, in the hills beyond the Tidbinbilla tracking station, has bushwalking tracks, some leading to interesting rock formations. There's also an animal reserve. The reserve is open from 9 am to 6 pm; the animal enclosures from 11 am to 5 pm. South-west of here in the Corin Forest, there's a one-km-long metal 'bobsled' run; rides are $3.

Other good walking areas include **Mt Ainslie**, on the north-east side of the city, and **Mt Majura** behind it (the combined area is called Canberra Nature Park); the Stromlo pine forests out to the west of the city; and Molonglo Gorge, to the east, near Queanbeyan.

The **Namadgi National Park**, occupying the whole south-west of the ACT and partly bordering New South Wales' mountainous Kosciusko National Park, has seven peaks over 1600 metres and offers more challenging bushwalking. The partly-surfaced Boboyan Rd crosses the park, going south from Tharwa in the ACT to Adaminaby on the eastern edge of the Snowy Mountains in New South Wales. The park visitor information centre (☎ 273 5222) is on this road, 24 km from Tharwa, and there are picnic and camping facilities in the park at the Orroral River crossing and Mt Clear.

Observatories & Tracking Stations

The ANU's Mt Stromlo Observatory is 16 km west of Canberra and has a 188-cm telescope plus a visitors' annexe open from 9.30 am to 4 pm daily. The Canberra Deep Space Communication Complex (usually called the Tidbinbilla tracking station), at Tidbinbilla, 40 km south-west of Canberra, is a joint US-Australian deep space tracking station. The visitors centre has displays of spacecraft and tracking technology. It's free, and open from 9 am to 5 pm daily. The area is popular for bushwalks and barbecues.

Old Homesteads

The beautifully restored Lanyon Homestead is 26 km south of the city, on the Murrumbidgee River near Tharwa. The early stone cottage on the site was built by convicts and the grand homestead was completed in 1859. This National Trust homestead, which now documents the life of the region before Canberra existed, is open from 10 am to 4 pm from Tuesday to Sunday. A major attraction is the collection of 24 Sidney Nolan paintings. Admission to the main homestead is $2; the Nolan gallery costs another $1.

Cuppacumbalong, also near Tharwa, is another old homestead, although neither as grand nor of such importance as Lanyon. It is now a craft studio and gallery and is open from 11 am to 5 pm Wednesday to Sunday.

Other Attractions

Mugga Lane Zoo, in Red Hill about seven km south of the city centre, is open from 9 am to 4 pm weekdays, and to 5 pm on weekends. Some No 352 buses will get you there, and admission is $5.50. **Rehwinkel's Animal Park** is on Macks Reef Rd, off the Federal Highway, 24 km north of Canberra and actually across the New South Wales border. It's open daily from 10 am to 5 pm, and admission is $6. **Australia Park**, seven km out on the Federal Highway at Watson, is a funfair in an imitation colonial setting.

North of Canberra, on the Barton Highway, is the **Old Canberra Inn**, built in 1850 and now restored as a restaurant and bistro. **Ginninderra Village**, also on the Barton Highway, about 14 km out, has a collection of craft workshops and galleries, and a school built in 1883 that has been converted to a store. It's open from 10 am to 5 pm daily and is free. Next door is **Cockington Green**, a miniature replica of an English village, open from 10 am to 5 pm daily, and to 6 pm in summer. Admission is $5.25. **Bywong Historic Village** is a re-creation of a mining settlement, about 20 km north of Canberra. It's open daily between 10 am and 4 pm and there are tours at 11 am, 1 pm and 3 pm. Entry is about $5.

Day Trips

A popular drive is east into New South Wales, past Bungendore, to **Braidwood** (an hour or so) with its many antique shops, craft stores and restaurants. There's an old hotel where you can get a pub lunch. **Lake George**, north of Bungendore, is known for its mysterious, periodic disappearing act. The village square in **Bungendore** has shops, crafts, foods and a display that tells the story of bushranger William Westwood, famous in the mid-1800s.

Another good route takes in **Tharwa** (see the Old Homesteads section) in fine, hilly grazing lands. There is a coffee shop at the historic site and a grocery store with 'hot pies, cold beer'. From here the route goes north-west to **Gibraltar Falls** (good walking) and **Tidbinbilla Nature Reserve**. The Tidbinbilla Space Tracking Station is on the way back into town along a slow, winding, scenic road.

QUEANBEYAN (population 25,500)

Just across the New South Wales border east of Canberra is Queanbeyan, now virtually a suburb of the capital it predates. Until 1838 it was known as 'Queen Bean'. There's a history museum in the town and good lookouts on Jerrabomberra Hill five km west and Bungendore Hill four km east.

New South Wales

Area   802,000 sq km
Population 5,500,000

New South Wales is the site of Captain Cook's original landing in Australia, the place where the first permanent settlement was established; and today it is both the most populous state and has the country's largest city – Sydney. Of course New South Wales is much more than Sydney with its glistening Opera House and equally well-known (if far less attractive) harbour bridge – but Sydney is certainly a good place to start.

It was down at Sydney Cove, where the ferries run from today, that the first settlement was made in 1788, so it is not surprising that Sydney has an air of history which is missing from most Australian cities. That doesn't stop Sydney from being a far brasher and more lively-looking city than its younger rival Melbourne. With a setting like Port Jackson (the harbour) to build around, it would be hard for Sydney to be unattractive.

Sydney has more than the central city going for it; Paddington is one of the most attractive inner-city residential areas in the world, and the Pacific shoreline is dotted with famous beaches like Bondi and Manly. Furthermore there are two good national parks marking the southern and northern boundaries of the city – Royal National Park and Ku-ring-gai Chase. Inland, it is a short drive to the Blue Mountains with some of the most spectacular scenery in Australia.

The Pacific Highway runs north and south from the capital, with great beaches, surf and scenery all along the coast. To the north Newcastle is the second city of New South Wales, a major industrial centre (but with fine beaches), and the nearby Hunter Valley is one of Australia's premier wine-producing areas with a popular annual wine festival. There are coastal resorts like Port Macquarie, Nambucca Heads and Coffs Harbour, and close to the Queensland border Byron Bay is one of the best travellers' stops on the whole eastern seaboard – a small, relaxed but lively surfers' favourite with strong links to the 1960s/70s counterculture that has taken root in the nearby hinterland. All the way up there are also long, empty, unspoiled stretches of coast, some protected as national parks. Further north are spectacular rainforest ranges reaching up to the high plateau of the New England region.

South of Sydney and inland are the southern highlands with beautiful scenery and good bushwalks. There is more good coastline on the way down to Victoria, plus Wollongong, the third city of New South Wales and another major industrial centre. In the south the Great Dividing Range climbs up into the heights of the Snowy Mountains, Australia's highest, with excellent summer bushwalking and winter skiing.

Further inland, the Great Divide rolls down to the vast inland plains, sweeping expanses of agricultural and grazing land, broken only by occasional ranges like the Warrumbungles, and finally dwindling into the harsh New South Wales outback. There's some fascinating history in the old towns and settlements including, in the far west, the mining town of Broken Hill, which is almost

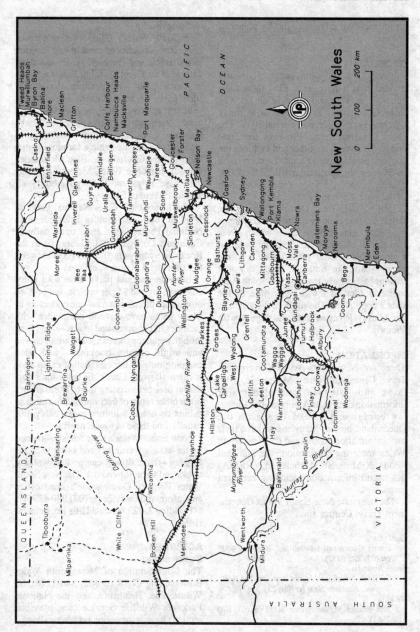

New South Wales

an independent city-state, run by powerful unions.

GEOGRAPHY

Australia's most populous state can be neatly divided into four regions. First there's the narrow coastal region, running all the way from Queensland to Victoria with many beaches, parks, inlets and coastal lakes. The Great Dividing Range also runs from one end of the state to the other and includes the cool and pleasant New England section north of Sydney, the spectacular Blue Mountains directly inland from Sydney and, in the south of the state, the Snowy Mountains.

Behind the Great Dividing Range the fertile farming country of the western slopes gradually fades into the plains which cover two-thirds of the state. This far western region is New South Wales's stretch of the great Australian outback, often dry and barren, particularly towards the South Australian border, and with very little of the state's population. The south of the state has the Murray River as a natural border with Victoria.

INFORMATION

There are New South Wales Government Travel Centres in Sydney, Melbourne, Adelaide and Brisbane, and also major information centres at Albury on the Victorian border and Tweed Heads on the Queensland border. Many towns have their own information centres and the New South Wales motoring association, the National Roads & Motorists Association, (NRMA) has useful information including excellent maps.

The interstate New South Wales Government Travel Centres are:

Queensland
    corner Queen and Edward Sts, Brisbane 4000 (☎ (07) 229 8833)
South Australia
    7th floor, Australian Airlines Building, 144 North Terrace, Adelaide 5000 (☎ (08) 231 3167)
Victoria
    388 Bourke St, Melbourne 3000 (☎ (03) 670 7461)

National Parks

New South Wales's 60-odd national parks range from stretches of coast to vast forested inland tracts and the high peaks and deep valleys of the Great Dividing Range, including some pretty empty slices of outback. Most parks can be reached by conventional vehicles in reasonable weather, although public transport into parks is scarce. Parks that are accessible without resorting to walking or a private vehicle for more than a short distance include the Blue Mountains, Bouddi, Brisbane Water, Morton, Ku-ring-gai Chase, Royal and Sydney Harbour – all within 150 km of Sydney.

The New South Wales National Parks & Wildlife Service (usually referred to as National Parks) has a shop open daily in Cadman's Cottage at 110 George St in the Rocks, in Sydney (☎ (02) 583 6333 between 8.30 am and 4.30 pm weekdays).

In some national parks there's an entry charge of around $5 per vehicle, but outside busy times there's often no-one collecting it. Many parks have drive-in camp sites with facilities like showers and toilets – often free, though popular parks can levy a small charge and might require booking – and bush camping outside the established camp sites is often allowed. Check the rules for a particular park before going there. There are not often other types of accommodation such as cabins or hotels within a park, but you'll usually find these in towns nearby.

New South Wales's state forests – owned by the state government and often used for logging – have drives, camp sites, walking tracks and so on for visitors. The New South Wales Forestry Commission's head office and information service (☎ (02) 980 4296) is at Building 2, 423 Pennant Hills Rd, Pennant Hills.

ACTIVITIES
Bushwalking

The Confederation of New South Wales Bushwalking Clubs (☎ (02) 548 1228), 82 Wilson Pde, Heathcote, and the National Parks & Wildlife Service (see previous section) have information on bushwalking.

Top: New Parliament House, Canberra, ACT (PS)
Bottom: High Court building by Lake Burley Griffin, Canberra, ACT (TW)

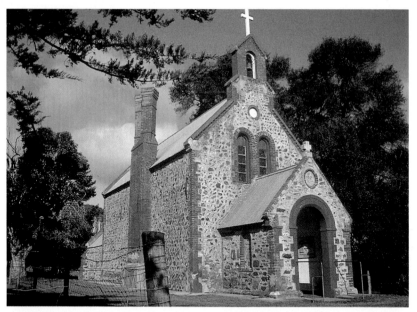

Top: Church with a chimney, Poonindie, Eyre Peninsula, SA (RN)
Left: Rialto building, Melbourne, Vic (TW)
Right: The Rocks, Sydney, NSW (RN)

Closest to the city are walks like the clifftop paths in the Royal National Park or the walks in Ku-ring-gai Chase National Park. Inland, the Blue Mountains and the adjoining Kanangra Boyd National Park have walks and some spectacular scenery. Morton National Park in the southern highlands is also spectacular and within easy reach of the city.

Further south, Kosciusko National Park in the Snowy Mountains has excellent longer walks, camping facilities and wildflowers in summer. It's best to let the snow have plenty of time to thaw after the winter. Barrington Tops National Park, north of Sydney near the New England tableland, and Warrumbungle National Park, further west near Coonabarabran, are just two of the other national parks offering excellent bushwalking. Lonely Planet's *Bushwalking in Australia* describes in detail some longer walks in New South Wales National Parks. Another useful book is *Walks in New South Wales* by Tyrone Thomas. The National Parks & Wildlife Service produces a good guide, *Bushwalks in the Sydney Region*, for $12.95.

The 250-km Great North Walk links Sydney with the Hunter Valley and takes about two weeks, or you can walk various sections. For more information contact the Department of Lands, 23-33 Bridge St, Sydney (☎ (02) 228 6111). Great Oz Walks (☎ (02) 810 6429) at 81 Elliot St, Balmain, Sydney, offers guided walks along sections of the route.

Water Sports

Diving & Snorkelling Excellent scuba diving and snorkelling can be found at a number of places. North of Sydney popular spots include Terrigal (96 km), Port Stephens (235 km), Seal Rocks (325 km) and Byron Bay (850 km). Head south to Jervis Bay in the Royal National Park, to Wattamolia (198 km) or Eden (488 km). You can take diving courses in a number of centres including Sydney and Byron Bay, though most people heading up to Queensland wait till they reach the Great Barrier Reef.

White-Water Rafting & Canoeing Rafting takes place on the upper Murray and Snowy rivers in the south of the state, and on the Nymboida and Gwydir in the north. Jindabyne and Thredbo in the Snowy Mountains are jumping-off points for the southern rivers; Coffs Harbour and Nambucca Heads for the northern. A day trip usually costs about $70.

With dams, rivers, lakes and coastal lakes there are plenty of opportunities to go canoeing in New South Wales. If you are after white-water, head for the Richmond and Murray rivers. The New South Wales Canoe Association (☎ (02) 251 3472) has information.

Swimming & Surfing This is the true-blue Sydney and New South Wales activity. All the beaches around Sydney have good swimming and/or surfing – see the Sydney section for details. The beaches in the Royal National Park are also popular.

Surf carnivals – competing lifesavers, surf rescue boats, all that stuff – start in December. Phone the Surf Life Saving Association for dates and venues, or contact the New South Wales Travel Centre.

Officially, Sydney has 34 surf beaches and there are many more along the New South Wales coast. The warmer north coast is more popular during the winter months at places like Seal Rocks (325 km), Crescent Head (497 km), Scotts Head (538 km), Angourie (744 km) and Lennox Heads (823 km). Byron Bay has been a surfing Mecca for almost as long as Australia has had surfies.

South of Sydney there is Stanwell Park (56 km), Wollongong (82 km), Huskisson (187 km) and Mollymook (222 km). Nat Young's *Surfing Australia's East Coast* (Castle Books) details the 'wheres and whens'.

Sailing Sydney Harbour and the Pittwater are both excellent for sailing and the sport is very popular. Check with the Australian Yachting Federation about clubs and sailing instructions.

Running & Cycling

There are tracks and facilities at Narrabeen Lakes north of Sydney. Wollongong is another city with a good bike track network. The Bicycle Institute of New South Wales (☎ (02) 212 5628), GPO Box 272, 82 Campbell St, Surry Hills, can provide information, including cycling routes throughout the state.

Sydney joggers do their stuff at Centennial Park which is also popular with cyclists. In August, the City to Surf Fun Run is Australia's biggest foot race.

Skiing

See the Snowy Mountains section for information about skiing in New South Wales.

GETTING THERE & AWAY

Transport into New South Wales is discussed mainly in the Sydney section.

GETTING AROUND

Note that student and other concessions on the government trains, buses and ferries apply only to Australian residents.

Air

Smaller airlines like East-West, Ansett Express and Eastern Australia Airlines operate comprehensive networks, mostly within the state, and other airlines serve particular regions. The chart shows some of the routes and the normal fares – but there are often special deals.

Bus

Within the state it can still be expensive to make short bus trips, so look for cheap stopover deals if you want to make a few stops on the way. Buses are often a little quicker and cheaper than trains but not always so.

Once you've reached your destination, there are usually local bus lines, though services may not be very frequent.

Train

The State Rail Authority (SRA) has the most comprehensive rail service in Australia. It will take you quite quickly to almost any

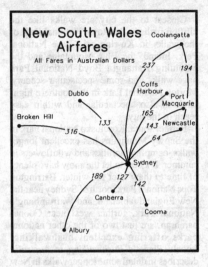

New South Wales Airfares

All Fares in Australian Dollars

sizable town in the state, but the frequency and value for money is variable: always compare with bus services. The SRA's network increasingly relies on co-ordinated train/bus services – the service as a whole is called Countrylink. (☎ (02) 217 8812 or 008 043 126, toll-free outside Sydney, between 6.30 am and 10 pm daily). There's an information centre at 11-31 York St in Sydney. Some main railway lines are served by high speed XPTs (Express Passenger Trains), which can top 160 km/h.

Intrastate services and economy fares from Sydney (many of which are combined rail/coach services) include Cooma, 446 km, seven hours, $44; Bathurst, 240 km, 4½ hours, $28; Broken Hill, 1125 km, about 17 hours (direct rail), $78; Tamworth, 455 km, $48 (direct rail), $42 (coach); Bourke, 841 km, about 12 hours, $65; Coffs Harbour, 608 km, $57; Byron Bay, 883 km, 13 to 16 hours, $65 (direct rail), $69 (combined rail/coach); Armidale, 530 km, $50; Orange, 323 km, $29; Dubbo, 431 km, $44; Griffith, 631 km, $57; Albury, 643 km, $57.

There are a variety of day-tour fares and holiday packages, and there's the good-value

Budget Seven Pass which gives a week's unlimited economy travel for $115.

Sydney

Population 3,400,000

As Australia's oldest and largest city Sydney (Sinney to the locals) has plenty to offer. The harbour, around which the city is built, was named Port Jackson by Captain Cook in 1770 but he actually anchored in Botany Bay, a few km to the south, and only passed by the narrow entrance to the harbour. In 1788 when the convict 'First Fleet' arrived in Sydney it too went first to Botany Bay, but after a few days moved north to Port Jackson. These first White settlers established themselves at Sydney Cove, still the centre of harbour shipping, and down near the waterfront in the area known as the Rocks are some of the earliest buildings in Australia.

Because Sydney grew in a piecemeal fashion, unlike later Australian cities which were planned from the start, it's a tighter, more congested centre without wide boulevards. It's also a dazzlingly modern city, with the most energy and style in Australia. In Sydney the buildings soar higher, the colours are brighter, the nightlife's more exciting, the drivers more aggressive and the consumption more conspicuous!

It all comes back to that stupendous harbour though. It's more than just the centrepiece for the city; everything in Sydney revolves around the harbour. Would the Opera House, for example, be anything like the place it is, if it wasn't perched right beside the harbour?

Orientation

Sydney came into existence before the era of grand plans that was to characterise most later Australian cities, and the layout is further complicated by the harbour with its numerous arms and inlets and by the hilly nature of the city.

The harbour divides Sydney into north and south, the Harbour Bridge joining the two. The city centre and most other places of interest are south of the harbour. The central city area is relatively long and narrow, although only George and Pitt Sts (the main commercial and shopping streets) run the whole three km from the waterfront Rocks area south to Central Railway Station.

The Rocks and the Sydney Cove waterfront mark the northern boundary of the centre, Central Railway Station is on the southern edge, the inlet of Darling Harbour is the western boundary and a string of pleasant parks border Elizabeth and Macquarie Sts on the east.

Beyond this park strip are some of the oldest and most interesting inner suburbs of Sydney – Woolloomooloo, Kings Cross and Paddington. Further east again are some of the more exclusive suburbs south of the harbour and then beachfront suburbs like Bondi. The airport is south of this area, beside Botany Bay, which is Sydney's second great harbour.

Suburbs stretch a good 25 km south, west and north from the centre. To the north and south they're limited by national parks, but to the west outlying towns like Penrith and Campbelltown are almost part of the urban sprawl.

Information

Tourist Information Excellent places for cheap travel tips and help are areas where budget travellers stay – in particular Victoria St in Kings Cross where hostel notice boards offer everything from flat-shares to unused air tickets.

The New South Wales Government Travel Centre (☎ 231 4444) is at 19 Castlereagh St. It's open Monday to Friday 9 am to 5 pm and has the usual range of brochures, leaflets and accommodation and tour details. They can make bookings. The Sydney Information Booth (☎ 235 2424) is in Martin Place and is open the same hours as the New South Wales centre.

The Tourist Information Service (☎ 669 5111) answers phone enquiries from 8 am to 6 pm daily. Some areas like the Rocks,

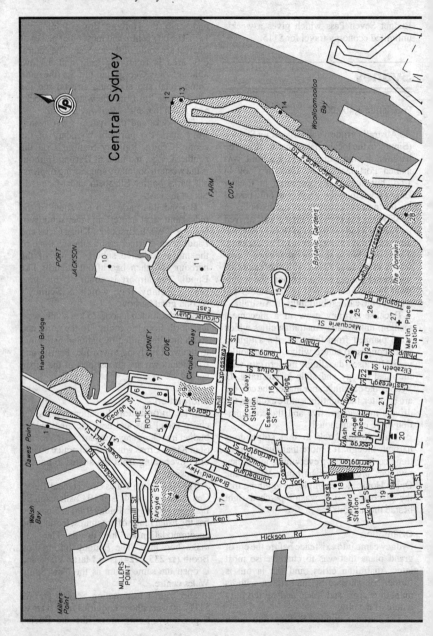

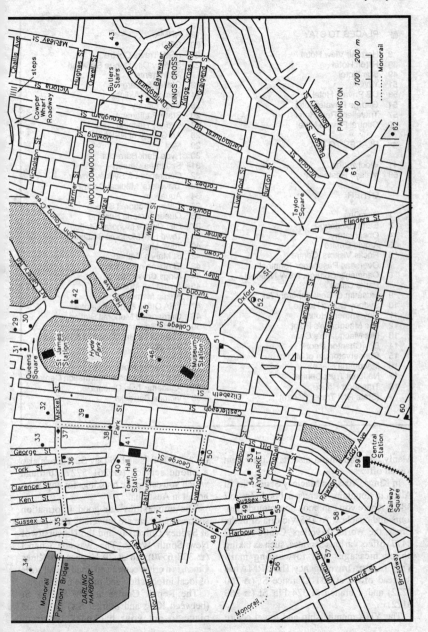

■ PLACES TO STAY

3   Harbour View Hotel
39 Hilton Hotel
49 Star Hotel
51 YWCA
53 CB Private Hotel
54 George Private Hotel
57 Travellers Rest Hotel
60 Central Private Hotel

▼ PLACES TO EAT

41 Woolworths
58 Malaya Restaurant

OTHER

1   Pier One
2   Earth Exchange
4   Observatory
5   Argyle Centre
6   Rocks Visitors' Centre
7   Overseas Passenger Terminal
8   Cadman's Cottage, NSW National
    Parks Office
9   Museum of Contemporary Art
10 Sydney Opera House
11 Government House
12 Mrs Macquarie's Point
13 Mrs Macquarie's Chair
14 Boy Charlton Pool
15 Conservatorium of Music
16 Macquarie Place
17 National Trust Centre
18 Transport House
    (State Rail Travel Centre)

19 NRMA
20 GPO
21 NSW Travel Centre
22 Sydney City Centre Serviced
    Apartments
23 Chifley Square
24 Australian Airlines
25 State Library
26 State Parliament
27 Sydney Hospital
28 Art Gallery of NSW
29 Mint
30 Hyde Park Barracks
31 St James Church
32 Centrepoint & Sydney Tower
33 Travellers' Medical Centre
34 Aquarium
35 Casino Monorail Station
36 Queen Victoria Building
37 City Centre Monorail Station
38 Town Hall Monorail Station
40 Town Hall
42 St Mary's Cathedral
43 El Alamein Fountain
44 Kings Cross Station
45 Australian Museum
46 Anzac Memorial
47 YHA Office & Travel Centre
48 Gardenside Monorail Station
50 World Square Monorail Station
52 Greyhound Bus Australia & Pioneer
    Bus Station
55 Chinatown
56 Haymarket Monorail Station
59 Bus Companies & Information Centre
61 Academy Twin Cinema
62 Victoria Barracks

Manly and Parramatta also have their own tourist offices.

In Kings Cross, on Macleay St near the El Alamein fountain, there's a booth (☎ 357 3883) where you can book accommodation, tours and coaches. At 185 Victoria St in the Cross, the World Travellers' Centre (☎ 357 4477) offers various services, such as taking phone messages and forwarding mail. They're also a travel agency. The NRMA has its head office at 151 Clarence St (☎ 260 9222) and a branch at 324 Pitt St (☎ 260 8122).

The YHA membership and travel centre (☎ 267 3044) is at 176 Day St. There's also a phone service (☎ 261 5727), through which you can make bookings for any YHA hostel in Australia.

The universities are good information sources and there are university newspapers at Sydney University and the University of New South Wales. The Wayside Chapel (☎ 358 6570), up at 29 Hughes St, Kings Cross, is a crisis centre and good for all sorts of local information and problem solving.

The Repair Centre at 140 Sussex St (between King and Market Sts) is a good place to get your backpack repaired.

Cameras which are playing up could be taken to Whilton Camera Service, Shop 533, Royal Arcade, for fast repairs.

Post & Telecommunications The GPO, the main post office, with its very busy poste restante where you may queue for over half an hour to pick up mail, is on Martin Place on the corner of Pitt St. Several travellers have reported delayed mail and other frustrations here, but all suburban post offices will hold mail and even if yours is going to the GPO you can have it redirected for a fee.

The Telecom Phone Centre at 100 King St just north of the Pitt St Mall is open 24 hours and some of the phones take major credit cards.

Sydney's STD area code is 02.

Books The best Sydney guide was *Roland Hughes Wraps Up Sydney*, but a new edition is a long time coming. Gregory's *Inside Sydney* is reasonable and costs $6.95. Heritage Field Guides such as *Sydney by Ferry & Foot*, *Sydney Walks* and *Sydney by Bicycle* cost $12.95. Lonely Planet's *Sydney City Guide* at $11.95 is a handy pocket guide to the city. *Blair's Travel Guide to New South Wales, Sydney & ACT* costs $14.95. So does *Aird's Guide to Sydney*. See Things to Buy for information on bookshops. For the seamy side of the city, read Peter Corris's Cliff Hardy thrillers – *White Meat* is a good example.

Medical Services & Emergencies The Traveller's Medical & Vaccination Centre (☎ 221 7133) on the 7th floor of the Dymocks Building, 428 George St, is a useful place. It's open from 8.30 am to 6 pm on weekdays, 9 am to noon on Saturday and you don't need an appointment. The Kings Cross Travellers' Clinic (☎ 358 3066) at Suite 1, 13 Springfield Ave, Kings Cross, is open from 10 am to 6 pm weekdays, 10 am to noon on Saturdays. Some useful addresses and phone numbers include:

Chemist
    Emergency Prescription Service 24 hours (☎ 438 3333)
Dentist
    Dental Emergency Information Service after hours (☎ 267 5919)
Rape
    Rape Crisis Centre 24 hours (☎ 819 6565)
Life Crisis
    Life Line (☎ 264 2222)
Interpreter Service
    Telephone Interpreter Service (☎ 221 1111)

The Rocks

Sydney's first settlement was made on the rocky spur of land on the west side of Sydney Cove from which the Harbour Bridge now leaps to the north shore. A pretty squalid place it was too, with overcrowding, open sewers and notoriously raucous residents. In the 1820s and '30s the *nouveaux riches* built their three-storey houses where Lower Fort St is today; their outlook was to the slums below.

In the 1870s and '80s the notorious Rocks 'pushes' were gangs of larrikins (a great Australian word) who used to haunt the area, snatching purses, robbing pedestrians, feuding and generally creating havoc. It became an area of warehouses and bond stores, then declined as more modern shipping and storage facilities were opened. An outbreak of bubonic plague at the turn of the century led to whole streets of the Rocks being razed and the construction of the Harbour Bridge also resulted in much demolition.

Since the 1970s redevelopment has made the Rocks into a most interesting area of Sydney, and imaginative restorations have converted the decrepit old warehouses into places like the busy Argyle Arts Centre. Redevelopment has gone far enough for some people and local residents are fighting to prevent the loss of old homes. The Rocks is still a wonderful area to wander around, full of narrow cobbled streets, fine colonial buildings and countless historical touches. Old pubs, restaurants and cafes provide good excuses to stop and take in the atmosphere.

Get a walking tour map of the area from

the Rocks Visitors' Centre (☎ 247 4972), 104 George St. A full walk round the area will take you under the Bradfield Highway, which divides the Rocks, to the Millers Point, Walsh Bay and Dawes Point areas just west of the Harbour Bridge. The centre is open weekdays 8.30 am to 5.30 pm, weekends 10 am to 5 pm.

The **Argyle Centre**, on the corner of Argyle and Playfair Sts, was originally built as bond stores between 1826 and 1881. Today it has a collection of shops, boutiques, studios and eating places. Everything seems geared to rich tourists but it's still worth a browse.

Just beyond the arts centre is the **Argyle Cut**, an old tunnel through the hill to the other side of the peninsula. At the far end of the cut is **Millers Point**, a delightful district of early colonial homes, some around a real village green. Close at hand are the Lord Nelson Hotel in Argyle St and the Hero of Waterloo Hotel on the corner of Windmill and Lower Fort Sts which vie for the title of Sydney's oldest pub. Also on Lower Fort St is the **Colonial House Museum** at No 53, open daily from 10 am to 5 pm.

On George St, close to the visitor centre, is **Cadman's Cottage** (1816), the oldest house in Sydney. When the cottage was built this was where the waterfront was, and the arches to the south of it once housed long boats; this was the home of the last Government Coxswain, John Cadman. The cottage now houses a National Parks & Wildlife information centre.

The **Earth Exchange** at 36-64 George St is an interactive geological museum. It's open daily between 10 am and 5 pm and admission is $6.50. At 100 George St **The Story of Sydney** recreates incidents in the city's history. It's open daily from 9 am with the last show at 5 pm; each show lasts an hour. Entry is $10 for adults, $7 concession, $22.50 family (two adults/two children, with $6 per extra child).

The **Australian Wine Centre** in Campbell's Storehouse at Circular Quay West has wines from all the major growing areas. You can take a tour and get a free tasting and it's open daily from 10 am to 5 pm.

The fine new **Museum of Contemporary Art** is on George St overlooking Circular Quay. Admission is $6 and it's open daily except Tuesday from 11 am to 7 pm.

You can find the site of the public gallows on Essex St, near the corner of Harrington St up towards St Patrick's Church. In the pleasant park on Observatory Hill, the **Sydney Observatory** has an interesting free museum open on weekends and weekday afternoons. Nightly, except Wednesdays, you can look through a telescope for $5.00 (concessions $2); bookings (☎ 241 2478) are necessary. Close by, the **National Trust Centre** in the old military hospital houses a museum, art gallery, bookshop and tea-rooms. The interesting exhibitions change every six weeks and admission is around $3 (students $1.50).

At Dawes Point on Walsh Bay, just beneath the bridge on this side, **Pier One** is a tourist, shopping and leisure complex with specialist shops, several expensive restaurants, a tavern, and an amusement centre.

Sydney Harbour Bridge

From the end of the Rocks the 'old coat hanger' rises up on its route to the north shore. It was a far from elegant, but very functional, symbol for the city until the Opera House came along. The bridge was completed in 1932 at a cost of $20 million, quite a bargain in modern terms, but it took until 1988 to pay off!

Crossing the bridge by car costs $2, southbound only; there is no toll in the other direction. There's a cycleway across the bridge and a pedestrian walkway – with stairs up to it from Cumberland St in the Rocks – and you can climb up inside one of the stone pylons (see City Views). (The pylons are purely decorative; they don't help to hold the bridge up in any way.) At rush hours the bridge gets very crowded and a harbour tunnel is being built to ease congestion. It begins about half a km south of the Opera House and meets the bridge road on the north side.

On the north shore is the grinning mouth-piece of another Sydney symbol – the Luna Park funfair. It is currently closed, awaiting the outcome of a battle between pre-servationists and developers who want its prime site.

At the end of Kirribilli Point east of the bridge stand **Admiralty House** and **Kirribilli House**, the Sydney pieds-à-terre of the Governor General and the Prime Minister respectively (Admiralty House is the one nearer the bridge).

Sydney Opera House

From the past symbol to the present one is a short walk around Sydney Cove – to the controversial Sydney Opera House. After countless delays and technical difficulties the Opera House opened in 1973, 14 years after work began. During a free Sunday afternoon concert or sitting in the open-air restaurant with a carafe of wine, watching the harbour life, it's a truly memorable place.

There are tours of the building and although the inside is nowhere near as spectacular as the outside, they are worth taking. They cost $7 (students $4) and operate from 9 am to 4 pm. There are also 90-minute tours of the backstage area for $10 on Sunday only (☎ 250 7250).

The Opera House has four auditoriums and puts on plays, concerts and films as well as opera. Popular performances sell out quickly, but there are often 'restricted view' and standing room tickets available. For operas these cost $15 and go on sale at 9 am of the performance day – you might have to start queuing much earlier than that, though. These tickets are always available for operas but not for other shows if they've sold out. On Sunday afternoons there are free performances on the outer walk of the building. You can also often catch a free lunch-time film or organ recital in the concert hall.

Before the Opera House was built the site was used as a tram depot. The designer, John Utzon, a Dane, won an international contest with his design but at the height of the cost overruns and construction difficulties and hassles, he quit in disgust and the building

was completed by a consortium of Australian architects. How were the enormous additional costs covered? – not by the taxpayer but in true-blue Aussie fashion by a series of Opera House lotteries. The Opera House looks fine from any angle, but the view from a ferry coming into Circular Quay is one of the best.

Circular Quay

Circular Quay is a busy hub for harbour ferry commuters. There is no finer way of getting around Sydney than these creaky old ships, or the sleeker new vessels.

Circular Quay was the original landing point for the First Fleet because of the deep water, and it was made semicircular during the 1830s. Settlement grew around the Tank Stream, a creek which provided early Sydney's water supply and ran into the harbour here. Later this was the shipping centre for Sydney, and early photographs show a forest of masts crowding the skyline. Across Circular Quay from the Opera House, beside the Rocks, is the overseas passenger terminal where cruise ships and visiting liners moor.

Macquarie Place

Narrow lanes, with some colourful early-opening pubs, lead back from Circular Quay towards the centre of the city. At the corner of Loftus and Bridge Sts, under the shady Moreton Bay figs in little Macquarie Place, are a cannon and anchor from the First Fleet flagship HMS *Sirius*. There are several other pieces of colonial memorabilia in this square, including an 1857 drinking fountain, an obelisk indicating distances to various points in the colony and a National-Trust-classified gentlemen's convenience.

City Centre

Central Sydney stretches from Central Railway Station in the south up to Circular Quay in the north. The business hub is towards the north end, and if anywhere is Sydney's centre it's **Martin Place**, a pedestrian mall extending from Macquarie St to George St beside the massive GPO. This is a popular lunch-time entertainment spot with buskers and more organised acts. In December a Christmas tree appears here in the summer heat.

The city has some attractive and imaginative shopping complexes including the old **Strand Arcade** between Pitt and George Sts just south of King St. The **Queen Victoria Building** on the corner of George and Market Sts, built in the style of a Byzantine palace in 1898 and once a fruit and vegetable market, has been restored to house about 200 shops, cafes and restaurants. The MLC Centre, Centrepoint and the Royal Arcade are just three of the other, modern centres off George and Pitt Sts.

In the basement of the Hilton Hotel, under the Royal Arcade between George and Pitt south of Market St, is the **Marble Bar**, a Victorian extravaganza built by George Adams, the fellow with the prescience to foresee Australia's gambling lust, who founded Tattersall's lotteries (Tattslotto). When the old Adams Hotel (originally O'Brien's Pub) was torn down to build the Hilton, the bar was carefully dismantled and reassembled like some archaeological wonder.

Half a block further south along George St is the 1874 **Town Hall** on the corner of Park St. Inside there's the impressive Grand Organ. Unfortunately, it is said that the acoustics are not as grand. Across the open space to the south, **St Andrew's Cathedral** was built about the same time. It today houses an unusual two-part organ with computerised sections. Recitals are held weekly.

From here the centre begins to fade, becoming rather grotty and ripe for the developers, before you reach Central Railway Station and the inner suburb of Glebe. Just west off George St, before the station, is the colourful Chinatown around Dixon St.

City Views

Sydney is becoming a mini-Manhattan and from up top you can look down on the convoluted streets that are a relic of the unplanned convict past.

Highest is the **Sydney Tower** on top of the Centrepoint complex on the corner of Pitt and Market Sts. This is a tower built purely for the sake of being high – it's nothing more than a gigantic column with a viewing gallery and revolving restaurant on the summit, 305 metres above street level. The tower is open from 9.30 am to 9.30 pm daily, except Sundays and holidays when it's open 10.30 am to 6.30 pm. Admission is $5 for the observation deck. You can see as far as the Blue Mountains to the west or Wollongong to the south, and there are various displays. Reservations for either of the restaurants are a good idea, but there's also a snack and coffee bar.

The **Harbour Bridge** is a good vantage point. You can climb up inside the south-east pylon daily from 10 am to 5 pm from mid-October to mid-February and at other times during school and public holidays. Entry is $1. You enter the pylon from the bridge's pedestrian walkway and climb 200 stairs for a panoramic view of the city. A stone staircase leads up to the bridge and walkway from Cumberland St in the Rocks.

For a view of the Opera House, harbour and bridge from sea level, either take a trip on the harbour or go to **Mrs Macquarie's Point**, one headland east of the Opera House. It has been a lookout point since at least 1810 when Elizabeth Macquarie, wife of one of the best early governors of New South Wales, had a stone chair hewn in the rock at the end of the point, where she would watch for ships entering the harbour or keep an eye on hubby's construction projects just across Farm Cove. The seat is still there today.

There are more excellent panoramas of the city centre from the north shore of the harbour. There is a good view from the rooftop of the Australian Museum and it too is free.

Darling Harbour

This inlet, half a km west of the city centre, has been turned into a huge waterfront leisure and tourist park. The $2 billion transformation was completed in 1988, not without a series of rows over the cost.

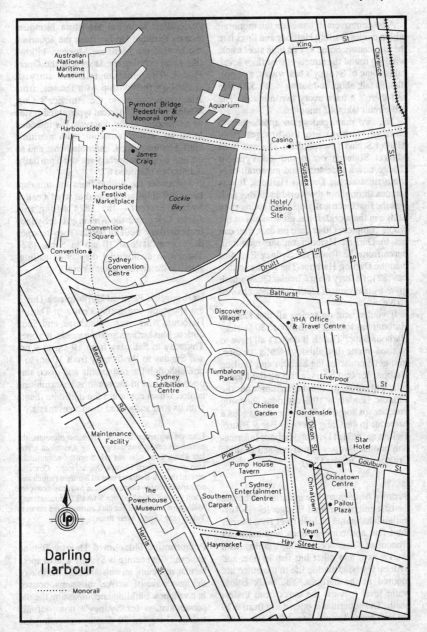

Darling Harbour

.... Monorail

Also controversial has been the monorail which circles Darling Harbour and links it to the city centre. Some say its blue steel track, winding round the streets at first floor level, ruins some of Sydney's best vistas, and politicians talk about re-routing it. It's $2 a ride and there's a train every two minutes. The full circuit takes 12 minutes.

The two main pedestrian approaches to Darling Harbour are footbridges from Market St and Liverpool St. The one from Market St leads on to the old Pyrmont Bridge, now a pedestrian-and-monorail-only route right across Darling Harbour. It was famous throughout the world in its day as it was the first electrically operated swing span bridge in the world. It has great views of the whole complex. Other than on foot, you can get to Darling Harbour on the monorail, buses from the Town, the Sydney Explorer bus, the Darling Harbour-The Rocks shuttle bus ($2) or a ferry from Circular Quay which gives a great view of Darling Harbour as you arrive.

If you're bent on seeing all that Darling Harbour has to offer, consider a $30 Darling Harbour Super Ticket. It doesn't all have to be used in one day, although that's the idea. You get a cruise of the harbour and Darling Harbour for two hours, a trip on the Monorail, entrance to the aquarium and the Chinese Garden, a 10% discount shopping voucher for some Harbourside stores plus a barbecue in the Craig Brewery Bar & Bistro. Tickets are sold at Darling Harbour Information booths, Sydney Aquarium and Matilda Cruises on Circular Quay.

Sydney Aquarium The aquarium is beside the east end of Pyrmont Bridge. Its all-Australian inhabitants include river fish, Barrier Reef fish and coral gardens, and saltwater crocodiles. Two 'oceanarium' tanks, with sharks, rays and other big fish in one, and Sydney Harbour marine life in the other, are moored in the harbour. You walk below water level to view the tanks from underneath. The aquarium is open daily from 9.30 am to 9 pm and admission is $12.50.

Australian National Maritime Museum Across Pyrmont Bridge from the aquarium the roof of the Maritime Museum billows like sails, echoing the shapes of the Opera House. The museum tells the story of Australia's relationship with the sea, from Aboriginal canoes to the America's Cup. Vessels of many different types stand inside or are moored at the wharves. It's intended to be an 'active' museum, with maritime craft demonstrations, entertainments and so on, and is open between 9 am and 5 pm daily. Admission is around $7.

Just under the bridge from the museum two more ships are moored at what's called Sydney Seaport – the 1874 sailing ship *James Craig* and the *Kanangra*, a Sydney harbour ferry built in 1912. They're open daily from at least 10 am to 5 pm ($2). There's an audiovisual display of sailing-ship life inside the *James Craig*.

Harbourside Festival Marketplace This is the shopping and eating centre of Darling Harbour, with over 200 shops and food outlets, plus buskers and live music. It's open Thursday to Saturday from 10 am to 9 pm and Sunday to Wednesday from 10 am to 7 pm, although the restaurants and disco stay open late. Just to the south is an exhibition centre, which continues the maritime theme with its roof suspended from steel masts.

Like the aquarium and the maritime museum, the exhibition centre was designed by Australian architect Philip Cox, who has taken up the adventurous lead given by Jorn Utzon's Opera House. Cox also created the new Sydney Football Stadium (which was perhaps a little too adventurous, as patrons discovered when the roof failed to cope with its first rainstorm), Melbourne's National Tennis Centre and the resort at Yulara near Uluru (Ayers Rock).

Powerhouse Museum & Nearby Behind the exhibition centre is Sydney's most spectacular museum, an outstanding example of the new wave of 'active' museums, housed in a vast new building encompassing the old power station for Sydney's now defunct trams. There are 30 displays covering the decorative arts, science and technology and social history.

It's a superbly displayed museum with lots to do besides just looking – video and computer activities, experiments, performances and demonstrations, films and so on. Major decorative art sections focus on childhood, Australian crafts, style, and 20th-century chairs; the science and technology hall includes working steam engines, a Catalina flying boat strung from the ceiling, and space travel exhibits; and the social history areas include a 1930s cinema and a pubs-and-brewing display. You can also reach the Powerhouse from Harris and Mary Ann Sts, Ultimo. It's open from 10 am to 5 pm daily and admission is free. Phone 11600 for recorded information.

In front of the exhibition centre, **Tumbalong Park** has playgrounds, an amphitheatre, lawns and trees. Across the park from the exhibition centre, **Discovery Village** will be a high-tech amusement park on Disneyland lines, while in another corner is the **Chinese Garden**, the biggest outside China, which was planned by landscape architects from New South Wales's sister province, Guangdong. Just south of the Chinese Garden, the old pump house which supplied hydraulic power for many Sydney lifts has been turned into the **Pump House Tavern**, with its own brewery. A little further south again is the 12,500 capacity **Sydney Entertainment Centre**, venue for big-name touring rock acts.

Early Central Buildings

After the founding governor Phillip left in 1792 the colony was run mainly by officials and soldiers more intent on making a quick fortune through the rum monopoly than anything else, and it was not until Lachlan Macquarie took over as governor in 1810 that order was restored. The narrow streets of parts of central Sydney are a reminder of the chaotic pre-Macquarie period.

Macquarie St Macquarie commissioned Francis Greenway, a convict transported for forgery, to design a series of public buildings, some of which are still among the finest in Sydney. Excellent views of all Greenway's buildings can be obtained from the 14th-floor cafeteria of the Law Courts building on the corner of Macquarie St and Queens Square.

St James Church and the **Hyde Park Barracks**, two of Greenway's early masterpieces, are on Queens Square at the northern end of Hyde Park, facing each other across Macquarie St. The Barracks, originally convict quarters, are now an interesting museum of Sydney's social history, complete with a reconstructed convict dormitory where the hammocks are far more comfortable than most Kings Cross hostel beds. The Barracks are open daily from 10 am to 5 pm except Tuesday mornings (free).

Next to the Barracks on Macquarie St is the **Mint Building**, originally built as a hospital in 1814 and known as the Rum Hospital because the builders constructed it in return for the lucrative monopoly on the rum trade. It became the Mint in 1853 and the northern end of the hospital is now the state **Parliament House**. When Parliament is sitting, 45-minute tours are given and the public is admitted to the galleries for question time (☎ 230 2111 for details). The Mint, with its collection of decorative arts, stamps and coins, is open from 10 am to 5 pm daily except Wednesday when it opens at noon. Admission is free.

Further up Macquarie St on the Botanic Gardens side, the **State Conservatorium of Music** was originally built, by Greenway again, as the stables and servants' quarters of a new government house for Macquarie. Macquarie was replaced as governor before the rest of the house could be finished, partly because of the perceived extravagance of this project. Greenway's life ended in poverty because he could never recoup the money of his own that he had put into the work. Today the building is a musical academy: on Wednesdays during term there are free lunch-time concerts.

Parks

Sydney has many parks which, together with

the harbour, make it one of the world's most spacious major cities. One string of parks borders the eastern side of the city centre. Stretching back from the harbour front, beside the Opera House, are the **Royal Botanic Gardens** with a magnificent collection of South Pacific plant life. The Gardens were established in 1816 and in one corner is a stone wall marking the site of the convict colony's first vegetable patch. There is also an Aboriginal plant trail. The tropical display, housed in the interconnecting Arc and Pyramid glasshouses, is worth the $5 admission. It's open daily from 10 am to 6 pm during summer and from 10 am to 4 pm the rest of the year. The gardens are open from 8 am to sunset daily. There's a visitor centre where guided walks start at 10 am every Wednesday and Friday.

Just east of the gardens, beside Woolloomooloo Bay, the **Boy Charlton Pool** is the nearest place to the city centre or Kings Cross where you can get a non-harbour swim. It's saltwater and open daily. The half km from here up to Mrs Macquarie's Point is also parkland (see the City Views section).

The Cahill Expressway separates the Botanic Gardens from the **Domain**, another open space to the south. You can cross the expressway on the Art Gallery Rd bridge. In the Domain on Sunday afternoons after 2 pm impassioned soapbox speakers entertain their listeners. Free events are held here during the Festival of Sydney in January, as well as the popular Carols by Candlelight. This is also a rallying place for usually peaceful public protests.

Hyde Park, between Elizabeth and College Sts, has delightful fountains and the Anzac Memorial. This is a popular place for a city sandwich lunch on the grass since it's only a few steps from the centre. **St Mary's Cathedral** overlooks the park from the east and the **Great Synagogue** is opposite to the western side: both are open for inspection and are worth a visit.

Sydney's biggest park, with running, cycling and horse tracks, duck ponds, barbecue sites and lots more, is **Centennial Park**,

five km from the centre and just east of Paddington. Black swans and many other birds nest here. You can hire bikes from several places on Clovelly Rd, Randwick, near the southern edge of the park (see Getting Around), or horses from Centennial Park Horse Hire at the Sydney Showgrounds on Lang Rd, just west of Centennial Park.

Balls Head Reserve, on the north shore of the harbour two headlands west of the Harbour Bridge, is a park with not only great views of the harbour, but also old Aboriginal rock paintings (in a cave) and carvings.

Apart from parks, Sydney also has wilder areas. Some of these, along the harbour shores, are described in the Harbour section. Another, **Davidson Park**, is an eight-km corridor of bushland in northern Sydney, stretching north-west from Bantry Bay on Middle Harbour up to the border of Ku-ring-gai Chase National Park at St Ives. There's also **Lane Cove River** recreation area, between the suburbs of Ryde and Chatswood, again north of the harbour. Both areas have extensive walking tracks and Lane Cove River has lots of picnic areas. You may see lyrebirds in Davidson Park; the males make their spectacular mating displays from May to August. You can pick up information sheets on these places at the national parks office in Cadman's Cottage in the Rocks.

Art Gallery of New South Wales

In the Domain, only a short walk from the centre, the art gallery has an excellent permanent display of Australian, European, Japanese and tribal art, and from time to time has some inspired temporary exhibits. It also has a good cafeteria, ideal for a genteel cup of tea. It's open from 10 am to 5 pm Monday to Saturday, noon to 5 pm Sunday. There's no entry charge but fees may apply for some major exhibitions. Free guided tours are available. Sydney is packed with other galleries, particularly in Paddington and Woollahra.

Australian Museum

The Australian Museum, on the corner of College and William Sts, right by Hyde Park, is a natural history museum with an excellent Australian wildlife collection, but it also has a good gallery tracing Aboriginal history from the Dreamtime to the present. See the latter before you head off into central Australia. There's a good bookshop with some outstanding publications on Aboriginal and Pacific arts & crafts. From its rooftop there are good views of Kings Cross to the east, the parks straight ahead, the city to the west and the Harbour Bridge in the distance. The museum is open from 10 am to 5 pm daily except Monday, when it opens from noon to 5 pm. Admission is $4 (concessions $1.50) but free after 4 pm and half price on Saturday.

Other Museums

On Macquarie St, just north of Parliament House, the **State Library** has one of the best collections of early records and works on Australia, including Captain Cook's and Joseph Banks's journals and Captain Bligh's log from the *Bounty* (the irascible Bligh recovered from that ordeal to become an early New South Wales governor where he suffered a second mutiny!). Many items are displayed in the library galleries, which are open from 10 am to 5 pm Monday to Saturday, 2 to 6 pm on Sunday. Free visiting exhibitions of various kinds are often shown here, too. There's also a general reference library. Other good museums include the **Nicholson** and **Macleay Museums** at Sydney University, with Greek, Assyrian, Egyptian and other antiquities at the former, and at the latter a curious collection ranging from stuffed birds and animals to anthropology to early computers and cameras. Both are free and open Monday to Friday, from 8.30 am to 4.15 or 4.30 pm. The university is about one km south-west of Central Railway Station, at the beginning of Parramatta Rd.

See the Rocks section for information on the Observatory, the Earth Exchange and The Story of Sydney.

On the Princes Highway at Loftus, about one km south of Sutherland, near Royal National Park, there's a **tramway museum** open on Sunday, Wednesday afternoon and public holidays – Sydney's last tram rumbled into the history books back in 1961. There's a 600-metre-long tram track and admission is $6. Out towards Parramatta, on Underwood Rd in Homebush, there's the State Sports Centre (☎ 763 0111), with its **Hall of Champions** featuring New South Wales sporting heroes from 1876 to the present. Sydney Cricket Ground has a **cricket museum**, open on match days.

Paddington

The inner-suburb of Paddington, four km east of the city centre, is one of the most attractive inner-city residential areas in the world. 'Paddo' is a tightly packed mass of terrace houses, built for aspiring artisans in the later years of the Victorian era. During the lemming-like rush to the dreary outer suburbs after WW II the area became a slum. A renewed interest in Victorian architecture (of which Australia has some gems) combined with a sudden recollection of the pleasures of inner-city life, led to the restoration of Paddo during the '60s.

Today it's a fascinating jumble of often

Terraced houses, Paddington

beautifully restored terraces, tumbling up and down the steeply sloping streets. Surprisingly there was an older Paddington of fine gentlemen's residences, a few of which still stand, although the once spacious gardens are now encroached upon by lesser buildings. Paddington is one of the world's finest examples of totally unplanned urban restoration and is full of trendy shops and restaurants, some fine art galleries and bookshops and interesting people. The best time to visit Paddo is Saturday when you can catch the 'Paddo Bazaar' at the corner of Newcombe and Oxford Sts with all sorts of eccentric market stalls.

Get a free copy of the 128-page *Paddington Book* (available from shops in the area) to find your way around. If you're in Paddington on a Tuesday morning you can visit the old **Victoria Barracks** on Oxford St where the impressive changing of the guards takes place at 10 or 11 am. Afterwards you'll get a free tour, which includes the Army Museum, once a jail within the grounds (the museum is also open on the first Sunday of the month from 1.30 to 4 pm). The barracks are closed to the public from mid-December to the end of January.

Among the many interesting buildings in Paddington is Juniper Hall, opposite the Town Hall at 250 Oxford St. It was built as a family home in 1824, and now contains the **Australian Museum of Childhood** which is appropriate as the building was once a child welfare institution. Much of the house is open for inspection daily from 10 am to 4 pm; entry is $3 for adults, $1.50 for kids. There is a National Trust gift shop and a cafe.

You can get to Paddo on bus No 378 from Central Railway Station, or bus Nos 380 or 389 from Circular Quay along Elizabeth St. The heart of Paddo is along **Oxford St** past the Barracks and in the streets north from there. A couple of blocks past the Barracks, you can turn up Underwood St, then follow Heeley St to reach **Five Ways**, a mass meeting of streets around which are some of Paddington's most interesting shops and places to eat, plus the lovely old Royal pub. **Paddington St**, further east, has some of the

finest-looking houses, while many of the antique shops are clustered along **Queen St**.

Kings Cross

'The Cross' has seedy strip joints, junkie teenage hookers, rambling, leafy old streets, lots of eateries; and it's the main travellers' centre in Sydney, with Australia's greatest concentration of hostels. Darlinghurst Rd is the Cross's main street and a good many of the hostels are on or near Victoria St, which diverges from Darlinghurst Rd just north of William St.

Kings Cross is close to the city centre, with lots of activity, and a great many travellers begin and end their Australian ventures in the Cross. It's a good place to swap information and buy or sell things. Numerous travellers' notice boards line the hostel and shop walls, and there's a car park where travellers buy and sell vehicles. The attractive (when it's working) thistle-like **El Alamein Fountain**, down in Fitzroy Gardens at the end of Darlinghurst Rd, is known locally as the 'elephant douche'! Next door, the Rex Hotel is probably Australia's greatest travellers' gathering place.

From the city you can walk straight up William St to the Cross (you can't miss the big Coca-Cola sign which marks the entrance to Darlinghurst Rd), or grab one of a multitude of buses which run there, or take the quick eastern suburbs train service right to the centre of the Cross. There's also a quieter pedestrian route from the city centre which you can find by ducking through Sydney Hospital from Macquarie St, crossing the Domain and descending the hill just on the right of the New South Wales Art Gallery, then going down Palmer St from its junction with Sir John Young Crescent, turning left along Harmer St, and following the paths and backstreets till you reach a flight of steps leading up to Victoria St, just south of its junction with Orwell St.

If you have a vehicle, there are usually empty spaces at the bottom (north) end of Victoria St where you can leave a vehicle for more than just a couple of hours. Another tip:

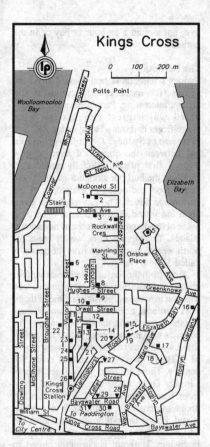

Kings Cross

0   100   200 m

Potts Point

Woolloomooloo Bay

Elizabeth Bay

Wharf Road

Wylde Street

Cowper Wharf Roadway

St Neot Ave

McDonald St

Stairs

Challis Ave

Macleay Street

Rockwall Cres

Manning St

Museum

Onslow Place

Onslow Ave

Tusculum Street

Greenknowe Ave

Hughes Street

Orwell Street

Victoria Street

Brougham Street

Elizabeth Bay Rd

Ward Ave

Roslyn Gardens

Roslyn St

Macleath Street

Darlinghurst Road

Kings Cross Station

Keller Street

Bayswater Road

Bayswater Ave

Ithaca Rd

To Paddington

Dowling Street

Mctthone Street

William St

Kings Cross Road

To City Centre

■ **PLACES TO STAY**

1   Backpackers Village
2   Rucksack Rest
3   Challis Lodge
4   Fairmont Hostel
6   Jackson Hotel
7   Boomerang Hostel
8   Macquarie Private Hotel
9   Downunder Backpackers
10 Jolly Swagman Backpackers (Orwell St)
11 Jolly Swagman Backpackers (Victoria St)
12 Jolly Swagman Backpackers (Springfield Mall)
13 Springfield Lodge
15 Rex Hotel
16 Young Travellers Hostel
17 Barncleuth House
21 Bernly Private Hotel
22 Kanga House
23 Travellers Rest
24 Kings Cross Backpackers
25 Highfield House Private Hotel
26 Plane Tree Lodge
30 Backpackers Headquarters

▼ **PLACES TO EAT**

20 Astoria
27 Geoffrey's Cafe
28 Bayswater Brasserie
29 Kardomah Cafe
31 Gado Gado (Cafe)

OTHER

5   Elizabeth Bay House
14 Springfield Avenue
18 Barncleuth Square
19 El Alamein Fountain/ Fitzroy Gardens

there are normally several *working* phone boxes in Kings Cross Station at the south end of Victoria St.

Between the city and the Cross is **Woolloomooloo**, the 'loo, one of Sydney's older areas with many narrow streets. This area, extremely run down in the early '70s, has gone through a complete restoration and is now very pleasant. But I bet you can't spell it without looking at it again. Does anywhere else in the world have four double-O's in its name? Near Cowper Wharf is Harry's Cafe de Wheels, a pie cart which opened in 1945 and is still going strong.

Beyond the Cross

The harbour front about half a km north-east of the Cross is called **Elizabeth Bay**. Here at 7 Onslow St is Elizabeth Bay House, one of Sydney's finest old homes, built in 1832 in Regency style, overlooking the harbour. It's open daily except Monday from 10 am to 4.30 pm, and admission is $4. Bus No 311 from Hunter St passes right by the house.

The next bay east – about half a km due

east from the Cross – is **Rushcutters Bay** which has a pleasant harbourside park and lots of boats at anchor. Then there's Darling Point and even trendier Double Bay – swish shops and lots of badly parked Porsches and Mercedes Benzes.

Next up in this direction is **Rose Bay**, then Nielsen Park (see Harbour Walks) and Vaucluse where Vaucluse House (open from 10 am to 4.30 pm except Monday, admission $5) on Wentworth Rd is an imposing turreted example of 19th-century Australiana in fine grounds. It was built in 1828 for the explorer William Wentworth. You can get there on bus No 325 from Edgecliff Station; get off a couple of stops past Nelson's Park.

At the end of the harbour is **Watsons Bay** with fashionable Doyles restaurant, a couple of Sydney's most 'be seen there' harbour beaches and the magnificent view across the Heads. All along this side of the harbour there are superb views back towards the city.

Other Suburbs

On the other side of the centre from Paddo and the Cross is **Balmain**, the arty centre of Sydney and in some ways rivalling Paddington in Victorian-era trendiness. **Glebe**, closer to the centre, has also been going up the social scale but it hasn't yet gone so far and still has a more studenty, Bohemian atmosphere, with lots of good-value restaurants.

Hunters Hill on the north shore, west of the centre, is full of elegant Victorian houses. The National Trust's Vienna Cottage at 38 Alexandra St, Hunters Hill, is a stone cottage built in 1871 by Jacob Hellman and is typical of the era. It's open Saturday from 2 to 4 pm and Sunday from 11 am to 4 pm.

While the eastern suburbs (the harbour to ocean area beyond the Cross) and the north shore (across the harbour) are the wealthy areas of Sydney, the western suburbs are the real suburbs. Heading west you come first to **Redfern**. Some parts of it are quite interesting, but others are Australia's closest approach to a real slum. Further out it's the red-tile-roofed, triple-front area of the 'slurbs', the dull Bankstowns of Sydney. It's in suburbs like these that most Australians live, not around a harbour or bay or in the outback.

The Harbour

Sydney's harbour is best viewed from the ferries. It's extravagantly colourful and always interesting. People have often wondered which great city has the most magnificent harbour – Hong Kong, Rio, San Francisco or Sydney? I've still to get to Rio, but between the others I'd have to give Sydney first place. Officially called Port Jackson, the harbour stretches about 20 km inland from the ocean to the mouth of the Parramatta River. The city centre is about eight km inland. The harbour is lined by a maze of headlands and inlets and has several islands. The biggest inlet, which heads off north-west a couple of km from the ocean, is called Middle Harbour.

Apart from the ferries and various harbour cruises (see Getting Around), you can take trips out to some of the islands. One of them, **Fort Denison**, or Pinchgut as it was uncomfortably named, was the site of a gallows for convicts who misbehaved, before it was fortified when Australians were having a bout of Russian fears back in the mid-19th century. There are tours there from Jetty 6, Circular Quay, at 10 am, 12.15 and 2 pm from Tuesday to Sunday. The trip takes 1½ hours and costs $8, including a tour of the island. Phone to book tours in advance (☎ 247 2733). **Goat Island**, the other tiny speck in Sydney Harbour, is currently closed to tours.

You can hire watercraft of various types from Balmoral Marine (☎ 969 6006) at 2 The Esplanade, Balmoral, on Middle Harbour. As an example of costs, windsurfers go for $15 an hour. There are several other harbour boat hire places.

At weekends the harbour is dotted with the sails of hundreds of yachts and a favourite activity is following the 18-footer yacht races on Sunday from September to March. Spectator ferries, complete with on-board bookies so you can bet on the outcome, follow the exciting races. Phone the Double Bay Sailing Club (☎ 363 5577) or the Royal

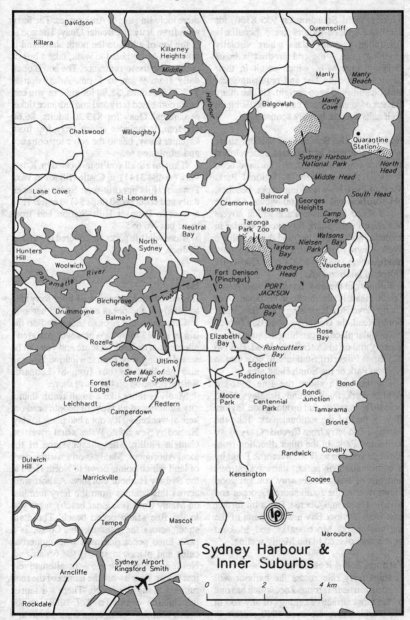

Sydney Harbour & Inner Suburbs

0   2   4 km

Sydney Yacht Squadron (☎ 955 8350) for details. Eighteen-footers are a peculiarly Australian yachting class where virtually anything goes – the end product is boats carrying huge sails, which result in their being fantastically fast and requiring great athletic ability to keep upright. Unlike many classes of yachts, these carry advertising on their sails and are heavily sponsored.

Harbour Walks Some of the harbour shore is still quite wild and several undeveloped stretches towards the ocean end have been declared Sydney Harbour National Park. Most of them have walking tracks, beaches, old fortifications and good views. On the south shore is Nielsen Park which covers Vaucluse Point, Shark Bay (very popular in summer, with a shark net) and the Hermitage Walk down round Hermit Bay. The park headquarters (☎ 337 5511) is at Greycliffe House in Nielsen Park.

Further out there's a fine short walk round South Head at the harbour entrance from Camp Cove Beach, passing Lady Bay, Inner South Head, the Gap at Watsons Bay (which is a popular place for catching the sunrise and sunset), and on to Outer South Head. Bus No 325 from Edgecliff Station will take you to Nielsen Park or the South Head area.

On the north shore the fine four-km Ashton Park track, round Bradleys Head below Taronga Zoo and up alongside Taylors Bay, is part of the national park. Take the Taronga Zoo ferry from Circular Quay to get to Ashton Park. In the other direction from Taronga you can walk to Cremorne Point by a combination of parks, stairways, streets and bits of bush. Either way you get good views over to the south shore. Georges and Middle Heads and Obelisk Bay a bit further east from Taylors Bay are also parts of the national park. More walks and lookout points are covered in the Manly section.

Taronga Zoo & Koala Park
A short ferry ride across the harbour will deposit you near Taronga Zoo, which has one of the most attractive settings of any zoo in the world. There are over 4000 critters in

there including lots of Aussie ones. The ferry goes from Jetty 5, Circular Quay. The zoo is at the top of a hill on the north shore and if you can't be bothered to walk, take a bus or cable car to the top entrance. The zoo is open daily from 9 am to 5 pm. Admission is $12.70 for adults, $5.80 for kids, or you can buy a combined ferry and zoo entrance ticket at Circular Quay for $13.20 adults, $6.60 children. It includes return ferry trip from Circular Quay, bus to the zoo's top entrance and admission fee.

If koalas are all you're interested in, Koala Park (☎ 484 3141) on Castle Hill Rd in West Pennant Hills in north-west Sydney is open daily and costs $6.50 (kids $4) to enter. Take a train to Pennant Hills Station and from there bus No 655.

More wildlife parks are covered in Around Sydney.

Manly
It is an excellent, cheap, half-hour ferry ride to Manly at the ocean edge of the harbour. JetCats cost a dollar or so more, and do the trip in just 15 minutes – however you aren't allowed out on deck on these and you can be seated a long way from a window. You can also get there by bus from St Leonards Railway Station on the north shore.

Manly is more like a small resort than a city suburb, and all types of people head out here at weekends. It's not a bad place to stay. Named by New South Wales's first governor, Captain Phillip, after the physique of the local Aborigines, Manly is on a narrow neck of land which points down to North Head at the Sydney Harbour entrance. A short walk across this isthmus from the ferry terminal on Manly Cove (the inner beach), takes you to the fine sandy ocean beach. The main street across the isthmus, the Corso, is a palm-lined pedestrian mall with numerous cafes and places to sit. At the ocean end, North and South Steyne – or alternatively just Ocean Beach – are the names of the road running along the beach. There's a tourist information centre (☎ 977 1088) on the beach near the Corso, open from 10 am to 4 pm daily. Here there are lockers where you can leave your valuables while swimming.

The **Manly Museum & Art Gallery** on West Esplanade (just to the left when you come off the ferry) has Australian paintings and intriguing temporary exhibitions on things like the history of surfing or swimming costumes. **Manly Underwater World** is an oceanarium also on West Esplanade, at the end of the beach. For about $12 you can get a close-up view of sharks and stingrays, and coral and kelp communities.

You can continue past Undersea World to join a 10-km walking track, the **Manly Scenic Walkway**, which follows the shoreline all the way back to the Spit bridge over Middle Harbour. Points of interest on the way, from the Manly end, include Fairlight, Forty Baskets and Reef beaches (the latter, a nude beach, involves a slight detour from the main track), great views between Dobroyd Head and Grotto Point, and ancient Aboriginal rock carvings on a sandstone platform between the Cutler Rd Lookout and Grotto Point. Collect a leaflet detailing the walk from the information centre. Bus Nos 182 and 241 go from the Spit bridge to Sydney city centre.

South of Manly, it's about three km to spectacular **North Head** at the Sydney Harbour entrance. Most of the headland is included in Sydney Harbour National Park – including the old quarantine station which housed suspected disease carriers from 1832 until 1984. From the ferry wharf a private bus heading for Manly Hospital will take you to near North Head.

North of Manly

A string of oceanfront suburbs stretches north up the coast from Manly, ending in beautiful, wealthy Palm Beach and the spectacular Barranjoey Heads at the mouth of Broken Bay, 30 km from Manly. There are lots of beaches along the way and buses do the route. From Palm Beach you can take cruises on the Pittwater, a fine inlet off Broken Bay, or the Hawkesbury River, or get ferries to Ku-ring-gai Chase or across Broken Bay to Patonga. The latter is part of

an interesting alternative route north: from Patonga there are buses to Gosford, where you can get a bus or train heading up the coast.

Beaches

Sydney's beaches are one of its greatest assets – they're easily accessible and usually very good. However, recently they've been having problems with pollution and in a number of places you're advised not to swim. Check out the situation when you're there.

There are two sorts of beaches in Sydney – harbour beaches and ocean beaches. The harbour beaches are sheltered and calm and generally smaller. The ocean beaches often have quite good surf.

Although they get crowded on hot summer weekends Sydney's beaches are never really shoulder to shoulder. Swimming is generally safe – at the ocean beaches you're only allowed to swim within the 'flagged' areas patrolled by the famed lifeguards. Efforts are made to keep the surfers separate from the swimmers. A high point of Sydney's beach life is the surf-lifesaving competitions at various beaches throughout the summer. Shark patrols are operated through the summer months and the ocean beaches are generally netted – Sydney has only had one fatal shark attack since 1937. The shark proof nets do not, incidentally, enclose the beaches – they run at right angles to the coast to dissuade sharks from patrolling along the beaches.

Many of Sydney's beaches are 'topless', but on some beaches this is not approved of so women should observe what other people are doing before forgetting their bikini tops. There are also a couple of nude beaches. Following is a brief resumé of some of the beaches:

Harbour Beaches On the south side, out near the heads (the harbour entrance), is trendy Camp Cove, a small but pleasant sliver of sand popular with families, and also topless. This was the place where Governor Phillip first landed in Sydney. Just north from Camp Cove and immediately inside the heads, tiny Lady Bay Beach achieved some notoriety in the process of becoming a nude beach. It's mainly a gay scene. There's another nude beach on the north shore of the harbour, Reef Beach (see the earlier Harbour Walks section).

Over on the ocean side from Camp Cove is Watsons Bay with the delightful outdoor seafood restaurant Doyles, where you can gaze back along the harbour towards the city.

Two other popular harbour beaches are Balmoral, with its little 'island', on the north side of the harbour and Nielsen Park on the south side at Vaucluse (see Harbour Walks).

South Ocean Beaches South of the heads there's a string of ocean beaches all the way to the entry to Botany Bay. Bondi, with its crowds, surfies and even fibreglass mermaids is probably the best-known beach in Australia. Bondi is rather like Earls Court is (or was) for young Australians in London, only, in this case, Bondi is a favourite with New Zealanders and other young visitors to Sydney. It's a popular gathering place, with a selection of cheap accommodation.

Some of Australia's easiest-reached Aboriginal carvings are a short walk north of the beach – outlines of fish on a flat rock on the golf course.

Tamarama, a little south of Bondi, is another beautiful sweep of sand with strong surf. Take bus No 391 from Bondi Junction Station to get there. Then there's Bronte, a wide beach popular with families (bus No 378 from Bondi Junction), and Coogee another wide, sweeping beach where you'll also find the popular Coogee Bay Hotel with its beer garden overlooking the beach. Other beaches towards Botany Bay, which is more for sailing than swimming due to the sharks, include Maroubra.

North Ocean Beaches The 30-km coast up to Barranjoey Heads is dotted with beaches beginning at Manly. Freshwater, first up from Manly, attracts a lot of teenagers, then there's Curl Curl (families and surfers), Dee Why and Collaroy (family beaches), the long sweep of Narrabeen which has some of Sydney's best surf as well as the Narrabeen Lakes which are home to many water birds, and further up the very safe Newport (families again). Up towards Barranjoey Heads three of the best are Avalon, Whale Beach and Palm Beach. Bus Nos 134 and 139 depart from Manly for Freshwater and Curl Curl. To get to Palm Beach from Manly take bus No 155, 156 or 157 to Narrabeen and from there take a No 190. Bus No 190 from York St in the city centre will take you to Newport and north.

Surf Beaches Surfing is a popular pastime in Sydney, and with the large number of good beaches close at hand, it's easy to see why. Apart from Bondi and Tamarama, there's Maroubra south of the heads. Beyond Botany Bay, Cronulla is another serious surf

beach. North of the heads there's another dozen or so dotted about 30 km up from Manly, the best being Narrabeen, North Avalon and Palm Beach, the north end of which is a nude beach.

Organised Tours
City There's a vast array of conventional city and area tours. Ask at the Travel Centre of New South Wales in Castlereagh St for details, and check out the give-away magazines from hotels and so on.

Australian Pacific, Ansett Pioneer, AAT King's, Newmans, Murrays and Clipper carry most of the tourists around town. You can join a half-day city or koala-cuddling tour for $30 to $35, a full-day city tour for $57 to $80.

Further Afield Longer day tours include the Blue Mountains and koala-cuddling ($42 to $50), the Blue Mountains and Jenolan Caves ($55), Hawkesbury River cruises plus Old Sydney Town (around $60), the Hunter Valley ($67) and Canberra ($66).

The YHA's 'Wonderbus' has a day tour of the Blue Mountains for under $30 daily except Sunday. Contact YHA Travel (☎ 267 3044) or the Glebe or Hereford hostels. Oztrek (☎ 360 3444), PO Box 1328, Darlinghurst, run popular day trips and camping tours, designed for backpackers. They'll pick you up from several hostels in Surry Hills, the city and Kings Cross or the YHAs in Glebe and Forest Lodge.

John Anderson's Gem Opal Outback Tours (☎ (068) 29 0143 in Lightening Ridge or book through Sydney YHA) will get you from Sydney to Brisbane in a week, via the outback, for about $380 – several travellers have written to recommend this trip. Countrylink also has some interesting packages.

Festivals
The Festival of Sydney is mainly devoted to the arts and lasts for most of January. Features include open-air opera and music in the parks and the Sydney Harbour ferry race. Sydney's Chinese celebrate their new year in Chinatown in January or February. A bit later, the highlight of the Gay Mardi Gras

festivities is the highly colourful parade from the city to the showgrounds in Moore Park one night in late February or early March, plus an incredible party in Oxford St. The showgrounds are also the venue for the Royal Easter Show, with its livestock displays, sideshows and rodeos.

In June in even-numbered years, the Sydney Biennale is a modern art festival. Also in June, but annually, there is the Sydney Film Festival.

In May you can catch the Bathtub Regatta across the Heads. On Boxing Day the Harbour is a fantastic sight, as boats of all shapes and sizes crowd its waters to farewell the competitors in the Sydney to Hobart Yacht Race.

Places to Stay

There's a wide variety of accommodation in Sydney including an excellent selection of very cheap hostels. The information that follows is subdivided by location as well as type so decide where you want to stay first of all. If you want to book a hotel or motel room, the New South Wales Travel Centre (☎ 231 4444) at 19 Castlereagh St performs this service. In Kings Cross, on Macleay St near the El Alamein fountain, there's an information booth (☎ 357 3883) which has daily accommodation specials. You can book tours and coaches here as well. There are cheap places in the 'flats to let' and 'share accommodation' ads in the *Sydney Morning Herald*, particularly on Wednesdays and Saturdays. Many travellers also find flat shares through other travellers whom they meet in Kings Cross. Bed & Breakfast Sydneyside (☎ 449 4430), PO Box 555, Turramurra, NSW 2074, is an organisation which will find you accommodation in a private home in Sydney for about $35 to $60 a night for a single, $55 to $90 a double.

When Maureen and I first set up Lonely Planet we lived in the basement of a Paddington terrace in Sydney, and since then we've made lots of trips and visits to the harbour city and tried out all sorts of areas around the city, either staying with friends or in a variety of places, more than a few of which feature here. The Cross is the backpacker centre and is great

fun if you like a little raucous squalor. Bondi is Sydney's best known beach and like the Cross there's lots of activity and lots of places to eat. If you'd like something quieter the distance to Manly is no big deal because you ride back and forth on the best transport Sydney has to offer – a harbour ferry.

– Tony Wheeler

Hostels Sydney has several YHA hostels and an enormous number of backpacker hostels. The backpacker places vary, so you may have to jump around until you find one that suits you. Although Sydney's backpacker hostels have been great value for years, new fire regulations may force many of them to raise their prices or shut down. Some backpacker hostels discourage or even ban Australians.

A few backpacker hostels have set hours for checking in or out, normally a couple of hours round 9 am and again around 6 pm, but once you're in you usually get a key so you can come and go whenever you like. In most places you're asked to be quiet after 10 or 11 pm. There are often cheap rates if you stay a week, and in winter prices can drop a little.

YHA Hostels As with most of Australia's YHAs, Sydney's no longer close during the day and they're cleaner and better run than many backpackers' hostels. You have to be a YHA member to stay at the Sydney hostels, although there are 'trial offers' and the like available from time to time.

In Glebe, *Hereford Lodge* (☎ 660 5577) at 51 Hereford St (off Glebe Point Rd) is the best YHA in town and charges $14 in six-bed dorms, $16 in four-bed dorms and $19 in two-bed dorms. Big motel-style rooms cost $65/75/80 for singles/doubles/triples and $90 for four people. It has a cafeteria, laundry, all the usual facilities plus a roof-top swimming pool and sauna. The *Glebe Point YHA Hostel* (☎ 692 8418) is at 262-264 Glebe Point Rd, about three km west of Central Railway Station. Dorm beds cost from $14 and twins $19 per person. Bus Nos 431 and 433 from Railway Square go along Glebe Point Rd and will drop you outside the YHA.

The *Dulwich Hill YHA Hostel* (☎ 569 0272) is at 407 Marrickville Rd, Dulwich Hill, on the corner of Wardell Rd, about six km south-west of the centre. It has twin rooms only for $14 per person ($77 per week). To get there take the 15- minute train ride from Central Railway Station to Dulwich Hill and walk about 750 metres north to Marrickville Rd. Bus No 426 from Circular Quay or Railway Square, and bus No 490 (daytime only and not Sundays) from behind the Queen Victoria building on York St, will both take you to the corner of Marrickville and Wardell Rds.

City The YMCA has long-term plans to open a new hostel to replace the one that burned down, but they haven't yet decided on a site (☎ 264 1011 to check on developments). The *CB Private Hotel* (☎ 211 5115) at 417 Pitt St has hotel rooms and dorm beds from $10 a night. There aren't any cooking facilities but there is a laundry.

The large and comfortable *YWCA* (☎ 264 2451) takes women, married couples and families and is at 5-11 Wentworth Ave, at the corner of Liverpool St across from Hyde Park. There's a cheap cafeteria. Beds in female-only bunkrooms go for $15, single rooms for $36 ($60 with private bathroom), twins $60 ($85), triples $85 ($110). Maximum stay in the dorms is one week.

Kings Cross 'The Cross' has several decent hostels but also Sydney's dirtiest, noisiest and most crowded ones. To get to Kings Cross, take the quick train ride from Central Railway Station or other city centre stations. Kings Cross Station has exits on both Darlinghurst Rd and Victoria St.

The place most people start looking is Victoria St but the better places are often full. The best time to get there is about 9 or 10 am, when people check out. Heading down Victoria St from Kings Cross Station or from the corner of Darlinghurst Rd, one of the first places you reach is *Plane Tree Lodge* (☎ 356 4551) at No 172. Dorm beds are $11 and twin rooms cost from $28. It's quite strictly run, but it's clean with good facilities. There's a

restaurant, open till late, where you can get an omelette for $5 or steaks from $10.50.

Highfield House Private Hotel (☎ 358 1552) at 166 Victoria St (the street sign says 'Budget Hotel') has small dormitories at $12 ($75 per week) and twins with bathroom for $30 ($180). It's clean and offers more privacy than normal hostels. The good value *Criss Cross Cafe* is here.

At No 162, *Kings Cross Backpackers* (☎ 356 3232) is a large and well-established hostel which runs several nearby houses. Prices per person are $10 in a dormitory or a single-sex four-person flat ($65 per week), $13 in a double room ($80 each per week). The doubles are quite roomy. Kitchens in the main houses are communal; as in most Kings Cross hostels they can get a bit scruffy but at least there's an adequate supply of pots, pans, cutlery, etc. Probably the best building is the main one at 162. There's a good notice board here.

Travellers Rest (☎ 358 4606) at No 156 is one of the cleaner hostels. Dorm beds are $12 in small rooms and there are also singles/doubles at $27/32. Weekly rates are six times the daily cost. All rooms have a TV and most have their own bathrooms. Check-out time is 9 am, an hour earlier than usual.

Across the road at No 141, *Kanga House* has dorms for $10 ($60 per week) and singles/doubles for $15/26 ($100/140). It's pretty standard but at least it should be around for a while, as they've bitten the bullet and spent a lot of money on meeting the fire safety standards. The *Boomerang Hostel* (☎ 358 2099) at No 110 is a little run-down but it's small and friendly. Dorm beds cost from $10 ($65 per week) and twins with bathroom are $30 ($180 per week).

Jolly Swagman Backpackers has three nearby locations – 144 Victoria St (☎ 358 6400), 16 Orwell St (☎ 358 6600) and 14 Springfield Mall (☎ 358 3330). Orwell St is off Victoria St just down from 144, Springfield Mall is a couple of turns off Orwell St. Dorm beds at Victoria St are $10 a night ($60 a week), double rooms are $24 ($144). At Orwell St dorm beds are $8 ($50) and singles/doubles are $17/20 ($100/120). At

Springfield Mall dorm beds are $10 and singles/doubles are $18/24. Each room has its own fridge, stove, sink and cooking gear; bathrooms and toilets are shared.

Also in Orwell St, at No 6, *Network Travellers' Hostel* has dorm beds for $12 and singles/doubles for $15/30. Doubles with bathroom are $40. Another popular place is at 25 Hughes St – *Downunder Backpackers* (☎ 358 1433), where dorm beds are $11 a night ($70 per week), double rooms $26 ($156) and flats $10 per person ($60). There are sizable cooking, dining and TV areas. Bed linen is provided, all bathrooms are shared and the office is open 24 hours. Things can get lively here.

North, on Macleay St, the *Fairmont Hostel* (☎ 357 1113) has dorms for $11 ($70 per week) and singles/twins for $14/24 ($72/85). Some of the rooms have balconies. There are a couple of places in McDonald St, a cul-de- sac off Macleay St just north of Challis Ave. *Rucksack Rest* (☎ 358 2348) at No 9 has dorm beds for $11 (but no Aussies allowed) and *Backpackers' Village* (☎ 358 2808) at No 3 with dorms for $10 ($6 for the first night) and doubles for $24, with cheaper four-day and weekly rates. Each room has a fridge and cooking facilities.

One of the most relaxed Kings Cross hostels is the pink *Barncleuth House* (☎ 358 1689) which is slightly away from the main drag, in a quieter street at 6 Barncleuth Square, east of Darlinghurst Rd. It has a courtyard garden and log fires when it's cold. Dorm beds or small doubles are $11 per person (around $70), and larger doubles are $13. Some of the dorms have double-bed bunks. A good vegetarian dinner costs $4.

The *Young Travellers Hostel* at Roslyn Gardens (☎ 357 3509) was a big place which had to fold because it couldn't meet the fire regulations, but a pleasant woman is running the house as a private hostel. There are now only three dorms and three double rooms in this fine old terrace – dorm beds cost $10 ($60 per week) and doubles are $25 ($130). Get there by following Elizabeth Bay Rd off Darlinghurst Rd then turning right into Roslyn Gardens.

Backpackers' Headquarters (☎ 331 2520) at 79 Bayswater Rd is a big place with dorm beds for $12 ($70 per week) and just one double, which goes for $25 ($160). It's popular, open 24 hours and has a cheap restaurant. It's currently for sale, so things might change.

Inner Suburbs At 665 South Dowling St, Surry Hills, opposite Moore Park, just north of the Cleveland St corner, is *Kangaroo Bakpak* (☎ 319 5915). It's a friendly place with dorm beds for $11 a night. If you're staying a couple of nights or more they'll refund the taxi fare from Central Railway Station. *Beethoven Lodge* (☎ 698 4203) a few doors north at No 641 is similar, with dorm beds for $10 ($65 per week) and a few twins for $12 per person. To get here from Central take bus Nos 372, 393 or 395, or it's about a 15-minute walk.

Also in Surry Hills, but closer to Central Railway Station, is *Backpackers' Headquarters* (☎ 698 8839) on the corner of Cleveland and Elizabeth Sts. Dorm beds are around $11 and there are a few private rooms, but it's a noisy location and pretty run down.

In Glebe, next to the YHA Hostel on Glebe Point Rd is *Glebe Point Village* (☎ 660 8878), with beds in shared rooms from $10 to $15 and doubles from $35. They also have longer-term flats. Also in Glebe, *Wattle House Hostel* (☎ 692 0879) is a friendly little hostel with beds in small shared rooms at $12 ($80 per week) or twins for $28 ($180). It's at 44 Hereford St, opposite the other YHA.

The *Harbourside Hotel* on Cremorne Point has dorm beds and great views, only a few minutes from Circular Quay by ferry – see the North Shore Hotels section.

Bondi The most famous of Sydney's beaches, Bondi has a fair range of accommodation – see also the Hotel section. Buses run all the way from the city to Bondi Beach, but it's quicker to take a train to Bondi Junction and bus No 380 from there. A combined ticket is slightly cheaper than paying two fares.

The comfortable *Lamrock Hostel* (☎ 365

0221) is at 7 Lamrock Ave, just back from the south end of Bondi Beach. It's a bright house with rooms for six to eight people at $15 each ($70 per week), or twin rooms at $45. Some have bathrooms. There's a barbecue, and Mokes for hire. Also just back from the beach is *Bondi Beach Travellers' Hostel* (☎ 365 4934) at 124 Curlewis St. It's less comfortable and bigger than the Lamrock but cheaper at $12, and still a decent typical hostel, with a fairly relaxed atmosphere and a garden.

Coogee Coogee Beach Backpackers (the name might be changing to *Sydney Beachside Budget Accommodation)* (☎ 665 7735) at 94 Beach St, is close to the beach. It's spacious, clean, bright and comfortable with dorm beds at $12 ($75 per week), doubles at $30, a garden, good kitchens, washing machines, a big sitting room with TV and stereo, and views. You pay $2.50 for sheet hire for your stay. They'll collect you if you call.

Nearby, *Indy's Beachside Backpackers* (☎ 664 2775) at 302 Arden St is a small, friendly place, and also good value with dorms about $12 and good doubles at $30. *Aaronbrook Lodge* (☎ 665 7798) at 116 Brook St (parallel to Arden St, a block further from the beach) is a new place with dorm beds for $12. The *Aegean* (☎ 398 4999) at 40 Coogee Bay Rd is further from the beach (although closer to public transport) and has shared accommodation in self-contained flats from about $10 per night. Bus No 373 from Circular Quay, No 372 from Railway Square and No 314 from Bondi Junction terminate within walking distance of these hostels, or phone to be picked up.

Back on Beach St, on the corner of Carr St, the *Grand Pacific Private Hotel* (☎ 665 6301) has shared rooms for about $11 per person as well as private rooms – see the Hotels section.

Manly Consider Manly if you want a bit of space, sea breeze, sea, surf, sand, and good eating and drinking without having to tread

concrete all the time. There is a good range of accommodation from backpacker hostels to four-star hotels overlooking a wonderful sweep of beach.

The *Manly Beach Backpackers Hostel* (☎ 977 2092), also known as the *Astra* (but hard to find because there's no sign) at 68-70 Pittwater Rd, Manly, charges $13 ($78 per week) in dorms and is close to the beach. Also in Manly is the *Kangaroo Lodge* (☎ 977 5859) at 53 Kangaroo St, a fair way from the beach, with dorm beds for $12 and full weekly board for $95. There are a number of permanent residents here.

North of Manly, at the top end of the northern beach strip and near the Pittwater and some good ocean beaches, the *Avalon Beach Hostel* (☎ 918 9709) at 59 Avalon Parade is a good place. The nightly cost in shared rooms for two or four varies as to whether you are willing to do a chore ($10) or not ($15). The office is open from 8 to 11 am and 5 to 9 pm; at other times there's a recorded message which tells you how to get there.

Hotels, Motels, Guesthouses, Flats & Serviced Apartments The main areas are the city, Kings Cross, Bondi Beach and Manly, but there are a few more places about the North Shore and elsewhere.

City The clutch of big old hotels in the south of the centre is convenient for Central Railway Station and the bus terminals. Nearest of all to the station is the *Central Private Hotel* (☎ 212 1068) at 356-358 Elizabeth St; turn right at the top end of Eddy Ave. All rooms have hot and cold water and a refrigerator. Singles/doubles are from $25/30 or $120/180 a week.

The *West End Hotel* (☎ 211 4822) at 412 Pitt St is a big place with a variety of rooms. Singles/doubles/triples/quads with common bathroom start at $25/40/50/55. Singles/doubles with bathroom are from $70/80. A full breakfast is $6 and there are lunch specials. Across the road at 417 Pitt St, the *CB Private Hotel* (☎ 211 5115) is run by the same people and is large, clean and very plain. Daily rates are $25/40/50 for singles/doubles/triples with common bathroom. They also have backpackers' rooms – see the hostels section. Weekly rates are about five times the daily rates.

A block west at 700A George St, the *George Private Hotel* (☎ 211 1800) has singles/doubles/triples from $26/40/54, all with common bathrooms. The weekly rate is six times the daily rate. It's clean and there's a guests' kitchen (but no pots, pans, etc) plus a launderette and a cafeteria.

The *Great Southern Hotel* (☎ 211 4311) at 717 George St has singles/doubles from $35/48, with a few small singles for $25. Close to Chinatown and Darling Harbour, the *Travellers Rest Hotel* (☎ 281 5555) at 37 Ultimo Rd in Haymarket is newly renovated and has singles/doubles from $55/65 or $65/75 with attached bathroom. There are also dorm beds, but at $24 they're way over-priced.

South of Central Railway Station, at 207 Cleveland St, the *Alfred Park Private Hotel* (☎ 699 4031) has small but clean rooms with fridge and TV from $30/40 for singles/doubles. Bathrooms are communal and there are cooking facilities. A big plus is that there's some secure car parking. It's fair value but note that their brochure's 'singles from $15' refers to dorm beds.

At the other end of the city centre, on the corner of Lower Fort St and Cumberland St, the *Harbour View Hotel* (☎ 252 3769) should have been renamed the 'Bridge View' in 1932 – it's right next to one of the approach pylons and a hundred metres from the Rocks. There's some noise from trains on the bridge and much more from the bands in the bar, but with clean rooms at $30/40 for singles/doubles (including light breakfast) it's amazing value for the location.

Nearby but without the noise, the National Trust has two self-contained *townhouses* in an historic terrace on Agar Steps. Each sleeps up to six people and costs around $130 per night (minimum two nights). Phone 258 0141 for more information. Right in the Rocks is the *Lord Nelson Brewery Hotel* (☎ 251 4044), on the corner of Kent and

Argyle Sts, where singles/doubles with breakfast cost $60 to $100 in one of the six rooms.

In the heart of the business district and only a few blocks from Circular Quay, *Sydney City Centre Serviced Apartments* (☎ 223 3529) in a tower block at 7 Elizabeth St, between Hunter St and Martin Place, has open-plan apartments from $60 a night.

The *Wynyard Travelodge* (☎ 299 3000), 7 York St near Wynyard Station, has rooms from $140, while the *Koala Park Regis* (☎ 267 6511), on the corner of Castlereagh and Park Sts, has singles/doubles at $95/105. *Harbour Rocks* (☎ 251 8944), 34 Harrington St, The Rocks, is a small hotel with rooms (which sleep up to six) from $80/150.

Kings Cross This area has almost as many hotels and flats as hostels, and many are in the budget range. The places to look are Darlinghurst Rd, Victoria St and the lanes between.

Springfield Lodge (☎ 358 3222) is pretty much in the centre of things at 9 Springfield Ave, just off Darlinghurst Rd. It's good in a simple, straightforward manner. The 72 rooms all have fridges, TV and tea-making facilities. Rooms with share bathrooms are $30/36 single/double ($140/150 per week); a third person pays $10 ($56 per week). Rooms with bathroom cost $42/44.

Close by at 15 Springfield Ave the *Bernly Private Hotel* (☎ 358 3122) is a bit more comfortable and a few dollars more expensive. All rooms have a TV, washbasin, fridge and tea/coffee making facilities. Some have showers, though all toilets are shared. Singles/doubles/triples cost $40/50/60, or $45/55/65 with shower; it's cheaper by the week. It's open 24 hours a day and has a roof terrace with views over to the harbour and city centre.

Orwell Lodge (☎ 358 1745) at 20 Orwell St is a bit musty but clean and quiet and has rooms for $30/40 ($140/160 per week) with shared bathrooms, and a three-bed suite with bathroom for $50 ($200). All rooms have a TV, fridge, stove and running water.

Off the bottom end of Victoria St at 21-23

Challis Ave, *Challis Lodge* (☎ 358 5422) is a private hotel charging from $26/32 ($140/168 per week) with shared bathroom, from $36/42 ($182/210) with private bathroom. An extra person costs $10. Most rooms have TV, fridge and tea/coffee-making facilities.

The *Plaza Hotel* (☎ 358 6455) is right in the heart of noisy Kings Cross at 23 Darlinghurst Rd. The entrance is just off the main street, in Llankelly Place, one block west of the Alamein Fountain. The cost is $19/27 for singles/doubles ($95/135 per week). It's a very plain and basic place with one shared bathroom for each floor, but it is quite OK. At No 40 there's *Budget Accommodation* (☎ 357 4730) with dorm beds for $10 and doubles for $25.

There are some classier budget hotels around Kings Cross, one of the best known being the comfortable *Macquarie Private Hotel* (☎ 358 4122) on the corner of Hughes and Tusculum Sts. Singles/doubles cost $50/55, or from $70/75 with a bathroom and kitchenette. There's a surcharge of 10% for smokers! There's also a restaurant with pasta from $8 and main courses from $12. Another place in this range is the *Holiday Lodge Private Hotel* (☎ 356 3955) at 55 Macleay St charging from $66.

The *Jackson Hotel* (☎ 358 5144) at 94 Victoria St has B&B rates of $70/80 – travellers have found this place comfortable and friendly. The *Roslyn Gardens Motor Inn* (☎ 358 1944), 4 Roslyn Gardens, Kings Cross, charges $69/79.

Slightly out of the area at Darling Point but still close to Kings Cross is *Bersens Cosmopolitan* (☎ 327 3207), 2B Mona Rd, Darling Point. Singles and doubles cost $99 per night and suites have cooking facilities. There's a rooftop terrace with spa and sauna and views of the city across Rushcutters Bay.

There are a number of serviced apartment places in the Cross too. They include the *Metro Motor Inn* (☎ 356 3511) at 40 Bayswater Rd at $92 per night; and *Kings Cross Holiday Apartments* (☎ 361 0637), 59 William St, $70 per day and $450 per week.

North Shore There are a few good possibilities a short way north of the Harbour Bridge – away from the crowds of travellers, but surprisingly close to the city centre with some different views of the city. The *Harbourside Hotel* (☎ 953 7977) at 41 Cremorne Rd in Cremorne is superbly situated (although a traveller complained that it's a long way from supermarkets) and has singles/doubles for $20/40, including a light breakfast and soup at night! Take a Milsons Point ferry from Circular Quay, get off at Cremorne Wharf and the hotel is a short way up the road. The *Travellers Rest* people who run one of the better hostels in Kings Cross have a second place at 7 Park Rd, St Leonards (☎ 436 3146), 500 metres from St Leonards Station, which is about a 10-minute train ride from the centre. They no longer have dorms but rooms are good value at $20/30, or $23/40 with bathroom.

In Kirribilli, a short ferry ride from Circular Quay, is the *Glenferrie Private Hotel* (☎ 955 1685) at 12A Carabella St. They have singles/doubles at $125/180 a week and twins at $200, including two meals a day. *Kirribilli Bed & Breakfast* (☎ 922 3134) is at 12 Parkes St and costs from $55/85.

In Neutral Bay, just north of Kirribilli, the *Neutral Bay Motor Lodge* (☎ 953 4199) is at 45 Kurraba Rd, on the corner of Hayes St. Motel units cost $55/60 (less by the week) and there are some guesthouse rooms with shared bathroom and kitchen from $120 a week. It's a clean, friendly, well-equipped place and a few rooms even have harbour views. It's often full but you can book ahead.

Inner Suburbs *Alishan International* (☎ 660 1001) at 100 Glebe Point Rd, Glebe, is a newly renovated place with dorm beds for $18, singles with shared bathroom from $50, and singles/doubles with bathroom from $65/75. Four-bed family rooms with bathroom cost $90 per night. There's a spa, kitchen, recreation room, garden and barbecue area.

The most central motel with anything like a reasonable tariff is the *Crown-Lodge Motel* (☎ 331 2433) at 289 Crown St, Surry Hills, between Campbell and Albion Sts, with rooms from $70. The *Esron Motel* (☎ 398 7022) at the corner of St Pauls and Dudley Sts, Randwick – near the racecourse – has rooms from $65.

The *Metro Motor Inn* (☎ 699 4133) at 1 Meagher St, Chippendale (three km from the city centre) costs $92 and has undercover parking. In Paddington, the *Paddington Terrace Motel* (☎ 361 0211) at 21 Oxford St, just east of South Dowling St, has rooms from $90/100.

Bondi Beach The *Bondi Beach Guest House* (☎ 389 8309) at 11 Consett Ave is clean and has singles/doubles for $30/35. There are fridges, tea/coffee-making facilities and a TV in all the rooms plus a kitchen and laundry. A few rooms have private bathrooms. Next door at No 11A *Thelellen Lodge* (☎ 30 1521) charges $30/40 for pleasant rooms with similar facilities, plus air-con.

A few metres up the hill from the south end of the beach, the *Beach Inn* (☎ 30 5333), run by the same people as the Thelellen Lodge, is a big, old Bondi hotel at 2 Campbell Parade on the corner of Francis St. Rooms with common bathroom cost from $30/37. Each room has a fridge, TV and tea/coffee-making facilities. Similar but a bit better is the *Hotel Bondi* (☎ 30 3271) at 178 Campbell Parade, where rooms cost from $30/35 with common bathroom and from $35/45 with attached bathroom.

The *Bondi Beach Motel* (☎ 30 5344) at 68 Gould St is quite modern and has been recommended. Rooms are around $52/64, variable with the season.

Serviced apartments or holiday units abound and include two under the name of *Enochs*: at 92 Campbell Parade (☎ 365 0423) and at 25 Wallis Parade in North Bondi (☎ 365 0472). Both let by the week only and begin from $315 in Bondi and $350 in North Bondi.

Coogee The *Grand Pacific Private Hotel* (☎ 665 6301) at the corner of Carr and Beach Sts, has singles/doubles from $17/24 ($85/140 per week), as well as dorm beds for

$11. These rates fluctuate depending on demand. There's a kitchen and laundry, and it's very close to the beach.

Manly As at Bondi prices change depending how busy the place is – December to March is worst.

At 27-29 Victoria Parade, two blocks to the right along the Esplanade from the ferry landing, the *Eversham Private Hotel* (☎ 977 2423) is a clean, no-frills place close to the ocean beach. It usually only takes weekly customers. Small singles cost $123 per week, larger singles are $133 and doubles are $186. There's a big dining room and they have some deals which include meals.

The *Manly Lodge* (☎ 977 8655) is over the road at 22 Victoria Parade. It's a nice place with rooms from $50/60 per night and cheaper weekly rates. They also have dorm beds ($15) and doubles ($40) in a nearby building.

The *Periwinkle Guest House* (☎ 977 4668) at 18-19 East Esplanade overlooks the harbour side of Manly and is a restored Victorian-era home. Rooms with shared bathroom cost $66/72, including a light breakfast.

Colleges The usual rules apply – vacations only, students for preference. The following are at the University of New South Wales in Kensington, about four km south of the city centre. At *New College* (☎ 662 6066) non-students pay $25 a night room only, $28 with breakfast and $35 full board. Students pay less. Rates at the other colleges are a little higher, but all offer much cheaper rates if you are staying for a while, say more than a fortnight. Other colleges include *Warrane College* (☎ 662 6199), a Catholic college which offers accommodation with full board to men during the summer vacation, and *International House* (☎ 663 0418). For long-term stays try the University of New South Wales campus accommodation service (☎ 697 3166).

A lot of the colleges at the University of Sydney (☎ 692 2222), a couple of km west of the centre along the Parramatta road, tend to be booked out with conferences in the vacations, but may still be worth a try.

Camping Sydney's caravan parks are a long way out of town. Listed here are some within 30 km of the centre.

Meriton North Ryde (☎ 88 72177), corner Lane Cove and Fontenoy Rds, North Ryde, camping $16 double, on-site vans from $47. At about 14 km out, this is the closest to the city centre.
Sheralee Tourist Caravan Park (☎ 567 7161), 88 Bryant St, Rockdale, sites $16.
East's Van Park Lane Cove River (☎ 805 0500), Plassey Rd, North Ryde, sites $17 double.
Lakeside Caravan Park (☎ 913 7845), Lake Park Rd, Narrabeen, 26 km north, camping from $12, on-site vans from $50 double.
Ramsgate Beach Caravan Park (☎ 529 7329), 289 Grand Parade, Ramsgate, sites $17 double, on-site vans from $40 double.

Places to Eat

If you're going to explore seriously Sydney's ethnic variety in restaurants a useful book is *Cheap Eats in Sydney* – good value at under $10.

There are many places to eat in the city centre from Central Railway Station past Hyde Park to Martin Place, on the western edge of the central area in Chinatown and Darling Harbour, and around the Rocks and Circular Quay, just north of the centre. Kings Cross, Darlinghurst, Paddington, Balmain, Glebe, Newtown, Redfern and several beach suburbs all offer more good possibilities. For an excellent cheap lunch during term-time, try the *Catering College* in Blaxland Rd, Ryde. Take bus No 500 from Circular Quay or Central and get off where it terminates.

City Centre *Carriages*, the Central Railway Station restaurant, is open from 6 am to 8 pm daily, and has reasonable food. Breakfast costs from about $4 and main courses are about $6. A five-minute walk from the station at 761 George St, near where George and Pitt Sts meet, the licensed *Malaya* is popular for its reasonably cheap Malay-Chinese food, and it's open daily. Heading north, at No 735 *Herng Her Jai* is a vegetarian Chinese restaurant open daily for lunch

and dinner with soups at around $3 and main courses from $8. They don't use MSG and you can't use tobacco or alcohol. *Mekong* at No 711 is basic but cheap – four dishes cost about $6 and the servings are huge. It's open daily between 11 am and 9.30 pm. *Cafe Japon* at No 709 has $6 lunch specials.

A couple of reasonable places for breakfast are *Downtown Cafe* at 701 George St, with bacon and eggs for under $5; and across the road at No 760 (George St's numbering is disrupted by Central Railway Station) *City South Coffee Lounge*, which is slightly cheaper until 10 am, and the servings are large.

Just under the railway line from Hay St, at 202 Elizabeth St, the *Roma* is a great place for cakes, pastries, coffees and home-made pasta, at reasonable prices. It's open from 7.30 am Monday to Saturday and closes at 7 pm weekdays, 4.30 Saturday.

Closer to the centre, on Liverpool St and in the Hyde Park area, there are many more possibilities. At 152 Elizabeth St, just south of Liverpool St, the *Cyprus Hellene Club* is open Monday to Saturday. Their $10 mixed platter is good value. A little dearer is the *Hellenic Club*, upstairs at 251 Elizabeth St, across from Hyde Park. *Hing Wah* in the Remington Centre, opposite Hyde Park on Liverpool St, offers a takeaway Chinese lunch from $3.50.

For breakfasts at around $6 in this part of town, go to the *Selana Coffee Lounge,* north of Liverpool St at 367 Pitt St. Nearby in the basement at 336 Pitt St, *Diethnes* is a large and friendly Greek restaurant. Open Monday to Saturday, it has soups from $2.50 and main courses around $8. *Carruthers* at 359 Pitt St is a good health food takeaway open during the day.

On Liverpool St near the corner of Kent St there are several Spanish restaurants, cheapest of which are *Cafeteria Espana* and, if you choose carefully, *Captain Torres*, famous for its seafood. There's also a restaurant in the *Spanish Club* across the street.

On the corner of George and Park Sts, the 2nd floor cafeteria in *Woolworth's* has meals such as lasagna and salad for $7. Better value is the small food hall in the basement (enter from an arcade in Pitt St) where there's a variety of shops with dishes for under $5.

The *Centrepoint Tavern*, downstairs in the Centrepoint shopping complex, at the corner of Pitt and Market Sts, is popular for its large assortment of meals between $7 and $10.

The next cross street up from Market St is King St and at its eastern end the *Hyde Park Barracks* are open during the day and have a popular, but not cheap, three-course set menu and other choices if you're less hungry.

On King St between George and Pitt, *Beta Bite* is a takeaway health food stall. *El Sano* at shop 2 in the CML Arcade, Martin Place, has interesting vegetarian and South American meals and snacks at moderate prices. In Ash St at the end of Angel Arcade, just north of Martin Place at 121 Pitt St, the popular *Fuji Tempura Bar* is a very good place for Japanese food with good main meals under $10. It's open from Monday to Friday for lunches and Wednesday to Friday for dinners.

Chinatown A few minutes' walk north-west from Central Railway Station to the intersection of Hay and Dixon Sts brings you to the heart of Chinatown. Dixon St is a colourful pedestrian mall and around here are some of the best places in Sydney for a good cheap meal. Weekend yum cha brunch is popular in Sydney and you may have to queue to get into some of the many places offering it.

Try the food centre in *Pailou Plaza* at 60 Dixon St, halfway between Goulburn and Hay Sts. Stalls offer food from Japan, Vietnam, Thailand, Malaysia, Singapore and other Asian countries. Meals are $4.50 to $6 and the food is good. A similarly priced, perhaps even more comprehensive, food centre is downstairs in the *Chinatown Centre* just south of the corner of Dixon and Goulburn Sts.

On the 5th floor of the Chinatown Centre is the up-market *Chinatown Garden Restaurant* with excellent food and particularly good yum cha daily from 10 am.

Jing May Noodles is a great place for a meal, with nothing over $12 and much cheaper noodle dishes. It's in the Princes Centre at the corner of Thomas and Quay Sts – Thomas St heads south off Hay St between Dixon and Sussex Sts. Two places with interesting menus are *Hingara* at 82 Dixon St, and *China Sea* at 94 Hay St where most meals are under $10. Others worth checking out are the large *Tai Yuen* at 110 Hay St and *New Tai Yuen* at 31 Dixon St. Both have main courses around $10 to $12.

In Sussex St, parallel to Dixon St, *Marigold* at No 299 has been popular for many years. It is good value unless you go for seafood in which case you'd better check your wallet first.

Darling Harbour There are lots of good places to eat here, including a *food hall* at the Harbourside Festival Marketplace. The hi-tech *Virgin Video Cafe* has cocktails and dishes up to about $12. At 17 Little Pier St, near the Powerhouse Museum, the *Pump House Tavern* has good food, although only the cheapest dishes cost under $9.

The Rocks The Rocks has lots of eateries and given its huge tourist turnover there is a surprising number of relatively inexpensive places.

At the top of George St, just before it goes under the bridge, the *Mercantile Hotel* is a restored pub with counter meals. Keep going up George St, turn left after you've gone under the bridge, and you'll come to the unrestored *Harbour View Hotel* where meals are basic but good value.

At 101 George St, *Phillip's Foote* has a good barbecue where you cook your own steak or fish for $15; the price includes a glass of wine but salads are extra. Next door at No 99 *Rock's Cafe* has snacks and light meals from 8 am to 7 pm during the week and till late on Friday and Saturday nights. *G'Day Cafe* at No 83 is similar but cheaper. Further south on George St the *Bakehouse* has good coffee and cakes as well as takeaways.

At Circular Quay a string of restaurants, many with outdoor tables, face the waterfront near the ferry wharves. *Rossini*, between wharf Nos 5 and 6, has a wide choice of Italian food from about $7 for pasta, and is open between 7 am and 10 pm. Nearby is *City Extra*, which is open 24 hours a day. Service can be slow but buskers will keep you amused. Pasta costs around $7.50 and main meals $13-plus. The takeaway stall near the Manly ferry wharf has good fish & chips.

Behind Circular Quay on the corner of Alfred and Loftus Sts is the *Paragon Cafe*, upstairs in the Paragon Hotel. It isn't cheap, with starters from $7 and main courses at $17 but the food is good. On George St near Hickson St, *Pancakes on The Rocks* is open 24 hours a day, good for odd-hour coffees.

Gumnut Tea Garden at 28 Harrington St, the continuation of Playfair St over Argyle St, is a popular daytime eatery. It has tables in the garden and specialises in fancy salads, soups, pastas, pies and desserts.

On the other side of the Bradfield Highway which leads onto the Harbour Bridge, there are more places to eat in the glossy Pier One centre – expensive but with great views. The *Harbourside Brasserie* here is the exception with its more reasonably priced light meals and cheaper takeaway food, from Japanese to Mexican.

Kables at the Regent Hotel, 199 George St, is one of the best restaurants in Sydney, serving absolutely fresh food flown in from all over Australia. It's also one of the most expensive restaurants (you can spend $4500 on a bottle of wine!) but the lunch-time set menu might be within reach at about $45 a head.

Meals with a View If you're visiting the opera house and want to eat, the *Forecourt* is more reasonably priced than either the *Harbour Restaurant* or the exorbitant *Bennelong*. The view's almost as good and there's a large outside sitting area. Snacks and pastas cost under $12; others are about $16. The Forecourt is open from 11.30 am to midnight.

Between Circular Quay and the opera house, the *Sydney Cove Oyster Bar* at Circular Quay East has another great view, Aussie wine and beers, oysters for $14.50 a dozen and a mixed seafood plate for $11. It's open from 11.30 am to 8 pm during the week, later on the weekends and in summer. Next door, *Portobella Cafe*, with outdoor tables, has cheap snacks and takeaways.

For some of the best views and seafood in Sydney, splurge at *Doyle's on the Quay* in the Overseas Passenger Terminal on the west side of Circular Quay. Starters cost from $10 and main courses from $19 – there's a minimum food order of $15. Five generations of Doyles have been serving seafood, so they must have it right. *Bilson's*, upstairs in the same building is also very good and very expensive. Doyle's has another branch, *Doyle's on the Beach* at 11 Marine Pde in Watsons Bay. The food and views are equally good and there are cheaper takeaways. The *Watsons Bay Hotel* shares the view and has cheaper seafood and steaks.

Another place to consider for the setting as much as the food is the Sydney Tower atop the Centrepoint Tower, on the corner of Pitt and Market Sts. There are three places to eat up here, but the only tolerably priced one is the *Sydney Tower Sky Lounge* on level 3, with light meals, tea, coffee and snacks from about $6. Bookings are essential for the other two restaurants.

East Sydney At 81 Stanley St, near the corner of Crown St, is the *Arch Coffee Lounge*, but although there's good coffee here the main reason for coming is that upstairs is *No Names*, so called because it has no name, no sign, nothing but cheap and very filling spaghetti and a few other daily dishes. The starter is $5, main course $7.50, and it's BYO. It's open daily for lunch and dinner but you might have to queue. This is the original No Names – there are now two others, in Glebe and Surry Hills.

Kings Cross Restaurants and cafes have mushroomed in Kings Cross. The *Rex Hotel* on Macleay Rd, next to the El Alamein fountain, offers a big serve of steak, chips and salad for $7. In the same building, the *Marco Polo* restaurant has dishes from $6. Around

Top: Sydney Opera House at night, NSW (PS)
Left: Darling Harbour, Sydney, NSW (TW)
Right: Sydney Opera House, NSW (PS)

Top: Old steam engine at woolshed, NSW (BD)
Left: Cattle gate near Camerons Corner, northern NSW (BD)
Right: Three Sisters, Katoomba, Blue Mountains, NSW (RI'A)

the corner at 7 Darlinghurst Rd, the *Astoria* is famous for its Australian home-style cooking, and you can get a roast dinner for $5. 'Brilliant' reported one hungry traveller. It's open from 11 am to 2.30 pm and 4 to 8.30 pm Monday to Saturday.

Several places with outdoor tables are near the fountain, all serving coffee, breakfasts, snacks and moderately priced meals. Nearby on Darlinghurst Rd, *Bourbon & Beefsteak* is open 24 hours. Opposite, there's a Korean restaurant with dishes from $4.50. There are a couple of cheapies on Llankelly Place: *Sar Tor*, where $5 gets you two Thai dishes with rice, and *Yakitori* where Japanese dishes cost from $4.50.

On Springfield Mall, on the corner of Darlinghurst Rd, the *Old Vienna Inn* is open 24 hours and has steaks from $7.50. Breakfast here costs $4.50. At *Geoffrey's Cafe*, on Roslyn St near the corner of Darlinghurst Rd, meals cost from $7.50. A bit further down Roslyn St, *Young Fongs* has soups from $2.50 and main courses around $7.50.

Gado Gado at 57 Bayswater Rd is open Monday to Saturday nights and has good Indonesian food from $6.50 to $8.50. It's an old favourite. Further down Bayswater Rd, *Cafe 79* at Backpackers Headquarters has daily specials for about $4.50.

On Kellet St near the corner of Bayswater Rd, *New York* is a basic place with straightforward meals at low prices. *Dean's Cafe* at 15 Kellet St is neither basic nor cheap but it's open late and it's a friendly place. Three courses will cost you $30 but there are cheaper suppers after 11.30 pm.

Back on Darlinghurst Rd, *Pinnochio's Pizzeria* at No 87 has pizzas from $7 but its other dishes are more expensive. It's open until 3 am. *Singh Thai* at No 111 has specials for $5 and most main courses around $6.50.

There are a few places on Victoria St, including *Tuyet Hong* at No 194 with Vietnamese/Chinese dishes from $4, and *Cabrinis* at No 150 and *Ferrari Trattoria* at No 142 with Italian dishes from around $6. The *Criss Cross* cafe in front of Highfield House is good value, as is the cafe at the *Plane Tree Lodge*.

South of William St at 112 Darlinghurst Rd, the Hare Krishnas have *Govinda's*, offering very cheap and delicious Indian-inspired food and drinks, both eat in and takeaway. Smorgasbords cost $5 for lunch (Monday to Saturday) and $7 for dinner (every night until 9 pm).

Oxford St Oxford St from Hyde Park through Darlinghurst to Paddington has a variety of ethnic restaurants and several good cake and pastry shops, plus plenty of interesting shops and faces.

Bali Inn at 80 Oxford St, Darlinghurst is a popular Indonesian place with interesting dishes from $6 to around $12; the lumpia (spring roll) is great and they do takeaways. At 86 Oxford St *Tin Hong* does cheap Chinese food. *Old Saigon* at No 107 has interesting Vietnamese and other Asian dishes with main courses around $10.

Further up Oxford St towards Paddington at 203, the popular *Thai Silver Spoon* has 'seafood hot pot' with prawns, squid and pieces of fish in a chilli sauce for around $10. Tom Yum soup costs under $5.

The *Balkan* at 209 Oxford St specialises in those two basic Yugoslavian dishes – *raznjici* and *cevapcici*. Ask for a *pola pola* ($12.50) and you'll get half of each. It's very filling and definitely for real meat eaters only. It's open daily from 11 am. Next door is the more upmarket *Balkan II*.

Still in Darlinghurst *Afrilanka* at 237 Oxford St is run by an African/Sri Lankan couple and the menu combines their cuisines – the food is good but not particularly cheap. It's open for dinner only and except in summer it's closed on Sundays. At No 263, *Borobodur* is another good, reasonably priced Indonesian place, although if you're hungry enough to take on a *rijstaffel* you'll pay about $40 for two.

North of Oxford St at 26 Burton St, Darlinghurst, the *Metro Cafe* is a very good, cheap vegetarian place. It's very busy and open for dinner from Wednesday to Friday, plus Sunday. Slightly more expensive but open for dinner daily and for lunch on weekdays, *Laurie's Vegetarian Restaurant* on the corner of Burton and Victoria Sts, serves good, filling vegetarian meals.

In Paddington, Oxford St numbers start again just beyond the intersection with Barcom Ave, the first street after Victoria St. There are several good late-night cafes including *Cappuccino City* at 12 Oxford St, opposite the Academy Twin Cinema, *Flicks Cafe* over the road two doors from the cinema, and *Oddy's* at No 116. *La Passion du Fruit* at 100 Oxford St is popular but pricey and has great desserts. In Juniper Hall the *Juniper Hall Cafe* has snacks from $4.50 and main courses around $9.

Some way further along Oxford St at No 312, *Sloane Rangers* is a vegetarian restaurant with meals at no more than $10. The *New Edition Tea Rooms* at 328A Oxford St is a busy cafe which you enter through the attached bookshop. Both these are open days only.

Finally, not to be missed, if only for a drink, is Paddo's *Royal Hotel* at Five Ways – plain old Aussie-style food is the go. From Oxford St, turn left down Henley St, opposite the Town Hall, continue past Underwood St and keep going to the five-way intersection.

Surry Hills This inner suburban area east and south-east of Central Railway Station offers a big range of cuisines, and it's taking off as a new restaurant area. A third *No Names*, at the Shakespeare Hotel, 198 Devonshire St, is pretty good evidence of this.

There some good restaurants in Crown St north of the intersection with Cleveland St, including *Da Ly*, a Vietnamese/Malaysian place at No 559. Entrees are around $3.50 and the most expensive main course is under $11. On the other side of the road at No 628, *Thai Orchid* has a large menu and excellent food. *Azar* at No 527 is a good Lebanese place with main courses around $8. In the same block as all these there's also a Japanese place, *Sushi House*.

The other cluster of restaurants in Surry Hills consists of Lebanese places on Cleveland St, mostly near the corner of Elizabeth St. Try *Abdul's*, which offers excellent value

in unpretentious surroundings and a $14.50 set-price menu, as well as takeaways. *Nada's* at 270A Cleveland St is classier than Abdul's but not much more expensive. A few blocks away, actually in Redfern rather than Surry Hills, is *Wilson's*, near the corner of Redfern Rd at 91 Pitt St. It's an inexpensive Lebanese restaurant of long standing (despite the name) and the set menus are good value. It's open for lunch on weekdays and for dinner daily.

At 409 Cleveland St you can shift to Turkey at *Erciyes* to try *pide*, a sort of Turkish pizza. There are now quite a few other pide places nearby.

At 353 Cleveland St *L'Aubbergade* is a French place that's been here since the '50s. Main courses range from $14 but the three-course set menu is only $20. It's open from Monday to Saturday. *Casapueblo* at 650 Bourke St, just off Cleveland St, serves good, inexpensive South American food between 6.30 and 10 pm, Tuesday to Saturday.

About 750 metres north along Bourke St, around the corner at 57A Fitzroy St, *Johnnie's Fish Cafe* has some of the best fish & chips in town, both eat-in and takeaway. It can get very crowded.

Glebe The centre of the action is Glebe Point Rd, where there are over 40 restaurants and cafes in a one-km strip up from the Broadway.

At *Rose Blues*, 23 Glebe Point Rd (Broadway end), you can have anything from breakfast to supper from a very varied menu, but with $12 hamburgers it isn't cheap. A little further along at 37 Glebe Point Rd, is *Badde Manors*, a popular cafe known for its Sunday breakfasts which are served until 3.30 pm. Main courses are around $7 and it's open from 8 am weekdays (9.30 am weekends) till midnight except Friday and Saturday when it closes at 5 am.

Tanjore at No 34 has a good variety of Indian cooking, with South Indian vegetarian dishes at lunch times. Main courses at dinner are about $9.

Around the corner, *No Names 2* is in the

Friend in Hand Hotel at 58 Cowper St. A variety of pasta dishes go for $5, main courses for $7.50, salad and bread included. There's jazz on Friday nights.

At 95-97 Glebe Point Rd, *Lien* is a Vietnamese restaurant with a varied menu from $7 to $10. *Kim Van* at No 147 is reputedly one of the best Vietnamese places in Sydney. Soups and starters are around $5, main courses $9 to $14; it's open daily for dinner.

Cafe Troppo (☎ 666 7332) at 175 Glebe Point Rd is a busy, fashionable place with good food and high prices – snacks start at around $6, with main meals getting up to $25. A less expensive place for eating focaccia and drinking good coffee while watching pedestrians is *The Craven*, next to the Valhalla on the corner of Hereford St. Across the road at No 315, *The Italian Nest's* food is nothing special but it is cheap. *The Pudding Shop* is good for sticky, filling cakes. Down Hereford St, the *bistro* at the YHA Hereford Lodge is good value.

Off the main drag at 115 Wigram St is *Harold's Bar & Grill* in the Harold Park Hotel, with pasta from $7.50 and main courses around $13. Sunday breakfast is good value and starts at $6.

North-west of Glebe are the suburbs of Balmain and Birchgrove – and more restaurants! About one km back towards Glebe, at 189 Darling St, Balmain, between Colgate and Waterview Sts, *Razi Afghan* has Afghani food. It's open nightly and main courses cost from $9.50. Also along this thoroughfare are the Japanese *Zen* at No 336, Thai *Tanee Thai* at No 388, Italian *Sorrentino* at No 266, French *L'Ironique* at No 246 and Sri Lankan *Lanka Curry House* at No 235. Nearby at 9 Beattie St, is an Indian restaurant, *Jewel of India*, with main courses under $10. It's open for lunch from Wednesday to Sunday and for dinner daily.

In Rozelle, next suburb along from Dalmain, *Eve's Harvest* at 71 Evans St is another excellent vegetarian restaurant. Down towards the water at 37 Cameron St in Birchgrove, *Thai Yai* has good Thai food with main courses starting at less than $7.

Dulwich Hill If you're staying at the YHA out here, try *Minh*, a Vietnamese and Thai place at 508 Marrickville Rd, near the corner of New Canterbury Rd. Main courses are from $7 and they're open Wednesday to Sunday. Around the corner, north-east on New Canterbury, is *Ibrahim's*, a huge Lebanese cake shop (it even has a grand piano) where you can get coffee for $1.80 and cakes from 85c. It stays open late.

Beaches En route to Bondi Beach at 288 Oxford St at Bondi Junction, *Sennin* has an imaginative vegetarian menu. It's open for dinner from Monday to Saturday, and daytime main meals cost from $9 (more at dinner). Several blocks further east, at 570 Oxford St, still in Bondi Junction, the *Mekong*, a relative of the one on George St in the city centre, serves the same fantastically cheap Cambodian fare. *Wei Song* at 96 Bronte Rd, a couple of blocks south of Oxford St, is more expensive (it would be hard not to be) but it's great for nonsmoking vegetarians. *Ya Habibi* at 100 Campbell Parade has good, cheap Middle Eastern food. A couple of blocks back from the beach, on the corner of Hall and O'Brien Sts, is *Positive Vibrations*, open daily from noon to midnight with an offbeat menu of African-influenced meals. There are sometimes African drummers on weekends.

In Coogee Bay Rd there are lots of takeaway places and a couple of Chinese restaurants. Two places on Arden St, which faces the sea, are quite good – *Sari Rasa* at No 186 has Asian food with main meals from $9 to $15. *Zesamee's Eatery* at No 190 has good value vegetarian meals; main dishes are $8.

Manly, on the north shore, has loads of fast-food places and a variety of restaurants and cafes. *Manly Asian Kitchen* is at 80 The Corso but the door is around the back in the car park. Main dishes start at about $6 and the serves are large. *Dubrovnik* has been recommended as good value. At the more expensive and no-smoking *Hammonds* at 38 Pittwater Rd, French vegetarian meals are

$15. Both restaurants are open nightly for dinner.

Faulty Bowers is on the beach at 7 Marine and has good food at around $10 a dish. Breakfast here is popular. *Brazil Cafe* at 29 Belgrave St is an up-market cafe with $6 focaccia and an interesting dinner menu with most meals around $12. It's open from 9 am to 11 pm daily.

North of the harbour, at 334 Pacific Highway, Crows Nest, *Curry Bazaar* (☎ 436 3620) is so popular that it's wise to book. Open for lunch and dinner Tuesday to Saturday and for dinner Sunday and Monday, it has good Indian food with most curries $9 or a little more. Takeaways are cheaper.

Entertainment

Listen to the What's On service at 6.30 pm on Radio 2JJJ or check the listings in the *Telegraph Mirror* on Thursday or the *Sydney Morning Herald*'s Metro section on Friday.

A lot of Sydney evening entertainment takes place in the Leagues Clubs, where the profits from the assembled ranks of one-armed bandits (poker machines – 'pokies') enable the clubs to put on big-name acts at low prices. They may be 'members only' for locals but as an interstate or, even better, international visitor you're generally welcome. You can usually get a meal too. Simply ring ahead and ask, then wave your interstate driving licence or your passport at the door. They're a Sydney institution so if you get a chance, visit one. Acts vary from Val Doonican or Max Bygraves to good Australian rock, but whatever the show you'll see a good cross-section of Sydneysiders.

The most lavish of the lot is the St George Leagues Club on Princes Highway, Kogarah. More centrally there's the City of Sydney RSL Club on George St or the South Sydney Leagues Club at 263 Chalmers St, Redfern, which has 94 poker machines and a top jackpot of $100,000. Apart from that, Souths is the home of Les Girls, Sydney's premier drag revue show.

Music Sydney doesn't have the same pub music scene as Melbourne, but there are a fair few places where you can count on something most nights of the week. What Sydney does have is a number of clubs where you can catch a band and/or a disco, plus some pleasant wine bars/bistros where for a low entry charge (sometimes free) you can catch the music and get a meal. Friday and Saturday, and to a lesser extent Thursday and Sunday, are the big nights. Venues worth a visit include:

Kardomah Cafe, 22 Bayswater Rd, Kings Cross – bands and disco nightly, busy and lively, admission usually around $8 unless you want a meal. Dress up a bit. Open till very late. It's also the place to see celebrities doing jam sessions.
Oz Rock Hotel, corner Victoria and Darlinghurst Rds and William St, Kings Cross – three floors with different scenes, crowded with suburbanites, backpackers and singles. Open Monday to Saturday till 3 am, Sunday till midnight; $3 entry after 11 pm.
Richie's Caribbean Club, 154 Brougham St, Kings Cross – jazz-funk/Caribbean music.
Round Midnight, Roslyn St, Kings Cross – jazz, blues and funk. Meals/supper available, $5 admission, open from 9 pm to 3 am all week.
Golden Sheaf Hotel 429 New South Head Rd, Double Bay, two km east of Kings Cross – pub with free bands several nights. Good food, popular with travellers.
The Freezer, 110 Oxford St, Paddington – cocktails and restaurant upstairs and a downstairs disco; open 8 pm to 3 am, Wednesday to Sunday; weekends cover charge about $6.
Klub Kakadu, 163 Oxford St, Darlinghurst – combined jazz/supper club with downstairs disco/nightclub and cover charge of $6 from Wednesday to Saturday, open 9 pm to 3 am.
Kinselas, 383 Bourke St, Darlinghurst – a renovated funeral parlour, now a nightclub, cocktail bar and restaurant. Nightclub open till 3 am Monday to Saturday.
Sydney Brasserie, 9A Barrack St, City – good jazz.
Sydney Trade Union Club, Foveaux St, Surry Hills – live music on three floors most nights, good place to catch up-and-coming Aussie bands, usually $3 to $6.
Hopetoun Hotel, 416 Bourke St, Surry Hills – rock pub, bands usually Wednesday to Sunday nights, free. Also good for up-and-coming bands. Wear black!
Graphic Arts Club, 26 Regent St, Chippendale – reggae/African, Saturday nights.
Harold Park Hotel, Glebe – rock bands usually Thursday to Saturday nights till 11 pm or midnight, about $6.

Cat & Fiddle Hotel, corner Darling and Elliott Sts, Balmain – pub rock usually Friday to Sunday nights, free.

Rose, Shamrock & Thistle Hotel (also known as 'the three weeds') 139 Evans St, Rozelle – rock/ folk/jazz some nights. Jazz on Saturday afternoons.

Grand Hotel Cock 'n' Bull Tavern, corner Bronte & Ebley Sts, Bondi Junction – bands (often free) or disco most nights.

Royal Hotel, Bondi Rd at Bondi Beach – bands, free.

Selina's (in the Coogee Bay Hotel), Coogee Bay Rd, Coogee Bay – rock, often top Australian bands for which you can pay $20. Main nights Friday and Saturday, but sometimes cheaper bands other nights and there's a piano bar.

Hotel Manly, opposite Manly Wharf – bands or disco nightly, also bands Saturday and Sunday afternoons, often free, otherwise up to $8. Open till 3 am.

There are many, many other places. The Paddington and Balmain town halls are sometimes venues for 'alternative' fundraisers and the like, and there's generally something happening at Darling Harbour. Sunday afternoon is a popular time for jazz in several places round town.

Pubs Other than the places listed in the Music section, there are a number of pubs worth visiting just for a drink and to meet locals and other travellers. In Kings Cross try the Darlo Bar on Darlinghurst Rd or the Rex Hotel on Macleay St. In Paddington the Albury Hotel on Oxford St is popular with gays; Anglophiles should visit the Lord Dudley on Jersey Rd. The Lord Nelson in Argyle St in the Rocks has its own brewery. On Lower Fort St, the Hero of Waterloo is an old place that gets crowded with both travellers and local residents. In Surry Hills the Bat & Ball on the corner of Cleveland and South Dowling Sts is popular with backpackers. Out at Bondi, the Bondi Hotel on Campbell Parade is open 24 hours.

Theatre Sydney has a good selection of mainstream theatres plus fringe and cabaret places. Tickets for just about everything are available by credit card payment over the phone through Ticketek (☎ 266 4800), or through the theatres. The Halftix booth on

Martin Place (☎ 0055 20580), between Castlereagh and Elizabeth Sts, sells half-price tickets for performances the same day from noon to 6 pm Monday to Saturday.

The top mainstream company is the Sydney Theatre Company, which has its own theatres at the Wharf, Pier 4, Hickson Rd, Walsh Bay below the Rocks. At NIDA – The National Institute of Dramatic Art, at 215 Anzac Parade, Kensington – student shows are staged regularly. The Seymour Centre at the corner of Cleveland St and City Rd, Chippendale (near Sydney University), has varied and interesting productions. The Bay St Theatre at 73-79 Bay St in Ultimo has mostly experimental shows. The Belvoir Street Theatre at 25 Belvoir St, Surry Hills has a variety of innovative and offbeat shows.

Film Most mainstream films are half price on Tuesday, except during school holidays at the major city venues. For more unusual fare, you'll find films at the Mandolin Cinema at 150 Elizabeth St, between Liverpool and Goulburn Sts – Chinese and repertory-style films are regularly featured. Other independent cinemas include the Academy Twin at 3A Oxford St, Paddington; the Valhalla Cinema at 166 Glebe Point Rd, Glebe; and ABJ's Encore Cinema at 64 Devonshire St, Surry Hills (near the eastern entrance to the Central railway underground walkway) which specialises in old classics.

The Sydney University Union Theatre can always be counted on for something good at low prices. The Australian Film Institute screens interesting new work and classics at the old Chauvel Cinema, now called the AFI Cinema on the corner of Oxford St and Oatley Rd, Paddington. You can also catch interesting films at the Opera House and Paddington Town Hall.

Almost a sight in itself is the State Movie Theatre on Market St between Pitt and George Sts. Wow! They don't make them like this anymore. It's the main venue for the Sydney Film Festival in the first half of June.

Odds & Ends On summer weekends there

is free music in parks. There's music at lunch time in Martin Place and at Darling Harbour and the State Conservatorium of Music on Macquarie St has free lunch-time concerts on Wednesdays during term time.

The *Sydney Morning Herald*'s Metro section lists art exhibitions, or buy a copy of the monthly *Art Almanac* ($1) at galleries and some newsagents.

Try and see something at the Opera House – they have film shows, ballet, theatre, classical music, opera and even rock concerts. The Opera House is the main home of the Sydney Dance Company and the Sydney Symphony Orchestra, which are the top outfits in their fields.

Sport Sydney is Australia's rugby league (as opposed to rugby union) capital and home to most of the teams in the Winfield Cup competition, which produces the world's best club teams in this 13-a-side, professional version of rugby. The season is April to September. You can usually just turn up at the ground and pay at the turnstiles, but big clashes often sell out. The biggest games, including internationals and the end of season Grand Final, are played at the Sydney Cricket Ground (SCG) or the new Sydney Football Stadium, which are side by side in Moore Park, just south of Paddington.

The SCG is also the home of interstate (Sheffield Shield) and international (Test and World Series) cricket from about November to March. The liveliest and cheapest section of the ground is the Hill, a grassy bank beneath the scoreboard.

On the second Sunday in August about 25,000 runners take to their heels from Park St to Bondi Beach in the City to Surf Run. The sporting year ends with the Boxing Day (26 December) start of the Sydney to Hobart yacht race. A huge fleet of yachts compete frantically to be first out of the harbour, before turning south for the three-to-five-day voyage to Hobart in Tasmania. This is one of the world's greatest yacht races and can be seen at its best either from a boat on the harbour or at the Sydney Harbour heads.

Things to Buy

There are several shopping complexes in the city, including the Centrepoint Mid City Centre, the MLC Centre, the Royal, Strand and Imperial arcades and the impressive old Queen Victoria Building. The Rocks and the Harbourside Festival Marketplace at Darling Harbour teem with shops which are open daily, while Paddington, especially Oxford St, has many bookshops, boutiques, art galleries and antique shops. Then there are all the large suburban shopping complexes – Sydney has some good ones.

Aboriginal Art The Dreamtime Aboriginal Art Centre has two shops – in the Argyle Arts Centre in the Rocks (open daily), and at 7 Walker Lane, opposite 7A Liverpool St, in Paddington. They have a lot of bark paintings and, as usual, these are attractive but costly. Didgeridoo, also in the Argyle Arts Centre, has a good range of Aboriginal print T-shirts, didgeridoos, boomerangs and baskets.

The Aboriginal Artists Gallery in Civic House, 477 Kent St (behind the Town Hall), has a large range of traditional and contemporary Aborigine and Islander work. Quality is high, prices competitive. At 135 Bathurst St (between Pitt and Castlereagh Sts), the Bush Church Aid Shop sells artefacts made by Aborigines from communities all over Australia.

New Guinea Primitive Arts, on the 6th floor at 428 George St, and also at shop 42, Level 2, Queen Victoria Building, has a big range of artefacts from PNG and some Aborigine work. Ethnographics Primitive Art at 46 Oxford St also has both PNG and Aboriginal stuff.

Bennelong Boomerangs, at 29-31 Playfair St in the Rocks, is owned by a guy who's been the Australian Boomerang Throwing Champion a few times so he can tell you it isn't as easy as it looks. They have a large collection of boomerangs in many woods and styles. Duncan's Boomerang School in Kings Cross has two outlets – at 138 and 202 William St. They stock an excellent array of boomerangs and offer free lessons in a nearby park on Sunday mornings.

Australiana Australian arts & crafts, T-shirts, souvenirs, designer clothing, bushgear and the like are available in lots of places. Much of this stuff is high quality, with prices to match, though you can pick up the odd bargain. Places to try include the Argyle Arts Centre in the Rocks. Other places include Souvenirs of Australia & the Pacific, in shop 606, Royal Arcade, beside the Pitt St entrance to the Hilton; and Everything Australian at shop 311 George St in the Mid City Centre. The Queen Victoria Building has several good craft places including Blue Gum on Level 5 and the Handmade Shop on Level 2.

For bushgear, try Morrisons at 105 George St, The Rocks, Goodwood Saddlery at 237-9 The Broadway or the Bushman's Outfitters at 71 Castlereagh St in the city.

The Wilderness Shop at 57 Liverpool St has high quality wilderness posters and books on wilderness issues, as well as great T-shirts and other good souvenirs. It's open all week. At the Gardens Shop in the Royal Botanic Gardens Visitors' Centre there are souvenirs, posters and books with an Australian plant theme.

The Australian Design Centre at 70 George St has an interesting variety of original Australian designs and products. The Metcalfe Arcade at 80-84 George St, houses the Society of Arts & Crafts of New South Wales with a gallery and sales, and there's Australian Craftworks at 127 George St in the old police station.

The Strand Arcade on George St, between Market and King Sts has many places featuring Australia's leading fashion designers and craftspeople. More reasonably priced are the Australian print T-shirts at Call Us Names, 51 Imperial Arcade, on the Pitt St level.

Markets Sydney has lots of weekend 'flea' markets, the most interesting, Paddo Village Bazaar, is held in the grounds of the church on the corner of Oxford and Newcombe Sts on Saturday. It's quite a scene. Balmain's Saturday market is also good; it's in the church on Darling St, opposite Gladstone Park.

Both these markets are tiny in comparison to Paddy's Markets, now at the Eveleigh Railway Workshops, adjacent to Redfern Station and held on Saturday and Sunday. The markets are also held at Flemington on Friday and Sunday.

Bookshops If books are your weakness, buy a copy of *The Bookshops of Sydney* – a guide to the hundreds of bookshops around. There are quite a few bookshops in the Paddington area, including New Edition Bookshop at 328a Oxford St where Australian authors are well represented.

Shops in the city centre include Dymocks, which was established in 1881 and whose shop at 424 George St is said to be the largest bookshop in Australia; the big Angus & Robertson at 168 Pitt St in the Pitt St Mall; and Grahame's at the corner of Pitt and Hunter Sts. The Travel Bookshop (☎ 241 3554) at 20 Bridge St in the city is open daily and has books on Sydney and the rest of Australia and the world. For literature, including a wide range of second-hand titles, try Gleebooks at 191 Glebe Point Rd in Glebe.

Galleries & Antiques Paddington and Woollahra have some 30 art galleries, most featuring Australian art and artists. Of interest are the Australian Centre for Photography and the Contemporary Jewellery Gallery.

The Sydney Antique Centre is a conglomeration of 60 shops at 531 South Dowling St, Surry Hills. Open daily from 10.30 am to 6 pm, it has items ranging from movie posters to silver, junk to jewellery. There's a cafe too.

Getting There & Away

Air Sydney's Kingsford Smith Airport, better known as Mascot because that's where it is, is Australia's busiest. It's fairly central which makes getting to or from it easy, but it also means that jet flights have to stop at 11 pm due to noise regulations.

You can fly into Sydney from all the usual international points and from all over Australia. Australian Airlines (☎ 13 1313, toll-free) and Ansett (☎ 13 1300, toll-free) have frequent flights to other capital cities. The cheapest fares to Alice Springs and Darwin are currently $270 and $350, but the standard fares are much higher, at $432 and $583.

East-West (☎ 268 1166) flies to most other major cities from Sydney, at similar fares to the bigger airlines. Eastern Australia Airlines (☎ 13 1313, toll-free) and Ansett Express (☎ 268 1242) are subsidiaries of the two major airlines and between them cover most major towns within the state. Other New South Wales airlines include Singleton Air Service, Hazelton Air Services, Aeropelican and Oxley Airlines.

Cheap international flights are advertised in the Saturday *Sydney Morning Herald*. The cheapest tickets of all are sold by travellers around Kings Cross – check hostel notice boards – but there's a risk: most tickets are nontransferable, so the person whose name is on the ticket has to check in for the flight, and you then have to trust to luck that no-one checks your passport against the ticket. If the ticket involves a change of planes, a stop-over, or otherwise checking in more than once, there's a pretty high chance you'll be caught out.

Bus As well as checking out the private operators it's worth finding out what the government Countrylink network of trains and buses has on offer – see the following train section.

There's hot competition on the routes between Sydney and other capitals so it pays to shop around. If you're doing a lot of travel check out the excellent bus pass deals, although make sure you get enough time and stopovers.

On straight point-to-point tickets there are also varying stopover deals, and these tend to change. Some companies charge a $5 fee for each stopover, but this can be waived if you book through certain agents, notably some of the Kings Cross hostels. Intra-state travel on private buses was once severely restricted because of the railway's monopoly, but this has been lifted and there is now

a bewildering array of deals available. Check hostel noticeboards or contact Dial-A-Coach (☎ 231 3815) at Shop 33, Imperial Arcade, Pitt St and Shop 12A (☎ 262 2175), Wynyard Station.

The big companies are Bus Australia and Greyhound/Pioneer, with Kirklands and McCafferty's following close behind, although the last two don't run Australia-wide. There are quite a few other companies which crop up from time to time, and more local operators such as Lindsay's which only goes as far as Woolgoolga just north of Coffs Harbour.

The Sydney to Brisbane run has more competing bus lines than any other. By the main route, the coastal Pacific Highway, it takes 15 or 16 hours and can cost as little as $55; the 'standard' cheap fare is around $65. You often need to book ahead. Not all buses stop in all the main towns en route. Greyhound/Pioneer and McCafferty's also go between Sydney and Brisbane by the inland New England Highway which takes an hour or two longer.

Some typical fares from Sydney are Port Macquarie $35 (seven hours), Coffs Harbour $45 (9½ hours), Byron Bay $55 (13 hours), Surfers Paradise $65 (14½) hours. Companies operating the Pacific Highway route to Brisbane are Greyhound/Pioneer, Kirklands, McCafferty's and Skennars.

Canberra to Sydney takes about four hours and the cheapest service is by Murrays, which depart three times daily for $24. Pioneer has the most frequent service on this route, up to nine times daily in each direction, with a few services operating to and from Sydney Airport (international terminal) ($26) as well as the city centre.

Melbourne to Sydney takes 12 to 13 hours by the most direct route, the Hume Highway. Add another hour or two if your bus detours via Canberra. With Greyhound, $52 will get you on either this more direct route or via the prettier, but much longer (up to 18 hours), coastal Princes Highway route. Other companies have even cheaper fares, such as Firefly (☎ 211 1644) which charges $40.

Adelaide to Sydney takes 18 to 25 hours

and costs from about $90 depending on the company and the route. A few of the Pioneer services go via Broken Hill which is a pricey $125 and 15½ hours from Sydney. Firefly's Sydney to Adelaide via Melbourne fare is often a little cheaper than direct fares on the major lines.

Sydney to Perth costs about $225 for the 52 to 56-hour trip. The daily Pioneer bus to Alice Springs costs $265 and takes 43 hours. To the Snowy Mountains, Deanes/Pioneer Tours (book through Pioneer) have one or two daily services to Cooma ($36), Jindabyne ($45), Thredbo, Perisher and Smiggins (all $48).

A coach terminal (☎ 281 9366) seems to be developing on Eddy Ave, but many companies maintain their own depots, notably Bus Australia (☎ 261 1888 or 13 2323, toll-free) which operates from the corner of Castlereagh and Hay Sts, and Greyhound/ Pioneer (☎ 286 8600 or 13 2030, toll-free) which has a depot at the corner of Oxford and Riley Sts. McCafferty's (☎ 361 5125) has a depot in Kings Cross at 179 Darlinghurst Rd, but they also pick up on Eddy Ave. Many lines make stops in suburbs on the way in or out of the city centres and some have feeder services from the suburbs.

Train The government's Countrylink rail network has been complemented by coaches and they provide a good service. On point-to-point tickets prices can be comparable to the private bus lines, and there are some special deals. These aren't widely advertised, so you'll have to ask. For example, the Budget Seven pass allows a week's travel anywhere in New South Wales for $115. This is very handy for getting off the beaten track and seeing some of the inland places bypassed by the regular bus lines on their lemming-like runs up the coast.

All interstate and principal regional services operate to and from Sydney's Central Railway Station on Eddy Ave. For information and bookings in Sydney there are Rail Travel Centres at Transport House, 11-31 York St (☎ 224 4744) and at Central Railway Station (☎ 219 1808). For bookings you can

also call the Central Reservation Centre (☎ 217 8812 or 008 043 126, toll-free). Rail fares and journey times to major cities in other states are competitive with buses, and there are sometimes special offers. Caper fares are considerably cheaper and on some runs (eg to Melbourne) the seven-day advance purchase requirement has been waived for economy tickets, but there is always a limited number of Caper seats available so it pays to book. On interstate journeys you can generally stop over anywhere for no extra charge as long as you finish the trip within two months.

Between Melbourne and Sydney there's a night train which goes daily called the Sydney Express (if you're going from Melbourne) or the Melbourne Express (from Sydney). The trip takes about 13 hours and the fares are $49 in economy, $120 in 1st ($85 Caper) or $180 ($125 Caper) with a sleeper. The quality of the economy carriages varies a lot, and in winter the heating is unreliable. An XPT service between Sydney and Melbourne is due to begin and this should improve the comfort and reduce travelling time.

There are a couple of trains daily to Canberra; the trip takes about five hours and costs around $45 in 1st class and $32 in economy. To Brisbane there's the daily overnight Brisbane Limited Express, which takes 16 hours and costs around $80 economy, $120 in 1st class, or $150 in 1st-class sleeper. In conjunction with this train there's a connecting bus from Casino to the New South Wales far north coast and the Queensland Gold Coast. You can also take the train between Sydney and Murwillumbah, just south of the Queensland border, from where there's a connecting bus to the Gold Coast.

You can travel between Sydney and Adelaide either via Melbourne (daily) or via Broken Hill on the Indian-Pacific (three times a week). Via Melbourne (changing trains at Sunshine) it's $91 economy, $170 1st class ($150 Caper), $270 ($230 Caper) with a sleeper. Via Broken Hill it's $100 economy, $226 ($158 Caper) economy sleeper, $307 ($215 Caper) 1st sleeper.

There's also the Speedlink – a bus/train connection which is not only cheaper but five or six hours faster. The 1st/economy fares are $98/$105.

Sydney to Perth is on the Indian-Pacific service – see the Perth section for more details.

There's an extensive rail network within New South Wales including frequent commuter-type train services to Sydney from Wollongong ($5.70 in economy), Katoomba ($8.50), Lithgow ($17) and Newcastle ($17). See the New South Wales introductory Getting Around section for details.

Buying a Car If you want to buy a car to travel round Australia, Sydney's a good place to do it. Parramatta Rd is lined with used car lots, but there are other setups geared specially to travellers. It's no longer legal to sell cars on the street in Kings Cross, and you risk a heavy fine and having your vehicle towed away if you do it. Instead, there are car markets: at the Kings Cross Parking Station on the corner of Ward Ave and Elizabeth Bay Rd, which charges sellers $5 a day or $25 a week (the excellent facilities include undercover phones, toilets, barbecue, TV etc, and the place is becoming something of a travellers' rendezvous underground); and the Sunday Flemington Car Market near Flemington Railway Station which charges $40. From the buyer's point of view, some of these vehicles have been around a fair bit – one north Queensland backpackers' hostel owner told us he'd seen the same ageing pink Holden three times in two years, under different ownership each time – but you can probably expect to get a more honest account of a vehicle's pros and cons from another traveller than from a professional salesperson.

Several places, including the odd hostel, will sell you a car with an undertaking to buy it back at an agreed price. A traveller has written to complain that when he returned to a hostel to sell the car, the manager didn't have enough money to buy it. He had to delay his flight home and sell it elsewhere at a big loss. A rule of thumb might be to allow yourself time, and deal with companies big enough to be worried about a complaint to the authorities – above all, ask other travellers about their experiences. Unless you're an experienced car mechanic, it's worth paying for an expert independent opinion on your choice of wheels. Always read the small print. We've heard of deals where the seller agreed to buy the vehicle back at 60% of sale price, minus 1% for every 1000km travelled, minus the cost of repairing any damage, and the buyer ended up with next to nothing.

One long-established place is Mach 1 Autos (☎ 569 3374) at 495 New Canterbury Rd, Dulwich Hill, which deals only with travellers and has 'sell and buy back' deals. They have cars and station wagons from about $2500. Registration fees and third-party insurance, which normally cost about $700 a year, are included in their prices, and you get a government roadworthiness certificate, legally required with the sale of any car. To reach Mach 1 take bus Nos 426 or 448 from Pitt St in central Sydney and get off at Dulwich Hill shopping centre, 150 metres from the car yard – or take a train to Dulwich Hill and call them from the station; they'll pick you up.

If you, or a friend, are a member of the NRMA you can get a vehicle checked over, for a fee, before you buy it. NRMA members can also get good deals on insurance, but they are now wary about insuring travellers, so you might have to shop around. Every vehicle's registration certificate includes third-party insurance, but it's a very good idea also to have extended third-party insurance, which covers you for damage to other vehicles, or even comprehensive insurance. For more on buying cars and on the motorists' associations, see the introductory Getting Around and Facts for the Visitor chapters.

Getting Around
For information on city trains, buses and ferries, call MetroTrips (☎ 954 4422), operated by the State Transit Authority (STA), from 6 am to 10 pm daily. The ferries also have their own number (☎ 256 4670). You

can pick up timetables at the bus, train and ferry information booths at Circular Quay.

To/From the Airport The international and domestic terminals at Sydney Airport are just across the runway from each other, and about a five-km bus trip apart.

Yellow Airport Express buses run every 20 or 30 minutes to/from the city and between the international and domestic terminals. Bus route No 300 goes to Circular Quay and No 350 goes to Kings Cross. Both stop at Central Railway Station and a few other stops along the way. From the airport to Central Railway Station the trip takes about 15 minutes, to Circular Quay or Kings Cross, 30 minutes. The fare is $5; between the two terminals it's $2. Buses leave the city from 5.15 am to 10 pm and the international terminal from 5.53 am to 10.55 pm. For Ansett passengers only, there's the $3 'Intershuttle' bus between the international and domestic terminals, every 20 minutes from 7 am to 9 pm.

A convenient alternative is the privately operated Sydney Airport bus which will take you between either airport terminal and any hotel or hostel in the city centre or Kings Cross for $4. It runs half-hourly from 6 am to 8 pm. For bookings call 667 3221 as far in advance as possible.

The YHA's 'Wonderbus' runs between the airport and the YHA Glebe hostel once a day (8 am from the airport, 7.15 am from Glebe) for $5. Book at the hostel or at the airport Travellers' Information desk.

There are some public bus services from the domestic terminals to the city (Nos 302 and 385 to Circular Quay) or Bondi Junction (No 064), but they operate mainly for airport workers and principally on weekdays.

A taxi between the airport and city will cost you about $17, depending on where you're going. There are several car rental desks at the airport. Luggage lockers at the airport cost $1 a day.

Bus There are extensive bus services in Sydney, but they are slow in comparison to the rail services. Some places – including Bondi Beach, Coogee and the north shore east of the Harbour Bridge – are not covered by trains so you do need buses (or ferries) to get there. Most buses are run by the STA, but some suburban services are run by private operators.

Circular Quay, Wynyard Park on York St, Central Railway Station and Railway Square are the main bus stops in the city centre. You can get 'Metro Ten' tickets, giving you 10 bus rides for the price of eight, at bus depots, the information booth at Circular Quay, railway stations near bus routes, and some newsagencies.

A useful city centre bus service is No 666. For $1.20, the bus goes on a loop from Wynyard Park on York St to the Art Gallery of New South Wales in the Domain and back, and it runs every half-hour from 10.10 am to 4.40 pm Monday to Saturday, 12.10 to 4.40 pm Sunday.

The Sydney Explorer is a tourist bus service which operates a continuous loop around the tourist sights of the city at roughly 15-minute intervals from 9.30 am to 5 pm daily. It costs $15, covers 20 km and 22 attractions, and you can hop on and off wherever you like. It would be much cheaper to get around these places by ordinary buses (in fact it's possible to walk around the places visited by the bus), but the Explorer's easy as you don't have to work out routes. Its 22 stops are marked by green and red signs and you can buy the ticket on the bus, at Circular Quay or the Travel Centre of New South Wales.

The route is from Circular Quay to the Opera House, down Macquarie St to Hyde Park, up to Mrs Macquarie Point, back down to the Art Gallery of New South Wales, across to Kings Cross and Elizabeth Bay, through Woolloomooloo, down to Central Railway Station, to several stops around Darling Harbour, back up George St and round the Rocks to Circular Quay. The Kings Cross stop is at the railway station near Darlinghurst Rd. You can also use the Explorer ticket on city buses between Central Railway Station and Circular Quay or the Rocks until midnight.

Train Quite a lot of Sydney is covered by the suburban rail service, which has frequent trains and is generally far quicker than the bus network.

If you have to change trains, buy a ticket to your ultimate destination before you board the first train – it's cheaper. Off-peak rail travel – after 9 am Monday to Friday or any time at weekends – is cheaper if you get a return ticket.

The rail system has a central City Circle and a number of lines radiating out from there to the suburbs. Trains round the City Circle go every couple of minutes in both directions and this is often the easiest way of hopping from one part of the centre to another. The stations on the City Circle, in clockwise order, are Central, Town Hall (on George St near Park St), Wynyard (York St at Wynyard Park), Circular Quay, St James (north end of Hyde Park) and Museum (south end of Hyde Park). A single trip anywhere on the City Circle or to a nearby suburb such as Kings Cross is $1.10.

Suburban trains all stop at Central Railway Station and usually one or more of the other City Circle stations too – most often Town Hall – so it's easy to get from the suburbs on to the City Circle. Trains generally run from around 4 am to about midnight, give or take an hour. You can get a train from Central Railway Station to Kings Cross, or vice versa, up to midnight any day.

Taxi Within the centre of Sydney and in the inner suburbs, taxis are easily flagged down on the street. You'll also find many (usually) in taxi ranks at Central, Wynyard and Circular Quay train stations, and at the large rank just off George St in Goulburn St. The four big taxi companies offer a pretty reliable telephone service: Taxis Combined (☎ 332 8888), RSL Taxis (☎ 699 0144), Legion (☎ 20 918) and Premier Radio Cabs (☎ 897 4000).

Boat Sydney's ferries are one of the nicest ways of getting around in Australia – and they're pretty cheap. Not only are there the fine harbour ferries (Manly $3.30, other places generally $2.50) but also JetCats to Manly ($4.50 – there's an off-peak return ticket for the same price). All the harbour ferries depart from Circular Quay. The STA, which runs most of the harbour ferries, puts out a free ferry and hydrofoil timetable. Many ferries have connecting bus services and the timetable lists these too. For instance, from the Taronga ferry you can hop straight onto bus No 238 to Taronga Zoo or Mosman Junction. Cheaper combined ferry-bus tickets are available.

In addition to the ferries there's a whole range of cruises from Circular Quay. Walk along the quay and you'll get leaflets detailing many of them. Best value are the three run by the STA. Two of these, the 10 am Harbour History Cruise and the 1 pm weekdays (1.30 pm weekends and holidays) Harbour Sights Cruise, go daily, last 2½ hours and cost $12 each. The STA also runs a 1½ hour Harbour Lights Cruise in the evening at 8 pm from Monday to Saturday for $10. Also interesting is the trip to Fort Denison (see the earlier Harbour section).

The Sydney Harbour Explorer, run by Captain Cook Cruises (☎ 251 5007), is a hop-on, hop-off service around the harbour with stops at Circular Quay (Jetty Six), the Opera House, Watsons Bay, Taronga and Darling Harbour. You get a $15 all-day ticket which allows you to get on and off whenever you like. The drawback is that it only makes four circuits, the first starting from Circular Quay at 9.30 am and the last getting back there at 5.30 pm. Captain Cook offers a range of other tours. Other ways of spending time and money on the harbour include disco cruises, gourmet cruises (breakfast, lunch or dinner) and cabaret cruises.

Combined Deals The STA has several special deals combining travel on its buses, trains and ferries. If you're planning some serious sightseeing, the $35 SydneyPass ($20 children/concession) gives you three consecutive days unlimited use of blue city buses between Central Railway Station and Circular Quay or the Rocks, Manly ferries except JetCats, the Sydney Explorer Bus and

STA Sydney Harbour Cruises. The SydneyPass also includes a trip to the airport on the Airport Express bus, and it does not have to be within the three days; however, it has to be your last trip as you must surrender the pass to the driver. The SydneyPass is on sale at the Travel Centre of New South Wales, 19 Castlereagh St, or the State Rail Travel Centre at 11-31 York St.

The CityHopper costs about $2.10, less from city stations, and gives a one-day train ride to/from your suburban station and unlimited travel around the city loop stations. It can only be used after 9 am on weekdays and all day Saturday and Sunday.

On the Eastern Suburbs line you can get a combination bus-rail ticket from some stations such as Kings Cross (but not Central) so that you can change to a bus for a destination such as Bondi Beach. This works out cheaper than buying the tickets separately.

Car Hire Avis, Budget, Thrifty and Hertz are on William St up from the city towards Kings Cross, together with a number of local operators. Car hire seems to be slightly more expensive in Sydney than elsewhere. The larger companies' metropolitan rates are typically about $75 a day for a small car (Ford Laser, Mitsubishi Lancer, Toyota Corolla, Nissan Pulsar); about $90 a day for a medium car (Holden Apollo, Toyota Camry, Nissan Pintara, Mitsubishi Magna); or about $100 ($80 in GA) a day for a big car (Holden Commodore, Ford Falcon). Some companies include insurance in their rates while others ask for a $200 excess paid upfront and refundable upon return of the car in good condition.

In the Telecom yellow pages there's a long list of agencies, but most of the cheap outfits won't let you take their cars very far afield, and if they do their rates often compare badly with the big operators. For new cars, Bargain Car Rental (☎ 648 4844), out at 185 Parramatta Rd, Auburn has good rates for week-long rentals – $45 a day including insurance and metropolitan kms.

Half Price Rent-A-Car (☎ 267 7177) at 29A Oxford St doesn't restrict you to the metropolitan area and it has some deals on one-way rentals. Rent-a-Bug (☎ 428 2322), north of the harbour in Lane Cove, has a fleet of Datsun 120Ys at under $20 per day, but only for use in Sydney. This deal is pretty standard with the cheaper operators. Two places worth checking are Betta Rent-A-Car (☎ 331 5333), 199A Darlinghurst Rd in Kings Cross; and Reliable Car Rentals (☎ 358 6011) at 18-36 Palmer St, Woolloomooloo.

Bicycle Hire The bike hire places tend to be in the suburbs. Centennial Park Cycles (☎ 398 5027) at 50 Clovelly Rd, Randwick, is one of a few places on Clovelly Rd. It charges $6 an hour, $10 for two hours, $14 for half a day, and $28 for a day. You must leave a $10 deposit and produce identification such as a driving licence. Another relatively central place is Tom's Bike Hire at 43 Jersey Rd, Woollahra. Over towards Manly, north of The Spit Bridge over Middle Harbour, you'll find Seaforth Cycles at 569 Sydney Rd, Seaforth, and Health Hire at 52 Balgowlah Rd, Balgowlah.

Around Sydney

There are superb national parks just to the north and south Sydney and other interesting places within easy reach. In the early days of European settlement small towns were established around the major centre, and although some have been engulfed by Sydney's urban sprawl, they're still of great interest.

ROYAL NATIONAL PARK
Thirty-six km south of the city, this is the second oldest national park in the world – only Yellowstone in the USA predates it. It stretches about 20 km south from Port Hacking and has a fine network of walking tracks through varied country including a two-day, 26-km trail along the coast, with spectacular clifftop stretches. There are good surfing and swimming beaches (although surfing at Marley is dangerous), a number of

pleasant, rocky swimming holes, and the Hacking River which runs right through the park. The park is carpeted with wild flowers in late winter and early spring. The visitor centre (☎ (02) 542 0666) is about two km from the park entrance. You can hire rowing boats on the river at Audley. Entry to the park is $5.50 per car, free for pedestrians.

Places to Stay

There's a camp site with showers, accessible by car, at Bonnie Vale near Bundeena on Port Hacking, and bush camping is allowed, with a permit from the visitor centre or the ranger, in many other areas – Burning Palms Beach towards the south is one of the best places. A few km up the coast from Burning Palms there's the small, basic (no electricity or phone) *Garie Beach Youth Hostel* near one of the best surfing beaches and one km from the nearest road. Beds cost $5. Book and collect the key from Mr or Mrs Gunnee (☎ (042) 94 3268) at 28 St Georges Rd in the nearby town of Otford or from the YHA in Sydney, either at the central office in Day St or from the Glebe Point Rd hostel – see the section on accommodation in Sydney for addresses.

Getting There & Away

By road you reach the park from the Princes Highway – from Sydney, turn off just south of Loftus – or from the coast road up from Wollongong through Stanwell Park. You can drive right through the park from end to end, and down to the coast in a few places. The Sydney to Wollongong railway forms the western edge of the park, but the Royal National Park Station at Audley has closed down, and the closest you can get is Loftus, from where it's about a four-km walk to the park entrance and another two km to the visitor centre.

An interesting way to reach the park is to take a train to Cronulla then a ferry (hourly) from Port Hacking to Bundeena. Bundeena has its own beaches, or you can walk 30 minutes to Jibbon nearer the ocean coast which has another good beach and some Aboriginal rock art. A private ferry runs once

a day from Cronulla's Tonkin St wharf all the way to Audley in the park and single/return tickets cost $5/8. Currently the ferry departs Cronulla at 11 am and Audley at 5 pm, with no services during winter, but phone (☎ (02) 528 2634) to check. There are Sunday afternoon river cruises from Audley.

BOTANY BAY

It's a common misconception amongst first-time visitors that Sydney is built around Botany Bay. Actually Sydney Harbour is Port Jackson and Botany Bay is 10 to 15 km to the south, although the city now encompasses Botany Bay too. Botany Bay was Captain Cook's first landing point in Australia and was named by Joseph Banks, the expedition's chief naturalist, for the many botanical specimens he found here.

In the **Botany Bay National Park** at Kurnell, on the south side of the bay, Captain Cook's landing place is marked with various monuments. The interesting Discovery Centre (☎ (02) 668 9923) relates to the good captain's life and explorations, as well as to the surrounding wetlands. The centre is open from 10.30 am to 4.30 or 5 pm daily; the rest of the historic site, with good bushland walking tracks and picnic areas, is open from 7.30 am to 7 or 8 pm. From Cronulla Station (10 km away) take bus No 67 or walk along Cronulla beach. If you're coming by car there's a $5.50 fee to enter the park.

On the northern side of the bay entrance, beyond the oil tankers heading for the Kurnell refinery, is La Perouse where the French explorer of that name turned up in 1788, just six days after the arrival of the First Fleet. He gave the poms a good scare as they weren't expecting the French to turn up at this part of their empire quite so soon. La Perouse and his men camped at Botany Bay for a few weeks then sailed off into the Pacific and totally disappeared. It was not until many years later that the wreck of their ship was discovered on a Pacific island near Vanuatu. At La Perouse there's a monument to him and a fort on small Bare Island, built in 1885 to discourage a feared Russian (yes Russian) invasion of Australia. The fort is

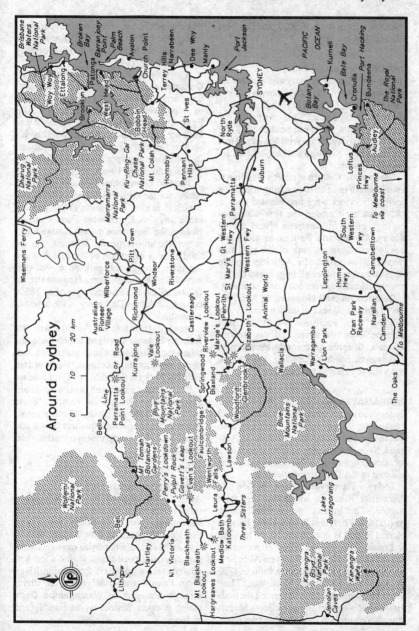

Around Sydney

0   10   20 km

PACIFIC OCEAN

open daily from 9 am to 3.30 pm. Bus Nos 393 and 394 run here.

CAMDEN (population 9000)

On the old Hume Highway and just across the new South-Eastern Freeway from Campbelltown, Camden is virtually an outer suburb of Sydney. This was one of Australia's first European settlements, and has many early buildings with National Trust classification – pick up a walking-tour leaflet from the library.

Gledswood Cellars at nearby Narellan is a winery built in an 1810 coaching house. It's open daily. Vines were first planted here in 1827, making Camden the first wine-producing centre in Australia. Next to the winery, **Australiana Park** is an all-in-one family entertainment park of the kind that crops up all over Australia. Activities include sheep shearing, water sliding, horse riding, rowing, dancing horses and koala cuddling.

Camden Aircraft Museum, at Narellan, has 17 old warplanes and is open Sunday and holidays only, admission $4. Buses from Campbelltown (the nearest railway station) run past. **Green's Motorcade Museum** in Leppington, north of Camden, has veteran and vintage cars and motorcycles.

PARRAMATTA (population 128,000)

Sydney today has sprawled out well beyond Parramatta, 24 km from the centre, which was the second European settlement in Australia. Sydney soon proved to be a poor area for farming and in 1788 Parramatta was selected as the first farm settlement.

Today's **Parramatta Park**, beside the Parramatta River, is where the first farm started. The tourist information centre (☎ (02) 630 3703) is at Prince Alfred Park on Market St and is open from 10 am to 4 pm weekdays, and shorter hours at weekends and holidays. **Elizabeth Farm** on Alice St is the oldest home in the country, built in 1793 by John and Elizabeth Macarthur. Their sheep breeding experiments formed the basis for Australia's wool industry. John Macarthur also controlled the lucrative rum trade,

and engineered the removal of several governors who tried to control him! You can visit the farmhouse from 10 am to 4.30 pm daily except Monday ($4).

A couple of blocks away **Hambledon Cottage** was built for the Macarthurs' daughters' governess. It's open from 11 am to 4 pm Wednesday to Sunday ($1.50). **Experiment Farm Cottage** at 9 Ruse St was built for James Ruse in the early 1800s; it's another fine early homestead, now furnished in 1840s style and open Tuesday to Thursday plus Sunday, from 10 am to 4 pm ($3).

The **Old Government House**, a country retreat for the early rulers, is in Parramatta Park and is now a museum ($4), open the same times as Experiment Farm Cottage. Nearby, the **Governor's Bath House** looks rather like an overgrown dovecote. On the third Sunday afternoon of the month, there are rides through the park on a well-preserved 1890s steam tram. **Roseneath**, in O'Connell St, is a fine example of an 1830s cottage. **St Johns Cemetery** is the oldest in Australia.

Near Parramatta in Auburn are the **Auburn Botanic Gardens** which include a billabong, Australian native plants and Japanese ornamental sections. **Featherdale Wildlife Park** (☎ (02) 622 1644) on Kildare Rd, Doonside, about halfway from Parramatta to Penrith, is another 'koala cuddlery'. There are plenty of other native fauna, in more spacious quarters than a zoo would provide. Featherdale is open daily and costs $6.

PENRITH (population 60,000)

Also on the edge of the capital's urban sprawl, Penrith is on the way to the Blue Mountains. The New South Wales Fire Service's **Museum of Fire** is open daily – here in the Hall of Flame you can experience simulated fire conditions. If that's too hot, you can take a cruise on the Nepean River. From Penrith you could reach the drive-through lion park at **Warragamba Dam**, which is open Wednesday to Sunday and holidays.

KU-RING-GAI CHASE NATIONAL PARK

Ku-ring-gai Chase is to the north, set between Sydney and the Hawkesbury River, 24 km from the city centre. Its east side borders that fine inlet, the Pittwater. There is over 100 km of shoreline, lots of forest and wildlife, many walking tracks and magnificent Aboriginal rock art. High points in the park offer superb views across deep inlets like Cowan Water and the wide Pittwater, and from West Head at the park's north-east tip there's another fantastic view across the Pittwater to Barranjoey Point at the end of Palm Beach. You may see lyre birds at West Head during their May to July mating period.

The popular **Waratah Park** (☎ (02) 450 2377) on Namba Rd, Terrey Hills, on the edge of the park, is another place where you can hold a koala. The TV series *Skippy the Bush Kangaroo* was filmed here. It's open daily and admission is $11.60, $5.80 for kids. For walks among native flora, visit the **Ku-ring-gai Wildflower Garden**, 420 Mona Vale Rd, St Ives. Both are open daily from 10 am.

Places to Stay

Camping is allowed only at the Basin, on the west side of the Pittwater, which is a walk of about two km from the West Head road, or a ferry ride from Palm Beach. These ferries (☎ (02) 918 2747) go hourly from 9 am to 4 pm (5 pm on weekends), $5 return. They also run to Mackerel Beach on the Pittwater. City buses go to Palm Beach. Book in advance for the Basin (☎ (02) 919 4036 from 9.30 to 10.30 am). The small *Pittwater Youth Hostel* (☎ (02) 99 2196) is a couple of km south of the camp site and is noted for friendly wildlife. Beds cost $12 and you must book in advance. Get there on the ferry from Church Point to Halls Wharf, from where it's a short walk. Several bus routes run from the city centre to Church Point.

Getting There & Away

There are four road entrances to the park – from Mt Colah (on the Pacific Highway) and Turramurra in the south-west, and Terrey Hills and Church Point in the south-east. The entry fee for a car is $5.

The Kalkari visitor centre (☎ (02) 457 9853), open from 9 am to 5 pm daily, is on Ku-ring-gai Chase Rd about four km into the park from Mt Colah, near Bobbin Head. There's an adjoining nature trail, with some wildlife. This road descends from the visitor centre to Bobbin Head on Cowan Water, where you can hire rowing boats, then goes round to the Turramurra entrance. Hornsby Buses (☎ (02) 457 8888) run from Turramurra Railway Station to the nearby park entrance ($1.90), with a few services continuing on to Bobbin Head.

There's a ferry between Palm Beach, the most northerly of Sydney's ocean beaches, and Bobbin Head via Patonga on the north side of the Hawkesbury River. It runs on weekends and daily during the September school holidays, $18 return. Contact the Palm Beach tourist office (☎ (02) 918 2747) for information.

At Akuna Bay on Coal and Candle Creek, off Cowan Water, there's a marina with a variety of craft, from rowing boats to cabin cruisers, for hire. Roads reach Akuna Bay and West Head from the Terrey Hills or Church Point entrances which are both served by city buses and Forest Coachlines (☎ (02) 450 2277).

HAWKESBURY RIVER

The Hawkesbury River enters the sea 30 km north of Sydney at Broken Bay. Dotted with coves, beaches, picnic spots and some fine riverside restaurants, it's one of the most attractive rivers in Australia and a popular centre for boating of all types. The Hawkesbury's final 20-odd km before it enters the ocean are fringed by deep inlets like Berowra Creek, Cowan Water and the Pittwater on the south side, and Brisbane Water on the north. The river flows between a succession of national parks – Marramarra and Ku-ring-gai to the south; Dharug, Brisbane Water and Bouddi to the north. About 100 km upstream are the towns of Windsor and Richmond.

An excellent way to get a feel for the river

is to take the river mail-boat (☎ (02) 985 7566) which runs up the river every weekday from Brooklyn on the south bank, about 13 km in from the coast, at 9.30 am and returns at 1.15 pm. There's also an afternoon run Wednesday to Friday. Passengers can come along for $16 and the 8.09 am train from Sydney's Central Railway Station will get you to Brooklyn in time to join the morning run.

The same people run other Hawkesbury trips including Brooklyn to Windsor cruises, Broken Bay cruises from Brooklyn and a daily ferry between Brooklyn and Patonga on the north shore ($4 one-way). There's a ferry from Brooklyn to Palm Beach and Avalon, on the narrow strip of land separating the Pittwater from the ocean, leaving Brooklyn at 8.30 am on Tuesday, Thursday and Sunday ($3 one-way). There are also cruises available from Wisemans Ferry on Sunday at 2 pm. The boat returns to Wisemans Ferry at 4 pm and the cost is $10.

Another interesting service is the weekend (daily in September school holidays) ferry (☎ (02) 918 2747) between Palm Beach, Patonga and Bobbin Head in Ku-ring-gai Chase National Park. From Patonga there are buses four times daily to Gosford, where you can pick up buses or trains going north. More Hawkesbury boat trips are covered in the Ku-ring-gai Chase National Park section.

The tiny settlement of **Wisemans Ferry** (where a ferry is still the only means of crossing the river) is a popular spot up the river – so much so that a large resort is due to open. There's also a guesthouse, *Wise Mans Folly* (☎ (045) 66 4566), which has rooms from $50. There are camping/caravan parks nearby but the only one with more than a handful of non-camping accommodation is *Del Rio Riverside Resort* (☎ (045) 66 4330), across the river and three km south at **Webbs Creek**. They have cabins from $45. You can hire houseboats (☎ (045) 66 4299 or 008 024 979, toll-free) and if you pick your time and hire for at least three days it can work out at under $100 a day – not bad between six people.

Across the river, **Dharug National Park**

is noted for its many Aboriginal rock carvings which date back nearly 10,000 years.

The **Great Northern Rd** which continues north from Wisemans Ferry is an example of early convict road building – it has scarcely changed since its original construction. The *Settlers Arms Inn* (☎ (045) 68 2111) at St Albans on this road dates from 1836 and the public bar is worth a beer. They have a few pleasant rooms but they're expensive at $60/80 for singles/doubles with bathroom. There are also four-bed rooms for $120 a night. There's a basic camp site opposite the pub.

WINDSOR AREA

Along with Richmond, Wilberforce, Castlereagh and Pitt Town, Windsor is one of the five 'Macquarie Towns' established by governor Lachlan Macquarie in the early 19th century on rich agricultural land on the upper Hawkesbury River. You can see them on the way to or from the Blue Mountains by the northern route along the Bells Line of Road. The drive from Windsor to Lithgow is spectacular and there are several viewpoint and picnic spots along the way.

The tourist information centre (☎ (045) 87 7388) just outside Windsor at McGraths Hill and open daily from 9 am to 5 pm, is the main information office for the upper Hawkesbury area. Windsor has its own tourist information centre which, together with the Hawkesbury Museum ($2.50), is in the 1843 **Daniel O'Connell Inn** in Thompson Square.

Other old buildings include the convict-built **St Matthew's Church** completed in 1822 and designed, like the courthouse, by the convict architect Francis Greenway. George St has more historic buildings and the 1815 **Macquarie Arms Hotel** is reckoned to be the oldest pub in Australia. The bushrangers Captain Thunderbolt and Bold Jack Donahue were brought up in Windsor. On the edge of town is the **Tebbit Observatory**, featured on the $100 note. There are day tours ($4), or you can have a look through the telescopes as part of the Friday and Saturday night tours ($10) (☎ 008 023 234, toll-free, or (045) 77 2485).

The **Australiana Pioneer Village** at Wilberforce is six km north of Windsor – it includes Rose's Cottage (1798), probably the oldest timber building in the country. The village is open daily, admission $10. At nearby **Ebenezer** the Presbyterian church, built in 1809, is said to be the oldest in Australia still in regular use.

Richmond, eight km west of Windsor, dates from 1810 and has a few more early buildings. There's a village-green-like park in the middle of town. St Peter's Church dates from 1841 and a number of notable pioneers are buried in its cemetery.

If you have a vehicle you can head north to Wisemans Ferry and from there drive 72 km along the Hawkesbury to the Pacific Highway near Gosford, or stay on small picturesque roads all the way north to Wollombi near Cessnock in the Hunter Valley.

Blue Mountains

The Blue Mountains, part of the Great Dividing Range, were once an impenetrable barrier to expansion inland from Sydney. Despite many attempts to find a route through the mountains, and a bizarre belief amongst many convicts that China, and freedom, was just on the other side, it was not until 1813 that a crossing was finally made and the western plains were opened up.

The Blue Mountains National Park has some truly fantastic scenery, excellent bushwalks and all the gorges, gum trees and cliffs you could ask for. The hills rise up just 65 km inland from Sydney and even a century ago this was a popular getaway for affluent Sydneysiders who came to escape the summer heat. Today it also attracts artists, and there are numerous galleries in the mountain towns. The mountains rise as high as 1100 metres and despite the intensive tourist development much of the area is so precipitous that it's still only open for bushwalkers. The blue haze, which gave the mountains their name, is a result of the fine mist of oil given off by eucalyptus trees.

Be prepared for the climatic difference between the Blue Mountains and the coast – you can swelter in Sydney but shiver in Katoomba. A lot of accommodation has heating.

Orientation

The Great Western Highway from Sydney follows a ridge line from east to west through the Blue Mountains. Along this less-than-beautiful road the Blue Mountains towns, none of them very big, often merge into each other – Glenbrook, Springwood, Woodford, Lawson, Wentworth Falls, Leura, Katoomba (the main accommodation centre), Medlow Bath, Blackheath, Mt Victoria, Hartley. On the western fringe of the mountains is Lithgow – see the later Central West section.

To the south and north of the Blue Mountains highway-ridge the country drops away into the precipitous valleys for which this region is famous, including the Grose Valley to the north, and the Jamison Valley south of Katoomba. There's a succession of turn-offs to waterfalls, lookout points or scenic alternative routes along the highway.

The old Bells Line of Road, much more scenic (and less congested) than the Great Western Highway, is a more northerly approach from Sydney; from Richmond it goes across north of the Grose Valley to bring you out on the main highway at either Lithgow or Mt Victoria.

Information

If you want to do more than just admire the Katoomba views visit the tourist information centre on the Great Western Highway at Glenbrook (☎ (047) 39 6266) or at Echo Point, Katoomba (☎ (047) 82 0756). The main visitor centre – the Blue Mountains Heritage Centre (☎ (047) 87 8877) – is on Govetts Leap Rd at Blackheath, about three km off the Great Western Highway. It's open daily and while good it's not very convenient if you're coming from Sydney. A second park visitor centre at Bruce Rd, Glenbrook

(☎ (047) 39 2950) is usually open only at weekends.

Good books on the Blue Mountains include *Exploring the Blue Mountains* by M E Hungerford and J K Donald (Kangaroo Press) and, for walkers, *Walks in the Blue Mountains* by Neil Paton (Kangaroo Press) and *How to See the Blue Mountains* by Jim Smith (Megalong Books).

It snows most years sometime between June and August, and the region has a Yule Festival, when many of the restaurants and guesthouses have good deals on 'Christmas' dinners.

National Parks

Large areas to the north and south of the Great Western Highway make up the **Blue Mountains National Park. Wollemi National Park**, north of Bells Line of Road, is the state's largest forested wilderness area, stretching almost up to Denman in the Hunter Valley and entered by no paved roads but offering good rugged bushwalking. It has lots of wildlife and similar landscape to the Blue Mountains. The virtually abandoned town of Newnes is on the western edge of Wollemi.

Kanangra Boyd National Park, west of the southern part of Blue Mountains National Park, has more bushwalking possibilities and grand scenery, and includes the spectacular Kanangra Walls Plateau which is entirely surrounded by sheer cliffs and can be reached by unsealed roads from Oberon or Jenolan Caves.

Walking

There are walks lasting from a few minutes to several days in the Blue Mountains and adjacent areas. The two most popular areas, spectacular from the tops of the cliffs or the bottoms of the valleys, are the Jamison Valley immediately south of Katoomba and the Grose Valley area, which is north-east of Katoomba and Blackheath. The area south of Glenbrook is another good place.

Visit a National Park visitor centre for information or, for shorter walks, ask at one of the tourist information centres. It's very rugged country and walkers sometimes get lost, so it's highly advisable to seek information from the visitor centres, not to go alone, and to tell someone where you're going. Most Blue Mountains watercourses are polluted, so you have to take your own water. And be prepared for rapid weather changes.

Places to Stay

There's plenty of accommodation in the Blue Mountains, but many places charge more at weekends and, in Katoomba especially, guesthouses tend to be booked out on long weekends. The places mentioned in the various sections are just a small selection of what's available; Katoomba is the main centre. You usually need a permit to camp and in some parts of the parks camping is banned, so check first.

Getting There & Away

Katoomba is now almost an outer suburb of Sydney, 109 km from the centre, and trains run frequently. There are one-day rail/bus packages for $37, including sightseeing. The standard one-way fare to Katoomba is $8.50 – it takes about two hours. See the Sydney section for other Blue Mountains day tours.

Getting Around

The Katoomba-Leura Bus Service (☎ (047) 82 3333) connects those two places (including stops opposite the old Carrington Hotel at the top end of Katoomba St, Katoomba, and at Echo Point) about 10 times on weekdays plus a few times on Saturday morning. It also has buses from Katoomba (opposite the Carrington) to Medlow Bath, Blackheath and Mt Victoria west along the Great Western Highway. Buses run about five times daily on weekdays from Blackheath along Hat Hill Rd and Govetts Leap Rd, which lead respectively to Perrys Lookdown and Govetts Leap, two of the most spectacular lookouts over the Grose Valley. The buses don't go all the way to these lookouts; they'll take you within about one km of Govetts Leap, but for Perrys Lookdown you'd have to walk several km from the last stop.

The Katoomba Woodford Bus Company

(☎ (047) 82 4213) runs between Leura and Katoomba and east as far as Woodford. They run from the Skyway and Katoomba Railway Station daily except for public holidays, although Sunday services are rather sparse.

On weekends and holidays the Blue Mountains Explorer Bus around Katoomba and Leura is a hop on, hop off service for which you buy an all-day ticket ($12.50). Contact Golden West Tours (☎ (047) 82 1866) of 283 Main St, Katoomba; the same people run Blue Mountains and Jenolan Caves tours from Katoomba.

Out & About Bush Experiences (☎ (047) 84 2361) at 49 Jersey Ave, Leura, has mountain bike tours and wilderness walks in the national park for about $100 a person for five days. Pedal Rentals (☎ (047) 51 3259) in Springwood rents good mountain bikes for $20 a day, less for longer rentals, and can give advice on routes. Even if you aren't in Springwood give them a call as they have agents in various places.

GLENBROOK TO KATOOMBA

From Marge's and Elizabeth's Lookouts just north of Glenbrook there are good views back to Sydney. The section of the Blue Mountains National Park south of Glenbrook contains **Red Hand Cave**, an old Aboriginal shelter with hand stencils on the walls.

The famous (and infamous) artist and author Norman Lindsay lived in **Springwood** from 1912 until he died in 1969. His home at 128 Chapman Parade is now a gallery and museum with exhibits of his paintings, cartoons, illustrations and, in the garden, sculptures. It's open from 11 am to 5 pm Friday to Sunday and public holidays, admission $5. The streets in the new housing developments nearby are named after characters from Lindsay's children's masterpiece *The Magic Pudding* – just the sort of kitsch that Lindsay hated.

Just south of the town of **Wentworth Falls** there are great views of the Jamison Valley, and of the 300-metre Wentworth Falls themselves, from Falls Reserve, which is the starting point for a network of walking tracks. In Wentworth Falls Yester Grange is a restored 19th-century premier's home, open from Wednesday to Sunday from 10 am to 5 pm. Wentworth Falls Zoo, on Horden Rd, is open daily except Monday and is known for its herd of deer.

Sublime Point, south of Leura, is another great lookout point. In **Leura**, Leuralla is an art deco mansion with a fine collection of 19th-century Australian art and a model railway museum. The house is a memorial to H V 'Doc' Evatt, the former Australian Labor Party leader who also, in the 1940s, was the first president of the United Nations. Leuralla is open from 10 am to 5 pm Wednesday to Sunday. Nearby Gordon Falls Reserve is a popular picnic spot and from here you can follow the road back past Leuralla, then take the Cliff Drive or the even more scenic Prince Henry Cliff Walk to Katoomba (it's about four km to Echo Point).

Places to Stay

At North Springwood there's a small, simple *Youth Hostel* (☎ (047) 54 1213 – phone first to arrange to collect the key) which costs $7. Though a bit off the beaten track it has great views. It's 10 km from Springwood Station but buses from there will drop you on Coromandel Ave, three km from the hostel. At Wentworth Falls, there's a B&B place (☎ (047) 57 1968) at 18A Asquith Ave charging $23 per person. Watch out for the Doberman. The *Leura Village Caravan Park* (☎ (047) 84 1552) has tent sites and on-site vans at the corner of the Great Western Highway and Leura Mall. There's also hotel, motel and guesthouse accommodation in the $60-and-up bracket.

There are national park camping areas which can be reached by car at Euroka Clearing near Glenbrook and Murphys Glen near Woodford. For Euroka Clearing you need to book by calling the Glenbrook office (☎ (049) 39 2950) which is open only at weekends. The dirt track to Murphys Glen is bad in wet weather and sometimes becomes impassable.

KATOOMBA (population 7300)

With its adjacent centres of Wentworth Falls and Leura this is the tourist centre of the Blue Mountains. It has always catered to visitors, being an Australian equivalent of an Indian 'hill station', where plains-dwellers escape the summer heat. Despite the almost continuous lines of tour buses passing through, Katoomba retains the atmosphere of a town from another time and place, with its art-deco and art-nouveau guesthouses and cafes, and its regular thick mists and occasional snow.

The Cliff Drive from Leura passes Honeymoon Lookout then reaches Echo Point about two km south of Katoomba centre. **Echo Point** has some of the best views of the Jamison Valley including the magnificent **Three Sisters** rock formation. Some good longer walks start from here. To reach Echo Point from Katoomba centre go down Lurline St then Echo Point Rd. A tourist information centre is here. The Three Sisters floodlit at night make an awesome sight, not to be missed.

A **scenic railway** runs 310 metres round

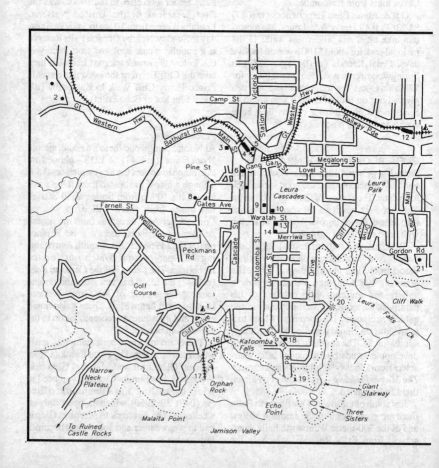

1	Convict Graves	13	Clarendon Hotel/Motel
2	Explorers Tree	14	RSL Club
3	Walkabout Backpackers	15	Katoomba Falls Caravan Park
4	Katoomba Railway Station	16	Skyway
5	Hotel Gearin	17	Scenic Railway
6	Hotel Katoomba	18	Echo Point Motor Inn
7	Parke St	19	Tourist Information
8	Swimming Pool	20	Honeymoon Lookout
9	Katoomba Mountain Lodge	21	Leuralla
10	Youth Hostel	22	Conservation Hut
11	Leura Village Caravan Park	23	Kiosk
12	Leura Railway Station		

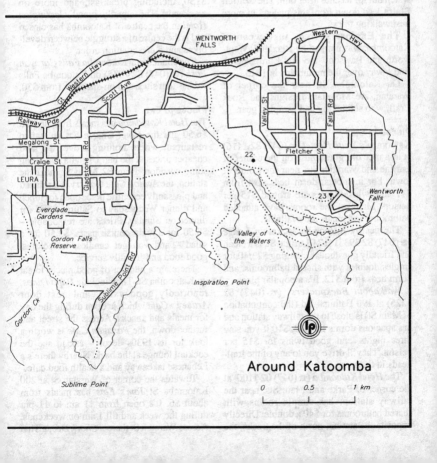

Around Katoomba

0   0.5   1 km

the cliff line west of Echo Point, down to the base of the Jamison Valley (one-way $2, return $3, extra for backpacks) and there's bushwalking in the area. The railway was built in the 1880s to transport miners to a coal mine, and its 45° incline is one of the steepest in the world. There is also the **Scenic Skyway**, a cable car crossing a gorge with views of Katoomba Falls, Orphan Rock and the Jamison Valley.

The walk to the **Ruined Castle** rock formation on Narrow Neck Plateau, dividing the Jamison and Megalong Valleys another couple of km west, is one of the best, but watch out for leeches after rain. The **Golden Stairs** lead down from this plateau to more bushwalking tracks.

The **Explorers Tree**, just west of Katoomba, was marked by Blaxland, Wentworth and Lawson, the first Europeans to find a way over the mountains in 1813.

On Katoomba St, near the corner of Waratah, are Mountain Designs and Rock Craft, who sell hiking and camping gear.

Places to Stay

Katoomba's *Youth Hostel* (☎ (047) 82 1416) is in a nice old guesthouse on the corner of Lurline and Waratah Sts, near the centre of town. For members, dorm beds cost from $11 and twins/doubles are around $15 per person. Many of the rooms have attached bathrooms and meals are available.

The nearby *Katoomba Mountain Lodge* (☎ (047) 82 3933) at 31 Lurline St, is a clean and friendly guesthouse charging $23/40 for singles/doubles with shared bathrooms, and dorm beds from $12. It's a popular place.

Walkabout Backpackers (☎ (047) 82 4226) at 190 Bathurst Rd (the continuation of Main St) is close to the railway station and has spacious dorms for $12, $10 if you stay three nights, and good twins for $15 per person. They'll drive you to any of the trailheads in the area.

The *Hotel Katoomba* (☎ (047) 82 1106) at the corner of Parke and Main Sts, near the railway station, has simple rooms with shared bathrooms for $40 a double. Directly opposite the station, north of the tracks, the

recently renovated *Hotel Gearin* (☎ (047) 82 4395) has singles/doubles for $25/45. The *Clarendon Hotel/Motel* (☎ (047) 82 1322), at the corner of Lurline and Waratah Sts, has a few twin rooms which they let at $20 per person, but they're usually booked out. The standard rates start at $60 a double for B&B. There's a theatre restaurant/ cabaret here with shows on Friday and Saturday nights – some of the acts are big names.

At the top of the hotel scale is the *Hydro Majestic Hotel* (☎ (047) 88 1002) a few km west of Katoomba at Medlow Bath, a superb relic of an earlier era. Doubles cost around $130, including breakfast, and more on weekends. The equally grand *Carrington Hotel* in the centre of Katoomba has closed and is the centre of a struggle between developers and a preservation order.

The council-run *Katoomba Falls Caravan Park* (☎ (047) 82 1835) on Katoomba Falls Rd has tent sites, and on-site vans from $30.

Places to Eat

The *Hotel Katoomba* has meals from around $6.50 and the *Hotel Gearin* has an Italian restaurant where nothing's over $8, and cheaper prices at the bar. Upstairs and along some corridors from 82 Main St, near the station, the *Avalon Cafe Gallery* is a relaxed and pleasantly eccentric place open for lunch and dinner Wednesday to Saturday and for dinner on Sunday. Prices are reasonable – $8.50 for a main course pasta, $3.50 for a salad – and you get candles, tablecloths, good food and friendly service.

There are a number of good places to eat on Katoomba St. They include *Papa Dinos*, reportedly good value, and next door *Aruney's Cafe* which is open during the day for meals and snacks. Across the street and further down, the *Paragon Cafe* is worth a look for its 1930s decor – ask to see the cocktail lounge at the back. Nearby there's a Lebanese takeaway and a health food cafe.

Towards the corner of Waratah St at 200 Katoomba St *Tom's Eats* has meals from about $6. It's open from 11 am to 11 pm during the week and till 1 am on weekends. Across Waratah St there's *Chork Dee*, a Thai restaurant open evenings except Monday with main courses around $9.

Quite a way down Waratah St, at No 94 in a residential area, *Memsahib's Kitchen* is an Indian BYO open for dinner from Friday to Sunday and Sunday lunches. Curries start at $8.50.

There are a couple of eateries off the Great Western Highway, still in Katoomba. The *Renaissance Restaurant* in the International School (still commonly known as the Renaissance Centre), 227 Great Western Highway, has main courses from $6.50 at lunch time, dearer in the evenings. At 13 Cliff Drive, near the highway towards Blackheath, the *Arjuna Cafe* has Indian and Asian food, vegetarian meals and home-made cakes. It's a pleasant place with mountain views, open from noon to 10 pm, Thursday to Monday.

Getting Around
You can hire geared mountain bikes at the youth hostel on the corner of Waratah and Lurline for $20 a day ($15 if you're staying there, and that includes a light meal at the Blues Cafe) and $12 for a half day ($10 for guests). If all their bikes are out, try the Cecil Guest House, further up Lurline St; the rates are similar.

There's a bus service (☎ (047) 82 4213) linking Katoomba Station, the scenic railway and Goyder Ave near Echo Point. It runs roughly hourly till about 4.30 pm on weekdays and a few times on Saturday and Sunday. There are also buses between central Katoomba and Echo Point.

BLACKHEATH (population 4500)
This little town on the main rail line from Sydney and the Great Western Highway is a good base for visiting – or looking at – the Grose Valley. There are superb lookouts a few km east of Blackheath, among them **Govetts Leap** with the adjacent **Bridal Veil Falls** (the Blue Mountains' highest), **Evans Lookout** to the south and **Pulpit Rock**, **Perrys Lookdown** and **Anvil Rock** to the

north. The last three are all reached from Hat Hill Rd.

A long cliff-edge track leads from Evans Lookout to Pulpit Rock and there are walks down into the Grose Valley itself and on the valley bottom – all involve at least a 300-metre descent and ascent. Get details on walks from the Blue Mountains' main national parks information centre, about three km out of Blackheath on Govetts Leap Rd, shortly before Govetts Leap itself. Perrys Lookdown is one of the few places where national park camping is allowed in this area. It's the beginning of the shortest route to the beautiful Blue Gum Forest in the valley bottom – about four hours return.

Places to Stay
Gardners Inn (☎ (047) 87 8347) on the highway in Blackheath, just north of the Govetts Leap Rd corner, is the oldest hotel in the Blue Mountains, dating from 1831, and is a clean, pleasant place charging $30 a night per person, including breakfast, $35 on Saturday.

The council-run *Blackheath Caravan Park* (☎ (047) 87 8101), with tent sites for $9 double and on-site vans from $30 a double, is on Prince Edward St, which is off Govetts Leap Rd about 600 metres from the highway. The *Lakeview Holiday Park* (☎ (047) 87 8532) on Prince Edward St has cabins from $30 a double. There is bush camping in the Grose Valley near Acacia Flat, about two hours walk from Blackheath Railway Station, via Govetts Leap – ask the National Parks office for details.

BEYOND BLACKHEATH
To the west and south-west of Blackheath lie the Kanimbla and Megalong valleys with yet more spectacular views from places like Hargreaves Lookout.

A couple of km along, at the top of the mountain, is the pretty National-Trust-classified town of **Mt Victoria**. The historical museum at the railway station is open from 2 to 5 pm on weekends and holidays. Interesting buildings include the Victoria & Albert Guesthouse, the 1849 Tollkeeper's

Cottage, the 1870s church and the Grand guesthouse. Off the highway at **Mt York** there's a memorial to the explorers who first found a way across the Blue Mountains. There's a short stretch of the original road across the mountains here.

About 11 km past Mt Victoria is the tiny village of **Hartley** which flourished in the 1830s and '40s as an administrative centre, but dwindled after 1887 when it was bypassed by the railway. There are still 17 buildings of historic significance which can be viewed. The National Parks office in the former Hartley post office is open daily except Wednesday from 10 am to 1 pm and 2 to 5 pm. Tours are available on weekdays.

Off Bells Line of Road, between Lithgow and Bell, is the Zig Zag Railway – see the Central West section later. Between Bell and Richmond the **Mt Tomah Botanic Gardens** are the cool climate annexe of Sydney's Royal Botanic Gardens. They're open daily from 10.30 am to 4 or 6 pm, and admission is $5 per car or $2 for pedestrians.

Places to Stay

At Mt Victoria the *Hotel Imperial* (☎ (047) 87 1233) on the highway has singles/doubles from $25/40, more on weekends. *Cedar Lodge Cabins* (☎ (047) 87 1256), on the highway in Mt Victoria, has comfortable cabins from $45 a night for doubles and $5 for each additional adult.

JENOLAN CAVES

South-west of Katoomba and on the west edge of Kanangra Boyd National Park are the best-known limestone caves in Australia. One cave has been open to the public since 1867 although parts of the system are still unexplored. Three caves are open for independent viewing, and you can visit a further nine by guided tours which go about 10 times a day from 10 am to 4 pm, with an evening tour at 8 pm. Tours last 1½ to two hours. Prices vary up to about $12 but the Lucas Cave, one of the best, costs $8. At holiday time arrive early as the best caves can be 'sold out' by 10 am. There's a network of walking trails outside the caves.

Near Jenolan Caves there are a few cabin setups in the $50 bracket. *Jenolan Caves House* does a four-course buffet lunch for $19.50.

There are various day-tour packages from Sydney, such as a rail/bus tour for $49, including a quick look at the Three Sisters, near Katoomba. Book at Sydney inner-city stations or on (02) 281 7499. This tour doesn't cover the cost of entry to the caves.

Jenolan Caves

YERRANDERIE

On the opposite (south-east) edge of Kanangra Boyd from Jenolan, Yerranderie is a remote, privately owned ghost town slowly being restored. For more information phone (02) 955 8083. Tent sites cost $7.50 and lodges from $30. You might have trouble getting here without a 4WD, but Kings Tours run expensive overnight trips from Sydney.

North Coast

The north coastal area of New South Wales is extremely popular – and with good reason. There are excellent fishing and surfing opportunities on the coast itself, and the hinterland with its numerous national parks offers wildlife, challenging bushwalks and some superb scenery.

The Pacific Highway runs all the way north along the coast into Queensland, and along it you'll find some great places to stay, including Byron Bay – a surfing Mecca and long-time travellers' favourite.

SYDNEY TO NEWCASTLE

Two main roads follow similar courses for some of the way from Sydney, but diverge as they approach Newcastle. The faster is the excellent Sydney to Newcastle Freeway, but just as scenic are the curves of the Pacific Highway which, once across the Hawkesbury River, runs nearer to the coast and the two large coastal lakes of Tuggerah and Macquarie. There are some interesting spots along the coast itself, off the highways.

Gosford (population 38,000)

Less than 100 km north of Sydney this is the centre for visiting the Brisbane Water National Park.

There are pubs, motels and a caravan park, and a backpackers' hostel might open soon – ask the tourist office (☎ (043) 25 2835), on Mann St near the railway station.

Old Sydney Town

On the Pacific Highway nine km south of Gosford, Old Sydney Town is a major reconstruction of early Sydney, including replicas of early ships, plus nonstop street theatre retelling events from the colony's early history. Children love the duels, hangings and floggings!

It's open from 10 am to 5 pm Wednesday to Sunday and daily during school holidays. Admission for adults is $12.80. There are

many tours here from Sydney, some including the Riverboat Postman.

National Parks

The Bouddi National Park is an attractive coastal park extending north from the Hawkesbury River mouth, 17 km from Gosford, with excellent bushwalking, camping and swimming. The beautiful Brisbane Water National Park offers similar attractions south-west of Gosford, just in from the mouth of the Hawkesbury. It has many old Aboriginal rock engravings.

GOSFORD TO NEWCASTLE

From Gosford you have the three options of going up the Pacific Highway or the Sydney to Newcastle Freeway or taking a coastal route around the saltwater Tuggerah Lake. All three are scenic but the coastal way – along what's known as the Central Coast – is probably the most interesting if you have time. There are hosts of caravan parks, camp sites and motels along the way. **Terrigal**, on the coastal route, is a popular surfing centre.

Further north, **Lake Macquarie** is Australia's biggest saltwater lake, popular for sailing, water-skiing and fishing. The Pacific Highway runs between it and the ocean. In **Wangi Wangi**, south of Toronto, you can visit the home of artist William Dobell. There are cruises on the lake in the *Wangi Queen* (☎ (049) 58 3211 for bookings) from Toronto and Belmont. There are train services to Toronto, and buses to Belmont and Speers Point.

NEWCASTLE (population 259,000)

New South Wales's second largest city, Newcastle is also one of Australia's largest ports. At the mouth of the Hunter River, 167 km north of Sydney, it's a major industrial and commercial centre, with the massive BHP steelworks and other heavy industries. It's also the export port for the Hunter Valley coalfields; coal exports are still Newcastle's lifeblood. Despite the city's industrial base, its centre with its wide leafy streets has a pleasant feel, and surf beaches are only a few hundred metres away.

In late 1989, Newcastle suffered Australia's most destructive earthquake, with 12 people killed and a lot of property damage. Around town you can still see signs of it – props holding up facades and buildings being restored or demolished.

Originally named Coal River, the city was founded in 1804 as a place for the most intractable of Sydney's convicts and was known as the 'hell of New South Wales'. The breakwater out to Nobbys Head with its lighthouse was built by convicts and the Bogey Hole, a swimming pool cut into the rock on the ocean's edge below the pleasant King Edward Park, was built for Major Morriset, a strict disciplinarian. It's still a great place for a dip.

Information & Orientation

The centre of Newcastle is a peninsula bordered by the ocean on one side and the Hunter River on the other. It tapers down to the long sandspit leading to Nobbys Head. Hunter St is the three-km-long main street. Between Newcomen and Perkins Sts it's a pedestrian mall.

There are left-luggage lockers at the railway station – for one-day use only. Not far from the station, the helpful tourist information centre (☎ (049) 29 9299; 008 025 929, toll-free) is at Queens Wharf on Wharf Rd by the river, open from 9 am to 5 pm Monday to Friday, 9.30 am to 3 pm weekends. They'll also book accommodation for you.

The Scout Outdoor Centre at 518 Hunter St, opposite the Casbah Hotel, is a good place for outdoor gear. The Wilderness Society, with an excellent range of T-shirts and other flora-&-fauna-inspired items, is on Hunter St next to the post office. Pick up a copy of the newsletter for information on organised walks and activities.

Around the City

The good **Newcastle Regional Art Gallery** is on Laman St next to Civic Park. It's open Monday to Friday from 10 am to 5 pm plus weekend afternoons, and admission is free. The nearby **Cooks Hill** area has several private galleries.

The new **Newcastle Regional Museum** at 787 Hunter St is open daily except Monday, and admission is $3. They also show occasional films. There is also a maritime museum (open daily except Monday) and a military museum (open weekends and holidays only) in **Fort Scratchley** out towards Nobbys Head, which dates from the 1880s. The fort is open from noon to 4 pm except on Monday, and admission to it and the museums is free.

North of the city across the Hunter River is the Stockton breakwater which is built over a sandbank known as **Oyster Bank** where many ships were once wrecked. The last was a four-masted barque, the *Adolphe*, in 1904. Its hull and various other wrecks are now built into the breakwater; the *Adolphe* is the only one visible today.

At the **Shortlands Wetlands Reserve** (near Sandgate Railway Station) there are walks and canoe trails.

Beaches

Newcastle is well-endowed with clean beaches, many with good surf, and several are patrolled. The main beach, **Newcastle Beach**, is only a couple of hundred metres from the centre of town; it has an ocean pool which is open at night, and usually good surf. **Merewether Beach**, further south, also has a pool which is open at night. **Bar Beach** is floodlit at night and the beach is protected by a rocky bar. **Nobbys Beach** is north of the centre and more sheltered from the southerlies. It's often open when other beaches are closed.

Blackbutt Reserve

At New Lambton Heights in the west of the city, this 166-hectare bushland reserve has a variety of bushwalks as well as aviaries, wildlife enclosures (including koalas) and fern houses. Bus No 216 runs there from the city centre.

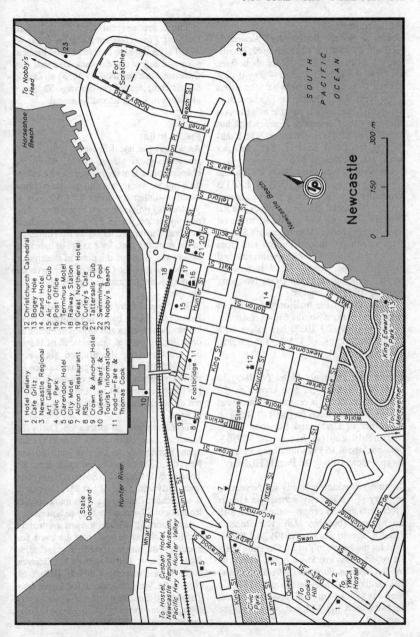

Newcastle

1 Hotel Delany
2 Cafe Gritz
3 Newcastle Regional
   Art Gallery
4 Civic Park
5 Clarendon Hotel
6 City Motel
7 Alcron Restaurant
8 RSL
9 Crown & Anchor Hotel
10 Queens Wharf &
   Tourist Information
11 Food-a-Fare &
   Thomas Cook
12 Christchurch Cathedral
13 Bogey Hole
14 Grand Hotel
15 Air Force Club
16 Post Office
17 Terminus Motel
18 Railway Station
19 Great Northern Hotel
20 Curleys Cafe
21 Tattersalls Club
22 Swimming Pool
23 Nobby's Beach

Places to Stay

Hostel & Hotels *Backpackers Newcastle* (☎ (049) 69 3436) at 42 Denison St, Hamilton, is a clean and friendly place about three km from the railway station – they'll pick you up if you ring. Otherwise take a bus going west along Hunter St; Denison St is the second intersection past the museum, on your left – the *Cambridge Hotel* (which has rooms from $20) is on the corner. The Backpackers has dorm beds for $11 ($60 per week) and doubles for $26.

On Scott St near the railway station, the *Great Northern Hotel* (☎ (049) 29 4961) is terminally past its prime but there are still hints of provincial grandeur – check out the murals in the lobby and take the lift to the 1st floor lounge. Fairly clean rooms are $24 for singles with common bathroom and from $31/45 for singles/doubles with attached bathroom. The George Hotel is now an empty block opposite the Great Northern, courtesy of the earthquake.

At the end of the mall on the corner of Hunter and Perkins Sts, the *Crown & Anchor Hotel* (☎ (049) 29 1027) has rooms with shared bathrooms at $25/35 for singles/ doubles.

Motels The *Terminus Motel* (☎ (049) 26 3244) at 107 Scott St, also known as the Harbourside Motel, is central with rooms at $42/48. The *City Motel* (☎ (049) 29 5855) on the corner of Darby and Burwood Sts, is reasonably central but costs $57/63. Belmont, about 15 km south, has a string of cheaper motels along the Pacific Highway.

Camping Stockton is handy for Newcastle by ferry – it's directly across the Hunter River from the city centre – otherwise it's 19 km by road (bus No 118). The *Stockton Beach Caravan Park* (☎ (049) 28 1393) is right on the beach in Pitt St. Camping costs $8, on-site vans are $34 a night. The *Newcastle Caravan Park* (☎ (049) 68 1394) at 293 Maitland Rd, Mayfield West (the Pacific Highway), is two km from Newcastle centre. Tent sites are a high $14, and on-site vans are from $30.

There are several sites at Belmont. *Belmont Pines Tourist Park* (☎ (049) 45 4750) is on the lake in Ethel St and has tent sites and a few on-site vans. *Belmont Bay Caravan Park* (☎ (049) 45 3653) on Gerald St, has camping and on-site vans. There are also sites in Redhead and Swansea.

Places to Eat

As well as the usual fast-food outlets there are some good places to eat. About the cheapest place is at the *Hunter TAFE College* on King St, where you can get three-course lunch or dinner for under $5 – Monday to Wednesday only. On Scott St just west of the railway station, the *Air Force Club* has cheap lunches. During the day head for Hunter St, in the mall and east, for a range of cafes and takeaways. Most of the pubs in the area do counter meals – the *Crown & Anchor* on the corner of Hunter and Perkins is one of the cheapest.

The *Food-A-Fare* food hall upstairs in the Hunter St Mall has international food, kebabs, sandwiches and more. On Pacific St, opposite the park at the east end of Hunter St, *Curley's* (the illuminated sign says 'Vienna Cafe') is a small, pleasant place for snacks or meals with main courses from $7. It's open between 10 am and at least 11.30 pm all week, except Sunday when it opens at 5 pm.

There are lots of places on Darby St. Mexican *Taco Bill's* at No 80 is BYO and open Wednesday to Sunday until 10 pm. Next door, *Taters* has baked spuds from $3. The *Darby St Cafe* at No 86 is a relaxed place open daily until late. At No 131, *Cafe Gritz* is a pleasant little place with main courses from about $7, open Tuesday to Saturday.

Beaumont St, in Hamilton just south of the Pacific Highway as you enter the town, has a cluster of Italian restaurants, including *Little Swallow*. The *Maharaja* is a licensed north Indian restaurant at 653 Hunter St, Newcastle West. It's open for lunch from Tuesday to Saturday and for dinner every night. Takeaways are available. Also in Newcastle West, at 32 Marketown Shopping

Centre, the *Istana Malaysia* is raved about by locals.

There is a Chinese and a Thai restaurant by the rock pool in the Star Complex at 569 Hunter St, and a coffee shop or two nearby. *Clams* at 87 Frederick St, Merewether, is famous for its seafood. It's next to the Beach Hotel and is closed on Sunday.

Entertainment

There's something on most nights; get the Wednesday *Newcastle Herald* for an entertainment lift-out, or the *Star* for daily listings.

Quay 1 on Wharf Rd has bands (sometimes quite big Aussie touring bands) two or three nights a week. Fannies is a glittery disco in the same complex. The popular Newcastle Workers Club on the corner of Union and King Sts also has regular bands – often quite big names. Tattersalls Club on Watt St between Scott and Hunter also has touring bands.

Pubs The Hotel Delany is a relaxed little pub on the corner of Council and Darby Sts, Cooks Hill, with music most nights. The Cricketers Arms, on the corner of Bull and Bruce Sts in Cooks Hill, is also popular. The Grand Hotel on the corner of Church and Bolton Sts has poetry readings, rock or jazz most nights.

In Merewether the Beach Hotel has music (usually rock) mainly on Wednesday, Saturday and Sunday nights. This is one of the most popular places in the area.

Getting There & Away

Air Aeropelican (☎ (049) 69 3444) flies several times a day between Sydney ($64) and Belmont, just south of Newcastle, and Eastern (☎ (049) 69 3055 or 13 1313, toll-free) flies to Sydney, the Gold Coast ($194) and Brisbane, and several towns en route.

Bus From Sydney to Newcastle you're better off taking the train. Going north from Newcastle, however, buses offer a much better service than trains. Newcastle to Port Macquarie costs about $28, to Byron Bay

$47, to Brisbane $50. Jayes Travel (☎ (049) 26 2000) at 285 Hunter St, is the main booking office. Sid Fogg's (☎ (049) 26 3199) runs to Canberra ($39) and Dubbo ($39.50).

There's Rover Motors' bus to Cessnock and from there to Maitland, but to many places in the Hunter region you have to go by train.

Train Trains to and from Sydney run about 20 times daily, and cost $17. A few trains a day are fast 'Flyers', but you must book a seat on these. Heading north, trains are far from frequent.

Getting Around

Bus STA buses cover all of Newcastle and the eastern side of Lake Macquarie. The bus information booth at the west end of the mall, on the corner of Perkins St, has timetables. For sightseeing try route No 348 or 358 to Swansea or No 306, 307 or 327 to Speers Point. Newcastle has similar special local transport deals to Sydney.

Trains run to the western side of Lake Macquarie with connecting buses to the south-western shores. A private bus company runs to Stockton – but much quicker is the STA ferry from Wharf Rd, between Merewether St and Queens Wharf. It runs frequently till 11 pm Monday to Thursday, midnight on Friday and Saturday and 8.30 pm on Sunday and holidays. The fare is $1.20.

Car As well as the regular places, you can hire used cars from Cheep Heep (☎ (049) 61 3144) at 107 Tudor St, Hamilton from $24 a day, including insurance. Bargain Wheels (☎ (049) 60 2165) charges from $20 a day, including insurance.

Bicycle Bike hire places come and go – the tourist information centre will know if one is operating currently.

HUNTER VALLEY

The Hunter Valley has two curiously diverse products – coal and wine. Steam trains still take coal to Hexham on the Hunter River near Newcastle. Singleton, 77 km inland from Newcastle, and Muswellbrook, a further 47 km, are two wine-producing/coal-mining areas (see the later New England section for more on these places). The centre of the Hunter Valley vineyards is the Pokolbin area near Cessnock and some wineries date back to the 1860s. You'll find many of Australia's best-known wine names. The Hunter Valley Vintage Festival attracts hordes of wine enthusiasts every February, for wine tasting, and grape-picking and treading contests.

The Upper Hunter Valley near Muswellbrook and Denman, less well known than the lower valley, is wilder country but has vineyards and a regular wine festival. The main road through the Hunter Valley is the New England Highway from Tamworth down to Newcastle. The 300-km-long Hunter River comes from further west and doesn't meet the highway until Singleton.

Wineries

There are about 30 vineyards in the Lower Hunter, and others in the Upper Hunter, where you can sample and buy wines. Generally they're open for tasting from Monday to Saturday, and with slightly reduced hours on Sunday. Many have picnic and barbecue facilities. Several wineries run tours – McWilliams Mt Pleasant is one (at 11 am and 2 pm on weekdays) and the Cessnock tourist information centre (☎ (049) 90 4477) can tell you of others. For the Upper Hunter, contact the Muswellbrook information centre on (☎ 065) 43 4024.

Hungerford Hill bills itself as a 'wine village'. It has a restaurant, handicrafts shop, 'farmers' market' and wine tours as well as the usual tasting and wine sales facilities – commercial but interesting. Nearby, Tyrrells is one of the oldest vineyard names in the Hunter.

Getting There & Around

Unless you have a bus pass or a long-distance ticket with stopovers it's cheaper to get to the Hunter by train or local buses, rather than with the major companies. Batterhams's buses (☎ (049) 90 5000) run between Cessnock and Sydney daily for $17. Maitland is the main train station for the Lower Hunter, with services from Newcastle and Sydney.

From Maitland there are buses to Cessnock. Rover Motors (☎ (049) 90 1175) at 231 Vincent St in Cessnock (opposite the Black Opal Hotel) has several services a day from Newcastle and Maitland to Cessnock, but fewer on weekends.

To explore the vineyards you can join a tour with Hunter Vineyard Tours (☎ (049) 91 1659). These cost $45 with lunch, $27 without, and they'll pick you up from Newcastle, Cessnock or Maitland. The tour covers some of the smaller vineyards with plenty of tasting and buying opportunities.

You can hire bicycles from the general store at Pokolbin Village (☎ (049) 98 7670) for $15 for a half day and $23 for a full day, less for rentals of more than one day. A balloon flight costs from $170.

Cessnock (population 17,000)

Cessnock is the main town and accommodation centre for the vineyards, a few km from Pokolbin and in the centre of the wineries. There's a useful tourist information centre (☎ (049) 90 4477) on the corner of Wollombi and Mount View Rds, open from 9 am to 5 pm daily weekdays and shorter hours on weekends.

Wollombi, a tiny town 31 km south of Cessnock, has some interesting old buildings and there are good lookouts around the valley.

Places to Stay There's a basic associate *Youth Hostel* (☎ (049) 90 1070) in the back of the Black Opal Hotel at 216 Vincent St, on the corner of Cessnock St. Bunks in small dorms are $11 for YHA members, $15 for others. Rooms in the hotel are $27 with breakfast.

Other hotels include the *Royal Oak* (☎ (049) 90 2366) on the corner of Vincent and Snape Sts, which has rooms at $15/30 for singles/doubles; the *Wentworth* (☎ (049)

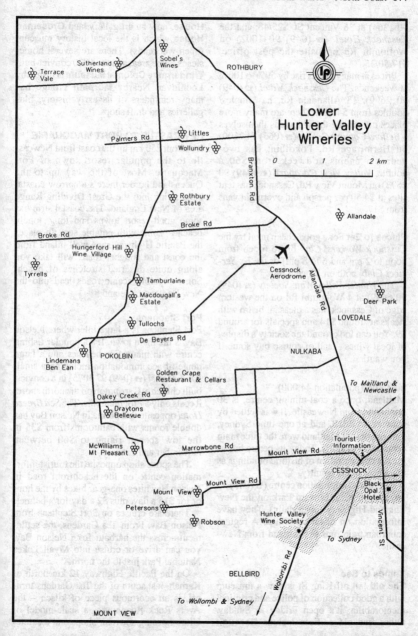

Lower Hunter Valley Wineries

0   1   2 km

Terrace Vale
Sutherland Wines
Sobel's Wines
ROTHBURY

Palmers Rd
Littles
Wollundry

Branxton Rd

Rothbury Estate

Broke Rd

Allandale

Broke Rd

Hungerford Hill Wine Village

Tyrrells

Tamburlaine

Macdougall's Estate

Cessnock Aerodrome

Allandale Rd

Tullochs

De Beyers Rd

Deer Park

LOVEDALE

Lindemans Ben Ean

POKOLBIN

Golden Grape Restaurant & Cellars

NULKABA

Oakey Creek Rd

To Maitland & Newcastle

Draytons Bellevue

McWilliams Mt Pleasant

Marrowbone Rd

Mount View Rd

Tourist Information

CESSNOCK

Mount View

Mount View Rd

Black Opal Hotel

Petersons

Robson

Hunter Valley Wine Society

Vincent St

To Sydney

BELLBIRD

To Wollombi & Sydney

MOUNT VIEW

90 1364) at 36 Vincent St, $25/48; and the *Cessnock Hotel* (☎ (049) 90 1002) on Wollombi Rd opposite the post office, $17.50/35.

Prices at many places rise by 50% to 100% at weekends. The *Cessnock Motel* (☎ (049) 90 2699), 13 Allandale Rd, has singles/doubles from $40/50. There are many more places out among the vineyards themselves – *Belford Country Cabins* (☎ (065) 74 7100) on Hermitage Rd, Pokolbin, has two-bedroom cabins midweek from $60 a double. *Valley View Carapark* (☎ (049) 90 2573) on Mount View Rd, Cessnock has tent sites at $4.50 per person and overnight vans from $17.

Places to Eat For a good cheap meal try the *Cessnock Workers' Club* bistro (open from noon to 2 pm and 6 to 8 pm) or the *Ex-Services Club*, both on Vincent St.

The *Hunter Valley Wine Society* (☎ (049) 90 6699) at 4 Wollombi Rd on the western edge of Cessnock, has a pleasant bistro with steaks at around $14 and specials for around $9. You can look round the society's display of local wines – and of course buy some if you want!

Maitland (population 44,000)

Maitland, once a coal-mining centre, is 30 km inland from Newcastle. It was settled by convicts in 1818, and at one time Sydney, Parramatta and Maitland were the three main centres in Australia. Today its centre has as great a concentration of historic buildings as anywhere in the country.

The tourist information centre (☎ (049) 33 2611) is in King Edward Park on the New England Highway (open daily). They have information on historical walks. A regular suburban train runs to Maitland from Newcastle.

Things to See

The **old jail** off King St is now a museum with a good collection of police and criminal memorabilia; it's open Friday to Sunday. Other fine old edifices include **Borough House,** now an art gallery, and **Grossman House** which is the local history museum (open weekends). There are several homesteads in the area; and the 1820 convict-built **Windermere Colonial Museum** is in nearby Lochinvar. Nearby **Morpeth** village has many reminders of its early history, plus galleries and craft shops.

NEWCASTLE TO PORT MACQUARIE

It's about 250 km up the coast from Newcastle to the popular resort town of Port Macquarie. Most of the way up to the Queensland border there's a narrow coastal band rising into the Great Dividing Range area of New England. The coastal strip has some good resort towns and long, lonely beaches, some with notable surf. In places the Pacific Highway runs well inland from the coast and rougher roads will take you along quite deserted stretches of beach. Some superbly scenic roads lead into the New England tableland.

Port Stephens

Port Stephens is a large inlet where Nelson Bay is the main town. It's a popular fishing centre with many fine beaches and a large range of accommodation including a small *Youth Hostel* (☎ (049) 97 3075) in a convict-built church at Carrington on the north shore; it costs only $7 for members. The *Sea Breeze Hotel* opposite the marina in Nelson Bay has double rooms with bathrooms from $35 in the low season rising to $60 between November and January.

The sports shop opposite the tourist information centre on the beachfront road in Nelson Bay hires one-gear bikes by the hour or for $15 a day, plus $2 a day for a helmet.

There are cruises on Port Stephens from Nelson Bay. From Tea Gardens, the settlement across the harbour from Nelson Bay, you can drive or cruise into Myall Lakes National Park just to the north.

On the Pacific Highway 12 km north of Karuah, just south of the Tea Gardens turn-off, is an enormous piece of kitsch – the Ayers Rock Roadhouse, a scale-model of Uluru housing souvenir shops and a cafeteria. This monstrosity is open 24 hours a day and entry is free.

Port Stephens Buses (☎ (049) 81 1207) runs buses between Nelson Bay and Sydney daily ($20), around the Port Stephens townships and to/from Newcastle.

Myall Lakes National Park

This park combines some beautiful lakes with ocean beaches and is one of the few remaining coastal lagoon systems in New South Wales. The main access points to the park are via the Lakes Way running south from Forster-Tuncurry, via Tea Gardens at the south of the park and from Bulahdelah on the Pacific Highway to the west. From Bulahdelah to the national park is 11 km. Just past the park entrance take the road signposted to Legges Camp at Bombah Point, another five km on.

At *Myall Shores* (ex Legges Camp) (☎ (049) 97 4495) at Bombah Point you can camp (from $12.50 for two people) or stay in a shared four-bed cabin for $12.50. A cabin to yourself costs from $40. Prices for the shared accommodation stay the same year-round; for the rest there's the normal summer price-hike. If you need a lift from Bulahdelah they'll take you for free at about 9 am and 3.30 pm during school terms and for $5 at other times. There's a restaurant and a shop at Bombah Point.

From Bombah Point a punt across to the coastal side of the park departs at least hourly between 8 am and 6 pm (cars $2.50, pedestrians 50c). There are camp sites at Mungo Brush and Seal Rocks, a tiny fishing and surfing village superbly situated on the ocean at the north-east edge of the park.

The Mungo Track is a walking trail through the park, which can be tackled as a one or two-day walk or in half-day sections. You can begin the walk at the southern edge of the park at Hawks Nest, near Tea Gardens.

Forster-Tuncurry (population 15,500)

Between the top end of Myall Lakes National Park and Taree, on a coastal loop road from Bulahdelah, the twin towns of Forster-Tuncurry are connected by a bridge at the sea entrance to Wallis Lake. This would be a good base for visiting the Myall Lakes National Park, and there are 13 other beaches close to town. There's a helpful visitor centre (☎ (065) 54 8799) on Little St.

Cheaper places to stay include *Lakes & Ocean Hotel* (☎ (065) 54 6005) at 10 Little St, Forster (singles/doubles without bathroom from $25/28); *Bali Hai Motel* (☎ (065) 54 6537), 132 Manning St, Tuncurry (from $24); and *Beachcourt Holiday Units* (☎ (065) 54 7562), 25 Beach St, Tuncurry. Most of the caravan parks have on-site vans.

Great Lakes Coaches (☎ (065) 54 5111) runs daily buses from Forster to Newcastle ($27) and Sydney ($30).

Barrington Tops National Park

On the inland side of the Great Dividing Rage, Dungog is a main access point to the Barrington Tops National Park, which contains two 1600-metre alpine plateaus that fall away steeply to just 400 metres. The park is noted for its wildlife and some unusual local flora, and has a variety of walking trails and picnic areas.

Forty-three km from Dungog you reach the park boundary at *Barrington Guest House* (☎ (049) 95 3212), which is the nearest accommodation to the park. There's a car-camp site in the park's eastern Gloucester River area, approached from the Stroud to Gloucester road.

Camden Haven

Fifty km north of Taree at Kew you can turn off the Pacific Highway and take a coastal route to Port Macquarie. The fishing towns of Laurieton, North Haven and Dunbogan, immediately north of **Crowdy Bay National Park** (good for fishing, surfing, walking and viewing spring wild flowers), are collectively known as Camden Haven, and a bit further north is the small township of **Lake Cathie**, from where Lighthouse Beach stretches 10 km up to the Port Macquarie Lighthouse. There's excellent fishing along the coast here, plus a range of accommodation and some fine bushwalks around the lakes close to the coast.

Diamond Head is near Laurieton at the north end of the national park. There's a basic (but pretty) camp site by the beach which costs $4 a night. You'll need to bring your own water.

PORT MACQUARIE (population 27,000)

One of the bigger resort centres on the New South Wales north coast, Port Macquarie makes a good stopping point on the journey from Sydney (430 km south). It was founded in 1821, making it one of the oldest towns in the state, and was a convict settlement until 1840. There is a wide range of accommodation and places to eat and a spot of nightlife, and the competition tends to keep prices down.

'Port' has been blessed with both a river frontage (the Hastings River enters the sea here) and a beautiful series of ocean beaches starting right in the town. It's a small enough place to find everything you need within reasonable walking distance of the centre.

Information

The information centre (☎ (065) 83 1077), open 8.30 am to 5 pm Monday to Friday, to 4.30 pm on weekends, is at the waterfront end of Horton St (the main street). You can rent canoes, windsurfers and boats at the marina on Park St, one km west of the centre. A traveller reports being able to use all the facilities at the RSL – pool, spa, sauna, exercise classes – for a fee of $4.50.

Things to See

Roto, off Lord St about two km from the town centre, is a grand 1891 homestead surrounded by a nature reserve which includes a very popular koala hospital. Entry is free and the house and hospital are open from 9 am to 4.30 pm daily. Feeding time is 3.30 pm.

The excellent **Hastings Historical Museum** on Clarence St, 1½ blocks east of Horton St, tells the story of Port Macquarie's early years with numerous convict artefacts.

It's open from 9.30 am to 4.30 pm Monday to Saturday, 1 to 4.30 pm Sunday, admission $3. On Wednesday and Sunday nights (7.30 in winter, 8.15 in summer) you can observe heavenly bodies from the **observatory** near Town Beach ($2).

Five km south of the town centre, between Miners Beach and Pacific Drive, **Sea Acres Rainforest Centre** is a 30-hectare flora & fauna reserve protecting a pocket of coastal rainforest. There's an ecology centre with displays and a 1.3 km raised boardwalk. Entry is $8.50.

Across the Hastings River

The 50c vehicle ferry across Hastings River at Settlement Point just out of Port Macquarie leads to two interesting roads north. A very rough dirt road right along the coast, past Limeburners Creek Nature Reserve with its saltwater lake, will take you to Point Plomer and Crescent Head, from where you can rejoin the highway at Kempsey.

The second road north from the Settlement Point Ferry – better and gravelled – takes a more inland route to meet the Crescent Head to Kempsey road.

Places to Stay

There are three hostels and lots of hotels, motels, holiday flats and camp sites. The competition keeps the costs down but in non-hostel places there's a 20% to 40% price variation between winter and summer, with school holiday times more expensive again, especially Christmas/New Year.

Hostels The three hostels are in hot competition and deals are possible during non-peak times. All have cooking facilities and discount deals with local businesses. Most central is *Backpackers Headquarters* (☎ (065) 83 1913) at 135 Horton St which has beds in small dorms for $10 and doubles/twins for $25/22. If there are five or more of you dorm beds are $8. You can hire bikes and tricycles for a small fee and there's a boat and car available. It has recently been totally renovated and a cafe and laundromat are being built.

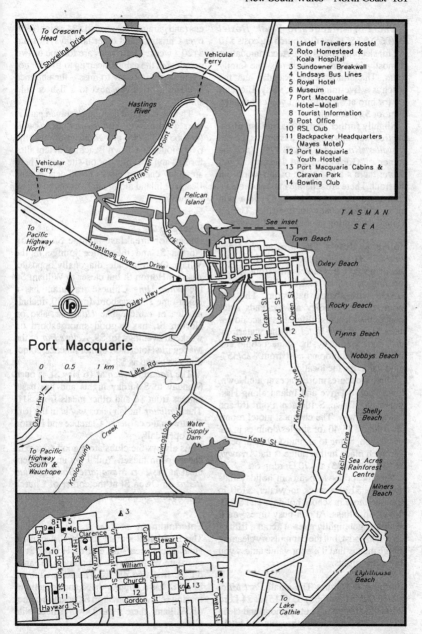

1 Lindel Travellers Hostel
2 Roto Homestead &
  Koala Hospital
3 Sundowner Breakwall
4 Lindsays Bus Lines
5 Royal Hotel
6 Museum
7 Port Macquarie
  Hotel–Motel
8 Tourist Information
9 Post Office
10 RSL Club
11 Backpacker Headquarters
   (Mayes Motel)
12 Port Macquarie
   Youth Hostel
13 Port Macquarie Cabins &
   Caravan Park
14 Bowling Club

Port Macquarie

0   0.5   1 km

The Port Macquarie *Youth Hostel* (☎ (065) 83 5512) at 40 Church St, costs $10 ($2 for sleeping sheet hire). Accommodation is mostly in dorms, but there's one family room. The atmosphere's friendly and the beach is a five-minute walk away. Bicycles are for hire at $2 a day and you can use the gym for $2 a session.

Slightly further from the centre but offering free pick-ups from the bus depots, *Lindel Travellers Hostel* (☎ (065) 83 1791) is on the corner of Gordon St and Hastings River Drive; there's a big globe of the world out the front. There are separate male and female dorms and the cost is $10, or $11 in a twin room, with a $1 charge for linen hire. There's a small swimming pool and free bicycles.

Hotels & Motels The *Macquarie Hotel* (☎ (065) 83 1011) at the end of Horton St, the main street, has motel units from $35/45 for singles/doubles and hotel rooms from $25/35 with shared bathroom. The pub rooms could be noisy at weekends since most of the local nightlife takes place downstairs. The *Royal Hotel* on the waterfront next door is run by the same people and rooms with bathrooms cost from $25/35 – good value for the location.

There are scores more places around town, down Pacific Drive and inland along Hastings River Drive, Settlement Point Rd and Oxley Highway. The cheapest motel rooms are around $35/40 for singles/doubles in the low season, rising to around $40/55 at peak. One such place in this range is the *Arrowyn* (☎ (065) 83 1633) at 170 Gordon St.

The cheapest two-bedroom holiday flats are about $120 a week in winter, $150 in summer, more in school holidays and $400-plus at Christmas. At non-busy times you'll be able to get nightly rates at about a fifth of the weekly cost, but the compulsory cleaning charge means that it's poor value unless you stay a few nights.

Camping & Cabins The small *Port Macquarie Cabins* (☎ (065) 83 1115) at 24 Lord St has old-fashioned but spacious and clean cabins with their own bathrooms and kitch-

ens (and garages) for around $24 a night ($38 over Christmas and other holidays) or from $120 a week. These rates are for one or two people, but the cabins sleep up to five for not much more. It's easy to miss – the entrance is down a driveway next to a fish & chip shop.

The most central camping/caravan park is the expensive *Sundowner Breakwall* (☎ (065) 83 2755) at 1 Munster St, near the river mouth and Town Beach, with tent sites for $14 and $30-plus for on-site vans. There are many cheaper places down near Flynns Beach or inland along the river or the Oxley highway.

Places to Eat

Places for breakfast include *Shades* on Horton St and the coffee lounge in the Village Centre arcade, diagonally opposite. Also on Horton St but closer to William St, the *Whar Hing* Chinese restaurant has a lunch-time smorgasbord for $6.50, including tea or coffee. The *Hot Wok*, also on Horton St, has a good smorgasbord on weekend evenings for $9. *Kelly's Bar* at the Macquarie Hotel has counter lunches, sometimes as cheap as $3.

The *Italian Kitchen* at 16 Hay St, is open Monday to Saturday nights and has pasta entrees from $6 and other meals from $11. The *Shalimar* Indian takeaway is in the Ritz Centre on the corner of Clarence and Horton Sts, open daily.

As always the clubs are a good source of cheap, plain tucker. You'll get an excellent meal at the *Port Macquarie Bowling Club Bistro* on Owen St at the corner of Church St. The *RSL Club*, on Short St, is good value.

Entertainment

The Lachlan Room in the Port Macquarie Hotel-Motel near the end of Horton St is open late Wednesday to Saturday, with bands on the first two nights. The RSL Club on Short St has a popular disco and sometimes touring acts. Also on Short St, near the corner of William, there's the Down Under Nite Club.

Getting There & Away
Air Oxley Airlines (☎ (065) 83 1955) flies daily to Sydney. The standard fare is $143 but there are many specials. Other standard fares include Lord Howe Island $154 and Brisbane $174. Check their agents at the corner of Horton and Bay Sts.

Bus Long-distance bus lines include Port Macquarie on their Sydney to Brisbane route, though not every service stops here. Lindsays (☎ (065) 83 1488 or 008 02 7944, toll-free) on Clarence St near the corner of Horton St has buses to Newcastle ($29), Sydney ($33), Brisbane ($45), Armidale ($30), Tamworth ($44) and various other destinations. Prices to destinations closer to Port Macquarie are high – $30 to Coffs Harbour.

Train The nearest station is Wauchope, 19 km inland, with four services daily northbound to Byron Bay and Murwillumbah, and southbound to Sydney ($48).

Getting Around
The Port Macquarie Bus Service (☎ (065) 83 2161) runs buses to Wauchope five times on weekdays, twice on Saturday and Sunday; to Lake Cathie and Kempsey; and a service around the town.

There are several car hire firms – the usual big names plus Rag-Top Rentals on the corner of Horton and Hayward Sts. *Port Venture* runs a two-hour river cruise, usually daily at 2 pm, from the wharf at the end of Clarence St.

PORT MACQUARIE TO COFFS HARBOUR
Wauchope (population 4200)
Nineteen km inland from Port Macquarie, Wauchope (pronounced 'war hope') is on the Hastings River west of Port Macquarie.

Timbertown is an interesting working replica of an 1880s timber town. It's open from 9 am to 5 pm daily and entry is $11 including rides (children $6). Lilybank Canoe Hire (☎ (065) 85 1600), on the river one km east of the town, has two-person

canoes for hire by the hour, day or week and can advise you on camping spots, etc, up the river. The **Big Bull**, a piece of kitsch billed as 'the world's biggest fibreglass bull', is three km east of Wauchope and houses educational displays, an animal nursery and a restaurant. It's open daily and entry is $5.

Wauchope has a range of accommodation including an associate *Youth Hostel* (☎ (065) 85 6134) at Rainbow Ridge, 11 km west on the Oxley Highway towards Tamworth. It costs $8 a night or you can pitch a tent in the grounds.

Oxley Wild Rivers National Park
North along the highway from Wauchope, 18 km before Walcha, the spectacular **Apsley Falls** are about one km off the highway. The falls, and the Apsley Gorge downstream, are part of the Oxley Wild Rivers National Park, and there are basic camping facilities near the falls. This national park is composed of several separate sections covering 300 sq km of the upper Apsley and Macleay Rivers and their tributaries. The northern part of the park is close to the Dorrigo to Armidale road. In the township of **Walcha** there is pub accommodation, a couple of motels and a caravan park with on-site vans.

Kempsey Area
North along the Pacific Highway from Wauchope is **Kempsey**, which is the home of the Akubra hat and has the Macleay River Historical Museum & Cultural Centre (entry $1) next to the tourist information centre (☎ (065) 62 5444) by the highway on the south side of town. This is worth a visit for the architecture alone – simple corrugated-iron structures which show that Australian architecture need not slavishly follow the lowest common denominator of overseas styles. There are some cheap on-site vans in caravan parks here – $16 at the *Willow Brook Caravan Park* (☎ (065) 62 7666) – but it's worth diverting off the highway to the coast at Hat Head, South West Rocks or Crescent Head.

Hat Head is a village with a caravan park and holiday flats at the foot of Hat Hill

Headland. There are good beaches and walks and part of the nearby coast is a national park. **South West Rocks** is another coastal resort village, near the mouth of the Macleay River, with good beaches and quite a range of accommodation. A big attraction is **Trial Bay Gaol** on the headland three km east of South West Rocks. This imposing edifice was a civil prison in the late 19th century and housed German POWs in WW I. It's now a museum with wonderful views, open daily from 9 am to 5 pm ($2.50). An attractive camping area surrounds the jail and there's a cafe in the grounds. Trial Bay is named after the brig *The Trial* which was stolen from Sydney by convicts in 1816 and wrecked here. **Smoky Cape Lighthouse**, a few km down the coast from the jail, can be inspected on Thursday (and Tuesday in school holidays) from 10 to 11.45 am and 1 to 2.45 pm. Mercury Roadlines (☎ (065) 62 4724) run buses from Kempsey to South West Rocks.

Crescent Head has a fine beach with famous surf, plus a camp site, other accommodation and restaurants, including a good health-food cafe. *Bush & Beach Retreat* (☎ (065) 66 0552) on Belmore River Rd sometimes has backpackers' beds, and during the low season it's worth checking the estate agents (☎ (065) 66 0500) as they might let houses for less than a week. This could be cheaper than on-site vans, which cost from $35. There's no daily letting in the summer and a van for a week costs $370 then. Camping costs $9 to $13.50.

Nambucca Heads (population 4900)
Just in from the mouth of the Nambucca (pronounced 'Nambucka') River, this little resort town is one of the better stops on the north coast. It's a laid-back place with good coastal scenery – great views from the headland above the river mouth.

On the river you can take a cruise, swim (at Bellwood) or hire windsurfers, canoes, boats or fishing tackle, while Nambucca Main Beach is one of several good surf spots. You can take white-water rafting trips with Wildwater Adventures (☎ (065) 53 4469) –

normally $70 for a day, but less for standby if you call after 4 pm the day before. Dive courses include those run by Mark Asquith (☎ (066) 55 2382). If worm racing interests you, visit the Worm Farm at Valla, seven km north along the highway.

Places to Stay *Nambucca Backpackers Hostel* (☎ (065) 68 6360) at 3 Newman St is a friendly place charging $9 in excellent four-bed dorms or double rooms. The amiable Norwegian-English couple who run it offer a variety of trips, from half-day outings to Taylors Arm or the impressive Bellingen bat colony and winery, to full-day visits to Dorrigo National Park. They'll pick you up on arrival and lend snorkel gear and boogie boards. From here it's a one-km walk through thick bush to the beach. You might come across wallabies in the evening.

On the highway not far from the bus stop is the *Last Resort* hostel (☎ (065) 68 8075), run by a couple of enthusiastic travellers who are getting the place together after a period of dubious management. It's relaxed and friendly and they offer sea-fishing trips ($20) and a beach barbecue ($10). Dorm beds go for $9 and there are twins at $10 a person. Their cafe selling affordable meals should be open by now.

The *Max Motel* (☎ (065) 68 6138) on Fraser St, the southern half of the town's main street, has rooms with glorious views of the river and ocean (but thin walls) from $30, and others for $28. Next door the *Blue Dolphin Motel* (☎ (065) 68 6700) is slightly more expensive. There is a clutch of caravan parks, most with tent sites and on-site vans, including the *White Albatross* (☎ (065) 68 6469)) by the river mouth, and the *Headland Caravan Park* (☎ (065) 68 6547)) which overlooks Main Beach. Holiday flats include *Marcel Towers* (☎ (065) 68 7041) on Wellington Drive by the river, which has flats from about $30 in the low season.

Places to Eat *Nambucca Heads Bowling Club* on Nelson St and the *RSL* on Fraser St both have restaurants with good-value meals – the bowling club's are cheaper. The *Golden*

Sands has pub meals, and *Midnight Express* opposite the pub is worth trying. *A Pizza This A Pizza That* at 40 Bowra St, the upper half of the main street, has pasta dishes from $9, pizzas from $8.50.

Getting There & Away Nambucca Heads is on the main rail route from Sydney to the north – the station is three km from town. Most bus companies go into the town on at least some of their Sydney to Brisbane runs – it's about $45 from Sydney or Brisbane, and $35 from Byron Bay. The company servicing the immediate area is Pells (☎ (065) 68 6106).

Inland from Nambucca Heads

The small town of **Bowraville** has a folk museum and many craft shops as well as a Saturday morning market. South of here is **Taylors Arm** where you'll find the 1903 Cosmopolitan, the hotel immortalised in that sad song *Pub with No Beer*.

Bellingen is a small, pleasant town on the banks of the Bellingen River, reached by turning off the Pacific Highway near **Urunga**, a popular fishing spot with a coastal lagoon, about halfway from Nambucca Heads to Coffs Harbour. At Bellingen you can hire canoes at the Oasis Cafe on the eastern edge of town. At **Thora**, 12 km west, Bushwhacker Expeditions (☎ (066) 55 8607) has day trips in canoes for $55 and rainforest treks.

From here the road climbs steeply up to Dorrigo. The rainforest of **Dorrigo National Park** is known for its orchids. There are several good walking tracks and it's well worth making the drive through dense forest to the Never Never picnic area, from where you can walk to waterfalls. Camping isn't allowed in the park but there's a range of accommodation, including camp sites, in Dorrigo. The new Dorrigo Rainforest Centre has an elevated walkway and good displays; take the park turn-off about one km east of Dorrigo. The park visitor centre (☎ (066) 57 2309) is a few km further on towards Bellingen.

Around Ebor, west of Dorrigo, the road to Armidale passes between two national parks on the eastern slopes of the New England plateau – **New England National Park**, with rainforest, heaths, valleys, escarpments and a 30-km walking track network; and **Cathedral Rock National Park** with spectacular rock formations. In the New England park there is a camp site and cabins on the Little Styx River in the Point Lookout area near the park entrance. The cabins sleep up to 10 and cost $35 for the first six people and $5 a head for the other four. For bookings phone (067) 75 9158) or contact the Dorrigo visitor centre.

North of Ebor and reached from the Grafton to Ebor or Grafton to Newton Boyd roads, **Guy Fawkes River National Park** is a vast wild area of the New England foothills – great if you like bushwalking for days without seeing anyone.

COFFS HARBOUR (population 44,300)

With Port Macquarie, Coffs Harbour (originally Koffs Harbour) is the major central north coast resort. The town centre is busy and nothing to write home about, but there's a harbour and some interesting headlands, and a string of good beaches stretch north. If you don't have your own transport it's a bit of a chore getting around the relatively long distances.

Information & Orientation

The Pacific Highway runs through town and it's called Grafton St in the middle. High St, the other main street in town, intersects with Grafton St at a pedestrian mall, and most of this end of town's accommodation, restaurants and nightlife is nearby. High St runs three km east, down to the harbour after which the town is named. This area is known as the Jetty.

The tourist office (☎ (066) 52 1522) is in Urana Park on Grafton St, near where Moonee St branches off.

Things to See

In town, **North Coast Botanic Gardens** on Hardacre St off High St focuses on the flora

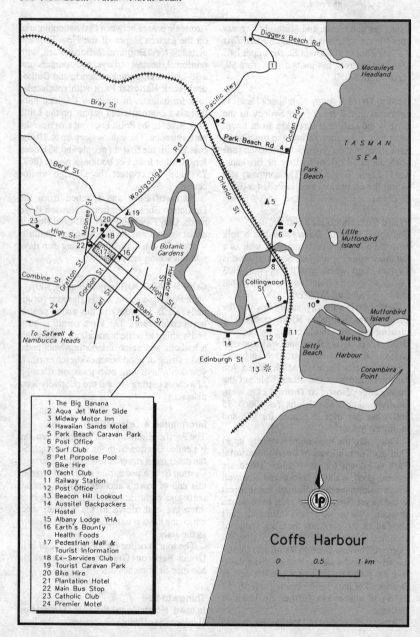

1   The Big Banana
2   Aqua Jet Water Slide
3   Midway Motor Inn
4   Hawaiian Sands Motel
5   Park Beach Caravan Park
6   Post Office
7   Surf Club
8   Pet Porpoise Pool
9   Bike Hire
10 Yacht Club
11 Railway Station
12 Post Office
13 Beacon Hill Lookout
14 Aussitel Backpackers
    Hostel
15 Albany Lodge YHA
16 Earth's Bounty
    Health Foods
17 Pedestrian Mall &
    Tourist Information
18 Ex–Services Club
19 Tourist Caravan Park
20 Bike Hire
21 Plantation Hotel
22 Main Bus Stop
23 Catholic Club
24 Premier Motel

Coffs Harbour

0   0.5   1 km

of the subtropical coast and is open daily from 10 am to 5 pm. Down at the end of High St the old timber-loading jetty still stands in the harbour. There are good views from **Beacon Hill Lookout** above the harbour up at the top of Edinburgh St, or from **Corambirra Point** on the south side of the harbour. You can walk out along the northern harbour wall to **Muttonbird Island**, a nature reserve where mutton birds (more formally called wedge-tailed shearwaters) breed. They lay eggs in underground burrows.

On Orlando St (the continuation of High St as it curves away from the harbour) there's a Pet Porpoise Pool, with shows twice daily. On Park Beach Rd near the corner of the Pacific Highway, the Aquajet is Coffs' water slide. **Bruxner Park Flora Reserve** with a nature trail, walking tracks and fine views over the coast, is nine km north-west in Orara East State Forest near Korora.

Beaches

Diggers Beach, protected by two headlands about three km north of the centre and reached by turning opposite the Big Banana, is worth travelling to. It has a nude section. North of Diggers there's another good beach at **Korora** and then a string of them up to Woolgoolga.

Activities

Coffs is a centre for 'adventure' activities like white-water rafting on the Nymboida River (medium hard standard, but no experience needed) and canoeing. The season for white-water rafting is November to May and several outfits run day trips from Coffs – you'd pay around $80 including two meals.

There's interesting scuba diving at the Solitary Islands, a few km up the coast, and Solitary Islands Diver Services (☎ 52 2422) are at 396 High St in Coffs. There are several dive courses available. Fishing is popular and it's possible to charter boats at the harbour. In June and July migrating humpback whales are often spotted. If you can't get out on the water, Muttonbird Island is a good place to watch from.

If you want to try abseiling (☎ 066) 51 4066), a full day includes instruction and meals and costs $71.

Places to Stay

Except in the hostels, expect prices in school holidays to rise by about 50% in midwinter and about 100% for Easter and Christmas/New Year.

Hostels Both hostels here are in good modern buildings. *Aussitel Backpackers Hostel* (☎ (066) 51 1871) at 312 High St, about 1½ km from the town centre and 500 metres from the harbour, is a lively place with dorm beds at $11 and $13 per person in doubles. It has all the usual hostel facilities plus good spacious communal areas and a pool. The enthusiastic management will help fix up white-water rafting, diving and other trips, and will pick you up on arrival and give rides to the beach during the day or the pub at night. There's a nice stretch of river over the road and canoes are free. Their discounts around town include $3 off entry to the Big Banana.

Albany Lodge (☎ (066) 52 6462), the YHA hostel at 110 Albany St, a block off High St and only one km from the town centre, is a friendly place. Dorm beds cost $10 and there are a few double rooms for $22. You can hire bicycles for $6 a day and surfboards for $5. The hostel is open all day and will pick you up if you arrive at a 'reasonable hour' – at night phone in advance to ask. You can fix up trips and activities here and they run excursions such as day trips to the Dorrigo area for $25.

Hotels Many of the town's hotels have accommodation and for singles it's fair value. Officially on Moonee St (although it looks to be on Grafton St) the *Fitzroy Hotel* (☎ (066) 52 3007) has singles/doubles for $15/30. Further down Grafton St, opposite the Ex-Services Club, the *Plantation Hotel* (☎ (066) 52 3855) has rooms from $20/25 for singles/doubles.

Motels & Holiday Flats There's a bunch of motels on Grafton St across from the tourist office; in the low season there might be price-cutting wars, although you'd be lucky to get below $30. They include *Bells* (☎ (066) 521493), *Toreador* (☎ (066) 52 3887), *Safari* (☎ (066) 521900) and *Golden Glow* (☎ (066) 52 2644).

If you want to be near the ocean, there's a second motel area on Ocean Parade and Park Beach Rd. *Park Beach Hotel/Motel* (the Hoey Moey) (☎ (066) 52 3833) on Park Beach Rd has singles/doubles from $25/32 and around the corner on Ocean Parade *Hawaiian Sands Motel* (☎ (066) 52 2666) is similar. They'll collect you from the airport, bus terminal or railway station. There are quite a few others in this area, all liable to sudden price-drops if business is slow.

The tourist information centre can tell you about holiday flats. These generally cost $40-plus per night and usually demand a seven day minimum booking in the high season.

Camping & Cabins The huge *Park Beach Caravan Park* (☎ (066) 52 3204) on Ocean Parade, one km north of the harbour and just north of the mouth of Coffs Harbour Creek, is right next to the beach and has tent sites at $10 a double, on-site vans for $25 and cabins from $33. The *Tourist Caravan Park* on the highway a couple of blocks on from the Ex-Services club has vans from $18 and cabins from $28. There are plenty of other places along the Pacific Highway north or south of town.

Island View Holiday Cabins (☎ (066) 53 6753) on Split Solitary Rd, North Sapphire, are pleasant, fully equipped, only 200 metres from the beach and cost $32 a double outside school holidays, when prices rise and you have to rent by the week.

Places to Eat
Some of the best cheap eats can be found in the various clubs – once you get past the massed ranks of poker machines by which they earn their living! The large Coffs *Ex-Services Club* on the corner of Grafton and Vernon Sts, has lunches and dinners for around $10 in its bistro. The *Catholic Club*

on High St, about one km inland from Grafton St, offers even better quality lunches and dinners at reasonable prices, and cheap beer.

Cafe Cezanne at 18 Elizabeth St, close to where Grafton St meets the Pacific Highway, has good French food but it's pricey. On Grafton St, near the corner of High St, the choice includes a Chinese restaurant, the *New Red Rose* (with lunch specials) and two pizza places. On Gordon St at the other end of the mall, *Earth's Bounty Health Foods* sells good takeaways. Among the many places to eat during the day on the mall, *Arons* is a stand which does good coffee and toasted sandwiches and is open for breakfast. Counter meals at *Hotel Coffs Harbour* are cheap, with daily specials under $6.

There's a string of restaurants at the Jetty, the harbour end of High St, a few blocks from the backpackers' hostel. In the same block there are Chinese, Mexican, Italian and French restaurants – plus the excellent *Fisherman's Katch* where a slap-up seafood meal will set you back around $25. Best value here are the meals at the *Pier Hotel*.

South of Coffs, the *Sawtell Hotel* has good, cheap seafood meals.

Entertainment
Nightclubs come and go quickly, but most are open until early morning every night. Currently popular are High St 66 and Oscars, both on the mall. The Hoey Moey has bands at weekends, sometimes quite big touring bands. Crystal's Night Club in the Ex-Services Club has bands and/or a disco and when top names come to Coffs this is usually where they play. Karaoke is booming and you have the opportunity to make a fool of yourself most nights at one of the clubs or pubs.

Getting There & Away
Air Ansett Express has direct flights from Sydney ($165), Ballina and Casino; Eastern from Brisbane, the Gold Coast, Lismore, Newcastle, Port Macquarie, Taree and Armidale; and Oxley Airlines from Brisbane and the Gold Coast.

Bus All the long-distance lines on the Sydney to Brisbane route stop at Coffs. The main stop is in Moonee St just west of the Pacific Highway in the town centre. It's about $44 to Sydney and $41 to Brisbane. There are also services to New England. As usual, it pays to ask for special deals, and check notice boards at the hostels.

Local buses (☎ (066) 54 1590) run to Woolgoolga ($4) and Grafton ($8) but only Monday to Friday.

Train The railway station (☎ (066) 52 2312) is down by the harbour near the end of High St. To Sydney it's $57; Brisbane $42.

Boat Coffs is a good place to pick up a ride along the coast on a yacht or cruiser. Ask around, or put a notice in the yacht club at the harbour – sometimes the hostels know of boat owners who are looking for people to help out.

Getting Around
There's a local bus service connecting the Jetty, the centre and Park Beach, but services are infrequent; none on Sunday. Bicycles are available for rent from Bob Wallis Bicycle Centre (☎ (066) 52 5102) on the corner of Collingwood and Orlando Sts.

COFFS HARBOUR TO TWEED HEADS
Woolgoolga (population 2300)
Twenty-six km north of Coffs, Woolgoolga is a pleasant fishing port and small resort with a fine surf beach. It has a sizable Indian Sikh population who have a gurdwara (place of worship), the **Guru Nanak Temple**, on River St, just off the highway at the south end of town. The restaurant across the road has good Indian food. More obvious than the temple is the Raj Mahal tourist trap at the northern turn-off, where there's a tandoori restaurant.

At the *Woolgoolga Beach reserve* (☎ (066) 54 1373) tent sites are $8, vans are $22, and cabins $32, rising to $9, $32 and $49 over Christmas. There are other camp sites further from the beach which are slightly cheaper.

Yuraygir National Park
Red Rock, off the highway but on the coast 10 km north of Woolgoolga, is on the edge of the southern section of the coastal Yuraygir National Park. Yuraygir covers 60 km of coast in three separate sections, the northern one reaching nearly to Yamba at the mouth of the Clarence River. The park's varied coastal landscape includes quiet beaches, lakes and waterways and there's plenty of scope for activities like fishing, surfing, swimming, canoeing, walking or just lying on beaches. There are several camp sites in the park, plus a range of accommodation in small coastal resorts nearby.

The central section of Yuraygir can be reached from the Wooli Rd off the Pacific Highway 15 km south of Grafton, or from the Maclean to Brooms Head road, north of Grafton. You can reach the northern section through Angourie, south of Yamba, or from the Maclean to Brooms Head road.

Grafton (population 16,350)
Grafton, a quiet country town on the Clarence River which flows down from the New England highlands near the Queensland border, is noted for its jacaranda and other tropical trees. There's a Jacaranda Festival in late October. The 1880 **Prentice House** on Fitzroy St is now an art gallery, and nearby **Schaeffer House** is a historical museum.

Grafton is on the main bus and rail routes north – though it's now bypassed by the Pacific Highway. There's a tourist information centre (☎ (066) 42 4677) on the Pacific Highway. You can take cruises on the Clarence River and the tourist information centre can tell you about local farms and timber mills which run regular tours. There are several interesting national parks in the area and a national parks district office (☎ (066) 42 0613) at 50 Victoria St.

Places to Stay There are several pubs with beds under $20, but much better value is the *Rathgar Guest House* (☎ (066) 42 7930) on the Pacific Highway south of town, next to the Caltex station. Built in 1865, it's being carefully restored and for $10 a person (spacious dorms and a few single and double rooms) you get high ceilings, cedar floors, and free brewed coffee. It's a million miles from the standard tacky hostel. There are $6 evening meals or you can cook in the communal kitchen.

Grafton to Ballina

From Grafton the highway follows the Clarence River north-east and the fishing port of **Maclean** is just off the highway close to the river mouth. Maclean celebrates its Scottish early settlers with a Highland Gathering each Easter.

East of Maclean, off the highway and at the river mouth, **Yamba** is a fishing town and a small but busy resort with good beaches and some cheap motels and caravan parks. A ferry ($2.50, four daily) links Yamba with Iluka on the north side of the river mouth. There are buses from Grafton (☎ (066) 42 2779) and Maclean to Yamba. Just south of Yamba, **Angourie** is one of the coast's top spots for experienced surfers, but beware rip tides. After the Clarence River, **Bundjalung National Park** lies between the highway and the coast. There are good beaches, canoeing, surfing and fishing in the park, plus lots of wildlife and some old Aboriginal camp sites. The main access points are Iluka and Evans Head at the south and north ends of the park. Both places have camp sites, van parks and motels.

Woodburn is where you turn off the highway for Evans Head, or turn inland for Casino and Lismore. Those with an interest in Papua New Guinea's history may want to see the monument and remains of New Italy, a settlement formed from the tattered remnants of the Marquis de Ray's plan to colonise the New Guinea island of New Ireland.

Ballina (population 12,500)

This busy town, on both the Pacific Highway and an island at the mouth of the Richmond River, is popular for sailing and fishing and has some ocean beaches too. There's often good surf nearby at Black Rock and Speed Reef.

The information centre (☎ (066) 86 3484), by the river at the south end of Norton St, contains one of the three balsa wood rafts from the La Balsa expedition that drifted across the Pacific from Ecuador to Ballina in 177 days in 1973. The museum is open daily and a video about the raft voyage plays constantly. They rent bikes for $6 a half day or $11 for the whole day.

Ballina has the historic **Shaws Bay Hotel** in Brighton St, East Ballina, and a busy little shipbuilding yard. Eleven km west on the Bruxner Highway there is a **Tropical Fruit Research Station**, open for visits on Mondays and Thursdays at 10 am.

Sunray Car Rentals (☎ (066) 86 7315) at 268 River St have cars from $30 a day, plus insurance. All the long-distance bus companies stop here, and there's a local service (☎ (066) 86 2024) stopping at the Esso station on Cherry St which runs to Lennox Head and Byron Bay.

Places to Stay & Eat On the highway west of town, next to where the long-distance buses (except Kirklands) stop and diagonally opposite the Big Prawn, *Oasis* (☎ (066) 86 2575) is a converted motel with dorm beds for $12 and doubles for $28. The manager will run you into town or you can hire bikes for $2 a day.

The *Ballina Travellers Lodge* (☎ (066) 86 6737) is a modern YHA hostel in town at 36-38 Tamar St and has single ($11), double ($25) and family ($34) rooms. There are also motel units. Bikes and boogie boards cost 50c an hour to hire and there's a pool. *Flat Rock Camping Park* on Coast Rd just north of the town is a good tent-only camp site, next to a surfing beach. There are numerous motels and a camping/caravan park too.

At *Popeye's* hamburger bar on River St you can have a sit-down curry for under $5, and they do breakfast as well. Nearby, *Local Motion* is an above-average pasta place. The *Ex-Services Club* has good food and river views. Twice a week the *Bowling Club* has a big seafood dinner for $17.

Lennox Head (population 2200)

From Ballina the Pacific Highway again runs a little inland but you'll hardly add one km to the journey if you follow the coast road from Ballina to Byron Bay. Long-distance buses take this route.

Lennox Head is the name of both the small, pleasant town with a fine beach and of the dramatic headland that overlooks it, 11 km out of Ballina and 18 km from Byron Bay. A number of travellers have written to say that they've enjoyed their stay here. It has some of the best surf on the coast, particularly in winter. Lake Ainsworth just back from the beach is a freshwater lake, good for swimming and windsurfing. Its dark colour is due to tea-tree oil, supposedly good for the skin and hair, seeping in from the surrounding vegetation.

Places to Stay & Eat

Lennox Beach House Hostel (☎ (066) 87 7636), very close to the lake and beach at Lot 2 & 3 Ross St, is a good, purpose-built hostel and the management is competent and friendly. Dorm beds cost $12 and there's a double room for $27. For $5 you get the use of the catamaran for as long as you stay, and bicycles, boards and other gear are free. Ring and see if they can give you a lift from Byron Bay. Across the road is *Lake Ainsworth Caravan Park* (☎ (066) 87 7249) with tent sites (from $9) and cabins ($22; $30 in the high season). You can get a good meal for $6 to $7 in the *Bowling Club Bistro*. *Lennox Health & Bulk Foods*, on the main street, has excellent takeaways and eat-in meals such as Indonesian food cooked in banana leaves. The *Lennox Point Hotel* has bands three nights a week.

BYRON BAY (population 3500)

Byron Bay is one of the most attractive stops on the whole east coast: a relaxed little seaside town with superb beaches and a great climate – warm in winter, hot in summer. Tourism is low key and Byron is a meeting place of alternative cultures: it's a surfing Mecca thanks to the superb surf below Cape Byron, and is also close to the 'back to the land' lifestyles pursued in the beautiful far north coast hinterland. There are good music venues, wholefood and vegetarian eateries, off-beat people, distinctive craft and clothes shops, a thriving fashion and surf industry, and numerous opportunities to learn yogic dance, take a massage or naturopathic therapy, have your stars read and so on. The Byron Bay market, in Butler St on the first Sunday of each month, is one of a series around the area at which the counterculture (almost establishment up here!) gets a chance to meet and sell its wares.

Information & Orientation

Byron Bay is six km east of the Pacific Highway. The tourist information centre (☎ (066) 85 8050) is in the muralled community centre on Jonson St, about 200 metres south of the roundabout. You can leave packs here between 10 am and 4 pm on weekdays for $1. Pick up a copy of the quirky weekly paper *Echo* to get an idea of the way of life around here.

Cape Byron

Cape Byron was named by Captain Cook after the poet Byron's grandfather, who had sailed round the world in the 1760s. One spur of the cape is the most easterly point of the Australian mainland. You can drive right up to the picturesque 1901 lighthouse on top of the cape. The lighthouse is one of the most powerful in the southern hemisphere. There's a fine 3½-km walking track right round the cape from the Captain Cook Lookout on Lighthouse Rd. It's circular, so you can leave bikes at the start. There's a good chance of seeing wallabies in the final rainforest stretch.

Beaches

The Byron area has a glorious collection of beaches, ranging from 10 km stretches of empty sand to secluded little coves, popular sunsoakers' strips to fine surf beaches. **Main Beach** immediately in front of the town is a good swimming beach and sometimes has decent surf. To the west and north the sand stretches 50 km plus, all the way to the Gold

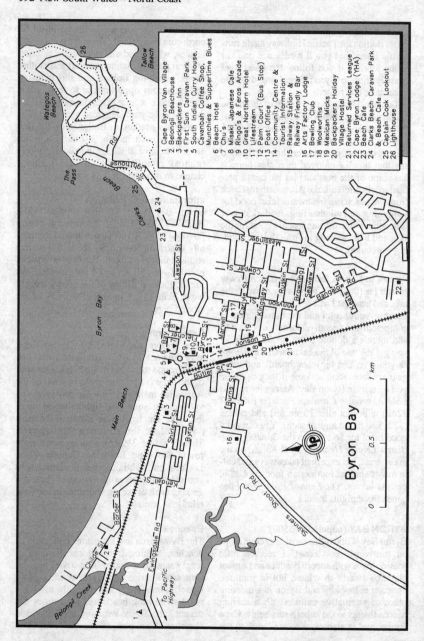

1 Cape Byron Van Village
2 Belongil Beachhouse
3 Backpackers Inn
4 First Sun Caravan Park
5 South Indian Curry House,
  Cavanbah Coffee Shop,
  Munchies & Suppertime Blues
6 Beach Hotel
7 Chu's
8 Misaki Japanese Cafe
9 Ringo's & Feros Arcade
10 Great Northern Hotel
11 Lifestream
12 Palm Court (Bus Stop)
13 Post Office
14 Community Centre &
  Tourist Information
15 Railway Station &
  Railway Friendly Bar
16 Arts Factory Lodge
17 Bowling Club
18 Woolworths
19 Mexican Micks
20 Backpackers Holiday
  Village Hostel
21 Returned Services League
22 Cape Byron Lodge (YHA)
23 Beach Cafe
24 Clarks Beach Caravan Park
  & Beach Cafe
25 Captain Cook Lookout
26 Lighthouse

Byron Bay

Coast, interrupted only by river or creek entrances and a few small headlands.

The eastern end of Main Beach, curving away towards Cape Byron, is known as **Clarks Beach** and can be good for surfers. The headland at the end of Clarks is called the Pass and the best surf is to be found off here and the next beach, **Watego's Beach**. **Little Watego's Beach** is a bit further round, almost at the tip of the cape. It's about three km from the town centre to Watego's and a road runs all the way. Dolphins are quite a common sight, particularly in the surf off Watego's and Little Watego's beaches, and a whale watch is mounted on Cape Byron in June and July each year to count humpback whales, which can sometimes be seen on their annual journey from Antarctica to the Great Barrier Reef.

South of Cape Byron, **Tallow Beach** stretches seven km down to a rockier stretch of shore around Broken Head, where a succession of small beaches (clothes optional) dot the coast before opening on to **Seven Mile Beach** which goes all the way to Lennox Head, a further 10 km south. You can reach Tallow from various points along the Byron Bay to Lennox Head road, which is parallel to the beach about 750 metres inland. The turning to the small settlement of **Suffolk Park** (with more good surf, particularly in winter, and a camping/caravan park) is five km from Byron Bay.

A further km down the Byron to Lennox road is the turning into the 1¾-km side road leading to the Broken Head Caravan Park at the south end of Tallow Beach. About 200 metres before the caravan park on this side road, the unsurfaced Seven Mile Beach Rd turns off south and runs along the back of the Broken Head coastal rainforest, a nature reserve. Seven Mile Beach Rd ends after five km (at the north end of Seven Mile Beach), but several tracks lead down from it through the forest to the Broken Head beaches – **Kings Beach** (for which there's a car park 750 metres down Seven Mile Beach Rd) and **Whites Beach** (a foot track after about 3¼ km) are just two good ones. Kings Beach is a nude beach.

Activities

Day trips in a 4WD to hinterland highlights like Minyon Falls, Mt Warning and the Border Ranges cost around $35 with operators like Damien Wilkinson's Big Scrub Tours (contact Byron Transit & Travel (☎ (066) 85 6554). Byron Bus & Coach in Marvel St does some coach tours such as to the Border Ranges and the Sunday markets at Nimbin and the Channon for $25.

Julian Rocks, three km offshore, is a meeting point of cold southerly currents and warm northerly ones, with a profusion of marine species from both. You can take diving courses or trips from Byron with Oz Dive (☎ (066) 85 6197) on Jonson St near the roundabout or Byron Bay Dive Centre (☎ (066) 85 7149) at 9 Lawson St. Sundive (☎ (066) 85 7755) on the corner of Lawson and Fletcher Sts has been recommended. There are also cheaper snorkelling trips.

Some hostels supply surfboards to their guests – or you can hire them from Maddog (☎ (066) 85 6395) at 91 Jonson St – $10 for a half day or $20 for the whole day. Boogie boards (free at all hostels) are $6 and $12.

Cape Byron is good for hang-gliding, and tandem flights (ie inexperienced you and a competent pilot) are possible (☎ (066) 84 7328). Tandem parachute jumps are available, but are expensive (☎ (066) 80 1448).

Places to Stay

Prices are higher at holiday times, particularly in summer. Some cafes – especially Suppertime Blues – have notice boards where longer-term places are advertised.

Hostels *Backpackers Holiday Village Hostel* (☎ 85 7660), at 116 Jonson St, close to the bus stop, is a clean, friendly, well-equipped place with a small pool – it does, however, feel a bit cramped and it's quite strictly run. Beds cost $11 or $26 for a double, and there's one double with bathroom for $33. Bicycles, surfboards and boogie boards are free.

To reach the *Arts Factory Lodge* (☎ (066) 85 7709) turn left at the 'Skinners Shoot Rd' sign just west of the railway crossing and follow the road (initially called Butler St) for one km. Turn left onto Burns St, left onto Wordsworth, then almost immediately right onto Gordon and follow the signs. Rooms are around a good-sized pool and dorms are $10 and doubles $25. Camping on a small island in the lodge garden costs $6. Bikes, boogie boards and snorkelling gear are free. It's a relaxed and friendly place in a good setting. They will pick you up from the bus stop.

The *Backpackers Inn* (☎ (066) 85 8231) is at 29 Shirley St, the main road out to the Pacific Highway, about half a km from the town centre. It's a modern hostel with a pool, and only a couple of minutes' walk from Main Beach. Rooms have ceiling fans and mostly have one double bed and one bunk. It's $11 per person or around $30 a double. The hostel is well equipped and clean, and bikes and boogie boards are free. They'll meet you at the bus stop.

Belongil Beachouse (☎ (066) 85 7868) is on Childe St, two km out by road but a shorter walk along the beach. It's just across a quiet road from the beach dunes and is excellent value at $11 a bed or about $30 a double. All rooms have ceiling fans and running water. It's a well-designed place and more than just a bed for the night. There's a good cafe with a nightly half-price special for guests – big servings of good food for around $3.50. To reach it by road follow Shirley St west about one km from the centre, then turn right along Kendall St for about 700 metres (Kendall St changes its name to Border St then Childe St). Phone to arrange a free taxi on arrival.

Byron Bay's associate YHA is the *Cape Byron Lodge* (☎ (066) 85 6445) about two km south of the centre at 78 Bangalow Rd. This is the cheapest in town with dorms at $10.50 for nonmembers and doubles for $29. It's popular, friendly, open all day, doesn't impose duties and offers free surfboards and bikes. It has a small pool and is less than 10 minutes' walk from Tallow Beach. The manager can pick you up from the centre on arrival if you ring.

Camping & Caravan Parks The best sites can be full in summer and at Easter. There are a number of council-run places. *First Sun Caravan Park* (☎ (066) 85 6544) is right by Main Beach, one minute's walk from the town centre. *Clarks Beach Caravan Park* (☎ (066) 85 3353) is one km east of the town centre. Both places levy a charge for day visitors, and Clarks Beach in particular is not known for its friendliness to suspected 'hippies'. The shady *Suffolk Park Caravan Park* (☎ (066) 85 3353) is beside Tallow Beach, five km south of Byron Bay centre, and *Broken Head Caravan Park* (☎ (066) 85 3245) is three km further south. See the earlier Beaches section for directions. All these have tent sites from $9; on-site vans and cabins cost about $24 and up.

Cape Byron Van Village (☎ (066) 85 7378), two km out of town on the road to the Pacific Highway, costs about the same as the council places. *Glen Villa Mobile Home Park* (☎ (066) 85 7382), on Butler St close to the town centre charges from $10 for tents and $30 for on-site vans.

Hotels, Motels, Flats & Resorts The *Great Northern Hotel* on Jonson St has singles/doubles for $15/25. Cheaper motels include *Glen Villa Village* (☎ (066) 85 7382) on Butler St near the post office and *Sunaway Motel* (☎ (066) 85 3369) in Suffolk Park at 42 Alcorn St. Most motels and holiday flats are on Bay St, facing Main Beach, or Lawson St out towards Cape Byron. Their prices are generally high but a week of wet weather will send them tumbling.

For holiday flats you often have to book ahead and commit yourself to several days, but at slack times you'll probably find something on the spot by asking in the tourist information centre or estate agents. Expect to pay at least $60 a night or $280 a week.

The *Byron Bay Beach Resort* (☎ (066) 85 8000) out on Bayshore Drive, three km out of town towards the Pacific Highway then 1½ km north, fronts the beach and has tennis, golf and horse riding. A 'chalet' costs from $79 a double, but there are sometimes off-season specials.

Places to Eat

Byron Bay has a wide variety of restaurants, and vegetarians are particularly well catered for.

Working south down Jonson St away from the beach, the big new *Beach Hotel* has main courses from $8 and burgers from $3.50. The very popular *South Indian Curry House* is open every evening till 10 pm with main courses from around $8. Just a few doors down, *Cavanbah Coffee Shop* with a few outdoor tables is a busy daytime place with excellent coffee, reasonably priced snacks and breakfast and lunch bargains.

On the same block *Munchies* and the newer *Suppertime Blues* offer similar vegetarian fare, almost side by side. Both are open daily until 6 pm, later in the summer. Munchies has at least 10 'no smoking' signs; Summertime Blues has a good notice board. Prices are small; servings big.

By the roundabout at the corner of Jonson and Lawson Sts, *Earth & Sea Pizzas* has a large range of pizzas, pasta and salads with prices ranging between $7.50 and $9.90. It's one of the best eateries in town. Across the road, *Ringo's* has snacks and meals, including breakfast, has a notice board and plays good background music. In Feros Arcade, *Annabella's* is a spaghetti bar open to 10 pm in summer, 5 pm on weekdays in winter, later on weekends. Next door *Mykonos Taverna* is open from 6 pm and has main courses at around $14. The cheap and busy *Indian Curry House* is also in the arcade.

On Jonson St, between the Earth & Sea Pizza and the railway station, are several places, including *Fondue Inn*. The idea here is to share main dishes – good value for a group. Another few doors down, *Lifestream* is a large health food eatery with excellent and cheap food, although it's only open from 9.30 am to 5 pm. Nearby in Palm Court, *Network Brasserie* is open from 6.30 pm until late daily except Sunday. The have cocktails and a wide range of beers (pricey), and pastas start at about $7.50; steaks at $14. To get served in the bar you have to express 'an intention to dine'.

Counter meals at the *Great Northern*

Hotel aren't especially cheap. The *Railway Friendly Bar*, in what used to be part of the station, is a fine watering hole with outdoor tables and snacks and meals. They have backpackers' specials. Opposite Woolworth's the long-standing and licensed *Mexican Micks* is still reasonably priced with most main meals less than $12 and weekly backpackers 'all you can eat' deals. Down Jonson St, the *Returned Services League* has a weekly seafood smorgasbord for $17.

At 11 Lawson St, a few metres in the Cape Byron direction from the central roundabout, *Chu's* Chinese restaurant has good cheap food with many main meals under $8.

The *Byron Bay Chinese Restaurant* in the Marvel St bowling club has lunch specials and $7.50 smorgasbords on Thursday between 5.30 and 7.30 pm. None of their main courses are over $9 and a large fried rice is only $3.50.

Fletcher St runs the short distance from Lawson St to the beach and here the relaxed *Misaki Japanese Cafe* (☎ (066) 85 7966) serves delicious food but portions are small. It's open for lunch and dinner most days; main meals start at $9.50. They prefer you to book. On the beach near the Clarks Beach caravan park the *Beach Cafe* serves breakfast from 7.30 am and does a variety of good snacks. It's not cheap – bacon and eggs cost from $6.50 – but the views are superb.

Entertainment

The Railway Friendly Bar has music most nights. It's a good place for a beer or two in any case, and is popular with locals and visitors. The Beach Hotel has bands several nights a week. The Returned Services League has bands (often touring) on Friday and Saturday (from rock to Kenny Ball) and free films on Sunday at 8 pm. The Piggery, near the Arts Factory Lodge, was a popular venue but has been recently sold. Check to see whether it has re-opened.

Getting There & Away

Bus Numerous buses go through Byron Bay northbound and southbound. To Brisbane it costs $21 with Kirklands and to Sydney it's

$58 with Kirklands or Greyhound/Pioneer. To Coffs Harbour costs about $35, to Surfers Paradise it's about $15.

Kirklands runs short distances around Byron Bay – to Murwillumbah, Ballina or Tweed Heads for instance. There are services several times daily to/from Lismore ($7), sometimes via Ballina. The main booking agent is Byron Bay Travel Centre (☎ (066) 85 6733) in Palm Court, opposite the Great Northern Hotel on Jonson St and near the bus stops.

You can get direct buses to Melbourne or Adelaide from Byron Bay – for more details see the Brisbane section.

Train Byron is on the Sydney to Murwillumbah coastal line, but only one train a day comes through in each direction. However there are several co-ordinated rail-bus services in each direction daily. From Sydney ($65) the quickest is the 7.15 am XPT, reaching Byron at 7.30 pm. This train continues to Murwillumbah ($5.40) and connects with a bus to Brisbane (total cost from Byron $20.50).

Getting Around

Bus Hitching is an accepted part of the scene around the area, but there are a few local bus services, including Kirklands (☎ (066) 21 2755) (see Getting There & Away) and Blanch's Bus Service (☎ (066) 85 6430). Byron Bus and Coach (☎ (066) 85 6533) on Marvel St, has a bus to and from Mullumbimby four times daily Monday to Friday. They run a $15 day tour to The Channon market and Protesters Falls on the second Sunday of each month.

Car & Motorcycle Byron Bay Motor Rentals (☎ (066) 85 8140) costs a little less than the majors. The repair shop opposite Woolworths hires motorbikes for $45 for 24 hours, but you must have a motorbike licence.

Bicycle All the hostels lend bikes to guests and Backpackers Holiday Village Hostel also rent them to nonguests. Let's Go Bikes (next to Maddog on Jonson St), rents good bikes at $3.50 an hour or $12 a day.

BYRON BAY TO MURWILLUMBAH

The Pacific Highway continues north from the Byron Bay turn-off to the state border at Tweed Heads. Just after the Mullumbimby turn-off is **Brunswick Heads**, a river-mouth town with a small fishing fleet and several caravan parks and motels.

A few more km up the highway the *New Brighton Hotel*, the old village pub of **Billinudgel**, is a friendly place for a beer and a counter meal. If you take the next turn to the right off the highway (the sign says South Golden Beach) and work your way through the housing estate to the shore, there's a rough dirt road running north behind the beach, up to Wooyung, and any number of sheltered free camp sites behind the dunes along the way.

A paved road runs right up the coast from Wooyung nearly all the way to Tweed Heads and makes an alternative to the Pacific Highway for this stretch. This coast is known as the Tweed Coast, and is much less developed than the Gold Coast to the north. **Bogangar/Cabarita** and **Kingscliff** are two small laid-back resorts. At Cabarita is the *Emu Park Backpackers Resort* (☎ (066) 76 1190), a new purpose-built hostel. Dorm beds are $12 and doubles are $27. They have free bikes, boogie boards and surfboards and it's a minute to the beach. They will collect you from the Coolangatta Transit Centre or Murwillumbah if you phone. Tweed Bus Service runs down the coast to Pottsville about four times a day during the week, once on Saturday (11 am from the tourist office stop) and none on Sunday. More frequent services run as far as Kingscliff.

MURWILLUMBAH (population 7800)

The last sizable town on the Pacific Highway before you reach the Gold Coast, Murwillumbah is in a banana and sugar-cane-growing area in the broad Tweed Valley. It's a 15-minute drive to the coast. There are several communes and 'back to the earth' centres in this area and you're within reach of Mt Warning and the spectacular New South Wales-Queensland border ranges. You can cross into Queensland by the Numinbah Rd through the ranges between the Springbrook and Lamington areas (see the Queensland chapter for more details). The excellent **Tweed River Gallery** is just up the road from the hostel. The tourist information centre (☎ (066) 72 1340) is on the Pacific Highway near the railway station.

Places to Stay & Eat
The YHA associate *Backpackers Lodge* (☎ (066) 72 3763) is at 1 Tumbulgum Rd beside the Tweed River – you'll see it on the right as you cross the bridge into town. It's a friendly place in a good location and some meals are communal. There are free canoes and rowing boats, plus evening river trips and outings to some of the area's many natural highlights, as well as to the weekly Sunday feast at the large Hare Krishna Farm a few km away on Tyalgum Rd, Eungella. Dorm beds are $11 and doubles are $24.

The *Riverview Hotel* on the highway has singles $15 or $17 with bathroom and doubles with bathroom for $25. Rooms at the front are noisy.

Getting There & Away
Murwillumbah is served by nearly all the buses on the Sydney (about $65) to Brisbane ($18) coastal run and is the end of the coastal rail line from Sydney. There's an XPT daily ($69), arriving at 10.30 pm and this connects with buses to the Gold Coast ($7 to Coolangatta, and $13 to Surfers Paradise) and Brisbane ($18). Heading for Sydney the train leaves at 9.15 pm.

TWEED HEADS (population 44,750)
Tweed Heads, at the mouth of the Tweed River, marks the southern end of the Gold Coast strip. The south side of Boundary St, which runs along a short peninsula to Point Danger above the river mouth, is in Tweed Heads and New South Wales, while the north side is in Coolangatta and Queensland. This end of the Gold Coast is a quieter place to stay than the resorts closer to Surfers Paradise.

The New South Wales Government Travel Centre (☎ (075) 36 4244) on Wharf St (the Pacific Highway) in the middle of town is open from 9 am to 5 pm daily.

Things to See
At Point Danger the towering **Captain Cook Memorial** straddles the state border. The 18-metre-high monument was completed in 1970 (the bicentenary of Cook's visit) and is topped by a laser beam lighthouse visible 35 km out to sea. The replica of the *Endeavour*'s capstan is made from ballast dumped by Cook after the *Endeavour* ran aground on the Great Barrier Reef, and recovered along with the ship's cannons in 1968. Point Danger was named by Cook after he nearly ran aground there too. Three km from Tweed Heads there are views over the Tweed Valley and the Gold Coast from the **Razorback Lookout**.

Places to Stay
Accommodation in Tweed Heads spills over into Coolangatta and up the Gold Coast, and the choice is more varied as well. See the Gold Coast section for more details. In Tweed there are motels, holiday flats and caravan parks with the usual prices and facilities.

Places to Eat
Meals at the *Rowing & Aquatic Club* on Coral St cost between $3.50 and $7.50. *Fisherman's Cove*, next door, is an excellent seafood specialist, but it's pricey. On Marine Parade, *Doyles on the Beach* is also good and has main courses at about $19. Upstairs at the Surf Lifesaving Club next to Doyles, the *Romano Room* has seafood from about $15 for main courses and a Friday night luau (Hawaian feast) and a pig-out smorgasbord for $15. Again, see also the Coolangatta entries in the Gold Coast section of the Queensland chapter.

Entertainment
The large Twin Towns Services Club on the

corner of Wharf St and Boundary St, and Seagulls Rugby Club on Gollan Drive in West Tweed Heads have regular touring acts. The new Bowling Club south on Wharf street from the Services Club also has entertainment.

Getting There & Away

Tweed Bus Service (☎ (075) 36 2500) has daily services to Murwillumbah, and daily except Sunday to Kingscliff (some continue on to Cabarita Beach and Pottsville). There's a stop outside the Tourist Information Centre.

See the Gold Coast section for details of local buses from Coolangatta as far north as Southport.

Far North Coast Hinterland

The area stretching 60 km or so inland from the Pacific Highway in far north New South Wales is full of interest for the beauty of its green rolling farmland, broken by spectacular forested mountains, and its high population of 'alternative lifestylers', 'back to the landers', 'freaks', 'hippies', whatever label you care to apply. These settlers, the first of whom were attracted to the area by the Aquarius Festival at Nimbin in 1973, have become an accepted part of the community – although there are still occasional run-ins with the Drug Squad.

Markets & Music

The weekend markets listed here are one place where the colourful alternative community is to be seen in force. The biggest market is at the Channon, between Lismore and Nimbin.

Ballina
    3rd Sunday, Fawcett Park
Bangalow
    4th Sunday, Showground
Brunswick Heads
    1st Sunday, behind Ampol petrol station

Byron Bay
    1st Sunday, Butler St Reserve
The Channon
    2nd Sunday, Coronation Park
Lennox Head
    5th Sunday, Lake Ainsworth
Nimbin
    4th Sunday, Showground

There are many accomplished musicians in the area and sometimes they play at the markets or in the village pub after the market (notably at Uki but never at the Channon, which doesn't have a pub). Other places where you can catch good music include the Chincogan Tavern at Mullumbimby and the Kohinur Hall at Main Arm which has a regular weekly musicians' club. The *Brunswick Byron Echo* newspaper has an informative weekly music column telling who's playing what where.

Getting Around

A web of country roads covers the area and you can nearly always approach a place by one route and leave by another. Nimbin, for instance, can be reached from Lismore, Mullumbimby or Murwillumbah. If you're planning to explore the area get the Forestry Commission's excellent Casino area map ($5) – the tourist information centre in Byron Bay is one place that sells it. There are a few local bus services emanating from Byron Bay, Lismore and Murwillumbah, but hitching is by far the commonest form of public transport.

LISMORE (population 38,250)

Thirty-five km inland from Ballina on the Bruxner Highway to New England, or 48 km in from Byron Bay, Lismore is the 'capital' of the state's far north – the centre of a productive rural district, with a student population from the Northern Rivers College of Advanced Education, and influenced by the alternative community in the country to the north. The rolling landscape between Lismore and the coast was covered in tall subtropical rainforest, known as the Big Scrub, until it was cleared for farming in the late 19th century.

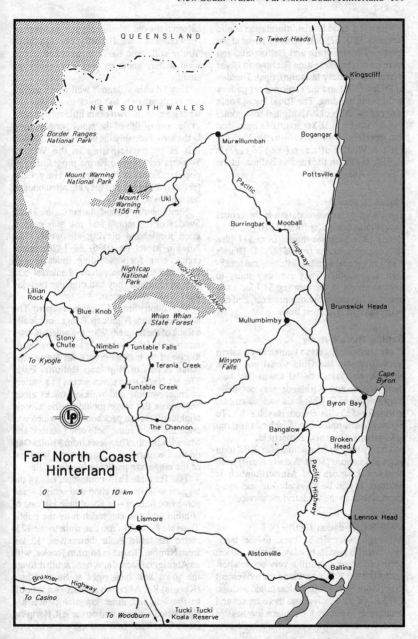

Far North Coast Hinterland

0   5   10 km

There is a good tourist information centre
(☎ (066) 22 0122) near Wilsons River at the
corner of Molesworth and Ballina Sts, and
there's also the interesting **Richmond River
Historical Society Museum**, open Tuesday
to Friday (50c) and the **regional art gallery**
in the same building. The **Tucki Tucki koala
reserve**, with an old Aboriginal ceremonial
ground nearby, is 16 km south of Lismore on
the Woodburn road. The district's National
Parks & Wildlife office (☎ (066) 28 1177) is
at Alstonville, on the road to Ballina, in the
Colonial Arcade.

Places to Stay
The cheapest accommodation is the central
Currendina Lodge (☎ (066) 21 6118), at 14
Ewing St, which has dorms from $11 plus
single/double rooms from $14/$24. There's
a TV lounge and a guests' kitchen, and breakfast is available. They run day tours to
interest points in the area (eg $10 for a trip
to one of the area's Sunday markets) and can
help organise rainforest treks.

Getting There & Away
There are daily flights to Lismore by Eastern
from Brisbane, the Gold Coast and some
New South Wales coastal towns. By bus,
there are several Kirklands services daily
from Ballina to Brisbane via various coastal
towns for $23. To Byron Bay it's $7. To
Sydney costs around $55. Kirklands also run
to Casino, Kyogle and Tenterfield.

The Sydney to Murwillumbah XPT train
stops at Lismore ($66). A daily tourist train
between Lismore and Murwillumbah is
planned; it will be privately run and more
expensive than the Countrylink service.

NIMBIN (population 1300)
Although Australia's 'back to the land'
movement is past its heyday, Nimbin, 30 km
north of Lismore, is still a very active alternative centre. This was where the movement
to northern New South Wales started with the
1973 Aquarius Festival and there are several
communes in the area. Despite a few hassles
from the cops and bureaucrats, relations

between the old inhabitants and multivaried
'newcomers' are friendly enough now.
You're still quite likely to be asked if you
want to buy ganja as you walk along the
street.

Tiny Nimbin village is well worth a visit,
but locals are only too quick to tell you that
what goes on in town bears little relationship
to the way of life of the many people living
in the area. Probably the best way to discover
this is by participating in the Willing
Workers on Organic Farms programme. A
popular farm in the area is Holy Goat
(☎ (066) 89 5344), but they are often booked
out well in advance.

Nimbin holds a good market on the fourth
Sunday of the month and you may catch a
good local band playing afterwards. The
Nimbin Motel (☎ (066) 89 1420) is the
contact point for horse riding. Rides through
the forest to various places of interest cost
$10 an hour and they can organise two-day
treks down to the coast.

The country around Nimbin is superb. The
800-metre-plus Nightcap Range, originally
a flank of the huge Mt Warning volcano, rises
north-east of the town and a sealed road leads
to one of its highest points, **Mt Nardi**. The
range is part of **Nightcap National Park**.
The Mt Nardi road gives access to a variety
of other vehicle and walking tracks along
and across the range including the historic
Nightcap Track, a packhorse trail which was
once the main route between Lismore and
Murwillumbah. The views from **Pholis Gap**
on the Googarna road, towards the west end
of the range, are particularly spectacular.

The Tuntable Falls commune, one of the
biggest with its own shop and school – and
some fine houses – is about nine km east of
Nimbin and you can reach it by the public
Tuntable Falls Rd. You can walk to the 123-
metre **Tuntable Falls** themselves, 13 km
from Nimbin. To get to **Nimbin Rocks**, with
an Aboriginal sacred site, head south through
the town and turn right at Stony Chute
(Kyogle) Rd. After two km there's a turn-off
to the left and three km along there's a
signposted walking trail on the left. **Hanging
Rock Creek** has falls and a good swimming

hole; take the road through Stoney Chute for 14 km, turn right at the Barker's Vale sign, then left onto Williams Rd; the falls are nearby on the right.

The Channon, a tiny village off the Nimbin to Lismore road, hosts the biggest of the region's markets on the second Sunday of each month. There's a good cafe here and a holiday farm (☎ (066) 88 6230) which also has tent sites and cabins. There's also a municipal camp site (☎ (066) 88 6321). About 15 km north up Terania Creek Rd is the rainforest of Nightcap National Park, from where a 750-metre walk leads to **Protesters' Falls**, named after the environmentalists whose 1979 campaign to stop logging was a major factor in the creation of the park.

Places to Stay

Granny's Farm (☎ (066) 89 1333), an associate YHA hostel, is a pleasant relaxed place surrounded by farmland, with platypuses in the nearby creek. There are dorms (with beds, not bunks) for $11 and doubles for $26, less for members. The friendly managers will sometimes give you rides to local places of interest. To reach the hostel go north along Cullen St from the centre and turn left just before the bridge over the creek.

The *Freemasons Hotel* in the centre is a lively pub with singles/doubles for $17/34. There's a caravan park beside the bowling club, a couple of hundred metres along the road that runs beside the pub; for two people camping is $8, on-site vans are $25.

Just out of town heading north, Crofton Rd branches off Blue Knob Rd, and four km along it is the quiet and pleasant *Nimbin Motel* (☎ (066) 89 1420) with singles/doubles for $20/$35.

Places to Eat

The *Rainbow Cafe* in the middle of town has a pleasant shady garden out the back. Wholesome meals cost from $4, and delicious cakes are around $1.50. They do breakfasts, as does the nearby *Copper Hood*, much more a standard country-town cafe. The *Freemasons Hotel* has counter meals.

Three km along Lillian Rock Rd (the turnoff is eight km from Nimbin on Blue Knob Rd), *Calurla Tea Garden* (☎ (066) 89 7297) is open between 10 am and 6 pm daily except Thursday. Dinner is available on weekends but give them a couple of days notice. The food is farmhouse style, the views of Mt Warning and the Border Ranges excellent and the owners very friendly. Ask them about arts & crafts in the area.

Getting There & Away

Hitching is pretty easy in this part of the world. On weekdays there are five buses daily each way between Lismore and Nimbin. On Saturday there are three buses each way, all departing Lismore before 8.45 am; there are none on Sunday. There's the daily Fulton's school bus which goes to/from Murwillumbah on weekdays (leaving Murwillumbah at 7 am, returning in the afternoon). It's a slow two hours and costs $10.

The nearest railway station is at Lismore.

MULLUMBIMBY (population 2500)

This little town, known simply as Mullum, is in subtropical countryside five km off the Pacific Highway between Bangalow and Brunswick Heads. Perhaps best known for its marijuana – 'Mullumbimby Madness' – it's a centre for the long-established farming community and for the alternative folk from nearby areas like Main Arm. There's nothing like the cultural frontier mentality of Nimbin here, and it's a very pleasant place. Perhaps the most obvious sign that the area's community is of a different mix from the usual rural Australian variety is that there's a good bookshop and several other places selling second-hand books, so if you need a used copy of *The Hobbit*, this is the place to come.

There's a tourist information centre (☎ (066) 84 1286) at the north end of Dalley St, near the library, and an **art gallery** at the corner of Burringbar and Stuart Sts. **Cedar House** is an old station agent's home in the town, now full of antiques. It's open daily.

West of Mullum in the Whian Whian State

Forest, **Minyon Falls** drop 100 metres into a rainforest gorge. There are good walking tracks around the falls and you can get within a couple of minutes' walk by conventional vehicle from Repentance Creek on one of the back roads between Mullum and Lismore. The eastern end of the historic Nightcap Track (see Nimbin) emerges at the north of Whian Whian State Forest.

Places to Stay & Eat
The *Mullumbimby Motel* (☎ 84 2387) at 121 Dalley St (the south end) has good rooms at $33. The *Lyrebird* (☎ (066) 84 1725) at the other end of Dalley St is a little dearer.

Mullum has a good collection of health food shops and cafes. A good place to hang out is the *Popular Cafe* on Burringbar St. The *Chincogan Tavern* on Burringbar St does good counter meals and has live music a couple of nights a week. *Mullum House* at 103 Stuart St is a good Chinese restaurant with main courses between $5.50 and $8.80.

Getting There & Away
There's a four times daily bus service from Byron Bay on weekdays by the Byron Bus & Coach company, and most Kirklands buses go through Mullum on their Lismore ($7.50) to Brisbane ($18.50) run. Mullum is on the Sydney to Murwillumbah railway. The XPT to Sydney departs at 9.15 am and costs $65.

MT WARNING
The dramatic peak of this 1156-metre mountain is a landmark dominating the whole New South Wales far north region. Mt Warning is solidified volcanic lava – the remains of the central vent of a volcano 20 million years old. Erosion has since carved out the deep Tweed and Oxley Valleys around Mt Warning, but on the far sides of those valleys outer flanks of the volcano remain as the Nightcap Range in the south and parts of the border ranges to the north. Mt Warning was named by Captain Cook as a landmark for avoiding Point Danger off Tweed Heads.

A six-km sealed road leads part of the way up the mountain from the Murwillumbah to Uki to Nimbin road: it's a great four-hour walk through rainforest to the summit and back. It's a marked trail, but sections are pretty steep. Take water. If you're on the summit at dawn you'll be the first person on the Australian mainland to see the sun's rays that day!

Places to Stay & Eat
Mt Warning is a national park and camping isn't allowed, but *Wollumbin Refuge Caravan Park* (☎ (066) 79 5120), four km down the hill on the Mt Warning approach road, has tent sites, cabins and on-site vans – and lots of wildlife. *Mt Warning Forest Hideaway* (☎ (066) 79 7139), 12 km southwest of Uki on Byrrill Creek Rd, has motel units with everything supplied including cooking gear, from $36/44 for singles/doubles. Meals are available.

The little village of Uki just below the mountain holds a mellow hippie/country market on the third Sunday of the month, and there are counter lunches at Uki's *Mt Warning Hotel*.

Getting There & Away
Fulton's (☎ (066) 79 5267 in Lismore) runs a bus on weekdays from Murwillumbah to Uki, Nimbin and Lismore, leaving Murwillumbah at 7 am and returning in the afternoon. It passes the foot of the six-km Mt Warning approach road.

BORDER RANGES NATIONAL PARK
The Border Ranges National Park covers the New South Wales side of the McPherson Range along the New South Wales-Queensland border and some of its outlying spurs. The Tweed Range Scenic Drive – gravel but usable in all weathers – loops through the park about 100 km from Lillian Rock (on the Uki to Kyogle road) to Wiangaree (on the Kyogle to Woodenbong road). It's well worth the effort of finding this fine drive which goes through mountain forest most of the way, with some steep hills and really breathtaking lookouts over the Tweed Valley to Mt Warning, and the coast 40 km away.

The adrenalin-charging walk out to the crag called the Pinnacle – about an hour from the road and back – is not for vertigo sufferers! There's a free camp site at the western edge of the park, about 12 km north of Wiangaree.

New England

New England is the area along the Great Dividing Range stretching north from around Newcastle to the Queensland border. It's a vast tableland of valuable sheep and cattle country with many good fishing and bushwalking areas, photogenic scenery and, unlike much of Australia, four distinct seasons. If you're travelling up and down the eastern seaboard it's worth taking a longer route through an inland area like New England now and then, to get a glimpse of non-coastal Australia – which has a different way of life, is at least as scenic as the coast, and suffers from a great deal less tourist hype.

The New England Highway, running north from Newcastle up to Warwick in Queensland, is an alternative to the coastal Pacific Highway. Scenically the several roads climbing up to New England, particularly on the eastern side, are more spectacular than the tableland itself, where large numbers of trees have unfortunately been cut down.

Getting There & Away
Air East-West Airlines and to a lesser extent Eastern Airlines have flights to New England towns. Norfolk Airlines (book through Ansett) flies between Armidale, Tamworth and Brisbane.

Bus Countrylink buses run direct to Sydney ($51) or connect with the XPT train to Sydney at Tamworth ($53). Several major companies run through New England on some of their Melbourne to Brisbane or Sydney to Brisbane services. Regional services include Skennars to Brisbane and the Coffs Harbour to Port Macquarie coastal strip. Lindsays run to Coffs then south to Port Macquarie. Border Coaches (☎ (067) 72 5774) run daily between the New England towns and Brisbane – slightly slower and cheaper than the major operators. Kirklands has a Lismore to Tenterfield service on weekdays only.

NEWCASTLE TO TAMWORTH
Singleton is a coal-mining town in the Hunter Valley and one of the oldest towns in the state. At Burdekin Park there's a historical museum in the 1841 jail. Lake Liddell, north-west of the town, is a water sports centre. You're still in the coal-mining area at Muswellbrook. Aberdeen overlooks the Liverpool Plains.

Scone is in beautiful country and has a Historical Society Museum. With over 40 horse studs in the area, the town describes itself as 'the horse capital of Australia', and there's an annual Horse Week in May. The rural *Scone Youth Hostel* (☎ (065) 45 2072) is actually 10 km east at Segenhoe; in Scone the *Belmore Hotel* (☎ (065) 45 2078) on Kelly St has rooms for $15 per person. There's a coal seam at nearby Burning Mountain, Wingen, which has been burning for over 5000 years.

Quirindi is high in the Liverpool Ranges, slightly off the New England Highway which continues north to Tamworth. It has a big racecourse, with the Quirindi Cup on the last Saturday in February the top event.

TAMWORTH (population 35,000)
Spend much time driving the country roads of Australia and listening to a radio and you'll soon realise that country music has a big following. Tamworth is the country music centre of the nation: an antipodean Nashville. Each January there's a week-long country music festival culminating in the Australia Day weekend when the Australasian country music awards are handed out. Much of the music is pretty derivative of the more redneck 'Grand Ol' Oprey' style, but there's also bluegrass and more Australian styles, including some good ratbag bands. At

CWA Park there's the Country Music Hands of Fame memorial with the hand imprints of many Australian country and western singers, and you can see wax models of some of them at Treloar's Menswear Store on Brisbane St. The tourist information centre (☎ (067) 68 4462) is in the park, on the corner of the New England Highway and Kable Ave. Tamworth also has numerous craft workshops and galleries.

Nundle is a historic gold-mining town, 63 km south-east, where you can still fossick. North of the Tamworth to Gunnedah road, Lake Keepit is a popular water sports centre. **Gunnedah** has a council caravan park with on-site vans from $20 and tent sites at $9, plus hotels and motels. All animals at the Waterways Wildlife Park, seven km west of Gunnedah, are reportedly treated like pets – just to make up for all those roadside kangaroo corpses!

Places to Stay

The *Central Hotel* (☎ (067) 66 2160) on the corner of Peel and Brisbane Sts in the city centre has shared rooms for $8 ($15 with breakfast) and singles/doubles from $28/48, with breakfast. The best value of the many motels are on the New England Highway (Newcastle road) on the south side of town, but they are still pricey.

TAMWORTH TO ARMIDALE

Walcha is off the New England Highway on the eastern slope of the Great Dividing Range, on the winding Oxley Highway route to the coast at Port Macquarie. There's a Tiger Moth, the first aircraft used in Australia for crop dusting, on display at the Pioneer Cottage. East of the town is the Apsley Gorge with magnificent waterfalls.

Back on the highway, **Uralla** is where the noted bushranger Captain Thunderbolt was buried in 1870. Thunderbolt's Rock, by the highway seven km south of town, was one of his hide-outs. In the 1850s there was a gold rush in this area, and some fossicking is still carried on near the Rocky River diggings.

ARMIDALE (population 22,000)

The main centre in the region and site of the New England University, Armidale is a popular halting point. The 1000-metre altitude means it's pleasantly cool in summer and frosty (but often sunny) in winter. The town centre is attractive with a pedestrian mall and some well-kept old buildings. The enthusiastic tourist information centre (☎ (067) 73 8527) and bus station are close by on the corner of Marsh and Dumaresq Sts.

Centrally placed on the corner of Rusden and Faulkner Sts, the **Armidale Folk Museum** is in an 1863 building and is open daily from 1 to 4 pm. The excellent **New England Regional Art Museum** is on Kentucky St, south of the town centre, and is also open daily. Off the Armidale to Kempsey road you can visit **Hillgrove**, a gold-mining ghost town 27 km east of Armidale, on the edge of an impressive gorge area. **Saumarez Homestead**, on the New England Highway between Armidale and Uralla, is a beautiful house which still contains the effects of the rich pastoralists who built it. The Armidale area is noted for its magnificent gorges, many of which contain impressive waterfalls when it rains enough. **Apsley Falls** rarely dry up. The **Wollomombi Falls** are 39 km east of Armidale and close to the Armidale to Kempsey road, and the 457-metre drop makes them the highest in Australia. Wollomombi Falls are part of the Oxley Wild Rivers National Park and there are walking trails around and to the bottom of the gorge here. Other falls include the fine **Chandler and Dangar Falls**. See the Port Macquarie to Coffs Harbour section for more information on national parks east of Armidale.

Places to Stay

Wicklow's Hotel (☎ (067) 72 2421), also known as the Pink Pub, is on the corner of Marsh and Dumaresq Sts near the bus station and has dorm beds from $8 ($12 with bed linen) and singles from $15. There's a YHA associate hostel at *Pembroke Caravan Park* (☎ (067) 72 6470) on Grafton Rd ($10 a night) and several other caravan parks with on-site vans. In the town centre there are a few old hotels like *Tattersalls* (☎ (067) 72 2247) on the mall and the *Royal Hotel* (☎ (067) 72 2259) on the corner of Marsh and Beardy Sts, both with rooms from $20/28 for singles/doubles – at Tattersalls you have the option of paying more and having a private bathroom, at the Royal continental breakfast is free.

Motels are expensive. About the only places you'll get a double for under $50 is the *Rosevilla Motel* (☎ (067) 72 3872) where singles/doubles cost $34/38, and the *Armidale Motel* (☎ (067) 72 8122) where they're from $42/45. Both are on the New England Highway north of town. No cheaper than the motels but more pleasant (and with a free breakfast) are a couple of B&B places in nice old houses: *Monivea* (☎ (067) 72 8001) at 172 Brown St and *Comeytrowe* (☎ (067) 72 5869) at 184 Marsh St.

Getting Around
Realistic Car Rentals (☎ (067) 72 8078) on the corner of Rusden and Dangar Sts has cars from $35 a day, including insurance and 100 free km – you must be over 23 and you can't go more than 100 km from Armidale, which rules out trips to the coast.

NORTH OF ARMIDALE
Guyra
Guyra is at an altitude of 1300 metres making it one of the highest towns in the state. There's a museum here, open only on Sunday afternoons, and a lagoon named Mother of Ducks. There are fine views from Chandlers Peak and, 12 km before Glen Innes, unusual 'balancing rocks' at Stonehenge.

Glen Innes
You're still at over 1000 metres at Glen Innes, which was a good place to meet bushrangers a century ago. The town's old hospital now houses a huge folk museum named **Land of the Beardies**. It's open between 2 and 5 pm daily and also between 10 and 11 am on weekdays. Glen Innes is still a centre for sapphire mining and you can

fossick at **Dunvegan Sapphire Reserve** on Reddeston Creek. The Gwydir Highway down from Glen Innes to Grafton passes through the Gibraltar Range National Park and close to the Washpool National Park – see the Grafton section.

Tenterfield
Tenterfield is the last town of any size before the Queensland border. In the town you can visit **Centenary Cottage**, dating from 1871, now the centre of a local museum complex; and **Hillview Doll Museum** with more than 1000 dolls on display. The Sir Henry Parkes Memorial School of Arts is where Parkes launched the national federation movement in 1889.

Tenterfield Lodge & Caravan Park (☎ (067) 36 1477) at 2 Manners Rd, close to the railway station, is an associate YHA hostel as well, charging $12.

Thunderbolt's Hideout, where bushranger Captain Thunderbolt did just that, is 11 km out of town.

National Parks
The rough Mt Lindesay Highway gives access to two small national parks in the spectacular granite boulder country north of Tenterfield. In **Boonoo Boonoo National Park** (pronounced something like 'bunna b'noo'), entered 22 km from Tenterfield, the Boonoo Boonoo River plunges 210 metres into a gorge at the falls of the same name. In **Bald Rock National Park**, 35 km from Tenterfield, 213-metre-high Bald Rock is the main feature. It's a relatively easy walk to the top where you'll enjoy superb views over Queensland and New South Wales. You can camp near its base.

South Coast

Though much less well known than the north coast between Sydney and Queensland, the south coast from Sydney to the Victorian border has a number of attractive spots including some excellent beaches, of both the secluded and sociable types, good surf and diving in many places, some interesting little fishing towns and bushland both lovely and spectacularly wild. There are a number of small resorts – this is a popular area for Victorian holiday-makers – and, inland, fine mountain national parks like Morton, Deua and Wadbilliga. The Snowy Mountains, Australia's highest, are 150 km in from the southern part of the coast.

The Princes Highway runs right along the south coast from Sydney through Wollongong and on to the Victorian border. Although this is a longer and slower route between Sydney and Melbourne than the Hume Highway, it's infinitely more interesting. South of Nowra the sandstone of the Sydney area gives way to granite and good soils, and the forests start to soar.

Getting There & Away

Ansett Express flies to Merimbula from Sydney, Kendell Airlines from Melbourne. Hazelton Airlines flies to Moruya. The railway from Sydney only goes as far south as Nowra (160 km). There are rail-coach co-ordinated services to most towns further south, but they aren't very frequent and involve a circuitous inland route. By bus, Greyhound/Pioneer travels the Princes Highway route. Typical fares to Sydney include Bega $52 (eight hours), Narooma $38 (seven hours), Batemans Bay $38 (six hours).

Pioneer Motor Service (a local company) runs buses between Eden and Sydney, often a couple of dollars cheaper than the bigger lines. Murrays' has daily buses between Canberra and the coastal strip from Nowra to Narooma, and Pioneer has a thrice-weekly Canberra to Bega service.

WOLLONGONG (population 209,000)

Only 80 km south of Sydney is the state's third largest city, an industrial centre which includes the biggest steelworks in Australia at Port Kembla. Wollongong also has some superb surf beaches, and the hills soar up behind, giving a fine backdrop, great views

over the city and coast, and good walks. The name Illawarra is often applied to Wollongong and its surrounds – it refers specifically to the hills behind the city (the Illawarra Escarpment) and the coastal Lake Illawarra to the south.

Information & Orientation

The tourist information centre (☎ (042) 28 0300) is on the corner of Crown and Kembla Sts, and is open from 9 am to 5 pm Monday to Friday, 10 am to 4 pm at weekends. Here, Crown St becomes a pedestrian mall for two blocks, emerging at the top on Keira St which is another important street, part of the Princes Highway. Through traffic bypasses the city on the Southern Freeway which runs from near Shellharbour, south of Wollongong, to Royal National Park in the north.

The GPO is at 296-98 Crown St near the railway station, but you might find the Wollongong East post office, lower down Crown St near the tourist centre, more convenient. The NRMA (☎ (042) 29 8133) is on the corner of Burelli and Kembla Sts. Wollongong Saddlery & Bushcraft Equipment at 90 Burelli St has bushwalking gear.

Things to See

BHP runs tours of its **Port Kembla steelworks**, mainly geared to groups but you may be able to tag along (☎ 042) 75 7802. Wollongong has an interesting harbour, with the fishing fleet based in the southern part called Belmore Basin, which was cut from solid rock in 1868. There's a fish market, a couple of fish restaurants and an 1872 lighthouse beside the harbour. The **old lighthouse** is open weekends from midday to 4 pm (1 pm to 5 pm during Daylight Saving); don't confuse it with the larger, newer lighthouse on the headland. The string of parks along the city shoreline make Wollongong a surprisingly attractive place.

The **Illawarra Historical Society's museum** is on Market St, open Wednesday from 10 am to 1 pm, Saturdays, Sundays and public holidays from 1.30 to 4.30 pm, admission is $1.50. The museum includes a

Wollongong

0   0.5   1 km

```
 1  Hospital
 2  Plant Room Restaurant
 3  Main Post Office
 4  Tattersalls Hotel
 5  Railway Station
 6  Hotel Illawarra
 7  Bus Station
 8  Art Gallery
 9  Australian Airlines
10  Ansett Airlines
11  Tourist Information Centre
12  Wollongong East Post Office
13  NRMA
14  International Centre
15  Historical Museum
16  City Bus Station
17  New Lighthouse
18  Old Lighthouse
```

reconstruction of the 1902 Mt Kembla village mining disaster. Wollongong's North Beach, north of the harbour, generally has better surf than the south beach. The harbour itself has beaches which are good for children. The **Wollongong Botanic Garden** on Northfields Ave, Keiraville, has both tropical and temperate plants and a lily lake.

If you're interested in seeing a rugby league match, check whether the Illawarra Steelers, members of the Sydney competition, are playing a home game in front of adoring fans.

Places to Stay

Hotels Several hotels have fairly cheap accommodation. The *Tattersalls Hotel* (☎ (042) 29 1952) at 333 Crown St, just down from the station, has decent rooms for $25/40/50 for singles/doubles/triples, and you can get reasonably priced food. On the corner of Keira and Market Sts the marginally dowdier *Hotel Illawarra* (☎ (042) 29 5411) also charges $20/30.

Motels About the only inexpensive motel in the area is the *Cabbage Tree Motel* (☎ (042)

84 4000) at Fairy Meadow, 3½ km north of Wollongong. The basic rate for singles/doubles is $36 a night, slightly more for twins, but there are various reduced rates for longer stays. Bring along your bargaining skills – the manager's motto is 'We deal'. Just about any bus heading north from the railway station will get you to Fairy Meadow.

Guesthouses Many of Wollongong's guesthouses won't take casual visitors, but you could try the *Excelsior Guest House* (☎ (042) 28 9320) at 5 Parkinson St, off the top end of Crown St near the hospital. The weekly rate is from just $70 per person including breakfast.

Colleges *International House* (☎ (042) 29 9711) on the Princes Highway in North Wollongong has accommodation during the vacations.

Camping You have to go a little way out before you can camp. The council runs camping areas on the beach at Corrimal (☎ (042) 84 4255), near the beach on Farrell Rd in Bulli (☎ (042) 84 8433) and in Fern St Windang (☎ (042) 95 1665), with beach and lake frontage. Bulli is 11 km north, Corrimal about halfway there and Windang is 15 km south, between Lake Illawarra and the sea. All charge $9 for camp sites (two people) and from $35 for vans or cabins, with prices rising during school and Christmas holidays. Buses run from the railway station to within walking distance of all these. There are quite a few privately owned caravan parks in the area – the tourist office has information.

Places to Eat

The *Plant Room* on Crown St opposite the corner of Gladstone Ave, just up the hill from the railway station, opens seven nights a week. It has a relaxed atmosphere and a tasty, cosmopolitan menu. All meals cost between $5 and $12. This is a good place for a late night coffee.

Good-priced snacks and meals at breakfast and lunch time are available at *Tattersalls Hotel* at 333 Crown St near the railway station. *Hal's Tavern* on the corner of Keira and Burelli Sts does lunch specials. It's a clean, spacious place with a small beer garden. Across Burelli St from here there's an *Indian restaurant* which claims to be the best in town.

Topkapi Kebab Restaurant at 76 Crown St has been recommended for its kebabs, or you can try *City Kebabs* on Crown St, west of the mall. Nearby, at 303 Crown St *Wollongong Thai* has dishes for $5 and under, including rice. In the mall the *Crown St Chinese Restaurant* has smorgasbord specials at various times of the day and night. In Kembla St near the corner of Crown St there's the *Pot of Gold* (Mexican), the more expensive *La Taverna* (Spanish and Italian) and across the street *Il Faro* (pizzas).

Angelo's Trattoria at the International Centre, 28 Stewart St, between Kembla and Corrimal Sts, serves moderately priced Italian food plus steaks and seafood. It's open for lunch and dinner daily and there's a pleasant bar. There's no sign on the street – walk along the verandah to the back of the building.

Lorenzo's on the mall near the Kembla St corner is a very good northern Italian restaurant, with main courses starting around $15. For seafood down by the harbour there's the good but expensive *Harbour Front Restaurant* and a reasonably priced cafe with meals at around $6.50.

The *Panorama Hotel* up on Bulli Pass does meals that are almost as good as its fantastic view.

Entertainment

Wollongong activity is mainly in the suburbs – the Friday *Illawarra Mercury* (known as the 'Mockery') has details. The clubs – like the Leagues Club in Church St, the Berkeley Sports Club or the Dapto Leagues Club often have weekend bands and nonmembers can usually get in, except at Corrimal. The North Wollongong Hotel has bands, particularly popular on Sunday afternoons.

For Sunday afternoon jazz go to the Panorama Hotel up on Bulli Pass. Woolshed bushdances are held on Friday and Saturday nights at Albion Park, 20 minutes south near Shellharbour.

Wollongong's Performing Arts Centre on Burelli St has theatre, dance, music and more. The Wollongong Festival in the first week of the August-September school holidays offers all sorts of activities.

Getting There & Away

Air The local airport at Albion Park, south of town, has some services but generally people use Sydney Airport (Mascot). Watts Coaches (☎ (042) 29 5100) run the Airporter Express bus between Wollongong and Mascot ($12).

Bus The bus station (☎ (042) 26 1022) is on the corner of Keira and Campbell Sts. There are about four daily services to Sydney ($12) and one to Canberra ($32). Pioneer's Sydney to Melbourne coastal route runs through Wollongong. To Melbourne it's $52. Direct buses to Brisbane with Pioneer cost the same from Wollongong as they do from Sydney – $63. Pioneer Motor Service (☎ (044) 21 7722 – this is a Nowra company, not the national giant) runs through Wollongong along the south coast as far as Eden.

Train There are about 20 fast electric trains daily to/from Sydney (about 80 minutes, $5.70 – the Countrylink service costs much more), and about 10 a day south along the coast as far as Kiama, Gerringong and Nowra, where the line ends. There are also a few trains from Wollongong north to Moss Vale, inland near the Hume Highway and Morton National Park.

Getting Around

You can reach a lot of Wollongong from the railway line and trains are fairly frequent. Some of the beaches are accessible by rail and there's a service to Kiama. The main city bus terminal is in Crown St where it meets Marine Drive.

You can hire paddleboats, rowing boats, catamarans and power boats at Lake Illawarra, and at Brighton Beach in Wollongong harbour you can hire windsurfers at weekends. Half-day tours of Wollongong are available.

AROUND WOLLONGONG

The hills rise suddenly and dramatically behind Wollongong and there's a range of walking tracks and lookouts on Mt Kembla and Mt Keira less than 10 km from the city centre, but no buses go up there. You get spectacular views over the town and coast from the **Bulli Pass** ('bull eye') on the Princes Highway, just north of Wollongong. The country is equally spectacular to the south if you head inland through the **Macquarie Pass National Park** to Moss Vale or through the Kangaroo Valley. The Fitzroy Falls and other attractions of mountainous **Morton National Park** can be reached by either route. On the road to Moss Vale you can see a fine local example of Australian kitsch – a huge potato in the middle of town. Yes, this is spud country.

Up the coast there are several excellent beaches. Those with good surf include **Sandon Point, Austinmer, Headlands** (only for experienced surfers) and **Sharkies**.

On the road to Otford and Royal National Park, the **Lawrence Hargraves Lookout** at Bald Hill above Stanwell Park is a superb clifftop viewpoint. Hargraves, a pioneer aviator, made his first attempts at flying in the area early this century. Hang gliders hang out there today. If you want to try hang gliding, courses are offered by Aerial Technics (☎ (042) 94 2545). Just south of Wollongong, **Lake Illawarra** is popular for water sports and there are also a number of reservoirs and dams in the vicinity.

WOLLONGONG TO NOWRA
Shellharbour

South of Lake Illawarra, Shellharbour is a popular holiday resort. It's one of the oldest towns along the coast and back in 1830 was a thriving port, but it declined after the construction of railway lines. There are good beaches on the Windang Peninsula north of the town.

Kiama

Kiama is famous for its blowhole: it can spout up to 60 metres high and is illuminated at night. There is also a **Maritime Museum**, good beaches and surf, and the scenic **Cathedral Rock** at Jones Beach.

Gerringong

Just south of Kiama is Gerringong with fine beaches and surf. Pioneer aviator Charles Kingsford Smith took off from Seven Mile Beach, immediately south of Gerringong and now a national park, to fly to New Zealand in 1933. Take the time to have a look at the excellent **Hilltop Gallery** on Fern St.

Gerringong has the *Chittick Lodge* hostel (**☎** ((042) 34 1249) on Bridges Rd five minutes' walk back up the hill from Werri Beach. It's a modern associate YHA hostel with good facilities and charges $10.

Berry

Berry was an early settlement; it has a number of National-Trust-classified buildings and the almost inevitable **Historical Museum**. One of the finer buildings dates from 1889 and is now the *Bunyip Inn Guest House* (**☎** (044) 64 2064). It isn't cheap – from $70/80 for singles/doubles midweek – but it's a very nice place.

Coolangatta

Coolangatta (no, not the Queensland Coolangatta) has a group of buildings (now converted into a motel) which were constructed by convicts in 1822. For $8 you can ride Bigfoot, a strange 4WD contraption, to the summit of Mt Coolangatta. The less adventurous might prefer to spend their $8 (plus 50 cents) eating all they want at the *Crows Nest Tavern*, also in Coolangatta.

NOWRA AREA

The coastal strip south of Gerringong down to Durras lake, just north of Batemans Bay, is known as Shoalhaven. It stretches inland up to 50 km to include the Morton and Bundawang national parks, as well as some large chunks of state forest. Inland on Shoalhaven River, the twin towns of **Nowra** and **Bomaderry** form the main population centre, followed by Ulladulla. The region is popular for water sports, and there are whitewater rafting trips available – phone the Bomaderry tourist information centre (**☎** 044) 21 0778 or 008 02 4261, toll-free). There's a National Parks office (**☎** (044) 21 9969) at 24 Berry St in Nowra.

In Bomaderry there's the *Barracks Youth Hostel* (**☎** (044) 23 0495) near the railway station on Meroo St, where beds for members cost $10 a night, $12 for nonmembers. You can camp in Nowra at the riverside Nowra Animal Park. *Shoalhaven Caravan Village* (**☎** (044) 23 0770) on Terrara Rd has on-site vans from $25 a double.

Inland, on the way to Fitzroy Falls, is **Kangaroo Valley** with old buildings including the Friendly Inn, a pioneer farm museum and a reconstruction of an 1880 dairy farm.

On the coast near Nowra is **Culburra-Orient Point**, a quiet resort town with a prawning fleet. A bit further south most of the shores of **Jervis Bay** are untouched bushland and white-sand beaches. Huskisson is the main settlement on the bay, which is popular with catamaran sailors and windsurfers. South of here at Vincentia is a nude beach. The promontory which forms the southern shore of the bay is mostly a nature reserve – though there's also a naval college – and there are some good walks, beaches and beautiful camp sites, notably Green Patch. Wreck Bay village on the south side of the promontory is an Aboriginal settlement. There's also an annexe of Canberra's National Botanic Gardens here for plants which are susceptible to frost.

Ulladulla is in an area of beautiful lakes, lagoons and beaches. There's good swimming and surfing in the area or you can make the bushwalk to the top of Pigeon House Mountain (719 metres) in the impressive Budawang Range. It's about a three-hour return trip from the end of the road. The mountain is in the south-east of Morton National Park.

BATEMANS BAY AREA

Batemans Bay is a popular resort at the

mouth of the Clyde River – again there's good bushwalking and swimming. It's also a fishing and diving centre. The tourist office (☎ (044) 72 6900) is on the highway. Things to see include Birdland Animal Park, and river cruises start at $10. There are also white-water rafting, abseiling and bushwalking tours available. The *Bayview Hotel* (☎ (044) 72 4522) on Orient St has singles/doubles for $18/26. Local buses run between Batemans Bay and Moruya daily except Sunday.

Along the coast north of Batemans Bay is **Murramarang National Park** where there's a superb camp site (about $5 a vehicle) between eucalypt forest and beach at Pebbly Beach. Semi-tame kangaroos hop between the tents; rosellas and kookaburras are among the plentiful bird life. There are some good coast and forest walks in this small national park. It's about nine km off the highway and the turn-off is at East Lynne. There's no public transport. At the southern end of the park there's another camp site at North Head, south of Durras.

About 80 km inland from Batemans Bay on the route to Canberra is **Braidwood** with many old sandstone buildings classified by the National Trust and a historical museum. From here there's road access to the superb rugged bushwalking country of the northern Budawang Range. South of Morton the line of mountain national parks stretches south through Budawang, Deua and Wadbilliga National Parks – all wilderness areas good for rugged bushwalking. Like other towns along the coast **Moruya** is a dairy centre but oyster farming is carried on here too. The old Coomerang House is of interest, but south-west is the beautifully situated old gold town of Nerrigundah and the Eurobodalla Historic Museum. There's some fairly unspoiled coast down the side roads south of Moruya, with a good beachside camp site (about $5 a vehicle) at **Congo**, where there are beaches on both sides of a headland.

NAROOMA AREA

Narooma is another oyster town. There are many inlets and lakes nearby. *Narooma YHA & Backpackers' Hostel* (☎ (044) 76 2824) is a good associate YHA hostel in an idyllic bushland setting with a long water frontage. Dorm beds for members are $11, $12 for nonmembers. There's also some accommodation for couples and families and you can usually camp here, too. For $2 you get the use of bikes, canoes and rowing boats for the duration of your stay. If you're coming by bus from the south ask the driver to drop you at the Old Highway turn-off, a couple of km before town. From here the hostel is about a one km walk. Once you're at the hostel the town is accessible by boat or canoe on the other side of Forsters Bay. A great way to go shopping.

Central Tilba, just 15 km south of town, is a little town which has undergone remarkably little change this century. There are now several craft workshops and a cheese factory which gives tastings.

South of the coastal Wallaga Lake and off the Princes Highway, **Bermagui** is a fishing centre made famous 50 years ago by American cowboy-novelist Zane Grey. If you have time, the largely unsealed road between Bermagui and Tathra, on the coast 15 km south-east of Bega, is a more interesting route than the highway. The road runs through sections of the Mimosa Rocks National Park which begins about five km north of Tathra and runs up the coast for 17 km. You can camp at Gillards Beach and Araunnu Beach (a fee of around $5 is due to be introduced) but you'll need to take your own water.

Inland and on the Princes Highway is **Cobargo**, another remarkably unspoilt old town. The main 2WD access to the **Wadbilliga National Park** is from near here. It's a rugged park and the many species of animals and birds live in surroundings which haven't changed much in thousands of years. For more information on access and bushwalks contact the National Parks office (☎ (044) 76 2888) at 36 Pacific Highway, Narooma.

Bega, near the junction of the Princes and Snowy Mountains Highways, is a useful access point to the snow country and it has a small *Youth Hostel* (☎ (064) 92 3103) on Kirkland Crescent, with beds for $11.

SOUTH TO THE VICTORIAN BORDER

The coast here is quite undeveloped, and there are many good beaches and some rugged virgin forests full of wildlife.

Merimbula is a big resort town popular with Victorians, and the good beaches get crowded over summer. On Main St the Merimbula Old School Museum is just that; it's open Tuesday, Thursday and Friday. The tourist office (☎ (064) 95 1129) is on Beach St.

At **Eden** the road bends away from the coast into Victoria, running through more mighty forests, the logging of which has sharply divided opinion in the region's timber towns. Eden is an old whaling town on Twofold Bay, much less touristy than other towns further up the coast. There's an intriguing little Killer Whale Museum where you can learn about the whaler swallowed by a whale in 1891 and regurgitated, unharmed, 15 hours later. Well, almost unharmed. His hair turned white and fell out due to the whale's digestive juices. There's also the skeleton of a killer whale, nicknamed 'Old Tom', one of many killers who used to round up the baleen whales into Twofold Bay for the whalers. The museum is open 11 am to 4 pm daily, entry $2.50.

The *Australasia Hotel* (☎ (064) 96 1600) has singles/doubles for around $25/38.

To the north and south of Eden is the **Ben Boyd National Park** – good for walking, camping, swimming and surfing, especially at Long Beach in the north.

Boydtown, south of Eden, was founded by Benjamin Boyd – a flamboyant early settler whose land-holdings were once second only in size to the Crown's. His grandiose plans aimed at making Boydtown the capital of Australia but his fortune foundered and so did the town – later he did too, disappearing without trace somewhere in the Pacific. Some of his buildings still stand, and the Sea Horse Inn, built by convict labour, is still in use today.

Snowy Mountains

The first people to ski in Australia were the fur hunters of Tasmania in the 1830s, using three-foot boards. Norwegian miners introduced skiing in Kiandra in the 1860s, and it is the first town in the world where competitive ski races were held. The skis in those days were home-made, crude objects; the method of braking was a pole held between the two skis. Early this century the development of the sport began with lodges like the one at Charlotte Pass, and the import of European skis. It slowly developed into the big business and numerous resorts that exist today.

Australia's winter snowfields straddle the New South Wales-Victoria border, but Mt Kosciusko (pronounced 'kozzyosko' and named after a Polish hero of the American War of Independence) in the Snowy Mountains is in New South Wales and at 2228 metres its summit is Australia's highest. Much of the state's Snowies are within the boundaries of the large Kosciusko National Park, an area of year-round interest: skiing in winter, bushwalking and vivid wild flowers in summer. The main ski resorts and the highest country are in the south central part of the park, west of Jindabyne. Thredbo and the Perisher Valley/Smiggin Holes area are the main downhill skiing areas. Charlotte Pass, Guthega and Mt Blue Cow are smaller downhill areas, as is Mt Selwyn, near Kiandra and towards the northern end of the park.

The upper waters of the Murray River form the state and national park boundary in the south-west. Another of Australia's best known rivers – the Snowy, made famous by Banjo Paterson's poem *The Man from Snowy River* and the film based on it – rises just below the summit of Mt Kosciusko. The Murrumbidgee also rises in the national park. You can take white- water rafting trips on the Murray and Snowy Rivers in summer when the water is high enough, but the waters are gentler than some you'll find

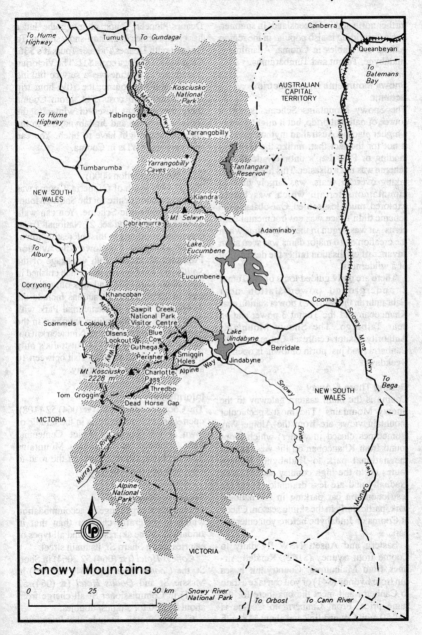

Snowy Mountains

0   25   50 km

To Orbost   To Cann River

Snowy River
National Park

further north and in Queensland. In summer, horse trail riding is also popular in the region – there are stables in Cooma, Adaminaby, Jindabyne, Tumut and Tumbarumba.

Snowy Mountains Hydroelectric Scheme

The Snowy Mountains Scheme is still a source of national pride, but it might occupy a higher place in Australian mythology were it not for the fact that, unlike the Gallipoli landing or Phar Lap's untimely death, the scheme was not a disaster. This huge project, taking over 25 years, was largely built in mountainous terrain which was barely explored, much less settled. One obstacle the scheme didn't face was environmental concerns – it was begun in the '50s, a time when the creation of 16 major dams was seen as an advance of civilisation rather the destruction of a wilderness.

There are daily guided tours of the Tumut 2 underground power station near Cabramurra, the Murray 1 power station near Khancoban and the Tumut 3 power station near Talbingo. The Snowy Mountains Authority visitor centre at Cooma, on the Canberra road just north of town, is open on weekdays.

Getting There & Away

Cooma is the main eastern gateway to the Snowy Mountains. The most spectacular mountain views are from the Alpine Way (sometimes closed in winter) which loops round from Khancoban on the west side of the national park to Jindabyne. Eastern routes up to the high country ascend more gradually and are less dramatic. There are restrictions on car parking in the national park, particularly in the skiing season. Check at Cooma or Jindabyne before you enter the park.

Eastern and Ansett NSW fly daily to Cooma from Sydney ($142), Kendell Airlines from Melbourne. Countrylink buses run from Sydney ($41) or you can take a train to Canberra and meet the bus there for the same price. From Canberra to Cooma is $11.50 with Countrylink and about $18 with

Deanes/Pioneer Tours, although the latter has cheaper rates in the non-snow season. To Sydney with Deanes/Pioneer Tours it's $36. Countrylink to Bega costs $11. The Victorian government's V/Line has a service linking Cooma and Melbourne; the 10½-hour trip by bus and train costs $44. From Cooma there are frequent buses in winter to the Skitube terminus and Jindabyne, but in the summer you might have to hitch. You can rent cars and 4WDs in Cooma.

COOMA (population 8000)

Just 114 km south of Canberra, Cooma was the construction centre for the Snowy Mountains Hydroelectric Scheme. You can walk down Lambie St and see 21 National-Trust-classified buildings in this interesting town.

Half a km west of the town is the **Aviation Pioneers Memorial** with wreckage of the *Southern Cloud*, an aircraft which crashed in the Snowies in 1931 and was only discovered in 1958. Other attractions include the **Avenue of Flags** in Centennial Park with flags of the 27 nationalities involved in the Snowy Mountains Scheme. Nineteen km out on the Adaminaby road is Australia's only llama farm, which you can visit between 10 am and 4 pm Friday to Sunday.

Information

The Cooma visitor centre (☎ (064) 52 1108), open 9 am to 5 pm daily, is in the middle of town at 119 Sharp St, beside Centennial Park. There's also a Snowy Mountains Scheme Information Centre on the road to Canberra just north of town.

Places to Stay & Eat

Cooma has a large range of accommodation which is generally cheaper than that in Jindabyne or the ski resorts, and all types of eateries along Sharp St, its main street.

Coffeys Hotel ((☎ (064) 52 2064) in Short St, the *Coomu Hotel* (☎ (064) 52 2003) in Massie St and *Dodds Hotel* (☎ (064) 52 2011) in Commissioner St all charge from about $17/30 for singles/ doubles.

Cheaper motels include the *Bunkhouse*

(☎ (064) 52 2983) on Soho St, and the *Swiss Motel* (☎ (064) 52 1950) and the *Family Motel* (☎ (064) 52 1414), both on Massie St. Singles/doubles are around $25/35. There are also three camping/caravan parks, all with on-site vans.

In **Nimmitabel**, a small town on the highway 37 km south-east of Cooma, the *Royal Arms* (☎ (064) 54 6422) is an old pub which has been converted into a guesthouse. Small singles/doubles cost $15/30, others are $32/44 and there's a suite for $63. It's a nice place.

JINDABYNE (population 1600)

Fifty-six km west of Cooma and a step nearer the mountains, Jindabyne is a new town on the shore of the artificial Lake Jindabyne which covers the old town. In summer you can swim or rent windsurfers or boats on the lake at Jindabyne. The Information Centre (☎ (064) 53 2003) is helpful.

Places to Stay

For accommodation inquiries contact the Jindabyne Reservation Centre (☎ (064) 56 2457 or 008 026 356, toll-free) on Petamin Plaza. Most visitors stay in holiday flats or units of which there are hundreds. In the winter high season there are three rates: midweek (five nights, Sunday to Thursday), weekend (Friday and Saturday nights) and weekly. Most places won't let by the night. Rates for a twin room range from about $500 midweek, $300 weekend and $800 per week. However, most places have six or eight-bed flats and these can work out at about $125/70/300 per person. There is also a handful of caravan parks, a couple of which are beside the lake.

KOSCIUSKO NATIONAL PARK

The 6900 sq km of New South Wales's largest national park includes caves, glacial lakes, forest and all of the state's ski resorts as well as the highest mountain in Australia. Although the park is most famous for its snow, it is also popular in summer when there are excellent bushwalks and marvel-lous alpine wild flowers. Outside the snow season you can drive to within eight km of the top of Mt Kosciusko, up the Kosciusko Rd from Jindabyne past Perisher and Char-lotte Valleys. The last section to the summit, from Charlotte Pass, is by road, then from the base of the mountain by footpath. There are other walking trails from Charlotte Pass, including the fantastic 20-km lakes walk which includes Blue, Albina and Club lakes.

Mt Kosciusko and the main ski resorts are in the south central part of the park. From Jindabyne the Kosciusko Rd leads to the national park headquarters and visitor centre (☎ (064) 56 1700, open from 8.30 am to 4.30 pm daily) about 15 km north-west at Sawpit Creek, then on to Smiggin Holes, Perisher Valley (33 km) and Charlotte Pass, with a turn-off before Perisher Valley to Guthega. A shuttle bus runs in winter from the visitor centre to Smiggin Holes and Perisher Valley. In winter you can normally drive as far as Perisher Valley, but snow chains must be carried and fitted where directed.

The *Alpine Accommodation Complex* (☎ (064) 56 2224) at Sawpit Creek has tent sites from $11 and cabins from $58 a double and $82 for six people. Prices go up during holiday and skiing seasons.

The Alpine Way to Thredbo (35 km from Jindabyne) and Khancoban turns off the Kosciusko Rd just outside Jindabyne. The Skitube is a tunnel railway up to Perisher Valley and Blue Cow from Bullocks Flats on the Jindabyne to Thredbo road. Travelling this way means you can avoid the hazards of driving on the Kosciusko Rd in winter. A return ticket costs $18, and there are deals on combined Skitube and lift tickets. You can hire skis and equipment at the terminal and there are luggage lockers (from $4 a day).

SKIING & SKI RESORTS

Snow skiing in Australia can be a marginal activity. The season is short (July, August and early September is really all there is) and good snow is by no means a safe bet. Nor are the mountains ideal for downhill skiing – their gently rounded shapes mean that most long runs are relatively easy, and the harder runs tend to be short and sharp. For a final bummer, the short seasons mean the operators have to get their returns quickly and costs can be high.

Having told you the bad, here's the good: when the snow's there and the sun's shining, the skiing can be just fine. You will find all the fun (not to mention 'heart in the mouth' fear) you could ask for. Further, the open slopes of the Australian alps are a ski-tourers' paradise – nordic (cross-country or langlauf) skiing is becoming increasingly popular and most resorts now offer lessons and hire equipment.

The national park includes some of the most famous trails – Kiandra to Kosciusko, the Grey Mare Range, Thredbo or Charlotte Pass to Kosciusko's summit and the Jagungal wilderness. The possibilities for nordic touring are endless, and often old cattle-farmers' huts are the only form of accommodation apart from your own tent.

In addition to touring, there is ample scope for cross-country racing (classic or skating) in the Perisher valley, and large citizen's races are held annually. On the steep slopes of the Main Range near Twynam and Carruthers the cross-country downhill (XCD) fanatics get their adrenalin rushes. In winter, the cliffs near Blue Lake become a practice ground for alpine climbers.

The cheapest (and by far the most fun) way to get out on the slopes is to gather a bunch of friends and rent a lodge or an apartment. Costs vary enormously but can be within the bounds of reason. Bring as much food and drink as you can, as supplies in the resorts are expensive.

There's cheaper accommodation in towns like Jindabyne and particularly Cooma, some distance below the ski slopes, than in the resorts like Thredbo and Perisher Valley where the snow's on your doorstep. There are buses every morning from Jindabyne and Cooma to the resorts, and back again in the afternoon. Jindabyne Reservation Centre (☎ 008 026 331, toll-free) can make reservations for all forms of accommodation in Jindabyne, Perisher Valley, Smiggin Holes, Guthega, Charlotte Pass and Thredbo. The

Thredbo Resort Centre (☎ (064) 52 6275) does much the same just for Thredbo. The Cooma visitor centre (☎ (064) 52 1108) will also make bookings. The New South Wales Travel Centres in Sydney (☎ (02) 231 4444) and other capital cities also make bookings.

Lift charges vary – see the following information on the various resorts. Class lessons cost from $25 or can be included in a package with lift tickets from about $40 to $60 a day, much less for five days. Boots, skis and stocks can be hired for about $25 a day, less for longer and less off the mountain. It's a trade-off whether to hire in the city and risk damage and adjustment problems or at the resort and possibly pay more. There are usually hire centres in towns close to the resorts, and many garages hire ski equipment as well as chains. Snow chains must be carried in the mountains during winter even if there is no snow – there are heavy penalties if you haven't got them, or you may not be allowed to drive into the alpine area.

Australian ski resorts are short of the frenetic nightlife of many European resorts, but compensate with lots of partying between the lodges. Nor is there a great variety of alternative activities apart from toboggan runs. Weekends tend to get crowded because the resorts are so convenient, particularly to Canberra.

During the season all the main resorts are connected by bus with Cooma which can be reached by road or air. For snow and road reports ring the various visitor centres, or in Sydney there's a recorded service on 11539. Thredbo also has its own number, 0055 34320.

Thredbo (1370 metres)

Thredbo has the longest runs (the longest is over three km through 670 metres of vertical drop) and the best and most expensive skiing in Australia. A day ticket costs $49, a five-day pass $225 and a five-day lift and lesson package costs $275. In summer Thredbo is still a good place to visit, unlike the other resorts which become ghost towns. It's a popular bushwalking centre with all sorts of excellent and scenic tracks. The chair lift to the top of Mt Crackenback runs right through the summer. From the top of the chair lift it's a two-km walk or cross-country ski to a good lookout point over Mt Kosciusko, or seven km to the top of the mountain itself. Remember to carry adequate clothing and be prepared for all conditions, even in summer.

Places to Stay There's a *Youth Hostel* (☎ (064) 57 6376), but during the ski season (early June to early October) it costs $39 on Saturday nights, $38 other nights *(if* they allow one-night stays) and $175 a week. At other times it's $12, or $32 in a twin room with bathroom. If you want to stay at the hostel in July, August or September, you should apply by April through the main Sydney YHA office. A ballot is held for places, but it's worth contacting the hostel or the YHA head office in Sydney to see if there are vacancies at short notice.

There's a pretty but very basic free camp site between Jindabyne and Thredbo, near the Skitube, called *Thredbo Diggers.*

Perisher Valley & Smiggin Holes (1680 metres)

Perisher Valley has a good selection of intermediate runs. Smiggin Holes is just down the road from Perisher and run by the same management so you can get a combined ski-tow ticket for both resorts. A shuttle bus runs between the two resorts and they are also joined by a lift system so it is possible to ski from one resort to the other.

Together they have over 100 km of runs and 30 ski lifts. You can reach Perisher Valley either by the Kosciusko Rd or by taking the Skitube. At Perisher/Smiggins a day ticket costs $49, a five-day pass costs $215, and a five-day lesson-and-lift package costs $220; $205 for beginners.

Charlotte Pass (1780 metres)

At the base of Mt Kosciusko this is the highest and one of the oldest and most isolated resorts in Australia. In winter you have to snowcat the last eight km from Perisher Valley. It has good ski-touring country. There are five lifts at the resort, that service

rather short but uncrowded runs. Many cross-country skiers start out for return trips to Thredbo from here.

Guthega (1630 metres)

This is mainly a day resort, best suited to intermediate and, to a lesser extent, beginner skiers. *Guthega Lodge* offers the only commercial accommodation. Guthega is smaller and less crowded than other places. Cross-country skiers head out for the Main Range or Rolling Ground from here.

Mt Selwyn (1492 metres)

This is the only ski resort in the northern end of the Kosciusko National Park, halfway between Tumut and Cooma. It has 13 lifts and is an ideal beginners' resort. One-day lift tickets are $38, five days costs $175 and five days plus lessons is $220, $199 for beginners. It's another day ski resort – the closest accommodation is at Adaminaby. The booking centre (☎ 008 020 777, toll- free) will book accommodation, some of which is relatively cheap – units for six people cost from $260 for five nights and there are onsite vans for $35 a double.

Mt Blue Cow (1640 metres)

Australia's newest ski resort, with beginner to intermediate skiing, is between Perisher Valley and Guthega in the Perisher Range. This is a day resort (no accommodation) accessible by the Skitube, but there are accommodation packages which include shuttles and Skitube tickets (☎ 008 251 354, toll-free). A day ticket costs $39, five days in seven costs $189. Lifts and lessons cost $59 per day ($44 for beginners) and $249 for five days ($199). You have to add the cost of using the Skitube to all these, but there are combined deals available.

ALPINE WAY

From Khancoban, on the western edge of the national park, the Alpine Way – partly unsealed and also sometimes closed in winter – loops round to the south past some good mountain viewpoints and the Murray 1 power station lookout, to Thredbo and

Jindabyne. Two of the best mountain views are from Olsen Lookout, 10 km off the Alpine Way on the Geehi Dam road, and Scammels Spur, just off the Alpine Way.

TUMUT AREA

Tumut is on the Snowy Mountains Highway on the north side of the national park. Australia's largest commercial trout farm is at nearby Blowering Dam. The tourist information centre can tell you about visits to the various centres of the Snowy Mountains Hydroelectric Scheme.

Talbingo Dam and the **Yarrangobilly limestone caves** (60 km east, about midway between Tumut and Kiandra) are other points to visit. The caves are only open at odd times – check at the tourist information centre. There's also a thermal pool at a constant temperature of 27°C and some beautiful country in the reserve around the caves.

Batlow is south of Tumut in a fruit-growing area. There's a 'Big Red Apple' centre if you're collecting Australian 'big' tourist attractions. Near Batlow is **Hume and Hovell's Lookout** where the two explorers did indeed pause for the view in 1824. **Paddy's River Dam** was built by Chinese gold miners back in the 1850s.

Continuing south from Batlow you reach **Tumbarumba**, site of the early exploits of bushranger Mad Dog Morgan. There's great mountain scenery and good bushwalks in the area and the Paddy's River Falls are only 16 km from the town.

South-West & the Murray

A number of roads run through the state's south-west – the Hume Highway being the obvious one. But there are alternative routes between Sydney and Melbourne, like the Olympic Way from Cowra to Wagga Wagga and Albury or the Mid Western and Newell Highways to West Wyalong and Narrandera.

Or there are routes to Adelaide like the Sturt Highway through Hay and Wentworth. You'll also come through the south-west if travelling direct between Brisbane and Melbourne. It's wide, rolling, sometimes hypnotic country with some of New South Wales's best farming areas and some interesting history if you have time to seek it out. The Murray River forms the boundary between New South Wales and Victoria, and although most of the interesting towns are on the Victorian side New South Wales has some too.

Getting There & Away

The Melbourne to Sydney bus services run on the Hume and the train services run close to it. There are several local and area bus services. Fearnes Coaches (☎ (069) 21 2316 or (02) 211 3328 in Sydney) run between Sydney and Wagga Wagga ($40), Gundagai ($37 from Sydney), Yass ($35), Goulburn ($30) and Mittagong ($20). See the warning in the Victorian Hume Highway section about the dangers of driving on this busy road.

Countrylink services reach most other towns in the area. The region is also criss-crossed by several major interstate bus routes – from Sydney and Brisbane to Melbourne and Adelaide. Airlines like Ansett Express and Kendell fly into the region and Macknight Airlines links Wagga Wagga, Hay, Deniliquin and Tocumwal.

ALONG THE HUME HIGHWAY

The Hume Highway is the main road between Australia's two largest cities. It's the fastest and shortest road and although it's not the most interesting there are interesting places along the way, as well as some worthwhile diversions off the Hume. One of the simplest is right at the beginning – instead of making the long, weary trek through Sydney's outer suburbs towards Camden and Campbelltown, take the coastal Princes Highway past the Royal National Park to Wollongong. Just after Wollongong you can cut inland on the Illawarra Highway through the picturesque Macquarie Pass and over rolling countryside to Moss Vale before rejoining the Hume. Further south you can leave the Hume to visit Canberra or continue beyond Canberra through the Snowy Mountains, rejoining the Hume in Victoria.

Sydney to Goulburn

The first 120 km or so out of Sydney can be done on the new South-Western Freeway, avoiding the old Hume. This way bypasses Camden (which with nearby Campbelltown is covered in the Around Sydney section), Picton and Thirlmere.

Picton is an early settlement with a tollkeeper's cottage, an old railway viaduct and the early St Mark's Church of England. The Thirlmere Rail Transport Museum, open weekends and holidays, has about 40 locomotives and other pieces, including an 1864 engine from railway pioneer Robert Stephenson. Wirrimbirra Fauna & Flora Sanctuary is 13 km south.

Mittagong is an agricultural centre with a tourist information centre (☎ (048) 71 2888) on the Hume. Thirty km west of Mittagong, **Joadja** is now a ghost town. It's on private property but it's open at certain times – check in Mittagong. Four km south of Mittagong a winding 65-km road leads west off the highway to the Wombeyan Caves, open from 10 am to 4 pm daily. The drive up is through superb mountain scenery. A little further south on the Hume, **Berrima** is a tiny town which was founded in 1829 and has changed remarkably little. It's a popular Sunday-drive destination for Sydneyites.

Bowral, just south of Mittagong off the highway, is another agricultural centre and from here you can visit the Mt Gibraltar Wildlife Reserve. Bowral was where cricketer Don Bradman, probably Australia's greatest sporting hero, spent his boyhood. In 1926, aged 17, he scored 300 runs for Bowral in a final against Moss Vale, averaging over 100 runs per innings for the season. There's now a cricket ground and museum dedicated to the 'Don'.

Moss Vale is an industrial town just south of Bowral. Throsby Park House, built between 1834 and 1837, is a fine old home built by the area's first settler. South of Moss Vale are **Bundanoon** and the large Morton National Park with deep gorges and high sandstone plateaus in the Budawang Range. There are several entry points to the park: two of the easiest are Fitzroy Falls and Bundanoon, both reachable by sealed road from Moss Vale. See the earlier South Coast section for full details of this excellent park.

Bundanoon is on the main Sydney to Yass railway and has buses from Moss Vale. The *Bundanoon Youth Hostel* (☎ (048) 83 6010) on Railway Ave is a good hostel with beds at $11. You can hire bicycles in the town.

Goulburn (population 24,000)

Goulburn was proclaimed a town in 1833. It's surrounded by sheep country and as a monument to the source of its wealth there's a three-storey-high **Big Merino** in town. It looks truly diabolic with its green eyes glowing at night: by day you can climb inside to see displays on wool or watch a 45-minute sheep show.

Buildings of interest include the 1840 **Riversdale coaching house** with its beautiful gardens (open daily except Tuesday) and **Garroorigang**, built in 1857, with bushranger, Aboriginal and Victorian displays (also open daily). There are several hotels, motels and caravan parks. In **Bradfordville**, 20 km away, the *Goulburn Yurtworks* (☎ (048) 21 5391) is an organic farm (and yurtworks) where you can stay for $10 a night, including meals, in return for a couple of hours' work. Longer stays can be negotiated. They'll pick you up from Goulburn if you give a day's notice.

Yass (population 4500)

Yass is closely connected with the early explorer Hume, for whom the highway is named. On Comur St, next to the tourist information centre (☎ (06) 226 2557), the **Hamilton Hume Museum** has exhibits relating to him. Near Yass at **Wee Jasper** are Careys Caves, open on Sunday afternoons from 1 pm.

Just east of Yass the Barton Highway

branches off the Hume for Canberra. Trans-border Buses (☎ (06) 226 1378) have frequent services.

Gundagai (population 2500)

Though now bypassed by the highway, Gundagai, 386 km from Sydney, is one of the more interesting small towns along the Hume. Between Gundagai and South Gundagai the long wooden Prince Alfred Bridge (now closed to traffic, but you can walk it) crosses the flood plain of the Murrumbidgee River, a reminder that in 1852 Gundagai suffered Australia's worst flood disaster when 89 people were drowned. Gold rushes and bushrangers were also part of its colourful early history and the notorious Captain Moonlight was tried in Gundagai's 1859 **courthouse**.

Other places of interest in town include the **Gabriel Gallery** of historic photos on the main street (Sheridan St), the **Historical Museum** on Homer St and the information centre on Sheridan St. Here there's the Marble Marvel, a 20,000-piece cathedral model. Is it art? Is it lunacy? Is it worth the $1 entry fee? Perhaps. You at least get to hear a snatch of *Along the Road to Gundagai* on the tape which plays while you visit the model.

Gundagai is known above all for featuring in a number of famous songs, including *Along the Road to Gundagai, My Mabel Waits for Me* and *When a Boy from Alabama Meets a Girl from Gundagai*. Its most famous monument is eight km east of town just off the highway. There, still sitting on his tuckerbox, is the **Dog on Tuckerbox memorial**, a sculpture of the dog who in a 19th-century bush ballad (and a more recent, perhaps even better known, poem by Jack Moses) 'sat on the tuckerbox, five miles from Gundagai', and refused to help while its owner's bullock team was bogged in the creek. A popular tale has it that the dog was even less helpful because in the original version it apparently shat on the tuckerbox.

The memorial is now a popular little tourist centre and roadside stop. Not far away is the Five Mile Pub, an equally popular place to break your journey back in the pioneer days.

Places to Stay & Eat There are plenty of motels including a number on West St, the northern entry to town from the Hume Highway. At the top of the hill on West St, *Gundagai Auto Cabins & Motel* (☎ (069) 44 1318) is one of the cheapest places with cabins (from $23), on-site vans (from $15) and motel units (from $35). It's a clean place. The *Gundagai River Caravan Park* is a pleasant spot, by the river near the south end of the Prince Alfred Bridge, with on-site vans for $16 and tent sites at $6. In the town on Sheridan St, the *Criterion Hotel* (☎ (069) 44 1048) and the *Royal Hotel* (☎ (069) 44 1024) have rooms for $15 per person.

There are several places to eat along Sheridan St and there are Chinese and Australian meals at the *RSL Club*. The *Niagara* restaurant and coffee lounge boasts the 'biggest menu between Sydney and Melbourne'.

Holbrook (population 1400)

Holbrook is the halfway point between Sydney and Melbourne, and was known as Germanton until WW I, during which it was renamed after a British war hero. In Holbrook Park there's a replica of the submarine in which he won a Victoria Cross. The local information centre is located in the interesting **Woolpack Inn Museum**, in an 1860 hotel.

Albury (population 41,000)

The New South Wales half of the Albury-Wodonga twin towns is on the north side of the Murray River. It's a busy and expanding industrial centre and an access point from Victoria to the New South Wales Snowy Mountains. The town dates from 1840 and has some historic buildings and botanic gardens.

There's a New South Wales Government Travel Centre (☎ (060) 21 2655) at Wodonga Place on the Hume Highway as you enter Albury and a larger one over the state border on the highway in Wodonga (☎ (060) 41 2255) which has information on the whole of New South Wales.

In summer there's good swimming in the Murray River in **Noreuil Park** behind the Albury information centre and you can take one-hour river cruises on the paddle-steamer *Cumberoona*. Also in the park is a tree marked by explorer William Hovell where he crossed the Murray on his 1824 expedition with Hamilton Hume from Sydney to Port Phillip (Melbourne wasn't there then). The **museum** is also in the park, and the **Arts Centre** is in a restored 1907 building on Dean St.

The **Ettamogah Wildlife Sanctuary**, 11 km north on the highway, has a collection of Aussie fauna, most of which arrived sick or injured, so this is a genuine sanctuary as opposed to the half-baked zoos which many so-called 'sanctuaries' are. It's open daily from 9 am to 5 pm ($4). Slightly further out the grotesque **Ettamogah Pub** looms up near the highway – a real-life recreation of a famous Aussie cartoon pub and proof that life (of a sort) follows art not vice versa. The **Jindera Pioneer Museum**, which includes several original buildings, is 16 km north-west of Albury, also open daily.

Places to Stay & Eat *Brady's Railway Hotel* (☎ (060) 21 4700), at 450 Smollett St has singles from $15. *Sodens Australia Hotel* (☎ (060) 21 2400) on the corner of David and Wilson Sts is a classified historic building and is a pleasant escape from motels, of which there are plenty in town. Pub rooms are $23/37 for singles/doubles and motel rooms are $40/48. The *Albury Central Caravan Park* (☎ (060) 21 8420) on North St has tent sites for $5 and cabins from $28.

The *Sailors, Soldiers & Airmen Club* on the corner of Dean and Olive Sts has a gym, bars, pokies, a disco, and a reasonably priced restaurant and bistro. There are several Chinese restaurants and pizza shops on Wagga Rd and Dean St. *Tiffins* in Dean St does good lunches. The *Commercial Club* on Dean St has fairly stiff dress regulations (a tie – for men only, presumably – is required in the dining room; jeans and runners aren't allowed anywhere) but also a reputation for very good food.

WAGGA WAGGA (population 50,000)

Wagga is a major city on the Murrumbidgee River. The name is pronounced 'wogga' not 'wagga' and is usually abbreviated to one word (although there's a literary group called Wagga Wagga Writers Writers). It's a busy farming centre with botanic gardens and a zoo. The Murray Cod Hatcheries & Fauna Park (entry $8), eight km from the city centre, has a 100-year-old, 52-kg fish.

The tourist office (☎ (069) 23 5402) is on Tarcutta St. The *St Vincent de Paul Formation Centre* (☎ (069) 31 3073) in San Isidor, six km from Wagga, has dorm beds for $7. You're more likely to get in with a YHA card.

Wallacetown Historical Arms Museum is 20 km south of Wagga. North of Wagga is **Junee** with some historic buildings including the lovely homestead Monte Cristo and some splendid pubs. The railway station and the buildings in the street nearby are well worth a look.

NARRANDERA (population 5000)

Near the junction of the Newell and Sturt Highways, Narrandera is in the Murrumbidgee Irrigation Area (MIA) – there's an MIA information centre in the town. The John Lake Centre ($5 entry) researches Murray/Darling aquatic life and has comprehensive aquarium displays, including a 50-kg Murray cod. There's a miniature zoo in town and there are swimming pools at Lake Talbot.

Leeton, 30 km away, was the first of the area's irrigation towns, dating from 1913. Like several of the MIA towns, Leeton was designed by Walter Burley Griffin (architect of Canberra) and is worth a walk around. There are weekday tours of one of Australia's biggest fruit canneries and of other food-processing plants.

South of Narrandera on the Newell Highway is **Jerilderie**, immortalised by the bushranger Ned Kelly who held up the whole town for two days in 1879. Kelly relics can be seen in the Telegraph Office Museum on Powell St.

Places to Stay

The *Youth Hostel* (☎ (069) 59 1768) is near the railway station, in an impressive old hotel. Dorm beds for members cost $11, and there's non-YHA guesthouse accommodation at $15/23 for singles/doubles. Cheapest of the hotels is the *Charles Sturt* (☎ (069) 59 2042) on the corner of East and Douglas Sts, at $16/26, and there are motels and a couple of caravan parks.

GRIFFITH (population 13,000)

This busy farming centre, another MIA town planned by Walter Burley Griffin, is in one of the state's biggest wine-producing areas, with around 10 wineries open most days. In odd-numbered years there's a wine and food festival at Easter. Griffith also has a reputation for large-scale marijuana production and for the unpleasant events that befall people who find out too much about it.

You can tour the **Griffith Rice Mill** at 10.30 am on weekdays. The large **Pioneer Park Museum** is just north of the town ($4). The tourist information centre is on the corner of Banna and Jondaryan Aves.

With the intensive irrigation in the area, Griffith is a good place to look for fruit-picking work from February to May.

National Parks

Cocoparra National Park, about 30 km away, via Yenda, has wild flowers in the spring and bush camping is permitted. **Willandra National Park**, 180 km northwest, via Hillston, centres on Willandra Billabong, an oasis in the dry plains. Contact the ranger (☎ (069) 67 8159) or the National Parks office in Griffith (☎ (069) 62 7755) about camping or basic accommodation in the old Willandra station's 'Men's Quarters'.

HAY (population 3000)

In flat, treeless country at the junction of three highways, Hay is a major merino sheep breeding centre. There are some fine beaches along the Murrumbidgee in this area, some interesting old buildings like the **Hay Gaol Museum**, and a plaque in Lachlan St marking Charles Sturt's journey on the Murrumbidgee and Murray Rivers in 1828-30.

DENILIQUIN (population 7800)

A sheep raising centre where much irrigated farming is also carried out, 'Deni' has the **Heritage Centre**, an 1879 school being restored as a museum and arts centre. A footbridge from Cressy St runs to the Island Wildlife Sanctuary. There's good river swimming at sandy McLean Beach.

The *Youth Hostel* (☎ (058) 81 2612) on the corner of Wood and Macauley Sts is a small place with beds for $7.

ALONG THE MURRAY

Most of the important river towns are on the Victorian side – see the Victoria chapter for more on the river. It's no problem to hop back and forth across the river as in many places roads run along both sides.

Albury (see the Hume Highway section) is the main New South Wales town on the Murray and also the first big town on the river down from its source. The Murray was once an important means of communication, with paddle-steamers splashing up and down stream, as though it was an antipodean Mississippi.

Corowa is a wine-producing centre downstream from Albury. The Lindeman winery has been here since 1860. You can have a meal at the popular services clubs in town or cross the river to visit the wineries in Rutherglen. On the second Sunday of each month and on public holidays there are train rides along the miniature Bangerang Railway.

Tocumwal on the Newell Highway is a quiet Murray town with a giant fibreglass codfish in the town square. The town has a sandy river beach and is a popular gliding centre. The Rocks is a popular picnic spot 11 km from town.

Close to the meeting of the Darling and the Murray, Australia's two longest rivers, **Wentworth** is overshadowed by nearby Mildura on the Victorian side of the Murray. The old paddle-steamer *Ruby* is on display near the Darling River bridge in Fotherby Park.

There's an interesting folk museum and the 1879-81 jail has a display of the sorts of things the authorities used when they wanted to be unpleasant to prisoners. Admission to the jail is $1.50. There are river cruises on a number of vessels including the 1914 riverboat *Loyalty*. The Cod River Aquarium displays many of the creatures found in the rivers.

About 70 km north, off the Silver City Highway to Broken Hill, is *Nindethana Station* (☎ (050) 27 0210), a working sheep station where you can stay for $40/60 for singles/doubles, with breakfast. There's a pool, and for $70 a day per person there's full board, horse-riding, and kayaking on the Anabranch River. Buses will drop you off nearby, but phone first to arrange a lift to the station.

Central West

The central west region starts inland from the Blue Mountains and continues for about 400 km, gradually fading from rolling agricultural land into New South Wales's harsh far west. This region has some of the earliest inland towns in Australia. From Sydney, Bathurst is the gateway to the region, and from here you can turn north-west through Orange and Dubbo or south-west through Cowra and West Wyalong. The Mid Western Highway, running from Bathurst through Cowra and Wagga Wagga to Albury, is an alternative Sydney to Melbourne route. It's longer than the Hume route but provides very different scenery.

Central west towns have the usual accommodation choices and there are YHA hostels at Dubbo and Orange.

Getting There & Away

Air Ansett Express flies from Sydney to a number of centres in the central west including Coonabarabran, Coonamble, Dubbo ($133), Mudgee and Walgett. Eastern serves other towns like Bathurst, Cowra, Parkes, Forbes, Young and Cootamundra. There are services from Dubbo to other locations in the central and far west of the state.

Bus Major lines have services through the region on routes between Sydney and Broken Hill or Adelaide, and from Brisbane to Melbourne or Adelaide. There are also local bus services including Bathurst to Orange (weekdays only).

Train Direct trains run from Sydney to Lithgow ($17), Bathurst ($25), Orange ($32), Dubbo ($61) and Parkes ($32). From those centres connecting buses run to most other towns including Cowra ($37 from Sydney), Forbes ($44), Grenfell ($39) and Mudgee ($30).

LITHGOW (population 14,700)

On the western fringe of the Blue Mountains, Lithgow is mainly an industrial town, a little bemused by its increasing number of visitors. The tourist information centre (☎ (063) 51 2307) is at 285 Main St. **Eskbank House** on Bennet St is a gracious 1841 home housing a pottery gallery and industrial museum. Admission is $2 and it's open daily between 10 am and 4 pm, except Tuesday and Wednesday. There are fine views from **Hassan Walls Lookout**, five km south of town.

The **Zig Zag Railway** by which, until 1910, trains descended from the Blue Mountains, was built in 1868 and was quite an engineering wonder in its day. Now it's restored and steam trains run in school holidays and on other Saturdays, Sundays and holidays from about 11 am to 4 pm. It's 10 km east of Lithgow (☎ 02) 858 1480 or (047) 57 3061.

See the earlier Blue Mountains section for information on the village of Hartley.

Newnes, about 50 km north of Lithgow on the edge of the wild Wollemi National Park, is a ghost town where the pub still functions. There's a five-km walk to a disused railway tunnel, now full of glow-worms.

Many of the pubs in Lithgow have accommodation from about $15/25 for singles/doubles. There's a frequent direct rail service to Sydney ($17), and some trains will take you to Bottom Points where you can catch the Zig Zag Railway.

BATHURST (population 25,500)

Bathurst, 208 km from Sydney, is Australia's oldest inland city. It can get cold here in winter, and snow is not unknown. The tourist information centre (☎ (063) 31 1622) is in the Civic Centre on Russell St.

It's a fine old town with many early buildings including the 1835 **Holy Trinity Church** and part of the **Old Government House** of 1817. The European street trees and the cold winter nights also help to give it a different feel to towns further north and west.

There is a good **museum** with Aboriginal artefacts as well as the usual pioneering exhibits, in the east wing of the impressive 1880 courthouse on Russell St. There is also an art gallery and the **Museum of Applied Arts & Sciences**. You can visit the home of the 1940s Labor Prime Minister Ben Chifley at 10 Busby St. Eight km out of town is **Abercrombie House**, a huge Gothic mansion of the 1870s. Tours begin at 3 pm on Wednesday except in June, July and December.

Close to Bathurst is the **Mt Panorama motor racing circuit**. Part of the track is only open during the races but the rest of it is normal public road. One of Australia's best-known races, the Bathurst 1000 km for production cars, takes place here each October. The track is only used twice each year, the other occasion being the Easter motorcycle events which, at one time, always seemed to be followed by an exciting bikie rampage.

Mt Panorama also has a couple of more permanent attractions: the **Sir Joseph Banks Nature Park** which has koalas, kangaroos and wallabies; and the **Bathurst Gold Diggings**, a reconstruction of an early gold-mining town.

There are plenty of expensive hotels and motels in Bathurst, but if you want to explore the region on a budget you might have to stay in one of the nearby small towns.

AROUND BATHURST

The **Abercrombie Caves** are 72 km south of the city. There are several guided tours each day. North of Bathurst the old mining town of **Hill End** was the scene for a gold rush from 1871 to 1874 and has many fine buildings from that era. It's now administered by the national parks as an historic site and is worth a visit. There are camp sites and rooms in the old *Royal Hotel* (☎ (063) 37 8261). Doubles with breakfast cost from $25. The information centre (☎ (063) 37 8206) is in the old Hill End Hospital.

Rockley, 34 km south of Bathurst, is another classified historic village. The *Club House Hotel* (☎ (063) 37 9203) has singles/doubles for $20/30. North-east of Bathurst is **Rylstone** where there are interesting Aboriginal rock paintings just outside the town (ask at the shire council) while 16 km north there are fine tree ferns in Fern Tree Gully.

MUDGEE AREA (population 6000)

Further north, 126 km from Bathurst, **Mudgee** is a pleasant town with many early buildings and the Colonial Inn Museum. In September there's a wine festival. The Mudgee Tourist Information Centre (☎ (063) 72 5875) is at 64 Market St, and here you can hire gold pans for $1.50.

There are many young and enthusiastic small wineries in the area, and people who find the Hunter Valley too commercial report that Mudgee wineries are a delight to visit. Around 18 wineries are open six or seven days a week. And they make some nice wine too. You can sample it with a meal at the *Wineglass Bar & Grill*, opposite the gardens on Perry St in Mudgee. The *Woolpack Hotel*, opposite the information centre has accommodation and might soon have backpackers' dorms. There are several caravan parks with on-site vans and cabins.

Gulgong, 30 km north-west, is an old gold town once described as 'the hub of the world'. It was also the boyhood home of poet Henry Lawson and there's a big collection of 'Lawsonia' in the art centre on Mayne St. Gulgong Pioneers Museum on Herbert St is good, and open daily from 9.30 am to 5 pm, admission $2. The *Centennial Hotel* (☎ (063) 74 1241) on Mayne St has singles/doubles with bathroom for $20/30. The *Heritage Centre* has very cheap dormitory accommodation, but it's often booked out by school groups. Phone (☎ (063) 74 1202) to check. At **Nagundie** 11 km north there's a rock five metres above the ground which is said always to hold water – it's an old Aboriginal water hole and you can camp there.

Further east towards New England is **Merriwa** at the western end of the Hunter with a number of historic buildings including an 1857 historical museum. Nearby **Cassilis** also has some old stone buildings and between there and Mudgee there are Aboriginal cave paintings just off the road.

Getting There & Away

This area isn't on any main highway (which is partly why it remains so pleasant) but there is a reasonable amount of public transport. By bus it's $28 to Sydney and $13.50 to Lithgow. There's one bus a day to and from Bathurst.

ORANGE (population 29,500)

This important fruit-growing centre does not, curiously enough, grow oranges! It was considered as a site for the federal capital before Canberra was eventually selected. This was the home town of pioneer poet Banjo Paterson (he wrote the words of *Waltzing Matilda*) and the foundations of his birthplace are now part of Banjo Paterson Park. There's an art gallery in the civic centre on Byng St while the historical museum on

Sale St includes a 300-year-old tree carved with Aboriginal designs.

Australia's first real gold rush took place at **Ophir**, 27 km north of Orange. The area is now a nature reserve and it's still popular with fossickers. You can borrow gold pans from the Orange visitor centre (☎ (063) 61 5226) on Byng St for a $3 deposit.

Lake Canobolas Park, with a camp site, is eight km south-west while a further six km brings you to the **Mt Canobolas Reserve** with hills, walking trails and camping. You can hire bicycles to get around the Mini-Bike Tourist Park, 10 km north.

Molong is north-west on the road to Wellington and four km south-east of the town is the grave of Yaranigh, the Aboriginal guide of explorer Sir Thomas Mitchell.

There's a *Youth Hostel* (☎ (063) 62 2444) in the historic Hotel Canobolas at 248 Summer St in the centre of town. Beds are $10. They have information on fruit-picking/processing work in the area.

Selwood's Coaches (☎ (063) 62 7963) run to Sydney ($25) via Bathurst ($10) and Katoomba ($12) daily, usually departing early in the morning.

DUBBO (population 32,000)

North of Parkes and Orange and 420 km from Sydney, Dubbo is an important travel crossroads. It's an agricultural and sheep and cattle raising town with some old buildings and a good **museum of colonial life** on Macquarie St. You can get tourist information from the museum or at the bus station (☎ (068) 84 1422) on the corner of Darling and Erskine Sts.

The **Old Dubbo Gaol** is another attraction, open daily. There is a fair amount of information on the Governor family, whose exploits are related in Thomas Keneally's novel *The Chant of Jimmy Blacksmith*.

Five km south-west of town, the **Western Plains Zoo** is the largest open-range zoo in Australia. You can hire bicycles there and ride around the exhibits. Entry is $11. In town, you can hire bicycles at Wheelers on the corner of Darling and Bultje Sts.

Places to Stay

Kurrajong House (☎ (068) 82 0922) is a pleasant YHA hostel at 87 Brisbane St, north of the railway line. From the bus station turn right up Erskine St and take the second right. Dorm beds are $10 ($11 for nonmembers and more during school holidays) and there are a few twin rooms.

On Talbragar St there are a number of pubs with accommodation, including the *Civic Hotel* (☎ (068) 82 3688) and the fine old *Pastoral Hotel* (☎ (068) 82 4219). The cheapest motel is the *John Oxley* (☎ (068) 82 4622), close to the centre at 199 Macquarie St. There are several caravan parks, all with on-site vans for around $21.

Getting There & Away

The air fare from Sydney is $133.

Dubbo is at the cross-roads of the Newell Highway (the main Melbourne/Brisbane route) and the Sydney/Adelaide route (via Broken Hill), and both New England and Bourke are easy to get to from here. Not a bad spot for long-distance hitching.

Most of the major bus companies pass through, but the local company Rendells (☎ (068) 87 8224) usually has the cheapest fares. Book at the bus station (☎ (068) 84 2411).

COWRA (population 8400)

On the alternative inland route to Melbourne the pleasant town of Cowra was the site of a Japanese prisoner-of-war camp during WW II. In 1944 an amazing mass prison break was made by the Japanese, resulting in the death of nearly 250 prisoners, many of them by suicide. Four prison guards were killed, but all the escapees were soon rounded up. The strange tale of this impossible escape attempt was told in the book and film titled *Die Like the Carp*. There's a Japanese war cemetery five km south of the town, and two km south-east of the cemetery a memorial marks the site of the break-out.

The Wyangala dam and recreation area, 40 km east of Cowra, has good water sport facilities. Canowindra, north of Cowra, has

a fine curving main street and is a big hot-air ballooning centre from April to October. In 1863 bushranger Ben Hall bailed up the whole town!

FORBES (population 8500)

Forbes is an oddly atmospheric place to wander round for a couple of hours. It has wide streets and a number of grand 19th-century buildings reflecting the wealth of its 1860s gold rush. Bushranger Ben Hall is buried in the town's cemetery – he was treacherously killed here in 1865, an event lamented in the bitter folk song *The Streets of Forbes*. Forbes has a museum with Hall relics and other memorabilia, open daily from 3 to 5 pm, in Cross St. The tourist information centre is at the old railway station just off the highway.

One km south of the centre is the **Lachlan Vintage Village**, a recreation of a 19th-century village, which is open daily with working demonstrations most days.

There are motels, pubs and various camp sites with on-site vans – cheapest is the *Lachlan View Caravan Park* (☎ (068) 52 1055) south of the centre on Flint St, with sites for $7 and vans from $20.

Between Forbes and Orange is **Eugowra** where one of early New South Wales's most spectacular gold-escort robberies took place. The town has a small museum and 15 km east there's rough bushwalking in Nangar National Park.

North-West

From Dubbo, roads radiate out to various parts of the state. The Newell Highway runs north-east right across the state, an excellent road which provides the quickest route between Melbourne and Brisbane. The Castlereagh Highway, forking off the Newell 66 km from Dubbo at Gilgandra, runs more or less directly north into the rugged opal country towards the Queensland border, its surfaced section ending soon after Lightning

Ridge. The Mitchell Highway heads off north-west to Bourke via Nyngan. At Nyngan the Barrier Highway forks off directly west to Broken Hill in New South Wales's far west.

Getting There & Away

Towns on the Newell Highway are served by Brisbane to Melbourne or Adelaide buses. Leslies Coaches (☎ 008 252 480, toll-free) run between Sydney and Lightning Ridge thrice weekly for $60; they have $5 stopovers on this interesting route via Katoomba, Gulgong and Walgett, as well as YHA discounts. Countrylink connects most other towns in the area with Sydney, usually with a train/bus combination via either Dubbo or Tamworth. Fares include Gunnedah $48, Coonabarabran $48 and Lightning Ridge $66. Eastern and Ansett Express fly to several of the main towns.

ALONG THE NEWELL

Gilgandra has the Gilgandra Observatory & Display Centre with an audiovisual of the moon landing and NASA Gemini flights, plus a historical display. Gilgandra is a junction town where the Newell and Castlereagh divide and a road also cuts across to the Mitchell.

Coonabarabran is the main access point for the spectacular mountain domes and spires of the Warrumbungle Range, a national park with superb walks and rock-climbing possibilities. There are camp sites in the park and you can get a walks map from the park headquarters at Canyon Camp, in the heart of the park 35 km west of Coonabarabran. The final 10 km of the road once you have entered the park is fairly rough.

The largest optical telescope in the southern hemisphere is at **Siding Spring**, 24 km west of the town at the edge of the park. You can visit it daily. Coonabarabran has a tourist information centre (☎ (068) 42 1441) on the Newell Highway at the south end of town. There's an associate YHA hostel ($11 a night) at the *Warrumbungles Mountain*

Motel (☎ (068) 42 1832) nine km out of town on the road to the national park.

Narrabri is a cotton-growing centre with the enormous Australia Telescope (actually five linked radio telescope dishes) 20 km west on the Yarrie Lake road. The visitor centre is open between 8 am and 4 pm daily. The **Mt Kaputar National Park**, good for walking, camping and climbing, is 53 km east of Narrabri by a steep gravel road. The huge dish of an OTC overseas communications antenna (tours given four times daily on weekdays) marks **Moree**. The town is on the flood-prone Gwydir River.

MOREE TO GLEN INNES

Between Moree and Glen Innes in New England is **Bingara**, a gemstone centre with an early gold-mining history. Turn off the Gwydir Highway at Warialda. The Bingara Historical Society Museum was probably the town's first hotel.

Inverell, further east, is a popular fossicking centre, particularly for sapphires. It's also a base for white-water rafting on the Gwydir River. The town has a National-Trust-classified courthouse and a pioneer village with buildings dating from the 1830s. A little south of Inverell is **Tingha** with the excellent Smith Museum of Mining & Natural History.

ALONG THE CASTLEREAGH

Coonamble, 98 north of Gilgandra, is at the edge of the Western Plains and from here you can travel west to the extensive **Macquarie Marshes** with their prolific bird life. The road continues north to **Walgett** in harsh, dry country near the Grawin and Glengarry opal fields.

A few km off the highway close to the Queensland border, **Lightning Ridge** is a huge opal field which is the only reliable source in the world of black opals. This remote centre is heavily into tourism with underground opal showrooms, an art gallery, a bottle museum, an opal mine which you can visit and much more. There are motels (none cheap) and a number of caravan parks with on-site vans. The *Tram-O-Tel* (☎ (068)

29 0448) on Morilla St has accommodation in converted trams for $20, or $15 per person sharing.

ALONG THE MITCHELL

From Dubbo the Mitchell Highway passes through the citrus-growing centre of **Narromine**. **Warren**, further north and off the Mitchell on the Macquarie Highway, is another access point for the Macquarie marshes, as is **Nyngan** where the Mitchell and Barrier Highways divide. The huge marshes are breeding grounds for ducks, water hens, swans, pelicans, ibis and herons. Nyngan was the scene of fierce resistance by Aborigines to early White encroachment.

The country north-west of Nyngan, the Western Plains which stretch away on the inland side of the Great Dividing Range, is a vast, tree-dotted plain eventually shelving off into the barren outback – the 'back of Bourke'. From Nyngan the highway and the railway both run arrow-straight for 206 km to Bourke, and further west really is the 'back of beyond'.

Outback

The far west of New South Wales is rough, rugged and sparsely populated, but it also produces a fair proportion of the state's wealth – particularly from the mines of Broken Hill. Although Broken Hill is far from everywhere, there are a number of places of great interest in the far west of the state.

BOURKE (population 3500)

Nearly 800 km north-west of ,Sydney, Bourke is known for nothing much apart from being on the edge of the outback – 'back of Bourke' is synonymous with the outback, the back of beyond. A glance at the map will show just how outback the area beyond Bourke is – there's no town of any size for far around, and the country is flat and featureless as far as the eye can see. Its very remoteness attracts a steady stream of visitors.

Bourke is on the Darling River as well as the Mitchell Highway, and before the roads came it was a major port. The courthouse (a fanciful building) has a crown on its spire, signifying that its jurisdiction includes maritime cases. There are other fine old administrative buildings around town.

The tourist information centre is at the bus depot (the old railway station) on Anson St. Here you can get a leaflet called *Swagman's Outback Mud Map Tours Bourke* detailing some drives to places like **Mt Gunderbooka** (with Aboriginal cave art and vivid wild flowers in spring), **Mt Oxley**, and **Fort Bourke Stockade**, just south of Bourke, where an early explorer tangled with Aborigines.

There is motel and pub accommodation in town, and the *Paddlewheel Caravan Park* (☎ (068) 72 2277) has tent sites ($7), vans (from $16), cabins and self-contained units (both from $30). Both the *Bowling Club* and the *Oxley Club* have Chinese menus.

Brewarrina is 95 km east of Bourke. The name is an Aboriginal word meaning 'good fishing' and there are Aboriginal stone fishing traps, known as the 'rocks' or the 'fisheries', just down from a weir they built in the Barwon River. If you visit here or one of the other outback attractions off the track around Bourke, visit a police station before leaving, to find out road conditions and also so they'll know where to start looking if you break down.

From Bourke the Mitchell Highway heads into Queensland at Barringum, with Cunnamulla 119 km over the border. Countrylink buses run between Dubbo and Bourke four times a week and connect with trains to Sydney ($66).

BACK OF BOURKE/CORNER COUNTRY

Back of Bourke really is just what the name says. There's no sealed road anywhere west of Bourke in New South Wales, and if you cared to drive the 713 km from Bourke to Broken Hill via Wanaaring and Milparinka it would be mostly on unsealed road. The far western corner of the state is a harsh, dry area of red plains, heat, dust and flies but with interesting physical features and prolific wildlife. The border between New South Wales and Queensland is marked by the dingo-proof fence, patrolled every day by boundary riders who each look after a 40 km section. Always seek local advice before setting off to travel in this area, particularly on secondary roads.

Milparinka

Milparinka, once a gold town, now consists of little more than a solitary hotel and some old sandstone buildings. In 1845 members of Charles Sturt's expedition from Adelaide, searching for an inland sea, were forced to camp near here for six months. The temperatures were high, the conditions terrible and their supplies inadequate. You can see the grave of James Poole, Sturt's second-in-command, about 14 km north-west of the settlement. Poole died of scurvy.

Tibooburra

Tibooburra, known as the hottest place in the state, is right in the north-west corner and has a number of stone buildings from the 1880s and '90s. Tibooburra used to be known as the Granites from the granite outcrops nearby – these are good to visit on a sunset walk. Although the town is so isolated, international flights bound for Sydney go right overhead and you often see them passing over. You can normally reach Tibooburra from Bourke or Broken Hill in a conventional vehicle except after rain (which is pretty rare!). There's a good National Parks office in town.

Places to Stay & Eat There's a national park camp site just north of town at *Dead Horse Gully*, where sites cost $4. In town, the *Granites Caravan Park* (☎ (080) 91 3305) has camping at $8, cabins at $30 and motel units at $35 to $50. Also, there are two fine old hotels – the *Family Hotel* (☎ (080) 91 3314) and the *Tibooburra Hotel* (☎ (080) 92 3310) (known as 'the two storey'), both with doubles at $30 to $35. The hotels do good

counter meals and even have tables outside where you can sit and watch the occasional 4WD pass by; very pleasant in the cooler months.

Sturt National Park

Tibooburra is an entry point for the Sturt National Park in the very corner of the state. The park has 300 km of driveable tracks, camping areas and even some walks – on the Jump Up Loop drive and to the top of Mt Wood. It is recommended that you inform the park ranger at Tibooburra before venturing into the park, however.

At Camerons Corner there's a post to mark the place where Queensland, South Australia and New South Wales meet. It's a favourite goal for visitors and a 4WD is not necessary to get there. Here (in the Queensland corner) the *Corner Sore* (!) does good sandwiches, homemade pies and even ice cream. Everybody coming by the Corner stops here and they have good advice on road conditions.

Country Race Meets

Some of the country race meetings are real occasions – the one at Louth, about 100 km south-west of Bourke, is particularly revered. The town's population is only about 50 and one year they recorded 29 planes 'flying in for the day'!

BARRIER HIGHWAY

The Barrier Highway is the main route in New South Wales's west. It heads west from Nyngan, and it's 594 km from there to Broken Hill. This road is an alternative route between Sydney and Adelaide and is the most direct route between Sydney and Western Australia.

Cobar (population 5500)

Cobar has a modern and highly productive copper mine but it also has an earlier history as evidenced by its old buildings, like the fine Great Western Hotel with its endless stretch of iron lacework ornamenting the verandah. There's a good museum; ask at the tourist information centre (☎ (068) 36 2448) in the main street about mine tours. There's a caravan park (☎ (068) 36 2425), pub accommodation and several motels, cheapest of which is the *Cross Roads* (☎ (068) 36 2711) on the corner of Bourke and Louth Rds, with singles/doubles from $38/46.

Near Cobar you can see 'Towser's Huts' – mud and stone huts rented out to miners in the 1890s. Weather balloons are released at 9 am and 3 pm daily from the meteorological station near Cobar. The important Mt Grenfell Aboriginal cave paintings are 40 km west of Cobar then 32 km north off the highway. You can't camp here but there are toilets and tank water. For more information contact National Parks in Cobar (☎ (068) 36 2692).

Wilcannia

Wilcannia is on the Darling River and in the days of paddle-steamers was an important river port. It's a much quieter place today, but you can still see buildings from that era – including the Athenaeum Chambers where the tourist information centre is located.

Wilcannia has a couple of motels costing around $50 a double. The local pub may provide meals, but it is best avoided unless you are an experienced bar room brawler.

White Cliffs

About 100 km north-west of Wilcannia is White Cliffs, an old opal-mining settlement. For a taste of life in a small outback community, it's worth the drive on a dirt road. You can fossick for opals around the old diggings, and there are a number of opal showrooms and underground homes open for inspection. Jock's Place is worth seeing – he has old relics collected in the area and can tell you about opal mining. Rosavilla is another, and they also offer horse-drawn wagon tours. A tourist pamphlet is available from the general store or the showrooms.

As you enter White Cliffs you pass the high-tech dishes of the solar energy research station, where emus often graze out the front. The station is open for inspection every day at 2 pm.

Places to Stay The *White Cliffs Hotel* (☎ (080) 91 6606) has basic rooms, but they

are air-con and good value at $22 a double. The management is friendly, all meals are available (although they're pricey) and there is a 4WD for guests' use – around town only. Of course the pub is also the centre of the town's social activity and the place to hear a few yarns over a beer. The *Post Office Family Inn* (☎ (080) 91 6645) has rooms for $12 per person and $3.50 breakfasts. The *White Cliffs Underground Motel* (☎ (080) 91 6677) has singles/doubles for $48/68. There is also a caravan park.

Mootwingee National Park

In the Bynguano Range, 131 km north of Broken Hill, there is an Aboriginal tribal ground with rock carvings and cave paintings – a national historic site which has been badly defaced by vandals. The major site is now controlled by the Aboriginal community and was closed to visitors for years but now there are two-hour ranger-escorted tours on Wednesdays and Saturdays at 11 am. The park is teeming with kangaroos and other wildlife and it is a place of quite exceptional beauty. It is well worth the 1½ to two-hour drive from Broken Hill, though be warned that it involves travelling on an isolated dirt road.

There are walks through the crumbling sandstone hills to rock pools, which usually have enough water for swimming, and rock paintings can still be seen in the areas that are not off limits. There is a camp site with toilets and water for washing, but drinking water might not be always available.

Silverton

Silverton, 25 km west of Broken Hill, is an old silver-mining town with historic buildings and a museum. Mining in the area dates from 1875 and developed further with the establishment of the mine at Umberumberka. Silverton peaked in 1885 when it had a population of 3000 and solid public buildings designed to last for centuries. In 1889 the mines at Silverton were closed and the population (and many of the houses) moved to Broken Hill.

Today it's an interesting little ghost town,

used as a setting in the films *Mad Max II*, *A Town Like Alice* and *Razorback*. A number of buildings still stand, including the old jail, now an historical museum (admission $1) and the Silverton Hotel. The hotel displays photographs taken on the film sets. There are also a couple of artists, Peter Brown and Albert Woodroffe, whose galleries are worth viewing.

The road beyond Silverton becomes bleak and lonely almost immediately but the **Umberumberka Reservoir**, 10 km from Silverton, is a popular picnic spot and **Penrose Park** has animal and bird life.

Bill Canard runs a variety of camel tours from Silverton, including a 15-minute tour of the town for $5 and a two-hour sunset trek for $40. The camels are often hitched up near the hotel or the School Craft Centre, or phone (080) 88 5327 or (080) 88 5306 after hours.

BROKEN HILL (population 27,000)

Out in the far west, Broken Hill is an oasis in the wilderness. It's a fascinating town not only for its comfortable existence in an extremely unwelcoming environment, but also for the fact that it was once a one-company town which spawned one equally strong union.

The Broken Hill Proprietary Company (BHP), after which the town was named, was formed in 1885 after a boundary rider, Charles Rasp, discovered a silver lode. Miners working on other finds in the area had failed to notice the real wealth. Other mining claims were staked, but BHP was always the 'big mine' and dominated the town. Charles Rasp went on to amass a personal fortune, and BHP, which later diversified into steel production, became Australia's largest company.

Early conditions in the mine were appalling. Hundreds of miners died and many more suffered from lead poisoning and lung disease. This gave rise to the other great force in Broken Hill, the unions. Many miners were immigrants – from Ireland, Germany, Italy and Malta – but all were united in their efforts to improve mining conditions.

The first 35 years of Broken Hill saw a militancy rarely matched in Australian industrial relations. Many campaigns were fought, police were called in to break strikes, and though there was a gradual improvement in conditions, the miners lost many confrontations. The turning point was the Big Strike of 1919 and 1920 lasting for over 18 months. The miners won a great victory, achieving a 35-hour week and the end of dry drilling, responsible for the dust that afflicted so many miners.

The concept of 'one big union', which had helped to win the strike, was formalised in 1923 with the formation of the Barrier Industrial Council, which still largely runs the town.

Today the richest silver/lead/zinc deposit in the world is still being worked, but lead and zinc have assumed a greater importance in the Silver City, as Broken Hill is known. There is enough ore left to ensure at least another 20 years of mining, but the new technology has greatly reduced the number of jobs in the mines.

In many ways Broken Hill is closer to South Australia than New South Wales. Broken Hill is 1170 km west of Sydney, but only 509 km from Adelaide and the clocks are set on Adelaide (central) rather than Sydney (eastern) time – half an hour behind.

Information

The city is laid out in a straightforward grid pattern, and the central area is easy to get around on foot. The impressive visitor centre (☎ (080) 87 6077) on the corner of Bromide and Blende Sts is open daily from 8.30 am to 5 pm. This building houses the main bus station, car rental desks and a good cafeteria. The National Parks office (☎ (080) 88 5933) is at 5 Oxide St. The Royal Automobile Association of South Australia (☎ (080) 88 4999) is at 261 Argent St and provides reciprocal service to other autoclub members. The swimming pool is on the corner of Sulphide and Wolfram Sts.

There's always a chance of power cuts in Broken Hill, as a huge flock of corellas has taken up residence near the power station

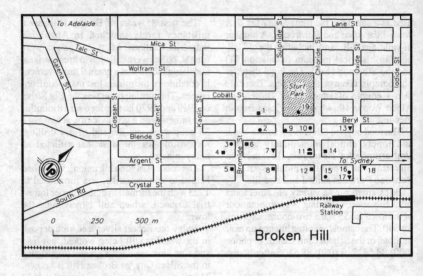

Broken Hill

1 Mario's Motel
2 Railway Museum
3 Tourist & Travel Centre
4 Tourist Lodge
5 Silver Spade Motel
6 Black Lion Inn
7 Champion Pizza
   & Chinese Take-Away
8 Mario's Palace Hotel
9 Trades Hall
10 Entertainment Centre
11 Post Office
12 Grand Private Hotel
13 International Store Deli
14 Royal Exchange Hotel
15 RSL Club
16 National Parks Office
17 Chinese Restaurant
18 Papa Joe's Pizza
19 City Art Gallery

and the birds amuse (and fry) themselves by
gnawing at the cables.

Mines

There are four working mines, controlled by
two companies. The deepest mine is the
North Mine, which goes down 1600 metres.

At that depth it can reach 60°C and massive
refrigeration plants are needed to control the
temperature. Unfortunately the working
mines can no longer be visited, but there are
two good tours of old mines.

Delprat's Mine (☎ (080) 88 1064) has an
excellent underground tour daily except
Sunday, where you don miners' gear and
descend 130 metres for a tour lasting nearly
two hours. It costs $18 (students $15).
Nobody under 12 years of age is allowed. To
get there go up Iodide St, cross the railway
tracks and follow the signs – it's about a
five-minute drive.

The Day Dream Mine, begun in 1881, is
33 km from Broken Hill, off the Silverton
Rd. A one-hour tour costs $10 for adults, $5
for children (or about $20 and $8.50 including transport from Broken Hill). Sturdy
footwear is essential. Contact the tourist
information centre for bookings.

The Gladstone Mining Museum on the
corner of South and Morish Sts in South
Broken Hill has life-size working exhibits in
an old hotel. It's open from 2 to 5 pm on
Monday, Wednesday, Friday and Saturday,
and school holidays. Admission is $4.
Follow South Rd around from the west end

of Crystal St and turn left at Eyre St; South St is on the right.

Artists

Broken Hill seems to inspire artists and there is a plethora of galleries in the town. They include the Broken Hill City Art Gallery in the Entertainment Centre, the Pro Hart Gallery at 108 Wyman St, and Jack Absalom's Gallery at 683 Chapple St. Wyman and Chapple STs run parallel to Mica St to the north-west of the town centre. Pro Hart, a former miner, is Broken Hill's best known artist and a local personality. Apart from his own work, his gallery displays minor works of major artists (Picasso, Dali, Roualt), but his collection of Australian art is superb. He charges admission ($2), but many others don't.

Some of the artists are friendly characters willing to chat with visitors. Try Hugh Schulz's Gallery at 52 Morgan St – the style of his paintings is naive and he's an interesting man to talk with. The Ant Hill Gallery on Bromide St opposite the information centre features local and major Australian artists. In the City Art Gallery is the 'Silver Tree', an intricate silver sculpture commissioned by Charles Rasp. Other paintings of various eras are displayed, and one gallery is devoted to the artists of Broken Hill.

Flying Doctor & School of the Air

You can visit the Royal Flying Doctor Service at the airport. Bookings must be made through the tourist information centre. The tour includes a film, and you inspect the headquarters, aircraft and the radio room that handles calls from remote towns and stations. Tour times are Monday to Friday, 10.30 am and 3.30 pm, and weekends at 10.30 am. The cost is $2 for adults, free for children under 12.

You can sit in on School of the Air broadcasts to kids in isolated homesteads, on weekdays at 8.30 am during school terms. The one-hour session costs $1 and must be booked through the information centre.

Afghani Mosque

There's a relic of the Afghani camel trains of the last century in the Afghani Mosque, built in 1891. The Afghani cameleers helped to open up the outback and the mosque was built on the site of a camel camp. It's on the corner of William and Buck Sts in North Broken Hill. Those wishing to visit are welcome on Sunday from about 2 pm.

Other Attractions

The new **Broken Hill Interpretive Centre**, in the same building as the visitor centre, is a good place to begin – here there are displays on all aspects of Broken Hill and the area and information on heritage walks around the city. The new **Geo-Interpretive Centre** in the old Bond Store has displays on the mineral wealth of the area and its exploitation.

At **White's Mineral Art Gallery & Mining Museum**, 1 Allendale St, you can walk into a mining stope and see mining memorabilia and minerals. It has a craft shop and sells crushed mineral collages. Follow Galena St out to the north-west for two km or so.

Organised Tours

Walking tours of the city are organised from Monday to Friday at 10.30 am, Sunday at 10.30 am and 2.30 pm. Enquire at the information centre. There are also self-drive tours of the city and a sundown nature trail in the hills north of the city; the information centre has brochures.

Silver City Tours (☎ (080) 87 6956) is one of the larger operators, with tours of the city and mines ($14), art galleries ($16), Royal Flying Doctor Service ($6), Silverton ($20), and further afield to White Cliffs ($90), Mootwingee ($60) and Menindee Lakes ($60), among others. All tours can be booked through the information centre and they can provide a full list of the many tours that run from Broken Hill to as far afield as the Flinders Ranges and the Sturt National Park.

A really interesting way to see some of the country beyond Broken Hill is to go along on an outback mail run. Contact Lindon Aviation (☎ (080) 88 5257), as far in advance as possible as these flights can be heavily booked. Their Saturday mail run departs at 7 am and takes you to approximately 16 outback stations and stops in White Cliffs before arriving back at Broken Hill at about 4 pm. The cost is $165 including lunch. On Tuesday the mail run stops at fewer stations, so you get four hours in White Cliffs. They also do various outback air tours – you can make a day trip to the Bourke and Wills 'dig' tree and Innamincka for $340 (minimum four passengers). Their wildlife tour for $165 (minimum three passengers) is popular.

Places to Stay

Close to the bus station there are a couple of accommodation possibilities. At 100 Argent St the *Tourist Lodge* (☎ (080) 88 2086) is YHA-associated and has dorm beds at $12 for YHA members only and spartan singles/doubles at $20/32. There's a lounge with a TV and pool table and a basic kitchen, all a bit musty. Across the road from the information centre the *Black Lion Inn* (☎ (080) 87 4801) is good value at $18/28 for singles/doubles with common bathroom. The rooms are old-fashioned but well kept.

Along Argent St there is a string of hotels, some of them very grand old places like *Mario's Palace Hotel* (☎ (080) 88 1699) at No 227 with its foyer and stairs painted with garish frescoes by local artists. The rooms are nothing special but OK for $22/30 for singles/doubles or $35/40 for better rooms with bathrooms. The place certainly has atmosphere (it's worth a look even if you don't stay there) but one traveller found it noisy all night. Further down at 320 Argent St, on the corner of Chloride St, the *Royal Exchange* (☎ (080) 87 2308) is another grand old place with large, comfortable singles/doubles at $34/48 with bathroom, $25 without. The *Grand Private Hotel* (☎ (080) 87 5305) at No 317 has had a face-lift and costs $38/45 in comfortable rooms with TV, and including a light breakfast. There are lots more hotels around town.

Broken Hill also has plenty of motels, although most of them are expensive. *Mario's Motel* (☎ (080) 88 5944) at 172 Beryl St, two blocks from Mario's Palace Hotel, has singles/doubles for $30/40, but it's a bit run down. The *Sturt Motel* (☎ (086) 87 3558), on the Adelaide road a little way from the centre, has specials from about $35. Most of the other motels are in the $50 to $70 bracket.

Camping The *Broken Hill Caravan Park* (☎ (080) 87 3841) on Rakow St to the north-west and the *Lake View Caravan Park* (☎ (080) 88 2250) at 1 Mann St to the east both have camp sites for $8 a double and on-site vans from around $23.

Places to Eat

Broken Hill is club town if ever there was one. They welcome visitors and in most cases you just sign the book at the front door and walk in. Background music consists of the continuous rattle of one-armed bandits (poker machines), but most have reasonably priced, reasonably good, very filling food. The *Barrier Social Democratic Club*, 218 Argent St, has good value counter meals, and an $8.50 breakfast (from 6 am) will keep you going all day. The *Musician's Club* at 267 Crystal St, is slightly cheaper, while the *RSL* is a bit more up-market.

There are lots of pubs too – this is a mining town – like the *Royal Exchange Hotel* at the corner of Argent St and Chloride St. Here, the *Pepinella Grill Room* is in a nice old dining room and has main courses in the $9 to $12 bracket and a superb serve-yourself salad table. They sometimes fly in fresh seafood. There are also cheaper counter meals in the bar.

The cafeteria in the information centre isn't bad value. *Papa Joe's* on Argent St has pasta and pizzas, although it doesn't stay open as late as the *Champion Pizza & Chinese Takeaway* on Sulphide St. Around the corner from Papa Joe's is the *Lobster Pot*, a fish & chip shop where you can eat in if you want. The *deli* on Oxide St near Beryl St is good for late-night supplies, and is worth a look at any time for its range of cheeses and cold meats.

Getting There & Away
Air Standard fares (check for specials) from Broken Hill include $145 to Adelaide with Kendall and Sunstate, $316 to Sydney with Hazelton, $95 to Mildura and $193 to Melbourne with Sunstate. With the major domestic airlines involved in a price war, it might be cheaper to go by bus to Adelaide and catch their flights there.

Bus Greyhound/Pioneer run daily to Adelaide for $40, to Mildura for $38 and to Sydney for $125. Buses depart from the tourist information centre, where you can book seats.

Train Broken Hill is on the Sydney to Perth railway line so the Indian Pacific passes through. To Sydney (Tuesday, Thursday and Saturday) it's $78 in 2nd class or $108 with a sleeping berth. There's also the 5 am daily Laser service for $78 – you take a Countrylink bus to Dubbo and an XPT train from there. To Adelaide the Indian Pacific costs $40 and takes seven hours. It leaves on Monday, Thursday and Saturday. To Melbourne, the Victorian government V/Line service runs on Monday, Wednesday, Friday and Sunday and costs $77. This involves taking a bus to Mildura and there connecting with a train.

Getting Around
There are plenty of taxis around Broken Hill. The major rental companies have offices here, but their 'remote region' rates can work out to be very expensive as the maximum free km allowance is 100 km per day. The Caltex station (☎ (080) 87 7512) at 190 Argent St might be marginally cheaper than the majors.

SOUTH OF BROKEN HILL
Menindee Lakes
This water storage development on the Darling River, 112 km south-east of Broken Hill, offers a variety of water sport facilities. Menindee is the town for the area. Bourke and Wills stayed in the Maiden's Hotel on their ill-fated trip north in 1860. The hotel was built in 1854 and has been with the same family for nearly 100 years. The Kinchega National Park is close to the town and the lakes, overflowing from the Darling River, are a haven for bird life.

Mungo National Park
North-east of Mildura and south of Menindee is Lake Mungo, site of the oldest archaeological finds in Australia – human skeletons and artefacts dating back 40,000 years. On the huge sand dunes on the edge of the lake even beginners can find evidence of ancient visitors, especially with the help of tours run by the park rangers. There's a visitor centre by the huge old Mungo woolshed and limited camping facilities. The park is part of the Willandra Lakes World Heritage Region.

A road leads across the dry lake bed to the dunes, known as the Great Wall of China or the Mungo Lunette. With 4WD you can make a complete 60-km loop of the dunes, and there are tours running from Mildura, in Victoria.

The Mungo Lodge is 2km outside the park on the road to Mildura. Motel rooms are $58.00 a double, or they have self-contained cottages sleeping four to six for $68.00.

Lord Howe Island

Only 11 km long and 2½ km wide, beautiful Lord Howe Island is a long way out in the Pacific, virtually due east of Port Macquarie and 600 km north-east of Sydney.

Lord Howe is really off the budget track, and apart from the expense of getting there you won't find much by the way of cheap accommodation. Most visitors to Lord Howe are on package tours.

It's heavily forested and has beautiful walks, a wide lagoon sheltered by a coral reef, and some fine beaches. It's small enough to get around on foot or by bicycle. The southern end is dominated by towering Mt Lidgbird (808 metres) and Mt Gower

(875 metres). You can climb Mt Gower in around six hours, round trip.

The lagoon has good snorkelling, and you can also inspect the sealife from glass-bottomed boats. On the other side of the island there's surf at Blinky Beach. The Lord Howe Island Historical Museum is usually open from 8 to 10 pm each evening. There's a shell museum, open Monday to Friday from 10 am to 4 pm and movies are shown in the public hall on Saturday and Tuesday.

Information
For more information on Lord Howe Island check with the Pacific Island Tourist Centre (☎ (02) 262 6011), 7th floor, 39-41 York St, Sydney.

Places to Stay
There are no camping grounds on the island. You can stay in full-board lodges or in apartments, usually with facilities for preparing your own food. Prices rise over Christmas/January, but even in the low season they're in the $200-dollar-a-day range. Food is more expensive than on the Australian mainland.

Getting There & Away
You used to get to Lord Howe by romantic old four-engined flying boats from Sydney. Today they've been retired and a small airport has been built on the island. One-way fares with Eastern Australia Airlines (an Australian Airlines subsidiary) are $337 from Sydney and $488 from Port Macquarie. With Oxley Airlines it's $330 from Port Macquarie or Coffs Harbour. There is no discounting on these routes unless you happen to be a Lord Howe resident.

Getting Around
You can hire bicycles from a number of places for $3 a day. There are motorcycles and a few rental cars on the island too, but a bike is all you need. There is an overall 25 kph speed limit.

Northern Territory

Area 1,346,000 sq km
Population 158,500

The fascinating Northern Territory is the least populated and most barren area of Australia. The populated parts of Australia are predominantly urban and coastal, but it is in the centre – the Red Heart – that the picture-book, untamed, sometimes surreal Australia exists.

The Red Centre is not just Ayers Rock, bang in the middle of nowhere. There are meteorite craters, eerie canyons, lost valleys of palms and noisy Alice Springs festivals. Where else is there an annual boat regatta on a river that hardly ever has any water? The red, incidentally, is evident as soon as you arrive – in the soil, the rocks and in Ayers Rock itself.

At the other end of the Track – the 1500 km of bitumen that connects Alice Springs to the north coast – is Darwin, probably the most cosmopolitan city in Australia, not to mention the heaviest-drinking city in the world. There is an annual boat race in Darwin for boats constructed entirely of beer cans – they have to use up the empties somehow.

Even that long, empty road between Alice Springs and Darwin isn't dull – there are plenty of interesting places along the way. As you travel up or down that single link you'll notice another of the Territory's real surprises – the contrast between the Centre's amazing aridity and the humid, tropical wetness of the Top End in the monsoon season. The wetlands and escarpments of Kakadu National Park are a treasure house of wildlife and Aboriginal rock painting.

With a small population and a more fragile economy than other parts of Australia, the Northern Territory isn't classified as a state. It was formerly administered by New South Wales and then by South Australia, but it has been controlled directly by the Federal Government since 1911. Since 1978 the Territory has been self-governing, although Canberra still has more say over its internal affairs than over those of the states.

NORTHERN TERRITORY ABORIGINES

About a quarter of the Territory's population is Aboriginal – a higher proportion than in most southern states.

The process of White settlement in the Northern Territory was just as troubled and violent as elsewhere in Australia, with Aboriginal groups vainly trying to resist the takeover of lands on which their way of life depended. By the early 20th century, most Aborigines were confined to government-allotted reserves or Christian missions. Others lived on cattle stations where they were employed as skilful and poorly paid stockmen or domestic servants, or were living a half-life on the edges of towns, attracted there by food and tobacco, sometimes finding low-paid work, too often acquiring an alcohol habit. Only a few – some of those on reserves, a few on cattle stations, and those in the remote outback – maintained much of their traditional way of life.

This situation largely persisted despite a

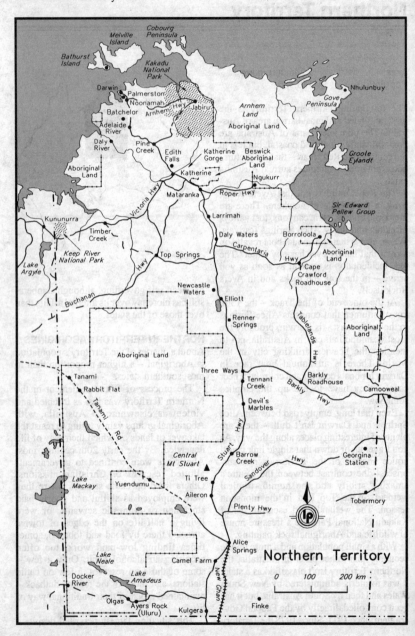

later shift in government policy to 'assimilation' – the belief that Aborigines should become fully integrated into White society. This, among other things, led to the gathering of many bush people, sometimes from different and mutually hostile clans, into settlements for education, welfare, etc.

In the 1960s, Northern Territory Aborigines began to demand more rights. In 1963 the people of Yirrkala on the Gove Peninsula, part of the Arnhem Land reserve, protested against plans for bauxite mining. In 1966 the Gurindji people on Wave Hill cattle station went on strike and asked for their tribal land, which formed part of the station, to be returned to them. Eventually the Gurindji were given 3238 sq km in a government-negotiated deal with the station owners. The Yirrkala people failed to stop the mining, but the way they presented their case, by producing sacred objects and bark paintings that showed their right to the land under Aboriginal custom, was a milestone.

In 1968, Aborigines gained the vote. In 1976 the Aboriginal Land (Northern Territory) Act was passed in Canberra. It handed over all reserves and mission lands in the Territory to Aboriginal ownership, and allowed Aboriginal groups to claim government land with which they have traditional ties (unless the land is already leased to someone, or in a town, or set aside for some other special purpose). Today, despite one or two tricks by unsympathetic authorities, Aborigines own more than one-third of the Northern Territory. This includes Uluru National Park, which was handed over to its original Pitjantjatjara owners in 1985 and immediately leased back to the national government for use as a national park. Minerals on Aboriginal land are still government property – though the landowners' permission for exploration and mining is usually required and has to be paid for.

The Northern Territory land rights laws have improved the lot of many Aborigines and encouraged the Outstation Movement that started in the 1970s. Aborigines began to leave the settlements and return to a more traditional, nomadic lifestyle on their own

land. Many, however, still remain in depressing conditions on the fringes of towns. Ironically, equal-pay laws in the 1960s deprived Aborigines of a major source of work, as many cattle station owners reacted by employing White stockmen instead.

While White goodwill is still on the increase, and more Aborigines are able to deal effectively with Whites, there are still many yawning gulfs between the cultures. White racism persists, as exhibited in the 'dress regulations' posted on the doors of many Northern Territory pubs. Finding a mode of harmonious coexistence remains a serious and long-term problem.

For these and other reasons it's usually hard for short-term visitors to make real contact with Aborigines, who often prefer to be left to themselves. This reticence can also exist between Aboriginal clans, who may speak different languages – there are about 70 separate Aboriginal languages in the Northern Territory.

Many Aborigines do not appreciate their photos being taken by strangers, even at a distance.

Aboriginal Art

You'll see lots of Aboriginal art in Alice Springs, Darwin and other towns. Art for sale is a modern development from sacred traditions like body and rock painting, and designs laid out on the earth.

Best known among the Northern Territory Aboriginal artists is Albert Namatjira (1902-59) whose European-style watercolour landscapes rank among the best of all Australian painting.

The Aboriginal 'dot' painters began their work in the early 1970s at Papunya, 258 km west of Alice Springs. They came from several tribes, and had been moved to Papunya against their will. They found a way of keeping traditions alive by depicting Dreamtime stories in paint. Their works look abstract, but in fact usually show, in a kind of map or code form, events from the journeys of the Dreamtime beings who travelled across the land creating its natural features and culture. Aborigines associate themselves and their traditional lands closely with these beings, whose special places have to be protected.

Paintings from the Papunya 'school' now hang in galleries in Australia and overseas, and artists elsewhere in the Territory are also painting in acrylic paint on canvas. The best examples change hands for five, sometimes six-figure sums. Such a success story has its down side – intermediaries sometimes make most of the profit and a lot of inferior work is flooding onto the market. Increasingly, however, the artists' co-operatives are marketing their work themselves. The less accomplished work has the merit of being cheaper – and it's also making money and creating work for the community. You can pick up good poster prints of some paintings, and several reasonably priced books with lots of colour plates and explanatory write-ups are available.

From the Centre come some attractive carved wooden animals, with designs burnt into them. Some of these can be picked up for $20 or less in shops and aren't too big for a backpack. More expensive is the batik which has been produced in recent years by women in several places in the Territory – notably Utopia, 250 km north-east of Alice Springs. Some of this work has found its way into major city galleries.

Among the treasures of the Top End are the rock paintings of Arnhem Land and Kakadu, which in some cases are more than 20,000 years old; they are among the world's most important ancient works of art.

Another art form in the north is painting on tree bark, which originated in western Arnhem Land. It was introduced to central and east Arnhem Land by missionaries earlier this century. Many of the designs from body painting and rock painting now appear on bark. The painters of western Arnhem Land turn out figures on plain backgrounds either in the distinctive X-ray style showing animals' bones and internal organs, or in *Mimi* style developed from ancient 'stick figure' rock art. East and central Arnhem Land artists produce more detailed, narrative-style pictures.

From Arnhem Land, notably the north-east, come excellent painted woodcarvings, mainly of birds – distinguishable from central Australian carvings by their designs and by the use of softer wood. Some of these aren't too pricey – or too big. Arnhem Landers also turn out appealing baskets made of pandanus leaf, coloured and patterned with vegetable dyes. Maningrida in north-central Arnhem Land is one of the chief sources of these. Didgeridoos and boomerangs are also available. Arnhem Land artists are also working on canvas, and some are developing a more personal, transitional, contemporary style.

The Tiwi people of Bathurst and Melville islands, north of Darwin, also produce bark paintings and fine, painted woodcarvings – carved poles showing mythological beings. These poles have developed from *pukamani* burial poles which are erected around graves. The Tiwi also make good pottery, batik and screen-printed fabric. They produce probably the best of the many Aboriginal-design T-shirts on the market. (Try to avoid the many commercially produced imitations of Aboriginal designs – your money will not get back to the real artists.)

Permits

You need a permit to enter Aboriginal land and in general these aren't granted unless you have friends or relatives working there, or you're on an organised tour. The exception to this rule is travel along public roads through Aboriginal land – though if you want to stop, even for fuel or provisions, you need a permit. If you stick to the main highways, there's no problem.

Three land councils deal with all requests for permits: ask the permits officer of the appropriate council for an application form. The Northern Land Council (☎ (089) 81 7011) is at 47 Stuart Highway, Stuart Park, Darwin (postal address: PO Box 39843, Winnellie, NT 0820); the Tiwi Land Council (☎ (089) 78 3991), for Bathurst and Melville islands, is at Nguiu, Bathurst Island, via Darwin, NT 0800; and the Central Land Council (☎ (089) 52 3800) is at 33 Stuart

Highway, Alice Springs (postal address: PO Box 3321, Alice Springs, NT 0871). Permits take around four to six weeks to be processed.

CLIMATE

The Top End thinks in terms of Dry and Wet rather than winter and summer. Roughly, the Dry is April to September, and the Wet is October to March, with the heaviest rain falling from January on. April, with the rains tapering off, and October to December, with uncomfortably high humidity and that 'waiting for the rains' feeling, are transition periods. The Top End is the most thundery part of Australia: Darwin has over 90 'thunderdays' a year, all between September and March.

In the Centre the temperatures are much more variable – plummeting below freezing on winter nights (July to August), and soaring into the high 40s on summer days (December to January). Come prepared for both extremes, and for intense sun and the occasional rainstorm at any time of year. When it rains, dirt roads quickly become quagmires.

INFORMATION

The Northern Territory Government Tourist Bureau (NTGTB) has offices in Alice Springs, Tennant Creek, Katherine, Darwin and in most state capitals. Addresses of the NTGTB state offices are:

New South Wales
    Corner Barrack and George Sts, Sydney (☎ (02) 262 3744)
Queensland
    48 Queen St, Brisbane (☎ (07) 229 5799)
South Australia
    9 Hindley St, Adelaide (☎ (08) 212 1133)
Victoria
    415 Bourke St, Melbourne (☎ (03) 670 6948)
Western Australia
    799 Hay St, Perth (☎ (09) 322 4255)

The NTGTB puts out several useful publications including the *Northern Territory Holiday Planner*.

National Parks

For detailed information on Uluru and Kakadu national parks contact the Australian National Parks & Wildlife Service (☎ (089) 81 5299) in Darwin, which administers these two parks. NTGTB offices also have details on them and there are information offices in the parks themselves. Other parks and natural and historic reserves are run by the Conservation Commission of the Northern Territory, which has offices at Alice Springs, Yulara, Katherine and Darwin, plus an information desk in the NTGTB office in Darwin. The Conservation Commission puts out leaflets on individual parks – usually available in NTGTB offices or from the parks themselves.

ACTIVITIES
Bushwalking

There are interesting bushwalking trails in the Northern Territory, but take care if you venture off the beaten track. You can climb the ranges surrounding Alice Springs, but wear stout shoes (the spinifex grass and burrs are very sharp). In summer, wear a hat and carry water even for short walks. Walking is best in the Dry, although shorter walks are possible in the Wet when the patches of monsoon rainforest are at their best. The Darwin Bushwalking Club (☎ (089) 85 1484) makes weekend expeditions all year round and welcomes visitors.

Swimming

Stay out of the sea during the Wet because box jellyfish stings can be fatal. Darwin beaches are popular, however, during the safe months. Beware too, of saltwater crocodiles in both salt and fresh waters in the Top End – though there are quite a few safe, natural swimming holes. Take local advice – and if in doubt, don't take a risk.

Fishing

This is good, particularly for barramundi, a perch that often grows to over a metre long and is great to eat. Barramundi is found both offshore and inland and there are fishing tours out of Darwin for the express purpose of catching it.

Fossicking

There are many places in the Northern Territory for the fossicker – check in advance with the NTGTB about where the best places are to go and if permission is required. Look around the Harts Range (72 km north-east of Alice Springs) for beryls, garnets and quartz; Eastern MacDonnell Ranges (east of Alice Springs) for beryls and garnets; Tennant Creek for gold and jasper; Anthony Lagoon (215 km east of the Stuart Highway, north of Tennant Creek) for ribbonstone; Pine Creek for gold; and Brock's Creek (37 km south-west of Adelaide River, south of Darwin) for topaz, tourmaline, garnet and zircon.

The Northern Territory Department of Mines & Energy publishes *A Guide to Fossicking in the Northern Territory*. One place you can get it is the Arts & Sciences Museum in Darwin.

Gliding & Parachuting

The thermals created by the dry heat of the Centre are fantastic for gliding. There is a gliding club at Bond Springs, 25 km north of Alice Springs; and a parachuting club at Batchelor, 88 km south of Darwin.

GETTING THERE & AWAY

Transport into the Northern Territory by bus, train, car and air is discussed mainly in the Alice Springs, Darwin and Ayers Rock sections.

GETTING AROUND

Air

Ansett NT has a denser flight network than Ansett or Australian Airlines and, on a couple of routes, slightly cheaper fares. There are also two small airlines: Air North flying between Darwin, Kakadu and Arnhem Land, and between Bathurst and Melville islands; and Tillair which operates between Alice Springs, Tennant Creek, Katherine and Darwin. The chart details regular (and standby) fares.

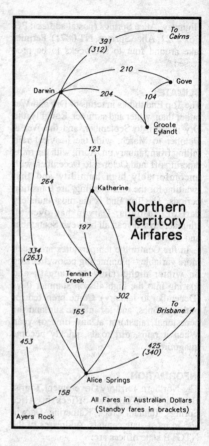

Northern Territory Airfares

All Fares in Australian Dollars (Standby fares in brackets)

Bus

Within the Territory, there's a fairly good bus network by the big national companies. See the Getting There & Away sections for the various towns.

Car

Off the beaten track, 'with care' is the thought to bear in mind, and all the usual precautions apply. You can get up-to-date information on road conditions by phone (☎ (089) 52 3833 in Alice Springs; (089) 84 4455 in Darwin). The offices of the NTGTB will advise you on which roads require a 4WD, all year round or just in the Wet.

It's wise to carry a basic kit of spare parts in case of breakdown. It may not be a matter of life or death, but it can save a lot of time, trouble and expense. Carry spare water, and if you do break down off the main roads, remain with the vehicle; you're more likely to be found and you'll have shade and protection from the heat.

Traffic may be fairly light, but a lot of people still manage to run into things, so watch out for the two great Northern Territory road hazards – road trains and animals. Road trains are huge trucks, which can only be used on the long outback roads of central and northern Australia – they're not allowed into the southern cities. A road train is very long and very big. If you try to overtake one make sure you have plenty of room to complete the manoeuvre. If you pass one travelling in the opposite direction give it plenty of room – if a road train puts its wheels off the road to pass you, the shower of stones and rocks that results will not do you or your windscreen any good.

At night, dusk and dawn the Territory's wildlife comes out to play. Hitting a kangaroo is all too easy and the damage to your vehicle, not to mention the kangaroo, can be severe. There are also buffaloes, cattle, wild horses and a number of other driving hazards which you are wise to avoid. There's really only one sensible way to deal with these night-time road hazards – don't drive at night. If you must drive at night, keep your speed right down, and remember that most animals travel in groups!

An added hazard in the Territory is the fact that there is no speed limit on the open roads, and so the temptation is to travel faster than the road conditions allow.

Hitching

Hitching is possible, but traffic can be scarce outside the towns. Three Ways, where the road to Mt Isa branches off the Darwin to Alice Springs road, is a point notorious for long waits for lifts.

Darwin

Population 73,000

The 'capital' of northern Australia comes as a surprise to many people. Instead of the hard-bitten, rough-and-ready town you might expect, Darwin is a lively, modern place with a young population, easy-going lifestyle and cosmopolitan atmosphere.

In part this is thanks to Cyclone Tracy, which did a comprehensive job of flattening Darwin on Christmas Day 1974. People who were there during the reconstruction say a new spirit grew up with the new buildings, as Darwinites, showing true Top End resilience, took the chance to make their city one of which to be proud. Darwin became a brighter, smarter, sturdier place, and development has continued into the 'post-post-cyclone' phase.

Darwin is still a frontier town, with a fairly transient population and a hard-drinking one at that – it's not easy to resist a beer or two after a day in the heat – but these days there are the full trappings of civilisation too. Darwin's also ethnically diverse with anywhere between 45 and 60 ethnic groups represented, depending on who you listen to. Asian and European accents are almost as thick in the air as the Aussie drawl.

A lot of people only live here for a year or two – it's surprising how many people you meet elsewhere who used to live in Darwin. It's reckoned you can consider yourself a 'Territorian' if you've stuck the climate and remoteness for five years. There is a constant flow of travellers coming and going from Asia, or making their way round Australia. Backpacks seem part of the everyday scene and people always appear to be heading somewhere else.

Darwin is an obvious base for trips to Kakadu and other Top End natural attractions such as Litchfield Park. It's a bit of an oasis too – whether you're travelling south to Alice Springs, west to Western Australia or east to Queensland, there are a lot of km to be covered before you get anywhere, and having reached Darwin many people rest a bit before leaving.

History

It took a long time to decide on Darwin as the site for the region's main centre and even after the city became established growth was slow and troubled. Early attempts to settle the Top End were mainly due to British fears that the French or Dutch might get a foothold in Australia. Between 1824 and 1829 Fort Dundas on Melville Island and Fort Wellington on the Cobourg Peninsula, 200 km north-east of Darwin, were settled then abandoned. Victoria, a further settlement in 1838 on Cobourg's Port Essington harbour, survived a cyclone and malaria, but was abandoned in 1849.

In 1845 the explorer Leichhardt reached Port Essington overland from Brisbane, and this aroused persistent interest in the Top End. The region came under the control of South Australia in 1863, and more ambitious development plans were made. A settlement was established in 1864 at Escape Cliffs at the mouth of the Adelaide River, not too far from Darwin's present locale, but it was abandoned in 1866. Finally Darwin was founded at its present site in 1869. The harbour had been discovered back in 1839 by John Lort Stokes in the *Beagle*, who named it Port Darwin after a former shipmate – the evolutionist Charles Darwin. At first the settlement was called Palmerston, but soon became unofficially known as Port Darwin, and in 1911 the name was officially changed.

Darwin's growth was accelerated by the discovery of gold at Pine Creek, about 200 km south, in 1871, but once the gold fever had run its course Darwin's development slowed down, due to the harsh, unpredictable climate (including occasional cyclones), and its poor communications with other Australian cities.

WW II put Darwin permanently on the map when the town became an important base for Allied action against the Japanese in the Pacific. The road south to the railhead at Alice Springs was surfaced, finally putting the city in direct contact with the rest of the country. Darwin was attacked 64 times during the war and 243 people lost their lives; it was the only place in Australia to suffer prolonged attacks.

Modern Darwin has an important role as the front door to Australia's northern region and as a centre for administration and mining. The port facilities have been expanded – but hopes of a railway line to Alice Springs have receded for the time being. Darwin's population, after rising rapidly, has steadied in the past few years, but the place still has a go-ahead feel.

Orientation

Darwin's centre is a fairly compact area at the end of a peninsula. The Stuart Highway does a big loop entering the city and finally heads south until it ends under the name Daly St. The city centre peninsula stretches southeast from here, and the main city centre shopping area, Smith St and its mall, is about half a km from Daly St.

Long-distance buses arrive at the transit centre at 69 Mitchell St, and there is accommodation a few minutes' walk away. Most of what you'll want in central Darwin is within two or three blocks of the transit centre or Smith St Mall. The suburbs spread a good 12 to 15 km away to the north and east, but the airport is conveniently central.

Information

Tourist Information The NTGTB (☎ 81 6611) is at 31 Smith St, in the mall. It's open from 8.45 am to 5 pm Monday to Friday, from 9 am to 12.30 pm on Saturdays and 10 am to 1 pm Sundays. It has free maps of the city and several decent booklets, and can book just about any tour or accommodation in the Territory. There's also a tourist information desk at the airport.

The NT Government Information Centre (☎ 89 7972) at 13 Smith St, open from Monday to Friday from 9 am to 4 pm, is more for locals, but if you're interested in delving into some aspect of the Northern Territory it may be able to help.

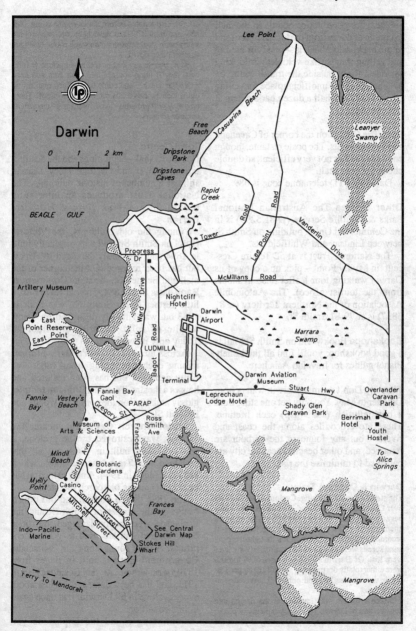

Darwin

0   1   2 km

Lee Point

Free Beach

Casuarina Beach

Leanyer Swamp

Dripstone Park

Dripstone Caves

Rapid Creek

BEAGLE GULF

Tower Road

Lee Point Road

Vanderlin Drive

Progress Dr

McMillans Road

Artillery Museum

Dick Ward Drive

Nightcliff Hotel

Darwin Airport

Marrara Swamp

East Point Reserve

East Point

East Point Road

Bagot Road

LUDMILLA

Terminal

Darwin Aviation Museum

Stuart Hwy

Overlander Caravan Park

Fannie Bay

Vestey's Beach

Fannie Bay Gaol

Gregory St

PARAP

Ross Smith Ave

Leprechaun Lodge Motel

Shady Glen Caravan Park

Berrimah Hotel

Youth Hostel

Museum of Arts & Sciences

Frances Bay Dr

To Alice Springs

Mindil Beach

Gilruth Ave

Botanic Gardens

Myilly Point

Casino

Gardens Rd

Smith Street

Mitchell Street

Frances Bay

Indo–Pacific Marine

See Central Darwin Map

Stokes Hill Wharf

Mangrove

Ferry To Mandorah

Mangrove

There are good notice boards in the mall (a couple of doors from the tourist office) and in the backpacker hostels – good for buying and selling things (like vehicles) or looking for rides. Right outside the transit centre on Mitchell St is the unofficial place for selling cars – you'll see half a dozen parked here at any one time.

Post The GPO is on the corner of Cavenagh and Edmunds Sts. The poste restante, though computerised, is not very efficient, so double check for your mail.

Darwin's STD telephone code is 089.

Other Offices The Australian National Parks & Wildlife Service (☎ 81 5299) is in the Commercial Union building on Smith St between Lindsay and Whitfield Sts.

The National Trust is at 52 Temira Crescent in Myilly Point – pick up a copy of its Darwin walking tour leaflet (also available from the tourist office). The Automobile Association of the Northern Territory (☎ 81 3837) is at 79-81 Smith St.

Bookshops Bookworld on Smith St Mall is a good bookshop; you'll find all the Lonely Planet guides for travel to Asia here.

Warning Don't swim in Darwin waters from October to May. You only get one sting from a box jellyfish (sea wasp) each lifetime. There are crocodiles along the coast and rivers – but any found in the harbour are removed, and other beaches near the city are patrolled to minimise the risk.

Darwin & Cyclone Tracy
The statistics are frightening. Cyclone Tracy built up over Christmas Eve 1974 and by midnight the winds began to reach their full fury. At 3.05 am the airport's anemometer cried 'enough', failing just after it recorded a speed of 217 km/h. It's thought the peak wind speeds were as high as 280 km/h. Sixty-six lives were lost. Of Darwin's 11,200 houses 50% to 60% were either totally destroyed or so badly damaged that repair was impossible, and only 400 survived relatively intact.

Much criticism was levelled at the design and construction of Darwin's houses, but plenty of places a century or more old, and built as solidly as you could ask for, also toppled before the awesome winds. The new and rebuilt houses have been cyclone-proofed with strong steel reinforcements and roofs which are firmly pinned down.

Most people say that next time a cyclone is forecast, they'll jump straight into their cars and head down the Track – and come back afterwards to find out if their houses really were cyclone-proof! Those who stay will probably take advantage of the official cyclone shelters.

Town Centre
Despite its shaky beginnings and the destruction of WW II and Cyclone Tracy, Darwin still has a number of historic buildings. The National Trust produces an interesting booklet titled *A Walk Through Historical Darwin*.

Among the old buildings, the **Victoria Hotel** on Smith St Mall was originally built in 1894 and was badly damaged by Tracy, but has been restored. On the corner of the mall and Bennett St, the stone **Commercial Bank** dates from 1884. The old **town hall**, a little further down Smith St, was built in 1883 but was virtually destroyed by Tracy, despite its solid Victorian construction. Today only its walls remain.

Across the road, **Brown's Mart**, a former mining exchange dating from 1885, was badly damaged but has been restored and houses a theatre. There's a **Chinese temple**, glossy and new, on the corner of Woods and Bennett Sts.

Christ Church Cathedral, nearer the harbour, was destroyed by the cyclone. It was originally built in 1902, but all that remained after Tracy was the porch, which had been added in 1944. A new cathedral has been built and the old porch retained.

The 1884 **police station** and **old courthouse** at the corner of Smith St and the Esplanade were badly damaged, but have been restored and are used as government offices. A little south along the Esplanade, **Government House**, built in stages from 1870, was known as the Residency until 1911, and has been damaged by just about every cyclone to hit Darwin. It is once again in fine condition.

Continuing round the Esplanade you

reach a **memorial** marking where the telegraph cable once ran from Darwin into the sea on its crossing to Banyuwangi in Java. This put Australia into instant communication with Britain for the first time.

Other buildings of interest along the Esplanade include the agreeably tropical **Darwin Hotel**, and **Admiralty House** at the corner of Knuckey St, which houses an arts & crafts gallery showing work by professional Top End artists, both White and Aboriginal. There is a pleasant cafe downstairs.

Across the street at 74 The Esplanade, in Lyons Cottage, is the **British-Australian Telegraph Residence Museum**. It's free and open daily from 10 am to noon and 12.30 to 5 pm. There are displays on pre-1911 north Australian history. About 500 metres further along the Esplanade is modern Darwin's architectural talking point: the pink and blue **Beaufort Darwin Centre**, housing a luxury hotel, a couple of up-market cafes, and the Performing Arts Centre.

The Esplanade is fronted by an expanse of grass and trees, and a pleasant pathway runs along near the sea from the Hotel Darwin to Daly St.

Aquascene

This is one tourist attraction actually worth the cost of admission. At Doctor's Gully, near the corner of Daly St and the Esplanade, fish come in for a feed every day at high tide. Half the stale bread in Darwin gets dispensed to a horde of milkfish, mullet, catfish and batfish. Some are quite big – the milkfish grow to over a metre and will demolish a whole slice of bread in one go. It's a great sight and children love it – the fish will take bread right out of your hand. Feeding times depend on the tides (☎ 81 7837 for tide times). Admission is $3 for adults; the bread is free.

Botanic Gardens

The gardens' site was used to grow vegetables during the earliest days of Darwin. Tracy severely damaged the gardens, uprooting three-quarters of the plants. Fortunately,

vegetation grows fast in Darwin's climate and the Botanic Gardens, with their good collection of tropical flora, were well restored. There's a coastal section over the road, between Gilruth Ave and Fannie Bay. It's an easy bicycle ride out to the gardens from the centre.

Indo-Pacific Marine

This small aquarium is a successful attempt to display living coral and its associated life. Each small tank is a complete ecosystem, with only the occasional extra fish introduced as food for some of the carnivores such as stonefish or angler fish.

They sometimes have box jellyfish, as well as more attractive creatures like sea horses, clown fish and butterfly fish. The aquarium is in Temira House, Lambell Terrace, near the corner of Smith St West and Gilruth Ave, about 1½ km from Smith St Mall. Admission is $5 for adults and it's open Wednesdays, Saturdays and Sundays from noon to 4 pm.

Museum of Arts & Sciences

This excellent museum and art gallery is on Conacher St, Fannie Bay, about four km from the city centre. It's bright, spacious, well laid out, not too big and full of interesting displays. A highlight is the Northern Territory Aboriginal art collection, with just the right mix of exhibits and information to help you start to understand the purpose of this art, its history and regional differences. It's particularly strong on carvings and bark paintings from Bathurst and Melville islands and Arnhem Land.

There's also a good collection on the art of the Pacific and Asian nations closest to Australia, including Indonesian *ikat* (woven cloth) and gamelan instruments; and a sea gypsies' floating home *(prahu)* from Sabah, Malaysia.

Pride of place among the stuffed Northern Territory birds and animals undoubtedly goes to 'Sweetheart', a five-metre, 780 kg saltwater crocodile, who became quite a Top End personality after numerous encounters with fishing dinghies on the Finnis River

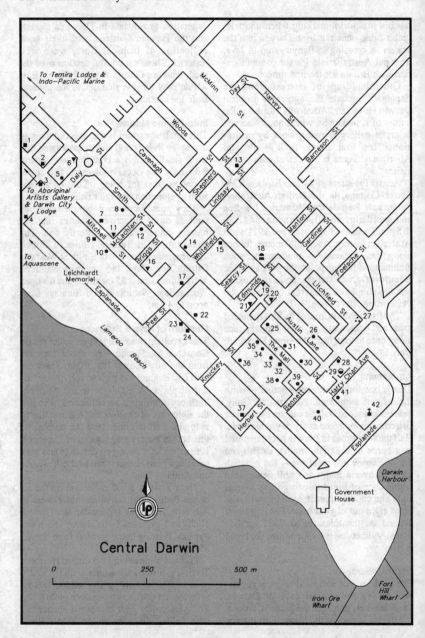

To Temira Lodge &
Indo-Pacific Marine

To Aboriginal
Artists Gallery
& Darwin City
Lodge

To Aquascene

Leichhardt
Memorial

Larrakeeyah Beach

Central Darwin

0   250   500 m

Government
House

Darwin
Harbour

Iron Ore
Wharf

Fort
Hill
Wharf

■ PLACES TO STAY

1 CWA Hostel
2 Inner City Lodge
3 YWCA Hostel
4 YMCA
7 Ivan's Backpackers Hostel
9 Darwin Motor Inn
13 Frogshollow Backpackers
15 Tiwi Lodge
17 Sherwood Lodge
22 Larrakeyah Lodge
23 Transit Centre & Transit Inn
24 Darwin City Youth Hostel
32 Victoria Hotel
37 Darwin Hotel

▼ PLACES TO EAT

6 Thai Garden Restaurant
11 Peppi's Restaurant & Poinciana Inn
16 Sizzler Restaurant
19 Inshore Water Gardens Restaurant
20 Simply Foods & Maharajah
   Indian Restaurant
21 Squire's Tavern & 1990s Nightclub

OTHER

5 Rent-a-Rocket
8 Thrifty Rent-a-Car
10 Performing Arts Centre
12 Rent-a-Dent *
14 Australian National Parks
   & Wildlife Service
18 GPO
25 Paspalis Centrepoint Arcade
   & Singapore Airlines
26 Garuda
27 Chinese Temple
28 Australian Airlines
29 City Bus Depot
30 Bookworld
31 Natrabu Travel Agency
33 NT Government Tourist Bureau
34 Galleria Shopping Centre
35 Darwin Plaza
36 Malaysian Airlines
38 Ansett Airlines
39 Qantas
40 Old Town Hall
41 Brown's Mart
42 Christ Church Cathedral

south of Darwin. Apparently he had a taste for outboard motors. He died during capture in 1979. You can also see a box jellyfish – safely dead – in a jar.

The non-Aboriginal Australian art collection includes works by top names like Nolan, Lindsay and Boyd. The museum has a good little bookshop and, outside, an old pearling lugger, a Vietnamese refugee boat and a plant trail explaining the Aboriginal uses for over 50 species.

Admission is free and it's open from Monday to Friday from 9 am to 5 pm, Saturday and Sunday 10 am to 6 pm. You can get there on bus Nos 4 or 6.

Fannie Bay Gaol Museum
Another interesting museum is a little further out of town at the corner of East Point Rd and Ross Smith Ave. This was Darwin's main jail from 1883 to 1979, when a new maximum security lockup opened at Berrimah. You can look round the old cells

and see the gallows used in the Territory's last hanging in 1952. There are also good displays on Cyclone Tracy, transport, technology and industrial archaeology. The museum is open daily from 10 am to 5 pm; admission is free. Take bus Nos 4 or 6 from the city centre.

East Point
This spit of undeveloped land north of Fannie Bay is good to visit in the late afternoon when wallabies come out to feed, cool breezes spring up and you can watch the sunset across the bay. There are some walking and riding trails as well as a road to the tip of the point. On the north side of the point is a series of wartime gun emplacements and the **Royal Australian Artillery Museum**, devoted to Darwin's WW II activity, open daily from 9.30 am to 5 pm. Bus Nos 4 or 6 will take you five km from the city centre to the corner of East Point Rd and

Ross Smith Ave; from there it's three km to the tip of the point.

Aviation Museum

Darwin's new aviation museum would be unspectacular were it not for the American B52 bomber. This truly mammoth aircraft, one of only two displayed outside the USA, dominates the other displays, which include the wreck of a Japanese Zero fighter shot down in 1942 and other items of historical interest. The museum is on the Stuart Highway in Winellie, about five km from the centre. It is open daily from 10 to 4 pm; entry is $5.

Beaches

Darwin has plenty of beaches, but you're wise to keep out of the water during the October to May wet season because of deadly box jellyfish ('stingers'). Popular beaches include **Mindil** and **Vestey's** on Fannie Bay, and **Mandorah**, across the bay from the town (see Around Darwin).

In north Darwin, there's a stinger net protecting part of **Nightcliff** beach off Casuarina Drive, and a stretch of the seven-km **Casuarina** beach further east is an official nude beach. This is a good beach but at low tide it's a long walk to the water's edge.

Like so many places in tropical Australia, Darwin has a waterslide – it's at **Parap Pool** on Ross Smith Ave and is open daily.

Organised Tours

There are innumerable tours in and around Darwin offered by a host of companies. NTGTB offices have a booklet, *Northern Territory Holiday Planner*, which helpfully lists brief details of most of them. Many tours go less frequently (if at all) in the wet season. Some of the longer or more adventurous ones have only a few departures a year: enquire beforehand if you're interested.

Local Among the Darwin city tours, Darwin Day Tours' four-hour trip is pretty comprehensive ($32). The same company also does 2½-hour trips to the crocodile farm at feeding times ($24). Coop & Co run dry-season horse-and-carriage city tours from $5 to $20. The Billy J harbour cruise costs $24 including a stopover at Mandorah. Another more expensive (around $55) harbour cruise by Billy J offers visitors a seafood meal, a 'corroboree' and sunset.

The *Sonny K* is a 20-seater hovercraft which makes one-hour trips around Darwin Harbour for $35. Dry-season departures are at 10 am daily from Frances Bay, about 500 metres from the centre of town.

Adelaide River Queen Wildlife River Tours run a $55, six-hour trip from Darwin to see Fogg Dam, the Adelaide River jumping crocodiles and Reptile World.

Further Afield You can take tours from Darwin to just about anywhere of interest in the Northern Territory. With money to burn, you could combine several major destinations or even make it to the Kimberley in Western Australia.

There are plenty of day trips (and longer) to places such as Litchfield Park and the Daly River, but one of the more interesting ones is a four-day canoe safari ($460) on the Daly River (dry season only) with Breakwater Canoe Tours (☎ 84 4899).

For bushwalkers, Willis's Walkabouts (☎ 85 2134) have been recommended. Organised by an ex-president of Darwin Bushwalking Club, these are guided hikes in small groups (usually four to eight people). You can join a prearranged walk of 11 to 21 days, or a group can set its own itinerary of two or more days. Some of Willis's Walkabouts are mentioned under Kakadu National Park, but others include Keep River and the Bungle Bungles (16 days), and the Mitchell Plateau in the Kimberley. Prices for 'choose-your-own' bushwalks start at $40 a day per person depending on the season and length of walk.

Brolga Air has scenic flights over Darwin and further afield from $85. Other interesting – but not cheap – tour destinations from Darwin include Bathurst and Melville islands, the Cobourg Peninsula, Arnhem Land and Gove. See the sections on those places.

Festivals

Aside from the Beer Can Regatta in June, with its sports and contests, there is the Bougainvillea Festival leading up to it, earlier in June. It's a week of concerts, dances, a picnic in the Botanic Gardens and a parade on the final day. Darwin also goes into festive mood for May Day (International Labour Day), regarded as the start of the 'no-box-jellyfish season' and the occasion of big beach parties, rock concerts the night before, etc. Unfortunately the jellyfish don't always leave on time. Darwinites are as fond of horse races as other Australians, and two big days at the Fannie Bay track are St Patrick's Day (17 March) and the Darwin Cup (October). The Royal Show takes place in July, and the Rodeo and Mud Crab Tying Competition in August.

Places to Stay

Darwin has hostels, guesthouses, motels, holiday flats, and a clutch of up-market hotels. The city's many caravan parks/camp sites are unfortunately all several km out.

Hostels There's a host of choices in this bracket, with several of the cheapest places on or near Mitchell St, conveniently close to the transit centre. Most places have guest kitchens, and the showers and toilets are almost always communal.

The 180-bed *Darwin City Youth Hostel* (☎ 81 3995) is at 69A Mitchell St next to the transit centre. Its rooms are all fan-cooled twins and cost $12 per person plus $1 for a sleeping sheet. In the dry season it's YHA members only here, and there's a three-day limit; in the Wet nonmembers can pay a $6 'introductory membership' fee. The building has reasonably new kitchens, bathrooms and an open-air sitting area.

Ivan's Backpackers Hostel (☎ 81 5385) at 88 Mitchell St has a pool, two kitchens, frequent barbecues, and camping gear for rent. A dormitory bunk is $13 in a four or six-bed room, $12.50 in a 10 or 12-bed room. It's friendly and informal, if a little cramped.

The *Darwin Transit Inn* (☎ 81 9733) at 69 Mitchell St has its reception actually in the transit centre. This place has definitely seen better days, but still gets a steady stream of travellers. There's a small pool, and it costs $12.50 per person in twin rooms, some with bathroom.

Very popular among travellers is the purpose-built *Frogshollow Backpackers* (☎ 41 2600) at 27 Lindsay St, about 10 minutes' walk from the transit centre but still close to the centre of town. It's a new, spacious and clean place, and has three spas which guests can use. The charge is $13 a night in an eight-bed dorm ($11.50 in the Wet), or $35 a double.

The smaller *Sherwood Lodge* (☎ 41 1994) is at 15 Peel St, with a breezy kitchen and sitting area upstairs. The cost is $11 per person, which gets you a bed in a cramped six-bed dorm, or you can pay $13 for a twin room. The place is clean, all rooms have fans, and sheets are supplied.

Further north along Mitchell St, about a 10-minute walk from the centre, is the family-run *Darwin City Lodge* (☎ 41 1295) at 151 Mitchell St. Formerly a family home, this place is one of the Cyclone Tracy survivors and is certainly a bit rough around the edges. It's clean, however, there's a pool and the owners are friendly. The cost is $11 in a dorm, or $24/33 for singles/doubles.

The Ys The YWCA, YMCA and the Country Women's Association also have hostels. The big, popular *YWCA* (☎ 81 8644) is at 119 Mitchell St. It takes women and men and has no curfew. Rooms have fans and fridges, are clean and well kept, and there are two TV lounges and a kitchen. The charge is $10 per person for a twin share, $20/34 for singles/doubles, or $25/40 for a room with bath and cooking facilities.

The small *CWA Hostel* (☎ 41 1536) is nearby, at the corner of Mitchell St and Packard Place, and takes women and men. It has two four-bed units with private bathrooms, fridge, kettle and toaster for $10 per person, or you can pay $16/28 for singles/doubles. There's a shared kitchen, a big garden and a TV room. You don't have to be a CWA member to stay.

The *YMCA* (☎ 81 8377) is at Doctor's Gully, just past the end of the Esplanade. It too takes men and women, but is not so good for solo women; most of the clients are semi-permanents. A dorm bed (three nights maximum) costs $10, while singles/ doubles go for $28/38. Weekly rates are cheaper.

Guesthouses Darwin has several small guesthouses – good for longer as well as short stays. Among those which aren't too far from the centre is the friendly *Park Lodge* (☎ 81 5692) at 42 Coronation Drive, Stuart Park. All rooms have fan, air-con and fridge; bathrooms, kitchen, sitting/TV room and laundry are communal. Air-con doubles cost $38. Weekly rates are cheaper. Numerous city buses, including Nos 5 and 8, run to this part of Darwin along the highway; ask the driver where to get off.

In Parap, just a few km from the city centre, the *Ross Smith Guest House* (☎ 81 8457) at 49 Parap Rd, is uninspiring. A single/double room with fan costs $16/21.

Motels, Hotels & Holiday Flats There are plenty of modern places in Darwin. Prices in this range often vary between the Dry and the cheaper Wet. Many of them give discounts if you stay a week or more – usually of the 7th-night-free variety. Typically these places have air-con and swimming pools.

Three older and cheaper places in central Darwin lack pools, however. The *Larrakeyah Lodge* (☎ 81 7550) at 50 Mitchell St, right opposite the transit centre, offers comfortable air-con rooms with fridge and shared facilities for $25 a twin, or $35/50 for singles/doubles. There is a TV lounge, laundry and coffee shop. In the centre at 35 Cavenagh St, the *Air Raid City Lodge* (☎ 81 9214) has air-con rooms – all with shower and toilet, fridge and tea/coffee-making facilities – for $40/50. At 53 Cavenagh St, on the corner of Whitefield St, the *Tiwi Lodge* (☎ 81 6471) is a motel with rooms at $60, with the usual facilities.

Another city centre place worth consider-ing is *Crest Townhouses* (☎ 81 1922) at 88 Woods St, which offers 'studios' for three adults or a family for $77. There are also bigger (two bedroom) 'town houses' for $97. *Peninsular Apartments* (☎ 81 1922) at 115 Smith St West has studios for three adults or a family at $77.

There's a good deal to be had sometimes at the *Boulevard Apartment Motel* (☎ 81 1544) at 38 Gardens Rd, the continuation of Cavenagh St beyond Daly St. Comfortable modern motel rooms, which normally cost $67 for one, two or three people, are let for $47 when the place isn't busy (more likely in the Wet). Rooms have private bathroom, fridge and TV and there's a pool, tennis court and restaurant. It's worth checking other motels for similar deals in the off-peak season – or ask in the tourist office.

If you have a vehicle there are places worth considering in the suburbs. The *Parap Village Apartments* (☎ 41 0301) at 39 Parap Rd, Fannie Bay has three-bedroom flats for $120 and two-bedroom flats for $105. The *Capricornia Motel* (☎ 81 4055) at 3 Kellaway St, Fannie Bay, has singles/twins for $55/65. Directly across from the airport on the Stuart Highway the *Leprechaun Lodge Motel* (☎ 84 3400) costs $43/54 for singles/twins. It's convenient for early morning departures, but not much else.

Other than these places, you're generally into the $80-plus bracket. The most expensive are the big modern hotels on Mitchell St and the Esplanade. You'll pay $140-plus for a single room at the *Atrium, Sheraton, Beaufort* or *Travelodge*.

Camping Sadly, Darwin takes no advantage of what could be fine camp sites on its many open spaces. East Point, for instance, would be superb. To camp or get an on-site van you must go to one of the privately run caravan parks in the outer city. A second drawback is that a number of the more conveniently sit-uated caravan parks don't take tent campers. The closest place to the city is the *Leprechaun Lodge Motel* which has a limited number of camping/caravan sites at the rear – enquire at reception.

Shady Glen Caravan Park (☎ 84 3330), 10 km east, at the corner of Stuart Highway and Farrell Crescent, Winnellie, camp sites at $10 for two, on-site vans $33 for two, cabins $35 for two.

Overlander Caravan Park (☎ 84 3025), 13 km east at 1064 McMillans Rd, Berrimah, camp sites at $7 for two, on-site vans $26 to $30.

Palms Caravan Park (☎ 32 2891), 17 km south of town on the Stuart Highway at Berrimah, camp sites at $8 for two.

Also consider camping at Howard Springs, 26 km out, where there are three caravan parks taking campers (see Around Darwin).

Places to Eat

Darwin's closeness to Asia is obvious in its large number of fine Asian eateries, but on the whole eating out is expensive. Takeaway places, a growing number of lunch spots in and around Smith St Mall and the excellent Asian-style markets – held two or three times a week at various sites around the city – are the cheapest.

City Centre – cafes, pubs & takeaways

Next to the transit centre on Mitchell St there's a small food centre with a couple of reasonably priced stalls and open-air tables to sit at. *Graham's*, at the far end, is popular with travellers and serves roast dinners in the evenings for $5, or full-on cholesterol breakfasts for $4.

A host of snack bars and cafes in Smith St Mall offer lots of choice during the day – but, except for Thursday, the late shopping night, they're virtually all closed from about 5 pm and on Saturday afternoons and Sundays.

There's a good collection of fast-food counters in Darwin Plaza towards the Knuckey St end of the mall – the *Sheik's Tent* for Lebanese, the *Taco House* for Mexican, *Odette's* for Asian, *Energy Foods* and *La Veg* for health foods, and *Roseland* for yoghurt, fruit salads and ice cream.

Opposite Darwin Plaza in the Paspalis Centrepoint arcade, the *Little Lark* is a popular BYO lunch spot. As well as the usual fast food, it has a Chinese takeaway or sit-down menu. Most main dishes are $6 including rice, and it's open from 8 am.

Further up the mall, the fancy new Galleria shopping centre has a few good places: *Satay King* specialises in Malaysian food and serves that excellent Nyonya dish, curry laksa; *Mamma Bella* serves predictable Italian food; *Chok's Place* has good Chinese dishes; and the *Galleria* is a straightforward burger place. There's a good seating area in the centre, although at lunch times it can be difficult to find a spare table.

Further up the mall is Anthony Plaza where the *French Bakehouse* is one of the few places you can get a coffee and snack every day. The *Cosmopolitan Cafe* next door is a busy breakfast and lunch spot – a healthy breakfast of fresh fruit, muesli, juice and toast costs $6.

Opposite Anthony Plaza is the Victoria Arcade, where the *Victoria Hotel* has lunch or dinner for around $6 in its upstairs Essington Carvery. Downstairs in the bar the barramundi burgers ($7 including chips and salad) are excellent, as are the steaks. In the arcade the *Sate House* has good cheap Indonesian fare. The popular *Brasserie* at the top of the mall is a licensed restaurant with both indoor and outdoor tables. Meals are quite cheap, and it's open for breakfast from 9 am.

Simply Foods at 37 Knuckey St is a busy health-food place. It's a good spot with appealing decor, music and friendly service. At 17 Cavenagh St, the *Tudor House Antiques & Fine Art Gallery* has a coffee lounge, with delicious home-made cakes and freshly ground coffee. Its double role gives it the most interesting decor of any Darwin cafe!

In Admiralty House, the open-air *Garden Cafe* provides a welcome breeze in Darwin's heat and humidity. Meals are around $10 and everything is fresh and home-made. It's open daily.

The *Darwin Hotel*, stretching from the Esplanade to Mitchell St, has a daily barbecue lunch for $10. Evening meals in its *Banjo* restaurant are $13 to $21.

City Centre – restaurants

The *Maharajah Indian Restaurant* at 37 Knuckey St has a

good $7 lunch special including a glass of wine. The menu is extensive with dishes from $9 to $13. The *Pancake Palace* on Cavenagh St near Knuckey St is open daily for lunch and in the evening until 1 am. Conveniently close to many of Darwin's night spots, it has sweet and savoury pancakes from $5. Cheap pasta meals are hard to find in Darwin.

Other restaurants include steakhouses, seafood specialists, and French, Greek and Italian cuisine. The numerous Chinese places are generally rather up-market. The *Jade Garden* on Smith St Mall (upstairs, roughly opposite the Victoria Arcade) offers a nine-course meal for $13 a head.

The *Pasta Joint Restaurant* at 21 Cavenagh St has a two-course lunch special at $7. At 40 Cavenagh St the *Arabian Nights* is a BYO place serving good Middle Eastern food in the $7 to $10 range, and there's a $3 discount on main courses at lunch times.

The *Sizzler* restaurant on Mitchell St is one of the chain found in Queensland. It's amazingly popular, with queues out onto the footpath every night. The reason is that it's very good value; for around $10 you can fill your plate from a wide range of dishes, and have a dessert too.

Probably the best restaurant in the city centre area is *Peppi's*, at 84 Mitchell St. It's fully licensed, and a two-course meal for two will set you back around $80 with drinks.

Out of the Centre On Smith St, just beyond Daly St, the *Thai Garden Restaurant* serves not only delicious and reasonably priced Thai food but pizzas too! They have a few outdoor tables. There's a takeaway Chinese place across the road, and a 24-hour fast-food joint next door.

Further out, the *Parap Hotel* on Parap Rd between Gregory and Hingston Sts does counter meals. It also has *Jessie's Bistro* where buffalo and beef steaks are around $10. It's open for lunch and dinner Monday to Saturday, and from 2 pm on Sundays. Locals recommend the food here. There are two other Jessie's Bistro locations – one in

the *Casuarina Tavern* and the other in the *Berrimah Hotel* on the Stuart Highway at Berrimah. There's a bakery in Gregory St, Parap, with the unlikely name of *Filthey McNastey's*, which does wonderful bread and other whole foods.

In the Botanic Gardens, the *Holtze Cottage* restaurant is a carnivore's delight. It's fully licensed and specialises in buffalo, kangaroo, crocodile and camel meats. It is open daily for lunch and dinner.

Markets Easily the best all-round eating experience in Darwin is the bustling Asian-style market at Mindil Beach on Thursday nights during the dry season. People begin arriving from 5.30 pm, bringing tables, chairs, rugs, grog and kids to settle under the coconut palms for sunset and decide which of the tantalising food-stall smells has the greatest allure. It's difficult to know whether to choose Thai, Sri Lankan, Indian, Malaysian, Chinese, Greek or Portuguese. You'll even find Indonesian black rice pudding. All prices are reasonable – around $2 to $5 for a meal. There are cake stalls, fruit-salad bars, arts & crafts stalls – and sometimes entertainment in the form of a band or street theatre.

Similar food stalls can be found at the Parap market on Saturday mornings and the one at Rapid Creek on Sunday mornings, but Mindil Beach is the best for atmosphere and closeness to town. It's about two km from the city centre, off Gilruth Ave. During the Wet, it transfers to Rapid Creek. Bus Nos 4 and 6 go past Mindil Beach: No 4 goes on to Rapid Creek, No 6 to Parap.

The Darwin Thirst

Darwin has a reputation for being one of the hardest-drinking towns in the world. In a dry year an average of 230 litres of the amber fluid disappears down each Darwinian throat. The Darwin thirst is summed up by the famed 'Darwin stubby' – a beer bottle that looks just like any other stubby, except that it contains two litres instead of 375 ml. The record for downing a Darwin stubby is one minute two seconds – but that was the pre-1983 Darwin stubby which was a mite larger at 2.25 litres! That's half an imperial gallon, more than half a US gallon!

The Darwin beer thirst is celebrated at the annual Beer Can Regatta in June. A series of boat races are held for boats constructed entirely of beer cans. Apart from the racing boats some unusual special entries generally turn up – like a beer-can Viking longboat or a beer-can submarine. Constructed by an Australian navy contingent the submarine actually submerged! The races also have their controversial elements – on one occasion a boat turned up made entirely of brand new cans, delivered straight from the brewery, sealed but empty. Unfair, cried other competitors, the beer must be drunk!

Entertainment

Darwin is a lively city with bands at several venues and many clubs and discos. More sophisticated tastes are catered for too – there's theatre, film, concerts and a casino.

Live bands play in Ellie's Balcony Bar upstairs at the Victoria Hotel, from 9 pm Wednesday to Saturday nights. The Billabong Bar in the Atrium Hotel, on the corner of the Esplanade and Peel St, has live bands on Friday and Saturday nights until 1 am. Take a look at the hotel's spectacular seven-storey glass-roofed atrium while you're there. The Billabong Bar also has a comedy night on Wednesdays.

The Darwin Hotel is pleasant in the evening for a quiet drink. There's a patio section by the pool. It's livelier on Friday nights, when there's a band in the Green Room, and on Sunday afternoons at the poolside jazz barbecue – $15 a head. There's also a nightclub in the Kakadu Bar here.

The Brewery Bar in the Frontier Hotel on the corner of Mitchell and Daly Sts is another popular venue.

Popular clubs and discos, often with live bands, include 1990s, Dix, Sweethearts and Circles. They're open nightly, with cover charges only on Saturdays. Some stay open all night, and midweek they offer cheap drinks to early arrivals. There's lots of entertainment on Sunday afternoons. Very popular is the Beachfront Hotel at Rapid Creek, where you can alternate between two bands – one in the outdoor bar known as the Cage, the other in the air-con Colonial Bar.

There are bands on Sundays at the Humpty Doo Hotel 10 km along the Arnhem Highway (33 km from Darwin) and at the Howard Springs Tavern on Whitewood Rd, Howard Springs.

The Nightcliff Hotel at the corner of Bagot and Trower Rds, about 10 km north of the city centre, has live music every night except Monday and Tuesday. It's a wild place with one of the longest bars in the Northern Territory, and on Wednesday nights it's 'fun night', with some bizarre entertainment. More laid back is the Top End Folk Club which meets every second Sunday of the month at the Gun Turret at East Point Reserve. Visitors are welcome, and you're welcome to perform also, in which case the $5 admission is waived.

The Performing Arts Centre (☎ 81 1222) on Mitchell St, opposite McLachlan St, hosts a variety of events from fashion award nights to plays, rock operas, pantomimes and concerts. There are sometimes bands and other shows in the amphitheatre in the Botanic Gardens.

There are several cinemas in town and the Darwin Film Society (☎ 81 2215) has regular showings of offbeat/artistic films at the Museum Theatrette in the Museum of Arts & Sciences, Conacher St, Bullocky Point.

Finally, there's the Diamond Beach Casino on Mindil Beach off Gilruth Ave – as long as you're 'properly dressed'. It's quite good entertainment to watch people cast away large sums of money. Callow youths at the door adjudicate whether the style of your shirt collar and the cut of your trousers is to their master's liking.

Two-up

The Alice and Darwin casinos offer plenty of opportunity to watch the Australian gambling mania in full flight. You can also observe a part of Australia's true cultural heritage, the all-Australian game of two-up.

The essential idea of two-up is to toss two coins and obtain two heads. The players stand around a circular playing area and bet on the coins showing either two heads or two tails when they fall. The 'spinner' uses a 'kip' to toss the coins and the house pays out and takes in as the coins fall – except that nothing happens on 'odd' tosses (one head, one tail) unless they're thrown five times in a row. In this case you lose unless you have also bet on this possibility. The spinner continues tossing until he or she either throws tails, throws five odds or throws three heads. If the spinner manages three heads then he or she also wins at 7½ to one on any bet placed on that possibility, then starts tossing all over again. When the spinner finally loses, the next player in the circle takes over as spinner.

Things to Buy

Aboriginal art is generally cheaper in Alice Springs, but Darwin has greater variety. Easily the best shop is the Aboriginal Artists' Gallery at 153 Mitchell St. It's open from 9 am to 5 pm Monday to Friday, and 10 am to 1 pm on Saturdays during the Dry. The gallery has excellent bark paintings from Arnhem Land, and interesting carvings by the Tiwi people of Bathurst and Melville islands and by the peoples of central Australia. Also for sale are beautiful woven baskets, dilly bags, dot paintings, clothing, Aboriginal literature and postcards. The Raintree Gallery at 29 Knuckey St has a similar collection on a smaller scale. You won't want the more widely available cheap commercial imitations once you've seen this stuff.

T-shirts printed with Aboriginal designs are popular but quality and prices vary. Riji Dij at 11 Knuckey St has a large range of T-shirts ($25). They are printed by Tiwi Designs and Territoriana, both local companies using Aboriginal designs and, to a large extent, Aboriginal labour. It stocks Tiwi printed fabric and clothing made from fabric printed by central Australian Aborigines.

You can find Balinese and Indian clothing at Darwin's markets – Mindil Beach (Thursday evening, dry season only), Parap (Saturday morning) and Rapid Creek (Sunday morning, and Thursday evening in the wet season). Local arts & crafts (the market at Parap is said to be the best), jewellery and bric-a-brac are on sale too. The Esplanade Gallery, upstairs in Admiralty House, has beautiful local jewellery – not cheap, but you may find something special. For pottery, try the Mango Pottery at 35 Gregory St, Parap, or Pandanus Pottery at 10 Litchfield St (☎ 81 7610, ring before turning up).

Getting There & Away

Air Darwin is becoming increasingly busy as an international as well as domestic gateway to the top of Australia.

International A popular international route is to/from Indonesia with the Indonesian airlines Merpati or Garuda. You can book Merpati at Natrabu (☎ 81 3695), an Indonesian government travel agency, at 16 Westlane Arcade (behind the Victoria Hotel on Smith St Mall). Merpati flies twice a week to/from Kupang in Timor ($198 one-way, $330 return), and from there it has further flights to numerous other places in Indonesia. Kupang is a 'designated entry port' in Indonesia which means you get the normal two-month visitor permit on arrival. Garuda (☎ 81 1103), on Cavenagh St, has direct flights to Denpasar (Bali) for $367 one-way, $671 return.

Royal Brunei Airlines (☎ 41 0966), also on Cavenagh St, flies twice weekly between Darwin and Bandar Seri Begawan, and on to Manila and Hong Kong.

Qantas and Singapore Airlines both fly to Darwin. Qantas (☎ 82 3355) is at the corner of Smith St Mall and Bennett St; Singapore Airlines is in the Paspalis Centrepoint building at the corner of Smith St Mall and Knuckey St.

Malaysian Airlines (☎ 41 2323) are on the 2nd floor of 38 Mitchell St.

Domestic Within Australia, you can fly to Darwin from other states with Australian Airlines and Ansett (which includes Ansett NT and Ansett WA). The post-deregulation cheap fares didn't reach Darwin, mainly because Compass didn't fly there. Watch out for the arrival of more competitors in the domestic air-travel market, as prices may tumble some time soon.

There are often stops or transfers at Alice Springs, Mt Isa or Adelaide on longer flights. Some flights from Queensland stop at Gove or Groote Eylandt. One-way fares include

Top: Jim Jim Falls, Kakadu National Park, NT (RI'A)
Left: Garden of Eden, Kings Canyon, NT (TW)
Right: Ayers Rock, NT (TW)

Top: Lubra's Leap, Katherine Gorge, NT (TW)
Bottom: Corroboree Rock, near Alice Springs, NT (TW)

Adelaide $503 ($402 standby), Alice Springs $329 ($263), Perth $572 ($458), Broome $334, Cairns $391 ($313), Mt Isa $328 ($262), Brisbane $551 ($441 standby) and Sydney $583 ($466). In Darwin, Australian Airlines (☎ 82 3333) is at 16 Bennett St; Ansett (☎ 80 3333) are in shop 14, Smith St Mall.

For air travel within the Northern Territory see the airfares chart in the introductory Getting Around section to this chapter. Air North's office (☎ 81 7477) is at Darwin Airport.

Bus You can reach Darwin by bus on three routes – the Western Australia route from Broome, Derby and Kununurra; the Queensland route through Mt Isa to Three Ways and up the Track from Alice Springs.

Bus Australia and Greyhound/Pioneer usually run daily up and down the Track to/from Alice Springs. Some buses connect in Alice Springs for Adelaide. Both companies have daily services to/from Townsville via Mt Isa, frequently with connections for Brisbane or Cairns. On Queensland services you often have to change buses at Three Ways or Tennant Creek and Mt Isa. For Western Australia, Greyhound/Pioneer go daily to/from Perth through Kununurra, Broome and Port Hedland, while Bus Australia does this trip every second day. With Greyhound/Pioneer you have the option once or twice a week of taking the Western Australia inland route south of Port Hedland, along the Great Northern Highway through Newman. Otherwise Western Australia buses follow the coastal route. All buses stop at Katherine.

Fares only vary by a couple of dollars between the companies and travel times are very similar, but beware of services that schedule long waits for connections in Tennant Creek or Mt Isa. For example, you pay around $80 one-way to Darwin from Tennant Creek (13 hours), $130 from Mt Isa (21 hours), $230 from Townsville (32 hours), $290 from Brisbane (51 hours), $150 from Alice Springs (19 hours), $145 from

Broome (22 hours), and $295 from Perth (57 hours). In Darwin both Greyhound/Pioneer (☎ 81 8700) and Bus Australia (☎ 81 3377) operate from the transit centre at 69 Mitchell St.

Getting Around

To/From the Airport Darwin's busy airport, only about six km from the centre of town, handles international flights as well as domestic ones. Hertz, Budget, Thrifty and Letz have desks at the airport. The taxi fare into the centre is about $12.

There is an airport shuttle bus (☎ 41 1656) for $5, which will pick up or drop off almost anywhere in the centre. When leaving Darwin book a day before departure. City bus Nos 5 and 8 also go along the Stuart Highway past the airport, and it's about 200 metres' walk to the terminal.

Bus Darwin has a fairly good city bus service – Monday to Friday. On Saturdays, services cease around lunch time and on Sundays and holidays they shut down completely. The city services start from the small terminal (☎ 89 7513) on Harry Chan Ave, near the corner of Smith St. Buses enter the city along Mitchell St and leave along Cavenagh St.

Fares are on a zone system – shorter trips are 90c or $1.20, the longest $1.70. Bus No 4 (to Fannie Bay, Nightcliff, Rapid Creek and Casuarina) and No 6 (Fannie Bay, Parap, Stuart Park) are useful for getting to Aquascene, Botanic Gardens, Mindil Beach, the Museum of Arts & Sciences, Fannie Bay Gaol Museum and East Point. Bus Nos 5 and 8 go up the Stuart Highway past the airport to Berrimah, from where No 5 goes north to Casuarina and No 8 continues along the highway to Palmerston.

On weekdays three buses a day go to Humpty Doo.

The Tour Tub is a private bus which does a circuit of the city, calling at the major places of interest, and you can hop on or off anywhere. In the city centre it leaves from Knuckey St, at the end of the Smith St mall. The set fare is $12.50, and the buses operate hourly from 9 am to 4 pm. Sites visited include Aquascene (only at fish-feeding times), Indo-Pacific Marine, Diamond Beach Casino, the museum and art gallery, East Point Military Museum, Fanny Bay Gaol and the Botanic Gardens.

Car Darwin has two 'backpacker special' car-rental operators, as well as several of the national companies.

Rent a Rocket (☎ 81 6977) at 9 Daly St, and Rent a Dent (☎ 81 1411) at the corner of Smith and McLachlan Sts, offer very similar deals on their mostly 1970s and early 1980s cars. Costs depend on whether you're staying near Darwin, or going further afield to Kakadu, Katherine, Litchfield Park and so on. For local trips, with Rent a Dent you pay $35 a day, depending on the vehicle, and must stay within 70 km of Darwin. This includes 200 free km, with a charge of 35c per km beyond that distance. With these deals you can't go beyond Humpty Doo or Acacia Store (about 70 km down the track).

The bigger companies usually class Darwin as 'remote', which means that cars cost about $10 a day more than they do elsewhere. Cheapa (☎ 81 8400), at 64 Stuart Highway, Parap, is probably the best value. Some of these companies offer three-day packages which include 900 free km, which means you can get out to Kakadu and back without any excess charges. The rates vary on the type of vehicle but Thrifty (☎ 81 8555) do a typical deal of $256 for a Toyota Corolla. One of the advantages of deals such as this is that you get a newer, faster and more reliable car.

Other deals to look for include cheaper rates for four or more days' hire, weekend specials (three days for roughly the price of two), and one-way hires (to Jabiru, Katherine or Alice Springs).

There are also 4WD vehicles in Darwin, but you usually have to book ahead, and fees and deposits can be hefty. The best place to start looking is probably Cheapa, which has several different models – the cheapest, a Suzuki four-seater, costs around $80 a day

including insurance, plus 35c a km over 100 km.

Rental companies, including the cut-price ones, generally operate a free towing or replacement service if the vehicle breaks down. But, especially with the cheaper operators, check the paperwork to see exactly what you're covered for in terms of damage to vehicles and injuries to passengers. The usual age and insurance requirements apply in Darwin and there may be restrictions on off-bitumen driving, or on the distance you're allowed to go from the city. Even with the big firms, the insurance does not cover you when driving off the bitumen.

Most rental companies are open every day and have agents in the city centre to save you trekking out to the Stuart Highway. Budget (☎ 84 4388), Hertz (☎ 41 0944) and Thrifty also have offices at the airport.

Moped & Bicycle Darwin has a fairly extensive network of bike tracks. It's a pleasant ride out from the city to the Botanical Gardens, Fannie Bay, East Point or even, if you're feeling fit, all the way to Nightcliff and Casuarina.

Darwin Bike Rentals in Top End Travel at 57 Mitchell St, has bikes from $8 a day (from 8 am to 5 pm), or $10 for 24 hours – plus tandems and mountain bikes, and hourly, weekly and monthly rates. Rent a Rocket is cheaper at $5 for half a day, $8 for 24 hours. They also rent out mopeds (for which you only need a car licence) at $15 for a half day, $20 for 24 hours.

The Top End

There are a number of places of interest close to Darwin, and several remoter and more spectacular Top End areas are becoming increasingly accessible. The chief glory among the latter is Kakadu National Park. Litchfield Park, a national park to the south of Darwin, and Melville and Bathurst islands to the north are other places that are worth the effort if you have the time and dollars.

A group of people can hire a vehicle in Darwin and get to most of the mainland places quite economically. There are also tours from Darwin to many of these places (see the Darwin Getting Around section). Some additional places that can be reached from Darwin are covered in the Down the Track section.

Crocodiles

The Top End has a fair population of crocodiles. After a century of being hunted, wild crocodiles became protected in the Northern Territory in 1971 and their numbers have increased to an estimated 100,000. There are two types of crocodile in Australia – freshwater and saltwater – and both are present in the Territory.

The smaller freshwater-dwelling crocodile is found in freshwater rivers and billabongs, while the larger saltwater crocodile can be found in or near almost any body of water, fresh or salt. Freshwater crocodiles, which have narrower snouts and rarely exceed three metres in length, are harmless to people unless provoked, but saltwater crocodiles can definitely be dangerous.

Ask locally before swimming or even paddling in any rivers or billabongs in the Top End – attacks on humans by salties happen more often than you might think. The beasts are apparently partial to dogs and can be attracted by barking some distance away. Since becoming protected, crocodiles are growing less afraid. Warning signs are posted alongside many dangerous stretches of water.

Crocodiles have become a major tourist attraction (eating the odd tourist certainly helps in this respect) and the Northern Territory is very big on crocodile humour. Darwin shops have a plentiful supply of crocodile T-shirts including the Darwin Crocodile Wrestling Club shirt, complete with gory blood stains and a large hole 'bitten' out of one side.

AROUND DARWIN

All the places listed here are within a couple of hours' travel from the city.

Mandorah

It's only 10 km across the harbour by boat to this popular beach resort on the tip of Cox Peninsula – you can reach it by road, but that's nearly 140 km, about half of it on unsealed roads. The return ferry trip is $30, with the first departure from Darwin at 10 am and the last one from Mandorah at 5 pm. The crossing takes about 30 minutes. The *Darwin Duchess* leaves the main Stokes Hill Wharf in Darwin three or four times a day Monday to Friday and on weekends in the tourist season.

Howard Springs

The springs, with crocodile-free swimming, are 27 km from the city. Turn off 23 km down the Stuart Highway, beyond Palmerston. The forest-surrounded swimming hole can get uncomfortably crowded because it's so convenient for the city. Nevertheless on a quiet day it's a pleasant spot for an excursion and there are short walking tracks and lots of bird life.

Places to Stay There are three nearby caravan parks. The *Coolalinga* (☎ (089) 83 1026), on the Stuart Highway four km beyond the Howard Springs turning, and the *Howard Springs Caravan Park* (☎ (089) 83 1169) at Whitewood Rd, Howard Springs, have tent and caravan sites only; while the *Nook* (☎ (089) 83 1048) at 17 Morgan Rd, Howard Springs, has tent sites, on-site vans ($25) and cabins ($40).

Arnhem Highway

The Arnhem Highway branches off southeast towards Kakadu 33 km south of Darwin. Only 10 km along this road you come to the small town of **Humpty Doo**, where the *Humpty Doo Hotel* is a colourful pub with some real character. They do counter lunches and teas all week. Sunday, when local bands usually play, is particularly popular. Graeme Gow's Reptile World has a big collection of Australian snakes and a knowledgeable owner (open daily from 8.30 am to 6 pm).

About 15 km beyond Humpty Doo is the turn-off to **Fogg Dam**, great for watching

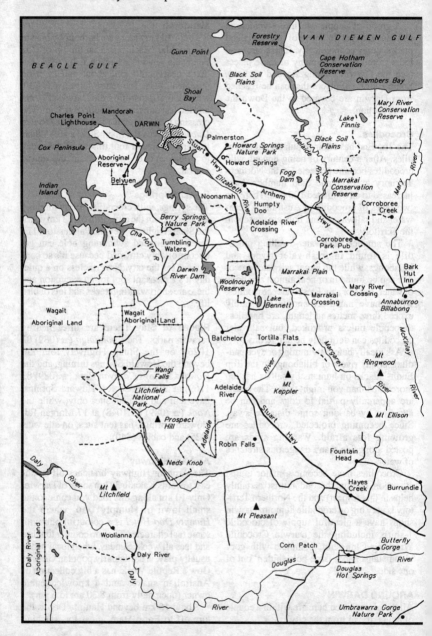

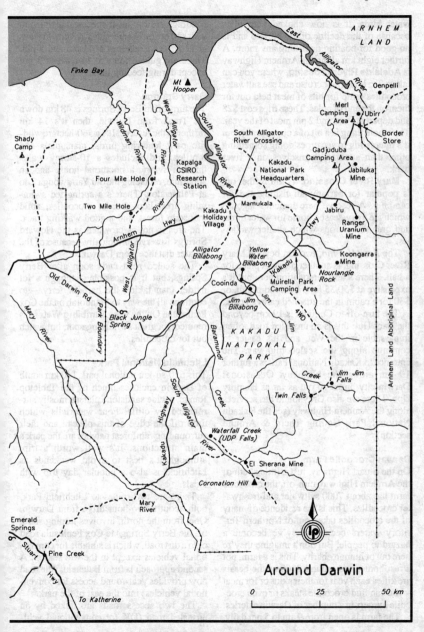

Around Darwin

0   25   50 km

water birds. It is now choked with lilies because of the decline of the buffalo and is no good for boating or fishing any more. A further eight km along the Arnhem Highway is **Adelaide River Crossing**, where you can take a 2½ hour river cruise and see saltwater crocodiles jump for bits of meat held out for them on the end of poles. These trips cost $28 and depart at 9 am and 2 pm most of the year. The whole thing is a bit of a circus really, but it's interesting to see crocs doing something other than sunning themselves on a river bank.

Mary River Crossing, 47 km further on, is popular for barramundi fishing and for camping. A reserve here includes lagoons which are a dry-season home for water birds, and granite outcrops which shelter wallabies.

The *Bark Hut Inn*, two km beyond Mary River Crossing, is another pleasant place for a halt. There's accommodation here but it's expensive at $50/55 for a twin room/unit, or $30 for a cabin in the attached caravan park.

The turn-off to Cooinda is 19 km beyond the Bark Hut: this is an unsealed road, often impassable in the Wet, and it's easier to continue along the sealed highway. The entrance to Kakadu National Park is a further 19 km along the highway. Occasional Darwin city buses go out as far as Humpty Doo. There are also Greyhound bus services along the Arnhem Highway (see the Kakadu National Park Getting There & Around section).

Darwin Crocodile Farm

On the Stuart Highway, just a little south of the Arnhem Highway turn-off, the crocodile farm has about 7000 saltwater and freshwater crocodiles. This is the residence of many of the crocodiles taken out of Northern Territory waters because they've become a hazard to people. But don't imagine they're here out of human charity. This is a farm, not a rest home, and around 2000 of the beasts are killed each year for their skins or for meat – you can find crocodile steaks or even crocodile burgers in a number of Darwin eateries.

The farm is open from 9 am to 5 pm daily.

Feedings are the most spectacular times to visit and are on Wednesdays at 3 pm, Fridays at 11 am, and Sundays at 11 am and 3 pm. There are guided tours at 11 am and 3 pm except during feeding times.

Berry Springs

The turn-off to Berry Springs is 48 km down the Track from Darwin, then it's 14 km further to the reserve. It's a 560-hectare wildlife park featuring birds, marsupials and reptiles, and includes a 10-storey walk-through aviary, a nocturnal house and an aquarium, replacing the old Yarrawonga Zoo at Palmerston. There's a spring-fed swimming area, kept free of crocodiles, amid monsoon forest, and a good walking track. The area is not as crowded as the Howard Springs Reserve, principally because of the greater distance from Darwin.

The sealed road ends soon after Berry Springs, but it is possible – though a lot harder than taking the harbour ferry – to continue all the way to Mandorah on the Cox Peninsula. On the way, **Tumbling Waters** is reputedly a great swimming spot, but watch out for crocodiles.

Litchfield National Park

This 650-sq-km national park 140 km south of Darwin encloses much of the Tabletop Range, a wide sandstone plateau mostly surrounded by cliffs. Four waterfalls which drop off the edge of this plateau and their surrounding rainforest patches are the park's main attractions. It's well worth a trip, although it's best to avoid weekends as Litchfield is also a popular day trip with locals.

There are two routes to Litchfield Park, both about a two-hour drive from Darwin. One, from the north, involves turning south off the Berry Springs to Cox Peninsula road onto a dirt road, which is suitable for conventional vehicles except in the wet season. A second approach is from Batchelor (the road now provides year-round access for conventional vehicles) into the east of the park.

The two access roads are linked by an unsealed road (OK for conventional vehicles) through the park. If you enter the park from Batchelor, it is 18 km from the park boundary to the **Florence Falls** turn-off on the eastern edge of the plateau. The falls lie five km off the road along a good track. This is an excellent swimming hole in the dry season, as is Buley Rockhole, a few km away, where you can also camp.

Eighteen km beyond the turning to Florence Falls is the turn-off to **Tolmer Falls**, which are a 400-metre walk off the road. There's also a 1½-km loop walking track here which gives you some excellent views of the area.

It's a further seven km along the main road to the turn-off to the most popular attraction in Litchfield – **Wangi Falls**, two km along a side road. The falls here flow year-round and fill a beautiful swimming hole. There are also extensive picnic and camping areas. From Wangi it's about 16 km to the ranger station near the park's northern access point.

Bush camping is also allowed at **Sandy Creek Falls** in a rainforest valley in the south of the park (4WD access only). There are several other 4WD tracks in the park, and plenty of bushwalking possibilities.

As usual in the Top End, it's easier to reach and get around the park from May to October.

Organised Tours There are plenty of companies offering day trips to Litchfield from Darwin. Cookes (☎ (089) 76 0140), based in Batchelor but with pick-ups in Darwin, is about the cheapest at $55 ($60 with lunch).

KAKADU NATIONAL PARK

Kakadu National Park is one of the natural marvels not just of the Northern Territory, but of Australia. The longer you stay, the more rewarding it is.

Kakadu stretches more than 200 km south from the coast and 100 km from east to west, with the main entrance 153 km by road east of Darwin. It encompasses a great variety of superb landscapes, swarms with wildlife and has some of Australia's best Aboriginal rock art.

Kakadu was proclaimed a national park in three stages. Stage One, the east-central part of the park including Ubirr, Nourlangie Rock, Jim Jim Falls, Twin Falls and Yellow Water Billabong, was declared in 1979 and is on the World Heritage list for both its natural and its cultural importance – a rare distinction. Stage Two, in the north, was declared in 1984 and won World Heritage listing for its natural importance. Stage Three, in the south, was finally listed in 1991, bringing virtually the whole South Alligator River system within the park.

The name Kakadu comes from Gagadju, one of the local Aboriginal languages, and part of Kakadu is Aboriginal land, leased to the government for use as a national park. There are several Aboriginal settlements in the park and about half the park rangers are Aborigines. Enclosed by the park, but not part of it, are a few tracts of land designated for other purposes – principally three uranium-mining leases in the east.

Geography & Vegetation

A straight line on the map separates Kakadu from the Arnhem Land Aboriginal Land to its east, which you can't enter without a permit. The Arnhem Land escarpment, a dramatic 100 to 200-metre-high sandstone cliffline, which provides the natural boundary of the very rugged Arnhem Land plateau, winds circuitously some 500 km through east and south-east Kakadu.

Creeks cut across the rocky plateau and tumble off the escarpment as thundering waterfalls in the wet season. They then flow across the lowlands to swamp the vast flood plains of Kakadu's four north-flowing rivers, turning the north of the park into a kind of huge vegetated lake. From west to east the rivers are the Wildman, the West Alligator, the South Alligator and the East Alligator. Such is the difference between dry and wet seasons that areas on river flood plains which are perfectly dry underfoot in September will be under three metres of water a few months later. As the waters recede in the Dry, some loops of wet season watercourses become cut off, but don't dry up. These are billabongs – and they're often carpeted with water lilies.

The coastline has long stretches of mangrove swamp, important for halting erosion and as a breeding ground for marine and bird species. The southern part of the park is drier, lowland hill country with open grassland and eucalypt woodland. Pockets of monsoon rainforest crop up here as well as in most of the park's other landscapes.

In all, Kakadu has over 1000 plant species, and a number of them are still used by the local Aborigines for food, bush medicine and other practical purposes.

Seasons

The great change between the Dry and the November-to-March Wet makes a big difference to visitors to Kakadu. Not only is the landscape transformed as the wetlands and waterfalls grow, but Kakadu's lesser roads become impassable in the Wet, cutting off some highlights like Jim Jim Falls. In the Wet and in the humid October 'build-up', temperatures rise (to 35°C or more) along with the humidity – and the number of mosquitoes, always high near water, rises to near plague proportions. Around 1300 mm of rain falls, mostly between January and March.

The most comfortable time is the late Dry, July to September. This is when wildlife, especially birds, congregates in big numbers around the shrinking billabongs and watercourses, but it's also when most tourists come to the park. May and June is quite a good time to visit – there aren't too many other visitors, the wetlands and waterfalls still have a lot of water and most of the tracks are open.

Wildlife

Kakadu has about 25 species of frog, 50 types of mammals, 55 fish species, 75 types of reptile, 275 bird species (one-third of all Australian bird species), and 4500 kinds of insect. There are frequent additions to the list, and a few of the rarer species are unique to the park. Kakadu's wetlands are on the UN list of Wetlands of International Importance,

principally because of their crucial significance to so many types of water bird.

You'll only see a tiny fraction of these creatures in a visit to the park since many of them are shy, nocturnal or few in numbers. Take advantage of talks and walks led by park rangers – mainly in the Dry – to get to know and see more of the wildlife (details from the park information centre). Cruises are run at South Alligator River and Yellow Water Billabong to enable you to see the water life.

Reptiles The park has both types of Australian crocodile: Twin and Jim Jim Falls for instance both have resident freshwater crocodiles, which are considered harmless, while there are about 3500 of the dangerous saltwater variety in the park. This beast ranges widely and is definitely not confined to salt water. Any expanse of water is quite likely to have a 'saltie' or two in it, and you're sure to see a few if you take a South Alligator or Yellow Water cruise. Take note of the plentiful crocodile warning signs: at least two people (a tourist and a fisherman) have been killed by saltwater crocodiles in Kakadu in recent years. Both ignored warnings.

Kakadu's other reptiles include several types of lizard, like the frilled lizard, and five freshwater turtle species of which the most common is the northern snake-necked turtle. The pig-nosed turtle, found here in 1973, was previously thought to live only in New Guinea. There are many snakes, including three highly poisonous types, but you're unlikely to see any. Oenpelli pythons, probably unique to the Kakadu escarpment, were only discovered in 1977.

Birds Kakadu's abundant water birds, in beautiful wetland settings, make a memorable sight. The park is one of the chief refuges in Australia for several species, among them the magpie goose, green pygmy goose and Burdekin duck. Kakadu is a staging post for birds migrating from the northern hemisphere around the beginning and end of the wet season. In September and October over 100,000 magpie geese gather at Mamukala.

Around 80% of the world population of this bird is in Kakadu at this time.

Other fine water birds include the jabiru stork with its distinctive red legs and long straight beak, pelicans and darters (also called snake birds for their snake-like movement as they swim for fish underwater).

Herons, egrets, ibis and cormorants are common. You're quite likely to see rainbow bee eaters and kingfishers (of which there are six types in inland Kakadu). Majestic white-breasted sea eagles are often seen near inland waterways too, and wedge-tailed eagles, whistling kites and black kites are common. At night you may hear barking owls calling – they sound just like dogs. Also spectacular is the red-tailed black cockatoo, and there are brolgas and bustards. A few bird species are unique to Kakadu, but they're rarely seen.

Mammals Several types of kangaroo and wallaby inhabit the park, and the shy black wallaroo is more or less unique to Kakadu. You might be lucky enough to see a sugar glider in wooded areas in the daytime. Kakadu is home to 25 bat species and a key refuge for four endangered varieties.

Water buffalo, which ran wild after being introduced to the Top End from Timor by European settlers in the first half of the 19th century, are being heavily reduced because they are potential carriers of cattle disease and damage the natural environment. By 1980 there were estimated to be well over 200,000 buffalo in the Northern Territory. Many are rounded up for slaughter or domestication by commercial contractors; some are shot humanely by park staff. They currently number about 2000 in Kakadu.

Fish You can't miss the silver barramundi, which creates a distinctive swirl near the water surface. It can grow well over a metre long and changes sex from male to female at the age of five or six years.

Rock Art

Kakadu has about 5000 Aboriginal rock painting sites dating from 20,000 or more years ago up to the 1960s. They range from hand prints to paintings of animals,

people, mythological beings and European ships, constituting one of the world's most important and fascinating rock-art collections. They provide a record of changing environments and Aboriginal lifestyles over the millennia.

In some places they are concentrated in large galleries, with paintings from different eras sometimes superimposed on one another. Some sites are kept secret – not only to protect them from damage, but also because they are private or sacred to the Aborigines. Some are even believed to be the residences of dangerous beings, who must not be approached by the ignorant. Two of the finest sites, however, have been opened up to visitors with access roads, walkways and explanatory signs. These are Ubirr and Nourlangie Rock. Park rangers conduct free art-site tours once or twice a day from May to October.

The dominant colours of all the art are yellow, red and white, obtained by grinding natural minerals to powder and mixing them with water.

Non-Aborigines owe much of their knowledge of the art to George Chaloupka, a Czechoslovakia-born Australian who devoted decades to studying it. Keep an eye open for his book on Nourlangie Rock. Chaloupka identified three main periods in Kakadu art – Pre-Estuarine, Estuarine and Post-Estuarine.

Pre-Estuarine From 20,000 or more years ago until 8000 or 10,000 years ago, Kakadu was probably a lot drier than today, with the coastline about 300 km further north, as much of the world's water was frozen in the larger polar ice caps. Rock paintings of this era show six main styles succeeding each other through time. Following the earliest hand or grass prints came a 'naturalistic' style, with large outline drawings of people or animals filled in with colour. Stick-like humans are shown hunting in this period. Some of the animals depicted, such as the thylacine (Tasmanian tiger) and the long-beaked echidna, have long been extinct in mainland Australia. Other paintings are thought to show large beasts wiped out worldwide millennia ago.

After the naturalistic style came the 'dynamic', in which motion is often cleverly depicted (a dotted line, for example, may show a spear's path through the air). Most humans shown are males with head-dresses, necklaces, armlets and so on, carrying weapons or dilly bags. Women are usually naked. In this era the first mythological beings appear – with human bodies and animal heads.

The fourth Pre-Estuarine style mainly shows simple, human silhouettes. They were followed by more 'stick figures' usually carrying fighting picks and wearing head adornments and skirts, and finally by the curious 'yam figures' in which people and animals are drawn in the shape of yams (or yams in the shape of people/animals!), with trailing roots and hairs. Yams must have been an important food source at this time, when the climate was probably increasingly damp.

Estuarine With the rising of the oceans about 8000 years ago much of Kakadu was covered with salt marshes. Many fish are depicted in the art of this period, and the X-ray style, showing the bones and internal organs, makes its appearance.

Post-Estuarine By about 1000 years ago, many of the salt marshes had turned into freshwater swamps and billabongs. The birds and plants which provided new food sources in this landscape appear in the art.

From around 400 years ago, Aboriginal artists also depicted the human newcomers to the region – Macassan fisherpeople from the south Celebes in present-day Indonesia, and later Europeans – and the things they brought, or their transport such as ships or horses.

In the last few decades the rock painting tradition has all but died out following the traumas that European settlement caused in Aboriginal society. Aborigines today devote artistic energy instead to painting on eucalyptus bark, often in traditional styles and usually for sale. But they still regard much of the rock art as important and take care to protect it.

Bark painting of long-necked turtle from
Western Arnhem Land.

Orientation – the Arnhem Highway

From where the Arnhem Highway to Kakadu turns east off the Stuart Highway, it's 120 km to the park entrance, and another 103 km east across the park to Jabiru, sealed all the way. The Kakadu Highway to Nourlangie Rock, Cooinda and Pine Creek turns south off the Arnhem Highway shortly before Jabiru.

A turn-off to the north, 18 km into the park along the Arnhem Highway, leads to camp sites at Two Mile Hole (eight km) and Four Mile Hole (38 km) on the Wildman River, popular for fishing. The track is not suitable for conventional vehicles except in the Dry, and then only as far as Two Mile Hole.

About 35 km further east along the highway, a turn-off to the south, again impassable to conventional vehicles in the Wet, leads to Alligator Billabong and the Kakadu Highway.

South Alligator River Crossing is on the highway 60 km into the park, about two km past Kakadu Holiday Village. The cruises on the tidal river here are a good opportunity for crocodile-spotting. Most days year-round there's a two-hour ($26.50) or five-hour ($56.50 including barbecue) cruise leaving at 10 am (☎ (089) 79 0166 for schedules or ask at Kakadu Holiday Village).

Seven km east of South Alligator, a short side road to the south leads to Mamukala, with a walking trail and bird-watching hides.

Information

The excellent Kakadu Park Information Centre (☎ (089) 79 2101), on the Kakadu Highway a couple of km south of where it turns off the Arnhem Highway, is open daily from 8 am to 5 pm. Here you'll find informative displays, including a special building devoted to birds, and a video room with several interesting films available – also details of guided art-site and wildlife walks. It's also where you pay the $8 entry fee. This entitles you to stay in the park for 14 days, and there are random checks at various places throughout the park to check tickets.

There's also an information centre at Jabiru Airport. In Darwin you can get information on Kakadu from the National Parks

& Wildlife Service. Top End tourist offices usually have copies of the *Kakadu Visitor Guide* leaflet, which includes a good map. Fuel is available at Kakadu Holiday Village, Border Store (no unleaded petrol or diesel), Jabiru and Cooinda. Jabiru also has a supermarket, post office and a Westpac bank.

Kakadu – A World Heritage of Unsurpassed Beauty, published by the Australian National Parks & Wildlife Service, is an informative and finely illustrated (but big) book on the park.

Walking

Kakadu is excellent but tough bushwalking country. Many people will be satisfied with the marked trails, which range from one km to 12 km long. For the more adventurous there are infinite possibilities especially in the drier south and east of the park, but take great care and prepare well. Tell people where you're going and don't go alone. You

need a permit from the park information centre to camp outside the established camp sites. The Darwin Bushwalking Club (☎ (089) 85 1484) welcomes visitors and may be able to help with information too. It has walks most weekends, often in Kakadu. Or you could join a Willis's Walkabout guided bushwalk (see Organised Tours under the Getting There & Around section).

Ubirr

This spectacular rock art site, also called Obiri Rock, lies 43 km north of the Arnhem Highway. The turn-off is 95 km from the park entrance and the road to Ubirr is sealed most of the way, but there are several creek crossings which make it impassable for a conventional vehicle for most of the wet season – sometimes for 4WD too. The rock-art site is open daily from 8.30 am to sunset from June to November.

Shortly before Ubirr you pass the Border

Mining

The Kakadu region contains nearly 10% of the world's known high-grade uranium ore. The national park surrounds three uranium-rich zones which are Aboriginal land, but which outside companies have the right to mine – Ranger, Jabiluka and Koongarra, all near the eastern border of the park. The federal government currently maintains a three-mine limit on the number of working uranium mines in Australia, and only Ranger of the Kakadu sites is being worked. (The other two working mines are Nabarlek in Arnhem Land, which has been mined out and is now simply a shrinking stockpile, and Roxby Downs in South Australia.)

You can tour the Ranger mine, opened in 1981. Jabiru town, close by, was built for the mine workers. The highly dubious uses of uranium and its potential damage to the local environment were not the only sources of controversy surrounding the granting of permission for mining here in the 1970s. The Northern Territory land rights laws had just been passed, and Aborigines were given the right to say no to mining on their lands, but the Ranger area was excluded from this provision. The Aborigines could, however, still negotiate the terms on which the mine companies would lease the land from them. Under pressure from the federal government and mine companies, the Aboriginal negotiators finally signed a deal in 1978, which brought them a decent share of the Ranger profits, but many felt that it didn't adequately protect their land or sacred sites.

By 1988 many of the Aboriginal owners of Jabiluka and Koongarra argued in favour of mining there, apparently impressed with the economic benefits brought by Ranger. It was estimated that the Aboriginal owners of the Ranger and Nabarlek mine sites had received about $100 million in royalties from the mine companies in less than a decade.

A large slice of Kakadu's Stage Three, declared national parkland in 1987, was temporarily set aside as a 'conservation zone', which means that the area was under national park protection except that mineral exploration was allowed. Mining companies were given five years to come to agreement with the Aboriginal landowners if they wanted to mine. In 1991, however, the Federal government refused permission for the Coronation Hill mine to go ahead, and Stage Three was given full national park status. ■

Store, near which are a couple of walking trails close to the East Alligator River, which forms the eastern boundary of the park here. There is a youth hostel and camp site nearby.

An easily followed path from the Ubirr car park takes you through the main galleries and up to a lookout with superb views – a 1½ km round trip. There are paintings on numerous rocks along the path, but the highlight is the main gallery with a large array of well-executed and preserved X-ray style wallabies, possums, goannas, tortoises and fish, plus a couple of *balanda* (white men) with hands on hips. Just round the corner from the main gallery, high on a rock face, is a Tasmanian tiger.

The Ubirr paintings are in many different styles. They were painted at times ranging from probably 20,000 or more years ago up to the 20th century. Allow plenty of time to seek out and study them.

Jabiru

The township, built to accommodate the Ranger mineworkers, has shops and a public swimming pool. Six km east is Jabiru Airport, and nearby the Ranger uranium mine. Minibus tours of the mine ($8) are available four times a day through Kakadu Air (☎ (089) 79 2411).

Nourlangie Rock

The sight of this looming, mysterious, isolated outlier of the Arnhem Land escarpment makes it easy to understand why it has been important to Aborigines for so long. Its long, red, sandstone bulk – striped in places with orange, white, even black – slopes up from surrounding woodland to fall away finally at one end in sheer, stepped cliffs, at the foot of which is Kakadu's best known collection of rock art.

The name Nourlangie is a corruption of *nawulandja*, an Aboriginal word which referred to an area bigger than the rock itself. The Aboriginal name of the rock is Burrunggui. You reach it at the end of a 12-km sealed road, which turns east off the Kakadu Highway, 22 km south of the Arnhem

Highway. Other interesting spots nearby make it worth spending a whole day in this corner of Kakadu. The last few km of the road are closed from around 5 pm daily.

From the main car park a round-trip walk of about two km takes you first to the Anbangbang shelter, which was used for 20,000 years as a refuge from heat, rain and the area's frequent wet-season thunderstorms. Namarrgon, the lightning man, appears in the rock art of the area as a skeletal white figure with stone axes attached to his head, elbows and knees. These strike the ground or clouds as he passes to make lightning.

Behind the shelter the path passes a rock painting of Namarrgon on the right before reaching two galleries. The first includes a group of dancing figures. The second is the Anbangbang gallery containing a famous group of paintings done in the 1960s by an artist called Najombolmi or Barramundi Charlie.

From the gallery you can walk onto a lookout where you can see the distant Arnhem Land cliff line, including Lightning Dreaming (Namarrgon Djadjam), which is the home of Namarrgon. There's a 12-km marked walk all the way round the rock, for which the park office has a leaflet.

Heading back towards the highway, you can take three turn-offs to further places of interest. The first, on the left about one km from the main car park, takes you to **Anbangbang Billabong**, with a dense carpet of lilies and a picnic site. The second, also on the left, leads to a short walk up to **Nawulandja Lookout**, with good views back over Nourlangie Rock.

The third turn-off, a dirt track on the right, takes you to another outstanding – but little visited – rock art gallery, **Nangaloar** or Nangaluwurr. You turn right off the track after about 1½ km to reach a small car park, from where it's an easily followed walk of about 1½ km to the paintings. There are many different styles and subjects here including a European ship, X-ray style fish, mythical beings and stick figures. A further six km along this road, followed by a three-km walk, brings you to **Gubara Pools**, an area of shaded pools set in monsoon forest.

Jim Jim & Twin Falls

These two spectacular waterfalls are down a 4WD-only dry-season track that turns south off the Kakadu Highway between the Nourlangie Rock and Cooinda turn-offs. It's about 60 km to Jim Jim Falls, with the last km on foot, and 70 km to Twin Falls, where the last few hundred metres are through the water up a snaking, forested gorge. Jim Jim – a sheer 215-metre drop – is awesome after the rains, but its waters can shrink to almost nothing at the end of the Dry. Twin Falls doesn't dry up.

Yellow Water & Cooinda

The turn-off to the Cooinda accommodation complex and the superb Yellow Water wetlands, with their big water bird population, is 48 km (sealed) down the Kakadu Highway from its junction with the Arnhem Highway. It's then about four km to Cooinda, and a couple more to the starting point for the boat trips on Yellow Water Billabong. These go several times daily year-round and cost $20 for two hours. This trip is one of the highlights of most people's visit to Kakadu. Early morning is the best time to go for then the bird life is most active. You're likely to see a saltwater crocodile or two. It's usually advisable to book your cruise the day before at Cooinda – particularly for the early departure.

Yellow Water is also an excellent place to watch the sunset from, particularly in the dry season when the smoke from the many bushfires which burn in the Top End at this time of year turns bright red in the setting sun. Bring plenty of insect repellent as the mosquitoes are voracious.

Cooinda to Pine Creek

Just south of the Yellow Water and Cooinda turn-off the Kakadu Highway ceases to be sealed. It heads south-west out of the park to Pine Creek on the Stuart Highway, about 160 km from Cooinda. This stretch is often closed to normal traffic in the Wet. If you're travelling up the Stuart Highway from the south, ask the police at Pine Creek for information on this route into Kakadu. On the way there are turn-offs to Waterfall Creek (also called Uranium Development Project or UDP Falls) which featured in *Crocodile Dundee*, and to the Arnhem Highway via the dry-season-only back road.

Places to Stay & Eat

Accommodation prices in Kakadu can vary tremendously depending on the season – dry-season prices (given here) are often as much as 50% above wet-season prices.

South Alligator Just a couple of km west of the South Alligator River on the Arnhem Highway is the *Kakadu Holiday Village* (☎ (089) 79 0166), which has four-bed share rooms for $28 per person, or singles/doubles for $113/144. The hotel has a restaurant and a basic shop.

Jabiru The *Four Seasons Kakadu* (☎ (089) 79 2800) is probably most famous for its design – it's set out in the shape of a crocodile, although this is only apparent from the air. There's nothing very exotic about the hotel itself, although it is comfortable enough. Room prices are $144/164.

The new *Kakadu Frontier Lodge* (☎ (089) 79 2422) has four-bed rooms at $23 per person, or $82 for a whole room. The only cooking facilities are a few barbecues.

Apart from the restaurants at the two resorts, the licensed *Jabiru Restaurant* in the town has takeaway burgers and a more expensive eat-in section with meals from $10. There's also a bakery across the road.

Ubirr The very basic YHA *Manbiyarra Youth Hostel* (☎ (089) 79 2985) has just 20 beds (in two-bed rooms), which cost $10 per person. The main problem with this place is that it's difficult to get to if you haven't got your own vehicle.

The Border Store has snack food and is open daily until 5 pm.

Cooinda This is by far the most popular

place to stay, mainly because of the proximity of the Yellow Water wetlands and the early morning boat cruises. It gets mighty crowded at times, mainly with camping tours. The *Four Seasons Cooinda* (☎ (089) 79 0145) has some comfortable units for $123/144, and much cheaper and more basic air-con 'budget rooms', which are just transportable huts of the type found on many building sites and more commonly known in the Territory as 'demountables', or 'dongas'. For $12 per person they are quite adequate, if a little cramped (two beds per room), although there are no cooking facilities.

The restaurant in the bar here serves unexciting but good-value meals, or there's the expensive *Mimi Restaurant*, with main courses at around $15.

Camping There are sites run by the national parks, and also some (with power) attached to the resorts :*Kakadu Holiday Village*, $20 for two with power, $14 without; *Four Seasons Cooinda*, $21/20; and *Kakadu Frontier Lodge*, $20/14.

The three main national park camp sites, with hot showers, flushing toilets and drinking water are: Merl, near the Border Store; Muirella Park, six km off the Kakadu Highway a few km south of the Nourlangie Rock turn-off; and Mardukal, just off the Kakadu Highway 1½ km south of the Cooinda turn-off. Only the Mardukal site is open during the Wet.

The national parks provide about 15 more basic camp sites around the park. The charge for camping at any site is $2 per person. To camp away from these you need a permit from the park information centre.

Getting There & Around

Ideally, take your own 4WD. The Arnhem Highway is sealed all the way to Jabiru. The Kakadu Highway is sealed from its junction with the Arnhem Highway, near Jabiru, to just beyond the Cooinda and Mardukal turn-offs. Sealed roads lead from the Kakadu Highway to Nourlangie Rock, the Muirella Park camping area and most of the way to Ubirr. Other roads are mostly dirt and blocked for varying periods during the Wet and early Dry.

Greyhound runs daily buses from Darwin to Kakadu and back. They leave Darwin at 7 am, and stop at Humpty Doo (one-way fare $19, 30 minutes), the Bark Hut ($24), Kakadu Holiday Village ($33), Jabiru ($41, 3¼ hours), Nourlangie Rock and Cooinda ($50, five hours). Aussiepass holders pay $50 return. The return service leaves Cooinda at 3 pm.

Organised Tours There are hosts of tours to Kakadu from Darwin and a few that start inside the park. Two-day tours typically take in Jim Jim Falls, Nourlangie Rock and the Yellow Water cruise, and cost from $170. Companies which aim at backpackers and seem to be popular include Hunter Safaris (☎ (089) 81 272), $170 for two days; Billy Can Tours (☎ (089) 81 2560), $195; Northern Adventure Safaris (☎ (089) 81 9733), $180 using Aussiepass to Jabiru, otherwise $198; and Ivan's Tours (☎ (089) 81 5524), two days and two nights $185.

A couple of operators offer deals such as use of a couple of video cameras amongst a small group. The idea is that you buy a copy of the resulting video. These trips are run by Kakadu Plus (☎ (089) 81 2560) and cost $208 for two days, plus $20 for the video at the end. There's a $20 discount for YHA members.

A one-day tour to Kakadu from Darwin is really too quick – but if you're short of time it's better than nothing. You could try Australian Kakadu Tours (☎ (089) 81 5144) who will whiz you to Yellow Water and Nourlangie Rock and back to Darwin for $88.

Longer tours usually cover most of the main sights plus a couple of extras. Some combine Kakadu with the Katherine Gorge. One of the popular ones are Katherine Adventure Tours (☎ (089) 71 0246) which charge $149 for two days, or $450 for a five-day trip, both from Katherine. Other interesting-looking trips are Australian Kakadu Tours's four-day $665 trip, which includes paddling to Twin Falls (May to

October only); Dial-a-Safari's four-day camping trips ($595), which focus on the south of the park or on Jim Jim and Twin Falls and little-visited art sites; and Terra Safari Tours's four-day camping trip for $520, which includes two nights at Koolpin Gorge in the south of the park (not January to March).

You can take 10-hour 4WD tours to Jim Jim and Twin Falls from Cooinda ($110, dry season) with Kakadu Gorge & Waterfall Tours (☎ (089) 79 2025).

Willis's Walkabouts (☎ (089) 85 2134) are bushwalks guided by knowledgeable Top End walkers, following your own or preset routes of two days or more. Many of the walks are in Kakadu: prices vary, but $750 for a two-week trip, including evening meals and return transport from Darwin, is fairly typical.

Flights Kakadu Air (☎ (089) 79 2411) does a number of flights over Kakadu. A half-hour flight from Jabiru costs $45, or it's $75 for an hour. From Cooinda half-hour flights are $75.

BATHURST & MELVILLE ISLANDS

These two large flat islands about 80 km north of Darwin are the home of the Tiwi Aborigines. You need a permit to visit them and though you might be given one if you gave tourism or curiosity as your reason, it's virtually impossible to get around the islands on your own. It's much better to go on a tour. Tiwi Tours (☎ (089) 81 5115), a company which employs many Tiwi among its staff, has been recommended.

The Tiwi people's island homes kept them fairly isolated from mainland developments until this century, and their culture has retained several unique features. Perhaps the best known are the pukamani burial poles, carved and painted with symbolic and mythological figures, which are erected around graves. More recently the Tiwi have turned their hand to art for sale – bark painting, textile screen printing, batik and pottery, using traditional designs and motifs.

The Tiwi had mixed relations with

Macassan fisherpeople, who came in search of the trepang, or sea cucumber. A British settlement in the 1820s at Fort Dundas, near Pularumpi on Melville Island, failed partly because of poor relations with the locals. The main settlement on the islands is **Nguiu** in the south-east of Bathurst Island, which was founded in 1911 as a Catholic mission.

Most Tiwi live on Bathurst Island and follow a non-traditional lifestyle. Some go back to their traditional lands on Melville Island for a few weeks each year. Melville

Figure carved in ironwood, Bathurst Island

Island also has descendants of Japanese pearl fisherpeople who regularly visited here early this century, and people of mixed Aboriginal and European parentage who were gathered here from around the Territory under government policy half a century ago.

A full-day Tiwi Tours trip costs $199 and includes your permit, a flight from Darwin to Nguiu, visits to the early Catholic mission buildings and craft workshops and tea with

Tiwi women, a boat crossing of the narrow Apsley Strait to Melville Island, swimming at Turacumbie Falls, a visit to the smaller community of Milikapiti on Melville's north coast, a trip to a pukamani burial site, and flight back to Darwin from Snake Bay on Melville. This tour is available from April to October. There are also day tours to Bathurst Island only ($169, March only).

Places to Stay
The only accommodation is on Melville Island, at the *Putjamirra Safari Camp*. It's in a beautiful setting right by the sea, and there are excellent bushwalking and fishing prospects. It's not a cheap place to stay, however, particularly with the cost of transport to the island. Australian Kakadu Tours (☎ (089) 81 5144) is currently offering a $250 weekend package which includes airfare, accommodation and meals.

COBOURG PENINSULA
This remote wilderness, 200 km north-east of Darwin, includes the Cobourg Marine Park and the Aboriginal-owned Gurig National Park. Entry to the latter is by permit, which has to be obtained in advance from the Cobourg Peninsula Sanctuary Board, PO Box 496, Palmerston, NT 0831.

The ruins of the early British settlement at Victoria can be visited on **Port Essington**, a superb 30-km-long natural harbour on the north side of the peninsula.

The track to Cobourg is accessible by 4WD vehicle only – and it's closed in the wet season. You pass through part of Arnhem Land and the Aboriginal owners there severely restrict the number of vehicles going through – so you're advised to apply up to a year ahead for the necessary permit (fee $10) from the Northern Territory Conservation Commission (☎ (089) 22 0211) at PO Box 38496, Palmerston, NT 0830. The drive from Jabiru takes about eight hours and the track is in reasonable condition, the roughest part coming in the hour or so after the turn-off from Murgenella.

There's a shady camp site about 100 metres from the shore at **Smith Point**, on the

north-east corner of Port Essington, with a shower and toilet, and a small store open a couple of hours a day. It costs about $20 a week to stay here.

You can fly to Cobourg from Darwin, but the camp site is some way from the airstrip, which makes things difficult if you're not on

Carving of straw-necked ibis,
Eastern Arnhem Land

a tour. Cobourg Marine (☎ (089) 79 0277) does $260 day trips from Darwin, which include a flight over Melville Island on the way, a cruise on Port Essington, visits to Aboriginal sacred sites, a tour of the Victoria ruins and game fishing.

ARNHEM LAND & GOVE

The entire eastern half of the Top End is the Arnhem Land Aboriginal Land which is spectacular, sparsely populated and the source of some good Aboriginal art. It's virtually closed to independent travellers apart from Gove, the peninsula at the north-east corner. One Darwin company, Arnhem Land Outback Expeditions (☎ (089) 48 0648), runs a three-day Arnhem Land tour for $595.

At **Nhulunbuy** on the Gove Peninsula there is a bauxite mining centre with a deep-

Ceremonial dillybag, Eastern Arnhem Land

water export port. The Aborigines of nearby Yirrkala made an important early step in the land rights movement in 1963 when they protested at the plans for this mining on their traditional land. They failed to stop it, but forced a government inquiry and won compensation, and their case caught the public eye.

You don't have to have a permit to visit Nhulunbuy and you can fly there direct from Darwin for $210 or from Cairns for $297 with Australian or Ansett. Travelling overland through Arnhem Land is impractical because of the number of different permits you need to get through different parts. Also, the tracks are extremely poor.

You can hire vehicles in Gove to explore the coastline (there are some fine beaches, but beware of crocodiles) and the local area. Get a permit to do this from the Northern Land Council in Gove (a formality).

Groote Eylandt, a large island off the east Arnhem Land coast, is also Aboriginal land, with a big manganese mining operation.

Down the Track

It's just over 1500 km south from Darwin to Alice Springs, and though at times it can be dreary there is an amazing variety of things to see or do along the road, or close to it.

Until WW II the Track really was just that – a dirt track – connecting the Territory's two main towns, Darwin and 'the Alice'. The need to supply Darwin quickly, which was under attack by Japanese aircraft from Timor, led to a rapid upgrading of the road – thanks in part to US troops. Although it is now sealed and well kept all the way, short, sharp floods during the Wet can cut the road and stop all traffic for days at a time.

The Stuart Highway takes its name from John McDouall Stuart, who made the first crossing of Australia from south to north. Twice he turned back due to lack of supplies, ill health and hostile Aborigines, but finally completed his epic trek in 1862. Only 10 years later the telegraph line to Darwin was laid along the route he had followed, and today the Stuart Highway between Darwin and Alice Springs follows the same path.

DARWIN TO KATHERINE

Some places along the Track south of Darwin (Howard Springs, Darwin Crocodile Farm and Litchfield Park) are covered in the Around Darwin section.

Lake Bennett

This is a popular camping, swimming, sailing and windsurfing spot among Darwinites. You can rent canoes. It's 80 km down the Track then seven km east. Camping is available for $5, or there are units for $9 per person. If you ring in advance (☎ (089) 76 0960) they'll pick you up from the highway.

Batchelor

This small town, 84 km down the Track from Darwin, then 13 km west, used to service the now-closed Rum Jungle uranium and copper mine nearby. In recent years it has received a boost from the growing popularity of nearby Litchfield National Park. Batchelor is the base of the Top End Gliding Club. It has a swimming pool open six days a week and an Aboriginal residential tertiary college. About an hour's walk away, or a shorter drive, is **Rum Jungle Lake** where you can canoe or swim, although this lake is close to an old tailings dump from the mine and the levels of radioactivity are supposedly high.

The *Batchelor Caravillage* (☎ (089) 76 0166) on Rum Jungle Rd has on-site vans for $48 a double, or tent sites for $13. The *Rum Jungle Motor Inn* (☎ (089) 76 0123) has singles/doubles for $58/68.

Adelaide River

Not to be confused with Adelaide River Crossing on the Arnhem Highway, this small settlement is on the Stuart Highway 111 km south of Darwin. It has a cemetery for those who died in the 1942-43 Japanese air raids. This whole stretch of the highway is dotted with a series of roadside WW II airstrips. Adelaide River has a pub, an Aboriginal art shop, the *Shady River View Caravan Park*

with tent sites, and the *Adelaide River Motor Inn* with singles from $25 to $35, doubles $45 to $60 (☎ (089) 76 7047 for both the above).

You can take tours from here or Batchelor to Litchfield Park, Daly River, Douglas Hot Springs and Butterfly Gorge – a bit cheaper than visiting the same places from Darwin.

Old Highway

South of Adelaide River, a sealed section of the old Stuart Highway, makes a loop to the south before rejoining the main road 52 km on. It's a scenic trip and leads to a number of pleasant spots, but access to them is often cut in the wet season.

The beautiful 12-metre **Robin Falls** are a short walk off this road, 17 km along. The falls, set in a monsoon-forested gorge, dwindle to a trickle in the dry season, but are spectacular in the Wet.

The turning to **Daly River** is 14 km further. Daly River is 109 km from the Stuart Highway. There's a Catholic mission (the ruins of an 1886 Jesuit mission) and the Daly River Nature Park where you can camp. Bird life is abundant at some times of the year, and quite a few saltwater and freshwater crocodiles inhabit the river.

To reach **Douglas Hot Springs**, turn south off the old highway just before it rejoins the Stuart Highway and go about 35 km. The nature park here includes a section of the Douglas River and several hot springs – a bit hot for bathing at 40°C.

Butterfly Gorge National Park is about 15 km beyond Douglas Hot Springs – you'll need a 4WD to get there. True to its name butterflies sometimes swarm in the gorge. Although it's generally safe to swim in these places, you should still watch out for crocs. There are camp sites with toilets and barbecues.

Pine Creek

This small town 245 km from Darwin was the scene of a gold rush in the 1870s and some of the old timber and corrugated iron buildings survive. The National Trust publishes a *Pine Creek Heritage Trail* leaflet with details of some of the more interesting buildings.

The old **railway station** has been restored and houses a visitors' information centre and a display on the Darwin to Pine Creek railway, opened in 1889 but now closed. **Pine Creek Museum** on Railway Parade near the post office has interesting displays on local history. The station and museum are usually open for an hour, each morning and afternoon. **Ah Toys General Store** is a reminder of the gold-rush days when Pine Creek's Chinese population heavily outnumbered the Europeans.

Pine Creek's *Youth Hostel* (☎ (089) 76 1254), close to the station, was built in the 1880s as quarters for railway workers. It hasn't changed much since. It's one of Australia's most basic hostels, but you get the feel of what Northern Territory pioneer life was like – no air-con, no hot water! The town has an unattractive caravan/camping park, and the *Pine Creek Hotel-Motel* (☎ (089) 76 1288) with air-con singles/doubles at $60/70.

In recent years gold mining has returned to Pine Creek with open-cut workings outside the town. Some visitors try panning for the precious stuff themselves. Back o' Beyond Tours (☎ (089) 76 1221) in Pine Creek offers two-hour trips round the town and old gold rush areas, with the chance to do some panning; or full-day tours towards Kakadu.

A dirt road goes north-east from Pine Creek to Kakadu National Park. It reaches the sealed Kakadu Highway after about 150 km, shortly before Cooinda. The dirt road is often closed in the Wet – check with Pine Creek police if you have any doubts. Along the way you can take an 80-km round-trip detour to **Waterfall Creek** (UDP Falls), a popular camping and swimming spot in Kakadu. About three km down the Stuart Highway south of Pine Creek is the turn-off to **Umbrawarra Gorge**, about 12 km west, where there's a camp site with toilets and barbecues, and you can swim in *normally* crocodile-free pools, one km from the car park.

Edith Falls

At the 293-km mark you can turn off to the beautiful Edith Falls, 19 km east of the road, where there's a free camp site with showers, toilets and barbecues. Swimming is possible in a clear, forest-surrounded pool at the bottom of the series of falls, and you may see freshwater crocodiles, the inoffensive variety, but be careful. There's a good walk up to rapids and more pools above the falls. Edith Falls is part of Katherine Gorge National Park.

KATHERINE (population 6100)

Apart from Tennant Creek this is the only town of any size between Darwin and Alice Springs. It's a bustling little place where the Victoria Highway branches off to the Kimberley and Western Australia. It's scheduled to grow to about 10,000 people in the 1990s, partly because of the big new airforce base at Tindal just south of town.

Katherine has long been an important stopping point, since the river it's built on and named after is the first permanent running water if you're coming north from Alice Springs. The town includes some historic old buildings, such as the **Sportsman's Arms**, featured in *We of the Never Never*, Jeannie Gunn's classic novel of turn-of-the-century outback life. The main interest here, however, is the spectacular Katherine Gorge 30 km to the north-east – a great place to camp, walk, swim, canoe, take a cruise or simply float along on an air mattress.

Orientation & Information

Katherine's main street, Katherine Terrace, is also the Stuart Highway running through the town. Coming from the north, you cross the Katherine River Bridge just before the town centre. The Victoria Highway to Western Australia branches off a further 300 metres on. After another 300 metres Giles St, the road to Katherine Gorge, branches off in the other direction. At the end of the town centre, is the NTGTB office (☎ (089) 72 2650), which is open from Monday to Friday from 9 am to 5 pm and Saturdays from 9 am to noon. The bus station is over the road from the NTGTB. There's a Northern Territory Conservation Commission office (☎ (089) 72 1799) on Katherine Terrace.

Town Centre

Katherine's old **railway station**, owned by the National Trust, houses a display on railway history and is open Monday to Friday from 11 am to 3 pm. Mimi Arts & Crafts on Pearce St is an Aboriginal-run shop, selling products made over a wide area – from the deserts in the west to the coast in the east.

Springvale Homestead, eight km southwest of town (turn right off the Victoria Highway after 3¾ km) claims to be the oldest cattle station in the Northern Territory. Today it's also a tourist accommodation centre, but free half-hour tours around the old homestead are given once or twice daily. From May to September, evening crocodile-spotting cruises ($29) are run from here, and three times a week there are night-time Aboriginal corroborees with demonstrations of fire making, traditional dance and spear throwing ($29 including barbecue).

Katherine has a good public swimming pool, beside the highway on the way out of town, about 750 metres past the bus station. There are also some pleasant thermal pools beside the river, down behind the youth hostel.

Organised Tours

Tours are available from Katherine taking in various combinations of the town and Springvale Homestead attractions, the gorge, Cutta Cutta Caves, Mataranka and Kakadu. Most accommodation places can book you on these and you'll be picked up from where you're staying – or ask at the NTGTB office or Travel North in the bus station.

Places to Stay

Kookaburra Lodge Backpackers (☎ (089) 71 0257) on the corner of Lindsay and Third Sts is just a few minutes' walk from the Transit Centre. It consists of old motel units with between six and 10 beds, and costs $11 a night. With so many people in each unit, the bathroom and cooking facilities can get overloaded at times.

Just around the corner is the *Palm Court Backpackers* (☎ (089) 72 2722) on the corner of Third and Giles Sts. It's in the most horrendously tasteless building, but the air-con rooms are uncrowded and have their own TV, fridge and bathroom. The problem here is that the communal cooking facilities are inadequate. The cost is $13 per person, or $42 to take a whole room (four beds).

The Katherine *Youth Hostel* (☎ (089) 72 2942) is two km along the Victoria Highway, on the right. It's a friendly place with 51 beds (no more than three in any room) and charges $8 a night, although the location is inconvenient.

The *Victoria Lodge Katherine* (☎ (089) 72 3464) is at 21 Victoria Highway. It's a good place with four-bed rooms at $8.50 to $11 per person (depending on the season), including a light breakfast.

There are several camping possibilities. One of the nicest is *Springvale Homestead* (☎ (089) 72 1355) with shady sites for $11. There's a swimming pool, you can rent canoes or rowing boats on the Katherine River nearby, or take a horse ride. Springvale also has budget rooms in a bunkhouse at $34/41 for singles/doubles. It has a licensed restaurant and a kiosk which doesn't serve meals. It's eight km out of Katherine; turn right off the Victoria Highway after four km and follow the signs.

On the road to Springvale, five km from town, is *Katherine Low Level Caravan Park* (☎ (089) 72 3962), a good place close to the river but a bit short of shade. Tent sites are $14.50 for two. Nearer town, 2½ km out along the Victoria Highway, the *Riverview Caravan Park* (☎ (089) 72 1011) has quite comfortable cabins for $35 singles/doubles, motel units for $39/48 and some tent sites. The thermal pools are five minutes' walk away.

The *Katherine Frontier Motor Inn* (☎ (089) 72 1744), four km south of town on the Stuart Highway, has tent sites at $5 a person, plus a pool, barbecue area and restaurant.

Among the motels, the *Beagle Motor Inn* (☎ (089) 72 3998) at the corner of Lindsay and Fourth Sts is probably the cheapest, with singles/doubles for $40/55.

Places to Eat

Basically Katherine has one or two of each of the usual types of Aussie eatery. Over the road from the Transit Centre, which has a 24-hour cafe, there's a *Big Rooster* fast-food place. The *Katherine Hotel-Motel*, just up the main street, has counter meals as well as the *Aussie's Bistro*, which is good value. Over the road there's the *Golden Bowl* Chinese restaurant, and the *Crossways Hotel*, a block further up on the corner of Warburton St, does good counter meals for around $7.

Getting There & Away

All buses between Darwin and Alice Springs, Queensland or Western Australia stop at Katherine, which means two or three daily to/from Western Australia, and usually four to/from Darwin, Alice Springs and Queensland. See the Darwin section for more details. Typical fares from Katherine are Darwin $40, Alice Springs $135, Three Ways $52, and Kununurra $43.

You can fly to Katherine from Darwin ($123) daily, or three times a week from Alice Springs ($302), both with Ansett NT. The Ansett office in Katherine is on the main street between Giles and Lindsay Sts (☎ (089) 72 1344). Katherine Airport is eight km south of town, just off the Stuart Highway.

Getting Around

You can rent bicycles at the youth hostel. Avis, Budget, Hertz and Territory Rent a Car all have car-rental offices in town.

Travel North has a six-times-daily bus service from the Transit Centre to the Gorge for $4 each way.

AROUND KATHERINE
Katherine Gorge (Nitmiluk)

Strictly speaking Katherine Gorge is 13 gorges, separated from each other by rapids of varying length. The gorge walls aren't high, but it is a remote, beautiful place. It is 12 km long and has been carved out by the Katherine River, which rises in Arnhem Land. Further downstream it becomes the Daly River before flowing into the Timor Sea 80 km south-west of Darwin. The difference in water levels between the Wet and Dry is staggering. During the dry season the gorge waters are calm, but from November to March they can become a raging torrent.

Swimming in the gorge is safe except when it's in flood. The only crocodiles around are the freshwater variety and they're more often seen in the cooler months. The country surrounding the gorge is excellent for walking.

It's 30 km by sealed road from Katherine to the visitors' centre and the camp site, and nearly one km further to the car park where the gorge begins and cruises start. The visitors' centre has displays and information on the national park, which spreads over 1800 sq km to include extensive back country and the Edith Falls to the north-west, as well as Katherine Gorge. There are details of a wide range of marked walking tracks starting here that go through the picturesque country south of the gorge, descending to the river at various points. Notice the smooth-barked salmon gums. Some of them pass Aboriginal rock paintings up to 7000 years old. You can walk to Edith Falls (76 km, five days) or points on the way. For the longer or more rugged walks, you need a permit from the visitors' centre. The Katherine Gorge Canoe Marathon, organised by the Red Cross, takes place in June.

Tours & Activities At the river you can rent one, two or three-person canoes (☎ (089) 71 0257 or call at the Kookaburra Backpackers). These cost $18/22/27 for a half day, or $25/35/45 for a whole day. This is a great way of exploring the gorge. You can also be adventurous and take the canoes out overnight, but you must book in advance as only a limited number of people are allowed to camp out in the gorges. You get a map with your canoe showing things of interest along the gorge sides – Aboriginal rock paintings, waterfalls, plant life and so on.

The alternative is a cruise. These depart daily and range from a two-hour run which includes a visit to some gorge-side rock paintings for $17, to an eight-hour trip to the fifth gorge (the most spectacular) for $55. All involve some walking between gorges (four km on the longest trip). In the wet season there are two-hour cruises only.

You can also take chopper flights over the gorge for $80.

Places to Stay The *Katherine Gorge Caravan Park* (☎ (089) 72 1253) has showers, toilets, barbecues and a store (open from 7 am to 7 pm) which also serves basic hot meals. Wallabies and goannas frequent the camp site. It costs $6.05 per adult to pitch a tent.

Getting There & Away The six-times-daily commuter bus costs $4 each way, and it picks up from anywhere in town. Kookaburra also runs a bus three times daily for $4.

Cutta Cutta Caves

Guided tours of these limestone caverns, 24 km south-east of Katherine along the Stuart Highway, are led by park rangers twice a day in the dry season, and cost $4.50. Orange horseshoe bats, a rare and endangered species, roost in the main cave. The rock formations outside the caves are impressive.

Beswick Aboriginal Land

This is a large area east of the Stuart Highway between Katherine and Mataranka. You normally need a permit to enter, except during the four-day festival in June or July at Barunga, 30 km off the highway. Aborigines from all over the Territory gather for dancing and sports, and you'll see lots of arts & crafts. The Sunday is the high point. Take a tent.

KATHERINE TO WESTERN AUSTRALIA

It's 513 km on the Victoria Highway from Katherine to Kununurra in Western Australia. The road is bitumen but very narrow: whenever two vehicles approach they have to edge off the road and inevitably stones shower everywhere. To preserve your windscreen and headlights pull well off and slow down. As you approach the Western Australian border you start to see the boab trees found in much of the north-west of Australia. There's a 1½-hour time change when you cross the border. There's also a quarantine inspection post, and all fruit and vegetables must be deposited here. This only applies when travelling from the Territory to Western Australia.

The highway is sometimes cut by floods – the wet season here is very wet. In the dry season if you stand on the **Victoria River Bridge** by the Victoria River Inn it's hard to imagine that the wide river, flowing far below your feet, can actually flow over the top of the bridge!

From April to October, daily boat trips are made on the river from here or from **Timber Creek**, further west. Max, the boat operator, is a local character and you'll be shown freshwater crocodiles, fish and turtles being fed – try some real billy tea, play the didgeridoo and light a fire using firesticks. Max has a good knowledge of the flora & fauna and local history.

Gregory National Park is a new park of over 10,000 sq km. At present, access is by 4WD only, but it is good bushwalking and canoeing country although it gets very hot – and wet – in the wet season. Just west of the Victoria River Inn there's a one-hour return walk up the escarpment, and more walking trails are being marked out. Gregory's Tree Historical Reserve is west of Timber Creek and you can see a boab marked by the early explorer.

Bordering Western Australia the **Keep River National Park** is noted for its sandstone landforms and has some excellent walking trails. You can reach the main points in the park by conventional vehicles during the dry season. Aboriginal art can be seen near the car park at the end of the road. By now a new park headquarters, roadhouse and camping facility, at the Northern Territory-Western Australia border post, may be more than just a plan.

MATARANKA

Mataranka is 103 km south-east of Katherine on the Stuart Highway. The attraction is **Mataranka Homestead**, seven km off the highway just south of the small town. The crystal-clear thermal pool here, in a pocket of rainforest, is a great place to wind down after a hot day on the road – though it can get crowded. There's no charge.

Just a short walk from the pool is the homestead accommodation area with a youth hostel, camp site and motel rooms – more relaxed than it sounds since you're a long way from anywhere else. A couple of hundred metres away is the **Waterhouse River**, where you can walk along the banks, or rent canoes and rowing boats for $5 an hour. Outside the homestead entrance is a replica of the Elsey Station Homestead which was made for the filming of *We of the Never Never* (whose story is set near Mataranka). There are historical displays inside the replica.

Places to Stay

At Mataranka Homestead (☎ (089) 75 4544), the *Youth Hostel* has 18 beds, is quite comfortable and has some twin rooms, though the kitchen is small. It costs $11 per person (YHA members only). There's also backpackers' accommodation available for $15. Camping is $6.50 per person, and air-con motel rooms with private bathroom are $55/70 for singles/doubles. In between there are self-contained budget cabins which cost $64 for up to five people. There's a store where you can get basic groceries, a bar with snacks and meals (not cheap), or you can use the camp site barbecues.

Also in Mataranka are the *Old Elsey Inn* (☎ (089) 75 4512) with a couple of rooms at $25 a head, and the *Territory Manor Motel* (☎ (089) 75 4516), a more luxurious place

with a swimming pool, restaurant and motel rooms at $52/56 for singles/doubles.

Getting There & Around

Long-distance buses travelling up and down the Stuart Highway call at Mataranka and the homestead.

MATARANKA TO THREE WAYS

Not far south of the Mataranka Homestead turn-off, the Roper Highway branches east off the Stuart Highway. It leads about 200 km to **Roper Bar**, near the Roper River on the edge of Aboriginal land, where there's a store with a camp site and a few rooms – mainly visited by fishing enthusiasts, though 4WD tours are available (☎ (089) 81 9455 in Darwin). All but about 40 km of the road is sealed. Shortly south of the Roper junction the **Elsey Cemetery** is not far off the highway. Here are the graves of characters like 'the Fizzer' who came to life in *We of the Never Never*.

Continuing south from Mataranka you pass through **Larrimah** – at one time the railway line from Darwin came as far as here, but it was abandoned after Cyclone Tracy. There are three camp sites. The one on the highway at the south end of town, *Green Park* (☎ (089) 75 9937), charges $9 per tent site. There's a swimming pool and a few crocodiles in fenced-off ponds – and basic air-con cabins cost $20 a double. You can also camp at the *Larrimah Wayside Inn* (☎ (089) 75 9931), 100 metres or so off the highway opposite the Green Park. The Wayside has singles/doubles from $15/25, on-site vans and cabins; it does counter meals and sells petrol several cents cheaper than the places on the highway.

Next is **Daly Waters**, three km off the highway, an important staging post in the early days of aviation – Amy Johnson landed here. The *Daly Waters Pub* (☎ (089) 75 9927), with air-con double rooms at $40, is not surprisingly the focus of local life – it also serves as police station, post office, bank and museum, and it's the main source of employment. It's an atmospheric place, dating from 1893 and said to be the oldest pub in the Territory, and good food's available. Daly Waters has a caravan park with tent sites at $6 per person – and another WW II airstrip.

Just south of Daly Waters the sealed Carpentaria Highway heads off east to **Borroloola** (on Aboriginal land, but visited by barramundi fishers) 378 km away near the Gulf of Carpentaria. After 267 km the Carpentaria Highway meets the Tablelands Highway, also sealed, at Cape Crawford Roadhouse. The Tablelands Highway runs 404 km south to meet the Barkly Highway at Barkly Roadhouse and there's no petrol between the two roadhouses.

Back on the Stuart Highway, after Daly Waters there's **Newcastle Waters** and **Elliott**, and the land gets drier and drier. Elliott has two caravan parks with tent sites and a hotel-motel. Lake Woods, 14 km west by dirt road, is a great spot for camping, though there are no facilities. Further south, a large rock known as **Lubra's Lookout** overlooks **Renner Springs**, and this is generally accepted as the dividing line between the seasonally wet Top End and the dry Centre.

About 50 km before Three Ways is **Churchill's Head**, a large rock said to look like Britain's wartime prime minister. Soon after, there's a memorial to Stuart at **Attack Creek**, where the explorer turned back on one of his attempts to cross Australia from south to north, reputedly after his party was attacked by a group of hostile Aborigines. The party was running low on supplies and this incident was the final straw.

THREE WAYS

Three Ways, 537 km north of the Alice, 988 km south of Darwin and 643 km west of Mt Isa, is basically a bloody long way from anywhere – apart from Tennant Creek, 26 km down the track. This is a classic 'get stuck' point for hitchhikers – anybody who has hitched around Australia seems to have a tale about Three Ways. The *Threeways Roadhouse* (☎ (089) 62 2744) at the junction has a friendly sign 'Hitch-hikers! No Loitering'. If you want to spend the night there you can

camp for $8 a double, or there are rooms at $25/35. The junction is marked by a memorial to John Flynn, the original flying doctor.

TENNANT CREEK (population 3300)

Apart from Katherine, this is the only town of any size between Darwin and Alice Springs. It's 26 km south of Three Ways, 511 km north of Alice Springs. A lot of travellers spend a night here and there are one or two attractions, mainly related to gold mining, to tempt you to stay a bit longer. The NTGTB office (☎ (089) 62 3388) is at the corner of the Stuart Highway and Davidson St, in the middle of town.

There's a tale that Tennant Creek was first settled when a wagonload of beer broke down here in the early 1930s and the drivers decided they might as well make themselves comfortable while they consumed the freight. Tennant Creek had a small gold rush around the same time. One of the major workings was **Noble's Nob**, 16 km east of the town along Peko Rd. It was discovered by a one-eyed man called John Noble who formed a surprisingly successful prospecting partnership with the blind William Weaber. This was the biggest open-cut gold mine in the country until mining ceased in 1985. Ore from other local mines is still processed and you can visit the open cut.

Along Peko Rd you can visit the old **Tennant Creek Battery**, where gold-bearing ore was crushed and treated. It's still in working order and guided tours are given one to four times daily from April to October (admission $1). Along the same road are the **One Tank Hill lookout** and the Argo mine, main operation of the Peko company which used to mine at Warrego, north-west of Tennant Creek.

The **National Trust Museum**, on Schmidt St near the corner of Windley St, houses six rooms of local memorabilia and reconstructed mining scenes. It's open daily from 10 am to 4 pm from April to October.

Anyinginyi is an interesting small Aboriginal arts & crafts shop on the highway in the centre of town. Most of the stuff sold is made locally and prices are lower than in Alice Springs.

Places to Stay

A basic *Youth Hostel* (☎ (089) 62 2719) at the corner of Leichhardt and Windley Sts has 26 beds. Windley St runs west off the Stuart Highway in the town centre, a block south of the NTGTB office. A bed in the hostel costs $8.

Camping is the only cheap alternative. The *Outback Caravan Park* (☎ (089) 62 2459) is one km along Peko Rd, which runs east off the Stuart Highway opposite Windley St. It has a swimming pool, tent sites at $15 a double and on-site vans or cabins (some air-con) for $25 to $34 double.

Motels aren't cheap. The *Safari Lodge Motel* (☎ (089) 62 2207) on the highway has singles/doubles for $56/66. There are also dormitory beds for $12. The *Goldfields Hotel-Motel* (☎ (089) 62 2030), also on the highway, has singles/doubles at $56/65.

TENNANT CREEK TO ALICE SPRINGS

About 90 km south of Tennant Creek are the **Devil's Marbles**, a haphazard pile of giant spherical boulders scattered on both sides of the road. According to Aboriginal mythology the Rainbow Serpent laid them. The Rainbow Serpent obviously got around because there is a similar collection of boulders on a South Island beach in New Zealand, and similar Devil's Pebbles 10 km north-west of Tennant Creek. At **Wauchope**, just to the south of the marbles, there's a camp site.

After the Devil's Marbles there are only a few places of interest to pause at on the trip south to the Alice. Near Barrow Creek the **Stuart Memorial** commemorates John McDouall Stuart. Visible to the east of the highway is **Central Mt Stuart**, the geographical centre of Australia. At **Barrow Creek** itself there is an old post office telegraph repeater station. It was attacked by Aborigines in 1874 and the station master and linesman were killed – their graves are by the road. A great number of Aborigines died in the inevitable reprisals.

The road continues through **Ti Tree** (which has a camp site) and finally **Aileron**, the last stop before the Alice. Although roadhouses and petrol are fairly plentiful (if expensive) along the track, it is wise to fill up regularly, particularly if you are on a motorcycle.

Alice Springs

Population 23,000

'The Alice', as it's usually known (never just Alice), was originally founded as a staging point for the overland telegraph line in the 1870s. A telegraph station was built near a permanent water hole in the bed of the dry Todd River. The river was named after Charles Todd, Superintendent of Telegraphs back in Adelaide, and a spring near the water hole was named after Alice, his wife.

A town, named Stuart, was first established in 1888, a few km south of the telegraph station, as a railhead for a proposed railway line. Because the railway didn't materialise, the town developed slowly. Not until 1933 did the town come to be known as Alice Springs.

The telegraph line through the Centre was built to connect with the undersea line from Darwin to Java, which on its completion put Australia in direct contact with Europe for the first time. It was a monumental task, but it was achieved in a remarkably short time.

Today Alice Springs is a pleasant, modern town with good shops and restaurants. It is a jumping-off point for the many tourist attractions of central Australia. There is also a major US communications base, Pine Gap, nearby and the US influence is very clear. It's a sobering thought that Alice Springs would be a priority target in the event of a nuclear war. The Alice Springs Peace Group (☎ (089) 52 1894) can tell you more about Pine Gap.

Alice Springs's growth to its present size has been recent and rapid. When the name was officially changed in 1933 the popula-

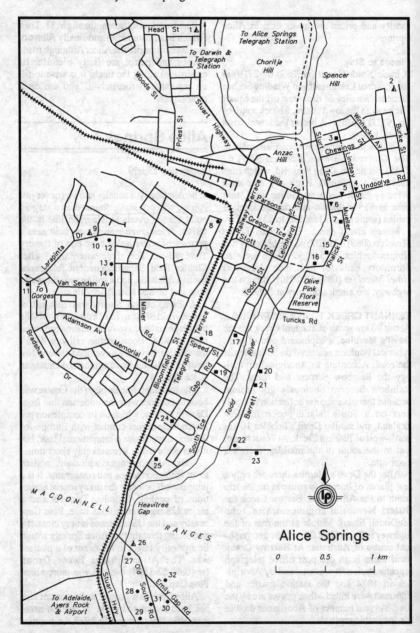

Alice Springs

0   0.5   1 km

■ PLACES TO STAY

1 Wintersun Caravan Park
2 Greenleaves Caravan Park
3 Arura Safari Lodge
7 Alice Lodge
9 Stuart Caravan Park
15 Sandrifter Safari Lodge
16 Alice Springs Pacific Resort
17 White Gums Holiday Units
19 Toddy's Backpackers
20 Desert Palms Resort
21 Sheraton Hotel
23 Four Seasons Motel
24 Alice Tourist Apartments
25 Gapview Resort Hotel
26 Heavitree Gap Caravan Park

▼ PLACES TO EAT

4 Fish Shop
5 Golden Inn Chinese Restaurant
6 Casa Nostra Pizza

OTHER

8 Pioneer Cemetery
10 Araluen Art Centre
11 Diorama
12 Strehlow Research Centre
13 Aviation Museum
14 Lasseter's & Namatjira's Graves
18 Swimming Pool
22 Lasseter's Casino
27 Pitchi Ritchi Sanctuary
28 Stuart Auto Museum
29 Old Timers' Museum
30 G'day Mate Tourist Park
31 Date Garden
32 MacDonnell Range Tourist Park

tion had only just reached 200! Even in the 1950s Alice Springs was still a tiny town with a population in the hundreds. Until WW II there was no sealed road leading there and it was only in 1987 that the old road south to Port Augusta and Adelaide was finally replaced by a new, shorter and fully sealed highway.

Recently some people have begun to think that Alice Springs's boom times have been too much of a good thing. When the Marron's Newsagency building on Todd St

Mall, the last remaining old verandahed building on Todd St, fell to the wreckers in mid-1988, people began to realise that the Alice was no longer the little outback town which readers of Neville Shute's famous novel expect to find. 'Surfer's Paradise in the desert' is a better description, according to some locals.

Orientation

The centre of Alice Springs is a conveniently compact area just five streets wide, bounded by the dry Todd River on one side and the Stuart Highway on the other. Anzac Hill forms a northern boundary to the central area while Stuart Terrace is the southern end. Many of the places to stay and virtually all of the places to eat are in this central rectangle. Todd St is the main shopping street of the town; from Wills Terrace to Gregory Terrace it is a pedestrian mall. The bus centre is on Hartley St at the back of Ford Plaza. If you arrive by bus you can walk through the plaza and come out on Todd St Mall.

Information

The NTGTB office (☎ (089) 52 1299) is in the glossy Ford Plaza building on Todd St Mall. It's open from 8.45 am to 5 pm Monday to Friday, and from 9 am to 12.30 pm and 1.15 to 4 pm on Saturdays, Sundays and holidays. Most tours can be booked here. The *Central Australian Visitors' Guide* is a useful monthly information booklet produced on the Alice Springs area.

The Northern Territory Conservation Commission (☎ (089) 51 8211) is on Todd St, just south of Stuart Terrace. There are maps, books and those popular 'No Swimming, Beware of Crocodiles' signs. The office is open Monday to Friday from 8 am to 4.20 pm. Information on the guided walks to the Telegraph Station, Finke Gorge and Simpson's Gap is available.

The *Centralian Advocate* is Alice Springs's twice-weekly newspaper. The Arunta Art Gallery on Todd St has a good selection of books.

Summer days can get very hot (up to 45°C) and even winter days are pretty warm.

However winter nights can freeze and a lot of people get caught off guard. In winter (June and July), five minutes after the sun goes down you can feel the heat disappear, and the average minimum nightly temperature is 4°C.

Despite Alice Springs's dry climate and low annual rainfall, the occasional rains can be heavy and the Todd River may flood.

Alice Events

The Alice has a string of colourful activities, particularly during the cool tourist months from May to August. The Camel Cup, a series of camel races, takes place in early May. At around the same time, Chateau Hornsby, the local winery, has a beerfest.

The Alice Springs Agricultural show takes place in early July, and the highlight is a fireworks display.

In August there's the Alice Springs Rodeo, when for one week the town is full of bow-legged stockmen, swaggering around in their 10-gallon hats, cowboy shirts, moleskin jeans, and R M Williams Cuban-heeled boots.

Finally in early October there's the event which probably draws the biggest crowds of all – the Henley-on-Todd Regatta. Having a series of boat races in the Todd River is slightly complicated by the fact that there is hardly ever any water in the river. Nevertheless a whole series of races are held for sailing boats, doubles, racing eights and every boat race class you could think of. The boats are all bottomless, the crews' legs stick out and they simply run down the course!

A Food & Wine Festival is held early in September, at the end of the regatta. Various restaurants, ethnic groups and local wineries provide a range of food and drink through the day. The Top Half Folk Festival changes location annually, but shows up in Alice every so often.

All through the cooler months there is also a string of country horse races at Alice Springs and surrounding outstations like Finke, Barrow Creek, Aileron or the Harts Range. They're colourful events and for the outstations they're the big turn-outs of the year.

Telegraph Station

Laying the telegraph line across the dry, harsh centre of Australia was no easy task, as the small museum at the old telegraph station, two km north of the town, shows. The original spring, which the town is named after, is also here. The station, one of 12 built along the telegraph line in the 1870s, was constructed of local stone in 1871-72 and continued in operation until 1932.

The station is open daily from 8 am throughout the year; entry is \$2.50. From April to October rangers give free guided tours several times daily; at other times you can use the informative self-guided brochure issued to all visitors.

The **Alice Springs** here are a great spot for a cooling dip, and the grassy picnic area by the station has barbecues, tables and some shady gum trees – a popular spot on weekends.

It's easy to walk or ride to the station from the Alice – just follow the path on the western (left hand) side of the riverbed; it takes about half an hour. The main road out to the station is signposted to the right off the Stuart Highway about one km north of the centre of town. There's another pleasant circular walk from the station out by the old cemetery and Trig Hill.

Anzac Hill

At the northern end of Todd St you can make the short, sharp ascent to the top of Anzac Hill (or you can drive there). From the top you have a fine view over modern Alice Springs and down to the MacDonnell Range that forms a southern boundary to the town. There are a number of other hills in and around Alice Springs which you can climb, but Anzac Hill is certainly the best known and most convenient.

Todd St

Right at the end of Todd St the signpost indicating how far Alice Springs is from almost anywhere makes a popular photographic subject.

The *Central Australian Visitors' Guide* booklet has an interesting heritage walk around the historic buildings concentrated in the compact central area. Before you stroll down Todd St Mall note the footbridge over the Todd River from Wills Terrace. The road here runs across a causeway, but until the bridge was built the Todd's infrequent flow could cut off one side of the town from the other.

Todd St is the main shopping street of the town, and most of it is a pleasant pedestrian mall. Along the street you can see Adelaide House, built in the early 1920s and now preserved as the **John Flynn Memorial Museum**. Originally it was Alice Springs's first hospital. It's open from 10 am to 4 pm Monday to Friday, and from 10 am to noon on Saturday. Admission is $1.50 (children 80c) and includes a cup of tea or coffee. Flynn, who was the founding flying doctor, is also commemorated by the **John Flynn Memorial Church** next door.

Other Old Buildings

There are a number of interesting old buildings along Hartley St including the **Stuart Town Gaol** built in 1907-08. It's open on Tuesday and Thursday from 10.30 am to 12.30 pm, and on Saturday mornings between 9.30 and 11.30 am. The **Old Courthouse**, which was in use until 1980, is on the corner of Hartley and Parsons Sts.

Across the road is the **Residency** which dates from 1926-27. It's now used for historical exhibits and is open from 9 am to 5 pm daily. Other old buildings include the **Hartley St School** beyond the post office and **Tunk's Store** on the corner of Hartley St and Stott Terrace.

Near the corner of Parsons St and Leichhardt Terrace the old **Pioneer Theatre**, is a former walk-in (rather than drive-in) cinema dating from 1944. These days it's a YHA hostel.

Spencer & Gillen Museum

Upstairs in Ford Plaza the Spencer & Gillen Museum of Central Australia has a fascinating collection, including some superb natural history displays. There's an interesting exhibition on meteors and meteorites (Henbury meteorites are on display). There are also exhibits on Aboriginal culture, some fine Papunya Tula sand paintings and displays of art of the Centre, including works by Albert Namatjira. Admission is $2 and it's open from 9 am to 5 pm daily.

Flying Doctor

The Royal Flying Doctor Base is close to the town centre in Stuart Terrace. It's open from 9 am to 3.30 pm Monday to Saturday, and from 1 to 4 pm on Sunday. The tours last half an hour and cost $1.50 (children 50c).

School of the Air

The School of the Air, which broadcasts school lessons to children on remote outback stations, is on Head St, about a km north of the centre. It's open from 1.30 to 3.30 pm Monday to Friday, but is closed, of course, during school holidays.

Aviation Museum

Alice Springs has an interesting little aviation museum housed in the former Connellan hangar on Memorial Ave, where the town's airport used to be in the early days. The museum includes a couple of poignant exhibits which pinpoint the dangers of outback aviation.

In 1929 pioneer aviator Charles Kingsford-Smith went missing in the north-west in his aircraft *Southern Cross*. Two other aviators, Anderson and Hitchcock, set off to search for Kingsford-Smith in their tiny aircraft *Kookaburra*. North of Alice Springs they struck engine trouble and made an emergency landing. Despite not having any tools they managed to fix the fault, but repeated attempts to take off failed due to the sandy, rocky soil. They had foolishly left Alice Springs not only without tools, but with minimal water and food. By the time an aerial search had been organised and their plane located both had died. Their bodies were recovered but the aircraft, intact and undamaged, was left. Kingsford-Smith turned up unharmed a few days later.

The aircraft was accidentally rediscovered by a mining surveyor in 1961, and in the '70s it was decided to collect the remains and exhibit them. They proved strangely elusive, however, and it took several years to find them again. They were finally located in 1978 by Sydney electronics whizz Dick Smith. Fifty years of exposure and bushfires had reduced the aircraft to a crumbled wreck. It is now displayed only a few steps from where the aircraft took off on its ill-fated mission. A short film tells the sad story of this misadventure.

The museum also displays a Wackett, which went missing in 1961 on a flight from Ceduna in South Australia. The pilot strayed no less than 42° off course and put down when he ran out of fuel. An enormous search failed to find him because he was so far from his expected route. The aircraft was discovered, again completely by accident, in 1965. The museum has a small booklet on this bizarre mishap.

The museum is not all tragedy – there are exhibits on pioneer aviation in the Territory and, of course, the famous Flying Doctor Service. The museum is open from Monday to Friday from 9 am to 4 pm, Saturday and Sunday from 10 am to 2 pm; admission is free.

Strehlow Research Centre

This new centre, on Larapinta Drive, commemorates the work of Professor Strehlow among the Aranda people of the district (see the Hermannsburg Mission section). The main function of the building is to house the most comprehensive collection of Aboriginal spirit items in the country. These were entrusted to Strehlow for safekeeping by the local Aborigines years ago when they realised their traditional life was under threat. Because the items are so important, and cannot be viewed by an uninitiated male or *any* female, they are kept in a vault in the centre. There is, however, a very good whizz-bang computer-controlled display on the works of Strehlow, and on the Aranda people. The building itself is something of a feature too – it has the largest rammed-earth wall in the southern hemisphere. The centre is open daily from 10 am to 5 pm; entry is $4.

Old Graves

Near the aviation museum there's a cemetery with a number of interesting graves including those of Albert Namatjira, and Harold Lasseter who perished while searching for the fabled gold of 'Lasseter's Reef'. Alice Springs has some pioneer graves in the small Stuart Memorial Cemetery on George Crescent, just across the railway lines.

Panorama Guth

Panorama Guth, at 65 Hartley St in the town centre, is a huge circular panorama which you view from an elevated, central observation point. It depicts almost all of the points of interest around the centre with uncanny realism. Painted by a Dutch artist, Henk Guth, it measures about 20 metres in diameter and admission is $3 (children $1) – whether you think it's worth paying money to see a reproduction of what you may see

for real is a different question! It's open from Monday to Saturday from 9 am to 5 pm, Sunday from 2 to 5 pm.

Diorama

On the outskirts of town on Larapinta Drive, the diorama is open from 10 am to 5 pm daily. Admission to this rather hokey collection of 3-D illustrations of various Aboriginal legends is $3 (children $1). Children love it.

Olive Pink Flora Reserve

Just across the Todd River from the centre, off Tuncks Rd, the Olive Pink Flora Reserve has a collection of shrubs and trees typical of the 200 km area around Alice Springs. This arid zone botanic garden is open from 10 am to 6 pm. There are some short walks in the reserve including the climb to the top of the Saladeen Range from where there's a fine view over the town.

Pitchi Ritchi Sanctuary

Just south of the Heavitree Gap causeway is Pitchi Ritchi ('gap in the range'), a flower and bird sanctuary and miniature folk museum with a collection of sculptures by Victorian artist William Ricketts – you can see more of his interesting work in the William Ricketts Sanctuary in the Dandenongs near Melbourne. The pleasant sanctuary is open from 9 am to 5 pm Monday to Saturday, 10 am to 4 pm Sunday, and the admission cost is $3 (children $1).

Date Garden & Camel Farm

On the Old South Rd, just beyond the Heavitree Gap, is Australia's only date garden. It's open daily from 9 am to 5 pm but is closed in November, December and January. There are tours on the hour.

The camel farm, on Emily Gap Rd, is open from 9 am to 5 pm daily, and here you have the chance to ride a camel. These strange 'ships of the desert', guided by their Afghani masters, were the main form of transport before the railways were built. There's a museum with displays about camels and early radio communications in the outback – admission is $6.50 (children $3.50). Graeme

Gow's Reptile World is here and the Weethalle Angora Goat Farm is adjacent.

Stuart Auto Museum
Just south of Heavitree Gap, the motor museum has a number of old cars and some interesting exhibits on pioneer motoring in the Territory. They include the tale of the first car to cross the Northern Territory, way back in 1907. The museum is open from 9 am to 5 pm daily and admission is $3.50 (children $2).

The Old Ghan
At the MacDonnell Siding, off the Stuart Highway 10 km south of Alice Springs, a group of local railway enthusiasts have restored a collection of Ghan locomotives and carriages on a stretch of disused siding from the old narrow-gauge Ghan railway track. You can wander round the equipment, watch the restoration work and learn more about this extraordinary railway line at the information centre. It's open from 9 am to 5 pm daily and admission is $3.

There are also trips on the old Ghan four days a week out to Ewaninga Siding, 23 km south of town. The trip takes 1½ hours and costs $12, and includes morning tea or a coldie in the bar car. MacDonnell Siding is on the Alice Wanderer bus route.

Chateau Hornsby
Alice Springs actually has a winery. It's 15 km out of town, five km off the road, before you get to the airport turn-off. The wine they produce here (moselle, riesling-semillon and shiraz) is not bad at all, although most of it gets sold to people intrigued at the novelty of a central Australian wine.

The pleasant restaurant here is open for lunch-time barbecues, and is a popular excursion from town. You can pedal out to Chateau Hornsby by bicycle – after tasting a little free wine the distance back seems much shorter. The easier option is to take the Alice Wanderer.

Organised Tours
The NTGTB can tell you about all sorts of organised tours from Alice Springs. There are the usual big-name operators and a host of small local operators. There are bus tours, 4WD tours, even balloon tours.

Note that although many of the tours don't operate daily, there is at least one trip a day to one or more of the major attractions – Ayers Rock and the Olgas, Kings Canyon, Palm Valley, both western and eastern Mac-Donnell Ranges, Simpson's Gap, Standley Chasm. Tours to less popular places – such as Rainbow Valley and Chambers Pillar – operate less often.

Most of the tours follow similar routes and you see much the same on them all, although the level of service and the degree of luxury will determine how much they cost. All the hostels can book tours, and they will also know exactly which company is offering the best deals. As long as the recession lasts and tourism numbers are down, it's likely that special discounts of up to 35% will continue to be offered.

Sahara Tours (☎ (089) 53 0881) offers very good daily camping trips to the Rock and elsewhere and these are popular with backpackers. They charge $165 for a two-day trip to the Rock and Olgas, or you can pay an extra $50 and spend an extra day taking in Kings Canyon – well worthwhile if you have the time. AKT and Landmark are other cheaper operators.

Rod Steinert (☎ (089) 55 5000) operates a variety of tours including his popular $56 Dreamtime & Bushtucker Tour. It's a half-day trip in which you meet some Aborigines and learn a little about their traditional life. There are demonstrations of weapons and foods and samples of barbecued witchetty grubs. AAT-Kings offer a similar trip.

Other tours include town tours, trips to the nearby gaps or longer day trips to Palm Valley, Chambers Pillar and other gorges. They start from $25 for the shorter half-day tours, and go up to $45 to $70 for longer day trips. Palm Valley is a popular day trip since it requires a 4WD, and these cost around $65.

Camel treks are another central Australian attraction. You can have a short ride for a few dollars at the camel farm or at Ross River, or take longer overnight, or two to seven-day camel treks costing from $125 to $700. Noel Fullerton's Camel Outback Safaris (☎ (089) 56 0925) is one operator.

You can see the Red Centre from the air as well – it's possible to go along on an outback mail run, dropping in on a string of outback stations to collect and deliver the mails. The trips with Chartair make seven to 14 calls and cost $205 (☎ (089) 52 3977). Sunrise balloon trips are also popular, and these cost from $88 which includes breakfast and 30-minute flight. Outback Ballooning (☎ (089) 52 8723) and Aussie Balloons (☎ (089) 53 0544) are two operators.

If your time is really limited, and your cash isn't, there are day trips to Ayers Rock which involve flying between Alice and the Rock; cost is typically $270.

Places to Stay

Hostels & Guesthouses There are plenty of hostels and guesthouses in Alice Springs. All the places catering to backpackers have the usual facilities and services – pool, courtesy bus, tour booking, bicycle hire, etc.

Right in the centre of town, on the corner of Leichhardt Terrace and Parsons St in the old Pioneer walk-in cinema, is the new YHA *Pioneer Hostel* (☎ (089) 52 8855). It has 64 beds in air-con dorms, and charges $12 ($1 more to exonerate you from the chores), but it only takes YHA members. It's open all day.

There's also the old YHA *Alice Springs Hostel* (☎ (089) 52 5016) on the corner of Todd St and Stott Terrace. It is cheaper at $9, and is pretty quiet these days. It's a friendly and well-run place, and a good source of information on local activities.

Also central is the *Melanka Lodge* (☎ (089) 52 2233) at 94 Todd St. This is a larger place with a variety of rooms, ranging from eight-bed dorms at $9 through to singles/doubles with bathroom for $52/59. The lodge has air-con, a swimming pool, a cafeteria and restaurant, and all modern facilities. It's a popular place, if soulless.

Over the river and still just a short walk from the centre, is the relaxed *Alice Lodge*

(☎ (089) 53 1975) at 4 Mueller St. This is a small, quiet and friendly hostel, with garden and pool. Nightly rates are $8 in the dorm, $20 for a single or $10 per person in a double, and $22 for an on-site van (prices include sheets, quilt hire is $1). There's a small kitchen, and barbecue and laundry facilities.

Back on the other side of the river, at 41 Gap Rd, is *Toddy's Backpackers* (☎ (089) 52 1322). This complex has laundry facilities and a communal kitchen for those not in the self-contained units. There's a swimming pool, barbecue and small shop on the site. Prices are $10 for dorms with shared facilities; $12 with TV and bathroom; $26 for doubles; $32 with bathroom.

Further along Gap Rd is the *Gapview Resort Hotel* (☎ 008 896 124). It's about one km from the centre, and charges $12 (less at quiet times). Accommodation is in six-bed units, each with bathroom, fridge and TV. Unfortunately the kitchen is poorly equipped and the restaurant charges around $10 for a meal, but most people who stay here seem to enjoy it.

The *Anglican Hostel* (☎ (089) 52 3108), also known as the Lodge, is on Bath St near Wills Terrace. It's good value with 'backpacker' beds for $9 and up, and singles/doubles for $23/33. There are also self-contained flats, a communal kitchen and a pool. The place is spotless but slightly institutional.

Hotels, Motels & Holiday Flats Right by the river at 1 Todd Mall is the *Old Alice Inn* (☎ (089) 52 1255). This pub gets noisy when there are bands playing on weekends, but is otherwise quite a reasonable place to stay. Room rates are $35 for singles/doubles, some with bath.

At 67 Gap Rd there's the *Swagman's Rest Motel* (☎ (089) 53 1333) with singles/doubles for $55/64, or from $72 for a family of four. The units are self-contained and there's a swimming pool.

The *Alice Tourist Apartments* (☎ (089) 52 2788) are on Gap Rd too and have rooms at $57/67 for singles/doubles or larger family rooms (up to six people) at $98.

Top: Aboriginal painting, Nourlangie Rock, Kakadu National Park, NT (DC)
Bottom: Supermarket mural, Alice Springs, NT (TW)

Top: Devils Marbles, Stuart Highway, NT (CLA)
Bottom: MacDonnell Ranges, Glen Helen Gorge, NT (RI'A)

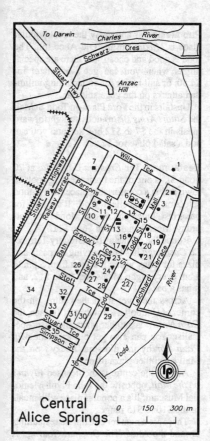

Central Alice Springs

0   150   300 m

■ **PLACES TO STAY**

2   Old Alice Inn
7   Anglican Hostel (The Lodge)
19 YHA Pioneer Hostel
25 Diplomat Motel
29 YHA Alice Springs Youth Hostel
30 Melanka Lodge
31 YWCA Stuart Lodge
33 Salvation Army Red Sheild Hostel

▼ **PLACES TO EAT**

8   Dog Rock Diner
11 Chopsticks Chinese Restaurant
17 Joanne's Cafe, Sweeties, Red Rock Cafe
20 Flynns on the Mall
21 Jolly Swagman
23 La Casalinga Italian Restaurant
24 Eranova Cafeteria
26 Overlander Steakhouse
32 Oriental Gourmet Chinese Restaurant

OTHER

1   Signpost
3   Springs Plaza
4   Ford Plaza
5   NT Government Tourist Bureau
6   Bus Terminus
9   Stuart Town Goal
10 Yeperenye Shopping Centre
12 Old Courthouse
13 GPO
14 The Residency
15 Ansett
16 John Flynn Memorial Museum
18 Australian Airlines
22 Library & Civic Centre
24 Arunta Art Gallery
27 Panorama Guth
28 Centre for Aboriginal Artists & Craftsmen
34 Billy Goat Hill
35 Royal Flying Doctor Base
36 NT Conservation Commission

There are plenty of motels, many of them fairly pricey, but there are often lower prices and special deals during the hot summer months.

On Barrett Drive, next to the Sheraton, the *Desert Palms Resort* (☎ (089) 52 5977) has spacious rooms, each with a small kitchen, at $62/72 for singles/doubles or $77 for four. There's a swimming pool. If you've got a car this is one of the best value motels in the Alice.

Some of the better priced places, virtually all of them with swimming pools, include:

Alice Sundown Motel (☎ (089) 52 8422), 39 Gap Rd – self-contained rooms at $57/72 for singles/doubles

Desert Rose Inn (☎ (089) 52 1411), 15 Railway Terrace – budget rooms at $47/62, or larger rooms at $76/86

Larapinta Lodge (☎ (089) 52 7255), 3 Larapinta Drive – singles/doubles/triples for $52/62/67

Camping Alice Springs's camp sites and their high season (winter) rates are:

G'Day Mate Tourist Park (☎ (089) 52 9589), Palm Circuit, near the date garden and Stuart Auto Museum – camping and cabins ($37)

Greenleaves Tourist Park (☎ (089) 52 8645), two km east on Burke St – camping and on-site vans ($32)

Heavitree Gap Caravan Park (☎ (089) 52 2370), Ross Highway, four km south of town – camping and on-site vans (from $30)

MacDonnell Range Tourist Park (☎ (089) 52 6111), Palm Place, five km from town – camping and on-site cabins ($45)

Stuart Caravan Park (☎ (089) 52 2547), two km west on Larapinta Drive – camping and on-site vans ($29)

Wintersun Caravan Park (☎ (089) 52 4080), two km north on the Stuart Highway – camping and on-site vans ($28).

Places to Eat

Snacks & Fast Food There are numerous places for a sandwich or light snack along Todd St Mall. Many of them put tables and chairs outside – ideal for a breakfast in the cool morning air.

The *Jolly Swagman* in Todd Plaza off the mall is a pleasant place for sandwiches and light snacks. Off the mall on the other side *Joanne's Cafe* offers similar fare. The *Red Rock Cafe* and *Sweeties* are side by side on the mall and open for breakfast, burgers, sandwiches, etc.

The big Ford Plaza has a lunch-time cafeteria-style eating place called *Fawlty's* with snacks, light meals, sandwiches and a salad bar. Across the mall, the Springs Plaza has *Golly It's Good*, with more sandwiches and snacks.

In the Yeperenye shopping centre on Hartley St there's the *Boomerang Coffee Shop*, the *Bakery* and a big Woolworths supermarket.

On Lindsay St, near the corner of Undoolya Rd, across the river, the *Fish Shop* is a good and reasonably cheap fish & chip shop.

Pub Meals Far and away the most popular place is *Maxim's* in the Old Alice Inn. The food is good and cheap, and there are special nights when you can get a schnitzel for $4.50, or spit roasts for $6 including unlimited attacks on the vegetable bar.

Upstairs in the Ford Plaza on Todd St Mall the *Stuart Arms Bistro* does straightforward meals in the $7 to $12 bracket, and you can add a salad plate for $2.

Restaurants The *Eranova Cafeteria*, at 70 Todd St, is one of the busiest eating spots in town and is a comfortable place with a good selection of excellent food. It's open for breakfast, lunch and dinner Monday to Saturday. Meals range from $6 to $11.

Round the corner at 105 Gregory Terrace, *La Casalinga* has been serving up pasta and pizza for many years; it's open from 5 pm to 1 am every night. Meals cost $8 to $12, and it has a bar.

Across the river from the centre, on the corner of Undoolya Rd and Sturt Terrace, the *Casa Nostra* is another pizza and pasta specialist. You can also get pizzas at the *Mia Pizza Bar* by the diorama. *Rocky's* on the Mall is another pizza place.

Also in the centre is the licensed *Flynn's on the Mall*, opposite the John Flynn Memorial Museum. It's a popular place with meals in the $10 to $15 range.

There are a number of Chinese restaurants around the Alice. The *Oriental Gourmet* is on Hartley St, near the corner of Stott Terrace. *Chopsticks*, on Hartley St at the Yeperenye shopping centre, is said to be good, and so is the bright yellow *Golden Inn* on Undoolya Rd, just over the bridge from the centre. Aside from the usual items you can sample some Malaysian and Sichuan dishes.

Of course the Alice has to have a steakhouse, so you can try the *Overlander Steakhouse* at 72 Hartley St. It features 'Territory food' such as beef and buffalo, and its Station Owner's Pie is a carnivore's delight – beef, buffalo, camel and kangaroo all in one! Quite a few of the restaurants in town have kangaroo and buffalo on the menu.

On Railway Terrace, opposite Coles, the *Dog Rock Diner* is an American-style place with main courses in the $10 range.

Out-of-town dining possibilities include the daily barbecue lunches at the *Chateau Hornsby* winery, or a late breakfast, lunch or tea at the *White Gums Park* opposite the Simpson's Gap National Park turn-off.

Another interesting possibility is an evening meal combined with a ride on the Old Ghan train at MacDonnell Siding (☎ (089) 55 5047). It operates weekly from April to October, and costs $39.

Entertainment

The Stuart Arms Bistro in Ford Plaza has music Wednesday, Thursday and Friday nights. At the Old Alice Inn, by the river on the corner of Wills and Leichhardt terraces, the Piano Bar has entertainment most nights, and sometimes features better known bands.

Bojangles is a restaurant and nightclub on Todd St, and the Alice Junction Tavern off Ross Highway has a disco on Friday and Saturday nights. The Overlander Steakhouse is the home of a good local bush band – Bloodwood.

If you want to watch the Australian gambling enthusiasm in a central Australian setting head for Lasseter's Casino, but dress up. Outback 'character' Ted Egan puts on a performance of tall tales and outback songs three nights a week at Chateau Hornsby ($15, or $33 with dinner). He also does occasional performances at his own place, Sinkatinny Downs.

There are all sorts of events at the glossy Araluen Art Centre on Larapinta Drive, including temporary art exhibits, theatre and music performances and regular films. The folk club meets here on Sunday nights. Bookings can be made at the Araluen booking office or through the NTGTB at Ford Plaza.

Things to Buy

Alice Springs has a number of art galleries and craft centres. If you've got an interest in central Australian art or you're looking for a piece to buy, then visit the Centre for Aboriginal Artists at 86-88 Todd St. It has a fine display of bark paintings, Papunya sand paintings, carvings, weapons, didgeridoos and much more, plus excellent descriptions of the development and meaning of the work. It's non-profit-making and designed both to preserve the crafts and to provide an outlet for quality work. The prices aren't necessarily low, but the artefacts are generally good.

The Papunya-Tula Artists Centre is a few doors up on Todd St and has a wide selection of Papunya sand paintings. The Central Australian Aboriginal Media Association shop on Hartley St by the Yeperenye shopping centre is another very good place, and prices are reasonable.

There are plenty of other, generally more commercial outlets for Aboriginal art including a good one in the Ford Plaza.

Getting There & Away

Air You can fly to Alice Springs with Australian Airlines or Ansett. Ansett (☎ (089) 50 4100) and Australian Airlines (☎ (089) 50 5222) face each other across Todd St at the Parson St intersection.

The discounting fever which saw the fares between the southern capitals tumble missed the Alice, but things may have changed by the time you read this. See the chart in the introductory Getting Around section to this chapter for details of airfares to other towns within the Northern Territory.

Alice Springs to Adelaide costs $331 ($265 standby), Darwin $329 ($263), Melbourne $411 ($329), Mt Isa $218 ($175), Perth $503 ($402) and Sydney $432 ($345). You can also fly direct to Ayers Rock from Adelaide, Sydney, Perth and Cairns. So if you're planning to fly to the Centre and visit Ayers Rock it would be more economical to fly straight to Ayers Rock, then continue to Alice Springs. See Getting There & Away under the Ayers Rock & the Olgas section for more details.

Bus Greyhound/Pioneer (☎ (089) 52 7888) and Bus Australia (☎ (089) 53 1022) have daily return services from Alice Springs to Ayers Rock, Darwin and Adelaide. It takes about 20 hours from Alice Springs to Darwin (1481 km) or Alice Springs to Adelaide (1543 km). You can connect to other places at various points up and down the Track – Three Ways for Mt Isa and the Queensland coast, Katherine for Western Australia, Erldunda for Ayers Rock, Port Augusta for Perth. Alice Springs to Darwin, Port Augusta or Adelaide is about $150; to Ayers Rock $60, Coober Pedy $75, Katherine $130.

In Alice Springs the buses all operate from the bus station at the Hartley St end of Ford Plaza.

Train The Ghan between Adelaide and Alice Springs costs $125 in coach class (no sleeper and no meals) or $395 in 1st, which includes meals and a sleeper. It departs from Adelaide on Monday and Thursday at 2 pm, arriving in Alice Springs the next morning at 11 am. From Alice Springs the departure is on Tuesday and Friday at 5.10 pm arriving in Adelaide the next afternoon at 4 pm.

You can also join it at Port Augusta, the connecting point on the Sydney to Perth route. Fares between Alice Springs and Port Augusta are $125 coach, and $296 1st-class sleeper.

You can transport cars between Alice Springs and Adelaide for $190, or between Alice Springs and Port Augusta for $180. Double check the times by which you need to have your car at the terminal for loading: they must be there several hours prior to departure for the train to be 'made up'. Unloading at the Adelaide end is slow so be prepared for a long wait.

The Ghan Australia's great railway adventure would have to be the Ghan. The Ghan went through a major change in 1980 and although it's now a rather more modern and comfortable (dare I say 'safe'?) adventure, it's still a great trip.

The Ghan saga started in 1877 when it was decided to build a railway line from Adelaide to Darwin. It eventually took over 50 years to reach Alice Springs, and they're still thinking about the final 1500 km to Darwin more than a century later. The basic problem was that they made a big mistake right at the start, a mistake that wasn't finally sorted out until 1980. They built the line in the wrong place.

The grand error was a result of concluding that,

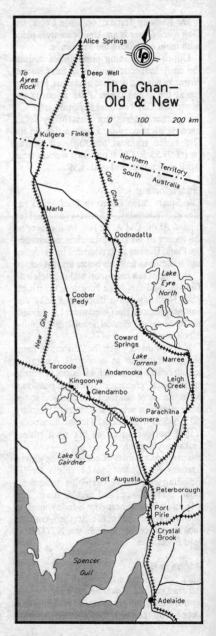

The Ghan—
Old & New

0   100   200 km

because all the creek beds north of Marree were bone dry, and because nobody had seen rain, there wasn't going to be rain in the future. In fact they laid the initial stretch of line right across a flood plain and when the rain came, even though it soon dried up, the line was simply washed away. In the century or so that the original Ghan line survived, it was a regular occurrence for the tracks to be washed away.

The wrong route was only part of the Ghan's problems. At first it was built wide gauge to Marree, then extended narrow gauge to Oodnadatta in 1884. And what a jerry-built line it was – the foundations were flimsy, the sleepers were too light, the grading was too steep and it meandered hopelessly. It was hardly surprising that right up to the end the top speed of the old Ghan was a flat-out 30 km/h!

Early rail travellers went from Adelaide to Marree on the broad-gauge line, changed there to narrow gauge as far as Oodnadatta, then had to make the final journey to Alice Springs by camel train. The Afghani-led camel trains had pioneered transport through the outback and it was from these Afghanis that the Ghan took its name.

Finally in 1929 the line was extended from Oodnadatta to Alice Springs. Though the Ghan was a great adventure, it simply didn't work. At the best of times it was chronically slow and uncomfortable as it bounced and bucked its way down the badly laid line. Worse, it was unreliable and expensive to run. And worst of all, a heavy rainfall could strand it at either end or even in the middle. Parachute drops of supplies to stranded train travellers became part of outback lore and on one occasion the Ghan rolled in 10 days late!

By the early '70s the South Australian state railway system was taken over by the Federal Government and a new line to Alice Springs was planned. The A$145 million line was to be standard gauge, laid from Tarcoola, north-west of Port Augusta on the transcontinental line, to Alice Springs – and it would be laid where rain would not wash it out. In 1980 the line was completed in circumstances that would be unusual for any major project today, let alone an Australian one – it was ahead of time and on budget.

In the late '80s the old Ghan made its last run and the old line was subsequently torn up. One of its last appearances was in the film *Mad Max III*.

Whereas the old train took 140 passengers and, under ideal conditions, made the trip in 50 hours, the new train takes twice as many passengers and does it in 24 hours. It's still the Ghan, but it's not the trip it once was.

At present the extension of the line further north from Alice Springs to Darwin is still under consideration. There's no way the line would make economic sense, but its value as a connection between the Top End and the rest of the country plus the smooth construction of the new Ghan line has kept the plan alive.

Car The basic thing to remember about getting to Alice Springs is that it's a very long way from anywhere, although at least roads to the north and south are both sealed. Coming in from Queensland it's 1180 km from Mt Isa to Alice Springs or 529 km from Three Ways, where the Mt Isa road meets the Darwin to Alice Springs road. Darwin to Alice Springs is 1481 km.

These are outback roads, but you're not in the *real* outer-outback where a breakdown can mean big trouble. Nevertheless, it's wise to have your vehicle well prepared since getting someone to come out to fix it if it breaks down is likely to be very expensive.

Similarly, you are unlikely to die of thirst waiting for a vehicle to come by if you do break down, but it's still wise to carry quite a bit of water. Roads can sometimes be made impassable by a short, sharp rainfall and you'll have to sit and wait for the water to recede. It usually won't take long on a sealed road, but you could sit and wait for a dirt road to dry out and become passable for rather a long time.

Petrol is readily available from stops along the road, but prices tend to be high. Some fuel stops are notorious for charging well over the odds, so carrying an extra can of fuel can save a few dollars by allowing you to go elsewhere.

Hitching Hitching to Alice is not the easiest trip in Australia, since traffic is light. For those going south, Three Ways is a notorious bottleneck where hitchers can spend a long time. The notice boards in the various Alice Springs hostels are good places to look for lifts.

Getting Around
Although there is a limited public bus system, Alice Springs is compact enough to get around on foot, and you can reach quite a few of the closer attractions by bicycle. If you want to go further afield you'll have to take a tour or rent a car.

To/From the Airport The brand new Alice

Springs airport is 14 km south of the town, about $20 by taxi.

There is an airport shuttle bus service (☎ 53 0310) which meets flights and takes passengers to all city accommodation and to the railway station. It costs $7.

Bus Asbus buses leave from outside the Yeperenye shopping centre on Hartley St. The south route runs along Gap Rd to the southern outskirts of town – useful for hitching.

The Alice Wanderer bus does a loop around the major sights – Chateau Hornsby, Camel Farm & Date Gardens, the Old Ghan, School of the Air and the Telegraph Station. You can get on and off wherever you like, and it runs hourly from around 9 am to 4 pm. The cost is $15 for a full day, $10 for half a day. The most convenient pick-up points are the Melanka Lodge and the bus terminus.

Car Avis, Budget, Hertz and Thrifty all have counters at Alice Springs Airport. Alice Springs is classified as a remote area so car hire can be expensive, particularly if you want to drive down to Ayers Rock or further afield.

Mokes are still popular in Alice Springs, but are usually restricted to a 50-km radius of the town and cannot be taken on dirt roads. Centre Car Rentals (☎ (089) 52 1405) in the Ford Plaza has Mokes for $18 a day, plus $10 insurance and 20c a km; other cars can be taken further afield. Cheapa Rent-a-Car (☎ (089) 52 9999), on the corner of Hartley St and Stott Terrace, is another place with Mokes, mopeds and cars.

Moped & Bicycle Alice Springs has a number of bicycle tracks and a bike is a great way of getting around town and out to the closer attractions, particularly in winter. The best place to rent a bike is from the hostel you're staying at. Typical rates are $10 per day.

Moke Rentals rent mopeds for $25 a day plus $5 insurance.

Around Alice Springs

Outside the town there are a great number of places within day-trip distance or with overnight stops thrown in. Generally they're found by heading east or west along the roads running parallel to the MacDonnell Ranges, which are directly south of Alice Springs. Places further south are usually visited on the way to Ayers Rock.

The scenery along the ranges is superb. There are many gorges that cut through the rocky cliffs and their sheer rock walls are spectacular. In the shaded gorges there are rocky water holes, a great deal of wildlife which can be seen if you're quiet and observant, and wild flowers in the spring.

You can get out to these gorges on group tours or with your own wheels. Some of the closer ones are accessible by bicycle or on foot. By yourself the Centre's eerie emptiness and peace can get through to you in a way that is impossible in a big group.

EASTERN MACDONNELL RANGES
Heading south from Alice Springs and just through the Heavitree Gap, a sign points to the road east by the Heavitree Gap camp site. The Ross Highway is sealed all the way to Trephina Gorge, about 75 km from Alice Springs. It's in pretty good condition most of the way to Arltunga, about 100 km from Alice Springs. From here the road bends back west and rejoins the Stuart Highway 50 km north of Alice Springs, but this section is a much rougher road and sometimes requires a 4WD.

Emily & Jessie Gaps
Emily Gap, 16 km out of town, is the next gap through the ranges east of the Heavitree Gap – it's narrow and often has water running through it.

Jessie Gap is only eight km further on and, like the previous gap, is a popular picnic and barbecue spot.

Corroboree Rock

Shortly after Jessie Gap there's the Undoolya Gap, another pass through the range, and the road continues 43 km to Corroboree Rock. There are many strangely shaped outcrops of rocks in the range and this one is said to have been used by Aborigines for their corroborees.

Trephina Gorge

About 75 km out, and a few km north of the road, is Trephina Gorge. It's wider and longer than the other gaps in the range – here you are well north of the main MacDonnell Ranges and in a new ridge. There's a good walk along the edge of the gorge, somewhat similar to the Kings Canyon walk (see South to Ayers Rock section). The trail then drops down to the sandy creek bed and loops back to the starting point. Keen walkers can follow a longer trail, which continues to the John Hayes Rockholes.

John Hayes Rockholes

A few km west of the gorge, reached by a track which can sometimes be unsuitable for conventional vehicles, are the delightful John Hayes Rockholes. A sheltered section of a deep gorge provides a series of water holes which retain water long after it has dried up in more exposed places. You can clamber around the rockholes or follow the path to one side up to a lookout above the gorge – perhaps you'll see why it is also called the Valley of the Eagles.

Ross River

Beyond Trephina Gorge it's another 10 km to the *Ross River Homestead* (☎ (089) 56 9711). It's much favoured by coach tours, but is an equally good place for independent visitors. Units cost $90/100, there are four-bed dorms for $12 per person or you can camp for $15 for two. There's a restaurant with good food and a very popular bar. It's a friendly sort of place, but the organisation is like an outback version of *Fawlty Towers*, so don't be surprised if bookings are forgotten or things don't work as planned!

There's lots to do including walks in the spectacular surrounding countryside, excursions to other attractions, short camel rides or safaris and horseback riding. Or simply lazing around with a cold one.

N'Dhala Gorge

The N'Dhala Gorge is about 10 km south of Ross River Homestead and has a number of ancient Aboriginal rock carvings. You may see rock wallabies. It's possible to turn off before the gorge and loop around it to return to Alice Springs by the Ringwood Homestead road, but this requires a 4WD.

Arltunga

At the eastern end of the MacDonnell Ranges, 92 km north-east of Alice Springs, Arltunga is an old gold-mining ghost town. Gold was discovered here in 1887 and 10 years later reef gold was discovered, but by 1912 the mining activity had petered out. Old buildings, a couple of cemeteries and the many deserted mine sites are all that remain. Alluvial (surface) gold has been completely worked out in the Arltunga Reserve, but there may still be gold further afield in the area. There are plenty of signs to explain things and some old mine shafts you can safely descend and explore a little way.

There's a small camp site and shop at Arltunga if you want to spend longer here. Most of the way to Arltunga is a graded track (a maintained dirt track), and rain can make the road impassable. You can loop right round and join the Stuart Highway 50 km north of Alice Springs, but this route is a graded track all the way and can be rough going. With side trips off the road a complete loop from Alice Springs to Arltunga and back would be something over 300 km – a fair drive on outback roads.

WESTERN MACDONNELL RANGES

Heading west from the Alice, Larapinta Drive divides just beyond Standley Chasm. Namatjira Drive continues slightly north of west and is sealed all the way to Glen Helen, 132 km from town. Beyond there the road continues to Haasts Bluff and Papunya, in Aboriginal land. From the fork near Standley

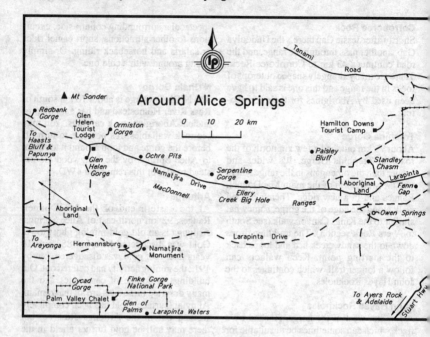

Around Alice Springs

Chasm, Larapinta Drive continues slightly south of west to Hermannsburg and beyond.

There are many spectacular gorges out in this direction and also some fine walks. A visit to Palm Valley, one of the prime attractions to the west of Alice Springs, requires a 4WD. See the Alice Springs Getting Around section for tour details.

The whole of the Western MacDonnells will be encompassed within the new Western MacDonnell Ranges National Park which is currently still in the planning stages. It is proposed that the park will cover an area between 1700 and 3000 sq km when it is established some time in the near future.

Simpson's Gap

Westbound from Alice Springs on Larapinta Drive you start on the northern side of the MacDonnell Ranges. You soon come to **Flynn's Grave**; the flying doctor's final resting place is topped by one of the Devil's

Marbles, brought down the Track from near Tennant Creek.

A little further on is the picturesque Simpson's Gap, 22 km out. Like the other gaps it is a thought-provoking example of nature's power and patience – for a river to cut a path through solid rock is amazing, but for a river that rarely ever runs to cut such a path is positively mind-boggling. There are often rock wallabies in the jumble of rocks on either side of the gap.

Larapinta Trail

The Larapinta Trail is a new and extended walking track which, when finally completed in the next few years, will offer walkers a 220-km trail along the backbone of the Western MacDonnell ranges, stretching from the Telegraph Station in Alice Springs to Mt Razorback, beyond Glen Helen. It will then be possible to choose anything from a two-day to a two-week trek, taking in a selection of the attractions in the

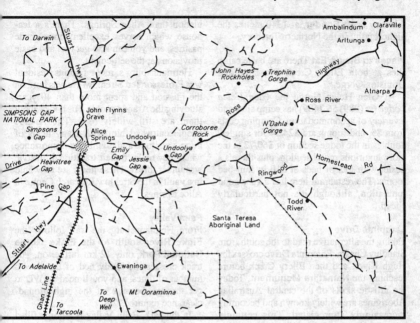

Western MacDonnells. At the time of writing the route was complete as far as Jay Creek, 24 km west of Simpsons Gap.

Contact the Northern Territory Conservation Commission (☎ (089) 50 8211) for further details.

Standley Chasm

Standley Chasm is 51 km out and is probably the most spectacular gap around Alice Springs. It is incredibly narrow – the near-vertical walls almost meet above you. Only for an instant each day does the noon sun illuminate the bottom of the gorge – at which moment the automatics click and a smile must appear on Mr Kodak's face!

Namatjira Drive

Not far beyond Standley Chasm you must choose whether to take the northerly Namatjira Drive or carry on along the more southerly Larapinta Drive. Further west along Namatjira Drive another series of gorges and gaps in the range awaits you. **Ellery Creek Big Hole** is 93 km from Alice Springs and has a large permanent water hole – just the place for a cooling dip, and there's a basic camp site close by. It's only 13 km further to **Serpentine Gorge**, a narrow gorge with a pleasant water hole at the entrance.

The large and rugged **Ormiston Gorge** also has a water hole and it leads to the enclosed valley of the Pound National Park. When the water holes of the Pound dry up, the fish that live there burrow into the sand, going into a sort of suspended animation, and reappear after rain. Ormiston has a camping area.

Only a couple of km further is the turn-off to the scenic **Glen Helen Gorge**, where the Finke River cuts through the MacDonnells The road is worse beyond this point, but if you continue west you'll reach the red-walled **Redbank Gorge** with its permanent water, 161 km from Alice Springs. Also out this way is **Mt Sonder,** at 1340 metres the highest point in the Northern Territory.

Places to Stay & Eat There are basic camp sites at both Ellery Creek Big Hole and Ormiston Gorge.

At Glen Helen Gorge the *Glen Helen Lodge* (☎ (089) 56 7489) has camp sites and a variety of accommodation. Camping costs from $5, and rooms are $24/34 for singles/doubles in the lodge section or $60/72 in the more luxurious motel section, plus there's a hostel with lots of beds at $10 in four-bed rooms. The restaurant here has a very good reputation, although it's not particularly cheap.

Larapinta Drive

Taking the alternative road to the south from Standley Chasm, Larapinta Drive crosses the Hugh River, and then Ellery Creek before reaching the **Namatjira Monument.** Today the artistic skills of the central Australian Aborigines are widely known and becoming increasingly appreciated. This certainly wasn't the case when the artist Albert Namatjira started to paint his central Australian landscapes in 1936. He used European techniques and equipment, but had an Aboriginal eye for the colours and scenery of the Red Centre. His paintings spawned a host of imitators. Namatjira supported many of his people on the income from his work. Because of his fame, he was allowed to buy alcohol at a time when this was otherwise illegal for Aborigines. In 1958, he was jailed for six months for supplying alcohol to Aborigines, and he died the following year, aged only 57.

Hermannsburg Mission

Only eight km beyond the Namatjira monument you reach the Hermannsburg Mission, 125 km from Alice Springs. This mission was established by German Lutheran missionaries in the middle of the last century. These days it's an Aboriginal settlement. Many of the buildings are still intact, and it's well worth a stroll through. Not long after it was set up, Hermannsburg had a bigger population than Alice Springs. There's a teahouse which serves excellent home-made pastries, and you can also get fuel and basic provisions at the settlement.

Hermannsburg's most famous resident was Professor Ted Strehlow. He was born on the mission and spent more than 40 years studying the Aranda people. His books about them are still widely read. The Aranda people entrusted him with many items of huge spiritual and symbolic importance when they realised their traditional lifestyle was under threat. These items are now held in a vault in the Strehlow Research Centre in Alice Springs.

Palm Valley

From Hermannsburg the trail follows the Finke River south to the **Finke Gorge National Park,** only 12 km further on. The track crosses the sandy bed of the river a number of times, and you'll need a 4WD to get through because of the high ground-clearance required.

In the park, Palm Valley is a gorge filled with some geographically misplaced palm trees unique to this part of the globe – a strangely tropical find in the dry Red Centre, and a popular day-trip destination.

There's a beautiful shady camping area with some long-drop toilets, and there's a couple of signposted walks.

South to Ayers Rock

You can make some interesting diversions off the road south to Ayers Rock. The Henbury Meteorite Craters are only a few km off the road, but you've got further to go to get to Ewaninga, Chambers Pillar, Finke or Kings Canyon.

Ewaninga & Chambers Pillar

Following the 'old south road' which runs close to the old Ghan railway line, it's only 35 km from Alice Springs to Ewaninga, with its prehistoric Aboriginal rock carvings. The carvings found here and at N'Dhala Gorge

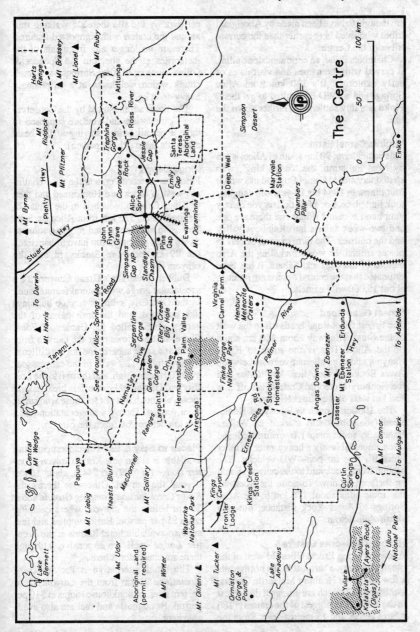

are thought to have been made by Aboriginal tribes who lived here earlier than the current tribes of the Centre.

Chambers Pillar, an eerie sandstone pillar, is carved with the names and visit dates of early explorers. It's 130 km from Alice Springs and a 4WD is required to get there. **Finke** is a tiny settlement, further down the line.

Virginia Camel Farm

This camel farm, 90 km south of Alice, is run by Noel Fullerton, the 'camel king', who started the annual Camel Cup and has won it four times. In 1984 his 12-year-old daughter took first place. For a few dollars you can try your hand at camel riding and there are one and two-week safaris into Rainbow Valley and the outback. The farm exports camels to places around the world including the Arab nations of the Gulf and Sahara. It has been estimated that the central deserts are home to about 15,000 wild camels.

Ernest Giles Road

The Ernest Giles Road heads off to the west of the Stuart Highway about 140 km south of the Alice. This is the route to Kings Canyon, and is an alternative route between Ayers Rock and the Alice. You'll also find the Henbury Meteorite Craters just off it, a few km west of the Stuart Highway.

The 100-km stretch to Stockyard Homestead (sometimes still marked as Wallara Ranch on some maps) is unsurfaced and often impassable after heavy rain; at other times it's fine for non-4WD vehicles. The section from Stockyard to the canyon should be surfaced by now. To go to the Rock via this route adds about 170 km to the Alice Springs to Ayers Rock distance, but is a worthwhile detour.

Henbury Meteorite Craters

A few km along Ernest Giles Rd west of the Stuart Highway, a turn-off to the north leads a few km to the Henbury Meteorite Craters, a cluster of 12 which are amongst the largest in the world. The biggest of the craters is 180 metres across and 15 metres deep. From the car park by the site there's a walking trail around the craters with signposted features. There are no longer any fragments of the meteorites at the site, but the Spencer & Gillen Museum in Alice Springs has a small chunk which weighs in at a surprisingly heavy 46½ kg.

The site is administered by the Conservation Commission and you are supposed to have a permit before staying at the basic camp site there ($1 per person).

Kings Canyon

From the meteorite craters the road continues west to Stockyard Homestead and then to Kings Canyon, which is in the Watarrka National Park, 323 km from Alice Springs. This is an alternative, and rougher, route to Ayers Rock although you have to backtrack the 89 km between Stockyard and the canyon.

Dubbed 'Australia's Grand Canyon' it's a spectacular gorge with natural features such as the Lost City, with its strange building-like outcrops, and the lush palms of the narrow gorge called the Garden of Eden. There are fine views over the canyon from its rim and some superb, and not too difficult, walking trails. The walls of the canyon soar over 200 metres high, and the trail to the Lost City and Garden of Eden offers breathtaking views, although it is not for those who suffer from vertigo. There's a ranger station just a few km before you reach the canyon.

Places to Stay & Eat The closest camping available is at the new *Kings Canyon Frontier Lodge* (☎ (089) 56 7442), about 10 km beyond the canyon. Otherwise there's the *Kings Creek Station Camping Ground* about 35 km before the canyon, where camping costs $5 per person. Basic supplies and fuel are also available here. Rooms at the *Frontier Lodge* itself are expensive, although there are cheap dorm beds.

The other alternative is the *Stockyard Homestead* 95 km from the canyon. There are tent sites, or bunkhouse rooms at $10 per person. Basic meals and fuel are also available here.

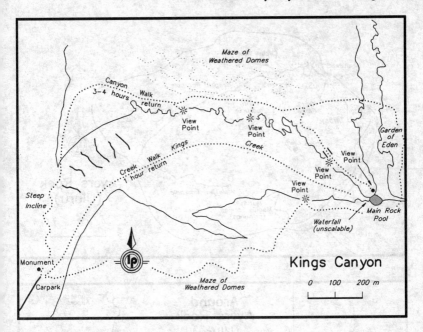

Kings Canyon

0   100   200 m

(Map labels: Maze of Weathered Domes; Canyon 3–4 hours Walk return; View Point; View Point; Garden of Eden; Kings Creek; Kings Creek Walk 1 hour return; View Point; View Point; View Point; Steep Incline; Main Rock Pool; Waterfall (unscalable); Monument; Carpark; Maze of Weathered Domes)

Ayers Rock & the Olgas

AYERS ROCK (ULURU)

The world-famous Ayers Rock, known to the Aborigines as Uluru, is 3.6 km long and rises a towering 348 metres from the pancake-flat surrounding scrub. It's believed that two-thirds of the Rock is beneath the sand. Everybody knows how its colour changes as the setting sun turns it a series of deeper and darker reds before it fades into grey. A performance in reverse, with fewer spectators, is performed at dawn each day.

The mighty Rock offers much more than a heavy-breathing scramble to the top and some pretty colours – it has a whole series of strange caves and eroded gullies. The entire area is of deep cultural significance to the Aborigines. To them it is known as Uluru – the name given to the Rock and the national park which surrounds it. The Aborigines now officially own the national park, although it is leased permanently to the Commonwealth Government. Disputes continue to rumble on over the effectiveness of this compromise.

It is not difficult at all to spend several days here. There are walking trails around the Rock and free, ranger-conducted walks delving into the plants, wildlife, geology and mythology of the area. It can take five hours to make the nine-km walk around the base of Ayers Rock looking at caves and paintings. **Maggie Springs**, at the base, is a permanent water hole, but after rain, water appears in holes all over and around the Rock and in countless waterfalls. Note that there are several Aboriginal sacred sites around the base of the Rock. They're clearly fenced off and signposted and to enter these areas is a grave offence, not just for non-Aborigines but for 'ineligible' Aborigines as well.

The entrance fee to the park is $10, and this is valid for a stay of three days. It is

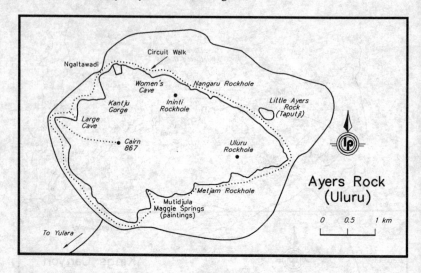

Ayers Rock (Uluru)

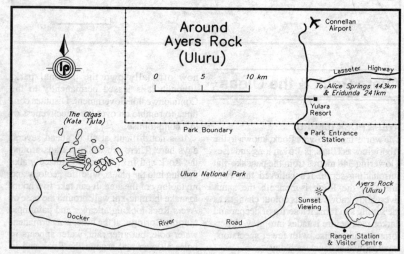

Around Ayers Rock (Uluru)

payable at the park entrance station, on the road between Yulara and the Rock.

Climbing the Rock

Those climbing either Ayers Rock or peaks in the Olgas should take care – numerous people have met their maker doing so, usually by having a heart attack, but some by taking a fatal tumble. It's equally easy to fall off the Olgas and there's the additional danger there of getting lost. Carry at least one litre of drinking water per person at all times, and one litre per person *per hour* of walking in summer. Such is the heat and its effect on people that the Rock is closed to climbing from 10 am to 4 pm on days when the temperature is forecast to reach 38°C or more. Too many people have ignored warnings and suffered the consequences.

The climb itself is 1.6 km and takes about two hours up and back with a good rest at the top. The first part of the walk is by far the steepest and most arduous, and there's a chain to hold on to. It's often very windy at the top, even when it isn't at the base, so make sure hats are well tied on.

It's worth noting that it goes against Aboriginal spiritual beliefs to climb the Rock, and they would prefer that people didn't. However, the traditional owners are pragmatic enough to realise that if climbing the Rock was prohibited, there would be far fewer visitors here.

THE OLGAS (KATA TJUTA)

The Olgas, a collection of smaller, more rounded rocks, stand 32 km to the west. Though less well known, the Olgas are equally impressive – indeed many people find them more captivating. They are known as Kata Tjuta to the Aborigines, meaning 'many heads', and are of Dreamtime significance.

Mt Olga, at 546 metres, is higher than Ayers Rock, and here too there are a couple of walking trails, the main one being to the **Valley of the Winds**, a six-km circuit track which takes from 2½ to four hours to cover. It's not particularly arduous but, as with the Rock climb, be prepared with water, and sun protection. There is also a short signposted track into the **Olga Gorge**.

There's a picnic and sunset-viewing area with toilet facilities just off the access road a few km west of the base of the Olgas.

A lonely sign at the western end of the Olgas access road points out that there is a hell of a lot of nothing if you travel west – although, suitably equipped, you can travel all the way to Kalgoorlie and on to Perth in Western Australia. It's 200 km to Docker River, an Aboriginal settlement on the road west, and about 1500 km all the way to Kalgoorlie. See the Warburton Road information in the Getting Around chapter. The *Perth to Alice Springs via Gunbarrel*

Highway or Warburton Road map, published by the RAC of Western Australia, is interesting and informative.

YULARA

Yulara, the service village for the national park, has effectively turned one of the world's least hospitable regions into an easy and comfortable place for outsiders to visit. Lying just outside the national park, 18 km from the Rock and 37 km from the Olgas, the $260 million complex, administered by the government Yulara Corporation, makes an excellent and surprisingly democratic base for exploring the area's renowned attractions. Opened in 1984, it supplies the only accommodation, food outlets and other services available in the region. The village incorporates the Ayers Rock Resort, and it combines futuristic flair with low, earth-toned foundations, fitting unobtrusively into the duned landscape.

By the 1970s it was clear that planning was required for the development of the area. Between 1931 and 1946 only 22 people were known to have climbed the Rock. In 1969 about 23,000 people visited Ayers Rock. Ten years later the figure was 65,000 and now the annual visitor figures are approaching 300,000!

It was intended when Yulara was built that the ugly cluster of motels, restaurants and other commercial enterprises at the eastern base of the Rock would all be demolished, leaving the prime attraction pleasingly alone in its age-old setting. It's never mentioned in any of the Yulara literature, but some of the original buildings are still there, because they were turned over to the local Aborigines. Nobody notices them because all access to the Rock is now from the west and the Aboriginal community is now off limits to the public.

Orientation & Information

In the spacious village area where everything is within 15 minutes' walk, there is a visitor centre, two international hotels, a medium-priced lodge, two camp sites, a bank, post office, petrol station, newsagency, numerous restaurants, a supermarket, craft gallery, a pub (of course), and even a police station (probably the only pink police station in the country!).

The Visitor Centre (open 8 am to 10 pm daily) contains good displays on the geography, flora & fauna and history of the region. The information available includes the *Yulara Ayers Rock Visitors' Guide* booklet.

Information is also available at the ranger station at the Rock, and there's a display of Aboriginal crafts outside in the Maruku Arts & Crafts complex where you can talk to the craftspeople.

The shopping square complex includes a supermarket, newsagency, post office and travel agency. You can get colour film processed at Territory Colour's same-day service. The only bank at Yulara is ANZ, but for $2 you can use the electronic funds transfer (EFTPOS) facility in the pub bottle shop to withdraw up to $200 with most credit cards.

There's a child-care centre in the village, and this operates from 7.30 am to 5.30 pm daily.

Walks & Talks

The rangers at Yulara give a series of walks and talks. There's a 'Living Desert' slide show and talk on the Centre's wildlife (2 pm Monday to Friday, free) while 'Feast or Famine' covers the foods of the desert (4 pm Monday to Friday, free).

The 'Edible Desert' walk ($10, children $5) shows you natural foods and medicines known to the Aborigines. The cost includes bus transport from Yulara, and the walk leaves at 8.30 am on Mondays, Wednesdays and Fridays. Bookings are necessary (☎ 56 2240).

A night walk to see the stars and constellations (Star Talk) leaves from the Visitor Centre every evening at 7, 8 or 9 pm, depending on the season ($10).

Walks at the Rock depart every morning from the ranger station or car park and are free.

There's a regular 15-minute slide show about the Uluru National Park in the visitors'

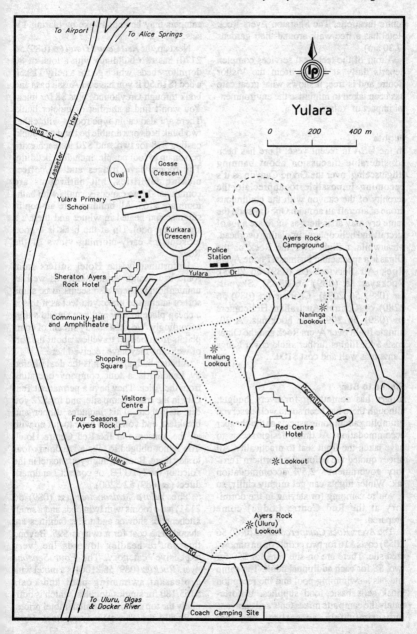

Yulara

0   200   400 m

To Airport   To Alice Springs

Giles St

Lasseter

Oval   Gosse
Crescent

Yulara Primary
School

Kurkara
Crescent

Police
Station

Sheraton Ayers
Rock Hotel

Yulara   Dr

Ayers Rock
Campground

Naninga
Lookout

Community Hall
and Amphitheatre

Imalung
Lookout

Shopping
Square

Visitors
Centre

Four Seasons
Ayers Rock

Parentie Rd

Red Centre
Hotel

Yulara   Dr

Lookout

Ayers Rock
(Uluru)
Lookout

Napala Rd

To Uluru, Olgas
& Docker River

Coach Camping Site

centre theatrette. The Sheraton Ayers Rock Hotel has a free walk around their gardens (7.30 am).

A tour of the technical services complex departs daily at 10 am from the Visitor Centre and is free; it shows what great care has been taken to minimise the environmental impact of Yulara.

Flights

In the USA in recent years there has been considerable discussion about banning 'flightseeing' over the Grand Canyon as it's becoming impossible to appreciate the serenity of the canyon with the continuous drone of aircraft all around. One day soon the same cry may arise here as there are a lot of aircraft and helicopters circulating overhead. Meanwhile a flight over the Rock or the Olgas is a spectacular business. Phone Ayers Rock Air Services (☎ (089) 56 2093), Rockayer (☎ (089) 56 2345), Skyport (☎ (089) 56 2093), Chartair (☎ (089) 56 2280) or Central Australian Helicopters (☎ (089) 56 2093) for bookings. A 30-minute flight over Ayers Rock and the Olgas costs $45; flights further afield cover Kings Canyon as well and cost $100.

Places to Stay

Yulara has something for every budget, although there has been some well-deserved grumbling about some aspects of the cheaper accommodation. At times design seems to have taken the front seat to practicality. All prices quoted are before the Northern Territory government's 2.5% accommodation tax. Winter nights can get mighty chilly, so if you're camping (or staying in the dormitory at the Red Centre Lodge) come prepared.

The *Ayers Rock Campground* (☎ (089) 56 2055) costs $16 for two people on an unpowered site. There are on-site vans for $59 for two, $8 for each additional adult. The camp site has a swimming pool and the reception kiosk sells basic food supplies. Unfortunately the camp site mixes tents and caravans indiscriminately, so early-to-bed tent campers may be kept awake by blaring TV sets.

Next up, the *Red Centre Hotel* (☎ (089) 56 2170) has two buildings with a total of 80 dormitory beds, which go for a hefty $19.50 a bed ($16.50 if you have an Aussiepass and book through Greyhound) plus $8 for linen. You won't find a sturdier or quieter bunk. There are also cabin-type rooms with either two bunk beds or a double bed and one bunk, costing $78 for two, and $20 for each extra person up to four people, including bedding. The rooms have fridges and tea/coffee-making facilities, but bathrooms are communal. More expensive units with bathroom are $165. All buildings are air-con in summer and heated in winter and there's a swimming pool. Up at the back is a good lookout for early-morning views of the Rock.

Unfortunately the Hotel suffers from some bad design – intentional as well as unintentional. There also seems to be some sort of attempt to make you feel as if this is a cheap place to stay and you should suffer accordingly. We get a steady stream of complaints from budget travellers about the sort of welcome they have received here.

A better budget option is the deal offered by Landmark, a tour company operating from the Alice. They have a permanent Tent City in the coach camp site, and for $22 you can stay there. This includes dinner and breakfast, and you don't have to put up with all the nonsense at the Red Centre Hotel. You're not obliged to take a Landmark tour to stay there. Book through your hostel in the Alice or the NTGTB, or contact Landmark direct (☎ (089) 52 5200).

The *Yulara Maisonettes* (☎ (089) 56 2131) have rooms with twin beds and a small kitchenette; shower and toilet facilities are shared. The cost for a twin is $95. Beyond this you're heading towards the 'very expensive' category. The *Four Seasons Ayers Rock* (☎ (089) 56 2100) is a motel with a pleasant swimming pool and costs $165/180 for singles/doubles, which is definitely the top end of Australian motel prices.

Finally the *Sheraton Ayers Rock Hotel*

(☎ (089) 56 2200) has 230 rooms costing from $212 to $260 depending on whether you have a courtyard view, garden view, desert view or (top price) Rock view! If that isn't enough there are some suites as well.

Places to Eat

The *Red Centre Hotel* has a takeaway counter offering breakfasts at high prices, lunch-time sandwiches from around $3 and cheaper dinners, like stew, for around $10. There are no kitchen facilities other than fridges and electric barbecues which you must feed with 20c coins. Packs of steak and sausages are $6. Altogether the food situation is not ideal and the charge for a cup of hot water became instantly infamous on the travellers' circuit from the moment the hotel opened for business!

The camp site kiosk sells canned goods, drinks, tea, coffee, breakfast cereals and the like. Over at the shopping square there is a fairly big supermarket which sells frozen pizzas and other fast foods – you can try to heat them up on the hotel's barbecues!

Also at the shopping square, the bistro in the *Yulara Tavern* does reasonable counter meals like steak or fish for about $12 to $14, or pasta for $9. The portions are not bad and this is a good place for a proper sit-down meal. Beer and wine are reasonably priced and the place is busy at night, when there is also music. Across the square, the takeaway place has burgers, sandwiches and pizzas for $6 to $10. There are also more expensive restaurants in the hotels.

Getting There & Away

Air Connellan Airport, about five km from Yulara, was part of the development scheme and takes Fokker F28s. This airport has made longer range flights into Ayers Rock possible – you can now fly directly to Ayers Rock from various major centres as well as from Alice Springs, which remains the popular starting point for the Rock. Ansett (☎ (089) 56 2155) has at least two flights daily for the 45-minute, $158 hop from Alice to the Rock.

The numerous flights direct to the Rock can be money-savers. If, for example, you

were intending to fly to the Centre from Adelaide it makes a lot more sense to go Adelaide-Ayers Rock-Alice Springs rather than Adelaide-Alice Springs-Ayers Rock-Alice Springs. You can fly direct between Ayers Rock and Perth ($417), Adelaide ($484) and Darwin ($453) with Ansett, and to Coober Pedy ($159) with Kendell. Day trips to Ayers Rock by air from Alice Springs cost from about $260.

Bus Apart from hitching, the cheapest way to get to the Rock is to take a bus or a tour. The big operators all have regular services between Alice Springs and Ayers Rock for about $60. The 441-km trip takes about 6½ hours. There are also direct services between Adelaide and Ayers Rock, although this actually means connecting with another bus at Erldunda, the turn-off from the Stuart Highway. Adelaide to Ayers Rock takes about 22 hours for the 1720-km trip and costs $200.

An interesting and unusual way to get to or from Yulara is to catch the weekly service which runs from Yulara to Perth ($216) via Docker River ($17 from Yulara), Warburton ($63), Leonora ($140), Kalgoorlie ($163) and the Great Eastern Highway. It departs Yulara at 1 pm on Saturdays, and from Perth at 6.45 pm Wednesdays, and the journey takes a shade over 30 hours. The route is operated by Transcontinental Coachlines WA (☎ (09) 250 2838).

Car If you haven't got your own wheels, renting a car in Alice Springs to go down to the Rock and back can be expensive. You're looking at $70 to $100 a day for a car from the big operators since they usually load on $10 a day as a 'remote rate' surcharge, which only includes 100 km a day, each extra km costing 25c. So if you spent three days and covered 1000 km (the bare minimum) you're up for around $450 including insurance and petrol costs. Still, between four people that's not much worse than taking a bus there and back. Cheaper deals are available from the smaller Alice Springs rent-a-car operators.

The road from Alice to Yulara is sealed

and there are regular food and petrol stops along the way. Yulara is 441 km from Alice, 241 km west of Erldunda on the Stuart Highway, and the whole journey takes about six to seven hours. Mt Connor, which is seen on the left shortly before Curtin Springs, is often mistaken for the Rock itself. Along the way you may see kangaroos and dingoes or, at night, cows fast asleep on the warm bitumen.

Organised Tours Tours from Alice Springs start at about $130 for a two-day trip (with Bus Australia) but this is a basic transport-only package which doesn't include either accommodation or meals. Once you include these costs it's actually cheaper to take an all-inclusive tour for around $165.

These all-inclusive two-day bus tours generally include the trip there and back, guided walks around sections of Ayers Rock, a trip to the Olgas and a stop at the sunset-viewing area known as Sunset Strip. There are also trips for three days, some including Kings Canyon.

You have to shop around a bit because different tours run on different days and you may not want to wait for a particular one. Other things to check for include: the time it gets to the Rock and the Olgas, whether the return is done early or late in the day and how fast the bus is. Prices can vary with the season and demand, and sometimes there may be cheaper 'stand-by' fares available. Bus pass travellers should note that the bus service to the Rock is often heavily booked

– if your schedule is tight it's best to plan ahead.

Getting Around

To/From the Airport There's an airport bus service connecting with Ansett flights. The fare is $7.

Around Yulara The village may sprawl a bit, but it's not too large to get around on foot. Walking trails lead across the dunes to little lookouts overlooking the village and surrounding terrain. Bicycles ($18) and mopeds ($30) can be rented by the day from the village (☎ (089) 56 2131).

Around Uluru National Park Several options are available if you want to go further afield from the Yulara resort to Ayers Rock or the Olgas in the Uluru National Park. Both Bus Australia and AAT-Kings offer transport from Yulara to the Rock and the Olgas, but these are all in the form of tours. Bus Australia is the cheaper of the two and the tours include Sunrise & Climb ($24), Base ($20) and Olgas & Sunset ($29), or there's a three-day Rock Pass for $47.

There are taxis at Yulara which operate on a multiple-hire basis. Costs include Yulara to the airport for $7 per person or Yulara to Ayers Rock and return for $20 per person.

Or you can hire a car – Avis, Budget, Thrifty and Hertz are all represented at Yulara. Their regular 'remote area' rates apply. The Mobil service station hires out mopeds which are fine for scooting between Yulara and the Rock.

Queensland

Area	1,727,000 sq km
Population	2,600,000

Queensland is Australia's holiday state. You're certain to find something to suit whether you prefer glossy, neon-lit Surfers Paradise, or long deserted beaches, or the island resorts and excellent diving of the Great Barrier Reef, or wild, remote national parks.

Brisbane, the state capital, is an increasingly lively city and the third biggest in Australia. In the north, Cairns is a busy travellers' centre and base for a whole range of side trips and activities. Between Brisbane and Cairns are scattered a string of towns and islands offering virtually every pastime you can imagine connected with the sea. Inland, several spectacular national parks are scattered over the ranges and between the isolated towns and cattle stations. In the far south-west corner of the state you'll find one of the most isolated towns of all, Birdsville, with the famous Birdsville Track.

North of Cairns, the Cape York Peninsula remains a wilderness against which people still test themselves. You can get an easy taste of this first frontier in Cooktown, Australia's first British settlement and once a riotous gold-rush town. Just inland from Cairns is the lush Atherton Tableland with countless beautiful waterfalls and scenic spots. Further inland, on the main route across Queensland to the Northern Territory, is the outback mining town of Mt Isa and, south-east of here, the town of Longreach with its Stockman's Hall of Fame.

Queensland started as yet another penal colony in 1824. As usual, the free settlers soon followed and Queensland became a separate colony independent of New South Wales in 1859. Queensland's early White settlers indulged in one of the greatest land grabs of all time and encountered fiercer Aboriginal opposition than in other states.

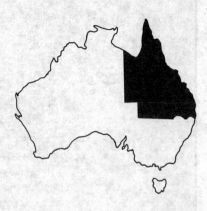

For much of the 19th century, what amounted to a guerrilla war took place along the frontiers of the White advance. A good, widely available book on the incredible adventures of the Queensland pioneers is *Queensland Frontier* (Pinevale Publications, Mareeba, 1982) by Glenville Pike.

Traditionally, agriculture and mining have been the backbone of the Queensland economy: the state contains a substantial chunk of Australia's mineral wealth. More recently, vast amounts of money have been invested in tourism, which is on the verge of becoming the state's leading money earner.

For many years, Queensland also had Australia's most controversial state government. The right-wing National Party was led by Sir Johannes Bjelke-Petersen (universally known as Joh) until 1987, when even Joh's own party decided he was a liability and replaced him. Whether it was views on rainforests, on Aboriginal land rights, or even on whether condom machines should be allowed in universities, you could count on the Queensland government to take the opposite stand to just about everybody else. Under the Nationals, the state also had more than its fair share of corruption scandals.

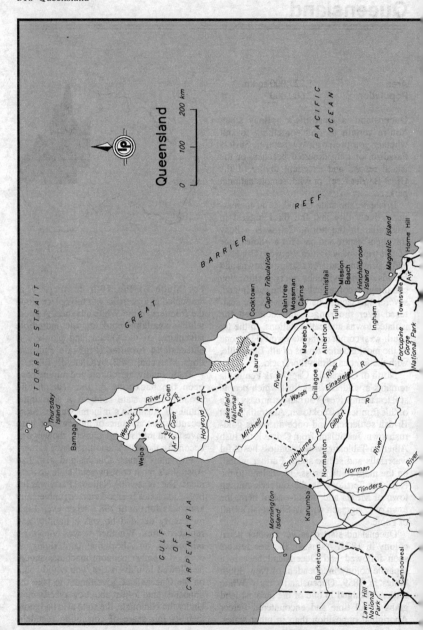

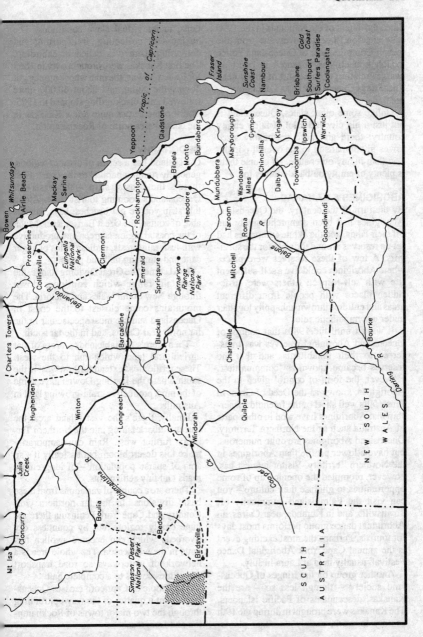

Since the defeat of the Nationals in the 1990 state election, it seems everyone from the former Commissioner of Queensland Police to Joh himself has appeared in court on charges relating to some sort of shady deal. These days Queensland has a Labor government.

Unlike some other states, Queensland is not just a big city and a lot of fairly empty country; there are more reasonably sized towns in comparison to the overall population than in any other state. Of course there is plenty of empty outback country too.

ABORIGINES & KANAKAS

By the turn of the century, the Queensland Aborigines had been comprehensively run off their lands, and the White authorities had set up reserves around the state for the survivors. A few of these reserves were places where Aborigines could live a self-sufficient life with self-respect; others were strife-ridden places with people from different areas and cultures thrown unhappily together under unsympathetic rule.

It wasn't until the 1980s that control of Queensland Aboriginal reserves was transferred to their inhabitants, and that the reserves became known as 'communities'. However, the form of control given to the Aborigines, known as the Deed of Grant in Trust, falls well short of the freehold ownership that Aborigines have won in other parts of Australia such as the Northern Territory. Queensland Aborigines are quite numerous, but have a lower profile than Aborigines in the Northern Territory. Visitor interest has, however, prompted the opening up of some opportunities to glimpse their culture – you can visit the Palm Island community off Townsville, and in Kuranda, near Cairns, an Aboriginal dance group performs most days for tourists. Perhaps the most exciting event is the annual Cape York Aboriginal Dance Festival, usually held at Laura in July.

Another group on the fringes of Queensland society – though less so – are the Kanakas, descendants of Pacific Islanders. The Kanakas were brought in during the 19th century to work, mainly on sugar planta-tions, under virtual slave conditions. The business of collecting, transporting and delivering them was called blackbirding. The first Kanakas were brought over in 1863 for Robert Towns, the man whose money got Townsville going, and about 60,000 more followed until blackbirding stopped in 1905. You'll come across quite a few Kanakas in the coastal area north of Rockhampton.

GEOGRAPHY

Queensland has a series of distinct regions, generally running parallel to the coast. First there's the coastal strip – the basis for Queensland's booming tourist trade. Along this strip you've got beaches, bays, islands and, of course, the Great Barrier Reef. Much of the coastal region is green and productive with lush rainforests, endless fields of sugar cane and stunning national parks.

Next comes the Great Dividing Range, the mountain range which continues down through New South Wales and Victoria. The mountains come closest to the coast in Queensland and are most spectacular in the far north near Cairns, and in the far south.

Then there's the tablelands – areas of flat agricultural land which run to the west. These fertile areas extend furthest west in the south where the Darling Downs have some of the most productive grain-growing land in Australia.

Finally, there's the vast inland area, the barren outback fading into the Northern Territory further west. Rain can temporarily make this desert bloom but basically it's an area of sparse population – of long empty roads and tiny settlements.

There are a couple of variations from these basic divisions. In the far northern Gulf Country and Cape York Peninsula there are huge empty regions cut by countless dry riverbeds which can become swollen torrents in the wet season. The whole area is a network of waterways so road transport sometimes comes to a complete halt.

The Tropic of Capricorn crosses Queensland about a quarter of the way up, running through the two major towns of Rockhampton and Longreach.

CLIMATE

The Queensland seasons are more a case of hotter and wetter or cooler and drier than of summer and winter. November/December to April/May is the wetter, hotter half of the year, while the real Wet, particularly affecting northern coastal areas, is January to March. Cairns usually gets about 1300 mm of rain in these three months, with daily temperatures in the high 30s. This is also the season for cyclones, and if one hits, the main road north, the Bruce Highway, can be blocked by the ensuing floods.

In the south, Brisbane and Rockhampton both get about 450 mm of rain from January to March, and temperatures in Brisbane rarely drop below 20°C. Queensland doesn't really get 'cold weather', except at night inland or upland from about May to September. Inland, of course, there's also a lot less rain than near the coast.

INFORMATION

Queensland has none of the state-run tourist information offices that you find in other states. Instead there are tourism offices, often privately run, which act as booking agents for the various hotels, tour companies and so on that sponsor them. You may not always get full or straightforward answers to your questions.

The Queensland Government Travel Centres are primarily booking offices, not information centres, but may prove useful. It's a good idea to check with these offices when planning a trip to Queensland as the cost of food and accommodation can vary greatly with the season, and high and low seasons often differ from one part of the coast to another. The interstate Travel Centre offices are:

Australian Capital Territory
    25 Garema Place, Canberra City, 2601
    (☎ (06) 248 8411)
New South Wales
    Shop 3, 133-135 King St, Newcastle, 2300
    (☎ (049) 26 2800)
    75 Castlereagh St, Sydney, 2000
    (☎ (02) 232 1788)

    Shop 11, Mayfair Mall Arcade, Cnr Church & St
    George Sts, Parramatta, 2150 (☎ (02) 891 1866)
South Australia
    10 Grenfell St, Adelaide, 5000 (☎ (08) 212 2399)
Victoria
    257 Collins St, Melbourne, 3000
    (☎ (03) 654 3866)
Western Australia
    55 St George's Terrace, Perth (☎ (09) 325 1600)

The Royal Automobile Club of Queensland (RACQ) has a series of excellent, detailed road maps covering the whole state, region by region. RACQ offices are a very helpful source of information about road and weather conditions. Also good is the Sunmap series of area maps, published by the state government. There are Sunmap shops in most big towns.

NATIONAL PARKS

Queensland has more than 200 national parks, and while some just cover a single hill or lake, others are major wilderness areas. Many islands and stretches of coast are national parks, while inland three of the most spectacular are: Lamington, on the forested rim of an ancient volcano on the New South Wales border; Carnarvon with its 30-km gorge south-west of Rockhampton; and rainforested Eungella, near Mackay, which is swarming with wildlife. Many parks have camping grounds with water, toilets and showers and there are often privately run camping grounds, motels or lodges on the park fringes. Sizeable parks usually have a network of walking tracks.

The Queensland National Parks & Wildlife Service operates four main information centres: at Gold Coast Highway, Burleigh Heads (☎ (075) 35 3032); 160 Ann St, Brisbane (☎ (07) 227 8185); Bruce Highway, Monkland in Gympie (☎ (074) 82 4189); and Bruce Highway, Cardwell (☎ (070) 66 8601). It's worth calling at one of these to find out what's where, and to get the rundown on camping in the national parks. You can also get info from the national parks offices in most major towns, and from the park rangers. Pick up a copy of *Ringtail* – the useful quarterly national parks newspaper.

To camp in a national park – whether in a fixed camping ground or in the bush – you need a permit which you can either get in advance by writing or calling in at the appropriate national parks office, or from the ranger at the park itself. Camping in national parks costs up to $7.50 a night for a site for up to six people. Some camping grounds fill up at holiday times, so you may need to book well ahead; you can usually book sites six to 12 weeks ahead by writing to the appropriate office. Lists of camping grounds are available from national parks offices, or look in *Ringtail*.

STATE FORESTS

There are also camping areas, walking trails and scenic drives in some state forests which can be just as scenic and wild as national parks. You can get information on state forest camping sites and facilities from tourist offices or from state forestry offices – the Queensland head office (☎ (07) 224 6018) is in Mineral House, 41 George St, Brisbane. Some others are at Fraser Rd, Two Mile, near Gympie; 11 Lannercost St, Ingham; Gregory St, Cardwell; and at Atherton.

ACTIVITIES
Bushwalking

This is a popular activity in Queensland year-round. There are bushwalking clubs in the state and several useful guidebooks. Lonely Planet's *Bushwalking in Australia* includes three walks in Queensland, which range between two and five days in length. National parks and state forests are some of the best places for walking, often with marked trails. You can get full information on walking in national parks and state forests from their respective offices.

There are excellent bushwalking possibilities in many parts of the state, including on several of the larger coastal islands such as Fraser and Hinchinbrook. Favourite bushwalkers' national parks on the mainland include Lamington in the southern Border Ranges, Main Range in the Great Divide, Cooloola just north of the Sunshine Coast, and Bellenden Ker south of Cairns, which contains Queensland's highest peak, Mt Bartle Frere (1657 metres).

Water Sports
Diving & Snorkelling The Great Barrier Reef provides some of the world's best diving and there's ample opportunity to learn and pursue this activity. The Queensland coast is probably the world's cheapest place to learn to scuba dive in tropical water – a five-day course leading to a recognised open water certificate usually costs somewhere between $250 and $390 and you almost always do a good part of your learning out on the Barrier Reef itself. These courses are now very popular and almost every town along the coast has one or more dive schools. The three most popular places are Airlie Beach, Townsville and Cairns.

Important factors to consider when choosing a course include the school's reputation, the relative amounts of time spent on pool/classroom training and out in the ocean, and whether your open-water time is spent on the outer reef as opposed to reefs around islands or even just off the mainland. The outer reef is usually more spectacular. Normally you have to show you can tread water for 10 minutes, and swim 200 metres, before you can start a course. Some schools also require a medical which will usually cost extra.

For certified divers, trips and equipment hire are available just about everywhere. You usually have to show evidence of qualifications. You can snorkel just about everywhere too. There are coral reefs off some mainland beaches and around several of the islands, and many day trips out to the Barrier Reef provide snorkelling gear free.

During the wet season, usually January to March, floods can wash a lot of mud out into the ocean and visibility for divers and snorkellers is sometimes affected.

White-Water Rafting & Canoeing The Tully and North Johnstone rivers between Townsville and Cairns are the big ones for white-water rafting. You can do day trips for about $65 to $85, or longer expeditions.

Coastal Queensland is full of waterways and lakes so there's no shortage of canoeing territory. You can rent canoes or join canoe tours in several places – among them Noosa, Townsville and Cairns.

Swimming & Surfing There are plenty of swimming beaches close to Brisbane on sheltered Moreton Bay. Popular surfing beaches are south of the capital on the Gold Coast and north on the Sunshine Coast. North of Fraser Island the beaches are sheltered by the Great Barrier Reef so they're great for swimming but no good for surf. The clear, sheltered waters of the reef hardly need to be mentioned. There are also innumerable, good, freshwater swimming spots around the state.

Other Water Sports Sailing enthusiasts will also find plenty of opportunities to practise their sport and many places which hire boats, both along the coast and inland. Airlie Beach and the Whitsunday Islands are probably the biggest centres and you can find almost any type of boating or sailing you want there. Fishing is probably Queensland's biggest participant sport and you can rent gear or boats for this in many places. Sailboards can also be hired in many spots along the coast.

Warning From around November to April, avoid swimming on unprotected northern beaches where deadly box jellyfish may lurk. If in any doubt, check with a local. If you're still in doubt, don't swim – you only get stung once in a lifetime. Great Keppel Island is usually the most northerly safe place in the box jellyfish season. Also in northern waters, saltwater crocodiles are a hazard. They may be found in the open sea or near creeks and rivers – especially tidal ones – sometimes surprising distances inland.

Fossicking
There are lots of good fossicking areas in Queensland – see the *Gem Field* brochure, published by the Queensland Government Travel Centre. It tells you the places where you have a fair chance of finding gems and the types you'll find. You'll need a 'miners right' before you set out.

GETTING AROUND
The peak tourist seasons are from mid-December to late January, 10 days either side of Easter, and mid-June to mid-October. The low season is February and March.

Air
Ansett and Australian Airlines both fly to Queensland's major cities, connecting them to the southern states and across to the Northern Territory. East-West flies to Brisbane, the Gold and Sunshine coasts and Cairns. There's also a multitude of smaller airlines operating up and down the coast, across the Cape York Peninsula and into the outback. During the wet season, such flights are often the only means of getting around the Gulf of Carpentaria or the Cape York Peninsula. These smaller airlines include Sunstate, Australian Regional (both closely linked to Australian Airlines), Sunbird and Flight West.

Bus
There are numerous bus services up the coast to Cairns and inland from Townsville through Mt Isa to the Northern Territory. The main companies on these routes are Greyhound/Pioneer, Bus Australia and McCafferty's. Prices are fairly similar, although McCafferty's tends to be a dollar or two cheaper. There's also a range of stopover deals. Generally you can get a free stopover at Brisbane with most companies, while McCafferty's and Bus Australia also allow one at Mt Isa, and Pioneer/Greyhound at the Gold Coast. Of course, if you have a bus pass you can stop wherever you want.

You can catch a Greyhound bus inland from Brisbane to Roma, Charleville, Longreach and up to Mt Isa, or you can go with McCafferty's from Rockhampton to Longreach. There are also many local services like Cairns to Cooktown or Brisbane to the Gold Coast.

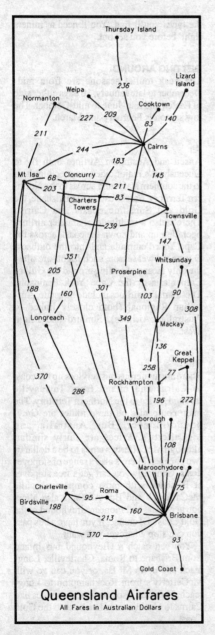

Queensland Airfares
All Fares in Australian Dollars

Train

There are four major rail routes in Queensland. The main one is Brisbane to Cairns, with a local extension on the scenic route into the Atherton Tableland. Inland from Brisbane, a service runs to Roma, Charleville and Quilpie; from Rockhampton you can go to Emerald, Longreach and Winton; and from Townsville there is a service to Mt Isa. There are other local and outback lines too. The Sunshine Rail Pass provides unlimited rail on all services in Queensland. Fares in economy/1st class are: 14 days for $242/351, 21 days for $280/432, and one month for $351/528.

Queensland trains are slower than buses but are similarly priced if you travel economy class. They're almost all air-con and you can get sleeping berths on most trains for $20 a night in economy, $34 in 1st class. You can break your journey on most services for no extra cost provided you complete the trip within five days (on a journey of up to 500 km), 10 days (501 to 1000 km) or 14 days (over 1000 km). The only interstate rail connection from Queensland is between Brisbane and Sydney.

Hitching

This is perfectly practicable and common, but take care: the police sometimes give hitchhikers a hard time, and there are long, lonely stretches of road where strange people are said to pick up unwary hitchhikers. Women should be particularly careful.

Boat

It's possible to make your way along the coast or even over to Papua New Guinea or Darwin by crewing on the numerous yachts and cruisers that sail Queensland waters. Ask at harbours, marinas, yacht or sailing clubs. Great Keppel Island, Airlie Beach, Townsville and Cairns are good places to try. Sometimes you'll get a free ride in exchange for your help, but it's more common for owners to ask $10 to $15 a day for food, etc.

Brisbane

Population 1,171,340

When Sydney and the colony of New South Wales needed a better place to store its more recalcitrant 'cons', the tropical country further north seemed a good place to drop them. Accordingly, in 1824, a penal settlement was established at Redcliffe on Moreton Bay, but was soon abandoned due to lack of water and hostile Aborigines. The settlement was moved south and inland to Brisbane, a town grew up, and although the penal settlement was abandoned in 1839, Brisbane's future was assured when the area was thrown open to free settlers in 1842. As Queensland's huge agricultural potential and then its mineral riches were developed, Brisbane grew to be a city, and today it is the third largest in Australia.

Brisbane is a scenic city, surrounded by hills and fine lookouts, and has some impressive bridges and squares. The terraced house architecture of the southern capitals only pops up in odd, isolated pockets here, but you'll find the tropical Queensland stilt houses with their wide verandahs all over the place.

Several of Queensland's major attractions can be reached on day trips from Brisbane. The Gold and Sunshine coasts and their mountainous hinterlands are easy drives from the city, and you can also visit the islands of Moreton Bay or head inland towards the Great Dividing Range and the Darling Downs.

Orientation

Brisbane is built along and between the looping meanders of the Brisbane River, about 25 km upstream from the river mouth. The Brisbane Transit Centre, where you'll arrive if you're coming by bus or train, is on Roma St about half a km west of the city centre. Head left as you leave the centre's main entrance and you'll find King George Square, the large open area in front of City Hall; it's a popular place to sit and watch the world pass by.

About one km west of the centre is the suburb of Paddington, where there's some cheap accommodation and several restaurants. South-west of the centre, across the river, are the Queensland Cultural Centre and the suburbs of West End and Highgate Hill, the latter also with some good accommodation possibilities. North-east up Ann St from the city, you arrive in Fortitude Valley which has a large ethnic population and lots more restaurants. Heading south-west along Brunswick St from Fortitude Valley will bring you to another river-looped part of the city at New Farm; this area has the greatest concentration of hostels, and is about three km from the centre.

Information

Tourist Offices The Tourism Brisbane information desk (☎ 221 8411) is in the City Hall. It's open Monday to Friday from 8.30 am to 5 pm. There's also the Brisbane Information Centre (☎ 229 5918) in the Queen St Mall, between Albert and Edward Sts; it's open Monday to Thursday from 8.30 am to 5 pm, Friday from 8.30 am to 8.30 pm, and Saturday from 8.30 to 11.30 am. The Greater Brisbane Tourist Association (☎ 236 2020) has a helpful office on level 2 of the Transit Centre; it provides information on the city and surrounding area. The Queensland Government Travel Centre (☎ 221 6111), on the corner of Adelaide and Edward Sts, is more a booking office than an information centre but may be able to answer some queries. It's open Monday to Friday from 9 am to 5 pm, Saturday from 9 to 11 am.

There are a number of giveaway information guides circulated in Brisbane including the useful entertainment guide *Time Off*. Another, *This Week in Brisbane*, contains a list of foreign consulates in the city.

The STD telephone area code for Brisbane is 07.

Other Offices The RACQ (☎ 361 2444) is at 190 Edward St. The National Parks & Wildlife Service (☎ 227 8185), open from

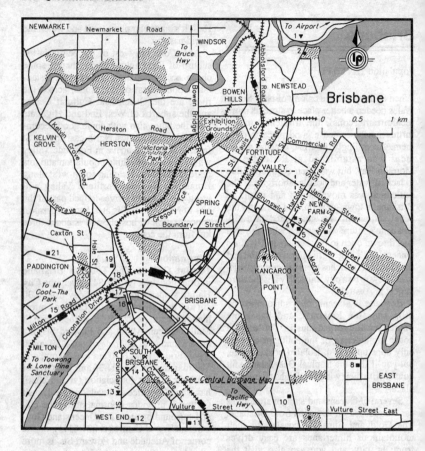

Monday to Friday, is at 160 Ann St. The Queensland Conservation Council Environment Centre (☎ 221 0188), with a library and information desk open to the public on weekdays from 9 am to 5 pm, is on the 2nd floor of the School of Arts building at 166 Ann St. The YHA membership office (☎ 236 1680) is at 154 Roma St, not far from the Transit Centre. The GPO is on Queen St.

Bookshops The Queensland Book Depot, on Adelaide St opposite the City Hall, is the city's biggest traditional bookshop. Other good ones include the Book Nook in the Metro Arts building at 109 Edward St; the Mansions Bookshop on George St; and the Billabong Bookshop, immediately east of Victoria Bridge, which is good for environmental and 'green' books, and also has a good section on Aboriginal books. Hema Maps, at 239 George St, specialises in travel books and maps.

City Hall

Brisbane's City Hall, on the corner of Adelaide and Albert Sts, has gradually been surrounded by skyscrapers but the observation platform still provides one of the best

1	Breakfast Creek Hotel
2	Newstead House
3	Back-Packers Down Under
4	Brunswick Hotel
5	Globe Trekkers Hostel
6	Queenslander Hostel
7	Backpackers Brisbane Central
8	Courtney Place Backpackers
9	Brisbane Cricket Ground (The Gabba)
10	Carmel Lodge Holiday Flats
11	Durham Villa Hostel
12	Somewhere to Stay Hostel
13	Qan Heng's Restaurant
14	Squirrels Restaurant
15	Brewery
16	William Jolly Bridge
17	Brisbane City Youth Hostel
18	The Brisbane Underground
19	Banana Benders & Aussie Way Backpackers
20	Lang Park
21	Backpackers Paddington

views across the city. There's a lift to the observation deck, which runs Monday to Friday from 8.30 am to 3.30 pm. The City Hall also houses a museum and art gallery on the ground floor; it's open Monday to Friday from 10 am to 4 pm and admission is free.

Queen St Mall

Running two blocks from Edward St to George St, this attractive mall is the shopping hub of the city. In addition to the 250-odd shops, there's an underground bus interchange, a Hilton Hotel, eight cinemas and even an indoor funfair.

The mall is bustling and alive, and is where Brisbanites try to look their best, particularly on Friday nights.

Early Buildings – city centre

The **Old Observatory & Windmill** on Wickham Terrace, just north of the city centre, is one of Brisbane's earliest buildings, dating from 1829. It was intended to grind grain for the early convict colony but due to a fundamental design error, it did not work properly. In 1837 it was made to work

as originally intended but the building was then converted to a signal post and later a meteorological observatory.

The National Trust's *Historic Walks* brochure will guide you around the city's most interesting early buildings. The National Trust has its headquarters in **Old Government House** (1862), the former state governor's residence at the southern end of George St. Nearby, **Parliament House**, overlooking the city Botanic Gardens, dates from 1868, and was built in French Renaissance style; the roof is made from Mt Isa copper. Tours are given seven times a day Monday to Friday when Parliament isn't sitting.

More of Brisbane's best old buildings line George St – notably the **Mansions** and **Harris Terrace**, Victorian town houses on the Margaret St corner.

On Elizabeth St, the Gothic-style **Old St Stephen's** (1850) is the oldest church in Brisbane. The **GPO** is an impressive neoclassical edifice dating from the 1870s. Across Queen St and on the corner of Creek St, the **National Bank building** (1885) is reckoned to be one of the finest examples of Italian Renaissance style in Australia! Its front doors were made from a single Queensland cedar log.

St John's Cathedral is still under construction – work started in 1901. You can take a guided tour at 11 am on Wednesday or Friday. Queensland's first **Government House**, built in 1853, is now the deanery for the cathedral. The declaration of Queensland's separation from the colony of New South Wales was read here.

The 1828 **Commissariat Stores** building, at 115 William St, was used as a government store right up until 1962. Today it houses the Royal Historical Society of Queensland, and can be visited for $1, Tuesday to Friday from 11 am to 2 pm, and Sunday from 11 am to 4 pm.

Early Buildings – suburbs

There are a number of interesting old houses and period recreations around Brisbane. **Newstead House**, four km north-east of the centre on Breakfast Creek Rd, Newstead, is the oldest surviving home in Brisbane. Built in 1846, overlooking the river, it is a stately mansion fully fitted with Victorian furnishings. The house is open from 11 am to 3 pm Monday to Thursday and from 2 to 5 pm on Sundays and public holidays. You can get there on bus Nos 160, 180 or 190 from the yellow stop on Edward St between Adelaide and Queen Sts. You can also get there on the Brisbane City Ferries cruise.

Earlystreet Historical Village is on McIlwraith Ave, off Bennetts Rd in Norman Park, four km east of the centre and south of the river. It's a re-creation of early Queensland colonial life with genuine old buildings in a garden setting. Entry is $6 and it's open from 9.30 am to 4.30 pm Monday to Friday, 10.30 am to 4.30 pm on weekends. You can get there on bus Nos 8A, 8B, 8C, 8D or 8E from Ann St by King George Square, or by train to Norman Park.

Miegunyah Folk Museum, at 31 Jordan Terrace, Bowen Hills, just north of Fortitude Valley, is housed in an 1884 building, a fine example of early Brisbane architecture. It's been furnished and decorated in period style as a memorial to the pioneer women of Queensland and is open from 10.30 am to 3 pm Tuesday and Wednesday, and to 4 pm on weekends. To get there, take an airport bus No 160 or Toombul bus Nos 170, 171 or 190.

Wolston House at Grindle Rd, Wacol, 18 km west of the centre, is an early colonial country residence, built in 1852 of local materials. It's open from 10 am to 4.30 pm, Wednesday to Sunday and on holidays.

Queensland Cultural Centre

This superb complex (☎ 11 632) spans a block either side of Melbourne St in South Brisbane, just across Victoria Bridge from the city centre. It houses the Queensland Art Gallery, the Queensland Museum and the State Library, all on the north side of Melbourne St, and, to the south, a **Performing Arts Complex** with two theatres, a concert hall and an auditorium which seats 4700 people. There are also cafeterias, restaurants and shops.

The **Queensland Museum** is intended to be a 'hands-on' place. Its large collection features a dinosaur garden and biplanes strung from the ceiling, and includes the 'Avian Cirrus' in which Queensland's Bert Hinkler made the first England to Australia solo flight in 1928. The museum is open daily from 9 am to 5 pm, except on Good Friday and Christmas and Anzac days. It also stays open until 8 pm on Wednesdays. Admission is free.

The **Queensland Art Gallery** shows visiting exhibitions as well as its impressive permanent collection which includes many Australian and international big names. It's open daily from 10 am to 5 pm and on Wednesdays till 8 pm, again except for Good Friday and Christmas and Anzac days. Admission is free except for some special exhibitions.

There are daily tours of the three buildings at 10 am and 2 pm, but these are not worth the $9.50. On weekdays, the gallery and arts complex both have free tours at 11 am, 1 and 2 pm. On weekends, there are free tours of the gallery at 2 and 3 pm, and of the arts complex at noon.

Other Museums

The **Queensland Maritime Museum**, on Stanley St, South Brisbane, has an 1881 dry dock, working models, and the WW II frigate HMAS *Diamantina*. It's open from 10 am to 5 pm daily; admission is $4.

Postal enthusiasts could try the **GPO Museum** at 261-285 Queen St. It's open Tuesday to Thursday from 10 am to 3 pm and admission is free. Out in St Lucia, the **Queensland University** on Sir Fred Schonell Drive has anthropology, antiquities and art museums.

Brisbane's trams no longer operate, but you can ride some early examples at the **Tramway Museum** on 2 McGinn Rd, Ferny Grove. The museum is 11 km from the city centre, and is open from 1.30 to 4 pm Sundays and most public holidays.

Southbank Site

Formerly the site of Expo 88, the southbank

area is now being extensively redeveloped, after much typical Queensland-style wrangling, wheeling and dealing. The World Expo Park funfair, with its roller coasters, spaceage ghost trains, etc, has been retained in plans for the site, and the area is currently under construction. When complete, it will be a development along the lines of Darling Harbour in Sydney.

Swimming Pools

The Spring Hill Baths in Torrington St are probably the oldest in the southern hemisphere! Built in 1886 for £2400, the pool is 23.43 metres long, and surrounded by colourfully painted, old-style changing cubicles. It's open from 6 am to 7 pm Monday to Friday and from 8 am to 6 pm on weekends.

The most central Olympic-sized pool is Centenary Pool (☎ 831 8259), on Gregory Terrace. It's open daily from 6 am to 6 or 8.30 pm, September to April.

Brewery

There are free tours of the XXXX (pronounced fourex) brewery (☎ 368 7597) on Milton Rd, Milton, about 1½ km west of the centre, Monday to Wednesday. You need to get a small group together to book, although most hostels organise groups to go through. The tour lasts about an hour, and is followed by about 40 minutes worth of free beer.

City Parks & Gardens

Brisbane has a number of parks and gardens including the original Botanic Gardens, established in 1855 on a loop of the Brisbane River, almost in the centre of the city. The park occupies 18 hectares, is open from sunrise to sunset and is a good spot for bike riding.

There are good views from **Wickham Park** and **Albert Park** on the hill just north of the city centre. **New Farm Park**, by the river at the southern end of Brunswick St, is noted for its rose displays, jacaranda trees and Devonshire teas. **Captain John Burke Park** is a nice little place underneath the

towering Story Bridge at the top of Kangaroo Point.

Mt Coot-tha Park

This large park with a lookout and an excellent botanic garden is just eight km west of the city centre. The views from the top are superb. On a clear day you can see the distant line of Moreton and Stradbroke islands, the Glasshouse Mountains to the north, the mountains behind the Gold Coast to the south and Brisbane, with the river winding through, at your feet. There's a restaurant serving Devonshire teas at one of the best lookout points.

There are some good walks around Mt Coot-tha and its foothills, like the one to J C Slaughter Falls on Simpsons Rd.

The **Mt Coot-tha Botanic Gardens**, at the foot of the mountain, are open daily from 8.30 am to 5 pm. The gardens concentrate on native Australian plants and include an enclosed tropical display dome, an arid zone collection and a teahouse. There are free guided walks through the gardens at 11 am and 1 pm daily except Monday. You'll also find the **Sir Thomas Brisbane Planetarium** here; it's the largest in Australia. Admission is $7 and there are shows at 3.30 and 7.30 pm Wednesday to Friday; 1.30, 3.30 and 7.30 pm Saturday; 1.30 and 3.30 pm Sunday.

There are buses to the lookout and botanic gardens at Mt Coot-tha. Bus No 10C to the lookout leaves from the green stops on Adelaide and George Sts once daily (twice on Sundays). Bus No 39 to the gardens leaves from Ann St at King George Square.

Brisbane Forest Park

Musgrave, Waterworks and Mt Nebo Rds lead out through the suburbs to the 750-metre-high D'Aguilar Range, about 20 km north-west of the city centre. The drive is well worthwhile for its great views, forest and hill scenery, bird life and away-from-it-all feeling.

Some 250 sq km of the range is protected in the Brisbane Forest Park. There are several walking tracks and lookouts and there's an information centre (☎ 300 4855), open Monday to Friday from 8.30 am to 4.30 pm, a few km after the Gap. There's a national park camping area at Manorina between Mts Nebo and Glorious. The closest you can get to Brisbane Forest Park by public transport is by bus to the Gap.

Wildlife Sanctuaries

The **Lone Pine Koala Sanctuary** at Fig Tree Pocket, 11 km south-west of the centre, is one of Australia's best known and most popular animal sanctuaries. It has more than 100 koalas plus other Australian animals. It's open from 9.30 am to 5 pm daily but not cheap at $9.

You can get to the sanctuary by bus, river cruise or bus tour. Cityxpress bus No 518 leaves from the Queen St underground bus station hourly to 5.35 pm Monday to Friday, or bus Nos 84 or 84A leave from green stops on Adelaide and George Sts four or five times daily.

Koala Cruises (☎ 229 7055) runs a tour to the sanctuary. It departs from the Riverside Centre at 1 pm daily and from North Quay 25 minutes later and takes about 1½ hours. There's an extra trip on Sunday. The $24 fare includes entrance to the sanctuary, and for an extra $8 you can take a bus tour to the gardens and lookout at Mt Coot-tha, instead of coming back by boat.

Bunya Park on Bunya Park Drive, Eatons Hill, has more koalas to cuddle and plenty more native flora & fauna. It's about 16 km north of the centre, and is open daily from 9.30 am to 5 pm. **Alma Park Zoo** at Kallangur has a large collection of palms, native fauna and some imported wildlife. It's 28 km north of the city centre and is open daily.

Australian Woolshed

This attraction, at 148 Stamford St, Ferny Hills, 15 km north of the centre, has regular shearing demonstrations and other activities such as a water slide ($2.95 for 30 minutes). There's also a restaurant which has dinner dances on Friday and Saturday nights ($26). Entry to the woolshed itself is $8.

Activities

For information about bushwalking near Brisbane, contact the Brisbane Bushwalkers Club (☎ 856 4050), at 2 Alderley Ave, Alderley. Scuba World (☎ 870 9030) at 36A High St, Toowong runs diving trips from $100 a day – it's cheaper further north on the Great Barrier Reef.

City Tours Some of the best value trips are run by the backpackers' hostels. The Brisbane City Council's 'Discover Brisbane' bus (☎ 225 4444) makes a 20-stop trip around the city sights; the 55-km trip takes half a day and costs $9. You can book by phone or by calling in at 69 Ann St. Admission fees to attractions aren't included, but you can get off the bus anywhere and return free to the centre on any city bus.

Most other tours take in the city centre, and then Mt Coot-tha, the Lone Pine Koala Sanctuary, and the Australian Woolshed, and cost from $20 for half a day up to around $35 for a full day.

Some operators include: Aladdin's (☎ 236 2727), Baxway's (☎ 862 1373), Boomerang (☎ 236 3614), and Sunstate (☎ 236 3355).

Other Tours You can also take day trips to the Gold or Sunshine coasts, Tamborine Mountain, Lamington National Park or the Darling Downs, typically for $30 to $35.

Aus-Trail (☎ 285 1711) at PO Box 109, Stafford, offers a range of trips designed for budget travellers, including an 11-day venture that takes in a cattle station near Roma, Carnarvon Gorge National Park, the Anakie gem fields, Blackdown Tableland and Noosa. The $460 cost includes food and camping equipment.

Festivals

The Warana Festival is a cultural, theatrical, educational and children's festival, with many outdoor events. It's held in the city Botanic Gardens, King George Square and Albert Park, around mid-September. Mid-August sees the Royal National Exhibition at the Gregory Terrace exhibition grounds. It developed from an old-style agricultural show.

Places to Stay

Brisbane has plenty of hostels and there are also several well-priced hotels, guesthouses and motels within easy reach of the centre.

Hostels Brisbane's hostel scene has changed dramatically in the last few years, largely because of new government regulations which laid down guidelines about the number of people in rooms, etc. Since these new laws are still not ratified by state parliament as we go to print, some of the older hostels are still operating, but don't be surprised if they have closed by the time you get there.

The hostels are concentrated in four areas: Petrie Terrace/Paddington, just west of the city centre and within walking distance of the Transit Centre; Fortitude Valley/New Farm, north-east of the city centre and accessible by train, bus and ferry; east across the river in Kangaroo Point, also accessible by bus and ferry; and south of the river in Highgate Hill. Most hostels do pick-ups on request.

There's a backpackers' accommodation desk on the 3rd floor of the Transit Centre. This desk is run by about six hostels in the city, and so by no means offers a comprehensive or necessarily unbiased service.

Petrie Terrace/Paddington The first offering here is the new *Brisbane City Youth Hostel* (☎ 236 1004) at 56 Quay St, just south of Upper Roma St. The facilities are excellent, although it's still very much a youth hostel. The cost is $12 per person in a four to six-bed dorm, or $30 for a twin room. Nonmembers pay a once-only temporary membership fee of $3. The hostel has a restaurant which serves good breakfasts, and dinner for $5.

Up to the right along Petrie Terrace, on the corner of Jessie St, is the new *Banana Benders Backpackers* (☎ 367 1157). It's poorly signposted but is painted bright yellow so you can't miss it. This is a small place with the usual facilities, and has good views over to the west. Dorm beds are $11, doubles $26. The only hassle here is that Petrie Terrace can get noisy during peak hours.

Down the side street past Banana Benders is the small *Aussie Way Backpackers* (☎ 369 0711) at 34 Cricket St. It's in a rambling old house in a residential area; dorm beds are the standard $11, doubles $26. Each four-bed dorm has its own kitchenette, and there's a small backyard.

Moving west of the city, the long-running *Backpackers Paddington* (☎ 368 1047) is at 175 Given Terrace, the continuation of Caxton St. This is a very relaxed, old-style hostel, with a cosy atmosphere, though it's a bit rough around the edges these days. Dorm beds are $11, doubles $26. Although this place is clean, quiet and well-run, it may not survive the stringent new regulations, *if* these are introduced and policed.

Fortitude Valley/New Farm In Fortitude Valley, the only hostel is the YHA-associated *Balmoral House* (☎ 252 1397) at 33 Amelia St, near the intersection of St Paul's Terrace and Brunswick St. The building has just been renovated, so the facilities are excellent, and the location is good (it's an easy train ride from the Transit Centre). However, it lacks a decent-sized communal area, and therefore, atmosphere. A bed in a spacious four-bed dorm costs $12, while singles/doubles with shared bathroom cost $20/30. Big discounts are offered on weekly rates.

Moving down Brunswick St towards New Farm, you'll find four good hostels in side streets. At 71 Kent St, the friendly *Backpackers Down Under* (☎ 358 4504) charges $10 a dorm bed and $25 a double. It's in an old house and has adequate facilities.

A bit further along is the *Globe Trekkers Hostel* (☎ 358 1251) at 35 Balfour St. This is a new hostel in a renovated house, and the good atmosphere and small size make it quite popular. Dorm beds are $11.

The *Queenslander* (☎ 358 3538), at 57 Annie St, is run by an amiable Irishman and has recently had an extension built at the rear.

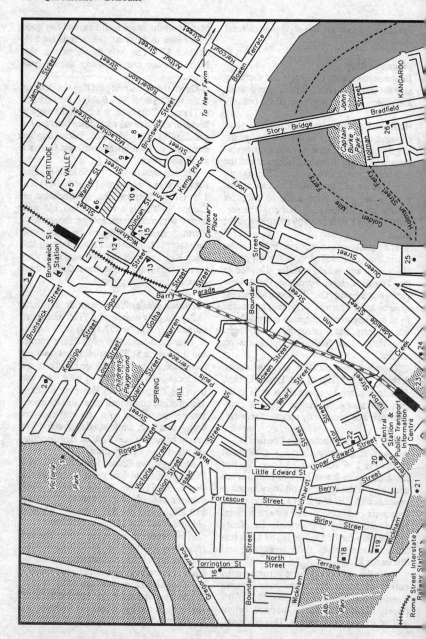

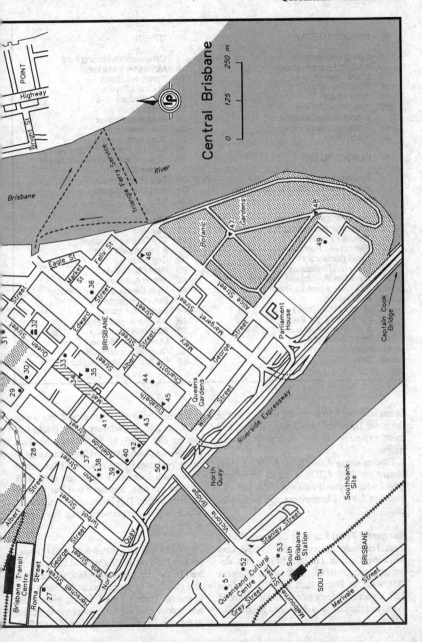

Central Brisbane

0 125 250 m

POINT

Highway

Bright St

Brisbane

River

Triangle Ferry Service

Eagle St

Felix St

Market St

36

BRISBANE

Edward Street

Queen Street

32

30

33

34

35

29

Albert Street

Mall

Adelaide Street

41

40

42

43

44

45

28

Ann Street

37

38

39

50

Albert Street

Turbot Street

Roma Street

George Street

Herschell Street

Tank Street

North Quay

27

Brisbane Transit Centre

Alice Street

Margaret Street

George Street

William Street

Mary Street

Charlotte Street

Elizabeth Street

Botanic Gardens

47

48

49

46

Parliament House

Queens Gardens

Riverside Expressway

Victoria Bridge

North Quay

Captain Cook Bridge

Southbank Site

SOUTH BRISBANE

Stanley Street

Grey Street

Melbourne Street

Merivale Street

South Brisbane Station

Queensland Cultural Centre

5

52

53

■ PLACES TO STAY

2 Spring Hill Terraces
3 Balmoral House Hostel
18 Marrs Town House
19 Soho Club Motel
20 Astor Motel
22 Yale Inner-City Inn
& Annie's Shandon Inn
27 Transcontinental Hotel
35 Hilton Hotel

▼ PLACES TO EAT

4 Shamrock Hotel
5 Home Made Chinese Meal Kitchen
7 Lucky's Trattoria
8 Dooley's Hotel
9 Giardinetto's Restaurant
10 Mayflower Restaurant
11 Chopstix Food Hall
12 Vietnamese Restaurant
13 Seoul Restaurant
14 Enjoy Inn Restaurant
15 Vung Tan Vietnamese Seafood
& Universal Noodle Restaurants
34 McDonald's
41 Jo Jo's Food Centre
45 Bohemian Cafe, Parrots
& Govinda's Restaurant
46 Port Office Hotel
47 Kiosk
48 Cafe

OTHER

1 Centenary Swimming Pool
6 McWhirter's Market
16 Spring Hill Baths
17 St Paul's Tavern
21 Old Windmill
23 Anzac Square
24 Australian Airlines
25 Riverside Centre
26 Story Bridge Hotel
28 National Parks & Wildlife Service
29 Queensland Government Tourist
Centre (QGTC)
30 East-West Airlines
31 Post Office Square
32 GPO
33 RACQ
36 Metro Arts Centre
37 City Hall
38 City Council Transport
& Information Centre
39 City Plaza
40 Hema Bookshop
42 Ansett Airlines
43 Myer Centre & Underground
Bus Interchange
44 Elizabeth Arcade
49 Old Government House
50 Billabong Bookshop
51 Queensland Museum
52 Queensland Art Gallery
53 Performing Arts Complex

Dorm beds are $10 in the old section, $12 in the new. There are also double rooms, and more expensive rooms with private bathroom.

Further along Annie St, at No 95, is *Atoa House* (☎ 358 4507), a small travellers' hostel with singles/doubles for $24, and a $1 discount for YHA members and backpackers.

Kangaroo Point Just over the Story Bridge from Fortitude Valley is the *Backpackers Brisbane Central* (☎ 891 1434), in a de-licensed section of the Story Bridge Hotel at 200 Main St. Dorm beds are $10, doubles $25. It's an easy ferry ride from the centre of town, and the pub next door does good cheap meals.

Further from the centre, and out along Shafston Ave, is *Courtney Place Backpackers* (☎ 891 5166) at 50 Geelong St. This family-run place is housed in a mansion built many years ago by a dentist with 18 children! A bed in a four or six-bed dorm costs $10, doubles are $24, and each bed has its own security locker. This is one of the few hostels which will make pick-ups from the airport, at any hour.

Highgate Hill The *Somewhere to Stay* hostel (☎ 846 2858) at 45 Brighton Rd is among the best in the city. It's a new place with a range and standard of accommodation that's hard to match. There's a pool, a good garden and an outdoor area with excellent views across to the city. Dorm beds range from $10 to $12, the more expensive ones having a TV and fridge. Single rooms cost $21 to $25, while doubles are generally $28 to $30. More expensive doubles with private bathroom cost $45, and the rooms with balconies get the views. The hostel runs a regular bus service to the Transit Centre, or you can get there on bus No 178 from Adelaide St, opposite Anzac Square.

A short distance away is *Durham Villa* (☎ 844 6853) at 17 Laura St. This hostel also has a pool and spacious gardens; dorm beds are $10, and singles/doubles cost $20/25.

Hotels & Motels Some guesthouses and holiday flats are included in this category. Prices may be cheaper on a weekly basis.

City Probably the best known cheap hotel among international travellers is the *Yale Inner-City Inn* (☎ 832 1663), at 413 Upper Edward St. It's a 10-minute uphill walk from the city centre. Singles/doubles are $30/40, including a continental breakfast. It's a modern building, with a laundry and a TV room. All rooms have fans and tea/coffee-making equipment; there are some with private bathrooms.

Annie's Shandon Inn (☎ 831 8684), next door at No 405, is a comfortable small hotel, with singles/doubles for $35/45 including breakfast and free tea/coffee throughout the day. There are a few rooms with private bathroom for $45/55. The hotel has laundry facilities, a TV room and a small car park at the rear.

Another option in the same area is the *Dorchester Holiday Units* (☎ 831 2967) at 484 Upper Edward St. Double rooms with cooking facilities, utensils, and private bathroom cost $48.

Just down the hill, there's a string of motels, some decently priced. The *Astor Motel* (☎ 831 9522), at 193 Wickham Terrace, has air-con singles/doubles at $35/39 with shared bathroom, or $59/69 with private bathroom. Rooms have tea/coffee-making facilities and breakfast is available. A little further along at No 333, the

Soho Club Motel (☎ 831 7722) charges $42/49 for singles/doubles.

Marrs Town House (☎ 831 5388), at 391 Wickham Terrace, is a little more expensive; singles/doubles start at $55/65. The management is helpful, and there are good views, but the rooms facing the road can be noisy.

About 1½ km from King George Square, at 260 Water St, Spring Hill, *Spring Hill Terraces* (☎ 854 1048) is an attractive place built in 1986. It offers self-contained, two-bedroom terraced houses from $49 to $62 for singles or doubles. There are also budget rooms at $37.

Suburbs In New Farm, the *Elizabeth Private Hotel* (☎ 358 1866), at 14 Harcourt St, has singles/doubles with shared bathroom for $32/35, including light breakfast. Just past Breakfast Creek on the way to the airport, the *Kingsford Hall Private Hotel* (☎ 862 1317), at 144 Kingsford Smith Drive, Hamilton (corner of Cooksley St) charges $32/35 for singles/doubles with shared bathroom. It has a guest kitchen.

In Highgate Hill, south of the old Expo site at 180 Gladstone Rd, the *Ambassador Brisbane Motel* (☎ 844 5661) costs $47/52 for rooms with private bathroom.

There are several motels and holiday flats in Kangaroo Point, including *Carmel Lodge Holiday Flats* (☎ 391 6855), at 819 Main St, which has rooms at $45 a double; and *Kangaroo Motel* (☎ 391 1145), at 624 Main St, which has similar prices.

About 13 km north of the city in Aspley, is the *Aspley Motor Inn* (☎ 263 5400), at 1159 Gympie Rd (the Bruce Highway), with singles/doubles from $40/45. Further on, at 1434 Gympie Rd, *Alpha Accommodation Centre Motel* (☎ 263 4011) charges $38/40.

Colleges *International House* (☎ 870 9593) at 5 Rock St, St Lucia, offers B&B for $34/56 during the university vacation periods. Other colleges offer similar deals.

Camping Curious Brisbane City Council regulations forbid tent camping within a 22-km radius of the centre, and there are no caravan sites close to the city either. In any case, many caravan parks are full up with permanent residents. All in all, the camping picture around Brisbane is miserable. It's a much better story south on the Gold Coast or north on the Sunshine Coast. You could try the following:

Aspley Acres Caravan Park (☎ 263 2668), 1420 Gympie Rd, Aspley – 13 km north, no camping but on-site vans for $35
Riviera Caravan Park (☎ 288 3644), 213 Brisbane Terrace, Goodna – 25 km south-west, sites $8 double, on-site vans from $25
Arizona Pines Van Park (☎ 888 1343), Boundary Rd, Kallangur North – 28 km north, sites $8.50, on-site vans $15
Springtime Gardens Caravan Park (☎ 208 8184), corner Pacific Highway & Old Chatswood Rd, Springwood – 24 km south, camping $8 double, on-site vans from $25

Places to Eat

Although Brisbane hasn't got the reputation of Sydney or Melbourne as a city for eating out, there's a fast-growing number of good places, many of them experimenting with local seafood and tropical fruits. More cafes and restaurants stay open past 9 pm, some even 24 hours (but don't expect to eat after 8.30 pm in most pubs), and many places are beginning to take advantage of the balmy climate by providing outdoor eating areas.

City You'll find a bit of everything around the central area. Four of the best city areas are the Queen St Mall, Edward St, the streets south and north of the mall between Charlotte and Adelaide Sts, and at the eastern end of Queen and Elizabeth Sts.

Queen St Mall teems with possibilities. *Jo Jo's*, a large food centre upstairs in the Pavilion shopping centre at 130 Queen St, is very popular. It has a collection of fast-food counters – Greek/Mediterranean, Chinese, European and Middle Eastern. Tables are scattered about and prices are from $6. It's open daily until midnight.

There are more possibilities in the ritzy *Myer Centre*, bounded by Queen St Mall, Albert, Elizabeth and George Sts. The lower level has fast-food outlets with everything from pizza to seafood, all at moderate prices.

Jimmy's on the Mall has three excellent open-air, licensed cafes – one at the Edward St end of the mall (open 24 hours), one in the middle, the other near the Albert St corner. Coffee is expensive but there are plenty of reasonably priced snacks, meals and desserts.

Towards the Edward St end of the mall, on the 2nd level of the Wintergarden shopping complex, the *New Orleans Food Centre* is open from 10 am until 2 am, and until 10.30 pm on Sundays. You can choose from various cuisines. Most meals cost upwards of $10 and often there's live music. On the ground floor of the Wintergarden, near the Elizabeth St entrance, there's another busy food centre with meals for $8 to $10.

Downstairs on Edward St, a couple of doors north of the mall, the *Capri Cafe* is another good lunch spot, open from 9.30 am to 4 pm, Monday to Friday. It has a good selection of home-made healthy meals.

For a good, cheap feed, *Govinda's Restaurant* at 99 Elizabeth St, offers filling vegetarian lunches for $5; it's run by the Hare Krishnas. Almost next door is the *Bohemian Cafe*, an interesting place which has evening poetry readings and live music. Nearby is *Parrots*, a stylish, licensed gourmet burger restaurant, open daily from 11.30 am to 11 pm. McDonald's certainly wouldn't recognise the fare that's dished up in this popular place. The burgers are a substantial meal, cost from $7.50 to $11.50 and come in a variety of forms.

Cafe Cubana, in the Wallace Bishop Arcade at 239 Albert St, is open Monday to Saturday and has good meals in the $12 to $15 range. You can also get a three-course set meal for $19, or for $24, a meal and a Greater Union cinema ticket.

There are a few Chinese places south along Edward St, near the Elizabeth St corner. The busy *Basement Cafe*, at 109 Edward St (downstairs in the Metro Arts building), is open for breakfast, lunch and dinner on weekdays and offers cheap, wholesome food.

A great place for lunch is the *Port Office Hotel* at 38 Edward St, near the Margaret St corner. It's extremely popular with office workers on weekdays and is open from 10 am to 11 pm Monday to Friday (6 pm on Saturdays), and has Sunday lunches to 4 pm. Dishes start from $8, and there's often live jazz on Sunday afternoons.

The City Plaza, on the corner of George and Adelaide Sts, has a handful of restaurants, some with tables outside by the fountain. *Tracks* has pub/bistro lunches for $12 from Monday to Friday, as well as some cheaper specials.

Michael's Bistro, at the eastern end of Elizabeth St in the Riverside Centre, has two sections, one offering French cuisine and seafood; the other – the *Waterfront Cafe* – offering Italian food. The food is expensive but the river view is terrific. There's also a pub and cafes at the Riverside Centre.

Spring Hill The *Spring Hill Hotel*, on the corner of Upper Edward and Leichhardt Sts, has good, cheap pub food and a backyard barbecue. The *Federal Hotel*, close to the same corner at 100 Leichhardt St, and the *Sportsmans*, a little east along Leichhardt St, do simple and cheap pub food.

There are two good restaurants in Spring Hill. The popular *Primavera* (☎ 831 3132), at 500 Boundary St, has probably the best Italian food in town as well as Lebanese food. Pasta and Lebanese dishes are reasonably priced, while other main meals are more expensive (from $15). You usually need to book and it's closed on Sundays. In the same block, *Harold's Posh Cafe*, at 466 Boundary St, has a good gourmet takeaway section, open from 10 am to 10 pm Monday to Saturday. In the restaurant section, meals start at $12.

Fortitude Valley East and uphill from the city centre lies Fortitude Valley, an area with lots of interesting eating spots around Brunswick, Ann and Wickham Sts. The many Chinese restaurants on little Duncan St include the excellent *Enjoy Inn*, on the corner of Wickham St, open daily until midnight.

It's not cheap but its banquet (around $24) is a bargain. Opposite Duncan St at 194 Wickham St, the *Vietnamese Restaurant* serves main meals at $7. The *Seoul Restaurant*, at 146 Wickham St, serves fairly authentic Korean dishes.

Chopstix is a food hall in an arcade between Brunswick and Wickham Sts, and the food is mainly Asian. Most main courses are around $8, but there are lots of cheaper snacks. The deservedly popular *Home Made Chinese Meal Kitchen*, at 257 Wickham St, has excellent food at moderate prices; main meals cost from around $10. It's open for lunch and dinner until 10 pm Monday to Saturday, but only for dinner on Sundays. The *Sala Thai*, at shop 56 in the Valley Plaza Centre on Wickham St, is a good, reasonably priced Thai restaurant with a four-course lunch for $10. It's open Monday to Friday, and nightly for dinner.

Brunswick St itself has more of an Italian flavour. *Cafe Europe*, in the mall (which runs between Ann and Wickham Sts), is a very good place for a coffee and/or breakfast. The popular *Giardinetto's* next door at No 366, is a small, pleasant Italian place, which does pasta dishes from $10. You can eat indoors or outside, and it's open for lunch Tuesday to Friday and dinner Tuesday to Sunday. The buffet dinner for $10 on Sunday nights is very good value.

Around the corner at 683 Ann St, the atmosphere is equally pleasant in *Lucky's Trattoria*, a fine Italian restaurant where two people can eat for around $40. It's only open in the evenings.

New Farm Continuing down Brunswick St from Fortitude Valley you hit New Farm with good eating possibilities near the backpackers' hostels. The *Brunswick Hotel* on the corner of Brunswick and Kent Sts, has good, cheap counter meals, and special entertainment nights for backpackers.

A bit further down Brunswick St at No 630, the *Baan Thai* is a reasonably priced Thai restaurant. Main meals are $12 – less for takeaway. It's open Tuesday to Sunday from 6 to 10 pm. *Jonny's Pizza Parlour*, at

669 Brunswick St, is a cheerful place, open nightly, with cheap pizzas and pasta. *Cafe Lunar*, at 681 Brunswick St, is a good place for a quiet coffee. The popular *Cafe Le Mer*, at 878 Brunswick St, offers 'gourmet' fish, chips and salad for around $12.

Breakfast Creek Breakfast Creek is about four km north-east of the city centre, just past Newstead House; bus Nos 160, 180 or 190 will get you there.

Breakfast Creek Wharf is right beside the creek at 190 Breakfast Creek Rd. The wharf building has an expensive but very good seafood restaurant plus an excellent cheaper takeaway section. There is also an Indian restaurant, plus *Ned Kelly's Australian Restaurant*.

The nearby *Breakfast Creek Hotel*, a great rambling building dating from 1899, at 2 Kingsford Smith Drive, is a real Brisbane institution. It's long been a Labor Party and trade union hang-out. In the public bar, the beer is still drawn from a wooden keg. The pub's *Spanish Garden Steak House* is renowned for its steaks.

Morningside In the eastern suburbs, Morningside has one of Brisbane's best Indian restaurants – *Scherhazade* – at 668 Wynnum Rd. It has main course curries at around $15, and is closed on Mondays.

Paddington West of the city centre, this is becoming a trendy area with lots of places to eat.

On Given Terrace, you can't miss the *Paddington Tavern*. It's a large pub with indoor and outdoor eating areas. Bistro-style meals, steaks and seafood are served daily, except on Sundays. *Masakan Indonesia* is an excellent, reasonably priced Indonesian restaurant at 215 Given Terrace. Rice and noodle dishes cost from $8, and seafood and meat dishes start at $14.

The *Sultan's Kitchen* (☎ 368 2194), at 163 Given Terrace, is an excellent Indian restaurant with great curries and a Sunday smorgasbord. It's open for lunch and dinner

daily except for Saturday lunch time, but it's pretty popular, so book on weekends.

The trendy *Caxton St Brasserie*, at 111 Caxton St, is a very popular nightspot. It's open nightly from 6 pm until late, and serves reasonably priced snacks and meals.

On the corner of Caxton St and Petrie Terrace, *Paddington Barracks Hotel* has cheap pasta meals for $5 or so. *Gambaros Seafood Takeaway*, on Caxton St near Petrie Terrace, does excellent fish & chips, and has more exotic seafood as well, with exotic prices to match. Right opposite the Paddington Barracks is the atmospheric *Michel Bonet*, an up-market French restaurant where main dishes start at around $20.

West End A couple of km south-west of the city centre and across the river is West End, where there are a number of restaurants. *Kim Thanh*, at 93 Hardgrave Rd, is a popular Chinese/Vietnamese place. It's open daily, and the menu is long and varied, with main meals from around $10. *Qan Heng's*, at 151 Boundary St (parallel to Hardgrave St), has similar food and prices, and is very busy.

Enzo's Place, at 70 Boundary St, is a good Italian spot with reasonably priced pasta, pizza, meat and seafood. It's open nightly for dinner and from Tuesday to Friday for lunches. The *Lounge Lizard Cafe*, at 69 Boundary St, is an offbeat place in the West End markets. It's open daily from 10 am until 11 or 12 at night, except for Sundays when it's only open in the evening. The menu is international, with main dishes around $10 to $15, and on weekends there's a cabaret.

Back towards the city centre, on the corner of Melbourne and Edmondstone Sts, South Brisbane, *Squirrels* is a good vegetarian restaurant open daily for lunch and dinner. From the buffet, a small plateful is $9, a large one $10 – or you can order from the menu with main dishes for around $11.

Toowong/St Lucia There are lots of possibilities in these suburbs near the university. *Pasta Pasta*, at 242 Hawken Drive, offers what its name suggests, and is cheap. A small serve is $5, a large $8. This is another popular place with students, open daily from 8 am to midnight.

Entertainment

Brisbane pubs generally stay open until 11 pm or midnight, particularly on Friday nights. Many pubs feature live music and there are several nightclubs. For a list of what's on, see the weekend papers, or the giveaway entertainment paper *Time Off*.

Pubs & Live Music

The Metro in the Treasury Hotel on the corner of George and Elizabeth Sts, is open Friday and Saturday nights until late. Tracks, in the City Plaza Tavern on the corner of George and Adelaide Sts, has a couple of bars with live bands as well as its very popular disco/nightclub. It's open nightly until late, and there's a cover charge.

For live rock, the Brisbane Tavern, on the corner of Ann and Wharf Sts, is good on Wednesday, Friday and Sunday nights. On some nights the Club Afro-Carib hosts bands here. Or try the Queen Ann Hotel, on the corner of Queen and Ann Sts on a Friday or Saturday night. The Port Office Hotel, on the corner of Edward and Margaret Sts, has bands on Wednesday and Friday nights, jazz and blues on Saturday and Sunday.

A short walk from the city centre, the Jubilee Hotel on St Paul's Terrace, Spring Hill, has musicians on Friday nights, Saturday and Sunday afternoons, and rock bands on Sunday nights. It has a 'dance bar' from Wednesday to Saturday nights, open until late. Also in Spring Hill, St Paul's Tavern, on the corner of Leichhardt and Wharf Sts, has live rock on Friday night, Saturday afternoon and Sunday night.

In Fortitude Valley, Bonaparte's Hotel, on the corner of Gipps St and St Paul's Terrace, has rock bands from Thursday to Saturday, 8 pm until 1 am. The Outpost, on the corner of Ann and Warner Sts, calls itself an alternative spot and hosts several bands nightly. You can get discounted drinks here. The Beat Nightclub is a punky, trendy place with live bands, near the Outpost.

Further down Brunswick St in New Farm,

the Brunswick Hotel has weekly entertainment nights for backpackers (with competitions and prizes), and live music on other nights. On the far edge of Fortitude Valley, at the corner of Ann and Commercial Sts, the Waterloo Hotel brews its own beer and offers free transport to backpackers staying in the area.

Over at Kangaroo Point, the Story Bridge Hotel (☎ 391 2266), at 200 Main St, is very popular, with live music most nights and jazz on Sunday afternoons. On Sunday nights there are informal gatherings with perhaps a jam session or poetry reading. Also in this area is the Pineapple Hotel, at 706 Main St, with bands every night. The Brisbane Jazz Club, at 1 Annie St, Kangaroo Point, has shows on weekends.

In Paddington, the Caxton Hotel on Caxton St has free jazz on Saturday afternoons and more live music at other times. The Paddington Tavern, on Given Terrace, is good for live music on a Thursday night.

Two popular places for a beer in Toowong near the University of Queensland are the Regatta, on the corner of Coronation Drive and Sylvan Rd, and the Royal Exchange.

Discos & Nightclubs

Brisbane's most popular nightclub, the Brisbane Underground, is over in Paddington, on the corner of Caxton and Hale Sts. Others are mainly in the city centre. The Move, in the Majestic Hotel at 382 George St, is a dance spot with recorded music and a $6 cover charge; it's open Friday and Saturday nights until 3 am. Most other nightclubs are open similar hours (Wednesday to Saturday nights until late, Sunday night until midnight). They include the Court Jester in the Criterion Tavern, which is in the MLC building on the corner of George and Adelaide Sts; Reflections in the Sheraton Hotel at 249 Turbot St; and the City Gardens Point Club at the Queensland Institute of Technology on George St.

Culture

Saturday's *Courier Mail* is good for information about what's on where.

The Performing Arts Complex in the Queensland Cultural Centre in South Brisbane, has a constant flow of events in its three venues, including concerts, plays, dance performances and film screenings. Concerts featuring classical music, ethnic music and jazz are held on Sunday afternoons. The Brisbane Arts Theatre, at 210 Petrie Terrace, has some interesting productions.

For alternative/offbeat cinema, you have three choices: the Schonell (☎ 371 1879), at the University of Queensland in St Lucia; the Classic (☎ 393 1066), at 963 Stanley St, East Brisbane; and the Metro Arts Cinema (☎ 221 8361), at 109 Edward St. Metro Arts has an 'alternative' theatre/dance centre and a South American arts & crafts gallery. It's a good spot for information on what's on around the city in the way of poetry readings, art exhibitions, Indian dance performances, belly-dancing lessons and even more esoteric stuff.

Sport You can see interstate cricket matches and international test cricket at the Brisbane Cricket Ground (the Gabba) in Woolloongabba, just south of Kangaroo Point. The cricket season runs between October and March.

During the other half of the year, rugby league is the big spectator sport. Local heroes Brisbane Broncos play their home games at Lang Park. Brisbane also has an Australian Rules football club, the Brisbane Bears, although their home base is Carrara on the Gold Coast. Like every other town and city in Australia, Brisbane has horse racing; the major tracks are at Doomben and Eagle Farm.

Things to Buy

The Caxton St Market is held Saturday morning in Paddington, about two km west of the city centre. Also on Saturday, from 10 am to 3 pm, the Spring Hill Village Market is just a few minutes from the city centre. Both markets are popular meeting places. Paddy's Markets on the corner of Florence and Commercial Rds, New Farm, are open daily from 9 am to 3 pm, with a huge variety of goods. At weekends, there's an extra flea market here.

Also on Saturdays, the Fortitude Valley Market is held in the Brunswick St Mall.

On Sundays, the Riverside Centre Market has 150 stalls, including glass blowing, weaving, leather work and children's activities. Also on Sunday, the Closeburn Country Market, 26 km out of town, is a similar arts & crafts affair and makes a good day's outing.

Getting There & Away

Arriving in and leaving Brisbane has been simplified by the Transit Centre on Roma St, about half a km west of the central King George Square. The Transit Centre is the main terminus and booking point for all long-distance buses and trains, as well as the airport bus. The centre has shops, banks, a post office, and plenty of places to eat and drink. There's also a foreign exchange counter, open from 6 am to 9 pm daily, at the Skennars bus desk on level 3, and a tourist information office on level 2. Left-luggage lockers are on level 3: they cost $1 but you have to remove your gear by 9 pm each day.

Air There are numerous Ansett and Australian Airlines flights from the southern capitals and north to the main Queensland centres like Rockhampton, Mackay, Townsville and Cairns. East-West flies from Sydney and Cairns. Air NSW flies daily from Sydney. Both Ansett and Australian have direct flights every week to Mt Isa and Darwin.

One-way fares include Sydney $232 ($155 stand-by), Melbourne $341 ($273 stand-by), and Adelaide $399 direct (more expensive via Sydney or Melbourne; $320 stand-by).

There are numerous connections by smaller airlines with smaller centres. East-West, Air NSW and Oxley Airlines link Brisbane with a string of places on the New South Wales north coast and New England. Sunstate, Sungold and Lloyd Air between them serve south-east Queensland as far north as Townsville and inland as far as Toowoomba and Emerald. The little outback airline Flight West goes to Roma ($160),

Charleville ($213), Quilpie, Blackall, Barcaldine, Longreach ($286), Winton, Cloncurry ($351), Mt Isa ($370), and to Windorah and Birdsville ($370).

Brisbane is also a busy international arrival and departure point with frequent flights to Asia, Europe, the Pacific islands, North America, New Zealand and Papua New Guinea.

Airline offices include: Australian and Sunstate (☎ 260 3311); Ansett, Sungold and Air NSW (☎ 854 2828); Qantas (☎ 833 3747); East-West (☎ 221 8444); and Flight West (☎ 252 1152).

Bus Numerous bus companies run between Sydney and Brisbane and up the Queensland coast to Cairns. Sydney to Brisbane via the Pacific Highway, takes 15 or 16 hours and costs around $65.

Companies operating the Pacific Highway route, with their Brisbane telephone numbers, are: Greyhound (☎ 844 3300); Bus Australia (☎ 236 1033); Kirklands (☎ 236 4444); McCafferty's (☎ 236 3033); Pioneer (☎ 846 3633); Border Coaches (☎ 236 2800); and Skennars (☎ 236 3013). All the lines have booking offices at the Brisbane Transit Centre.

Bus Australia, Greyhound/Pioneer and McCafferty's also run between Sydney and Brisbane by the inland New England Highway which takes an hour or two longer. The usual fare is around $68, but Border Coaches does it for $50 for YHA members and backpackers.

Between Brisbane and Melbourne, the most direct route is the Newell Highway which takes 20 to 23 hours. McCafferty's, Bus Australia, and Greyhound/Pioneer all follow this route daily. The fare between Brisbane and Melbourne is around $115, although again, Border Coaches does it for $85 one-way.

Between Adelaide and Brisbane, the trip takes around 29 hours and is covered by Bus Australia and Greyhound/Pioneer. The fare is around $170.

North to Cairns, Greyhound/Pioneer, Bus Australia and McCafferty's run about nine

buses a day. Ask about stopovers – different lines offer different deals. The fares and journey times to places up the coast are as follows:

Destination	Time	Cost
Noosa Heads	3 hours	$25
Hervey Bay	4 hours	$31
Rockhampton	9 hours	$63
Mackay	13 hours	$90
Townsville	19 hours	$118
Cairns	24 hours	$139

To get to Longreach, Mt Isa and the Northern Territory, McCafferty's and Greyhound both operate daily services between Brisbane and Mt Isa (24 hours, $135), via Longreach (17 hours, $85).

Train – interstate You can reach Brisbane by rail from Sydney and continue north to Cairns or inland to Roma and Charleville. The daily XPT takes 14 hours between Sydney and Brisbane. Fares are $130 in 1st class, $90 in economy; there are no sleepers in either class on this train. A Caper (Customer Advance Purchase Excursion Rail) ticket, which you have to buy at least seven days in advance, cuts about 30% off the price. You can, as on all major interstate trains, break the journey anywhere provided you arrange it in advance and complete the journey within two months (with a one-way ticket) or six months (return ticket).

Train – within Queensland North from Brisbane, the Spirit of Capricorn runs the 639 km to Rockhampton daily (9½ hours; $94.20 1st class, $58.90 2nd class). The Capricornian covers the same route three times a week, but travels through the night. Sleepers cost an extra $40 in 1st class, $25 in 2nd.

The Sunlander departs three days a week for the 1631-km journey to Cairns (33 hours; $193.50 1st class, $126.70 2nd class), via Rockhampton, Mackay (18 hours; $156.20/ 101.70), and Townsville (26 hours; $179/ 117). The fares include sleeping berths in both classes.

On Sundays only, a motorail service (the

Queenslander) runs to Cairns. Passengers travelling 1st class have a special bar and also get sleeping berths and all meals included in their fare, which is nearly twice the usual 1st-class fare. You can travel economy on the Queenslander but there are no economy-class sleepers. To Mackay, the 1st class/economy fares are $254.70/88.10; to Townsville $300.60/104.40, and to Cairns $342.10/114.70.

The Westlander runs on the inland route to Roma, Charleville and Cunnamulla twice a week.

Main-line departures in Brisbane are from the Brisbane Transit Centre. For reservations, telephone Queensland Rail (☎ 235 1122) or call into its office at 208 Adelaide St next to Anzac Square.

Getting Around

The best place for bus information is the City Council Transport Information Centre (☎ 225 4444) in the Brisbane Administration Centre at 69 Ann St; it's open Monday to Friday from 8.15 am to 5.45 pm. The Public Transport Information Centre (☎ 225 0211) in Central Station covers local trains, ferries and buses. It's open Monday to Friday from 8.15 am to 5 pm. There's also a ferry information service (☎ 399 4768).

To/From the Airport Brisbane's Eagle Farm Airport is north-east of the centre, near the coast. The international terminal is about nine km by road from the domestic terminal. Coachtrans (☎ 236 1730) runs a shuttle bus from the Transit Centre to both terminals and back, every half hour from 5 am to 11 pm. The buses will also stop at various points in the city centre and Fortitude Valley. The fare is $6. There are also a few daily direct buses between the airport and the Gold and Sunshine coasts.

A taxi to the centre costs about $9.50 from the international terminal, $13 from the domestic. Avis, Budget, Hertz and Thrifty have car rental desks at the airport.

Bus In addition to the normal city buses, there are Cityxpress services which run between the suburbs and centre, and Rockets which are fast peak-hour commuter buses. From the Transit Centre, you need to walk into the city centre to pick up some buses. Most above-ground bus stops in the city are colour coded to help you find the right one. The underground bus station beneath the Myer Centre is used mainly by Cityxpresses and buses to/from the south of the city. There is a map of the station, above ground in the mall on the corner of Queen and Albert Sts.

In the area between Wharf St and the Queensland Cultural Centre, buses cost just 45c a trip. Other fares are on a zone system costing 90c, $1.30 or $1.80 for zones 1, 2 or 3 respectively, or $2.20 for a journey across all three zones. Special deals include the unlimited travel Day Rover ($5.50 from a bus driver, $5 from newsagents or shops with a yellow 'fare deal' sign in their window). The RoverLink is a one-day ticket providing unlimited travel on any buses or trains for $7.50.

Buses run every 10 to 20 minutes Monday to Friday till about 6 pm, and on Saturday mornings. Services are less frequent on weekday evenings, Saturday afternoons and evenings, and Sundays. On Sundays, buses stop at 7 pm, and on other days at 11 pm. City Circle bus No 333 does a clockwise loop round the area along George, Adelaide, Wharf, Eagle and Mary Sts every five minutes until 5.45 pm Monday to Friday.

Useful buses from the city centre include Nos 177 or 178 to Fortitude Valley and New Farm (from the brown stops on Adelaide St between King George Square and Edward St). Bardon bus No 144 to Paddington leaves from the red stops opposite the Transit Centre or from outside the Coles store on Adelaide St.

Bus Nos 160, 180 or 190 to Fortitude Valley, Newstead House and Breakfast Creek leave from the yellow stops on Edward St between Adelaide and Queen Sts. Bus No 177 to West End leaves from the brown stop on Edward St, opposite Anzac Square.

Bayside Buslines (☎ 893 1047) runs between Brisbane and the southern Bayside

(Capalaba Park, Wellington Point, Cleveland, Koala Park and Redland Bay). Hornibrook Bus Lines (☎ 284 1622) runs between Brisbane and the northern Bayside (Sandgate, Clontarf, Redcliffe and Scarborough).

Train The fast Citytrain network has seven lines, out to Ipswich, Beenleigh and Cleveland in the south and Pinkenba, Shorncliffe, Caboolture and Ferny Grove in the north. You can buy Day Rover tickets ($8) a day ahead, from any station. These give you unlimited train travel for one day (after 9 am on weekdays).

All trains go through Roma St, Central and Brunswick St stations, and a journey in the city central area is 90c.

Car The big firms have offices in Brisbane and there are a number of smaller operators, including Cut Rate Rentals (☎ 350 2081), AA Bargain Inedell Car Rentals (☎ 350 2353), Betta (☎ 221 7787), Crown Rent A Car (☎ 854 1848), Low Price Hire Cars (☎ 393 1657), Roadway Rent a Car (☎ 868 1500) and Half-Price (☎ 229 3544). Half-Price does one-way rentals to Cairns and southern capitals: two days to Cairns costs between $160 and $240, depending on the season.

You can hire 4WDs from Brisbane 4WD Hire (☎ 269 4869) at 139 Connaught St, Sandgate, for $55 a day and upwards, including insurance. Low Price Hire Cars also has 4WDs.

Bicycle A good way to spend a day is to ride the riverside bicycle track from the city Botanic Gardens out to Queensland University. It's about seven km one-way: you can stop for a beer at the Regatta pub in Toowong, use the cheap swimming pool or hire a tennis court at the university, and have a meal in one of the reasonably priced eateries in Toowong on the way back.

At 50 Albert St, Brisbane Bicycle Sales (☎ 229 2433) is open seven days a week and charges $6 per hour or $15 for eight-hour hire.

Boat Brisbane makes good use of its river and there are cruises as well as the regular ferries. Cross-river ferries cost 80c one-way and generally run every 15 minutes until after 11 pm Monday to Saturday; there are shorter hours on Sunday. You can take a bicycle on the ferry for 50c.

The most central routes are: the Holman St Ferry, from the Riverside Centre to Holman St on the tip of Kangaroo Point; and the Triangle Ferry Service, which travels in a loop from Edward St to the Waterfront Place at the end of Charlotte St in the city and across to Thornton St on Kangaroo Point; and the Dockside Ferry, which runs from the Riverside Centre around to Dockside on the south-east side of Kangaroo Point.

One interesting trip is the Brisbane City Ferries cruise from Edward St (corner of the Botanic Gardens) to Newstead House and the university (3½ hours, $8). It leaves at 1 pm on Saturdays and Sundays and in school holidays. On some days, the ferry stops to let you look around the Queensland Cultural Centre, or Newstead House. It's advisable to book (☎ 399 4768).

You can take more expensive trips on the *Kookaburra Queen* and *Kookaburra Queen II* paddle steamers from the Waterfront Place, or with Brisbane Paddlewheeler Cruises (jazz and disco cruises), or Adai Cruises ('rage on the river' night cruises from Breakfast Creek).

Moreton Bay

Moreton Bay, at the mouth of the Brisbane River, is said to have 365 islands. The larger islands shelter a long stretch of coast: South Stradbroke Island is only just north of the Gold Coast, while Bribie Island is only just south of the Sunshine Coast. In between are North Stradbroke and Moreton islands.

THE BAYSIDE
Redcliffe, 35 km north of Brisbane, was the first White settlement in Queensland. The Aborigines called the place Humpybong or

'Dead Houses' and the name is still applied to the peninsula. Redcliffe is now an outer suburb of Brisbane and a popular retirement place. South of Redcliffe, **Sandgate** is another long-running seaside resort, now more of an outer suburb.

Coastal towns south of the Brisbane River mouth include **Wynnum, Ormiston, Cleveland** and **Redland Bay**. Cleveland is the main access point for North Stradbroke Island. The Redland Bay area is a fertile market garden for Brisbane and a Strawberry Festival is held on the first weekend in September. There's an 1864 lighthouse at Cleveland Point and the 1853 Cleveland Courthouse is now a restaurant.

Ormiston House in Wellington St, Ormiston, is a very fine home built in 1862 and open for inspection Sunday afternoons between March and November. The first commercially grown sugar cane in Queensland came from this site. Whepstead on Main Rd, Wellington Point, is another early home, built in 1874. It's now also a restaurant.

STRADBROKE ISLAND

Until 1896, the two Stradbroke islands were one but in that year a storm cut the sand spit joining the two at Jumpinpin. Today, South Stradbroke is virtually uninhabited but it's a popular day trip from the Gold Coast.

North Stradbroke is a larger island with a permanent population, and although a popular escape from Brisbane is still relatively unspoilt. 'Straddie' is a sand island, and despite the sand-mining operations in the south, there's plenty of vegetation and beautiful scenery in the north. There are three budget-priced hostels and several camping grounds.

In 1828, Dunwich was established on the west coast of the island as a quarantine station for immigrants but in 1850 a ship brought cholera and the cemetery tells the sad story of the 28 victims of the outbreak that followed. Dunwich, Amity Point and Point Lookout, the three small centres on the island, are all in the north and connected by paved roads. Most of the southern part of the island is closed to visitors due to ongoing

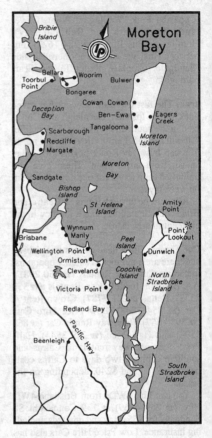

sand mining; the only road into this swampier, more remote area is a private mining company road.

Straddie has plenty of lovely beaches, good surfing, some bays and inlets around Point Lookout, lots of wildlife and good bushwalking around Blue Lake, Brown Lake and Eighteen Mile Swamp. On the ocean side you may even spot a humpback whale or two on their northward migration to the Great Barrier Reef where they breed during the winter months. Dolphins and porpoises are common.

Activities

Apart from beach activities, there's the island to explore. Sealed roads only run between the three centres in the north and across from Dunwich to Blue Lake; in any case you have to walk the last 2.7 km to the lake. You can swim in the freshwater **Blue Lake** or nearby **Tortoise Lagoon**, or walk along the track and watch for snakes, goannas, golden wallabies and birds.

If you're staying at one of the Point Lookout hostels, you may be able to join a tour to investigate some of the island. Otherwise, you could walk from Point Lookout down the beach then 2½ km inland to Blue Lake – 11 km one-way in all. If this sounds too much, catch the local bus to Dunwich and then hitch or walk the eight km to Blue Lake. **Brown Lake**, about three km along the Blue Lake road from Dunwich, also offers deep freshwater swimming, and is more easily accessible.

If you want to hike the 15 to 20 km across the island from Dunwich to Point Lookout, a number of dirt track loops break the monotony of the bitumen road. A pleasant diversion is to **Myora Springs**, surrounded by lush vegetation and walking tracks, near the coast about four km north of Dunwich.

Places to Stay

Dunwich, Amity Point and Point Lookout have caravan parks, all with tent sites. Foreshore camping at $2 per person is allowed at designated areas on the east and north coasts, but you can't camp in the Blue Lake National Park. Both Dunwich and Amity Point have a general store but no pub, restaurant or supermarket.

At Point Lookout, the *Stradbroke Island Carapark* (☎ (07) 409 8127) has fully self-contained cabins at $38 a double, and some on-site vans for $22.

Point Lookout also has places offering share accommodation. Follow the main road around the corner from the Stradbroke Hotel (the only pub on the island) to the first of these. On the left, perched on a hill, is *Point Lookout Backpackers Hostel* (☎ (07) 409 8279). At $11 a night, with space for 32, it has good self-contained dorms. Tea and coffee are free. Tours of the island and fishing/boat trips are offered. If you call from Dunwich, someone from the hostel may come and pick you up.

A little further up the road on the right-hand side, the *Headland Chalet* (☎ (07) 409 8252) is an old guesthouse, with motel-style rooms, overlooking beautiful Main Beach. These have a fridge, tea and coffee-making gear, a maximum of four beds and cost $12.50 per person, or $30 a double. There's a pool, a games and TV room, free washing machines and a small kitchen plus a budget-priced restaurant with a fantastic view.

Downhill to the left is *Samarinda Holiday Village* (☎ (07) 409 8213) with shared cabin accommodation from $11 per night, and singles/doubles at $24. There's a licensed restaurant, TV room and laundry. Some of the cabins are self-contained and all have tea-making facilities.

Places to Eat

At Point Lookout, the *Stradbroke Hotel* has meals (the Sunday smorgasbord is especially good), a great beer garden with an ocean outlook, and a two-metre pet carpet snake. *Samarinda Holiday Village* has cheap meals, and on Thursdays a party night with live music and a three-course meal for $18. The *Headland Chalet* specialises in local seafood at budget prices.

The general stores in each of the three centres have some supplies and a few takeaways. If you're fixing your own meals bring basic supplies and alcohol as the mark-up on the island is significant.

Getting There & Around

Cleveland, on the southern Bayside, is the departure point from the mainland and there are numerous ways of getting from central Brisbane to the island: a train or bus and water taxi or ferry; a through-bus; your own vehicle; or a hostel tour from Brisbane.

Cheapest is the Southern Cross Bus Company (☎ (07) 376 3791) which runs a daily return service direct between Brisbane and the island. Buses leave from stop 1 outside the Transit Centre, calling at 190 Ann St about 10 minutes later. The return fare is $16, including the ferry, and the bus stops at all three centres on North Stradbroke. Although the ferry trip takes an hour, the advantage of this service is that you stay on the bus from start to finish – a total of about 2½ hours from the city to Point Lookout.

If you're going independently, note that the last water taxis and ferries leave Cleveland at 6.30 pm most days. Trains leave Brisbane for Cleveland about every half hour from 5 am. The journey takes about an hour. Bayside Buslines (☎ (07) 396 8055) runs a weekday and Saturday morning 45-minute service between Brisbane and Cleveland on the Bayside Bullet (Nos 621 and 622), as well as a regular service (Nos 600, 611, 615, 625) which takes about an hour ($2.90). Both depart about every half hour (less frequently at weekends) from Elizabeth St in central Brisbane.

In Cleveland, the buses stop at the railway station, a km or so from the water taxi and ferry terminals. There's a free bus service between the station and terminals; buses leave about 15 minutes before water taxis are due to depart for Straddie. Two water-taxi companies operate between Cleveland and Dunwich – the *Spirit of Stradbroke* (☎ (07) 286 2666) and the *Stradbroke Flyer* (☎ (07) 286 1964). The *Spirit* charges $8 return and the *Flyer* $9. The water-taxi trip takes 20 minutes and, with both companies, you get a dollar or so discount on a return ticket. Water taxis depart hourly from 6 am to 6 pm every day, with a break from noon to 2 pm.

Stradbroke Ferries (☎ (07) 286 2666) run the vehicle ferry from Cleveland to Dunwich about 12 times a day, less often on Saturdays. It costs $56 return for a vehicle plus passengers, and $6 return for pedestrians. Last departures from Cleveland are normally at 6 pm but there are late ferries at 7.15 and 8 pm on Friday.

Green's Bus Service (☎ (07) 409 9228) plies between the three centres on the island and meets most water taxis and ferries. If you get stuck at Dunwich, you can hitch or call Stradbroke Taxi Service (☎ (07) 409 9124).

It's roughly 20 km from Dunwich to Point Lookout. It's possible to rent a 4WD vehicle on the island for around $65 per day. Ask at the hostels.

MORETON ISLAND (population 200)

North of Stradbroke, Moreton Island is less visited and still almost a wilderness. Apart from a few rocky headlands, it's all sand, with Mt Tempest, towering to 280 metres, probably the highest sand hill in the world. It's a strange landscape, alternating between bare sand, forest, lakes and swamps, with a 30-km surf beach along the eastern side. The island's bird life is prolific, and at its northern tip is a **lighthouse**, built in 1857. Sand mining on the island is being phased out and 89% of the island is now a national park. There are several wrecks off the west coast.

Moreton Island has no paved roads but 4WD vehicles can travel along beaches and a few cross-island tracks – seek local advice about tides and creek crossings. The National Parks & Wildlife Service publishes a map of the island, which you can get on the ferry, or from the national parks office at False Patch Wrecks.

Tangalooma, halfway down the western side of the island, is a popular tourist resort sited at an old whaling station. The only other settlements, all on the west coast, are **Bulwer** near the north-west tip, **Cowan Cowan** between Bulwer and Tangalooma, and **Kooringal** near the southern tip. The shops at Kooringal and Bulwer are expensive, so bring what you can from the mainland. For a bit of shark spotting, go to the Tangalooma Resort at 5 pm, when resort staff dump garbage off the end of the jetty.

Without your own vehicle, walking is the only way to get around, and you'll need several days to explore the island. There are some trails around the resort area and it's about 14 km from Tangalooma or the Ben-Ewa camp ground on the west side to Eagers Creek camp ground on the east, then seven km up the beach to Blue Lagoon and a further six to Cape Moreton at the north-eastern tip.

Mt Tempest is about three km inland from

Eagers Creek. A similar distance south and inland from Tangalooma is an area of bare sand known as the **Desert**, while the **Big Sandhills** and the **Little Sandhills** are towards the narrow southern end of the island. The biggest lakes and some swamps are in the north-east, and the west coast from Cowan Cowan past Bulwer is also swampy.

Places to Stay

A twin room at the *Tangalooma Resort* (☎ (07) 268 6333) costs from $90 per night.

National park camping sites, with water, toilets and cold showers are at Ben-Ewa and False Patch Wrecks, both between Cowan Cowan and Tangalooma, and at Eagers Creek and Blue Lagoon on the northern half of the ocean coast. Camping is allowed behind coastal dunes in many places. For information and camping permits, contact the National Parks & Wildlife Service (☎ (07) 227 8185) at 160 Ann St in Brisbane, or the ranger at False Patch Wrecks (☎ (07) 408 2710). It's also possible to pitch a tent under the trees by the beach at Reeders Point. There are a few holiday flats or houses for rent at Kooringal, Cowan Cowan or Bulwer.

Getting There & Away

The *Tangalooma Flyer* (☎ (07) 268 6333) a fast catamaran operated by the resort, leaves from Brisbane every day except Thursday. You can use it for a day trip to the island or as a ferry if you're going to camp. A day trip from Brisbane, including barbecue lunch, costs $42; for any trip, it's advisable to book a day in advance. In Brisbane, the dock is at Holt St, off Kingsford Smith Drive in Eagle Farm.

The *Moreton Venture* (☎ (07) 895 1000) is a vehicle ferry which runs four days a week to Tangalooma or to Reeders Point at the southern tip of the island. The ferry leaves from Whyte Island, which is joined to the mainland by road, at the southern side of the Brisbane River mouth. You can take your own 4WD across or, for $20, take the ferry trip there and back plus a 4WD tour to places

of interest on the island. You get back to the mainland at 4 pm.

Other ferries include the *Combie Trader* (☎ (07) 203 6399), with daily services between Scarborough and Bulwer (except Tuesday). Fares are $45 one-way ($75 return) for an average vehicle with a driver and three passengers, and $15 one-way ($20 return) for pedestrians. The ferry also does day trips on Wednesday and Sunday for $18.

Bribie-Moreton Ferry Services (☎ (07) 888 2209) runs a daily ferry to Bulwer and Cowan Cowan from near Spinnaker Sound, Bribie Island. Bribie Island Barge Services (☎ (07) 408 1499) go to Bulwer from Toorbul Point, Bribie Island. Ferry crossings take 1½ to two hours, and it's advisable to book.

ST HELENA ISLAND

Just six km from the mouth of the Brisbane River, little St Helena Island used to be a high-security prison from 1867 to 1932. There are remains of several prison buildings on the island, plus the first passenger tramway in Brisbane which, when built in 1884, had horse-drawn cars. Sandy beaches and mangroves alternate around the island's coast.

Several outfits run day trips to St Helena, including guided tours on the island. Adai Cruises (☎ (07) 262 6978) leaves from the BP Marina on Kingsford Smith Drive, Breakfast Creek, at 9 am on Saturdays and Sundays, returning at 5 pm. The $25 price includes lunch, but it costs an extra $3 to get onto the island. St Helena Ferries (☎ (07) 393 3726) leaves from Manly Harbour, opposite Cardigan Parade, on the south Bayside ($15). You can reach Manly from central Brisbane in about 35 minutes by train.

OTHER ISLANDS
Bishop Island

Tiny Bishop Island, almost in the river mouth, has a series of hulks along its beaches to combat erosion. It has a tavern, swimming pool, picnic/barbecue areas and some cabin accommodation. There's a small mangrove swamp with some bird life. Yulara Marine Tours (☎ (07) 283 4334) runs a ferry service to Bishop Island from the Brisbane Riverside Centre on Wednesdays, Fridays and Sundays; the fare is $12.

Coochie Island

Coochie Island is a 10-minute ferry ride from Victoria Point on the southern Bayside. It's a popular outing from the mainland, with good beaches, but more built-up than most other Moreton Bay islands you can visit. You can rent bicycles, boats, catamarans and surf skis on the island. The ferry runs continuously from 8 am to 5.30 or 6 pm on weekends and holidays, less often on other days.

Russell Island

Russell Island, between the southern end of North Stradbroke and the mainland, is also inhabited. It's about seven km long. The interesting Green Dragon Museum is in the north-west of the island. St Helena Ferries (☎ (07) 393 3726) runs cruises to Russell Island from Manly Harbour on the southern Bayside. There's a ferry service (☎ (07) 286 2666) from the Banana St ramp in Redland Bay, which does a loop around Russell and nearby **Lamb**, **Macleay** and **Karragarra** islands three or four times a day.

Bribie Island

Bribie Island, at the northern end of Moreton Bay, is 31 km long but apart from the southern end, where there are a couple of small towns, the island is largely untouched. There's a bridge across Pumicestone Passage from the mainland to Bellara on the south-west coast. Bongaree, just south of Bellara, is the main town. Buses run there from Caboolture and Brisbane. There's good surfing on the ocean side and a calm channel towards the mainland. Bongaree and Bellara, and Woorim on the south-east coast, have a few motels and holiday flats from about $50 a double, and there are some restaurants too.

Gold Coast

Population 235,000

The Gold Coast is a 35-km strip of beaches running north from the New South Wales-Queensland border. It's the most thoroughly commercialised resort in Australia and is virtually one continuous development culminating in the high-rise splendour of Surfers Paradise.

This coast has been a holiday spot since the 1880s but only after WW II did developers start taking serious notice of Surfers. More than two million visitors a year come to the Gold Coast. Japanese companies own a large slice of the coast's prime real estate, including 40% of hotel rooms.

You can stay on the Gold Coast pretty cheaply, and there's quite a range of things to do – good surf beaches, excellent eating and entertainment possibilities and a hinterland with some fine natural features. Although the beaches are good, the artificial 'attractions' are generally somewhat contrived, and often fiercely expensive.

Orientation

The whole coast from Tweed Heads in New South Wales up to Main Beach, north of Surfers Paradise, is developed, but most of the real action is around Surfers itself. Tweed Heads and Coolangatta at the southern end are older, quieter, cheaper resorts. Moving north from there you pass through Bilinga, Tugun, Currumbin, Palm Beach, Burleigh Heads, Miami, Nobby Beach, Mermaid Beach and Broadbeach – all lower key resorts.

Southport, the oldest town in the area, is north and just inland from Surfers, behind the sheltered expanse of the Broadwater which is fed by the Nerang and Coomera rivers. The Gold Coast Highway runs right along the coastal strip, leaving the Pacific Highway just north of Coolangatta and rejoining it inland from Southport.

The Gold Coast airport is at Coolangatta.

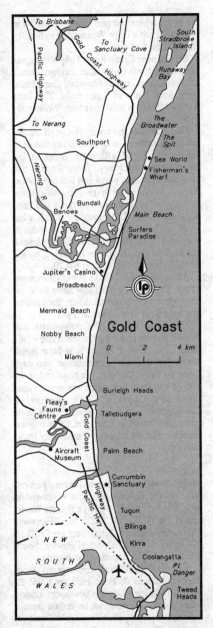

To Brisbane
To Sanctuary Cove
South Stradbroke Island
Pacific Highway
Gold Coast Highway
Runaway Bay
To Nerang
The Broadwater
The Spit
Southport
Sea World
Fisherman's Wharf
Nerang R.
Bundall
Benowa
Main Beach
Surfers Paradise
Jupiter's Casino
Broadbeach
Mermaid Beach
Nobby Beach
Gold Coast
0   2   4 km
Miami
Burleigh Heads
Fleay's Fauna Centre
Tallebudgera
Aircraft Museum
Gold Coast Highway
Palm Beach
Currumbin Sanctuary
Tugun
Pacific Hwy
Bilinga
Kirra
NEW
SOUTH
WALES
Coolangatta
Pt Danger
Tweed Heads

Most buses to the Gold Coast travel the full length of the strip.

Information

The Gold Coast Visitors Bureau (☎ (075) 38 4419), on Cavill Ave Mall, in the heart of Surfers Paradise, is open from 8 am to 4 pm Monday to Friday, 9 am to 3 pm Saturday and 9 am to 1.30 pm Sunday. There's another office (☎ (075) 36 7765) in the Beach House Plaza on the corner of Marine Parade and McLean St in Coolangatta.

At Burleigh Heads, on the Gold Coast Highway, there's a national parks information centre (☎ (075) 35 3032), a useful place to call in if you're planning to visit some of the state's national parks. It's open daily.

There are at least four glossy giveaway booklets available, including *Wot's On, Today* and *This Week* – these have street plans of the whole strip, as well as entertainment and eating details, although it must be said that they are mostly full of ads. Another source of info is a 24-hour recorded telephone service (☎ 0055 227 20).

Surfers Paradise

The centre of the Gold Coast is a real highrise jungle; in fact there is such a skyscraper conglomeration that in the afternoon, much of the beach is in shadow! Still, people pack in for the lights, activities, nightlife, shopping, restaurants, attractions and that strip of ocean sand.

Surfers has come a long way since 1936 when there was just the brand new Surfers Paradise Hotel, a little hideaway nine km from Southport. The hotel has now been swallowed up by a shopping/eating complex called the Paradise Centre. Cavill Ave, with a pedestrian mall at its beach end, is the heart of Surfers. Yet, despite all the changes and growth, at most times of year you don't usually have to go very far north or south to find a relatively open, quiet, sunny beach.

The Gold Coast Highway runs right through Surfers, only a block back from the beach. It takes the southbound traffic, while Remembrance Drive and Ferny Ave, a further block back from the beach, take the northbound traffic. Another block back is the looping Nerang River. The Surfers rich live around the surrounding canals.

Main Beach & The Spit

North of Surfers is Main Beach, and beyond that the Spit – a narrow, three-km-long tongue of sand dividing the ocean from the Broadwater.

On the Broadwater side of the Spit, **Fisherman's Wharf** is the departure point for most pleasure cruises, with a pub, a restaurant, swimming pool and shops. Across on the ocean front is the Sheraton Mirage, while up from Fisherman's Wharf is **Sea World**, a huge aquatic amusement centre. Sea World has dolphin shows, sea lion shows, water ski shows, a monorail, an *Endeavour* replica, roller coasters and so on. It's open daily from 10 am to 5 pm and admission is $29 for adults and $16 for kids. The beach at the northern end of the Spit is not developed and is good for relatively secluded sunbathing.

Southport & North

Sheltered from the ocean by the Spit, Southport was the original town on the Gold Coast but it's now modern and rather nondescript. The built-up area continues north of Southport through Labrador, Anglers Paradise and Runaway Bay to Paradise Point. Sanctuary Cove, about 10 km north of Southport on Hope Island, is an up-market resort with a Hyatt hotel, two golf courses, a marina, flats and houses.

Southern Gold Coast

Just south of Surfers at **Broadbeach**, Jupiter's Casino is a Gold Coast landmark – it was Queensland's first legal casino and is open 24 hours a day. The small **Burleigh Head National Park**, on the north side of the mouth of Tallebudgera Creek, has picnic tables, a walking track around the headland, wallabies and some *wild* koalas. **West Burleigh** is just back along the creek from the heads, and here Fleay's Fauna Centre has an excellent collection of native wildlife along four km of walking tracks. This was

the place where the platypus was first bred in captivity. It's open Wednesday to Sunday from 10 am to 4 pm.

On Guineas Creek Rd at **Tally Valley**, six km inland from Currumbin Bridge, there's an aircraft museum at Chewing Gum Field, open from 9 am to 5 pm daily. The Tally Valley Market is held near here Wednesday to Sunday.

Back towards the coast, flocks of technicoloured lorikeets and other birds flutter in for morning and afternoon feeds at the **Currumbin Sanctuary**. There are also tree kangaroos, koalas, emus and lots more Australian fauna, plus a two-km miniature railway, an adventure playground and craft demonstrations. The sanctuary is half a km south of Currumbin Creek, on both sides of the Gold Coast Highway, open daily from 8 am to 5.30 pm. If you're travelling by the Surfside bus, get off at stop No 20.

About eight km inland along Currumbin Creek Rd, **Olson's Bird Gardens** have yet more exotic feathered creatures; the gardens are open daily from 9 am to 5 pm.

The 'twin towns' of **Coolangatta** and **Tweed Heads** mark the southern end of the Gold Coast. Tweed Heads is in New South Wales but the two places merge into each other. At **Point Danger**, the headland at the end of the state line, there are good views from the Captain Cook memorial. Coolangatta is a friendly, laid-back little place, the beach is fine, and its two good hostels make it a very popular stop for backpackers.

Activities

Water Sports Numerous places, particularly on the Broadwater, rent water-sports gear. For sailboards, try Max Brown Watersports (☎ (075) 32 7722) on Waterways Drive, Main Beach. Kirra Surf (☎ (075) 36 3922), at 57 Gold Coast Highway, South Kirra, is one place renting surfboards.

You can hire small motorboats from Popeye Marine & Boat Hire (☎ (075) 32 5822) at Mariners Cove in Southport, among other places. Jet skis can be rented from a number of places, including Gold Coast Jet

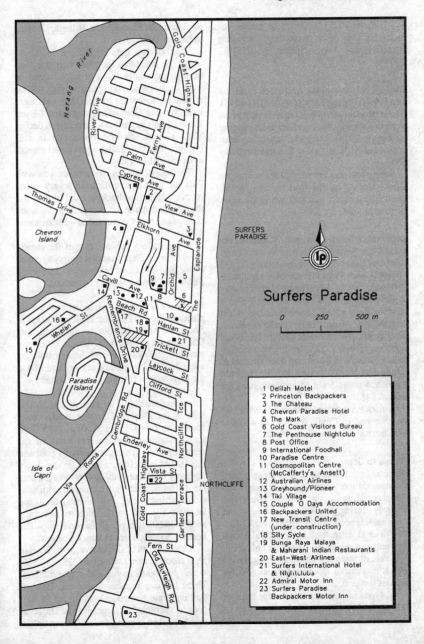

Surfers Paradise

0   250   500 m

1 Delilah Motel
2 Princeton Backpackers
3 The Chateau
4 Chevron Paradise Hotel
5 The Mark
6 Gold Coast Visitors Bureau
7 The Penthouse Nightclub
8 Post Office
9 International Foodhall
10 Paradise Centre
11 Cosmopolitan Centre
   (McCafferty's, Ansett)
12 Australian Airlines
13 Greyhound/Pioneer
14 Tiki Village
15 Couple 'O Days Accommodation
16 Backpackers United
17 New Transit Centre
   (under construction)
18 Silly Sycle
19 Bunga Raya Malaya
   & Maharani Indian Restaurants
20 East–West Airlines
21 Surfers International Hotel
   & Nightclubs
22 Admiral Motor Inn
23 Surfers Paradise
   Backpackers Motor Inn

Ski Hire (☎ (075) 92 2415). A number of operators also offer parasailing, including Budds Beach Water Sports (☎ (075) 92 0644).

Other There are horse trail rides from the Gold Coast Riding Ranch (☎ (075) 94 4255), on the Broadbeach to Nerang road next to the Surfers Raceway, or Gum Nuts Horse Riding Resort (☎ (075) 43 0191), where an hour costs from $15, half a day $35 and a full day $55.

Bungy jumpers are catered for at Bungee Down Under, on the Spit by Sea World. First-time jumpers pay $69, while for experienced jumpers it's $45.

Organised Tours Tours run by some of the hostels are probably the best value. Otherwise, bus trips up into the mountains behind the coast cost $25 to Tamborine Mountain, $30 further afield. River or canal cruises may include refreshments only, or lunch plus a floating floor show. In the evening you'll probably get music, dancing and dinner. A straight couple of hours along the inland waterways costs $25, while an evening dinner cruise will be around $35. Cruises to South Stradbroke Island usually include lunch and some form of entertainment for around $45.

Cruises leave from Fisherman's Wharf, or the river end of Cavill Ave, or the wharf at the Chevron Hotel on Ferny Ave.

Places to Stay

Hostels and backpackers' places apart, accommodation prices are extremely variable according to the season. They rise severely during the school holidays and some motels push prices higher over Christmas than at other holiday peaks although they may not rise at all if there's a cold snap. As a rule of thumb, a little searching should find a reasonable double room at $50 for most of the year.

All types of accommodation are cheaper outside Surfers. You'll find a selection of cheap motels at the southern end of the coast at places like Palm Beach, Bilinga, Coolangatta and Tweed Heads.

The holiday flats which are found all along the coast can be better bargains than motels, especially for a group of three or four. In peak seasons especially, flats will be rented on a weekly rather than overnight basis, but don't let that frighten you off. Even if they won't negotiate a daily rate, a decent $225-a-week, two-bedroom flat is still cheaper than two $30-a-night motel rooms, even for just four days.

The tourist offices can provide you with lists of accommodation in every price bracket, including backpackers' places, but they can't hope to be comprehensive since there are so many possibilities – an estimated 3000 in all.

If you have a vehicle, one of the easiest ways to find a place to stay is simply to cruise along the Gold Coast Highway and try a few places that have 'vacancy' signs out.

Hostels There are a number of hostel-style places in Surfers Paradise itself and others in Southport and Labrador to the north, and Coolangatta to the south. Unless otherwise stated, nightly costs for all these hostels are a standard $12 in the low season, and $14 in the high season (December and January).

Surfers Paradise The best of the hostels here is the *Surfers Paradise Backpackers Motor Inn* (☎ (075) 38 7250) at 2835 Gold Coast Highway, about a km south of the centre of town. It's clean and has a pool and basement parking, although the busy highway right out front is very noisy. There are 16 units, each self-contained with spacious sitting areas, full kitchen facilities, laundry, TV and video; most of the units accommodate four people in two rooms. The hostel also runs tours to various places.

A block south of Cavill Ave, at 40 Whelan St, is *Backpackers United* (☎ (075) 38 5346) which has bunk rooms and a few doubles. There are two sections – one has 19 units (with private bathroom) taking up to four people; the other has larger dorms. The communal kitchen is small and only open until 8 pm, but there's a good pool with plenty of space for sunbathing and outdoor eating.

At 18 Whelan St, the friendly *Couple 'o' Days Accommodation* (☎ (075) 92 4200) is in a quiet part of town and has 30 beds. Each unit is self-contained, with its own kitchen, lounge and bathroom. There's also a pool, and a small garden.

The *Princeton Backpackers* (☎ (075) 92 3166), at 69 Ferny Ave, is another block of holiday flats converted to self-contained four-bed units; but as there are no shared areas, the place lacks any real communal atmosphere.

North of the town centre, at 3323 Gold Coast Highway, *Surf & Sun* (☎ (075) 38 7305) has four-bed units with bath, TV and fridge. There's a new communal kitchen, and a pool. Of all the Surfers hostels, this one is closest to the beach. Double rooms are available in the low season for $30.

Southport/Labrador Southport has one of the nicest hostels on the south coast – the *Trekkers Guest House* (☎ (075) 91 5616) at 22 White St, Southport, about four km north of Surfers. It's in an old house which has been well renovated and furnished, and has all the usual facilities – laundry, kitchens, pool, TV lounge, courtesy bus – and accommodation is in three or four-bed rooms, most with bathroom. The atmosphere is very appealing and the staff organise trips to nightclubs and other events most evenings. The twice-weekly $5 barbecues are also popular.

At Labrador, a km further north again, is the *Gold Coast International Backpackers* (☎ (075) 91 1661) at 62 Frank St, close to Marine Parade. Dorm beds here cost $12.

Coolangatta The popular *Backpackers Inn* (☎ (075) 36 2422), at 45 McLean St, is a short walk from the post office end of Griffith St. Accommodation in three to six-bed dorms costs $12, while single/double rooms are $16/25. The hostel lacks cooking facilities but has a bar, a restaurant serving dinner and breakfast, and barbecues twice a week. There's a pool, and the management

organises beach parties and trips to the hinterland mountains.

The 80-bed *Gold Coast Youth Hostel* (☎ (075) 36 7644) on Coolangatta Rd, Bilinga, is about three km from central Coolangatta. It's a newish building, mainly with dorms but there are three twin rooms. The nightly cost for YHA members is $9; nonmembers pay an 'introductory fee' of $3. There's a TV/sitting room, a good kitchen and dining room, a swimming pool and a pool table. The hostel bus will often give you a free ride into Coolangatta.

Motels & Flats As you might imagine, there are dozens of motels and holiday flats up and down the coast, and these are usually quite good value in the low season.

Surfers Paradise Most of the central motels disappeared during the renovation of Cavill Ave Mall. At 2985 Gold Coast Highway, the *Silver Sands Motel* (☎ (075) 38 6041) has singles/doubles from $40/45. Close by at No 2965, the *Admiral Motor Inn* (☎ (075) 39 8759) has units with cooking facilities from $35.

Another survivor is the *Delilah Motel* (☎ (075) 38 1722) on the corner of Ferny and Cypress Aves, just north of the centre. Units here start at $40/45. *Camelot Holiday Apartments* (☎ (075) 39 9380), at 33 Cypress Ave, has self-contained four-bed units at $40 a double and $54 for four, including linen. There's a minimum stay of three days.

The huge *Sands Courtesy Inn* (☎ (075) 39 8433), on the waterfront at 40 The Esplanade, has one and two-bedroom flats which sleep two to six people; costs range from $45 to $85.

Southern Gold Coast In Broadbeach, the *Motel Casa Blanca* (☎ (075) 50 3511), at 2649 Gold Coast Highway, has units from $55. At Mermaid Beach, the *Red Emu Motel* (☎ (075) 55 2748), on the corner of the Gold Coast Highway and Peerless Ave, has doubles from $28 in the low season. Also in Mermaid Beach, the small *Van Diemen Motel* (☎ (075) 52 7611), at 2267 Gold Coast

Highway, has units from $28 a night. In Miami the *Miami Inn Motel* (☎ (075) 56 3211), at 1910 Gold Coast Highway, has units starting at $35/40.

Coolangatta has another cluster of accommodation. The old *Coolangatta Sands Hotel* (☎ (075) 36 3066), at the corner of Griffith and McLean Sts, has rooms from $25/35, and meals are available downstairs. Over at Rainbow Bay in Coolangatta, there are holiday flats like *Rainbow Place* (☎ (075) 36 9144), at 180 Marine Parade, charging $380 a week for two people.

Camping Several caravan/camping parks are along the Gold Coast strip, most with on-site vans, cabins and holiday flats. The *Main Beach Caravan Park* (☎ (075) 31 4225), just north of Surfers on Main Beach Parade, doesn't allow camping, but has powered van sites for $11, and on-site cabins for $35.

To the south, the *Miami Caravan Park* (☎ (075) 52 7533), at 2200 Gold Coast Highway, charges $12 for tent sites, and has on-site accommodation from $20.

There are more sites at Burleigh, Palm Beach and Kirra.

Places to Eat

There are plenty of fast-food places along the Gold Coast. A sensible and pleasant development has been the growing number of restaurants and cafes with outdoor eating areas. In the off season, many Gold Coast restaurants close early, so outside Surfers Paradise it's often a case of eat early or starve.

Surfers Paradise There's plenty of choice in and around the Cavill Ave Mall. *Charlie's*, at the beach end, has outdoor tables under umbrellas and is reasonably priced; it's open 24 hours. There are others also around the mall's busy giant chess set, like *Tamari Bistro* and *Confetti*, both serving more expensive Italian food. Tamari's pasta dishes and specials are $9, other main meals are $12 to $15.

Along the mall and away from the beach, the busy *Shell Bar* on the corner of Orchid Ave offers good-value snacks and meals. Breakfasts for $7 include juice, one of five

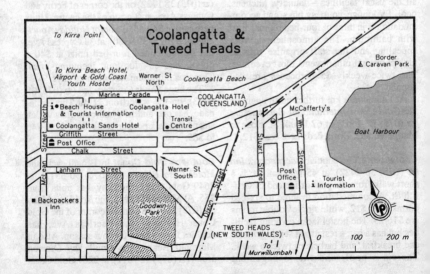

hot dishes, toast, and a bottomless cup of tea or coffee. Opposite, *Surfers Tavern Beergarden* has good cheap pub lunches for $5, including a pot of beer.

On the corner of Cavill Ave and the inland side of the Gold Coast Highway, the very popular *Bavarian Steakhouse* has straightforward steak & chips style food, and also a pasta and salad buffet bar with lunch for $8 and dinner $10.

A block north, along Elkhorn Ave, there are several places to eat, including the small *Boonchu* Thai restaurant which has mixed Asian dishes for around $8. Next door, the *Beachhouse Cafe* is open 24 hours with hamburgers for $4 and pasta for $7. On the corner of Elkhorn Ave and the Esplanade, the *Montmartre French Patisserie* is good for breakfasts and lunches. On the adjacent corner, The *Chateau* has an all-you-can-eat breakfast buffet for $5.

Orchid Ave is another good place to look. *Jenny's Coffee Shop*, in the Monte Carlo Arcade, is a good daytime place with wholesome meals. Just along Orchid Ave in the Mark complex, the *Curry Pot* is a longrunning BYO Indian place with meat and seafood dishes for $10 and vegetarian dishes for $8. It's open from 5.30 pm. Next door is the excellent and popular *Sweethearts*, which offers a huge array of health foods. It's open daily from 8.30 am to 8.30 pm.

On the highway, near Beach St, is the *Bunga Raya Malaya Restaurant* and the *Maharani Indian Restaurant*. Both are quite expensive, with main courses around $12 to $18, but are worth a try. The Bunga Raya has another branch a few km along the highway at Broadbeach.

Fisherman's Wharf, on The Spit, has a wonderful view and quite a few eating options. At the southern end, a food hall sells snacks and meals.

Southern Gold Coast There are heaps of places along the highway between Surfers and Burleigh Heads. *Sizzler*, on the Gold Coast Highway at Mermaid Beach, is a very popular place; meals cost around $10, and you can attack the salad bar for an extra $4.

The *Pizza Hut*, on the highway at Miami Beach, has a Tuesday night feast for $5. The *Seaview Room* of the Miami Hotel-Motel on the beachfront at Miami has a daily lunch and dinner seafood platter special for $9.

In Burleigh Heads, the *Masakan Indonesia*, at 1837 Gold Coast Highway, has reasonably priced Indonesian dishes. Around the corner, facing the beach, the Burleigh Hotel has the *Four Seasons Bistro*, with good pub fare.

Coolangatta A walk along Griffith St will turn up plenty of places for a meal. There are a few more places in McLean St between Griffith St and Marine Parade, including a creperie and, next door, pub bistro meals up to $7 in the *Coolangatta Sands Hotel*.

On the corner of McLean St and Marine Parade, the Beach House shopping complex has a number of eateries and a couple tucked away in the arcade running between Griffith St and Marine Parade. *Farley's Coffee Lounge* is good for breakfasts. Also here is the *Jungle, Mexican Cantina, Andalos Lebanese* and the *Aussie Eatery*, which has breakfast for $4, and other snack-type meals for $5 to $7.

The *Coolangatta Pie Shop*, on Griffith St, has a variety of pies and pasties, as well as fresh bread.

Entertainment
With more than 30 nightclubs around Surfers alone, entertainment is what it's all about on the Gold Coast. In addition, there's Jupiter's Casino, live-music venues, plenty of cinemas, and even a cultural centre. Most places have fairly strict dress codes. Lots of the nightclubs give away free entry passes, both at their doors and on the streets. Some of the hostels organise nights out at clubs, with $2 drink nights and free entry.

Benson's Nite Club, at 22 Orchid Ave, has all sorts of deals to help you avoid the cover charge and/or get cheap drinks. The Penthouse Nightclub, also on Orchid Ave, has four floors of nightlife with a piano bar, an over-25s disco and more. The lively Player's in the Surfers International Hotel, at 7

Trickett St, is open from 8 pm to 5 am. The Megadrome in the same building specialises in fairly raunchy male and female revues. Player's can also be pretty crass, with 'wet t-shirt' and 'wet jocks' competitions on Friday nights.

The Tok H, at 19A Cavill Ave, has a disco, plus live entertainment some nights; happy hours are from 6 pm to midnight Monday to Wednesday, and from 6 to 9 pm Thursday to Saturday. Rumours, with a casual atmosphere and great music, on level 1 of the Mark, is open Tuesday to Sunday until late.

Jupiter's Casino in Broadbeach has a restaurant and a good disco called Fortunes, with mixed music and age groups. Similar 'classy' nightspots include Twains International in the Mark on Orchid Ave, and Traders in the Gold Coast International Hotel.

The Benowa Tavern on Ashmore Rd, Benowa, has reasonable bands and a casual atmosphere, and on some nights entry is free. The Surfers Beergarden on Cavill Ave has live rock Sunday nights and sometimes during the week. There's also live music at Fisherman's Wharf most days.

Quite a few restaurants also provide music or entertainment during meals. A popular cabaret restaurant is Dracula's at 1 Sunshine Blvd, Miami Keys. Dracula's offers a four-course meal served by waiters and waitresses who throw themselves into the Dracula theme. The night climaxes in a disco.

In Coolangatta, the Penthouse on Hill St is a nightclub open most nights with a variety of entertainment. Premieres, on Warner St, is a fun nightclub/disco, with a $5 cover charge on weekends. Live music can be heard several nights at the Coolangatta Sands Hotel. Much of the entertainment on the southern Gold Coast revolves around the clubs and pokies in Tweed Heads.

After all this, it may be a relief to know that there is the Centre, the Gold Coast's arts complex, beside the Nerang River at Bundall. It houses theatres, galleries, a restaurant and bar. Shows include musicals, concerts, plays, dance performances, and exhibitions, which are listed under Entertainment in some of the Gold Coast tourist publications.

Getting There & Away

Air The Gold Coast is only a couple of hours by road from the centre of Brisbane but has its own busy airport at Coolangatta.

Ansett and Australian airlines fly direct from the southern capitals. Fares include Sydney $219 ($175 stand-by), Melbourne $333 ($266), Adelaide $375 ($300) and Perth $635. East-West also flies daily from Albury, Brisbane, Cairns, Hobart and Sydney, while Eastern flies daily from Brisbane ($93) and several New South Wales coastal towns.

If you need to contact airlines while on the Gold Coast, ring Ansett (☎ (075) 38 3699), Australian and Eastern (☎ (075) 38 1188) or East-West (☎ (075) 50 3800).

Bus All Sydney to Brisbane services along the Pacific Highway route detour along the full length of the Gold Coast. From Sydney to the Gold Coast costs around $60.

Some companies, including Greyhound/Pioneer and Bus Australia, will allow you a free stopover on the Gold Coast if you have a through ticket. Nearly all buses between Brisbane and Melbourne or Adelaide also start from or continue on to the Gold Coast. Many Greyhound and Pioneer services out of Brisbane to Cairns and Melbourne (via the inland route) actually start from Coolangatta.

Between Brisbane and Coolangatta, Coachtrans operates buses almost every half hour from around 4.30 am to 9 pm. The trip takes three hours and costs $11.30. Some services go all the way to or from Brisbane's international airport. In Coolangatta, the Transit Centre is on Warner St, while the Surfers Transit Centre is still being built. In the meantime, all long-distance buses leave from Beach Rd in Surfers.

The main bus terminals in Surfers Paradise are McCafferty's and Kirklands (☎ (075) 38 2700), Bus Australia (☎ (075) 38 0000), Pioneer (☎ (075) 61 6400) and Greyhound (☎ (075) 31 6677).

In Coolangatta the main bus terminals are: Greyhound/Pioneer (☎ (075) 36 6600) and McCafferty's (☎ (075) 36 1700).

Train There's no railway station on the Gold Coast but there are connecting bus services once daily to Murwillumbah (one hour) and Casino (three hours) in northern New South Wales; from there you can take a train to Sydney. There's a Queensland Rail booking office (☎ (075) 39 9280) in the Cavill Park building on the corner of Beach Rd and the Gold Coast Highway in Surfers Paradise.

Getting Around

To/From the Airport Coolangatta Airport is the seventh busiest in Australia. Several different bus companies run airport shuttle buses. Kenny's Coaches (☎ (075) 34 4554) goes to Coolangatta and Tweed Heads for $3 one-way. Gold Coast Airport Transit (☎ (075) 36 6841) from Surfers Paradise meets every Australian Airlines arrival and departure. It costs $8 between the airport and Surfers and will do pick-ups or drop-offs from your accommodation. Silverbray (☎ (075) 76 4000) meets all Ansett arrivals and departures, leaving Surfers 75 minutes before take-off. If there's three or more of you it's cheaper to take a taxi.

Bus Surfside Buslines (☎ (075) 36 7666) runs a frequent service up and down the Gold Coast Highway between Southport and Tweed Heads. Last buses leave Tweed Heads at 11.45 pm and Southport at 1.10 am (on weekends 11.15 pm from Tweed Heads, midnight from Southport). You can get a Day Rover ticket for $6.35, or a weekly one for $23.10.

Car & Moped There are stacks of car-rental firms along the Gold Coast, particularly in Surfers – pick up any of the giveaway Gold Coast guides or scan the Yellow Pages. All the big companies are represented, plus a host of local operators in the small car and rent-a-wreck categories. Rent-A-Bomb (☎ (075) 38 8007) in the Chevron Hotel Arcade, Surfers, is one of the cheapest, and

has cars, Mokes and mopeds. Others you could try are Bargain Wheels (☎ (075) 34 4281) or Red Rocket (☎ (075) 38 9074) at Shop 28, The Forum, Orchid Ave, Surfers.

For mopeds, go to Gold Coast Moped Hire (☎ (075) 38 0111) at 3 Beach Rd in Surfers, or Vespa Moped Hire (☎ (075) 38 3483) in Shop 3, Surfers International Arcade.

Bicycle In Surfers, try Silly Sycle (☎ (075) 38 6991) in the Islander building on Beach Rd.

GOLD COAST HINTERLAND

The mountains of the **McPherson Range**, about 20 km inland from Coolangatta and stretching about 60 km back along the New South Wales border to meet the Great Dividing Range, are a paradise for walkers. The great views and beautiful natural features are easily accessible if you just fancy driving around for a day or two. Expect a lot of rain in the mountains from December to March, and in winter the nights can be cold.

Pacific Highway

This, the main road from Coolangatta to Brisbane, runs behind the Gold Coast. **Nerang**, nine km inland from Southport on the Pacific Highway, has almost become a suburb of the coastal strip. From Nerang and from Mudgeeraba, a bit further south on the Pacific Highway, roads lead south-west up to the fine national parks in the McPherson Range.

Several of the Gold Coast's artificial 'attractions' are on the Pacific Highway at **Oxenford** and **Coomera**: the Wet 'n' Wild Water Park, with one-metre artificial surf; Koala Town; Dreamworld, a Disneyland-style creation with a $27 admission fee; and Movie World, a re-creation of the Warner Brothers film studios in Hollywood ($29) – what next?

A three-hour horse-riding trek through beautiful rainforest and river scenery in the **Numinbah Valley** near Nerang (☎ (075) 33 4137) will cost you $25. The staff do pick-ups from the Gold Coast.

Beenleigh is about halfway from the

Gold Coast to Brisbane. The rum distillery here dates from 1884 and is open for tours ($4) from 10.30 am to 3.30 pm.

Tamborine Mountain

Just 45 km north-west of the Gold Coast, this 600-metre-high plateau is on a northern spur of the McPherson Range. Patches of the area's original forests remain in nine small national parks. There are gorges, spectacular waterfalls like Witches Falls and Cedar Creek Falls, great views inland or over the coast, and walking tracks. There's a visitor information centre (☎ (075) 45 1171) at Doughty Park, North Tamborine.

The main turn-off to the mountain is at Oxenford on the Pacific Highway. Some of the best lookouts are in **Witches Falls National Park**, south-west of North Tamborine, and at **Cameron Falls**, north-west of North Tamborine. **Macrozamia Grove National Park**, near Mt Tamborine township, has some extremely old macrozamia palms. Other places of interest on the mountain or on the way up include **Jasper Farm**, a commercial fossicking site at Upper Coomera; **Thunderbird World** where you can ride horses or fossick for thunder eggs; and huge trees in **MacDonald National Park**.

Thunder Eggs

Thunder eggs are spherical rocks of volcanic origin which contain quartz crystals or semi-precious gems such as agate. The 'eggs', which range in size from a cm in diameter to about the size of a cricket ball, were formed when gas cavities in hardened lava filled with mineral deposits or crystal, and weathering of the rock created the smooth, rounded shape.

There's a handful of reasonably priced motels and guesthouses in Mt Tamborine township and Eagle Heights, and a camping ground with on-site vans at *Thunderbird Park* (☎ (075) 45 1468) in Mt Tamborine.

Springbrook Plateau

This forested 900-metre-high plateau, like the rest of the McPherson Range, is a remnant of the huge volcano which used to be centred on Mt Warning in New South

Wales. It's reached by paved roads from Nerang or Mudgeeraba, or from Murwillumbah in New South Wales, which are all between 30 and 40 km away.

There are five small national parks in the Springbrook area, with gorges, cliffs, forests, waterfalls, walking tracks and several picnic areas. In **Gwongorella National Park**, just off the Mudgeeraba to Springbrook road, the Purling Brook Falls drop 109 metres into rainforest. Downstream, Waringa Pool is a beautiful summer swimming hole. There's a national park camping area beside the Gwongorella picnic area, a short walk from the falls.

Natural Arch National Park, in the valley to the west of Springbrook Plateau, is just off the Nerang to Murwillumbah road. A one-km walking circuit takes you to a rock arch spanning a water-formed cave which is home to a huge colony of glow-worms.

There are rangers' offices and information centres at Natural Arch and Springbrook. Pick up a copy of the national parks walking tracks leaflet. Camping permits for Gwongorella are available from the ranger at Springbrook (☎ (075) 33 5147, between 3 and 4 pm weekdays only). Springbrook village itself has a number of restored pioneer buildings and memorabilia including Nerang's original 1889 railway station.

Lamington National Park

West of Springbrook, this large, 200-sq-km park covers more of the McPherson Range and adjoins the Border Ranges National Park in New South Wales. It includes thickly wooded valleys, 1100-metre-high ranges, plus most of the Lamington Plateau. Much of the vegetation is subtropical rainforest. There are beautiful gorges, caves, superb views, a great many waterfalls and pools, and lots of wildlife. Bower birds are quite common and pademelons, a type of small wallaby, can be seen on the grassy forest verges in late afternoon.

The park has 160 km of walking tracks ranging from a 'senses trail' for the blind at **Binna Burra**, to the Border Track which leads from Binna Burra to **O'Reillys** via the crest of the range.

Places to Stay Visitors to Lamington usually head first for either Binna Burra, or Green Mountains (also called O'Reillys). Many of the walking tracks start at these two places.

Binna Burra, 35 km from Nerang by paved road, has the *Binna Burra Mountain Lodge* (☎ (075) 33 3622) with a small camping ground. It's advisable to book if you want to camp. Accommodation in the lodge is normally from $91 per person per night, but that includes all meals, free hiking and climbing gear, and activities like guided walks, bus trips and abseiling. There's a kiosk selling basic supplies.

Green Mountains is 32 km south of Canungra by a mostly paved road. *O'Reilly's Mountain Resort* (☎ (075) 44 0644), at Green Mountains, has similar prices and facilities to Binna Burra. There's also a kiosk, and a national parks camping ground about 600 metres away.

It's quite possible to camp in Lamington, but there are restrictions. You can get information from the national parks offices at Burleigh Heads or Brisbane, but camping permits must be obtained from the ranger at Green Mountains (☎ (075) 44 0634).

Getting There & Away The Mountain Coach Company (☎ 008 077 423, toll-free) in Brisbane runs a daily bus service from the Brisbane Transit Centre to Binna Burra. It leaves Brisbane in the afternoon and stops at the Commercial Hotel in Nerang on the way. The company also runs a service from the Gold Coast. Departures from Binna Burra are at 7.15 am daily, except for Sundays (3 pm).

Allstate Scenic Tours (☎ (07) 285 1777) runs a bus service six times a week between the Brisbane Transit Centre and Green Mountains (O'Reillys). The one-way trip takes about three hours and costs $16. Book at the Skennars desk in the Transit Centre.

Mt Lindesay Highway

This road runs south from Brisbane, across the Great Dividing Range west of Lamington, and into New South Wales at Woodenbong. **Beaudesert**, in cattle country 66 km from Brisbane, is just 20 km south-west of Tamborine Mountain. It has a pioneer museum and tourist information centre on Jane St.

West of Beaudesert is the stretch of the Great Dividing Range known as the **Scenic Rim** (see the Darling Downs section). Further south, **Mt Barney National Park** is undeveloped but popular with bushwalkers and climbers. It's in the Great Dividing Range just north of the state border. You reach it from the Rathdowney to Boonah road. There's a tourist information office (☎ (075) 44 1222) on the highway at Rathdowney.

Sunshine Coast

The stretch of coast from the top of Bribie Island to Noosa is known as the Sunshine Coast. It's much less neon-lit and commercial than the Gold Coast and is renowned for fine beaches and surfing. The northern half of the Sunshine Coast from Maroochydore is less built-up than the southern half.

North of Noosa is the Cooloola National Park and Rainbow Beach, an access point for Fraser Island. Inland from the Sunshine Coast the towns along the Bruce Highway (the main road north) have a series of artificial tourist attractions.

Getting There & Away

Air The Sunshine Coast has airports at Maroochydore and Noosa. Sunstate flies from Brisbane ($75), Air NSW and East-West from Sydney.

Bus Sunshine Coast Coaches (☎ (07) 236 1901) runs about 10 buses daily connecting Brisbane with the Sunshine Coast and its hinterland towns. It's about two hours from Brisbane to Maroochydore and three hours

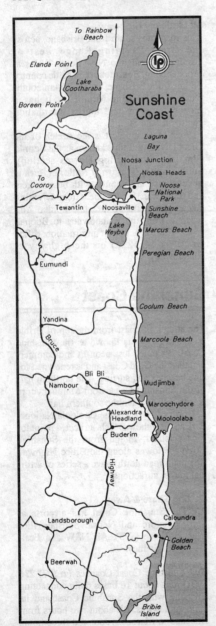

to Noosa. In Brisbane the buses leave from the Transit Centre. To head north up the Bruce Highway from the Sunshine Coast, you first take a bus to Nambour or Cooroy on the highway. The last bus from Noosa to Cooroy leaves at 10.30 pm. From Cooroy to Noosa, the last departure is 3.40 pm. There's also the local Noosa District Bus Lines which links Noosa with towns on the Bruce Highway.

Train The most convenient stations for the Sunshine Coast are Nambour and Cooroy. There are services daily to these places from Brisbane and from the north.

CABOOLTURE (population 6451)

This region, 49 km north of Brisbane, once had a large Aboriginal population. Nowadays, it's a prosperous dairy centre famous for its yoghurt. It also has two of the most interesting of the numerous attractions which line the Bruce Highway heading north.

The **Abbey Museum** on Old Toorbul Point Rd is a world social history museum, looked after by a monastic movement and open on Tuesdays, Thursdays and Saturdays. Its 4500-item collection had been housed in London, Cyprus, Egypt and Sri Lanka before finding its home in Australia.

Caboolture Historical Village on Beerburrum Rd, open daily from 10 am to 3 pm, has about 30 early Australian buildings in a bush setting.

GLASSHOUSE MOUNTAINS

Shortly after Caboolture, the Glasshouse Mountains are a dramatic visual starting point for the Sunshine Coast. They're a bizarre series of volcanic crags rising abruptly out of the plain to 300 metres or more. They were named by Captain Cook and, depending on whose story you believe, he either noted the reflections of the glass-smooth rock sides of the mountains, or he thought they looked like glass furnaces in his native Yorkshire. The mountains are popular with rock climbers, although you can walk up some of them, with some scrambling.

The Bruce Highway today veers away from the Glasshouse Mountains after Caboolture, but you can take the slightly longer Old Bruce Highway loop through Beerburrum, Glasshouse Mountains village, Beerwah and Landsborough. From Glasshouse Mountains village, a road leads 10 km west to a good lookout point.

There are a few caravan/camping parks, hotels and motels in the area.

CALOUNDRA (population 45,000)

At the southern end of the Sunshine Coast strip, Caloundra has some decent beaches but compared with places further north, it's a bit faded these days. Bulcock Beach, good for windsurfing, is just down from the main street, overlooking the northern end of Bribie Island.

Points of interest include the **Queensland Air Museum** at Caloundra Aerodrome, which is open Wednesday, Saturday and Sunday from 10 am to 4 pm. There's a two-thirds scale replica of Captain Cook's ship the *Endeavour*, on display from 9 am to 4.45 pm daily at 3 Landsborough Parade, Seafarer's Wharf. You can take cruises around the channels and Bribie Island from Caloundra.

There's a tourist information office (☎ (074) 91 0202) on Caloundra Rd.

Places to Stay

Between Bulcock St and the beach, at 27-29 Leeding Terrace, there's a good hostel, *Back Packers United* (☎ (074) 91 6278). The *Caloundra Holiday Resort* at Dicky Beach also has backpackers' accommodation at $10. The *Caloundra Motel* (☎ (074) 91 1411), at 30 Bowman Rd, has air-con singles/doubles for $28/34. Caloundra has at least six caravan parks with on-site vans and cabins.

MAROOCHYDORE (population 70,000)

North from Caloundra, the coast is built up most of the way to the triple towns of Mooloolaba, Alexandra Headland and Maroochydore. **Mooloolaba** has the brightest atmosphere, with a beach, a couple of lively seafront pubs and eateries, the odd nightspot (live bands at weekends in the Mooloolaba Hotel) and a smattering of Bali boutiques. **Alexandra Headland** has a long sandy beach.

Maroochydore, the main centre, has both an ocean beach and the Maroochy River with lots of pelicans and a few islands. There's decent surf in several spots.

Information

Tourist information is available at the Sunshine Coast Tourism & Development Board (☎ 008 072 041, toll-free) on Alexandra Parade, the main road passing through Alexandra Headland. You can also get information and free maps from the Cotton Tree Tourist Centre (☎ (074) 43 1629) at 22 King St, Cotton Tree, Maroochydore.

Places to Stay

The YHA *Holiday Hostel* (☎ (074) 43 3151) is at 24 Schirrmann Drive, a couple of turns off Bradman Ave. Nightly cost is $10 in a dorm, and $22 for a double. *Zords Backpackers* (☎ (074) 43 1755) is at 15 The Esplanade, opposite the river. There's dorm accommodation for $10 as well as normal motel doubles for $30.

There's also the usual selection of caravan/camping parks and motels, with most of the caravan parks in Maroochydore. One of the most popular with travellers is the *Cotton Tree Caravan Park* (☎ (074) 43 1253) on the Esplanade beside the river. In Mooloolaba there's the *Parkyn Parade Caravan Park* (☎ (074) 44 1201). Neither place has on-site vans. For these try the *Alexandra Gardens Caravan Park* (☎ (074) 43 23568) on Okinja Rd, Maroochydore.

Motels are generally rather expensive. You could try the *Kyamba Court Motel* (☎ (074) 44 0202) at 94 Brisbane Rd, Mooloolaba.

Getting Around

The *Sandpiper* water taxi crosses the Maroochy River three times a day to the north shore, where there's a recreation reserve. You can hire boats at several places in Maroochydore and Mooloolaba, or take river cruises at Maroochydore.

Mokes can be hired from the Moke Bloke (☎ (074) 43 5777) at the corner of Third Ave and Aerodrome Rd in Maroochydore. Trusty Car Hire (☎ (074) 43 6100), at 24 Aerodrome Rd, has Mokes, 4WDs and cars.

NOOSA (population 24,500)

A surfers' Mecca since the early 1960s, Noosa has now become a resort for the fashionable – with beaches, nightlife, the fine coastal Noosa National Park and, just to the north, the walks, waterways and beaches of the Cooloola National Park. Noosa remains a far cry from the hype of the Gold Coast, and has more character than the rest of the Sunshine Coast.

Orientation

Noosa is actually a string of small linked centres – with confusingly similar names – stretching back from the mouth of the Noosa River and along its maze of tributary creeks and lakes. The slickest resort area is Noosa Heads, on the coast between the river mouth and rocky Noosa Head. From Noosa Heads two roads lead back to Noosaville, about three km away. One goes across an island known as Noosa Sound, the other circles round to the south through Noosa Junction where you'll find most of the area's shops and cheaper restaurants. Noosaville is the departure point for most river cruises.

Further inland, beyond Noosaville, you reach Tewantin, six km from Noosa Heads. Another centre, on the coast three km southeast of Noosa Heads and Noosa Junction, is Sunshine Beach, which has a cheap backpackers' hostel.

Information

The tourist information office on Hastings St in Noosa Heads has a range of brochures and the staff are helpful.

There are also a number of privately run tourist information offices which double as booking agents for accommodation, trips, tours and so on. Typical of these is Australia House (☎ (074) 47 3798) on Sunshine Beach Rd, Noosa Junction.

Written Dimension is a good bookshop on Sunshine Beach Rd, Noosa Junction.

Noosa National Park

The spectacular cape at Noosa Head marks the northern end of the Sunshine Coast. The national park extends for about two km in each direction from the headland, and has fine walks, great coastal scenery and a string of bays on the north side with waves which draw surfers from all over. Alexandria Bay on the eastern side is the best sandy beach.

The main vehicle access to the national park is from Hastings St in Noosa Heads, from where you can drive about one km into the park. You can also drive up to Laguna Lookout in the park from Viewland Drive in Noosa Junction, or walk into the park from McAnally Drive or Parkedge Rd in Sunshine Beach.

Activities

Water Sports Noosa Dive & Sports Centre, on Hastings St, offers dive trips and courses, as well as renting sailboards, snorkelling gear, surf mats, and mopeds.

Noosa Sailboards (☎ (074) 47 5890) rents sailboards at the river mouth. Seawind Charters (☎ (074) 47 3042) in Sunshine Beach has sailboards, jet skis, and yachts for hire. Several places on the river in Noosaville and Tewantin also rent out boats, sailboards, jet skis, and other equipment, and offer tours up the river.

Organised Tours & Cruises Most cruises up the Noosa River to Lakes Cooroibah and Cootharaba leave from the river beside Gympie Terrace in Noosaville.

There are also 4WD trips along the coloured sands to Fraser Island. A day trip is typically $65. Check out the hostels in Noosaville to see if a trip is being organised. From Noosa, a three-day Fraser Island trip costs around $110.

Places to Stay

Except for hostels, accommodation prices can rise as much as 50% in busy times, even 100% in the December to January peak season. If you're going to stay a few days, it's worth asking at information offices and estate agents about holiday flats or units. These can be economical, especially for a group. In the off season, some estate agents rent private holiday homes at bargain rates, or advertise for caretakers – look on Sunshine Beach Rd in Noosa Junction or Hastings St in Noosa Heads.

Hostels The *Noosa Backpackers Resort* (☎ (074) 49 8151) at 9 William St, Munna Point, Noosaville, is a popular hostel with good cooking and sitting areas, a garden and a pool. Nightly cost is $11 a head in dorms or double rooms, and the owners will help you fix up cheap trips on the river or north to the Cooloola area or Fraser Island. There's also a good cafe, and a courtesy bus for pick-ups.

Also in Noosaville is the new *Adventure Affairs Backpackers* (☎ (074) 49 8055) at 173 Gympie Terrace. The dorms here are large, but the facilities are still very good, and there's a swimming pool in the backyard. A bed here will cost you $12, and there's a courtesy bus.

In Sunshine Beach, the small *Noosa Hostel* (☎ (074) 47 4739), at 26 Stevens St, is conveniently close to the beach, but is quite a way from anywhere else. Dorm beds in self-contained units cost $10, and the hostel bus usually meets incoming buses in Hastings St, Noosa Heads.

Melaluka Units (☎ (074) 47 3663), also in Sunshine Beach at 7 Selene St, is only a couple of minutes' walk from the beach. There are single and double rooms available, and a bed costs $12. You'll have to make your own way here, but it's very close to the main road if you're travelling by local bus.

In Noosa Heads itself, *Halse Lodge* (☎ (074) 47 3254) is an immaculately kept place, run by the Anglican church. It's housed in a beautiful old building, complete with polished wooden floors, and there are

views over the town and sea. The staff are friendly, and although the lodge has an institutional air, it's excellent value at $15 for B&B, $6 more if you need linen, and may be convenient if you're just stopping overnight. Smoking is not permitted here.

Motels & Holiday Units The best area for cheaper motels is along Gympie Terrace and Hilton Terrace, the main road through Noosaville. The *Noosa Riverside Motel* (☎ (074) 49 7551), at 175 Gympie Terrace, is about as cheap as you'll get. In the low season, singles/doubles are $35/40 in rooms with their own well-equipped kitchens. The *Noosa Lakes Motel*, at 3 Hilton Terrace, has similar prices.

In Noosa Heads, the *Claribe Motel* (☎ (074) 47 3486), at 263 David Low Way, also charges $35/40.

Holiday units to try in Noosaville, charging between $35 and $50 for a double, include *Noosa River Beach* (☎ (074) 49 7873) at 281 Gympie Terrace; and *River Palms* (☎ (074) 49 7318) at 137 Gympie Terrace.

Most of the accommodation in Noosa Heads is of the expensive variety, either resorts or holiday flats. Cheapest of the bunch are *Tingirana* (☎ (074) 47 3274) at 25 Hastings St, with units from $55; and *Vi Ash Wa* (☎ (074) 47 4467) at 36 Grant St, where units start at $35.

Camping The caravan parks all tend to spread out away from the centre. The *Noosa River Caravan Park* (☎ (074) 49 8950) in Robert St, the *Content Caravan Park* (☎ (074) 49 7746) on Weyba Rd, both in Noosaville, and the *Sunrise Holiday Village* (☎ (074) 47 3294) in Sunshine Beach all have tent sites, as well as on-site vans and cabins – book ahead in peak times.

Places to Eat

Most of the cheaper places are on Sunshine Beach Rd, the main street in Noosa Junction. *Roma Pizza*, at the southern end of the street, is a sit-down restaurant which has pizzas from $6, as well as other dishes. *Thai House*

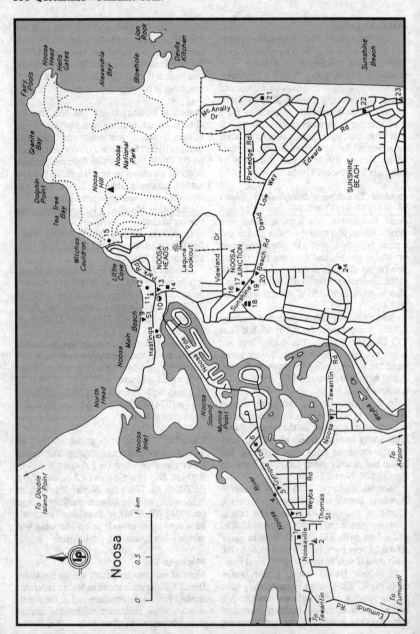

Sunshine Beach

Lion Rock

Devils Kitchen

Blowhole

Alexandria Bay

Noosa Head

Hells Gates

Fairy Pools

Mc Anally Dr

21

22 23

Parkedge Rd

Edward Rd

SUNSHINE BEACH

Granite Bay

Dolphin Point

Tea Tree Bay

Noosa Hill

Noosa National Park

Witches Cauldron

Little Cove

15

David Low Way

Beach Rd

24

North Head

Noosa Main Beach

Park Rd

12

11

9

10

8

Hastings St

NOOSA HEADS

Laguna Lookout

Viewland Dr

NOOSA JUNCTION

16

17

13

14

18

19

20

Sunshine

Noosa Pde

Noosa Sound

Noosa Inlet

Munna Point

Noosa River

Gympie Tce

5

4

3

1

2

Noosaville

Thomas St

Weyba Rd

Tewantin Rd

Weyba Ck

7

6

To Airport

To Tewantin

Eumundi Rd

To Eumundi

To Double Island Point

Noosa

0   0.5   1 km

1	Adventure Affairs Backpackers & Noosa Riverside Motel
2	Noosa River Caravan Park
3	Scandals Restaurant
4	Noosa Yacht & Rowing Club
5	Mexican Cantina
6	Noosa Backpackers Resort
7	Maharanii Indian Restaurant
8	Bike & Moped Hire & Dive Shop
9	Eduardo's Restaurant
10	Long-Distance Bus Stop
11	Tourist Information Office
12	Noosa Surf Life Saving Club
13	Cafe Le Monde
14	Halse Lodge & Moke Hire
15	National Parks Office
16	Suntop Cafe
17	Noosa 3 Cinemas
18	Post Office
19	Thai House Restaurant
20	Pizza Roma
21	Noosa Hostel
22	Melaluka Units
23	Sunrise Holiday Village Caravan Park
24	Police & Fire Department

is a reasonably priced Thai restaurant, upstairs at the Sunshine Centre on Sunshine Beach Rd. On the same road, the *Suntop Cafe*, in the Suntop Plaza, is good for breakfast or light meals.

In Noosa Heads, trendy Hastings St has a collection of smart, expensive and surprisingly good restaurants. *Eduardo's*, right on the beach, has excellent food; ask for a table on the beachfront deck. Standards are even higher at *La Plage* although it's definitely expensive. Across the road is the pleasant *Aqua Bar*, but *Cafe Le Monde* near the roundabout is probably the most popular Hastings St restaurant. Above it is the more expensive *Palmers*.

Hastings St also has some cheaper cafes in a couple of arcades. *Nikki's Chicken & Seafood Bar* is reasonably priced, and the *Bay Village Food Court* has a selection of lunch-time stalls with good food.

In Noosaville there are several choices. *Scandals* is a good little BYO place on the corner of Thomas St and Gympie Terrace,

while a little further along, at 247 Gympie Terrace, the *Mexican Cantina* is another BYO place with good food and prices. The *Bratpackers Cafe*, in the Noosa Backpackers Resort, is good for light meals. About a km out along Weyba Rd, the road which connects Noosaville with Noosa Junction, the *Maharanii* is an Indian restaurant which is open nightly.

Two cheaper places to eat in Noosa are the *Noosa Surf Life Saving Club*, right on the beach at Noosa Heads, and the *Noosa Yacht & Rowing Club* on the river by the tennis courts at Noosaville. Both offer standard, pub-style meals.

Entertainment
The Underground, opposite Coles supermarket on Lanyana Way, Noosa Junction, is the most popular disco. The dress regulations are quite strict here.

The Noosa 3 Cinemas on Sunshine Beach Rd, Noosa Junction, show mainstream, general-release movies.

Getting Around
Noosa District Bus Lines (☎ (074) 42 8649) runs a local service between Noosa, Cooroy, Eumundi and Nambour. Monday to Friday there are about 11 services in each direction between Sunshine Beach, Noosa Junction, Hastings St in Noosa Heads, Noosa Sound, Thomas St in Noosaville, and Tewantin.

Mokes are available from Noosa Car Rental (☎ (074) 47 3777), right opposite the bus stop in Noosa Heads. There are a number of other local operators, plus national firms like Avis and Thrifty. If you want to drive up the Cooloola Coast beach to the wreck of the *Cherry Venture* and to Double Island Point, Sunshine Rentals beside the Noosa Junction post office rent 4WDs for $100 to $150 a day.

Noosa Dive & Sports Centre, at the end of Hastings St, rents mopeds at $25 for half a day and $35 a full day. Adventure Affairs Backpackers rents bikes ($5 for half a day, $8 a day) and canoes ($15 for half a day, $20 a day).

COOLOOLA COAST

A couple of km upstream from Noosaville, the Noosa River takes a northward bend at Tewantin and widens out into Lake Cooroibah then Lake Cootharaba, which is at the southern end of Cooloola National Park. The park stretches about 50 km north to Rainbow Beach (see the later Rainbow Beach section). It's a varied wilderness area of mangrove-lined waterways, forest, heathland and lakes, all of it featuring plentiful bird life and lots of wild flowers in spring. The Teewah coloured sands are on this coast.

From Tewantin, you can take a vehicle ferry across the Noosa River to reach the 50-km stretch of beach along Laguna Bay. Ferries leave from 6 am to 9 pm Sunday to Thursday (to midnight Friday and Saturday) and cost $4.50 per car. In a 4WD, you can go right up this beach to Double Island Point, then across to the small town of Rainbow Beach, one of the access points for Fraser Island. It's quite possible to hitch to Rainbow Beach this way.

On the way up to Double Island Point along the beach, you pass high dunes and the Teewah coloured sand cliffs, which are 200 metres high in some places. Shortly south of Double Island Point, the rusting *Cherry Venture*, a 3000-ton freighter swept ashore by a cyclone in 1973, sits in the sand.

Lake Cootharaba

This 90-sq-km lake is about 20 km upstream from Tewantin. You can reach it by river from Noosaville or Tewantin. By land there's a 20-km direct road (eight km of it unsealed) from Tewantin to Boreen Point on the western shore of the lake, or a longer paved route via Cooroy on the Bruce Highway and Pomona. Boreen Point has two caravan/camping parks (one of them with on-site vans), plus a couple of motels and holiday units.

From Boreen Point, the road continues five km north to Elanda Point, where there's a lovely lakeside camping ground, but beware of the sandflies and mosquitoes. The ranger (☎ (074) 85 3165) for the Cooloola National Park is also here.

Southern Cooloola

From Elanda Point, the Cooloola Wilderness Trail, a 4WD track, heads 46 km north to meet the Gympie to Rainbow Beach road. There's also a seven-km walking trail to the Cooloola National Park visitor centre at Kinaba Island (☎ (074) 49 7364) near the northern end of Lake Cootharaba. This is the only land route to the visitor centre – most people reach it by boat.

You can explore further north along the Noosa River, beyond Lake Cootharaba, by walking trail or canoe; it's OK to camp in some places.

Northern Cooloola

The easiest way to reach this part of the national park is from the Rainbow Beach area. Northern Cooloola has camping grounds between Freshwater Lake and the eastern beach, and near Double Island Point on the north facing beach (both 4WD or foot access only). There are several walking tracks, and the main vehicle access is from the Gympie to Rainbow Beach road, four km south of Rainbow Beach. You can get information and camping permits for northern Cooloola from the national parks information centre in Rainbow Beach (☎ (074) 86 3160).

NAMBOUR (population 9579)

You often see sugar-cane trains crossing the main street of this sugar-growing town. Pineapples and other tropical fruit are also grown in the area, and the 'Big Pineapple' is one of Nambour's two superbly kitsch 'big' creations. It looms by the highway at Woombye, about six km south of the town, and you can climb up inside this 15-metre fibreglass wonder to see the full story of pineapple cultivation. As if that wasn't enough, six km north of Nambour at Yandina is the 'Big Cow'.

Further up the highway at Eumundi, you can fossick for thunder eggs at Thunder Egg Farm, or you could try the locally brewed beer.

SUNSHINE COAST HINTERLAND
Blackall Range

The mountains rise fairly close behind the coast and west of Nambour or Landsborough you can take the scenic Mapleton to Maleny road right along the ridge line of the Blackall Range. **Mapleton Falls National Park** is four km west of Mapleton and **Kondalilla National Park** is three km off the Mapleton to Montville stretch of the road. Both have rainforest, and the Kondalilla Falls drop 80 metres into a rainforest valley, while at Mapleton Falls, Pencil Creek plunges 120 metres. This is a great area for exploring – there's lots of bird life and several walking tracks in the parks. The *Mapleton Hotel* is a good place for a counter meal or a cold beer.

South Burnett

Further inland, the South Burnett region includes Australia's most important peanut-growing area. **Kingaroy** almost means 'peanuts' in Australia, not least because the well-known ex-premier of Queensland, Joh Bjelke-Petersen, hails from here. There's a tourist office (☎ (071) 62 3199) at 128 Haly St, Kingaroy. You can inspect the peanut storage silos on weekdays at 10.30 am and 1.30 pm.

South-east of Kingaroy, **Nanango** is another peanut town but with an earlier history of gold mining. You can fossick for gold at **Seven Mile Diggings**, 11 km from Nanango. **Murgon** is the main town of the region north of Kingaroy. It has the Queensland Dairy Industry Museum, on Gayndah Rd. Six km south of Murgon the **Cherbourg** Aboriginal community runs a pottery and craft shop, open from Monday to Friday.

The **Bunya Mountains**, isolated outliers of the Great Dividing Range, rise abruptly to over 1000 metres, and are accessible by sealed road about 50 km south-west of Kingaroy. The mountains are a national park, with a variety of vegetation from rainforest to heathland. There are two camping grounds in the park, plus a network of walking tracks to numerous waterfalls and lookouts. The ranger (☎ (071) 68 3127) is at Dandabah.

Darling Downs

West of the Great Dividing Range in southern Queensland stretch the rolling plains of the Darling Downs, some of the most fertile and productive agricultural land in Australia. In the state's early history, the Darling Downs were something of a back door into the region. Nobody was allowed within an 80-km radius of the penal colony of Brisbane but settlers gradually pushed their way north from New South Wales through this area.

West of the Darling Downs, the population becomes more scattered as you move out of the crop-producing area into sheep and cattle country centred on towns like Roma, Charleville and Cunnamulla.

From Ipswich, just inland from Brisbane, there are two main routes west: a southern one through Warwick and Goondiwindi to Cunnamulla, and a northern one through Toowoomba and Roma to Charleville. From Charleville you can continue west to the Channel Country or turn north for Longreach (see the Outback Queensland section).

The Darling Downs region is linked to New South Wales by two main trunk roads: the New England Highway from Warwick down to Tamworth and the Newell Highway from Goondiwindi to Dubbo. Further west, the Mitchell Highway from Charleville and Cunnamulla is the main trunk road into New South Wales.

Getting There & Away

Air Sunstate (☎ (076) 38 1199, in Toowoomba) and Sabair both fly between Brisbane and Toowoomba at least once daily. Flight West (☎ (07) 229 1177) flies Brisbane to Charleville and back six days a week, with stops at Roma five days a week.

Bus Many long-distance buses between Brisbane and Sydney or Victoria go through the Darling Downs. Ipswich, Toowoomba and Warwick are on the New England Highway route. Similarly Ipswich, Toowoomba and Goondiwindi are on the Newell Highway route.

Greyhound runs a variety of buses west into Queensland from Brisbane: to Mt Isa daily (24½ hours, $135) through Ipswich, Toowoomba (2½ hours, $14), Roma (seven hours, $44), Charleville (11 hours, $52) and Longreach (17 hours, $85).

Skennars has daily buses from Brisbane to Ipswich, Toowoomba, Warwick, Goondiwindi, Roma and Charleville, also between Toowoomba and Warwick twice daily, and five days a week between Warwick and the Gold Coast.

McCafferty's runs a bus service between Ipswich and Toowoomba several times a day to co-ordinate with the suburban trains between Brisbane and Ipswich. There are also McCafferty's buses between Toowoomba and the Gold Coast, Toowoomba and Mt Isa, and between Brisbane and Rockhampton via Ipswich, Toowoomba and Miles.

Train The air-con Westlander runs twice a week from Brisbane to Cunnamulla and Quilpie, through Ipswich, Toowoomba, Roma and Charleville. The 777-km journey from Brisbane to Charleville takes about 17 hours.

Non air-con trains run twice weekly between Brisbane and Dirranbandi, through Ipswich, Toowoomba, Warwick and Goondiwindi. Going back to Brisbane you have to change to a co-ordinated bus service between Toowoomba and Ipswich and then get on a suburban train from Ipswich.

IPSWICH (population 75,000)

Virtually an outer suburb of Brisbane now, Ipswich was a convict settlement as early as 1827 and one of the most important early Queensland towns. It's the main gateway to the Darling Downs. On the way from Brisbane to Ipswich, **Wolston House** at Wacol is an 1850s country house with a collection of early Australian furniture; it's open from 10 or 11 am to 4.30 pm Wednesday to Sunday.

Ipswich has many fine old houses and public buildings: if you're interested in Queensland's distinctive architecture, pick up the excellent *Ipswich City Heritage Trails* leaflet which will guide you around a great diversity of buildings. The kiosk in Queens Park, above the town centre, doubles as a tourist information office (☎ (07) 281 5167).

IPSWICH TO WARWICK

South-west of Ipswich, the Cunningham Highway to Warwick crosses the Great Dividing Range at **Cunningham's Gap**, with 1100-metre mountains rising either side of the road. **Main Range National Park**, which covers the Great Dividing Range for about 20 km north and south of Cunningham's Gap, is great walking country, with a variety of walks starting from the car park at the crest of Cunningham's Gap. Much of the range is covered in rainforest. There's a camping area by the road on the west side of the gap: contact the ranger (☎ (076) 66 1133) for permits. **Spicer's Gap**, in the range south of Cunningham's Gap, has excellent views and another camping area. To reach it you turn off the highway five km west of Aratula, back towards Ipswich.

WARWICK AREA

South-west of Brisbane, 162 km inland and near the New South Wales border, Warwick is the oldest town in Queensland after Brisbane. It's a busy Darling Downs farming centre noted for roses, and for its rodeo on the last weekend in October. **Pringle Cottage** on Dragon St, dating from 1863, is a museum, open daily. There's a tourist office (☎ (076) 61 3686) on Palmerin St. The *Warwick Youth Hostel* (☎ (076) 61 2698), with 18 beds at $8.50 a night, is at 6 Palmerin St.

Killarney, south-east of Warwick near the New South Wales border, is a pretty little town in an area of fine mountain scenery. Among the many lovely waterfalls in the area is Queen Mary Falls, tumbling 40 metres into a rainforested gorge 10 km east of Killarney. There's a caravan/camping park (☎ (076) 64 7151) on the road near the falls.

South of Warwick on the New England Highway is **Stanthorpe**, near the New South Wales border. At 915 metres it's the coolest town in the state and a centre for fruit production and wine making, with more than 20 vineyards, some of which you can tour. There's a tourist office (☎ (076) 81 1799) at 61 Marsh St.

From the highway 26 km south of Stanthorpe, a paved road leads nine km east up to **Girraween National Park**, an area of 1000-metre- high hills, valleys and huge granite outcrops. The park has a visitor centre (☎ (076) 84 5157), two camping grounds with hot showers, and several walking tracks of varying length. Girraween adjoins Bald Rock National Park over the border in New South Wales. It can fall below freezing on winter nights up here, but summer days are warm. Call the park's visitor centre to book camping sites in advance.

GOONDIWINDI & FURTHER WEST
West of Warwick, **Goondiwindi** is on the New South Wales border and the Macintyre River. It's a popular stop on the Newell Highway between Melbourne and Brisbane. There's a small museum in the old customs house and a wildlife sanctuary at the Boobera Lagoon. If you continue inland from Goondiwindi you reach **St George**, where cotton is grown on irrigated land.

Much further west is **Cunnamulla**, 254 km north of Bourke in New South Wales and very definitely in the outback. This is another sheep-raising centre, noted for its wild flowers. The **Yowah** opal fields are about 150 km further west.

TOOWOOMBA (population 80,000)
On the edge of the Great Dividing Range and the Darling Downs, 138 km inland from Brisbane, this is the largest city in the region. It's a gracious city with parks, tree-lined streets, several art galleries and many early buildings. The old **Bull's Head Inn** on Bris-

bane St, Drayton, six km west, dates from 1847 and you can visit it from 10 am to 4 pm, Thursday to Monday, for $2. In Toowoomba itself there's the **Cobb & Co Museum** on the corner of James and Water Sts, and **Botanical Gardens** in Queens Park on the corner of Margaret and Lindsay Sts. The tourist information centre (☎ (076) 32 1988) is at 541 Ruthven St.

Places to Stay
The two cheapest hotels in town are the *Ruthven Hotel*, near the information centre, and the *Law Courts Hotel*, on the corner of Margaret and Neil Sts. Both are pretty basic.

Three km south of Jondaryan, which is about 45 km out of Toowoomba, there's a YHA-associated *Youth Hostel* in the 1859 *Jondaryan Woolshed* (☎ (076) 92 2229). The building is also a wool pioneer complex with museums, and daily shearing and blacksmithing demonstrations. Nightly cost in the hostel is $5.

ROMA (population 5706)
An early Queensland settlement, and now the centre for a huge sheep and cattle-raising district, Roma also has some curious small industries. There's enough oil in the area to support a small refinery, which produces just enough petroleum for local use. Gas deposits are rather larger, and Roma supplies Brisbane through a 450-km pipeline. There's also the small Romavilla Winery which is open daily; a wine festival is held in November.

Hervey Bay Area

North of the Sunshine and Cooloola coasts is 120-km-long Fraser Island. The two mainland departure points for the island are **Rainbow Beach** in the south and Hervey Bay opposite Fraser's west coast. Inland on the Bruce Highway are Gympie, where you turn off for Rainbow Beach, and Maryborough, where you turn off for Hervey Bay.

GYMPIE (population 10,800)

Gympie came into existence with an 1867 gold rush, and gold continued to be mined here right up to 1920. A week-long Gold Rush Festival is held in Gympie every October.

One of the four main national parks information centres in Queensland (☎ (074) 82 4189) is on the Bruce Highway as you enter Gympie from the south. In the same building there's a tourist information office (☎ (074) 82 5444), open daily from 8.30 am to 3.30 pm, and nearby is the interesting **Gympie Gold Mining & Historical Museum.**

A few km north of the town on Fraser Rd, Two Mile, a second museum is devoted to another source of Queensland's early wealth – the timber industry. The **Woodworks Forestry & Timber Museum** is open Monday to Friday from 10 am to 4 pm, Sundays 1 to 4 pm. You can get information on camping in nearby state forests here.

Gympie has several motels and caravan parks, and it's on the main bus and train routes north from Brisbane.

RAINBOW BEACH (population 726)

This little town, on the coast 70 km from Gympie, is an access point for Fraser Island and a base for visiting the northern part of Cooloola National Park.

From Rainbow Beach it's a 13-km drive north along the beach to Inskip Point, where ferries leave for Fraser Island. South-east of the town, the beach curves away 13 km to Double Island Point at the top of the Cooloola coast. One km along this beach is the 120-metre-high **Carlo sand blow,** and beyond it, the coloured sand cliffs after which the town is named. You can walk behind or along the beach all the way from the town and up to the lighthouse on Double Island Point.

The privately run Rainbow Beach Tourist Information Centre (☎ (074) 86 3227) has a list of other walks in the area. In a 4WD it's possible to drive to Noosa, 70 km south, along the beach most of the way. (See the earlier Cooloola Coast section.) The Rainbow Beach Backpackers also has a privately run tourist information centre.

The national parks office (☎ (074) 86 3160), for Fraser Island vehicle and camping permits and northern Cooloola National Park camping permits, is beside the main road as you enter Rainbow Beach.

Places to Stay

Rainbow Beach Backpackers (☎ (074) 86 3288), at 66 Rainbow Beach Rd, charges $10 per person per night in self-contained units.

Rainbow Beach Hotel-Motel (☎ (074) 86 3125) near the beachfront has rooms from $35/40 during the week, and there are two other slightly more expensive motels.

The *Rainbow Beach Holiday Village* (☎ (074) 86 3222) by the main road in the town has tent sites and on-site vans.

Getting There & Away

A school bus leaves Polley's Depot in Gympie at 6 am and 3 pm for Rainbow Beach, and heads back from Rainbow Beach at 7.20 am and 4.45 pm. It's open to all comers and runs Monday to Friday, usually in the school holidays too.

Another way to Rainbow Beach is to hitchhike along the beaches up from Noosa or on to Fraser Island. If you have a 4WD vehicle you can drive this way too.

Getting Around

In Rainbow Beach, the tourist information centre (☎ (071) 86 3227), at 8 Rainbow Beach Rd, and Jeep City (☎ (071) 86 3223), at 10 Karounda Court, both rent 4WDs.

There are also tours to Fraser Island, plus half-day trips to combinations of places like the Carlo sand blow, the coloured sand cliffs, Double Island Point, Lake Freshwater, Cooloola rainforest and the *Cherry Venture* wreck.

MARYBOROUGH (population 20,111)

Today, timber and sugar are Maryborough's major industries, but the town's earlier importance as an industrial centre and port on the Mary River led to the construction of a series of imposing Victorian buildings.

The greatest concentration of old buildings is on Wharf St. The post office, built in 1869, is just one of the buildings which reflect Maryborough's early prosperity; some of the old hotels are also fine examples of Victoriana. A street market is held every Thursday in the town centre. Maryborough also has a **railway museum** in the old railway station on Lennox St.

There are several motels and camping/caravan parks in the town, plus budget accommodation in some of the old hotels, such as the *Criterion* in Wharf St.

HERVEY BAY (population 13,600)

The five small settlements which make up the town of Hervey Bay, on the bay of the same name, are popular family holiday spots with safe beaches and a huge number of caravan parks. Of more interest is Fraser Island, for which Hervey Bay is a main access point. There's no surf at Hervey Bay, and the best beach is at Torquay.

Orientation

The five little towns are strung along a 10-km-long, north-facing stretch of coast. From west to east they are Point Vernon, Pialba, Scarness, Torquay and Urangan. Pialba is the main centre and the stopping point for long-distance buses. Fraser Island is 12 km across the Great Sandy Strait from Urangan, with Woody Island in between. River Heads, the departure point for the main Fraser Island ferries, is 15 km south of Urangan.

Things to See

The **Hervey Bay Wildlife Park**, on the corner of Maryborough Rd and Fairway Drive, Pialba, has native Australian fauna from wedge-tailed eagles to koalas as well as introduced species like camels and water buffaloes. Crocodiles are fed at 11.30 am and lorikeets at 3 pm.

Urangan Pier, a little further along the Esplanade, is 1.4 km long. Once used for sugar and oil handling, it's a popular fishing spot, since the far end stands in 25 to 30 metres of water.

One km east of the pier, at **Dayman Point**, there are good views over to Woody and Fraser islands, and monuments to Matthew Flinders and the Z Force WW II commandos who sank Japanese ships in Singapore Harbour in 1943.

Organised Tours

A number of companies run whale-watching tours from Hervey Bay and from the tip of Fraser Island. There are half and full-day tours between August and October. The tours cost around $45 and include lunch on board. *Fraser Flyer* (☎ (071) 25 1655) and MV *Islander* (☎ (071) 28 9370) are among the boats that offer cruises.

Places to Stay

Hostels Hervey Bay had, at last count, four hostels, spread between Scarness and Urangan. All do pick-ups from the main bus stop in Pialba, and all organise trips to Fraser Island.

First up is the very friendly *Mango Tourist Hostel* (☎ (071) 242382) at 110 Torquay Rd, Scarness. It's a small place, with just six beds ($9), but is clean and quiet, and the young couple running it really look after you.

A little further along, at 408 The Esplanade, Torquay, is the 100-bed *Koala Backpackers* (☎ (071) 25 3601). The beach is just across the road, and there are plenty of shops and eating possibilities close by. Dorm beds and double rooms cost $10 per person, and for every four to six beds there's a separate kitchen and bathroom. The hostel also has a pool and recreation room.

The *Hervey Bay Backpackers* (☎ (071) 28 1458), at 195 Torquay Terrace, is 2½ km from the bus stop. It has the usual hostel facilities and a pool. A bunk in a fan-cooled room with shared bathroom is $10. There are also a few slightly more expensive rooms with private bathroom and TV.

At Urangan, the *Colonial Log Cabin & Backpackers Resort* (☎ (071) 25 1844), on the corner of Pulgul St and Boat Harbour Drive, is a very well set-up place, but is quite

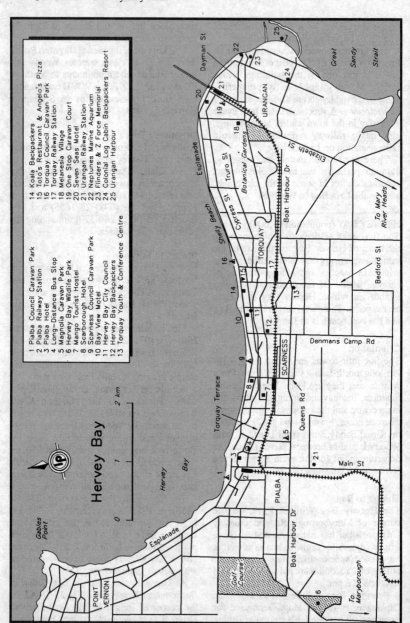

Hervey Bay

1 Pialba Council Caravan Park
2 Pialba Railway Station
3 Pialba Hotel
4 Long-Distance Bus Stop
5 Magnolia Caravan Park
6 Hervey Bay Wildlife Park
7 Mango Tourist Hostel
8 Scarborough Hotel
9 Scarness Council Caravan Park
10 Bay View Motel
11 Hervey Bay City Council
12 Hervey Bay Backpackers
13 Torquay Youth & Conference Centre
14 Koala Backpackers
15 Toto's Restaurant & Angelo's Pizza
16 Torquay Council Caravan Park
17 Torquay Railway Station
18 Melanesia Village
19 One Stop Caravan Court
20 Seven Seas Motel
21 Urangan Railway Station
22 Neptunes Marine Aquarium
23 Flinders & Z Force Memorial
24 Colonial Log Cabin Backpackers Resort
25 Urangan Harbour

a way from the centre of things. All accommodation is in twin rooms, and this costs $10 per person. The kitchen's a little cramped when busy, but is well equipped and spotless. You have free use of bicycles, and there's a good pool and tennis court.

Another possibility is the *Seven Seas Motel* (☎ (071) 28 9699) which has share units with four or six beds at $10 per person. It's at 573 The Esplanade, Urangan, close to the pier.

Motels & Holiday Flats There are plenty of these too. The *Bay View Motel* (☎ (071) 28 1134), at 399 The Esplanade, Torquay, between Tavistock St and Dennis Camp Rd, has units from $28/30 with TV, fan, fridge and tea/coffee facilities.

Calypso Holiday Units (☎ (074) 25 2688), at 480 The Esplanade in Torquay, has fully self-contained units for $45, and these can sleep up to four people.

Camping There are at least a dozen caravan/camping parks in Hervey Bay. Some of the best are the council-run parks along the Esplanade at Scarness (☎ (071) 28 1274), Torquay (☎ (074) 25 1578) and Pialba (☎ (071) 28 1399). These parks have tent sites and just a few on-site vans – book ahead.

The *Magnolia Caravan Park* (☎ (071) 28 1700), on the corner of Boat Harbour Drive and Taylor St, has a variety of on-site accommodation.

Places to Eat

Despite being the 'business' centre, Pialba has few places to eat. The *Pialba Hotel* has excellent meals for around $8, and also has live music some nights. The *RSL Club* on Torquay Rd is slightly cheaper.

The Esplanade in Torquay is the food focus in Hervey Bay. *Willy's (Manfred's)*, next to Koala Backpackers, is a popular place, again with live music some nights; there are backpackers' specials for $5. *Toto's*, on Fraser St, has good pizza and pasta, while *Gringo's Mexican Cantina*, at 449 The Esplanade, needs no explanation. The pub in

Torquay has the *China Garden* restaurant and you can sit outside to eat, often with musical accompaniment.

Seven Seas, at 573 The Esplanade, Urangan, is said to be the best seafood restaurant in Hervey Bay. It's open from 6 pm daily. In Urangan, *Melanesia Village*, on Elizabeth St, has a restaurant with two-course Thursday lunch specials in its garden lounge.

Getting There & Away

Sunstate and Sungold both fly to and from Brisbane six or seven days a week. Hervey Bay Airport is off Booral Rd, Urangan.

Hervey Bay is on the major bus route. It's about 4½ hours from Brisbane (around $30), and about 5½ hours from Rockhampton ($50).

Hervey Bay's main bus stop is a shelter by a church on the corner of Bryant St and Torquay Rd in Pialba. You can make bus bookings and get timetable information through any of the hostels, or through Bezants Travel on the corner of Bryant St and Torquay Rd in Pialba.

Getting Around

Maryborough-Hervey Bay Coaches (☎ (071) 21 3719) runs a service between the two centres several times daily Monday to Friday. On weekends, there's just one bus on Saturday morning.

There are a couple of good local 4WD hire places. Wide Bay Renta Centa (☎ (071) 25 1766) has two locations – 430 The Esplanade in Torquay, and the Shell service station on the corner of Bryant St and Torquay Rd in Pialba. This friendly outfit has good, reliable vehicles and can also arrange camping gear. Bay City Rentals (☎ (071) 24 3488), at 4 Fraser St in Torquay, is also reliable. Apart from these, you could always try Avis or Budget.

FRASER ISLAND

Fraser Island, the world's largest sand island, is 120 km long by about 15 km wide and rises to 200 metres above sea level in places. Apart from three or four small rock outcrops, it's all sand – mostly covered in vegetation. Here and there the cover is broken by sand blows – dunes that grow, shrink or move as the wind pushes them. The island also has about 200 lakes, some of them superb for swimming. Nearly all its northern third forms the Great Sandy National Park.

Fraser Island is a delight for those who love fishing, walking, exploring by 4WD or trail bike, and for those who simply enjoy nature. There are superb beaches (though swimming in the ocean can be dangerous due to severe undertows), towering dunes, thick forests, walking tracks, interesting wildlife and clear freshwater lakes and streams for swimming. You can camp or stay in accommodation. The island is sparsely populated and although more than 20,000 vehicles a year pile on to it, it remains wild. A network of sandy tracks crisscrosses the island and you can drive along great stretches of beach – but it's 4WD or trail bike only; there are no paved roads.

The island takes its name from Eliza Fraser, the wife of the captain of a ship which was wrecked further north in 1836. Making their way south to look for help, a group from the ship fell among Aborigines on Fraser Island. Some of the group died during their two-month wait for rescue, but others, including Eliza Fraser, survived with Aboriginal help.

The Butchulla Aborigines who used Fraser Island as a seasonal home were driven out onto missions when timber cutters moved on to the island in the 1860s. The cutters were after satinay, a rainforest tree almost unique to Fraser Island which is highly resistant to marine borer; this timber was used to line the Suez Canal. It was not until 1991 that logging on the island ceased.

In the mid-1970s, Fraser Island was the subject of a bitter struggle between conservationists and industry – in this case a sand-mining company. The decision went to the conservationists.

Information

There's a visitor centre on the east coast of the island at Eurong, and rangers at

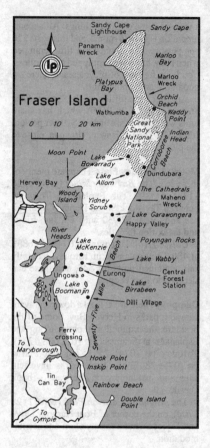

Dundubura and Waddy Point. The national parks office at Eurong has plenty of leaflets detailing walking trails and the flora & fauna found on the island.

At Central Forest Station there's a small display on the history of exploration and logging on the island.

A good map is essential if you will be spending a few days exploring. The Sunmap 1:125,000 provides all the detail you need, and is widely available in Hervey Bay.

General supplies are available from stores at Eurong, Happy Valley and Cathedral Beach, but as you might expect, prices are high. There are also public telephones at these sites.

It's possible to leave your car at the Esso service station in River Heads for $2 per day.

Permits You'll need a permit to take a vehicle onto the island, and to camp. The most convenient place to get permits is the Esso service station at River Heads, just half a km from the ferry to Wanggoolba Creek. Vehicles cost $15, and camping costs $7.50 per site per night. If you're staying in some of the island's cabin accommodation, or camping in one of the private camping grounds, there's no need to pay the $7.50.

Permits can also be obtained from the national parks office in Rainbow Beach; the Hervey Bay City Council (☎ (071) 25 1855) in Bideford St, Torquay; or from the national parks offices in Maryborough, Brisbane or Gympie.

Driving on the Island The only thing stopping you taking a conventional (non-4WD) vehicle onto the island is the fact that you probably won't get more than half a km before you get bogged in sand. Small 4WD sedans are OK, but you may have ground-clearance problems on some of the inland tracks – a 'proper' 4WD gives maximum mobility.

Ask on the mainland about island driving conditions before renting a 4WD vehicle. Sometimes rain and storms can make beaches and tracks very heavy going, if not impassable. The best sources of such information are probably the offices issuing the vehicle permits.

Driving on the island requires a good deal of care, to protect not only yourself but the fragile environment. Apart from the beaches, where you are free to drive at will, all tracks are obvious and you should stick to them. Most major junctions are signposted, but only the two dedicated 'scenic routes' are signposted along their length. When driving, you should have 4WD engaged at all times, not so much because of the danger of getting stuck, but because your wheels are less likely to spin and damage the sandy tracks.

When driving on the beaches, keep an eye out for washouts at the many creek outlets, especially after heavy rain. Use turn indicators to show oncoming vehicles which side you intend passing on. Low tide is the best time to travel as large expanses of smooth hard sand are exposed. An additional hazard is that the beach directly outside the resorts is used as a landing strip for small aircraft. At high tide it is much more difficult, and quite slow going. The speed limit on the beaches is 80 km/h, and on the inland tracks it's 35 km/h, although there's little opportunity to reach that speed.

Drive slowly when passing pedestrians and people fishing, as they probably won't hear you coming above the roar of the surf.

Driving on the eastern beach is fairly straightforward; the western beach is more treacherous and has swamps and holes – avoid it.

Around the Island

Starting from the south at Hook Point, you cross a number of creeks and get to Dilli Village, the former sand-mining centre. After the settlements of Eurong and Happy Valley, you cross Eli Creek, the largest on the east coast. About 65 km from Hook Point are the remains of the *Maheno*, a former passenger liner which was wrecked here in 1935 as it was being towed to a Japanese scrap yard.

Two marked vehicle tracks lead inland from Happy Valley: one goes to **Lake Garawongera** then south to the beach again at Poyungan Valley (15 km); the other heads to **Yidney Scrub** and a number of lakes before returning to the ocean beach north of the *Maheno* (45 km). The latter route will take you to some fine lakes and good lookout points among the highest dunes on the island.

Four km beyond Eurong is a signposted walking trail to the beautiful **Lake Wabby**, which is being slowly filled by a massive sand blow that advances about three metres a year. It's a 45-minute walk (rewarded by a swim in the lake), or you can drive a further 2.6 km north on the beach and there's a scenic route which will take you to a lookout on the inland side of the lake.

Not far north of the *Maheno* you enter the national park and pass the **Cathedrals**, 25 km of coloured sand cliffs. Dundubara has a ranger's hut, and probably the best camp ground on the island. Then there's a 20-km stretch of beach before you come to the rock outcrops of Indian Head, Middle Rocks and Waddy Point. Just past here is **Orchid Beach** with its resort, and it's a further 30 km of beach up to **Sandy Cape**, the northern tip, with its lighthouse a few km to the west.

A popular inland area for visitors is the south-central lake and rainforest country around Central Forest Station and lakes McKenzie, Jennings, Birrabeen and Boomanjin. **Lake McKenzie** is unbelievably clear. Known as a 'window' lake, the water here is actually part of the water table, and so has not flowed anywhere over land.

Walking Tracks There are a number of 'walkers-only' tracks ranging from the one-km Wungul Sand Blow Track at Dundubara to the 13-km trail between lakes Wabby and McKenzie. The useful *Fraser Island Recreation Area* leaflet put out by the National Parks & Wildlife Service lists several more.

Places to Stay & Eat
Come well equipped since supplies on the island are limited and only available in a few places. And be prepared for mosquitoes and horseflies.

Camping This is the cheapest way to stay on the island and gives you the chance to get closer to Fraser Island's unique natural environment. The national parks service and forestry department operate 11 camping areas on the island, some accessible only by boat or on foot. Those in the north at Dundubara, Waddy Point and Wathumba and in the south at Central Forest Station, Lake Boomanjin and Lake McKenzie all have toilets and showers. You can also camp on some stretches of beach. To camp in any of these public areas you need a permit.

There are also two privately owned camping grounds on the east coast, at *Eurong Beach Resort* (☎ (071) 28 3411), 35 km

north of Hook Point; and *Cathedral Beach Resort & Camping Park* (☎ (071) 28 4988), 34 km north of Eurong. A site at Cathedral Beach, which has a store, costs $14 for two people. At Eurong, camping is free if you've come across on the *Fraser Venture* or *Rainbow Venture* ferries, otherwise it's $1. The Eurong Beach Resort has a store, bar and restaurant which campers can use.

Other Accommodation *Dilli Village Recreation Camp* (☎ (071) 27 9130) is 200 metres from the east coast, 24 km from Hook Point and nine km from Eurong. A four-bed cabin with shower and equipped kitchen costs $10 per person per night. Doubles/twins with shared bathroom are $40. If you're in these standard rooms you have to eat at the camp catering service where breakfast and lunch are $5 each, and dinner is $7.

The *Eurong Beach Resort* (☎ (071) 27 9122), 35 km north of Hook Point on the east coast, has rooms and flats from $58, as well as a camping ground.

Just south of Happy Valley, the low-key *Yidney Rocks Cabins* (☎ (071) 27 9167) are right on the edge of the beach. They're old but comfortable, and sleep from six to eight people. The nightly rate is $65, but, as with all accommodation on the island, three-day or longer bookings are preferred.

The *Happy Valley Resort* (☎ (071) 27 9144) itself has motel rooms at $100 for a double, and self-contained units at $295 per week for four people. The *Cathedral Beach Camping Ground* also has a few on-site vans at $50 per night.

The *Orchid Beach Resort* (☎ (071) 27 9185), about 100 km up the east coast from Hook Point, is the most luxurious place on Fraser Island with doubles at $150 per person for full board. There's also a restaurant, bar and store here.

Getting There & Around
See the Hervey Bay and Rainbow Beach sections for details of 4WD hire from the mainland. The only vehicles available on the island are a couple of small Suzukis at Shorty's Car Hire, Eurong, for $90 per day.

On the island you can get fuel at Eurong, Happy Valley, Cathedral Beach and Orchid Beach.

Vehicle ferries (known locally as barges) operate to the southern end of Fraser Island from Inskip Point near Rainbow Beach, and to the west coast of the island from River Heads south of Urangan. There's also a ferry, the *Fraser II*, from Urangan to Moon Point on the island, but this is an inconvenient place to land as it's a long drive across to the other side.

The *Rainbow Venture* operates the 10-minute crossing from Inskip Point to Hook Point on Fraser Island. It makes this crossing regularly from about 7 am to about 4.30 pm daily. The price is $25 return per vehicle, and you can get tickets either in Rainbow Beach or on board the ferry.

The *Fraser Venture* makes the 30-minute crossing from River Heads to Wanggoolba Creek (also called Woongoolber Creek) on the west coast of Fraser Island. Departures from River Heads are at 9 am and 3.30 pm, and from the island at 9.30 am and 4 pm. The barge takes 22 vehicles but it's still advisable to book, through Bezants Travel (☎ (071) 24 1900) in Hervey Bay. The return fare for vehicle and driver is $32, plus $5 for each extra passenger.

It's quite possible to make your own way around the island, and hitching along the main tracks and beaches is pretty common practice. River Heads is probably the best place to try your luck, as this is where most of the island's traffic starts its journey.

Organised Tours Most 'day tours' to Fraser Island allow you to split the trip and stay a few days on the island before coming back.

There are several 4WD bus tour operators in Rainbow Beach and Hervey Bay. Prices for day tours range upwards from $45. Each outfit follows a different route but a typical tour might take in a trip up the east coast to the *Maheno* wreck and the Cathedrals, plus Central Forest Station and a couple of the lakes in the centre of the island.

Self-drive tours organised from the hostels are popular, and currently cost around $75 per person for a three-day trip. This doesn't include food or fuel but all the gear is organised for you. Find out how many will be in the group, as some places take up to nine people, which can be a bit unwieldy – five is much better.

BUNDABERG (population 55,000)
At the northern end of Hervey Bay, Bundaberg is a major sugar-growing, processing and exporting centre near the mouth of the Burnett River. Some of the sugar ends up in the famous Bundaberg Rum. The town is 50 km off the Bruce Highway and is the departure point for Lady Elliot and Lady Musgrave islands.

In summer, Bundaberg attracts a steady stream of travellers looking for work picking tomatoes.

Orientation & Information
Bundaberg Tourist Information Centre (☎ (071) 52 2406) is on the corner of Isis Highway, the main road as you enter the town from the south, and Bourbong St. It's open daily from 9 am to 5 pm. The town centre and post office are about a km east along Bourbong St from the tourist office.

Things to See
You can tour the **rum distillery** (☎ (071) 72 1333) on Avenue St in East Bundaberg at 10 am, 12.30 pm and 2.30 pm Monday to Friday – $4 including a drink. It's not far off the eastern end of Bourbong St. Tours of the bulk sugar terminal at Burnett Heads are held at 3.15 pm weekdays.

Aviator Bert Hinkler, who in 1928 made the first solo flight between England and Australia, was born and raised in Bundaberg. The house in Southampton, England, which he lived in for his last years was dismantled and shipped brick by brick to the corner of Young St and Perry Rd in North Bundaberg. It's an **aviation museum**, open daily from 10 am to 4 pm.

On the Bruce Highway near Bundaberg, Gin Gin is an old pastoral town. The strange **Mystery Craters** – 35 small craters in a big sandstone slab said to be at least 25 million years old – are 17 km along the Bundaberg road from Gin Gin.

Beaches

Moore Park and **Bargara** are good surf beaches, and turtles nest at the beach at Mon Repos. Local buses go to Bargara and Moore Park a few times on weekdays from Bundaberg post office. Four types of turtle – loggerhead, green, flatback and leatherback – have been known to nest at **Mon Repos** from late November to January, but it's predominantly the loggerhead which lays its eggs here. The rookery is unusual, since turtles generally prefer sandy islands off the coast. The young emerge and quickly make their way to the sea from mid-January to March. You're most likely to see the turtles laying their eggs around midnight when the tide is high. Observation of the turtles is controlled by national parks staff.

Places to Stay

Bundaberg has three backpackers' places: *Bundaberg Backpackers & Travellers Lodge* (☎ (071) 52 2080), at Targo St; *Bargara Beach Backpackers* (☎ (071) 59 2295), in the Linksview Motel at 13 See St; and *City Centre Backpackers* (☎ (071) 51 3501), in the Grosvenor Hotel at 216 Bourbong St. All offer the usual hostel facilities, and may be able to help you find work.

The *Royal Hotel* (☎ (071) 51 2201), on the corner of Barolin and Bourbong Sts, has singles/doubles for $23/30. The town also has plenty of motels and caravan/camping parks.

Getting There & Away

Air services are by Sunstate (from Brisbane, Gladstone, Rockhampton, Mackay and Townsville daily) and Lloyd Air (daily from Brisbane and Gladstone). All the main bus companies serve Bundaberg on the main north-south route. The main stop is Stewart's Coach Terminal (☎ (071) 52 9700) at 66 Targo St. Bundaberg is also a stop for trains between Brisbane and Rockhampton or Cairns.

Capricorn Coast

This central coastal area of Queensland takes its name from its position straddling the Tropic of Capricorn. Rockhampton is the major population centre in the area, and just off the coast lies Great Keppel Island (a popular island getaway) and the Capricornia Marine Park, the southernmost part of the Great Barrier Reef.

There are some good beaches on the coast itself, and a few small towns, most of them minor resorts with a variety of accommodation.

SOUTHERN REEF ISLANDS

The southernmost part of the Great Barrier Reef, known as the Capricornia section, begins north-east of Bundaberg. From Lady Elliot Island, 80 km off Bundaberg, this string of coral reefs and cays dots the ocean for about 140 km up to Tryon Island east of Rockhampton.

Several cays in this part of the reef are excellent for reef walking, snorkelling, diving and just getting back to nature – though reaching them is generally more expensive than reaching islands nearer the coast. Access is from Bundaberg, Gladstone or Rosslyn Bay near Rockhampton. A few of the islands are important breeding grounds for turtles and sea birds.

On the four national park islands where camping is allowed (Lady Musgrave, Masthead, Tryon and North West) campers must be totally self-sufficient. Numbers of campers are limited so it's advisable to apply well ahead for a camping permit. You can book six months ahead for these islands instead of the usual six to 12 weeks for other Queensland national parks. Contact the Queensland National Parks & Wildlife Service (☎ (079) 76 1621) on Roseberry St in Gladstone. If you get a permit you'll also receive information on any rules, such as restrictions on the use of generators, and on how not to harm the wildlife.

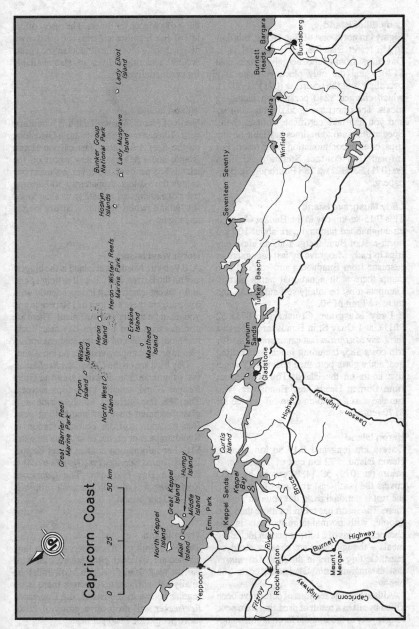

Capricorn Coast

0   25   50 km

Great Barrier Reef Marine Park

North Keppel Island
Great Keppel Island
Miall Island
Middle Island
Humpy Island
Keppel Park

Tryon Island
Wilson Island
North West Island
Heron Island
Erskine Island
Heron–Wistari Reefs Marine Park
Masthead Island

Hoskyn Islands
Lady Musgrave Island
Bunker Group National Park

Lady Elliot Island

Yeppoon
Emu Park
Keppel Sands
Keppel Bay

Rockhampton

Curtis Island

Gladstone
Tannum Sands
Turkey Beach

Seventeen Seventy

Winfield
Miara
Burnett Heads
Bargara
Bundaberg

Fitzroy River
Bruce
Highway
Dawson Highway
Burnett Highway
Capricorn Highway
Mount Morgan

Lady Elliot Island

Eighty km north-east of Bundaberg, this 0.4-sq-km resort island is not a national park. Day trips from Bundaberg by plane cost $170 – and the only place you can stay overnight is at the resort (☎ (071) 51 6077), which charges $240 per person including meals. The resort has good diving facilities and you can take certificate courses there. Special deals are sometimes available on day trips, or on accommodation at the resort. For information contact Sunstate Airlines (☎ (071) 52 2322) at 188 Bourbong St, Bundaberg.

Lady Musgrave Island

This 0.15-sq-km cay in the Bunker Group is an uninhabited national park about 100 km north-east of Bundaberg. You can make day trips to Lady Musgrave by fast catamaran or seaplane from Bundaberg and you can also camp there with a national parks permit. Campers must be totally self-sufficient, and there's a limit of 50.

Lady Musgrave Cruises (☎ (071) 52 9011), at 1 Quay St in Bundaberg, operates the *Lady Musgrave* fast catamaran. The day trip costs $85, including lunch, snorkelling gear and a glass-bottomed boat ride. You get five hours on the island. The boat leaves from Burnett Heads near Bundaberg. You can use it as a camping drop-off service for $170 return.

Heron Island

Only a km long and 0.17 sq km in area, Heron Island is 72 km east of Gladstone. A resort (☎ (079) 58 1488) owned by P&O covers the north-eastern third of the island; the rest is national park, but you can't camp there. The resort has room for more than 250 people, with normal nightly costs in the cheapest rooms of $100 per person including meals – though there are cheaper stand-by rates. Getting there, in the *Reef Adventurer* fast catamaran from Gladstone, costs $65 one-way.

Although large sections of coral have been killed by silt as a result of dredging for a new, longer jetty at the island, Heron is still some-thing of a Mecca for divers. The resort offers lots of dive facilities and trips and has its own dive school – a certificate course for guests is $280, and single dives are also available for certified divers.

Wilson Island

North of Heron, Wilson Island is a national park. You can make day trips from Gladstone on the *Reef Adventurer* fast cat via Heron Island, and P&O has a new resort on the island ($85 per day). However, not everyone enjoys the visitors. Apparently 300 nesting pairs of endangered roseate terns abandoned the island when regular visitors began turning up.

North West Island

At 0.9 sq km, North West Island is the biggest cay on the Barrier Reef. It's all national park, and you can camp there independently with a permit, but there's a limit of 150 people and you must be totally self-sufficient. There are also day trips from Rosslyn Bay near Rockhampton, and several commercial enterprises plan to set up camping ventures on the island.

Day trips are on the *Capricorn Reefseeker* fast catamaran from Rosslyn Bay and Great Keppel Island, usually three trips a week. The $88 fare includes lunch, a ride in a glass-bottomed boat and snorkelling gear. Bus transport to/from accommodation in Rockhampton or on the coast costs an extra $10. For information contact Great Keppel Island Tourist Services (☎ (079) 33 6744) at Rosslyn Bay Harbour. The *Capricorn Reefseeker* will also do camping drop-offs for $120 per person.

Tryon Island

There's a limit of 30 campers on this tiny, six-hectare national park island, north of North West Island. Again, you must be totally self-sufficient. Although there is no regular access to the island, the *Capricorn Reefseeker* will drop off a group of 20 or more people for $120 per head.

GLADSTONE (population 22,083)

Twenty km off the highway, Gladstone is one of the busiest ports in Australia. It handles agricultural, mineral and coal exports from central Queensland, plus the alumina which is processed in Gladstone from bauxite ore shipped from Weipa on the Cape York Peninsula.

Gladstone is the main departure point for boats to Heron, Masthead and Wilson islands on the Barrier Reef. Its own harbour, Port Curtis, has many islands. It has plenty of motels and caravan parks. There's a tourist information office (☎ (079) 72 4000) in Shop 6, City Centre Plaza, Goondoon St.

Most coast buses stop at Gladstone and it's also on the Brisbane to Rockhampton rail route. Air services include Sunstate's daily coastal hop and daily flights by Lloyd Air from Bundaberg and Brisbane. Ansett flies from Brisbane once a week.

ROCKHAMPTON (population 50,146)

Australia's 'beef capital' sits astride the Tropic of Capricorn. First settled by Europeans in 1855, Rockhampton had a relatively small, early gold rush but cattle soon became the big industry.

Rockhampton is an access point for Great Keppel and other islands. The boats leave from Rosslyn Bay on the coast about 50 km away but transport from Rocky is easy. There's also plenty of accommodation on the coast itself.

Orientation

Rockhampton is about 40 km from the coast, straddling the Fitzroy River. The long Fitzroy Bridge connects the old central part of Rockhampton with the newer suburbs to the north.

The Bruce Highway skirts the town centre and crosses the river upstream from the Fitzroy Bridge. Coming from the south, turn right up Denham or Fitzroy Sts to reach the centre of town.

Information

The Capricorn Information Centre (☎ (079)

27 2055), on the highway as you enter Rocky from the south, is beside the Tropic of Capricorn marker and three km from the town centre. There's a more central but smaller tourist information office on the East St Mall between Denham and William Sts. The RACQ (☎ (079) 27 2255) is at 134 William St. The national parks district office (☎ (079) 27 6511) is at 194 Quay St.

Things to See

There are many fine buildings in the town, particularly on **Quay St**, where you'll find one of the best Victorian street frontages in Australia. You can pick up tourist leaflets and magazines which map out town walking trails.

The **Botanic Gardens** at the end of Spencer St, in the south of the city, were established in 1869 and have an excellent tropical collection and walk-through aviary.

Places to Stay

Hostels The *Rockhampton Youth Hostel* (☎ (079) 27 5288), at 60 MacFarlane St, costs $10. It's a spacious hostel with good facilities, and is a 20-minute walk north of the centre. Except on weekends, you can get there on a High St bus. The hostel is just around the corner from the Greyhound/Pioneer terminal, and five minutes' walk from McCafferty's terminal. The Rocky hostel is a good place to organise trips to Great Keppel Island, and to book the popular hostel there. Discounts on tours to the Koorana Crocodile Farm and Cammoo Caves are available too.

Hotels & Motels There are plenty of old-fashioned hotels around the centre but nothing of great value in the motel line. On Quay St, the old *Criterion Hotel* (☎ (079) 22 1225) is one of Rockhampton's most magnificent old buildings. Hotel rooms are $24/28 for singles/doubles, and motel rooms are $38/43.

North of the river, if you can't get into the youth hostel, try the *Post Office Hotel-Motel* on Musgrave St, a block north of the Transit Centre. It has singles/doubles at $25/35. Or

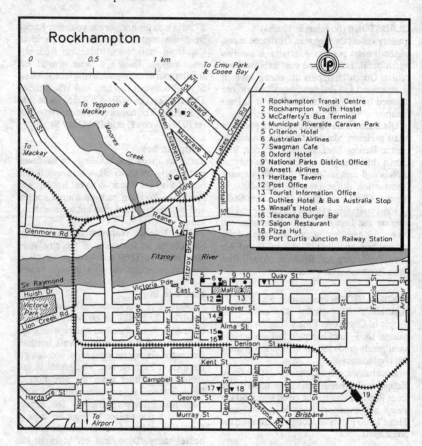

Rockhampton

0   0.5   1 km

To Emu Park
& Cooee Bay

To Yeppoon &
Mackay

Moores Creek

To Mackay

Albert St
Queen Elizabeth Drive
Musgrave St
Fitzroy Bridge
Jardine St
Painswick St
Edward St
Goodsall St
Yaamba Creek Rd

Glenmore Rd

Reaney St

Fitzroy   River

1 Rockhampton Transit Centre
2 Rockhampton Youth Hostel
3 McCafferty's Bus Terminal
4 Municipal Riverside Caravan Park
5 Criterion Hotel
6 Australian Airlines
7 Swagman Cafe
8 Oxford Hotel
9 National Parks District Office
10 Ansett Airlines
11 Heritage Tavern
12 Post Office
13 Tourist Information Office
14 Duthies Hotel & Bus Australia Stop
15 Winsall's Hotel
16 Texacana Burger Bar
17 Saigon Restaurant
18 Pizza Hut
19 Port Curtis Junction Railway Station

Sir Raymond
Huish Dr
Victoria Park
Lion Creek Rd

Victoria Pde
East St
Mall
Quay St
Bolsover St
Alma St
Denison St
Kent St
Campbell St
George St
Murray St

Cambridge St
Archer St
Fitzroy St
Denham St
William St
Derby St
Stanley St
South St
Francis St
Arthur St
Gladstone Rd

Harda Cre St
North St
Albert St

To Airport

To Brisbane

there are some motel rooms with private bathrooms and cooking facilities at the *Ramblers Caravan Park* (☎ (079) 28 2084) a km further north on the Bruce Highway.

You'll find lots of motels on the Bruce Highway as you come into Rockhampton from both the north and south.

Camping There are several camping grounds in Rocky, including the *Municipal Riverside Caravan Park* (☎ (079) 22 3779), just across the bridge from the city centre, which has tent sites but no on-site vans. Most of the other grounds have on-site vans and

cabins, as well as camping facilities. *Southside Caravan Village* (☎ (079) 27 3013), across the Bruce Highway from the Capricorn Information Centre, on the southern approach to Rocky, is a well-kept place with a shop and pool. You can get buses to the town centre.

Places to Eat

Several of the pubs have bistro sections as well as bar meals. The *Criterion Hotel* does counter meals from $6, and also has a seafood and steak restaurant where main meals are from $10. There's a smorgasbord lunch from Wednesday to Friday for $11. The *Heritage Tavern*, on the corner of Quay and William Sts, *Winsall's Hotel* on the corner of Denham and Alma Sts, and the *Savoy Hotel* all have similar set-ups.

Pacino's, on the corner of Fitzroy and George Sts, about a km south of the Fitzroy Bridge, is a good Italian restaurant if you're in the mood for a minor splash-out. The *Swagman Cafe*, at 8 Denham St, is good for cooked breakfasts at $5 to $7.

The *Tropical Fruit & Juice Bar*, on the mall across from the post office, has good fruit salads and smoothies. There's a clutch of burger, juice and hot-dog places open late at night at the Fitzroy St end of the mall.

More substantial eateries, all open quite late, are scattered along Denham St. Near the corner of Alma St there's *Vijay's Curry House*, open till 9 pm Monday to Saturday. The *Texacana Burger Bar*, also near this corner, stays open until 9 or 10 pm. Further along are three Chinese restaurants where you can sit down or take away.

Entertainment
The Criterion Hotel has a busy but relaxed scene in its little Newsroom Bar where local musicians and groups play on Wednesday, Thursday and Friday nights. There's also live rock in the beer garden on Sunday afternoons.

On Sundays, from 4 to 8 pm, there's live jazz at the Savoy Hotel. Rockhampton has a small collection of clubs. The Flamingo, on Quay St between William and Derby Sts, has touring bands and dress rules.

Getting There & Away
Air You can fly to Rocky from all the usual places along the coast with Ansett or Australian. Sunstate includes Rockhampton on its daily coastal hop from Brisbane ($196 from Rockhampton) to Mackay ($136) and back. Australian Regional Airlines also has flights between Rockhampton, Mackay and Proserpine.

Australian, Sunstate and Australian Regional (☎ 008 177 245, toll-free) are at

107 East St, and Ansett (☎ 008 177 576, toll-free) is at 137 East St.

Bus The major bus companies all pass through Rockhampton on the coastal route. McCafferty's also runs to Longreach ($51) via Emerald ($28) three times a week. From Rockhampton to Cairns is 13 hours ($90); to Mackay, four hours ($40); and to Brisbane, 10 hours ($70).

Greyhound/Pioneer (☎ (079) 22 5811) operate from the Transit Centre on Musgrave St, 500 metres north of the bridge. McCafferty's (☎ (079) 27 2844) has a terminal just north of the bridge, also on Musgrave St. Bus Australia stops outside Duthies Hotel on the corner of Bolsover and Denham Sts.

Duthies Travel (☎ (079) 27 6288), on Denham St, handles tickets for most destinations.

Train Both the Sunlander (four times a week) and Queenslander (once a week) travel between Brisbane and Cairns, stopping at Rockhampton. The Capricornian (a night train, three times a week) and the Spirit of Capricorn (six times a week) travel between Rockhampton and Brisbane. Twice weekly, the Midlander runs between Rockhampton, Emerald, Longreach and Winton. For more information, contact the Queensland Rail office in Rockhampton (☎ (079) 32 0211).

Getting Around
Rockhampton Airport is five km south of the centre. The Port Curtis Junction Railway Station is about 1½ km from the centre.

There's a reasonably comprehensive city bus network. Young's Bus Service runs day trips to Mt Morgan, and Rotherys Coaches (☎ (079) 22 4320) does trips to Koorana Crocodile Farm and the Capricorn Coast, the town sights and the Cammoo and Capricorn caves.

AROUND ROCKHAMPTON
Berserker Range
This rugged range, which starts 26 km north of Rocky, is noted for its spectacular limestone caves and passages. Several tours a day

are taken through **Olsen's Capricorn Caverns** and **Cammoo Caves**, near the Caves township, east off the Bruce Highway.

Mt Morgan (population 3700)

The open-cut gold and copper mine at Mt Morgan, 38 km south-west of Rockhampton on the Burnett Highway, was worked (off and on) from the 1880s until 1981. You can still visit the 325-metre-deep mine – tours (☎ (079) 38 1550) leave the mine car park at 1.30 pm on Monday, Wednesday, Friday and Saturday – and some of the town buildings are reminders of its more exciting past. There's quite a good museum on the corner of Morgan and East Sts (open daily) and a tourist information centre in the library on Morgan St.

Young's Bus Service (☎ (079) 22 3813) operates a regular bus from Rockhampton to Mt Morgan four times daily on weekdays, twice on Saturdays. In Rockhampton, the buses leave from the corner of East and William Sts.

YEPPOON (population 9000)

This small seaside resort, on the coast 43 km north-east of Rockhampton, is much cooler than Rocky in summer. It's also where you come to catch ferries to Great Keppel Island. If you can't afford to stay at Great Keppel, there are a couple of good hostels in Yeppoon, and the beaches in the area are quite good too.

Places to Stay

The pleasant *Yeppoon Backpackers Hostel* (☎ (079) 39 2122) is on the seafront at 12 Anzac Parade. Accommodation is in eight-bed units with bathroom, sitting room, balcony and kitchen. The nightly cost is $10 and the hostel also has a sun deck and pool.

Up on the hill behind the town, the *Barrier Reef Backpackers*, at 30 Queen St, has good views of the town. There's also the *Keppel Bay Backpackers*, one block back from the waterfront on Barry St.

Also on Normanby St is the pleasant *Tidewater Motel* (☎ (079) 39 1632). It's probably the cheapest motel in town. Normally singles/doubles are $28/30, although like everywhere in Yeppoon, prices can rise by about one-third in the peak holiday seasons. There's a pool and a laundry, and breakfast is available.

Places to Eat

Most places are on Normanby and James Sts. On Normanby St, near the seafront, the *Hong Kong Cafe* does a $7 meal including starters, main dish, rice and tea or coffee. *Sandy's Cafe*, open from 7.30 am to 9 pm, has a variety of meals from $8.

Entertainment

The Strand Hotel, on the corner of Anzac Parade and Normanby St, is a popular pub with live bands on Friday and Saturday nights. Back along James St there's the Nightowl disco in the Railway Hotel-Motel, and on Hill St is the flashier La Bamba disco/nightspot.

Getting There & Away

If you're heading for Great Keppel or the reef, most of the cruise and ferry operators will transport you – often free – between your accommodation (in Rockhampton or on the coast) and Rosslyn Bay Harbour. Young's Bus Service (☎ (079) 22 3813) also runs several buses a day between Rockhampton, Yeppoon and the rest of the Capricorn Coast. Departures in Rockhampton are from Denham St near the corner of Bolsover St.

If you're driving to Rosslyn Bay you can leave your vehicle for $3 a day at the harbour, or there's the Kempsea lock-up car park on the main road just north of the harbour turn-off. The Kempsea car park charges $5 a day ($2 for motorbikes) and runs a free bus to and from the harbour.

YEPPOON TO EMU PARK

There are beaches dotted all along the 19-km coast from Yeppoon south to Emu Park. At **Cooee Bay**, a couple of km from Yeppoon, the annual Australian 'Cooee' Championships are held each August.

Rosslyn Bay Harbour, reached by a short side road about seven km south of Yeppoon, is the departure point for trips to the Keppel Bay islands and North West Island.

South of Rosslyn Bay are three fine headlands with good views – **Double Head, Bluff Point** and **Pinnacle Point**. After Pinnacle Point the road crosses **Causeway Lake**, a saltwater inlet where you can rent canoes and sailboards. Further south at **Emu Park** there are more good views and the 'Singing Ship' – a series of drilled tubes and pipes which emit whistling or moaning sounds when there's a breeze blowing. It's a memorial to Captain Cook. Emu Park also has a museum which doubles as a tourist information centre.

Koorana Crocodile Farm is five km off the Emu Park to Rockhampton road. The turn-off is 15 km from Emu Park. The farm has hundreds of crocs, and tours are given at 1 pm three or four days a week.

Places to Stay

There are many possibilities, including several caravan/camping parks, along this stretch of coast. At Cooee Bay, the *Poinciana Tourist Park* (☎ (079) 39 1601) has tent sites and on-site cabins. Further along, at Lammermoor Beach just before the turn-off to Rosslyn Bay Harbour, *Golden Sands* (☎ (079) 33 6193) has pleasant holiday flats at $40. It's just across the road from the beach.

A couple of km south of the Rosslyn Bay turn-off, *Capricorn Palms Caravan Park* (☎ (079) 33 6144) is a modern, well-kept place set back from the road at Mulambin Beach. Further south, the *Coolwaters Holiday Village* (☎ (079) 39 6102) has tent sites and on-site vans.

Finally, at Emu Park, the council-run *Bell Park Caravan Park* (☎ (079) 39 6202) is shady and very close to the beach.

GREAT KEPPEL ISLAND

Owned by Australian Airlines, Great Keppel has recently undergone a $14 million upgrade and is now a very popular resort, especially among young families and couples. The airline has a variety of package tours to Great Keppel: depending where you start from, seven days there will cost you at least $1500 per person including airfares, food and facilities.

The good news about Great Keppel is that, unlike many of the resort islands, there are some good budget accommodation alternatives, and it's also one of the cheapest and easiest Queensland islands to reach. Daytrippers to the resort have access to a pool, a bar, outdoor tables and umbrellas, horseriding and a barbecue lunch on weekends.

Although it's not actually on the reef, Great Keppel is the equal of most islands up the coast. It's 13 km offshore, and is big enough that you won't see all of it in an afternoon but small enough to explore over a few days. It covers 14 sq km and boasts 18 km of very fine beaches.

Things to See & Do

It only takes a short stroll from the main resort area to find your own deserted stretch of white-sand beach. The water's clear, warm and beautiful. There is good coral at many points around the island, especially between Great Keppel and Humpy Island to the south. A 20-minute walk around the headland south of the resort brings you to **Monkey Beach** where there's good snorkelling.

There are a number of bushwalking tracks from Fishermans Beach, the main beach. The longest, and one of the more difficult, goes across to the lighthouse near Bald Rock Point on the far side of the island (2½ hours one-way). Some beaches, like Red Beach near the lighthouse, are only accessible by boat.

There's a fine **underwater observatory** by Middle Island, close to Great Keppel. A confiscated Taiwanese fishing junk was sunk next to the observatory to provide a haven for fish. A visit to the observatory costs $10, which includes the boat trip. Boats leave hourly from 11.15 am daily. You can buy tickets at the Wapparaburra Kiosk. Tours on the *Seafari* from Rosslyn Bay also take in the observatory.

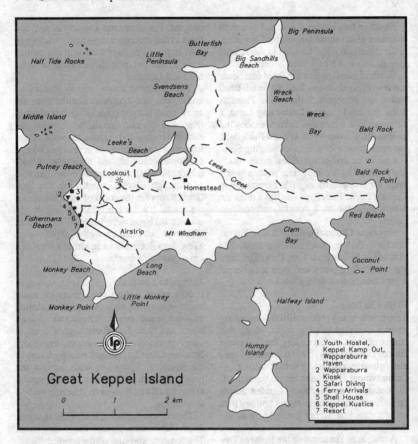

Great Keppel Island

1	Youth Hostel, Keppel Kamp Out, Wapparaburra Haven
2	Wapparaburra Kiosk
3	Safari Diving
4	Ferry Arrivals
5	Shell House
6	Keppel Kuatics
7	Resort

0   1   2 km

Horse rides organised by the resort go to the restored homestead in the middle of the island. Hour-long rides head off two or three times a day and cost $18 if you're a resort guest, $3 more if you're not.

Water Sports Capricorn Reef Diving and Wapparaburra Haven & Water Sports, both on Fishermans Beach, hire out jet skis, sailboards, catamarans, motorboats, fuel, tackle and bait. You can also try parasailing with Capricorn Reef Diving ($30 for 10 minutes).

The *Tropic Diva* (☎ (079) 28 0433) runs snorkelling, fishing and diving trips from Rosslyn Bay to various locations around the islands. For divers, a day trip costs $60 including all diving gear and two air fills, and you can be dropped on Great Keppel at the end of the day if you wish. You can also do an open-water certificate course for $195. For snorkelling and fishing, a day trip costs $35.

Several other vessels are available for diving, fishing or cruising trips – ask at the Capricorn Information Centre in Rockhampton or at Rosslyn Bay. Two possibilities are Keppel Isles Yacht Charters (☎ (079) 39

4939) and Keppel Island Cruises (☎ (079) 33 6622).

Places to Stay & Eat

Most people take package tours, but there are terrific alternatives for the budget traveller. The *Great Keppel Youth Hostel* (☎ (079) 27 5288) costs $9 a night and has two kitchens, a laundry and a barbecue area. Book through the Rockhampton Youth Hostel or well ahead through the Brisbane YHA.

At *Wapparaburra Haven* (☎ (079) 39 1907) you can camp close to the beach for $8, rent a mattress in a tent for $12, or sleep in a cabin at $75 for singles/doubles plus $10 for each extra person. The tents have electric lighting and hold four people each. The tent village has a stove and washing-up facilities under cover but no fridge or kitchen gear.

Next door to Wapparaburra Haven is *Keppel Kamp Out*, which is geared to the 18-35 age bracket, and has organised activities. The cost – $38 per person – includes twin-share tents, three meals and activities like water sports, parties and video nights.

If you want to cook it's best to bring a few basic supplies. Fruit, vegetables, groceries and dairy foods are sold at the pricey Wapparaburra Kiosk, which also does evening meals from $8.

The resort has day-trippers' facilities plus the *Keppel Cafe* with burgers from $2.60, meat pies, etc. There's a daily lunch smorgasbord at $19.50 for nonguests, and a $7 barbecue on weekends only.

Halfway along the path between the resort and the kiosk, the *Shell House* not only has a shell or two, but also does excellent Devonshire teas. The friendly owner has lived on Keppel for many years. His tropical garden offers a pleasant break from the sun.

Getting There & Away

Air Australian Airlines flies at least twice daily between Rockhampton and Great Keppel ($77 one-way).

Boat Ferries for Great Keppel leave from Rosslyn Bay Harbour on the Capricorn Coast. Three boats, the *Seafari*, *Aquajet* and *Reefseeker*, make the crossing daily. You can book the ferries through your accommodation or agents in Rockhampton or the Capricorn Coast. The youth hostel in Rockhampton often has bargains. All the boats are operated by Great Keppel Island Tourist Services (☎ (079) 33 6744) at Rosslyn Bay.

The *Reefseeker* costs $27 for a return trip to the island, the *Aquajet* is $22, and the *Seafari* is $25. If you want to do a day trip to the reef, the *Reefseeker* continues after dropping off at Great Keppel. The day trip costs $80 and includes diving and a smorgasbord lunch. The *Seafari* continues on a three-hour trip around the island, which includes boom netting and snorkelling. This is free if you have come across on either of the other two boats; resort guests pay $10. This then gives you three hours on the island before the return to Rosslyn Bay.

The *Aquajet* leaves Rosslyn Bay at 9.30, 11 am and 3.30 pm, and from Great Keppel at 10 am, 2.45 and 4.15 pm. The *Reefseeker* leaves at 9 am, and returns at 4.30 pm from Great Keppel. The *Seafari* leaves Rosslyn at 9 am and Great Keppel at 3.45 pm.

OTHER KEPPEL BAY ISLANDS

Great Keppel is only the biggest of the 18 continental islands dotted around Keppel Bay, all within 20 km of the coast. You may get to visit **Middle Island**, with its underwater observatory, or **Halfway** or **Humpy** islands if you're staying on Great Keppel. Most of the islands have clean white beaches and several, notably Halfway, have excellent fringing coral reefs. Some, including Middle and **Miall**, are national parks where you can maroon yourself for a few days' camping. To camp on a national park island, you need to take all your own supplies including water. Numbers of campers on each island are restricted – for example, eight on Middle and six on Miall. You can get information and permits from the national parks regional office at 194 Quay St in Rockhampton (☎ (079) 27 6511) or the ranger's office at Rosslyn Bay Harbour (☎ (079) 33 6608).

North Keppel is the second largest of the group and one of the most northerly. It covers

GREAT BARRIER REEF

Facts & Figures

The Great Barrier Reef is 2000 km in length. It starts slightly south of the Tropic of Capricorn, somewhere out from Bundaberg or Gladstone, and ends in the Torres Strait, just south of Papua New Guinea. This huge length makes it not only the most extensive reef system in the world, but also the biggest structure made by living organisms. At its southern end, the reef is up to 300 km from the mainland, while at the northern end it runs nearer to the coast, is much less broken and can be up to 80 km wide. In the 'lagoon' between the outer reef and the coast, the waters are dotted with smaller reefs, cays and islands. Drilling on the reef has indicated that the coral can be more than 500 metres thick. Most of the reef is around two million years old, but there are sections dating back 18 million years.

What is It?

Coral is formed by a small, primitive animal, a marine polyp of the family Coelenterata. Some polyps, known as hard corals, form a hard surface by excreting lime. When they die, the hard 'skeletons' remain and these gradually build up the reef. New polyps grow on their dead predecessors and continually add to the reef. The skeletons of hard corals are white and the colours of reefs come from living polyps.

Coral needs a number of preconditions for healthy growth. First the water temperature must not drop below 17.5°C – thus the Barrier Reef does not continue further south into cooler waters. The water must be clear to allow sunlight to penetrate, and it must be salty. Coral will not grow below depths of 30 metres because the sunlight does not penetrate sufficiently, nor does it grow around river mouths. The Barrier Reef ends near Papua New Guinea because the Fly River's enormous water flow is both fresh and muddy.

One of the most spectacular sights of the Barrier Reef occurs for a few nights after a full moon in late spring or early summer each year, when vast numbers of corals spawn at the same time. The tiny bundles of sperm and eggs are visible to the naked eye and the event has been likened to a gigantic underwater snowstorm.

Reef Types

What's known as the Great Barrier Reef is not one reef but about 2600 separate ones. Basically, reefs are either fringing or barrier. You will find fringing reefs off sloping sides of islands or the mainland coast. Barrier reefs are further out to sea: the 'real' Great Barrier Reef, or outer reef, is at the edge of the Australian continental shelf, and the channel between the reef and the coast can be 60 metres deep. In places, the reef rises straight up from that depth. This raises the question of how the reef built up from that depth when coral cannot survive below 30 metres? One theory is that the reef gradually grew as the sea bed subsided, implying that the reef was able to keep pace with the rate of subsidence. Another theory is that the sea level gradually rose, and again the coral growth was able to keep pace.

Reef Inhabitants

There are about 400 different types of coral on the Great Barrier Reef. Equally colourful are the many clams which appear to be embedded in the coral. Other reef inhabitants include about 1500 species of fish, 4000 types of mollusc (clams, snails, etc), 350 echinoderms (sea urchins, starfish, sea cucumbers and so on, all with a five-arm body plan), and countless thousands of species of crustaceans (crabs, shrimps and their relatives), sponges and worms.

Reef waters are also home to dugong (the sea cows which gave rise to the mermaid myth) and breeding grounds for humpback whales, which migrate every winter from Antarctica. The reef's islands form important nesting colonies for many types of sea bird, and six of the world's seven species of sea turtle lay eggs on the islands' sandy beaches in spring or summer.

Crown-of-Thorns Starfish One reef inhabitant which has enjoyed enormous publicity is the crown-of-thorns starfish – notorious because it appeared to be chewing through large areas of the Great Barrier Reef. It's thought that the crown-of-thorns develops a taste for coral when the reef ecology is upset – as, for example, when the supply of bivalves (oysters, clams), which comprise its normal diet, is diminished.

Dangerous Creatures Hungry sharks are the usual idea of an aquatic nasty but the Barrier Reef's most unpleasant creatures are generally less dramatic. For a start, there are scorpion fish with highly venomous spines. The butterfly cod is a very beautiful scorpion fish and relies on its colourful, slow-moving appearance to warn off possible enemies. In contrast, the stonefish lies hidden on the bottom, looking just like a rock, and is very dangerous to step on. Although they're rather rare, it's a good idea to wear shoes when walking on the reef – this is sensible anyway to protect yourself against sharp coral and rocks.

Stinging jellyfish are a danger only in coastal waters and only in certain seasons. The deadly 'sea wasp' is in fact a box jellyfish (see the Warning at the beginning of this chapter). As for sharks, there has been no recorded case of a visitor to the reef islands meeting a hungry one.

Viewing the Reef

The best way of seeing the reef is by diving or snorkelling in it. Otherwise you can walk on it, view it through the floor of glass-bottomed boats or the windows of semisubmersibles, or descend below the ocean surface inside 'underwater observatories'. You can also see a living coral reef and its accompanying life forms without leaving dry land, at the Great Barrier Reef Wonderland aquarium in Townsville.

Innumerable tour operators run day trips to the outer reef and to coral-fringed islands from towns on the Queensland coast. The cost depends on how much reef-viewing paraphernalia is used, how far the reef is from the coast, how luxurious the vessel that takes you there is, and whether lunch is included. Usually, free use of snorkelling gear is part of the package. Some islands have good reefs too: they're usually cheaper to reach and you can stay on quite a few of them.

The Great Barrier Reef Marine Park Authority (GBRMPA) is the body looking after the welfare of most of the reef. Its address is PO Box 1379, Townsville, Queensland 4810 (☎ (077) 81 8811). It also has an office in Great Barrier Reef Wonderland in Townsville.

Islands

There are three types of island off the Queensland coast. In the south, before you reach the Barrier Reef, are several large vegetated sand islands like North Stradbroke, Moreton and Fraser islands. These are interesting to visit for a variety of reasons but not for coral. Strung along the whole coast, mostly close inshore, are continental islands like Great Keppel, most of the Whitsundays, Hinchinbrook and Dunk. At one time, these would have been the peaks of coastal ranges, but rising sea levels submerged the mountains. The islands' vegetation is similar to that of the adjacent mainland.

The true coral islands, or cays, may be on the outer reef, or may be isolated between it and the mainland. Green Island near Cairns, the Low Isles near Port Douglas and Heron Island off Gladstone are all cays. Cays are formed when a reef is above sea level, even at high tide. Dead coral is ground down by water action to form sand and, in some cases, eventually vegetation takes root. Coral cays are low-lying, unlike the often hilly islands closer to the coast. There are about 300 cays on the reef, 69 of them vegetated.

The Queensland islands are extremely variable so don't let the catchword 'reef island' suck you in. Most of the popular resort islands are actually continental islands and some are well south of the Great Barrier Reef. Being a reef island is not necessarily important, since many continental islands will still have fringing reefs as well as other attractions that a tiny dot-on-the-map coral cay is simply too small for – like hills to climb, bushwalks, and secluded beaches where you can get away from other island lovers.

The islands also vary considerably in their accessibility – Lady Elliot for instance is a $170 return flight, others are just a few dollars by ferry. If you want to stay on an island rather than make a day trip from the mainland, this too can vary widely in cost. Accommodation is generally in the form of expensive resorts, where most visitors will be on an all-inclusive package holiday. But there are a few exceptions to this rule, plus on some islands it's possible to camp. A few islands have proper camping areas with toilets and fresh water on tap while, at the other extreme, on some you'll even have to bring drinking water with you.

For more information on individual islands, see under the Capricorn Coast, Whitsunday Coast, North Coast and Far North Queensland sections of this chapter. Also good is Lonely Planet's *Islands of Australia's Great Barrier Reef.* ∎

six sq km and is a national park. The most popular camping spot is Considine Beach on the north-west coast, which has well water for washing, and toilets. Take insect repellent.

Just south of North Keppel, tiny **Pumpkin Island** has five cabins (☎ (079) 39 2431) which accommodate either five or six people each at a cost of $80 to $110 per cabin. There's water and solar electricity, and each cabin has a stove, fridge, and a bathroom with shower. Bedding is provided.

CAPRICORN HINTERLAND
The Capricorn Highway runs inland, virtually along the tropic, across the central Queensland highlands to Barcaldine, from where you can continue west and north-west along the Landsborough Highway to meet the Townsville to Mt Isa road.

The area was first opened up by miners chasing gold and copper around Emerald, and sapphires around Anakie, but cattle, grain crops and coal provide its main living today. Carnarvon National Park, south of Emerald, is one of Australia's most spectacular and interesting.

Getting There & Away
Sunstate and Sungold link Brisbane with Blackwater and Emerald, and Sunstate also flies to Clermont. Flight West has flights from Brisbane to Townsville, Rockhampton and Mackay; and from Mt Isa to Blackall, Longreach ($188 from Mt Isa, $286 from Brisbane), Winton and Barcaldine.

McCafferty's has a Rockhampton to Longreach service three times a week which calls at all towns along the Capricorn Highway. The twice-weekly Midlander train runs between Rockhampton and Winton, following the same route as the highway.

Blackdown Tableland National Park
On the way to Emerald from Rocky you pass through the coal-mining centre of **Blackwater**. About 30 km before Blackwater and 11 km west of Dingo is the turn-off for Blackdown Tableland National Park. The tableland is around 800 metres high, with spectacular sandstone scenery plus some unique wildlife and plant species. The 20-km gravel road leading on to the tableland can be unsafe in wet weather, and is not suitable for caravans at any time.

In the park, you can bushwalk to waterfalls and lookout points, study Aboriginal rock art, and swim. There's a camping area at **Mimosa Creek**, about 10 km into the park. Camping permits for the park are available from the ranger at Blackdown (☎ (079) 89 1964). Bring a gas stove for cooking.

Coal Mines
Several of the massive open-cut Queensland coal mines, about 200 km inland from Rockhampton and Mackay, give free tours lasting about 1½ hours; book ahead. The Blackwater mine tour (☎ (079) 82 5166), off the Rockhampton to Emerald road, leaves the main mine office on Wednesdays at 10 am. For the Goonyella (☎ (079) 42 3224) and Peak Downs (☎ (079) 41 6233) mines near Moranbah, buses depart Moranbah town square at 10 am on Tuesdays and Thursdays. Tours of Blair Athol mine (☎ (079) 83 1866) near Clermont start on Tuesdays at 9 am.

Gem Fields
West of Emerald, about 270 km inland from Rockhampton, the gem fields around Anakie, Sapphire, Rubyvale and Willows Gemfield are known for sapphires, zircons, amethysts, rubies, topaz, jasper, even diamonds and gold. To go fossicking, you need a 'fossicking licence', sold from the Emerald Courthouse or on the gem field.

Anakie, 42 km west of Emerald on the Capricorn Highway, has the Gemfields Information Centre where you can find out how to go fossicking and pick up maps of the fossicking areas. **Sapphire** is 10 km north of Anakie on a sealed road. There's large-scale open-cut mining between here and **Rubyvale**, seven km further north, but plenty of room for fossickers as well. Sapphire has an associate YHA hostel and camping at *Sunrise Cabins* (☎ (079) 85 4281), about a km out of town on the road to Rubyvale. At the hostel you can get information, licences and maps, hire fossicking gear or arrange a gem-field tour. There are also caravan/camping parks at Anakie, Rubyvale and Willows Gemfield.

Sapphires are found close to the surface at **Willows Gemfield**, 38 km west of Anakie.

Clermont (population 1700)

North of Emerald is Clermont, with the huge Blair Athol open-cut coal mine. Clermont is Queensland's oldest tropical inland town, founded on copper, gold, sheep and cattle. It was the scene of gold-field race riots in the 1880s, and a military takeover of the town in 1891 after a confrontation between striking sheep shearers and non-union labour.

The town has a couple of pubs and a caravan park with on-site vans.

Springsure (population 800)

Springsure, south of Emerald, has two historical museums and some attractive surrounding countryside, with granite mountains and sunflower fields (the sunflowers are used to produce oil and seed). Nearby is the **Old Rainworth Fort** at Burnside, built following the Wills Massacre of 1861 when Aborigines killed 19 Whites on Cullin-La-Ringo Station north-west of Springsure.

For accommodation you have the choice of a motel and a caravan park.

Carnarvon National Park

Rugged Carnarvon National Park, in the middle of the Great Dividing Range, has dramatic gorge scenery and many Aboriginal rock paintings and carvings. It's reached from Rolleston, south-east of Springsure, or from Injune, north of Roma. The impressive Carnarvon Gorge is all that most people see of the park, which is pretty inaccessible.

From Rolleston to Carnarvon Gorge, the road is bitumen for 27 km and unsealed for 69 km. From Roma via Injune and Wyseby, the road is good bitumen for 170 km then unsealed and fairly rough for 67 km. After rain, both roads become impassable.

Carnarvon Gorge is stunning, partly because it's an oasis surrounded by drier plains and partly due to its scenic variety, which includes sandstone cliffs, moss gardens, deep pools, and rare palms and ferns. There's also lots of wildlife. You can drive to the nearby camping ground, but the gorge itself is only accessible on foot. Aboriginal art can be viewed at three main sites – **Baloon Cave**, the **Art Gallery**, and **Cathedral Cave**. It's believed Aborigines lived here as long as 19,000 years ago.

To get into the more westerly and rugged Mt Moffatt section of Carnarvon National Park, there are two unsealed roads from Injune: one through Womblebank Station, the other via Westgrove Station; both are passable by conventional vehicle, except after heavy rain. There are no through roads from Mt Moffatt to Carnarvon Gorge or to the third and fourth remote sections of the park – Salvator Rosa and Ka Ka Mundi. Mt Moffatt has some beautiful scenery, diverse vegetation and wildlife, and **Kenniff Cave**, an important Aboriginal archaeological site.

Places to Stay The *Oasis Lodge* (☎ (079) 84 4503), near the entrance to the Carnarvon Gorge section of the park, offers cabins or 'safari tents' from $138 a night per person, including full board and organised activities. There's a general store with fuel.

The national park camping ground is about three km into the Carnarvon Gorge section of the park and has an information centre, showers and toilets. Wood for cooking is not plentiful, so you should provide your own gas cooking equipment. You need a permit to camp, and it's usually advisable to book by phoning the Carnarvon Gorge rangers (☎ (079) 84 4505).

You can also camp at Big Ben camping area, 500 metres upstream from Cathedral Cave – a 12-km walk up the gorge. Again, permits are required. This enables the side gorges to be explored unhurriedly.

In the Mt Moffatt section, camping with a permit is allowed at six sites but you need to be completely self-sufficient, and a 4WD is advisable; telephone the Mt Moffatt rangers for details (☎ (076) 26 3581).

Whitsunday Coast

The Whitsunday Islands, which lie just off the coast between Mackay and Bowen, are probably the best known in Queensland. Mackay itself is a major regional centre, while the main access point for the islands themselves is Airlie Beach (Shute Harbour). Airlie Beach is a very popular travellers' hangout, mainly because many companies offering dive courses operate from here.

MACKAY (population 48,725)
Mackay is surrounded by sugar cane and processes a third of Australia's sugar crop. The sugar, loaded at the world's largest sugar-loading terminal at Port Mackay, has been grown here since 1865.

Mackay is nothing special, yet its town centre is attractively planted, and there are some good beaches a bus ride away. It's also an access point for the national parks at Cape Hillsborough and Eungella, and for the Great Barrier Reef; there are some interesting islands just an hour or two away.

Orientation
Mackay is on the Pioneer River and its main streets are laid out in a simple grid on the south side of the river. The main intersecting streets are Wood and Victoria. The railway and bus stations are only a few blocks from the centre and the airport is also fairly close. The newer suburbs are north of the river. Most of the popular beaches are still further north.

Information
Mackay's tourist information centre (☎ (079) 52 2677) is about three km south of the centre on Nebo Rd (the Bruce Highway). It's open from 9 am to 5 pm Monday to Friday, and from 9 am to 4 pm Saturday and Sunday. Next to it stands a Taiwanese fishing junk which was seized in 1976 when it was caught poaching giant clams within Australian waters. The RACQ (☎ (079) 57 2198) is at 214 Victoria St, and the national parks

district office (☎ (079) 51 8788) is on the corner of Wood and River Sts.

Things to See & Do
There are botanic gardens and an orchid house in **Queen's Park**, towards the eastern end of Gordon St. At the harbour in Port Mackay, six km north of the town centre, the small **Mackay Maritime Museum** is open daily Thursday to Monday from 10 am to 3 pm. There are good views over the harbour from **Mt Basset**, and at **Rotary Lookout** on Mt Oscar in North Mackay.

There's a town beach at the eastern end of Shakespeare St, two km from the centre. Other beaches include Far Beach, six km south of the river mouth; Harbour Beach, just south of the harbour wall; and Lamberts Beach, north of the harbour. But the best beaches are about 16 km north of Mackay at Blacks Beach, Eimeo and Bucasia. You turn right at the 'Northern Beaches' sign four km north of town on the Bruce Highway to reach them.

In the July to mid-November cane-crushing season, you can visit the Racecourse Sugar Mill (☎ (079) 57 4727) at 1.30 pm on weekdays for a tour. Polstone Sugar Farm gives tours for about $10 twice a week. In the crushing season you can tour the Mackay Harbour bulk sugar terminals at 10.30 am on weekdays. The 19th-century home of Mackay's founder, John Mackay, is at **Greenmount Homestead**, 20 km from town along the Peak Downs Highway towards Clermont. It's open to visitors from 9.30 am to 12.30 pm Monday to Friday, and from 10 am to 4 pm on Sundays.

Brumby Bob's Trail Rides, at 10 Jansen St, Slade Point, are only 10 minutes from town and offer three-hour trail rides across sand dunes, along the beach and through melaleuca forests. The $30 cost includes a drink at the local pub, billy tea and damper and transport there and back.

Organised Tours Roylen Cruises (☎ (079) 55 3066) runs fast catamaran day trips from Mackay Harbour to Brampton Island, Credlin Reef on the Barrier Reef, and Ham-

Top: Brisbane city from the Brisbane River, Qld (PS)
Left: Brisbane Town Hall, Qld (TW)
Right: Ramsay Bay, Hinchinbrook Island, Qld (TW)

Top: Sunset at Great Keppell Island, Qld (TW)
Left: Burrawangs growing on South Molle Island, Whitsundays, Qld (TW)
Right: Arthur Bay, Magnetic Island, Qld (CLA)

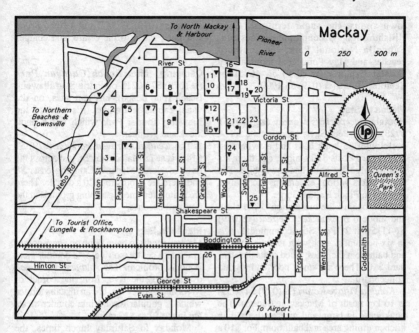

	PLACES TO STAY		
3	Backpackers Mackay		
8	Hotel Whitsunday		
9	International Lodge		
17	McGuire's Hotel		
18	Ambassador Hotel		
19	Palace Hotel		

	PLACES TO EAT		
1	Pizza Hut		
4	Le Cafe Carverie		
7	Hotel Mackay		
10	Wilkinson's Hotel		
11	Woody's Bakehouse		
14	Creperie Restaurant		

15	Tourist Chicken Bar
20	Tropical Salad Bar
21	Mandarin China Restaurant
24	Top Spot Coffee Lounge
25	Alpapa's Italian Restaurant

	OTHER
2	Mackay Bus Station
5	Austral Hotel
6	RACQ
12	Australian Airlines
13	Ansett
16	Post Office
22	RSL Club
23	Town Hall
26	Railway Station

ilton Island in the Whitsundays. The Credlin trip, four days a week, takes you to a pontoon on the reef with an underwater observatory. You also get a semisubmersible ride, and you can hire snorkelling or diving gear.

The tourist office has details of other trips including Air Pioneer's flights out to the Barrier Reef for snorkelling and reef walking.

Day trips by various operators go to the

town sights, the sugar terminal, Cape Hillsborough, Greenmount Homestead, Eungella National Park, the southern beaches and Hay Point coal terminal; try Coastal Explorer (☎ (079) 56 4606), or Reeforest Tours (☎ (079) 53 1000).

Places to Stay

Hostels *Backpackers Mackay* (☎ (079) 51 3728) at 32 Peel St, is an associate YHA hostel with 35 bunk beds and a swimming pool. A bed costs $10 a night, and there's a small charge for linen and towel hire. The hostel offers various excursions including a day trip to Finch Hatton Gorge.

Right behind the bus station is the clean and modern *Backpackers Retreat* (☎ (079) 51 1115), at 21 Peel St. Accommodation is in six-bed units, each with its own kitchen and bathroom facilities; a bed costs the standard $10. There's a small pool and a good noticeboard.

Kohuna Village Resort (☎ (079) 54 8555) is 16 km north of Mackay at Bucasia. The bunkhouse is large and airy, with its own kitchen/dining area and bathroom. For $10 a night, you can also use the three pools, buy meals and drinks at the resort, hire canoes and sailboards or play tennis. There's a courtesy bus, but it doesn't meet all buses. The Northern Beaches bus comes to Kohuna twice a day Monday to Friday.

Also in the beach suburbs, at Eimeo, is *Beachcomber Backpackers* (☎ (079) 54 6204), at Sunset Bay. The facilities are good and a lot of travellers have good things to say about this place. Beds cost $10 per night.

Hotels & Motels Back in the town centre, *Central Lodge* (☎ (079) 57 3654), at 231 Alfred St, has good clean singles/doubles at $25/30, and motel-style rooms at $30/35.

The *Ambassador Hotel* (☎ (079) 57 2368) at 2 Sydney St, is quite pleasant and has a balcony and rooftop bar; singles/doubles are $25/30. The *Paradise Lodge Motel* (☎ (079) 51 3644) is just behind the bus station at 19 Peel St, and costs $39/49 for singles/doubles.

There's a whole string of motels south along Nebo Rd (the Bruce Highway). *Cool*

Palms (☎ (079) 57 5477), at 4 Nebo Rd, is still fairly close to the centre, and charges $32/34.

Camping The *Beach Caravan Park* (☎ (079) 57 4021), on Petrie St at Illawong Beach (Far Beach), has tent sites, on-site vans, cabins and villas. It's next to the Illawong Tourist Park which has a pool, kiosk and grill bar.

The *Central Caravan Park* (☎ (079) 57 6141) is at 15 Malcomson St, just across the river in North Mackay. Camping costs $8 and there are cabins for $20 a double. There are quite a few more camping grounds at the northern beaches.

Places to Eat

Mackay seems to have a pub on every corner in the city centre, so finding a counter meal is not a problem. The *Ambassador Hotel*, overlooking the river from the corner of River and Sydney Sts, has an upstairs terrace which is popular for a drink; counter meals are in the $7 to $12 range.

Monday to Saturday lunch times, the *Hotel Mackay*, on the corner of Wellington and Victoria Sts, has a daily special for $3, and steak or seafood meals from $8. For something a bit more up-market, the Wilkinson Hotel has *Wilkie's Balcony Restaurant*, which is open in the evenings.

Woody's Bakehouse, in an arcade off Wood St, has a variety of home-made pies, cakes and breads. For fast food, the *Tourist Chicken Bar*, at 94 Wood St, is open daily to 8 pm. The *7 Wood St Cafe*, between Victoria and River Sts, is a very cheap sandwich bar/coffee shop.

Further along Wood St, at No 73, the *Top Spot Coffee Lounge* in Jamor House, does good home-made meals, including a range of vegetarian dishes. It's a pity this place is so tucked away.

On the corner of Alfred and Sydney Sts, *Alpapa's Italian Restaurant* is a pleasant little place with really good, reasonably priced pizza and other dishes. The *Creperie*, on Gregory St, serves excellent savoury pancakes for around $10, and cheaper sweet ones as well. *Pee Bees*, at 27 Sydney St, is a licensed Mexican place open nightly.

For Chinese food, try the *Lychee Gardens*, on the corner of Victoria and Wellington Sts. It's close to the hostels and has a bargain lunch smorgasbord from Monday to Friday for $7.

For 24-hour greasy spoon, the cafe in the bus station does the usual stuff, including a fried breakfast – worth its weight in cholesterol.

Entertainment
The Oriental Hotel has a variety of live entertainment Thursdays to Sundays, and cabaret some nights. The Prince of Wales, on River St, has bands Friday and Saturday and a disco other nights. In the Austral Hotel you'll catch Saturday afternoon jazz once a fortnight, and guitar nights on Wednesdays and Saturdays.

Nightclubs, often with live bands as well as discos, include Illusions at 45 River St, Valentino's at 99 Victoria St, and Paradise Nights in Toucan's Arcade, 85 Victoria St.

Getting There & Away
Air Ansett has direct flights most days between Mackay and Brisbane ($258), Cairns, Hamilton Island, Rockhampton ($136) and Sydney, and less often to Proserpine ($103). Australian Airlines flies daily direct to/from Brisbane and Rockhampton.

Australian Regional Airlines flies to/from Rockhampton, Proserpine and Brampton Island; Helijet Air Services to/from Lindeman Island, Hamilton Island and Whitsunday Airport; and Sunstate to/from Townsville, Rockhampton, Gladstone, Bundaberg and Brisbane.

In Mackay, Ansett and Sungold offices (☎ (079) 57 1571) are on the corner of Victoria and Macalister Sts; Australian, Sunstate and Australian Regional (☎ (079) 57 1411) are at 105 Victoria St.

Bus All buses travelling along the coast stop at Mackay. The bus station is on Milton St, about a 10-minute walk west of the town centre. Average journey times and typical

fares are: Cairns, 10½ hours ($70); Townsville, four hours ($48); Airlie Beach, two hours ($26); and Brisbane, 12 hours ($90).

Train The Sunlander and Queenslander (both from Brisbane to Cairns) stop at Mackay. The economy fare from Brisbane is $101.70 for both trains, while in 1st class the Sunlander costs $156.20 and the Queenslander $254.70. Mackay Railway Station (☎ (079) 57 2551) is on Boddington St.

Getting Around
Count on about $6 for a taxi from Mackay Airport to the city. Avis, Budget and Hertz have counters at the airport, but rental cars in Mackay are neither cheap nor plentiful.

Seaforth's runs the bus service to the northern beaches twice daily on weekdays at 1.20 and 3.05 pm. Buses leave from outside the RSL on Sydney St. It's about an hour from Mackay to most of the northern beaches, and the fare is around $2.

AROUND MACKAY
Eungella National Park
Most days of the year you can be pretty sure to see platypuses close to the Broken River camping ground in this large national park 74 km west of Mackay. Eungella covers nearly 500 sq km of the Clarke Range, climbing to 1280 metres at Mt Dalrymple.

Eungella has been cut off from other rainforest areas for probably 30,000 years and has at least six life forms which exist nowhere else – the Eungella honeyeater (a bird), the orange-sided skink (a lizard), the Mackay tulip oak (a tall buttressed rainforest tree) and three species of frog of which the Eungella gastric brooding frog is unusual for incubating its eggs in its stomach and giving birth by spitting out the tadpoles!

Two walking tracks lead from the camping ground to spectacular waterfalls and swimming holes in the **Finch Hatton Gorge**. The last two or three km of the 10-km drive from the main road to the camping ground involve several creek crossings and 4WD is necessary after heavy rain.

There's a ranger's office, camping

ground, picnic area and kiosk near the bridge over **Broken River**, five km from Eungella village.

Platypuses are usually seen in pools near the Broken River bridge and upstream. The best times are the hours immediately after dawn and before dark, and you must remain patiently still and silent.

Several walking tracks start from Broken River bridge, and a short walk downstream there's a good swimming hole. Near the bridge colourful birds are prolific, while at night the rufous bettong, a small kangaroo, is quite common. You might also see two types of brushtail possum and two species of glider. Park rangers sometimes lead wildlife-watching sessions, or night spotlighting trips to pick out nocturnal animals.

Places to Stay There are three national park camping grounds. You'll need to get camping permits from the ranger (☎ (079) 58 4552) at Broken River. During school holiday periods it's advisable to check in advance whether there's room.

Also beside the bridge here, the *Broken River Mountain Retreat* (☎ 58 4528) has fully equipped units sleeping up to six for $50 a double and $9 for each extra person.

In Eungella village the *Valley View Caravan Park* has tent sites and on-site vans.

Just a couple of km from the gorge itself is the *Platypus Bush Camp* (☎ (079) 583204). It's a beautiful retreat, with bush huts and camping sites. You need to bring all your own food, and cooking facilities are provided, even though there's no electricity. If you phone from Eungella village, someone will pick you up.

Getting There & Away There are no buses to Eungella, but hitching is quite possible. Reeforest Adventure Tours (☎ (079) 53 1000) runs day trips from Mackay, plus a drop-off service for $20 return.

Cape Hillsborough National Park

This coastal park, 54 km north of Mackay, takes in the rocky Cape Hillsborough, 300 metres high, and nearby Andrews Point and Wedge Island, which are joined by a causeway at low tide. There are beaches and several walking tracks and the scenery ranges from cliffs, rocky coast, dunes and scrub to rainforest and woodland. Kangaroos, wallabies, sugar gliders and turtles are quite common.

Places to Stay The *Cape Hillsborough Resort* (☎ (079) 59 0152) has tent sites, on-site vans and cabins, and some motel rooms.

In the park itself is the Smalleys Beach camping area, but you'll need a permit (☎ (079) 59 0410). Near Seaforth is the *Halliday Bay Resort* (☎ (079) 59 0121) with a shop, pool, tennis court, water sports, tent sites, and self-contained rooms from $52.

Getting There & Away A school bus, which anyone can take, leaves Mackay post office at 2.45 pm Monday to Friday during the school term. It only goes to Seaforth, but if you're staying at Cape Hillsborough Resort, the driver might drop you there.

Brampton & Carlisle Islands

These two mountainous national park islands are in the Cumberland Group, 32 km north-east of Mackay. Both are about five sq km in area, and are joined by a sand bank which you can walk across at low tide. Carlisle's highest point is 389-metre Skiddaw Peak, Brampton's is 219-metre Brampton Peak. Both islands have forested slopes, sandy beaches, good walks and fringing coral reefs with good snorkelling.

Brampton has an Australian-Airlines-owned resort (☎ (079) 51 4499) on its north-east coast, opposite Carlisle Island. It's in the luxury class at $800 per person per week with breakfast, tennis, golf, water sports and so on. Carlisle Island is uninhabited; you can camp but there are no facilities and you must even bring water.

The *Spirit of Roylen* fast catamaran leaves Mackay Harbour daily for Brampton Island ($40 return), and you can use it for a day trip. You can also fly daily from Mackay ($59 one-way with Australian Regional).

Most other islands in the Cumberland

Group and the Sir James Smith Group to the north are also national parks; if you fancy a spot of Robinson Crusoeing and can afford to charter a boat or seaplane, Goldsmith and Scawfell are good bets. Contact the national parks offices in Mackay (☎ (079) 57 6292) or Seaforth (☎ (079) 59 0410) for all camping permits and information.

Newry & Rabbit Islands

These small, little-known tropical islands are two of a cluster of tiny islands just off the coast about 40 km north-west of Mackay. Newry Island, one km long, has a small resort (☎ (079) 59 0214) where camping is $7 per person, and a bunk is $15. There are also cabins, sleeping up to five, with their own bathrooms and cooking facilities, and these cost $60 for two plus $20 for each extra person. All guests can use the resort restaurant.

Rabbit Island, the largest of the group at 4.5 sq km, has a national park camping ground with toilets and a rainwater tank which can be empty in dry times. It also has the only sandy beaches in the group. From November to January sea turtles nest here. Contact the Mackay (☎ (078) 51 8788) or Seaforth (☎ (079) 59 0410) national parks offices for permits and information.

The Newry resort picks up guests from Victor Creek, four km west of Seaforth, for $10.

Sugar Growing

Sugar is easily the most visible crop from Mackay north, past Cairns, up the Queensland coast. Sugar was a success almost from the day it was introduced in the region back in 1865, but its early days had a distinctly unsavoury air as the plantations were worked by Pacific Islanders who were often forced from their homes to come and work on Australian cane fields. 'Blackbirding', as this virtual slave trading was known, took a long time to be stamped out.

Today, cane growing is a highly mechanised business and visitors are welcome to inspect the crushing plants during the harvesting season from about August to December. The most spectacular part of the operation is the firing of the cane fields, when rubbish is burnt off by night fires. Mechanical harvesters cut and gather the cane which is then transported to the sugar mills, often on narrow-gauge railway lines laid through the cane fields. These lines are a familiar sight throughout cane country. The cane is then shredded and passed through a series of crushers. The extracted juice is heated and cleaned of impurities and then evaporated to form a syrup. The next process reduces the syrup to molasses and low-grade sugar. Further refining stages end with the sugar loaded into bulk containers for export.

Sugar production is a remarkably efficient process. The crushed fibres, known as bagasse, are burnt as fuel; impurities separated from the juice are used as fertilisers; and the molasses is used either to produce ethanol or as stock feed.

AIRLIE BEACH & SHUTE HARBOUR

It's 25 km from the Bruce Highway at Proserpine to Airlie Beach, which is the main accommodation centre opposite the Whitsunday Islands. Most boats to the islands leave from Shute Harbour, eight km from Airlie Beach.

Airlie Beach has grown phenomenally over the past 10 years and is now a bustling place. The area is one of the pleasure boating capitals of Australia. Apart from Shute Harbour itself, which is packed with craft, lots of boats anchor in Airlie Bay. Airlie Beach is also developing a reputation as a centre for learning to scuba dive. Yet, despite all of this development, it's still a small place maintaining a relaxed air.

The road between Airlie Beach and Shute Harbour passes through **Conway National Park** which stretches away north and south along the coast. The southern end of the park separates the Whitsunday Passage from Repulse Bay, named by Captain Cook who strayed into it thinking it was the main passage. Most of the park is rugged ranges and valleys covered in rainforest, but there is a camping ground and ranger's office near the road, and a few walking tracks in the surrounding area. The two-km walk up to Mt Rooper lookout, north of the road, gives good views of the Whitsunday Passage and islands.

Another pleasant walk is along Mandalay Rd, about three km east of Airlie Beach, up to **Mandalay Point**.

To reach the beautiful **Cedar Creek Falls**, turn off the Proserpine to Airlie Beach road

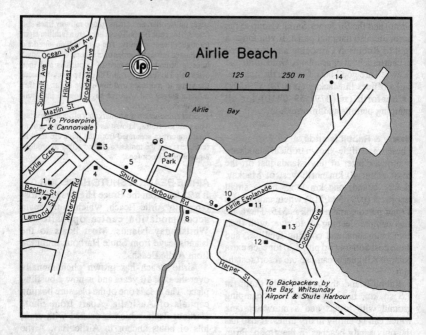

1 Club 13 Begley St
   (Whitsunday Backpackers)
2 Market Mopeds
3 Post Office
4 Whitsunday Wanderers Resort
5 Whitsunday Travel Centre
6 Long-Distance Bus Stop
7 Australian Airlines & Newsagent
8 Club Magnums
9 Mandy's Mine of Information
10 Pinky's
11 Annie's Place
12 Club Habitat
13 Airlie Beach Hotel
14 Sailing Club

on to Conway Rd, eight km from Proserpine. It's then about 15 km to the falls – the roads are well signposted. At the end of Conway Rd, 27 km from the turn-off, is the small settlement of **Conway** with a beach, the

Black Stump Caravan Park and a pleasant pub.

Beware of stingers in the waters from October to April.

Information

Nearly everything of importance in Airlie Beach is on the main road, Shute Harbour Rd. The Whitsunday Information Centre (☎ (079) 46 6673), in the same building as the national parks office, is on the corner of Mandalay and Shute Harbour Rds, about two km from the centre. There are hosts of booking agencies and ticket offices and the notice board outside the newsagent on the main street lists rides, rooms to rent and so on. Many people come to Airlie Beach looking for casual work in hotels, restaurants or on the boats.

The national parks office (☎ (079) 46 7022), is open from 8 am to 5 pm Monday to Friday and at varying weekend hours. This office deals with camping bookings and permits for Conway and the island national parks.

Activities

Diving At least four outfits in and around Airlie Beach offer five to six-day scuba-diving certificate courses. Standard costs vary from $260 to $390 but sometimes discounts are available. Most involve three days' tuition on the mainland and two days' diving on the Great Barrier Reef. All the firms also offer diving trips for certified divers. Book where you are staying, or at one of the agencies on the main road in Airlie Beach.

The companies include: Oceania Dive (☎ (079) 46 6032), Shute Harbour Rd, Airlie Beach; Down Under Dive (☎ (079) 46 6137), based at the Reef Oceania Village at Cannes; Pro-Dive, (☎ (079) 46 6508), 303 Shute Harbour Rd, Airlie Beach; and Barrier Reef Diving Services (☎ (079) 46 6204), The Esplanade, Airlie Beach.

Other Activities The 25-metre freshwater pool at the Coral Sea Resort on Ocean View Ave is open to the public daily from 8 am to 6 pm.

You can take half-day horseback trail rides ($30) with Brandy Creek Trail Rides (☎ (079) 46 6848), 12 km from Airlie Beach back towards Proserpine. They can pick you up from your accommodation.

Festivals

Airlie Beach is the centre of activities during the annual Whitsunday Village Fun Race (for cruising yachts) each September. The festivities include a Miss Figurehead competition where the contestants traditionally compete topless.

Places to Stay

Hostels There's been such a proliferation of hostels in recent years that the competition to get bodies on beds is fierce. Some places offer deals, such as the first night free if you stay for more than one night, and the $5 bed is not unheard of. At the main bus stop there's

a row of booths where the hostel reps tout for trade when the buses arrive. This saves you the sort of circus that exists at places such as Hervey Bay where you get leaflets thrust at you while trying to get off the bus and retrieve your luggage.

Right in the centre of Airlie Beach, *Club Magnums* (☎ (079) 46 6266) is a huge place, with cabins set out in a very pleasant tropical garden. The emphasis is on partying, and there's a restaurant and bar with activities each night. A bed in a four or six-bed unit is $10.

Also in the centre is *Club Habitat* (☎ (079) 46 6312), an old motel converted to back-packers' accommodation. A night in a four to six-bed room with bathroom costs $10. There's a pool, good communal kitchen and lounge, and the atmosphere is friendly. *Club 13 Begley St* (☎ (079) 46 7376), also called *Whitsunday Backpackers*, overlooks the bay from the hill just above the centre. This multilevel place consists of five three-bedroom 'clubs'. Each air-con bedroom has a bathroom (some with spa) and four or six beds, while each 'club' has its own cooking and laundry facilities, and a balcony with tremendous views. Beds are $10, but the first night is free if you stay more than one night.

Half a km out of town, towards Shute Harbour, is *Backpackers by the Bay* (☎ (079) 46 7267) at Lot 5, Hermitage Drive. It's a small, relaxed hostel with a good atmosphere, and is probably quieter than those in the centre. The nightly cost in a four-bed dorm is $10.

Back the other way from the centre, the *Whitsunday Motel Backpackers* (☎ (079) 46 6306) is on the old road which follows the shoreline, about 1½ km from Airlie Beach. There are 10 fan-cooled units, each with kitchen, bathroom and TV. The nightly cost in a four-bed unit is $9, and in a six-bed unit $6.

Further along towards Cannonvale, 2.2 km from Airlie Beach, is the *Bush Village Youth Hostel* (☎ (079) 46 6177) in St Martin's Lane. It has self-contained four-bed units at $9 per person. Each unit has cooking facilities, fridge, bathroom and TV. The units are a bit old-fashioned but clean, and the owners are very helpful.

Finally, there's the huge *Reef Oceania Village* (☎ (079) 46 6137), at Cannonvale, three km from Airlie Beach. It's well set out and has good facilities, but gets mixed reports from travellers. If you like a big place with a gregarious atmosphere and lots of activities, you'll like this place. There's a range of accommodation: basic eight-bed dorms for $5; larger six-bed units with TV and bathroom; and double rooms with bathroom for $25. There's the obligatory pool, and also a bar and restaurant. The courtesy bus meets all buses, even those arriving at some bloody awful hour of the night.

Hotels & Motels The *Airlie Beach Hotel* (☎ (079) 46 6233), on Shute Harbour Rd, near the corner of Coconut Grove, has air-con rooms with TV and private bathroom for around $40 a double, although you can sometimes get a discount if things are quiet.

Motels are pretty expensive: about the cheapest is the *Airlie Beach Motor Lodge* (☎ (079) 46 6418) on Lamond St which has singles/doubles from $40/45.

Resorts & Holiday Flats Outside the peak seasons, some of the resorts are much cheaper. *Whitsunday Wanderers* (☎ (079) 46 6446), on Shute Harbour Rd in Airlie Beach, offers stand-by accommodation for $49 a double including breakfast. It has four pools, tennis, landscaped gardens, bar, restaurant and nightly live entertainment. You might have to stay a few nights to qualify for these offers. Normally a double in this place is $90 or more.

Generally, you'll find better value in some of the holiday flats. The notice board outside the newsagency in Airlie Beach usually has notices for long-term share accommodation. Four people sharing a flat will pay $17 each or less in these places and all bed linen and cooking equipment, etc, is supplied. *Sunlit Waters* (☎ (079) 46 6352), at the corner of Begley St and Airlie Crescent in Airlie Beach, has a pool and charges $30 to $38 for two people, $8 for each extra person.

Other holiday flats in Airlie Beach include *Rogers* (☎ (079) 46 6224), at 265 Shute Harbour Rd, with doubles from $40; and *McDowalls* (☎ (079) 46 6176) at 32 Airlie Crescent, which has similar prices. Neither of these places has a pool, however.

Camping There are quite a few camping/caravan parks strung along the main road from Cannonvale to Shute Harbour, which although packed out during the school holidays are OK the rest of the time. A tent site at the Conway National Park camping ground, close to Shute Harbour, is $7.50 a night for up to six people, but there's a maximum stay of four nights in peak season. There are a couple more sites at Swamp Bay, reached by a 4½-km walking track. For information, camping permits and bookings, contact the national park's office (☎ (079) 46 7022) on Shute Harbour Rd, two km from Airlie Beach.

Privately run van parks usually have pools and will rent you bed linen. The parks often have tent sites as well as a choice of two or three types of on-site vans or units. Three or four people can share one of these quite economically. Places include: *Island Gateway Caravan Village* (☎ (079) 46 6228); *Flame Tree Tourist Village* (☎ (079) 46 9388); and *Shute Harbour Gardens Caravan Park* (☎ (079) 46 6483).

Places to Eat

Most of the eating possibilities are on, or just off, Shute Harbour Rd in Airlie Beach. If you're preparing your own food, there are a couple of small supermarkets on the main street, and a good fruit & vegie shop on Begley St.

The *Airlie Beach Hotel* has a bistro with pub meals from $6. *La Perouse*, tucked away in an arcade between Coconut Grove and Airlie Esplanade, is expensive, with steaks at around $14, but there's a dinner special.

On Airlie Esplanade, *Annie's Place* is a budget-priced eatery serving excellent hamburgers and other snacks. Don't miss *Pinky's*, a popular, moderately priced little place on the corner. Its varied menu starts with sandwiches from $3 and meals from $7. It has budget evening meals from $6 to $8.

Across Shute Harbour Rd, next to Club Habitat, is *Bongo Congo*, a popular licensed place with good meals from $8 to $12 and a good sound system, and it's open until quite late.

Club Magnums has a restaurant right on Shute Harbour Rd, which often has theme cuisine, such as Caribbean; meals are generally around $5.

Just by the main car park, the small *Cafe Le Mignon* is a popular, reasonably priced place open from 8 am to 5 pm, closing earlier on weekends. Sandwiches and croissants with fancy fillings cost from $4.

If you feel like Italian food, there are two places either side of Shute Harbour Rd near the post office. *Romeo's*, open daily from 7 am to midnight, has two sections: a gourmet takeaway and a more expensive restaurant with a sea view. *Chianti's*, across the road, has less in the budget range although you get garlic bread, salad and a glass of wine or a soft drink with a meal which makes it worth considering. It's open from 6 to 10 pm Monday to Saturday.

Entertainment

The Airlie Beach Hotel has toad races on Tuesday and Thursday nights at 7.30 pm. There are good prizes for the winners of each race (usually boat cruises), and all proceeds go to charity. You can rent a steed for $3 and the whole evening is a rowdy, fun event. This pub is also the place to go for live rock music, and there's a disco most nights, as well as Saturday and Sunday afternoons.

Club Magnums also has a nightclub, just up from the Whitsunday Travel Centre on Shute Harbour Rd.

There are regular bands in the Reef Gateway Hotel at Cannonvale, with a free bus sometimes provided from Airlie Beach. You can also try night party cruises to a couple of resort islands.

Getting There & Away

Air Helijet Air Services (☎ (079) 46 9133) has flights to/from Mackay and Whitsunday Airport (via Lindeman and Hamilton islands) for $90 one-way if you fly direct.

Bus All the main bus companies make detours to Airlie Beach and Shute Harbour. There are buses to/from Airlie Beach and Brisbane (18 hours, $97), Mackay (two hours), Rockhampton (six hours), Townsville (four hours) and Cairns (nine hours).

Unless you have a pass with a major bus company, to travel between Proserpine and Airlie Beach or Shute Harbour you have to get a Sampsons bus (☎ (079) 45 2377); these run several times daily between Proserpine Airport, Mill St in Proserpine, Airlie Beach and Shute Harbour.

None of the main bus companies have offices in Airlie Beach, but any booking agency along Shute Harbour Rd can help. The main bus stop is in the car park behind the shops, about halfway along Shute Harbour Rd.

Boat The sailing club at the end of Airlie Beach Esplanade has a notice board showing when rides or crewing are available. Ask around Airlie Beach or Shute Harbour.

Getting Around

Several car rental agencies operate locally, with Avis and National opposite each other on Shute Harbour Rd, Airlie Beach. Market Mopeds (☎ (079) 46 7004), one block back from the main street, has scooters and cars for rent.

WHITSUNDAY ISLANDS

The 74 Whitsunday Islands are probably the best known Queensland islands. The group was named by Captain Cook who sailed through here on 3 July 1770. They're scattered on both sides of the Whitsunday Passage and are all within 50 km of Shute Harbour. The Whitsundays are mostly continental islands, the tips of underwater mountains, but many of them have fringing coral reefs. The actual barrier reef is at least 60 km out from Shute Harbour; Hook Reef is the nearest part of it.

The islands – mostly hilly and wooded –

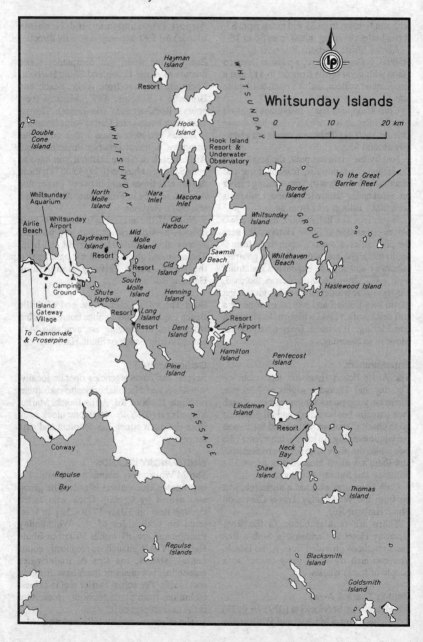

Whitsunday Islands

and the passages between them are certainly beautiful, and while a few are developed with tourist resorts, most are uninhabited and several offer the chance of some back-to-nature beach camping and bushwalking. All but five of the Whitsundays are predominantly or completely national park. The exceptions include Dent Island, which has a grazing lease, and the resort islands of Hamilton, Daydream and Hayman. The other main resorts are on South Molle and Lindeman islands, and at Happy Bay on Long Island.

Most people staying in the resorts are on package holidays and, with the exceptions of some cabins and resort camping on Long and Hook Islands, resort accommodation is beyond the reach of the shoestring traveller.

Curiously, the Whitsundays are misnamed – Captain Cook didn't really sail through them on Whit Sunday. When he got back to England, his meticulously kept log was a day out because he had not allowed for crossing the international date line! As he sailed through the Whitsundays and further north, Cook was also unaware of the existence of the Barrier Reef, although he realised there was something to the east of his ship making the water unusually calm. It wasn't until he ran aground on the Endeavour Reef, near Cooktown, that he finally found out about the Great Barrier Reef.

Camping on the Islands

Although accommodation in the island resorts is mostly expensive, it's possible to camp on several islands. Long and Hook islands have privately run camping grounds, and on North Molle, Whitsunday, Henning, Border, Haslewood, Shaw, Thomas, Repulse and Hook islands you can camp cheaply at national parks sites. Self-sufficiency is the key to camping in national park sites; some have toilets, but only a few have drinking water, and then not always year-round. You're advised to take five litres of water per person per day, plus three days' extra supply in case you get stuck. You should also have a fuel stove – wood fires are banned on some islands and unwelcome on the others. There's a national parks leaflet which describes the various sites, and provides

detailed information on what to take and do. The national parks district office (☎ (079) 46 7022) is in Airlie Beach, on Shute Harbour Rd.

For information on boat transport to/from the islands, contact one of the many booking agencies in Airlie Beach. For $30 to $50 return per person, a number of the regular day-trip boats will drop you off at the end of a cruise and pick you up again on an agreed date. Generally the day-tour boats are better for this than the island resort boats. Some boat operators will rent you water containers or help you organise other gear.

The water taxi (☎ (079) 46 9202) from Shute Harbour is slow and expensive; it costs from $120 to $440 return, depending on the island.

Contact the national parks office to arrange a camping permit ($2 per person per night); sites take up to six people and numbers are limited for each camping area.

The possibilities for camping in national parks in the Whitsundays are summarised in the table.

Island	Location	Sites	Drinking Water
Shute	northern end	2	no
North Molle	Hannah Point	5	seasonal
	Cockatoo Beach	10	seasonal
Whitsunday	Whitehaven Beach (southern end)	20	no
	Scrub Hen Beach	10	no
	Dugong Beach	15	yes, but may be seasonal
	Sawmill Beach	5	seasonal
	Joe's Beach	4	no
Hook	Curlew Beach	10	no
Thomas	Sea Eagle Beach	10	no
Shaw	Neck Bay Beach	3	no
South Repulse	western beach	3	no
Gloucester*	Bona Bay	10	no
Armit*	western beach	5	no
Saddleback*	western side	5	no
Grassy	south-west point	2	no

* Northern islands like Armit, Gloucester and Saddleback are harder to reach since the water taxi and cruises from Shute Harbour don't usually go there. Gloucester and Saddleback are best reached from Earlando, Dingo Beach or Bowen.

Long Island

One of the closer and less commercial of the resort islands, Long Island is nearly all national park. The 16.5 sq km island has lots of rainforest, 13 km of walking tracks and some fine lookouts.

The *Island Resort* (☎ (079) 46 9400), where the cruise boats stop, has a long expanse of genuine tropical island beach. The resort has two pools, tennis, archery, water sports and so on, as well as the obligatory disco. The standard rate is $130/150, but stand-by rates are often available. Meals can be arranged for $32 per day.

Palm Bay (☎ (079) 46 9233), about a km south of Happy Bay, is one of the two cheapest island resorts. There are nine simple cabins, with cooking facilities and fridges, and you can either get some supplies here or bring them over from the mainland. Prices range from $30 to $100 per person. There's good snorkelling, a glass-bottomed boat, and dinghies, catamarans and sailboards for hire. It's wise to book well ahead. The return launch fare from Shute Harbour is $20.

Hook Island

Second largest of the Whitsundays, Hook Island is 53 sq km and rises to 450 metres at Hook Peak. There are a number of beaches dotted around the island. It's mainly national park, with a camping area at Curlew Beach in the southern Macona Inlet, but there's also the *Hook Island Resort* facing Whitsunday Island in the south.

The island also has an underwater observatory ($8.50). The return launch trip to the resort is $20.

The beautiful, fjord-like Nara Inlet on Hook Island is a very popular deep-water anchorage for visiting yachts.

Daydream Island

This small, two-km-long island is only a couple of hundred metres across at its widest point. It's the nearest resort island to Shute Harbour and has one of the best swimming pools. The totally rebuilt resort (☎ (079) 46 9200) aims to create a party atmosphere. Accommodation per person is normally from $95 a day including meals, non-powered water activities and tennis, but there's a stand-by rate of $70 including the return trip from Shute Harbour. You can also spend a day on Daydream for $25 including boat transfers, lunch and water-sport facilities.

South Molle Island

Largest of the Molle group of islands at four sq km, South Molle is virtually joined to Mid Molle and North Molle islands. It has long stretches of beach and is crisscrossed by walking tracks. The highest point is 198-metre Mt Jeffreys, but the climb up Spion Kop is also worthwhile. You can spend a day walking on the island for the cost of the $25 ferry trip.

Most of South Molle is national park but there's the *South Molle Island Resort* (☎ (079) 46 9433) in the north, where the boats come in, with nightly costs from $115 per person including all meals. Stand-by rates of $70 are offered out of peak season. The resort has a big pool, a small golf course and a gym and offers tennis, squash, archery, snorkelling and windsurfing, all included in the price. Hundreds of rainbow lorikeets fly in to feed every day at 3 pm.

Hamilton Island

This privately owned island, the most flamboyant resort island in the Whitsundays, has its own jet airport, a 400-boat marina and accommodation for more than 1000, including one tower block. The range of entertainment possibilities, not surprisingly, is extensive (and expensive): helicopter joy rides, game fishing, parasailing, cruising, scuba diving, about seven restaurants, shops, squash courts, even a dolphin pool and a hill-top fauna reserve with wombats, crocodiles and koalas. The cheapest double room costs $200, but stand-by rates cut about one-third off these prices. Hamilton is more like a small town than a resort, so there are a variety of restaurants, takeaways and even a small supermarket.

Hamilton is about five sq km in area and rises to 200 metres at Passage Peak. It can make an interesting day trip from Shute Harbour ($30 return for the launch only).

The airport is used mainly by people jetting between resort islands, with launches and helicopters laid on to whisk them off to their chosen spots. Ansett flies nonstop to Hamilton from Brisbane ($270 one-way), Cairns ($202), Melbourne ($436) and Sydney ($375). Stand-by is available on some routes. But there's little point flying to Hamilton if you're on a budget since you'll probably be staying at Airlie Beach or on one of the islands which are easily – and more cheaply – reached from Shute Harbour.

Hayman Island

Owned by Ansett, Hayman has been remodelled into such an exclusive resort that day trips no longer call there. The nearest you'll probably get is some of the reefs or small islands nearby such as Black Island (also called Bali Hai) or Arkhurst, Langford or Bird islands.

Hayman, the most northerly of the Whitsunday Group, has an area of four sq km, and rises to 250 metres above sea level. It has forested hills, valleys and beaches. The resort, in the south, is fronted by a wide, shallow reef which emerges from the water at low tide. Rooms start at $250 a night, and food is equally expensive.

Lindeman Island

One of the most southerly of the Whitsundays, Lindeman covers eight sq km, most of which is national park. The island has 20 km of walking trails and the highest point is 210-metre Mt Oldfield.

The resort, in the south, has a golf course, tennis and lots of water activities. Double rooms cost around $300 including meals, and there are launches from Shute Harbour. Lindeman also has its own airstrip: Reef World Airlines flies from Mackay ($51), Whitsunday Airport near Shute Harbour ($42) and Proserpine ($42).

With plenty of little beaches and secluded bays on Lindeman it's no hassle at all to find one to yourself. There are also a lot of small islands dotted around, some of which are easy to get across to. Lindeman is pleasant because it's somewhat smaller than the big, crowded resorts and also far enough from the centre of the Whitsundays to avoid the day-trippers.

Whitsunday Island

The largest of the Whitsunday Group, this island covers 109 sq km and rises to 438 metres at Whitsunday Peak. There's no resort, but six-km Whitehaven Beach on the south-east coast is probably the longest and finest beach in the group, with good snorkelling off its southern end. There are national park camping areas at Whitehaven Beach, Scrub Hen Beach in the north-west, Dugong and Sawmill beaches on the west, and Joe's Beach.

Cid Harbour

Between Hook and Whitsunday islands, Cid Harbour was the anchorage for part of the US Navy before the Battle of the Coral Sea, turning point in the Pacific theatre of WW II. Today, visiting ocean cruise liners anchor here.

Getting Around

Air Helijet Air Services (☎ (079) 46 9133), based at Whitsunday Airport, near Shute Harbour, makes scenic flights over the islands and/or reef (minimum two adults) from $40 for 15 minutes to $100 for an hour. It will also land seaplanes on the reef for semisubmersible rides, glass-bottomed boating, reef walking or snorkelling; prices start at $100.

Boat There's a bamboozling array of boat trips, and all the hostels and agencies have dozens of brochures. Mandy's Mine of Information, on Shute Harbour Rd in Airlie Beach, prints a useful list dividing the trips into manageable categories. You can make bookings at Mandy's or any of the other agents in Airlie Beach.

Most boats depart from Shute Harbour, the end of the road from Airlie Beach. You can bus there from Airlie Beach – some of the cruise operators do coach pick-ups from

Airlie Beach – or you can leave your car in the Shute Harbour car park for $3 for 24 hours. There's a lock-up car park a few hundred metres back along the road by the Shell service station, costing $5 from 8 am to 5 pm or $8 for 24 hours. To avoid busy Shute Harbour, a few boats now leave from Airlie Beach.

There are day trips to one or more islands from $20 to $50; day-long sailing trips from $30 to $42; three-day sailing trips from around $160 to $200; sailing trips which include diving; day cruises to the Great Barrier Reef from $40 to $80; fishing trips from $45; night cruises from $40; and self-skippered yachts from $260 per week.

BOWEN (population 7663)

This agreeable town, founded in 1861, was the first coastal settlement north of Rockhampton. Although soon overshadowed by Mackay to the south and Townsville to the north, Bowen survived, and today is a thriving fruit and vegetable-growing centre which attracts hundreds of people for seasonal picking work.

There's a good museum at 22 Gordon St with displays relating to the town's early history. It's open weekdays and Sunday mornings. Just north of Bowen, a string of sandy beaches, some of them quite secluded, dot the coast around the cape.

Places to Stay

Bowen Backpackers (☎ (077) 86 3433) is at 56 Herbert St, on the main road. Cooking, eating and sitting areas and some bedrooms are in a renovated, old-style Queensland house, and there's more accommodation in a newer section. The nightly cost is $10, plus $2 for bed linen. The hostel is a pleasant place to take a breather from the more hectic scene elsewhere on the coast.

Bowen has a long list of motels, holiday flats, caravan/camping parks; most are on the Bruce Highway, in the town or up near Queens and Horseshoe Bay beaches. Cheaper motels on the highway include the *Big Mango Motel* and the *Ocean View*.

Places to Eat

The *Club Hotel* and the *Central Hotel*, a block or two down Herbert St from the backpackers, both do counter meals. Near the Central, the *Bowen Tuckerbox* does a range of decently priced snacks and meals for around $7, as well as pizzas. You can also get pizza at *Francos* on Herbert St. The *Denison Hotel* on Powell St, has a char grill from 6 to 8 pm.

Getting There & Away

Buses between Rockhampton and Townsville stop at Bowen. Typical travelling times and fares are Rockhampton, 6½ hours ($68); Airlie Beach, two hours ($12) and Townsville, 2½ hours ($20). The Sunlander and Queenslander trains also stop at Bowen. The economy fare from Brisbane is $109.60. If you're sick of driving, there's also a motorail service between Bowen and Townsville.

North Coast

AYR (population 8787)

This sugar town is on the delta of one of the biggest rivers in Queensland, the Burdekin. Rice is also grown in the area. On Wilmington St, the **House of Australian Nature** has displays of orchids, shells and butterflies; it's open from 8 am to 5 pm daily.

Across the Burdekin River is **Home Hill** with an historical museum. Between Ayr and Townsville you pass the **Australian Institute of Marine Science** on Cape Ferguson. You can visit it from 8 am to 4 pm Monday to Friday, with guided tours given on Fridays.

Twenty-eight km south of Townsville, or 72 km north of Ayr, along the Bruce Highway, then six km south by paved road, there's a good camp ground by Alligator Creek in the big **Bowling Green Bay National Park**. Swimming holes in the creek are good during the wet season and some walking tracks start from the camp ground. Alligator Creek tumbles down between two rugged ranges which rise steeply from the coastal plains. The taller range peaks in Mt Elliot (1234 metres), whose higher slopes harbour some of Queensland's most southerly tropical rainforest. There's no public transport to the park.

TOWNSVILLE (population 86,000)

The third largest city in Queensland and the main centre in the north of the state, Townsville is the port city for the agricultural and mining production of the vast inland region of northern Queensland. Founded in 1864 by the efforts of a Scot, John Melton Black, and the money of Robert Towns, a Sydney-based sea captain and financier, Townsville developed mainly on the back of Chinese and Kanaka labour.

Today Townsville is a working city, a major armed forces base, and the site of James Cook University. It's the start of the main road from Queensland to the Northern Territory. It's the only departure point for Magnetic Island (20 minutes away by ferry), while the Barrier Reef is about 1¾ hours away by fast catamaran.

In recent years, millions of dollars have been spent in an effort to attract more visitors to stay for a time in Townsville rather than go straight through to Cairns. A Sheraton hotel-casino and a marina have been built on Townsville's ocean front, and the Flinders East area fronting Ross Creek is being redeveloped, while retaining many of its 19th-century buildings. The centrepiece here is the Great Barrier Reef Wonderland complex. Along with these big money efforts, there's been a boom in budget accommodation and in the eating and entertainment scene; yet the visitors are still staying away in droves.

Orientation

Townsville centres on Ross Creek and is dominated by 290-metre Castle Hill with a lookout perched on top. The city sprawls a long way, but the centre's a fairly compact area that you can easily get around on foot.

Most of the accommodation is in the centre. The Transit Centre, the arrival and departure point for long-distance buses, is on Palmer St, just south of Ross Creek. The city centre is immediately to the north of the creek, over the Dean St bridge. Flinders St Mall stretches to the left from the north side of the bridge, towards the railway station. To the right of the bridge is the Flinders St East area, which contains many of the town's oldest buildings, several cafes and restaurants, the Great Barrier Reef Wonderland and the ferry departure points.

Information

The Magnetic North Information Centre (☎ (077) 71 2724) is in the middle of Flinders St Mall, between Stokes and Dean Sts. It's open Monday to Friday from 9 am to 5 pm, Saturdays and Sundays from 9 am to noon. The RACQ (☎ (077) 75 3999) is at 202 Ross River Rd, in the suburb of Aitkenvale.

Apart from the main post office on Flinders St, there's a branch in the Barrier Reef Wonderland which is open weekends as well as weekdays.

Townsville holds an interesting Sunday morning crafts and food market in the Flinders St Mall.

There are a lot of rodeos in Queensland, a number of them in the small towns inland from Townsville. The season is May to October and the tourist office should have details.

Great Barrier Reef Wonderland

Townsville's top attraction is at the end of Flinders St East beside Ross Creek. While its impressive aquarium is the highlight, there are several other sections including a theatre, the Queensland Museum, shops, a good national parks information office, and a terminal for ferries to Magnetic Island.

A combined ticket to the aquarium, theatre and museum costs $17.50, or you can pay for each individually, but this works out more expensive.

Aquarium The huge main tank has a living coral reef and hundreds of reef fish and other life. To maintain the natural conditions needed to keep this community alive, 'tides'

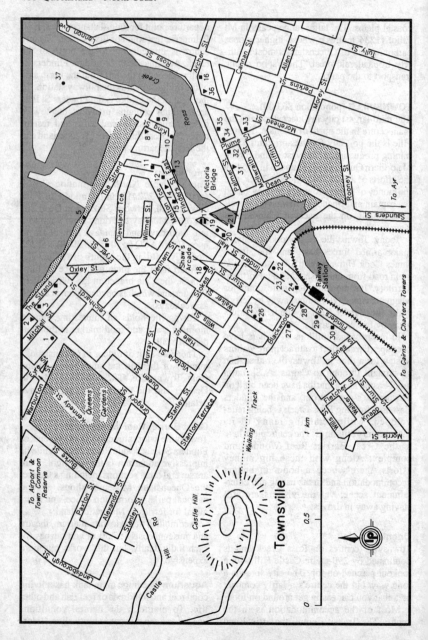

Townsville

are imitated by raising and lowering the water level, a wave machine simulates the ebb and flow of the ocean, and marine algae are used in the purification system. The aquarium also has several smaller tanks,

extensive displays on the history and life of the reef, and a theatrette where films on the reef are shown. It's open daily from 9.30 am to 5 pm and admission is $10.

Omnimax Theatre This is a cinema with angled seating and a dome-shaped screen for a 3-D effect. Hour-long films on the reef and outer space alternate through the day from 9.30 am till 5.30 pm. There are also some evening sessions. Admission to one film is $8.50.

Queensland Museum This museum has displays focusing on north Queensland, including wetland birds and other wildlife, rainforest, ocean wrecks and Aboriginal artefacts. The museum is open daily from 9 am to 5 pm (Fridays until 8 pm) and admission is $2.

Other Museums & Galleries
The **Townsville Museum** on the corner of Sturt and Stokes Sts has a permanent display on early Townsville and the North Queensland independence campaigns, as well as temporary exhibitions. It's open daily from 10 am to 1 or 3 pm.

The **Jezzine Military Museum** is just off the northern end of The Strand. There's also a **Maritime Museum** on Benwell Rd, in South Townsville; and the **Perc Tucker Regional Gallery**, at the Denham St end of the Flinders St Mall, is one of the best regional art galleries in Australia.

Parks, Gardens & Sanctuaries
Behind the Strand, **Queens Gardens** on Gregory St, a km from the town centre, are the original botanic gardens in Townsville, dating from 1878. The new botanic gardens, **Anderson Park**, are six km south-west of the centre on Gulliver St, Mundingburra.

For a chance to see some wildlife, make your way out to the **Town Common Reserve**, five km north of the centre, just off Cape Pallarenda Rd. This 32-sq-km area ranges from mangrove swamps and salt marsh to dry grassland and pockets of woodland and forest. The common is best known for water birds such as magpie geese, which herald the start of the wet season, and stately brolgas, which gather in the Dry. Early morning is the best time to see them.

The **Billabong Sanctuary**, 17 km south on the Bruce Highway, is a zoo of Australian animals. It's open daily, with shows (including crocodile or giant eel feeding) at 11.30 am, plus 2.30 pm on weekends and holidays.

Other Attractions

The **Flinders St Mall** is bright, breezy and full of interest. Giant games of chess, backgammon and snakes & ladders are part of the mall activities. Just down from the mall, the old Victoria swing bridge has been turned into shops and eateries.

East of the mall you can stroll along **Flinders St East** beside the creek. Many of the best 19th-century buildings are in this part of town, while further out, on a breakwater at the mouth of Ross Creek, is the casino. A more pleasant walk is north along the **Strand**, a long beachfront drive with a marina, gardens, some awesome banyan trees, the Tobruk swimming pool and a big artificial waterfall.

There's a road up to the top of **Castle Hill**, where there are good views over the town and coast, and you can also walk up from Stanton Terrace.

Activities

Diving Townsville has four or five diving schools, including one of Australia's best – Mike Ball Watersports (☎ (077) 72 3022), at 252 Walker St. Five-day certificate courses start twice a week and cost around $360 with five trips to the reef – plus two nights there on the more expensive option. You have to take a $30 medical before you start the course.

Pro-Dive, another well-regarded dive school, also runs courses in Townsville. Its office (☎ (077) 21 1760) is in Great Barrier Reef Wonderland. Pro-Dive's five-day certificate course costs $340, starts twice a week, and includes one night and two days on the reef, with a total of seven dives.

You can get cheap or free accommodation

at some hostels if you book a dive course from that hostel.

For experienced divers, the wreck of the *Yongala*, a passenger liner which sank off Cape Bowling Green in 1911 with 122 lives lost, is more of an attraction than the John Brewer Reef, the destination for many day trips. The *Yongala* has huge numbers of fish and large marine life like turtles and rays. John Brewer Reef has been damaged by the crown-of-thorns starfish and cyclones, and parts of the reef have little live coral. Mike Ball and Pro-Dive both run trips out to the *Yongala*.

Beware of box jellyfish off the beaches from October to May.

Places to Stay

Hostels Townsville's hostel scene is probably the best example of large operators jumping on the budget accommodation bandwagon. The result is an oversupply of hostels, and it's quite within the bounds of possibility that some of the places listed here will be closed by the time you visit.

Palmer St, in the area of the Transit Centre, has three hostels. Upstairs in the Transit Centre itself is the *Transit Centre Backpackers* (☎ (077) 21 2322), a huge air-con place with more than 200 beds. Although convenient for bus departures, the place lacks atmosphere. Dorm beds are $10.

Much better is the smaller hostel in the *Globetrotters Harbourside Inn* (☎ (077) 71 3242), at 45 Palmer St. This hostel has all the usual facilities – kitchen area, lounge, pool, laundry facilities – and is clean and well run. Dorm beds are $10, while good singles/doubles cost $20/26.

Townsville's other huge offering is the 300-plus-bed *Adventurers Resort* (☎ (077) 21 1522) at 79 Palmer St. Accommodation is in rooms taking two, four or 10 people, and there's a kitchen, dining and sitting area, garden, takeaway kiosk and budget licensed restaurant. Dorm beds are $11 ($14 with air-con), while singles/doubles cost $20/28.

Also on this side of the river is *Southbank Village Backpackers* (☎ (077) 72 2122), at 33 Plume St, just a minute or so from the

Transit Centre. Dorm beds (not bunks) in this small place are $10.

There are more places north of Ross Creek. One of the best of these is the *Backpackers Hostel* (☎ (077) 72 2820), up a flight of steps at 23 Wills St, opposite the law courts. It's a small, cosy and friendly place with excellent views over the town. Beds in clean and spacious dorms cost $10, there's a courtesy coach to meet incoming buses, free laundry facilities and free tea and coffee. Quite a few travellers end up here after finding the big Palmer St places too anonymous and crowded.

Next up is *Civic House Backpackers Inn* (☎ (077) 71 5381) at 262 Walker St. This very easy-going hostel has modern six-bed dorms, each with bathroom, as well as some older rooms. Dorm beds cost $10, and double rooms are $26. On Friday nights there's a free barbecue for guests.

The busy *Backpackers International* (☎ (077) 72 4340), at 205 Flinders St East, has about 140 beds in a rambling collection of rooms behind a fine balconied Victorian front. It's a clean place, if a bit rundown and gloomy, and beds cost $10.

The *Reef Lodge* (☎ (077) 21 1112) at 4 Wickham St, has dorm beds for $11, or there are singles/doubles for $24/30 with coin-in-the-slot air-con. It's another small place with the usual facilities, although the stoves in the kitchen also require coins.

The *Pioneer Backpacker Hostel* (☎ (077) 21 1691) is at 537 Flinders St, opposite the railway station. It's cheap ($10) and cheerful, with bunks in two large dorms. This place also promotes itself as an art expo, and you can sell any handicrafts you make on their Sunday market stall in the Flinders St Mall.

Hotels & Guesthouses The *Sunseeker Private Hotel* (☎ (077) 71 3409), at 10 Blackwood St, near Sturt St, has small dorms, as well as singles/doubles at $30/38.

There are also a number of traditional old hotels like the *Great Northern* (☎ (077) 71 6191) at 500 Flinders St down by the railway

station. Nightly cost is $24/30; some doubles have private bathrooms for an extra $5. The *Seaview Hotel* (☎ (077) 71 5005), at 56 The Strand, has singles/doubles at $22/30.

Motels Cheaper motels include the central *Rex City Motel* (☎ (077) 71 6048), at 143 Wills St, with rooms at $49/50; and the *Strand Motel* (☎ (077) 72 1977), at 51 The Strand, with rooms at $36/40.

Yongala Lodge (☎ (070) 72 4633), at 11 Fryer St, has singles/doubles for $45/60. A two-bedroom flat with fully equipped kitchenette, sitting area and balcony costs $70. At the front, in a lovely 19th-century building, is a Greek restaurant, and there are displays of period furniture, memorabilia, and finds from the *Yongala* wreck. Numerous motels are on the two roads leading into Townsville from the Bruce Highway to the south.

Some holiday flats offer similar prices to the cheaper motels. *Seagren Holiday Apartments* (☎ (077) 72 5867), at 94 The Strand, charges $50 to $60 for two people.

Camping There are two caravan parks which are only about two km from town, and both have on-site vans as well as tent sites. *Rowes Bay Caravan Park* (☎ (077) 71 3576) is just over the road from the beach on Heatley Parade, Rowes Bay; and the *Showground Caravan Park* (☎ (077) 72 1487) is at 16 Kings Rd, West End.

Places to Eat

The *Exchange Hotel* on Flinders St has a courtyard restaurant with steaks from $10, and the Melton Black's Piano Bar upstairs with more expensive food. The *Crown Tavern*, on the corner of Palmer and Morehead Sts, just south of Ross Creek, has very good counter lunches and dinners from around $9.

On the Strand, the *Seaview Hotel* is a popular place to eat and has steaks, seafood and other meals from $5. In the evening from Wednesday to Saturday there's live music.

The *Criterion Tavern*, on the corner of The Strand and King St, also has counter meals and a steakhouse/bistro; live bands play in the beer garden on weekends.

Over on Palmer St, the cafe in the Transit Centre serves quite substantial meals and is open from 5 am to 11 pm. At the front of the centre, *Andy's Bistro*, open daily from 6 pm, has a $6 fill-your-plate special. Also on Palmer St is *Cactus Jack's*, a licensed Mexican bistro. It's a lively place with main courses in the $10 range.

Flinders St offers plenty of choices. The *Thai International Restaurant*, upstairs on Flinders St East, has fine soups for $6, and imaginative main courses for $10 to $13. On the ground floor here is the *Metro Eastside Cafe*, a pleasant place with dishes such as lasagna and moussaka for $4.

Also in this area is the licensed *Capitol* Chinese restaurant. Apart from the à la carte menu, they do an excellent $12.50 buffet each night, and there's a good range of well-prepared dishes to tuck into. Also here is *Luvit*, which does very good filled savoury pancakes.

Further along Flinders St, past the southern end of the mall, is *Mariners Seafood Restaurant* at No 428. Here you can also dine buffet-style for around $20. Almost next door is the *Jun Japanese Restaurant*, which is nothing special but is moderately priced at $12 to $15 for main courses. The *Cafe Nova*, on Blackwood St near the corner of Flinders St, is open from 7 pm till late every night except Monday; it has snacks and light meals from $7 and is BYO. It also features live music.

Just off the Strand, near the Seaview Hotel, is the *Rasa Pinang* Malaysian restaurant. All the dishes on the menu are less than $10, and the $5 takeaway dishes are very good value.

Beside Ross Creek, near the bottom of Stokes St and just down from the mall, there's an inviting collection of food stalls and open-air tables known as the *Boardwalk Food Fare*, at the northern end of Victoria Bridge. Cuisines featured include Italian, seafood, Mexican, health food and more, all at reasonable prices, and you can buy alcohol but only if you are eating.

Entertainment

Townsville's nightlife is just as lively as Cairns's and ranges from pub bands to flashy clubs and, of course, the casino. Much of the action is on Flinders St. The James Cook Tavern, at 273 Flinders St East, has live music on Friday and Saturday nights. There's a blues club on Friday nights from 7 pm until late.

Nightclubs include the Bank at 169 Flinders St East, and the Terrace Cabaret on the corner of Flinders and Denham Sts. Dress regulations apply at both clubs. Further along Flinders St, past the mall, are the disco/nightclubs Opus 1 Cabaret and Shaboom.

The Criterion Tavern, at 10 The Strand, has live bands and entertainment in its outdoor section. Moving along the Strand, the Seaview Hotel has rock music on Wednesday to Saturday nights. For a change of pace, the Hotel Allen on Gregory St has a guitarist in its beer garden on Friday nights and Sunday afternoons. The Crown Tavern on Palmer St, just south of Ross Creek, offers jazz and toad racing on Sunday afternoons.

The Civic Theatre (☎ (077) 72 2677), on Boundary St in South Townsville, is the regional centre for performing arts and varied cultural pursuits. If you have the right clothes and fancy trying your luck on the spin of the wheel, the Sheraton Breakwater Casino is down at the end of Sir Leslie Thiess Drive, beyond Flinders St East.

Getting There & Away

Air You can fly to Townsville from Cairns ($145), Brisbane ($308), Sydney or Melbourne several times a day with Ansett or Australian Airlines – and from other major centres usually once or twice a day. You can also get to Mt Isa ($239), Darwin or Alice Springs from Townsville with either airline. Australian Regional Airlines has services to Cairns and Dunk Island; Sunstate flies to Mackay ($147), Rockhampton, Gladstone and Bundaberg; and Sungold to Mackay.

Flight West (☎ (077) 25 1622) has flights to/from Mt Isa ($239) at least once a day, often with stops at small places on the way. It also flies to Cairns ($145), Mackay ($147), Rockhampton ($193) and Brisbane ($308).

Bus Greyhound/Pioneer (☎ (077) 71 2134), McCafferty's (☎ (077) 72 5100), and Bus Australia (☎ (077) 71 6688) all have services at least once a day between Brisbane and Cairns, stopping in Townsville en route. It's 18 to 21 hours from Brisbane ($118), 10 to 11 hours from Rockhampton ($73), about six hours from Mackay ($48), 3½ hours from Airlie Beach ($30), three hours from Mission Beach ($31) and 4½ hours from Cairns ($40). To Mt Isa the trip takes 11 hours and costs $81.

All the bus companies use the Townsville Transit Centre on Palmer St.

Train The Brisbane to Cairns Sunlander travels through Townsville three times a week. From Brisbane to Townsville takes 26 hours ($117 in economy, $179 in 1st class). From Townsville, Proserpine is a five-hour journey, Rockhampton is 14½ hours and Cairns, seven hours. The Queenslander does the same Brisbane to Cairns run once a week (leaving Brisbane on Sunday mornings and Cairns on Tuesday mornings). It's a bit faster than the Sunlander and has a special bar for 1st-class passengers where movies are shown. Economy fares are the same as on the Sunlander: 1st class from Brisbane to Townsville is $300 which includes all meals and a sleeping compartment.

The Inlander operates twice weekly from Townsville to Mt Isa (18 hours; $113.10 in economy, $172.20 in 1st class). Townsville to Charters Towers takes three hours ($16.60 in economy only).

Getting Around

To/From the Airport Townsville Airport is five km north-west of the city at Garbutt. A taxi is $8. The Brolga Airport Shuttle Bus (☎ (077) 79 7799) services all main arrivals and departures. It costs $4.50 one-way and

will drop you or pick you up almost anywhere fairly central.

Bus The City Explorer (☎ (077) 71 5024) is one of those hop-off hop-on services. The bus does a 32-km loop with stops near main attractions ($8). Services are usually hourly, and the bus normally runs Tuesday to Saturday in the main tourist season, less frequently the rest of the year.

Car The larger car-rental agencies are all represented in Townsville, as well as smaller firms like Brolga Mini-Vehicle Hire (☎ (077) 71 4261) at the corner of Hanran and Ogden Sts. Other smaller operators include Rent-a-Rocket (☎ (077) 72 6880), 14 Dean St, South Townsville, and Sun City Rent-a-Moke (☎ (077) 72 2702) at 27 Eyre St, North Ward.

MAGNETIC ISLAND (population 2500)

Magnetic is one of the most popular islands for travellers because it's so cheap and convenient to get to. It's big enough to offer plenty of things to see and do, including some fine bushwalks.

Only 13 km offshore from Townsville, Magnetic Island was named by Captain Cook, who thought his ship's compass went funny when he sailed by in 1770. The island has some fine beaches, lots of bird life, bushwalking tracks, a koala sanctuary and an aquarium. It's dominated by 500-metre Mt Cook.

There are several small towns along the coast and the island has quite a different atmosphere to the purely resort islands along the reef. Magnetic is one of the larger reef islands (52 sq km) and about 70% of it is national park.

Orientation & Information

Magnetic Island is roughly triangular in shape with Picnic Bay, the main town and ferry pier, at the southern corner. There's a road up the eastern side of the island to Horseshoe Bay and a rough track along the west coast. Along the north coast it's walking only. The best place for information is Magnetic Travel & Accommodation (☎ (077) 78 5099) at 4 The Esplanade, Picnic Bay. You can rent bicycles here, book tours (some with special backpackers' rates), and arrange accommodation and flights.

Walks

The national parks service produces a leaflet for Magnetic Island's excellent bushwalking tracks. Possible walks include:

1	Nelly Bay to Arcadia	6 km	1½ hours
2	Picnic Bay to West Point	8 km	2½ hours
3	Horseshoe Bay road to Arthur Bay	2 km	½ hour
	Arthur Bay to Florence Bay	2 km	½ hour
	Horseshoe Bay road to the Forts	2 km	¾ hour
4	Horseshoe Bay to Balding Bay	3 km	¾ hour
	Horseshoe Bay to Radical Bay	3 km	¾ hour
5	Mt Cook ascent	8 km	all day

Except for the long Mt Cook ascent, none of the walks require special preparation.

You can string several walks together to make an excellent full day's outing. Starting from Nelly Bay, walk directly inland along Mandalay Ave and follow the signpost to the Horseshoe Bay lookout, from where the trail drops down and around to Arcadia. This part is about a six-km walk taking 1½ hours. Towards the end of this track there's a choice of routes. Take the longer track, via a quick detour to Sphinx Lookout, to the Horseshoe Bay road beyond Arcadia. You've then only got a short walk to the Radical Bay junction from where you can walk to the Forts and on down to Radical Bay. From here it's up and over to Horseshoe Bay, via Balding Bay if you wish. From Horseshoe Bay you can take the bus back to the other end of the island.

If you want to climb 506-metre Mt Cook, a compass and adequate water supply should be carried. There is no marked trail but it's fairly easy to follow a ridge line from the saddle on the Nelly Bay to Arcadia track. After heavy rain there's a waterfall on Petersen Creek. You can also hike along the

west coast from Picnic Bay to Young Bay and West Point.

Picnic Bay to Nelly Bay

Picnic Bay is convenient for the ferry and has a good selection of shops and places to stay and eat. There's a lookout above the town and just to the west of Picnic Bay is **Cockle Bay** with the wreck of the *City of Adelaide*. Heading around the coast from Picnic Bay you soon come to **Rocky Bay** where there's a short, steep walk down to its beautiful beach.

Next around the coast is **Nelly Bay** with the Shark World aquarium, which has coral displays, tropical fish aquariums, tortoises and sharks. The sharks are fed daily at 2 pm. There's also a snack bar, and a licensed restaurant, open from 9 am to 9 pm. Nelly Bay has a good beach with shade, and a reef at low tide. At the far end of the bay there are some pioneer graves, and the beginnings of the controversial Magnetic Quay development, but the developer has gone into receivership and quite possibly the resort will get no further. If this is the case, the unfinished works will have damaged a large part of the small reef here, and will remain an ugly blot on the landscape.

Arcadia

Round the headland you come to **Geoffrey Bay** with shops, a walking track, and an interesting 400-metre low-tide trail over the fringing coral reef from the southern end of the beach; a board indicates the start of the trail. Then there's Arcadia, with the Arcadia Holiday Resort (where there are live bands at weekends and the pool is open to the public) and, just around the headland, the very pleasant Alma Bay beach. The Magnetic Marine ferry comes to Arcadia three times on weekdays and six times daily on weekends.

Radical Bay & the Forts

The road runs back from the coast until you reach the junction of the road to Radical Bay. There's a choice of routes here if you don't want to go straight to Horseshoe Bay. You

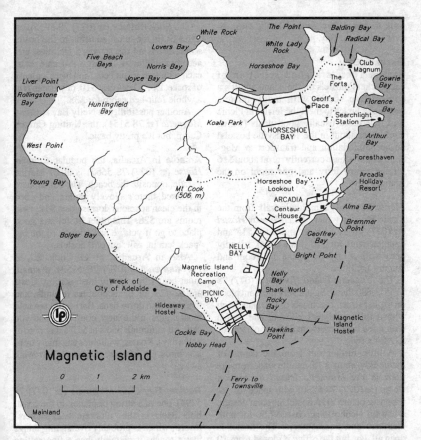

Magnetic Island

0   1   2 km

Mainland

can either take the track via the Forts, or you can take the road to Radical Bay, with tracks leading off it to secluded Arthur and Florence bays and the old **Searchlight Station** on the headland between the two.

The track to the Forts (which date from WW II) is driveable most of the way, but is also a pleasant stroll. If you're on foot, as an alternative to backtracking to the road junction, you can continue downhill from the forts and rejoin the Radical Bay road just before the resort. From here you can walk across the headland to the beautiful **Balding Bay** (an unofficial nude bathing beach) and Horseshoe Bay.

Horseshoe Bay

Horseshoe Bay is the end of the road. It has more shops and accommodation and a long stretch of beach. There's a lagoon **bird sanctuary** a few hundred metres from the beach, the **Koala Park** which is quite a long drive off the main road, and a **mango plantation** which you can visit. At the beach there are boats, sailboards and canoes for hire and you can also parasail. From the beach you can walk to Maud Bay, around to the west, or over to Radical Bay.

Places to Stay

Hostels There's a good selection of backpackers' hostels on the island and it's a competitive scene, with many hostels sending vehicles to meet the ferries at Picnic Bay. There are usually good deals (which you'll hear about in the Townsville hostels) on accommodation and transport to Magnetic Island – these currently run at about $16 for the return ferry and one night on the island.

Picnic Bay Only a minute's walk from the Picnic Bay ferry pier, the *Hideaway Hostel* (☎ (077) 78 5110) has singles for $15 and doubles/twins for $20. It's a clean, friendly place with a tiny kitchen, a TV room and laundry facilities.

The *Magnetic Island Hostel* (☎ (077) 78 5755), at 80 Picnic St, is a very pleasant place on a quiet street. It consists of two flats, each with a fully equipped kitchen, and rooms with three beds; costs are $10 per person, or $22 for a twin.

A little further out from the centre of Picnic Bay, about a 15-minute walk from the pier, is the *Magnetic Island Recreation Camp* (☎ (077) 78 5280) with space for 36. It's an associate YHA hostel, popular despite a ban on alcohol, and costs $7.50 for both members and nonmembers. The hostel is open all day, but the office is closed from 10 am to 5 pm. There's a tennis court and you can hire bicycles and snorkelling gear. To get there, walk along the Esplanade away from town to Granite St, then straight up to the top and turn right. The local bus will take you there free.

Nelly Bay As you round the corner into Nelly Bay, you'll notice the blue-and-white-striped 'Camp-O-Tel' accommodation (a cross between a cabin and a tent with beds or bunks) at *Shark World* (☎ (077) 78 5187). It cost $6 per person to camp in your own tent and $12 per head in the Camp-O-Tels, which apparently get unbearably hot in summer.

The *Rock Wallaby* (☎ (077) 78 5955), on Yates St, is the latest addition to the hostel scene. It has all the standard facilities, and accommodation is in large A-frame huts, each with four to six beds, and there's plenty of space. Dorm beds cost $10, or you can rent a whole four-bed cabin for $38.

Another possibility in Nelly Bay is *Camp Magnetic* (☎ 78 5151), the Uniting Church Camp, but it's pretty basic.

Arcadia In Arcadia, the popular *Centaur House* (☎ (077) 78 5668) is at 27 Marine Parade, opposite the beach. The atmosphere is relaxed, there's a lovely garden, and a bed in the clean spacious dorms costs $12; twin rooms are $28. This quiet hostel is a good place to go if you've had enough of the big 'pack 'em in, spit 'em out' hostels.

Also in Arcadia, at 11 Cook Rd, is *Foresthaven* (☎ (077) 78 5153), a small, quiet hostel in a lovely bush setting. Costs are $24/28 for twins/doubles in units, and there are also dorm beds. Barbecues are held most nights in the large courtyard, and you can rent mountain bikes at $10 a day ($6 for half a day). Koalas, wallabies and many tropical birds are often seen just a short walk away.

Radical Bay *Club Magnums* (☎ (077) 78 5294), one of a string of places up the coast, bills itself as the 'ultimate backpackers' resort', which is probably overstating things just a touch. It certainly has a fine setting right on the beach, but is a bit isolated, being at the end of the road and away from any shops. Still, if you're the sort of traveller who has enjoyed the other Magnums places, you won't be disappointed here. Cost is $12 per night, and there's a bar and restaurant.

Horseshoe Bay *Geoff's Place* (☎ (077) 78 5577), is one of the island's most popular places for young travellers. There are extensive grounds in which you can camp for $5 per person, take a bunk in a marquee for $6 or share a cabin for $10 – although all prices are $2 higher the first night. There are also A-frame cedar cabins, each with a double bed and a bunk. In these you pay $12 per person ($15 the first night). There's a kitchen, plus a bar and a restaurant offering breakfast and dinner, where you get a good meal for $5 to $7.50. You can hire mountain bikes for $12 a day, or ride horses at a nearby ranch. You can use the courtesy bus, which shuttles between here and Picnic Bay six times a day, for exploring other bays on the island.

Hotels & Holiday Flats There are hotels, motels, resorts and more than a dozen holiday flats on the island. At certain times, these can be rather packed, so it's wise to phone ahead and book if necessary.

Holiday flats mostly quote weekly rates. Prices vary with demand – even in peak season, you may find bargains if there happens to be a flat vacant. Single-bedroom flats are mostly $250 to $350 per week, two-bedroom flats $300 to $450. Among the cheapest is *Ti-Tree Lodge Flats*, at 20 Barbara St in Picnic Bay, where daily costs are $40 to $50 for doubles and twins.

At Arcadia, the *Arcadia Resort* (☎ (077) 78 5177) has poolside rooms for $35/55, or terrace rooms for $40/65. All rooms have bathroom, air-con, TV, fridge and tea/coffee-making equipment. On Hayles Ave, also in Arcadia, the *Magnetic Retreat* (☎ (077) 78 5357) has modern, fully equipped one and two-bedroom flats, and charges from $65 to $75 for doubles.

At Alma Bay, the *Alma Den Beach Resort* (☎ (077)) has units for two at $75.

Places to Eat
Picnic Bay In this area, all the places to eat are along the Esplanade. The *Picnic Bay Pub* has counter meals from $6 to $10, and there are cheaper snacks. Further along, *Crusoe's* is a straightforward restaurant with a good reputation and evening meals from $6 to $12. The *Greek Grill* has good prices, with dishes such as souvlaki for $3.50 and moussaka for $4.

The popular *Taste of Paradise*, at the far end of the Esplanade, is open seven days and has meals from $6.

Nelly Bay *Mexican Munchies* runs the gamut from enchiladas to tacos, and is open daily from 6 pm. There's a blackboard outside where you can chalk up your reservation during the day. Nearby, in the small shopping centre on Sooning St, is *Possums*, good for snacks and takeaways.

Arcadia The Arcadia Holiday Resort has a number of eating possibilities, with outdoor meals by the pool from $8 to $10. *Skippers Restaurant* has more expensive meals.

Alla Capri on Hayles Ave has pizzas for around $9, and a pleasant outdoor eating area with visiting possums for entertainment.

In the small shopping centre, the *Bake-house* opens early and is a good place for a coffee and croissant breakfast. Next door is *Banister's Seafood* which is a high-quality fish & chips place with an open-air dining area; it is BYO.

Horseshoe Bay The *Bounty Snack Bar* has takeaways. Other than that, the only place to eat is *Geoff's Place*, about a km back along the main road. There's also a small store if you're preparing your own food.

Getting There & Away
Two companies, Magnetic Marine (☎ (077) 72 7122) and Magnetic Link (☎ (077) 78 5130), both run 10 or 11 ferries a day to and from Townsville for $12 return ($10 with a student card). All ferries go to Picnic Bay (a 20-minute ride) and some of Magnetic Marine's continue to Arcadia.

In Townsville, Magnetic Marine departs from three places: Flinders St East, the Great Barrier Reef Wonderland and the breakwater on Sir Leslie Thiess Drive, near the Sheraton Casino. Magnetic Link goes from Flinders St East and from the Great Barrier Reef Wonderland.

Last ferries leave Townsville around 6.30 pm, except for Magnetic Link's late services on Friday at 9.30 pm and Saturdays at 11.30 pm.

Both companies offer package deals which include transport around the island

and/or lunch, and there are also deals with the hostels.

Magnetic Barge services (☎ (077) 72 5090) also runs a vehicle ferry to Picnic Bay from the south side of Ross Creek three times a day during the week and twice a day on weekends. It's $70 return for a car, so for a short stay it's probably not worth it.

Getting Around

Bus The Magnetic Island Bus Service operates between Picnic Bay and Horseshoe Bay six to 10 times a day. Some bus trips include Radical Bay, others the Koala Park. You can either get tickets from place to place or a full-day pass ($5).

Moke You soon get the impression that 90% of the vehicles on Magnetic Island are Mokes. At times there seems to be nothing else. There are at least two companies which rent out Mokes in Picnic Bay.

Magnetic Island Rent-a-Moke (☎ (077) 78 5377) is the biggest operator, with more than 100 vehicles. Daily charges are around $30, and there's an additional charge of 20c per km.

Holiday Moke Hire (☎ (077) 78 5703) is another Moke agent, and has its office in the TAB on the Esplanade.

Moped The main place for 50cc machines is Roadrunner Scooter Hire (☎ (077) 78 5222) at Shop 2, Picnic Bay Arcade. Day hire is $25, half-day hire $19, and 24-hour hire $35. All rates include unlimited km, insurance and use of a helmet. To hire a scooter you don't need a motorbike licence, just a car licence that you have held for six months, and a $50 deposit.

Bicycle Magnetic Island is ideal for cycling, and there are new mountain bikes available for rent at various places – the Esplanade in Picnic Bay, Foresthaven Resort in Arcadia and Geoff's Place in Horseshoe Bay. Although the bikes all belong to the same outfit, costs vary depending on where you rent them: the average is $10 for a day, $6 for half a day.

Tours Places along the Esplanade handle tours of the island, as well as trips to nearby Orpheus Island.

TOWNSVILLE TO CAIRNS
Mt Spec National Park

This national park, which straddles the 1000-metre-plus Paluma Range, west of the Bruce Highway, has Australia's most southerly pocket of tropical rainforest. Sixty-five km north of Townsville, a paved road turns off the highway and winds up along the southern edge of the park, passing **Little Crystal Creek** and **McClelland's Lookout** on the way to the small village of Paluma. Pioneer runs day trips from Townsville ($30).

Big Crystal Creek, also in the park, is another good place to swim, and there's a camping site. For a permit, contact the park ranger (☎ (077) 70 8526), or the Townsville or Ingham national parks offices. Bower birds are relatively common in the park. To get there, turn off the Bruce Highway two km after the Paluma turn-off, and take the four-km road to the site.

Jourama National Park

Jourama National Park is nine unpaved km off the highway, 89 km north of Townsville. There are more good swimming holes here, along with waterfalls, a short walking track, a camping ground (permits as for Big Crystal Creek) and a lookout.

For camping permits, get in touch with the national parks office in Ingham (☎ (077) 76 1700).

Ingham (population 6100)

There's a lot of Spanish and Italian influence in this sugar-producing town. **Lucinda**, a port town 24 km from Ingham, has a six-km jetty used for shipping the sugar.

In Ingham, most of the accommodation is on Lannercost St. The *Hinchinbrook Hotel* (☎ (077) 76 2227), at 85 Lannercost St, offers beds to backpackers at $10 each. The national parks district office (☎ (077) 76 1700), at 11 Lannercost St, deals with camping permits for Mt Spec, Wallaman

Falls, Jourama National Park, and Orpheus Island.

There are a number of places to visit around Ingham including **Wallaman Falls**, 48 km inland, where a tributary of the Herbert River cascades for 305 metres, the longest single drop in Australia. The falls are much more spectacular in the wet season. You can normally reach them by conventional vehicle along an unpaved road; there's a national parks camping area with a swimming hole nearby.

Only seven km off the highway is the **Victoria Mill**, the largest sugar mill in the southern hemisphere. Free tours are given in the crushing season.

Orpheus Island

Lying off the coast between Townsville and Ingham, Orpheus is a narrow 14-sq-km granite island surrounded by coral reefs. One of the Palm Group, it's a quiet, secluded island which is good for camping, snorkelling and diving. Orpheus is mostly national park and is heavily forested, with lots of bird life; turtles also nest here. Camping is allowed in two places (permits from Ingham) but take your own water. Also on the island are a giant clam research station and a small resort with rooms at \$280-plus per person.

If you want to camp, you can get there by charter boat from Taylor's Beach (25 km from Ingham) or Lucinda, or you can get the Westmark (☎ (077) 21 1913) people in Townsville to drop you off on one of their day trips.

Cardwell (population 1249)

South of Cardwell, the Bruce Highway climbs high above the coast with tremendous views down across the winding, mangrove-lined waterways known as the Everglades, which separate Hinchinbrook Island from the coast.

Cardwell is one of north Queensland's very earliest towns, dating from 1864, and is the only town on the highway between Brisbane and Cairns which is actually on the coast. It's more or less a one-street place and

is the departure point for Hinchinbrook and other continental islands. It also has one of Queensland's four main national parks information centres (☎ (070) 66 8601) on the highway in the middle of town. The office is open daily, and deals with camping permits for nearby national parks.

There are several good places for freshwater swimming a short drive from the town. Most of the coastal forest north of Cardwell is protected as the **Edmund Kennedy National Park**. At the southern end of the park, there's a camping site close to the beach and some walking tracks – turn down Clifts Rd four km north of Cardwell to reach them.

The **Murray Falls** with fine rock pools for swimming, and a free camping ground, are 22 km west of the highway – turn off at the 'Murray Upper Road' sign about 27 km north of Cardwell.

Places to Stay The *Cardwell Backpackers Hostel* (☎ (070) 66 8922) is at 178 Bowen St, towards the northern end of town. It has a sizeable dorm and a couple of smaller rooms plus the usual kitchen and bathroom facilities. Cost is \$10 a night. Bed linen is provided, there are bicycles for rent and breakfast is available.

The YHA *Hinchinbrook Hostel* (☎ (070) 66 8648), at 175 Bruce Highway, charges \$10 for a dorm bed and \$24 a double.

There are several motel, camping and on-site van possibilities. *Kookaburra Park* (☎ (070) 66 8648), on the highway roughly in the middle of town, has tent sites and a range of on-site accommodation.

Getting There & Away All buses between Townsville and Cairns stop at Cardwell. The fare is around \$20 from either place. Cardwell is also on the main Brisbane to Cairns railway.

Hinchinbrook Island

The entire large island of Hinchinbrook is national park. There's a low-key resort on Hinchinbrook's northern peninsula, Cape Richards, and 12 national park camping areas. Hinchinbrook is popular with bushwalkers and has several good tracks.

The terrain of the island is varied – lush tropical forest on the mainland side, towering mountains in the middle and long sandy beaches and secluded bays on the eastern side. Hinchinbrook covers 635 sq km and rugged Mt Bowen, at 1142 metres, is the highest peak. There's plenty of wildlife, especially pretty-faced wallabies and the iridescent blue Ulysses butterfly.

There's a five-km walking trail from the resort to Macushla via Shepherd Bay, and a fairly hard 30 km track down the east coast from Ramsay Bay to Zoe Bay and on to George Point. Zoe Bay, with its beautiful waterfall, is one of the most scenic spots on the island. Walkers are warned to take plenty of insect repellent; the sandflies on Hinchinbrook can be a real pest.

The resort has rooms for around 60 people but it's not cheap at $170 a day per person, including excellent meals and transfer from Cardwell.

The camp grounds are at the Haven opposite Cardwell (water available from Pages Creek), Macushla on Missionary Bay in the north (bring drinking water with you), and at nine spots along the east coast (water available at most). The east coast trail camping areas include Nina Bay, Little Ramsay Bay, Zoe Bay, Mulligan Bay and George Point. Numbers for each camping area are limited (anywhere from 10 to 35) and depend on the total number of walkers on the island. For camping permits, and detailed trail information, contact the national parks office in Cardwell (☎ (070) 66 8601).

An excellent way of seeing the island is by sea kayak. R'n'R (☎ 008 07 9039, toll-free) operate four-day expeditions along the east coast of Hinchinbrook from Lucinda every two weeks. The $460 cost includes all meals and equipment.

Getting There & Away You can book for the Hinchinbrook resort and various island trips at the Hinchinbrook Booking Office (☎ (070) 66 8539) at 91 Bruce Highway, Cardwell. The MV *Reef Adventure II* or *Hinchinbrook Explorer* leave Cardwell for Hinchinbrook daily except Monday at 9 am, returning at 4 pm. It'll drop you at Macushla if you like.

Tully (population 2800)

The wettest place in Australia gets a drenching average of 440 cm a year. Tully is the cheapest place to start from if you're doing a white-water rafting trip on the Tully River. The town is a regular stop for buses and trains between Townsville and Cairns, and there are a couple of caravan/camping parks and a motel. Nearby Mission Beach, however, is a much more appealing place to stay, and the rafting operators will pick you up from there.

Mission Beach (population 640)

This name covers a string of small settlements dotted along a 14-km beach east of Tully. Rainforest comes right down to the coast in places. From south to north, the settlements are: South Mission Beach, Wongaling Beach, Mission Beach, Clump Point, Bingil Bay and Garners Beach. Mission Beach is named after an Aboriginal mission which was founded here in 1914 but destroyed by a cyclone in 1918.

Tam O'Shanter Point, beyond South Mission Beach, was the starting point for the ill-fated 1848 overland expedition to Cape York led by 30-year-old Edmund Kennedy. All but three of the party's 13 members, including Kennedy, died. There's a memorial to the expedition at Tam O'Shanter Point.

Walks The rainforest around Mission Beach is a haunt of cassowaries but unfortunately the population has been depleted by road accidents and the destruction of rainforest by logging and cyclones. A four-km rainforest walking track leads from the Tully road, about two km west of the South Mission Beach turn-off, to the El Arish road, crossing Luff Hill with fine views on the way. Another rainforest track leads up to Bicton Hill from the Bingil Bay car park. It's a four-km circuit with several good lookouts.

Boat Trips Raging Thunder (☎ (070) 51 4911 in Mission Beach) and R'n'R (☎ 008 07 9039, toll-free) are white-water rafting companies which charge $99 from Mission Beach for trips on the Tully River.

Raging Thunder also offers three-day sea kayak expeditions to the Family Islands for $360 including meals and equipment (except sleeping bags). R'n'R runs three-day sea kayak trips from Kurrimine Beach, 10 km north of Mission Beach, to the Barnard Islands for $350.

From Clump Point you can take boat trips out to Beaver Cay on the Barrier Reef. These usually include snorkelling and a ride in a glass-bottomed boat for around $80. Services can be reduced during the wet season (roughly January to March). Edmund Kennedy Adventure Cruises (☎ (070) 68 7250) runs trips along the Hull River from South Mission Beach, about three times weekly. You may see saltwater crocodiles.

Places to Stay There are three hostels in Mission Beach, and all do pick-ups from the bus stop in Mission Beach proper. *Mission Beach Backpackers Lodge* (☎ (070) 68 8317), at 28 Wongaling Beach Rd, 650 metres from the beach, is a modern, well-equipped place with a pool and garden. You sleep in spacious dorms for $10.

Treehouse (☎ (070) 68 7137), an associate YHA hostel, is a wooden stilt house with good views over rainforest and the coast. It's off Bingil Bay Rd and signposted from the El Arish to Mission Beach road. The kitchen and the rooms, which house four or six bunks, are on the small side but the views make up for that. The cost is $11 per night.

Scotty's Mission Beach House (☎ (070) 688 676), at 167 Reid Rd, has room for 50; dorm beds are $12 and doubles $27. There's a pool, and every second day a barbecue on the beach.

The *Hideaway Caravan Park* (☎ (070) 68 7104), on Porter Promenade, has tent sites and on-site vans. There are at least two other caravan parks with similar facilities and prices. Other accommodation includes a scattering of motels, holiday units and three fairly low-key resorts. The cheapest is the *Mission Beach Village Motel* (☎ (070) 68 7212) at 7 Porter Promenade in Mission Beach proper, with rooms from $50.

Places to Eat For a full meal, you'd probably have to go to one of the resorts. Otherwise, there are a couple of Chinese places in Mission Beach proper. There's a small shopping centre, including a supermarket, open seven days a week, at Mission Beach proper and another supermarket in the resort on Wongaling Beach Rd.

Getting There & Away Around four buses a day in each direction between Townsville and Cairns make the detour off the Bruce Highway down to Mission Beach. The average fare is around $13 from Cairns, and $30 from Townsville.

Dunk Island & the Family Islands

One of the more interesting Barrier Reef resorts is 4½ km off Mission Beach at Brammo Bay on the northern end of heavily wooded, 10-sq-km Dunk Island. There's also a national park camping ground close to the resort (permits are available from the national parks office in Cardwell). A couple of places in Mission Beach rent camping gear.

From 1897 to 1923 E J Banfield lived on Dunk and wrote his book *The Confessions of a Beachcomber*; the island is remarkably little changed from his early description. Today it has a small artist colony centred around Bruce Arthur, a tapestry maker and former Olympic wrestler. Dunk is noted for prolific bird life (nearly 150 species) and many butterflies. There are superb views over the entrances to the Hinchinbrook Channel from the top of 271-metre Mt Kootaloo. Thirteen km of walking tracks lead from the camping ground area to headlands and beaches.

South of Dunk are the seven tiny Family Islands. One of them, Bedarra, has a very exclusive resort, where costs start around $400 a day per person! Five of the other Family Islands are national parks and you can bush camp on three of them – Wheeler, Combe and Bowden (permits from Cardwell, take your own water).

Getting There & Away Water taxis operate from Wongaling Beach and South Mission Beach several times daily, and these cost $7 one-way. Day trips to the island from Mission Beach cost around $20 with lunch on the *Quick Cat*.

You can fly to Dunk with Australian Regional Airlines from Townsville ($105) or Cairns ($95).

Innisfail

Innisfail is at the junction of the North and South Johnstone rivers. The North Johnstone, flowing down from the Atherton Tableland, is good for white-water rafting and canoeing. There are a few reasonably priced motels in Innisfail and a handful of caravan parks, where you can also camp. Flying Fish Point, on the north side of the Johnstone River mouth, is reportedly a good camping spot.

Innisfail has been a sugar city for over a century. It's a busy place, with a large Italian population – although on Owen St you can also find a Chinese temple (open daily from 7 am to 5 pm). The Italians first arrived early this century to work the cane fields: some became plantation owners themselves and in the 1930s there was even a local 'mafia' called the Black Hand!

At **Mourilyan**, seven km south of Innisfail, there's the Australian Sugar Museum, open from 9 am to 4.30 pm daily. An export terminal on the coast east of Mourilyan handles the sugar produced in Innisfail, Tully and Mourilyan.

Twenty-eight km north-west of Innisfail at **Nerada** is one of Australia's few tea plantations and factories (☎ (070) 64 5177). It's open daily from 10 am to 4 pm. The Palmerston Highway winds up to the Atherton Tableland, passing through the rainforest of the **Palmerston National Park**, which has a number of creeks, waterfalls, scenic walking tracks and a camping ground at Henrietta Creek just off the road. The ranger's office (☎ (070) 64 5115) is at the eastern entrance to the park, 33 km from Innisfail.

Babinda

Babinda is the next place on the Bruce Highway north of Innisfail, but before you reach it there's a turning to **Josephine Falls**, a popular picnic spot eight km inland from the highway. The falls are at the foot of the Bellenden Ker range which includes Queensland's highest peak, **Mt Bartle Frere** (1657 metres). A trail leads to the Bartle Frere summit from the ranger's hut near Josephine Falls. The ascent is for fit and experienced walkers – it's a 15-km, two-day return trip, and rain and cloud can close in suddenly.

Babinda Boulders, where a creek rushes between enormous rocks, is another good picnic place, seven km inland from Babinda. From the boulders you can walk the **Goldfield Track** – first opened up in the 1930s when there was a minor gold rush. It leads 10 km to the Goldsborough Valley, across a saddle in the Bellenden Ker range. The track ends at a causeway on the Mulgrave River, from where a forestry road leads eight km to a camping ground in the **Goldsborough Valley State Forest Park**. From there it's 15 km on to the Gillies Highway between Gordonvale and Atherton.

Gordonvale

Back on the Bruce Highway, Gordonvale is almost at Cairns. It has two Sikh gurdwaras (places of worship). The winding Gillies Highway leads from here up on to the Atherton Tableland.

Also at Gordonvale is the **Mulgrave Rambler**, a steam train which runs daily along the course of the Little Mulgrave River through sugar country. The $24 cost includes a sugar mill tour; departure is at 11.30 am.

NORTH COAST HINTERLAND

The Flinders Highway heads inland from Townsville and runs virtually due west for its entire length – almost 800 km from Townsville to Cloncurry.

Ravenswood

At Mingela, 83 km from Townsville, a paved road leads 40 km south to Ravenswood, once a gold-rush centre. Two pubs, a church, a school and a couple of hundred people linger on amid the old mines and near-abandoned streets.

Eighty km on down the road past Ravenswood, the big **Burdekin Falls Dam**, completed in 1987, holds back more than 200 sq km of water.

Charters Towers (population 6900)

This busy town, 130 km inland from Townsville, was Queensland's fabulously rich second city in the gold-rush days. Many old houses with classic verandahs and lace work, and imposing public buildings and mining structures remain. It's possible to make a day trip here from Townsville and get a glimpse of outback Queensland on the way.

At 336 metres above sea level, the dry air of Charters Towers makes a welcome change from the humid coast. The gleam of gold was first spotted in 1871, in a creek bed at the foot of Towers Hill, by an Aboriginal boy called Jupiter Mosman. Within a few years, the surrounding area was peppered with diggings and a large town had grown. In its heyday (around the turn of the century), Charters Towers had a population of 30,000, nearly 100 mines, and even its own stock exchange. It attracted wealth seekers from far and wide and came to be known as 'The World'. Mosman St, the main street in those days, had 25 pubs.

When the gold ran out in the 1920s, the city shrank, but survived as a centre for the beef industry. Since the mid-1980s, Charters Towers has seen a bit of a gold revival as modern processes enable companies to work deposits in previously uneconomical areas.

Orientation & Information Central Charters Towers is basically two streets, Gill St and Mosman St, which meet at right angles. Towers Hill stands over the town to the south. Buses arrive and depart at the Goldfield Star service station on the corner of Gill and Church Sts. The railway station (☎ (077) 87 2239) is on Enterprise Rd, 2½ km east along Gill St from the centre.

There are two tourist offices – one, privately run, at 61 Gill St (☎ (077) 87 1280) which is open from Monday to Friday and Saturday mornings; and another in the Stock Exchange Arcade on Mosman St. Pick up the free *Guide to Charters Towers* booklet and a copy of the National Trust's walking tour leaflet.

Things to See On Mosman St a few metres up the hill from the corner of Gill St is the picturesque **Stock Exchange Arcade**, built in 1887 and restored in 1972. Today it houses the National Trust office, a tourist office, a couple of galleries and shops and a poorly displayed mining museum. There are a number of other interesting old buildings on Gill St.

At 62 Mosman St there's the **Zara Clark Museum**, with an interesting collection focusing on transport and lifestyles in early Charters Towers.

On Gill St, **Stan Pollard's Store** (1906), near the Mosman St end, has an ancient 'flying fox' – a sort of aerial runway which transports cash from the counters to the central till. There's also a great selection of country hats.

Probably the finest of the town's old houses is Frederick Pfeiffer's, on Paul St. It's now a Mormon chapel, but you can walk around the outside. Pfeiffer was a gold miner who became Queensland's first millionaire.

Five km from town is the **Venus Battery**, where gold-bearing ore was crushed and processed from 1872 until as recently as 1972. The battery has been restored to working order and is open from 9 am to 5 pm daily, with guided tours at 10 am and 2 pm. Entry is $3.

Festivals During the Australia Day weekend in late January, more than 100 cricket teams and their supporters converge on Charters Towers

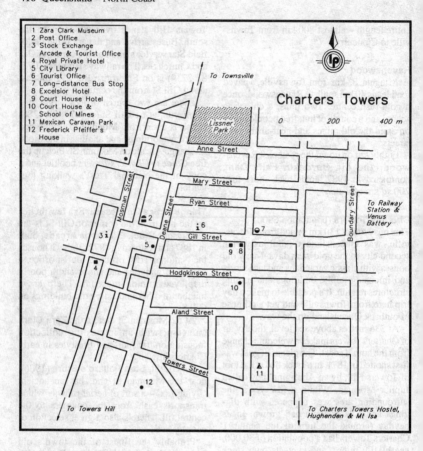

1 Zara Clark Museum
2 Post Office
3 Stock Exchange
   Arcade & Tourist Office
4 Royal Private Hotel
5 City Library
6 Tourist Office
7 Long-distance Bus Stop
8 Excelsior Hotel
9 Court House Hotel
10 Court House &
   School of Mines
11 Mexican Caravan Park
12 Frederick Pfeiffer's
   House

Charters Towers

0   200   400 m

To Townsville

Lissner Park

Anne Street

Mary Street

Ryan Street

Gill Street

Hodgkinson Street

Aland Street

Towers Street

Mosman Street

Deane Street

Boundary Street

To Railway
Station &
Venus
Battery

To Towers Hill

To Charters Towers Hostel,
Hughenden & Mt Isa

for a competition known as the Goldfield Ashes. The town also hosts one of Australia's biggest annual country music festivals on the May Day weekend each year.

Places to Stay The excellent little *Charters Towers Hostel* (☎ (077) 87 1028) is at 58 York St, two km south of the town centre. It's a renovated old wooden house with pleasant breezy verandahs and sitting areas, and there's room for about 30 people in beds or bunks. The cost is $12 a night and you can rent bedding for $1. There are bikes for rent

and you can get a cheap combined ticket for some of the town's museums and the Venus Battery. Canoe trips are also organised through cattle stations along the Burdekin River – when the river's flowing.

The *Mexican Caravan Park* (☎ (077) 87 1161) is fairly central, south of Gill St at 75 Church St. As well as tent sites, it has on-site vans and units, plus a swimming pool and store. The next cheapest beds in town are in the old *Court House Hotel* (☎ (077) 87 1187) at 120 Gill St.

The *Park Motel* (☎ (077) 87 1022), at 1

Top: Coral Cay, Rainbow Beach, Qld (RI'A)
Left: Keogh's Run, Mt Hotham, Vic (RN)
Right: Bridal Veil Falls, Blue Mountains, NSW (CLA)

Top: Hot springs, Mataranka, NT (BW)
Left: Opal miner, Coober Pedy, SA (PS)
Right: Moomba gas fields, Strzelecki Track, SA (BD)

Mosman St, has pleasant grounds and a good restaurant and costs $52/60.

Places to Eat Nearly all the pubs have decent meals and most of them have hot 'daily special' lunches. For atmosphere, try the *Excelsior* or *Court House* hotels on Gill St. The *Billabong Coffee Lounge*, in the Stock Exchange Arcade, is good for drinks and light eats. There are a few takeaway places on Mosman St.

Other cafes and restaurants are mainly along Gill St. The *Heritage Restaurant*, above the library, is a classy place; it's open for lunch daily, and for dinner Friday and Saturday.

Getting There & Around Flight West Airlines has three departures a week to Townsville ($83) and Mt Isa ($203). You can make transport bookings and inquiries at the helpful Towers Travel (☎ (077) 87 1546) at 114 Gill St.

There are buses from Townsville to Charters Towers (1¾ hours, $16) and from Charters Towers on to Mt Isa (nine hours, $76).

By train, the journey from Charters Towers to Townsville takes three hours and costs $15.60, economy only. As well as the twice-weekly Inlander running between Townsville and Mt Isa, there's a once-weekly motorail service from Charters Towers to Townsville.

The hostel hires bikes, and Gold Nugget Scenic Tours (☎ (077) 87 1568) runs city tours most weekdays.

Charters Towers to Hughenden

There are a few small towns, mostly with caravan/camping parks and a single motel, along this 243-km stretch. Around Hughenden, sheep begin to take over from cattle on the stations. Grass seed, which is abundant to the east, ruins sheep's wool.

The *Allan Terry Caravan Park* (☎ (077) 41 119) on Resolution St, Hughenden, has a large swimming pool next door but the railway yard over the road is a bit noisy. There are tent sites and on-site vans.

Porcupine Gorge

If the weather has been dry, and you're not in a hurry and have a vehicle, take a trip out to Porcupine Gorge National Park, an oasis in the dry country north of Hughenden off the mostly unpaved, often corrugated Kennedy Developmental Road.

The best spot to drive to is **Pyramid Lookout**, about 80 km from Hughenden. You can camp here and it's an easy 30-minute walk down into the gorge, with some fine rock formations and a permanently running creek. Few people come here and there's a fair bit of wildlife. The Kennedy Developmental Road would eventually take you to the Atherton Tableland, but it would be a pretty rough trip, particularly during the wet season.

Hughenden to Cloncurry

Keep your eyes open for wild emus and brolgas on this stretch. **Richmond**, 112 km from Hughenden, and **Julia Creek**, 144 km further on, are small towns both with motels and caravan/camping parks. From Julia Creek, a surfaced road turns off north to Normanton (420 km) and Karumba (494 km) near the Gulf. You can also reach Burketown (467 km) this way; see the Cape York & the Gulf section for more information on these towns.

Far North Queensland

Queensland's far north is one of the most popular tourist destinations in the country, especially in winter when sun-starved southerners flock here in droves.

Cairns, with its international airport, is the major centre for the region. It's a place where most travellers spend a few days before heading off – north to the superb rainforests of Daintree and Cape Tribulation and the historic town of Cooktown; west to the cool air of the Atherton Tableland; or east to the islands and the Barrier Reef.

CAIRNS (population 68,000)

The 'capital' of the far north and perhaps the best known city on the Queensland coast, Cairns has become one of Australia's top travellers' destinations in recent years.

Cairns is a centre for a whole host of activities – not just scuba diving but also white-water rafting, canoeing, horse-riding and, of course, the latest lunatic crazes – bungy jumping and rap jumping. On the debit side, Cairns' rapid tourist growth has destroyed much of its laid-back tropical atmosphere. It also lacks a beach, but there are some good ones not far north.

Cairns marks the end of the Bruce Highway and the railway line from Brisbane. The town came into existence in 1876, a beachhead in the mangroves intended as a port for the Hodgkinson River gold field 100 km inland. Initially, it struggled under rivalry from Smithfield 12 km north, a rowdy frontier town that was washed away by a flood in 1879 (it's now an outer Cairns suburb), then from Port Douglas, founded in 1877

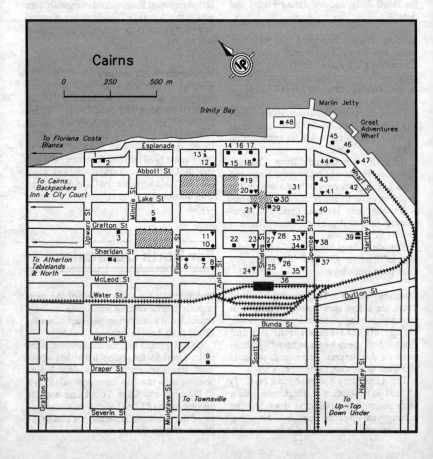

after Christie Palmerston discovered an easier route from there to the gold field. What saved Cairns was the Atherton Tableland 'tin rush' from 1880. Cairns became the starting point of the railway to the tableland, built a few years later.

Cairns is at its climatic best – and busiest – from May to October; in summer it gets rather sticky (to put it mildly!).

Orientation

The centre of Cairns is a relatively compact area running back from the Esplanade. Off Wharf St (the southern continuation of the Esplanade), you'll find Marlin Jetty, Great Adventures Wharf and the Pier – the main departure points for reef trips. Further round

is Trinity Wharf (a cruise-liner dock with shops and cafes) and the Transit Centre, where long-distance buses arrive and depart.

Back from the waterfront is City Place, a pedestrian mall at the meeting of Shields and Lake Sts.

Cairns is surrounded to the south and north by mangrove swamps, and the sea in front of the town is shallow and at low tide becomes a long sweep of mud, although there are lots of interesting water birds.

Information

Tourist Information There's no shortage of tourist information in Cairns – if anything, it's the opposite. The Cairns Tourist Information Centre (☎ (070) 31 1751), at 99 The

---

■ **PLACES TO STAY**

1 Bel-Air Backpackers & Silver Palm Guesthouse
2 Caravella's 149 Hostel
3 Tracks Hostel
4 Inn the Tropics
5 Parkview Tourist Hostel
9 Gone Walkabout Hostel
12 Wintersun Apartments
14 Action Backpackers, Hostel 89 Bellview
16 Jimmy's Hostel, Caravella's 77 Hostel & Rapture of the Deep Hostel
17 International Budget Accommodation
22 Pacific Coast Budget Accommodation
25 Grand Hotel
29 Hides Hotel
32 Aussie II Hostel
36 McLeod St Youth Hostel
37 Coconut Palm Hostel
45 Hilton Hotel
48 The Pier & Radisson Plaza Hotel

▼ **PLACES TO EAT**

8 Roma Roulette Restaurant
11 Rio's Restaurant
15 Magnums Restaurant
20 Backpackers Restaurant
21 Swagman's Restaurant
23 Omar Khayam Restaurant
24 Surf 'n Turf Restaurant

26 John & Diana's Breakfast & Burger House
27 La Fettucini Restaurant
28 Fiorelli's Deli
33 Mozart Bakery & Willem Tell Restaurant
35 Bangkok Room Thai Restaurant
38 Taj Indian Restaurant
41 Creme de la Creme

OTHER

6 Johno's Blues Bar
7 RACQ
10 Far North Queensland Promotion Bureau
11 Magnums Nightclub
13 Cairns Tourist Information Centre
15 End of the World Nightclub
18 Air Niugini
19 Blue Horizon Divers
20 Australian Airlines
21 Cairns Museum
30 Lake St Transit Bus Stop & City Place
31 Orchid Plaza & Australia Post Shop
34 Rusty's Pub
39 GPO
40 Tropical Paradise Travel Centre
42 East-West Airlines
43 Qantas
44 National Parks & Wildlife Service
46 Great Adventures Office
47 Trinity Wharf & Transit Centre

Esplanade, is right in the thick of things and has a good range of leaflets. A second source is the Far North Queensland Promotion Bureau (☎ (070) 51 3588), on the corner of Sheridan and Aplin Sts.

Also good for information are the various backpackers' hostels, as most have a separate tour-booking service, and these are open much longer hours than the official places. The only problem here is that each hostel will be selling different tours, depending on the commission deal they have with the tour companies – so shop around.

The Community Information Service (☎ (070) 51 4953) in Tropical Arcade off Shields St, half a block back from the Esplanade, is good for some tourist information plus more offbeat things like where you can play croquet or do t'ai chi. It also has details on foreign consulates in Cairns and health services.

Post The GPO, on the corner of Grafton and Hartley Sts, has a poste restante service. For general business (stamps, etc), there's also an Australia Post shop in the Orchid Plaza on Lake St.

Other Offices The RACQ office (☎ (070) 51 4788), at 112 Sheridan St, is a good place to get information on road conditions, especially if you're driving up to Cooktown or the Cape York Peninsula, or across to the Gulf of Carpentaria. The National Parks & Wildlife Service (☎ (070) 51 9811), at 41 The Esplanade, deals with camping permits for Davies Creek, the Frankland Islands, Lizard Island and Jardine River.

Bookshops Proudmans, in the Pier complex, is probably the best bookshop in town. The Green Possum Environmental Bookshop, in an arcade off Grafton St right by Rusty's Bazaar, is also interesting. For maps, check out Sunmap at 36 Shields St.

Things to See
A walk around the town centre turns up a few points of historical interest, although with the spate of recent development, the older

buildings are now few and far between. The oldest part of town is the **Trinity Wharf** area, but even this has been redeveloped. There are still some imposing neoclassical buildings from the 1920s on Abbott St, and the frontages around the corner of Spence and Lake Sts date from 1909 to 1926. A walk along the **Esplanade**, with views over to rainforested mountains across the estuary and cool evening breezes, is very agreeable.

The **Pier** is a spanking new plaza with expensive boutiques and souvenir shops downstairs, and some interesting eating possibilities upstairs. On Saturday mornings there's a food market inside, and on Sundays, a craft market. These are known as the Mud Markets. The up-market Radisson Plaza Hotel, also in the complex, has the most amazing lobby – it's a mock-up of some north Queensland rainforest, but the effect is like something straight out of Disneyland!

Right in the centre of town, on the corner of Lake and Shields Sts, the **Cairns Museum** is housed in the 1907 School of Arts building, a fine example of early Cairns architecture. It has Aboriginal artefacts, a display on the construction of the Cairns to Kuranda railway, the contents of a now demolished Grafton St joss house, exhibits on the old Palmer River and Hodgkinson gold fields, and material on the early timber industry. It's open daily from 10 am to 3 pm and entry costs $1.

A colourful part of town on weekends is the **Rusty's Bazaar** area bounded by Grafton, Spence, Sheridan and Shields Sts. There are some interesting shops, a couple of cafes and restaurants, and the open area becomes a very busy market selling arts & crafts and lots of food. This part of Grafton St used to be the Cairns Chinatown and also a red-light district.

North-west of town, in Edge Hill, are the **Flecker Botanic Gardens** on Collins Ave. Over the road from the gardens, a boardwalk leads through a patch of rainforest to **Saltwater Creek** and the two small **Centenary Lakes**. Collins Ave turns west off Sheridan St (the Cook Highway) three km from the centre of Cairns. The gardens are 700 metres from the turning. Just before the gardens is the entrance to the **Whitfield Range Environmental Park**, with walking tracks which give good views over the city and coast. You can get there on the Northland Bus Service or the Red Explorer.

Also in Edge Hill, the **Royal Flying Doctor Service** regional office, at 1 Junction St, is open to visitors daily from 9 am to 4.30 pm; entry is $2.30.

Activities

Most of the courses and trips mentioned here can be booked through your accommodation or through a variety of agents, as well as from the operators themselves.

Diving & Snorkelling Cairns is the scuba-diving capital of the Barrier Reef and the reef is closer to the coast here than it is further south. The competition is cutthroat – and the company offering the cheapest deal one week may be old news the next.

Most people look for a course which takes them to the outer Barrier Reef rather than the reefs around Green or Fitzroy islands. Some places give you more time on the reef than others – but you may prefer an extra day in the pool and classroom before venturing out. A chat with people who have already done a course can tell you some of the pros and cons. A good teacher can make all the difference to your confidence and the amount of fun you have. Another factor is how big the groups are – the smaller the better if you want personal attention.

Two schools with good reputations are Deep Sea Divers Den (☎ (070) 51 2223) at 319 Draper St, and Pro-Dive (☎ (070) 51 9915) at Marlin Jetty. But that's not to dismiss the others, which include: South Pacific Dive Centre (☎ (070) 51 7933) at 77B Lake St near the centre of the mall; Down Under Dive (☎ (070) 31 1288) at 155 Sheridan St; Peter Tibbs Scuba School (☎ (070) 52 1266/51 2604) at Trinity Wharf; Ausdive (☎ (070) 31 1255) at 5 Digger St; and Peter Boundy's Fitzroy Island Dive Centre (☎ (070) 51 0294). Most of these places can be booked through the hostels.

Reef Care (☎ (070) 31 6266), at 25 Spence St, offers dives for experienced divers and also has excellent lectures given by a marine biologist, so you can better appreciate the reef before you set off.

Prices differ quite a bit between schools but usually one or other of them has a discount going. Expect to pay around $350 to $400 for two days in the pool and classroom, one day trip to the reef and back, and two more days on the reef with an overnight stay on board.

White-Water Rafting & Kayaking Three of the rivers flowing down from the Atherton Tableland make for some excellent white-water rafting. Most popular is a day in the rainforested gorges of the Tully River, 150 km south of Cairns. So many people do this trip that there can be 20 or more craft on the river at once, meaning you may have to queue up to shoot each section of rapids – yet despite this, most people are exhilarated at the end of the day. The Tully day trips leave daily year-round. Two companies running them from Cairns are Raging Thunder (☎ (070) 31 1466) at 111 Spence St, and R 'n' R (☎ (070) 51 7777 or 008 07 9039, toll-free) at 49 Abbott St. Day trips on the Tully cost around $110. There are cheaper half-day trips on the Barron River ($55), not far inland from Cairns, or you can make longer expeditions on the remote North Johnstone River which rises near Malanda and enters the sea at Innisfail.

Outrageous Russell (☎ (070) 51 7777) offers white-water rafting for $39 on the Russell River, south of Bellenden Ker National Park.

Butler's Canoe Adventures (☎ (070) 51 4055) offer day trips on the Mulgrave River for $60; these are not white-water trips, but sedate and pleasant paddles through the rainforest.

Raging Thunder and R'n'R also offer a range of sea kayaking expeditions from Cairns. R'n'R runs a day trip from Palm Cove, just north of Cairns to Double Island for $85.

Other Activities Bungy jumping has hit Cairns, and there are a couple of possibilities. The closest is A J Hacketts on the Cook Highway just past the Kuranda turn-off. There's another opposite the market at Kuranda where, for $50, you can fling yourself from a cage suspended from a crane. Rap jumping (☎ (070) 51 3464) is basically free-fall abseiling and yet another thrill for adrenalin junkies; check at the hostel booking offices for details.

For something a bit more sedate, but equally expensive, try a chopper ride over the reef (☎ (070) 35 9002), a scenic glider flight (☎ (070) 53 7936), or a hot-air balloon flight over the tablelands for just $99 including champagne breakfast (☎ (070) 51 7366). For a bit of airborne nostalgia, DC3 Queensland have daily DC3 flights to Cooktown for $125 return, while Cairns Tiger Moth Scenic Flights (☎ (070) 35 9400) start at $75.

Organised Tours

As you'd expect, there are hundreds of tours available from Cairns. Some are specially aimed at backpackers and many of these are pretty good value. You can make bookings through your accommodation or at travel agencies which specialise in this type of trip. Agencies include Tropical Paradise Travel (☎ (070) 51 9533), at 25 Spence St, and Going Places (☎ (070) 51 4055) at 26 Abbott St.

Cairns Half-day trips around the city sights, or two-hour cruises from Marlin Jetty up along Trinity Inlet and around Admiralty Island, cost $18.

Atherton Tableland As a guide, some typical tours with any of the cheaper operators are as follows: around $30 for a full day trip to Kuranda and the Atherton Tableland, including a swim in Lake Eacham and a short bushwalk.

A visit to Nerada tea plantation combined with Atherton Tableland waterfalls and lakes, is offered by several 'conventional' tour companies; the trip costs around $40.

Daintree, Cape Tribulation & Cooktown
A trip to Mossman Gorge and Port Douglas (return) will cost $35 without meals. A day trip to Cape Tribulation and back is $40 to $80 depending on how small the group is and how comfortable the vehicle. You get stops at a few places on the way and often a guided bushwalk thrown in. Some of the longer trips are better value; expect to pay around $50 for two days to Cape Trib, including Mossman Gorge and accommodation at Crocodylus Village (Daintree) and/or Jungle Lodge (Cape Trib), and $60 for three days.

Outback Bike Expeditions (☎ (070) 93 8851) runs two-day trips from Kuranda to Cooktown via Cape Trib, and shorter tableland trips. There are also rainforest tours by mountain bike from $48 per day (☎ (070) 55 3089).

Barrier Reef Several options are available for day trips to the reef. Great Adventures (☎ (070) 51 0455) does a nine-hour, $100 outer reef trip which includes a two-hour stop on Green Island. You get three hours on the reef itself, lunch, snorkelling gear, and a semisubmersible and glass-bottomed boat ride thrown in. Great Adventures also does day trips to Michaelmas Cay, again including two hours on Green Island, for $80. Cheaper is their nine-hour 'no frills' cruise to Fitzroy Island and Moore Reef for $48 with free use of snorkelling gear. Great Adventures has its own wharf.

The *Big Cat* offers a return trip to Green Island for $20 taking about 1½ hours, while the *Reef Jet* does the journey in half that time and operates twice daily ($26). Sunlover Cruises (☎ (070) 31 1055) has the cheapest trip to Fitzroy Island ($15), and also does outer reef day trips for $39.

Noah's Ark Cruises (☎ (070) 51 7777) offers a day trip to Hastings Reef and Michaelmas Cay for $35, including boom netting and snorkelling gear. Certified divers can take two dives for an extra $40.

Ocean Free (☎ (070) 31 2920) is an ocean-going schooner which sails out to Upolu Cay or Green Island daily for $39, while *Quickcat III* (☎ (070) 31 1255) takes

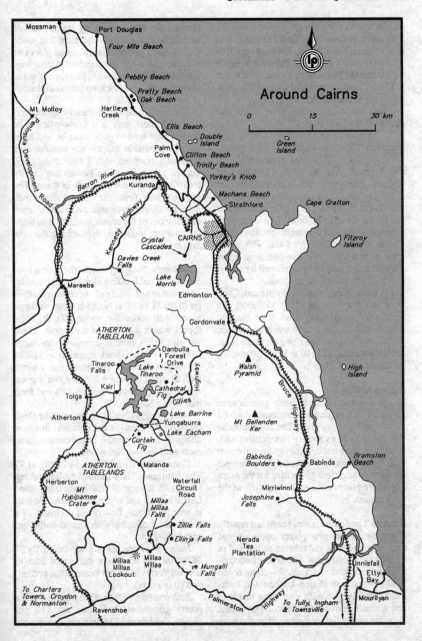

Around Cairns

0   15   30 km

Mossman
Port Douglas
Four Mile Beach
Pebbly Beach
Pretty Beach
Oak Beach
Hartleys Creek
Mt Molloy
Ellis Beach
Double Island
Green Island
Palm Cove
Clifton Beach
Trinity Beach
Yorkey's Knob
Kuranda
Machans Beach
Strathford
Cape Grafton
Peninsula Development Road
Barron River
Kennedy Highway
Crystal Cascades
CAIRNS
Davies Creek
Fitzroy Island
Mareeba
Lake Morris
Edmonton
ATHERTON TABLELAND
Danbulla Forest Drive
Gordonvale
Tinaroo Falls
Lake Tinaroo
Walsh Pyramid
High Island
Kairi
Cathedral Fig
Gillies
Tolga
Lake Barrine
Yungaburra
Lake Eacham
Mt Bellenden Ker
Bruce Highway
Atherton
Curtain Fig
Malanda
Babinda Boulders
Babinda
Bramston Beach
ATHERTON TABLELANDS
Herberton
Mt Hypipamee Crater
Waterfall Circuit Road
Mirriwinni
Josephine Falls
Millaa Millaa Falls
Zillie Falls
Nerada Tea Plantation
Ellinja Falls
Millaa Millaa Lookout
Millaa Millaa
Mungalli Falls
Innisfail
Etty Bay
To Charters Towers, Croydon & Normanton
Ravenshoe
Palmerston Highway
To Tully, Ingham & Townsville
Mourilyan

snorkellers to the outer edge of the reef for $90, and certified divers for $125 (including gear). Ocean Deep Diving Services (☎ (070) 31 6465) runs trips out to Paradise Reef on the catamaran *Passions of Paradise*; the cost is $38 including lunch and snorkelling gear; scuba dives cost extra.

There are many, many other boats and operators, so shop around.

Outback There are a number of companies which operate 4WD trips between Cairns and Darwin, via the Gulf Country and Kakadu. The typical cost is around $500 for a 10-day trip. One company is Frontier Safaris (☎ (070) 31 1751. Overland Safaris (☎ (070) 54 5252) does five-day trips through some very remote country from Cairns to Ayers Rock for $450. This outfit cops quite a bit of negative flak from some travellers, but may have improved by now – check on the travellers' grapevine.

For something completely different, Cape York Air Services (☎ (070) 35 9399), the local mail contractor, does mail runs to remote outback stations on weekdays. Space permitting, you can go along on these runs, but it's not cheap at $140 to $275, depending on the length of the trip.

Places to Stay

Cairns has hostels and cheap guesthouses galore as well as plenty of reasonably priced motels and holiday flats. The accommodation business is extremely competitive and, apart from the hostels, prices go up and down with the seasons. Lower weekly rates are par for the course. Prices given here for the more expensive places can rise 30% or 40% in the peak season.

Hostels The Cairns hostel scene is a rapidly changing one as new places open up, old ones change hands and others rise and fall in quality and popularity. The type of accommodation is pretty standard – fan-cooled bunk rooms with shared kitchen and bathroom, usually also with a washing machine and a smallish swimming pool. The dorms are often pretty tightly packed, though many

places have spacious sitting areas. Most of the kitchens are small and tatty, but since Cairns has a good range of cheap places to eat out, that's not too much of a problem. Unfortunately, you have to beware of theft in some places – use lock-up rooms and safes if they're available.

The Esplanade has the greatest concentration of hostels, and is a lively place. The hostels here tend to pack them in, and have very little outside space – any outdoor area is usually cramped with a swimming pool. On the plus side, these hostels are ideally located and are the cheapest in town. The hostels away from the centre offer much more breathing space, and the inconvenience of being out of the centre is minimal as there are courtesy buses which make regular runs into town.

Esplanade Starting from the corner of Shields St and heading along the Esplanade, *International Budget Accommodation* (☎ (070) 31 1424) at No 67 is a big, well-run place with room for about 200, in bunk rooms which take two to six people. There are also a few double rooms. Prices range from $10 in a six-bunk room up to $17/24 for singles/doubles. The hostel has a kiosk with diving equipment for hire and a good notice board. Downstairs is a 140-seat food hall with a bar.

Next along, at No 73, *Rapture of the Deep* (☎ (070) 51 2866) is the cheapest in town, charging $7 per person in six-bunk rooms, each with its own bathroom.

Caravella's Hostel 77 (☎ 51 2159), at 77 The Esplanade, is a rambling place taking about 150. It's one of the longest established Cairns hostels and kept pretty clean. The cost in four to 10-bed, fan-cooled dorms is $9 a head, while doubles with shared bathroom cost $20.

Jimmy's on the Esplanade (☎ (070) 51 5670), at No 83, has a variety of four to six-bed dorms at $8 per person (fan-cooled) or $10 (air-con).

Bellview (☎ (070) 51 9385), at No 85, is a pretty good hostel. Dorms are $12 per person, twin rooms $14, and some rooms are air-conditioned. The kitchen facilities are good, and there's a small pool and outdoor tables. There are also air-con motel rooms with fridge, TV and private bathroom at $30/38 for singles/doubles.

Hostel 89 (☎ (070) 31 2237), at No 89, is one of the best kept hostels on the Esplanade. It's smallish, with room for about 50 in dorms of various sizes, some with private bathrooms, and nightly costs are $9 per person, or doubles for $22. Security is good, with a locked grille at the street entrance.

On the corner of Aplin St, at 93 The Esplanade, *Action Backpackers* (☎ (070) 31 1919) is a lively, friendly place. Doubles are $22 and there are several six to 12-bed dorms at $9 a head.

Three blocks further along the Esplanade at No 149 is another bigger hostel, *Caravella's 149* (☎ (070) 51 2431). Its popularity means that even the big cooking/sitting/TV/pool/games area at the back can get pretty busy. You pay $8 in a 14-bed dorm, $10 in a four-bed room. A few six-bunk rooms have air-con and bathroom. The doubles at the back behind the pool are probably the most spacious rooms.

A couple of doors down at No 157, *Bel-Air* (☎ (070) 31 4790) is a bright new place, although some of the rooms have no outside windows and so are a bit dingy.

Around Town Over at 255 Lake St, *Cairns Backpackers Inn* (☎ (070) 51 9166) occupies three houses, with entrances on both Lake and Digger Sts. The hostel runs a free bus to and from the town centre several times a day. Beds and bunks are squeezed pretty tightly into the rooms, but there's plenty of space in the other areas. You pay $9 in a dorm or there are singles/doubles for $16/22. Meals are served three or four nights a week, and there are bicycles for hire.

On the corner of Spence and Sheridan Sts, the *Coconut Palm Hostel* (☎ (070) 51 6946), has dorm beds for $8 and double rooms for $22.

Closer to the centre, *Parkview Tourist Hostel* (☎ (070) 51 3700) is at 174 Grafton St, three blocks back from the Esplanade.

Cost is $8 a night in dorms, $10 per person in double or twin rooms. The hostel is clean and spacious with a large garden. It has a restaurant with cheap breakfasts and dinners, as well as a couple of small kitchens.

At 72 Grafton St, the *Aussie II Hostel* (☎ (070) 51 7620) is clean and roomy with space for about 80 people. You pay $8 for a dorm bed, with a maximum of six people in each room. There are also twin and double rooms at $10 per person. Slightly better rooms are available for a couple of dollars more. The hostel has two kitchens and a TV room. There's no pool but you can use the pools at the two Caravella hostels.

Two blocks west of the station at 274 Draper St, *Gone Walkabout Hostel* (☎ (070) 51 6160) is one of the best in Cairns but it's small and at times hard to get into. The rooms aren't big and there's no pool but it's a comfortable, clean and friendly place. You pay $10 whether you're in a dorm or one of the little doubles. It's not a place for late partying however.

The YHA *McLeod St Youth Hostel* (☎ (070) 51 0772), at 20-24 McLeod St, has dorm beds for $10, twin rooms for $10 per person and singles/doubles for $16/24. Non-members pay $1 extra. The facilities are good and the hostel has car parking spaces.

The *Up-Top Down Under Holiday Lodge* (☎ (070) 51 3636) at 164-170 Spence St, 1½ km from the town centre, has a large, well-equipped kitchen, two TV lounges and a pool. Dorm beds are $10.50 and singles/doubles $25, all with shared bathroom.

Lastly there's the popular *Tracks Hostel* (☎ (070) 31 1474) at 149 Grafton St. It spans three houses and so has a number of kitchens and plenty of other facilities. Costs are $8 in four-bed rooms, or $9 per person in twin rooms.

Guesthouses & Hotels A couple of places in this bracket are almost in the hostel price range, the difference being that their emphasis is on rooms rather than dorms.

On the Esplanade, the *Silver Palm Guesthouse* (☎ 51 2059) at No 153, between Upward and Minnie Sts, is a clean guesthouse with singles/doubles at $19/28, including use of a kitchen, laundry and TV room.

Inn The Tropics (☎ (070) 31 1088), at 141 Sheridan St, between Minnie and Upward Sts, is a relatively new place with a good pool, a small guests' kitchen and an open-air courtyard with tables. For $15 you get a bed in a double or twin room with fridge, sink and dollar-in-the-slot air-con. There are family rooms for $39. Bathrooms are communal, but the place is kept very clean.

Also on Sheridan St, at No 100, is *Pacific Coast Budget Accommodation* (☎ (070) 51 1264), one of a chain of places along the east coast. Clean, fan-cooled singles/doubles are $22/32, or $32/36 with air-con; all prices include continental breakfast. Bathrooms are shared, and there's a smallish kitchen, a dining room (offering cheap dinners) and laundry facilities.

City Court Garden Apartments (☎ (070) 51 7642), at 13 Charles St, has clean rooms, each with its own kitchen and bathroom. Although small, this place has a spacious feel, unlike the other Esplanade places. Dorm beds are $10, doubles $25, and there's a one-bedroom apartment for $40. The hostel has a pool and jacuzzi, and the obligatory courtesy coach.

Motels & Holiday Flats Holiday flats are well worth considering, especially for a group of three or four people who are staying a few days or more. Expect pools, air-con and laundry facilities in this category. Holiday flats generally supply all bedding, cooking utensils, etc.

Wintersun Motel Holiday Apartments (☎ (070) 51 2933), at 84 Abbott St, is quite a good place. Large, fully equipped, one-bedroom flats with immaculate '60s decor and air-con cost $45.

The somewhat grotty *Cairns Motel* (☎ (070) 51 2771), at 48 Spence St, is about as central as you could ask for. The 15 fan-cooled rooms cost $40/45 for singles/doubles. Eight newer air-con rooms are $50/55. It's very noisy here when there's music at nearby Rusty's Pub.

Sunshine Villa (☎ (070) 51 5288), at 161 Grafton St, has excellent fully equipped flats. For brief stays the prices aren't worthwhile, but for five or more nights they start to look more reasonable. In the low season, three people sharing a one-bedroom flat for a week would pay $190 each, while five people in a two-bedroom flat pay $150 each for a week.

Sheridan St has numerous motels. *Captain Cook Endeavour Inns* (☎ (070) 51 6811) is at No 204, with singles/doubles from $40/55 and backpackers' accommodation too.

Camping There are about a dozen caravan parks in and around Cairns, though none really central. Almost without exception they take campers as well as caravans. The more conveniently located ones include:

At *Cairns Coconut Caravan Village* (☎ (070) 54 6644), on the Bruce Highway, camp sites cost $10 for two, Camp-O-Tel units $18 a double, and cabin vans $32. The *City Caravan Park* (☎ (070) 51 1467), on the corner of Little & James Sts, has tent sites for $11, and on-site vans for $28.

Places to Eat

For a town of its size, Cairns has quite an amazing number and variety of restaurants. Opening hours are long, and more places are taking advantage of the climate by providing open-air dining. Most newer places are on the Esplanade, the Pier or around City Place at the centre of the mall.

Most of the hostels have giveaway vouchers for cheap, and even free meals, at various spots around town, ask about them.

Cafes & Takeaways The Esplanade has a growing collection of fast-food and takeaway joints – the stretch between Shields and Aplin Sts is virtually wall-to-wall eateries, most of them takeaways. The *International Hostel*, at No 67, has an Asian-style food hall with a bar plus good-value Indian, Mexican, Chinese and Italian food. Between here and the corner of Aplin St you'll find more places serving Italian and

Chinese food, burgers, kebabs, pizzas, seafood and ice cream – at all hours.

Greens, on the Esplanade, is a popular vegetarian and health food takeaway – the vegie burgers for $3.80 should keep you going for a while.

Just back from the Esplanade, on Aplin St, the *Galloping Gourmet Takeaway* offers a full breakfast for $5, and has a lunch deal of $3 – both good value.

For a breakfast croissant and coffee there's *Mozarts* on the corner of Grafton and Spence Sts, or try the *Boardwalk Cafe* in the Pier.

On Sheridan St, between Spence and Shields Sts, the *Mouth Trap* serves cheap breakfasts all day, while *John & Diana's Breakfast & Burger House*, at 35 Sheridan St, has virtually every combination of cooked breakfast imaginable for $5 or less. In the Andrejic Arcade, which runs from 55 Lake St through to Grafton St, are two good lunch places. *Nibbles* has sandwiches, rolls and pitta breads. The *Hibiscus Coffee Lounge* has a Chinese smorgasbord.

Pubs Right in the town centre, on City Place, *Hides Hotel* has some of the best pub food in Cairns; prices start at $4, and the hotel is also open for lunch. The *Barrier Reef Hotel*, on the corner of Abbott and Wharf Sts, also does good, cheap counter meals.

On the Esplanade, just along from the hostel strip, the *RSL Club* has counter meals, such as steak and schnitzel, and nothing is over $10.

Restaurants The extremely popular *Backpackers' Restaurant*, upstairs at 24 Shields St, is open from lunch time until late and offers a buffet-style selection of hot meals and salads for $6 for as much as you can get on your plate. The food wins no prizes but there's plenty of it; the restaurant also has a bar.

The *Budget Bistro*, at 96 Lake St, in the small arcade near Australian Airlines, has an excellent array of hot dishes, salads and fruits. A full plate is $7 in the evening; $5 at lunch time.

Magnums Restaurant, on Abbott St, is a

popular place, and the $1 Sunday evening barbecue certainly pulls in the crowds. *End of the World*, a nightclub on the corner of Abbott and Aplin Sts, has very basic food, but it's cheap and a lot of people seem to eat here, often with hostel meal vouchers.

At the Pier, there are two bistro restaurants (run by the same people) which are pretty good value – the *Pearl at the Pier* and *Pumpernic's*. The menus are virtually identical, the only difference being that the Pearl has harbour views and so slightly higher prices. Main courses at Pumpernics are $7.90, including unlimited attacks on the salad bar; the same deal at the Pearl costs $9.90. Kids' meals at both these places are only $1.

If you fancy Lebanese food, there's the BYO *Omar Khayam* at 82A Sheridan St but at $20 per person for a mixed plate it's not good value. There are cheaper takeaways from $7. The *Toko Baru*, at 42 Spence St, is a very good, slightly expensive Indonesian restaurant. The food is authentically spicy; it's open nightly and is BYO. On Spence St, almost opposite the Coconut Palm Hostel is the *Bangkok Room Thai Restaurant*. Further along Spence St, the *Taj* serves pretty good Indian food for $8 and up.

Damari's, at 64 Shields St, is a pleasantly atmospheric Italian restaurant with pasta at around $8 for starters and $14 for main course.

If you're at one of the hostels and would like a pizza delivered, *Friendly's Pizza Villa* (☎ 31 1433) has medium pizzas for about $11.

The *Cosmos Restaurant*, at 89 The Esplanade, has good seafood, a bar and live music each night.

Entertainment

The licensed Backpackers' Restaurant is packed with travellers every night. It's a good meeting place where you're almost bound to run into someone you've met elsewhere. Cairns doesn't have as big a pub rock scene as you might expect but things have improved in recent years. Radio 4CA (to be found on 846 KHz) has the rundown on who is playing where; so does the Friday *Cairns Post*.

End of the World, a nightclub on the corner of Abbott and Aplin Sts, is a popular place for a drink and a bop. There's a huge video screen, low lighting, loud music and usually some sort of deal going where you get cheap drinks. Just around the corner on Abbott St, Magnums has live music most nights and is another backpackers' favourite.

Johno's Blues Bar, at 101 Sheridan St, has live music, is open early for meals and kicks on until late at night; there are usually good deals for cheap drinks.

The Crown Hotel, at 35 Shields St, has live bands several nights a week. Hideaways, a popular nightspot in the Great Northern Hotel, has live bands every night, except Sunday, from 9 pm until 2 am.

Another popular place is Oscar's Bar, in the Great Northern Hotel, with live rock nightly except Sunday. Trinity Wharf is good for live music on Saturday and Sunday afternoons and the Trinity Wharf Tavern is popular on a Friday night.

Playpen International, at 3 Lake St, often has big-name bands and is open until late. It's a huge place with plenty of room to move. Tropos, on the corner of Lake and Spence Sts is a good disco, and the DJ will usually oblige with requests.

Things to Buy

Many artists live in the Cairns region, so there's a wide range of local handicrafts available – pottery, clothing, stained glass, jewellery, leather work and so on. Aboriginal art is also for sale in a few places, as are crafts from Papua New Guinea and places further afield in the Pacific. Apart from the many souvenir shops dotted around the town centre, the weekend markets at Rusty's Bazaar and the Pier are all worth a visit.

Getting There & Away

Air In Cairns, Australian and Australian Regional (☎ (070) 50 3777) are on the corner of Shields and Lake Sts, Ansett (☎ (070) 50 2211) is at 84 Lake St, and East-West (☎ (070) 51 5477) is on Lake St, near Wharf St.

Domestic Flights Being such a popular destination, there is fierce competition to get bums on seats. Since deregulation, prices have tumbled to something approaching a sensible level for the first time. There are often promotional fares available, and these offer substantial savings over regular fares.

Airlines serving Cairns include Ansett, Australian and East-West. Regular one-way fares include Melbourne $474 (stand-by $379), Sydney $431 ($345), Brisbane $349 ($279), Townsville $137, Mt Isa $244 ($195), Darwin $391 ($313) and Alice Springs $365. Fares of around $350 return from Melbourne were on offer recently, and it seems deals such as this will remain fairly common.

Flights inland and up the Cape York Peninsula from Cairns are shared amongst a number of small feeder airlines. Australian Regional flies to Bamaga, Lizard Island ($140), Weipa ($209) and Thursday Island ($236). Sunbird Airlines (☎ (070) 53 4899 at the airport or book through Australian) covers a big network of places on the Cape York Peninsula, Torres Strait Islands and the Gulf, and its flights include Cooktown ($83). It also makes interesting flights to/from Mt Isa ($244) via various stops on the Gulf. Flight West (☎ (070) 35 9511 or through Ansett) operates a similar service through the Gulf, Cape York and Mt Isa.

International Flights Cairns International Airport has regular flights to and from North America, Papua New Guinea and Asia. Air Niugini (☎ (070) 51 4177) is at 4 Shields St; the Port Moresby flight costs $378 one-way and goes five times a week. Qantas, at 13 Spence St (☎ (070) 51 0100) also flies to Port Moresby, and twice weekly direct to the US west coast.

Bus All the bus companies operate from the Transit Centre at Trinity Wharf.

Greyhound/Pioneer (☎ (070) 51 2411), McCafferty's (☎ (070) 51 5899)), and Bus Australia (☎ (070) 31 1677) all run at least one bus a day up the coast from Brisbane and Townsville to Cairns. Journey times and fares are: from Brisbane, 23 to 27 hours ($130); from Rockhampton, 14 to 16 hours ($86); Mackay, 10 to 12 hours ($65) and Townsville, 4½ hours ($36).

Train The Sunlander between Brisbane and Cairns runs three times a week, and the Queenslander motorail service goes once a week (leaving Brisbane on Sunday and Cairns on Tuesday). The 1681-km trip from Brisbane takes about 33 hours. The economy fare from Brisbane is $112.75 on both trains, while 1st-class fares are $193.50 on the Sunlander and $342.10 (including sleeping berth and all meals) on the Queenslander. For bookings and information, call Queensland Rail in Cairns (☎ (070) 51 1111).

Getting Around
To/From the Airport The airport in Cairns has two sections, both off the Captain Cook Highway north of the town. The main domestic and international airlines use the new section, officially called Cairns International Airport. This is reached by an approach road that turns off the highway about 3½ km from central Cairns. The other part of the airport, which some people still call Cairns Airport, is reached from a second turning off the highway, 1½ km north of the main one. Sunbird is one of the airlines using this old section.

The shuttle bus (☎ (070) 35 9555) from the main terminal costs $4 and will drop you almost anywhere central in Cairns; ring when you're leaving. A taxi is about $10. Avis, Budget, Hertz and Thrifty have desks at the international terminal.

Bus There are a number of local bus services in and around Cairns. Schedules for most of them are posted at the main city stop (known as the Lake St Transit) in City Place. Buses on most routes leave hourly from 7 am to 5 pm, Monday to Friday. On weekends, services are less frequent and some routes close down from Saturday lunch time to Monday morning. Bus No 208, run by Marlin Coast Buslines (☎ (070) 55 3709), goes up to Trinity and Clifton beaches, Wild World,

Palm Cove and Ellis Beach. The last buses back to Cairns leave Ellis Beach at 4.40 pm Monday to Friday, 3 pm Saturday and 4 pm Sunday.

Cairns Trans (☎ (070) 35 2600), to Yorkeys Knob and Holloways Beach, has last buses leaving Yorkeys Knob at 6.15 pm Monday to Friday and 1.10 pm on Saturday. From Holloways Beach, last buses are at 5.55 pm on weekdays, 12.50 pm on Saturdays. There are no services on Sundays. Southern Cross Bus Services (☎ (070) 55 1240), which run to Machans Beach, has last buses to Cairns at 4.45 pm Monday to Friday and 10 am Saturday; there's no service on Sunday.

The Red Explorer (☎ (070) 55 1240) is an air-con service which plies a circular route around the city, and you can get on or off at any of the nine stops. It runs hourly from 9 am to 4 pm daily except Sundays from 85 Lake St, and a day ticket costs a hefty $18. The main stops of interest are No 4 (Freshwater Creek swimming hole), No 5 (Freshwater Connection), No 6 (Mangrove Boardwalk near the airport), No 7 (Botanic Gardens) and No 8 (Royal Flying Doctor Complex).

Car It's well worth considering renting a car. There's plenty to see and do on land around Cairns, whether it's making the beach crawl up to Port Douglas or exploring the Atherton Tableland. Mokes are about the cheapest cars to rent and ideal for relaxed, open-air sightseeing. Most of the car-rental firms in Cairns have Mokes. While the major firms are along Lake St, local firms have mushroomed all over Cairns and some of them offer good deals, particularly for weekly rental. However, don't be taken in by cut-rates advertising – once you add in all the hidden costs, prices are fairly similar everywhere. Shop around and find the deal that suits. Generally, Mokes are around $40 per day, VW convertibles $45, and regular cars from $45 up. It's also possible to rent 4WDs from around $75.

Note that most Cairns rental firms specifically prohibit you from taking most of their cars up the Cape Tribulation road, on the road to Cooktown, or on the Chillagoe Caves road. A sign in the car will usually announce this prohibition and the contract will threaten dire unhappiness if you do so. Of course, lots of people ignore these prohibitions, but if you get stuck in the mud halfway to Cape Tribulation, it could be a little embarrassing. Be warned that these roads are fairly rough and sometimes impassable in conventional vehicles. Also note that a sizeable deposit is generally required for car rental, anything from $100 to $250 in Cairns, although this is waived if you're paying with a credit card.

Bicycle & Motorcycle Several hostels rent bicycles so, as with most things in Cairns, there's no problem tracking one down. You'll notice mopeds for hire out the front of some hotels. Either inquire there or ring Skeeter Skooter Hire (☎ (018) 77 4254). Jolly Frog (☎ (070) 31 2379) at 101 The Esplanade has scooters from $40 and larger bikes from $55 per day.

ISLANDS OFF CAIRNS

Green and Fitzroy are wooded islands off Cairns which attract hordes of day-trippers. North of Green Island and 40 km from Cairns, tiny **Michaelmas Cay** is a national park and home to thousands of sea birds. In summer, during the peak nesting season, 30,000 or more birds cram on to the cay; some day trips from Cairns call here.

Getting There & Away

Great Adventures (☎ (070) 51 0455) is one of a number of outfits running ferries from Cairns to Green and Fitzroy islands. It has its own wharf in Cairns, near Trinity Wharf, and offers a wide choice of services. The high-speed cats cost $22 return to Fitzroy or $35 return to Green. You can visit both for $38. Other operators include the Big Cat (☎ (070) 51 0444) or the Reef Jet (☎ (070) 31 5559).

Green Island

Green Island, 27 km north-east of Cairns, is a true coral cay 660 metres long by 260 metres wide. The beautiful island and its surrounding reef are all national park but marred by shonky development. Nevertheless, a 10-minute stroll to the far end of the island will remind you that the beach is beautiful, the water fine, the snorkelling good and the fish prolific.

The artificial attractions start at the end of the pier with the underwater observatory ($4). Glass-bottomed boats go from the pier too, while on the island there's the Barrier Reef Theatre and Marineland Melanesia with fish and corals in tanks, larger creatures (sharks, turtles, crocodiles) in pools or enclosures, and a display of art from Papua New Guinea. The more expensive day trips to Green Island include entry to all these 'wonders'. You can hire sailboards or canoes.

Places to Stay & Eat The *Green Island Reef Resort* (☎ (070) 51 4644) isn't in the budget range – regular nightly costs are $140 per person or more, including all meals and use of snorkelling and other beach equipment. The proposed multimillion dollar redevelopment of the island, in the planning stages for years, still hasn't started, but when it does, prices are likely to jump considerably.

Fitzroy Island

Six km off the coast and 26 km south-east of Cairns, Fitzroy is a larger continental island with coral-covered beaches which are good for snorkelling, but not ideal for swimming and sunbaking. Snorkellers will find good coral only 50 metres off the beach in the resort area, and the island has its own dive school. There are some fine walks, including one to the island's high point.

Places to Stay Unlike Green Island, Fitzroy (☎ (070) 51 9588) has a variety of accommodation. There are hostel-style units accommodating four people in bunks at $24 each ($85 for the whole unit), with shared kitchen and bathroom. The 'villa units' cost $158/210 singles/doubles including breakfast and dinner. There's a pool, snack bar with fish & chips and pizza, a bar, a couple of shops and also a laundromat.

ATHERTON TABLELAND

Inland from the coast between Innisfail and Cairns, the land rises sharply then rolls gently across the lush Atherton Tableland towards the Great Dividing Range. The tableland's altitude, more than 900 metres in places, tempers the tropical heat, and the abundant rainfall and rich volcanic soil combine to make this one of the greenest places in Queensland. In the south are Queensland's two highest mountains – Bartle Frere (1657 metres) and Bellenden Ker (1591 metres).

Little more than a century ago, this peaceful, pastoral region was still wild jungle. The first pioneers came in the 1870s, looking for a repeat of the Palmer River gold rush, further north. As elsewhere in Queensland, the Aboriginal population was violently opposed to this intrusion but was soon overrun. Some gold was found and rather more tin, but although mining spurred the development of roads and railways through the rugged, difficult land of the plateau, farming and timber soon became the chief activities.

Getting There & Around

The train ride from Cairns to Kuranda is a major tableland attraction – but without a car the rest of the tableland can be hard to reach. From south to north, the four good roads from the coast are: the Palmerston Highway from Innisfail to Millaa Millaa and Ravenshoe; the Gillies Highway from Gordonvale up past Lakes Tinaroo, Barrine and Eacham to Yungaburra and Atherton; the Kennedy Highway from Cairns to Kuranda and Mareeba; and the Peninsula Developmental Road from Mossman through Mt Molloy to Mareeba.

Kuranda (population 300)

This beautiful town, with its tropical vegetation, is surrounded by spectacular scenery and has one of Queensland's most attractive hostels. There is no bank in Kuranda.

Things to See The **Sunday Market** has produce and arts & crafts (including Aboriginal and imported goods) on sale. Everyone comes out of the woodwork on this day and it's well worth the trip up from Cairns, although things quieten after about 2 pm. The market is also held on Friday and Wednesday, but it's on a much smaller scale; on other days, Kuranda reverts to its normal sleepy character.

Near the market area, the **Australian Butterfly Sanctuary** ($8.50) has guided tours hourly from 10 am to 3 pm. On Coondoo St, the **Kuranda Wildlife Noctarium** ($7), where you can see nocturnal rainforest animals like gliders, fruit bats and echidnas, is open from 10 am to 4 pm daily.

Also on Coondoo St, the **Tjapukai Dance Theatre**, a local Aboriginal dance troupe, goes through its paces daily at 11 am and 1.30 pm ($13). The hour-long performance tells you a few basic things about Aboriginal culture with song, dance and humour and features didgeridoo playing and dancing. Almost across the road is the **Jilli Binna Aboriginal Crafts & Museum**; there's a small display (admission free) on Aboriginal culture and the old Mona Mona mission near Kuranda, many of whose people and their descendants live on in the area.

Over the footbridge behind the railway station you can hire canoes on the Barron River, take a one-hour river cruise ($7.50) or a forest walking tour (10.15 am).

There are several picturesque walks starting with short signed tracks down through the market. **Jumrum Creek Environmental Park**, off the Barron Falls road, 700 metres from the bottom of Thongon St, has a short walking track and a big population of fruit bats. Further down, the Barron Falls road divides: the left fork takes you to a lookout over the falls, while a further 1½ km along the right fork brings you to Wrights Lookout where you can see back down the Barron Gorge to Cairns.

Places to Stay The friendly and atmospheric *Kuranda Hostel* (☎ (070) 93 7355), also known as *Mrs Miller's*, is at 6 Arara St, near the railway station. It's a rambling old

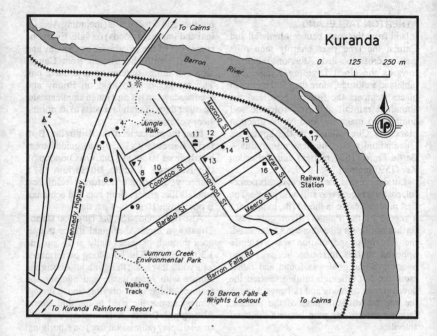

Kuranda

0   125   250 m

1 Pioneer Cemetery
2 Kuranda Van Park
3 Lookout
4 Market
5 Kuranda Bungy
6 Australian Butterfly Sanctuary
7 Annabel's Bakery
8 Down to Earth Foods
9 Kuranda Wildlife Noctarium
10 Frogs Restaurant
11 Post Office
12 Tjapukai Dance Theatre
   & Kuranda Village Bistro
13 Top Pub (Fitzpatrick's Tavern)
14 Jilli Binna Aboriginal Crafts
   & Museum
15 Bottom Pub (Kuranda Hotel)
16 Mrs Miller's Kuranda Hostel
17 Canoe Hire & River Cruises

room. Dorm accommodation is $10 (plus $1 extra the first night for a sheet) and there are double rooms for $25 (sheets provided). Hostel guests can get worthwhile discounts on most Kuranda attractions, and the $28-day tour of the tablelands is particularly popular.

A couple of km out of town, back on the Kennedy Highway towards Mareeba, the modern up-market *Kuranda Rainforest Resort* (☎ (070) 93 7567) has a backpackers' section where the nightly cost in a four-bed room is $12. The facilities are excellent and include a bar, restaurant, swimming pool and tennis courts, but some travellers have felt peeved at the second-class citizen status they were afforded (the hostel is around the back and hidden from the main part of the resort). Regular motel rooms are $60, one-bedroom cabins are $40 for doubles/twins (unserviced) and two-bedroom serviced units are $75, or $15 more with cooking facilities. The resort has a free courtesy bus

place with a huge garden, a small salt-water pool, a restaurant/sitting/video room, an enlightening graffiti room and a separate TV which picks up three times daily from Trinity Wharf in Cairns.

The *Bottom Pub/Kuranda Hotel* (☎ (070) 93 7206) at the corner of Coondoo and Arara Sts, has a pool and 12 motel-style rooms at $28/38. For campers, the *Kuranda Van Park* (☎ (070) 93 7316) is a few km out of town, up the road directly opposite the Kuranda turn-off on the Kennedy Highway. It has camp sites for $11 or outrageously priced on-site vans at $65.

Places to Eat The Bottom Pub has the *Garden Bar & Grill*, with burgers and snags from $2 to $6. The *Top Pub* has lunch and dinner, from $4 for burgers through to $10 for a fisherman's basket. At the hostel, the *Rainforest Restaurant* has excellent dinners and light lunches.

Next to the Tjapukai Theatre on Coondoo St, the *Kuranda Village Bistro* is a popular spot, although is not particularly cheap. A better bet is the licensed *Frogs Restaurant*, a bit further along. It is reasonably good value with full breakfasts, home-made pies and main meals from around $8. *Down to Earth Foods*, on the corner of Coondoo and Therwine Sts, does cheap snacks, smoothies and juices. And just a few doors along, the excellent *Annabel's Bakery* has a large range of pastries.

Getting There & Away White Car Coaches (☎ (070) 51 9533) has buses three or four times daily (twice on weekends) from outside Tropical Paradise Travel at 25 Spence St Cairns. The fare is $4.40 one-way, $8.80 return.

The most popular way of getting to Kuranda is on the incredibly scenic railway that winds 34 km from Cairns to Kuranda. This line, which took five years to build, was opened in 1891 and goes through 15 tunnels, climbing more than 300 metres in the last 21 km. Kuranda's railway station, decked out in tropical flowers and ferns, is justly famous.

There are two services on this line – the local trains, and the tourist train, known as the Kuranda Commentary Train. The local costs $11.20 one-way ($19.20 return), and

runs daily at 8.30 and 9.30 am, although there's no 9.30 service on Saturday.

The commentary train operates daily and costs $16 one-way, $25 return. There are uniformed hostesses, free orange juice, and a commentary. You also get a booklet on the line's history and a photo stop at the 260-metre Barron Falls. The commentary train has its own ticket office (☎ (070) 55 2222) at Cairns Railway Station – or you can board at Freshwater Connection, 10 km out of Cairns.

Mareeba (population 6600)
From Kuranda, the Kennedy Highway runs west across the tableland to Mareeba, the centre of a tobacco and rice-growing area, then continues south to Atherton in the centre of the tableland. From Mareeba, the Peninsula Developmental Road heads 40 km north to Mt Molloy where it forks for Mossman and the coast one way, Cooktown and Cape York the other. This is the main road from Cairns to the north. Mareeba has a range of accommodation and in July hosts one of Australia's biggest rodeos.

Chillagoe (population 250)
From Mareeba, you can continue 140 km west to Chillagoe. After Dimbulah (42 km), the road is gravel and although it may be impassable in the Wet, for most of the year you can make this interesting trip in a conventional vehicle. At Chillagoe you can visit impressive limestone caves and rock pinnacles, Aboriginal rock-art galleries, ruins of smelters from early this century, a working mine and a museum.

The caves are a national park and there are guided tours of some of them, usually given at 9 am and 1.30 pm. For more information, ask the ranger (☎ (070) 94 7163) on Queen St in the town, or contact the Cairns national parks office. The rangers can also tell you about other caves with self-guiding trails, for which you'll need a torch.

Places to Stay There's a small national park camping ground at Chillagoe, and the

Chillagoe Caravan Park (☎ (070) 94 7177) on Queen St has tent sites. *Chillagoe Caves Lodge* (☎ (070) 94 7106), at 7 King St, has hostel accommodation with cooking facilities at $9, or rooms at $20/35 for singles/doubles. It also has an inexpensive restaurant.

Getting There & Away The once-weekly Cairns to Chillagoe train takes 12 hours and leaves Cairns on Wednesdays, Chillagoe on Thursdays. White Car Coaches runs buses to Chillagoe twice a week – one from Cairns, one from Atherton, and both travel via Mareeba. Cairns to Chillagoe takes about four hours and costs around $40 return. There are day tours from Cairns for about $85.

Atherton (population 4600)

Although it's a pleasant, prosperous town, Atherton has little of interest in its own right. On the Herberton road, about a km from the centre, is Atherton's old post office, now an art gallery and information office, and the restored Chinese joss house. *Atherton Backpackers* (☎ (070) 91 3552) at 37 Alice St, not far from the centre of town, is quite a good place and has dorm beds for $9, and singles/doubles for $15/25.

Lake Tinaroo

From Atherton or nearby Tolga it's a short drive to this large lake created for the Barron River hydroelectric power scheme. Tinaroo Falls, at the north-western corner of the lake, has a motel and a caravan park which offers tent sites, self-contained cabins and motel rooms. You can rent sailboards over the road from the caravan park. A restaurant and kiosk overlook the dam.

The road continues over the dam as a gravel track which does a 31-km circuit of the lake, finally emerging on the Gillies Highway at Boar Pocket Rd, four km east of Lake Barrine. This is called the **Danbulla Forest Drive** and it's a pleasant trip – though sometimes impassable for conventional vehicles after heavy rain. It passes several

free lakeside camping grounds, run by the Queensland forestry department (there are showers and toilets). **Lake Euramoo**, about halfway along, is in a double volcanic crater; there's a short botanical walk around the lake. There is another crater at **Mobo Creek**, a short walk off the drive. Then, 25 km from the dam, it's a short walk to the **Cathedral Fig**, a truly gigantic strangler fig tree.

Yungaburra

This pretty village is 13 km east of Atherton along the Gillies Highway. The central streets of the town have been classified by the National Trust and are quite atmospheric.

Three km out of Yungaburra on the Malanda road is the strangler fig known as the **Curtain Fig** for its aerial roots which form a 15-metre-high hanging screen.

The *Lake Eacham Hotel* (☎ (070) 95 3515), in Yungaburra, is a fine old village centre pub with rooms at $30/40. Or there's the *Kookaburra Motel* at $33/38. The *Burra Bun* is a small gourmet restaurant opposite the pub. The food is excellent and the servings generous – the deep-fried camembert with a tropical salad and home-made bread is a treat ($9).

Four km away, on the southern shores of Lake Tinaroo, you can camp at the *Lakeside Motor Inn*.

Lakes Eacham & Barrine

These two lovely crater lakes are off the Gillies Highway shortly east of Yungaburra. Both are reached by paved roads, and are great swimming spots. There are rainforest walking tracks around their perimeters – 6½ km around Lake Barrine, four km around Lake Eacham.

At Lake Barrine there's a restaurant and most of the year you can take a 45-minute cruise (twice a day). Lake Eacham is quieter and more beautiful – an excellent place for a picnic or a swim, and there's a small floating kids' pool.

Both lakes are national parks and camping is not allowed. However, there are camp sites at *Lake Eacham Tourist Park* (☎ (070) 95 3730), two km down the Malanda road from

Lake Eacham. *Chambers Rainforest Holiday Apartments* (☎ (070) 95 3754) has self-contained one-bedroom apartments at $195 for three nights (doubles or twins).

Malanda

About 15 km south of Lake Eacham, Malanda is one of the most pleasant spots to stay on the tableland – a small town with some old buildings in its centre, a couple of pubs and some good places to eat and stay. Malanda also has a huge dairy and claims to have the longest milk run in Australia since it supplies milk all the way to Darwin and the north of Western Australia.

Places to Stay The *Gondwanaland Hostel* (☎ (070) 96 5046) at 17 Mary St, behind the park in the middle of town, was a good place, but it may or may not be open – ring and check.

The *Malanda Falls Caravan Park* (☎ (070) 96 5314) is at 38 Park Ave, beside the Atherton road on the edge of town. It's spacious and next to a swimming hole where the upper waters of the North Johnstone River tumble over Malanda Falls. There are tent sites, cabins and on-site vans. In the town centre, the *Malanda Hotel-Motel* (☎ (070) 96 5101), on the corner of James and English Sts, has motel-style rooms.

Millaa Millaa (population 350)

The 16-km 'waterfall circuit' road, near this small town, 24 km south of Malanda, passes some of the most picturesque falls on the tableland. You enter the circuit by taking Theresa Creek Rd one km east of Millaa Millaa on the Palmerston Highway. **Millaa Millaa Falls**, the first you reach, are the most spectacular, and have the best swimming hole.

Continuing around the circuit, you reach **Zillie Falls** and then **Ellinjaa Falls** before returning to the Palmerston Highway just 2½ km out of Millaa Millaa. A further 5½ km down the Palmerston Highway there's a turning to **Mungalli Falls**, five km off the highway, with a teahouse/restaurant and a

few self-contained units (☎ (070) 97 2358). The Palmerston Highway continues through Palmerston National Park to Innisfail.

Millaa Millaa itself has a caravan park with tent sites and cabins, and the *Millaa Millaa Hotel* has accommodation and meals. The **Eacham Historical Society Museum** is on the main street.

A few km west of Millaa Millaa, the East Evelyn road passes the **Millaa Millaa lookout** with its superb panoramic view.

Mt Hypipamee

The Kennedy Highway between Atherton and Ravenshoe passes the eerie Mt Hypipamee crater. It's a scenic 400-metre walk from the picnic area, past **Dinner Falls**, to this narrow, 138-metre-deep crater with its spooky, evil-looking lake far below. You can camp at the picnic area – permits are available from the national parks office in Yungaburra (☎ (070) 95 3768).

Herberton (population 1500)

On a slightly longer alternative route between Atherton and Ravenshoe, this old tin-mining town holds a colourful Tin Festival each September. On Holdcroft Drive is the **Herberton Historical Village**, with about 30 old buildings which have been transported here from around the tableland.

Ravenshoe

At an altitude of 915 metres, Ravenshoe is a forestry centre on the western edge of the tablelands. It has the usual caravan/camping park and a couple of pubs and motels.

Little Millstream Falls are a few km south of Ravenshoe on the Tully Gorge road.

The Kennedy Highway continues southwest from Ravenshoe for 114 km, from where you can head south to Charters Towers by paved road all the way, or west by the Gulf Developmental Road to Croydon and Normanton.

Six km past Ravenshoe and one km off the road are the **Millstream Falls**, the widest in Australia although only 13 metres high. You can camp here, but you must get a permit from the national parks office at Yungaburra (☎ (070) 95 3768).

The small mining town of **Mt Garnet**, 47 km west of Ravenshoe, comes alive one weekend every May when it hosts one of Queensland's top outback race meetings. About 60 km past Mt Garnet, the road passes through **Forty Mile Scrub National Park**, where the semi-evergreen vine thicket is a descendant of the vegetation that covered much of the Gondwana super-continent 300 million years ago – before Australia, South America, India, Africa and Antarctica drifted apart.

Gulf Developmental Road

From the Kennedy Highway to Normanton, the 460-km road is mostly paved, but some rough stretches west of Georgetown make it a dry-weather route only. The road passes through Mt Surprise, Georgetown and Croydon. There are hotels or motels and caravan/camping parks at Mt Surprise, Georgetown, Einasleigh and Forsayth. The region crossed by the road has many ruined gold mines and settlements, and attracts some gem fossickers.

The **Elizabeth Creek** gem field, 42 km west of Mt Surprise and accessible by conventional vehicle in the Dry, is Australia's best topaz field. Information on the field is available at the Mt Surprise service station (☎ (070) 62 3153). Between Mt Surprise and Georgetown, an unpaved road leads south to tiny **Einasleigh**, from where you could reach Kidston, Australia's richest gold mine. Einasleigh Gorge, good for swimming, is just across the road from the Einasleigh pub.

CAIRNS TO PORT DOUGLAS

The Bruce Highway, which runs nearly 2000 km north from Brisbane, ends in Cairns, but the surfaced coastal road continues another 110 km north to Mossman and Daintree. This final stretch, the Cook Highway, is a treat because it often runs right along the shore and there are some superb beaches.

Heading out of Cairns, towards the airport, you'll find an interesting and informative elevated **mangrove boardwalk** a couple of hundred metres before you reach the airport. There are explanatory signs at regular intervals, and these give some insight into the surprising ecological complexities of swamp vegetation. There's also a small observation platform.

Kamerunga Rd, off the Cook Highway just north of the airport turning, leads inland to the **Freshwater Connection**, a railway museum complex where you can also catch the Kuranda Commentary Train. It's 10 km from the centre of town. Just beyond Freshwater is the turning south along Redlynch Intake Rd to **Crystal Cascades**, a popular outing with waterfalls and swimming holes 22 km from Cairns.

North along the Cook Highway are the Cairns northern beaches, which are really a string of suburbs. In order, these are **Machans, Holloways, Yorkeys Knob, Trinity, Kewarra**, and **Clifton** beaches and **Palm Cove**. Holloways and Trinity are the best for a short beach trip from Cairns. At Palm Cove, 22 km from Cairns, **Wild World** has lots of crocodiles and snakes, tame kangaroos and Australian birds; there are shows daily.

Round the headland past Palm Cove and Double Island, **Ellis Beach** is a lovely spot. Its southern end is an unofficial nude bathing beach and the central part of the beach has a good camping ground.

Soon after Ellis Beach, **Hartleys Creek Crocodile Farm**, 40 km from Cairns, has a collection of far north Australian wildlife. Most of the enclosures are a bit shoddy but showmanship makes it one of the most interesting 'animal places' in Australia. When they feed Charlie the crocodile in the 'Crocodile Attack Show' you know for certain why it's not wise to get bitten by one! And you've never seen anything eat apples until you've seen a cassowary knock back a dozen of them. The park is open daily but it's best to go at crocodile feeding time which is 3 pm; entry is $8.

Shortly before Mossman there's a turn-off to fashionable Port Douglas, the departure point for the delightful Low Isles. Then just before Daintree village is the gravel turn-off to the Cape Tribulation rainforests. From Cape Tribulation, it's possible to continue up to historic Cooktown by 4WD along the controversial Bloomfield Track. Alternatively, there's the partly surfaced inland road from Cairns, but both roads to Cooktown can be cut after periods of heavy rain.

PORT DOUGLAS (population 1300)

In the early days of far north Queensland's development, Port Douglas was a rival for Cairns, but when Cairns eventually got the upper hand, Port Douglas became a sleepy little backwater. Recently, however, people began to realise what a delightful place it was, and up went the multimillion dollar Sheraton Mirage and Radisson Royal Palms resorts. These were quickly followed by a golf course, a heliport, hovercraft services from Cairns, a marina and shopping complex, and an avenue of palms lining the road from the Cook Highway to Port Douglas – all the ingredients of a retreat for the rich and fashionable. Yet, despite all this development, 'Port' has managed to keep its original charm and there is still cheap accommodation. Many travellers arrive here and soon wonder why they spent so long in Cairns – Port is much more relaxed, and there's plenty to do.

The little town has a couple of good central pubs with outdoor sitting areas, and a string of interesting little shops and restaurants to wander around when the beach, the boats and the lookout get dull. You can make trips to the Low Isles, the Barrier Reef, Mossman and Cape Tribulation.

Orientation & Information

It's six km from the highway along a long, low spit of land to Port Douglas. The Sheraton Mirage resort occupies a long stretch of Four Mile Beach and Port Douglas proper is just a few streets on the western half of the end of the spit, beside and back from Dickson's Inlet. There's a fine view over the coastline and sea from Flagstaff Hill lookout.

The helpful Port Douglas Tourist Informa-

tion Centre (☎ (070) 99 3211) is at 27 Macrossan St.

Things to See

On the pier off Anzac Park, Ben Cropp's **Shipwreck Museum** is quite interesting and open from 9 am to 5 pm daily; admission is $3.50. The **Rainforest Habitat**, where the Port Douglas road leaves the main highway, is an all-new, whiz-bang attraction on which large sums have been lavished. The end result is without doubt impressive – a huge enclosed canopy forms an artificial rainforest environment beneath, and this is home to at least 30 species of birds and as many of butterflies. It's all very wonderful, but a bit over the top at $10 per person.

Activities

The Port Douglas Dive Centre (☎ (070) 99 5327), with a shop down near the public wharf at the end of Anzac Park, runs openwater diving certificate courses, as does Haba Dive (☎ (070) 99 5254) in the Marina.

Reef Trips *Quicksilver* fast cats do daily trips to Agincourt Reef on the outer reef. For $158 you get snorkelling gear, a semisubmersible ride, underwater observatory viewing and lunch. For certified divers, two 40-minute dives will cost an extra $65 with all gear provided.

There are a number of other local operators, all of which start at the Marina – take a wander around and see what's on offer.

Organised Tours The Mossman Gorge trip run by the Port 'o' Call Lodge – an afternoon including a swim and rainforest walk – is good value at $8. With the regular operators, a day trip to Cape Tribulation is around $50. A two-day 4WD Cooktown loop – up via the inland road, back by the Bloomfield Track – is about $160. Bally Hooley Rail Tours (☎ (070) 98 5899) at the Marina runs trips in a miniature steam train to Mossman sugar mill and Drumsara sugar plantation beyond Mossman.

Places to Stay

The best backpackers' accommodation in Port is the *Port 'o' Call Lodge* (☎ (070) 99 5422), about one km from the centre, along the main road (Davidson St). This is a modern place with four-bed dorms at $12 per person, and a few double rooms at $39; all rooms have bathroom. There's a pool, cooking facilities, a restaurant with cheap and filling food, a bar and a daily free courtesy coach to Cairns. The lodge also runs trips to Mossman Gorge for $8, and hooks up with a couple of the hostel tours which operate between Cairns and Cape Trib.

The *Port Douglas Travellers Hostel* (☎ (070) 98 5922) at 111 Davidson St, about 1½ km from the town centre, is well kept with pleasant open-sided cooking and sitting areas, a small store, garden and pool. Accommodation is in bunk rooms for $11 a night and there are bicycles for hire. The hostel runs diving courses and the prices include accommodation at the hostel – a one-week open-water course costs $450.

Port Douglas also has a number of caravan parks, mostly along Davidson St, all with pools, tent sites and on-site vans or cabins.

Most of the motels and holiday flats are expensive. The *Travellers Palm Motel* (☎ (070) 98 5198) and the *Coconut Grove Motel* (☎ (070) 98 5124), both on Macrossan St near the corner of Davidson St, have some singles/doubles for $55/65.There's a couple of reasonably priced medium-range resorts: *Whispering Palms* and *Ti-Tree*, both just off the road between the main highway and the centre of town. Whispering Palms has a pool, restaurant and beach access with self-contained flats from $65, while Ti-Tree has a pool and tennis courts, and similar prices.

At the top of the range are the *Radisson Royal Palms* (☎ (070) 99 5577) and the *Sheraton Mirage* resorts, both of which have prices which will singe your hand as you reach for your credit card, but have excellent facilities.

Places to Eat

Port Douglas has a surprisingly good array of restaurants for such a small town. At the bottom of the scale is *Mocka's Pies* on Macrossan St, while both the pubs offer standard pub meals for around $8 – the *Court House Hotel* has an outdoor eating area and a pleasantly breezy lounge bar.

Shoestrings Restaurant, at the Port 'o' Call Lodge, serves good breakfasts and cheap pub-style meals in the evenings. It's quite popular with locals as well as travellers.

Also on Macrossan St, not far from the Davidson St corner, the *Bodensee Cafe* does delicious pastries and meals at $10 to $15, including German and vegetarian specials. A couple of doors along, *Bandito's* has nachos and other snacks which are a bit cheaper. Over the road, *Thai Cuisine* has absolutely superb food, and is well worth a splurge – main courses are $12 to $15. It's open only on Friday, Saturday, Monday and Tuesday evenings from 5 pm, and it's a good idea to drop by early and reserve a table as this place is justifiably popular. Also on this side of the road is the *Jade Inn*, a good place for takeaway Chinese tucker.

Further along Macrossan St, on the other side, is the *Mata Bubu*, which specialises in interesting vegetarian dishes. The menu changes regularly and it's a good place for lunch or breakfast. On the corner of Macrossan and Wharf Sts is the flash new *Oskars Seafood Restaurant*, complete with fake cave decor. The menu is varied and main courses range in price from $12 to $16.

There's also a few choices in the Marina Mirage complex, including a couple of up-market restaurants (such as *Fiorelli's*) and some cheaper cafes and ice-cream parlours.

Entertainment

The Central Hotel has live bands at weekends (more often during the peak tourist season), while in the Marina Mirage, there's FJs Nightspot, which is open until 3 am.

Getting There & Away

Bus Coral Coaches (☎ (070) 98 1611) is a Mossman-based bus company which covers the Cairns to Cooktown coastal route via Port Douglas, Mossman, Daintree, Cape

Tribulation and Bloomfield. Bookings and departures in Cairns are from Tropical Paradise Travel (☎ (070) 51 9533) at 25 Spence St. Coral Coaches runs several buses daily between Cairns and Port Douglas (1¼ hours, $13.40), Mossman ($14.50), and on to Daintree village ($17.20). From Mossman you can get connections to Mossman Gorge ($4). Road conditions permitting, services from Cairns to Cape Tribulation go two or three times daily ($23.70), and on to Cooktown via the Bloomfield Track three days a week ($46.30).

Coral Coaches usually lets you stop over as often as you like along the route, so they're as good as any tour. Owing to the ruggedness of some of the roads, the possibility of delays, and the frequent hopping in and out of the variety of vehicles which cover different sections of the route, riding with Coral Coaches is about as close as Australia comes to travelling in the Third World – and it's fun.

Boat Apart from the Coral Coaches buses, there's the daily *Quicksilver* fast catamaran service from Port Douglas to Cairns and back. It's $15 one-way, $25 return. The *Quicksilver* booking office (☎ (070) 99 5050) in Port Douglas is in the Marina Mirage complex.

Getting Around
Avis, National and Budget all have offices on Macrossan St, but there are smaller and cheaper local firms around too.

Both the hostels have bikes for hire, or the Port Douglas Tour Services office on Macrossan also has them.

AROUND PORT DOUGLAS
Low Isles
Offshore from Port Douglas is a fine little coral cay surrounded by a lagoon and topped by an old lighthouse. This is a very different sort of reef island from hyped-up Green Island off Cairns. *Hardy's Courier* (a regular catamaran) makes daily trips to the Low Isles from Port Douglas, and the price ($45) includes lunch, snorkelling gear and boom

netting. The *Quicksilver* fast catamarans from Port Douglas do Low Isles trips for $95, including lunch, snorkelling gear, a guided snorkelling tour and a glass-bottomed boat ride.

Mossman & Daintree
Mossman, the most northerly sugar town, has a big Italian population and is becoming a centre for tropical fruit growing. At beautiful **Mossman Gorge**, five km west, a three-km circuit walking track leads through rainforest to swimming holes and rapids. Coral Coaches run buses up to the gorge from Mossman, or you can take one of the hostel tours from Port Douglas.

The highway continues 35 km beyond Mossman to the village of Daintree, passing the gravel turn-off to the Daintree River ferry after 24 km. In Daintree village, the **Butterfly Farm** at Barratt Creek is open from 10 am to 4 pm daily. The small **Timber Museum** is worth a look, although the pieces for sale carry astronomical price tags.

Five km beyond Daintree village, along Stewarts Creek Rd, is a coffee plantation which, apart from coffee, also has an extensive range of exotic fruit and nut trees, and a signposted rainforest walk. It's open daily from 10 am to 4.30 pm, entry is $4, and it's owned by a very friendly old hippie.

Daintree River Tours A number of operators offer river trips on the Daintree from various points between the ferry and Daintree village. It's certainly a worthwhile activity, as croc sightings are common, especially on sunny days when the tide is low, as they love to sun themselves on the exposed banks.

The two tours which depart from the ferry crossing are very much in it for the quick buck, and their boats reflect this – gimmicky colours, and one even calls itself a 'train'. Best of the bunch is the low-key Daintree River & Cruise Centre, four km beyond the ferry turn-off on the Mossman to Daintree road. Knowledgeable guides take small groups up less-frequented parts of the river, and the price includes the use of a pair of binoculars for each person. The trips take one hour, cost $8 and depart daily at 9.50 am, 1.10 and 2.15 pm. A longer tour (1½ hours) departs daily at 11.10 am and costs $12.

Places to Stay & Eat There are several accommodation possibilities in Mossman, including a creekside caravan/camping park next to the swimming pool at the northern end of town. You can get good cheap meals in the *Post Office Hotel* on Mill St and the *Exchange Hotel*.

As yet, the tiny town of Daintree only has a caravan/camping park, a modest coffee shop and the flashy new *Barramundi Garden* at the Timber Museum. The *Daintree Tea House*, a couple of km back along the Mossman road, boasts barramundi with trimmings for $9.

CAPE TRIBULATION AREA

After crossing the Daintree River by ferry, it's another 34 km of gravel road, with a few hills and creek crossings, to Cape Tribulation. Unless there has been exceptionally heavy rain, conventional vehicles can usually make it, with care, to Cape Trib.

Cape Tribulation was named by Captain Cook, since it was a little north of here that his troubles started when his ship ran on to the Endeavour Reef. Mt Sorrow was also named by Cook.

In the '70s, much of this coast was a seldom-visited hippie outpost, with settlements like Cedar Bay, north of Cape Trib between Bloomfield and Cooktown. These days, Cape Tribulation is becoming more and more popular with visitors. It's an incredibly beautiful stretch of coast, and is one of the few places in Australia where tropical rainforest meets the sea.

Remember, however, that this is rainforest – you'll need to take mosquito repellent with you. Approaching Cape Trib from the south,

---

Rainforest

Nearly all of Australia was covered in rainforest 50 million years ago, but by the time Europeans arrived, only about 1% of the rainforest was left. Today, logging and clearing for farms have reduced that to less than 0.3% – about 20,000 sq km. More than half of this, and nearly all the *tropical* rainforest, is in Queensland.

The biggest surviving virgin rainforest area covers the ranges from south of Mossman up to Cooktown. It's called the Greater Daintree. This is one of the few places on earth where evolution has continued, virtually uninterrupted, since flowering plants first appeared about 130 million years ago. Conservationists argue that apart from the normal reasons for saving rainforests – such as combating the greenhouse effect and preserving species habitats – this forest is extra valuable as it's such a diverse genetic storehouse.

To the timber industry, the idea of total protection of the Greater Daintree is like a red rag to a bull. Their case, aside from job losses, is that more than 90% of Queensland's remaining rainforest is on government land and only 19% of that is used for timber – and then not destructively, since cutting is selective and time is left for the forest to regenerate before being logged again.

In 1983, the local Douglas Shire Council decided to bulldoze a gravel road 22 km through the forest from just north of Cape Tribulation to the Bloomfield River. Cape Trib became the scene of a classic 'greenies versus bulldozers' blockade. Several months and numerous arrests later, the road builders won and the Bloomfield Track was opened. The road works have caused large amounts of soil to wash out into the ocean, raising serious fears for the Barrier Reef.

However, Cape Trib was not the only Queensland issue preoccupying conservationists: in 1987 the Australian government agreed to propose the 'Queensland Wet Tropics' – 9000 sq km of rainforest from north of Bloomfield down to near Townsville – for World Heritage listing.

Despite strenuous resistance by the Queensland timber industry and state government, it seems certain that the Greater Daintree and most of the rest of north Queensland's rainforest will be saved. It's an issue that has set not only timber workers against conservationists, but longer term residents against more recent arrivals, northern country people against 'southern city intellectuals', and independent-minded Queenslanders against 'interfering Canberra'! ∎

the last bank is at Mossman. You can get petrol at two or three places between Mossman and Cooktown by this coastal route.

Getting There & Away

See the Port Douglas section for details of the buses between Cairns, Port Douglas and Cape Trib.

Some excellent deals can be found at most of the hostels in Cairns combining transport to Cape Tribulation with hostel accommodation – for instance $39 including two nights at Crocodylus Village, or $49 with one night at Crocodylus and one at the Jungle Lodge.

It's quite easy to hitch, since beyond the Daintree ferry, all vehicles *have* to head to Cape Trib, there's nowhere else to go!

Daintree River to Cape Tribulation

Ten km back from Daintree village, on the Mossman to Daintree road, is the five-km gravel road to the Daintree River ferry and Cape Trib. Ferries operate every few minutes from 6 am to midnight and cost $2 for a car, $1.70 for a motorbike, plus $1 for each passenger.

Three km beyond the ferry, Cape Kimberley Rd leads down to Cape Kimberley beach, five km away. About nine km from the ferry, just after you cross the spectacular Heights of Alexandra range, is the **Daintree Rainforest Environmental Centre** (☎ (070) 98 9171) – an excellent information centre with rainforest displays, a self-guided forest boardwalk and an audiovisual show. It's open daily from 9 am to 4 pm; entry is $6.

About 12 km from the ferry you reach Buchanan Creek Rd, which is the turn-off for **Cow Bay** (5½ km).

Further on, the road strikes the shore at **Thornton Beach**, then passes the Bouncing Stones, where the unusually smooth pebbles bounce to a great height if thrown down. **Noah Beach**, with a national park camping ground, is eight km before Cape Trib.

Places to Stay & Eat At Cape Kimberley beach, the *Daintree Rainforest Resort* (☎ (070) 90 7500) has camp sites for $5 per

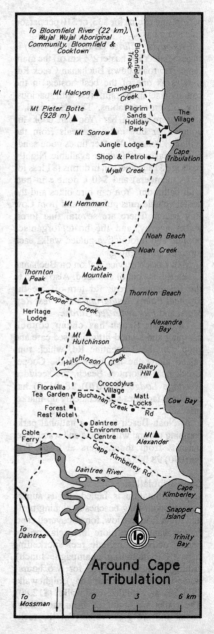

Around Cape Tribulation

person, and cabins for $35, or $10 per person on a share basis.

Crocodylus Village (☎ (070) 98 9166) is an associate YHA hostel 2½ km off the main Cape Trib road, down Buchanan Creek Rd. It rates as one of the best hostels in the country – set in the rainforest with spacious, airy, off-ground cabins. There's a pool, a small store and a bar. You can cook for yourself or buy evening meals from the 'village kitchen'. At other times good sandwiches, cakes and fruit are available. Nightly costs are $13 per person in dorms ($1 less for YHA members) and $40 a double in huts with bathroom. You can hire bikes and the hostel vehicle runs guests to and from Cow Bay beach. There are several fine forest walks nearby, and the hostel organises popular and informative guided walks each morning and evening.

Matt Lock's service station on Buchanan Creek Rd has petrol and food. Also close to the Buchanan Creek Rd turn-off are the *Tropical Palms Restaurant*, the *Forest Rest Motel* and *Floravilla Tea Garden*.

Thornton Beach has cheap council camping and a good little licensed cafe and shop. On the Turpentine Rd, which runs inland along the left bank of the Cooper Creek near Thornton Beach, the secluded *Heritage Lodge* (☎ (070) 98 9138) has excellent facilities and decidedly up-market prices.

At Noah Beach there's a national parks camping ground with toilets and water – get permits from the rangers at Cape Trib (☎ (070) 98 0052).

Cape Tribulation

Cape Tribulation is famed for its superb scenery, with long beaches stretching north and south from the low, forest-covered cape. If you want to do more than relax on the beach, activities include reef snorkelling trips ($59 including champagne lunch), fishing, windsurfing ($15 for two hours), horse-riding ($35 for half a day), night walks ($11.50) and guided bushwalks ($12.80). The walks are organised from the Village hostel and are great value. For the really energetic, there are also mountain bikes for hire.

Places to Stay & Eat Cape Tribulation's two hostels are a few hundred metres apart. The *Jungle Lodge* (☎ (070) 98 0086), off the road just before the cape, has six-bed dorms at $12 per night. Its Drysdale Arms bar and restaurant is a convivial meeting spot, with a pool just outside. There's a strong party atmosphere here, so if you're looking for peace and quiet, you're better off at the Village, or the Pilgrim Sands Holiday Park.

The *Village* (☎ (070) 98 0040) is a slightly more up-market hostel with quite comfortable log cabins, a pool, bar and a restaurant with à la carte menu. The nightly cost is $12.50 per person and there are also double rooms for $34.

Just off the road, 1½ km north of Cape Trib, the *Pilgrim Sands Holiday Park* (☎ (070) 98 0030) has camp sites for $9.50, a self-contained four-bed cabin for $38, and two-bedroom units (five beds) with bathroom for $53. Bed linen can be supplied for a small charge.

Cape Tribulation also has a takeaway food place which makes great hamburgers.

CAPE TRIBULATION TO COOKTOWN

Just north of Cape Tribulation, the Bloomfield Track (4WD only) heads through the forest as far as **Wujal Wujal** Aboriginal community 22 km north, on the far side of the Bloomfield River crossing. Even for 4WD vehicles, the Bloomfield River and some of the Track are impassable after heavy rain.

From Wujal Wujal another dirt road – rough but usually passable in a conventional vehicle in the Dry – heads 46 km north through the tiny settlements of **Bloomfield**, **Rossville** and **Helenvale** to meet the main Cairns to Cooktown road (also dirt) 28 km before Cooktown.

Places to Stay & Eat

At the *Roadhouse* at Bloomfield you can camp or sleep in very basic bunk rooms for $10 (bedding extra). Bloomfield River cruises and trail rides are offered. At Helenvale, the *Lion's Den* is a good place to halt – it's a colourful 1875 bush pub. You can camp beside the river or the pub has a few rooms.

The *Home Rule Rainforest Lodge* (☎ (070) 51 7046) is a couple of km towards the coast from Rossville. It has cheap share accommodation ($10) and cooking facilities, or you can buy meals for $8. The lodge also has cheap packages from Cairns. The *Bloomfield Wilderness Lodge* (☎ (070) 33 2002) is close to the mouth of the Bloomfield River and aims to make holes in fat wallets – $495/750 for a single/double for three nights (minimum stay), and children are 'not encouraged'.

CAIRNS TO COOKTOWN – THE INLAND ROAD

The 'main' road up from Cairns loops through Kuranda, Mareeba, Mt Molloy, the wolfram mining town of Mt Carbine, Palmer River crossing and Lakeland, where the road up to Cape York Peninsula splits off. Most of the second half of this 341-km road is unpaved, and often corrugated.

In **Mt Molloy**, the *National Hotel* (☎ (070) 94 1133) has cheap accommodation. James Venture Mulligan, the man who started both the Palmer River and Hodgkinson River gold rushes, is buried in the Mt Molloy cemetery. At the **Palmer River** crossing there's a cafe/petrol station and a camping ground. The 1873 to 1883 gold rush, for which the Palmer River is famous, happened in very remote country about 70 km west of here. Its main towns were Palmerville and Maytown, of which very little is left today.

Shortly before Cooktown, the road passes **Black Mountain**, a pile of thousands of granite boulders. It's said there are ways between the huge rocks which will take you under the hill from one side to the other, but people have died trying to find them. Black Mountain is known to Aborigines as Kalcajagga – 'Place of the Spears'. The colour comes not from the rocks themselves, but from lichen which grow on them.

COOKTOWN (population 913)

Cooktown can claim to have been Australia's first British settlement. From June to August 1770, Captain Cook beached his barque *Endeavour* there, and during that time, Joseph Banks, the chief naturalist, took the chance to study Australian flora & fauna along the banks of the Endeavour River. Banks collected 186 plant species and wrote the first European description of a kangaroo. The north side of the river has scarcely changed since then.

The explorers had amicable contacts with the local Aborigines, but race relations in the area turned sour a century later when Cooktown was founded as the unruly port for the 1873 to 1883 Palmer River gold rush 140 km south-west. Hell's Gate, a narrow pass on the track between Cooktown and the Palmer River, was the scene of frequent ambushes as Aborigines tried to stop their lands being overrun. Battle Camp, about 60 km inland from Cooktown, was the site of a major battle between Whites and Cape York Aborigines.

In 1874, before Cairns was even thought of, Cooktown was the second biggest town in Queensland. At its peak there were no less than 94 pubs, almost as many brothels, and the population was over 30,000! As many as half of these were Chinese, whose industrious presence led to some wild race riots.

After the gold rush ended, cyclones and a WW II evacuation came close to killing Cooktown. The opening of the excellent James Cook Historical Museum in 1970 started to bring in some visitor dollars although Cooktown's population is still less than 1000 and just three pubs remain.

The effort of getting to Cooktown is rewarded not just by the atmosphere but by some fascinating reminders of the area's past. With a vehicle, you could use the town as a base for visiting the Quinkan rock art near Laura or even Lakefield National Park.

Orientation & Information

Cooktown is on the inland side of a north-pointing headland sheltering the mouth of

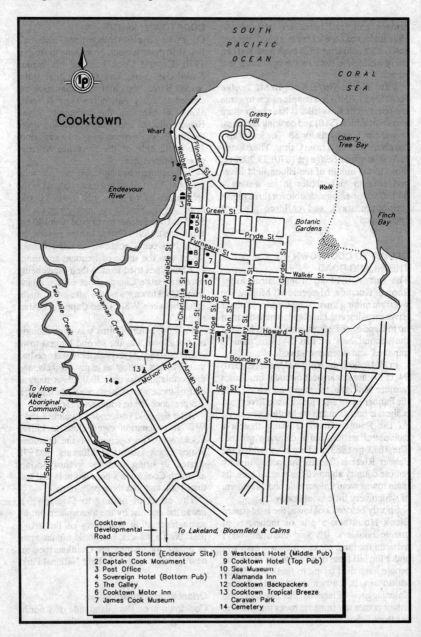

Cooktown

SOUTH
PACIFIC
OCEAN

CORAL
SEA

Grassy
Hill

Cherry
Tree Bay

Walk

Finch
Bay

Botanic
Gardens

Wharf

Endeavour River

Two Mile Creek

Chinaman Creek

To Hope Vale Aboriginal Community

South Rd

McIvor Rd

Annan St

Adelaide St

Charlotte St

Helen St

Hope St

John St

May St

May St

Garden St

Webber Esplanade

Flinders St

Green St

Furneaux St

Pryde St

Walker St

Hogg St

Howard St

Boundary St

Ida St

Cooktown Developmental Road

To Lakeland, Bloomfield & Cairns

1 Inscribed Stone (Endeavour Site)
2 Captain Cook Monument
3 Post Office
4 Sovereign Hotel (Bottom Pub)
5 The Galley
6 Cooktown Motor Inn
7 James Cook Museum
8 Westcoast Hotel (Middle Pub)
9 Cooktown Hotel (Top Pub)
10 Sea Museum
11 Alamanda Inn
12 Cooktown Backpackers
13 Cooktown Tropical Breeze Caravan Park
14 Cemetery

the Endeavour River. Charlotte St runs south from the wharf, and along it are three pubs, a post office, a bank and a tourist information office (☎ (070) 69 5555) near the Sovereign Hotel.

Things to See

Charlotte St has a number of interesting monuments starting with one to the tragic Mary Watson (see the Lizard Island section) opposite the Sovereign Hotel. She is buried in Cooktown cemetery. A little further towards the wharf are memorials to the equally tragic explorer Edmund Kennedy and to Captain Cook. Behind these stands a cannon, which was sent from Brisbane in 1885 along with three cannonballs, two rifles and one officer in response to Cooktown's plea for defences against a feared Russian invasion! Right by the waterside, a stone with an inscription marks the spot where the *Endeavour* was careened.

The **James Cook Historical Museum** on Helen St, a block up from Charlotte St near the corner of Furneaux St, has displays relating to all aspects of Cooktown's past – Aborigines, Cook's voyages, the Palmer River gold rush and the Chinese community. The museum is open daily. There's a good **Sea Museum** a block away on Walker St – open daily from 9 am to 4 pm.

The Cooktown cemetery, a few hundred metres along McIvor Rd from the top end of Charlotte St, is worth a visit. There are many interesting graves including those of Mary Watson and the 'Normanby Woman' – thought to have been a north European who survived a shipwreck as a child and lived with Aborigines for years until 'rescued' by white people. She died soon after.

Organised Tours

Endeavour River Mangrove Cruises (☎ (070) 69 5377) do just what their name suggests twice daily and three nights a week in an eight-seater craft. The fare is reasonable and you stand a good chance of catching your evening meal with the fishing lines and bait supplied.

Cook's Landing Bus Tours (☎ (070) 69 5101) does morning tours, three days a week, to Black Mountain, the Lion's Den bush pub, and the prawn farm and gorges on the Annan River.

Strikie's Feral Safaris run a variety of good-fun 4WD trips to places like Black Mountain, the Lion's Den and Cedar Bay National Park, Hope Vale Aboriginal community north of Cooktown, Aboriginal rock-art sites, waterfalls and Normanby. A day outing costs $65 or more.

It's possible to join tour groups to Cape York in Cooktown – probably at a bit of a saving on the price from Cairns. You can also make diving and fishing trips from Cooktown.

Places to Stay

Cooktown Backpackers (☎ (070) 69 5166), on the corner of Charlotte and Boundary Sts, is a comfortable, well-equipped place. There's a good kitchen, dining area, pool, garden, TV lounge and great views. A bunk is $12 a night and there are bicycles for hire. The Sunday night barbecue is excellent value.

The *Cooktown Motor Inn* (☎ (070) 69 5357), on Charlotte St in the centre, has singles/doubles from $25/45 including a light breakfast. Some rooms have cooking facilities. The 1874 *Sovereign Hotel* (☎ (070) 69 5400) is in the middle of town on the corner of Charlotte and Green Sts. Also known as the Bottom Pub, it has a superb pool, and accommodation includes 'budget' rooms at $32/43 with bathroom, twin beds, fan and tea/coffee facilities; most of the other rooms have air-con.

The *Tropical Breeze Caravan Park* (☎ (070) 69 5417) has tent sites and on-site vans.

Places to Eat

All three pubs serve counter meals. The *Cooktown Hotel* (Top Pub) has lunches and dinners, Monday to Saturday, from around $4, plus meals in the slightly more expensive Tavern Restaurant/Garden Lounge; it also has a great beer garden.

On Friday nights, people descend on the

Westcoast Hotel (Middle Pub) from miles around for the area's only regular live band.

The *Galley*, a takeaway coffee shop/restaurant in Sovereign Square next to the hotel, has a variety of good-value food including pizzas, salads and curries; a large pizza is about $11.

The *Endeavour Inn*, just beyond the Reef Cafe, is a more up-market licensed restaurant, open for breakfast, lunch and dinner.

Getting There & Away
Air Sunbird (☎ (070) 53 4899 in Cairns) operates flights between Cairns and Cooktown six days a week which cost $83 one-way. Cooktown Backpackers and Hinterland Aviation in Cairns (☎ (070) 53 7323 or ask at the Tropical Paradise Travel Centre) operate 'Backpackers Charters' which makes scenic flights between Cairns and Cooktown, with drop-offs at Cow Bay. You need at least four people, but the price per head is a worthwhile saving on the scheduled flights.

Bus Coral Coaches travels between Cooktown and Bloomfield three days a week and you can get connections to Cape Trib and Cairns the same day. Cairns to Cooktown is $46.30 and takes about nine hours.

The Cooktown Bus Service (☎ (070) 51 1064) runs two or three times a week each way between Cairns and Cooktown along the main (inland) road. It takes six or seven hours and costs $45. Buses depart from outside the Tropical Paradise Travel Centre in Cairns.

Boat The expensive *Quicksilver* 'wave piercer' catamaran runs daily except Tuesday from Port Douglas to Cooktown and back (2½ hours one-way).

Getting Around
You can rent bicycles from Cooktown Backpackers or the Sovereign Hotel. The Cooktown Motor Inn has Mokes and 4WDs.

LIZARD ISLAND
Lizard Island, the furthest north of the Barrier Reef resort islands, is about 100 km from Cooktown. It was named by Joseph Banks after Captain Cook spent a day there, trying to find a way out through the reef to the open sea.

A Queensland tragedy took place here in 1881 when a settler's wife, Mary Watson, took to sea in a large metal pot with her son and a Chinese servant, after Aborigines killed her other servant while her husband was away fishing. The three eventually died of thirst on a barren island to the north, Mary leaving a diary of their terrible last days. Their tragic story is told at the Cooktown museum.

The island has superb beaches, great swimming and snorkelling, the remains of the Watsons' cottage, a pricey resort and a national parks camping ground. There are plenty of bushwalks and bird life, and great views from Cook's Look, the highest point on the island, from where Captain Cook surveyed the area in search of a passage through the reef.

Places to Stay
In the resort, accommodation including all meals and use of the facilities costs from a mere $275 per day. As the island is relatively isolated, it's been a favourite retreat for celebrities, and a popular stop for yachties, for many years.

The small national park camping ground is at Watson's Bay. It has a fireplace, pit toilet, picnic table and a hand-pumped water supply 250 metres away. Camping permits are available from the national parks office (☎ (070) 51 9811) at 41 The Esplanade in Cairns, and you must take all supplies with you as the resort won't sell you any. You can't take stove fuel on the plane but there's enough driftwood on the beach to use for cooking.

Getting There & Away
Australian Regional flies from Cairns for $140 one-way.

Cape York & the Gulf

CAPE YORK PENINSULA

The Cape York Peninsula is one of the wildest and least populated parts of Australia. The Tip, as it is called, is the most northerly point on the mainland of Australia, and between here and Papua New Guinea, just 150 km away, a scatter of islands dot the Torres Strait.

Getting up to the north along the rough and rugged Peninsula Developmental Road is still one of Australia's great road adventures. It's a trip for the tough and experienced since the roads are *all* dirt, and even at the height of the Dry there are some difficult river crossings. In the last few years, several tour operators have sprung up to offer this adventure to those who can't or don't want to go it alone.

Ron and Viv Moon's book *Cape York, An Adventurer's Guide* provides all the necessary detail. It costs about $20 and is available from many Queensland bookshops.

Getting There & Away

Air Australian Regional Airlines, owned by Australian Airlines, flies from Cairns to Weipa ($209), and Bamaga several days a week. Sunbird Airlines, based at Cairns Airport (☎ (070) 53 4899), also has an extensive network around the peninsula and the Torres Strait Islands. Sunbird also flies from Cairns to Cooktown and Lockhart. Flight West (☎ (070) 53 5511) goes to Aurukun ($274), on the coast south of Weipa, via Coen ($207) and back three times a week from Cairns.

Driving to the Top Every year, more and more hardy travellers equipped with their own 4WD vehicles or trail bikes, make the long haul up to the top of Cape York. Apart from being able to say you have been as far north as you can get in Australia, you also test yourself against some pretty hard going and see some wild and wonderful country

into the bargain. It's no easy trip, and during the wet season nothing moves by road at all.

The travelling season is from mid-May to mid-November but the beginning and end of that period are borderline, depending on how late or early the wet season is. The best time is June to September. Conventional vehicles can usually reach Coen and even, with care and skill, get across to Weipa on the Gulf of Carpentaria but it's *very* rough going. If you want to continue north from the Weipa turn-off to Cape York, you'll need 4WD, a winch and plenty of strong steel wire.

The major problem is the many river crossings; even as late as June or July they will still be swift-flowing and frequently alter their course. The rivers often have very steep banks. The Great Dividing Range runs right up the spine of the peninsula and rivers run east and west off it. Although the rivers in the south of the peninsula only flow in the wet season, those further north flow year-round.

The ideal set-up for a Cape York expedition is two 4WD vehicles travelling together – one can haul the other out where necessary. You can also make it to the top on motorcycles, floating the machines across the wider rivers. There are usually large truck inner tubes left at the river crossings for this purpose. Beware of crocodiles!

After the Archer River Roadhouse, 65 km beyond Coen, Weipa (on the coast) and usually Bamaga (just south of the Tip) are the only places for a regular supply of petrol and mechanical repairs. Visits to the RACQ and the national parks office in Cairns are well worthwhile before you head north.

You no longer need a permit to visit Aboriginal communities on the peninsula or traverse their land, but it's advisable to make contact beforehand by letter or radio phone. The same applies to Torres Strait Islander communities. Apart from Bamaga, most of the mainland Aboriginal communities are well off the main track north, and do not have any facilities or accommodation for travellers.

Organised Tours A host of companies operates 4WD tours from Cairns to Cape York. The trips typically take seven to 14 days, cost from $500, and take in Laura, the Quinkan rock-art galleries, Lakefield National Park, Coen, Weipa, Indian Head Falls, Bamaga, Somerset and Cape York itself. Most trips also visit Thursday Island, as well as taking in Cape Tribulation, Cooktown and/or the Palmer River gold fields at the start or end of the odyssey.

Travel on standard tours is in 4WDs with five to 12 passengers, accommodation is in tents and all food is supplied. Some 4WD tour companies include Oz Tours Safaris, Down Under Tours, New Look Adventures and Wild Track Adventure Safaris, the last two being among the most experienced operators with excellent reputations.

An alternative package is to fly one way, and travel overland the other, which generally takes seven to 14 days. Two companies which do these are New Look Adventures and Wild Track. Both include Thursday Island and cost from $1225 to $1675.

The MV *Queen of the Isles* operates a weekly return trip to Thursday Island leaving Cairns on Sunday evening and getting back on Saturday. Stops are made at Lizard Island, Thursday Island, Cooktown and a couple of uninhabited islands. Per-person costs, including all meals, snorkelling gear and fishing tackle range from around $600 in a six-berth cabin to $1300 in a double with bathroom. Contact Royal Tropic Cruise Line (☎ (070) 31 1844) in Cairns for bookings. It's possible to sail one way and travel overland the other – check with Oz Tours Safaris for details.

Finally, the airborne Peninsula Mail Run, claimed to be the longest in the world, takes visitors to a different area each weekday. For more details, contact Cape York Air Services (☎ (070) 53 5858).

Lakeland & Laura

The Peninsula Developmental Road turns off the Cairns to Cooktown inland road at Lakeland. Facilities here include a general store with food, petrol and diesel, a small caravan/camping park and a hotel-motel.

From Lakeland it's 734 km to Bamaga, almost at the top of the peninsula. The first stretch to Laura is not too bad, just some corrugations, potholes, grids and causeways – the creek crossings are bridged. It gets worse.

About 48 km from Lakeland is the turn-off to the **Quinkan Aboriginal rock-art galleries** at Split Rock in spectacular sandstone country. The art was executed by Aboriginal tribes which were decimated during the Palmer River gold rush of the 1870s. The four main galleries at Quinkan – the only ones open to visitors – contain some superb examples of well-preserved rock paintings dating back 13,000 to 14,000 years. You'll need a permit to visit the site – from the ranger's office in Laura or organise it beforehand in Cairns at the Department of Community Services, 6 Abbott St (☎ (070) 51 4777).

At Laura, you can also pick up a guided tour to the galleries, run by the Trezise Bush Guide Service (☎ (070) 60 3236). Some tours from Cairns also come here.

Laura has a general store with food and fuel, a place for minor mechanical repairs, a post office, a Commonwealth Bank agency, a pleasant pub, an airstrip and a museum with Aboriginal art.

The major annual event is the two-day Cape York Aboriginal Dance Festival, normally held at the beginning of July. All the Cape York Aboriginal communities assemble for this festival, which is a great opportunity for outsiders to witness living Aboriginal culture. Coral Coaches runs buses from Cairns for $60. The entrance is $30, which includes the Laura rodeo (Aboriginal riders only).

Lakefield National Park

The main turn-off to Lakefield National Park is just past Laura and it's only about a 45-minute drive from Laura into the park. Conventional vehicles can get as far as the ranger station at New Laura, and possibly well into the northern section of the park during the dry season.

Lakefield is the second-largest national

Cape York Peninsula

0   50   100 km

park in Queensland and the most accessible of those on the Cape York Peninsula. It's best known for its wetlands and associated wildlife. The park's extensive river system drains into Princess Charlotte Bay on its northern perimeter. This is the only national park on the peninsula where fishing is permitted, and a canoe is a good way to investigate the park. Watch out for the crocs! You can bush camp at a number of sites – get permits from the rangers at New Laura (PMB 79, Cairns) or Lakefield, further north in the park.

The wide sweep of Princess Charlotte Bay, which includes the coastal section of Lakefield National Park, is the site of some of Australia's biggest rock-art galleries. Unfortunately, this stretch of coast is extremely hard to reach except from the sea.

Laura to Archer River Roadhouse

It's 135 km from Laura to **Musgrave** with its historic fortress telegraph station, built in 1887. Before Musgrave, there's the Hann River crossing and a roadhouse at the 75-km mark. Musgrave itself has petrol, diesel, food, beer, an STD phone, cafe and an airstrip.

Coen, 245 km north of Laura, is virtually the capital of the peninsula with a pub, a general store, a hospital, school and police station. You can get mechanical repairs done here. Coen has an airstrip and a racecourse where picnic races are held each August. The whole peninsula closes down for this event, even the mining town of Weipa. There are a few free camping sites both in and around town.

Apart from a few telegraph stations, the only habitation on the 402-km stretch from Coen to Bamaga is the **Archer River Roadhouse**, 65 km north of Coen. This is the final stop for regular petrol and mechanical repairs; you can also camp and get a hot shower and buy your last supplies before Bamaga.

Northern National Parks

Four national parks can be reached from the main track north of Coen. To stay at any of them, you must be totally self-sufficient. Only a few km north of Coen, before Archer River Roadhouse, you can turn west to **Rokeby/Croll Creek National Park** and **Archer Bend National Park** – the ranger station is in Rokeby, about 45 km off the main track. Access is for 4WD only.

These little-visited parks cover a large area including the McIlwraith Range in Rokeby and, in the west of very remote Archer Bend, the junction of the Coen and Archer rivers. There are no facilities but bush camping is permitted at a number of river sites in Rokeby. These parks are best explored by bushwalkers.

Around 21 km north of the Archer River Roadhouse is the turn-off to Portland Roads, the Lockhart River Aboriginal community and **Iron Range National Park**. The 150-km road into the tiny coastal settlement of Portland Roads passes through the national park. While still pretty rough, this track has been improved. If you visit the national park, register with the ranger on arrival. It has the rugged hills of the Janet and Tozer ranges, beautiful coastal scenery and Australia's largest area of lowland rainforest, plus some animals which are also found in New Guinea but no further south in Australia. Bush camping is permitted.

The fourth of the northern national parks is the **Jardine**.

Weipa (population 2500)

Weipa is 135 km from the main track. The southern turn-off to it is about 20 km north of the Iron Range turn-off, and this road has recently been upgraded – you can cover the distance in just a couple of hours. You can also get to Weipa from Batavia Downs, which is a little further up the main track and has a 19th-century homestead. The two approaches converge about halfway along.

Weipa is a modern mining town which works the world's largest deposits of bauxite (the ore from which aluminium is processed). The mining company, Comalco, runs regular tours of its operations from May to December. The town has a wide range of facilities including a motel, a hotel and a camp ground.

In the vicinity, there's interesting country to explore, good fishing and some pleasant camping sites. There is talk of an international space launch station being established at Port Musgrave, north of Weipa.

North to the Jardine

Back on the main track, after Batavia Downs there are almost 200 km of rough road and numerous river crossings (the Wenlock and the Dulhunty being the two major ones) before you reach the Jardine River ferry crossing. Between the Wenlock River and the Jardine ferry there are two possible routes: the more direct but rougher old route (116 km), and the more circuitous but quicker new route (159 km), which branches off the old route about one km past the South Alice Creek crossing.

If you intend camping further north, you'll need to get a permit from the ranger at **Heathlands**, about 80 km north of the Wenlock, and about 12 km from both the old and new roads.

The **Jardine River National Park** stretches east to the coast from the main track. The Jardine River spills more fresh water into the sea than any other river in Australia. It's wild impenetrable country. There's a good camping spot on the banks of the Jardine at the crossing, and permits must be obtained from the ranger at Heathlands.

The Top

The first settlement north of the Jardine River, **Bamaga** is a mainly Torres Strait Islander community. There's a motel (advance bookings required) and camping grounds at nearby Seisa and Cowral Creek. The town has postal facilities, a hospital, a Commonwealth Bank agency, STD phones, a supermarket and some petrol (closed Saturday afternoon and Sunday). It's only about 40 km from Bamaga to the very northern tip. Daily ferries run between Bamaga and Thursday Island.

Beyond Bamaga, off the Cape York track

but only about 11 km south-east of the cape, is **Somerset** which was established in 1863 as a haven for shipwrecked sailors and a signal to the rest of the world that this was British territory. It was hoped at one time that it might become a major trading centre, a sort of Singapore of north Queensland, but it was closed in 1879 when its functions were moved to Thursday Island, which was also thought more suitable for a pearling industry. The story of Somerset is inextricably linked with the adventurous Jardine family, one of whom stayed on after Somerset was officially closed to run his own cattle stations, coconut plantation and pearling business. He married a Samoan princess and entertained passing British dignitaries. He and his wife are buried at Somerset. Sadly, apart from a few of Jardine's coconut trees, there's nothing much left at Somerset now, but the fishing is good and there are lovely views.

At **Cape York** itself are two resorts. *Cape York Wilderness Lodge* (☎ (070) 69 1444), 400 metres from the Tip, is a luxury resort costing $165-plus per night. It also has a small camping ground with a kiosk, toilets and showers. *Punsand Bay Private Reserve* provides more modest accommodation on the western side of the cape. There are permanent tents or you can pitch your own in the camping ground. You can book in Cairns at the Going Places tour agency. A ferry runs from Punsand Bay to Thursday Island daily at 7.30 am.

Torres Strait Islands (population 5000)

The Torres Strait Islands have been a part of Queensland since 1879, the best known of them being Thursday Island. The 70 other islands are sprinkled from Cape York in the south almost to New Guinea in the north but only 17 of them are inhabited, and all but three are set aside for islanders. Most visitors to Cape York take a look at Thursday Island or the nearby islands.

Torres Strait Islanders came from Melanesia and Polynesia about 2000 years ago, bringing with them a more material culture than that of the mainland Aborigines. The strait saw violence from early days right through to WW II, including head-hunters, marauding pirates, greedy men in pursuit of pearls, 'blackbirders' and Japanese bombs. Christianity, replacing warlike islander cults, has done well this century. **Possession Island**, an uninhabited national park close to Cape York, was where Captain Cook 'claimed' all the east coast of Australia for England in 1770.

The islands' economy is based on fishing but it's hard to compete with the technology used by outfits on Australia's east coast. There is high islander unemployment and economic difficulties have led to cries for compensation, even independence. In the past, the islanders have not been allowed to share in managing the area's few resources nor have they been provided with adequate education. The cries for secession will probably bring more autonomy, but not independence.

Thursday Island is hilly, just over three sq km in area and 39 km off Cape York. At one time, it was a major pearling centre and the pearlers' cemeteries tell the hard tale of what a dangerous occupation it was. Some pearls are still produced here from seeded 'culture farms' which don't offer much employment to the locals. The island has also lost its importance as a halt for vessels but it's still a popular pause for passing yachties.

Thursday Island is an attractive, easy-going place and its main appeal is its cultural mix – Asians, Europeans and Pacific Islanders have all contributed to its history.

Places to Stay & Eat Accommodation and food are available in Thursday Island's four hotels and one motel. The airport is on nearby Horn Island and a ferry links the two islands. There's a camping ground near the wharf on Horn Island, but none on Thursday Island. You can hire boats for fishing trips and cruises. You might be able to find accommodation on other islands by asking around.

Getting There & Around Sunbird Airlines regularly flies to most of the inhabited islands. At least two ferry services operate from Bamaga and Punsand Bay to Thursday Island, both taking roughly an hour one-way and costing about $50 return.

GULF OF CARPENTARIA

North of Mt Isa and Cloncurry, the Gulf is a sparsely populated region cut by a great number of rivers. During the Wet, the dirt roads turn to mud and even the surfaced roads can be flooded, so June to September is the safest time to visit this area.

Although Burke and Wills were the first Europeans to pass through the Gulf Country (see the History section of the Facts about the Country chapter), the coast of the Gulf of Carpentaria had been charted by Dutch explorers even before Captain Cook's visit to Australia. The actual coastline of the Gulf is mainly mangrove swamps which is why there is little habitation there.

Two of the settlements in the region, Burketown and Normanton, were founded in the 1860s, before better known places on the Pacific coast like Cairns and Cooktown came into existence. Europeans settled the area as sheep and cattle country, also in the hope of providing a western port for produce from further east and south in Queensland.

Today the Gulf Country is mainly cattle country. It's a remote, hot, tough region with excellent fishing and a large crocodile population. Mornington Island, in the Gulf itself 120 km north of Burketown, is an Aboriginal community.

The main road into the Gulf region is from Cloncurry to Normanton (378 km, surfaced all the way) with a turn-off to Burketown at the Burke & Wills Roadhouse, which is also the junction of the surfaced road from Julia Creek. Between Cloncurry and Normanton, the flat plain is interrupted by a solitary hill beside the road – Bang Bang Jump-up. There's also an unpaved 332-km road from Camooweal, west of Mt Isa, to Burketown, with a turn-off at the Gregory Downs supply stop to **Lawn Hill National Park**. If you're driving any of these roads, make sure to ask about fuel stops and carry water with you.

For tourist information, advice on road conditions and general inquiries, contact the

Gulf Local Authorities Development Association, 91 Digger St, Cairns (☎ (070) 51 1420).

Activities

Fishing There are a number of places set up especially to cater for people who have become addicted to barramundi fishing, and other cheaper places where the fishing is good. These include: *Sweers Island Resort* (☎ (077) 43 7887, ask for Sweers Island Resort), which charges $110 per person per day; *Sweers Island Houseboats* (☎ (077) 43 9690), $80; *Birri Fishing Resort* (☎ (077) 17 2031), Mornington Island, which costs $195 per day including all tackle and boat hire; and *Hells Gate Roadhouse* (☎ (077) 43 7887, ask for Hells Gate), 50 km east of the Northern Territory border, which has B&B for $25.

Savannah Guides The Savannah Guides (☎ (070) 51 4658 in Cairns) are a network of professionals who staff guide posts at strategic locations throughout the Gulf. They are people with good local knowledge, and have access to points of interest, many of which are on private property and would be difficult to visit unaccompanied. For more information, phone the guides or write to PO Box 2291, Cairns.

Getting There & Away

Air Flight West Airlines (☎ (077) 43 9333) flies a few times a week between Mt Isa and Cairns ($244) with stops at various places in the Gulf Country, including Normanton ($211), Karumba ($213), Julia Creek ($92), Burketown ($183), and Mornington Island ($207).

Bus Campbell's Coaches (☎ (077) 43 2006) has a weekly bus service between Mt Isa, Normanton and Karumba. Karumba Coachline (☎ (070) 51 8311), operated by Cairns Tours Service, has a twice-weekly service from Cairns to Karumba ($105) via Georgetown ($55) and Normanton ($95).

Train From the Atherton Tableland, the Gulf Developmental Road runs to Normanton through Georgetown and Croydon. The last stretch into Normanton on this route can be made on the famous Gulflander train which runs just once weekly in each direction between Croydon and Normanton. The 151-km trip, in a very vintage-looking train, is made from Croydon on Thursday and from Normanton on Wednesday (four hours, $21). It's also possible to travel by train from Cairns to Forsayth, about 50 km south of Georgetown.

Burketown (population 235)

This tiny town is probably best known for its isolation. In the centre of a cattle-raising area, Burketown is 25 km south of the Gulf and can be reached by road from Cloncurry, Julia Creek or Camooweal. You've got at least 150 km of unpaved road to cover to reach Burketown, whichever direction you come from. Some of Nevil Shute's famous novel *A Town Like Alice* is set here.

Burketown is an excellent place for bird watching, and is also one of the places to view the phenomenon known as 'Morning Glory' – weird tubular cloud formations extending the full length of the horizon which roll out of the Gulf in the early morning, often in lines of three or four. This only happens from September to November.

The Gregory Downs Hotel, 117 km south of town, is the focal point of the annual North-West Canoe Race in May; the swimming hole in Gregory Downs is superb.

The town has a caravan park (no on-site vans) or you can get rooms in the *Albert Hotel* (☎ (077) 45 5104) for $50/70. *Escott Lodge* (☎ (077) 45 5108) 17 km west of Burketown, has singles/doubles for $45/75, and a camping ground; meals are available.

Normanton (population 1100)

Normanton was first set up as a port for the Cloncurry copper fields but then became Croydon's gold-rush port, its population peaking at 3000 in 1891. The huge railway station on the edge of town, a monument to the gold era, still functions twice a week. The centre of town life today is the Albion Hotel, especially on Friday night when people crowd in from the surrounding area.

You can get rooms in the *Albion Hotel* (☎ (077) 45 1218) for $45/55, or there's a motel, and a caravan park with on-site vans.

Karumba (population 550)

Karumba, 69 km from Normanton by paved road and actually on the Gulf at the mangrove-fringed mouth of the **Norman River**, is a prawn, barramundi and crab-fishing centre. It's possible to charter boats for fishing trips from here, and there's a regular vehicle barge between Karumba and Weipa.

The town has quite an interesting history. At one time it was a refuelling station for the flying boats which used to connect Sydney and the UK. The RAAF has also had Catalina flying boats based here.

The *Karumba Lodge Hotel-Motel* (☎ (077) 45 9143) charges $55/66 for singles/doubles, and the *Gulf Country Caravan Park* (☎ (077) 45 9148) has on-site cabins.

Croydon (population 220)

Connected to Normanton by the curious-looking Gulflander train, this old gold-mining town was once the biggest in the Gulf and has many interesting buildings. It's reckoned there were once 50,000 gold mines in the area and reminders of them are scattered all around the country. Such was the prosperity of the town that it had its own aerated water factory, gas street lamps, a foundry and coach builders.

The **Courthouse** and **Mining Warden's Office** have their original furnishings, while the **Club Hotel** also dates back to the mining days. There's a bit of a resurgence of gold mining in the area again today, with new technology making it feasible to rework the old diggings.

The Croydon General Store has a small museum, and there's an open-air display of old mining and steam equipment.

For accommodation, the town has the *Club Hotel* (☎ (077) 45 6184) at $25/35, meals are available and it's possible to camp.

The *Gulf Gate Roadhouse* (☎ (077) 45 6169) has air-con motel units.

Other Gulf Towns

There are accommodation possibilities in other Gulf towns: including Georgetown; Mt Surprise; Tallaroo Station (☎ (070) 62 3021), 50 km west of Georgetown; Dorunda Station (☎ (070) 53 4500), 200 km north-east of Normanton; Forsayth; Einasleigh; and the *Heartbreak Hotel* (☎ (089) 75 9928) at Cape Crawford, 110 km south-west of Borroloola at the junction of the Carpentaria and Tableland highways (actually in the Northern Territory).

At Lawn Hill National Park, on the road between Camooweal and Burketown, there are camp sites for $7.50; contact the national parks office in Mt Isa (☎ (070) 43 2055) for permits, or write to the Ranger, PMB 12, MS 1463, Mt Isa. The *Burke & Wills Roadhouse* (☎ 011, ask for Gulf public telephone 47811L2), on the Cloncurry to Normanton road, has four air-con rooms and a few camping sites.

Outback

Heading west from the Queensland coast, it's not long after crossing the Great Dividing Range that the land starts to become drier, and the towns smaller and further apart.

The area, although sparsely settled, is well serviced by major roads – the Flinders Highway connects northern Queensland with the Northern Territory, meeting the Barkly Highway at the mining town of Mt Isa; while the Landsborough and Mitchell highways run from the New South Wales border south of Cunnamulla right up to Mt Isa. Longreach, with its Stockman's Hall of Fame, is a major destination for trips through outback Queensland.

Once off these major arteries, however, road conditions deteriorate rapidly, services are virtually nonexistent and you need to be fully self-sufficient, carrying spare parts, fuel and water. With the correct preparation, it's possible to make the great outback journeys down the tracks which connect Queensland with South Australia – the Strzelecki and Birdsville tracks.

CLONCURRY (population 2000)

The centre for a copper boom in the last century, Cloncurry was the largest copper producer in the British empire in 1916. Today it's a pastoral centre and base for the Royal Flying Doctor Service.

Cloncurry's museum, just off the highway on the east side of town, is partly housed in buildings transported from Mary Kathleen. The collection includes relics of the Burke & Wills expedition and a big collection of local rocks and minerals. You can see steam engines outside for free. The John Flynn Place Museum in Daintree St houses exhibits on mining, the Flying Doctor Service and the School of the Air.

The cheapest motel in Cloncurry is the *Wagon Wheel Motel* (☎ (077) 42 1866) at 54 Ramsay St with singles/doubles at $32/45. You can camp in the *Cloncurry Caravan Park* opposite the museum or take an on-site van.

The Burke Developmental Road, north from Cloncurry, is paved all the way to Normanton (375 km) and Karumba (449 km) near the Gulf of Carpentaria. Burketown is 443 km from Cloncurry.

CLONCURRY TO MT ISA

This 124-km stretch of the Flinders Highway has a number of interesting stops. At **Corella River**, 41 km west of Cloncurry, there's a memorial cairn to the Burke & Wills expedition, which passed here in 1861. Ten km beyond this is the site of **Mary Kathleen**, a uranium mining town from the 1950s to 1982. It has been completely demolished.

The turning to **Lake Julius**, Mt Isa's reserve water supply, is 36 km beyond Mary Kathleen. There's a camp ground at the lake and **Battle Mountain**, north of the Lake Julius dam wall, was the scene of the last stand of the Kalkadoon people, a rare pitched battle between Aborigines and Europeans in 1884.

MT ISA (population 25,000)

The mining town of Mt Isa owes its existence to an immensely rich copper, silver, lead and zinc mine, and the skyline is dominated by the massive 270-metre-high exhaust stack from the lead smelter. 'The Isa', as the town is known locally, also lays claim to being the largest city in the world – it covers an area of 41,255 sq km!

It's a rough and ready though prosperous town, and the job opportunities here have attracted people from about 60 different ethnic groups. There's plenty of low-cost accommodation for travellers stopping over here, and you can tour the mine.

The first Mt Isa deposits were discovered in 1923 by a prospector called John Campbell Miles who gave Mt Isa its name – a corruption of Mt Ida, a gold field in Western Australia. Since the ore deposits were large and low grade, working them required the sort of investment only a company could make. Mt Isa Mines was founded in 1924 but it was during and after WW II that Mt Isa really took off and today it's the Western world's biggest silver and lead producer. Virtually the whole town is run by Mt Isa Mines, and the ore is railed 900 km to Townsville on the coast.

Orientation & Information

The town centre, a fairly compact area, is immediately east of the Leichhardt River which separates it from the mining area. Greyhound/Pioneer buses stop right in the centre on Miles St, while McCafferty's use the Campbell's Coaches depot on Pamela St.

There's a tourist office (☎ (077) 43 7966) on Marian St between Corbould and Mullan Sts. It's open Monday to Friday from 8 am to 5 pm, plus Saturdays and Sundays (between April and September) from 8.30 am to 1.30 pm.

The Crusade Bookshop, at 11 Simpson St, is the best between Townsville and Darwin.

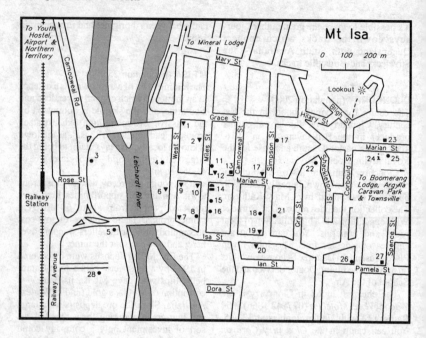

The Mine

The mine is the major attraction and there are two tours available. Make bookings for both at the tourist office.

The three-hour underground tour, on which you don a hard hat and miner's suit, takes you down into some of the 4600 km of tunnels. Since only nine people are allowed on each tour, it's advisable to book as far ahead as possible by phoning the tourist office. Tours leave the tourist office at 8 and 11.45 am Monday to Friday and cost $20.

The two-hour surface tours (by bus) leave twice a day Monday to Friday year-round, and once on Saturday and Sunday mornings from April to September. The bus picks up from both the tourist office and the Greyhound/Pioneer terminal on request and costs $10. It's well worth the money, especially as the bus takes you right through the major workshops and mine site, and the price includes a visit to the visitors centre (see below).

The mine company also runs a mining display and visitors centre on Church St near the town centre. It's open daily from 9 am to noon and from 1 to 4 pm, and from 10 am to 2 pm Saturday and Sunday. The $2 entry fee (students $1) includes a film.

Other Attractions

Also interesting is the **Frank Aston Museum**, a part underground complex on a hill close to the town centre at the corner of Shackleton and Marian Sts. This rambling place has a very diverse collection ranging from old mining gear to ageing flying doctor radios, and displays on the Lardil Aborigines of Mornington Island in the Gulf of Carpentaria and the Kalkadoon people from the Mt Isa area. It's open daily from 10 am to 3 pm.

You can visit the **Royal Flying Doctor Service** base at the corner of Grace St and Camooweal Rd, Monday to Saturday from 10 am to 4 pm. The $2.50 admission includes

■ PLACES TO STAY

13 Verona Motel & Restaurant
23 Budget Accommodation
27 Travellers Haven

▼ PLACES TO EAT

1 Western Steakhouse
2 Bazza's Cafe
6 Clicks Cafe
7 Argent Hotel
9 Boyd Hotel
10 Mt Isa Hotel
12 Flamenco Cafe & Good Frenz
   Coffee Shop
17 Kentucky Fried Chicken
19 Red Lantern Chinese Restaurant
20 The Tavern

OTHER

3 School of the Air & Royal Flying
  Doctor Service
4 Civic Centre
5 Swimming Pool
8 Australian Airlines
11 Greyhound/Pioneer Bus Terminal
14 Post Office
15 Flight West Airlines
16 Ansett Airlines
18 Crusade Bookshop
21 Curly Dann's Outdoor World
22 Frank Aston Museum
24 Tourist Office
25 Kalkadoon Tribal Centre
26 Campbell's Coaches
   & McCafferty's Terminal
28 Mining Display & Visitors Centre

a film. Next door the **School of the Air**, which brings education by radio to children in remote places, is open Monday to Friday from 10 am to noon (admission $1).

The National-Trust-classified **Tent House**, at 16 Fourth Ave, is one of the last surviving houses typical of the early days of Mt Isa. It is open weekdays from 9 am to 3 pm.

The **Kalkadoon Tribal Centre & Culture-Keeping Place**, on Marian St next to the tourist office, is open most weekdays (admission $1). It's partly a museum and you can see some artefacts.

Mt Isa has a big, clean swimming pool on Isa St next to the tennis courts, and the small entrance fee includes use of showers.

Mt Isa's August rodeo is the biggest in Australia.

Organised Tours

Outback Tracks runs tours to isolated rock-art sites. These leave daily from the tourist office, which you can contact for details.

In the winter season, Copper City Tours (☎ (077) 43 7966) offers full-day outback trips which visit Aboriginal rock paintings, an old copper mine and Mary Kathleen; and three-day camping trips to Lawn Hill gorge

and Riversleigh, the site of 15-million-year-old fossils which have revealed much about Australia's prehistoric animals.

Places to Stay

Hostels About half a km from the town centre, the *Travellers Haven* (☎ (077) 43 0313), on the corner of Spence and Pamela Sts, is a fully air-con place with bunk beds from $11, and singles/doubles from $18/26.

Mt Isa's 28-bed *Youth Hostel* (☎ (077) 43 5557), in the shadow of the mines at Wellington Park Rd, about a two-km walk from the town centre, is pretty basic. Although it's open all day and only charges $8 a night, it's hard to think of any other reason for walking all this way.

Motels & Guesthouses *Budget Accommodation* (☎ (077) 43 4004), opposite the tourist office at 28 Marian St, has a few air-con motel-type rooms, with TV and tea/coffee-making facilities, for $15 per person, including breakfast. This place is more for permanent residents, but overnighters are made welcome if there's room.

The *Welcome Inn* (☎ (077) 43 2241), at 118 Camooweal St, has air-con singles/doubles at $20/27, or shared accommodation for $14. Bathrooms and toilets are communal. There's no guest kitchen but rooms have a fridge, and breakfast is available. Camooweal St runs through the town centre a block east of Miles St – don't confuse it with Camooweal Rd.

Boomerang Lodge (☎ (077) 43 2019) is outside the centre, hidden away at 11 Boyd Parade. Air-con doubles with bathroom are $40, but the rooms will also take three or four people at $46. There's a communal kitchen, a TV lounge and a swimming pool.

Other motels include the *Inland Oasis Motel* (☎ (077) 43 3433) at 195 Barkly Highway, with room-only singles/doubles at $45/53, and the *Copper City Motel* (☎ (077) 43 2033), at 105 Butler St, which costs $43/48 for a room only.

Camping Mt Isa has a string of caravan/ camping parks, some along the Barkly Highway going east, others in the north of town and all about two km from the centre. Tent sites cost $5 per person and on-site vans $27 a double.

Two caravan parks with nice big swimming pools are the *Mt Isa Caravan Park* (☎ (077) 43 3252) and the *Argylla Caravan Park* (☎ (077) 43 4733) which is the first one you reach coming from the east. Probably the best spot, however is four km out of town going west, at *Moondarra Caravan Park* (☎ (077) 43 9780).

Places to Eat
The *Tavern*, on Isa St, has excellent counter meals at lunch times and evenings. Cheap 'workers' specials' for $3 are available in the public bar, and more expensive fare in its bistro. *Boydie's Fair Dinkum Steakhouse* (!) at the Boyd Hotel, serves good grills from $5 to $10.

There are also good but slightly more expensive bistro meals in the *Silver Bar* of the Argent Hotel on Isa St near the corner of West St.

There are a number of centrally located pizzerias, cafes and snack bars, including *Clicks* on West St, which offers a variety of burgers, and *Bazza's* on Miles St. *Flamenco*, on Marian St near the corner of Miles St, has burgers, sandwiches and 20 flavours of ice cream.

For a substantial feed, the *Western Steakhouse*, on the corner of West and Grace Sts, is a glossy, American-style place where, as the name suggests, the emphasis is on meat. In the south of town, the *Irish Club* (☎ (077) 43 2577) on the corner of Buckley and Nineteenth Aves reportedly serves good-value meals.

If you've just stepped off an early morning bus, the *Mt Isa Hotel*, on the corner of Marian and Miles Sts, serves good breakfasts from 7 am, but there's a minimum charge of $4.70 per person.

Entertainment
There are bands in the Boyd Hotel on weekend evenings. Also popular is the Cave nightclub in the Mt Isa Hotel, the Irish Club (live rock & roll Friday and Saturday nights, disco on Saturday) and the Buffalo Club on Grace St.

Getting There & Away
Air Ansett and Ansett NT (☎ (077) 44 1767), Australian (☎ (077) 44 1222) and Flight West Airlines (☎ (077) 43 9333) are all on Miles St, half a block south of Marian St.

Ansett and Australian Airlines both have nonstop flights two to four times weekly from Alice Springs at $218 ($175 stand-by), Brisbane $370 ($296), Cairns $244 ($195) and Darwin $328 ($262). Flight West links Mt Isa with Cairns ($244), Townsville ($239), Normanton ($211), Karumba ($213) and various places along the Flinders Highway every day. From Mt Isa it also flies three times weekly to Brisbane ($370), via Longreach ($188) and Winton ($152).

Bus Pioneer (☎ (077) 43 4888) and Greyhound (☎ (077) 43 6655) are both at 24 Miles St in Mt Isa, near the corner of Marian St. McCafferty's operates from the Campbell's Coaches terminal (☎ (077) 43 2006) at the corner of Pamela and Stanley Sts.

Greyhound, Pioneer, and McCafferty's all run daily between Townsville and Three

Ways, passing through Mt Isa. Townsville to Mt Isa takes 11 hours ($81), while on to Three Ways or Tennant Creek takes another six or seven hours ($34). All the companies have connections at Three Ways or Tennant Creek for Alice Springs ($225) and Darwin ($259).

Greyhound and McCafferty's operate daily to Brisbane (about 24 hours) by the inland route through Winton ($50) and Longreach ($56).

Campbell's Coaches goes to Normanton ($64) and Karumba ($70) once a week. Greyhound Getaway Pass holders can use this service on payment of a supplement.

Train The air-con Inlander operates twice weekly between Townsville and Mt Isa, via Charters Towers, Hughenden and Cloncurry. The full journey takes about 18 hours and costs $124.20 in 1st class, $82.70 in economy.

MT ISA TO THREE WAYS

There's nothing much for the whole 650 km to the Three Ways junction in the Northern Territory. Camooweal is 188 km from Mt Isa, just before the Queensland-Northern Territory border and it's the only place of any size at all. West of Camooweal, the next petrol station (and the most expensive petrol anywhere between Townsville and Darwin) is 270 km along at *Barkly Homestead* (☎ (077) 64 4549). You can camp here for $3 per person. Motel rooms are $50/57.

Lawn Hill National Park

Amid arid country 400 km from Mt Isa and 100 km west of Gregory Downs on the Camooweal to Burketown road, this is an oasis of gorges, creeks, ponds and tropical vegetation that the Aborigines have enjoyed for perhaps 30,000 years. Their paintings and old camping sites abound. Two rock-art sites have been made accessible to visitors. There are freshwater crocodiles – the inoffensive variety – in the creek. Also in the park are extensive and virtually unexplored limestone formations.

Getting there is the problem – it's a beautiful, pristine place that's miles from anywhere or anybody. The last 300 km or so from Mt Isa – after you leave the Barkly Highway – are unsealed and often impassable after rain. Four-wheel-drive vehicles are recommended, though not always necessary in the dry season. There's a camping ground with showers and toilets in the park, and 17 km of walking tracks. The nearest place to buy petrol is at Gregory Downs. There's accommodation at the *Gregory Downs Hotel* and you can camp beside the Gregory River.

MT ISA TO LONGREACH

Fourteen km east of Cloncurry, the narrow Landsborough Highway turns off south-east to McKinlay (91 km), Kynuna (165 km), Winton (328 km) and Longreach (501 km).

McKinlay is a tiny settlement which would probably have been doomed to eternal insignificance were it not for the fact this is the location of the Walkabout Creek Hotel, which featured in the amazingly successful movie *Crocodile Dundee*. Greyhound buses between Mt Isa and Brisbane via Longreach make a refreshment stop here when they come through. The *Blue Heeler* at **Kynuna** is another renowned old outback pub, and even has its own surf life saving club!

Winton (population 1300)

Winton is a sheep-raising centre and also the railhead from which cattle are transported after being brought from the Channel Country by road train. The road north to Cloncurry is fully paved, but still gets washed out during a really bad wet season.

Around Winton

At **Combo Waterhole** on Dagworth Station, between Winton and Kynuna, Australia's most famous poet/songwriter, Banjo Paterson, is said to have written *Waltzing Matilda*, way back in 1895. Later, Qantas was founded at Winton in 1920. These two diverse influences are united in Winton's Qantilda pioneer museum!

The country around Winton is rough and rugged, with much wildlife, notably brolgas.

There are also Aboriginal sites with paintings, carvings and artefacts.

At **Lark Quarry Environmental Park**, 120 km south-west of Winton, dinosaur footprints 100 million years old have been perfectly preserved in limestone. It takes around two hours to drive from Winton to Lark Quarry in a conventional vehicle but the dirt road is impassable in wet weather. You can get directions at the Winton Shire Council offices (☎ (076) 57 1188)) at 78 Vindex St. There's no water at the site or along the road from Winton, so take your own.

LONGREACH (population 3000)

This prosperous outback town was the home of Qantas earlier this century, but these days is just as famous for the Australian Stockman's Hall of Fame & Outback Heritage Centre, one of the biggest attractions in outback Queensland.

Longreach's human population is vastly outnumbered by the sheep population which is over a million; there are a fair few cattle too.

It was here that the Queensland & Northern Territory Aerial Service, better known as Qantas, was based in its early days in the 1920s. The original Qantas hangar, which still stands at Longreach Airport (almost opposite the Hall of Fame), was also the first aircraft 'factory' in Australia – six DH-50 biplanes were assembled here in 1926. There are plans to build an aviation museum alongside the original hangar, but in the meantime there's a 'preview' display housed in the Longreach tourist office, itself a replica of the first Qantas booking office. It's on the corner of Duck and Eagle Sts, and is open daily.

Longreach was also the starting point for one of Queensland's most colourful early crimes when, in 1870, a bushranger sporting the title 'Captain Starlight' stole 1000 head of cattle and trotted them 2400 km south to South Australia where he sold them. He then made his way back to Queensland, where he was arrested and, unbelievably, acquitted.

Stockman's Hall of Fame

The centre is housed in a beautifully conceived building, two km east of town along the road to Barcaldine. The excellent displays are divided into periods from the first White settlement through to today; and these deal with all aspects of the pioneering pastoral days. Although the crucial roles played by the pioneer women, Aboriginal stockmen and Aboriginal women are poorly represented, there are plans to remedy this when funds become available.

It's well worth visiting the Hall of Fame, as it gives a fascinating insight into this side of the European development of Australia. Admission is $14 ($10 concession), and the centre is open daily from 9 am to 5 pm. Allow yourself half a day to take it all in. Greyhound operate a twice-daily service from the terminal on Eagle St (8.45 am and 1 pm, returning at 1.15 and 5 pm), for $3; free if you have an Aussie Pass. Otherwise it's a half-hour walk.

Organised Tours

There is a surprising number of tours available in Longreach. Transwest Tours (☎ 008 077 002, toll-free), at 113 Eagle St, does half-day town tours, while Yellowbelly Express (book at Greyhound) do popular river trips on the nearby Norman River. Outback Aussie Tours (☎ 008 016 200, toll-free), which operate from the youth hostel, also do some interesting boat and bus trips.

Quite a few of the sheep stations in the area have realised that tourism can bring in a bit of money when times are tough in the wool industry, and visiting these stations can be an interesting activity. Stations currently open include: Toobrack (☎ (076) 58 9158), 68 km south; Whitehill (☎ (076) 58 2175), 38 km south-west; Oakley (☎ Transwest); Longway (☎ (076) 58 2191), 17 km north; Lorraine (☎ (076) 57 1693), between Longreach and Winton; and Avington (☎ (076) 57 5952), 75 km west of Blackall. Some of these places are only open for day trips while others offer accommodation and a range of activities. Avington, for example, has beds in its shearers' quarters for $15 as well as rooms in its homestead for $40/50, including B&B and dinner. Activities include horse-riding, trail-bike riding, canoeing and barge cruises. For any visit to a sheep station you'll need to ring before you arrive.

Longreach Air Charters (☎ (076) 58 9156) run day trips to Birdsville.

Places to Stay & Eat

The *Longreach Swaggies Backpackers* (☎ (076) 58 2777) is on the corner of Womproo and Thrush Sts, about one km east of the centre. It's quite well set up, with a bed in a four-bed dorm costing $11 or $13. There are cooking facilities and a TV lounge. Closer to the centre is the *Longreach Youth Hostel* (☎ (076) 58 1350) at 120 Galah St, two blocks south of the railway station. It's quite OK and charges $12 per night for a dorm bed, and there are family rooms available.

If neither of these suit, there's a choice of at least four pubs on Eagle St (the *Welcome Home* has rooms for $20/26), as well as many motels and a caravan park.

The *Bush Verandah* is a good little restaurant on Eagle St, while *Smithy's* is a licensed bistro on the road out towards the Hall of Fame. For breakfast or a snack, there's the *Stockman's Hall of Food* on Eagle St.

Getting There & Away

Flight West have flights three times a week which connect Longreach with Mt Isa ($188), Winton ($80) and Brisbane ($286).

Greyhound (☎ (076) 58 1776) and McCafferty's (☎ (076) 58 1155) both have daily services to Mt Isa (7½ hours, $56), and Brisbane (17 hours, $85). McCafferty's also operate three times a week to Rockhampton (nine hours, $51).

The twice-weekly Midlander train connects Longreach with Rockhampton (14 hours, $59.10).

LONGREACH TO CHARLEVILLE
Barcaldine (population 1500)
Barcaldine, between Emerald and Longreach, is another sheep and cattle centre. It was the scene of a major step towards the 1902 formation of the Australian

Labor Party when, in 1891, striking shearers met under a ghost gum tree, before marching to Clermont to continue their struggle. At the same time dock workers in Sydney rioted, refusing to handle bales of wool sheared by non-union labour.

The tree is now called the Tree of Knowledge, and still stands in the centre of town. Following the Labor Party centenary celebration in Barcaldine in 1991, a heritage centre is now being built, and this should be quite impressive when complete. In the meantime, there's a temporary display.

South of Barcaldine is Blackall, supposedly the site of the famous Black Stump. Not far from here is **Black's Palace**, an Aboriginal site with burial caves and impressive rock paintings. It's on private property but can be visited with the permission of the warden (☎ (076) 57 4455, 57 4663).

Charleville (population 3523)
About 800 km from the coast, Charleville is the end of the Warrego Highway and the centre of another huge cattle and sheep-raising region. This was an important centre for early explorers and something of an oasis in the outback, being on the Warrego River. There are various reminders around the town of the early explorers, and a historical museum in the 1880 Queensland National Bank building on Albert St.

THE CHANNEL COUNTRY
The remote and sparsely populated southwest corner of Queensland, bordering the Northern Territory, South Australia and New South Wales, takes its name from the myriad channels which crisscross the area. In this inhospitable region it hardly ever rains, but water from the summer monsoon further north pours into the Channel Country along the Georgina, Hamilton and Diamantina rivers and Cooper's Creek. Flooding towards the great depression of Lake Eyre in South Australia, the mass of water arrives on this huge plain, eventually drying up in water holes or salt pans.

Only on rare occasions (the early '70s and

1989 during this century) does the vast amount of water actually reach Lake Eyre and fill it. For a short period after each wet season, however, the Channel Country does become fertile, and cattle are grazed here.

Getting There & Around

Some roads from the east and north to the fringes of the Channel Country are paved, but during the October to May wet season even these can be cut – and the dirt roads become quagmires. In addition, the summer heat is unbearable so a visit is best made in the cooler winter from May to September. Visiting this area requires a sturdy vehicle (4WD if you want to get off the beaten track) and some experience of outback driving. Anywhere west of Cunnamulla or Quilpie, always carry plenty of petrol and drinking water and notify the police, so that if you don't turn up at the next town, the necessary steps can be taken.

You can reach Quilpie on the Westlander train from Brisbane twice a week. Flight West Airlines (☎ (07) 229 1177 in Brisbane) flies once weekly from Brisbane to Birdsville and back, via Charleville, Quilpie and Windorah. Augusta Airways flies from Port Augusta in South Australia to Birdsville, Bedourie and Boulia on Saturdays, and back on Sundays.

Diamantina Developmental Road

The main road through the Channel Country is the Diamantina Developmental Road that runs south from Mt Isa through Boulia to Bedourie and then turns east through Windorah and Quilpie to Charleville. In all, it's a long and lonely 1340 km, a little over half of which is surfaced.

Boulia is the 'capital' of the Channel Country; Burke and Wills passed through here on their long trek. There's a museum in a restored 1888 stone house in the little town. Near Boulia, the mysterious Min Min Light, a sort of earthbound UFO, is sometimes seen. It's said to resemble the headlights of a car and can hover a metre or two above the ground before vanishing and reappearing in a different place.

Boulia has the *Australian Motel-Hotel* (☎ (077) 46 3144) with singles/doubles at $27/32, or $37/42 with private bathroom. There's also a caravan park (no on-site vans) and a couple of cafes.

Windorah is either very dry or very wet and has a pub and a caravan/camping park. **Quilpie** is an opal-mining town and the rail-head from which cattle, grazed here during the fertile wet season, are railed to the coast. It has two pubs with rooms, and a motel.

Other Routes The Kennedy Developmental Road runs from Winton to Boulia and is mostly surfaced with a couple of fuel and accommodation stops, at **Middleton** and **Hamilton**, on the way.

From Quilpie to Birdsville you follow the Diamantina road through Windorah but then branch off south to Betoota. It's 394 dull km from Windorah to Birdsville. **Betoota**, with one store and one pub, is all there is along the way.

South of Quilpie and west of Cunnamulla is **Thargomindah**, with a pub and a motel. From here camel trains used to cross to Bourke in New South Wales. **Noccundra**, further west, was once a busy little community. It now has just a hotel (with fuel, food and accommodation) and a population of three!

Birdsville

This tiny settlement, with a population of about 30, is the most remote place in Queensland and possesses one of Australia's most famous pubs – the *Birdsville Hotel* (☎ (00717) 8244), which dates from 1884. You can stay there for $38/60 for a single/double. There's also a caravan park with camp sites.

Birdsville, only 12 km from the South Australian border, is the northern end of the 481-km Birdsville Track which leads down to Marree in South Australia. In the late 19th century, Birdsville was quite a busy place as cattle were driven south to South Australia and a customs charge was made on each head of cattle leaving Queensland. With Federation, the charge was abolished, and as cattle are now moved by rail and road, Birdsville has become almost ghost-like. Its big moment today is the annual Birdsville Races on the first weekend in September, when as many as 3000 racing and boozing enthusiasts make the trip to Birdsville.

Birdsville gets its water from a 1219-metre-deep artesian well which delivers the water at 65°C.

Birdsville Track

To the south, the Birdsville Track passes between the Simpson Desert to the west and Sturt's Stony Desert to the east. The first stretch from Birdsville has two alternative routes. Ask local advice about which is better. The Inner Track – marked 'not recommended' on most maps – crosses the Goyder Lagoon (the 'end' of the Diamantina River) and a big Wet will sometimes cut this route. The longer, more easterly Outside Track crosses sandy country at the edge of

the desert where it is sometimes difficult to find the track. Travellers driving the Birdsville Track must fill in a 'destination' card with Birdsville police and then report to the police at the other end of the track.

Simpson Desert National Park

West of Birdsville, the waterless Simpson Desert National Park is Queensland's biggest at 5000 sq km. Conventional cars can tackle the Birdsville Track quite easily but the Simpson requires far more preparation. Official advice is that crossings should only be tackled by parties of at least three 4WD vehicles and that you should have a radio to call for help if necessary. Permits are required before you can traverse the park, and you should advise the Birdsville police of your intended movements. For permits, contact national parks offices in Longreach (☎ (076) 58 1761), Emerald (☎ (079) 82 2246) or Charleville (☎ (076) 54 1255).

South Australia

Area	984,277 sq km
Population	1,390,000

South Australia is the driest of the states –
even Western Australia doesn't have such a
large proportion of desert. It is also the most
urbanised. Adelaide, the capital, once had a
reputation as the wowsers' capital and is
often referred to as 'the city of churches'.
The churches may still be there, but otherwise times have changed.

Today the city's cultural spirit is
epitomised by the biennial Adelaide Arts
Festival. The death of wowserism is nowhere
better seen than in the Barossa Valley Wine
Festival held every two years and Adelaide's
annual Formula One Grand Prix. An
example of the state's relatively liberal
attitude is Australia's first legal nudist beach
just a short drive south of the city. South
Australia also has progressive legislation on
Aboriginal land rights, national parks, can-
nabis and homosexuality.

Outside Adelaide, the state is best known
for its vineyards and wineries. The Barossa
Valley is probably the best known wine-producing area in the country, even though the
amount of 'Barossa wine' produced annually
far exceeds the grape-growing capacity of
the valley! The state also has the fine Clare
and Coonawarra valleys, and the southern
vineyards are only a short drive from the city.
Wine festivals in South Australia are frequent and fun.

Further north, the rugged Flinders Ranges
make an ideal area for all sorts of outdoor
activities. The far north and west of the state
have some of the most inhospitable land in
Australia. The long drive west across the
Nullarbor starts in South Australia; the road
runs close to dramatic cliffs along the Great
Australian Bight.

That still leaves the Murray River, the
interesting coast towards the Victorian
border, fascinating Kangaroo Island and the
Eyre, Yorke and Fleurieu peninsulas.

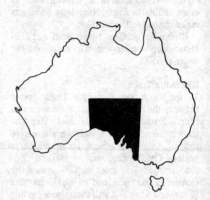

William Light landed at Holdfast Bay
(today Glenelg) in 1836, proclaimed the area
a British colony and chose a site about 10 km
inland for the capital, which he named Adelaide after his wife. At first, progress was
slow and only British government funds
saved the independently managed colony
from bankruptcy. The colony became self-
supporting by the mid-1840s and self-
governing in 1856. Steamers on the Murray
River linked the state with the east, and
agricultural and pastoral activity became the
main industry.

ABORIGINES

It is estimated that there were 12,000 Aborigines in South Australia at the beginning of
the 19th century. Many were killed by the
White settlers or died from introduced diseases; the survivors were pushed off their
lands to the more barren and inhospitable
parts of the state. Today most of the state's
5000 Aborigines live on remote reserves or
settlements.

GEOGRAPHY

The state is sparsely settled. Adelaide, the
Fleurieu Peninsula to the south, and the area

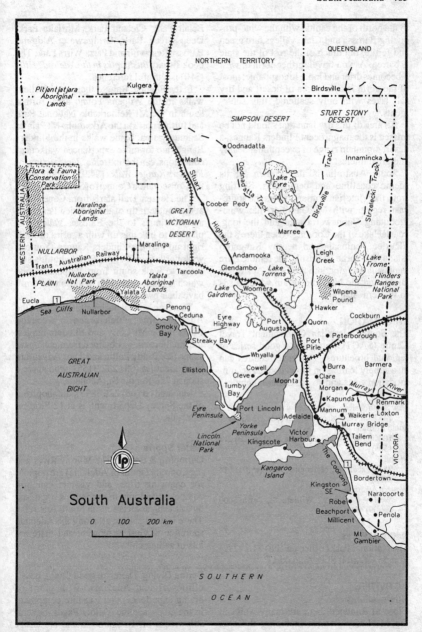

South Australia

0   100   200 km

to the north of the capital with the wine-producing Barossa and Clare valleys, are green and fertile, but much of the rest of the state is barren. As you travel further north or west it becomes drier and more inhospitable; most of the north is a vast area of desert and dry salt lakes with only scattered, tiny settlements.

An area of this dry land that should not be missed is the magnificent Flinders Ranges, a desert mountain range of exceptional beauty and great interest.

South Australia is also known for its scenic coastline and peninsulas. Starting from the Victorian border, there's the south-east region with Mt Gambier, the wine-producing Coonawarra area and the long, coastal lake of the Coorong. Then there's the Fleurieu Peninsula and nearby Kangaroo Island, the Yorke Peninsula, the remote Eyre Peninsula merging into the Great Australian Bight, and the Nullarbor Plain which leads to Western Australia.

INFORMATION

The South Australian Government Travel Centre (SAGTC) produces a good series of regional brochures. The travel centres can also supply leaflets on travel details, accommodation costs and so on. Offices include:

New South Wales
    143 King St, Sydney 2000 (☎ (02) 232 8388)
South Australia
    18 King William St, Adelaide 5000 (☎ (08) 212 1505)
Victoria
    25 Elizabeth St, Melbourne 3000 (☎ (03) 614 6522)
Western Australia
    Wesley Centre, 93 William St, Perth 6000 (☎ (09) 481 1268)

National Parks

The National Parks office (☎ (08) 216 7777) is at 55 Grenfell St in Adelaide.

ACTIVITIES
Bushwalking

Close to Adelaide there are many walks in the Mt Lofty Ranges including those at Belair Park, Cleland Park, Morialta Park, Deep Creek Park, Bridgewater-Aldgate, Barossa Reservoir and Parra Wirra Park. The book *Twenty Bushwalks in the Adelaide Hills* ($10) is a useful reference.

In the Flinders Ranges there are excellent walks in the Wilpena Pound area, further south in the Mt Remarkable National Park and further north in the Arkaroola-Mt Painter Sanctuary area. Some walks in the Flinders Ranges are for more experienced walkers as conditions can be extreme. Get a copy of *Flinders Ranges Walks* ($4.95), produced by the Conservation Council of South Australia.

The Heysen Trail starts from Cape Jervis at the southern tip of the Fleurieu Peninsula and continues to the Barossa Valley. It's planned to link this up with a series of trails right up into the Flinders Ranges. You can walk north from Crystal Brook, but it's still easier to walk south from Wilpena Pound which is more accessible to those who don't have their own transport.

There are several bushwalking clubs in the Adelaide area which organise weekend walks in the Mt Lofty and Flinders ranges. Information can be obtained from bush-gear shops like Paddy Pallin and Thor Adventure Equipment (☎ (08) 232 3155), who share a shop at 228 Rundle St, Adelaide.

Mapland (☎ (08) 226 3895), the shopfront of the Survey Department, is at 12 Pirie St, Adelaide.

Water Sports

Canoeing & Sailing The Murray River and the Coorong (south of Adelaide) are popular for canoeing trips, and visitors can hire equipment and join in canoe trips organised by canoeing associations in South Australia. There is good sailing all along the Adelaide shoreline of Gulf St Vincent and there are lots of sailing clubs.

Scuba Diving There are good diving possibilities around Adelaide. With proof of diving experience, you can hire equipment in the city – see the Yellow Pages. Several shipwrecks off Kangaroo Island are easily accessible to scuba divers. Port Noarlunga Reef Marine Reserve (18 km south of Adelaide) and Aldinga (43 km south) are good centres for boat diving. The reefs around Snapper Point (42 km south) are suitable for snorkelling.

At Rapid Bay (88 km south of Adelaide), there's abundant marine life; you can dive from the jetty. Wallaroo on the Yorke Peninsula, Port Lincoln on the Eyre Peninsula and Second Valley (65 km south of Adelaide) are other good areas.

Swimming & Surfing Seacliff, Brighton, Somerton, Glenelg, West Beach, Henley Beach, Grange, West Lake, Semaphore, Glanville and Largs Bay are all popular city beaches. Further south there are plenty of beaches with good surf. Skinny-dipping is permitted at Maslins Beach, 40 km south of the city.

You have to get over to Pondalowie on the Yorke Peninsula for the state's best board riding. Other good surf areas can be found along the Eyre Peninsula – close to Adelaide at Boomer and Chiton, between Victor Harbor and Port Elliot, and near Goolwa. Cactus Beach, on remote Point Sinclair west of Ceduna, is famous for its surf.

GETTING THERE & AWAY

See the Adelaide Getting There & Away section for details on transport to South Australia. It is worth noting that if you're travelling to Western Australia you can't take honey, plants, fruit or vegetables past the Norseman checkpoint; travelling into South Australia from Victoria between Mildura and Renmark you'll come across a similar roadblock.

GETTING AROUND
Air

Kendell Airlines (book through Ansett ☎ (08) 233 3322) is the main regional operator with flights fanning out from Adelaide to Mt Gambier, Kangaroo Island, Port

Lincoln, Streaky Bay, Ceduna, Coober Pedy and Broken Hill. Other local operators include State Air and Lincoln Airlines. There are flights to Oodnadatta, Innamincka, Birdsville, Hawker and Kangaroo Island. See the South Australian airfares chart for the prices of flights within the state.

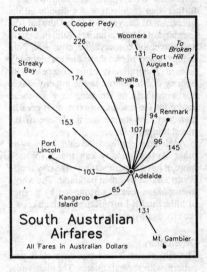

Bus

As well as the major interstate companies, services within the state include Stateliner (☎ (08) 223 2777) (the main operator), Premier (☎ (08) 223 2744), Yorke Peninsula (☎ (08) 391 2977) and smaller local companies.

Train

Intrastate passenger services were unfortunately discontinued after Australian National Railways took over the state's railways. You can still, however, travel within South Australia on interstate trains – the Indian Pacific and the Trans-Australian (Sydney to Perth), the Ghan (Adelaide to Alice Springs) and the Overland (Adelaide to Melbourne).

Adelaide

Population 1,003,000

Adelaide is a solid, dare I say gracious, city – when the early colonists built they generally built with stone. The solidity goes further than architecture, for despite all the liberalism of the years of Don Dunstan (the flamboyant former premier), Adelaide is still an inherently conservative city – an 'old money' place. In part that's due to Adelaide's role in Australia. It can't compete with Sydney or Melbourne in the big city stakes nor with Perth or Brisbane as a go-ahead centre for the resources boom, so it goes its own way; for the visitor that's one of the nicest things about it.

Adelaide is civilised and calm in a way no other Australian city can match. What's more, it has a superb setting – the city centre is surrounded by green parkland. The whole metropolitan area is surrounded by a range of hills, the Mt Lofty Ranges, which crowd the city against the sea.

Orientation

The city centre is laid out on a clear grid pattern, with several squares. The main street is King William St, with Victoria Square at the heart of the city. The GPO is on King William St by Victoria Square. Continue north up King William St and you'll find the tourist bureau on the other side of the road. Most cross streets change their name at King William St.

The most interesting streets are Rundle Mall and Hindley St. Rundle Mall was one of Australia's first city malls and one of the most successful. It's colourful, always a hive of activity and most of the big shops are here.

Just across King William St, Rundle Mall becomes Hindley St. This is Adelaide's left bank/sin centre – if a place like Adelaide can be imagined to have such a centre. Well, you'll find the odd strip club and adult bookshop, together with plenty of reasonably priced restaurants and snack bars, and an increasing number of glitzy bars and dance clubs.

The next street north of Hindley St is North Terrace, with the casino and local railway station just to the west of King William St, and a string of major public buildings including the art gallery, museum and university to the east.

Continue north and you're in the North Parklands with the Festival Centre; then it's across the Torrens River and into North Adelaide, also laid out in a grid pattern.

Information

Tourist Information The South Australian Government Travel Centre (☎ 212 1505, or 008 882 092, toll-free) is at 18 King William St. It's open from 8.45 am to 5.30 pm on weekdays, and from 9 am to 2 pm on weekends and public holidays. There's a recorded message service on 11688.

A good source of information is the Backpackers' Information Centre (☎ 232 4774) at 314 Gilles St, close to many hostels and often open late. If you phone from the bus or railway station, David, the friendly manager, will probably be able to pick you up. As well as giving information and advice on Adelaide, the centre puts together tours to Kangaroo Island and the Flinders Ranges. They also have bikes for hire ($15 per day), and sometimes know of great deals on driving rented cars back to their home bases.

The STD telephone area code for Adelaide is 08.

Useful Organisations The Royal Automobile Association of South Australia (☎ 223 4555) is central at 41 Hindmarsh Square – they also have a good bookshop section. Morphett Auto Repairs (☎ 231 5056) at 42 Stafford St (off O'Halloran St) has been recommended for repairs and advice.

The YHA office (☎ 231 5583) at 38 Sturt St is open from 9.30 am to 4.30 pm on weekdays. The National Parks office (☎ 216 7777) is at 55 Grenfell St. The government Department of Recreation (☎ 234 0844) is also a good source of maps and information.

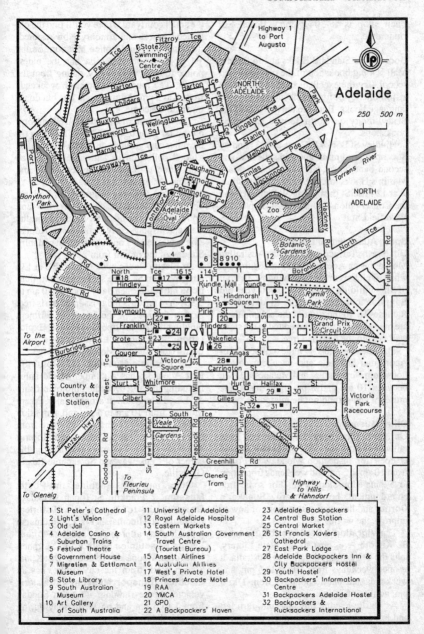

Adelaide

0   250   500 m

1 St Peter's Cathedral
2 Light's Vision
3 Old Jail
4 Adelaide Casino &
   Suburban Trains
5 Festival Theatre
6 Government House
7 Migration & Settlement
   Museum
8 State Library
9 South Australian
   Museum
10 Art Gallery
   of South Australia
11 University of Adelaide
12 Royal Adelaide Hospital
13 Eastern Markets
14 South Australian Government
   Travel Centre
   (Tourist Bureau)
15 Ansett Airlines
16 Australian Airlines
17 West's Private Hotel
18 Princes Arcade Motel
19 RAA
20 YMCA
21 GPO
22 A Backpackers' Haven
23 Adelaide Backpackers
24 Central Bus Station
25 Central Market
26 St Francis Xaviers
   Cathedral
27 East Park Lodge
28 Adelaide Backpackers Inn &
   City Backpackers Hostel
29 Youth Hostel
30 Backpackers' Information
   Centre
31 Backpackers Adelaide Hostel
32 Backpackers &
   Rucksackers International

Their shop is at 304 Henley Beach Rd, Underdale.

Bookshops Standard Books at 136 Rundle Mall is a big bookshop of the old-fashioned school. Try the excellent Europa Bookshop at 16 Pulteney St for its selection of foreign-language books. Both the university and the State Library on North Terrace have good bookshops.

Hindley St Books & Cards at 103 Hindley St is open until midnight, and sells new and second-hand books, tapes and records. Mary Martin's Bookshop, an Adelaide institution, is at 12 Pirie St (near King William St), and the Conservation Council has a shop at 120 Wakefield St.

South Australian Museum

On North Terrace, the South Australian Museum is an Adelaide landmark with huge whale skeletons in the front window. In front of the building, there's a 3000-year-old Egyptian column thought to date from Rameses II. To the right of the column there are many small fossils embedded in the stone wall next to the petrified tree.

The museum has a huge collection of Aboriginal artefacts and excellent collections from New Guinea and Melanesia. Open between 10 am and 5 pm daily, it's a fine museum and should not be missed.

Other Museums

On North Terrace by the casino and local railway station, the old **Parliament House** is open for inspection Monday to Friday from 10 am to 5 pm and weekends from noon to 5 pm; admission is $3. For some free entertainment, head to nearby **Speaker's Corner** and hear various versions of how to improve the world.

The **Migration & Settlement Museum** at 82 Kintore Ave, next to the State Library, tells the story of immigration to Australia. It is open weekdays from 10 am to 5 pm, and weekends and public holidays from 1 to 5 pm; admission is free.

As you're leaving this museum, turn left and left again, and walk through the lane to the small courtyard where you'll find the old police barracks and armoury. Now restored, it houses the small **Police Museum** on the 1st floor. South Australia has the oldest police force in the country, dating from the 1860s. The museum is open on weekends from 1 to 5 pm. Admission is free but donations are welcome.

The **Museum of Classical Archaeology** on the 1st floor of the Mitchell Building (in the university grounds on North Terrace) has a good collection of antiquities. It's open from noon to 3 pm during term time and weekends; admission is free.

There's a **Railway Museum** on Railway Terrace off West Beach Rd at Mile End South. It tells the history of railways in the state and displays early locomotives. Admission is 60c and it's open on the first and third Sunday of the month from 2 to 5 pm.

At Electra House, next to the GPO at 131 King William St, there's a **Telecommunications Museum** open daily from 10.30 am to 3.30 pm (4 pm on Sunday); admission is free. Across the road in the Lands Department building there's the free **Museum of Exploration, Surveying & Land Heritage**, open from 10 am to 4 pm Monday to Friday.

The **Maritime Museum**, 117 Lipson St, Port Adelaide, has a number of old ships including the *Nelcebee*, the third oldest ship on Lloyd's register. It's open daily except Monday from 10 am to 5 pm and admission is $6. Bus Nos 154 and 155 go there from North Terrace. There's also the **Shipping Museum** (open by appointment) on the corner of Causeway and Semaphore Rds in Glanville.

Other museums include: the **Postal Museum**, 2 Franklin St (open weekdays from 11 am to 2 pm); the **Historical Museum** at Hindmarsh Place, Hindmarsh (open Sunday afternoons); and the **Pioneer Village Museum** on South Rd in Morphett Vale (open Wednesday to Sunday). St Kilda, 30 km north from the city centre, has an **Electrical Transport Museum** with historic vehicles, some running; it's open Sunday from 1 to 5 pm and on Wednesday during school holidays. Admission is $4.

Tandanya

Tandanya at 253 Grenfell St is an Aboriginal cultural institute (owned and run by Aborigines) containing galleries, arts & crafts workshops, performance spaces, a cafe and a good gift shop. It's open weekdays and weekend afternoons.

State Library

Displays at the State Library on North Terrace include Colonel Light's surveying equipment, an 1865 photographic panorama of Adelaide and, in the Mortlock Library in the same complex, memorabilia of cricket star Sir Donald Bradman. The reading room (where there are often displays) is open daily until at least 5 pm (closed Sunday morning); the Mortlock Library is closed on Wednesday and Sunday.

Art Galleries

On North Terrace, the **Art Gallery of South Australia** has a good selection from contemporary Australian and overseas artists, as well as fine minor works from many periods. The South-East Asian ceramic collection is of particular note. The gallery has a pleasant little coffee shop with outside tables. It is open daily from 10 am to 5 pm, admission is free and there are tours at 11 am.

The gallery of the **Royal South Australian Society of Art**, 1st floor on the corner of North Terrace and Kintore Ave, hosts frequent visiting exhibitions. It's open weekdays from 11 am to 5 pm and weekends from 2 to 5 pm; admission is free. Other galleries include the **Union Gallery** on the top floor of the Adelaide University Union Building (open weekdays) and the **Festival Centre Gallery** near the Playhouse.

Ayers House & Edmund Wright House

Ayers House is on North Terrace close to the city centre. This fine old mansion was originally constructed in 1846 but was added to over the next 30 years. Now completely restored, it houses two restaurants but is open for visitors from Tuesday to Friday between 10 am and 4 pm and on weekends between 2 and 4 pm. Admission is $3 and on week-

days there are tours. The elegant bluestone building serves as the headquarters of the South Australian National Trust (☎ 223 1655).

At 59 King William St, Edmund Wright House (1876) was originally built in an elaborate Renaissance style with intricate decoration for the Bishop of South Australia. It is now used as government offices and for official functions.

Other City Buildings

The imposing **town hall**, built from 1863-66 in 16th-century Renaissance style, looks out on King William St between Flinders and Pirie Sts. The faces of Queen Victoria and Prince Albert are carved into the facade. The post office across the road is almost as imposing.

On North Terrace, **Government House** was built between 1838 and 1840 with further additions in 1855. The earliest section is one of the oldest buildings in Adelaide. **Parliament House** on North Terrace has a facade with 10 marble Corinthian columns. Building commenced in 1883 but was not completed until 1939.

Holy Trinity Church, also on North Terrace (near Montefiore Rd), was the first Anglican church in the state; it was built in 1838. Other early churches are **St Francis Xavier Cathedral** on Wakefield St (built around 1856) and **St Peter's Cathedral** in Pennington Terrace, North Adelaide (built between 1869 and 1876). St Francis Xavier Cathedral is beside Victoria Square, where you will also find a number of other important early buildings: the **Magistrate's Court** 0f 1847-50 (originally used as the Supreme Court); the 1869 **Supreme Court**; and the **Treasury Building**.

Festival Centre

The Adelaide Festival Centre is close to the Torrens River. Looking uncannily like a squared-off version of the vastly more expensive Sydney Opera House, it performs a similar function with its variety of auditoriums and theatres. The complex was completed in 1977, and there are tours from

Monday to Saturday at 11 am and 2 pm costing $3. More tours are sometimes added (☎ 216 8713).

One of the most pleasant aspects of the Festival Theatre is its riverside setting; people picnic on the grass in front of the theatre and there are several places to eat. You can also hire pedal boats nearby or enjoy free concerts and exhibitions here. In the Piano Room, top pianists play during happy hour on Friday between 4.30 and 6 pm; admission is free. On Saturday nights from 10.30 pm till late, a free band plays anything from romantic jazz to contemporary, energetic pop.

Living Arts Centre

On the corner of Morphett St and North Terrace, the Living Arts Centre with galleries, stage areas, artists' studios, craft workshops and cinemas is the home of the Fringe Festival administration (☎ 231 7760) and a broad spectrum of arts-related activities.

Grand Prix

The Australian Formula One Grand Prix takes place in Adelaide in late October or early November each year and is the final race of the international Grand Prix season. The track is along city streets immediately to the east of the city centre. The cars reach 300 km/h down Dequetteville Terrace.

With practice sessions and supporting races, the event goes on for five days and all Adelaide gets into it. This must be one of the easiest Grands Prix in the world to get to since you can easily find a place to park (if you don't mind a 10-minute walk to the track) and there's plenty of public transport. Big improvements in the spectator embankments and viewing areas mean good views without the expense of a seat in the stands.

Botanic Gardens & Other Parks

The central city is completely surrounded by green parkland, and the Torrens River, itself bordered by park, separates Adelaide from North Adelaide which is also surrounded by park.

On North Terrace, the Botanic Gardens have pleasant artificial lakes and are only a short stroll from the city centre. The glass Palm House was made in Germany in 1871. Every Tuesday and Friday at 10.30 am, free guided tours of the Gardens, taking about 1½ hours, leave from the kiosk. The Gardens are open weekdays from 7 am to sunset, and on the weekends and public holidays from 9 am to sunset. The Conservatory in the gardens is open between 10 am and 4 pm; admission is $2.

Rymill Park in the East Parkland has a boating lake and a 600-metre jogging track. The South Parkland contains **Veale Gardens** with streams and flower beds. To the west are a number of sports grounds while the **North Parkland** borders the Torrens and surrounds North Adelaide. The **Adelaide Oval**, site for interstate and international cricket matches, is north of the Torrens River in this part of the park. The North Parkland also contains **Bonython Park**, **Pinky Flat**, and **Elder Park** which adjoins the university and Festival Centre.

Light's Vision

On Montefiore Hill, north of the city centre across the Torrens River, stands the statue of Light's Vision. Adelaide's founder is said to have stood here and mapped out his plan for the city. It is a good place to start your exploration of the city centre since you get a bird's-eye view of the modern city, with green parkland and the gleaming white Festival Centre at your feet. Another fine Adelaide view, particularly at night, can be enjoyed from Windy Point Lookout in Belair Rd, a continuation of Unley Rd.

Adelaide Zoo

On Frome Rd, the zoo has a noted collection of Australian birds as well as other important exhibits including sloths, giant anteaters, spider monkeys and ring-tailed lemurs. The zoo is open daily from 9.30 am to 5 pm; admission is $7.50. The best way of getting there is to take a cruise on the *Popeye* ($2) which departs from Elder Park in front of the

Festival Centre. You can also catch bus Nos 272 or 273 from Currey St.

North Adelaide

Interesting old bluestone buildings and pubs abound in North Adelaide, only a short bus ride through the park to the north of the city centre. It's one of the oldest parts of Adelaide, and Melbourne St is Adelaide's swankiest shopping street with lots of interesting little shops and expensive restaurants.

Markets

Three km north-west of town at 36 South Rd, Thebarton, there's the large **Brickworks Market**, open Friday to Monday from 9 am to 5 pm, which includes a leisure complex and sells food, arts, crafts, clothes, books and plain old junk. It's not a bad place to stroll around. To get there from the city take bus Nos 112, 114, 116 or 118 to stop 8 from Grenfell St. The similar **Adelaide Sunday Market** is held on East Terrace between Rundle and Grenfell Sts.

In town, the **Central Market** on Grote St sells produce, fish and crafts. It's open on Tuesday, Thursday, Friday and Saturday mornings. The revamped **East End Markets** near Rundle St are open from Friday to Sunday and have produce and other stalls.

West Beach Airport

The airport is centrally located west of the city. The Vickers Vimy which made the first flight between England and Australia way back in 1919 is on display in a showroom in the car park. At the controls were Sir Keith and Sir Ross Smith; the flight took 27 days with numerous stops along the way. A similar aircraft made the first nonstop Atlantic crossing in the same year. (The Vimy was a surprisingly large WW I twin-engined biplane bomber.)

Glenelg

Glenelg, one of the most popular of the beaches stretching in a long chain south of Adelaide, is a suburban seaside resort with a couple of attractions. First of all, it's an excellent place to stay – there are many guesthouses, hotels and holiday flats here if you can't find something suitable in the city.

Secondly, it's one of the oldest parts of Adelaide – the first South Australian colonists actually landed in Glenelg – so there are a number of places of historic interest. As a bonus, Glenelg is exceptionally easy to get to. Adelaide's only tram runs from Victoria Square in the city centre right to Glenelg Beach. It costs $2.30 (less between 9 am and 3 pm) and is commendably fast (taking about 30 minutes) as its route keeps it separate from the road traffic.

At the jetty in front of the town hall and by the beach is **Bay World**; you can't miss the camel out the front. Pick up a map or a walking or cycling-tour brochure from the helpful information desk. As well as the souvenirs sold here there is a museum and aquarium with sea life in tanks and apparently a shrunken human head amongst the curios; admission is $2. You can also rent bicycles here.

On MacFarlane St, the **Old Gum Tree** marks the spot where the proclamation of South Australia was read in 1836. Governor Hindmarsh and the first colonists landed on the beach nearby and bus Nos 167 or 168 will take you there.

Apart from Glenelg's fine collection of early buildings, it also has a popular **amusement park**, including a waterslide, behind the beach.

The boat harbour shelters a large number of yachts and Glenelg's premier attraction, a reproduction of **HMS Buffalo**, the original settlers' conveyance. The original *Buffalo* was built in 1813 in India. Also a seafood restaurant (main courses around $15), the ship and a museum are open to visitors for $2.50 from 10 am to 5 pm on weekdays and from 9 am on weekends. There's also an aquarium featuring South Australian fish.

Jetty Rd, the main street, is lined with shops and restaurants and the tram line goes right down the centre.

Other Suburbs

In Jetty St, Grange (west of the city centre), is **Sturt's Cottage**, the home of the famous early Australian explorer. Preserved as a museum, it's open Wednesday to Sunday and public holidays from 1 to 5 pm. In Semaphore (north-west of the city centre), there's **Fort Glanville**, built in 1878 when Australia was having its phase of Russophobia as a result of the Crimean War. It's open during the summer.

In **Port Adelaide** (north-west of the city), you can make boat trips from North Parade Wharf except during July. **Carrick Hill** at 590 Fullarton Rd, Springfield (south of the city), is built in the style of an Elizabethan manor house set in an English-style garden.

Organised Tours

Several companies offer sightseeing trips; check at the tourist office or on hostel notice boards.

Half-day city tours with Premier (☎ 233 2744) cost $19. You can go further afield to Hahndorf in the Adelaide Hills, to Birdwood Mills and the Torrens Gorge, or to the Mt Lofty Ranges and the Cleland Reserve (where there's a koala cuddlery) for $22. For $14 you get a day pass on the Adelaide Explorer ('Adelaide's only road registered tram replica') which does a continuous circuit of a number of attractions, including Glenelg. The only problem is that it's a long circuit and you have to wait over two hours for the next 'tram' to come past.

E&K Mini-Tours (☎ 337 8739) are popular with travellers. They have a Barossa day tour for $18, including lunch, and a two-hour Adelaide by Night tour for $10. Other companies offering Barossa tours include True Blue (☎ 296 0938), who also travel further afield, and Premier (☎ 233 2774). There are also day tours to Goolwa and the Murray Mouth, and various tours of the Fleurieu Peninsula and Kangaroo Island.

You can take a day trip to Kangaroo Island with Kendell Airlines (☎ (08) 233 3322), but you'd have to be pretty short of time and long on cash for it to be an option. There are any number of trips to the Flinders Ranges – True Blue (☎ 296 0938) has a three-day package for $160; and Barry's Tours (☎ 266 1236) charges about $220 for four days.

Freewheeling Cycle Tours (☎ 373 3482) have a variety of rides, including day tours of Adelaide ($20 including a barbecue) and the McLaren Vale wineries ($35). Bike Moves (☎ 293 2922) also run good tours, mainly longer trips around the Flinders Ranges and Kangaroo Island.

Adelaide Arts Festival

South Australia enjoys two of Australia's major festivals: the Barossa Valley Vintage Festival on odd-numbered years and the Adelaide Arts Festival in February-March of the even-numbered years. The three-week festival of the arts attracts culture vultures from all over Australia to drama, dance, music and other live performances. There is also a writers' week, art exhibitions, poetry readings and other activities with guest speakers and performers from all over the world. The Fringe Festival, which takes place at the same time as the main festival, is also interesting.

Places to Stay

Many motel and some hotel prices rise between Christmas and the end of January, and almost all are higher during the Grand Prix, when accommodation is extremely scarce. As one manager put it, 'It's the only time anyone makes any money', so expect no mercy.

Hostels There are a couple of hostels near the bus station. Turn left out of the bus station along Franklin St and on the next corner, Morphett St, is *Adelaide Backpackers* (☎ 231 2430). It's a lively, friendly place which has been newly renovated. You can book tours here and the office opens at 5.30 am.

At 11 Cannon St, a laneway running off Franklin St opposite the bus station, *A Backpackers' Haven* (☎ 410 1218) has dorm beds for $9 ($10 in four-bed rooms) and singles/doubles for $14/25. You can hire bikes here for $12 a day. *Backpack Australia* (☎ 231 0639) is a new place at 128 Grote St, opposite the Central Market. Beds cost from $10 and meals are available.

Most of the other hostels are clustered in the south-east corner of the city centre. Get there on bus Nos 191 to 198 from Pulteney St or take any bus going to the South Terrace area, although it's not really that far to walk. Most of the hostels do pick-ups.

The *Youth Hostel* (☎ 223 6007) is at 290 Gilles St. Beds, for members only, cost $11. The hostel is closed between 9.30 am and 1 pm. Nearby is the pleasant, low-key *Backpackers Adelaide Hostel* (☎ 223 5680) at 263 Gilles St, with another house a few doors along. Dorm beds cost from $11. At 275 Gilles St there's another hostel, *Backpackers & Rucksackers International* (☎ 232 0823), with dorm beds from $10.

Two streets closer to the city centre on Carrington St, there are another couple of hostels. *City Backpackers Hostel* (☎ 223 2715) at No 118 advertises itself as 'the hottest joint in town', but it's actually a small, friendly place with dorm beds for $10 and doubles for $22. There's some off-street parking. Nearby at 112 Carrington St, *Adelaide Backpackers Inn* (☎ 223 6635) is an old pub with dorm beds from $12 and doubles from $26. They've got a a coin laundry and you can book tours and hire bikes here ($8 a day).

At the east end of Angas St, *East Park Lodge* (☎ 223 1228) at No 341 is in the big old Salvation Army hostel building. It's renovated, clean and well run. Dorm beds cost $10, with singles/doubles from $12.50/22. There are good views from the roof and it's close to parkland (and the Grand Prix circuit).

The large *YMCA* (☎ 223 1611) at 76 Flinders St is central and takes guests of either sex. Dorms are $11 and singles/twins are $18/30. Office hours are 9 am to 9 pm Monday to Friday, and 9 am to noon and 4 to 8 pm on weekends and holidays. Dorms open at 4 pm.

The *Princes Arcade Motel* (☎ 231 5471) at 262 Hindley St in the city centre has a few dorm beds for about $10. They don't take bookings for the dorm so there's a chance you'll get in here if you're stuck for somewhere to stay.

Hotels The *Metropolitan Hotel* (☎ 231 5471) at 46 Grote St is central and has singles/doubles/triples for $20/28/39. *West's Private Hotel* (☎ 231 7575) at 110B Hindley St is also central, and singles/doubles/triples cost $25/35/45. All rooms have fans and tea/coffee-making facilities. It's a reasonable place, although you might want to choose a room on the top floor to avoid noise from the disco at street level.

Other central hotels include the *Plaza Private Hotel* (☎ 231 6371) at 85 Hindley St, an old but well-kept place built around a palm-filled courtyard. Rooms with washbasins cost from $25/35. At 205 Rundle St the *Austral Hotel* (☎ 223 4660) has singles/doubles for $25/35 – one traveller found the bar below to be noisy and rough. Both these places lift their prices during the Grand Prix.

The *Afton Private Hotel* (☎ 223 3416) at 260 South Terrace is good value at $70 a week (no shorter stays) with a full English breakfast. The catch is that it's almost always full. If you plan to arrive after 8 pm, phone ahead.

Motels All these places increase their prices during the Grand Prix. The *Adelaide City Centre Motel* (☎ 231 4040) is right in the city centre at 23 Hindley St, near the corner of King William St. The rooms are small, but at $49/54 for singles/doubles with a light breakfast and standard motel facilities, it's reasonable value. At 262 Hindley St the *Princes Arcade Motel* (☎ 231 9524) has motel rooms from $45/55 and some rooms with shared bathroom from $35/45.

On the corner of Franklin St and Gawler Place, near the YMCA, the *Earl of Zetland Hotel* (☎ 223 5500) has some motel-style rooms from $45/59. The rooms are large and in good condition. The *Clarice City Motel* (☎ 223 3560) is at 220 Hutt St, around the corner from the youth hostel. There are cheaper rooms with shared facilities from $25/42; motel units are $47/59, including a light breakfast.

Although there are motels all over Adelaide there's a 'motel alley' along Glen Osmond Rd, the road that leads in to the city centre from the south-east. This is quite a busy road so some places are a bit noisy.

Powell's Court (☎ 271 7995) is two km south of the city centre at 2 Glen Osmond Rd, Parkside. Rooms cost from $40/45, they all have kitchens and there are rooms big enough for three or four for not much more than the price of a double.

The *Sunny South Motel* (☎ 79 1621), four km south of the city at 190 Glen Osmond Rd, Fullarton, costs from $32/38. Nearby is *Princes Highway* (☎ 79 9253) at 199 Glen Osmond Rd, Frewville, which costs from $42/47.

Colleges At Adelaide University, *St Ann's College* (☎ 267 1478) operates as a hostel from the second week in December through to the end of January; beds are around $13. At other colleges, accommodation generally includes meals and is much more expensive.

Camping There are quite a few caravan parks around Adelaide. The following are some within 10 km of the city centre – check the tourist office for others. All prices given are for two people; all prices rise around Christmas and during the Grand Prix, when most are booked out.

Adelaide Caravan Park (☎ 363 1566), Bruton St, Hackney, is only two km north-east of the city centre by the Torrens River. On-site vans cost from $34, and there are no tent sites.
Windsor Gardens Caravan Park (☎ 261 1091), 78 Windsor Grove, Windsor Gardens, is six km north-east (take bus No 281 from North Terrace); camping costs $8 and cabins are $25.
West Beach Caravan Park (☎ 356 7654), Military Rd, West Beach, is eight km west of the city; camping costs $10, on-site vans $29 (plus $3 for each additional person) and cabins $45 (plus $4). This park is close to the beach and only a couple of km from Glenelg. Get there on bus No 276 or 277 from Grenfell St in the city.
Beachfront Van & Tourist Park (☎ 49 7726), 349 Military Rd, Semaphore Park, is on the beach about 10 km from the city centre (bus No 139 from Grenfell gets you fairly close). This park has tent sites from $11, on-site vans from $28 and cabins from $42.

Glenelg There's a lot of accommodation in Glenelg, but prices can rise, sometimes dramatically, around Christmas and during the Grand Prix. There's a tourist office on the foreshore (☎ 294 5833) which can help with accommodation.

Glenelg Beach Headquarters (☎ 376 0007) at 7 Mosely St is around the corner from the tram terminus. It's a clean and friendly hostel in three big renovated terrace houses with a spa, bar, pool room and an inexpensive restaurant. Some rooms have marble fireplaces and some private rooms have a small fridge. Comfortable beds (not bunks) are $12 in dorms and $15 per person in doubles. If you stay more than three nights they'll refund your taxi fare from the city centre, but they can often collect you from the train or bus station if you ring.

Further south from the tram line but on the sea at 16 South Esplanade is *Albert Hall* (☎ 294 1966), a restored mansion. Dorm beds cost from $10 and there are some private rooms for around $30/35. They can usually pick you up from the city.

The *St Vincent Hotel* (☎ 294 4377) at 28 Jetty Rd has singles/doubles for $26/48, or $35/55 with bathroom – all with a light breakfast. These prices stay the same all year round.

There are a lot of holiday flats and serviced apartments; most quote weekly rather than daily rates. The friendly *Glenelg Seaway Apartments* (☎ 295 8503) at 18 Durham St charge about $12 per person in the low season and have been recommended.

At 7 North Esplanade the *Alkoomi Holiday Motel* (☎ 294 6624) has rooms for $44, rising to $82. The adjoining *Wambini Lodge* (☎ 295 4689), the same price, is run by the same people. The *Norfolk Motel* (☎ 295 6354) is at 69-71 Broadway, a few blocks south of Jetty Rd. It's a fairly small motel with 20 units from $44 to $55.

Places to Eat
Although Adelaide does not have the variety of cuisines of Melbourne or Sydney, it has quite enough to ensure survival with style!

Licensing laws are liberal in South Australia so a high proportion of restaurants are licensed. Those which claim to be BYO are often just licensed restaurants which allow you to bring your own alcohol if you wish.

For about $6, *Cheap Eats in Adelaide* is a good guide to the constantly changing food scene.

Hindley St If Adelaide has a food centre, it has to be Hindley St, where you'll find a range of cuisines, interspersed with Adelaide's small and seedy collection of strip clubs and an increasing number of glittery bars and discos.

In the basement at 33 Hindley St is the *Chinatown Restaurant*. Most dishes are in the $8 to $12 range but the food really is good. Lunches are cheaper. At No 79, *Food for Life*, a Hare Krishna restaurant, has free food between noon and 2 pm, Monday to Saturday. *Central Pizza* at 139 Hindley St has Italian fare and is open daily from noon to midnight; meals start from $5.50. Abdul and Jamil's friendly *Quiet Waters* downstairs at No 75 is a pleasant Lebanese coffee lounge serving good food; vegetarian side dishes cost from around $3.50 with main courses from $6.50 and meat dishes from $8.

Pagana's at 101 Hindley St does main-course pastas from $8.50, with daily specials for around $7.50. It's good authentic Italian food and there's wine by the glass. There is a string of Middle Eastern takeaways, most with yiros (kebabs) at about $4. *Noah's Ark* at No 116 stays open all night. There are several Greek places like *Hindley's Olympic Restaurant* at No 139 which serves souvlaki and spiced lamb, although it's getting pricey with main courses from $9 and fish from $13.

For Indian food, the *Madras Cafe* at 142 Hindley St is open nightly except Monday and has main courses from $8. At No 77, *Beanstalk* is a cooperative cafe offering good, cheap vegetarian food. It's open weekdays only, until about 8 pm. *Aspara* at No 160A is a basic place selling Cambodian and Thai food, with satays for $4 and main courses around $6.

Still on Hindley St but across Morphett St, the *Peaceful Vegetarian Restaurant* at No 167 serves healthy Asian dishes. Entrees are about $2 and main courses are all $6. A little further along, the *Traditional Fish & Chip Cafe* has specials at around $5, but most other dishes are much dearer. At 273 Hindley St *Marcellina* has Italian food and all-you-can-eat deals for about $5.

On Gilbert Place, which dog-legs between Hindley St and King William St, the *Pancake Place* is open 24 hours and main-course specials are under $7. Next door the *Penang Chinese Coffee Shop* is open Monday to Saturday until 11 pm and has main courses for under $5. Round the corner is *D'Angelo's Restaurant* – a pleasant Italian place with main dishes in the $9 range with pastas a bit cheaper.

Also close to Hindley St one of the best Indian restaurants would have to be *Taj Tandoor* at 76 Light Square.

Around the City Gouger St is another street of restaurants with some long-standing fish and seafood places. Try *Paul's* at 79 Gouger St, *George's* at No 113 or *Stanley's* at No 76. There are now a lot of other cuisines available along the street. *Star of Siam* at No 83A serves good Thai food; a three-course lunch costs about $16. *Mamma Getta Restaurant* at No 55 is Italian and most dishes are under $7, with pasta cheaper. *Ming's Palace* at 201 Gouger St is open daily and has yum cha. Main courses cost from $6. At No 167, the Japanese *Matsuri* has excellent sushi from $2 and stone-grilled seafood dishes for about $19.

Downstairs at 107 King William St, near the GPO, *Governor Wallen's Restaurant* is open for lunch and dinner and has meals from $4. Near the bus station at 114 Grote St, the *Angkor Wat* has Thai and Cambodian food, with good lunch-time specials such as two courses and rice for $4.

There are several Italian places at the east end of Rundle St. Also here is *Mezes*, a small, casual Greek place at No 287 with an open-view kitchen and tables on the street. Main courses are about $12 and it's open till late.

At 69 Grote St, *Ellinis* is a Greek restaurant which specialises in seafood and serves excellent and reasonably priced food. At 242A Rundle St there's *Tapas*, which serves snacks until late every day.

Adelaide University's union building is close to the city centre – try the *Bistro* there. It's open Monday to Friday from noon to 2.30 pm and from 5.30 to 8.30 pm. Their main courses start from just $5. The *Union Cafeteria* on the ground floor is cheaper; a cup of coffee is bottomless.

The *Central Market* between Gouger and Grote Sts near Victoria Square is good value for food, fruit, vegetables and bread. A bit further away at 131 Pirie St *Fasta Pasta* is a cheap, popular Italian restaurant. The *Venezia Italian* restaurant at 121 Pirie St has pastas from $6.50. The *Volga*, upstairs at 116 Flinders St, is a Russian restaurant. It's quite a formal place with live music at night, but the lunch-time prices aren't bad, with main courses around $7.50 – or you can spend $70 on pancakes with caviar.

Nearby at 63 Hughes St *Seoul* is a Korean restaurant open for lunch and dinner, with dishes from $5. The *Pullman Adelaide Casino Restaurant* has a good-value smorgasbord. *Cactus* is a Mexican cafe at 121 Grenfell St.

On Pulteney St, near the corner of Carrington St, *Food & Friends* is a fish & chip shop with cheap sit-down meals, such as calamari, salad and chips for under $5. It closes at 8.30 pm. On Gilles St near the hostels, *Gilles Snacks* has inexpensive breakfasts and takeaways.

The *Witches Brew* on the corner of Sturt St and Whitmore Square has main courses from $4.50 – the entertainment is psychic readings.

If you're after late-night eats, then look for the *Pie Carts* which appear every night from 6 pm till the early hours; they're an institution. If a pie floater (the great Australian meat pie floating on a thick pea soup, completely covered in tomato sauce) is your thing then look for the vans at the corner by the GPO and on North Terrace near the railway station. Floaters cost $2.60. If they don't sound like your thing (and I sincerely hope they don't for your stomach's sake!) then there are also more straightforward pies, as well as tea and coffee.

Halifax Lounge at 65 Flinders St is run by one of the local churches and offers a place to go from 10 am to 4 pm. There's tea and coffee and you can hang around reading and writing if you like.

Food Centres As in other Australian cities, Singapore-style food centres (where a group of kitchens share a communal eating area) are excellent, inexpensive places to eat.

On Grote St, a block south of the bus station, the *Chinatown* centre has a good collection of places. Also good is the *Hawker's Corner* on the corner of West Terrace and Wright St. It's open for lunch and dinner daily except Monday and has Chinese, Vietnamese, Thai and Indian food.

The *City Cross Arcade* off Grenfell St has European and Asian food, as does *Food Affair* at the Gallerie Shopping Centre, which runs from North Terrace through to Gawler Place (on the basement level beside the John Martins department store). On the corner of Hindley and Leigh Sts, the *Underground Diner* has mainly Asian stalls; dishes start at $4.50 and there's a bar. There's also a *Food Court* at the new East End Markets with European and Asian stalls.

Counter Meals Adelaide is very well represented in this category, particularly at lunch time. Just look for those telltale blackboards standing outside. You don't have to look far to find one with meals under $5. There are plenty of cheap 'counteries' to be had in Hindley and Rundle Sts and elsewhere around the city. Across in North Adelaide, The *British* at 58 Finniss St has a 'touch of the British' about it, plus a pleasant beer garden where you can grill the food yourself at the barbecue. Main courses are about $11 ($1 less if you cook your own).

Open Air & Lunch Adelaide is one of the best cities in Australia for *alfresco* dining;

the climate is dry, it's sunny and it usually isn't so hot that you risk sunstroke.

Hindmarsh Square is a good place to start looking for lunch in the sun. On the north Pulteney St corner *Carrots* is a long-running health-food place. It's a nice, airy place to sit and look out over the square. It's open weekdays from 10 am to 4 pm. At 37 Pulteney St on the west side of the square, the *Indonesian House of Food* has lunch specials at around $7. Next door is the *Jasmin Indian Restaurant* with good main courses for around $10. There's a second location nearby but they're closed on Sunday.

Another outdoor place is the *Festival Bistro* in the Festival Centre overlooking the Torrens River. It has sandwiches and snacks and is open late into the evenings (it is closed on Sunday). The gardens around the Festival Centre are a good place for a picnic.

La Strada on the corner of North Terrace and Austin St is a cafeteria that also serves pizzas, pasta and other Italian food from $5.50.

The *Al Fresco Gelateria* at 260 Rundle St has tables out on the footpath; it is a good place for a gelati, cappuccino or a variety of sweets.

Away from the City Centre A good cheapie is the *Bengal Kitchen* at 151 Marion Rd, Richmond West. The food is good, the garlic content is high and it's inexpensive. There's a free feast on Sunday at the *Hare Krishna Temple*, 74 Semaphore Rd, Semaphore, and on Saturday (4.30 pm) at the *Food for Life* restaurant, 79 Hindley St.

There are quite a few eating places along O'Connell St and elsewhere in North Adelaide, most of them on the pricey side. *African Rakuba* at 33 O'Connell St has a Sudanese flavour. A three-course meal with meat and vegetarian dishes costs about $12 and the portions are large. *Bacall's* at 149 Melbourne St has creole and cajun food with three-course lunches for $15 on weekdays and specials at dinner.

Entertainment

Casino The Adelaide Casino is housed in the old railway station on North Terrace and, with the new Convention Centre and the Hyatt Regency Hotel, it's part of the Adelaide Plaza complex. Apart from gambling facilities (including a two-up game, of course) there are five bars and a restaurant. It's open from 10 am to 4 am on weekdays, for 24 hours on weekends and smart casual dress is required.

Cinemas There are a number of commercial cinemas around town, particularly on Hindley St. Alternative cinemas include the Chelsea Cinema at 275 Kensington Rd, Kensington, and the Piccadilly at 181 O'Connell St, North Adelaide, or the Capri at 141 Goodwood Rd, Goodwood, which has an organist from Tuesday to Saturday. The university film club often shows good films in the union. There are free lunch-time films at the State Film & Video Library.

Mt Thebarton Adelaide's ice-skating rink (☎ 352 7977) also has an artificial indoor snow-skiing centre. The 150-metre-long slope is called Mt Thebarton. It's open seven days a week and you can also ice skate and toboggan. It's at 23 East Terrace, Thebarton. Get there on any bus Nos 154 to 157 departing from in front of the railway station on North Terrace.

Pubs & Music There are lots of pubs with entertainment. Check Thursday's *Advertiser* newspaper or ring the radio station SA FM (☎ 272 1990) for a recorded gig guide. The free music paper *Rip it Up* is worth picking up for its listings. For theatre and gallery reviews check the free monthly paper, *Adelaide Review*.

Most discos and dance clubs demand 'smart casual dress' and even some not-so-up-market venues have strict dress codes – as well as the usual ban on singlets, thongs and exposed tattoos. In some places, even 'black or dark T-shirts or windcheaters' are banned.

Several pubs brew their own beer. The best of these is the Port Dock Brewery Hotel at 10 Todd Place in Port Adelaide. Their beer is sold in 13 other hotels around town. Black Diamond Bitter is their best. The Earl of Aberdeen on Light Square is a more up-market place which brews good beer.

There's the usual rock pub circuit. Better pubs include the Austral and the Exeter (which has real ale and boasts 'no renovations, no bullshit, no karaoke') in Rundle St at Nos 205 and 246 respectively. The Commercial Hotel on the corner of Morphett and Hindley Sts is open late but it's rough. The Saracen's Head on Carrington St, near King William St, has bands on Wednesday and Friday nights, as does the King's Head, nearby in King William St, on Wednesday and Thursday nights.

The Old Lion Hotel is an up-market place on trendy Melbourne St, North Adelaide. It brews its own beer and has an expensive dining room and a disco. Adelaide University often has big-name rock bands on at the union. Every Friday lunch time during term, there is a free band playing upstairs in the union bar.

There is a string of places with folk and jazz, particularly on Friday and Saturday nights. You'll find them in the 'what's on' guides too. The Union Bistro in Adelaide University's Union each Friday night has free jazz bands playing until 10.30 pm; you can get a good cheap dinner until 8.30 pm.

There's always something on at the Adelaide Festival Centre; the South Australian Government Travel Centre's (SAGTC) *What's On* guide tells all. There are usually free concerts in the amphitheatre at the Festival Centre on Sunday from 2 to 4 pm. Also check the Piano Bar here for free shows.

Every Sunday night the Irish Club at 11 Carrington St has music and what they claim to be the 'best Guinness in town'. If you prefer the products of the other Celtic minority group, the Earl of Zetland pub on Flinders St near the YMCA claims to have the world's largest collection of malt whiskeys available by the nip.

Things to Buy

Tandanya, the large centre run by the Aboriginal Cultural Institute at 253 Grenfell St,

includes a crafts and souvenir shop; it is open daily and there's also a cafe. The Jam Factory, a centre for the production and sale of crafts, is in the Living Arts Centre on the corner of Morphett St and North Terrace.

For camping equipment, see Paddy Pallin and Thor Adventure Equipment (☎ (08) 232 3155) who share a shop at 228 Rundle St. Trims on the corner of King William and Carrington Sts has less hi-tech camping gear and is a good place to buy work clothes (good for bushwalking and cheaper than the designer stuff) and other odds and ends.

Getting There & Away

Air Adelaide is the major departure point from the southern states for Alice Springs and Darwin. Many flights from Melbourne and Sydney to the Northern Territory go via Adelaide. Note that the Darwin route is often heavily booked. Australian Airlines (☎ 217 3333) is at 144 North Terrace and Ansett (☎ 233 3322) is at 142 North Terrace.

Airlines can quote higher standard fares, but all have a range of specials and advance-purchase deals so it's always worth checking around. Discount fares from Adelaide start around $352 to Brisbane, $250 to Sydney, $174 to Melbourne and $360 to Perth.

For airfares within the state, refer to the airfares chart in the introductory Getting Around section in this chapter.

Bus Dial-a-Coach (☎ 410 0088) has an office at Shop 7 in the underpass at the railway station. They're agents for just about every company in Australia and they have specials, although it's still worth checking around the hostels for cheaper deals.

Bus Australia and Greyhound/Pioneer run to Adelaide from Sydney, Melbourne, Perth, Alice Springs and other main centres. From Melbourne it's 9½ hours and around $40, Sydney is 21 hours and $89, Perth 34 hours and $160, and Alice Springs 21 hours and $153.

Firefly Express runs to Melbourne and is usually a little cheaper than the others. An Adelaide-Melbourne-Sydney ticket on Firefly is often cheaper than a direct Adelaide to Sydney ticket with other companies, although the trip takes longer. There are various bus operators, particularly on the Perth route, and there are frequent special deals on offer.

If you're going to Melbourne, a good alternative to the major bus lines is to spend three days and two nights on the trip with the Wayward Bus Company (☎ 371 2492, or 008 882 823, toll-free) which runs a 22-seater bus along a scenic route, including Victoria's spectacular Great Ocean Road, visiting a winery or two along the way.

The $110 fare (10% off for students and YHA members) includes lunches but not accommodation or other meals – they have camping gear for hire if you need it but they always stop where cheap accommodation is available. Departures from Adelaide are on Wednesday at 8 am; from Melbourne they depart on Saturday at 8 am. If demand is high a second departure each week is added. This trip gets good comments from travellers.

Bus Australia (☎ 212 7999), Pioneer (☎ 233 2733) and Greyhound (☎ 233 2777) depart from the central bus station at 101-111 Franklin St. Firefly Express (☎ 231 1488) is at 185 Victoria Square, near the corner of Franklin St.

Stateliner (☎ 233 2777), Premier (☎ 233 2744) and other South Australian operators are at the central bus station. Stateliner have services to Alice Springs, the Eyre Peninsula, Arkaroola, the Riverland area and to Broken Hill in New South Wales. Premier go to Victor Harbor, Moonta and Murray Bridge. See the appropriate Getting There & Away sections in this chapter for details.

Yorke Peninsula bus service (☎ 391 2977) has services to the east coast and the centre of Yorke Peninsula. The depot is opposite the bus station. Mt Barker buses runs from the same depot and they have frequent buses going to Hahndorf and Mt Barker for about $3.50.

Train There are two stations in Adelaide: the large one on North Terrace, now only for suburban trains; and the new interstate terminal on Railway Terrace, Keswick (☎ 231 7699 for information and bookings), just south-west of the city centre. It's wise to book ahead, particularly on the very popular Ghan.

Seven-day advance purchase fares (Caper fares) are considerably cheaper than the standard fares. Because of competition from buses and cheap flights, the advance purchase requirement has been waived for economy fares between Adelaide and Sydney or Melbourne (and on all fares between Melbourne and Sydney).

Adelaide is connected by rail with Sydney, Melbourne, Perth, Broken Hill, Alice Springs and other centres. To Melbourne the daily overnight Overland takes about 13 hours and costs $42 in economy, or $85 ($60 Caper) in 1st class and $145 with sleeper ($102 Caper).

You can travel between Sydney and Adelaide either via Melbourne (daily) or via Broken Hill on the Indian-Pacific (three times a week). Via Melbourne (changing trains at Sunshine) it's $127 economy, $205 1st class and $325 ($215 Caper) with a sleeper. Via Broken Hill it's $100 economy, $226 ($158 Caper) economy sleeper and $307 ($215 Caper) 1st-class sleeper.

There's also the Speedlink – a bus-train connection which is not only cheaper but five or six hours faster. You travel from Sydney to Albury on the XPT train, and from Albury to Adelaide on a V/Line bus. Travel time is under 20 hours – the 1st class/economy fares are $98/$105.

Between Adelaide and Perth there is the Indian-Pacific which runs three times a week and the once-weekly Trans-Australian. The Adelaide to Perth trip takes about 42 hours. Fares are $165 ($150 Caper) for an economy seat, $412 ($289 Caper) for an economy sleeping berth with meals or $545 ($382 Caper) in a 1st-class sleeping berth with meals.

The Ghan between Adelaide and Alice Springs runs weekly (twice weekly from April to October) and takes 23 hours. The fare is $125 in economy and $395 ($277 Caper) in a 1st-class sleeper with meals. From Port Augusta to Alice Springs it's 18 hours and $125 in economy and $296 ($277 Caper – yes, the same as from Adelaide) in a sleeper.

Car It's worth contacting the Backpackers' Information Centre (☎ 232 4774) at 314 Gilles St to see if they know of any hire cars that need to be driven back to their home bases – this can be a remarkably cheap way of covering long distances.

Hitching For Melbourne take bus Nos 164, 165 or 166 from Pulteney St to stop 21 on Mt Barker Rd and thumb from there. To Port Augusta and Perth take bus No 224 from King William St to Port Wakefield Rd in Gepps Cross, and then walk or get a lift to Carvans Petrol Station and start from there.

Hitching across the Nullarbor from Adelaide to Perth

Many people start hitching in Port Augusta from the petrol station furthest away from Adelaide on the Eyre Highway. While this hitching spot is popular, many people have waited 48 hours for a ride. The traffic is light. Cars and trucks are accelerating as they leave town and are not inclined to stop. The petrol station closer to the town centre is a better alternative. Staff at most petrol stations don't like hitchhikers chatting up potential rides.

You might get a lift all the way across to Perth, but many people beginning that long trip don't want to risk being stuck with a less than sparkling personality all the way, so there's a fair chance that the cars that do stop will be going to towns on the highway in South Australia. These can take time to get out of and they won't necessarily have a bank, although most have post offices for Commonwealth Bank customers.

It's a good idea to carry something out of which you can make a sign. My 'third day' sign finally got me out of Eucla – in a Holden containing two tripping shearers, three other hitchhikers and a few kelpie puppies.

The best time to hitch and get rides with truckies from Adelaide is on Friday evening or Saturday morning, and coming back from Perth on Tuesday evening and Wednesday morning.

Boat MV *Island Seaway* runs a passenger service from Port Adelaide to Kingscote (Kangaroo Island). See the Kangaroo Island section later in this chapter for details.

Getting Around

To/From the Airport Adelaide's modern international airport is conveniently located 8 km west of the city centre. There's an airport bus service (☎ 381 5311) operating between hotels at least hourly from around 7 am to 8 pm for $3.50. From Victoria Square to the domestic terminal takes about 35 minutes; slightly less to the international terminal. If you're catching a flight on one of the smaller airlines (eg to Kangaroo Island) let the driver know, as the drop-off point is different. A taxi costs about $10. You can travel between the city and the airport entrance on bus Nos 276 or 277.

Budget, Hertz, Avis and Thrifty have rent-a-car desks at the airport.

Car Rental The major companies are represented in Adelaide. Budget places include Rent-a-Bug (☎ 234 0911), with cars under $20 a day including insurance, and Cut Price Rentals (☎ 43 7788) which has cars from $15 a day, plus $10 insurance or $150 a week including insurance. Check the Yellow Pages for other cheapies.

Moped & Bicycle Rental Action Moped (☎ 211 7060) at 400 King William St rent mopeds for $50 per day, bicycles for $15 and tandems for $25. Several of the hostels around the city rent bikes. Pulteney St Cycles at No 309, near Carrington St, rent one-speed mountain-type bikes at $10 for the first day and $5 for following days. Out at Glenelg there's a bike-hire place right next door to the information centre.

Bike Moves (☎ 293 2922) rent mountain bikes for $18 per day ($65 per week), standard 10-speeds for $15 ($55) and quality lightweights for $28 ($100). They also have panniers, tents and other touring equipment for hire, and they'll deliver the bike to you.

Local Transport Adelaide has an integrated local transport system operated by the STA (State Transport Authority) (☎ 210 1000 until 7.30 pm daily, until 4 pm on Sunday). The office, where you can get timetables and buy a transport map for 30c, is on the corner of King William and Grenfell Sts.

Adelaide is divided into three zones: travel within one or two sections costs $1.20, one or two zones $2.30 or three zones $3.10. From the city to Glenelg is a one-zone trip. Travel between 9 am and 3 pm on weekdays is considerably cheaper. Three-zone Day-trip tickets (usable from 9 am) cost $3.50. Multitrip tickets for the various zones give 10 rides for the price of seven. Tickets cost more if they are bought on board – get them from railway stations, bus depots and some newsagents and delicatessens. Multitrip and Day-trip tickets are also available from post offices.

In the city centre there is a free bus service: the Bee Line service basically runs down King William St from the Glenelg tram terminus at Victoria Square and round the corner to the railway station. It operates every five minutes from 8 am to 6 pm weekdays, to 9 pm on Friday and from 8 am to 12.15 pm on Saturday.

Four buses a day run between the Ansett building on North Terrace and the interstate train station for about $3 (☎ 217 4444). For two or more people, a taxi is no dearer.

There's a solitary tram service which will whisk you out to Glenelg from Victoria Square for $2.30 (it is cheaper between 9 am and 3 pm).

Around Adelaide

Adelaide is fortunate to have so much that is easily accessible to the city: the Barossa is an easy day trip; the wineries of the Southern Vales are a morning or afternoon visit; and the Adelaide Hills are less than half an hour from the city.

ADELAIDE HILLS

Adelaide is flanked by hills to the south and east. The highest point, **Mt Lofty** at 771 metres, is a 30-minute drive from the city and offers spectacular views over Adelaide, particularly from Windy Point at night. The hills

are scenic and varied with tiny villages which look as though they are straight from Europe. The **Montacute Scenic Route** is one of the best drives through the hills. Walking tracks, 1000 km of them altogether, crisscross the hills. Ambelong Tours (☎ (08) 274 1222) have half and full-day walks in the hills.

Parks in the hills include the **Cleland Conservation Park**, 19 km from the city on the slopes of Mt Lofty. There's a wide variety of wildlife in the park and it's open from 9 am to 5 pm daily. There are walking tracks, barbecues, waterfalls and a rugged gorge at the **Morialta Park** near Rostrevor. Other parks include the **Parra Wirra Park** to the north of the city and the **Belair Recreation Park** to the south. The **Warrawong Sanctuary** (☎ 388 5380) on Williams Rd, Mylor, has a variety of wildlife including some rarely seen nocturnal animals. Nightly guided walks must be booked and cost $10; on weekends there are day walks for $5.

Heading out south-east of Adelaide on the Princes Highway, you'll pass the **Old Toll House** in Glen Osmond at the foot of the hills. Tolls were collected here for just five years from 1841.

Places to Stay

The YHA has five 'limited access' hostels for members in the Mt Lofty Ranges at Para Wirra, Norton Summit, Mt Lofty, Mylor and Kuitpo. These hostels are on the Heysen Trail. You must book in advance and obtain the key from the YHA office in Adelaide. They each cost $5 or $6 a night, plus a key deposit.

The friendly *Fuzzie's Farm* (☎ (08) 390 1111) at Norton Summit is a developing 'eco-village' on 15 hectares next to the Morialta Conservation Park, about 15 km east of Adelaide. There are various farm animals, vegetable gardens and craft studios, as well as a restaurant, spa and pool. Hostel-style accommodation costs $12 – if you want to join in and help run the farm or build the hamlet, you pay $8 with all meals included, although they'd prefer you to stay at least a week with this deal.

BIRDWOOD

The **Birdwood Hill Museum** has the largest collection of old cars and motorcycles in Australia. It's open daily from 9 am to 5 pm and costs $6. The town was once a gold-mining centre and has various other old buildings. You can get to Birdwood (50 km east from Adelaide) via Chain of Ponds and Gumeracha or via Lobethal, passing through the spectacular **Torrens River Gorge** en route.

There isn't much accommodation – the *Blumberg Inn* has just one expensive room and the pub no longer takes guests. Nor is there any regular public transport. Phone the museum (☎ (08) 68 5006) and they might be able to advise you on getting a lift up.

Gumeracha has a toy factory with a 20-metre-high rocking horse – yes, another of those Australian 'big' attractions. **Lobethal** has a fine little historical museum open on Tuesday and Sunday afternoons. The **Gorge Wildlife Park** at Cudlee Creek is surrounded in natural bushland and has one of the largest private wildlife collections in Australia.

In Gumeracha (40 km east of Adelaide), the *Gumeracha Hotel* (☎ (08) 389 1001) has rooms for $20 per person.

HAHNDORF (population 1300)

The oldest surviving German settlement in Australia, Hahndorf, 29 km south-east of Adelaide, is a popular day trip. Settled in 1839 by Lutherans who left Prussia to escape religious persecution, the town took its name from the ship's captain Hahn; *dorf* is German for 'village'. Hahndorf still has an honorary Burgermeister.

The information centre (☎ (08) 388 1185) on the main street is open daily. Various German festivals are held in the town including the annual mid-January Scheutzenfest beer festival. The **German Arms Hotel** at 50 Main St dates from 1834. The **Hahndorf Academy**, established in 1857, houses an art gallery and museum. The **Antique Clock Museum** at 91 Main St has a fine collection of timepieces, including a very large cuckoo clock; admission is $3.

Places to Stay & Eat

The *Hahndorf Holiday Village* caravan park (☎ (08) 388 7361) is 1½ km out of town on Main St. Camp sites are $10 and on-site vans are $39 for two. Other than this and a couple of expensive motels, the only option is to take up the offer of 'emergency accommodation for stuck backpackers' (☎ (08) 388 7079) – it's very cheap but there's only one room and a tent, so don't rely on it.

Hahndorf restaurants have good, solid German food, of course; they include the *German Arms* and the *Cottage Kitchen* on Main St. There's also a Chinese restaurant and a few takeaways.

Getting There & Away

Mt Barker bus service runs frequently from opposite the central bus station in Adelaide. The one-way fare is $3.20.

Fleurieu Peninsula

South of Adelaide is the Fleurieu Peninsula, so close that most places can be visited on day trips from the city. Gulf St Vincent has a series of fine beaches down to Cape Jervis. The southern coast, from Cape Jervis to the mouth of the Murray River, is pounded by the Southern Ocean.

The peninsula was named by Frenchman Nicholas Baudin after Napoleon's Minister for the Navy, who financed Baudin's expedition to Australia. In the early days, settlers on the peninsula ran a busy smuggling business but in 1837 the first whaling station was established at Encounter Bay. This grew to become the colony's first successful industry.

There are good surfing beaches along this rugged coastline. Inland there's rolling countryside and the vineyards of the McLaren Vale area.

Getting There & Away

Premier (☎ (08) 233 2744) has up to three services daily on the two-hour Adelaide to

McLaren Vale ($4.10), Port Elliot ($8.70) and Victor Harbor ($8.70) route.

The Kangaroo Island Connection (☎ (08) 384 6860) runs twice a day to Cape Jervis from Adelaide. The fares are Aldinga $4.80, Yankalilla $8.90 and Cape Jervis $11. You can also travel to Goolwa with Johnsons (☎ (08) 339 2488) for $8.90; they're at Adelaide's central bus station, near Bus Australia.

There's no direct service between Cape Jervis and Victor Harbor, but the owner of the Warringa Guesthouse in Victor Harbor will run you across for $8; coming the other way he'll pick you up from Port Jervis if you make arrangements through the youth hostel in Penneshaw.

To Strathalbyn, the Mt Barker bus service (☎ (08) 391 2977) runs from Adelaide (changing at Mt Barker) on weekdays for $4.80.

The Steam Ranger, a tourist steam train, runs between Adelaide and Victor Harbor on Sundays during May and from mid-August to the end of November – these dates can change (☎ (08) 231 1701 to check). Return tickets cost around $35. The Cockle Train runs on Sunday all year round (more frequently during January) between Victor Harbor and Goolwa for $10 return. It doesn't run on very hot days because of the fire danger.

GULF ST VINCENT BEACHES

There is a string of fine beaches south of Adelaide along the Gulf St Vincent coast of the peninsula. The beaches extend from **Christie's Beach** through **Port Noarlunga**, **Seaford Beach** and **Moana Beach** before you reach **Maslin Beach**, the southern end of which became the first legal nude beach in Australia.

Further south, beyond **Aldinga Beach** and **Sellicks Beach**, the coastline is rockier

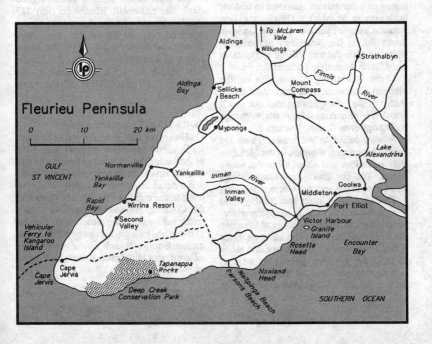

but there are still good swimming beaches at **Myponga**, **Normanville** and several other places. The coast road ends at **Cape Jervis** at the tip of the peninsula. From here you can look across the narrow Backstairs Passage to Kangaroo Island, 13 km away. Near Cape Jervis there's a 12-hectare fauna park. The cape is a popular spot for hang-gliding.

Places to Stay

In Yankalilla, four km east of Normanville, *Jack & Jillaroo* (☎ (085) 58 2926) has beds from $15 including food. They also do pick ups from Adelaide's central bus station and have horse-riding packages.

The *Cape Jervis Tavern* (☎ (085) 98 0276), the only place to stay in Cape Jervis, has rooms for $40/49 and also serves food – the fish has been highly recommended.

SOUTHERN VALES

Adelaide has sprawled so far that the small town of **Morphett Vale** (south of Adelaide) is now an outer suburb. Amongst its historic buildings is St Mary's (1846), the first Roman Catholic church in the state. On Main South Rd, at the Noarlunga turn-off, the Morphett Vale Pioneer Village recreates an early South Australian settlement.

There is a string of wineries on the Fleurieu Peninsula; **McLaren Vale** is the centre of the wine-growing area but you'll also find wine makers at **Reynella**, **Willunga** and **Langhorne Creek**. The area is particularly well suited to red wines. There are around two dozen wineries in the McLaren Vale area alone and about 40 in the whole region. You can make a pleasant tastings crawl around the various wineries.

The first winery in the area (in Reynella) was established in 1838; some of the wineries date back to the last century and have fine old buildings. Most of them are open to the public from Monday to Saturday, and many of them are open on Sunday as well. A number have picnic or barbecue areas close to the cellar sales. Some good small wineries are Wirra Wirra, Coriole and Hardy's Chateau Reynella.

The McLaren Vale Wine Bushing Festival takes place over a week in late October to early November each year. It's a busy time of wine tastings and tours, and the whole thing is topped by a grand Elizabethan Feast.

A great way to visit a few wineries is on a camel with the Outback Camel Co (☎ (085) 567 236). A one-day trek costs $75, and there are other shorter rides available. These tours only operate between October and April.

Willunga, in the south of the Southern Vales winery area, has a long history and a collection of fine buildings from the colonial era. It is the centre for Australian almond growing, and the Almond Blossom Festival is held in July. At the **Mt Magnificent Conservation Park**, 12 km east of Willunga, you can see kangaroos and take pleasant walks.

Places to Stay & Eat

The *Hotel McLaren* in McLaren Vale has single/double rooms for $35/50 including a light breakfast.

The wine tasters' lunches can be a good deal; the *Oliverhill Winery* (☎ (08) 323 8922) at Seaview Rd has Italian and Chinese main courses for $6 or less, but *James Haselgrove Wines* (☎ (08) 323 8706) on the corner of Kangarilla and Foggo Rds has the best meals from $8. In Willunga, the *Willunga Hotel* (☎ (085) 56 2135) has rooms for $30/40.

PORT ELLIOT (population 800)

On Horseshoe Bay, a smaller part of Encounter Bay, Port Elliot was established in 1854 as the seaport for the Murray River trade and was the first town on Encounter Bay. Today it is a resort town with fine views along the coast to the mouth of the Murray River and the Coorong. **Horseshoe Bay** has a sheltered, safe swimming beach with a good cliff-top walk above it. Nearby surf beaches include **Boomer Beach**, on the western edge of town, and **Middleton Beach**, to the east of town.

Places to Stay

The *Royal Family Hotel* (☎ (085) 54 2219) at 32 North Terrace has rooms for $15 per person (although this might rise when the renovations are completed) and reasonable counter meals. You can camp or stay in on-site vans at the *Port Elliot Caravan Park* in Horseshoe Bay.

VICTOR HARBOR (population 4500)

The main town on the peninsula, 84 km south of Adelaide, Victor Harbor looks out on to Encounter Bay where Flinders and Baudin had their historic meeting in 1802. Up on the headland known as the Bluff, there's a memorial to the 'encounter' which took place on the bay below. It's a steep climb up to the Bluff for the fine views.

Victor, as the town is often called, was founded early in South Australia's history as a sealing and whaling centre. South of the town at Rosetta Bay, below the Bluff, is **Whaler's Haven** with many interesting reminders of those early whaling days. The first whaling station was established here in 1837 and another followed soon after on Granite Island, but whaling ceased in 1864. After that, Victor became the main seaside resort for Adelaide; it still retains something of that atmosphere with some grand pubs, public buildings and a small foreshore funfair.

Historic buildings include **St Augustine's Church of England** (1869), the **Telegraph Station** (1869), the **Fountain Inn** (1840), the **Museum of Historical Art** ($1 admission) and the **Cornhill Museum & Art Gallery**.

The tourist office is on Torrens St, diagonally opposite the police station.

The port is protected from the high southern seas by **Granite Island**, a small island connected to the mainland by a causeway. You can ride out there on a double-decker tram pulled by Clydesdale draught-horses for $2. On the island there are good views across the bay, and if you're feeling lazy you can ride to the top of the hill on a chair lift.

Seals are common on the shores, and southern right whales are visiting more often these days. If you come out at night with a torch you'll probably see (and hear) fairy penguins.

Places to Stay

The *Warringa Guesthouse* (☎ (085) 52 1028) at 16 Flinders Parade, near the railway station, is an associate youth hostel. It has a prime seafront location and a friendly atmosphere. A bed in the hostel is $10 ($8 for YHA members) while singles/doubles in the guesthouse cost $25/40 – less in the off-season. They also have a restaurant serving breakfast, lunch and dinner, a pleasant little bar and bikes for hire. The owner is a good source of local information, and if you're heading for Kangaroo Island, he'll take you to Cape Jervis for $8.

The *Grosvenor Hotel* (☎ (085) 52 1011), a block away on Ocean St, is reasonable at $23/35, or $40 for a three-bed room. The council *caravan park* (☎ (085) 52 1142) has tent sites and on-site vans.

There's a *Youth Hostel* (☎ (085) 58 8277) on the Heysen Trail in the Inman Valley, near Glacier Rock, 20 km west from Victor Harbor; beds are $7 a night.

Places to Eat

The *Original Fish & Chip Shop* on Ocean St has good fish & chips, although prices for sit-down meals are high. The *Hotel Victor* has tasty counter meals from about $6, while the *Ocean Chinese Restaurant* on Ocean St has good meals at around $8. A three-course dinner at the classier *Apollon Restaurant* on Torrens St is about $25.

GOOLWA (population 1600)

On Lake Alexandrina near the mouth of the Murray River, Goolwa initially grew with the developing trade along the mighty Murray. The Murray mouth silted up and large ships were unable to get up to Goolwa, so a railway line, the first in the state, was built from Goolwa to nearby Port Elliot. In the 1880s a new railway line to Adelaide spelt the end for Goolwa as a port town.

Today Goolwa is a resort with some interesting old buildings. The **museum** on Porter St ($1 admission) is open every afternoon except Monday. Two km away at the **Malleebaa Woolshed**, you can see 18 breeds of sheep and other sheep-related displays – it's only open on long weekends and during school holidays.

The **Sir Richard Peninsula** is a long stretch of beach leading to the mouth of the Murray. You can drive along it (if your car is up to it) but there's no way across to the similar beaches of the Coorong which begin on the other side of the Murray River mouth.

There are cruises on Lake Alexandrina on the MV *Aroona* or PS *Mundoo* from $15. Possibly more amusing is a trip with the Coorong Pirate (☎ (085) 52 1221), a large and irredeemably ocker gentleman who runs fun trips from about $15.

Goolwa is the departure point for upriver cruises on the *Murray River Queen*. **Milang** on Lake Alexandrina was a centre for the river trade even before Goolwa. In the early days of the river-shipping business, bullock wagons carried goods overland between here and Adelaide.

The tourist office (☎ (085) 55 1144) is in the centre of Goolwa near Signal Point. At Signal Point itself there's a large display on the Murray River, including a film, which costs $5.

There's a free, 24-hour vehicle ferry crossing over to **Hindmarsh Island**.

Places to Stay

The *Corio Hotel* (☎ (085) 55 1136) on Railway Terrace has singles/doubles for $20/40 with breakfast. The *Camping & Tourist Park* (☎ (085) 55 2144) on Kessell Rd has tent sites and on-site vans.

On Hindmarsh Island, *Narnu Pioneer Holiday Farm* (☎ (085) 55 2002) has cottages for about $60; some have four bedrooms. There's a surcharge if you stay less than three days.

STRATHALBYN (population 1750)

On the Angas River, this picturesque town was settled in 1839 by Scottish immigrants. Unlike most country towns, it isn't strung out along a highway and there's a lot more than the main street worth seeing. The tourist office (☎ (085) 36 3212) is on Albyn Terrace.

Among the many interesting old buildings in this classified 'heritage town' is **St Andrew's Church**, one of the best known country churches in Australia.

Places to Stay & Eat

The *Terminus Hotel* (☎ (085) 36 2026) on Rankine St has singles/doubles for $20/35; it was the first building in Strathalbyn. The council *caravan park* (☎ (085) 36 3681) is a basic, shady place by the cricket ground.

The *Terminus* and the *Commercial* hotels have reasonable counter meals or there's *Strath Eats*, a cafe and pizza bar. Eat early – in winter you can find everything shut by 7 pm.

Kangaroo Island

Population 4000

The third biggest island in Australia (after Tasmania and Melville Island, off Darwin), Kangaroo Island is a holiday resort for many Adelaide vacationers. About 150 km long and 30 km wide, the island is sparsely populated and offers superb scenery, pleasant sheltered beaches along the north coast, a rugged and wave-swept south coast plus lots of native wildlife and excellent fishing.

Like other islands off the south coast of Australia, Kangaroo Island had a rough and ready early history with sealers, whalers and escaped convicts all playing their often ruthless part. Many of the place names on the island have a French flavour since it was first charted by the French explorer Nicholas Baudin. Matthew Flinders had already named the island after the many kangaroos he saw there, but Baudin named many other prominent features.

Apart from beaches, bushwalks and wildlife, the island also has more than its fair share of shipwrecks. A number are of interest to scuba divers.

The main National Parks office (which doubles as the tourist office) is in Kingscote (☎ (0848) 22 381).

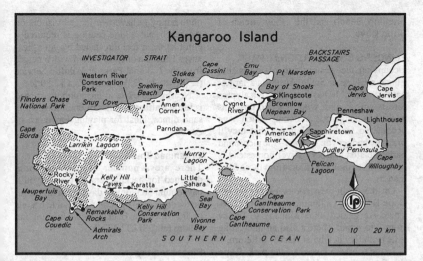

Kangaroo Island

KINGSCOTE (population 1400)

The main town on the island, Kingscote is also the arrival point for the ferries and flights. This was the first White settlement in South Australia, although it was soon superseded by Adelaide and other mainland centres. Although there had been other Europeans on the island many years earlier, Kingscote was only formally settled in 1836 and was all but abandoned just a few years later.

The rock pool and **Brownlow Beach** are good places for swimming. The old cottage, Hope (built in 1858), is a museum and the headstones in Kingscote's cemetery make interesting reading. **St Alban's Church** (built in 1884) has beautiful stained-glass windows.

AMERICAN RIVER (population 120)

Between Kingscote and Penneshaw, the small settlement of American River takes its name from the American sealers who built a boat here in 1803-4. The town is on a small peninsula and shelters an inner bay, named **Pelican Lagoon** by Flinders, which is now a bird sanctuary.

PENNESHAW

Looking across the narrow Backstairs Passage to the Fleurieu Peninsula, Penneshaw is a quiet little resort town with a pleasant beach at **Hog's Bay** and the tiny inlet of **Christmas Cove** which is used as a boat harbour. You can sometimes see penguins on the rocks below the town. **Frenchman's Rock** is a monument housing a replica of the rock Baudin inscribed in 1803. The original is in the South Australian Art Gallery. The **Old Penneshaw School** houses a folk museum.

The Dudley Peninsula, the knob of land on the eastern end of the island on which Penneshaw is located, has several other points of interest. There's surf at **Pennington Bay** and the sheltered waters of **Chapman River** are popular for canoeing. The **Cape Willoughby Lighthouse**, the oldest in the state, first operated in 1852; it's open from 1 to 3.30 pm Monday to Friday.

NORTH COAST

There are a series of fine sheltered beaches along the north coast. Near Kingscote, **Emu Bay** has a beautiful, long sweep of sand. Other good beaches include **Stokes Bay**,

Snelling Beach and the sandy stretch of **Snug Cove**.

FLINDERS CHASE NATIONAL PARK

Occupying the western end of the island, Flinders Chase is South Australia's largest national park. It has beautiful eucalyptus forests with koalas, wild pigs and possums as well as kangaroos and emus which have become so fearless of humans that they'll brazenly badger you for food – the picnic and barbecue area at Rocky River homestead is fenced off to protect visitors from these free-loaders.

On the north-west corner of the island, **Cape Borda** has a lighthouse built in 1858. There are guided tours Monday to Friday from 2 to 4 pm. There's also an interesting little cemetery nearby at Harvey's Return.

In the southern corner of the park, **Cape du Couedic** is wild and remote. An extremely picturesque lighthouse built in 1906 tops the cape; you can follow the path from the car park down to Admirals Arch – a natural archway pounded by towering seas. You can often see seals and penguins here.

At Kirkpatrick Point, a couple of km east of Cape du Couedic, the **Remarkable Rocks** are a series of bizarre granite rocks on a huge dome stretching 75 metres down to the sea.

SOUTH COAST

The south coast is rough and wave-swept compared with the north coast. At **Hanson Bay**, close to Cape du Couedic at the western end of the coast, there's a colony of fairy penguins. A little further east you come to **Kelly Hill Caves**, a series of limestone caves discovered in the 1880s when a horse – named Ned Kelly – fell through a hole in the ground. There are six tours daily ($2) between 10 am and 3 pm, but sometimes less often in winter (☎ (0848) 37231).

Vivonne Bay has a long and beautiful sweep of beach. There is excellent fishing but bathers should take great care; the undertows are fierce and swimmers are advised to stick close to the jetty or the river mouth. **Seal Bay** is another sweeping beach, with plenty of resident seals. They're generally

quite happy to have two-legged visitors on the beach, but a little caution is required – don't let them feel threatened by your presence. They can only be visited with a ranger from the National Parks & Wildlife Service (☎ (0848) 28 233) and there's a $2.50 fee.

Nearby and close to the south coast road is **Little Sahara**, a series of enormous white sand dunes, ideal for playing Lawrence of Arabia.

Organised Tours

There are a number of package tours designed for backpackers. Typically you'll pay around $85 for two days and a night, but better deals crop up. Check Adelaide hostels or the Adelaide Backpackers' Information Centre (☎ (08) 232 4774).

Places to Stay

Hostels *Penneshaw Youth Hostel* (☎ (0848) 31 173) costs $10 in dorms or $12 per person in twin rooms. They also offer a $55 accommodation and tour package. The *Penguin Hostel* (☎ (0848) 31 018), also in Penneshaw, has beds in self-contained units for $12, or $15 with linen; doubles cost about $35. They also have a tour package. The same people have *Gull Cottage* which sleeps nine and costs $75 a night. The *Hill Farm Hostel* (☎ (0848) 22 778) in Kingscote charges around $10 a bed.

Hotels & Motels In American River *Linnetts Island Club* (☎ (0848) 33 053) has rooms from $22/42. In Kingscote *Ellsons Seaview* (☎ (0848) 22 030) on Chapman Terrace has rooms from $55/65 and a few guesthouse-style rooms at $30/36. In Penneshaw the *Sorrento Resort Motel* (☎ (0848) 31 028) has rooms from $55/70.

Camping, Cabins & Holiday Flats There are numerous camp sites and a wide selection of cabins and holiday flats, many charging about $40 a night for a room sleeping four to six. Weekly costs are much lower, and peak times are more expensive.

One of the best deals is at *Coranda Farm* (☎ (0840) 31 019) in Penneshaw which has a 'tent city' and charges $6 per person in two-person tents.

Other places with cabins in the $20 to $40 range include: the *Ravine Wildlife Park* (☎ (0848) 93 256) at Flinders Chase; *Beachfront Cottages* (☎ (08) 332 1083 in Adelaide) or the *Hoey House* (☎ (08) 47 5837 in Adelaide) in Penneshaw; *Eleanor River Holiday Cabins* (☎ (0848) 94 250) in Vivonne Bay; and *Casaurina Coastal Units* (☎ (0848) 33 020) in American River.

In Flinders Chase you can camp at the Rocky River park headquarters, or elsewhere with a permit. There's a $1.50 entry fee to the national park, but a $10 pass covers all entry and camping fees for the whole island.

Watch out for kangaroos if you are camping at Flinders Chase. They get into tents looking for food and can cause a lot of damage. The National Parks service has houses for rent at Rocky River, Cape Borda and Cape du Couedic. They sleep at least four people and cost between $20 and $50 a night – good value; phone ☎ (0848) 22 381 for bookings.

Getting There & Away
Air Air Kangaroo Island (☎ (08) 234 4177) has daily services from Adelaide to American River ($51 one-way), Penneshaw ($51), Kingscote ($65) and Pandana ($53). If you fly into American River you must arrange a transfer into town. Albatross Airlines (☎ (08) 234 3399) fly from Adelaide to Kingscote three times daily ($58 one-way).

Ferry The *Island Seaway* crosses to Kingscote from Port Adelaide every Monday. The crossing takes 6½ hours and costs $26 one-way. Accompanied bicycles cost $4.20, motorcycles $35 and cars $106 (including the driver). The service between Kingscote and Port Lincoln has been discontinued but might start up again. Contact the agents, R W Miller (☎ (08) 47 5577), 3 Todd St, Port Adelaide, for more information. In Kingscote contact Patrick Sleigh Shipping (☎ (0848) 22 273) on Commercial St.

Most people cross from Cape Jervis,

opposite Kangaroo Island on the end of the Fleurieu Peninsula. The *Valerie Jane* (☎ (0848) 31 233) is a nonvehicle ferry which runs to Penneshaw twice daily for $24 and does the trip in half an hour – during July the service takes a break.

Sealink (☎ 008 088 836, toll-free) operates two vehicle ferries, *Philanderer III* and *Island Navigator*, which now run all year, taking an hour to Penneshaw. There are at least a couple of sailings each day, with more in January. One-way fares are $26 for passengers, $4 for bicycles, $20 for motorbikes and $58 for cars.

The Kangaroo Island Connection (☎ (08) 384 6860), a bus service from Adelaide, costs $11 one-way and connects with most Sealink services. It departs from the central bus station.

See the Fleurieu Peninsula Getting There & Away section for information on getting to Victor Harbor from Cape Jervis.

Getting Around
There's an airport bus running from the Kangaroo Island Airport to Kingscote for about $6. Kingscote Taxi & Tours Service (☎ (0848) 22 640) provides a daily service between American River, Kingscote (town and airport) and Penneshaw; advance booking is usually necessary. The Sealink Shuttle (☎ 008 088 836, toll-free, or (0848) 31 122) connects with ferries and links Penneshaw with Kingscote ($10) and American River ($6). You have to book in advance.

There are a variety of rental cars and motorcycles; the SAGTC has a car-hire leaflet for the island. The 'big three' have agencies and there are a number of independent operators. None are cheap. Kingscote Car Hire (☎ (0848) 28 186) charges $55 a day with 200 free km; Kangaroo Island Rental Cars (☎ (0848) 22 390) in Kingscote is similar.

You can hire mopeds in Kingscote at the Country Cottage Shop (☎ (0848) 22 148) and from the Penneshaw Youth Hostel (☎ (0848) 31 173) for $30 a day. You can't take them on unsealed roads – which isn't a bad idea, as people who ride motorbikes on the island's unsealed roads have a fairly high accident rate, and mopeds are even less stable.

You can, with difficulty, hitch around the island. It's especially difficult in the off-season. Bicycling is also hard work as the roads are unsealed. Also, the distances are large; from Penneshaw to Cape Borda is 140 km. Bicycles can be hired from Kingscote Takeaway (☎ (0848) 22 585) in Kingscote, Linnett's Island Club (☎ (0848) 33 053) in American River and the Sorrento Motel (☎ (0848) 31 028) in Penneshaw.

Barossa Valley

South Australia's famous valley vies with the Hunter Valley in New South Wales as the best known wine-producing area in Australia. The gently sloping valley is about 40 km long and five to 11 km wide. The Barossa turns out a quarter of all the wine in Australia, and since it is only about 50 km north-east from Adelaide, it's a very popular place to visit.

The Barossa still has some of the German flavour from its original settlement in 1842. Fleeing religious persecution in Prussia and Silesia, those first settlers weren't wine makers, but fortunately someone soon came along and recognised the valley's potential. The name is actually a misspelling of Barrosa in Spain, close to where Spanish sherry comes from. Prior to WW I place names in the Barossa probably sounded even more Germanic but during the war many German names were patriotically anglicised. When the fervour died down some were changed back.

A leisurely tastings crawl around the wineries is a popular activity for visitors. On first impressions, this area is a little disappointing since it's rather wide and flat; from the central road it doesn't appear valley-like at all. Furthermore, the main road through Lyndoch, Tanunda and Nuriootpa (the main towns) is rather busy and noisy – not at all like the peaceful valley you might expect.

You must get off the main road to begin to appreciate the Barossa Valley. Take the scenic drive between Angaston and Tanunda, the palm-fringed road to Seppeltsfield and Marananga or wander through the sleepy historic settlement of Bethany.

There's a tourist information centre (☎ (085) 62 1866) in Coulthard House at 66 Murray St, Nuriootpa.

Wineries

The Barossa has over 50 wineries; many of them are open to the public and offer guided tours or free wine tastings. Get a copy of the SAGTC's Barossa leaflet for full details of locations and opening hours.

Some of the most interesting wineries are listed here.

Chateau Yaldara at Lyndoch was established in 1947 in the ruins of a 19th-century winery and flour mill. It has a notable art collection which can be seen on conducted tours.

Kaiser Stuhl and *Penfolds* in Nuriootpa have recently combined, becoming one of the largest wineries in the southern hemisphere. The imposing building fronts the main road. This is a large, commercial winery although they do have an excellent winery tour.

Krondorf at Tanunda is currently one of the glamour wine makers with a high reputation for their wine.

Leo Buring Chateau Leonay, Tanunda, is another winery fantasy with turrets and towers although it dates only from 1945.

Orlando at Rowland Flat, between Lyndoch and Tanunda, was established in 1847 and is one of the oldest wineries in the valley.

Saltrams in Angaston is another old winery. Established in 1859, it has friendly and informative staff.

Seppelts in Seppeltsfield was founded in 1852; the old bluestone buildings are surrounded by gardens and date palms. The extensive complex includes a picnic area with gas barbecues. There is also a family mausoleum.

Tanunda in Tanunda is a magnificent old bluestone building built in 1889 but it is not open to the public.

Wolf Blass out beyond Nuriootpa was only founded in 1973, but by a combination of excellent wines and clever marketing they've quickly become one of the best known wine makers in Australia.

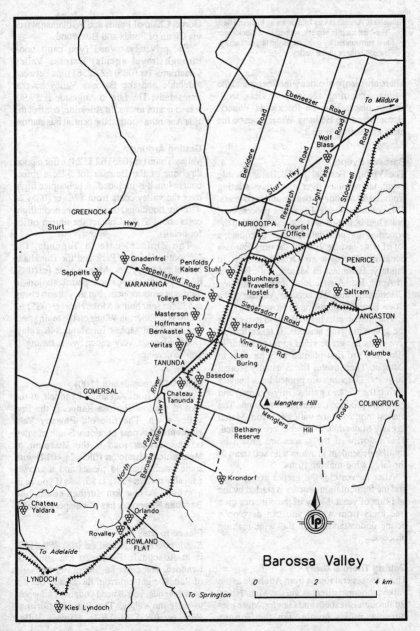

To Mildura

Ebeneezer Road

Belvidere Road

Wolf Blass

Sturt Hwy

Research Road

Light Pass Road

Stockwell Road

GREENOCK

Sturt Hwy

NURIOOTPA

Tourist Office

PENRICE

Gnadenfrei

Penfolds/ Kaiser Stuhl

Seppelts

Seppeltsfield Road

MARANANGA

Bunkhaus Travellers Hostel

Saltram

Tolleys Pedare

Siegersdorf Road

ANGASTON

Masterson

Hardys

Hoffmanns

Bernkastel

Vine Vale Rd

Veritas

Yalumba

TANUNDA

Leo Buring

Basedow

GOMERSAL

River

Menglers Hill

COLINGROVE

Chateau Tanunda

Menglers Hill Road

Bethany Reserve

Para Valley Hwy

Barossa Valley Hwy

North Para River

Krondorf

Chateau Yaldara

Orlando

Rovalley

ROWLAND FLAT

To Adelaide

LYNDOCH

Kies Lyndoch

To Springton

Barossa Valley

0   2   4 km

Yalumba in Angaston was founded way back in 1849. The blue marble winery, topped by a clocktower and surrounded by gardens, is the largest family-owned winery in the valley.

There are plenty of other wineries around the valley, and often the smaller, less well-known places like the Rockfords Winery, Henschke or the Bethany Winery can be the most interesting to visit.

Barossa Events

The Vintage Festival is the Barossa's big event, taking place over seven days starting from Easter Monday in odd-numbered years. The colourful festival features processions, brass bands, tug-of-war contests between the wineries, maypole dancing and, of course, a lot of wine tasting. It's not the only Barossa occasion: there is an Oom Pah Fest in January; Essenfest in March; Folk Festival in April; Hot Air Balloon Regatta in May; Classic Gourmet Weekend in August; and a Brass Band Competition in November.

The main events in the Barossa move with the grape-growing seasons. It takes four to five years for grape vines to reach maturity after they are first planted in September to October. Their useful life is usually around 40 years. The vines are pruned back heavily during the winter months (July-August) and grow and produce fruit over the summer. The busiest months in the valley are from March to early May when the grapes are harvested. The majority of the grapes are grown by small independent growers who sell them to the large wine-making firms.

After harvesting, the grapes are crushed and the fermentation process is started by the addition of yeast. Many of the wineries give free tours from which you can develop a better understanding of the wine-making process.

Getting There & Away

There are several routes from Adelaide to the valley; the most direct is via the Main North Rd through Elizabeth and Gawler. More picturesque routes go through the Torrens Gorge, Chain of Ponds and Williamstown or via Chain of Ponds and Birdwood.

The privately owned (you can't book through travel agents) Barossa Valley Coachlines (☎ (085) 62 6258) runs between Adelaide and the Barossa Valley several times daily. The fare to Angaston is $7.90, less to nearer towns. In Adelaide, contact the Bus Australia booth at the central bus station.

Getting Around

Valley Tours (☎ (085) 62 1524) offer a good day tour of the Barossa for $25; a three-course lunch is included. A helicopter flight over the valley costs from $26 (☎ (085) 24 4209 for bookings) or a hot-air balloon flight costs about $180. Contact the tourist office for details.

The Zinfadel cafe in Tanunda, the Nuriootpa Caravan Park and the Bunkhaus Hostel rent bicycles. Moped Hire (☎ (085) 63 2677) at the Caltex petrol station in Tanunda rents mopeds, but they aren't cheap at $32 for four hours. Moke Hire (☎ (085) 62 1058) is at Elderton Wines on the main street and has Mini Mokes for about $40 a day. Don't plan on very much wine tasting if you're driving.

LYNDOCH (population 1500)

Coming up from Adelaide, Lyndoch, at the foot of the low Barossa Range, is the first valley town. The fine old **Pewsey Vale Homestead** is near Lyndoch. South of town on the Gawler road is the **Museum of Mechanical Music** (☎ (085) 24 4014) with some fascinating old pieces and a knowledgeable owner. Entry is $5, less if you're in a group. A few km further south, the **Barossa Reservoir** has a 'whispering wall'.

Places to Stay

Kersbrook Youth Hostel (☎ (08) 389 3185) is at Roachdale Farm, 20 km south of Lyndoch, and costs $6. Buses run to Chain of Ponds, eight km from the hostel, but not on weekends; you'll need your own transport to visit the valley. The *Barossa Caravan Park* (☎ (085) 24 4262), Barossa Valley

Highway, Lyndoch, has tent sites from $6, on-site vans from $24 and cabins from $26.

Places to Eat

The valley's only true German-style bakery is the *Lyndoch Bakery & Restaurant* off the Barossa Valley Highway in Lyndoch. They have many varieties of rye, wheat and other breads and rolls. The restaurant's menu features traditional Bavarian dishes from $6.90 to $10.90 and huge and very filling cakes. It's open daily except Monday, from breakfast until 6 pm.

TANUNDA (population 3200)

In the centre of the valley is Tanunda, the most Germanic of the towns. You can still see early cottages around **Goat Square**, the site of the original Ziegenmarkt. At 47 Murray St the **Barossa Valley Historical Museum** has exhibits on the valley's early settlement; it's open Monday to Friday from 1 to 5 pm and on weekends from 2 to 5 pm. **Storybook Cottage** (admission $3.50) on Oak St is a park created for children.

The **Kev Rohrlach Collection** on the main road between Nuriootpa and Tanunda is a private museum of transport and technology. It's open daily from 10 am to 5 pm; admission is $5. There are also a number of arts & crafts galleries around the town.

There are fine old churches in all the valley towns but Tanunda has some of the most interesting. The Lutheran **Tabor church** dates from 1849, and the 1868 Lutheran **St John's Church** has life-size wooden statues of Christ, Moses, and the apostles Peter, Paul and John.

From Tanunda, turn off the main road and take the scenic drive through Bethany and via Mengler Hill to Angaston. It runs through beautiful, peaceful country; the view over the valley from Mengler Hill is especially good.

Places to Stay

Tanunda has the reasonable *Tanunda Hotel* (☎ (085) 63 2030) at 51 Murray St with singles/doubles from $38/48 and the *Valley Hotel* (☎ (086) 63 2039), also on Murray St, which has rooms from $18/30. The tourist office has a list of 'alternative' (generally B&B) accommodation in the valley, most fairly pricey.

The *Langmeil Rd Caravan Park* (no phone), two km from the Tanunda post office, is a basic place by a stream. Camping is around $7 for two.

The *Tanunda Caravan & Tourist Park* (☎ (085) 63 2784), Barossa Valley Highway, Tanunda has camping at $9 for two, on-site vans from $26 and air-con cabins from $29.

Places to Eat

The valley is renowned for its solid, German-style eating places but they tend to be expensive. One exception is the *Heinemann Park Restaurant*, just on the Adelaide side of Tanunda, directly opposite the caravan park. It's simple and reasonably priced with main courses from $8.50 to $14.

Crackers Restaurant provides, according to one traveller, 'gastronomic orgasms'. The *Zinfandel Tea Rooms* at 58 Murray St specialises in light lunches and continental cakes. *Giovannis* at the Barossa Junction Resort has reasonably priced Italian food. *Bergmans* on the main street is a large gallery and restaurant which sometimes has a disco in the cellar at weekends.

At 51 Murray St the *Tanunda Hotel* has a nice lounge with counter meals in the $7 to $9 bracket; they also have cheaper snacks. In an arcade across the road there's *Fortune Garden*, a Chinese place with meals from $5.50. The *Apex Bakery* on Elizabeth St still uses wood-fired ovens.

NURIOOTPA (population 3200)

At the north end of the valley Nuriootpa, known locally as 'Nuri', is the commercial centre of the Barossa Valley. **Coulthard House**, the home of a pioneer settler in the 1840s, is now used as the local tourist information centre (☎ (085) 62 1866). Check out the amazing 'mobile home' out the front – it looks like a refugee from a Disney cartoon but it travelled the outback before there were roads. There are several pleasant picnic grounds and a swimming pool in the park.

Places to Stay
The *Bunkhaus Travellers Hostel* (☎ (085) 62 2260) is one km outside Nuriootpa on the main highway between Nuriootpa and Tanunda (look for the keg on the corner). It's a pleasant, well-kept little place with a room for 12 ($10 per night) plus a double unit. You can even drink your Barossa wine with dinner. The helpful owners have bicycles for hire and the Adelaide bus stops at the door on request. Some backpackers' tours of the Barossa from Adelaide will drop you off here and you can make the return journey when you like.

The *Angas Park Hotel* (☎ (085) 62 1050) at 22 Murray St in Nuriootpa charges $20 per person, including a light breakfast. The nearby *Vine Inn Hotel/Motel* (☎ (085) 62 2133) has motel units from $55/65. Also in Nuriootpa is the *Karawatha Guesthouse* (☎ (085) 62 1746) on Greenock Rd, which costs $30/44 including breakfast.

The *Barossa Valley Tourist Park* (☎ (085) 62 1404), Penrice Rd, Nuriootpa, has camping at $9 for two and cabins from $30. West of Nuriootpa, the *Seppeltsfield Holiday Cabins* (☎ (085) 62 8240) in Seppeltsfield has self-contained cabins for $50.

Places to Eat
The *Vine Inn Hotel* at 14 Murray St is good for reasonably priced counter meals. *Die Weinstube Restaurant*, south of Nuriootpa, is pleasant with its outdoor eating area. The valley is famed for its fine bakeries and bread. *Linke's Bakery* at 40 Murray St, one of the best, is a good place for breakfast. There are cheap counter meals at the *Angas Park Hotel*.

ANGASTON (population 1900)
On the eastern side of the valley, this town was named after George Fife Angas, one of the area's pioneers. **Collingrove** homestead, built by his son in 1853, is owned by the National Trust; it's open from 11 am to 4 pm daily and admission is $3.

Places to Stay
Angaston has the *Barossa Brauhaus* (☎ (085) 64 2014) at 41 Murray St, a fine hotel with B&B rates of $18 per person. Just down the street at No 59 is the *Angaston Hotel* (☎ (085) 64 2428) with B&B at $20 per person. Good for a splurge in Angaston is the National Trust's 1856 *Collingrove Homestead* (☎ (085) 64 2061). The four rooms are part of the old servants' quarters and cost $60/85, including breakfast.

OTHER PLACES
Bethany, near Tanunda, was the first German settlement in the valley. There's an arts & crafts gallery in a restored cottage. Old cottages still stand around the Bethany reserve and the Landhaus is claimed to be the smallest hotel in the world. **Gomersal** is also near Tanunda, and trained sheepdogs go through their paces here at Breezy Gully on Monday, Wednesday and Saturday at 2 pm.

Springton, in the south-east of the valley, has the Herbig Tree – an enormous hollow gum tree where a pioneer settler lived with his family from 1855 to 1860.

Mid-North

The area between Adelaide and Port Augusta is generally known as the Mid-North. Two main routes run north of Adelaide through the area. The first runs to Gawler where you can turn east to the Barossa Valley and the Riverland area, or continue north through Burra to Peterborough. From there you have the option of turning north-west to the Flinders Ranges or continuing on the Barrier Highway to the north-east for the long run to Broken Hill in New South Wales.

The second route heads off slightly north-west through Wakefield and then to Port Pirie and Port Augusta on the Spencer Gulf. You can then travel to the Flinders or the Eyre Peninsula or head west towards the Nullarbor and Western Australia. As well as the two main routes, a network of smaller roads covers this region.

The mid-north area includes some of the most fertile land in the state. Sunshine, rainfall and excellent soil combine to make this a prosperous agricultural region with excellent wine-making areas like the Clare Valley.

KAPUNDA (population 1350)

About 80 km north of Adelaide and a little north of the Barossa Valley, Kapunda is off the main roads which head north, but you can take a pleasant backroads route from the valley through the town and join the Barrier Highway a little further north. Copper was found at Kapunda in 1842 and it became the first mining town in Australia – for a while it was the biggest country town in the state. At its peak, it had a population of 10,000 with 22 hotels but the mines closed in 1888.

There's a lookout point in the town with views over the old open-cut mines and mine chimneys. There's a historical museum, and an eight-metre-high bronze statue of 'Map Kernow' (the Son of Cornwall in old Cornish) stands at the Adelaide end of town as a tribute to pioneer miners. It's a pleasant drive 42 km north-east of Kapunda to Eudunda.

CLARE (population 2400)

This pleasant little town, 135 km north of Adelaide, is another big wine-producing centre although far less commercial than the Barossa Valley. It was settled in 1842 and named after County Clare in Ireland. Over Easter, there's the Irish Affair Festival with art exhibitions, horse races, wine tastings and other events. The tourist office (☎ (088) 42 2131) is in the town hall on the main street. They have information about various tours of the district.

The first vines were planted in 1848 by Jesuit priests and communion wine is still produced. The Jesuit **St Aloysius Church** dates from 1875 and the associated Sevenhill Cellars produces some fine wines. There are many other wineries in the valley including the well-known Stanley Wine Company, dating from 1894.

The town has a number of interesting buildings including an impressive Catholic church and, in what seems to be a South Australian norm, a police station and courthouse dating from 1850 which are preserved as a **museum**. The **Wolta Wolta Homestead** dates from 1864 and is open on weekends.

Bungaree Station, a working property 12 km north of Clare with many historical exhibits, can only be seen on a tour prebooked for a minimum of eight people (☎ (088) 42 2677). There's accommodation in the shearers' quarters for about $10 a bed, but groups have precedence. *Geralka Farm* (☎ (088) 45 8081), 25 km north of Clare, is another working farm which caters for visitors. You can camp or stay in on-site vans.

Mintaro, a small town 18 km south-east of Clare, has many architectural gems, including **Martindale Hall**, an imposing mansion which offers accommodation at imposing prices. There are tours of Mintaro; (☎ 008 439 011, toll-free).

Places to Stay

On Main St the *Taminga Hotel* (☎ (088) 42 2808) and the *Clare Hotel* (☎ (088) 42 2816) are basic country hotels with single rooms from about $12 and doubles costing considerably more than double that. *Bentley's Hotel/Motel* (☎ (088) 42 2815) on the main street has pub rooms with bathroom for $25/35 and motel units from $32/45.

The *Christison Park Caravan Park* (☎ (088) 42 2724) is the closest camping ground to town and has sites for $9, on-site vans for $25 and self-contained cabins for $40. B&B accommodation in the district is mostly quite expensive. The tourist office has a complete list.

Getting There & Away

You can visit the Barossa Valley on your way north to the Clare Valley, and in turn the Clare Valley can be visited en route to the Flinders Ranges. Driving from Adelaide, turn off at Watervale for the scenic 22-km drive to Clare. The daily Stateliner bus to Adelaide costs $10.

BURRA (population 1200)

This pretty little town was a copper-mining centre from 1847 to 1877, with various British ethnic groups forming their own communities (the Cornish being the most numerous). The district Burra Burra takes it name from the Hindi word for 'great' by one account, and from the Aboriginal name of the creek by another.

Information

The tourist office (☎ (088) 92 2154) in Market Square is open from 10 am to 4 pm daily. They have an interesting *Burra Historic Tour* booklet and have keys to the miners dugouts, the old jail and the powder magazine. They also offer twice-daily (if enough people show up) tours of the town for $12.50, or you can buy a Burra Passport which gives entry to most attractions.

Things to See

There's an 11-km Heritage Trail around the town. There are many solid, old stone buildings, tiny Cornish cottages and numerous reminders of the mining days. The **Market**

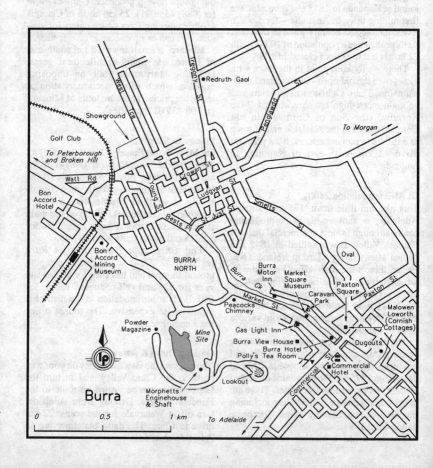

Burra

Square Museum (admission $1) is across from the tourist office.

The 33 cottages at **Paxton Square** were built for Cornish miners in the 1850s and one has been furnished in 1850s style – others are available for accommodation. In Burra's early days nearly 1500 people lived in dugouts by the creek and a couple of these old miners' dugouts have been preserved. The historic tour booklet describes many other interesting old buildings, including Redruth Gaol and more Cornish cottages on Truro St, north of the town centre.

The National Trust **Bon Accord Museum** is on the site of an original mine. It's open weekdays and Sundays from 10.30 am to 3.30 pm, and Saturdays from 12.30 to 3.30 pm; admission is $2.50. There's a lookout over the town at the old mine site, near the powder magazine and Morphett's engine house and mineshaft. Mining ceased in Burra in 1877 and the town became an agricultural centre, but in 1969 mining recommenced and continued until 1981. The open-cut site by the lookout is from that second period of mining.

Burra Gorge and picnic area is 27 km south-east from town on the Morgan road.

Places to Stay & Eat

You can stay at the historic *Paxton Square Cottages* (☎ (088) 92 2622). Cottages sleeping four cost from $33, and there are six-person cottages for $42. Linen hire is extra. There's quite a lot of pub accommodation including the *Burra Hotel* (☎ (088) 92 2389) on Market Square which has singles/doubles at $25/44 (including full breakfast); the *Royal Exchange Hotel* (☎ (088) 92 2390), Bests Place, with rooms for $15/25; and the *Bon Accord Hotel* (☎ (088) 92 2382), Park Lane, $22/36 (including breakfast).

There's also a motel and several B&B places – check with the tourist office for addresses. The small *caravan park* (☎ (088) 92 2442) has tent sites but they're all gravel.

The *Burra Hotel* has good counter meals and you can get a good lunch at *Polly's Tea Rooms*.

Getting There & Away

Pioneer's Adelaide to Sydney service passes through Burra, and it's $12.60 to Adelaide. The Mobil station is the agency. ABM Coaches (☎ (08) 349 5551) pass through Burra on their Adelaide to Orroroo run, but not every day. There is no public transport between Burra and Clare, only 43 km away.

PORT PIRIE (population 14,700)

Port Pirie, 84 km south of Port Augusta, is an industrial centre with lead smelters that handle the output from Broken Hill. There are smelter tours on Wednesday and Saturday which depart at 10 am from the tourist office (☎ (086) 33 0439), 10 Jubilee Place. It's also a major port for the shipping of agricultural produce and is the home of country & western music in South Australia, with a festival over a long weekend each October.

There are many interesting buildings including some fine hotels. On Ellen St, the **National Trust Museum** (admission $2) includes the old railway station, police station and customs house (open daily). **Carn Brae** in Florence St is an old house with turn-of-the-century furniture, paintings and memorabilia. Near Port Pirie there's a museum on **Weerona Island**, 13 km out, and the **Telowie Gorge** park is also within easy reach.

Places to Stay & Eat

The *International Hotel* (☎ (086) 32 2422) on Ellen St has singles/doubles/triples for $20/32/39 and motel units for $45/50/54. The *Port Pirie Hotel* (☎ (086) 32 446), near the grain silos, has rooms for $20/30. The *Abaccy Motel* (☎ (086) 32 3701) on Florence St charges $35/40/45. The *Port Pirie Caravan Park* (☎ (086) 32 4275) has sites for $6.70 and on-site vans for $24.

There are a few cafes around town and hotel counter meals are available – but nowhere special. If you're hungry in the evening and don't want an expensive meal at the *Chelsea Restaurant* in the Jubilee Tavern, one of *Angelo's* unimpressive pizzas or a Chinese meal at *Toledo*, there's often a pie cart parked near the post office.

OTHER MID-NORTH TOWNS
Jamestown, north of the Clare Valley at the southern edge of the Flinders Ranges, is a country town with a Railway Station Museum open Sunday from 2 to 4 pm.

Peterborough is another gateway town to the Flinders Ranges. This is an important railway centre and also a place where the problems railway engineers in Australia have to cope with are clearly illustrated. The colonial bungling which led to Australia's mixed-up railway system managed to run three different railway gauges through Peterborough! **Steamtown** is a working railway museum – on holiday weekends between April and October and some school holidays, narrow-gauge steam-trains run between Peterborough and Orroroo to the north-west. The old town hall in Peterborough is now a museum and art gallery.

North from here into the Flinders Ranges, a land boom took place in the 1870s as settlers, encouraged by easy credit from the government, established farming towns. Sturdy farms and towns sprung up, but the wet seasons that had encouraged hopes of wheat farming soon gave way to the normal dry conditions and the towns tumbled into ruins. Some of the most interesting reminders of those days can be seen in the southern Flinders Ranges.

South-East

Most travellers between Melbourne and Adelaide pass through the south-east of South Australia. The Western and Dukes highways form the most direct route between the two cities (729 km) but the South Australian stretch is not terribly exciting, although south of this route there is more interesting country and you can take detours. The Princes Highway along the coast is of greater interest. Along this road you pass through Mt Gambier with its impressive crater lakes and then along the Coorong, an extensive coastal lagoon system.

Getting There & Away
Air Kendell Airlines (☎ (08) 233 3322) fly Melbourne-Mt Gambier-Adelaide most days. The fare from Mt Gambier to either city is $131. O'Conners Air Services (☎ (087) 23 0666) also fly between Adelaide and Mt Gambier.

Bus Bonds Mt Gambier Motor Service (☎ (08) 231 9090 in Adelaide, (087) 25 5037 in Mt Gambier) run from the central bus station in Adelaide to Mt Gambier daily except Saturday (coming from Mt Gambier the service is daily). The trip takes about six hours.

Fares from Adelaide are: Meningie $19, Kingston SE $26, Robe $30 and Mt Gambier $30. From Mt Gambier to Kingston SE costs $19. The Victorian government's V/Line bus runs to Melbourne on weekdays, taking about six hours ($42).

THE COORONG
The Coorong is a unique national park – a long, narrow strip curving along the coast for 145 km. The northern end is at Lake Alexandrina where the Murray River reaches the sea; the southern end is at Kingston SE. It's a narrow, shallow lagoon and a complex series of salt pans, separated from the sea by the huge sand dunes of the Younghusband Peninsula, more usually known as the Hummocks.

The area is a superb natural bird sanctuary with vast numbers of water birds. *Storm Boy*, a film about a young boy's friendship with a pelican, was shot on the Coorong. At Salt Creek you can take the nature trail turn-off from the Princes Highway and follow the old road which runs along the shore of the Coorong for some distance.

Camping is permitted in most areas of the park, but you need a permit from the National Parks office at Salt Creek (try a service station if the office is closed) or Noonameena.

KINGSTON SE (population 1300)

At the southern end of the Coorong, Kingston is a small beach resort and a good base for visiting the Coorong. The town was originally named Maria Creek after a ship wrecked at Cape Jaffa in 1840. No lives were lost in the shipwreck, but as the 27 crew and passengers made their way south towards Lake Albert they were all killed by Aborigines. There's a memorial to the *Maria* in Kingston, but it's said that Policeman's Point was named as the place where European retribution caught up with the Aborigines.

Other attractions are the **Pioneer Museum** and the nearby **Cape Jaffa Lighthouse** which is open from 2 to 5 pm daily. Kingston is a centre for rock-lobster fishing but Kingston's best known lobster is hardly edible. Towering by the roadside, **Larry the Big Lobster** is a superb piece of Australian kitsch. The amazingly realistic lobster, made of fibreglass and steel, fronts a tourist centre. You can buy real crayfish, freshly cooked, at the jetty.

The **Jip Jip National Park**, 45 km northeast of Kingston, features huge granite outcrops in the bush. From Kingston conventional vehicles can drive 16 km along the beach to the **Granites**, while with 4WD you can continue right along the beach to the mouth of the Murray River.

In Kingston the *Kingston Bunkers* (☎ (087) 67 2185) at 21 Holland St has dorm beds for $10.

ROBE (population 600)

Robe, a small port dating from 1845, was one of the state's first settlements. Its citizens made a fortune in the late 1850s as a result of the Victorian gold rush. The Victorian government instituted a £10 head tax on Chinese gold miners, and many Chinese circumvented the tax by getting to Victoria via Robe; 10,000 arrived in 1857 alone. The **Chinamen's Wells** in the region are a reminder of that time.

Early buildings include the 1863 **Customs House** which is now a museum. There's also an old jail up on the cliffs and a small arts & crafts gallery. Nearby **Long Beach** is good for windsurfing, offering a variety of conditions. If you fancy eating part of the Australian coat of arms, the *Caledonian Inn* offers fillet of kangaroo for about $14.

BEACHPORT (population 400)

South of Robe this quiet little seaside town is, like other places along the coast, a crayfishing centre. There's a small museum and a couple of other old buildings. There's good surfing at the blowhole, and the nearby salt lake is called the Pool of Siloam.

Beachport Youth Hostel (☎ (087) 35 8197), right on the beach, has beds at $7. During the winter it isn't always open.

MILLICENT (population 5250)

At Millicent the 'Alternative 1' route through Robe and Beachport rejoins the main road. The town has a central swimming lake, and on George St there's a museum and the **Admella Gallery**. A narrow-gauge steam engine is on display nearby. There's also a **Historical & Maritime Museum** in the town.

The **Canunda National Park** with its giant sand dunes is 13 km west of town. You can camp near Southend – contact the ranger at Southend (☎ (087) 35 6053) for details. In **Tantanoola**, 21 km to the south-east, the stuffed 'Tantanoola Tiger' is on display at the Tantanoola Tiger Hotel. This beast, actually an Assyrian wolf, was shot in 1895 after a lot of publicity. It was presumed to have escaped from a shipwreck, but quite why a ship would have a wolf on board is not clear!

The **Tantanoola Caves** are nearby. The caves' visitor centre (☎ (087) 34 4153) runs tours for a minimum of four people ($15 each, including hire of helmet and light). You aren't allowed in wearing sandals or thongs and you can expect to get dirty. They'll sell you a pair of overalls for $8.

MT GAMBIER (population 20,000)

The major town and commercial centre of the south-east, Mt Gambier is 486 km from

Adelaide. It is built on the slopes of the volcano from which the town takes its name.

There are three craters, each with its own lake – the beautiful **Blue Lake** is the best known, although from about March to November the lake is more grey than blue. In November it mysteriously changes back to blue again, just in time for the holiday season! The lake is 70 metres deep and there's a five-km scenic drive around it. Mt Gambier also has many parks including the **Cave Park** with its deep 'cave' (more of a steep-sided hole) behind the city hall.

The town is in a rich agricultural area, but timber and limestone (cut in blocks for use as a building material) are the main products. Even a pine-plantation hater might be impressed by the forests of mature trees on the Glenelg Highway between Mt Gambier and the Victorian border.

On Sunday afternoons you can visit the museum in the old courthouse. There are also tours of the district's sawmills – check with the Lady Nelson Tourist Information & Interpretive Centre (☎ (087) 24 1730) on the highway, or the Woods & Forests Visitors' Information Centre (☎ (087) 24 2711), on the highway further east.

Places to Stay & Eat
The *Blue Lake Motel* (☎ (087) 25 5211) at 1 Kennedy Ave, just off the highway, has some dorm rooms, each with bathrooms, for $12 per person. Further east on the highway, at the edge of town, the *Jubilee Holiday Park* (☎ (087) 25 5109) has some dorm beds in cabins from $10. A local bus from the Target shopping centre will get you near here. There are several other caravan parks with cabins and on-site vans.

Jens Hotel on Commercial St next to the city hall claims to have the cheapest counter meals in town, with specials for around $3. Further west on Commercial St, the *Hitching Rail* is a cafe and bakery with meals, takeaways and good cakes and pies.

PORT MACDONNELL (population 700)
South of Mt Gambier, this quiet fishing port

was once a busy shipping port, hence the surprisingly big 1863 **customs house**, now housing a restaurant. There's a **Maritime Museum**, and the poet Adam Lindsay Gordon's home, **Dingley Dell**, is now a museum.

There are some fine walks in the area, including the path to the top of **Mt Schank**, an extinct volcano crater. Closer to town, the rugged coastline to the west is worth a look.

ALONG THE DUKES HIGHWAY
The Dukes Highway, the main Melbourne to Adelaide route, is not terribly exciting, particularly from Tailem Bend through to the Victorian border.

Just on the South Australian side of the border, **Bordertown** is in a prosperous agricultural area. Former Prime Minister Bob Hawke was born in Bordertown and lived here for the first six years of his life. There's a bust of Bob outside the town hall.

Keith is another farming town; it has a small museum and the **Mt Rescue Conservation Park** 16 km north. This area was once known as the 90 Mile Desert. **Tintinara** is the only other town of any size; it's also an access point to the Mt Rescue Park. **Coonalpyn**, a tiny township, is an access point for the **Mt Boothby Conservation Park**.

NARACOORTE (population 4750)
Settled in the 1840s, Naracoorte is one of the oldest towns in the state and one of the largest in the south east. The tourist office (☎ (087) 62 2798) is at the **Sheep's Back Wool Museum** on MacDonnell St; there's also an **art gallery** on Smith St. On Jenkins Terrace, the **Home of a Hundred Collections** museum has a range of displays and a $4 entry fee. **Pioneer Park** has restored locomotives and the town also has a swimming lake.

The **Naracoorte Caves** (open daily) are 11 km out of town – Fossil Cave has ice-age fossils. There are three other caves with stalactites and stalagmites. **Bat Cave**, from which bats make a spectacular departure on summer evenings, is 17 km out of town. There are adventure tours, involving climbing and crawling, and you can camp nearby.

There are numerous water birds at the **Bool Lagoon Reserve**, 24 km to the south. There's a camp site near the park office in the Hacks Lagoon area, but you have to take your own water.

COONAWARRA

This very compact (only 12 km by two km) wine-producing area is 10 km north of Penola. Wynn's Coonawarra Estate is the area's best known winery and there are about 14 others which offer cellar-door sales. Most are open from Monday to Friday, some (including Wynn's) also on Saturday and Sunday. **Penola** is the main town in the area. The **Bushman's Inn** in Penola North has displays of coins and Aboriginal artefacts.

Murray River

Australia's greatest river starts in the Snowy Mountains in the Australian Alps and for most of its length forms the boundary between New South Wales and Victoria. However, it's in South Australia that the Murray comes into its own.

First, it flows west through the Riverland area where irrigation has turned unproductive land into an important wine-making and fruit-growing region. Although names like the Barossa and Hunter are better known, the Riverland produces a large proportion of Australia's wine.

Then at Morgan the river turns sharply south and flows through the Lower Murray region to the sea. In all, the river flows 650 km from the border of South Australia with New South Wales and Victoria to the sea.

The Murray has lots of watersport possibilities, plenty of wildlife (particularly water birds), and in the Riverland section a positive surfeit of wineries to visit.

This is also a river with a history. Before the advent of the railways, the Murray was the Mississippi of Australia with paddle steamers carrying trade from the interior down to the coast. Many of the river towns still have a strong flavour of those riverboat days. If you've the cash and inclination, you can still ride a paddle steamer forging its leisurely way on a cruise down the mighty Murray.

The Murray River region has plenty of conventional accommodation, including a hostel in Berri, but if you're with a group of people, a very pleasant way to explore the Murray is to rent a houseboat and set off along the river. Houseboats can be hired in Morgan, Waikerie, Loxton, Berri, Renmark and other river centres, but they are popular so it's wise to book well ahead.

The SAGTC can advise you about prices and make bookings, or you can contact the Riverland Holiday Booking Centre (☎ (085) 86 6621) in Renmark. The cost depends on what you hire, where you hire it and, more importantly, when you hire it. Typical prices are around $600 a week for a four-berth houseboat, and around $950 for eight or 10-berth boats. These costs can drop in winter.

For the well-heeled there are the trips on riverboats such as the huge paddle steamer PS *Murray River Queen* which makes 13-day trips between Mildura (Victoria) to the river mouth at Goolwa (about $2000 per person). Or the MV *Murray Princess* has three and six-day cruises that depart from Renmark from about $525 (three days) and $1000 (six days) per person in single accommodation, cheaper in the winter and for doubles.

There are plenty of day trips. From Renmark, for example, you can make short day trips on the MV *Barrangul*, and, on the Lower Murray at Goolwa, the PS *Mundoo*.

Getting There & Away
Air Sunstate Airlines (☎ (08) 217 3333) flights can be booked through Australian Airlines, 144 North Terrace, Adelaide. They fly to Renmark from Adelaide ($96) twice daily from Monday to Friday and once on Sunday.

Bus Stateliner runs from Adelaide via Blanche Town and Waikerie, and the fare to Berri, Loxton and Renmark is $23.50. Bus Australia and Greyhound/Pioneer pass through on their Adelaide to Sydney journey. The cheapest bus is the local Trans City at $20.

RENMARK (population 7900)

In the centre of the Riverland irrigation area and 254 km east from Adelaide, Renmark was a starting point for the great irrigation projects that revolutionised the area, and was the first of the river towns. Irrigation was begun in 1887 by the Canadian Chaffey brothers; you can see one of their wood-burning irrigation pumps on Renmark Ave. **Olivewood**, Charles Chaffey's home, is also on Renmark Ave; it is open daily except Wednesday from 2.30 to 4 pm.

The area produces grapes and other fruit, and there are plenty of wineries which offer free tastings. In the town, you can inspect the 1911 paddle steamer *Industry*, now restored and with various components working – if you put a coin in the slot. Among the many river cruises offered, there are 1½-hour trips on the MV *Barrangul* for $25. There are several art galleries in town, and koalas and other wildlife on **Goat Island** in the river.

The tourist office (☎ (085) 86 6703) is on Murray Ave. Riverland Sports, also on Murray Ave, hires bicycles.

Places to Stay & Eat

Grays Caravan Village (☎ (085) 86 6522) is close to the town centre and has the cheapest tent sites, but you'd do much better to walk about a km east to the *Renmark Caravan Park* (☎ (085) 86 6315), idyllically situated on a bend in the river. Camp sites cost $8 and on-site vans range from $26. Further along the river, the *Riverbend Caravan Park* (☎ (085) 85 5131) is slightly cheaper and hires canoes and bicycles.

The *Renmark Hotel/Motel* (☎ (085) 86 6755) has pub rooms from $20/25 ($35/40 with bathroom) and motel units from $45/50. There are counter meals available or you could try *Sophia's Restaurant*, which has good Greek food and a takeaway service downstairs.

BERRI (population 7400)

At one time a refuelling stop for the wood-burning paddle steamers, the town takes its name from the Aboriginal words *berri berri*, or big bend in the river. It's the economic centre of the Riverland and there are several wineries nearby. **Berri Estates Winery** at Glossop, 13 km west of Berri, is one of the biggest wineries in Australia, if not the whole southern hemisphere.

Berri also has a large fruit-juice factory with four tours a day on weekends. Lovers of Australian kitsch should visit the **Big Orange** (50c entry), four km out of Berri on the road to Renmark. There are exhibits telling the economic story of the Riverland area. The adjacent Riverland Display Centre, open from 9 am to 5 pm daily, has vintage cars and motorcycles. The tourist office (☎ (085) 82 1655) is on Vaughan Terrace.

In town, the lookout on Fiedler St has views over the town and river. Near the ferry wharf there's a monument to Jimmy James, an Aboriginal tracker, with some interesting information on tracking. There's also a **koala sanctuary** near the Martins Bend recreation area on the river. Near Berri, the small town of **Monash** has a huge children's playground with no less than 180 different amusements. The big event in Berri is the rodeo each Easter Monday.

Punts still cross the river from the Berri Hotel on Riverside Ave to Loxton.

Places to Stay

There's a new hostel, *Berri Backpackers* (☎ (085) 82 3144), on the Sturt Highway. It's run by a couple of experienced travellers and you can ask here about fruit-picking work. Dorm beds are $12, and singles/doubles cost $14/25.

The *Berri Caravan Park* (☎ (085) 82 1718) on Riverview Drive has tent sites and on-site vans. At the *Berri Hotel/Motel* (☎ (085) 82 1411) on Riverview Drive, singles/doubles in the pub cost from $30/34, and from $50/56 in the motel.

LOXTON (population 3400)

From Berri the Murray makes a large loop south of the Sturt Highway. Loxton, at the bottom of this loop, is involved in the usual Riverland activities of fruit growing and wine making. The **Katarapko Game Reserve** occupies much of the area within the loop; you can camp here with a permit. Contact the National Parks office (☎ (085) 85 2177) in Berri.

The tourist office (☎ (085) 84 7919) is in front of the Loxton Hotel on East Terrace. Loxton's major attraction is the riverside **Historical Village**; it's open daily from 10 am to 4 pm on weekdays and to 5 pm on weekends – admission is $3.50. There are two-hour river cruises on the MV *River Rambler* for $7, and **Penfolds** winery is open daily except Sunday. Riverland Canoeing Adventures (☎ (085) 84 1494) on Alamein Ave rent one/two-person canoes for $15/20 a day; they also rent bicycles.

Places to Stay & Eat

The *Loxton Riverfront Caravan Park* (☎ (085) 84 7862) has a hostel, but it's only cheap for groups – individuals pay $25 a room. Tent sites are $8.50 and on-site vans cost from $25.

The *Loxton Hotel/Motel* (☎ (085) 84 7266) on East Terrace has rooms from $16/24 and good motel units from $46/50. The hotel has a couple of dining rooms, plus counter meals. Otherwise there's a Chinese restaurant and several coffee shops and takeaways.

BARMERA (population 2000)

On the shores of Lake Bonney (where Donald Campbell made an attempt on the world water-speed record in 1964), Barmera was once on the overland stock route along which cattle were driven from New South Wales.

The ruins of **Napper's Old Accommodation House**, built in 1850 at the mouth of Chambers Creek, are a reminder of that era, as is the **Overland Corner Hotel** on the Morgan road, 19 km out of town. It takes its name from a bend in the Murray River where overlanders, travellers and explorers once stopped. Later, drovers paused here, and the hotel (built in 1859) is now a museum. It is open Wednesday to Sunday from 10 am to 5 pm and additional days during holiday periods. There's also an **art gallery & museum** in the town.

Lake Bonney, which has sandy beaches, is popular for swimming and water sports. There's even a nude beach at **Pelican Point**. On the Sturt Highway five km west of Barmera, the **Cobdogla Irrigation Museum** (☎ (085) 82 2289) has the world's only working Humphrey Pump – a sort of giant water cannon – and working steam trains and traction engines. Display and operating days are infrequent (generally during school and public holidays) so phone first; admission is $4. There's a conservation area at **Moorook** (head south from Kingston-on-Murray), which has nature trails.

Riverland Canoe Tours (☎ (085) 88 2869) offers various guided trips from two hours ($12) to two days ($100). Fishing and yabbying trips cost about $40 a day from a boat, and $20 by bus. Contact the tourist office (☎ (085) 84 7919) for details – it's in the new bus station on Barwell Ave.

Places to Stay

The *Barmera Hotel Motor Inn* (☎ (085) 88 2111) has rooms from $25/35/45 for singles/doubles/triples, or $48/55/65 in the motel. Singles and doubles at the *Lake Vista Holiday Flats* (☎ (085) 88 2326) cost from $35, and there are several caravan parks, including *Lake Bonney* (☎ (085) 88 2234).

Orchard Farm Stay (☎ (085) 88 2052) offers B&B for $35/50.

WAIKERIE (population 1600)

The town takes its name from the Aboriginal word for 'anything that flies', after the teeming bird life on the lagoons and river around Waikerie. Curiously, Waikerie also has the most active gliding centre in Australia (☎ (085) 41 2644).

Other attractions in and around the town are wine tasting, the **Pooginook Conservation Park** (12 km north-east), which has echidnas and hairy-nosed wombats, the **Kangaroo Park, Holder Bend Reserve** and the **Waikerie Producers Co-op**, which is the largest citrus packing house in the southern hemisphere. There is a tourist centre (☎ (085) 41 2295) at 20 McCoy St. The *Waikerie Hotel* (☎ (085) 41 2999) has accommodation.

MORGAN (population 400)

In its prime this was the busiest river port in Australia, with wharves towering 12 metres high. There's a car ferry across the Murray here. Morgan is off the Sturt Highway to the north and from here a pipeline pumps water to Whyalla on Spencer Gulf.

The *Commercial Hotel* (☎ (085) 40 2107) has single/double rooms from $15/30, or there's *Morgan Riverside Caravan Park* (☎ (085) 40 2207) with tent sites and cabins.

SWAN REACH (population 200)

This sleepy old town, 70 km south-west of Waikerie, has picturesque river scenery and, hardly surprisingly, lots of swans. Just downriver the Murray makes a long, gentle curve for 11 km in all. The bend is appropriately known as Big Bend; there's a picnic reserve here and many sulphur-crested cockatoos.

MANNUM (population 2000)

The *Mary Ann*, Australia's first riverboat, was built here and made the first paddle steamer trip up the Murray from Mannum in 1853. The river is very wide here and there are many relics of the pioneering days on the river, including the 1898 paddle steamer *Marion*, now a floating museum (open daily from 10 am to 4 pm). You can also see a replica of Sturt's whaleboat and relics of the *Mary Ann*.

The **Haldon Rd Bird Sanctuary** has pelicans, ducks, swans and other water birds.

The **Cascade Waterfalls**, 11 km from Mannum on Reedy Creek, are also worth visiting. Off Purnong Rd there's a lookout tower.

MURRAY BRIDGE (population 8700)

South Australia's largest river town, only 82 km south-east from Adelaide, is named for the long 1879 bridge, reputedly the first to span the Murray. It's a popular area for fishing, swimming, water-skiing and barbecues. From here you can make day cruises on the MV *Kookaburra*.

If you're stuck in Murray Bridge, you can arrange to see antique doll collections, a pipe collection or chocolate manufacturing, or you can pay a visit to **Mary the Blacksmith** at 41 Doyle Rd, three km from town on the Mannum road. This entertaining woman forges iron over a 200-year-old anvil; admission is $3. Turn up on a Sunday afternoon or make an appointment on (065) 32 5526. In the **Sturt Reserve** by the river, there's a coin-in-the-slot bunyip and a very long children's slide. Sometimes during summer there's bungy jumping from the bridge – check with the helpful tourist office (☎ (065) 32 6660) on South Terrace.

Near Murray Bridge is **Monarto** – the town that never was. A grandiose plan was drawn up to build a second major city for South Australia by the turn of the century. This site was chosen and land purchased in the early 1970s, but nothing further happened and the project was totally abandoned.

Places to Stay & Eat

The Balcony Private Hotel (☎ (065) 32 3830) is right in the town centre and costs $15/30 for singles/doubles and $45 for a five-person family room. The friendly owners are knowledgeable about the area. The *Oval Caravan Park* (☎ (065) 32 2388) has tent sites and on-site vans.

You can eat at the *Oriental Garden* or the *Murray Bridge Hotel* which has good counter meals. The *Bridgeport Hotel* has also been recommended. The *Butterfly House* on Jervois Rd has $6 barbecues and the *Italian Club* on Lincoln Rd serves dinner between 6 and 8 pm, Friday to Sunday.

Getting There & Away
Buses to Adelaide cost $9, and you can pick up a bus to Melbourne ($40) or Sydney ($89). Getting to the south-east of the state from here by bus isn't easy. You have to connect with a bus leaving Tailem Bend for Mount Gambier ($26) at around 9.30 am and the only way to get there from Murray Bridge is on the Pinnaroo service, which departs Murray Bridge in the early evening.

TAILEM BEND (population 1700)
At a sharp bend in the river, Tailem Bend is near the mouth of the Murray River. **Old Tailem Town** is a re-creation of a pioneer village; it's open daily and costs $5. After Wellington, south of Tailem Bend, the Murray opens into huge **Lake Alexandrina**; there are lots of water birds, but sometimes boating is tricky. The river mouth is near Goolwa – see the previous Fleurieu Peninsula section in this chapter for more information on this area. You can take a ferry across the river at Jervis from where it's 11 km to the interesting old town of Wellington.

Yorke Peninsula

The Yorke Peninsula is a popular holiday area within easy driving distance from Adelaide. There are pleasant beaches along both sides, the Innes National Park on the tip of the peninsula and plenty of opportunities for fishing. The area's economy was originally based on the copper mines of Little Cornwall (the name given to the copper mining areas of Yorke Peninsula). As the mines declined, agriculture developed and much of the land now grows barley and other grains.

Cornwall & Copper Mines
In the early 1860s, copper was discovered in the Moonta-Kadina-Wallaroo area (known as the 'Copper Triangle') and within a few

years a full-scale copper rush was on. Most of the miners were from Cornwall in England, and the area still has a strong Cornish influence, with many old cottages and churches looking as if they have been transplanted straight from Cornwall. The boom peaked around the turn of the century, but in the early 1920s a slump in copper prices and rising labour costs closed all the peninsula's mines.

Over a long weekend in May of odd-numbered years, the Kernewek Lowender festival is held in Little Cornwall. It's a

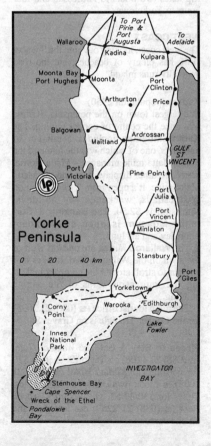

chance to try Cornish pasties or watch a wheelbarrow race.

Getting There & Away

Premier (☎ (08) 233 2744) operates a daily Adelaide-Kadina-Wallaroo-Moonta-Port Hughes-Moonta Bay bus. It takes about three hours to Moonta and costs $12.80.

Yorke Peninsula bus service runs from Adelaide to Yorketown daily, but the route alternates daily between the east coast and down the centre of the peninsula. Examples of fares from Adelaide are: Yorketown $21, Edithburgh $21 and Port Vincent $20. The trip takes two hours to Ardrossan and four hours to Yorketown.

WEST COAST

The west coast, looking out onto the Spencer Gulf, has plenty of beaches, but the road generally runs inland.

Kadina (population 2950)

The largest town on the peninsula, Kadina was once the centre of copper mining. The **Kadina Museum** includes a number of buildings, one of which was the home of the Matta Matta mine manager – Matta House. There are other displays here and the Matta Matta mine. It's open from 2 to 4.30 pm on Wednesdays, weekends and holidays; admission is $2.50. The **Banking & Currency Museum** is open daily except Thursday and all June.

The **Wallaroo Mines** are one km west of the town on the Wallaroo road. It takes half an hour to stroll around the complex including the impressive ruins of the engine building.

The main tourist office (☎ (088) 21 2093) for the Copper Triangle is on Graves St.

Places to Stay & Eat The *Wombat Hotel* (☎ (088) 21 1108) on Taylor St charges $19 per person. The *Kadina Hotel* (☎ (088) 21 2008), a block away, has singles/doubles/triples for $30/47/62. The *Kadina Caravan Park* (☎ (088) 21 2259) has tent sites and on-site vans.

Cornish pasties are found in many shops; *Prices Bakery* has excellent ones. *Sarah's Place* is good for pancakes and Cornish cooking, and the *Dynasty Room* is a Chinese place on Goyander St; it has lunch specials, as do the pubs.

Wallaroo (population 2000)

The second point of the Copper Triangle, this port town was a major centre during the copper boom. The 'big stack', one of the great chimneys from the copper smelters (built in 1861), still stands, but today the port's main function is exporting agricultural products, and the grain terminal dwarfs the town. In the old post office there's a **Maritime Museum**, open on Wednesday, weekends and school holidays; admission is $2. There are other interesting buildings like the old railway station, now a restaurant, and some fair beaches.

Places to Stay & Eat The *Weerona Hotel* (☎ (088) 23 2008) on John Terrace has singles/doubles for about $25/35. *Sonbern Lodge* (☎ (088) 23 2291), also on John Terrace, is a nice old building and has singles/doubles/triples for $24/38/47 (or $31/46/55 with bathroom), and motel units in a new wing. On the beach near the grain terminal, the *Office Beach Caravan Park* (☎ (088) 23 2722) has tent sites and on-site vans.

Some of the hotels have counter meals and you can get snacks from *Prices Bakery* or more substantial meals in the pricey restaurant in the old railway station. *Samina's Pizza House* has takeaways and sit-down meals. Even if you aren't staying there, you can eat in the dining room at the Sonbern Lodge.

Moonta (population 1900)

At Moonta, 18 km south of Wallaroo, the copper mine was once said to be the richest mine in Australia. The town grew so fast that its school once had over 1000 students; the building now houses the largest country museum in the state (admission $2.50). It's part of the collection of mine-works' ruins at the **Moonta Heritage Site** which you can explore with a self-guiding map from the museum or from the tourist office in Kadina. On weekends only, the tourist railway will take you around the **Moonta Mines Complex**.

Places to Stay The *Cornwall Hotel* (☎ (088) 25 2304) on Ryan St has rooms for $20/30; at the *Royal* (☎ (088) 252108) nearby they're $25/25. Right on the beach three km away, the *Moonta Bay Caravan Park* (☎ (088) 25 2406) has tent sites and cabins.

Port Broughton

This port town has a pleasant harbour. *Port Broughton Caravan Park* (☎ (086) 35 2188) has tent sites and on-site vans. The old *Port Broughton Hotel* (☎ (088) 35 2004) by the foreshore has rooms at $20/25 and the bar serves cheap counter meals.

EAST COAST

The east coast road from the top of Gulf St Vincent down to Stenhouse Bay near Cape Spencer closely follows the coast. There are many sandy beaches and secluded coves. **Port Clinton** is the northernmost beach resort. A little south is **Price**, where salt is produced at salt pans just outside town. **Ardrossan** is the largest port on this coast. There's a museum on Fifth St, and ploughing enthusiasts will be delighted to hear that Ardrossan was the place where the stump-jump plough was invented.

Continuing south, the road runs through **Pine Point**, **Black Point**, **Port Julia** and **Port Vincent** (each has a sandy beach) in the next 50 km. Port Vincent has the *Tuckerway Youth Hostel* (☎ (088) 53 7285) which costs $5.50.

The road continues to hug the coast through **Stansbury**, **Wool Bay**, **Port Giles** and **Coobowie** until Edithburgh.

Edithburgh has a rock swimming pool in a small cove; from the clifftops you can look across to the islets of the **Troubridge Shoals** where there is good scuba diving. There's also a small maritime museum and nearby Sultana Bay is a good spot for swimming. The road from Edithburgh to Stenhouse Bay is very scenic.

Near Marion Bay is *Hillocks Drive* (☎ (088) 54 4002), a private property where you can camp or stay in on-site vans. There's superb scenery and lots of kangaroos, emus and native birds. For visitors there's a $3 entry fee.

INNES NATIONAL PARK

The southern tip of the peninsula, marked by Cape Spencer, is part of the Innes National Park ($2 entry fee). **Stenhouse Bay**, just outside the park, and **Pondalowie Bay**, within the park, are the principal settlements. The park has fine coastal scenery and there's good fishing and reef diving.

Pondalowie Bay is the base for a large cray-fishing fleet and also has a fine surf beach. All the other beaches, except for Browns Beach, are dangerous for swimming.

In the park is the wreck of the barque *Ethel*, a 711-ton ship which ran ashore in 1904. All that remains are the ribs of the hull rising forlornly from the sands. Her anchor is mounted in a memorial on the clifftop above the beach.

Just past the Cape Spencer turn-off is a marker which directs you to the six ruined buildings at the **Inneston Historic Site**.

Places to Stay

Stenhouse Bay has a *caravan park* with limited facilities. With a permit ($5 per group per night), you can camp in most places in the park. Phone the National Parks office in Stenhouse Bay (☎ (088) 54 4040) for more details.

Getting There & Away

There is no public transport to the end of the peninsula. Yorke Peninsula bus service will take you as far as Warooka and then you can try to hitch, but traffic is sparse.

Eyre Peninsula

The wide Eyre Peninsula points south between Spencer Gulf and the Great Australian Bight. It's bordered on the north side by the Eyre Highway from Port Augusta to Ceduna. The coastal run along the peninsula is in two parts: the Lincoln Highway southwest from Port Augusta to Port Lincoln; and the Flinders Highway north-west to Ceduna. It's 468 km from Port Augusta direct to Ceduna via the Eyre Highway – via the loop south it's 763 km.

This is a resort area with many good beaches, sheltered bays and pleasant little port towns. On the west coast there are superb surf beaches and spectacular coastal scenery. The area offshore further west is home to the great white shark. This is a favourite locale for making shark films – some scenes from *Jaws* were filmed here. The Eyre Peninsula also has a flourishing agricultural sector, while the iron ore deposits at Iron Knob and Iron Baron are processed and shipped from the busy port of Whyalla.

The stretch of coast from Port Lincoln to Streaky Bay had one of the earliest European contacts. In 1627 the Dutch explorer Peter Nuyts sailed right along the north and west coasts of Australia in his ship the *Gulden Zeepard*. He continued along the south coast and crossed the Great Australian Bight, but gave up at Streaky Bay and turned back to more hospitable climes.

Abel Tasman circumnavigated the continent 15 years later, but missed the mainland; he only saw Tasmania. It was more than a century later that Cook 'discovered' the fertile east coast. In 1802 Matthew Flinders charted the Eyre Peninsula and named many of its features during his epic circumnavigation of Australia. The peninsula takes its name from Edward John Eyre, the hardy explorer who made the first recorded east to west crossing of the continent in 1841.

Getting There & Away
Air Kendell Airlines (☎ (08) 233 3322) are booked through Ansett in Adelaide. They fly to Port Lincoln ($103), Whyalla ($107), Streaky Bay ($153) and Ceduna ($174) on the Eyre Peninsula. Lincoln Airlines (☎ (086) 82 5688) flies between Port Lincoln and Adelaide for $78.

Bus Stateliner (☎ (08) 233 2777) runs to many places on the peninsula from Adelaide, including Port Augusta ($25), Whyalla ($28), Port Lincoln ($49), Ceduna ($58) and Streaky Bay ($52). You can also travel to Port Augusta and Ceduna with the major companies on their Adelaide to Perth run. It takes 9½ hours from Adelaide to Ceduna.

Boat There's no longer a boat service between Adelaide and Port Lincoln (via Kangaroo Island) but it might start up again – contact the agents, W Miller (☎ (08) 47 5577), 3 Todd St, Port Adelaide, for more information.

PORT AUGUSTA (population 15,300)
Matthew Flinders was the first European to set foot in the area, but the town was not established until 1854. Today, this busy port city is the gateway to the outback region of South Australia. It's also a major crossroads for travellers.

From here, roads head west across the Nullarbor to Western Australia, north to Alice Springs and Darwin in the Northern Territory, south to Adelaide and east to Broken Hill and Sydney in New South Wales. The main railway line between the east and west coasts and the Adelaide to Alice Springs route both pass through. The town is also a major electricity-generating centre, burning coal from Leigh Creek.

There are tours of the **Thomas Playford Power Station** at 10 am, 11 am and 1 pm Monday to Friday, and tours of the **School of the Air** at 10 am on weekdays during school terms. You can climb the **water tower** on Mitchell Terrace for a good view of the town and across to the Flinders Ranges.

Other attractions include the **Curdnatta Art & Pottery Gallery**, in Port Augusta's first railway station, and the **Homestead Park Pioneer Museum** ($1.50). Old buildings include the **Greenbush Gaol** (1869), the old **town hall** and the **Grange** (1878).

Information
The Wadlata Outback Centre (☎ (086) 42 4511) at 41 Flinders Terrace is the tourist information centre; it also has an 'awe-inspiring hi-tech trip into the early outback' for $5.50.

Places to Stay & Eat
Port Augusta Backpackers (☎ (086) 41 1008) at 17 Trent St is a basic but friendly place with beds for $10. As the only hostel in this crossroads city, it's a good place to pick up information from other travellers. There's free tea and coffee, kangaroo meat most nights and tours of the Flinders Ranges.

The *Commonwealth Hotel* (☎ (086) 42 2844) at 73 Commercial Rd has rooms for $15/26, and the *Great Northern Hotel* (☎ (086) 42 3906) at 4 Tassie St has rooms for $20/28. *Fauna Caravan Park* (☎ (086) 42 2974) has sites and on-site vans. On the highway, *Tuckers Diner* is a truckies' eating place; it is open 24 hours.

Ridgi-Didge BBQ Steak House at 78 Commercial Rd has lunch specials and also cheap dinners. Near the backpackers' hostel, the *Pastoral Hotel* has good counter meals. *Price's Bakery* on Church St has good bread and takeaways. If you're struck by simultaneous desires to eat and wash your clothes, visit *Ian's Chicken Hut & Laundromat* on the highway.

Getting There & Away
Air Augusta Airways (☎ (086) 42 3100) flies to Adelaide on weekdays for $94. On Saturday you can take the mail plane to Boulia in outback Queensland, stopping in Birdsville and Innamincka on the way, for $300.

Bus The bus station (☎ (086) 42 5055) is at 21 Mackay St. Stateliner runs to Adelaide ($25), Coober Pedy ($53), Port Lincoln ($40), Ceduna ($45) and other places on the Eyre Peninsula. Greyhound/Pioneer destinations from Port Augusta include Perth ($160) and Alice Springs ($153).

Train By train Sydney is 32 hours away and a standard economy ticket costs $126 ($262 for a sleeper); Perth, 33 hours, $160 ($369); and Adelaide, four hours, $26.

WHYALLA (population 29,000)
The largest city in the state after Adelaide, Whyalla is a major steel-producing centre with a busy deep-water port. There are tours of the **BHP steel works** at 9.30 am on Monday, Wednesday and Saturday. They start from the tourist centre and cost $4 for adults, $1.50 for children and $10 for a family ticket. The tourist centre (☎ (086) 45 7900) is on the Lincoln Highway, near BHP. Next to the tourist centre is the **Maritime Museum** (which includes a big model railway) with tours at 11 am, noon, 1, 2 and 3 pm. Entry is $4 for adults.

Ore comes to Whyalla from Iron Knob, Iron Monarch and Iron Baron. **Iron Knob** was the first iron ore deposit in Australia to be exploited; there are tours ($2.50) of the mine at 10 am and 2 pm on weekdays and at 2 pm on Saturday. Visitors on either of the Whyalla area tours must not wear sandals, thongs or other open shoes.

Whyalla also has fine beaches and a **fauna & reptile park** on the Lincoln Highway near the airport; admission is $3. On Ekblom St, there are historical exhibits in the **Mt Laura Homestead Museum** ($1) which is open on Sunday and public holidays from 2 to 4 pm. The **Historical & Maritime Museum** (☎ (086) 49 1296), 26 Keats Crescent, is a diver's private collection – call for an appointment.

Places to Stay & Eat
The *Hotel Whyalla* (☎ (086) 45 7411) on Darling Terrace has self-contained single/double rooms from $20/30.

The *Spencer Hotel* (☎ (086) 45 8411), on the corner of Forsyth St and Darling Terrace near the bus terminal, is a big place with self-contained singles/twins from $22/34.

It's often heavily booked by gangs of contractors working in the area – you'll find it friendly or threatening depending on your gender and/or your attitude to bush workers.

The *Lord Gowrie Hotel* (☎ (086) 45 8955) on Gowrie Ave is a small place with similar facilities and prices.

The cheapest motel is *Airport Whyalla* (☎ (086) 45 2122) on the Lincoln Highway with rooms from $38/42. The *Whyalla Foreshore Caravan Park* (☎ (086) 45 7474) has tent sites and on-site vans.

The *Oriental Inn* Chinese restaurant on Essington Lewis Ave has been recommended; there's also the *King Po* on Carlton Parade which has a large menu with main courses from about $7.50.

WHYALLA TO PORT LINCOLN
Cowell (population 600)
Cowell is a pleasant little town near a large jade deposit. You can see cutting and polishing at the **Cowell Jade Factory** on Second St. There's a small **museum** in the old post office and an **agricultural museum**. There are good beaches on Franklin Harbour.

Places to Stay The impressive *Franklin Harbour Hotel* (☎ (086) 29 2015) is close to the beach and has rooms for $20/30. The *Schultz Farm* (☎ (086) 29 2194) guesthouse overlooks the sea (but is quite a long way from it) and has accommodation for $20 per person with breakfast. The *Cowell Foreshore Caravan Park* (☎ (086) 29 2307) has tent sites and on-site vans.

Further South
Cleve is 43 km inland from Cowell and while it's just a quiet country town the drive there is pleasant. There's a fauna park with a nocturnal house. Back on the coast, **Arno Bay** is another small beach resort. The *Arno Hotel* (☎ (086) 28 0001) is only 100 metres from a good beach and has rooms at $20/34, including breakfast. Close by is the *Arno Bay Caravan Park* (☎ (086) 28 0085).

South again is **Port Neill** and then **Tumby Bay** with its long, curving, white sand beach,

the C L Alexander Museum and a number of interesting old buildings around the town. The **Sir Joseph Banks Islands** are 15 km offshore; there are many attractive bays and reefs plus a wide variety of sea birds which nest on the islands.

North Shields is a very small settlement 13 km north of Port Lincoln on the shore of Boston Bay. The Karlinda Collection here has over 10,000 shells, rocks and examples of marine life. The hotel here has no rooms, and the youth hostel nearby is for groups only but there is the *Port Lincoln Caravan Park* (☎ (086) 84 3512) – despite its name it is actually in North Shields.

PORT LINCOLN (population 10,700)
At the southern end of the Eyre Peninsula, 662 km from Adelaide by road but only 250 km as the crow flies, Port Lincoln was named by Matthew Flinders in 1801. The first settlers arrived in 1839 and the town has grown to become the tuna fishing capital of Australia; the annual Tunarama Festival in January of each year signals the start of the tuna fishing season with boisterous merriment over the Australia Day weekend. Port Lincoln was once considered as an alternative to Adelaide as the state capital and is still an important deep-water port.

The town is pleasantly situated on Boston Bay. There are a number of historic buildings including the **Old Mill** on Dorset Place which houses a small pioneer museum. The Lincoln Hotel dates from 1840, making it the oldest hotel on the peninsula. On the Flinders Highway, **Mill Cottage** is another museum, open from 2 to 5 pm daily. The **Axel Stenross Maritime Museum** is a memorial to a local boat-building identity and includes his workshop. There are a number of islands off Boston Bay.

Fourteen km offshore is **Dangerous Reef**, the world's largest breeding area for the white pointer shark. Believe it or not, a charter company runs trips out here for divers looking for that extra little bite. Even at over $400 per person they're always fully booked.

Information

The tourist office (☎ (086) 82 6666) is at the Eyre Travel Centre on Tasman Terrace, the main street.

Places to Stay & Eat

Cheapest of the hotels are the *Boston Hotel* (☎ (086) 82 1311) on King St with single/double rooms for $17/26 ($28/35 with bathroom), and the *Pier Hotel* (☎ (086) 82 1322) at $18/26 ($26/35 with bathroom). *Westward Ho* holiday flats (☎ (086) 82 2425) have one-room flats (sleeps two) from about $40 and also a range of larger flats. The *Kirton Point Caravan Park* (☎ (086) 82 2537) has tent sites and four-person bunk cabins from $24.

Dial-a-Curry in Tasman Mall is a good cheap Indian restaurant, but it may not survive the planned renovation of the mall. The *Castle Family Restaurant* has good cheap meals at around $9 a main course. Counter meals at the *Lincoln* and *Pier* hotels are good value.

Getting There & Away

Daily Stateliner buses run from Adelaide via Cummins or Tumby Bay for $39, but there is no public transport between here and Streaky Bay. You either have to go back to Port Augusta for the Adelaide-Streaky Bay-Ceduna bus, or hitch.

Getting Around

There are various tours, including town tours ($15), a day tour of Whalers Way ($35) and the lower peninsula tour ($45). For details see the tourist office. You can hire bikes at Lincoln Cycles, 60 Liverpool St.

AROUND PORT LINCOLN

Cape Carnot, better known as Whalers' Way, is 32 km south of Port Lincoln and a permit ($12 plus key deposit) to enter the conservation reserve must be obtained in Port Lincoln. The Shell petrol station on the corner of Tasman and Mortlock Terraces issues permits, as do several other businesses in town.

A 15-km drive around the reserve takes you past stupendous cliffs pounded by huge surf. At **Sleaford Bay** there are the remains of an old whaling station. Camping is permitted at a couple of sites, but you have to buy a separate permit for each day you stay. You can also buy permits to visit **Mikkira Koala Sanctuary** from the Shell station – they cost $5.

Also south of Port Lincoln is the **Lincoln National Park**, again with a magnificent coastline. There are a few tent sites in the park, and a $3 permit from the ranger (☎ (086) 88 3173) or the National Parks office (☎ (086) 82 3936) is necessary. You can visit offshore islands like **Boston Island, Wedge Island** or **Thistle Island**; the tourist office in Port Lincoln will help you find a boat to get out to them.

PORT LINCOLN TO STREAKY BAY
Coffin Bay

Coffin Bay is a sheltered stretch of water with some fine beaches and Coffin Bay township. From here you can find spectacular coastal scenery at **Point Avoid, Almonta Beach** and **Yangie Bay**. Coffin Bay Peninsula is a national park and there's a 25-km trail to Yangie Bay but you need a 4WD from there to Point Sir Isaac on the tip the peninsula. You can see emus, Cape Barren geese and other wildlife at the **Kellidie Bay Conservation Park**.

Places to Stay There are motel units at the *Coffin Bay Hotel* (☎ (086) 85 4111) from $45/52. The *Coffin Bay Caravan Park* (☎ (086) 85 4170) is the only place in the nearby area where you can camp and they also have on-site vans – there's a 10% discount for backpackers. There are many units around town for rent. Bush camping (difficult access) is allowed at a few places on the peninsula. Contact the ranger at Coffin Bay township (☎ (086) 85 4047).

Coffin Bay to Point Labatt

Just past **Coulta**, 40 km north of Coffin Bay, there's good surfing at **Greenly Beach**. Near Coulta is *Wepowie Farm* (☎ (086) 87 2063) where you can camp or stay in the farm cottage for $12/24 for a single/double, plus a fee for linen if required.

Just north of **Elliston**, a small resort and fishing town with a nice bay, take the turn-off to **Anxious Bay** and **Salmon Point** for some great ocean scenery. It's a seven-km detour. There are a number of islands nearby but you'll have to charter a boat or plane to get there. There's accommodation on **Flinders Island** at $80 a night for four people. There are good swimming beaches around **Waterloo Bay**, while **Blackfellows** has fine surf. **Talia**, further up the coast, has impressive granite rock faces and the limestone **Talia Caves**.

At **Port Kenny** on Venus Bay, there are more beaches, and whales are often seen off the coast when they come to breed in October. **Venus Bay** has a fleet of prawn trawlers.

Shortly before Streaky Bay, the turn-off to **Point Labatt** takes you to the only permanent colony of sea lions on the Australian mainland. You look down on their rocks from the clifftop, 50 metres above. There's good coastal scenery from here to Streaky Bay.

STREAKY BAY (population 1000)

This little town takes it name from the 'streaky' water, caused by seaweed in the bay. The town is surrounded by bays, caves and high cliffs. The **Kelsh Pioneer Museum** is open on Friday from 2 to 5 pm and at other times by prior arrangement.

Curious granite outcrops known as inselbergs are found at numerous places around the Eyre Peninsula. You can see a good group known as **Murphy's Haystacks** near the highway about 20 km south-east of Streaky Bay. If you want to get closer you'll need to pick up the key from the council offices in Streaky Bay and pay $2 plus a deposit. **Perlubie Beach**, north of Streaky Bay, is another good surfing beach.

Places to Stay

Streaky Bay Community Hotel (☎ (086) 26 1008) has singles/doubles/triples for $25/30/39 and motel units for $40/48/60, or there's the *Foreshore Tourist Park* (☎ (086) 26 1666) with tent sites and on-site vans.

SMOKY BAY (population 100)

This tiny town has a rodeo at Easter which draws competitors and spectators from all over the country. The only place to stay is a friendly *Caravan Park* (☎ (086) 25 7030) with tent sites and cabins.

CEDUNA (population 2800)

Just past the junction of the Flinders and Eyre highways, Ceduna marks the end of the Eyre Peninsula area and the start of the long, empty stretch of highway across the Nullarbor Plain into Western Australia. The town was founded in 1896 although a whaling station had existed on St Peter Island, off nearby Cape Thevenard, back in 1850.

There's a friendly tourist office (☎ (086) 25 2972) in the main street. It's also a travel agency, and you might find yourself visiting to buy a bus ticket to Western Australia after a few days waiting for a lift. Pioneer charges $160 to Perth or $126 to Norseman.

You can also buy tickets for whale-spotting helicopter flights for $60 – they depart from the Nullarbor Roadhouse, 300 km further west (the National Parks Service warns that helicopters can cause whales distress – if you're on a flight which passes low over whales, *complain*). Whales have been spotted from the coast and the good news is that sightings are becoming more frequent. Whales visit the Great Australian Bight during their June to October breeding season.

The **Old Schoolhouse Museum** has pioneer exhibits and artefacts from the British atomic weapons programme at Maralinga. There is an **overseas telecommunications earth station** 34 km north of Ceduna where microwave communications are bounced off satellites. Tours depart at 11 am and 2 pm on weekdays.

There are many beaches and sheltered coves around Ceduna while 13 km out of town, you can see the old **McKenzie Ruin** at the earlier township site of Denial Bay. **Laura Bay**, off the road to Smoky Bay 20 km south-west of Ceduna, is a small conservation park with many species of birds.

Turn off the highway at **Penong** (famous for its numerous windmills), about 75 km west of Ceduna, and a 20-km dirt track gets you to **Point Sinclair**. Here you'll find **Cactus Beach** and some of Australia's best surf, as well as more sheltered beaches. The whole point is private property but you can camp for $3.50. Contact the general store (☎ (086) 25 1036) at Point Sinclair – open daily between 12.30 and 2.30 pm and the only place you can get drinking water (for a price).

Places to Stay

The *Ceduna Community Hotel* (☎ (086) 25 2008) has rooms from $25/29 and a good cheap bistro. There are also motel units and a couple of other motels in town. There are a number of caravan parks with on-site vans and cabins.

OTHER PLACES

Cummins, inland and north of Port Lincoln, is a small town with the good **Koppio Museum** showing early agricultural equipment. Admission is $1.50 and it's open daily except Monday. Along the Eyre Highway the road passes through **Kimba**, **Kyancutta** and **Wudinna**, all important agricultural centres but otherwise of little interest. Kimba is on the very edge of the outback and you can visit **Lake Gilles** and the **Gawler Ranges** from here.

Mt Wudinna, which is 10 km north-east of Wudinna, is the second-largest rock in the south of Australia.

Flinders Ranges

Rising from the northern end of Gulf St Vincent and running north for 800 km into the arid outback, the Flinders Ranges offer some of the most spectacular scenery in Aus-

tralia. It's a superb area for bushwalks, wildlife or taking in the ever-changing colours of the outback. In the far north of the Flinders region, the mountains are hemmed in by barren salt lakes.

The ranges, like so much of Australia, are geologically ancient, but worn though the peaks may be the colours are amazing – this area has always been a favourite of artists. Like other dry regions of Australia, the vegetation is surprisingly diverse and colourful. In the spring, when rain is most likely, the country is at its greenest and carpeted with wild flowers. In summer the nights are cool but the days can be searingly hot. Winter is probably the best time to visit, although there are attractions at any time of year.

In 1802, when Flinders first set foot in the ranges, there were a number of Aboriginal tribes in the region. You can visit some of their sites: the rock paintings at Yourambulla (near Hawker) and Arkaroo (near Wilpena); and the rock-cut patterns at Sacred Canyon (near Wilpena) and Chambers Gorge.

Bushwalking is one of the main attractions of the area. Campers can generally find water in rock pools during cooler months, but this is wild, rugged country and care should be taken before setting out. Wilpena Pound, the Arkaroola-Mt Painter Sanctuary and Mt Remarkable National Park all have excellent walks, many of them along marked trails.

In the early mornings and evenings, you've got a good chance of spotting wildlife including emus, a variety of kangaroos and many different lizards. The bird life is especially prolific with colourful parrots, galahs, rosellas and many others – often in great numbers.

Information

It's definitely worth getting a good map of the area as there are many back roads and a variety of road surfaces. The SAGTC's Flinders Ranges' leaflet is quite good and the RAA, SAGTC and the National Parks office all put out maps of the ranges area and Wilpena Pound. *Touring in the Flinders Ranges* is a good little book produced by the RAA and available from their offices. If

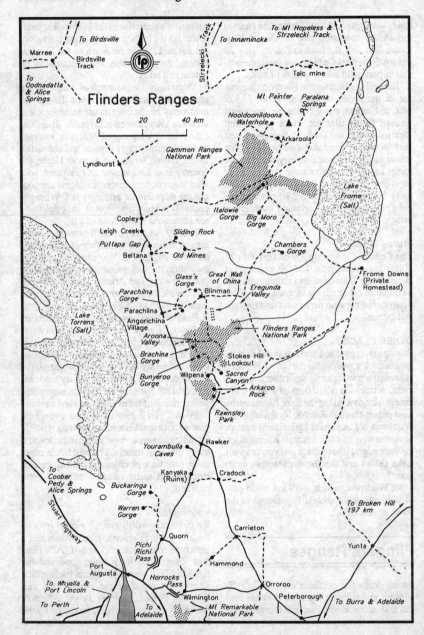

Flinders Ranges

0   20   40 km

To Birdsville

Marree

Birdsville Track

To Oodnadatta & Alice Springs

Strzelecki Track

To Innamincka

To Mt Hopeless & Strzelecki Track

Talc mine

Mt Painter

Paralana Springs

Nooldoonildoona Waterhole

Arkaroola

Gammon Ranges National Park

Lyndhurst

Lake Frome (Salt)

Copley

Leigh Creek

Puttapa Gap

Beltana

Italowie Gorge

Big Moro Gorge

Sliding Rock

Old Mines

Chambers Gorge

Glass's Gorge

Great Wall of China

Frome Downs (Private Homestead)

Parachilna Gorge

Blinman

Eregunda Valley

Parachilna

Angorichina Village

Aroona Valley

Flinders Ranges National Park

Brachina Gorge

Stokes Hill Lookout

Bunyeroo Gorge

Wilpena

Sacred Canyon

Lake Torrens (Salt)

Arkaroo Rock

Rawnsley Park

To Coober Pedy & Alice Springs

Yourambulla Caves

Hawker

Buckaringa Gorge

Kanyaka (Ruins)

Cradock

Warren Gorge

To Broken Hill 197 km

Carrieton

Stuart Highway

Quorn

Pichi Richi Pass

Hammond

Yunta

Port Augusta

Horrocks Pass

Orroroo

To Whyalla & Port Lincoln

Wilmington

Peterborough

To Perth

To Adelaide

Mt Remarkable National Park

To Burra & Adelaide

you're planning on doing more than just the standard walks in the Flinders, look for a copy of *Flinders Ranges Walks* ($7.95) and the *Walking Guide to the North Flinders Ranges* ($14.95).

The main National Parks office for the Flinders Ranges and the far north is at Hawker (☎ (086) 48 4244), in the old council offices. The office is open on weekdays only, but there's another office at Wilpena (☎ (086) 48 0048) which is open daily.

Organised Tours

There are plenty of tours from Adelaide to the ranges and also tours out from Wilpena Pound and Arkaroola. There are a few catering for backpackers – see hostel notice boards for current fares and itineraries.

The major bus companies also do tours and there are plenty of companies offering more adventurous 4WD tours, including Butlers Outback Safaris (☎ (086) 42 2188), Desert Trek (☎ (08) 264 7200), Intrepid Tours (☎ (086) 48 6277) and Gawler Outback Tours (☎ (085) 22 2254). Horse-riding treks are also available with Pichi Richi Saddle & Pack (☎ (086) 48 6075), Woodleigh Farm (☎ (088) 23 2334) and Melrose Mountain Rides (☎ (086) 66 2193).

There are camel treks from Blinman, ranging from 1½-hour rides ($20) to week-long treks ($700) (☎ (086) 48 4874). Outback Airways. who can be contacted via the Hawker Caravan Park ✈☎ (086) 48 4006), flies to most places in the far north and also has tours. Five people on a two-day tour would pay from about $450 each. At Wilpena you can take a scenic flight for about $30.

Places to Stay

There are hotels and caravan parks as well as many cottages and farms offering all sorts of accommodation. Contact the SAGTC in Adelaide (☎ (08) 212 1505, or 008 882 092, toll-free) for further details. In Quorn, Quornucopia (☎ (086) 486 282) has information about cottages, but none for overnight stays. Summer is the off-season

here, because of the heat, and some places have special deals then.

To camp in the national park (except at the private camping ground at Wilpena Pound) you need a permit from a National Parks office for $3 per night, valid for up to five people.

Getting There & Away

Bus Stateliner runs from Adelaide to Wilpena Pound ($43.90) on Friday (arriving after midnight); it returns on Sunday. On Wednesday and Friday they have a service via Quorn, Hawker and Parachilna to Arkaroola, returning on Sunday and Thursday. The fare for the 12-hour trip to Arkaroola is $66; the bus to Leigh Creek costs $43.

Car It's good surfaced road all the way north to Wilpena Pound, but from there the roads are dirt – quite good when they're dry but they can be closed by rain. Check with National Parks offices for current information. The Marree road skirting the western edge of the Flinders Ranges is surfaced up to Lyndhurst.

There are three routes to Arkaroola. The fastest is to continue up the Marree road beyond Parachilna and turn off at Copley, near Leigh Creek. An alternative is to travel up the Barrier Highway towards Broken Hill as far as Yunta and then turn north and follow the long (310 km) gravel road via Frome Downs, skirting the edge of Lake Frome and crossing the dingo-proof fence twice. There is no petrol or water available along this road and it's best to travel earlier in the day because the sun in your eyes can be unpleasant in the late afternoon.

Probably the most interesting route is to go via Wilpena Pound and take the road via Chambers Gorge, meeting the Frome Downs road south of Balcanoona. This road tends to be difficult after rain.

Getting Around

If you have a vehicle you can make a loop that takes you around an interesting section of the southern part of the Flinders. From

Port Augusta go through the Pichi Richi Pass to Quorn and Hawker and on up to Wilpena Pound. From Wilpena Pound, continue north through the Flinders Ranges National Park to Blinman then down through the Parachilna Gorge to Parachilna, back on to the plains and south to Hawker – thus looping right round Wilpena Pound.

Alternatively, on the way south from Parachilna, head back into the ranges on the Brachina Gorge road, about 20 km south, which will eventually lead you to Wilpena Pound. From Wilpena Pound, you can also loop north into the Flinders Ranges National Park through Bunyeroo Gorge and the Aroona Valley.

MT REMARKABLE NATIONAL PARK

South-east of Port Augusta and in the southern stretch of the Flinders Ranges, the Mt Remarkable National Park is near Wilmington and Melrose. From Wilmington you can drive into the park and walk through narrow **Alligator Gorge**; in places the walls of this spectacularly beautiful gorge are only two metres apart.

Hancocks Lookout, just north of the park near Horrocks Pass, offers excellent views of Spencer Gulf. There is a camping ground in the Mambray Creek section, and bush camping is permitted in some areas. There are rangers' offices (for camping permits) at Mambray Creek (☎ (086) 67 5181) and Alligator Gorge (☎ (086) 67 5181).

MELROSE

This tiny town is the oldest settlement in the Flinders Ranges. It's on the southern edge of the Mt Remarkable National Park, at the foot of Mt Remarkable (956 metres). There's a walking trail to the top of the mountain. The old police station and courthouse now houses a museum. The **Mt Remarkable Hotel** was built in 1846 and its exterior has scarcely changed since. West of town along Mt Remarkable Creek is **Cathedral Rock**.

Places to Stay

The *Mt Remarkable Hotel* (☎ (086) 66 2119) and the *North Star Hotel* (☎ 66 2110) both have single/double rooms at $17.50/25. The Mt Remarkable Hotel has more character; the floors slope, the doors won't close and you expect to see a ghost around every corner! There's now a ghost-free motel section with units from $25/32.

The *Melrose Caravan Park* (☎ (086) 66 2060) is in a picturesque spot along the creek and has tent sites and on-site vans and cabins.

OTHER SOUTHERN FLINDERS RANGES TOWNS

Other towns in the south of the Flinders Ranges include **Carrieton**, where a major rodeo is held each October, **Bruce** and **Hammond**, railheads which have faded away to ghost towns, and **Orroroo**, an agricultural centre. Nearby **Black Rock Peak** has good bushwalks and terrific views. You can see Aboriginal **rock carvings** at Pekina Creek and the nearby ruins of the **Pekina Station Homestead** are worth a visit.

Between Melrose and Port Germein you pass through the scenic **Germein Gorge**, while **Bangor** has the ruins of the Gorge Hotel. At **Port Germein** the *Casual Affair* (☎ (086) 34 5342) is a coffee shop, gallery and craft centre where there's some backpackers' accommodation. Dorm beds cost about $8 and meals start from about $3. Further south at **Wirrabara** there's a *Youth Hostel* (☎ (086) 68 4158) with beds for $6.

QUORN (population 1050)

The 'gateway to the Flinders' is about 330 km north of Adelaide and 46 km north-east from Port Augusta. It became an important railway town after the completion of the Great Northern Railway in 1878, and it still has some flavour of the pioneering days.

The railway was closed in 1957, but some of the line has reopened as a tourist railway. A vintage steam engine makes a 43-km round trip from Quorn to the scenic Pichi Richi Pass for $15. It runs on weekends and public holidays between March and mid-November, with extra services during the October school holiday (☎ (08) 213 4777).

The town, picturesquely sited in a valley,

has a couple of art galleries. **Quornucopia** offers a range of unusual crafts and gifts and there's the small **Quorn Mill Museum** and restaurant in an old bakery and flour mill. From Quorn you can make 4WD trips into the Flinders Ranges and visit the nearby **Warren Gorge** (which has good rock climbing), the **Buckaringa Gorge** (good for picnics) and the **Waukarie Creek Trail** which runs from Woolshed Flat to Waukarie Creek. Closer to the town, you can follow walking trails to the top of **Devil's Peak** and **Dutchman's Stern**.

Information is available at the District Council office, Seventh St.

Places to Stay & Eat

The *Transcontinental Hotel* (☎ (086) 48 6076) on Railway Terrace (the main street) is a friendly place with backpackers' beds at $10 a night (10% off if you're using this book) and cooking facilities. There is accommodation available at other pubs, including the *Grand Junction Hotel* (☎ (086) 48 6025) which has singles/doubles for $20/30. The *Quorn Caravan Park* (☎ (086) 48 6066) has tent sites and on-site vans. *Pichi Richi Pantry* sells good takeaways and some meals.

KANYAKA

North of Quorn, on the way to Hawker, are the ruins of the old Kanyaka settlement. It was founded in 1851 and up to 70 families lived here, but it was abandoned in the 1870s. Only the ruins of the stone houses remain of the high hopes that early settlers had for this harsh area.

If you're coming from the north, don't be fooled by the signs for the Kanyaka settlement; all there is here is a solitary gravestone by the creek bed. The ruins are further south, with a second group a couple of hundred metres away along the dirt road, behind a rise. The first group also has an old graveyard. Note the solid stone dunnies (toilets), clearly built to last.

It's about one km along the creek to the cookhouse and shearing shed. The track continues around 1½ km to a picturesque permanent water hole, overlooked by the **Kanyaka Death Rock**.

HAWKER (population 350)

There are a number of places of interest which can be conveniently visited from here, including the Kanyaka ruins to the south and Wilpena Pound, only a short drive north. **Willow Waters** is another old property abandoned in the 1890s when crops failed. There are Aboriginal rock paintings south of Hawker at **Yourambulla Cave**, a hollow in the rocks high up on the side of Yourambulla Peak, a half-hour walk from the road.

Places to Stay & Eat

The *Hawker Hotel* (☎ (086) 48 4102) costs $25/35 for pub-style singles/doubles. Motel units are $50/60. The counter meals here are certainly filling. There's another motel and a couple of caravan parks with on-site vans. The *Hawker Caravan Park* in town is the shadier.

The *Sightseers Cafe* has reasonably priced meals, or there's the more up-market *Old Ghan Restaurant* in the disused railway station.

Getting There & Away

Apart for the Stateliner bus service, which costs $10.80 from Adelaide and comes through late at night, you can get to Wilpena Pound on the 6 am newspaper run from in front of the Hawker Shopping Centre. It can only take one passenger.

WILPENA POUND

The best known feature of the ranges is the huge natural basin known as Wilpena Pound. Covering about 80 sq km, it is ringed by a circle of cliffs and is accessible only by the narrow opening at Sliding Rock through which Wilpena Creek sometimes flows. From outside Wilpena Pound the cliff face is almost sheer – soaring to 1000 metres – but inside the basin floor slopes gently away from the peaks.

There is plenty of wildlife in Wilpena Pound, particularly bird life which includes everything from rosellas, galahs and budgerigars to emus and wedge-tailed eagles. You can make scenic flights over Wilpena Pound for about $40 or excursions to other places of interest in the vicinity. **Sacred Canyon**, with rock-cut patterns, is off to the east. North of Wilpena Pound is the **Flinders Ranges National Park** where scenic attractions include the Bunyeroo and Brachina gorges and the Aroona Valley.

Walks

If you're planning to walk for more than about three hours, fill in the log book at the ranger's office – and don't forget to 'sign off' when you return!

There is a series of bushwalks in the park, clearly marked by blue triangles along the tracks. Pick up a copy of the Wilpena leaflet issued by the National Parks & Wildlife Service or the similar leaflet from the general store (which also sells more detailed maps)

– both have maps which are quite OK for day walks on the marked trails. It is recommended that you do not walk solo and that you are adequately equipped – particularly with drinking water and sun protection in the summer.

Most of the walks start from the camping ground and the walking times indicated are for a reasonably easy pace. The St Marys Peak walk is probably the most interesting, but there are plenty of others worth considering. They vary from short walks, suitable for those with small children, to longer ones taking more than a day.

You can take an excellent day-long walk from the camp site in Wilpena Pound to St Marys Peak and back – either as an up-and-down or a round-trip expedition. Up and back, it's faster and more interesting to take the route outside Wilpena Pound and then up to the Tanderra Saddle since the scenery is much more spectacular.

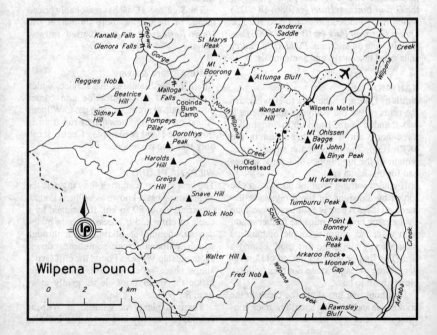

The final climb up to the saddle is fairly steep and the stretch to the top of the peak is a real scramble. The views are superb from the saddle and the peak; the white glimmer of Lake Torrens is visible off to the west and the long Aroona Valley stretches off to the north.

Descending from the peak to the saddle you can then head back down on the same direct route or take the longer round-trip walk through Wilpena Pound via the Old Homestead and Sliding Rock. This is the same track you take to get to Edeowie Gorge. Alternatively, you can take your time and stay at the Cooinda bush-camping site.

Places to Stay & Eat

Unless you've got a tent there is no cheap accommodation at Wilpena Pound. If you're equipped for camping there's a camping ground with facilities including a well-stocked store. Otherwise, the *Wilpena Pound Motel* (☎ (086) 48 0004, or (08) 212 6386 in Adelaide) has all mod cons including a restaurant and swimming pool but it costs $72/80 a night for singles/doubles. There is a plan to build a large accommodation complex near Wilpena Pound, but it has run into trouble with funding and environmentalists.

You can get pies, pasties and groceries in the general store. Counter lunches are available and there's also the motel restaurant.

Off the Hawker road, about 10 km south of Wilpena and close to the Pound's outer edge, *Rawnsley Park* (☎ (086) 48 0030) has tent sites for $7.50, dorm beds for $9, on-site vans for $28 and cabins from $36. The Stateliner bus will drop you at the turn-off and from there it's a four-km walk. You can also make overnight horse treks starting from here.

BLINMAN (population 100)

From the 1860s to the 1890s this was a busy copper town but today it's just a tiny country town on the circular route around Wilpena Pound. It's a useful starting point for visits to many of the scenic attractions in the area

and the delightful *Hotel North Blinman* has a real outback pub flavour – rooms cost $20 per person or $25 with bathroom. You can have a shower here for $1, and there's a swimming pool.

AROUND BLINMAN

The beautiful **Aroona Valley** and the ruins of the **Aroona Homestead** are to the south of Blinman. Further south is the **Brachina Gorge**, another typically spectacular Flinders Ranges' gorge. Between Blinman and Wilpena Pound is the **Great Wall of China**, a long ridge capped with ironstone. Between Parachilna and Blinman it's a scenic drive on a rough dirt road through the **Parachilna Gorge** where there are good picnic areas.

Angorichina Tourist Village (☎ (086) 48 4842), about halfway between Blinman and Parachilna in the Parachilna Gorge, has tent sites ($7), units ($40 a double and $6 extra per person – up to five people) and chalets (same prices as units – up to eight people). YHA members get a 10% discount. In peak periods you might have to stay a minimum of two nights. The owners are friendly and can advise on travel in this picturesque and rugged area. They can usually pick you up from Parachilna, which is on the Stateliner route, and drop you at trailheads.

At **Parachilna** there's the revamped *Prairie Hotel* (☎ (086) 48 4895) which has beds in a basic dorm for $5 and hotel accommodation for $20/35, including breakfast.

North of Blinman, on the Oodnadatta road, **Beltana** is almost a ghost town but you can turn east here and visit the **old copper mines** at Sliding Rock. At one time Beltana was a major camel-breeding station and much of the town is being restored. You can get a guide to the town from the museum in the old railway station.

It's a long drive from anywhere to **Chambers Gorge**, well to the north-east towards Lake Frome. The deep gorge has rock carvings and from Mt Chambers you can see Lake Frome and the Flinders Ranges all the way from Mt Painter to Wilpena. There are camping facilities at Mt Chambers.

LEIGH CREEK (population 1000)

North of Beltana, Leigh Creek's huge open-cut coal mine supplies the Port Augusta power station. Tree planting has transformed this once barren town; you can do a drive-yourself tour of the coal works by following the green arrow signs. In 1982 the whole town was shifted south a few km to allow mining on the site.

From Leigh Creek, you can visit the **Aroona Dam** and the **Gammon Ranges National Park** (64 km to the east), but it's a remote and rugged area for experienced bushwalkers only. For information contact the ranger on ☎ (086) 48 4829.

ARKAROOLA

The tiny settlement of Arkaroola, in the northern part of the Flinders Ranges, was established in 1968. It's a privately operated wildlife sanctuary in rugged and spectacular country. From the settlement you can take a 4WD trip along the 'ridge top' through rugged mountain country and there are also scenic flights and many walking tracks. The ridge-top tour costs $55 – expensive but it's a spectacular four-hour trip through amazing scenery.

This was a mining area and old tracks lead to rock pools at the **Barraranna Gorge** and **Echo Camp**, and to water holes at **Arkaroola** and **Nooldoonooldoona** (quite a mouthful!). Further on are the **Bolla Bollana Springs** and also the ruins of a copper smelter.

Mt Painter is a very scenic landmark, and there are fine views from **Freeling Heights** across Yudnamutana Gorge or **Siller's Lookout** from where you can see the salt flats of Lake Frome. This is real, red outback country and Mt Painter is a spectacular example of that landscape. **Paralana Hot Springs** is believed to be the site of the last volcanic activity to have taken place in Australia.

There are many interesting walks in this area, but take water – and care. You get out of sight of civilisation surprisingly fast and you'll quickly realise what an inhospitable place the outback can be, particularly when it's hot.

Places to Stay & Eat

The resort camp site costs $10 for two and there is a variety of other accommodation. Bunk beds are $10 but you have to book these in advance. Holiday-flat-style units cost $39 for twin rooms with shared facilities or there are motel units from $59 for a double. There's a small shop where you can buy basic supplies and a fairly pricey restaurant.

Getting There & Away

Stateliner runs from Adelaide ($66) on Wednesday and Friday, returning on Sunday and Thursday.

Outback

The area north of the Eyre Peninsula and the Flinders Ranges stretches into the vast, empty area of South Australia's far north. Although sparsely populated and difficult to travel through, it has much of interest. Large parts of the far north are prohibited areas (either Aboriginal land or the Woomera restricted area) and without 4WD or camels it's not possible to stray far from the main roads as there are virtually no other surfaced roads.

To visit the national parks up here (and much of the far north is national park) you need a desert parks' permit which costs $50 per vehicle. It's valid for a year and includes an excellent information book and detailed route and area maps.

Permits are available in many towns (although not from most National Parks offices, strangely) including: Adelaide (RAA and others), Alice Springs (Shell Todd service station), Birdsville, Broken Hill (RAA), Coober Pedy (Underground Books), Hawker, Innamincka, Kulgera, Leigh Creek, Marree, Mt Gambier (RAA), Oodnadatta, Port Augusta (National Parks office and the information centre) and William Creek.

If you want to visit the Dalhousie Mound warm springs in the Witjira National Park north of Oodnadatta, you need only buy a $15 day/night permit.

If you're camping, avoid creek beds because of the possibility of flash floods.

ROUTES NORTH

The last stretch of the sealed Stuart Highway was opened in 1987 so you can now drive on a smooth bitumen road all the way from Adelaide to Alice Springs. It's a long way – 933 km from Port Augusta to the Northern Territory border. The temptation to rush along that smooth road has resulted in more than a few high-speed meetings between cars and cattle. Take care.

For those who want to travel to the Northern Territory the hard way, there is still the **Oodnadatta Track**. This old road runs from Port Augusta through the Flinders Ranges to Leigh Creek, Lyndhurst, Marree, Oodnadatta and eventually joins the Stuart Highway not far south of the Territory border. For most of the way it runs close to the old railway line route. The road is surfaced as far as Lyndhurst, after that it's a typical outback track. There are a number of routes across from Oodnadatta to the Stuart Highway. From Oodnadatta to Coober Pedy is 195 km.

The two other routes of interest in the far north are the famous **Birdsville Track** and the **Strzelecki Track** – see the relevant sections later in this chapter. These days the tracks have been so much improved that during the winter season it's quite feasible to do them in any car that's in good condition – a 4WD is not necessary. Rain or summer heat can be quite a different story.

For more information on these outback routes check with the state automobile associations. *Outback Central & South Australia*, published by the South Australian Department of Lands, is an excellent tourist map with a lot of interesting information. Algona Publications (16 Charles St, Northcote, Victoria 3070) do a good *Simpson Desert South-Lake Eyre* map which covers all three tracks.

The South Australian outback includes much of the Simpson Desert and the harsh, rocky land of Sturt's Stony Desert. There are also huge salt lakes which every once in a long while fill with water. **Lake Eyre**, used by Donald Campbell for his attempt on the world's land-speed record in the '60s, filled up for a time in the '70s. It filled up again in 1989, only the third occasion since White people first reached this area.

When the infrequent rains do reach this dry land the effect is amazing – flowers bloom and plants grow at a breakneck pace in order to complete their life cycle before the dry returns. There is even a species of frog that goes into a sort of suspended animation, remaining in the ground for years on end, only to pop up with the first sign of rain.

On a much more mundane level, roads can be washed out and the surface turned into a sticky glue. Vehicles are often stuck for days – or even weeks.

WOOMERA

During the '50s and '60s Woomera was used to launch experimental British rockets and conduct tests in an abortive European project to send a satellite into orbit. The Woomera Prohibited Area occupies a vast stretch of land in the centre of the state. The town of Woomera, in the south-east corner of the Prohibited Area, is still a military base and there are US military personnel working here. About 2000 people live here today, as against 5000 at the town's peak. Still, it's a surprisingly large (and orderly) town for this part of the world.

A small **museum** has various local oddments and a collection of old aircraft and missiles. The museum tells you something about the missile testing in the past but little about what goes on today. The plutonium contamination of the '50s doesn't get a mention, although along the highway you'll see the signs warning you that the country west of the road is off limits.

Places to Stay

Woomera Travellers' Village (☎ (086) 73 7800), near the entrance to the town, has backpackers' accommodation for $12 a bed, tent sites for $5 per person and on-site vans from $24 a double. There's also a kiosk here. The *Eldo Hotel* (☎ (086) 73 7867) in town on Kotana Ave has backpackers' rooms at about $12 and singles/doubles for $15/24 ('Eldo' is the acronym for the European Launch Development Organisation).

Getting There & Away
Air Kendell Airlines (☎ (08) 233 3322) fly from Adelaide to Woomera most days of the week for $131.

Bus Woomera is seven km off the Stuart Highway from the tiny and scruffy little settlement of Pimba, 175 km north of Port Augusta. Stateliner and the long-distance bus lines pass through Woomera daily. It's about $40 to Adelaide, and $120 to Alice Springs.

ANDAMOOKA (population 400)
Off the Stuart Highway, north of Woomera and west of Lake Torrens, Andamooka is a rough-and-ready little opal-mining town. Many residents live underground to avoid the temperature extremes. It's about 115 km north from Pimba to Andamooka and although the road is fair it quickly becomes impassable after rain.

Olympic Dam is a huge uranium mine on Roxby Downs station near Andamooka. You can get to Andamooka and Roxby Downs with Stateliner.

The *Andamooka Motel* (☎ (086) 72 7186) has rooms for about $35/45, less in summer. You can camp at the caravan park, and the *Tuckerbox* does good meals.

GLENDAMBO
Glendambo is 113 km north of Pimba and 252 km south of Coober Pedy. It's a new store, pub, motel and caravan park, all developed since the completion of the new Stuart Highway – an indication of the increased traffic since the road was sealed.

COOBER PEDY (population 2000)
On the Stuart Highway, 860 km north of Adelaide, Coober Pedy is one of the best known outback towns. The name is Aboriginal and means 'white fellow's hole in the ground', which aptly describes the place, as a large proportion of the population live in dugouts to shelter from daytime temperatures that can soar to over 50°C and cold winter nights.

Coober Pedy is in an extremely inhospitable area and the town reflects this; even in the middle of winter it looks dried out and dusty with piles of junk everywhere. This is no attractive little settlement, in fact it's hardly surprising that much of *Mad Max III* was filmed here – the town looks like the end of the world!

Information
The tourist office (☎ (086) 72 5298) is in the council offices, opposite the Opal Inn as you enter the town. It is open weekdays and sometimes weekends. The Underground Bookshop is very good for information on the local area and the outback in general. They also sell second-hand books.

Around the town there are mine tours, opal-cutting demonstrations, and polished stones and jewellery on sale.

Dugout Homes
Many of the early dugout homes were simply worked-out mines but now they're often cut specifically as residences. Several homes are open to visitors – all you have to do is create an eccentric enough abode and you can charge admission! Harry's Crocodile Nest, about five km out of town, charges $2 and is definitely one of the more eccentric. It makes an appearance towards the end of *Mad Max III*. Various other homes are open for $1.50 to $2, including Faye's, which has an indoor swimming pool!

Other Attractions
These include the **Big Winch** (a lookout over the town), the **Underground Catacomb Church** and the **Old Timers Mine**, a tourist

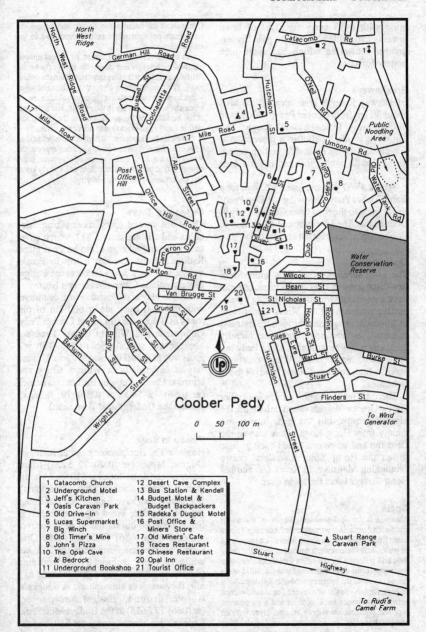

Coober Pedy

0   50   100 m

1 Catacomb Church	12 Desert Cave Complex
2 Underground Motel	13 Bus Station & Kendell
3 Jeff's Kitchen	14 Budget Motel &
4 Oasis Caravan Park	Budget Backpackers
5 Old Drive-In	15 Radeka's Dugout Motel
6 Lucas Supermarket	16 Post Office &
7 Big Winch	Miners' Store
8 Old Timer's Mine	17 Old Miners' Cafe
9 John's Pizza	18 Traces Restaurant
10 The Opal Cave	19 Chinese Restaurant
& Bedrock	20 Opal Inn
11 Underground Bookshop	21 Tourist Office

mine with a $3 entry fee. Out of town towards Crocodile Harry's you pass **Underground Potteries** which has some nice pottery for sale.

Breakaways

Breakaway Reserve is an area of low hills about 30 km from Coober Pedy, which have 'broken away' from the Stuart Range. You can drive to the lookout in a conventional vehicle and see the natural formation known as the **Castle**, which featured in *Mad Max III*.

With a 4WD you can make a 65-km loop from Coober Pedy, following the Dog Proof Fence back to the road from Coober Pedy to Oodnadatta. The Underground Bookshop in Coober Pedy has a leaflet and map.

Opal Mining

The town survives from opals which were first discovered in 1911. Keen fossickers can have a go themselves after acquiring a prospecting permit from the Mines Department in Adelaide. Fossicking through the outcasts is known as noodling. There are literally hundreds of mines around Coober Pedy but there are no big operators. When somebody makes a find, dozens of others head off to the same area.

There are many migrant groups in Coober Pedy – Greeks, Yugoslavs and Italians are the biggest groups, but the gem buyers are mainly from Hong Kong. They stay in the Opal Inn and when one heads back to base (often the Hong Kong travellers' centre Chungking Mansions in Kowloon) another Hong Konger takes the room over.

Opals

Australia is the opal-producing centre of the world and South Australia is where most of Australia's opals come from. Opals are hardened from silica suspended in water, and the colour is produced by light being split and reflected by the silica molecules. Valuable opals are cut in three different fashions: solid opals can be cut out of the rough into cabochons (domed-top stones); triplets consist of a layer of opal sandwiched between an opaque backing layer and a transparent cap; and doublets are simply an opal layer with an opaque backing. In addition, some opals from Queensland are found embedded in rock; these are sometimes polished while still incorporated in the surrounding rock.

An opal's value is determined by its colour and clarity – the brighter and clearer the colour the better. Brilliance of colour is more important than the colour itself. The type of opal is also a determinant of value – black and crystal opals are the most valuable, semiblack and semicrystal are in the middle, and milk opal at the bottom. The bigger the pattern the better, and visible flaws (like cracks) also affect the value.

Shape is also important – a high dome is better than a flat opal. Finally, given equality of other aspects, the size is important. As with any sort of gemstone, don't expect to find great bargains unless you clearly know and understand what you are buying.

Organised Tours

There are several tours, most taking three hours and costing around $12, which cover the sights and take you into an opal mine. Radeka's Tours includes a trip to Breakaways, and Joe's Tours (book at the Budget Motel) include Crocodile Harry's Nest.

On Monday and Thursday you can travel with the mail truck along 600 km of dirt roads as it does the trip round Coober Pedy, Oodnadatta and William Creek. There's a backpackers' special price of $45. This is a great way to get off the beaten track. You can stay at Oodnadatta or William Creek and return to Coober Pedy on the next mail truck (☎ (086) 72 5900 or (086) 70 7822, or contact the Underground Bookshop).

Places to Stay

Hostels The *Backpacker's Inn* at Radeka's Dugout Motel (☎ (086) 72 5223) offers underground dormitories at $10 for 24 hours (handy if you're catching a bus at odd hours). Some travellers have complained that things get too crowded, but a big new section is being tunnelled out so that should improve.

Bedrock (☎ (086) 72 5028) at the Opal Cave complex has dorm beds for $12, but while they are technically underground (they're in a tunnel bored into the side of a hill) they aren't as atmospheric as Radeka's. Above ground, *Budget Backpackers* (☎ (086) 72 5613) at the Budget Motel near Radeka's has shared rooms for $10, and the

Stuart Range Caravan Park, south of town, has backpackers' accommodation for $10.

Hotels & Motels There are a number of hotels and motels, some underground, some with big air-conditioners! Listed here are some of the cheaper places. *Umoona Opal Mine* (☎ (086) 72 5288) on Hutchison St has singles/doubles for $15/24. Bathrooms are communal but there are kitchen facilities. The *Budget Motel* (☎ (086) 72 5163) has rooms from $20/30 or from $38 with bathrooms. *Opal Inn Hotel/Motel* (☎ (086) 72 5054) has pub rooms for $25/35. *Radeka's Dugout Motel* costs from $40/55/60 for singles/doubles/triples in the low season (summer), rising steeply in the winter.

Camping There are several caravan parks. The *Oasis Caravan Park* (☎ (086) 72 5169) is good and has tent sites and on-site vans. The *Stuart Range Caravan Park* (☎ (086) 72 5179) has also been recommended but it's further from the town centre. Even further out (about five km), *Rudy's Camel Mine* (☎ (086) 72 5614) costs $2.50 per person.

Places to Eat
The *Last Resort Cafe*, next to the Underground Bookshop, does a good line in drinks and desserts as well as meals, including breakfast. Unfortunately it's open only during the day. *Jeff's Kitchen*, next to the Oasis Caravan Park, serves breakfast and other meals. *Sergio's* has Italian food, including spaghetti from $6, and there are a couple of Greek places, the *Taverna* and *Traces*. There are also a couple of pizza places, and the *Opal Inn* does counter meals. *Miners' Store*, next to the post office, is the best of the supermarkets. The Acropolis Cafe was a good place but it has closed down – because it was blown up! It's that sort of town.

Entertainment
The restaurant on top of the Mobil station in the centre of town doubles as a disco. Other than that, playing pool at the Oasis Inn seems to be main form of entertainment in town, although you could also see what's happening in the bars at the plush new Desert Inn Hotel complex.

Getting There & Away
Air Kendell Airlines (☎ (08) 233 3322) fly from Adelaide to Coober Pedy most days of the week ($226), and from Coober Pedy to Uluru (Ayers Rock) once a week ($184).

Bus It's 413 km from Coober Pedy to Kulgera, just across the border into the Northern Territory, and from there it's another 280 km to Alice Springs. Bus Australia and Greyhound/Pioneer pass through on the Adelaide-Alice Springs route. It's about $60 from Adelaide and $51 from Alice Springs. Stateliner run buses from Adelaide to Coober Pedy at least twice daily, arriving at a God-awful middle-of-the-night hour.

MARLA
Not far south of the Northern Territory border, Marla is a new settlement where the Ghan railway line crosses the new Stuart Highway. The opal mining fields of **Mintabie** are 35 km west. Marla has motel rooms, camping facilities, supplies and so on.

On the Stuart Highway 83 km south of Marla, *Cadney Homestead* (☎ (086) 70 7994) has tent sites for $5 per person and cabins for $28. If you're heading for Oodnadatta, turning off the highway here gives you a shorter run on dirt roads than going via Marla or Coober Pedy, and you pass through the **Painted Desert** on the way.

MARREE (population 400)
On the rugged alternate road north through Oodnadatta, Marree is a tiny township once used as a staging post for the Afghani-led camel trains of the last century. There are still a few old date palms here, and an incongruously large pub. Marree is also the southern end of the Birdsville track. Six km east of town is **Frome Creek**, a dry creek bed that with rain can cut the track for weeks on end.

Stateliner have a weekly bus from Adelaide to Marree for $66.

OODNADATTA (population 200)

The tiny town of Oodnadatta (like Marree, it got even tinier with the old Ghan track's closure) is at the point where the road and the old railway lines diverged. It was an important staging post during the construction of the overland telegraph line and later was the railhead for the line from Adelaide, from its original extension to Oodnadatta in 1884 until it finally reached Alice Springs in 1929.

Places to Stay

The *Oodnadatta Caravan Park* (☎ (086) 70 7822) has tent sites for $10.50, one on-site van for $25/30 a single/double and units (soon to have cooking facilities) for $35/40. Or there's the *Transcontinental Hotel* (☎ (086) 70 7804) with B&B at $33/61.

BIRDSVILLE TRACK

Years ago cattle from the south-west of Queensland were driven down the Birdsville Track to Marree where they were loaded onto trains – these days they're trucked out on the 'beef roads'. It's 520 km between Marree and Birdsville, just across the border.

Although non-4WD vehicles can manage the track without difficulty, it's worth bearing in mind that it's a long way to push if you break down – and that traffic along the road isn't exactly heavy. Petrol is available at Mungeranie, about 220 km north of Marree and 300 km south of Birdsville.

The track is more or less at the meeting point between the sand dunes of the Simpson Desert to the west and the desolate wastes of Sturt's Stony Desert to the east. There are ruins of a couple of homesteads along the track and artesian bores gush out boiling-hot salty water at many places. At **Clifton Hill**, about 200 km south of Birdsville, the track splits and the main route goes round the east side of Goyders Lagoon. The last travellers to die on the track took the wrong turning, got lost, ran out of petrol and died before they were discovered.

STRZELECKI TRACK

These days the Strzelecki Track can be handled by regular vehicles. It starts at Lyndhurst, about 80 km south of Marree, and runs 460 km to the tiny outpost of Innamincka. The discovery of natural gas deposits near Moomba has brought a great deal of development and improvement to the track. The new Moomba-Strzelecki track is better kept but longer and less interesting than the old track which follows the Strzelecki Creek. Fuel is available at Moomba in emergencies.

INNAMINCKA

At the northern end of the Strzelecki Track, Innamincka is on Cooper's Creek where the Burke & Wills expedition of 1860 came to its end. Near here is the Burke & Wills 'dig' tree, the memorials and markers where their bodies were found and the marker where King, the sole survivor, was found. He was cared for by Aborigines until his rescue.

There is also a memorial where Howitt, who led the rescue party, set up his depot on the creek. The dig tree is actually across the border in Queensland. The word 'dig' is no longer visible, but the expedition's camp number can still be made out.

Cooper's Creek only flows during floods but there are permanent water holes, so the area was important to Aborigines and was a base for the European explorers of the 1800s.

Algona Publications' *Innamincka-Coongie Lakes* map is a good source of information on the Innamincka area. For a moving account of the bumbling, foolhardy and tragic Burke & Wills expedition, read Alan Moorehead's *Cooper's Creek*.

Places to Stay

The *Innamincka Hotel* (☎ (086) 75 9901) has just four motel-style rooms at $30/50/75 for singles/doubles/triples. The *Innamincka Trading Post* (☎ (086) 75 9900) has cabins at $40 a double without linen, $50 with linen. There are plenty of places to camp along the creek.

THE GHAN

See the Northern Territory chapter for details of the famous train line from Adelaide to Alice Springs.

Tasmania

Area 68,000 sq km
Population 450,000

Tasmania is Australia's only island state and this has been a major influence on its historical, cultural and geographical development. Being an island, it was considered an ideal location for penal settlements, and convicts who reoffended on the Australian mainland were shipped there. Its isolation has also helped preserve its rich colonial heritage, and ensured that most of the state's wilderness areas (with a few notable exceptions) have remained relatively unspoiled.

The first European to see Tasmania was the famous Dutch navigator Abel Tasman who arrived in 1642 and called it Van Diemen's Land, after the Governor of the Dutch East Indies. In the 18th century, Tasmania was sighted and visited by a series of famous European seamen, including Captains Tobias Furneaux, James Cook and William Bligh, all of whom believed it to be part of the Australian mainland.

European contact with the Tasmanian coast became more frequent after the soldiers and convicts of the First Fleet settled at Sydney Cove in 1788, mainly because ships heading to the colony of New South Wales from the west had to sail around the island.

In 1798 Lieutenant Matthew Flinders circumnavigated Van Diemen's Land and proved that it was an island. He named the rough stretch of sea between the island and the mainland Bass Strait, after George Bass, the ship's surgeon. The discovery of Bass Strait shortened the journey to Sydney from India or the Cape of Good Hope by a week.

In the late 1790s Governor King of New South Wales decided to establish a second colony in Australia, south of Sydney Cove. Port Phillip Bay in Victoria was considered, but a site on the Derwent River in Tasmania was finally chosen and in 1804 Hobart Town was established. Although convicts were sent with the first settlers, penal settlements

were not built until later; at Macquarie Harbour in 1821, Maria Island in 1825 and at Port Arthur in 1832. For more than three decades, Van Diemen's Land was the most feared destination for British convicts.

In 1856 transportation to Van Diemen's Land was abolished and its first parliament elected. Also in 1856, in an effort to escape the stigma of its dreadful penal reputation, Van Diemen's Land became officially known as Tasmania, after its first European discoverer.

Reminders of the island's convict days and early history are everywhere. There are the penal settlement ruins at Port Arthur, many convict-built bridges, a host of beautifully preserved Georgian sandstone buildings and more than 20 historical towns or villages classified by the National Trust.

Tasmania is also renowned worldwide for its pristine wilderness areas and, during the last twenty or so years, has played an essential role in world environmental and conservation issues.

In the 1989 state elections, Tasmania's Green Independents gained 18% of the vote and held the balance of power in parliament until the 1992 election. For more information, see a book called *The Rest of the World is Watching – Tasmania and the Greens* (Pan Macmillan, Australia), edited by C Pybus and R Flanagan.

TASMANIAN ABORIGINES

Since European settlement, the story of Australia's Aborigines has not been a happy one and nowhere has it been more tragic than in Tasmania.

Tasmania's Aborigines became separated from the mainland over 10,000 years ago when rising ocean levels, caused by the thawing of the last ice age, cut the state off from the rest of the country. From that time on their culture diverged from that of the mainland population. They lived by hunting, fishing and gathering, sheltered in bark lean-tos and, despite Tasmania's cold weather, went naked apart from a coating of grease and charcoal. Their society was based on sharing and exchange – a concept the European invaders failed to come to terms with.

European settlers found Tasmania fertile and fenced it off to make farms. As the Aborigines lost more and more of their traditional hunting grounds, they realised that the Europeans had come to steal their land, not share it, and began to fight for what was rightfully theirs. By 1806 the killing on both sides was out of control. The Aborigines speared shepherds and their stock, and, in turn, were hunted and shot. Europeans abducted Aboriginal children to use as forced labour, raped and tortured Aboriginal women, gave poisoned flour to friendly tribes, and laid steel traps in the bush.

In 1828 martial law was proclaimed by Governor Arthur giving soldiers the right to arrest or shoot on sight any Aborigine found in an area of European settlement. Finally, in an attempt to flush out all Aborigines and corner them on the Tasman Peninsula, a human chain, known as the Black Line, was formed by the settlers and this moved for three weeks through the state. Ultimately unsuccessful, it did, however, manage to clear the tribes from settled districts.

Between 1829 and 1834 the remnants of this once proud and peaceful race were col-lected from all over the island and resettled in a reserve on Flinders Island – to be 'civilised' and Christianised. With nothing to do but exist, most of them died of despair, homesickness, poor food or respiratory disease. Of the 135 who came to the island, only 47 survivors were transferred to Oyster Cove in 1837. It's hard to believe, but during those first 35 years of European settlement, 183 Europeans and nearly 4000 Aborigines were killed.

European sealers had been working in Bass Strait since 1798 and, although they occasionally raided tribes along the coast, on the whole their contact with the Aborigines was based on trade. Aboriginal women were also traded and many sealers settled down on the Bass Strait islands with these women and had families.

By 1847 a new Aboriginal community, with a lifestyle based on both Aboriginal and European ways, had emerged on the Furneaux group of islands, saving the Tasmanian Aborigine from total extinction. Today there are more than 6500 of their descendants still living in Tasmania and still fighting for their rights.

GEOGRAPHY

Despite being a small state, Tasmania's geographical diversity ensures that it has something for everyone.

Tasmania's population is concentrated mainly on the north and south-east coasts where the undulating countryside is rich and fertile. The coast and its bays are accessible and inviting, with attractive coves and beaches. In winter, the midlands region is almost a re-creation of the green England so beloved of early settlers, and the sparsely populated lakes country in the central highlands is serenely beautiful.

By contrast, the south-west and west coasts are amazingly wild and virtually untouched. For much of the year, raging seas batter the length of the west coast, and rainfall is high. Inland, the forests and mountains of Tasmania's west and south-west form one of the world's last great wilderness areas,

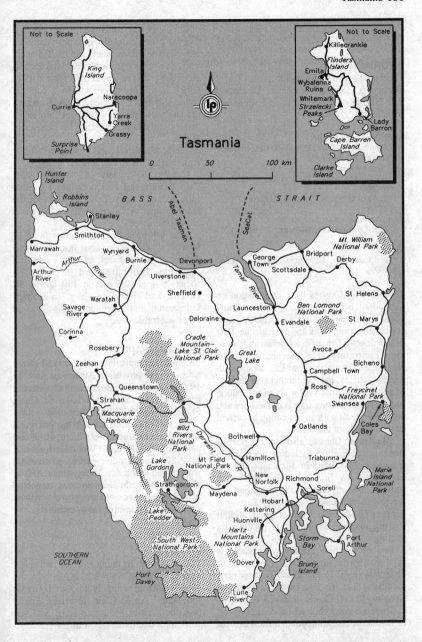

Tasmania

Not to Scale

King Island
Naracoopa
Currie
Yarra Creek
Grassy
Surprise Point

Not to Scale
Killiecrankie
Flinders Island
Emita
Wybalenna Ruins
Whitemark
Strzelecki Peaks
Lady Barron
Cape Barren Island
Clarke Island

0   50   100 km

Hunter Island
Robbins Island
Stanley
Smithton
Marrawah
Wynyard
Arthur River
Arthur River
Burnie
Waratah
Savage River
Corinna
Rosebery
Zeehan
Queenstown
Strahan
Macquarie Harbour
Wild Rivers National Park
Lake Gordon
Strathgordon
Lake Pedder
South West National Park
Port Davey
SOUTHERN OCEAN

BASS   STRAIT
Abel Tasman
SeaCat

Devonport
Ulverstone
Sheffield
George Town
Scottsdale
Bridport
Derby
Launceston
Deloraine
Cradle Mountain– Lake St Clair National Park
Great Lake
Evandale
Ben Lomond National Park
St Helens
St Marys
Avoca
Campbell Town
Bicheno
Ross
Freycinet National Park
Swansea
Coles Bay
Oatlands
Bothwell
Mt Field National Park
Hamilton
New Norfolk
Maydena
Richmond
Sorell
Triabunna
Maria Island National Park
Hobart
Kettering
Huonville
Hartz Mountains National Park
Dover
Storm Bay
Bruny Island
Port Arthur
Lune River

Mt William National Park

Tamar River

almost all of which are national parks which have been listed as World Heritage regions.

INFORMATION

There are government-run Tasmanian Travel Centres in Hobart, Launceston, Devonport and Burnie. On the mainland there are branches in:

Australian Capital Territory
  Shop 5, GIO House, City Walk, Canberra 2608 (☎ (06) 247 0888)
New South Wales
  149 King St, Sydney 2000 (☎ (02) 233 2500)
Queensland
  217-219 Queen St, Brisbane 4000 (☎ (07) 221 2744)
South Australia
  32 King William St, Adelaide 5000 (☎ (08) 211 7411)
Victoria
  256 Collins St, Melbourne 3000 (☎ (03) 653 7999)

These Travel Centres have information on just about everything you need to know about Tasmania and are also able to book accommodation, tours and even airline, boat or bus tickets. The offices publish an invaluable bimonthly free newspaper called *Tasmanian Travelways* which, along with feature articles, has comprehensive listings of accommodation, visitor activities, public transport, connecting transport facilities and vehicle hire, all with an indication of current costs throughout the state.

The Travel Centres also stock a host of free tourist literature, including the monthly magazine *This Week in Tasmania* and the excellent *Let's Talk About* leaflets which provide in-depth information about particular towns or areas. The annual *Tasmania Visitors Guide*, which has a good foldout touring map of Tasmania, is particularly useful.

One of the best maps of the island is produced by the Royal Automobile Club of Tasmania (RACT) and costs $1.50 for non-members, 50c for members. It's available from any Travel Centre or RACT office.

There's a good choice of accommodation in Tasmania, including youth hostels in most of the major towns and plenty of camping/caravan parks, most of which have tent sites as well as on-site vans and cabins. Tasmania also has a wide selection of colonial accommodation – that is, places built prior to 1901 which have been decorated in a colonial style. Although a bit pricey, colonial accommodation is a great way to savour Tasmania's history, and can be a real treat for a couple of nights.

For hotels, motels and most guesthouses, a private bathroom and toilet is standard.

Despite the variety of places to stay, Tasmania's major tourist centres are often fully booked in summer, so it's wise to make reservations. Accommodation also costs more in summer.

The Wilderness Society (☎ (002) 34 9366) has information about Tasmania's wilderness regions, as well as a good selection of books, brochures and leaflets. The society's head office is at 130 Davey St, Hobart, and there are shops in Hobart, Launceston and Devonport as well as in other Australian cities.

NATIONAL PARKS

Tasmania has more national parks and scenic reserves than any other Australian state. In 1982, Tasmania's three largest national parks, Cradle Mountain-Lake St Clair, Franklin-Gordon Wild Rivers and South-West, were declared among the last great temperate wilderness areas in the world and placed on the UNESCO World Heritage list. In 1989, several other parks and reserves were added to the list. Today, about 20% of Tasmania is World Heritage area, protected from logging, hydroelectric power schemes and, with a few simple rules, ourselves.

ACTIVITIES
Bushwalking

Tasmania, with its many national parks, has some of the finest bushwalks in Australia, the most famous of which is the superb Cradle Mountain-Lake St Clair 'Overland Track' (see the Cradle Mountain-Lake St Clair section for details on this walk).

Good books on the subject include *100 Walks in Tasmania* by Tyrone Thomas, *South West Tasmania* by John Chapman, and Lonely Planet's *Bushwalking in Australia* by John and Monica Chapman, which has a large section on some of Tasmania's best walks.

The Department of Parks, Wildlife & Heritage has a great deal of informative literature about the state's national parks and reserves, as well as several leaflets on particular aspects of bushwalking. It also publishes a booklet called *Welcome to the Wilderness – Bushwalking Trip Planner for Tasmania's World Heritage Area* which has sections on preplanning, minimal impact bushwalking and wilderness survival. Also included is a very useful equipment check list which is essential reading for bushwalkers unfamiliar with Tasmania's notoriously changeable weather. On long walks, it's important to remember that in any season a fine day can quickly become cold and stormy, so warm clothing, waterproof gear, a tent and a compass are vital. If you write to the Department of Parks, Wildlife & Heritage at GPO Box 44A, Hobart, 7001, you'll be sent this booklet and other leaflets for free. You can also pick up all the department's literature from its head office at 134 Macquarie St, Hobart; at Henty House, Civic Square, Launceston; or at any ranger station in the national parks.

The department also produces an excellent series of maps; again, these can be sent for or can be picked up at most bush outdoor equipment stores, Wilderness Society shops and newsagencies in Tasmania.

As bushwalking is so popular in Tasmania, there are many excellent shops selling bush gear, as well as several youth hostels which hire out equipment or take bushwalking tours. In the former category Paddy Pallin in Hobart and Launceston, Allgoods in Launceston and the Backpackers' Barn in Devonport all have a very good range of bushwalking gear and plenty of invaluable advice.

See under the national parks sections for more information on Tasmania's walks.

Water Sports

The north and east coasts have plenty of sheltered, white-sand beaches which are excellent for swimming. Although there are some pleasant beaches near Hobart, such as Bellerive and Sandy Bay, these tend to be polluted so it's better to head towards Kingston, Blackmans Bay or Seven Mile Beach for safe swimming. On the west coast there's some pretty ferocious surf but the beaches are unpatrolled.

Tasmania has plenty of good surf beaches, particularly on the east coast north of Bicheno. Closer to Hobart, Clifton Beach and the surf beach en route to South Arm are popular surfing spots. The southern beaches of Bruny Island, particularly Cloudy Bay, are also good.

On the east coast and around King and Flinders islands, there are some excellent scuba diving opportunities. Equipment can be rented in Hobart, Launceston or on the east coast, and dive courses in Tasmania are considerably cheaper than on the mainland.

With so many rivers and lakes, rafting, rowing and canoeing are all popular pastimes in Tasmania. The most challenging of rivers to raft is probably the Franklin (see the Franklin-Gordon Wild Rivers National Park section), although rafting trips are also organised on the Picton, upper Huon, Weld and Leven rivers. For information about tour operators etc, contact the Department of Parks, Wildlife & Heritage (☎ (002) 30 2620) in Hobart. Beautiful Lake Barrington, near Sheffield, hosted the World Rowing Championships in 1990.

Caving

Tasmania's caves are regarded as being some of the most impressive in Australia. The caves at Mole Creek and Hastings are open daily to the public but gems such as the Kubla Khan and Croesus caves (near Mole Creek) are only accessible to experienced cavers.

Skiing

There are two major ski resorts in Tasmania: Ben Lomond, 60 km from Launceston; and

Mt Mawson, in Mt Field National Park. Both offer cheaper, although less developed, ski facilities than the major resorts in Victoria and New South Wales but, despite the state's southerly latitude, snowfalls tend to be fairly light and unreliable. For more information see the chapters on the Ben Lomond and Mt Field national parks.

GETTING THERE & AWAY
Air
The domestic airlines that fly to Tassie are Ansett, Australian, Eastern, Kendell (☎ (03)

668 2222), Phillip Island (☎ (059) 56 7316), King Island (☎ (03) 580 3777), Airlines of Tasmania, Aus-Air (☎ (03) 580 6166), and Promair (☎ (056) 88 1487).

Ansett and Australian Airlines have flights to Tasmania from most Australian state capitals, while the other airlines operate from various airports in Victoria. Most flights are to Hobart, Launceston, Devonport, Wynyard (Burnie), Smithton, Flinders Island and King Island, although Airlines of Tasmania also has flights from Melbourne to Queenstown and Strahan.

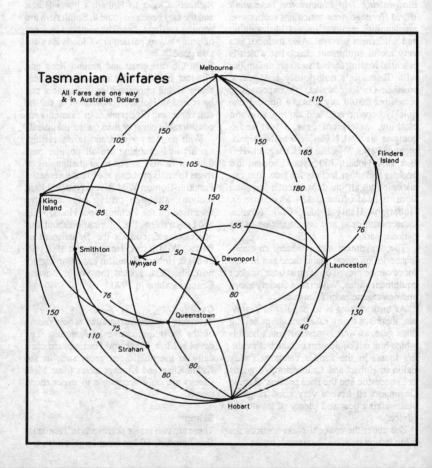

Tasmanian Airfares

All Fares are one way
& in Australian Dollars

Airfares to Tasmania are constantly changing but because of the number of operators prices are competitive and you can get some good deals – especially if you book well in advance or if you are planning a trip in the winter months. In addition, students under 25 years can get some good discounts on fares with the larger airlines.

To Hobart Ansett and Australian Airlines fly from Melbourne for around $300 return if you book in advance, although cheaper fares are often available (about $240). A full return economy fare is $425. From Sydney fares are slightly more expensive, and from Brisbane an advance purchase return ticket is around $450.

There's also a weekly Qantas/Air New Zealand flight between Christchurch, New Zealand, and Hobart.

To Launceston Ansett and Australian fly from Melbourne for around $230 return if you book in advance, or $370 if you don't. Slightly cheaper are Airlines of Tasmania who fly from Melbourne's Essendon Airport, Aus-Air who fly from Melbourne's Moorabbin Airport and Promair who operate out of either the Moorabbin or the eastern Victorian airports of Welshpool or Traralgon. Promair also offers a special 'Strait Sea/Air' package where, for around $209 or less, you can combine a one-way flight between Welshpool and Launceston with a one-way trip between George Town and Welshpool on the *SeaCat*.

To Devonport & Wynyard (Burnie) The cheapest flights from the mainland are to these airports. Eastern Airlines have deals from Melbourne to Devonport for around $200 return. Kendell Airlines and Aus-Air (flying from Moorabbin) are slightly cheaper.

Aus-Air also flies to Wynyard from Moorabbin ($190 advance purchase return or $270 full economy return). Phillip Island Airlines and Kendell Airlines both fly to Wynyard for around $230.

Other Destinations Airlines of Tasmania (flying from Essendon) and Aus-Air (from Moorabbin) fly to Smithton for around $210 return. Airlines of Tasmania, Aus-Air and Promair (from Moorabbin or Welshpool) all fly to Flinders Island for around $250, while Aus-Air and Kendell Airlines fly to King Island for around $220 return. King Island Airlines also flies from Moorabbin to King Island and offers slightly cheaper fares.

Boat

The *Abel Tasman*, which operates between Melbourne and Devonport, can accommodate 919 passengers and 260 cars. It has four decks and, with its swimming pool, saunas, restaurant and bars, is more like a cruise ship than a ferry.

It departs from the TT Line terminal (☎ (03) 644 5233) at Melbourne's Station Pier and from the terminal at Devonport's Esplanade (☎ (004) 23 0333) at 6 pm on alternate days, arriving 14½ hours later at 8.30 am. Its direction of sailing is determined by the month's odd or even dates; call TT Line (☎ 008 030 344, toll-free) for exact dates.

The fares depend on whether you're travelling in the bargain (late April to mid-September), shoulder (mid-September to mid-December and February to late April) or holiday (mid-December and January) seasons. One-way tickets range from hostel-style accommodation on C Deck for $74, $103 and $127 to suites on A Deck for $182, $254 and $295. There are pretty good discounts for children and students under 26 years.

The cost for accompanied vehicles depends on the size of the vehicle and the season. One-way rates start from around $96 for cars, while motorcycles cost $49 and bicycles $12.

The high-speed *SeaCat* between Port Welshpool in eastern Victoria and George Town in Tasmania crosses Bass Strait in just 4½ hours. Designed and built in Hobart to accommodate 350 passengers and 84 cars, it has been heralded as a major innovation in marine transport and similar models are now operating in Europe.

However, the *SeaCat* only operates between November and April, and the frequency of sailings depend on the season. During the peak period, between 1 December and 31 January, the *SeaCat* departs Port Welshpool daily at 2 pm and George Town daily at 6.30 pm. During November, and from 1 February to 30 April, there are departures daily except Tuesdays.

One-way passenger fares range from $114 to $120. Passengers are restricted to two pieces of luggage; extra items cost $5 each. One-way vehicle fares start from $145; motorcycles and bicycles cost from $72 and $18.

Neither Port Welshpool nor George Town are major centres, so the *SeaCat* runs in conjunction with a bus service called the RoadCat. On the mainland, the RoadCat takes passengers between Melbourne and Port Welshpool, and in Tasmania, it operates between George Town and Launceston. In Melbourne the RoadCat stops at Spencer St Station, Dandenong and Chadstone; and in Launceston it stops at the Hobart Coaches terminals. The service is not expensive and is included in your *SeaCat* fare.

The *SeaCat* has had a few teething problems and there are some who claim that the motion of the catamaran increases the risk of seasickness. For information and bookings, phone SeaCat Tasmania (☎ 008 030 131, toll-free).

GETTING AROUND
Air
Airlines of Tasmania (☎ (003) 91 8422) operate a fairly extensive network of domestic flights which can be booked at most travel agencies and any Tasmanian Travel Centre. The chart shows all their routes and prices. It's worth noting that the airline also has flights between Melbourne and Launceston via Flinders Island which are only a little more expensive than flying direct; these give you the option of a stopover on Flinders, more or less for free.

Bus
Tasmania has a good bus network connecting all major towns and centres, but weekend services are infrequent and this can be inconvenient for the traveller with only a limited time in the state. There are more buses in summer than in winter.

The three main bus companies – Tasmanian Redline Coaches, Hobart Coaches and Tasmanian Wilderness Transport (Invicta) – cover most of the state between them. All three have depots in the major centres of Hobart, Launceston and Devonport as well as agents in the stopover towns.

Each company also has its own special passes; you can't use a Greyhound/Pioneer Aussie Pass in Tasmania. Redline has the Super Tassie Pass, for seven, 14, 21 or 28 days, which gives you unrestricted travel on all their routes for $99, $120, $140 or $160 and is also valid for the small east coast services run by Peakes and Haley's. Hobart Coaches has a 30-day Explorer Travel Pass which is valid for 10 trips, costs $100 and can only be used on their services. Invicta has a Wilderness & Highway Pass for seven days ($120) or 14 days ($159) which is valid on all of their routes and those of Hobart Coaches.

If you are considering buying any of these passes, don't forget to check the weekend timetables. Also, make sure that you buy a pass with a company that has services to the areas that you want to visit; *Tasmanian Travelways* has details of timetables and fares. These passes can also be bought in advance on the mainland from either Greyhound/Pioneer or Bus Australia but generally, it's cheaper to buy them in Tasmania. To give you some idea of the costs, a one-way trip between Hobart and Launceston costs about $15, between Hobart and Queenstown $29, and between Launceston and Bicheno $18.

Train
For economic reasons there are no longer any passenger rail services in Tasmania, which probably accounts for the number of

railway models, displays and exhibitions in the state!

Car & Campervan

Although you can bring cars from the mainland to Tasmania, it might work out cheaper to rent one for your visit, particularly if your stay is a short one. Tasmania has a wide range of national and local car rental agencies and the rates (along with parking fines) are considerably lower than they are on the mainland.

Tasmanian Travelways lists many of the rental options but, before you decide on a company, don't forget to ask about any km limitations, what the insurance covers (is windscreen and tyre damage included?) and ensure that there are no hidden 'seasonal adjustments'. It is, however, quite normal for smaller rental companies to ask for a bond of around $200.

If you arrange your car rental with one of the large national firms like Budget, Hertz or Avis you should, with a bit of bargaining, be able to get a rate of under $60 a day for a small car (Corolla, Laser, Pulsar). Although this is more expensive than many smaller companies, there's no bond and you get unlimited km, comprehensive insurance and reliable cars. While many of the larger firms have offices at airports or docks, the smaller ones can often arrange for your car to be picked up at your point of arrival.

Small local firms like Advance Car Rentals, which has offices in Hobart, Launceston and Devonport, charge around $44 a day ($264 a week) for the same type of cars, but with varied conditions. Tasmania also has a number of companies renting older cars like VW beetles for around $20 a day. In this bracket Range/Rent-A-Bug, with offices in Hobart and Devonport, has a good reputation.

Tasmanian Travelways also has a listing of campervan rental companies. All the larger national firms have campervans for around $800 a week, but by far the cheapest and most popular is Touring Motor Homes (☎ (003) 95 1366) at 21 Glen Dhu St, which is near the Launceston City Youth Hostel.

While you're driving around the state, watch out for the wildlife which, all too often, ends up flattened on the roadside.

Hitching

Travel by thumb in Tassie is generally good but wrap up in winter and keep a raincoat handy. A good number of the state's roads are still unsurfaced and the traffic can be sparse, so although these roads often lead to interesting waterfalls etc, you might miss out if you're hitching.

Bicycle

Tasmania is a good size for exploring by bicycle and you can hire bikes throughout the state. If you plan to cycle between Hobart and Launceston, via either coast, then count on it taking around 10 to 14 days. For a full circuit of the island, you should allow 14 to 28 days.

The manager of the Launceston City Youth Hostel runs Rent-A-Cycle and has a good variety of touring and mountain bikes plus all the equipment you'll need for short or long trips. You should be able to hire a bike for between $10 and $15 a day or $60 to $70 a week. If you're planning on an extended ride it's worth considering buying a bike and reselling it at the end. Rent-A-Cycle has a very comprehensive leaflet called *Cycling in Tasmania* with some invaluable hints and advice. You can get hold of a copy before your visit by sending a stamped addressed envelope to Rent-A-Cycle, 36 Thistle St, Launceston, 7250. Don't forget that wearing a helmet is compulsory in Tasmania and if you're caught without one, it's a $20 on-the-spot fine.

If you bring a bike over on the *Abel Tasman* or the *SeaCat* it will cost you around $17 each way. By air, Ansett charges $10 to carry a bicycle one-way to Hobart and $8 to Launceston. Australian Airlines charges a flat $15 one-way to either city. It's easier to get your bike over to Tassie on flights to Hobart or Launceston than on those to smaller airports such as Wynyard or Devonport.

Hobart

Population 129,000

Hobart is Australia's second oldest capital city and also the smallest and most southerly. Straddling the mouth of the Derwent River and backed by mountains which offer fine views over the city, Hobart has managed to combine the progress and the benefits of a modern city with the rich heritage of its colonial past. The beautiful Georgian buildings, the busy harbour and the easy-going atmosphere all make Hobart one of the most enjoyable and engaging of Australia's cities.

Tasmania's first colony was founded in 1803 at Risdon Cove, but a year later Lieutenant-Colonel David Collins, governor of the new settlement in Van Diemen's Land, sailed down the Derwent River and decided that a cove about 10 km below Risdon on the opposite shore was a better place to settle. This became the site of Tasmania's future capital city which began as a village of tents and wattle-and-daub huts with a population of 178 convicts, 25 marines, 15 women, 21 children, 13 free settlers and 10 civil officers.

Hobart Town, as it was known until 1881, was proclaimed a city in 1842. Very important to its development was the Derwent River estuary, one of the world's finest deepwater harbours, and many merchants made their fortunes from the whaling trade, shipbuilding and the export of products like corn and merino wool.

Orientation
Being fairly small and simply laid out, Hobart is an easy city to find your way around. The streets in the city centre are arranged in a grid pattern around the Elizabeth St Mall. The Travel Centre and GPO are on Elizabeth St and Ansett Airlines has an office in the popular shopping area of Liverpool St. The Cat & Fiddle Arcade is another central shopping area and Australian Airlines has an office there.

Salamanca Place, the famous row of Geor-gian warehouses, is along the waterfront, while south of this is Battery Point, Hobart's delightfully well-preserved early colonial district. If you follow the river around from Battery Point you'll come to Sandy Bay, the site of Hobart's university and the Wrest Point Casino – one of Hobart's main landmarks.

The north side of the centre is bounded by the recreation area known locally as the Domain (short for the Queens Domain) which includes the Royal Botanical Gardens, and the Derwent River. From here the Tasman Bridge crosses the river to the eastern suburbs and the airport.

Information
The Tasmanian Travel Centre (☎ 30 0250) at 80 Elizabeth St is open weekdays from 8.45 am to 5 pm, and from 8.45 am to noon on weekends and holidays. You can also get tourist information from the travel section of Mures Fish Centre, Victoria Dock.

The Tasmanian YHA (☎ 34 9617) is at 28 Criterion St and is open weekdays from 9 am to 4.30 pm but is closed at the weekends. The RACT (☎ 38 2266) is on the corner of Murray and Patrick Sts. Paddy Pallin (☎ 31 0777) is at 76 Elizabeth St. The Wilderness Society's head office (☎ 34 9366) is at 130 Davey St and its shop is at The Galleria, Salamanca Place. The National Trust shop is in the same arcade.

The Department of Parks, Wildlife & Heritage (☎ 30 2620) has its head office at 134 Macquarie St; its Tasmap Centre (☎ 30 3382) is on the ground floor. The department has lots of information on Tasmania's parks and reserves and is an essential contact for would-be walkers.

Hobart's STD area telephone code is 002.

Historic Buildings
One of the things that makes Hobart so unusual among Australian cities is its wealth of old and remarkably well-preserved buildings. There are more than 90 buildings in Hobart that are classified by the National Trust and 60 of these, featuring some of Hobart's best Georgian architecture, are in

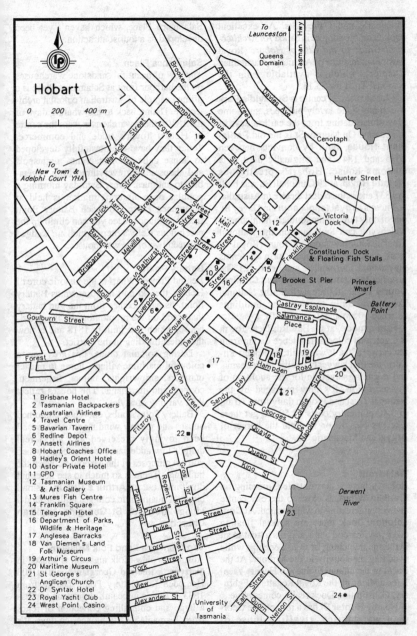

Hobart

0   200   400 m

To Launceston

To New Town &
Adelphi Court YHA

Queens
Domain

Cenotaph

Hunter Street

Victoria
Dock

Constitution Dock
& Floating Fish Stalls

Brooke St Pier

Princes
Wharf

Battery
Point

Castray Esplanade

Salamanca
Place

Derwent
River

University
of
Tasmania

1 Brisbane Hotel
2 Tasmanian Backpackers
3 Australian Airlines
4 Travel Centre
5 Bavarian Tavern
6 Redline Depot
7 Ansett Airlines
8 Hobart Coaches Office
9 Hadley's Orient Hotel
10 Astor Private Hotel
11 GPO
12 Tasmanian Museum
 & Art Gallery
13 Mures Fish Centre
14 Franklin Square
15 Telegraph Hotel
16 Department of Parks,
 Wildlife & Heritage
17 Anglesea Barracks
18 Van Diemen's Land
 Folk Museum
19 Arthur's Circus
20 Maritime Museum
21 St George's
 Anglican Church
22 Dr Syntax Hotel
23 Royal Yacht Club
24 Wrest Point Casino

Macquarie and Davey Sts. An excellent booklet on the subject is called *An Architectural Guide to the City of Hobart* (Royal Australian Institute of Architects, Tasmanian Chapter), which is available from the National Trust for $3.15.

Close to the city centre is **St David's Park** which has some lovely old trees, and some gravestones dating from the earliest days of the colony. On Murray St is the old **Parliament House**, built by convicts between 1835 and 1841 and originally used as a customs house. Hobart's prestigious **Theatre Royal**, at 29 Campbell St, was built in 1837 and is the oldest theatre in Australia.

There's a **royal tennis court** in Davey St, one of only three in the southern hemisphere, which you can look into on the National Trust's Saturday morning tour. (Royal or 'real' tennis is an ancient form of tennis played in a four-walled indoor court.) The historic **Penitentiary Chapel** and **Criminal Courts** are at 28 Campbell St; the National Trust runs daily tours of the buildings between 10 am and 2 pm ($2.50).

Runnymede, at 61 Bay Rd, New Town, is a gracious colonial residence dating from the early 1830s. It was built for Robert Pitcairn, the first lawyer to qualify in Tasmania, and a leading advocate for the abolition of transportation. It's now managed by the National Trust and is open daily from 10 am to 4.40 pm; entry costs $3.50. To get there take bus Nos 15 or 16 from the corner of Argyle and Macquarie Sts.

Waterfront

Hobart's busy waterfront area, focusing on **Franklin Wharf**, is close to the city centre and very interesting to walk around. At **Constitution Dock** there are several floating takeaway seafood stalls and it's a treat to sit in the sun munching fresh fish & chips while watching the activity in the harbour. At the finish of the annual Sydney to Hobart Yacht Race and during the Royal Regatta in February, Constitution Dock really comes alive.

Nearby **Hunter St** has a row of fine Georgian warehouses, rivalling those of Salamanca Place, which haven't yet been developed as a tourist attraction.

Salamanca Place

The row of beautiful sandstone warehouses on the harbour front at Salamanca Place is a prime example of Australian colonial architecture. Dating back to the whaling days of the 1830s, these warehouses were the centre of Hobart Town's trade and commerce. Today they have been tastefully developed to house galleries, restaurants, nightspots and shops selling everything from vegetables to antiques. Every Saturday morning a popular open-air craft market is held at Salamanca Place. To reach Battery Point from Salamanca Place you can climb up the precipitous Kelly's Steps which are wedged between two of the warehouses.

Battery Point

Behind Princes Wharf is the historic core of Hobart, the old port area known as Battery Point. Its name comes from the gun battery that stood on the promontory by the guardhouse, which was built in 1818 and is now the oldest building in the district.

During colonial times, this area was a colourful maritime village, home to master mariners, shipwrights, sailors, fishermen, coopers and merchants. The houses reflect their varying lifestyles.

Battery Point's pubs, churches, conjoined houses and narrow winding streets have all been lovingly preserved and are a real delight to wander around, especially when you get glimpses of the harbour between the buildings. There is so much to see here, but don't miss out on **Arthur's Circus**, a small circle of quaint little cottages built around a village green, or **St George's Anglican Church**.

Van Diemen's Land Folk Museum

Australia's oldest folk museum is housed in Narryna, a fine old Georgian home at 103 Hampden Rd, Battery Point. Dating from 1833, it stands in beautiful grounds and has a large and enthralling collection of relics from Tasmania's early pioneering days. It's open on weekdays from 10 am to 5 pm and on weekends from 2 to 5 pm; admission costs $3.50.

Maritime Museum of Australia

Secheron House, in Secheron Rd, Battery Point, was built in 1831 and is classified by the National Trust. It also houses the fascinating Maritime Museum which has an extensive collection of photos, paintings, models and relics depicting Tasmania's, and particularly Hobart's, colourful shipping history. Entry costs $2 and it's open daily from 1 to 4.40 pm except Saturdays, when it's open from 10 am to 5 pm.

Tasmanian Museum & Art Gallery

The excellent Tasmanian Museum & Art Gallery, at 5 Argyle St, incorporates Hobart's oldest building, the Commissariat Store, built in 1808. The museum section features a Tasmanian Aboriginal display and relics from the state's colonial heritage, while the gallery has a very good collection of Tasmanian colonial art. It's open daily from 10 am to 5 pm and admission is free.

Anglesea Barracks

Built in 1811, this is the oldest military establishment in Australia still used by the army. There's no admission fee to the museum, which is open weekdays from 9 am to 3.30 pm, and there are guided tours of the restored buildings and grounds on Tuesdays at 11 am.

Other Museums

The **Allport Museum & Library of Fine Arts** is based in the State Library at 91 Murray St. It has a collection of rare books on Australasia and the Pacific region and you can visit for free on weekdays from 9 am to 5 pm.

The **National Telecommunications & Postal Museum**, at 19-21 Castray Esplanade, is open weekdays from 8 am to 5 pm and on Saturdays from 9 am to 1 pm; entry costs $1.

Other museums include the **John Elliott Classics Museum** at the University of Tasmania, the **Tasmanian Transport Museum**

in Glenorchy, and Australia's first public museum, the **Lady Franklin Gallery**, in Lenah Valley Rd.

Other Attractions

Just by the Tasman Bridge is the recreation area called the **Queens Domain** and Tasmania's Royal Botanical Gardens which are very pleasant and definitely worth a visit.

Hobart is dominated by 1270-metre-high **Mt Wellington**, and there are many fine views and interesting walking tracks in the mountain area. There are also good views from the **Old Signal Station** on Mt Nelson, above Sandy Bay.

Organised Tours

Several boat cruise companies operate from the Brooke St Pier and Franklin Wharf and offer a variety of cruises in and around the harbour. One of the most popular is the four-hour Cadbury's Cruise, run by the Cruise Company (☎ 34 9294), which costs $30. You do a slow return cruise to the Cadbury Schweppes factory in Claremont where you disembark and tour the premises (this is a good place to stock up on chocolate if you are planning on any bushwalking). The cruise timetables are pretty changeable so it is best book in advance. For $8 you can tour the Cadbury Schweppes factory by yourself, but you must book beforehand at the Travel Centre.

You can also take a two-hour tour of the historic and beautiful Cascade Brewery (☎ 30 9111), in Cascade Rd, which is Australia's oldest brewery. During the week there are tours at 9.30 am and 1 pm which cost $6 and must be booked in advance.

One of the best ways to get a feel for Hobart's colonial history is to take the Saturday morning walking tour organised by the National Trust. The tour concentrates on the historic Battery Point area and departs at 9.30 am from the wishing well in Franklin Square – you don't have to book, just turn up. The walk costs $5 and takes 2½ hours. You could do a similar tour on your own with the help of a *Historic Village Battery Point* leaflet available from the Travel Centre.

Day and half-day bus tours in and around Hobart are operated by Redline and Hobart Coaches. Typical half-day tours include trips to Richmond ($22), the City Sights ($7.50) and Mt Wellington ($9). Full-day tour destinations include Port Arthur ($28), Hastings Caves & the Huon Valley ($40) and Maria Island ($34). Invicta also runs day and two-day excursions to places like Mt Field National Park, Cradle Mountain and Strahan.

There are three companies in Hobart offering scenic flights: Par Avion (☎ 48 5390), Tasair Pty Ltd (☎ 48 5088) and Wilderness Air (☎ 34 2336), which also airlifts bushwalkers into the more remote areas.

Festivals

From 29 December to 2 January, Hobart's waterfront area is alive with spectators and celebrating yachties at the finish of the annual New Year Sydney to Hobart Yacht Race. The Royal Hobart Regatta, in February, is a major aquatic carnival with boat races and other activites.

Places to Stay

Hostels Hobart has three youth hostels. The main one, *Adelphi Court* (☎ 28 4829), is 2½ km from the city at 17 Stoke St, New Town. It's an excellent hostel with good facilities and costs $12 for a dorm bed, or $15 each for a double room. To get there take Metro bus Nos 15 or 16 from Argyle St to stop No 8A, or bus Nos 25 to 42, 100 or 105 to 128 from outside the Travel Centre, Elizabeth St, to stop No 13. Redline also runs a daily drop-off and pick-up service between here and the airport.

The peaceful *Bellerive Hostel* (☎ 44 2552) is on the other side of the Derwent River at 52 King St, Bellerive, and costs $9 a night. The lovely old stone building used to be a schoolhouse and dates from 1869. To get there at the weekends, when the ferry doesn't run, you can catch any of the Bellerive buses (Nos 83 to 87) from outside Fitzgerald's store, Collins St, to stop Nos 17 or 19.

Woodlands Hostel (☎ 28 6720), at 7 Woodlands Ave, New Town, is a superb building and one of New Town's original homes, but is only used as an overflow hostel when Adelphi Court is full. It's best to turn up at nearby Adelphi first, and if there isn't any room you'll get directed here. A dorm bed costs $9.

Nearby, at 300 Park St, New Town, is the *Tower Motel* (☎ 28 0166) with backpackers' accommodation at $10 a night. Each dorm has its own bathroom, and the beds are well spaced out. You can have a room to yourself for $25, or a double for $30.

Right in the centre of town, on the first floor of the New Sydney Hotel at 87 Bathurst St, is *Tasmanian Backpackers* (☎ 34 4516). This is Tasmania's first backpackers' hostel and is very good value at $12 a night for dorm accommodation. Again, Redline runs a daily airport pick-up and drop-off service from here.

Guesthouses & Private Hotels *Adelphi Court* (☎ 28 4829), at 17 Stoke St, New Town, has guesthouse accommodation, in addition to the youth hostel, at $34/48 for singles/doubles; the price includes a cooked breakfast.

The *Imperial Private Hotel* (☎ 23 7509) is in the city centre at 138 Collins St. It's a big, rambling old place but is clean, has good beds and costs $29.50/46 for singles/doubles including a continental breakfast.

The *Astor Private Hotel* (☎ 34 6611), at 157 Macquarie St, is central and has nicely furnished rooms with a certain old-fashioned charm for $35/50 including a continental breakfast.

Hadley's Orient Hotel (☎ 23 4355), at 34 Murray St, is one of Hobart's best older style hotels. Compared to the large hotel chains, this hotel has a lot more charm and, at $75/90, is considerably cheaper.

In Sandy Bay there's *Red Chapel House* (☎ 25 2273) at 27 Red Chapel Ave, past the casino. Singles/doubles cost $42/55 including a cooked breakfast, and the place has a friendly, family-run atmosphere.

If you have the money, in Battery Point you can stay in some beautiful colonial guesthouses and cottages. *Old World Accommodation* (☎ 23 3743) at 25 Colville St is a bit difficult to find but is about the cheapest colonial guesthouse in Battery Point. It's very comfortable and costs $40/50 for singles/doubles with TV and a continental breakfast. The colonial cottages cost around $60/75 for B&B. In this range you could also try *Barton Cottage* (☎ 23 6808) at 72 Hampden Rd, or *Colville Cottage* (☎ 23 6968) at 32 Mona St.

If none of these appeal, there's always the wonderful *Lenna of Hobart* (☎ 23 2911), an old mansion at 20 Runnymede St, Battery Point, which is steeped in history and luxury and costs $120/140. Other 1st-class accommodation includes the *Wrest Point Hotel* (☎ 25 0112) at 410 Sandy Bay Rd, Sandy Bay, and the *Sheraton* (☎ 35 4535) at 1 Davey St on the waterfront.

Hotels The *Bavarian Tavern* (☎ 34 7977) at 281 Liverpool St offers about the cheapest hotel accommodation in Hobart. It is clean and costs $20/40 for singles/doubles with a self-serve continental breakfast.

At 67 Liverpool St, near the mall, the *Brunswick Hotel* (☎ 34 4981) is pretty central and has average rooms costing $25/40 with a continental breakfast. Across the road, at 72 Liverpool St, the *Alabama Hotel* (☎ 34 3737) is a little more comfortable and charges $27/44 for singles/doubles.

Two blocks up from the mall, at 145 Elizabeth St, is the *Black Prince* (☎ 34 3501) which has large, modern rooms with bathroom and TV for $34/46. The *Brisbane Hotel* (☎ 34 4920), at 3 Brisbane St, is quite good value. Comfortable singles/doubles with TV and a continental breakfast cost $30/48.

If you want to stay by the waterfront, the *Telegraph Hotel* (☎ 34 6254), at 19 Morrison St, is in the heart of Franklin Wharf and good value at $25/35 with a continental breakfast. A few doors away, the *Customs House Hotel* (☎ 34 6645), at 1 Murray St, has even better views of the waterfront and costs $30/50 with a continental breakfast.

There are also a couple of moderately priced hotels in Sandy Bay. *Dr Syntax Hotel*

(☎ 23 6258), at 139 Sandy Bay Rd, is very close to Battery Point. It has comfortable singles/doubles with TV for $32/45. The *Beach House Hotel* (☎ 25 1161), at 646 Sandy Bay Rd, is two km past the casino and has good rooms with TV and continental breakfast for $37/49.

Motels & Holiday Flats There are plenty of motels in Hobart but some are rather a long way out. The cheapest include the *Shoreline Motor Motel* (☎ 47 9504) on the corner of Rokeby Rd and Shoreline Drive, Howrah, which costs $40 a double; the *Marina Motel* (☎ 28 4748) at 153 Risdon Rd, Lutana, where singles/doubles cost $35/45; and the *Highway Village Motor Inn* (☎ 72 6721) at 897 Brooker Ave, Berriedale, which costs $43/48. For a motel closer to the city centre, you could try the *Mayfair Motel* (☎ 31 1188) at 17 Cavell St, West Hobart, which has rooms for $58/63.

Hobart has a number of self-contained holiday flats with fully equipped kitchens. Fairly close to town, the *Domain View Apartments* (☎ 34 1181) at 352 Argyle St, North Hobart, cost $42 a double and $6 for each extra person, with a one-night surcharge. *Knopwood Holiday Flat* (☎ 23 2290), at 6 Knopwood St, Battery Point, is a two-bedroom upstairs flat overlooking Salamanca Place. It costs $53 a double and $12 for each extra person, and has a one-night surcharge.

Colleges During the December to February summer vacation and the May and August holidays, you can stay at the University of Tasmania residential halls. *Christ College* (☎ 23 5190), College Rd, Sandy Bay, has rooms for $24 ($15 for under 18s). *Jane Franklin Hall* (☎ 23 2000; 6 Elboden St, South Hobart) costs $25/38 for singles/doubles with breakfast.

Camping The handiest camping ground is the *Sandy Bay Caravan Park* (☎ 25 1264), which is less than four km from the city, at 1 Peel St, Sandy Bay. It costs $8 a double for a tent site and on-site vans are $30 a double, excluding blankets and linen. To get there, take Metro bus Nos 54, 55 or 56 from Franklin Square. There are also parks a little further out at Elwick and Berriedale (north of the city) and at Mornington (in the eastern suburbs).

Places to Eat

Hobart has plenty of straightforward street cafes like the *Piccadilly* at 136 Collins St or the *Carlton Restaurant*, 50 Liverpool St. The *Criterion Coffee Lounge*, at 10 Criterion St, is recommended for an excellent cheap breakfast.

A good lunch-time cafe is *La Cuisine* at 85 Bathurst St and 79 Harrington St. There's a good selection of croissants, quiches and patés and you can get a quick, light meal for around $5.

A couple of good-fun places are *The Belfry* at 171 Elizabeth St, which is open till midnight on Saturdays and the *Retro Cafe* on the corner of Salamanca Place and Montpelier Retreat, which is open until midnight on Fridays.

Constitution Dock has a number of floating takeaway seafood stalls such as *Mako Quality Seafoods* and *Flippers*. Close by is *Mures Fish Centre* where you can get excellent fish & chips and other fishy fare at the bistro on Lower Deck, or an ice cream in the Polar Parlour.

A little more difficult to get to, but well worth the effort, is the historic *Mount Nelson Signal Station Tea House*, on the summit of Mt Nelson, which has spectacular 180° panoramic views of Hobart and the surrounding area.

Pub Meals For $6 you can get a very filling meal at the *New Sydney Hotel*, below Tasmanian Backpackers, at 87 Bathurst St. Many other hotels serve good counter meals and those in the $7 to $9 range include the *Brunswick* at 67 Liverpool St; the *Wheatsheaf Hotel* at 314 Macquarie St; and the *Telegraph Hotel* at 19 Morrison St.

Stoppy's Waterfront Tavern, on Salamanca Place, is a little trendier and has good counter meals for around $8 as well as bands from Thursday to Sunday nights.

Restaurants The *Aegean*, at 121 Collins St in the city, is a Greek restaurant which serves excellent food and often provides entertainment such as belly dancing, Greek music and the traditional smashing of plates.

At 84A Harrington St, the *Little Bali* is very small but has cheap, good-value Indonesian food to eat in or take away. It is only open for dinner on Saturdays and Sundays but does lunch from Monday to Friday.

The licensed *Hara Wholefood Cafe* at 181 Liverpool St has an extensive range of mouth-watering vegetarian dishes and is open from 10 am until late evening Monday to Saturday. For delicious home-made pasta dishes try either *La Suprema* at 255 Liverpool St or *Bertie's Pasta Restaurant* at 115 Collins St.

The suburb of North Hobart is developing a reputation for good-value, interesting places to eat. *Latinos* is at the Empire Hotel, 299 Elizabeth St, and has been highly recommended for cheap, filling South American cuisine. At 321 Elizabeth St is *Ali Akbar*, a very popular Lebanese restaurant. *Marti Zucco's*, at 364 Elizabeth St, has a great atmosphere, good food and is deservedly popular. Also worth checking out in North Hobart is the '50s style *Fish Cafe* at 340 Elizabeth St and the Chinese *Kan Wan* at 404 Elizabeth St.

At Salamanca Place, *Mr Wooby's* is a pleasant licensed eatery where you can get a three-course meal for under $20 or snacks for $5; it's open until quite late. Nearby, at 87 Salamanca Place, is the licensed *Ball & Chain Grill* which has a good reputation for grilled steaks. At No 39 there is *Rockerfeller's*, a trendy bar which also has good meals. For excellent Japanese food, try the licensed *Sakura* at 85 Salamanca Place. Good Japanese fare is also to be found at the *Sushi Bar*, Mures Fish Centre, Victoria Dock.

In Battery Point the licensed *Gur Pertab's*

Top: Adelaide Festival Centre, SA (TW)
Bottom: Supermarket mural, Coober Pedy, SA (TW)

Top: Sign on the Eyre Highway, Nullarbor Plain, SA (RN)
Left: Ghost gum, Wilpena Pound, Flinders Ranges, SA (TW)
Right: Glenelg, Adelaide, SA (TW)

(☎ 23 7011) at 47 Hampden Rd, serves very good Indian and Malaysian food.

In Sandy Bay the licensed Italian restaurant *Don Camillo* (☎ 34 1006), in the shopping centre, has an excellent reputation, and *Tarantella* (☎ 23 6652) at 16A Princes St has also been recommended for Italian food.

In the more expensive bracket, and owned by the same people, are the award-winning seafood restaurant *Little Mures* (☎ 23 6917) at 5 Knopwood St, Battery Point, and the famous *Upper Deck Restaurant* (☎ 31 2121) with the spectacular harbour view at Mures Fish Centre, Victoria Dock.

Also on the waterfront, the *Drunken Admiral* (☎ 34 1903) at 17 Hunter St has been highly recommended for good seafood and a great atmosphere.

Entertainment

The *Mercury* newspaper and *This Week in Tasmania* have details on most of Hobart's entertainment.

There are cover bands most nights of the week at the New Sydney Hotel, 87 Bathurst St, and the Duke of Wellington, 192 Macquarie St. For jazz, blues and rock 'n' roll, both the St Ives Hotel at 86 Sandy Bay Rd and the Travellers Rest, 394 Sandy Bay Rd, have bands from Wednesday to Sunday nights.

There is always a good scene to be found at Maloney's Hotel on the corner of Macquarie and Argyle Sts; there are bands on Friday and Saturday nights and a nightclub upstairs. Another recommended nightclub is Round Midnight at 39 Salamanca Place which is open until 4 am Tuesday to Saturday. Round Midnight is on the top floor of the building which houses the bar Knopwoods Retreat and the cafe/bar Rockerfeller's.

There are 17 bars at the Wrest Point Casino, and some, like the Birdcage, need to be seen to be believed. The casino also has a disco every night with a cover charge on Fridays and Saturdays only.

At 375 Elizabeth St, North Hobart, you'll find the State Cinema (☎ 34 6318) which screens alternative/offbeat films, while at 181 Collins St there's a large Village complex (☎ 34 7288) which shows the mainstream releases.

Getting There & Away

Air For information on international and domestic flights to and from Hobart see the Getting There & Away section at the beginning of this chapter. Ansett (☎ 38 0800) has an office at 178 Liverpool St; Australian Airlines (☎ 38 3511) is based at 160 Collins St; and Airlines of Tasmania (☎ 48 5030) has an office at Hobart Airport.

Bus The main bus companies operating from Hobart are Redline Coaches (☎ 34 4577) at 199 Collins St; Hobart Coaches (☎ 34 4077) at 60 Collins St; and Tasmanian Wilderness Transport, also known as Invicta (☎ 008 030 505, toll-free), at 60 Collins St. Hobart Coaches also has departure points at St David's Cathedral, on the corner of Macquarie and Murray Sts, and outside the treasury building in Murray St.

Hobart Coaches' destinations include New Norfolk ($3.40), Woodbridge, Cygnet ($5.30), Geeveston ($11), Dover, Cockle Creek and Port Arthur ($11). Both Redline and Hobart Coaches run to Bicheno, Swansea, St Marys, St Helens, Oatlands, Ross, Campbell Town, Launceston, Deloraine, Devonport and Burnie; Hobart Coaches is usually slightly cheaper. Redline also runs to Wynyard, Stanley and Smithton; and both Redline and Invicta run to Queenstown ($29.40) and Strahan ($34.20).

Car There are more than 20 car rental firms in Hobart. Some of the cheaper ones include Range/Rent-A-Bug (☎ 34 9435) at 105 Murray St, Advance Car Rentals (☎ 24 0822) at 277 Macquarie St; Bargain Car Rentals (☎ 34 6959) at 189A Harrington St; and Statewide Rent-A-Car (☎ 25 1204) at 388 Sandy Bay Rd, Sandy Bay.

Hitching To start hitching north, take a Bridgewater or Brighton bus from opposite the GPO in Elizabeth St. To hitch along the east coast, take a bus to Sorell first.

Getting Around

To/From the Airport The airport is in Hobart's eastern suburbs, 26 km from the city centre. Redline runs a pick-up and drop-off shuttle service between the city centre (via Adelphi Court and Tasmanian Backpackers) and the airport for $5.

Bus The local bus service is run by Metro. The main office is at 18 Elizabeth St, opposite the GPO. If you're planning to bus around Hobart, it's worth buying Metro's user-friendly timetable which only costs $1. For $2.20, you can also get a Day Rover ticket which can be used all day on weekends and between 9 am and 4.30 pm and after 6 pm on weekdays.

If you want to go to Mt Wellington without taking a tour, take bus No 48 from Franklin Square in Macquarie St; it will get you to Fern Tree at the base of the mountain, but from there it's a 13-km walk to the top!

Bicycle About the only place to hire bikes in Hobart is from Tasmanian Backpackers (☎ 34 4516), on the 1st floor of the New Sydney Hotel, 87 Bathurst St. At the time of writing, their biking facilities were limited, but they were expecting to improve. It costs about $3 to hire a bike for an hour or $15 for the day.

Boat On weekdays the ferry MV *Emmalisa* operates between the Brooke St Pier and Bellerive Wharf and is a very pleasant way to cross the Derwent River. It departs Hobart at 6.55, 7.40, 8.15 am and 4.35, 5.15 and 5.55 pm. From Bellerive there are services at 7.25, 8 and 8.35 am and at 4.50, 5.30 and 6.10 pm. A one-way ticket costs $1.40. There is no weekend service.

Around Hobart

TAROONA

Ten km from Hobart, on the Channel Highway, is Taroona's famous **Shot Tower**, completed in 1870. From the top of the 48-metre tower there are fine views over the Derwent River estuary. Lead shot was once produced in high towers like this by dropping molten lead from the top which, on its way down, formed a perfect sphere and solidified when it hit water at the bottom.

The tower, small museum, craft shop and beautiful grounds are open daily from 9 am to 5 pm and admission costs $3. There is also a tearoom which advertises 'convictshire' teas.

From Taroona Beach, you can walk around to Kingston Beach (about three km); at some points, the track runs close to rock cliffs and you get good views of the Derwent across to Opossum Bay.

KINGSTON

The town of Kingston, 11 km south of Hobart, is the headquarters of the Commonwealth Antarctic Division. The centre is open weekdays from 9 am to 5 pm and admission is free. There's a very pleasant picnic area along Browns River at the eastern end of Kingston Beach.

Close by there are also some good beaches including **Blackmans Bay**, which has a blowhole; **Tinderbox**, where there is good snorkelling; and **Howden**. There are good views across to Bruny Island from Piersons Point, near Tinderbox.

BRIDGEWATER

This town, 19 km north of Hobart, is so named because of the causeway built here by convicts in the 1830s. More than 150 convicts laboured in chains (moving two million tonnes of stone and clay) to build this main north-south crossing of the Derwent River. The old **Watch House**, on the other side of the river from the town, was built by convicts in 1838 to guard the causeway and is now a museum housing relics from the convict days. Admission is $1.50.

PONTVILLE

Further north, on the Midland Highway, is the historic town of Pontville which has a number of interesting buildings dating from the 1830s. Much of the freestone used in Tasmania's early buildings was supplied from quarries at Pontville.

In nearby Brighton, on Briggs Rd, is the **Bonorong Park Wildlife Centre** which is open daily from 8 am to 5 pm; entry costs $4.

NEW NORFOLK (population 6200)

Set in the lush rolling countryside of the Derwent Valley, New Norfolk is historically a very interesting town. It was first settled in 1803 and became an important hop-growing centre, which is why the area is dotted with old oast houses used in the drying of hops. Also distinctive are the rows of tall poplars planted to protect crops from the wind.

Originally called Elizabeth Town, New Norfolk was renamed after the arrival of settlers (1807 onwards) from the abandoned Pacific Ocean colony on Norfolk Island.

Things to See & Do

The **Visitors Historical & Information Centre**, next to the Council Chambers in Circle St, has an interesting photographic and memorabilia display. The key to the centre can be obtained from the council office during working hours.

The **Oast House** on Hobart Rd is both a unique museum devoted to the history of the hop industry and a tearoom. It's open daily except Tuesdays from 8 am to 5 pm (closed June and July) and admission costs $3. The building itself has been classified by the National Trust and is worth seeing from the outside, even if you don't go in.

Also interesting to visit are **St Matthew's Church of England**, built in 1823, which is Tasmania's oldest existing church, and the **Bush Inn**, claimed to be the oldest continuously licensed hotel in Australia. The **Old Colony Inn**, at 21 Montagu St, is a wonder-

ful museum of colonial furnishings and artefacts; there's also a tearoom where you can get some great homemade snacks. The inn is open from 9 am to 5 pm and admission costs $2.

Australian Newsprint Mills (☎ (002) 61 0433) is one of the area's major industries and tours can be arranged Tuesday to Friday if you give at least 24 hours' notice.

For around $28 you can also take a **jet-boat ride** on the Derwent River rapids. The 30-minute ride can be booked at the Devil Jet office (☎ (002) 61 3460), behind the Bush Inn.

In 1864, the first rainbow and brown trout in the southern hemisphere were bred in the **Salmon Ponds** at Plenty, 11 km west of New Norfolk. The ponds and museum on Lower Bushy Park Rd are open daily and there's also a restaurant (if you're ordering the fish you'll know it's fresh!).

Places to Stay

If you want to sample colonial accommodation but it's normally out of your price range, the *New Norfolk Youth Hostel* (☎ (002) 61 2591), on Boyer Rd, is a good place to stay. It's an historic bridge tollhouse, built in 1841, and a bed costs only $5. However, it's very small, so it's a good idea to turn up early. The *Bush Inn* (☎ (002) 61 2256), on Montagu St, was built in 1815 and has singles/doubles for $28/48 including a cooked breakfast, but there's a one-night surcharge. The *Friendship Lodge* (☎ (002) 61 1171), at 5 Oast St, is indeed friendly, and very comfortable. The rates are $30/50 and include a cooked breakfast.

Camp sites and on-site vans are also available at the *New Norfolk Caravan Park* (☎ (002) 61 1268), on the Esplanade.

Getting There & Away

Hobart Coaches (☎ (002) 34 4077) is the main operator between Hobart and New Norfolk and on weekdays there are eight or nine buses in both directions. At weekends there's a limited service and a one-way/return fare costs $3.40/6.80. In New Norfolk, the buses leave from 15 Stephen St.

MT FIELD NATIONAL PARK

Mt Field, only 80 km from Hobart, was declared a national park in 1916, which makes it one of Australia's oldest. The park is well known for its spectacular mountain scenery, alpine moorland, dense rainforest, lakes, abundant wildlife and spectacular waterfalls. The magnificent 40-metre **Russell Falls** is an easy 15-minute walk (the path is suitable for wheelchairs), and there are also easy walks to Lady Barron, Horseshoe and Marriotts falls as well as longer eight-hour bushwalks. With sufficient snow, there's cross-country and limited downhill skiing at **Mt Mawson**. For more information, contact the park ranger (☎ (002) 88 1149).

Places to Stay

Lake Dobson Cabins, 15 km into the park, has three very basic six-bunk cabins. The cost per cabin is $10 a night, regardless of numbers, and you must book ahead at the ranger's office. There's also a camping ground in the park run by the rangers; a site (for two) costs $5.

National Park Youth Hostel (☎ (002) 88 1369) is in the township of National Park, on the main road between Strathgordon and New Norfolk. The hostel is 200 metres past the turn-off to the park and costs $9 a night. The nearby *Russell Falls Holiday Cottages* (☎ (002) 88 1198) cost $40 a double.

Getting There & Away

On weekdays, the 4 pm Hobart Coaches bus from Hobart to New Norfolk continues on to Mt Field. A ticket to National Park costs $7.50 one-way and there is a return service to Hobart on weekdays at 7.55 am. Invicta (☎ 008 030 505, toll-free) also runs one bus to and from Scotts Peak via the park and Maydena (twice weekly and at weekends).

RICHMOND (population 587)

Richmond is just 24 km from Hobart and, with more than 50 buildings dating from the 19th century, is Tasmania's premier historic town. Straddling the Coal River, on the old route between Hobart and Port Arthur, Richmond was a strategic military post and convict station. Its famous and much-photographed bridge, built by convicts in 1823, is the oldest road bridge in Australia.

With the completion of the Sorell Causeway in 1872, traffic travelling to the Tasman Peninsula and the east coast by-passed Richmond, which is why the village is so well preserved today.

Things to See & Do

The northern wing of **Richmond Gaol** was built in 1825, five years before the settlement at Port Arthur, and is the best preserved convict jail in Australia. It features detailed records of the old penal system and convicts who were confined there, and is open daily from 9 am to 5 pm; entry costs $2.50.

Other places of interest include **St John's Church** (1836), the oldest Catholic church in Australia; **St Luke's Church of England** (1834); the **Courthouse** (1825); the **Old Post Office** (1826); the **Bridge Inn** (1817); the **Granary** (1829); and the **Richmond Arms Hotel** (1888). There's also a **model village** (designed from original plans) of Hobart Town as it was in the 1820s. It's open daily from 9 am to 5 pm and entry costs $4. The maze, on the main street, is quite fun (especially if you want to lose your children for a while) but is only made of wooden divides, not hedges.

Places to Stay & Eat

For those on a tight budget, try the *Trekkers Lodge* (☎ (002) 62 2451) at 26 Bridge St, opposite the maze. A bed in one of the three clean and pleasant dorms costs $10.

The *Richmond Country Bed & Breakfast* (☎ (002) 62 4238), on Prossers Rd, costs $35/50 for singles/doubles including a continental breakfast. The *Richmond Cabin & Tourist Park* (☎ (002) 62 2192), in Middle Tea Tree Rd, has camp sites, on-site vans and cabins.

You can get something to eat and drink at *Ashmore* or at the maze tearooms, which are both on Richmond's main street.

Getting There & Away

If you have your own car, Richmond is an easy day trip from Hobart. If you don't, both Redline and Hobart Coaches have bus tours to Richmond. Hobart Coaches runs about four buses a day on weekdays to and from Richmond ($6.20 return), most of which continue on to Bicheno. The Hobart Coaches agent in Richmond is the Richmond Store on the main street. There are no weekend services.

South-East Coast

South of Hobart are the scenic fruit-growing and timber areas of the Huon Peninsula, D'Entrecasteaux Channel and Esperance, as well as beautiful Bruny Island and the Hartz Mountains National Park. The area is known for its spectacular rainbows, which probably occur frequently here due to the southern latitude.

In the '60s, it was fruit growing (particularly apple growing) in the Huon Valley that put Tasmania on the international export map. Today, however, far less fruit is grown, and most of that is for the domestic market. Around the end of February and during March there is sometimes fruit-picking work, but competition for jobs is stiff.

KETTERING (population 288)

The small port of Kettering, on a sheltered bay 34 km south of Hobart, is the terminal for the Bruny Island car ferry. The nearby town of **Snug** has a walking track to Snug Falls, and you can visit the Channel Historical and Folk Museum. Just south of Snug is a good swimming beach at **Coningham**.

North of Kettering at **Margate** (20 km from Hobart) there's an old steam train, and its seven carriages have been made into interesting shops and offices. As you would expect, the old buffet car is a cafe serving pretty good Devonshire teas.

On weekdays, Hobart Coaches has about four buses a day to Woodbridge via Kingston, Margate, Snug and Kettering.

BRUNY ISLAND (population 400)

Bruny Island is almost two islands, joined by a narrow strip of land where mutton birds and other waterfowl breed, and is a peaceful and beautiful retreat. The sparsely populated island has five state reserves and is renowned for its varied wildlife, including fairy penguins and many species of reptiles. The island's coastal scenery is superb and there are plenty of fine swimming and surf beaches, as well as good sea and freshwater fishing.

The island was sighted by Abel Tasman in 1642 and later visited by Furneaux, Cook, Bligh and Cox between 1770 and 1790, but was named after Rear Admiral Bruny d'Entrecasteaux who explored and surveyed the area in 1792. Truganini, the last full-blooded Tasmanian Aboriginal to survive, was a member of Bruny Island's south-east tribe.

The island's history is recorded in the **Bligh Museum** at Adventure Bay, South Bruny, which is open daily from 9 am to 5 pm and costs $1. Also of historical interest is South Bruny's lighthouse which was built in 1836 and is the second oldest in Australia.

Places to Stay

On Lighthouse Rd, Lunawanna, South Bruny, the *Backpackers' Hostel* (☎ (002) 93 1271) has a very good reputation and costs $10 a night or $60 for seven nights. The hostel has some wonderful views over the D'Entrecasteaux Channel to the Hartz Mountains. In Adventure Bay, South Bruny, there is the *Lumeah Hostel* (☎ (002) 93 1265) which has dormitory beds for $13 and the *Captain James Cook Caravan Park* (☎ (002) 93 1128) where on-site vans cost $25 a double.

At Dennes Point on North Bruny the *Channel View Guest House* (☎ (002) 60 6266) has good-value accommodation at $20/30 for singles/doubles with breakfast. Also at Dennes Point is *House Sofia Holiday*

Accommodation (☎ (002) 60 6277) which costs $30/45 with a cooked breakfast.

Getting There & Away

On weekdays there are nine daily ferry services between Kettering and Roberts Point, on Bruny Island. On Fridays there is an extra crossing, and the weekend schedule can vary, so check the times in Hobart's *Mercury* newspaper. There's no charge for foot passengers or cyclists, but if you have a car it will cost $11 from Monday to Thursday, and $17 on Friday afternoons and weekends. Hobart Coaches has two buses on most days which connect with the ferry.

CYGNET (population 715)

This small township was originally named 'Port de Cygne Noir' (Port of the Black Swan) by the French Admiral D'Entrecasteaux because of the many swans seen on the bay. Now known as Cygnet, the town and surrounding area have many apple and other fruit orchards and offer excellent fishing, plenty of bushwalks and some fine beaches, particularly further south at Verona Sands. Close to Cygnet is the **Talune Wildlife Park & Koala Garden**, the **Elsewhere Vineyard** and the **Deepings** wood-turning workshop, which can all be visited.

Places to Stay

Balfes Hill Youth Hostel (☎ (002) 95 1551) is on Sandhills Rd, about five km from town. It costs $10 a night and can get crowded during the fruit-picking season. From December to April the manager organises rafting trips on the Huon River which are good fun and cost around $65 a day, including lunch.

The *Cygnet Hotel* (☎ (002) 95 1267) has singles/doubles for $25/50 with a cooked breakfast, while at 22 Channel Highway the *Wilfred Lodge* (☎ (002) 95 1604) charges $35/45 including a cooked breakfast. There's also a basic camping ground. If you are fruit picking, many of the hotels in Cygnet will rent you a room at a very reasonable weekly rate.

Getting There & Away

Hobart Coaches has a once-daily service to Gordon and Cygnet ($5.30) and Thorpe Coaches does two runs each weekday from Huonville to Cygnet.

GROVE

On the Huon Highway, about six km north of Huonville, is the **Huon Valley Apple & Heritage Museum** which is crammed with displays and machinery that take you back 100 years. It's open daily from 9.30 am to 5 pm and the $2.50 admission fee includes an apple prepared on the antique apple corer and peeler.

HUONVILLE (population 1347)

Named after Huon D'Kermandec, who was second in command to D'Entrecasteaux, this busy, small town on the picturesque Huon River is another apple-growing centre. The valuable softwood Huon pine was also first discovered here, though large stands are now found only around the Gordon River. For the visitor, one of Huonville's main attractions these days is a jet boat ride on the river or hiring pedal boats and aqua bikes from the office on the Esplanade (☎ (002) 64 1838).

GEEVESTON

Geeveston, 31 km south of Huonville, is the administrative centre for Esperance, Australia's most southerly municipality, and also the gateway to the wild Hartz Mountains National Park.

Hobart Coaches runs four buses a day between Hobart and Geeveston ($11 one-way) via Huonville ($5.60 one-way), but there are no weekend services. In Hobart, the buses depart from St David's Cathedral, and in Geeveston, from Geeveston Electrical in the main street.

HARTZ MOUNTAINS NATIONAL PARK

This national park, classified as a World Heritage area, is very popular with weekend walkers and day-trippers as it's only 84 km from Hobart. The park is renowned for its snow-capped rugged mountains, glacial lakes, deep gorges, high alpine moorlands and dense rainforest. Being on the edge of the South West National Park, it is subject to vicious changes in weather, so even on a day walk take waterproof gear and warm clothing. There are some great views from the **Waratah Lookout** (24 km from Geeveston) – look for the jagged peaks of the Snowy Range and the Devils Backbone. There are good walks in the park, including tracks to Hartz Peak (1255 metres), Mt Picton (1327 metres) and the Arthur Range, near Federation Peak (1224 metres). For information about walking in the area, visit the Wilderness Society or Paddy Pallin in Hobart; the Lune River Youth Hostel also has plenty of advice and information, as does the park ranger (☎ (002) 98 3198).

DOVER (population 570)

This picturesque fishing port, 20 km south of Geeveston on the Huon Highway, has some fine beaches and excellent bushwalks; the three small islands in the bay are known as Faith, Hope and Charity. Last century, the processing and exporting of Huon pine was Dover's major industry, and sleepers made here and in the nearby timber towns of Strathblane and Raminea were shipped to China, India and Germany. If you have your own car and are heading further south, it's a good idea to buy petrol and food supplies here.

Places to Stay

The *Dover Hotel* (☎ (002) 98 1210), on the Huon Highway, has backpackers' accommodation for $12 a night. A room in the hotel costs $26/52 for singles/doubles including a cooked breakfast. *Three Island Holiday Apartments* (☎ (002) 98 1396), on Jetty Rd, cost $40 a double. The *Dover Beachside Caravan Park* (☎ (002) 98 1301), on Esperance Coast Rd, has tent sites and on-site vans.

Getting There & Away

Hobart Coaches runs one bus a day to and from Dover on weekdays.

HASTINGS

Today, it's the spectacular **Newdegate Cave** that attracts visitors to the once thriving logging and wharf town of Hastings. The cave is found among the lush vegetation of the Hastings Caves State Reserve, and is well signposted from the Huon Highway. Daily tours ($6) leave promptly at 11.15 am and 1.15, 2.15 and 3.15 pm, with an extra tour at 4.15 pm from December to April. It's best to allow about 10 minutes for the delightful rainforest walk to the cave entrance.

About five km from the cave is a thermal swimming pool ($2), filled daily with warm water from a thermal spring. Near the pool there is a kiosk and a restaurant.

For those interested in a more adventurous exploration of the 20-km cave system at Hastings, Exit Cave Adventure Tours (☎ (002) 438 546) runs a 4½-hour expedition ($60 per person including transport from Hobart) which is suitable for beginners.

LUNE RIVER

A few km south-west of Hastings is Lune River, a haven for gem collectors and the site of Australia's most southerly post office and youth hostel. From here you can also take a scenic 16-km ride on the **Ida Bay Railway** to the lovely beach at Deep Hole Bay. The train departs daily at 11.30 am, 1 and 3 pm (in summer there are more services) and costs $9.

The most southerly drive you can make in Australia is along the secondary road from Lune River to **Cockle Creek** and beautiful **Recherche Bay**. This is an area of spectacular mountain peaks, endless beaches and secluded coves – ideal for camping and bushwalking.

Places to Stay

The *Lune River Youth Hostel* (☎ (002) 98 3163), also known as the Doing Place, costs $9 a night. It's very homely and there's certainly plenty to do – ask the managers about hiring mountain bikes or kayaks, or about bushwalking, fishing and caving. Don't forget to bring plenty of food with you as the hostel only has basic supplies.

About half a km further south, *Ida Bay Railway Cabins* (☎ (002) 98 3110) offers backpackers' accommodation for $11 a night.

Getting There & Away

Hobart Coaches makes a return trip from Hobart to Cockle Creek, via the Lune River Youth Hostel, three times a week ($35 one-way). The Lune River Hostel also runs a shuttle service every Tuesday from the Adelphi Court Youth Hostel in Hobart, to Lune River. The cost is $16 including your first night's accommodation at the hostel. A return trip leaves Lune River for Adelphi Court every Monday ($10).

Tasman Peninsula

The Arthur Highway runs from Hobart through Sorell and Copping to Port Arthur, 100 km away. As there is no bank on the Tasman Peninsula and the supermarkets are quite expensive, it's a good idea to take advantage of both the banking and shopping facilities at Sorell. And to get you into the convict mood, there's an excellent **Colonial Convict Exhibition** at Copping which features many objects once used at Port Arthur.

PORT ARTHUR

In 1830, Governor Arthur chose the Tasman Peninsula as the place to confine prisoners who had committed further crimes in the colony. He called the peninsula a 'natural penitentiary' because it was only connected to the mainland by a narrow strip of land, less than 100 metres wide, called Eaglehawk Neck. To deter convicts from escaping, a line of ferocious guard dogs were chained up across the isthmus and a rumour circulated that the waters on either side were infested with sharks.

Between 1830 and 1877, about 12,500 convicts served sentences at Port Arthur and for most of them it was a living hell. With its Model Prison, featuring a new system of solitary confinement, which replaced brutal

beatings, Port Arthur was seen as an advancement in prison reform. In reality, however, the punishment of total isolation and sensory deprivation sent the convicts mad.

The township of Port Arthur became the centre of a network of penal stations on the peninsula and was, itself, much more than just a prison town. It had fine buildings and thriving industries including timber milling, shipbuilding, coal mining, brick and nail production and shoemaking. Australia's first railway literally 'ran' the seven km between Norfolk Bay and Long Bay; convicts pushed the carriages along the tracks. A semaphore telegraph system allowed instant communication between Port Arthur, the penal outstations and Hobart. Convict farms provided fresh vegetables, a boys' prison was built at Point Puer to reform and educate juvenile convicts, and a church, one of the most readily recognised tourist sights in Australia, was erected.

The Isle of the Dead, in the middle of Carnavon Bay, was the cemetery for 1769 convicts and 180 free settlers and officers. Convicts were buried six or seven to a grave with no headstones, their bodies wrapped in sailcloth and covered with quicklime.

Today, the well-presented historic site of Port Arthur is Tasmania's premier tourist attraction. For a fee of $7.50 you can visit all the restored buildings including the Lunatic Asylum (now a museum) and the Model Prison. The ticket is valid for 24 hours and entitles you to free admission into the museum and a guided tour of the settlement. The tours are well worthwhile and leave hourly from the car park in front of the information office between 9.30 am and 3.30 pm. Once you've entered the site you can also take a cruise to the Isle of the Dead, or a historic tour in a horse-drawn carriage, but both cost extra.

Places to Stay

The *Port Arthur Youth Hostel* (☎ (002) 50 2311) is very well positioned on the edge of the historic site and costs $10 a night. To get there, continue half a km past the Port Arthur

Tasman Peninsula

turn-off and turn left at the sign for the hostel and the Port Arthur Motor Inn. You can buy your historic site entry ticket at the hostel, but you don't have to pay the $7.50 entry fee if you just want to walk through the ruins to the shop or cafes.

Apart from this, most of Port Arthur's accommodation is pricey. A good place to stay, however, is the *Seascape Guest House* (☎ (002) 50 2367) on Arthur Highway where singles/doubles cost $32/48, including a cooked breakfast.

The excellent *Garden Point Caravan Park* (☎ (002) 50 2340) is two km before Port Arthur and has good cooking shelters and a laundry. It costs $8 for two people to camp and $40 a double for a cabin.

Places to Eat

The licensed *Frances Langford Tea Rooms*, in the restored Policeman's Quarters inside the settlement, is a good place for a cuppa or for a light lunch, and is open from 10 am to 5 pm. Also at the historic site is the *Broad Arrow*, a cafeteria open from 9 am to 6 pm (5 pm in the off-season) which also sells souvenirs.

The *Port Arthur Motor Inn* next to the youth hostel, often has cheap specials on the menu, such as lasagna and a beer for $6.

Entertainment

During the high season there is some unique entertainment at Port Arthur. From October to May at 7.45 pm every evening the classic 1926 silent movie *For the Term of His Natural Life* is screened at the Broad Arrow cafe. This film, based on the Marcus Clarke novel about convict life and filmed on location in Port Arthur, costs $4 and finishes just in time to catch the Port Arthur Ghost Tour.

Ghostly apparitions, poltergeists and unexplained happenings have been recorded at Port Arthur since the 1870s and these nightly lantern-lit walking tours of the buildings and ruins are good fun but also pretty spooky. From December to April, two-hour Ghost Tours leave from the site car park at 9.30 pm, and are well worth the $4.

Getting There & Away

If you don't have your own transport, the only way to take a day trip to Port Arthur from Hobart is on an organised tour; with public transport you'll have to stay the night. Hobart Coaches has a weekday service once a day which travels via most towns on the Tasman Peninsula and costs $11 one-way. (There are buses back to Hobart daily except Tuesdays.) The Peninsula Coach Service (☎ (002) 50 3186), which must be booked in advance, also runs one bus a day, and visits many of the sights on the Peninsula ($9 one-way). It operates from 199 Collins St and also does a run from Port Arthur to Hobart on Sundays. All these buses will pick you up or drop you off at the youth hostel.

To get to the east coast from Port Arthur, take the morning Hobart Coaches bus as far as Sorell, and ask the bus driver to radio ahead to ensure that the connecting Hobart Coaches bus to Bicheno waits for you.

AROUND THE PENINSULA

The Tasman Peninsula has many bushwalks, superb scenery, delightful stretches of beach and beautiful bays. Near Eaglehawk Neck there are the incredible coastal formations of the **Tessellated Pavement**, the **Devils Kitchen**, the **Blowhole** and **Tasmans Arch**.

South of Port Arthur is **Remarkable Cave** which you can walk through when the tide is out. You can also visit the remains of the penal outstations at **Koonya**, **Premaydena** and **Saltwater River**, and the ruins of the dreaded **Coal Mines Station**. The **Tasmanian Devil Park** at Taranna is open daily and costs $6, and the **Bush Mill**, on the Arthur Highway, features a steam railway and pioneer settlement.

Organised Tours

Remarkable Tours (**☎** (002) 50 2359) runs five trips a day ($5) between 10 am and 3 pm to Remarkable Cave as well as twilight tours of the peninsula's other attractions, which should be booked in advance. Tours leave from the car park in front of Port Arthur's information office. Tasman Peninsula Detours (**☎** (002) 50 3355) also has full-day tours of the area for an all-inclusive price of $59, and these too should be booked in advance.

Places to Stay & Eat

At Eaglehawk Neck, 20 km before the penal settlement, is *Backpackers' Accommodation* (**☎** (002) 50 3248), on Old Jetty Rd. It's a small friendly hostel costing $10 a night, and a good base from which to do the many hikes in the area. You can buy delicious home-grown vegetables from the hostel managers.

In the pleasant seaside town of Nubeena, 11 km beyond Port Arthur, the *White Beach Caravan Park* (**☎** (002) 50 2142) has tent sites and on-site vans. Also worth checking out is *Parker's Holiday Cottages* (**☎** (002) 50 2138), where singles/doubles cost $30/40 and $5 for each additional person. The *Nubeena Tavern* (**☎** (002) 50 2250) in Nubeena has been recommended for its counter meals.

At Koonya there's bunkhouse accommodation at *Seaview Riding Ranch* (**☎** (002) 50 3110) but this definitely must be booked in advance.

There are also free but basic camping facilities at Lime Bay, Fortescue Bay and White Beach run by the Department of Parks, Wildlife & Heritage.

East Coast & North-East

Tasmania's scenic east coast, with its long sandy beaches, fine fishing and rare peacefulness, is known as the 'sun coast' because of its mild climate. The area boasts more than 2250 hours of sunshine a year.

Exploration and settlement of the region, which was found to be most suitable for grazing, proceeded rapidly after the establishment of Hobart in 1803. Offshore fishing and particularly whaling also became important, as did tin mining and timber cutting. Many of the convicts who served out their terms in the area stayed on to help the settlers lay the foundations of the fishing, wool, beef and grain industries which are still important today.

The largest town on the coast is St Helens, with a population of only 1000, and a leisurely trip up the Tasman Highway to this north-eastern town is highly recommended. The spectacular scenery around Coles Bay is not to be missed, and Bicheno and Swansea are pleasant seaside towns to spend a few restful days.

Banking facilities on the east coast are very limited and in some towns the banks are only open one or two days a week. There are agencies for the Commonwealth Bank at all post offices. If you get stuck for money on a weekend, the only key-card facility on the coast is at the Westpac bank in Bicheno.

Getting There & Around

Bus Redline and Hobart Coaches are the main bus companies operating on the east coast, but several smaller companies – Peakes Coach Service (**☎** (003) 72 2390), Bicheno Coach Services (**☎** (003) 75 1461), and Haley's Coaches (☎ (003) 76 1807) – also do runs between Swansea, Coles Bay, Bicheno, St Marys, St Helens and Derby. With all of these, you can buy your tickets when boarding. None of the smaller companies will accept a Hobart Coaches Explorer Travel Pass, but the Redline Super Tassie Pass can be used on services run by Peakes and Haley's.

Bus services are limited at weekends, so it might take a little longer to travel between towns than you anticipate.

Bicycle Cycling along the east coast is one of the most pleasant ways of appreciating this part of Tasmania. If you are planning to cycle between Swansea and Coles Bay, there's an informal boat service for cyclists and hikers which operates between the eastern end of Nine Mile Beach and Swanwick, just north of Coles Bay. The trip costs $9 and has to be booked in advance (☎ (002) 57 0239). The service only runs from October to mid-May, but will save you a 65-km ride.

BUCKLAND

This tiny township, 61 km from Hobart, was once a staging post for coaches. Ye Olde Buckland Inn, at 5 Kent St, welcomed coach drivers and travellers a century ago, and today, offers a very good counter lunch from Thursday to Sunday.

The stone **Church of St John the Baptist**, dating from 1846, is worth a visit. It has a stained-glass window which was rescued from a 14th-century abbey in England just before Cromwell sacked the building.

ORFORD (population 378)

Orford is a popular little seaside resort on the Prosser River (named after an escaped prisoner who was caught on its banks). There's good fishing, swimming and some excellent walks in the area.

There's plenty of accommodation in Orford, although the cheapest is probably *Sea Breeze Holiday Flats* (☎ (002) 57 1375).

It's on the corner of Rudd Ave and Walpole St and costs $30 a double, with a one-night surcharge. On the Tasman Highway, the *Blue Waters Motor Hotel* (☎ (002) 57 1102) has singles/doubles for $35/45, and the *Island View Motel* (☎ (002) 57 1114) costs $42/50.

TRIABUNNA (population 924)

The larger town of Triabunna, a little further north, was a whaling station and garrison town when nearby Maria Island was a penal settlement. Today its main industries are fishing and woodchip processing. You can charter boats for fishing and cruising and go bushwalking or horse riding at popular Woodstock Farm (☎ (002) 57 3186). The ferry to Maria Island also leaves from the jetty at Triabunna.

Places to Stay & Eat

The *Triabunna Youth Hostel* (☎ (002) 57 3439), in Spencer St, is a comfortable and quiet place to stay for $9 a night. The *Triabunna Caravan Park* (☎ (002) 57 3575), on the corner of Vicary and Melbourne Sts, also has a good reputation and has camp sites and on-site vans. The *Spring Bay Hotel* on Charles St has cheap counter meals.

MARIA ISLAND NATIONAL PARK

In 1971 Maria Island was declared a wildlife sanctuary and a year later became a national park. It's popular with bird-watchers, being the only national park in Tasmania where you can see all 11 of the state's native bird species. Forester kangaroos, Cape Barren geese and emus are also a common sight during the day.

This peaceful island features some magnificent scenery, including fossil-studded sandstone and limestone cliffs, beautiful white sandy beaches, forests and fern gullies. There are some lovely walks on the island, including the Bishop and Clerk Mountain Walk and the historical Fossil Cliffs Nature Walk; brochures are available for both. The marine life around the island is also diverse and plentiful, and for those with the equipment, the scuba diving is spectacular.

Historically, Maria Island is also very interesting – from 1825 to 1832, the settlement of Darlington was Tasmania's second penal colony (the first was Sarah Island near Strahan). The remains of the penal village, including the Commissariat Store (1825) and the Mill House (1846), are remarkably well preserved and easy to visit; in fact, you'll probably end up staying in one of the old buildings. There are no shops on the island so don't forget to bring your own supplies.

Places to Stay

The rooms in the penitentiary at Darlington and some of the other buildings have been converted into bunkhouses for visitors. These are called the *Parks, Wildlife & Heritage Penitentiary Units* (☎ (002) 57 1420) and cost $6 a night, but it's wise to book as the beds are sometimes taken by school groups. There are also three camp grounds on the island.

Getting There & Away

The ferry MV *Maria Lady* (☎ (002) 57 3264) operates once a day between the Triabunna Jetty and Darlington, on Maria Island. The return fare costs $16 for day visitors ($10 for children) and $19 for campers. Bad weather can sometimes delay the service so be prepared to stay a day or so longer on the island if necessary.

SWANSEA (population 428)

On the shores of Great Oyster Bay, with superb views across to the Freycinet Peninsula, Swansea is a popular place for camping, boating, fishing and surfing. It was first settled in the 1820s and is the administrative centre for Glamorgan, Australia's oldest rural municipality.

Swansea has a number of interesting historic buildings including the original Council Chambers, which are still in use, and the lovely red-brick Morris's General Store, built in 1838. The **Community Centre** dates from 1860 and houses a museum of local history and the only oversized billiard table

in Australia. The museum is open from Monday to Saturday and entry costs $2.

The **Swansea Bark Mill & East Coast Museum**, at 96 Tasman Highway, is also worth a look. In one section, the processing of black-wattle bark, a basic ingredient used in the tanning of heavy leathers, is demonstrated while the adjoining museum features displays of Swansea's early history including some superb old photographs. It's open daily from 9 am to 5 pm and admission is $4.50.

You can hire wave skis and sailboards from Seaside Enterprises, next to the youth hostel.

Places to Stay & Eat

The *Swansea Youth Hostel* (☎ (002) 57 8367), at 5 Franklin St, is in a lovely spot right by the sea and costs $9 a night. In the busy summer season, priority is given to YHA members. Almost opposite the hostel is the *Oyster Bay Guest House* (☎ (002) 57 8110) which was built in 1836 and offers friendly colonial accommodation at $35/60 for singles/doubles with a cooked breakfast.

The *Swansea Caravan Park* (☎ (002) 57 8177) on Shaw St, just by the beach, is very clean and has tent sites and on-site vans and cabins. The *Kenmore Caravan Park* (☎ (002) 57 8148), on Bridge St, also has a good reputation.

Just Maggies, at 26 Franklin St, has coffee, cakes and light lunches, but for breakfast go to the *Pier Milk Bar*, just along the road. The *Swan Motor Inn* does counter meals, or for something special try the licensed *Shy Albatross Restaurant* in the Oyster Bay Guest House.

Getting There & Away

Hobart coaches has at least one morning and afternoon service between Hobart and Bicheno ($17.90 one-way) via Swansea ($14.60) on most days except Saturday. The Hobart Coaches agent in Swansea is the Shell service station on Franklin St.

On weekdays only, Redline has one service between Launceston and Bicheno ($18) via Swansea ($14.40). The route runs through Campbell Town and past the Lake Leake turn-off. There's also a daily service between Hobart and Bicheno ($24.40) via Swansea ($21) from Monday to Friday. The Redline agent in Swansea is the Food Store at 8 Franklin St.

Peakes Coach Service runs a daily bus on weekdays between Swansea and St Marys ($8) via Bicheno ($4). The buses depart from Morris's General Store in Franklin St.

COLES BAY & FREYCINET NATIONAL PARK
On the way to Coles Bay, look out for **Moulting Lagoon** which is a breeding ground for black swans. The tiny township itself is both dominated and sheltered by the spectacular 300-metre-high pink granite mountains known as the Hazards. It's the gateway to many white-sand beaches, secluded coves, rocky cliffs and excellent bushwalks in the Freycinet National Park. The park, incorporating Freycinet Peninsula and beautiful Schouten Island, is noted for its coastal heaths, orchids and other wild flowers and for its wildlife, including black cockatoos, yellow wattle birds and Bennetts wallabies. Walks include a 27-km circuit of the park plus many other shorter tracks, one of the most beautiful being the walk to **Wineglass Bay**.

There is one general store in Coles Bay which sells groceries, basic supplies and petrol as well as hiring out small motor boats, a large speed boat (for which you need a licence) and scuba-diving tanks.

Places to Stay & Eat
Coles Bay Youth Hostel, in the national park, is mainly used by groups, and must be booked at the YHA state office in Hobart (☎ (002) 34 9617). For cheap accommodation, however, try the *Iluka Holiday Centre* (☎ (002) 57 0115) on Muirs Beach, which has a backpackers' cabin for $10 a night, on-site vans for $25 a double, and more expensive units, cabins and cottages. *Pine Lodge Cabins* (☎ (002) 57 0113) in Harold St has two cabins which sleep four to five

and these are good value at $40 per cabin, even with a one-night surcharge.

Actually in the national park, and looking nothing like a chateau, is the *Chateau* (☎ (002) 57 0101), a group of cabins leading down to the water's edge. Costs start at $37.50 per person, including a cooked breakfast, and reasonably priced evening meals are also available.

Sites at the national park camp ground (☎ (002) 57 0107) should be booked at the ranger station and cost $6 a double. The scenery at the free camping sites of Wineglass Bay (1½ to two hours), Hazards Beach (two to three hours) and Cooks Beach (about 4½ hours) are, however, well worth the walk.

The licensed *Freycinet Restaurant & Oyster Bay Takeaway* (☎ (002) 57 0255) is open daily from 8.30 am and has very reasonably priced meals, a spectacular view and a good atmosphere. You can also eat at the *Chateau* restaurant, but you must book.

Getting There & Away
Redline and Hobart Coaches can drop you at the Coles Bay turn-off en route to Bicheno and you can hitch the 28 km from there, but traffic may be scarce. Bicheno Coach Services runs two buses each weekday between Coles Bay and Bicheno, and one on Saturdays. In Bicheno, buses depart from the newsagent in Foster St, and in Coles Bay, from the general store; tickets are $5 per person and $2.50 for a bicycle.

BICHENO (population 700)
In the early 1800s, whalers and sealers used Bicheno's tiny picturesque harbour, called the Gulch, to shelter their boats. They also built lookouts in the hills to watch for passing whales. These days, fishing is still one of the town's major occupations, and if you are down at the Gulch around lunch time, when all the fishing boats return, you can buy fresh crayfish, abalone, oysters or anything else caught that night straight from the boats. Tourism is also very important to Bicheno; it's a lovely spot to stay for a few days.

Things to See & Do

An interesting three-km **foreshore walkway** from Redbill Point to the Blowhole continues south around the beach to Courlands Bay. For the views, you can also walk up to the **Whalers Lookout** and the **Freycinet Lookout**.

At nightfall you may be lucky enough to see the fairy penguins at the northern end of Redbill Beach and at low tide you can walk out to **Diamond Island**, opposite the youth hostel.

The Dive Centre (**☎** (003) 75 1138/43), opposite the Sea Life Centre on the foreshore, runs courses which are more reasonably priced than those in warmer waters, and you can also hire or buy diving equipment from its shop.

The Sea Life Centre is open daily from 9 am to 5 pm and features Tasmanian marine life swimming behind glass windows. There's also a restored trading ketch but, at $4 for admission, the centre is rather overpriced and a bit depressing. Seven km north of town is the 32-hectare East Coast Birdlife & Animal Park which is open daily from 9 am to 5.30 pm; entry costs $6.

Places to Stay

Three km north of town, on the beach opposite Diamond Island, is the *Bicheno Youth Hostel* (**☎** (003) 75 1293). It costs $8 a night and may be booked out in summer. The *Bicheno Dive Centre* (**☎** (003) 75 1138) has three self-contained cabins, each with six bunks. Although these are used mainly by divers, anyone can stay there. At $14 a person or $17 with linen, it's good value, especially if you get a cabin to yourself.

Wintersun Lodge Motel (**☎** (003) 75 1225), on the northern outskirts of town at 35 Gordon St, is a friendly place with singles/doubles at $40/50.

The *Bicheno Cabins & Tourist Park* (**☎** (003) 75 1117), at Champ St, has camp sites and expensive on-site vans. The *Bicheno Campervan Park* (**☎** (003) 75 1280), on the corner of Burgess and Tribe Sts, is a little cheaper: $8 a double to camp and $28 a double for an on-site van.

Places to Eat

On the Tasman Highway, the *Longboat Tavern* has been recommended for good counter meals and seafood. This is next to the Beachfront Family Resort which has a good restaurant called the *Whaler's Return*. Also on the highway is *Waubs Bay House* which has a good reputation for eat-in or takeaway pizzas. For lunch you can try the bistro at the *Sea Life Centre* which specialises in seafood but could give better value for money. Close by, the *Galleon Coffee Shop* has reasonably priced meals, but you have to leave your backpacks outside.

About 30 km north of Bicheno is the Chain of Lagoons where you can buy very reasonable fresh crayfish from a roadside stand called *Wardlaw's Picnic Crays*. If you continue on the Highway through Elephant Pass there are some great views, and very good food at *Mt Elephant Barn*, near Gray.

Getting There & Away

For information on the Bicheno services run by Redline, Hobart Coaches and Peakes Coach Service, see the Getting There & Away section for Swansea. The agent for Redline in Bicheno is Sam's Cut Price Store, 39 Foster St; for Hobart Coaches it's the Mobil service station on the Tasman Highway. The Peakes bus to Swansea and St Marys leaves from the BP service station on Foster St. The Bicheno Coach Services bus to Coles Bay leaves from the newsagent in Foster St.

ST MARYS (population 650)

St Marys is a charming little town, 10 km inland from the coast, near the Mt Nicholas range. There's not much to do there except enjoy the peacefulness of the countryside, visit a number of waterfalls in the area, and take walks in the state forest. St Marys is also an important road junction, as this is where the Tasman Highway meets the A4 which heads west through Fingal and Avoca to the Midland Highway.

Seventeen km north of St Marys is the resort town of **Scamander** which has excellent beaches for swimming and surfing, and is a popular fishing spot.

Places to Stay

The superbly positioned *St Marys Youth Hostel* (☎ (003) 72 2341), on a working sheep farm called Seaview, is surrounded by state forest. It's at the end of a dirt track, eight km from St Marys on German Town Rd, and commands magnificent views of the coast, ocean and mountains. It costs $8 a night to stay in the hostel (or $7.95 for a Super Saver!) and $25 a double in the new 'Gumppie' units (Green Upwardly Mobile Professional People Interested in the Environment). The hostel is a great place to stay and you can either hitch up there or the warden picks up hostellers from the post office between 10 and 11 am every day except Sunday.

There's also accommodation in the *St Marys Hotel* (☎ (003) 72 2181) where singles/doubles cost $20/36.

Getting There & Away

The Peakes bus between St Marys and Swansea via Bicheno departs from the newsagent on Gray Rd.

Redline has one service from Launceston ($13.40), and another from Hobart ($23.80) every day except Saturday – both continuing on to St Helens. The Redline agent in St Marys is the newsagent on Gray Rd.

You can also get to St Helens with Haley's Coaches; buses depart weekdays from the post office at 9 am ($3) and continue on to Derby to connect with the Redline bus to Launceston.

ST HELENS (population 1000)

St Helens, on Georges Bay, is the largest town on the east coast and a popular holiday destination. First settled in 1830, this old whaling town has an interesting and varied history which is recorded in the **History Room**, adjacent to the town's library. The room is open weekdays from 9 am to 12.30 pm and admission is $2.

Today, St Helens is Tasmania's largest

fishing port with a big fleet based in the bay. Visitors can charter boats for offshore game fishing or just a lazy cruise.

While the beaches in town are not very good for swimming, there are excellent scenic beaches at **Binalong Bay** (10 km from St Helens), **Sloop Rock** (12 km) and **Stieglitz** (7 km), as well as at St Helens and Humbug points. You can also visit **St Columba Falls**, near Pyengana, 24 km away.

Places to Stay

The *St Helens Youth Hostel* (☎ (003) 76 1661), at 5 Cameron St, is in a lovely quiet spot by the beach and costs $10 a night. The *St Helens Hotel Motel* (☎ (003) 76 1133), at 49 Cecilia St, has new and very clean backpackers' accommodation at $18 a night. There are also more up-market rooms at $40/45 for singles/doubles, and reasonably priced counter meals.

Both the *Hillcrest Caravan Inn* (☎ (003) 76 3298), at St Helens Point Rd, Stieglitz, and the *St Helens Caravan Park* (☎ (003) 76 1290), on Penelope St, are a little way out of town. Both have camping and on-site vans, and have very good reputations.

Getting There & Away

Redline has daily (except Saturday) connections to Launceston ($16.60) and Hobart ($27.40). The Redline agent in St Helens is the newsagent in Cecilia St. During the week you can get to St Marys, or Derby (to connect with the Redline bus to Launceston), and to Winnaleah on Haley's Coaches which depart from the BP service station on the main street.

WELDBOROUGH

The Weldborough Pass, with its mountain scenery and dense rainforests, is quite spectacular. During the tin-mining boom last century, hundreds of Chinese migrated to Tasmania and many made Weldborough their base. The famous Joss House, now in Launceston's Queen Victoria Museum & Art Gallery, was built in Weldborough.

The town's only hotel calls itself *The*

Worst Little Pub in Tassie and has 'leprechaun pea soup' and 'blowfly sponge' on the menu, but don't be put off – it's quite a nice place to stop for a drink.

GLADSTONE
About 25 km off the Tasman Highway, between St Helens and Scottsdale, is the tiny town of Gladstone. The town was one of the last tin-mining centres in north-eastern Tasmania, until the mine closed in 1982. At one time, there were a number of mining communities in the area and a large Chinese population. Today, many of the old mining settlements are just ghost towns and Gladstone shows signs of heading that way too.

Twelve km from Gladstone is the popular **Mt William National Park** where you can see large numbers of Forester kangaroos. From Gladstone, an unsurfaced road runs 42 km to the **Eddystone Lighthouse**, built in 1887. There are very basic camping facilities at Eddystone Point, the most eastern point of the Tasmanian mainland, and you will have to bring your own water supplies.

You can get to Gladstone on the mail run which departs daily from outside the post office in Derby.

DERBY
In 1874, tin was discovered in Derby and, due mainly to the famous Briseis Tin Mine, this little township flourished throughout the late 19th century. Today Derby is a classified historic town, and some of the old mine buildings are now part of the excellent **Tin Mine Centre** which features a mine museum of old photographs and mining implements, and a recreation of an old mining shanty town. The centre is open from 9 am to 5 pm (10 am to 4 pm during June, July and August) and admission costs $4.

Places to Stay & Eat
The *Dorset Hotel* (☎ (003) 54 2360) has singles/doubles for $20/35 with a continental breakfast, and also does good counter meals. The *Crib Shed Tea Rooms* (part of the mine museum) specialises in country cooking and serves delicious scones.

Six km from Winnaleah, near Derby, is the peaceful *Merlinkei Farm Hostel* (☎ (003) 54 2152) which costs $9 a night. If you are hitching, most vehicles will give you a lift or, if you ring from Winnaleah, the manager will pick you up. Being a dairy farm, there's an unlimited supply of fresh milk, and hostellers can help around the farm and even earn a 'milking certificate'.

Getting There & Away
On weekdays, Redline has a daily service between Launceston and Winnaleah via Derby ($11) and Scottsdale. There's only one service on Sundays, and none on Saturdays. The Redline agent is the general store in Derby's main street. On weekdays, you can get to St Helens and Winnaleah on the Haley's bus which departs from the post office.

SCOTTSDALE (population 2000)
Scottsdale, the major town in the north-east, serves some of Tasmania's richest agricultural and forestry country, and its setting is consequently quite beautiful. Of the two hotels in town, accommodation is cheaper at *Lords Hotel*, 2 King St, and a tent site at the nearby *North East Caravan Park* costs $5.

At Nabowla, 21 km west of Scottsdale, is the **Bridestowe Lavender Farm**. It's open daily from Boxing Day until the third week in January and is spectacular to visit when the lavender is in flower; entry costs $4. Twenty-one km north of Scottsdale is the popular beach resort of **Bridport**. From there, it's another 45 km to the unspoiled beaches and great diving and snorkelling at **Tomahawk**.

For bus services to Scottsdale, see the Getting There & Away section for Derby. To get to Bridport, you can take a local bus from Scottsdale; buses depart twice daily on weekdays from the Redline stop in Scottsdale ($7.50 one-way). You'll need your own transport to visit Tomahawk.

BEN LOMOND NATIONAL PARK
This 165-sq-km park, 50 km south-east of

Launceston, includes the entire Ben Lomond Range and is best known for its good snow coverage and skiing facilities. During the ski season, a kiosk, tavern and restaurant are open in the alpine village and there's accommodation at the *Creek Inn* (☎ (003) 72 2444). To check conditions for downhill or cross-country skiing, ring Ben Lomond Ski Rentals (☎ (003) 31 1312) or listen to 7LA radio for snow reports. A lift ticket is $20 and all ski equipment hire costs about half what it does on the mainland.

The scenery at Ben Lomond is magnificent all year round and the park is particularly noted for its alpine wild flowers which run riot in spring and summer. The park's highest point is Legges Tor (1572 metres), which is also the second highest peak in Tasmania. It can be reached via a good walking track from Carr Villa, on the slopes of Ben Lomond. The ranger's telephone number is (003) 90 6279.

Getting There & Away

During the ski season, Invicta (☎ 008 030 505, toll-free) has a daily return service ($25) between the ski fields and the rear entrance of Paddy Pallin at 59 Brisbane St, Launceston. Invicta also runs a shuttle service from the bottom of Jacobs Ladder to the alpine village ($6 one-way).

Midlands

Tasmania's midlands region has a definite English feel, due to the diligent efforts of early settlers who planted English trees and hedgerows. The agricultural potential of the area contributed to Tasmania's rapid settlement, and coach stations, garrison towns, stone villages and pastoral properties soon sprang up as convict gangs constructed the main road between Hobart and Launceston. Fine wool, beef cattle and timber milling put the midlands on the map and these, along with tourism, are still the main industries.

The course of the Midland Highway has changed slightly from its original route and many of the historic towns are now by-passed, but it's definitely worth making a few detours to see them.

Getting There & Away

Both Redline and Hobart Coaches have several daily services up and down the Midland Highway which can drop you off at any of the towns mentioned in this section. Fares from Hobart include Oatlands $8.40, Ross $11.40, Campbell Town $12.80 and Launceston $15.20.

OATLANDS (population 550)

With the largest collection of colonial architecture in Australia, and the largest number of buildings dating from before 1837, the town of Oatlands is not to be missed. In the main street alone, there are 87 historical buildings and the oldest is the 1829 convict-built **Courthouse**. Much of the sandstone for these early buildings came from the shores of **Lake Dulverton**, now a wildlife sanctuary, which is beside the town.

Today, one of Oatlands's main attractions is **Callington Mill**, the restoration of which was Tasmania's main Bicentennial project. The mill features a faithfully restored cap with a fantail attachment that automatically turns its sails into the wind, and you can climb up the middle. Entry is free.

An unusual way of seeing Oatlands's sights is to go on one of Peter Fielding's ghost or convict tours (☎ (002) 54 1135). The former starts at 8 pm from Callington Mill and the latter at 5 pm from Ye Olde Crooke Shoppe in the main street. Both tours cost $5 and it's best to book ahead.

Places to Stay & Eat

There's plenty of accommodation in Oatlands, although much of it is of the more expensive colonial type. The *Oatlands Youth Hostel* (☎ (002) 54 1320), at 9 Wellington St, has a reputation for being a 'home away from home' and costs $9 a night. The *Midland Hotel* (☎ (002) 54 1103), at 91 High St, costs $30/45 for singles/doubles, including a cooked breakfast.

Holyrood House, on the main street, dates from 1840. It's a good place for meals, which are served by staff in colonial dress.

ROSS (population 310)

This ex-garrison town, 120 km from Hobart, is steeped in colonial charm and history. It was established in 1812 to protect travellers on the main north-south road and was an important coach staging post.

Things to See

The town is famous for the unique convict-built **Ross Bridge**, the third oldest bridge in Australia. Daniel Herbert, a convict stone-mason, was granted a pardon for his detailed work on the 184 panels which decorate the arches.

In the heart of town is a crossroads which can lead you in one of four directions – 'temptation' (represented by the Man-O'-Ross Hotel), 'salvation' (the Catholic church), 'recreation' (the town hall) and 'damnation' (the old jail).

Other interesting historic buildings include the **Scotch Thistle Inn**, first licensed in 1840 as a coaching inn and now a licensed restaurant; the **Old Barracks**, restored by the National Trust; the **Uniting Church** (1885); **St John's Church of England** (1868); and the **Ross Post Office** (1896).

The **Tasmanian Wool Centre**, a museum and craft shop on Church St, is open daily from 9.30 am to 5.30 pm and entry costs $4. Also on Church St is a **militaria collection**, open from Saturday to Thursday ($3).

Places to Stay

The *Man-O'-Ross Hotel* (☎ (003) 81 5240), on Church St, has singles/doubles for $25/40. If you want to treat yourself, then stay in either *Apple Dumpling Cottage* (1880) or *Hudson Cottage* (1850). Both cost $75 a double and need to be booked in advance (☎ (003) 81 5354). Adjacent to the Ross Bridge is the caravan park (☎ (003) 81 5462), where there's camping and cheap on-site cabins.

CAMPBELL TOWN (population 879)

Twelve km from Ross is Campbell Town, another former garrison settlement which boasts plenty of examples of early colonial architecture. These include the convict-built **Red Bridge** (1836), the **Grange** (1847), **St Luke's Church of England** (1835), the **Campbell Town Inn** (1840), the building known as the **Fox Hunters Return** (1829), and the **Old School** (1878).

There's a secondary road from Campbell Town through the excellent fishing and bushwalking area around **Lake Leake** (32 km), to Swansea on the east coast. The daily Redline bus from Hobart to Bicheno travels via this route and can drop you at the Lake Leake turn-off – from here to the lake is another four km. From Conara Junction, 11 km north of Campbell Town, the A4 heads east from the Midland Highway to St Marys.

Launceston

Population 64,500

Officially founded by Lieutenant-Colonel William Paterson in 1805, Launceston is Australia's third oldest city and the commercial centre of northern Tasmania.

The Tamar River estuary was discovered in 1798 by Bass and Flinders who were circumnavigating Van Diemen's Land to find out if it was joined to the rest of Australia. Launceston was the third attempt at a settlement on the river and was originally called Patersonia, after its founder. In 1907, the city was renamed in honour of Governor King who was born in Launceston, England, a town settled 1000 years before on the Tamar River in the county of Cornwall.

Orientation

The city centre is arranged in a grid pattern around the Brisbane St Mall, between Charles and St John Sts. Two blocks north, on Cameron St, there's another pedestrian mall called the Civic Square. To the east of both malls is Yorktown Square, a charming and lively area of restored buildings which have been turned into shops and restaurants.

Although Launceston suffers from a lack of street signs, it's not difficult to find your way around. Launceston's main attractions are all within walking distance of the centre.

Information

The Tasmanian Travel Centre (☎ (003) 37 3111), on the corner of St John and Paterson Sts, is open weekdays from 8.45 am to 5 pm, and on Saturdays between 9 am and noon. You can also get tourist information from the Wilderness Shop at 174 Charles St and there's a Tasmap Centre at Henty House in the Civic Square.

For camping gear try Paddy Pallin, at 59 Brisbane St, and Allgoods, at 60 Elizabeth St – both are excellent. If you're in town on the weekend, there's a craft market in Yorktown Square.

Cataract Gorge

Only a ten-minute walk from the city centre is the magnificent Cataract Gorge. Here, almost vertical cliffs line the banks of the South Esk River as it enters the Tamar. The area around the gorge has been made a reserve for native flora & fauna, and is one of Launceston's best known tourist attractions.

Two walking tracks, one on either side of the gorge, lead up to **First Basin**, which is filled with water from the South Esk River (the northern trail is easier than the southern). The waters of First Basin are cold and very deep, so you may feel safer swimming in the concrete pool. The landscaped area around the basin features picnic spots, the Gorge Restaurant and a cafe. There's also a chair lift, which crosses the basin to the reserve on the other side; the breathtaking six-minute ride costs $3. A good walking track leads further up the gorge to **Second Basin** and Duck Reach. A little further on is the Trevallyn Dam quarry where, from November to April, you can do some 'simulated' hang-gliding for $5.

Penny Royal World

The Penny Royal entertainment complex, which claims to take you back to a 'world of yesteryear', has exhibits including working 19th-century water mills and windmills, gunpowder mills and model boats. You can take a ride on a barge, a restored city tram and, best of all, a 45-minute cruise up the gorge on the *Lady Stelfox* paddle steamer. Although some parts of the Penny Royal complex are interesting, overall it's not really worth the $15 admission fee. You can, however, just pay for one of the attractions; the cruise, for instance, only costs $5.

Queen Victoria Museum & Art Gallery

The Queen Victoria Museum & Art Gallery was built late last century and displays the splendour of the period both inside and out. It has a unique collection of Tasmanian fauna, Aboriginal artefacts, penal settlement relics and colonial paintings. A major attraction is the splendid joss house, donated by the descendants of Chinese settlers. The museum's Planetarium is also very popular. The centre is open Monday to Saturday from 10 am to 5 pm, and from 2 to 5 pm on Sundays. The gallery and museum are free, but it costs $1 to visit the Planetarium, which is open from 11 am to 2 pm on weekdays and from 2 to 3 pm on Saturdays.

Maritime Museum

The historic Johnstone & Wilmot warehouse, on the corner of Cimitiere and St John Sts, dates from 1842 and houses the Launceston Maritime Museum. The artefacts and displays concentrate on the maritime history of northern Tasmania, and the city's local history archives are also kept in this building. The museum is open from 10 am to 4 pm Monday to Saturday and from 2 to 4 pm on Sundays; admission is $2.

Historic Buildings

Macquarie House, in the Civic Square, was built in 1830 as a warehouse but was later used as a military barracks and office building. It now houses part of the Queen Victoria Museum & Art Gallery and is open from 10

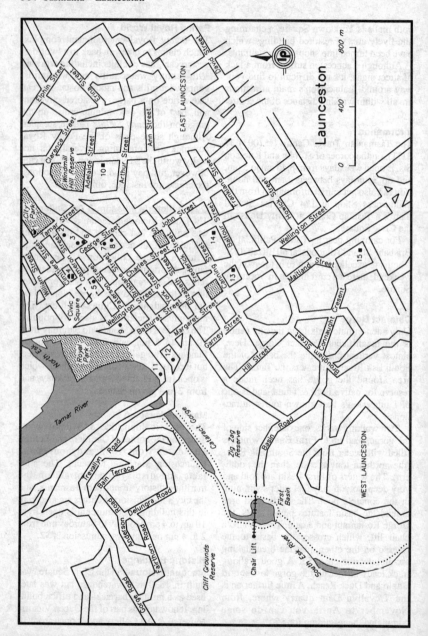

Launceston

am to 4 pm Monday to Saturday, and on Sunday afternoons.

The **Old Umbrella Shop**, at 60 George St, was built in the 1860s, and still houses a selection of umbrellas. Classified by the National Trust, it is the last genuine period shop in the state. The interior is lined with Tasmanian blackwood timber, and the shop sells a good range of National Trust items. It's open from 9 am to 5 pm on weekdays and from 9 am to noon on Saturdays.

On the Midland Highway, six km from the city, is **Franklin House**, one of Launceston's most attractive Georgian homes. It was built in 1838 and has been beautifully restored and furnished by the National Trust. An outstanding feature of its interior is the woodwork, which has been carved from New South Wales cedar. The house is open daily from 9 am to 5 pm (4 pm in winter) and admission is $4.

Parks & Gardens

Launceston is sometimes referred to as 'the garden city' and, with so many beautiful public squares, parks and reserves, it's easy to understand why.

The 13-hectare **City Park** is a fine example of a Victorian garden and features an elegant fountain, a bandstand, a monkey and wallaby enclosure and a conservatory.

Princes Square, between Charles and St John Sts, features a bronze fountain bought at the 1858 Paris Exhibition.

Other public parks and gardens include **Royal Park**, near the junction between the North Esk and Tamar rivers; the **Punchbowl Reserve** with its magnificent rhododendron garden; **Windmill Hill Reserve**; and the **Trevallyn Recreation Area**.

Other Attractions

Richies Mill Art Centre is a restored 1834 flour mill and miller's cottage on Bridge Rd near the Penny Royal. As the mill stands by the river in pleasant leafy grounds and has a good restaurant, it's a nice place to spend an hour or two.

The **Design Centre of Tasmania**, on the corner of Brisbane and Tamar Sts, is a retail outlet displaying work by the state's top artists and craftspeople.

The **Waverley Woollen Mills & National Automobile Museum** are on Waverley Rd, five km from the city centre. The mills were established in 1874 and are the oldest operating woollen mills in Australia. The mills and museum are open daily from 9 am to 4 pm, and admission costs $3 and $4 respectively.

The **Tamar Knitting Mills**, founded in 1926, are at 21 Hobart Rd and can also be inspected. They are open daily from 9 am to 4 pm, and admission is free.

Organised Tours

Redline Coaches (☎ (003) 31 9177) on George St, and Starline Coaches (☎ (003) 31 1411) on Forster Rd, have half and full-day tours of the Tamar Valley ($20), Mole Creek ($42) and the City Sights ($25). Invicta runs one to four-day tours to wilderness areas like Cradle Mountain and Lake St Clair.

Places to Stay

Hostels The *Launceston City Youth Hostel* (☎ (003) 44 9779), which is not a YHA hostel, is at 36 Thistle St, two km from the centre of town. It has dorm beds and family rooms for $10 a night. The building dates from the 1940s and used to be the canteen for the Coats Patons woollen mill. The hostel has mountain and touring bikes for hire as well as a comprehensive selection of bushwalking gear. The manager can also give you some useful tips on cycling and bushwalking in Tasmania.

Guesthouses & Private Hotels The *Ashton Gate Tourist Lodge* (☎ (003) 31 6180), at 32 High St, is very homely and costs $30/45 for singles/doubles with a continental breakfast. A few doors away, at 22 High St, the *Windmill Hill Tourist Lodge* (☎ (003) 31 9337) costs $25/35. The lodge also has a four-bed room which costs $15 per person, and self-contained holiday flats at $50 a double.

If you can afford the extra, there are some great guesthouses offering rather luxurious colonial accommodation such as *Airlie Dorset Terrace* (☎ (003) 34 2162), at 138 St John St, where singles/doubles cost $57/70, including a cooked breakfast.

For something really special, you could try renting your own fully-furnished two-bedroom colonial cottage. The wonderful *Ivy Cottage* and *Alice's Place* (☎ (003) 31 8431, 31 7481) are next door to each other at 17 York St. Both are only a short stroll from the city centre and have their own small gardens. At around $94 for two people, and $20 for each additional person, the price is not over the top.

Hotels Launceston has a good selection of hotels for a town of its size. One of the cheapest and quietest is the *Sportsman's Hall Hotel* (☎ (003) 31 3968), at 252 Charles St, where singles/doubles cost $20/30 with breakfast.

Close by, at 191 Charles St, is the *Hotel Tasmania* (☎ (003) 31 7355) which has rooms with a fridge, coffee/tea-making facilities and telephone for $37/52; the price includes a continental breakfast.

The *TRC Hotel* (☎ (003) 31 3424), adjacent to the Penny Royal Windmill at 131 Paterson St, has good, clean rooms with bathroom for $25/40, including a cooked breakfast. There are also dormitory-style rooms for $18 a night; the staff here are very friendly.

The *Royal Hotel* (☎ (003) 31 2526), at 90 George St, is pretty close to the Redline depot and costs $22/40 with a cooked breakfast. Be warned, however, that on Friday and Saturday nights, bands play until 2.30 am, which makes it rather difficult to sleep.

The *Centennial Hotel* (☎ (003) 31 4957), on the corner of Bathurst and Balfour Sts, has rooms for $30/50, including a cooked breakfast. The hotel is very popular, so it's a good idea to book in advance.

Motels & Holiday Flats Although fairly close to the city centre, the *Mews Mini Motel* (☎ (003) 31 2861), at 89 Margaret St, is in a quiet part of town. Rooms cost $41/55, including a cooked breakfast. The *Motel Maldon* (☎ (003) 31 3211), at 32 Brisbane St, is two minutes' walk from the city centre and costs $45/55, including breakfast.

Although a little difficult to find, *Clarke Holiday House* (☎ (003) 34 2237) at 19 Neika Ave, near the corner of Basin Rd and Brougham St, is good value at $35 a double.

Camping The *Treasure Island Caravan Park* (☎ (003) 44 2600) is on Glen Dhu St, past the Launceston City Youth Hostel. It has camping sites, on-site vans and cabins. The park gets crowded and is right next to the freeway, but it does have good facilities.

Places to Eat
Banjo's bakes all its own breads, pizzas, cakes etc and has two shops, one in Yorktown Square and one at 98 Brisbane St; both are open daily from 6 am to 6 pm. At Yorktown Square, you can also dine alfresco at *Molly York's Coffee Shoppe*.

The *Deli*, at the rear of the Identity Store, 40 St John St, is very popular with shoppers and has good coffee and quality cakes and snacks. The *Konditorei Cafe Manfred* has delicious inexpensive home-made German rolls and pastries. It's at 95 George St, near the Redline depot, and a good place to sit while waiting for a bus. *Ripples Restaurant*, in the Ritchies Mill Art Centre, specialises in light meals such as crepes and pancakes, and there's a lovely view of the boats on the Tamar River from the outdoor tables.

Most of Launceston's many hotels have filling, reasonably priced counter meals but you probably won't get cheaper than the $7 specials at the *Royal Oak*, on the corner of Brisbane and Tamar Sts.

There are a few good restaurants in Launceston charging $9 to $13 for a main meal. One of the most popular is *Calabrisella* (☎ (003) 31 1958), at 56 Wellington St, which serves excellent Italian food and is often packed, so bookings are advisable. It's open until the early hours on Fridays and Saturdays, and until midnight on other nights except Tuesdays. You can also get takeaway pizza.

The *Pasta House*, in Yorktown Square, is a licensed restaurant with pasta dishes for around $8.50; it's open until 9.30 pm Monday to Saturday.

Montezuma's, at 63 Brisbane St, is a good-fun Mexican restaurant with main courses at around $12.50, or a filling Mexican snack for $5. It's open until 3 am on Fridays and Saturdays. For Chinese food try the *Canton*, at 201 Charles St; it's one of the best moderately priced Chinese restaurants in town.

For $13 or more, there's the *Satay House* out at Kingscourt Shopping Centre, Kings Meadows, which serves excellent Indonesian fare. *Fee & Me*, a licensed brasserie at 36 The Kingsway, has a good selection of Tasmanian wines. *Shrimps*, at 72 George St, is a good choice for seafood and an intimate atmosphere, and *Dicky Whites*, at 107 Brisbane St, is the place for steaks. The *Gorge Restaurant*, at Cataract Gorge, has fairly good food and undoubtedly the best setting in Launceston.

Entertainment

There's quite a good choice of evening entertainment in Launceston, most of which is advertised either in the *Examiner* newspaper or in *This Week in Tasmania*.

The Batman Fawkner, at 35-39 Cameron St, has live music nightly (except Tuesdays), a disco on Friday and Saturday nights, free films every Wednesday night and a monthly Friday night showing of the film *The Blues Brothers*.

The Pavilion Tavern in Yorktown Square also has music Tuesday to Saturday nights and a cabaret-style nightclub called Twains. Rosies Tavern, at 158 George St, has music every night except Tuesdays and Sundays and nice comfy couches to lounge in. The Royal Hotel, also in George St, is another popular venue for live bands on Wednesday to Saturday nights. Alfresco's is a wine bar in the Victoria Hotel, 211 Brisbane St, which is also becoming quite a popular venue.

In the disco department, Hot Gossip, in the Launceston Hotel (107 Brisbane St) is open Wednesdays to Saturdays, while upstairs, Slates is an historic pool room, which is worth seeing.

If you want to risk a few dollars, or just observe how the rich play, check out the Launceston Federal Country Club Casino at Prospect, 10 km from the city centre. You don't have to pay to get in and about the only article of clothing disapproved of these days is track shoes. The disco at the casino, Regines, is also free and the drinks are not as expensive as you might expect.

Getting There & Away

Air For information on domestic flights to and from Launceston, see the Getting There & Away section at the beginning of this chapter. Ansett Airlines (☎ (003) 32 5101) is at 54 Brisbane St, Australian Airlines (☎ (003) 32 9911) is based on the corner of Brisbane and George Sts, and Airlines of Tasmania (☎ (003) 91 8422) has an office at the airport.

Bus The main bus companies operating out of Launceston are Redline (☎ (003) 31 9177), 112 George St; Hobart Coaches (☎ (003) 34 3600) 83 Cimitiere St; Invicta (☎ 008 030 505, toll-free) 59 Brisbane St, at the rear of Paddy Pallin; and Tamar Valley Coaches (☎ (003) 34 0828) at 26 Wellington St.

Both Redline and Hobart Coaches run buses to Deloraine ($5.40), Devonport

($10.60) and Burnie ($14.20). Redline also has services to Wynyard, Stanley, Smithton ($23.20), Queenstown ($44.60), Strahan ($49.50), George Town, St Marys ($13.40), St Helens ($16.60), Bicheno and Swansea. Invicta has services to Ben Lomond during the ski season ($25) and to Cradle Mountain ($65 return).

Car There are plenty of car rental firms in Launceston. Some of the cheaper ones are Apple Car Rentals (☎ (003) 31 1399), 201 Wellington St; Advance Car Rentals (☎ (003) 31 3022), 32 Cameron St; and Drive-Away Rent-A-Car (☎ (003) 31 6056), 50 York St.

Hitching To start hitching to Devonport and the north-west, catch the Prospect Casino bus from stop C on St John St. For Hobart and the east coast, catch a Franklin House bus from the same stop. For the Tasman Highway route to the east coast catch a Waverley bus from stop G on St John St.

Getting Around
To/From the Airport Redline operates an airport shuttle service which meets all incoming flights and picks up passengers an hour or so before all departures. The fare is $5 and Redline can pick you up or drop you off wherever you're staying. By taxi it costs about $15 to get into the city.

Bus The local bus service is run by Metro, and the main departure point is at Metro Central, on St John St, between Paterson and York Sts. For $2.20 you can buy an unlimited travel Day Rover ticket which can be used all day on weekends and between 9 am and 4.30 pm and after 6 pm on weekdays. Most routes, however, do not operate in the evenings, and Sunday services are very limited.

Bicycle Rent-A-Cycle, at the Launceston City Youth Hostel (☎ (003) 44 9779), has a huge range of 10-speed tourers and mountain bikes. The tourers cost $9 a day or $60 a week, including helmet and panniers; and the mountain bikes cost $90 a week. There's

a reducing rate for each additional week and a slight reduction if you're staying at the hostel. You can leave your luggage at the hostel, and it's also possible to do a one-way rental and send the bicycle back by bus.

Around Launceston

HADSPEN (population 900)
Entally House, 18 km from Launceston and just west of Hadspen, is one of Tasmania's best known historic homes. It was built in 1819 by Thomas Haydock Reibey but is now owned by the National Trust. Set in beautiful grounds, it creates a vivid picture of what life must have been like for the well-to-do on an early farming property. The home, its stables, church, coach house and grounds are open daily from 10 am to 12.30 pm and from 1 to 5 pm and admission costs $4. The Reibeys have quite an interesting family history which you can read about in a bro-chure on sale at the property ($1.50).

On the roadside two km west of Hadspen is **Carrick Mill**, a lovely ivy-covered blue-stone mill, which dates from 1810 and has been very well restored.

Places to Stay & Eat
In Hadspen, on the corner of Bass Highway and Main Rd, is the *Launceston Cabin & Tourist Park* (☎ (003) 93 6391). The park has good facilities and costs $9 to camp, $30 a double for an on-site van and $40 a double for well-equipped cabins.

The *Red Feather Inn* (☎ (003) 93 6331), built in 1844, has a good restaurant with main meals for around $13.50.

LIFFEY VALLEY
The Liffey Valley State Reserve protects the beautiful rainforested valley at the foot of the Great Western Tiers and features the impressive **Liffey Valley Falls**. It's a very popular destination for fishing or bushwalk-ing, and day-trippers are also attracted by an amazing fernery which has the largest

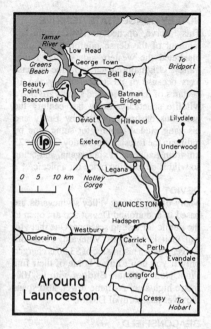

Around
Launceston

variety of native ferns for sale in the whole state.

The fernery, tearooms and gallery were built from wattle and pine. You can sit in the tearooms, enjoy freshly made scones and take in the view of Drys Bluff, which at 1297 metres is the highest peak in the Great Western Tiers. The fernery and tearooms are open from Wednesday to Sunday between 11 am and 5 pm but are closed during July. Liffey is 34 km south of Carrick, via Bracknell, and is a good day trip from Launceston.

EVANDALE (population 600)

Evandale, 19 km south of Launceston in the South Esk Valley, is another National-Trust-classified town. Many of its 19th-century buildings are in excellent condition. In keeping with its olde-worlde atmosphere, Evandale hosts a Penny Farthing Championships in February each year, which attracts national and international competitors.

Eight km south of Evandale is the National Trust property of **Clarendon**, which was completed in 1838 and is one of the grandest Georgian mansions in Australia. The house and its formal gardens are open daily from 10 am to 5 pm (closing an hour earlier in June, July and August) and admission is $4.

The *Clarendon Arms Hotel* (☎ (003) 91 8181), at 11 Russell St, has been licensed since 1847 and is a good place to stay. Singles/doubles with a cooked breakfast cost $30/40 and there are some interesting murals in the hallway depicting the area's history. The locals may encourage you to see if you can spot the well-concealed rabbit in the stagecoach mural; have a go, it really is there!

LONGFORD (population 2000)

Longford, also a National-Trust-classified town, is 27 km from Launceston, in the rich pastoral area watered by the South Esk and Macquarie rivers.

One of the best ways to explore this historic town is to follow the National Trust's *Longford Walkabout* brochure which will take you past many colonial buildings such as **Christ Church**, **Jessen Lodge** and **Noake's Cottages**.

If you want to stay overnight, the *Riverside Caravan Park* (☎ (003) 91 1470), on the banks of the Macquarie River, has tent sites and on-site vans.

The **Longford Wildlife Park**, on Pateena Rd, about 14 km from the town, provides a permanent conservation area for native Tasmanian flora & fauna. The 70 hectares of bush and pasture has kangaroos, wallabies, echidnas, Cape Barren geese, wild ducks and native birds. It's open Tuesdays to Thursdays and at the weekends from 10 am to 5 pm; admission is $4.

About eight km from Longford is the historic town of **Perth**, which has a number of noteworthy buildings. The distinctive octagonal Baptist Tabernacle, in Clarence St, was built in 1889 and is definitely well worth a look.

Tamar Valley

The Tamar River separates the east and west Tamar districts and links Launceston with its ocean port of Bell Bay. Crossing the river near Deviot is Batman Bridge, the only bridge on the lower reaches of the Tamar. The river is tidal for the 64 km to Launceston and wends its way through some lovely orchards, pastures, forests and vineyards. Black swans are seen here.

The Tamar Valley and nearby Pipers River are among Tasmania's main wine-producing areas and the tasty, dry premium wines produced here are starting to achieve world recognition.

European history of the region dates from 1798 when Bass and Flinders discovered the estuary. The valley then slowly developed, first as a port of call for sailors and sealers from the Bass Strait islands and then as a sanctuary for some of the desperate characters who took to the bush during the convict days.

In the late 1870s gold was discovered at Cabbage Tree Hill, now Beaconsfield, and the fortunes of the valley took a new turn. The region boomed and for a time Cabbage Tree Hill was the third largest town in Tasmania, with over six million dollars worth of gold being extracted before water seepage forced the mines to close in 1914.

Getting There & Away

On weekdays Tamar Valley Coaches (☎ (003) 34 0828) has at least three buses a day running up and down the West Tamar Valley, but there are no services at the weekends. A one-way ticket to Beaconsfield costs $4.80.

On most weekdays, and once a day on weekends, Redline has four buses a day that run up the East Tamar Valley between Launceston and George Town. The RoadCat bus also runs between Launceston and George Town, servicing all *SeaCat* departures and arrivals.

NOTLEY GORGE STATE RESERVE

This reserve, opened in 1940, is the last remnant of the dense rainforest that once blanketed the western side of the Tamar Valley. Originally saved from the settlers' axes because of its inaccessibility, the 10 hectares of ferns, trees and shrubs are also a wildlife sanctuary. Early last century the notorious bushranger Matthew Brady and his gang eluded capture for some time by hiding in the forests here. Notley Gorge is 23 km from Launceston via Legana, and being so wild is an exciting place for a picnic.

DEVIOT

Many of the Tamar Valley's vineyards are based in and around Deviot and are open to the public for tasting sessions. One that you can visit is Marion's Vineyard, Foreshore Drive, where a tasting fee of $3.50 is charged only if you don't buy a bottle of their fine Pinot Noir. **Batman Bridge**, with its 100-metre-high steel A-frame tower, also spans the river just north of Deviot.

BEACONSFIELD

The once-thriving gold-mining town of Beaconsfield is still dominated by the ruins of its three original mine buildings. One of these houses is the **Grubb Shaft Museum** complex, which is open daily from 10 am to 4 pm ($1.50). It has interesting displays of local memorabilia, and a reconstruction of a miner's cottage and old school. Beaconsfield Gold Mines Ltd has opened up the old Hart shaft next to the museum, and with today's technology overcoming the water seepage problem is hoping to strike some of the town's still plentiful gold reserves.

Further north is picturesque **Beauty Point** and, at the mouth of the Tamar River, the holiday and fishing resorts of **Greens Beach** and **Kelso** where there are good beaches and caravan parks.

LOW HEAD

It is notoriously difficult to navigate up the Tamar River, and the **Pilot Station** at Low Head, on the eastern shore, guides vessels safely through the waters. This convict-built station, dating from 1835, is the oldest in Australia and houses an interesting **maritime museum**, and a good cafe which is open daily. There are several navigational lead lights around town which date from 1881, and on Tuesdays and Thursdays, the **lighthouse** (built in 1888) can be inspected. For good surf, try **East Beach**, on Bass Strait, or there is safe swimming at **Lagoon Bay**, on the river.

Beach Pines Holiday Park (☎ (003) 82 2602) is right by the sea and has chalets for $53 a double, and camp sites for $5. The owners send a car to meet all *SeaCat* arrivals in George Town.

GEORGE TOWN (population 5600)

Before the age of the *SeaCat*, George Town was best known as the site where Colonel Paterson landed in 1804, leading to the settlement of northern Tasmania.

The *SeaCat* terminal is just south of town, and because the RoadCat is waiting to whisk you off to Launceston or Hobart on arrival, this is about all many people actually see of this small town. There are, however, some interesting attractions in George Town and the surrounding area.

On Cimitiere St, the **Grove** is a lovely Georgian stone residence dating from the 1830s which has been classified by the National Trust. It's open daily from 10 am to 5 pm and entry costs $2.50. Refreshments are available and lunch is served by staff in period costume.

The **Old Watch House** on Macquarie St dates from 1843 and has been turned into a museum; it's open on weekdays from 8 am to 5 pm and it costs nothing to look around. Also of interest is the **St Mary Magdalen Anglican Church** on Anne St.

Places to Stay

Gray's Hotel (☎ (003) 82 2655), at 77 Macquarie St, costs $70 a double and the *Pier Hotel Motel* (☎ (003) 82 1300), at 3 Elizabeth St, has singles from $30. A new YHA hostel opened in 1992; it's at 4 Elizabeth St

(☎ (003) 82 1399) and has beds for $12 ($15 nonmembers).

During the summer months, the *Furneaux Explorer* (☎ (003) 56 1699) is moored at the yacht club, opposite the *SeaCat* terminal, and does B&B for $25.

HILLWOOD

Further south is the attractive rural area of Hillwood, where from November to April you can pick your own strawberries, raspberries and apples and sample some Tasmanian fruit wines at the **Hillwood Strawberry Farm**. The village is also noted for its fishing and lovely river views.

LILYDALE

The small town of Lilydale, 27 km from Launceston, stands at the foot of Mt Arthur and is a convenient base for bushwalkers heading for the mountain or other scenic trails in the area. Three km from the town is the **Lilydale Falls Reserve** which has camping facilities and two easily accessible waterfalls. At the nearby town of Lalla, there's a **Rhododendron Reserve** which is spectacular in season.

North-Central

Between the northern coastal strip and the Great Western Tiers (which rise up to Tasmania's central plateau), there are some interesting towns and scenic spots. The Bass Highway continues west from Launceston to Deloraine, on the edge of the north-west region.

Getting There & Away

Redline has daily buses from Launceston, through Westbury and Deloraine to Smithton, as well as a service from Deloraine to Mole Creek; Hobart Coaches has services between Hobart, Launceston, Deloraine and Burnie; while Invicta buses run between Launceston, Devonport, Sheffield, Lake St Clair and Cradle Mountain.

WESTBURY (population 1200)

The historic town of Westbury, 28 km west of Launceston, is best known for its **White House**, a National-Trust-managed property built in 1841. The house features colonial furnishings and a collection of 19th-century toys, and is open from 10 am to 4 pm on Tuesdays, Thursdays and weekends; entry costs $4.

The **Westbury Gemstone, Mineral & Mural Display**, on the Bass Highway, is open daily from 9.30 am to 4.30 pm and costs $2. Next door is **Pearn's Steam World** which is open from 9 am to 4.30 pm; it costs $3 to inspect a wide range of steam engines.

DELORAINE (population 1920)

Deloraine is Tasmania's largest inland town, and with its lovely riverside picnic area, superb setting at the foot of the Great Western Tiers and good amenities, makes a great base from which to explore the surrounding area. Being so close to the Cradle Mountain-Lake St Clair area, and even closer to a number of impressive waterfalls and shorter walking tracks, Deloraine is fast becoming a major bushwalking centre. You'll find a Visitor Information Centre at 29 West Church St.

The town itself has a lot of charm, as many of its Georgian and Victorian buildings have been faithfully restored. Places of interest include the **Folk Museum, St Mark's Church of England**, and **Bonney's Inn**, which serves lunches and Devonshire teas. Two km out of town is the **Bowerbank Mill** which is classified by the National Trust. Although closed to the public, it's still worth a look from the outside.

Places to Stay & Eat

The *Highview Lodge Youth Hostel* (☎ (003) 62 2996), perched on the hillside at 8 Blake St, has magnificent views of the Great Western Tiers and costs $9 a night. The managers are experienced bushwalkers and organise very reasonably priced and well-equipped trips to Cradle Mountain, the Walls of Jerusalem and other destinations. The

hostel also offers bush transport, and rents mountain or touring bikes to guests. This hostel receives excellent reports from many travellers.

Kev's Kumphy Korner (☎ (003) 62 3408) is a new backpackers' hostel at 24 Bass Highway. It's clean and modern and costs $10 a night. Almost opposite is the *Bush Inn* (☎ (003) 62 2365), which also offers good backpackers' accommodation at $10 a night ($13 with breakfast).

The *Deloraine Hotel* (☎ (003) 62 2022), near the river on the main street, is a beautiful old-fashioned hotel with singles/doubles for $30/40 including a cooked breakfast. There is also a camping ground at West Parade.

One of the best places to eat in Deloraine is *Reuben's Restaurant*, on the main street, which is open daily from 8 am onwards. The atmosphere is relaxed and the cooking, whether you order a filling home-made soup for $4 or a more expensive meal, is delicious. The manager is a real character and enjoys the company of travellers.

Getting There & Away

See under Getting There & Away at the beginning of the North-Central section. Redline's agent in Deloraine is the visitor information centre at 29 West Church St; the Hobart Coaches agent is Sam's Supermarket at 1 Emu Bay Rd; and Invicta's agent is Sullivans Restaurant at 17 West Parade.

MOLE CREEK (population 360)

West of Deloraine is Mole Creek, where you'll find spectacular limestone caves, leatherwood honey and one of Tasmania's best wildlife parks.

Marakoopa Cave, from the Aboriginal word meaning 'handsome', is a wet cave 14 km from Mole Creek which features an incredible glow-worm display. In summer, tours leave at 10, 11.15 am, 2.30 and 4 pm and cost $6. **King Solomon Cave** is a dry cave with amazing calcite crystals that reflect light. In summer, tours leave at 10.30, 11.30 am, 12.30, 2, 3 and 4 pm and also cost $6. If you're visiting in winter, ring the ranger (☎ (003) 63 1245) to find out the tour times.

The leatherwood tree only grows in the damp western part of Tasmania, so honey made from its flower is unique to this state. From January to April, when the honey is being extracted, you can visit the **Stevens Leatherwood Honey Factory** and learn all about this fascinating industry. The factory is open during weekdays from 8 am to 4 pm, and admission is free.

Two km beyond Chudleigh, on the way to Mole Creek, is the **Tasmanian Wildlife Park & Koala Village** which is worth a visit. It's open daily from 9 am to 5 pm, and entry costs $6.50.

SHEFFIELD (population 950)

These days, Sheffield is either referred to as 'the town of murals' or 'the outdoor art gallery'. Since 1986, 23 murals depicting the history of the area have been painted in and around this little town, and these have become a major tourist attraction. At the **Diversity Murals Theatrette**, on the main street, you can see an interesting documentary explaining the history and meaning of the individual paintings. The theatrette is open all day from Monday to Saturday, and every Sunday afternoon; entry costs $1.50.

The scenery around Sheffield is also impressive, with **Mt Roland** (1234 metres) dominating the peaceful farmlands, thick forests, and rivers brimming with fish. Nearby is beautiful **Lake Barrington**, part of the Mersey-Forth hydroelectricity scheme, which is a major rowing venue and state recreation reserve.

Places to Stay

Paradise Cottage (☎ (004) 91 1613), owned by the Diversity Theatrette, and the *Carinya Host Farm* (☎ (004) 91 1593), on Staverton Rd, Roland, each cost $12.50 a night. Both are great out-of-the-way places to stay, and, if you ring from town, will come and pick you up. At 14 Main Rd, a little closer to town, is the new *Sheffield Hostel* (☎ (004) 91 1769) which costs $9 a night.

DEVONPORT (population 21,500)

Nestled behind the dramatic lighthouse-topped Mersey Bluff, Devonport is the terminal for the *Abel Tasman*, the vehicular ferry between Victoria and Tasmania.

The Bluff Lighthouse was built in 1889 to direct the colony's rapidly growing sea traffic, and its light can be seen from up to 27 km out to sea. Today, the port is still very important and handles much of the export produce from the rich agricultural areas around Devonport.

Devonport tries hard to attract tourists but its visitors are usually arriving or departing rather than actually staying. Indeed, the city is often referred to as the 'gateway to Tasmania'.

Information

The Tasmanian Travel Centres at 18 Rooke St (☎ (004) 24 1526) in the city centre and at the *Abel Tasman* ferry terminal in East Devonport, are not terribly helpful.

For any information about Devonport and Tasmania in general, head for the Back-packers' Barn (☎ (004) 24 3628) at 12 Edward St. The Barn is open daily from 8 am to 6 pm, and the staff can arrange transport, car rental, help organise itineraries or look after your backpack. There's a cafe, an excellent bushwalking shop, and a rest room with showers which travellers can use for $3 a day.

The Devonport Showcase, at 5 Best St, also has a complete range of tourist information with displays and workshop demonstrations of arts & crafts. The centre opens daily at 9 am, half an earlier when the ferry arrives, and closes at 5 pm. The Wilderness Shop is at 27 Stewart St.

Tiagarra

The Tasmanian Aboriginal Culture & Art Centre is at Mersey Bluff, on the road to the lighthouse. It's known as Tiagarra, which is the Tasmanian Aboriginal word for 'keep', and was set up to preserve the art and culture of the Tasmanian Aborigines. The centre has a rare collection of more than 250 rock

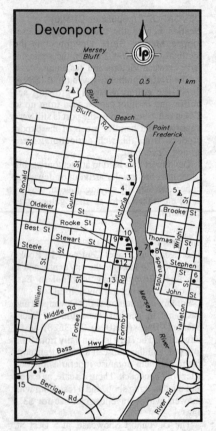

Devonport

1 Tiagarra
2 Mersey Bluff Caravan Park
3 River View Lodge
4 Elimatta Motor Inn
5 Abel Tasman Caravan Park
6 Radclyffe Hall
7 Mersey River Ferry Service
8 TT Line Abel Tasman Ferry Terminal
9 Invicta Office & Hobart
   Coaches Depot
10 Devonport Showcase
11 Post Office
12 Tasmanian Travel Centre
13 Wenvoe Heights
14 Home Hill
15 MacWright House Youth Hostel

ing museum. It's open daily from 10 am to 5 pm, and admission is $2.

The **Don River Railway & Museum**, out of town on the Bass Highway towards Ulverstone, features a collection of steam locomotives and passenger carriages, and you can take a ride on a vintage train along the banks of the Don River. It's open daily from 11 am to 4 pm and entry costs $6.

Other Attractions

The **Devonport Gallery & Art Centre**, at 45-47 Stewart St, is open from 10 am to 4.30 pm Tuesday to Friday and on Saturday morning and Sunday afternoon.

At 77 Middle Rd, not far from the youth hostel, is **Home Hill**, which used to be the residence of Joseph and Dame Enid Lyons. The house was built by them in 1916 and is now administered by the National Trust. Joseph Lyons is the only Australian to have been both the premier of his state and prime minister of Australia, and Dame Enid Lyons was the first woman to become a member of the House of Representatives. Home Hill is open Tuesday to Thursday and on weekends from 2 to 4 pm; admission is $4.

Organised Tours

Most of the tours operating out of Devonport are to Tasmania's wilderness areas and they vary from one-day trips to four-day tours.

engravings, and is open daily from 9 am to 4.30 pm; it's well worth the $2 admission fee.

Museums

The **Tasmanian Maritime & Folk Museum**, at 47 Victoria Parade, has a display of model sailing ships based on the vessels which visited Tasmania in the early days. It's open Tuesday to Sunday from 2 to 4 pm and admission is $1.

Taswegia, in the lovely old building at 56-57 Formby Rd, is a commercial printing house with a very interesting historic print-

The two main operators are Invicta's Tasmanian Wildnerness Transport and Maxwell's Charter Tour Coach & Taxi Service, whose agent is the Backpackers' Barn.

Places to Stay

Hostels *MacWright House* (☎ (004) 24 5696), 400 metres past Home Hill, is Devonport's youth hostel and costs $9 a night. It's a 40-minute walk from the town centre or else an Invicta bus can drop you off from the ferry terminal or airport.

At 139 Tarleton St, East Devonport, *Radclyffe Hall* (☎ (004) 27 9219) advertises itself as providing accommodation for women but, although women are given priority, men are permitted to stay if there's room. This small hostel has a cosy feel, and costs $14 a night in a dorm or $15 per person in a twin room.

Guesthouses & Hotels *River View Lodge* (☎ (004) 24 7357), at 18 Victoria Parade, has a friendly atmosphere and costs $30/40 for singles/doubles, including an excellent cooked breakfast; it's deservedly popular with travellers.

Wenvoe Heights (☎ (004) 24 1719), at 44 McFie St, is a beautiful two-storey Federation brick building. It has been completely renovated and costs $35.20/48.40 with a cooked breakfast, or slightly more if you take a room with its own facilities.

Two good hotels are the *Alexander Hotel* (☎ (004) 24 2252), at 78 Formby Rd, and the *Hotel Formby* (☎ (004) 24 1601), at 82 Formby Rd; both cost $30/40 with breakfast.

Motels There are quite a number of motels in east and central Devonport. The *Edgewater Motor Inn* (☎ (004) 27 8441), at 2 Thomas St in East Devonport, is not very attractive from the outside, but is close to the ferry terminal and costs $44/49 for singles/doubles. The *Argosy Motor Inn* (☎ (004) 27 8872), on Tarleton St, East Devonport, costs $70 a double.

At 15 Victoria Parade, on the other side of the Mersey, the *Elimatta Motor Inn* (☎ (004) 24 6555) costs $55/60; the rooms in the attached hotel are cheaper.

Camping The *Mersey Bluff Caravan Park* (☎ (004) 24 8655) is 2½ km from town, near Tiagarra. It's very pleasant and there are some good beaches nearby.

East Devonport has two caravan parks for visitors, both of which are close to the beach and have good reputations. The *Abel Tasman Caravan Park* (☎ (004) 27 8794), at 6 Wright St, has camp sites, bunkhouse accommodation for $12, on-site vans for $28 a double and cabins at $38 a double. *Devonport's Vacation Village* (☎ (004) 27 8886), on North Caroline St, has similar prices.

Places to Eat

There are plenty of coffee lounges and takeaways in the mall, but for a good atmosphere and great snacks try *Billy N Damper*, the cafe at the front of the Backpackers' Barn, 12 Edward St. It's open daily from 8 am to 6 pm, and will take party bookings in the evenings. The *Coffee Shop* in the Devonport Showcase is also open daily and is good for a drink or a snack.

Most hotels have good counter meals from around $7; try the *Tamahere* at 34 Best St, the *Alexander* at 78 Formby Rd, or the *Formby* at 82 Formby Rd. In East Devonport, the *Edgewater Hotel*, at 2 Thomas St, has cheap counter meals for around $5.

Devonport has a good selection of moderately priced restaurants. *Bandidos*, at 18-22 King St, is a good Mexican restaurant with an authentic atmosphere where main dishes cost around $11. *Greex*, at 159 Rooke St, has Greek and Lebanese food for around $13 a main dish, and good light-lunch specials for $7. For Italian food, try *Il Mondo Antico* at 142A William St, and for Chinese food, there's the *Silky Apple* at 33 King St. On Sundays the *Old Rectory*, at 71 Wright St, does a good, filling Sunday roast for only $10.

Entertainment

Check the *Advocate* newspaper for

Devonport's entertainment details. The Elimatta Motor Inn, at 15 Victoria Parade, occasionally has weekend bands, and on Wednesday, Friday and Saturday nights, a nightclub called Steps. At the Tamahere Hotel, there's a nightclub called Club One, while City Limits, at 18 King St, is also a popular nightspot.

Getting There & Away

Air For information on domestic flights to and from Devonport, see the Getting There & Away section at the beginning of this chapter.

Bus Redline's agent is the Backpackers' Barn (☎ (004) 24 3628) at 9 Edward St, and its depot is nearby, although all buses also stop at the ferry terminal. Redline has daily buses from Devonport to Hobart ($25.80), Launceston ($10.60), Burnie ($5.60) and Smithton ($9).

The agent for Hobart Coaches is the Invicta office (☎ 008 030 505, toll-free) at 9-11 Best St. Hobart Coaches has daily buses to Hobart and Burnie, and all towns en route.

The majority of Invicta's wilderness services depart daily from Devonport. Most days their buses can take you to Sheffield, Cradle Mountain ($35), Strahan ($50), Zeehan, Derwent Bridge, Lake St Clair ($45) or the Walls of Jerusalem.

If none of the scheduled wilderness services suit your particular needs, then you can charter a minibus from either Invicta or the Backpackers' Barn. For example, a bus from Devonport to Cradle Mountain costs $120 or, if there are five people or more, $30 each. Invicta has scheduled services to Cradle Mountain ($65 return), and also does charters for five times the per-person fare.

Car There are plenty of cheap car rental firms including Range/Rent-A-Bug (☎ (004) 27 9034), at 5 Murray St, East Devonport; and Advance Car Rentals (☎ (004) 24 8885) at the corner of William and Oldaker Sts.

Boat See the Getting There & Away section at the beginning of this chapter for details on

the *Abel Tasman* ferry service between Melbourne and Devonport. The TT Line terminal (☎ (004) 23 0333) is at the Esplanade, East Devonport.

Getting Around

Invicta runs an airport shuttle bus which services all flight departures and arrivals, and picks you up from or drops you off where you're staying ($5).

Invicta runs exactly the same shuttle service to and from the *Abel Tasman* ($3), while Redline has return trips between Hobart and the *Abel Tasman* via Launceston.

South of Best St, local buses are run by Invicta, while north of Best St and East Devonport is covered by Hobart Coaches. If this is confusing don't worry; most places in Devonport are within easy walking distance.

There's also a Mersey River ferry service linking central Devonport with East Devonport, which operates seven days a week. The one-way adult fare is $1 and bicycles cost 40c.

You can hire bicycles at the Backpackers' Barn or from Hire a Bike (☎ (004) 24 3889).

North-West

Tasmania's magnificent north-west coast is a land as rich in history as it is diverse in scenery. Its story goes back 37,000 years to a time when giant kangaroos and wombats roamed the area. Aboriginal tribes once took shelter in the caves along the coast, leaving a legacy of rock engravings and middens.

Europeans quickly realised the potential of the region and settlers moved further and further west, building towns along the coast and inland on the many rivers. The area was soon transformed into a vital part of the young colony's developing economy.

ULVERSTONE (population 9400)

Ulverstone, at the mouth of the Leven River, is a pleasant town with some fine beaches

Top: Ross Bridge, Ross, Tas (CH)
Bottom: Cataract Gorge, Launceston, Tas (CH)

Top: Pieman River, Tas (TT)
Left: Constitution Dock, Hobart, Tas (PS)
Right: Van Diemens Land Company Store, Stanley, Tas (PT)

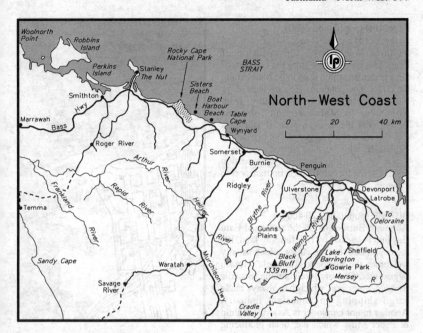

North-West Coast

and good amenities; it's a good base for exploring the surrounding area.

Just 30 km south is the **Gunns Plains Cave Reserve**; daily guided tours of the spectacular wet cave leave hourly from 10 am to 4 pm and cost \$4. Nearby is **Leven Canyon**, a magnificent gorge with a number of walking tracks. If you have your own transport, you can combine visits to both attractions in a 105-km round trip from Ulverstone through Sprent, Central Castra and Nietta to Leven Canyon, near Black Bluff (1339 metres), and back via Preston, Gunns Plains and North Motton.

Places to Stay & Eat
There's plenty of accommodation in Ulverstone, but for a great location try the *Ocean View Guest House* (☎ (004) 25 5401) at 1 Victoria St, 100 metres from the beach. It's a lovely old house where singles/doubles with a continental breakfast cost \$35/55. At

42 Reibey St, in the centre of town, there's the Federation-style *Furner's Hotel* (☎ (004) 25 1488) which costs \$35/50.

There are also plenty of camping grounds, including the *Apex Caravan Park* (☎ (004) 25 2935) on Queen St and the *Ulverstone Caravan Park* (☎ (004) 25 2624) on Water St, which also has on-site vans and units.

Pedro the Fisherman, down by the wharf, does extremely cheap but filling takeaway fish & chips or seafood & chips – and if you can't finish the packet there are plenty of obliging seagulls around!

If you're driving between Ulverstone and Penguin the old Bass Highway runs closer to the coast than the new one, and offers some fine views of three small islands known as the **Three Sisters**.

Getting There & Away
See the Burnie Getting There & Away section for details of transport to and from Ulverstone.

PENGUIN (population 2600)

At the foot of the Dial Range State Forest and on three lovely bays, the township of Penguin takes its name from the colonies of fairy penguins which used to be found along the coast. The penguins are rare these days but can be seen, if you're lucky, from November to March around Johnsons Beach, near the caravan park. If you miss out, there's a much larger model one on the Esplanade, which can be viewed any time.

See the Getting There & Away section under Burnie for information on transport to Penguin.

BURNIE (population 20,400)

Although Burnie sits on the shores of Emu Bay and is backed by rich farming land, it's factory smoke, not the views, which usually welcomes the visitor to Tasmania's fourth largest city. One of Burnie's main assets is its deep-water port which has always made cargo shipping an important industry. Another major employer is Associated Pulp & Paper Mills which has been producing paper in Burnie since 1938.

The town (named after William Burnie, a director of the Van Diemen's Land Company) started life quietly until the discovery of tin at Mt Bischoff in Waratah. In 1878, the Van Diemen's Land Company opened a wooden tramway between the mine at Waratah and the port of Burnie. This was the humble beginning of the important Emu Bay Railway which, in the 1900s, linked the port of Burnie to the rich silver fields of Zeehan and Rosebery. The Emu Bay Railway, which travels through some wild and impressive country, still operates today but, unfortunately, does not carry passengers.

The Tasmanian Travel Centre (☎ (004) 31 8111), at 48 Cattley St, is very helpful and a good source of information on Tasmania's north-west.

Things to See & Do

The **Burnie Pioneer Village Museum**, on High St, next to the Civic Plaza, has an

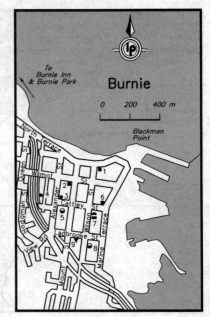

1   Beach Hotel
2   Club Hotel
3   Travel Centre
4   Pioneer Village Museum
5   Hobart Coaches Depot
6   Bay View Hotel
7   Post Office
8   Redline Depot
9   The Amourette Restaurant

authentic blacksmith's shop, printer, and boot shop. This impressive museum is open from 9 am to 5 pm Mondays to Fridays, and from 1.30 to 5 pm on weekends; admission is $3.

Burnie Park is quite pleasant and features an animal sanctuary and the oldest building in town, the Burnie Inn. The Inn was built in 1847 and moved from its original site to the park in 1973. It's classified by the National Trust and is open at the weekends.

From Monday to Thursday, at 2 pm, you can take a free tour of the Associated Pulp & Paper Mills complex. On weekdays you can also visit the Lactos cheese factory, on Old Surrey Rd, where you can taste and purchase the products. The **Burnie Regional Art Gallery**, in Wilmot St, is open daily and is also worth a look.

There are a number of waterfalls and viewpoints in the Burnie area including **Roundhill Lookout** and **Fern Glade**, just three km from the centre, and the impressive **Guide Falls** at Ridgley, 16 km away.

Places to Stay

There's no budget accommodation in Burnie and the nearest youth hostel is at Wynyard, 19 km away.

Reasonably priced hotels include the *Regent* (☎ (004) 31 1933), at 26 North Terrace, which costs $20/35 for singles/doubles; the *Club Hotel* (☎ (004) 31 2244), at 14 Mount St, which costs $25/45 with a continental breakfast; and the *Bay View Hotel* (☎ (004) 31 2711), 14 Marine Terrace, which costs $34/40 with a continental breakfast.

At Cooee, three km west of Burnie on the Bass Highway, the *Treasure Island Caravan Park* (☎ (004) 31 1925) has tent sites, cabins and on-site vans.

Places to Eat

There are plenty of cafes along Mount, Wilmot, Wilson and Cattley Sts. For cheap lunches try the *Zodiac* in Cattley St or the *Napoli* cafe above Fitzgerald's department store on the corner of Wilson and Cattley Sts.

Most hotels have reasonably priced counter meals from Monday to Saturday. The *Beach Hotel* at 1 Wilson St, on the waterfront, always has a good spread.

Ladbroke St, between Mount and Wilson Sts, is the area to go when you're hungry. The *Amourette Restaurant* (☎ (004) 31 5023) specialises in delicious continental-style cooking and has a changing menu with main meals from around $11 – it's a good idea to book. Next door is the *Kasbah Pizza Hut* and opposite is the *Li Yin* which has good Chinese food and an all-you-can-eat three-course meal for $12.

Not far away, at 104 Wilson St, the *Burnie Steak House* has meals for around $15. The *Rialto Gallery Restaurant*, at 46 Wilmot St, serves good Italian food and is open for dinner on Sunday nights.

Entertainment

Check the *Advocate* newspaper for entertainment listings. On Friday and Saturday nights there are discos at the Bay View Hotel and the Club Hotel. On Friday nights, the Beach Hotel is a popular place for a drink.

Getting There & Away

Air The nearest airport is at Wynyard, 20 km from Burnie. North West Travel (☎ (004) 31 2166), on the corner of Wilmot and Mount Sts in Burnie, is the agent for Kendell and Ansett Airlines.

Bus Redline has daily services to and from Smithton, Wynyard, Devonport, Launceston and Hobart. During the week, two of these services make the detour to Stanley. Redline also has at least one service between Burnie and Strahan via Queenstown ($25.60). The Redline agent in Burnie is at 117 Wilson St.

Hobart Coaches has daily services between Hobart and Burnie via Launceston, Deloraine, Devonport, Ulverstone and Penguin. Its agent in Burnie is the Rivoli Cafe at 54 Cattley St.

During the week, Metro Burnie (☎ (004) 31 3822), at 30 Strahan St, also has regular buses to Ulverstone, Penguin and Wynyard which depart from various stops in Cattley St.

WYNYARD (population 4600)

Sheltered by the impressive Table Cape and geologically fascinating Fossil Bluff, Wynyard sits both on the seafront and on the banks of the Inglis River. The town is surrounded by beautiful patchwork farmland which is best appreciated by flying into Wynyard Airport.

Although there's not much to see in the

town itself, Wynyard is a good base from which to explore the many attractions in the area. Good sources of tourist information include the Council Chambers on Saunders St, and most hotels or restaurants.

Places to Stay

The *Wynyard Youth Hostel* (☎ (004) 42 2013) is at 36 Dodgin St, one block south of the main shopping centre, and costs $9 a night. If you've arrived by air, take the airport road and turn right into Dodgin St – it's only a five-minute walk. The *Federal Hotel* (☎ (004) 42 2056) at 82 Goldie St, in the middle of town, costs $30/50 for singles/doubles with a cooked breakfast and also has good counter meals seven days a week.

Close to town, on the Esplanade, is the *Municipal Caravan Park* (☎ (004) 42 2740). East of Wynyard, on the scenic road to Burnie, the *Leisure Ville Caravan Park* (☎ (004) 42 2291) has camp sites, cabins and on-site vans.

Getting There & Away

For information on domestic flights to and from Wynyard, see the Getting There & Away section at the beginning of this chapter.

See the Burnie section for details on Redline and Metro Burnie bus services to Wynyard. The Redline agent is the BP service station next to the post office, and Metro Burnie buses depart from outside the Vincent de Paul shop in Jackson St.

AROUND WYNYARD

Seven km from Wynyard, beyond the golf course, is **Fossil Bluff**, where the oldest marsupial fossil found in Australia was unearthed. The soft sandstone here features numerous shell fossils deposited when the level of Bass Strait was much higher.

Other attractions in the area include the unforgettable views from **Table Cape** and its lighthouse. At **Boat Harbour Beach**, 14 km from Wynyard, there's a beautiful bay with white sand and crystal blue water – a lovely spot for rock-pool exploring and snorkelling.

If you want to stay the night, there's a caravan park, and motel-style accommodation.

Nearby, in the **Rocky Cape National Park**, Sisters Beach is an eight-km expanse of glistening white sand, safe swimming and good fishing. Also in the park is the 10-hectare **Birdland Native Gardens** which has information on more than 60 species of birds native to the area. You can also visit a number of waterfalls, including **Detention Falls**, three km south of Myalla, and **Dip Falls**, near Mawbanna. The **Hellyer Gorge**, 30 km from Wynyard on the Murchison Highway, has a lovely picnic area amid thick myrtle forest, and is worth a visit.

Unless you have your own transport, you will have to hitchhike to get to most of these places. Redline Coaches will drop you at the turn-off to Boat Harbour (three km) and Sisters Beach (nine km).

STANLEY (population 600)

Nestled at the foot of the extraordinary Circular Head (better known as the Nut), Stanley is a very appealing historical village which has changed little since its early days. In 1826 it became the headquarters of the London-based Van Diemen's Land Company which was granted a charter to settle and cultivate the Circular Head region.

The area really prospered when large quantities of mutton, beef and potatoes were shipped to Victoria's gold fields, and it continued to do so when settlers discovered the rich dairying land behind Sisters Hills and the tin reserves at Mt Bischoff.

Today, Stanley is a well-to-do fishing village with many historical buildings and great seascapes. To better appreciate Stanley's charm, pick up a walking tour map from De Jonge's Souvenirs or the Discovery Centre, both on Church St. The Plough Inn also has tourist information and rents bicycles for local use.

The Nut

This striking 152-metre basalt formation, thought to be 12½ million years old, can be seen for many km around Stanley. It's a hard 10-minute climb to the top, but the view is definitely worth it. For the less energetic, a chairlift operates from 9.30 am to 4.30 pm and costs $3.50.

Other Attractions

The old bluestone building on the seafront is the **Van Diemen's Land Company Store** which was designed by John Lee Archer, Tasmania's famous colonial architect, and dates from 1844. The company's actual headquarters were at Highfield, to the east of Stanley, and these are currently being restored.

Also near the wharf is a particularly fine old bluestone building which used to be a grain store and was built in 1843 from stones brought to Stanley as ship's ballast.

The **Plough Inn** (1840), on Church St, has been fully restored and furnished with period furniture. It's open daily and entry costs $3. Next door is a little folk museum called the **Discovery Centre** which is open daily from 10 am to 4.30 pm; entry costs $2.

Other buildings of historical interest include **Lyons Cottage**, on Church St, which was the birthplace of former Prime Minister Joseph Lyons and is open from 10 am to 4 pm; the **Union Hotel**, also on Church St, which dates from 1849; and the **Presbyterian Church** which was probably Australia's first prefabricated building, bought in England and transported to Stanley in 1853.

Places to Stay

Stanley has a wide selection of accommodation. The *Stanley Youth Hostel* (☎ (004) 58 1266) is near the beach in the *Wharf Rd Caravan Park* and costs $9 a night. The caravan park has tent sites and on-site vans and cabins.

Pol & Pen (☎ (004) 58 1334) are a pair of two-bedroom, self-contained cottages, which are very good value at $35 a double and $6 for each additional person. The *Union Hotel* (☎ (004) 58 1161), on Church St, has singles/doubles for $25/35. Also on Church St, *Touchwood Cottage* (☎ (004) 58 1348),

is a lovely colonial guesthouse which costs $40/55, including a cooked breakfast.

Places to Eat

Julie & Patrick's Seafood Restaurant is next door to Hursey Seafoods (where massive live crays, crabs and fish are kept in tanks in the shop). Both places are owned by the same people which means that the food served in the restaurant couldn't be fresher.

Sullivans, a licensed restaurant at 25 Church St, is open daily and serves light lunches, teas and dinner. At the Nut there is the *Nut Shop Tearooms*, and the *Union Hotel* has quite good counter meals.

Getting There & Away

Redline has two services a day on weekdays which run from Hobart to Smithton via Stanley, and three running via Stanley in the other direction. The Redline agent is the BP service station on the corner of Wharf Rd and Marine Esplanade.

AROUND STANLEY

Smithton, 22 km from Stanley, serves one of Tasmania's greatest forestry areas and is also the administrative centre for Circular Head. There's not much to see or do in the town itself, but the town's airport makes it an arrival point for some light aircraft flights from the mainland.

Woolnorth, on the north-western tip of Tasmania, near Cape Grim, is a 220-sq-km cattle and sheep property which is the only remaining holding of the Van Diemen's Land Company. You can only go there if you are part of a tour, and coaches to Woolnorth and the magnificent coastline in the area leave every even day at 9.30 am from the Bridge Hotel in Smithton. The tour, which includes a good lunch, costs $55 and can be booked by phone (☎ (004) 52 2577) or at any Tasmanian Travel Centre.

Allendale Gardens, on the B22 road to Edith Creek, is a good place to walk around or relax; the two-hectare property includes impressive botanical gardens, a rainforest walk, a wild-flower section and a cafe serving Devonshire teas. The centre is open daily from 10 am to 6 pm (closed June and July) and costs $5.

Massive ferns, myrtles, fungi and lichens are all found at **Milkshake Forest Reserve**, 45 km south of Smithton. A little further west of the reserve, set in beautiful rainforest, is tranquil **Lake Chisholm**.

MARRAWAH

Marrawah, at the end of the Bass Highway, is where the wild Indian Ocean occasionally throws up the remains of ships wrecked on the dangerous and rugged west coast. To visit Marrawah, the most westerly town in Tasmania, it is best to have your own vehicle, but from Monday to Saturday you can get a lift on the mail run from Smithton.

This part of the coast was once home to Tasmanian Aborigines and particular areas have been proclaimed reserves to protect the environment and remaining relics, including rock carvings, middens and hut depressions. The main Aboriginal sites are at **Mt Cameron West**, near Green Point, at **West Point** and **Sundown Point**.

The township of Marrawah consists of a hotel and a general store selling petrol and supplies. The hotel has meals, and no accommodation, but there is a very basic camping area at Green Point, two km from Marrawah. This region is good for fishing, camping and bushwalking, or just for getting away from it all. Marrawah's main attraction, however, is its enormous surf and the state's surfing championships are held here every year around Easter.

ARTHUR RIVER

The sleepy town of Arthur River, 14 km south of Marrawah, is mainly a collection of holiday houses for people who come here to fish. There is one kiosk with very basic supplies, no public transport and, apart from a camping area (with no facilities), only one place to stay. The *Arthur River Holiday Units* (☎ (004) 57 1288), on Gardiner St, have singles/doubles for $40/60.

Apart from the fishing, visitors come here to explore the Arthur-Pieman Protected Area and to take a cruise on the Arthur River. The attractions of the Protected Area include magnificent ocean beaches, waterfalls on the Nelson River, Rebecca Lagoon, Temma Harbour, the old mining town of Balfour, the Pieman River and the Norfolk Ranges.

If you are exploring south of Temma Harbour you really need a 4WD and if you are going south of Greens Creek you need to get a permit from the Arthur River Base Office (☎ (004) 57 1225) in Arthur River.

Arthur River Cruise

Paddy and Turk Porteous operate scenic day cruises on the Arthur River (☎ (004) 57 1158) which depart at 10 am and return at 3 pm. You sail up the river, feeding sea eagles on the way, to the confluence of the Arthur and Frankland rivers. Here you have lunch, with billy-tea, in a rainforest clearing which took Turk almost five years to clear. After lunch there is a one-hour guided walking tour through the dense vegetation. The $30 cruise runs most days in summer, but as a minimum of eight people is required it's best to book in advance; you can do this at any Tasmanian Travel Centre.

HELLYER GORGE

It's about 150 km on the Murchison Highway between Somerset, on the north coast, to Zeehan, close to the west coast. Hellyer Gorge is a serene myrtle forest reserve on the banks of the Hellyer River, halfway between Somerset and the turn-off to Waratah, Savage River and Corinna. The highway winds precariously through the impressive gorge, and there are plenty of rest and picnic areas.

The new Guildford Junction Highway, between Hampshire and Guildford, was built to shorten the trip from the north coast to the west, but it's also had the effect of diverting traffic from the peaceful recreational reserve at Hellyer Gorge. The new road follows part of the Emu Bay Railway route and links up with Burnie.

The Mt Bischoff mine, near Waratah, was once the world's richest tin mine, but these days it is the iron ore of Savage River that keeps mining alive in the region.

CORINNA

Corinna, 28 km south-west of Savage River, was once a thriving gold-mining settlement but is now little more than a ghost town. These days it's the scenery and the Pieman River Cruises (☎ (004) 35 7277) that attract the visitors. The cruise takes you through impressive forests of eucalypts, ferns and Huon pines to the Pieman Heads. Costing $25, which includes morning tea, the tours on the MV *Arcadia II* depart daily at 10.30 am and return at 2 pm. It's definitely best to book during the summer months, and if you are staying at the Savage River Motor Inn you can book there.

ROSEBERY (population 2700)

Mining began in Rosebery in 1900 with the completion of the Emu Bay Railway between Burnie and Zeehan, but when the Zeehan lead smelters closed in 1913 operations also shut here. The Electrolytic Zinc Company then bought and reopened the mine in 1936 and it has operated ever since. There's not much to see in Rosebery but if you want to stay overnight, the *Plandome* and *Rosebery* hotels have accommodation, and there's a caravan park.

West Coast

Nature at its most awe-inspiring is the attraction of Tasmania's rugged and magnificent west coast. Formidable mountains, buttongrass plains, ancient rivers, tranquil lakes, dense rainforests and a treacherous coast are all features of this compelling and beautiful region, much of which is now World Heritage area.

Centuries before the arrival of Europeans, this part of Tasmania was home to many of the state's Aborigines, and plenty of archaeological evidence, some of it more than 20,000 years old, has been found of these original inhabitants. Indeed, were it not for its vast mineral reserves and rich stands of

Huon pine, this region would probably have remained the domain of the Aborigines.

Prior to 1932, when the road from Hobart to Queenstown was built, the only way into the area was by sea, through the dangerously narrow Macquarie Harbour to Strahan. Despite such inaccessibility, early European settlement brought explorers, convicts, soldiers, loggers, prospectors, railway gangs and fishermen, while the 20th century has brought outdoor adventurers, naturalists and environmental crusaders.

It was over the wild rivers, beautiful lakes and lonely valleys of Tasmania's south-west that the battles between environmentalists and big business raged. This is the area that saw the flooding of Lake Pedder and the creation of a system of lakes on the upper reaches of the Pieman River to feed massive hydroelectric schemes. It was here, over the proposed damming of the Franklin and Lower Gordon rivers, that the greatest and longest environmental debate in Australia's history, culminating in an 11-week river blockade, took place.

While debate continues on questions of wilderness versus electricity and World Heritage area versus woodchip, nature herself has begun to reclaim what is hers. The rusting railways, abandoned mines and deserted towns of the early west-coast mining days are becoming mere spectres in the regeneration of the bush.

ZEEHAN (population 1750)

In 1882, rich deposits of silver and lead were discovered in the quiet little town of Zeehan and, by the turn of the century, it had become a booming mining centre with a population that peaked at nearly 10,000. In its heyday, Zeehan had 26 hotels and its Gaiety Theatre was the largest in Australia. In 1908, however, the mines began to fail and the town declined. With the reopening of the Renison Tin Mine at Renison Bell in the '70s, the town experienced a revival, but today, with the low price of tin, its future does not look bright.

The road from Zeehan to Strahan (47 km)

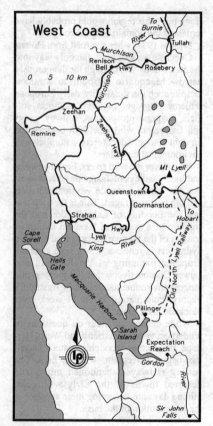

has been upgraded and is a good alternative to the highway route via Queenstown (75 km).

Things to See
Buildings that remain from the early boom days include the once famous **Grand Hotel**, the **Gaiety Theatre**, the **post office**, the **bank** and **St Luke's Church**.

For an excellent insight into the workings of a mine, visit the **West Coast Pioneers' Memorial Museum** on Main St. It's open daily from 8.30 am to 5 pm and is free (donations welcome). The museum also fea-

tures an interesting mineral collection and an exhibit of steam locomotives and carriages used on the early west-coast railways.

Places to Stay
The *Cecil Hotel* (☎ (004) 71 6221) on Main St has singles/doubles for $30/40. The *Treasure Island Caravan Park* (☎ (004) 71 6633) on Hurst St has tent sites, cabins and on-site vans.

Getting There & Away
On most days (except Sundays) there's at least one Redline service from Burnie to Strahan via Zeehan; the return bus travels from Strahan to Devonport via Zeehan. The Redline agent in Zeehan is Maines Milk Bar on Main St. Invicta's Strahan to Devonport service also stops in Zeehan. On weekdays, there's a school bus which departs for Queenstown in the morning and returns to Zeehan in the afternoon.

QUEENSTOWN (population 3700)
The final, winding descent into Queenstown from the Lyell Highway is an unforgettable experience. With deep eroded gullies and naked multicoloured hills, there is no escaping the fact that this is a mining town, and that the destruction of the surrounding area is a direct result of this industry.

In 1881, the discovery of alluvial gold in the Queen River valley first brought prospectors to the area. Two years later, mining began on the rich Mt Lyell deposits, and for nearly a decade miners extracted a few ounces of gold a day and ignored the mountain's rich copper reserves. In 1891, however, the Mt Lyell Mining Company began to concentrate on the copper and it soon became the most profitable mineral on the west coast.

In 1899, the company built a 35-km railway between Queenstown and Strahan to transport copper, and passengers, to the coast. It traversed spectacular terrain (48 bridges were built) and was so steep in some sections that the rack and pinion system had to be used to assist the two steam engines hauling the train.

At the turn of the century, Queenstown had a population of 5051 and was the third largest town in Tasmania. It had 14 hotels, there were 28 mining companies working the Mt Lyell deposits, and 11 furnaces were involved in the smelting process. The Mt Lyell Mining & Railway Company eventually acquired most of the mines or leases, and since 1933 has worked the area without a rival.

After 20 years of mining, the rainforested hills around Queenstown had been stripped bare: three million tonnes of timber had been felled to feed the furnaces. By 1900, uncontrolled pollution from the copper smelters was killing any vegetation that had not already been cut down, and bushfires raged through the hills every summer, fuelled by the sulphur-impregnated soils and dead stumps, until there was no regrowth left at all.

Today, mining is still Queenstown's major industry but there are concerns that the ore deposits may be dwindling. Recently, attempts have been made to reforest parts of Queenstown's famous lunar landscape but, because tourism is another important source of income, and the denudation is exactly what visitors come to see, a question mark hangs over the continuation of such projects.

Information

The RACT, at 18 Orr St, has plenty of tourist brochures and the staff are very helpful. You can also get visitor information at the Galley Museum on the corner of Sticht and Driffield Sts.

Galley Museum

The Galley Museum started life as the Imperial Hotel and was the first brick hotel in Queenstown. The building has since served many purposes, including a period as the single men's quarters for the Mt Lyell Company. The museum features a good collection of old photographs (recording the history of Queenstown and the west coast), as well as a display of early mining equip-

ment, personal effects and household goods from the town's pioneering days. The museum is open from 10 am to 12.30 pm and from 1.30 to 4.30 pm Monday to Friday, and from 1.30 to 4.30 pm on weekends; entry is $2.

Mt Lyell Mine

Mt Lyell Mine Tours (☎ (004) 71 2222) operates from the Western Arts & Crafts Centre on Driffield St and takes groups or individuals on a surface tour of the Mt Lyell Mine and the Mining Museum (1½ hours, $7). From October to April, tours depart daily at 9.15 am, 2.30 and 4.30 pm, and from May to September they leave at 9.15 am and 4 pm. These tours are very interesting and offer a real insight into both early and modern mining processes.

Other Attractions

There are good views from **Spion Kop Lookout**, in the centre of town (follow Bowes St). If you are wondering why the football oval on your left is brown instead of green, Queenstown's footy team is tough – they play on silica, not grass, and this is the only silica oval in the world.

Queenstown has a good *Historic Walk* brochure which guides you around the town from the Galley Museum to Spion Kop Lookout. You can pick up the leaflet and map in any shop or hotel and it is an excellent way to see all the sights.

The **Miner's Siding**, on Driffield St, is a public park featuring a restored ABT steam locomotive and a rock sculpture which tells the history of the Queenstown to Strahan railway.

The Hydro Electric Commission (HEC) is building a dam on the King River, near Crotty, which will be linked to the King Power Station at the junction between the King and Queen rivers. This power development scheme will create a 53-sq-km lake called Lake Durbury, which the HEC hopes will become a major tourist attraction.

Places to Stay & Eat

At 1 Penghana Rd, just over the bridge on

the way to Strahan, is *Mountain View Holiday Lodge* (☎ (004) 71 1163) which is the old single men's quarters for the Mt Lyell Mining Company. The hostel section is pretty basic, but for $8 a night you get your own room and there are cooking facilities. Many of the rooms have been renovated as motel-style units and cost $45 a double.

The *Queenstown Cabin & Tourist Park* (☎ (004) 71 1332), at 17 Grafton St, has bunkhouse accommodation for $17 a double or a space on the floor for $6. There are also on-site vans and cabins.

The *Empire Hotel* (☎ (004) 71 1699), at 2 Orr St, is a lovely old hotel with an imposing staircase classified by the National Trust. Clean and pleasant singles/doubles cost $18/28 and, for a little extra, you can get breakfast. *Hunter's Hotel* (☎ (004) 71 1531), further up Orr St, has exactly the same rates.

The *Mount Lyell Motor Hotel* (☎ (004) 71 1888), at 1 Orr St, has motel suites for $43.50/52.50; the staff are very friendly.

Apart from counter meals, which are pretty good at the *Mount Lyell Motor Inn*, Queenstown has very little to offer in the way of places to eat. On Orr St, *JJ's* has good cakes and light snacks, and nearby there's a chicken shop and a pizza place (which does a great pizza with a thin crusty base).

Getting There & Away

See the Airfares chart in the Getting Around section for an idea of airfares to and from Queenstown.

Redline has daily bus services (Monday to Saturday) between Queenstown and Strahan ($4.80), Hobart ($29.40), Burnie ($25.60) and Devonport. The Redline agent is on Orr St between the TAB and Commonwealth Bank.

If you are hitching, it can be a long wait between vehicles on both the Lyell and Murchison highways, and in winter it gets pretty cold.

When the HEC has completed its King River power development scheme, six km of the Lyell Highway will be relocated because the existing route will have become part of

Lake Burbury. The new highway will be south of the present one and will feature a 340-metre-long bridge across the new lake. When the nearby Anthony power development is complete, a new road will also be built between Queenstown and Tullah, offering a more scenic alternative to the Zeehan Highway.

STRAHAN (population 400)

Strahan, 40 km from Queenstown on Macquarie Harbour, is the only town on this rugged and dangerous coast. Though only a shadow of its former self, the town is rich in convict, logging and mining history.

Treacherous seas, the lack of natural harbours and high rainfall discouraged early settlement of the region until Macquarie Harbour was discovered by sailors searching for the source of the Huon pine that frequently washed up on the southern beaches.

In those days, the area was totally inaccessible by land and very difficult to reach by sea, and in 1821 these dubious assets prompted the establishment of a penal settlement on Sarah Island, in the middle of the harbour. Its main function was to isolate the worst of the colony's convicts and to use their muscle to harvest the huge stands of Huon pine. The convicts worked upriver 12 hours a day, often in leg irons, felling the pines and rafting them back to the island's saw-pits where they were used to build ships and furniture.

With its barbaric treatment of prisoners, Sarah Island became one of Australia's most notorious penal settlements. The most dreaded punishment was confinement on tiny Grummet Island, where up to 40 convicts at a time were held in appalling conditions on what was little more than a windswept rock – for some, death was a welcome release.

Sarah Island appeared in Marcus Clarke's graphic novel about convict life *For the Term of his Natural Life*. In 1834, however, after the establishment of the 'escape-proof' penal settlement at Port Arthur, Sarah Island was abandoned.

As the port for Queenstown, Strahan reached its peak of prosperity with the west-coast mining boom, and the completion of the Mt Lyell Mining Company's railway line in the 1890s. At the turn of the century, it was a bustling centre with a population of 2000. Steamers operated regularly between Strahan and Hobart, Launceston and Melbourne carrying copper, gold, silver, lead, timber and passengers. The closure of many of the west-coast mines and the opening of the Emu Bay Railway from Zeehan to Burnie led to the decline of Strahan as a port.

These days, Strahan is a charming seaside town which draws visitors in droves for cruises on the Gordon River and scenic flights over the area. The council has just approved a large wharf development scheme which, if it goes ahead, will bring some unfortunate changes to this as yet unspoiled fishing town.

Things to See

Probably the finest buildings on the west coast are Strahan's imposing **post office** and **Union Steam Ship Company building**. Next door to the post office is the historic **Customs House** which is open daily from 8 am to 5 pm and has detailed tourist information display boards. It is here that you can get information on Strahan's historic foreshore walk which links West Strahan Beach, the town centre and the old Regatta Point Railway Station.

The **lighthouse** at Cape Sorell, on the south head of the harbour, is the third largest in Tasmania. Opposite the caravan park is a **gemstone & mineral museum**. Strahan's **Hogarth Falls**, in Peoples Park, is definitely worth a look.

Six km from the town is the impressive 33-km **Ocean Beach** where the sunsets have to be seen to be believed. In October, when the birds return from their winter migration, the beach is also a mutton bird rookery.

Twelve km along the upgraded road from Strahan to Zeehan are some spectacular sand dunes, some of them more than 30 metres in height.

Organised Tours

Gordon River Cruise A traditional way of experiencing the indescribable beauty of the Gordon River is on one of the modern, comfortable launches owned by Gordon River Cruises (☎ (004) 71 7317) which operate from Strahan's wharf. Half-day trips operate year-round and, between September and April, there are full-day trips up the river to Expectation Reach. The $55 full-day cruise departs at 9 am, includes lunch and also visits Sarah Island and Hells Gates (the narrow entrance to Macquarie Harbour), returning at 3 pm. The $37 half-day cruise departs at 9 am and returns at 1.30 pm.

Seaplane Tour A highly recommended way to see the river and surrounding World Heritage area is on a seaplane tour with Wilderness Air (☎ (004) 71 7280). The planes take off from Strahan's wharf every 1½ hours from 9 am onwards and fly up the river to Sir John Falls, where they land so that you can take a walk in the rainforest, before flying back via Sarah Island, Cape Sorell, Hells Gates and Ocean Beach. The 80-minute flight is well worth the $90. Longer and shorter seaplane trips are available, and groups can even charter the planes and plan their own itinerary.

Jet-Boat Ride Wild Rivers Jet (☎ (004) 71 7174), also at the Wilderness Air office on the wharf, operates 40-minute jet-boat rides up the King River for $35.

Places to Stay

Although Strahan has a range of accommodation, places are often full, so it's best to book ahead.

At $10 a night, the *Strahan Youth Hostel* (☎ (004) 71 7255) in Harvey St is the cheapest accommodation in town. It also has two on-site vans which cost $30 a double.

Three km from town, on Ocean Beach Rd, is the historic *Strahan Lodge* (☎ (004) 71 7142) where singles/doubles with a continental breakfast cost $25/35. Unless you have your own transport, it may be a bit inconvenient.

Hamer's Hotel (☎ (004) 71 7191) is opposite the wharf right in the middle of town and has passable rooms for $25/50, including a continental breakfast.

On Ocean Beach Rd, *West Strahan Caravan Park* (☎ (004) 71 7239) charges $7 for a double tent site.

If you get stuck for somewhere to stay then you can try ringing Mrs Abel (☎ (004) 71 7271); she does B&B for $15/30. Or there's Mrs Giles (☎ (004) 71 7227), who has a home on the beach which she rents for $40.

Places to Eat

At the magnificent *Franklin Manor* (☎ (004) 71 7311) you can get an excellent three-course meal for $24 but it's best to book. *Hamer's Hotel*, *Regatta Point Tavern*, on the Esplanade, and the *Strahan Inn*, Jolly St, all have good meals. The *Harbour Cafe* has takeaways, but it's pleasant to eat on the premises as there are great views across the wharf.

Getting There & Away

See the Getting Around section at the beginning of this chapter for information on flights to Strahan.

Redline has daily (except Sunday) services from Hobart ($34.20), Burnie ($30.40), Devonport and Launceston ($49.40). The Redline agent is the newsagent on the main street.

Invicta also runs buses from Hobart and Devonport to Strahan; its agent is the Harbour Cafe on the main street.

FRANKLIN-GORDON WILD RIVERS NATIONAL PARK

This World-Heritage-listed park includes the catchment areas of the Franklin and Olga rivers and part of the Gordon River, as well as the excellent bushwalking region known as **Frenchmans Cap**. It has a number of unique plant species and a major Aboriginal archaeological site at **Kutikina Cave**.

Much of the park is impenetrable rainforest, but the Lyell Highway traverses its northern end and there are a few short walks which you can do from the road. These include hikes to **Donaghys Hill**, from which you can see the Franklin River and the magnificent white quartzite dome of Frenchmans Cap, a walk to **Nelson Falls** and several short walks around the Collingwood River area.

The three to five-day walk to Frenchmans Cap, which features a ride across the Franklin River on a pulley contraption called the Flying Fox, is probably the park's best known bushwalk. The best way, however, to see this magnificent park is not to cross the Franklin River but to raft down it.

Rafting the Franklin

The Franklin is a very wild river and rafting it can be a hazardous journey. Experienced rafters can tackle it if they are fully equipped and prepared, or there are tour companies who offer complete rafting packages. Whether you go with an independent group or a tour operator, it's a good idea to contact the Queenstown Department of Parks, Wildlife & Heritage (☎ (004) 71 2511; PO Box 21, Queenstown, 7467) for a copy of their excellent and up-to-date notes on the trip. Also worth contacting are Wilderness Guides (☎ (08) 296 7093; 60 Holder Rd, North Brighton, SA, 5048) who publish laminated, spiral-bound rafting maps of the Franklin River.

All expeditions should register at the booth at the junction between the Lyell Highway and the Collingwood River, 49 km west of Derwent Bridge. The trip, starting at Collingwood River and ending at Heritage Landing, on the Franklin, takes about 14 days (you can do a shorter eight-day one) and there are camp sites along the way. From your exit point, you can be picked up by a Gordon River Cruise boat or a Wilderness Air seaplane.

Tour companies that arrange complete rafting packages include Peregrine Adventures (☎ (03) 663 8611), 258 Lonsdale St, Melbourne; World Expeditions (☎ (02) 264 3366), 3rd Floor, 441 Kent St, Sydney; and Rafting Tasmania (☎ (002) 27 8295), 63 Channel Highway, Taroona, Tasmania. An all-inclusive rafting package deal, including transport from Hobart, costs around $120 a day.

SOUTH-WEST NATIONAL PARK

There are few places left in the world as isolated and untouched as Tasmania's south-west wilderness, the state's largest national park. It is the home of some of the world's last tracts of virgin temperate rainforest, and these contribute much to the grandeur and extraordinary diversity of this ancient area.

The south-west is the habitat of the endemic Huon pine, which lives for more than 3000 years, and of the swamp gum, the world's tallest hardwood and flowering plant. About 300 species of lichens, mosses and ferns, some rare and endangered, festoon the dense rainforest; superb glacial tarns decorate the jagged mountains; and in summer, the delicate alpine meadows are ablaze with wild flowers and flowering shrubs. Through it all are the wild rivers, with rapids tearing through deep gorges and waterfalls plunging over cliffs. Each year more and more people venture into the heart of this incredible part of Tasmania's World Heritage area, seeking the peace, isolation and challenge of a region as old as the last Ice Age.

The best known walk in the park is between Port Davey and Cockle Creek, near Recherche Bay. This takes about 10 days and should only be tackled by experienced hikers, well prepared for the often vicious weather conditions. Light planes are used to airlift bushwalkers into the south-west and there is vehicle access to Cockle Creek. A whole range of escorted wilderness adventures are possible, involving flying, hiking, rafting, canoeing, mountaineering, caving and camping; more information on these can be obtained from any Tasmanian Travel Centre or from the Wilderness Society. The ranger's telephone number is (002) 88 1283.

LAKE PEDDER

At the edge of the south-west wilderness lies Lake Pedder, once a spectacularly beautiful natural lake considered the crown jewel of the region. In 1972, however, it was flooded beyond all recognition to become part of the HEC's Gordon River power development, although its original name was retained. Together with nearby Lake Gordon, Pedder now holds 27 times the volume of water in Sydney Harbour and is the largest inland freshwater catchment in Australia. The underground Gordon Power Station is the largest in Tasmania and the HEC conduct daily tours around it. The visitors centre at the Gordon Dam site has plenty of information about the scheme.

The flooding of Lake Pedder was, and still is, very controversial. The beauty of the original lake was such that many are still campaigning to see the lake returned to its natural state, and in 1974 Edward St John, the QC on the National Lake Pedder Committee of Inquiry, voiced the opinion that they may be successful: 'Our children will undo what we so foolishly have done'.

STRATHGORDON

Built to service HEC employees, the township of Strathgordon is the base from which to visit lakes Pedder and Gordon, the Gordon Dam and the power station. Strathgordon is also becoming a popular bushwalking, trout fishing, boating and water-skiing resort. There's a camping ground, and accommodation at the *Lake Pedder Motor Inn* (☎ (002) 80 1166) where singles/doubles cost $47/52.

Cradle Mountain-Lake St Clair

Tasmania's best known national park is the superb 1262-sq-km World Heritage area of Cradle Mountain-Lake St Clair. The spectacular mountain peaks, deep gorges, lakes, tarns, wild open moorlands, and the reserve's incredible variety of flora & fauna, extend from the Great Western Tiers in Tasmania's north to Derwent Bridge, on the Lyell Highway in the south. It is one of the most glaciated areas in Australia and includes Mt Ossa (1617 metres), Tasmania's highest mountain, and Lake St Clair, Australia's deepest natural freshwater lake.

The preservation of this region as a national park is due, in part, to the Austrian Gustav Weindorfer who fell in love with the area and claimed, 'This must be a national park for all time. It is magnificent. Everyone should know about it, and come and enjoy it'. In 1912 he built a chalet out of King Billy pine called Waldheim ('Forest Home' in German), and from 1916 he lived there permanently. Today, eight bushwalkers' huts have been constructed near his original chalet, at the northern end of the park, and the area is named Waldheim, after his chalet.

There are plenty of day walks in both the Cradle Valley and Cynthia Bay (Lake St Clair) regions, but it is the spectacular 80-km walk between the two that has turned this park into a bushwalkers' Mecca. The Overland Track is one of the finest bushwalks in Australia, and in summer up to a hundred people a day can set off on it. The track can be walked in either direction, but most people walk from north to south, from Cradle Valley to Cynthia Bay.

At the northern park boundary, and built on the verge of an amazing rainforest, the visitor centre and ranger station (☎ (004) 92 1133) is open year-round from 8 am to 5 pm. All walkers must register here before setting out on any trip and those doing the Overland Track pay their fees here ($20 for adults, $10 for children, students and pensioners, and $50 a family). The centre is staffed by rangers who can advise you about weather conditions, walking gear, maximum and minimum walking groups, bush safety, and bush etiquette. The centre also has plenty of leaflets and videos for hikers on all aspects of walking, from the dangers of hypothermia to the skills of minimal impact bushwalking.

For visitors in wheelchairs, or with youngsters in prams, the centre also features an easy, but quite spectacular, 500-metre circular boardwalk through the adjacent rainforest called the **Rainforest-Pencil Pine Falls Walking Track**.

Cradle Mountain Scenic Flights (☎ (004) 92 1400), which operates from the Cradle View Restaurant, offers a much less energetic way to see all the sights. A 25-minute trip costs $120 for two or $40 each for three or more people.

Cynthia Bay, near the southern park boundary, also has a very informative ranger station (☎ (002) 89 1115) where you register to walk the Overland Track in the opposite direction. At the nearby kiosk you can book a seat on the *Ida Clair* ferry. The boat does a $16 return trip to Narcissus Hut, at the northern end of Lake St Clair, departing at 9 am and 1 and 3 pm and is also available for charter. From the same kiosk you can also hire dinghies for a spot of fishing or relaxing on the lake, but don't fall in – it's freezing!

The Overland Track

The best time to walk the Overland Track is during summer when the flowering plants are most prolific, although spring and autumn also have their attractions. You can walk the track in winter, but only if you're very experienced.

The trail is well marked for its entire length and, at an easy pace, takes around five or six days to walk. En route, however, there are many secondary paths leading up to mountains like Mt Ossa (only three km off the track) or other natural features, making it a great temptation to take a few more days to explore the region fully. In fact, the length of time you take is only limited by the amount of supplies you can carry. There are 12 unattended huts along the track which you can use for overnight accommodation, but in summer they can get full.

A detailed description of the walk is given in Lonely Planet's *Bushwalking in Australia*. The most dangerous part of the walk is the exposed high plateau between Waldheim and Pelion Creek. The south-west wind that blows across here can be bitterly cold and sometimes strong enough to knock you off your feet.

If you are walking from Cradle Valley to Cynthia Bay, you have the option of radioing from Narcissus Hut for the *Ida Clair* ferry to come and pick you up. This trip costs $13 and will save you a 5½-hour walk. The *Ida Clair* can also take you from Cynthia Bay to

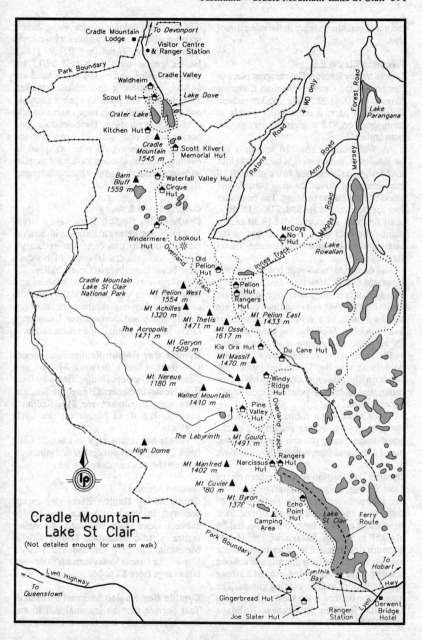

Cradle Mountain–
Lake St Clair
(Not detailed enough for use on walk)

the hut if you are walking in the other direction.

Places to Stay & Eat

Cradle Valley Region The cheapest place in this area is the *Cradle Mountain Camping Ground* (☎ (004) 92 1395), 2½ km outside the national park; it costs $10 a double to camp here or $15 a night to stay in the bunkhouse.

At Waldheim, about 10 km into the national park, there are eight basic huts (four four-bed, two six-bed and two eight-bed) all containing gas stoves, cooking utensils and wood heaters but no bedding. The minimum fees for these cabins are $38, $48 and $58 or, if all the beds are occupied, $13.50 each a night. The huts have to be booked at the camp ground (or at any Tasmanian Travel Centre).

Just on the national park boundary is the luxurious *Cradle Mountain Lodge* (☎ (004) 92 1303), where singles/doubles in the main chalet cost $76/90, self-contained cabins are $120 a double, or a deluxe spa cabin costs $156 a double. The lodge has good facilities for its guests and anyone is welcome to eat at the excellent restaurant (make sure you book first), visit the Tavern Bar (which has bands on Thursday nights) or buy basic groceries and unleaded petrol at the lodge's general store.

The *Cradle View Restaurant*, near the camping ground, serves reasonably priced home-made meals; you can also buy leaded petrol and diesel from outside the restaurant.

Cynthia Bay Region At the southern end of Lake St Clair, there are five huts (one 16-bed, one four-bed and three nine-bed), plenty of camp sites and a kiosk that sells basic food supplies. It costs $8 for two to camp and $6 a night to stay at *Milligania*, the 16-bed dormitory-style hut. The other huts contain a stove, fridge, cooking utensils and a wood heater but no bedding and cost $12.50 per person; they're mainly used by groups. The huts can be booked at the kiosk or by ringing Lakeside St Clair Wilderness Holidays (☎ (002) 89 1137).

At Derwent Bridge, five km away, there's accommodation at the wooden chalet-style *Derwent Bridge Hotel* (☎ (002) 89 1144). Heated cabins with linen cost $9/15 for singles/doubles, and rooms in the hotel are $45/65, including a continental breakfast. The manager has plans to open a camping and caravan park with inexpensive on-site vans and free camping. The hotel does good hearty meals and, with its open fire and friendly staff, is a good place to spend an evening. You can also buy food, basic supplies and maps, and rent fishing or bushwalking gear from here.

Getting There & Away

Cradle Valley Region Three days a week, Redline's bus between Burnie and Strahan (via Devonport) can drop you at Leary's Corner, and you can take one of Invicta's local buses from there to Cradle Valley.

Invicta services between Strahan and Devonport run via Cradle Valley, and the company also has return trips between Cradle Valley and Devonport or Launceston ($65). Invicta's agent is the visitor centre.

Cynthia Bay Region Redline has services five days a week between Hobart and Strahan via Derwent Bridge. One-way fares from Hobart to Derwent Bridge are $20, and from there to Strahan are $15. Redline's agent is the Road House on the Lyell Highway.

Invicta has return trips to Lake St Clair from Devonport, Launceston or Hobart; its agent is the kiosk at Lake St Clair.

Getting Around

Cradle Valley Region Every day except Sundays, Invicta runs a local bus service between Dove Lake, Waldheim, the visitor centre, Cradle Mountain Lodge, Cradle Mountain Camping Ground and Leary's Corner (the Cradle Valley turn-off); one-way fares range from $2 to $6.

Cynthia Bay Region Maxwell's Coach & Taxi Service runs an informal taxi to and from Cynthia Bay and Derwent Bridge for

$4. Maxwell's also meets the Redline buses at Derwent Bridge, on the Lyell Highway, which are heading to Hobart or Strahan.

Lake Country

The sparsely populated lake country of Tasmania's central plateau is a region of breathtaking scenery with steep mountains, hundreds of glacial lakes, crystal-clear streams, waterfalls and a good variety of flora & fauna. It's also known for its fine trout fishing, and for its ambitious hydro-electricity schemes which have seen the damming of rivers, the creation of artificial lakes, the building of power stations, both above and below ground, and the construction of km of massive silver pipelines over the rough terrain.

Tasmania has the largest hydroelectric power system in Australia, generating 95% of its own and 8% of Australia's total electricity output. The first dam was constructed on Great Lake in 1911. Subsequently, the Derwent, Mersey, South Esk, Forth, Gordon and Pieman rivers were also dammed, and work is now proceeding on the King and Anthony rivers, near Queenstown.

If you want to inspect the developments, go along to the Tungatinah, Tarraleah and Liapootah power stations on the extensive Derwent scheme between Queenstown and Hobart.

Over the years, dam building for the hydroelectric power stations has been a subject of considerable controversy. While conservationists have been greatly concerned over their potential to harm the environment, many Tasmanians have seen the dams and power stations as a welcome source of employment. The first public outcry against the uncontrolled damming of Tasmania's magnificent rivers was brought about by the flooding of Lake Pedder in the mid '70s. The most famous dispute was, of course, over the proposed damming of the Franklin and Lower Gordon rivers which was won, after seven long years, by the environmentalists. With the completion of the schemes on the King and Anthony rivers, however, the era of large dam building in Tasmania

will be just about over. Any other suitable sites are in World Heritage areas and cannot be touched.

Just south-east of Cradle Mountain is the **Walls of Jerusalem National Park**, which is a focal point for mountaineers, bush-walkers and cross-country skiers. There's excellent fishing at **Lake King William**, on the Derwent River, south of the Lyell Highway, as well as in **Lake Sorell, Lake Crescent, Arthurs Lake** and **Little Pine Lagoon**.

Places to Stay
The *Bronte Park Highland Village* (☎ (002) 89 1126) has a pleasant hostel which costs $10 a night; cottages from $52 a double; chalet rooms at $35/50 for singles/doubles and camp sites for $7 a double.

At Swan Bay, near Miena, the *Great Lake Hotel* (☎ (002) 59 8163) has singles/doubles for $35/55, including a continental breakfast; cabins at $15 each; and camping sites at $8.

In Poatina, the HEC's *Chalet* (☎ (003) 97 8245) costs $31/54.50 including a cooked breakfast, as does the *Chalet* at Tarraleah (☎ (002) 89 3128).

The *Lachlan Hotel* (☎ (002) 87 1215) in Ouse has rooms for $25/50 including a cooked breakfast.

BOTHWELL (population 360)
Bothwell, in the beautiful Clyde River valley, is a charming and historic town, with 53 buildings recognised or classified by the National Trust. Places of particular interest include the beautifully restored **Slate Cottage** (☎ (002) 59 5554) of 1835; a **bootmakers shop** (☎ (002) 59 5736), fitted out as it would have been in the 1890s; **Thorpe Mill** (☎ (002) 59 5580), a flour mill from the 1820s; the delightful **St Luke's Church** (1821); and the Castle Hotel, first licensed in 1821. Note that the places with telephone numbers must be rung in advance to arrange a visit. Bothwell is probably best known for its great trout fishing.

Accommodation in Bothwell can be expensive, but *Mrs Wood's Farmhouse*

(☎ (002) 59 5612), at Dennistoun, is highly recommended at $65 a double. There are also plans for some shearers' quarters in Dennistoun to be converted to backpackers' accommodation.

Getting There & Away
Public transport to this area is not good (and neither is the hitching). Invicta's services between Lake St Clair and Launceston or Devonport go via Bronte Park and Miena. Its agent is the Bronte Park Highland Village. Invicta also runs a limited return service to the Walls of Jerusalem from either Devonport or Launceston via Deloraine.

Bass Strait Islands

Tasmania has two main islands guarding the eastern and western entrances to Bass Strait. Once the temporary and sometimes violent home of sealers, sailors and prospectors, King and Flinders islands are now retreats of unspoiled natural beauty, rich in marine and wildlife.

KING ISLAND (population 2750)
At the western end of Bass Strait, this rugged island is 64 km across at its widest point, and has more than 145 km of unspoilt coastline with beautiful beaches and quiet lagoons.

Discovered in 1798, and named after Governor King of New South Wales, King Island quickly gained a reputation as a home and breeding ground for seals and sea elephants. Just as quickly, however, these animals were hunted close to extinction by brutal sealers and sailors known as the 'Straitsmen'.

Over the years, the stormy seas of Bass Strait have claimed many ships and there are at least 57 wrecks in the coastal waters around King Island. The island's worst shipwreck occurred in 1845 when the *Cataraqui*, an immigrant ship, went down with 399 people aboard.

King Island is probably best known for its dairy produce (particularly its rich Brie cheese and cream), although kelp and large crayfish are other valuable exports. Its other main industry was the production of scheelite (used in the manufacture of armaments) until the mine and factory at Grassy closed in December 1990.

For the visitor, King Island offers long deserted beaches with good swimming, and a coastline with exotic marine life and accessible shipwrecks which is ideal for scuba diving. Because of the treacherous seas, King Island has four lighthouses and the one at Currie is open to visitors between 2 and 4 pm on weekends. About half the island is still native bush which harbours a wide variety of wildlife including Bennetts wallabies, pheasants, platypuses, echidnas, turkeys, sea eagles and fairy penguins. Near **Surprise Bay**, in the south, an amazing calcified forest has the experts puzzling over whether the formations are of wood, coral or even kelp roots. There is excellent bushwalking on the island, particularly on the unpopulated north coast. Cycling is also popular because of the island's size and relative flatness.

King Island's main town is Currie, on the west coast. Top Tours, in Main St, conducts full and half-day tours around the island; it's also a good place for tourist information. Currie's **King Island Museum** has some interesting historical artefacts; admission is $2.

Places to Stay & Eat
Top Tours & Accommodation (☎ (004) 62 1245), at 13 Main St, has good accommodation at $35/45 for singles/doubles including a continental breakfast. *King Island A-Frame Holiday Homes* (☎ (004) 62 1563), on North Rd, cost $60 a double. The *Boomerang Motel* (☎ (004) 62 1288) is a little more expensive at $53/60, including a continental breakfast, and its restaurant has a very good reputation. The *Bass Caravan Park* (☎ (004) 62 1260) is also on North Rd and has on-site vans at $24 a double.

In Naracoopa, on the east coast, *Naracoopa Lodge* (☎ (004) 61 1294) has good hostel-style accommodation at $15 a night. *Naracoopa Holiday Units* (☎ (004) 61 1326) charges $45 a double. Further south on Yarra Creek Rd, *Yarra Creek Host Farm* (☎ (004) 61 1276) has singles/doubles for $20/35, including a cooked breakfast. Note, however, that the road from Currie to Naracoopa is only partly sealed, and that it's really only feasible to stay in this part of the island if you have a car.

Getting There & Around

See the Getting There & Away section at the beginning of this chapter for information on flights to and from King Island.

In Currie, you can rent cars from King Island Auto Rentals (☎ (004) 62 1297) from about $45 a day, or from Howell's Auto Rent (☎ (004) 62 1282) from about $60. Be warned that some King Island roads are very rough, so unless you have a 4WD you might need some digging gear.

You can also hire mountain bikes from Top Tours (☎ (004) 62 1245) for about $8 a day or $40 a week.

FLINDERS ISLAND (population 980)

Flinders Island is the largest of the Furneaux Group, a collection of islands which cover an area of 1969 sq km off the north-eastern tip of Tasmania. Flinders is approximately 60 km long and 20 km wide and is followed in size by Cape Barren and Clarke islands.

First chartered in 1798 by the navigator Matthew Flinders, the Furneaux Group became a base for the 'Straitsmen' who not only slaughtered seals in their tens of thousands but also indulged in a little piracy. Of the 120 or so ships wrecked on the islands' rocks, it is thought that quite a number were purposefully lured there by sealers displaying false lights.

The most tragic part of Flinders Island's history, however, was the role it played in the virtual annihilation of Tasmania's Aborigines. In 1831, those Aborigines who had survived the state's martial law (which gave soldiers the right to arrest or shoot any Aborigine found in a settled area) were brought to the island to be resettled. Of the 135 survivors who were transported to Wybalenna (an Aboriginal word meaning 'Black man's house') to be 'civilised' and educated, only 47 survived to make their final journey to Oyster Cove in 1847.

Today, all that remains of the unfortunate settlement is the **cemetery**, which tells the tragic story, and the **chapel**, which has been restored by the National Trust and is open to visitors. Nearby, there's also the **Emita Museum** which displays a variety of Aboriginal artefacts as well as old sealing and sailing relics.

On a brighter note, Flinders Island has many attractions for the visitor. Its beaches, especially on the western side, are beautiful, and the fishing and scuba diving are also good. Like King Island, there is no shortage of shipwrecks around the islands, some of which are clearly visible from shore. A more unusual pastime is fossicking for 'diamonds' (which are actually fragments of white topaz) on the beach and creek at **Killiecrankie Bay**. At one time there were plenty of stones to be found, but there are fewer now, and the locals have actually started to dive for them using special equipment.

Flinders Island has some great bushwalks, the most popular being the five-hour return walk to the granite peaks of **Mt Strzelecki** which affords some great views of the surrounding area. There are also a number of lookouts on the island including **Furneaux Lookout**, almost in the centre of the island, **Walkers Hill** and **Mt Tanner**.

The island's abundant vegetation supports a wide variety of wildlife, including more than 150 species of birds, the most well known being the Cape Barren goose (now protected) and the mutton bird.

The main industries on Flinders Island are farming, fishing and seasonal muttonbirding. The main administrative centre is Whitemark, and Lady Barron in the south is the main fishing area and deep-water port.

Each September, the mutton birds return to Flinders and other Bass Strait islands, after a summer in the northern hemisphere, to clean out and repair their burrows from the previous year. They then head out to sea again before returning in November for the breeding season which lasts until April. Eggs are then laid in one three-day period, and the parents take it in turns, two weeks at a time, to incubate them.

Once their single chick has hatched, both parents feed the fledgling until mid-April when all the adult birds depart, leaving the young to fend for themselves and hopefully to follow their parents north.

Unfortunately for the well-fed little mutton birds, they make good eating and once the adult birds leave the nests the 'birders', or mutton-bird hunters, move in.

Places to Stay

At Pats River, Whitemark, *Bluff House* (☎ (003) 59 2034) has singles/doubles with a cooked breakfast for $29/43.50, and in the centre of town the *Interstate Hotel* (☎ (003) 59 2114) has rooms for $20/35. On Bluff Rd, the *Flinders Island Cabin Park* (☎ (003) 59 2188) has cabins for $20/35.

At Emita, on Fairhaven Rd, the *Green-glades Host Farm* (☎ (003) 59 8506) offers three cooked meals a day plus lodging for $45 per person.

The rather luxurious *Furneaux Tavern* (☎ (003) 59 3521) at Lady Barron, has rooms for $70/95, including continental breakfast.

For longer stays, there's also a good selection of reasonable holiday houses and flats on the island.

Getting There & Around

For information on flights to and from Flinders Island see the Getting There & Away section at the beginning of this chapter.

In Whitemark, Bowman Transport Auto Rent (☎ (003) 59 2014) has cars from around $45 a day, while both Flinders Island Car Rentals (☎ (003) 59 2168) and Flinders Island Transport Services (☎ (003) 59 2060) rent cars from $50 a day.

Victoria

Area	228,000 sq km
Population	4,100,000

When White Australia's founders up in Sydney decided it was time to get a foothold on some other part of the continent they had a go at establishing a settlement on Port Phillip Bay in 1803. Through a combination of bad luck and bad management they soon decided it was a lousy place to live and moved down to Tasmania. So it is not surprising that when Melbourne did become established, a long-lasting rivalry with Sydney began.

In 1835 the first permanent European settlement was made at the present site of Melbourne, although whalers and sealers had used the Victorian coast for a number of years. The earliest settlers, John Batman and John Pascoe Fawkner, came to Melbourne in search of the land they had been unable to obtain in Tasmania. Not until 1837, by which time several hundred settlers had moved in, was the town named Melbourne and given an official seal of approval.

Their free-enterprise spirit naturally led to clashes with the staid powers of Sydney. The settlers were not interested in the convict system, for example, and on a number of occasions turned convict ships away. They wanted to form a breakaway colony, and their PR efforts included naming it after the Queen and the capital city after her Prime Minister, Lord Melbourne.

Finally, in 1851, the colony of Victoria was formed and separated from New South Wales. At about the same time gold was discovered, and the population doubled in little more than a year. As with a number of other Australian gold rushes, few people made fortunes but many stayed on to establish new settlements and work the land. Some of the most interesting historical areas in Victoria are associated with those gold-rush days.

Melbourne, as Australia's second city, is

naturally the state's prime attraction. Although it is not as intrinsically appealing as Sydney, it does lay claim to being the fashion, food and cultural centre of Australia and also the financial focus. Victoria is the most densely populated of the Australian states and also the most industrialised.

The failure of a number of Victorian financial institutions (both government and private) in the late 1980s and the state's generally low standing in the economic stakes fuelled the already rampant rivalry between Victoria and anywhere 'north of the border'. Unfortunately much of the recent criticism has been justified, and the state has become the butt of even more jokes.

Of course Victoria is much more than its capital city. The Great Ocean Rd runs southwest towards South Australia; it has some of the most spectacular coastal scenery in the world and evocative reminders of the whaling days in some of the small port towns that predate Melbourne. To the south-east of the capital is Phillip Island with its nightly penguin parade. Further south is Wilsons Promontory – the southernmost point on the Australian mainland and also one of the best loved national parks, with excellent scenery and bushwalks. Continuing east towards the New South Wales border there's more great coast and superb rainforests in the Gippsland region.

Victoria's stretch of the Great Dividing Range includes the Victorian Alps, which have some of the best ski fields in Australia and are much closer to Melbourne than New South Wales's fields are to Sydney. Skiing on weekends is easy for Melbournians, while in summer the mountains are popular for camping, walking and a whole host of outdoor activities. Of course you don't have to go all the way to the Alps to get into the hills; the ever-popular Dandenongs are less than an hour from the centre of Melbourne, while the spectacular Grampians, another popular mountain area, are further to the west.

Finally, there's the Murray River region in the north, which has many historic river towns, such as Swan Hill and Echuca. Victoria also has its wine-growing areas, particularly in the north on the slopes of the Great Dividing Range. And the gold country certainly shouldn't be forgotten – towns like Bendigo and Ballarat still have a strong flavour of those heady gold-rush days, and lucky prospectors are still finding gold today.

GEOGRAPHY

Victoria's geography is probably more diverse than that of any other Australian state, as it includes both the final stretch of the Great Dividing Range and associated outcrops plus a swath of the flatter country to the west. The Great Dividing Range reaches its greatest altitude across the Victoria-New South Wales border. The mountains run south-west from the New South Wales border, then bend around to run more directly west as the range crosses north of Melbourne and finally fades out before the South Australian border.

The Victorian coast is particularly varied. On the eastern side is the mountain-backed Gippsland region while to the west is spectacular coastline running to South Australia.

The north-west of the state, beyond the Great Divide, is flat plains. It is especially dry and empty in the extreme north-west of the state, where you'll find the eerie Sunset Country. For most of the length of the border between New South Wales and Victoria, the mighty Murray River forms the actual boundary.

CLIMATE

Victoria, and Melbourne in particular, has a single major drawback – the bloody climate. Statistically it's not that bad; the average temperature summer or winter is only a few degrees less than Sydney's and it's certainly far less humid than Sydney or Brisbane. The annual rainfall is also less than either of those damp cities. The trouble with Melbourne's climate is that it's totally unpredictable; you can boil one day and shiver the next. What the hell am I talking about – it's the next minute, not the next day! In Melbourne if you don't like the weather, so they say, just wait a minute. It's not that Melbourne has four distinct seasons, it's just that they often all come on the same day. You simply can't trust the sun to shine in summer or, for that matter, the winter to be cold; it's totally fickle.

Although the weather is basically somewhat cooler in Melbourne than elsewhere in continental Australia, you'll rarely need more than a light overcoat or jacket even in the depths of winter. Inland, however, in places like Ballarat, it can get really cold.

INFORMATION

The Victorian Tourism Commission operates the following offices around Australia:

Australian Capital Territory
     Jolimont Centre, corner of Northbourne Ave and Rudd St, Canberra 2601 (☎ (06) 47 6355)
New South Wales
     192 Pitt St, Sydney 2000 (☎ (02) 233 5499)
Queensland
     221 Queen St, Brisbane 4000 (☎ (07) 221 4300)
South Australia
     16 Grenfell St, Adelaide 5000 (☎ (08) 51 4129)
Tasmania
     126 Collins St, Hobart 7000 (☎ (002) 31 0499)
Western Australia
     56 William St, Perth 6000 (☎ (09) 481 1484)

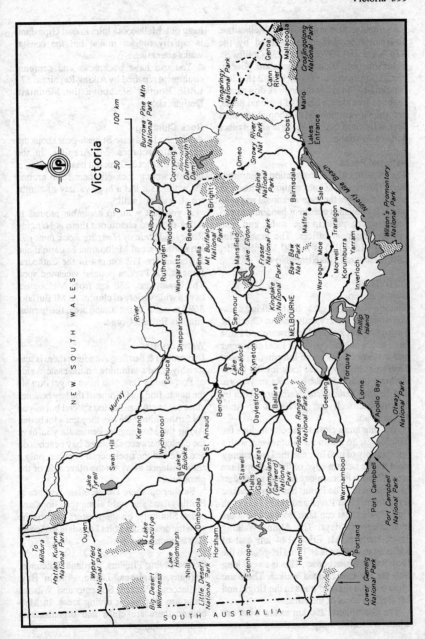

Remarkably, there is no office in Melbourne. Tourism information is handled by the RACV (☎ (03) 607 2137) at 230 Collins St.

Information Victoria, the state government's information centre, is at 318 Little Bourke St. The information desk downstairs supplies free sketch maps of national parks, and the Government Map Shop at the next desk sells maps both of Victoria and of other parts of Australia.

National Parks

The Department of Conservation & Environment (previously Conservation, Forests & Lands) manages the state's national and state parks. It publishes excellent handouts to virtually every park in the state, and also operates regional offices. The head office (☎ (03) 412 4011) is at 240 Victoria Pde, East Melbourne. Take tram No 42.

ACTIVITIES
Bushwalking

Victoria has some great bushwalking areas and a number of very active clubs. Check the bush-gear shops around Hardware and Little Bourke Sts in Melbourne for local club news and magazines. For more information about bushwalking in Victoria look for the handy walking guides *50 Bush Walks in Victoria* and *50 Day Walks Near Melbourne* both by Sandra Bardwell and published by Anne O'Donovan.

Walking areas close to the city include the You Yangs, 56 km to the south-west, with a wide variety of bird life; and the Dandenongs right on the eastern edge of the metropolitan area. Wilsons Promontory is to the south-east in Gippsland. 'The Prom' has many marked trails from Tidal River and from Telegraph Bay – walks that can take from a few hours to a couple of days. The Alpine Walking Track starts at Mt Erica, 144 km east of Melbourne, and ends at Tom Groggin on the New South Wales border. This is a very long trail for the experienced walker. There are other popular marked trails in the Bright and Mt Buffalo areas of the Alps.

The Grampians, 250 km to the west, are where Victoria's only remaining red roos

hang out. Mallacoota Inlet in east Gippsland is equally rugged inland but the coastal walks are easier.

You can have backpacks and camping equipment repaired by Aiking Repairs at 377 Little Bourke St, above the Mountain Designs shop.

Rock Climbing

Again, the Hardware St bush-gear shops are good info sources. Mt Arapiles, in the western district 330 km out near Natimuk, is famous among rock-climbers from around the world as it has a huge variety of climbs for all levels of skill.

If you just want to scramble around in rather crowded conditions there is Hanging Rock (of *Picnic of Hanging Rock* fame) 72 km north-west of Melbourne. Sugarloaf and Jawbones are 112 km out in the Cathedral Range State Park, a popular weekend spot. The Grampians, 250 km from Melbourne, have a wide variety of climbs. At Mt Buffalo, 369 km north in the alpine area, the hardest climb is Buffalo Gorge.

Water Sports

Swimming & Surfing Although there is reasonably good swimming on the eastern side of Port Phillip Bay, you have to get outside the bay to find surf. Some of the bay beaches close to the city are not too special but as you get further round the bay they get a lot better. Along the Mornington Peninsula you have the choice between sheltered bay beaches on one side and the open ocean beaches, only a short distance away on the other side of the peninsula.

Further out there are excellent beaches at Phillip Island and right along the Gippsland coast. Similarly, on the western side of the state the coast from Point Lonsdale to Apollo Bay is popular for surfing.

Scuba Diving Flinders, Portland, Kilcunda, Torquay, Anglesea, Lorne, Apollo Bay, Mallacoota, Portsea, Sorrento and Wilsons Prom are all popular diving areas. In Melbourne there are clubs and organisations renting equipment.

Boats & Sailing There are many sailing clubs all around Port Phillip Bay and on Albert Park Lake in Melbourne. Elsewhere around the state there are many lakes popular for sailing. On the large Gippsland Lakes system you can hire yachts and launches, which work out to be quite economical among a few people.

At Studley Park, in the Melbourne suburb of Kew, you can hire a whole selection of rowing boats, canoes and kayaks by the hour – good fun, although a fair few people seem to find themselves upside down in the muddy Yarra!

Further upstream at Fairfield Park, there is another boathouse, restored to its original Edwardian elegance, offering Devonshire teas and other snacks, and boats and canoes for hire. You might catch a performance in the outdoor amphitheatre on a bend in the river in the natural bushland.

Canoes can also be rented by Como Park, further down the Yarra towards the city. At Albert Park Lake you can hire rowing boats and sailing boats.

Houseboat holidays are also popular, and these can be arranged on Lake Eildon, or on the Murray River at Echuca or Mildura.

Running & Cycling

The four-km jogging track (popularly known as 'the Tan') around the Kings Domain and the Royal Botanic Gardens in central Melbourne is one of the most popular running circuits in Australia. Albert Park Lake is also busy. With its relatively flat terrain, Melbourne is very popular with bike riders – quite a few of us at Lonely Planet ride bicycles to work.

It's easy to hire bicycles on the popular Yarra-side bicycle track but not so easy to find them for longer term hire in Melbourne. Contact Bicycle Victoria (☎ (03) 670 9911) for information on tours and organised rides in Victoria. They also run the Great Victorian Bike Ride, held annually around November, in which thousands of cyclists take part. They may be able to tell you where you can hire a touring bike.

GETTING THERE & AWAY

See the Melbourne section for details of transport into Victoria.

GETTING AROUND

V/Line (☎ (03) 619 5000) has a fairly comprehensive rail network of metropolitan and country services. The rail services are supplemented by connecting V/Line buses. The principal rail routes radiating from Melbourne are:

West to Geelong then inland to Warrnambool; a bus runs along the Great Ocean Rd from Geelong through Lorne and Apollo Bay

North-west to Ballarat and on through Horsham in the central west to Adelaide in South Australia; buses connect from Stawell south-west to Halls Gap in the Grampians or north-west towards the Mallee

North-west through Ballarat and then to Mildura on the Murray River

North through Bendigo and the central highlands to Swan Hill on the Murray

North to Shepparton, Numurkah and Cobram along the Goulburn Valley

North along the Hume Highway route to Albury/ Wodonga on the route to Sydney; buses run from Wangaratta to Beechworth and Bright or north to Corowa

East through Traralgon and Sale to Bairnsdale in Gippsland; a branch line runs to Leongatha near Wilsons Prom. Buses connect from Bairnsdale to Lakes Entrance, Orbost, Cann River and Merimbula

V/Line have four regional timetables with details of all their services, and these are available from station bookstalls.

Melbourne

Population 2,900,000

Melbourne has always had a fierce rivalry with Sydney. It goes right back to their founding; Sydney had nearly 50 years' head start on its southern sister and even then the foundation of Melbourne was a rather haphazard affair. Not until 1835, following exploratory trips from Tasmania, was the

Melbourne area eventually settled by a group of Tasmanian entrepreneurs.

In 1851 the colony of Victoria became independent of New South Wales and almost immediately the small town of Melbourne became the centre for Australia's biggest and most prolonged gold rush. In just a few years Melbourne suddenly became a real place on the map, and the city's solid, substantial appearance essentially dates from those heady days. For a while last century Melbourne was the larger and more exciting city, known as 'Marvellous Melbourne', but Sydney gradually pulled ahead and Melbourne now ranks number two to its more glamorous northern sister.

In population there's little between them; they're both large cities in the three million bracket, but Sydney is more the metropolis than Melbourne. These days Melbourne is a big Australian city; Sydney's a big world one. This doesn't stop people liking Melbourne more. Many visitors find Melbourne a more easygoing, friendlier city where you can get a feel for the place as somewhere real people live, not just a glossy tourist attraction.

Orientation

Melbourne's city centre is apparently simple, with its grid of wide boulevards. However, these are interspersed with narrow streets from which run off a veritable maze of little alleys and lanes, giving the otherwise overpoweringly orderly and planned centre a little human chaos. The main streets are Collins and Bourke Sts (south-west to north-east) crossed by Swanston and Elizabeth Sts (south-east to north-west).

Swanston St crosses straight over the river to the south and runs right out of the city into Carlton to the north. Most traffic coming into the city from the south used to enter by Swanston St, but this all came to stop when the street was closed to traffic early in 1992. The result has been great for pedestrians and terrible for car users. Most traffic from the north comes in on parallel Elizabeth St, since this is the direct route in from the airport and from Sydney.

The Yarra River forms a southern boundary to the city area, with railway lines running between the river and Flinders St (the city centre street running closest to the river bank). Right beside the river on the corner of Swanston and Flinders Sts is the ornate old Flinders St Station. This is the main railway station for suburban railway services, and 'under the clocks' at the station entrance is a favourite Melbourne meeting place. The other Melbourne station, for country and interstate services, is Spencer St Station, and next to it you have the Spencer St bus terminal, from which V/Line and the interstate companies operate. The Spencer St end of town also has a number of old hotels and cheaper places to stay.

The Collins and Bourke St blocks between Swanston and Elizabeth Sts are Melbourne's shopping centre, the Bourke St block also being a pedestrian – and tram – mall. On the mall you'll find Myers (the biggest department store chain in Australia) and right next door on the Bourke and Elizabeth Sts corner is the GPO.

Most travellers will arrive in Melbourne at the north side of the city, on Franklin St. The Greyhound/Pioneer bus company and the Skybus airport bus service both operate from a terminal on this street. From the terminal you can turn right to Elizabeth St to get a tram to the YHA hostels or left to Swanston St to get tram No 15 to St Kilda. Or you can walk to the city hostels, which are only about ten minutes away.

Melbourne trams should be treated with some caution by car drivers. You can only overtake a tram on the left and must always stop behind one when it halts to drop or collect passengers (except where there are central 'islands' for passengers). In the city centre at most junctions a peculiar path must be followed to make right-hand turns, in order to accommodate the trams. Note that in rainy weather tram tracks are extremely slippery, motorcyclists should take special care. Cyclists must beware of tram tracks at all times; if you get a wheel into the track you're flat on your face immediately, and painfully.

Information

Tourist Information The National Trust (☎ 654 4711) publishes several walking-tour guides to Melbourne, some free. The National Trust is on Tasma Terrace, 6 Parliament Place, where they have a bookshop.

The YHA (☎ 670 7991) has its helpful Melbourne office at 205 King St, on the corner of Little Bourke St. It's quite close to Spencer St station. They handle membership inquiries and travel bookings.

Information Victoria (☎ 651 4100) at 318 Little Bourke St has a good range of maps and guidebooks.

The Bank of Melbourne, which has several branches, is open on Saturdays from 9 to 12 am.

Post & Telecommunications The Melbourne GPO is on the corner of Bourke and Elizabeth Sts. There's an efficient poste restante and phones for interstate and international calls. Phone centres can also be found behind the GPO on Little Bourke St and across the road on Elizabeth St.

The STD telephone area code for Melbourne is 03.

Books & Bookshops Melbourne has a lot of excellent bookshops including a big Angus & Robertson on Elizabeth St, several Collins Bookshops around the city, and the agreeably chaotic McGills on Elizabeth St opposite the GPO (good for interstate and overseas newspapers). Whole Earth at 83 Bourke St is more 'alternative' and is open late (there are other good bookshops nearby); Readings on Lygon St in Carlton is more literary and has an excellent window notice board where you'll find all sorts of offers to share accommodation or rides. There are several good bookshops on Brunswick St, Fitzroy.

Although not strictly a bookshop, the Environment Centre (☎ 654 4833) at 247 Flinders Lane has a wide variety of books, calendars, posters and magazines and is a good place for information about activities in the environment and conservation movements.

Among guides to Melbourne, de Lacy Lowe's *Exploring Melbourne by Tram* and the National Trust's *Walking Melbourne* are useful.

Foreign Consulates Quite a number of countries have diplomatic representation in Melbourne. Look up Consulates & Legations in the Yellow Pages for details.

Medical Services The Travellers' Medical & Vaccination Centre (☎ 602 5788) is at Level 2, 393 Little Bourke St in the city. They're open weekdays from 8.30 am to 5.30 pm, and later by appointment, and have excellent information on the latest vaccinations needed for most countries.

The Yarra River

Melbourne's prime natural feature, the Yarra, is a surprisingly pleasant river, with all the new parks, walks and bike tracks that have been built along its banks. Despite the cracks about it 'running upside down', it's just muddy, not particularly dirty.

When the racing rowing boats are gliding down the river on a sunny day, or you're driving along Alexandra Ave towards the city on a clear night, the Yarra can really look quite magical. Best of all you can bike it for km along the riverside without risking being wiped out by some nut in a Holden. The bike tracks have been gradually extended further upstream and hopefully will eventually start to move further downstream as well. On weekends you can hire bicycles – see Getting Around.

There are also barbecues beside the river and near **Como Park** in South Yarra, and you can hire canoes, kayaks and rowing boats further upstream. **Studley Park** in Kew is the most popular place for boating.

A more leisurely way to boat down the river is on one of the tour boats which operate on the river from Princes Walk beside Princes Bridge (across from Flinders St Station). 'Bar-b-boats' (☎ 696 1241) at 1 South Wharf Rd, opposite the World Trade Centre, offer cruising barbecues for up to 12 people. You supply the snags and they charge

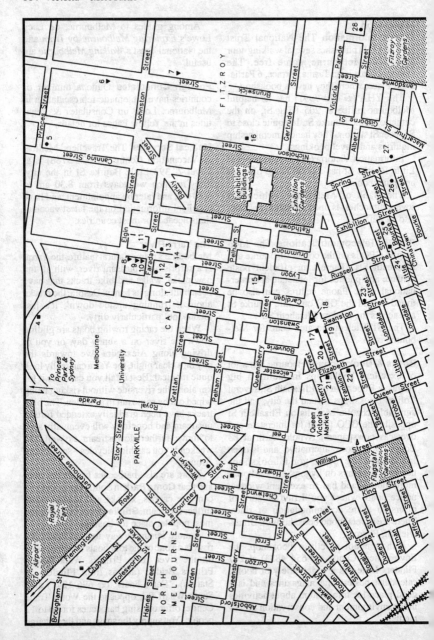

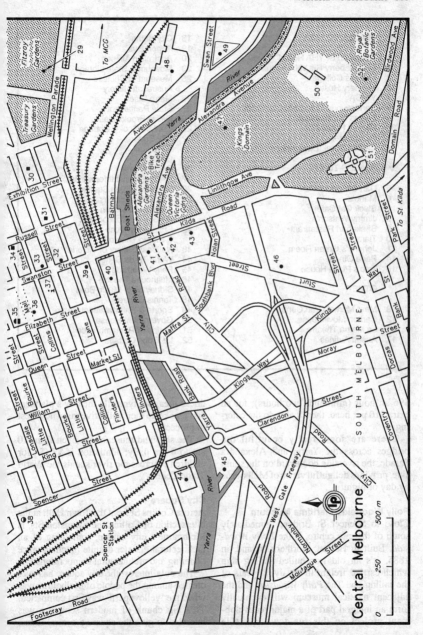

Central Melbourne

$96 an hour (minimum two hours); for an extra $10 per head, they'll also do the catering.

There are some really beautiful old bridges across the Yarra; and Alexandra Parade, the riverside boulevard on the south side, provides delightful views of Melbourne by day or night.

Polly Woodside Maritime Museum
Close to Spencer St Bridge, immediately south of the city centre, is the *Polly Woodside*. Built in Belfast, Northern Ireland, in 1885, it's an old iron-hulled sailing ship which carried freight in the dying years of the sailing era. The *Polly Woodside* and the adjacent nautical museum will eventually form an integral part of a major redevelopment project on this run-down riverside

docks area, but typically the city's planners can't make up their collective mind how best to proceed.

The ship and museum are open from 10 am to 4 pm daily; admission is $7 ($4 for children). Across the river stands the World Trade Centre.

City Square
Across Collins St from the Town Hall, at the intersection of Collins and Swanston Sts, is Melbourne's city square, something of an architectural disaster despite much advance planning and architectural competitions.

The only interest the city square has ever created among the people of Melbourne was when the 'yellow peril' was first completed. This big chunk of modern sculpture was intended to give the square a central focus, but unfortunately it was the sort of thing that makes the you-call-that-art brigade foam at the mouth. Even more unfortunately, Melbourne's city council at that time had absolutely nothing better to do than foam at the mouth too, and after endless arguments and veritable zeppelins full of hot air the council got the sack and the yellow peril was spirited away to a new (and obscure) home in a riverside park down towards Spencer St.

With the sculpture gone Melbournians appeared to lose interest completely in the square, the adjacent shops went broke, and now with the closure of the adjacent bit of Swanston St, plans are being formulated to tear it down and start yet again. Beside the square there's a derelict old theatre which has been a political football for many years and nobody dares to get rid of it. Still standing in the square in late '91 was a statue of the luckless explorers Burke and Wills, looking suitably heroic. This statue has had quite an interesting history of moving from place to place around the city and now looks set to move again.

Around the City

Continuing up Collins St beside the city square you come to the **'Paris End'**, where graceful trees shade the street and do give it something of a Parisian look, although many of the fine old buildings that used to line the street have now disappeared. Two big hotels on Collins St are popular meeting and eating places – see the Hyatt and Regent hotels under Places to Eat.

Up Collins St the other way you come to the **Melbourne Stock Exchange** at No 351. You can visit the 3rd-floor visitors' gallery from 9 am to noon and 2 to 5 pm, Monday to Friday, although with computerisation the 'floor' now has none of the frenetic activity which used to characterise stock exchanges across the developed world. Those interested in the forces of capitalism at work can also have a free tour of the exchange.

Bourke St has more shops but less style than Collins St. In the '70s, when every Australian city had to have a pedestrian mall, Melbourne got one too: the **Bourke St Mall**.

It's difficult for a pedestrian mall to work with 30-tonne trams barrelling through the middle of it every few minutes. However, after several multimillion dollar rearrangements of the potted plants and the benches, the mall has emerged as something of a focus for city shoppers, with its buskers, its missionaries and its big department stores.

Half a block up from Bourke St is **Chinatown** on Little Bourke St. This narrow lane was a thronging Chinese quarter even back in the gold-rush days and it's now a busy, crowded couple of blocks of often excellent Chinese restaurants, Asian supermarkets and shops. The successful touch here was the addition of decorative street lamps and Chinese tiled arches over the lane. Yes, I know they're artificial and garish but they look great. Another half block up to Lonsdale St brings you to the central city's Greek quarter.

City Buildings

Melbourne's an intriguing blend of the soaring new and the stately old. Carrying the 'new' banner are buildings like the **Melbourne Central** shopping and office complex on the corner of Latrobe and Elizabeth Sts. It was opened amid much fanfare in late 1991, and the centrepiece of the complex is the old **Shot Tower**, which still stands on its original site but is now enclosed within the new building. The **Rialto** on Collins St is another recent project. Its semi-reflective glass looks stunningly different under varying light – it's something of a city Ayer's Rock! When it was finished the Rialto was the tallest office building in Australia. Beside it is the imaginative Menzies at the Rialto Hotel which uses the facades of two old buildings and cleverly incorporates an old stone paved alleyway which used to run between them.

Or there's **Nauru House** on Exhibition St; Nauru is a tiny Pacific island whose entire population could comfortably be housed in this big office block. It is an extremely wealthy island since it's basically solid phosphate, hence the building's nickname of 'Birdshit House'. Only a sparrow hop away is the equally soaring **Regent Hotel**, with its 15-storey central atrium starting on the 35th floor. It's a great place to stay if you can stretch to $200 a night.

In the late 1980s there was a development boom in the city centre which saw the construction of a quite a number of state-of-the-art multistorey office blocks. Unfortunately with the recession the bubble burst and many of these buildings are standing empty, waiting for better times and new tenants.

On Spring St is a hotel of quite another era: the gracious old **Windsor Hotel**. Across the road from this is the imposing **State Parliament House**, a relic of Melbourne's gold-rush wealth. It served as the national parliament while Canberra was under construction.

Other old buildings in the centre include the 1853 **Treasury Building** in the Treasury Gardens, the 1872 **Old Royal Mint** and the 1842 **St James Cathedral**, both beside Flagstaff Gardens. Victoriana enthusiasts may also find some very small Melbourne buildings of interest – scattered around the city are a number of very fine cast-iron men's **urinals** (like French *pissoirs*). They mainly date from 1903 to 1914, and one on the corner of Exhibition and Lonsdale St is classified by the National Trust. Other good examples include one outside the North Melbourne Town Hall where there is also a very fine drinking fountain.

On the corner of Swanston and Flinders Sts is the main railway station for local trains in Melbourne, the grand old **Flinders St Station**. Across the road from the station is one of Melbourne's best known pubs, **Young & Jacksons**, which is famed mainly for the painting of Chloe hanging in the upstairs bar. Judged indecent at the Melbourne Exhibition of 1880, she has gone on to win affection among generations of Melbourne drinkers. The pub has been carefully restored.

The **Melbourne Club**, pillar of the Melbourne establishment, is off Spring St up at the Treasury Gardens end of town. This end block of Bourke St is popular and has some good restaurants, bookshops and record shops. **St Patrick's Cathedral**, one of the city's most imposing churches, is also at this end of town.

Over the other side of the city is the **Queen Victoria Market**, on the corner of Peel and Victoria Sts. It's the city's main retail produce centre, a popular multicultural scene on Tuesdays, Thursdays, Fridays and Saturday mornings, when the stall operators shout, yell and generally go all out to move the goods. On Sundays the fruit & vegies give way to general goods – everything from cut-price jeans to second-hand records.

National Museum & State Library

Extending for a block between Swanston St and Russell St beside Latrobe St is the National Museum plus the State Library and La Trobe Library. The State Library has a gracious, octagonal, domed reading room and any book lover will enjoy its atmosphere. Its collection of more than a million books and other reference material is particularly notable for its coverage of the humanities and social sciences, as well as art, music, performing arts, Australiana and rare books, including a 4000-year-old Mesopotamian tablet.

Exhibits at the museum range from the first car and aircraft in Australia to the stuffed remains of Phar Lap, the legendary racehorse which nearly disrupted Australian-American relations when it died a suspicious death in the USA. The complex also includes a planetarium.

The museum is open from 10 am to 5 pm every day and admission is free except to special exhibits. Some time in the future the museum is scheduled to move to a new home across the river in the redeveloped docklands, but until that development gets moving (some time in the next century, perhaps?) the museum stays where it is.

Old Melbourne Gaol

A block further up Russell St is this gruesome old prison and penal museum. It was built of bluestone in 1841 and was used right up to 1929. In all, over 100 prisoners were hanged there. It's a dark, dank, spooky place.

The museum displays include death masks of noted bushrangers and convicts, Ned Kelly's armour, the very scaffold from which Ned took his fatal plunge and some fascinating records of early 'transported' convicts, indicating just what flimsy excuses could be used to pack people off to Australia's unwelcoming shores. It's an unpleasant reminder of the brutality of Australia's early convict days. It is open from 9.30 am to 4.30 pm daily, and admission is $5.50 (children $2.50, family $13, students $3.20).

Royal Melbourne Zoo

Just north of the city centre in Parkville is Melbourne's excellent zoo. There are numerous walk-through enclosures in this well-planned zoo. You walk through the aviary, around the monkey enclosures and even over the lions' park on a bridge. The new butterfly enclosure and the gorilla forest are both excellent. This is the oldest zoo in Australia and one of the oldest in the world.

The zoo is open from 9 am to 5 pm every day of the week and admission is $9 (children $4.50, family $25). You can get to it on tram No 55 from William St in the city. The zoo is in Royal Park; a marker in the park indicates where the Burke & Wills expedition set off on its ill-fated journey in 1860.

Science Works Museum

Opened in mid-1992, this is Melbourne's newest museum. Many of the exhibits were mothballed for years as there was no room in the National Museum in Swanston St. It's at 2 Booker St, Spotswood, about five minutes walk from Spotswood Station, or just over the West Gate Bridge if you're driving.

The Melbourne Cup

If you happen to be in Melbourne in November you can catch the greatest horse race in Australia, the prestigious Melbourne Cup. Although its position as the bearer of the largest prize for an Australian horse race is constantly under challenge, no other race can bring the country to a standstill.

For about an hour during the lead-up to the race on the first Tuesday in November, a public holiday in Victoria, people all over the country get touched by Melbourne's spring racing fever.

Serious punters and fashion-conscious racegoers pack the grandstand and lawns of the Victoria Racing Club's beautiful Flemington Racecourse, once-a-year betters make their choice or organise Cup syndicates with friends, and the race is watched or listened to on TVs and radios in hotels, clubs and houses across the land. Australia virtually comes to a halt for the three or so minutes during which the race is actually run.

The two-mile (3.2 km) flat race has in recent years attracted horses and owners from Europe and the Middle East, breaking the stranglehold that New Zealand horses and trainers had on the coveted gold cup for many years.

Many people say that to be in Melbourne in November and not go to the Cup is like going to Paris and skipping the Louvre, or turning your back on the bulls in Pamplona!

Melbourne Cricket Ground

The MCG is one of Australia's biggest sporting stadiums and was the central stadium for the 1956 Melbourne Olympics. Set in Yarra Park, which stretches from the city and East Melbourne to Richmond, the huge stadium can accommodate over 100,000 spectators, and does so at least once a year. The big occasion is the annual Australian Rules football Grand Final in September. This is Australia's biggest sporting event and brings Melbourne, which engages in a winter of Aussie Rules football mania each year, to a fever pitch. The only other sporting event which generates the same sort of national interest in Australia is the Melbourne Cup horse race each November.

Cricket is, of course, the other major sport played in the MCG; international Test and one-day matches as well as interstate Sheffield Shield and other local district games take place here over the summer months, and draw big crowds.

On the city side of the stadium there's the **Australian Gallery of Sport & Olympic**

Museum, a museum dedicated to Australia's sporting passions. It's open from 10 am to 4 pm every day and admission is $5 (children $2).

Victorian Arts Centre

As you cross the river to the south of the city, Swanston St becomes St Kilda Rd, a very fine boulevard which runs straight out of the city towards the war memorial, takes a kink around the shrine and then continues to St Kilda. Beyond the memorial it's ad agency alley, with many office blocks lining the road.

Right by the river is Melbourne's large arts centre. The **National Gallery** was the first part of the complex to be completed, back in 1968, and it houses a very fine collection of art. The gallery has outstanding local and overseas collections, an excellent photography collection and many fascinating temporary exhibits from all over the world. There is usually a good display of Aboriginal art, and the 19th-century gallery is really worth a visit. The stained-glass ceiling in the Great Hall is superb – best viewed from a supine position. The gallery is open from 10 am to 5 pm except Mondays and the admission is $3 (students and children $1.50). There are additional charges for some special exhibits.

Beside the gallery is the **Concert Hall** complex. It may look rather like a grounded prison ship from *Star Wars* but it houses (mostly underground) an excellent concert hall, the state theatre, playhouse, studio and a performing arts museum, all topped by that tall pointy spire; well it does look nice at night. Inside it looks nice at any time and there's something on virtually every night. There are one-hour tours of the complex ($4) Monday to Saturday at noon and 2.30 pm, and on Sunday there are 1½-hour backstage tours ($9) at 12.15 and 2.15 pm, and for these you should make a booking (☎ 617 8151).

The **Performing Arts Museum** in the centre has changing exhibits on all aspects of the performing arts: it might be a display of rock musicians' outfits or an exhibit on horror in the theatre! Opening hours are weekdays 11 am to 5 pm and weekends noon to 5 pm, admission is $2.70 (children $1.40).

Parks & Gardens

Victoria has dubbed itself 'the garden state' and it's certainly true in Melbourne; the city has many swaths of green all around the central area. They're varied and delightful – formal central gardens like the Treasury and Flagstaff Gardens, wide empty parklands like Royal Park, the particularly fine Botanic Gardens and many others.

Royal Botanic Gardens Certainly the finest botanic garden in Australia and arguably among the finest in the world, this is one of the nicest spots in Melbourne. There's nothing more genteel to do in Melbourne than to have scones and cream by the lake on a Sunday afternoon. The beautifully laid out gardens are right beside the Yarra River; indeed the river once actually ran through the gardens and the lakes are the remains of curves of the river, cut off when the river was straightened out to lessen the annual flood damage. The garden site was chosen in 1845 but the real development took place when Baron Sir Ferdinand von Mueller took charge in 1852.

There's a surprising amount of fauna as well as flora in the gardens. Apart from the ever-present water fowl and the frequent visits from cockatoos you may also see rabbits and possums if you're lucky. In all, more than 50 varieties of birds can be seen in the gardens. A large contingent of fruit bats, usually found in the warmer climes of north Queensland, has taken up residence for the last ten summers or so – look for them high up the trees of the fern gully.

You can pick up guide-yourself leaflets at the park entrances; these are changed with the seasons and tell you what to look out for at the different times of year. The gardens are open daily from sunrise to sunset.

Kings Domain The Botanic Gardens form a corner of the Kings Domain, a park which also contains the Shrine of Remembrance, Governor La Trobe's Cottage and the Sidney

Myer Music Bowl. It's flanked by St Kilda Rd. The whole park is encircled by the Tan Track, a four-km running track which is probably Melbourne's favourite venue for joggers. The track has an amusing variety of exercise points – a mixture of the stations of the cross and miniature golf, someone once said.

Beside St Kilda Rd stands the massive **Shrine of Remembrance**, a WW I war memorial which took so long to build that WW II was well under way when it eventually opened. Huge though it is, the shrine somehow manages to look completely anonymous; you could almost forget it was there. It's worth climbing up to the top as there are fine views to the city along St Kilda Rd . The shrine's big day of the year is Anzac Day. Back during the Vietnam era some enterprising individuals managed to sneak up to the well-guarded shrine on the night before Anzac Day and paint 'PEACE' across the front in large letters. The shrine is open to visitors daily, except Sunday, from 10 am to 5 pm.

Across from the shrine is **Governor La Trobe's Cottage**, the original Victorian government house sent out from the UK in prefabricated form in 1840. It was originally sited in Jolimont, near the MCG, and was moved here when the decision was made to preserve this interesting piece of Melbourne's early history. The simple little cottage is open Monday and Wednesday from 10 am to 4 pm, weekends from 11 am to 4 pm, and admission is $3.50 (children $1.80, family $8).

The cottage is flanked by the **Old Observatory** and the **National Herbarium**. On some nights the observatory is open to the public for a free view of the heavens between 8 and 10 pm, but it is usually booked out months in advance. Phone the Museum of Victoria (☎ 669 9942) for details. Amongst other things the herbarium tests suspected marijuana samples to decide if they really are the dreaded weed.

The imposing building overlooking the Botanic Gardens is **Government House** where Victoria's governor resides. It's a copy of Queen Victoria's palace on England's Isle of Wight. There are guided tours on Monday, Wednesday and Saturday for $5 per person (☎ 654 4562).

Across the road from the herbarium on Dallas Brooks Drive is the **Australian Centre for Contemporary Art** which is open Tuesday to Friday from 11 am to 5 pm, weekends from 2 to 5 pm. It shows mainly the work of Australian artists. Up at the city end of the park is the **Sidney Myer Music Bowl**, an outdoor performance area in a natural bowl. It's used for concerts in the summer months but not rock concerts, due to trouble in the past from some younger members of the audience! In winter it turns into a skating rink.

Treasury & Fitzroy Gardens These two popular formal parks lie immediately to the east of the city centre, overshadowed by the Hilton Hotel. The Fitzroy Gardens, with its stately avenues lined with English elms, is a popular spot for wedding photographs; on virtually every Saturday afternoon there's a continuous procession of wedding cars pulling up for the participants to be snapped. The pathways in the park are actually laid out in the form of a Union Jack!

The gardens contain several points of interest including **Captain Cook's Cottage**, which was uprooted from its native Yorkshire and reassembled in the park in 1934. Actually it's not certain that the good captain ever did live in this house, but never mind, it looks very picturesque. The house is furnished in period style and has an interesting Captain Cook exhibit. It's open from 9 am to 5 pm daily and admission is $1.70 (children 60c).

In the centre of the gardens, by the kiosk, is a miniature Tudor village and a carved fairy-tale tree. Off in the north-west corner of the park is the people's pathway – a circular path paved with individually engraved bricks. Anybody who dropped by here on 5 February 1978 got to produce their own little bit of art for posterity and it's quite intriguing to wander around.

The two gardens have a large resident

population of possums; you may see them in the early evening or at night.

Other Parks The central **Flagstaff Gardens** were the first public gardens in Melbourne. From a lookout point here, ships arriving at the city were sighted in the early colonial days. A plaque in the gardens describes how the site was used for this purpose. Closer to the seafront is **Albert Park Lake,** a shallow lake created from a swamp area. The lake is popular for boating and there's another popular jogging track around the perimeter. You can hire boats on the lake, the Jolly Roger Boathouse is at the city end of the lake and rents rowing and sailing boats. On Saturday the two sailing clubs here have races on the lake. On the north side of the city, the Exhibition Gardens are the site of the **Exhibition Buildings**, a wonder of the southern hemisphere when they were built for the Great Exhibition of 1880. Later they were used by the Victorian Parliament for 27 years, while the Victorian parliament building was used by the national legislature until Canberra's parliament building was finally completed. They're still a major exhibition centre today and a new extension is one of the few successful uses of the 'mirror building' architectural craze which gripped Melbourne for a spell. There are some fine old fountains around the building, one of them well reflected in the mirror building.

To the north-east of the city, the Yarra is bordered by parkland, much loved by runners, rowers and cyclists. Rowing boats can be hired from the **Studley Park and Fairfield boathouses** – you can dawdle down the river with cockatoos screeching on the banks and the rush-hour traffic roaring along the Eastern Freeway overhead. In parts of Studley Park you could be out in the bush; it's hard to believe the city's all around you. The birds here are sometimes spectacular.

At 7 Templestowe Rd in the Melbourne suburb of Bulleen, **Heide Park & Gallery** is the former home of two prominent Australian artists, John and Sunday Reed, and houses an impressive collection of 20th-century Australian art. The sprawling park is an informal combination of deciduous and native trees, with a carefully tended kitchen garden and scattered sculpture gardens running right down to the banks of the Yarra. Heide is open from Tuesday to Friday between 10 am and 5 pm, and on Saturdays and Sundays between noon and 5 pm. Bus No 203 goes to Bulleen, and the Yarra bike path goes close by.

Melbourne Jogging

I've been a keen jogger for many years, and Melbourne provides some great routes for runners. Like many other Melbourne runners, my favourite is the Tan Track, the almost four-km circuit of the Botanic Gardens. If I get around in less than 16 minutes I'm happy, and I usually run the Tan first thing in the morning, four or five times a week. Incidentally every Tan regular has a favourite direction. I prefer to run up the steep Anderson St and get the tough bit over with quickly!

If I want a shorter run (from my home in Richmond, that is), then I run over to Fitzroy Gardens, the park beside the Hilton Hotel, and do a lap of that. Both these runs have great scenery as a plus point. The bicycle track beside the Yarra is another good run – from the boatsheds in the city to one of the Richmond/Hawthorn bridges is a good long riverside run, but watch out for the bike riders. A circuit of Albert Park Lake also makes a pleasant run, particularly when the sailboats are racing on Saturday afternoons.
- Tony Wheeler

Other Old Buildings

Como Overlooking the Yarra River from Como Park in South Yarra, Como was built between 1840 and 1859. The home with its extensive grounds has been authentically restored and furnished and is operated by the National Trust. Aboriginal rites and feasts were still being held on the banks of the Yarra when the house was first built, and an early occupant writes of seeing a cannibal rite from her bedroom window.

Como is open from 10 am to 5 pm every day and admission is $5.50 (students $3.75, children $2.75) and you can get there on tram No 8 from the city.

Ripponlea Ripponlea is at 192 Hotham St, Elsternwick, close to St Kilda. It's another fine old mansion with elegant gardens inhabited by peacocks. Ripponlea is open 10 am to 5 pm daily (8 pm in summer) and admission is $5.50 (students $3.75, children $2.75, family $15).

Montsalvat In Eltham, the mud-brick and alternative lifestylers suburb, Montsalvat on Hillcrest Ave (26 km out) is Justus Jorgensen's eclectic re-creation of a European artists' colony which today houses all manner of artists and artisans. It's open dawn to dusk daily. It's also the venue for Australia's biggest jazz festival, every January. It's a two-km walk from Eltham Station.

Other Museums
There are a number of smaller museums around Melbourne. In Chinatown in the city centre the **Museum of Chinese Australian History** is on Cohen Place, close to the corner of Lonsdale and Exhibition Sts. Housed in an 1890s Victorian warehouse, the museum traces the history of the Chinese in Australia. It's open Sunday to Thursday from noon to 5 pm; admission is $3 (children $1.50).

The **Melbourne Fire Brigade Museum** is at 8 Gisborne St, East Melbourne, and is open Fridays from 9 am to 3 pm and Sundays from 10 am to 4 pm; admission is $3 (children $1).

On Latrobe St near the corner of Russell St in the city is a small **Police Museum**, open weekdays from 10 am to 4 pm; free entry.

Out at Moorabbin Airport, Cheltenham, the **Moorabbin Air Museum** has a collection of old aircraft including a number from WW II. It's open daily from 10 to 5 pm.

Trams
If Melbourne has a symbol then it's a movable one – trams. Not those horrible, plastic-looking modern ones either; real Melbourne trams are green and yellow, ancient-looking and half the weight of an ocean liner. Trams are the standard means of public transport and they work remarkably well. More than a few cities which once had trams wish they still did today.

The old trams are gradually being replaced by new ones and some of the older trams have been turned into mobile works of art, painted from front to back by local artists. If you like old trams then watch out for them on weekends when some delightful vintage examples are rolled out on summer Sundays and used in place of the modern ones on the Hawthorn run from Princes Gate.

To come to grips with Melbourne and its trams try a ride on tram No 8. It starts off along Swanston St in the city, rolls down St Kilda Rd beside the Kings Domain, turns round by the war memorial and on to Toorak Rd through South Yarra and Toorak. Another popular tram ride is No 15 or No 16 which cruise right down St Kilda Rd to St Kilda.

There's a good little book *See Melbourne by Tram* by de Lacy Lowe, which will help you make the most of your season ticket.

Trams are such a part of Melbourne life they've even been used for a play – Act One of *Storming Mont Albert by Tram* took place from Mont Albert to the city, Act Two on the way back. The passengers were the audience, the actors got on and off along the way. It wasn't a bad play! There's even a tram restaurant: the Colonial Tramcar Restaurant cruises Melbourne every night and you can have dinner on the move for $40 to $75 including drinks, depending on the time and the night (☎ 696 4000 for reservations).

Melbourne Suburbs
Melbourne's inner-city suburbs have gone through the same 'trendification' process that has hit Sydney suburbs like Paddington and Balmain. Carlton is the most obvious example of this activity, but Parkville, Fitzroy, South Melbourne, Albert Park, Richmond and Hawthorn are other popular inner-city suburbs with a strong Victorian flavour.

Carlton & Fitzroy Carlton is one of Melbourne's most interesting inner-city suburbs – partly because here you'll find probably the most attractive collection of Victoriana, partly because the university is here and partly because Carlton is also the

Italian quarter of Melbourne with the biggest collection of Italian restaurants in Australia.

Lygon St, Carlton, is the backbone of Carlton and along here you'll find enough Italian restaurants, coffee houses, pizzerias and gelaterias to satisfy the most rabid pasta and cappuccino freak. The Lygon St Festa is held annually in November and always gets a good turn-out. The greasy-pole-climbing competition is popular.

Carlton is flanked by gracious Parkville and the seedy/trendy mixture of Fitzroy. **Brunswick St, Fitzroy** (recently headlined in the *Age* as the Street of Chic and Shame) displays both the most appalling inner-city poverty and the liveliest array of cafes, restaurants, young designer clothes shops and bookshops to be found in Melbourne. Any day now the developers will be moving in. **Johnston Street, Fitzroy,** is the home of the annual Hispanic Festival, every November.

South Yarra & Toorak South of the Yarra River (as the name indicates) South Yarra is one of the more frenetic Melbourne suburbs, Toorak one of the most exclusive. The two roads to remember here are Toorak Rd and Chapel St. **Toorak Rd** is one of Australia's classiest shopping streets, frequented by those well-known Toorak matrons in their Porsches, Mercedes Benzes and Range Rovers (otherwise known as 'Toorak tractors'). Apart from expensive shops and some of Australia's best (and most expensive) restaurants, Toorak Rd also has a number of very reasonably priced places to eat. Toorak Rd forms the main artery through both South Yarra and Toorak.

Running across Toorak Rd is **Chapel St, South Yarra**; if the word for Toorak Rd is 'exclusive' then for Chapel St it's 'trendy'. The street is virtually wall-to-wall boutiques ranging from punk to Indian bangles and beads, op-shop to antique, plus restaurants and the imaginative Jam Factory shopping centre, with the delightful Prahran Market off Commercial Rd nearby – a great place for fruit and vegetables. Chapel St trendiness fades as it gets further into Prahran, but turn right by the Prahran Town Hall and wander

along Greville St, at one time Melbourne's freak street, which still has some curious shops and a good Sunday market.

South Yarra also has one of Australia's finest colonial mansions, Como House, and the Royal Botanic Gardens flank the suburb.

Richmond As Carlton is to Italy so Richmond is to Greece; this suburb, just to the east of the city centre, is the Greek centre for the third largest Greek city in the world. That's right, after Athens and Thessaloniki, Melbourne is the next largest city in terms of Greek population. Richmond is, of course, the best place for a souvlaki in Melbourne! More recently Richmond became the centre for a huge influx of Vietnamese, and colourful **Victoria St** is known as 'Little Saigon'.

The suburb is another centre for Victorian architecture, much of it restored or currently in the process of restoration. **Bridge Rd** is something of a Melbourne fashion centre, with shops where many Australian fashion designers sell their seconds and rejects.

St Kilda This seaside suburb is Melbourne's most cosmopolitan and is very lively on weekends, particularly on Sundays. It's also the somewhat feeble excuse for a Melbourne sin centre; if you're after seedy nightlife you'll do better in Sydney's Kings Cross but if you want a meal late at night or some activity on the weekends then St Kilda is the place to be. Fitzroy and Acland Sts, with their numerous restaurants, snack bars and takeaways, are the main streets in St Kilda.

Sunday morning along the **Esplanade** features an interesting amateur art show and craft market, while along Acland St gluttons will have their minds blown by the amazing selection of cakes in the coffee shop windows. St Kilda has lots of local Jewish and ethnic colour. The huge old Palais Theatre and the raucous Luna Park amusement centre, with roller coasters and the like, can also be found here.

The St Kilda Festival is held on the second weekend in February. Acland St is usually turned into a mall with foodstalls and entertainment, and in Fitzroy St all the restaurants

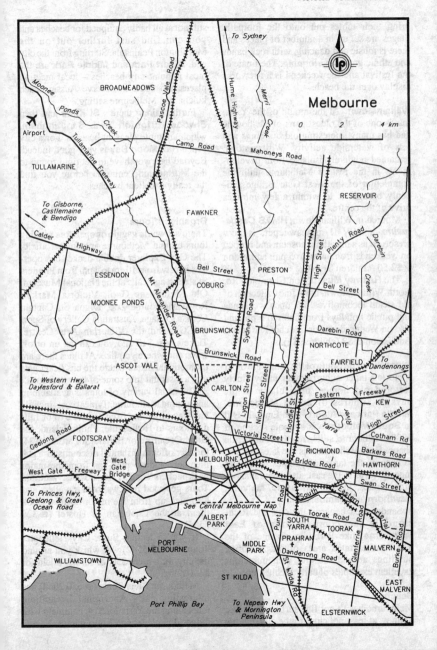

bring their tables out onto the footpath. Stages are set up in a number of places and there is music and dancing, with rock bands and ethnic groups performing. The finale of the festival and the weekend is a fireworks display over the beach.

Williamstown At the mouth of the Yarra, this is one of the oldest parts of Melbourne and has many interesting old buildings and lots of waterside activity. Williamstown remained relatively isolated from developments in the rest of Melbourne until the completion of the West Gate Bridge suddenly brought it to within a few minutes drive of the centre.

Moored in Williamstown, **HMAS Castlemaine**, a WW II minesweeper, is now preserved as a maritime museum and is open on weekends from noon to 5 pm; admission is $2.50 (children $1.50).

The **Railway Museum** on Champion Rd, North Williamstown, has a fine collection of old steam locomotives. It's open weekends and public holidays from noon to 5 pm and also on Wednesdays during school holidays. Admission is $2 (children $1).

Other Suburbs South of the centre are other Victorian inner suburbs with many finely restored old homes, particularly in the bayside suburbs of **South Melbourne, Middle Park** and **Albert Park**. Emerald Hill in **South Melbourne** is a whole section of 1880s Melbourne, still in relatively authentic shape. **Port Melbourne** is the latest suburb to become the target of yuppies. Wealthier inner suburbs to the east, also popular shopping centres, include **Armadale, Malvern, Hawthorn** and **Camberwell**.

Sandwiched between the city and Richmond is the compact area of **East Melbourne**; like Parkville it's one of the most concentrated areas of old Victorian buildings around the city with numerous excellent examples of early architecture.

Beaches

Melbourne hasn't got fine surf beaches like Sydney, at least not close to the city, but it's still not at all badly equipped for beaches and you can find surf further out on the Mornington Peninsula. Starting from the city end, **Albert Park** and **Middle Park** are the most popular city beaches – local meeting places and spots to observe Aussie beach kulcha in a Melbourne setting.

Further along there's **St Kilda** and then **Elwood, Brighton** and **Sandringham**, which are quite pleasant beaches. For a city beach **Half Moon Bay** is very good indeed. Beyond here you have to get right round to the Mornington Peninsula before you find the really excellent beaches.

Organised Tours

There's a whole gaggle of operators running tours around Melbourne and further afield. The City Explorer double-decker bus operates hourly from 10 am to 4 pm from Flinders St station and calls at the National Museum, Old Melbourne Gaol, Victoria Market, Royal Melbourne Zoo, Lygon St, Captain Cook's Cottage, Australian Gallery of Sport (MCG), and the Victorian Arts Centre. Tickets cost $13 and you can get on or off when and where you like. At times there are promotional offers where the bus ticket gets you a discount into some of the attractions.

The usual variety of tours is available in and around Melbourne. Typical costs include half-day city tours from around $13 or full-day tours to Healesville, Phillip Island, the Great Ocean Rd or Ballarat for around $34. Pioneer offers substantial discounts to YHA members and do pick-ups from the major backpackers' and YHA hostels. Autopia Tours get good reviews from travellers and also pick up from the major hostels. Book them at the Chapman St Hostel (☎ 328 3595).

If you're feeling flush, City Helicopter Tours (☎ 629 5542) will whisk you around the city for a mere $50, or further afield for a lot more.

Melbourne River Tours (☎ 650 2054) has interesting daily Aboriginal Dreamtime tours along the Yarra for $14, complete with didgeridoo player and Koori guides.

Festivals

Moomba is Melbourne's annual festival, held around the beginning of March. The weather is usually good and Melbournians let their hair down.

The **Melbourne Film Festival** is one of the world's oldest and best, although the catch is that it's held in June, the depths of winter.

Melbourne is Australia's comedy capital, and the **Comedy Festival** in April is an exciting time, with local acts (often en route to the Edinburgh Fringe) and international guests.

The **Melbourne International Festival** (formerly known as the Spoleto Festival as a similar festival was held in Spoleto, Italy) is an excellent arts festival with many and varied events, including the popular Fringe Festival. It's held in September. The world-famous Melbourne Cup is run on the first Tuesday in November each year.

Places to Stay

Melbourne has a fairly wide range of accommodation. It's not centred in any particular area although the old-fashioned hotels are found mainly in the city, particularly near Spencer St Station. The seaside suburb of St Kilda is probably the best general accommodation centre in Melbourne. There you'll find a wide variety of reasonably priced motels, private hotels, guesthouses, holiday flats and popular travellers' hostels.

For places to share, the notice boards in the universities, in the YHA office and in the front window of Readings bookshop in Carlton are all worth checking. The classified columns in the *Age* on Wednesdays and Saturdays are the place to look for longer term accommodation. It is much easier to find places to rent in Melbourne than in Sydney. Note that most of the cheaper hotels, guesthouses and the like will also offer cheaper weekly rates. These are typically about four times the daily rates so it soon becomes better value to stay for a week.

Hostels With the proliferation of back-packers' hostels in recent years, the competition is now fierce. Most offer similar facilities, although some are definitely better than others. Most places, particularly those out of the city centre, offer free pick-up from the bus and train stations, and when the interstate buses come in early in the morning there are sometimes more hostel minibuses than backpackers. It helps if you know where you want to stay, so you're not faced with a bewildering array of options when you step off a bus half-asleep after an uncomfortable night.

City Centre There are two YHA hostels, both in North Melbourne, about three km from the city centre. Both offer a 10% discount for a pre-booked five-day stay. From the airport you can ask the Skybus to drop you at the North Melbourne hostels.

The YHA showpiece is the *Queensberry Hill Hostel* (☎ 329 8599) at 78 Howard St, North Melbourne. This 348-bed place was only completed in mid-1991 and so has excellent facilities. Charges range from $17 for YHA members in a dorm ($3 more for nonmembers) up to $68 for a serviced room with private bathroom. There's a breakfast and dinner service available, and office hours are 7.30 am to 10.30 pm, although there is 24-hour access once you have checked in. Catch tram No 55 from William St, or tram No 59 from Elizabeth St, and get off at stop No 15.

The other YHA hostel in North Melbourne is the 100-bed *Chapman St Hostel* (☎ 328 3595) at 76 Chapman St. Accommodation in this nonsmoking hostel costs $15 per person in twin rooms. Both hostels have good notice boards if you're looking for people to travel with, share lifts, cheap airline tickets or just general information. There are a number of very good tours which operate out of the hostels, and destinations include Phillip Island, Wilsons Prom, the Great Ocean Road and the Grampians.

There are a number of backpacker hostel alternatives in the central city, although finding a bed in Melbourne in the middle of summer can still be difficult.

Many city backpackers' hostels have a

strong streak of opportunism to them, but never mind, they're central, quite comfortable if a little noisy and rundown, and the price is right. They are older pubs, the sort of places where for years the hotel rooms have been empty and unused. Suddenly, with the influx of travellers to Australia, they've got a use again!

The best of the city bunch is probably the *Rendezvous Travellers City Hotel* (☎ 329 7635) at 441 Elizabeth St, within easy walking distance of both the bus terminals and Spencer St Station. A bed in a four or six-bed dorm costs $15; single/double rooms cost from $30/36. The cooking facilities are adequate and the security is generally thought to be good.

The *Backpackers City Inn* (☎ 650 4379) is at 197 Bourke St (3rd floor of the Carlton Hotel) and charges $12 in a dorm, $14 per person in a twin room. It's not a bad place, and there's a bar on the 2nd floor.

The other city place is *Zanies Backpackers* (☎ 663 7862) at 230 Russell St on the corner of Lonsdale St. Despite the flash pub and bistro downstairs, the accommodation upstairs is very shabby, and it's generally rundown and gloomy. At $10 a night it is undeniably cheap, but only 'international' visitors are taken in – if you're just from interstate you ain't welcome here. Try practising that pommy accent.

On the fringe of the city at 116 Nicholson St, Fitzroy, is the fairly new *Nunnery* (☎ 419 8637), almost opposite the Exhibition Buildings. It's a large, spacious building with good facilities, including an excellent lounge with open fire. The bedrooms are definitely on the small side, but the furniture is new and the rooms have central heating. Beds in dorms with up to eight beds cost $14, twins and doubles $18 per person. Take tram No 96 heading east along Bourke St, and get off at stop No 11.

St Kilda It's very easy to get out to seaside St Kilda, just a straightforward tram ride. Nos 15 or 16 from Swanston St down the wide, tree-lined St Kilda Rd to Fitzroy St will get you there. Alternatively there's the light-rail service (No 96 from Spencer St & Bourke St) to the old St Kilda railway station and along Fitzroy and Acland Sts.

Apart from the travellers' hostels listed here, there are a number of longer term boarding houses in St Kilda, but these can be a little rough and probably wouldn't suit most travellers.

Probably the best known of the St Kilda hostels is the *Enfield House Backpackers* (☎ 534 8159) at 2 Enfield St. It's a huge old boarding house which has been turned into a backpackers' hostel with rooms for 100 people. It's in a good location, close to the St Kilda restaurants and easy to get to. Rooms generally have bunks for four people at $12 each but there are also singles/doubles at $16/28. There are also some nearby flats managed by the hostel which are good if you're intending to stay longer in Melbourne, costing $160 a week for up to four people. There is a courtesy van which picks up travellers from the airline terminal in Franklin St, Spencer St Station, and from Station Pier for the Tasmanian ferries. These people also operate the *Melbourne Workers Hostel* (☎ 534 8995) at 28 Grey St. This is older and smaller than Enfield House, but is also cheaper at $9 per night.

Right next door to the Workers Hostel is the other main place in St Kilda, the *St Kilda Backpackers Inn* (☎ 534 5283) at 24 Grey St. This place is also known as the Coffee Palace. It's fairly shabby but otherwise OK with dorm beds for $8 and twins at $10 per person. They also have the *Lola's Cottage Backpackers* at 56 Jackson St, just around the corner. This is a smaller place, but is similarly priced at $9 per night.

At 24 Mitford St is the *Backpackers by the Beach* (☎ 525 4355. It's a much smaller place with good facilities, although the kitchen is tiny. All dorm rooms have a fridge and colour TV. A bed here costs $10, or there are a few small double bungalows in the large back yard, which also has some picnic tables.

Victoria's Backpackers Hostel (☎ 525 5165) is at 46 Acland St; it has dormitory beds from $9 or doubles at $14 each.

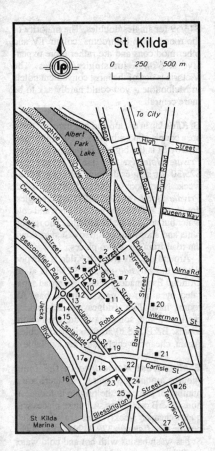

St Kilda

0   250   500 m

To City

Albert
Park
Lake

Aughtie Drive

Queens Road

High Street

St Kilda Road

Punt Road

Canterbury Road

Park Street

Beaconsfield Pde

Fitzroy Street

Princes Street

Grey Street

Acland Street

Robe St

Barkly Street

Queens Way

Alma Rd

Inkerman St

Carlisle St

Blessington Street

Tennyson St

Jacka Blvd

Esplanade

St Kilda
Marina

More up-market, but still good value, is the *Olembia Travellers Hotel* (☎ 537 1412; 008 032 635, toll-free) at 96 Barkly St. Here the carpets are less worn, the facilities better and the whole place has less of a boarding-house feel to it. Dorm beds cost $14, but there's also a $2 bed linen charge. Single/double rooms cost $30/44, with better deals available for longer stays. All rooms are centrally heated, and there's a comfortable lounge.

For longer term stays, the flats at 84 Blessington St (☎ 787 5720) cater to back-packers, and the charge is $110 per week.

Elsewhere *Andy's Backpackers Hostel* (☎ 489 1802) at 49 James St, Northcote, eight km north of the city centre, has beds from $8 to $12 in a variety of places in Northcote. The main hostel in James St is well set up and the atmosphere is very casual and friendly. It does the usual pick-ups from points in the city, and it's very close to tram Nos 86 or 87 from Bourke St; get off at stop No 31. If demand warrants it, Andy organises impromptu tours to various places, such as the Healesville Sanctuary, a country race meeting, or places that are generally harder to reach without your own transport.

It's a pretty good place and is popular with travellers, particularly those wanting a longer stay.

Further out in this direction is the *Terrace Travellers Hostel* (☎ 470 1006) at 418 Murray Rd, Preston – take trams Nos 10, 11 or 13 and get off at stop No 48. Although the facilities here are as good as at any of the other hostels, it is a long way from the centre of things, and it lacks atmosphere. Dorm beds are $10 with reductions for longer stays.

The Y The *YWCA Family Hotel* (☎ 329 5188) is conveniently central at 489 Elizabeth St, close to the bus terminals, and very competitively priced. Singles/doubles are $45/56 or there are four-bed bunk rooms for $60; all rooms have shower and toilet, air-con, and tea-making facilities. Outside it's very much '70s bare concrete but inside it's functional and well equipped. There's also a cafeteria here.

Hotels As with cheaper accommodation, you have a choice between the convenience of the city centre and the often more pleasant surroundings of the inner suburbs.

City Melbourne's cheap hotels tend to be concentrated at the Spencer St end of the city, near the railway station. At 44 Spencer St the *John Spencer Hotel* (☎ 629 6991) has rooms at $36/46 in the older hotel section or more expensive motel-style rooms from $74/84. It's rather brighter inside than its somewhat gloomy exterior would suggest.

Close by at 131 King St the *Kingsgate Hotel* (☎ 629 4171) is a big old place with more than 200 widely varying rooms – the most expensive have bathrooms, air-con, fridges, and so on. In between there are rooms with attached shower and toilet, or just a wash basin, and right at the bottom they're very bare and basic. Singles range from $28 to $39, doubles from $46 to $54.

The *Victoria Hotel* (☎ 653 0441) at 215 Little Collins St is a notch up-market from the cheapest city hotels. It's a big place with no less than 520 rooms. There are 135 basic rooms without private facilities which cost $46/59 for singles/doubles. The majority of the rooms have bathrooms, colour TV and other mod cons and are rather more expensive at $74/95 for singles/doubles. The Victoria is one of the most convenient hotels in Melbourne – you could hardly ask to be more central.

St Kilda Up at the top end of Fitzroy St there are a couple of possibilities. First of all at 151 Fitzroy St is the big old-fashioned *Majestic Private Hotel* (☎ 534 0561). Rooms cost $25/30 for singles/doubles, cheaper by the week. Next door at No 149 is the *Regal Private Hotel* (☎ 534 5603) with singles/doubles at $20/28. Rooms have hot and cold water but not private bathrooms. The restaurants and shops along Fitzroy St start down the road from these two places.

Around the bay from St Kilda is Elwood where the *Bayside* (☎ 531 9238) is at 65 Ormond Esplanade, a rather busy road separated by a narrow park from the bay. All rooms have TVs, fridges and tea-making facilities, and some have attached bathrooms. B&B is $30/50 for singles/doubles. Again, cheaper weekly rates are available.

East & West Melbourne In the inner suburbs around the central city there are a number of places in the private hotel/guesthouse/B&B categories. All these places will quote cheaper weekly rates. In West Melbourne the *Miami* (☎ 329 8499) at 13 Hawke St has wash basins with hot and cold water in all the rooms, and breakfast is included in the $31/34 nightly tariff. Although simple, the Miami is well kept, and it's an easy walk to the centre. It's a big, square block of a place with over 100 rooms.

The *Georgian Court* (☎ 419 6353) at 21 George St, East Melbourne, has rooms for $45/58, cheaper weekly rates and shared cooking facilities. George St is a quiet, tree-lined street and the genteel-looking Georgian Court is right across the road from the post office. Although East Melbourne is very close to the city centre it's generally a fairly quiet area. At 101 George St the *George Street* (☎ 419 1693) has serviced apartments, all with bathroom, fridge and cooking facilities at $65 a double including a light breakfast.

South Yarra Tram No 8 from the city runs right by the *West End* (☎ 866 5375) at 76 Toorak Rd West in South Yarra. This pleasant, small guesthouse looks across to Fawkner Park; the rooms have tea-making facilities and cost $28/44 including breakfast.

About midway between South Yarra Station and Chapel St, the *Toorak Private Hotel* (☎ 827 8652) is at 189 Toorak Rd. Nightly costs are just $20/25 for singles/doubles; weekly rates are $79/115. Most of the residents are long-term, however, and it's no longer popular with backpackers.

Motels & Serviced Apartments There's no real motel strip in Melbourne but you can find reasonably priced (ie doubles for around $50) and fairly central motels in several suburbs, South Yarra and St Kilda in particular. The *Domain* (☎ 866 3701), at 52 Darling St in South Yarra, has rooms at $55/62 with all the usual motel mod cons (although no bathroom). It's conveniently close to the tram lines for the centre and to the Yarra River. At No 26 on the same street the *St James Holiday Units* (☎ 866 4455) has one and two-bedroom units at $55 a double.

There has been a trend in recent years to convert blocks of flats in South Yarra into holiday apartments. Some of them are quite expensive but cheaper ones include the *Avoca St Apartments* (☎ 867 5200) at 23 Avoca St where self-contained units cost $65 a day or $395 a week. *South Yarra Place* (☎ 867 6595) at 41 Margaret St is $55 to $68, or there's the *Aston* (☎ 866 2953) at 42 Powell St with one-bedroom units at $75.

In St Kilda the *Carlisle Lodge Motel* (☎ 534 0316) at 32 Carlisle St has rooms at $55 per person. It's a plain, slightly older motel but rooms have fridges and a few have cooking facilities and air-con. Almost on the corner with Fitzroy St, directly opposite the station, the *Executive* (☎ 534 0303) is at 239 Canterbury Rd, St Kilda, and has rooms at $30 a double. It's a square, featureless box looking more like a block of flats than a motel, but is conveniently close to all the noise and colour of Fitzroy St.

Right on Fitzroy St at No 63 is *Pebble Court* (☎ 534 0524) which has motel rooms for $50/65 for singles/doubles and serviced apartments from $75. Their rates rise at peak times such as the AFL Grand Final and the Melbourne Cup.

Acland St has several places including the *Kingscourt Motor Inn* (☎ 534 0673) at No 15 where rooms cost $48/52. At 3 Acland St the *Spaceline Motel* (☎ 534 8074) has singles/doubles from $40/45. *City Gate Travel* (☎ 534 2650) at 6 Tennyson St has holiday flats from $42.

You'll also find some reasonably priced motels in less attractive suburbs on the main routes into and out of Melbourne. There are a number of motels in Coburg and Brunswick on Sydney Rd.

Colleges Melbourne has three universities: the long-established Melbourne University and two newer 'bush universities' – La Trobe and Monash. Visitors would probably find the latter two too far away from the centre to be worth considering.

Melbourne University, by contrast, is very central, just to the north of the city centre. The following colleges have accommodation in the vacation period from late November to mid-February; B&B ranges from $30 to $39, and there's a minimum stay of three nights: *International House* (☎ 347 6655); *Medley Hall* (☎ 663 5847); *Ridley College* (☎ 387 7555); *Ormond College* (☎ 348 1688); *Queen's College* (☎ 349 0500); *Trinity College* (☎ 347 1044); *University College* (☎ 347 3533); *Whitley College* (☎ 347 8388). There are cheaper rates for students at all these colleges.

Camping Melbourne is not too badly off for city camp sites although none of them are very close to the centre. The Coburg East site (10 km north) and the Footscray site (eight km west) are probably the most convenient. The Footscray site only has on-site vans but the Coburg one is quite comprehensively equipped. The following are some of Melbourne's closer sites:

Northside Caravan Park
Corner Hume Highway and Coopers Rd, Campbellfield, 14 km north, camping $12, cabin vans $35 (☎ 305 3614)

Melbourne Caravan Park
265 Elizabeth St, Coburg East, 10 km north, camping $10, on-site vans $28, flats $39 (☎ 354 3533)

Crystal Brook Holiday Centre
Corner Warrandyte and Andersons Creek Rd, Doncaster East, 21 km north-east, camping $14, on-site vans $46 (☎ 844 3637)

Footscray Caravan Park
163 Somerville Rd, West Footscray, eight km west, no camping, on-site vans $28 (☎ 314 6646)

Hobsons Bay Caravan Park
158 Kororoit Creek Rd, Williamstown, 17 km south, camping $12, cabin vans $30 (☎ 397 2395)

Places to Eat

Historically the Victorian licensing laws made it difficult and expensive to get a liquor licence but quite simple to obtain a BYO (bring-your-own) licence. The resulting plethora of BYOs is held by staunch Melbournians to be the cornerstone of Melbourne's culinary superiority. Recently these laws have been relaxed and many BYOs are now also becoming licensed, so you can choose to BYO or buy your liquor from the restaurant. There are lots of exclusively licensed restaurants too, some of which are actually cheap, but it's the BYOs which you will find everywhere around the city. It's rare to be charged 'corkage' when you bring your own wine to a Melbourne BYO.

There are over 30 pages of restaurants in the Melbourne Yellow Pages phone direc-

---

Melbourne Restaurants

Writing travel guides certainly gives you a taste for eating out, even in your own home town. Some of my Melbourne favourites are in Richmond, since that's where we live, particularly places along Bridge Rd which we can walk to in minutes. The *Uptown Deli* and the *Tofu Shop* are two familiar places while *Rajdoot* is our favourite local source for a good Indian curry. Bridge Rd also has one of the best pizzerias in Melbourne – *Silvio's* at No 270. If we want something fancier (and more expensive) we head for *Cafe Kanis* at No 138 where the food is rather like what Californians would call California Cuisine. Or we cross Punt Rd to *Il Duca* at 10 Wellington Parade, on the Richmond edge of East Melbourne. This is one of the nicest Italian restaurants in Melbourne, where the menu always features something a little different and delicious.

Of course we have some firm favourites on Victoria St, Richmond's 'Little Saigon'. It's amusing how so many of the Vietnamese restaurants here have double-barrelled names. Like the bare and basic (but cheap and delicious) *Thy Thy 1* at No 142 or the new, glossy and noisy (but still cheap) *Tho Tho* at No 66. Smack in the middle of the Richmond Greek quarter of Swan St there's an excellent Thai restaurant, *Erewan* at No 205.

In the city we often seem to be rushing to grab a meal before going to the cinema or theatre. A favourite for a quick meal is the Hyatt Hotel's superb *Food Court*. I've loved these multi-cuisine food centres ever since first coming across them in Singapore in the early '70s, and this one is a great place to eat; the Japanese food here is particularly good. There's also a good *Tapas Bar* upstairs, another good cuisine for a fast meal. Or just round the corner from the Hyatt is *Rosati's* on Flinders Lane – not cheap, but the food is always good.

In South Yarra, *Pieroni's* at 172 Toorak Rd is a close relation to Rosati's and a good place for excellent if slightly pricey Italian food. Australia is probably the world's cappucino capital, and it's easier to find an excellent cappucino in Melbourne than in Rome. The *Deli* at 26 Toorak Rd is a good place for a cappucino any time of the day or night. Lygon St in Carlton is Melbourne's cappucino centre, of course, but my favourite eatery on this predominantly Italian street is the Chinese-Malaysian *Nyonya*. Finally for the morning after all this great eating, head to the *Fitz* at 347 Brunswick St, Fitzroy, for the best breakfast in Melbourne. ■

Tony Wheeler

tory and two guidebooks, both titled *Cheap Eats*, if you're serious about searching out the best dining bargains. There are restaurants all over the place – go to Lygon St, Carlton, for Italian food; Swan St, Richmond, for Greek food; Victoria St, Richmond, for Vietnamese; Sydney Rd, Brunswick, for Turkish; Little Bourke St in the city for Chinese; or Johnston St, Fitzroy, for Spanish.

The restaurants we list are just a small selection of favourites which are near the city centre or are in the main areas where travellers may be staying in or visiting. For rock-bottom cheapness the best bargains can probably be found amongst the Vietnamese restaurants on Victoria St, Richmond, or the Turkish ones on Sydney Rd, Brunswick. For sheer variety head to Brunswick St, Fitzroy.

City The central city area offers a range of good-value eating possibilities, and although Chinese food is the specialty, there are many other cuisines.

Chinese You'll find a superb variety of Chinese food along Little Bourke St, the Chinatown of Melbourne. Most of the Little Bourke St Chinese restaurants tend to be more expensive, however. You have to dive off into the narrow lanes off Little Bourke, or abandon it altogether, to find the real bargains, like *Nam Loong* at 223 Russell St where even the blackboard menu is in Chinese. You almost feel like they're being condescending when they produce an English menu and you can certainly expect nothing but chopsticks. The prices are, however, something to smile about, with main dishes for around $6.50. Eat early though, Nam Loong closes at 9.30 pm.

At 30 Crossley St the *Malaya* does filling Malaysian-Chinese food, especially the soups and noodle dishes. Main courses are $6 to $12. *Peony Gardens* at 283 Little Lonsdale is more of a takeaway place, less a restaurant. It's patronised by Chinese students, and it's not only good but cheap too. Most dishes are $3 to $5 and at that price you really can't complain about plastic plates and

utensils or having to clear the table off after you've eaten. It's open for lunch Monday to Friday.

The crowded *Kunming Restaurant* at 212 Little Bourke St combines straightforward, no-frills decor with excellent food including 'the best Char Kwei Teow outside KL'. The authentic noodle and rice dishes are only about $7 and this is one of the best value Chinese restaurants in Melbourne. *King of Kings* at 209 Russell St also has very good and cheap food, and is open until 2 am.

The *Jan Bo Seafood Restaurant* at 40 Little Bourke St has a more expensive à la carte menu but their Sunday yum cha at 11 am or 1 pm is great, and most dishes are $2.20. At the other extreme the highly acclaimed *Flower Drum* in Market Lane has beautiful food, excellent service and incredibly high prices!

City – other Asian restaurants Malaysian food has become a firm favourite in Melbourne recently and it's generally very reasonably priced. The *Little Malaysia* at 26 Liverpool St, the *Rumah Penang* at No 11 on the same street, and the *Ipoh* at 272 Russell St are all worth trying.

There are plenty of Japanese places in the city including the *Toki Sushi Bar* at Zanies on the corner of Russell and Lonsdale Sts, where sushi meets pub food. It's an informal sushi bar in a city hotel with reasonable prices and good food.

Yamato is a tiny Japanese restaurant at 28 Corrs Lane, hidden away off Little Bourke St. It's been around for years and turns out excellent food at reasonable prices. Main courses cost from $9 and their banana tempura is definitely worth a try. The *Stone Garden (Sekitei)* at 169 Bourke St is another relatively inexpensive hidden-away Japanese restaurant.

India House, upstairs at 401-405 Swanston St, at the Carlton end of the city, has good Indian food and a relaxed atmosphere. The set lunch for $12 is excellent value. *Gopal's* at 139 Swanston St is run by the Hare Krishna sect, and like their other places around Australia, is pure, wholesome and very cheap.

The city also has Korean, Mongolian, Thai and Vietnamese places.

City – other cuisines Surprisingly, two of the city's most expensive hotels, both on Collins St, have good places for a reasonably priced meal. On the corner of Collins and Russell Sts the *Hyatt Food Court* has a choice of half a dozen dining styles including pasta and pizza, Mediterranean Turkish-cum-Greek, Japanese, Chinese and even straightforward Aussie steaks. It's very popular and at night can be very noisy. Further up Collins you come to the Regent Hotel and ANZ Bank towers; in the 'great space' between them you'll find *Babalu* with an interesting menu where you can make a meal of starters or mix Mexican and Chinese. It's licensed and also very popular.

Open from 7 am to midnight every day and 24 hours over the weekend, the *Pancake Parlour* is the place to go for a meal from breakfast to a late-night snack. It's at 25 Market Lane, is fairly fast-foodish in atmosphere and a bit expensive but very popular. There are other branches in Centrepoint on Bourke St and at 22 McKillop St.

Almost at the top of Bourke St is another Melbourne institution – *Pellegrini's* at No 66. It's a quick-meal sort of place with the usual pasta dishes. If you want to take things a little easier then go round the corner to their restaurant in Crossley St where you can relax over the same food at higher prices. Right across Bourke St at 20 Meyers Place the *Italian Waiters Restaurant* is another historic Melbourne institution. Simply knowing it's there, hidden away upstairs without a sign to announce its presence, is half the fun. It's open until late, and good cheap Italian food is the order of the day.

There's a small Greek enclave in the city along Lonsdale St from the corner with Russell St. *Stalactites*, right on the corner at 177 Lonsdale, is the best known, mainly for its bizarre stalactite decor and the fact that it's open 24 hours – the last time the front door was closed was in 1980! *Electra* at 195

Lonsdale St is more elegant than the average run of cheap Greeks, with main courses at around $12, and there's also the pleasant *Tsindos the Greek's Restaurant* at 197 Lonsdale.

Campari Bistro at 25 Hardware St, a hop, step and jump from the GPO, is a busy little Italian bistro which can get very crowded at lunch time; main courses are around $9. Nearby is the spacious and bright *McKillop Food Hall* at 21-27 McKillop St where lunch-time food possibilities include noodles from *Asian Fair*, a slice of pizza from *Alberto's* or even a pie and chips from *True Blue*.

The *Spaghetti Bazaar* at 13 The Causeway does plain and simple pasta at plain and simple prices. *Rosati's*, on Flinders Lane just around the corner from the Hyatt Hotel, is a huge and trendy place, somewhere to go to see and be seen as much as to eat or drink anything. Vegetarians can find other good places, particularly at lunch time at the host of *Pure & Natural Food Co* outlets dotted around the city, or try *Gopal's* (mentioned earlier). For a real change in the city, book lunch at the *William Angliss College* (☎ 606 2111) at 555 Latrobe St. For $15 you get an excellent three-course lunch prepared by the college's apprentice chefs and served by the apprentice waiters. You have to be there between 12 and 12.30 and it's only open during term time. Next door you can get a $5 haircut from the trainee hairdressers!

There's a good choice of pub food specialists around the city. You could try the *Sherlock Holmes* at 415 Collins St or the *Phoenix Hotel* at 82 Flinders St. The *Grosvenor Tavern* at 2a Equitable Place, off Little Collins St, is a little hard to find but worth the effort.

For a lunch-time sandwich or a range of delicious snacks the *Myers* department store food hall, on the ground floor between Little Bourke and Lonsdale Sts, has a very wide selection. The *David Jones* department store, in the basement of their Bourke St store (the one opposite, not next to, Myers), also has an excellent selection of goodies to satisfy even the most obscure craving.

St Kilda This has always been the late-night centre in Melbourne, and it's now the backpacker centre as well. Tram Nos 15 or 16 or the St Kilda light-rail (tram Nos 69 or 79) will get you here. Most of the eating places are along Fitzroy and Acland Sts. Starting from the seaside end at 1 Fitzroy St is *Cleopatra's*. This tiny Lebanese place, which mainly does takeaways, also produces some of the best quality Middle Eastern food in Melbourne, at very reasonable prices; large serves are around $5. Almost next door is *Mariners* at No 9, an excellent licensed and BYO seafood place with nothing over about $12, and it's open until 1 am. At 23 Fitzroy St there's the *Aztec Restaurant*, a good Mexican place with flamenco dancers on Thursday and Sunday nights.

At 55 Fitzroy St *Leo's Spaghetti Bar* is something of a St Kilda institution with pasta from around $6 to $8, excellent coffee and late opening hours. Leo's is divided into three parts and the prices rise as you move from the coffee bar at the front through the central bistro area to the restaurant section at the back. The *USA Dog House Cafe* at No 63 is a good place for a coffee and snack at a table on the footpath.

Topolino's at 87 Fitzroy St is noted not only for its excellent pizzas but also for its late opening hours. There are other traditional Italian dishes as well. Some distance further up is the *Bamff* at No 145 where the chef does amazing things with vegetables, although it closes at 10.30 pm.

Turn the corner from Fitzroy St into Acland St and you'll find a host of places to try including the very trendy *Caffe Maximus* at No 64. It's a stylish place which attracts the local stylish people and is good for an afternoon coffee or a late-night pasta. Style don't come cheap, however: pastas are $12 to $15, other main dishes $13 to $18; pretty mind-blowing desserts, though.

Right next door is *Greasy Joe's*, not quite as stylish as the Caffe Max but much more so than its name would suggest! Straightforward meals here are all under $10 and it's also licensed.

The *Amber* at No 73 is an Indian place

with excellent food and reasonable prices. Across the road at No 90, *Daniel Gerards* is a friendly place with a mildly eccentric owner (Daniel), who serves fine main dishes for $14 to $18.

The *Cafe Danube* at No 107 and *Scheherezade* at No 99 also do good, plain Central European food in large quantities. These are good places to come when you're really hungry.

Wild Rice at 211 Barkly St is a very good little cafe where the emphasis is on macrobiotic and other interesting snack food; the variety is excellent and the prices low.

There are quite a few other restaurants along Acland St but the street's crowning glory is its orgiastic cake shops. The displays in the shop windows emanate so many calories you're in danger of putting on kg just walking by them!

Finally there's *Jean-Jacques* at 40 Jacka Boulevard, right by the seafront. The restaurant section, *Jean-Jacques by the Sea*, is glossy, expensive and has some of the best seafood you'll find in Melbourne. Don't despair, for those of us without gold American Express cards there's a takeaway section where you can get fish for $2.60, calamari for $4.50, excellent chips for $1.60 or a 'fisherman's box' seafood assortment for $9. Then you can sit outside, watch the sea and share your meal with the ever-hungry seagulls.

Albert Park & Port Melbourne These beach suburbs have some interesting cheap dining possibilities. At 183 Victoria Ave, Albert Park, the *Stavros Tavern* is a very popular long-running Greek restaurant which has excellent food, and bazouki players on Friday and Saturday nights. The *Avenue Food Store* at 69 Victoria Ave does good home-made takeaway food.

Port Melbourne has a host of popular pub food possibilities including the *Clare Castle* at 354 Graham St, the *Rose & Crown* at 309 Bay St and *Roosters by the Bay* at 24 Bay St. Also on Bay St is the *Bay & Boundary Hotel* with its daily specials marked on a blackboard, and a friendly atmosphere. The

Albion Hotel at 146 Evans St has very good seafood at around $12 for a main course.

Williamstown As a final cheap eats possibility, cross the bridge to Williamstown where the remarkable *Yacht Club Hotel* at 207 Nelson Place has some of the cheapest pub food around, although it's pretty uninspiring. There's also good Indian food by the sea at *Kohinoor* at 233 Nelson Place.

North & West Melbourne North Melbourne, where the Melbourne YHA hostels are found, is not a great restaurant quarter although there are some possibilities along Victoria St. Try *Amiconi* at No 359. This traditional little Italian bistro has been going so long they must be doing something right. Or try *Dalat's* at No 270 for Vietnamese food or *Warung Agus* at 305 for truly superb Malaysian, Indonesian and vegetarian food.

The *Eldorado Hotel* at 46 Leveson St is famous for its cheap prices and generous serves.

The vibrant *Victoria Market*, on the corner of Victoria and Elizabeth Sts, sells produce on Tuesday, Thursday and Saturday mornings and all day Friday, and on Sundays sells clothes and cheap goods. It's a great place to pick up a sandwich or picnic supplies for lunch in the parks.

Carlton To get to Lygon St you can take tram Nos 1 or 21 from the centre, or walk – it's not far from central Melbourne. This is the Italian centre of Melbourne although it really isn't the great restaurant area it used to be. There's a certain 'been there, ate that' sameness about too many of the Lygon St regulars these days. Still, there are a few pleasant surprises scattered amongst them, and some interesting places nearby.

Starting from the city end, *Toto's Pizza House* at No 101 claims to be the first pizzeria in Australia. Toto's is licensed but drinks are very reasonably priced and pizzas are mostly $6 to $11. As a final plus it's open past midnight every night of the week. *Casa di Iorio* at No 141 is another long-running favourite.

Head on up Lygon St after your pizza for an excellent coffee and cake at *Notturno* at No 177. There are tables out on the pavement and it's open 24 hours a day. *Papa Gino's* at No 221 is another long-running pizza-and-pasta place with a good reputation. At No 303 *Tiamo's* is another old Lygon St campaigner. It's a straightforward pasta place and popular with students from Melbourne University, which is only a short stroll up Faraday St. You're not going to find any culinary thrills here but with pastas from $6 the prices are easy to live with and it's a calm and comfortable place for a meal.

There's a popular theory that hidden somewhere in the middle of Lygon St there's an enormous Italian kitchen that turns out all the food for all the restaurants in Carlton – they're that much alike! So the places that are different really stand out. One of Lygon St's pleasant surprises is *Nyonya* at No 191; the food originates from Singapore, and is a blend of Malay spices and ingredients with Chinese cooking styles. It's a bright and cheerful place to eat; main courses are mostly $7 to $10 – try the superb curry laksa.

Further down at 333 Lygon St, *Jimmy Watson's* is another Melbourne institution (Carlton has a few of them). Wine and talk are the order of the day at this see-and-be-seen wine bar but the food is good too. There are hot meals or you can make up a plate of excellent cold food for around $8. The house wine is around $8 a bottle and since the annual Jimmy Watson's wine award is probably the best known in Australia you can count on it being drinkable!

Nearby at No 329 *Shakahari* is one of Melbourne's longest running and most popular vegetarian restaurants with a really interesting menu. Main dishes are around $10 here – very reasonable given the standard of the food in this pleasantly relaxed restaurant. Across the road, *Trotters* at No 400 is popular at all hours of the day, including breakfast. Lygon St also has dark little coffee bars and tempting, calorie-stuffed cake shops.

For a taste of Melbourne nostalgia turn off Lygon St to *Johnny's Green Room* at 194

Faraday St. This is another place that's open 24 hours a day, a place where you can get a cheap bowl of spaghetti and a cup of strong coffee (a game of pool too if you want) at any hour of the night. Beside it at No 200 is *Brunettis* with delectable cakes, coffee and ice cream.

Head a block over from Lygon St to Rathdowne St where there are several interesting places to choose from. The *Carlton Curry House* at 204 Rathdowne St continues to please. It's plain and simple; you enter the restaurant proper through a busy takeaway area up front, but the curries are excellent and the prices are low – main courses around $7. It's very popular, so reservations are advisable (☎ 347 9632).

The *Fu Lu* at 172 Rathdowne is a very reasonably priced Chinese place – main dishes are only $5 to $7. Right next door is *Amritas*, a very relaxed Indian restaurant with main courses for around $10. They serve some interesting Goan dishes.

At 154 Rathdowne St the *Carlton Chinese Noodle Cafe* does a whole bunch of noodle dishes and some good curries. It's basically a takeaway place but you can eat there too. Head way further up Rathdowne St to the *Carlton Paragon Cafe* at No 651, the direct descendant of the gone but not forgotten Cafe Paradiso on Lygon St. The food's excellent from breakfast to dinner, there are lots of vegetarian dishes on the menu and come dessert time the trifle is still a knockout.

Fitzroy Brunswick St seemed suddenly to zoom from nowhere to somewhere in the restaurant business and for sheer variety this strip can't be beaten. Not only does Brunswick St have several of the best Thai restaurants in Melbourne it also has the only Ethiopian and Afghan restaurants!

Working our way up Brunswick St from the city end interesting places to try include *Nyala* at 113 Brunswick St, which does Ethiopian and other African food. The combination plate gives you an interesting variety of dishes to try, you scoop them up with the spongy bread known as *injera*. The Kenyan dishes are also interesting. *Tojo's*

next door is a very good place specialising in Thai and Malaysian food.

Annick's at 153 Brunswick St is a straightforward but comfortable little restaurant with very reasonable prices for excellent French food. Starters are around $8, main courses around $15, and desserts $7. It's deservedly popular and you must book (☎ 419 3007).

Further up towards Johnston St is the popular *Thai Thani* at No 293 and, just beyond Johnston St, *Patee's* at No 371. These are both excellent restaurants for lovers of hot and spicy Thai food. Patee's probably started the Melbourne Thai restaurant practice of taking your shoes off at the door and sitting cross legged on the floor.

The Fitz at No 347 and *Bakers* at No 384 are both very popular cafe-style places.

Afghanistan is not a place noted for its cuisine, but if you want to give it a go (steaks, kebabs, curries basically) then head for the *Afghan Gallery Restaurant* at 327 Brunswick St. Also not noted for the intricacies of its cuisine is the famous *Black Cat* at No 252, still an arty-trendy coffee bar, ideal for coffee and cake at late hours. Better for food, however, is *Mario's* at 303 Brunswick St. It's a vaguely old-fashioned cafe with straightforward food, vaguely Italian in flavour! Mario's opens early for breakfast but it isn't even BYO, no alcohol at all!

Round the corner on Johnston St you'll find Melbourne's Spanish quarter with restaurants like the very Spanish *Cafe Tapas* at No 36; although its food is good, it is almost equally well-known for its desert-scene decor. At No 60 the *Colmao Flamenco* (☎ 417 4131) also does wonders with the garlic and the seafood. It's not all that cheap, but there's a flamenco guitarist on Friday and Saturday nights. Paella for two at $26 is extremely good value. Also on Johnston St is *Carmen* at 74. There's live music most nights and the outdoor barbecue is popular – buy your meat or fish at the counter and cook it yourself.

At 15 Johnston St, near the corner of Nicholson St, *Chishti's* is well known for its excellent Indian food, some of the best

Indian food in Melbourne according to curry fanatics. It's especially good for vegetarian meals. Main courses are around $12 to $15 and the service is friendly and efficient. It's open seven nights a week.

North across Alexandra Parade at 477 Brunswick St is the wonderfully quirky *Bohemia Cafe* (☎ 489 9739), with some amazing interior design – something like a cross between a museum and a junkyard. It's open every day from 6 pm to 1 am for snacks and until 11 pm for Thai-style meals, with main dishes costing around $8. It's popular, so book.

Brunswick Head directly north of the city centre along that majestic avenue Royal Parade and you suddenly find yourself in the narrow, congested shopping street of Sydney Rd, Brunswick. This is indeed the road to Sydney but at rush-hour it's also one of the worst bottlenecks in Melbourne. In the evenings it's no problem at all. Sydney Rd is one of Melbourne's Turkish restaurant areas, and you can get there from Elizabeth St in the city centre on tram Nos 18, 19 or 20. The Turkish restaurants along Sydney Rd often bake their own delicious bread *(pide)* on the premises.

Alasya at 555 Sydney Rd is so popular that it's engulfed the places next door and spawned an identical offshoot, *Alasya 2*, closer to the city at 163 Sydney Rd. Here, as at most of the other Turkish places, you can choose from the menu or opt for a fixed price meal which gets you 10 (yes!) starters, a mixture of main courses, a selection of desserts, heaps of freshly baked bread and coffee all for a fixed $19.80. It's terrific value and you'd better bring a healthy appetite with you.

Quite a bit further up Sydney Rd, the *Golden Teras* (or Terrace) is at 803-805. It's quite spacious and classy-looking but the food is cheap and delicious – try the $12 banquet. Big and busy and with a belly dancer on Friday and Saturday nights the spacious *Sultan Ahmet* at No 835 is more of the same with a fixed price menu for just $14.50, or $18 with extras such as vine leaves and yet more dips.

Sydney Rd isn't all Turkish however; at No 217 you can head for Spain at *La Paella* and yes, their paella is superb and extra good value at $24 for two. Opposite La Paella is a large, popular Italian restaurant called *La Nostalgia*.

Richmond Richmond is Melbourne's Greek and Vietnamese centre. Take tram No 70 from Batman Ave, by the river in the city, and get off on Swan St at the Church St junction in Richmond. The 100 metres or so along Swan St away from the city past Church St is virtually wall-to-wall Greek restaurants.

For years the *Laikon* at No 272 was one of the best Greek food bargains in Melbourne. Inside, the Laikon is still plain and simple and the food straightforward and tasty but it's no longer top of the list. There's no menu so just go to the counter and order tzatziki and taramasalata (both dips), pitta bread to dip in it, and souvlaki (kebab) which comes with salad. With a sticky sweet dessert and coffee you'll pay about $15 a head. While you're at the counter you'd better grab the wine bottle opener to uncork your wine too – the bottle shop on the corner of Swan and Church Sts sells retsina. The Laikon does good takeaways too.

Some of the other Swan St Greek restaurants provide food at virtually rock-bottom prices but with somewhat brighter surroundings. Try *Elatos* at No 213 where the seafood is particularly good, or *Agapi* at No 262 with the standard assortment of dips and starters plus sardines, stuffed peppers, moussaka, souvlaki and all the other Greek favourites. At No 256, *Kaliva* looks a bit smarter and also has live music on Thursday to Sunday nights. Again seafood is a speciality here. And there's *Salona* at No 260A, with more of the standard Greek menu.

Greek food may have been Richmond's original claim to cheap eats popularity but these days it's just as well known for its bargain-priced Vietnamese restaurants. Richmond has a large Vietnamese population and Victoria St has become Melbourne's Little Saigon, packed with Vietnamese shops, businesses and some superb restaurants. At some of these places you may find you're the only non-Vietnamese diner in the house. No problem, they always have an English menu and you always get a friendly reception. Tram Nos 23 (peak hours only) or 42 will get you there from Victoria Parade, north of the city centre.

The two Thy Thys are possibly the best known Vietnamese restaurants in Victoria St. *Thy Thy I* at 142 Victoria St is hidden away upstairs and is popular, basic and dirt cheap. *Thy Thy 2* at No 116 is equally straightforward, crowded and noisy and equally good value. (If you want a drink first, go across the road to the *Bakers Arms* at No 355 for a distinctly un-Australian, trash-pop pub.)

One Victoria St favourite is the bare, basic but very friendly *Sanh Sanh* at No 270. *Vao Doi* at No 120 is not the cheapest along here but the decor is definitely somewhat flashier, not quite so cafe-like. Main courses are generally around $7 for the regular dishes so a couple can eat well here for less than $20. Steamboats are also good value at around $30.

Greek and Vietnamese food is not all Richmond has to offer. At 103 Swan St, *Mexicali Rose* is Mexican with a difference. They do indeed have all the usual tacos and tostadas but also a number of dishes which don't appear in every other Melbourne Mexican. Right in the middle of Little Saigon you can also find one of Melbourne's better Turkish restaurants, *Pamukkale* at 375 Victoria St. Great dips, kebabs and Turkish pizzas. Or at No 385 there's one of the better Mexican restaurants, *El Rincon*. Apart from the Mexican regulars they also offer a changing variety of South American dishes and there's Latin American music some nights.

Bridge Rd, the road out from the city midway between Swan and Victoria Sts, also has some great food possibilities. Take tram Nos 48 or 75 (or No 24 during rush hours) from Flinders St in the city to these restaurants. Starting at the city end of Bridge Rd there's the *Uptown Deli* at No 14. With pastas at around $10 it's not the cheapest eating around but the food is good and it's a bright, cheerful, convenient place. Close by

is *Chilli Padi* at 18 Bridge Rd. This place has a variety of Malay-Chinese dishes, as well as excellent juices and coffee.

At 78 Bridge Rd, the *Tofu Shop* is definitely one for those on a vegetarian/health kick. It can be a squeeze finding a stool at the counter at lunch time but never mind, the salads, vegetables, filled filo pastries and soyalaki (great invention) are tasty.

Sweet Jamaique at 127 Bridge Rd has a deli section downstairs and a more expensive restaurant area upstairs. Downstairs the food is reasonably priced and does indeed have some Caribbean curry with a creole touch. Nearby is *Rajdoot* at 142 Bridge Rd; if you've travelled in India you'll remember that as a popular Indian motorcycle brand! It's a small place with excellent Indian food including some great tandoori dishes.

The *London Tavern* at 238 Lennox St (midway between Swan St and Bridge Rd) used to be Lonely Planet's local pub, until we moved office. It rose to local pub food fame under a chef who liked India and curries and despite his departure the menu still has some interesting dishes, plus there's a bright and sunny courtyard where you can eat outside.

South Yarra Take tram No 8 from Swanston St in the city to South Yarra. Along Toorak Rd you'll find some of Melbourne's most expensive restaurants – places where a couple would have no trouble paying over $100 for a meal. Fortunately there are some more relevant places in between – like *Pinocchio's* at 152 Toorak Rd, which has a blackboard menu of standard Italian favourites. It's a pleasant and convenient place to eat and the pizzas are excellent; the takeaway prices are lower.

Only a couple of doors away at No 156 is *Tamani's*, Italian once again and something of a Melbourne institution. It's a popular restaurant with good pasta dishes and salads. Just across the railway tracks at No 164, *Alfio's* is almost too smoothly trendy-looking for its own good but the prices aren't bad, there's a nice sunny courtyard out back and their pasta can be superb. Backtrack down Toorak Rd to No 74 where you'll find a similar ambience and similar food at the *Barolo Bistro* – a pleasant little espresso bar with a blackboard menu, snappy service and a small courtyard out back. Or cross the road to the pleasantly relaxed and old-fashioned looking *Yarra's* at 97 Toorak Rd, directly opposite the post office. It's open from breakfast time right through to reasonably late at night.

South Yarra's not all Italian; there are also a number of the currently trendy deli places, in particular *The Deli* at 26 Toorak Rd. This large, airy place has good food, excellent salads and is fine for a late-night coffee or a not-too-early breakfast. Tables are also set out on the footpath and it's very much a place to be seen. Upstairs at 177 Toorak Rd the *Mt Lebanon* has excellent Lebanese food (and a belly dancer) but it's more expensive than the regular string of Middle East eateries.

Backtrack towards the city on Toorak Rd and just a short distance from St Kilda Rd you'll find the *Fawkner Club*, which isn't a club at all. The straightforward pub food is in the $12 to $14 bracket and it's a gathering place for local yuppies. The Fawkner is convenient for the Toorak Rd guesthouses, the Botanic Gardens and, most important, it has a big sunny courtyard with a sliding glass roof.

At 384 Punt Rd, *Percy's* is an unassuming little place with superb food. It's not cheap, at around $15 to $20 for a main course, but the food is excellent, as is the ambience. It's small and popular, so make a reservation (☎ 866 2960).

An eclectic blend of deli food, open-air eating and expensive restaurants can also be found along Chapel St. Turn right from Toorak Rd and there are places to try all the way. At No 571 there's *Spaghetti Graffiti* where the people are friendly, the pasta is quite good and, most important, it's open round the clock. Right next door at No 569 is *Kanpai*, a neat little Japanese restaurant with surprisingly modestly priced dishes. Further along at No 517 there's the *Tandoor* which has excellent Indian food but is definitely not cheap.

Across the road at 478 Chapel St, *Amigo's* offers standard Mexican fare from tacos to enchiladas. Cross back to *African Tukul* at No 425; Melbourne doesn't have many African restaurants and this is an interesting place to try, although it's not all that cheap. Continue down Chapel St almost to Commercial Rd and you'll find *Soda Sisters Drugstore* at 382. It's a facsimile of a '50s American soda fountain with ice-cream sodas, sundaes, hamburgers and other representatives of American kulcha, including waitresses on roller skates.

Patra at 359 Chapel St is a popular Greek restaurant with a pleasant courtyard. The immensely popular Prahran Market is back from the Chapel St-Commercial Rd junction – go here for some of the best fresh vegetables, fruit and fish in Melbourne.

Prahran If you continue across Commercial Rd you enter Prahran where at 310 Chapel St the *Ankara Restaurant* does a good fixed-price Turkish meal. Further down at 68 Chapel St, Windsor, the *Marmara* is even better with great marinated kebabs and delicious thick Turkish bread.

At 270 Chapel St the *Court Jester* serves slightly up-market pub food and some adventurous dishes amongst the usual counter meals; it has a truly artistic blackboard menu and reasonable prices. At 188 Chapel St *Himalaya* does Indian curries with some South-East Asian influence.

Turn into Greville St beside the town hall and down beside the railway tracks at No 95 you'll find the ever-popular *Feedwell Cafe*. This long-running but rather pricey vegetarian restaurant is open from 7.30 am for breakfast through to 5 pm and does great cakes and baked goodies. Soups, sandwiches, vegetarian pizza slices and the like cost around $5. On the way down Greville St check the curious collection of recycled clothes and furniture shops, and the train emerging from the pub wall opposite Feedwell.

South Melbourne At 331 Clarendon St is the *Chinese Noodle Shop*, with excellent authentic noodles dishes at around $7 to $10, pleasant surroundings and fast, friendly service. Further on, *Taco Bill's* at No 375 has strictly mass-market Mexican food but is good value for all that. There's a whole string of Taco Bills around Melbourne, all very similar; check the addresses in the phone directory. To any Americans out there: Taco Bill's is about 100 times better than Taco Bells!

If you're feeling financially flush and ready for a good night out check out *The Last Aussie Fishcaf* just off Clarendon St at 256 Park St. It's a sort of movie musical vision of a '50s fish & chips cafe with prices already in the '90s! Never mind, the food's good (how many '50s fishcafs had sushi on the menu?), and there's music and entertainment. The tiny *Cafe Goa* at 602 City Rd is also worth a try. As the name suggests, the emphasis is on Portuguese-Indian cooking, and they do it well. You don't want to give any cheek to the *maître d'* here or you'll be out on the footpath in no time.

Entertainment

The best source of 'what's on' info in Melbourne is the *Entertainment Guide* which comes out every Friday with the *Age* newspaper.

During the summer months watch out for the FEIPP (Fantastic Entertainment In Public Places) programme with activities put on in city parks and public places during weekday lunch times and at the weekends. There's also often something going on in the City Square.

Melbourne has a number of concert halls and other venues. Right by the river the Arts Centre concert hall is the focus for opera and concert music. There's also the Dallas Brooks Hall just north of Fitzroy Gardens and the outdoor Sidney Myer Music Bowl in the Kings Domain. Big rock concerts are usually held at the Arts Centre concert hall, the old and barn-like Festival Hall, the ex-swimming-pool Sports & Entertainment Centre with its quirky acoustics, or the new National Tennis Centre.

Half-Tix (☎ 650 9420) is a booth in the Bourke St Mall which sells heavily reduced tickets to various events, on the performance day only.

According to the Victorian licensing laws, clubs cannot refuse to serve travellers. Take a driving licence or your passport if you feel like explaining to the bouncers that you're from outside Victoria.

Rock Music A lot of Melbourne's night time scene is tied up with rock pubs – some of the big crowded places can afford the top Australian bands and it's for this reason that Melbourne is very much Australia's rock music centre. It's on the sweaty grind around the Melbourne rock pubs that Australia's best bands really prove themselves. The *Entertainment Guide* and FM stations like MMM (commercial, 105.1) or RRR (102.7) and PBS (106.7), both public, will tell you who's on and where, as will *Beat* and *Inpress* magazines, available free from the right kind of cafe or from any pub with bands. Cover charges at the pubs vary widely – some nights it's free, generally it's from around $6, big names on weekend nights can cost $10 or more. Music generally starts around 9.30 pm, although the bigger the name the later the show. Those that follow are just a few of the places offering a variety of music.

Although it's not what it once was the small Station Hotel on Greville St, Prahran still attracts the crowds. It's one of the longest running of the rock pubs, a place with a bit of a Melbourne rock history. This pub also brews its own beer, and the sculpture of the locomotive crashing through the house next door is quite arresting. The Saturday arvo sessions are popular. In St Kilda the Palace, next door to the Palais on the Lower Esplanade, is another big place which has popular bands. In Fitzroy St, St Kilda there is the Prince of Wales Hotel which also starts late. You can hear some good jazz and blues here as well as rock, new wave etc. Also in St Kilda is the well-known Esplanade Hotel, on the Esplanade of course, which has live music every night and Sunday afternoons, free of charge. It's also a great place just to sit with a beer and watch the sun set over the pier, with Williamstown and the West Gate Bridge in the background.

The Central Club Hotel in Richmond is a student-type pub which mainly caters for small bands – it's scruffy and the bar tends to close early, but the music's good. The Club in Smith St, Collingwood, and the Tote in Johnson St, Collingwood, are similar, attracting interesting fringe bands. Also in the category are the Royal Derby and the Punters Club, both in Brunswick St, Fitzroy.

Folk & Acoustic Music Yes there are also folk pubs. In the *Entertainment Guide* check the acoustic and folk music listings. One of the most popular is the Dan O'Connell Hotel, (the 'Dan') on the corner of Princes and Canning Sts in Carlton. For those interested in Irish music they claim 'we sell more Irish whiskey than Scotch' as proof of their Irish authenticity. Usually it's folk music on Wednesday and Thursday, Irish music on Friday and sometimes Saturday. O'Sullivan's Hotel at 442 Nicholson St in North Fitzroy often has good bands and performers.

At 1221 High St, Malvern the long-running Green Man Music Club is still a popular folk venue with shows over dinner or supper. The Cafe Yartz at 224 High St, Northcote, is another good place, as is Molly Bloom's in Bay St, Port Melbourne (though it can get a bit rough at times). The Melbourne Folk Club headquarters is the Brunswick East Club Hotel at 280 Lygon St.

Jazz Popular jazz pubs include the Fountain Inn Hotel in Bay St, Port Melbourne; the Limerick Arms in Clarendon St, South Melbourne; Bell's Hotel & Brewery at Moray St, South Melbourne; and the Bridge Hotel in Richmond.

Nightclubs & Discos Melbourne has Australia's biggest and most fiercely competitive selection of nightclubs and discos. In fact, and many a bet has been won on this fact, Melbourne has more discos than New York. There seems to be a continuous competition to create the next 'biggest, brashest,

most exclusive' club. There will be some sort of dress standards at all of them and the more 'exclusive' spots are likely to be selective about who they let in. Door charges are generally from $10 to $15.

Popular places include the sophisticated Metro nightclub at 20 Bourke St with no less than eight bars, in what used to be the Metro Theatre. The place was given a high-tech multimillion dollar renovation in '87 to become the biggest disco in the southern hemisphere. Long-running places include the three-level Inflation at 60 King St and the big and more middle-of-the-road Underground at 22 King St. In King St you will also find the Hippodrome, X and the Grainstore, making the 'King St Strip' *the* nightclub street of Melbourne.

One of Melbourne's places-to-be-seen-scene is Checkpoint Charlie's with post-holocaust decor at Commercial Rd, Prahran. Around the corner at 386 Chapel St is *Chasers*, another disco/nightclub with a flashy interior, which also has bands occasionally.

Hotels, Brewery Pubs & Wine Bars Apart from the music pubs there are quite a few other popular pubs and wine bars. Top of the wine bar list would have to be Jimmy Watson's on Lygon St, Carlton – very much a place to see and be seen, especially around lunch time Saturday, but a good place for a glass of wine anytime. It has a delightful (when the sun is shining) open courtyard out back.

Also in Carlton, the Lemon Tree Hotel at 10 Grattan St, by the Exhibition Gardens, is another popular gathering place with a pleasant courtyard and good food. In nearby Fitzroy the Lord Newry Hotel at 543 Brunswick St is a pub which puts effort into its wine list so it straddles the pub/wine bar category.

Other popular pubs, often with open courtyards, include the Fawkner Club at 52 Toorak Rd West, which has good jazz on Sunday afternoons, and the New Argo Inn at 64 Argo St, both in South Yarra. The Capitol

Wine Bar at 257 Toorak Rd in South Yarra is a comfortable modern place.

Or there's the Cricketer's Arms Hotel at 69 Cruickshank St in Port Melbourne. There's another Cricketer's Arms at 327 Punt Rd in Richmond, popular after a game at the MCG.

Lord Jim's (very much a place for pick-ups) is at 36 St George's Rd, North Fitzroy, and the Council Club is in South Melbourne. The Moonee Valley (known as the Punters' Club) in Brunswick St, Fitzroy, is a good sleazy place to hang out if you like wearing black.

Pubs which brew their own beer ('boutique beers') have become all the rage in the last few years. The beer is certainly not cheap, but is definitely a cut above the standard mass-produced stuff. For homesick Europeans, these are the places to look for some *real* bitter. Popular pubs include the Station Hotel, 96 Greville St, Prahran; the Redback, 75 Flemington Rd, North Melbourne; Bell's Hotel & Brewery, 157 Moray St, South Melbourne; and the Geebung Polo Club, 85 Auburn Rd, Auburn.

Theatre Restaurants No mention of Melbourne's eating/entertainment possibilities would be complete without a section on theatre restaurants. Melbourne's particular inspiration is combining eating out with fringe theatre and/or comedy. The peak days of the theatre restaurant revolution have passed and they're even a mite establishment these days, but never mind, they're still good fun.

Granddaddy of these places is the Last Laugh (☎ 419 8600) on the corner of Smith and Gertrude Sts in Collingwood. It's an old cinema/dole office, done up in a dazzling mishmash of styles from high kitsch up and down. Inside there's room for 200 people to have a good time. The food is reasonably good and there's a bar. Like other fringe places, vegetarians are well catered for. You have time to get through the appetisers, soup and main course before part one of the show and dessert comes up before part two. It costs, depending on the night and the show,

around $32 for dinner and show, and about $17 for show only.

Upstairs there's Le Joke, where smaller acts appear. It is slightly cheaper at around $28 for dinner and show, $15 for show only.

Comedy venues come and go at high speed; check the *Entertainment Guide* for the latest situation.

Cinema Melbourne's best alternative cinemas include the Valhalla at 89 High St, Northcote, which shows different films every night. They produce a superb six-month film calendar detailing all their shows. On Friday nights, the midnight showing of *Blues Brothers* has a cult following.

The Carlton Moviehouse at 235 Faraday St – under threat from 'developers' at the time of writing – has a similar programme. It's locally known as the 'bughouse'. Various other cinemas around Melbourne specialise in non-mainstream films. These include the Longford Cinema at 59 Toorak Rd, South Yarra; the Astor Theatre at 1 Chapel St on the corner of Dandenong Rd, St Kilda; the Brighton Bay cinema at 294 Bay St, Brighton; the Trak at 445 Toorak Rd, Toorak; and the Kino at Collins Place, 45 Collins St in the city. At the universities you can try the Agora at La Trobe, way out in Bundoora, or the Union Theatre at Melbourne University. In the wilds of West Coburg is the Progress Theatre at 236 Reynard St, which shows films on Friday, Saturday and Sunday nights and made a bijou appearance on screen itself in the recent *Death in Brunswick*. Finally, there's the excellent State Film Theatre at 1 Macarthur St, East Melbourne.

Theatre There's lots of theatre in Melbourne too, ranging from the commercial places up the east end of the central city area to the many and varied smaller and experimental theatres.

La Mama at 205 Faraday St, Carlton, has not only been brave, it's also been a long-term survivor where many of the big names of Australian theatre made their debut. Readings Bookshop in Lygon St handles tickets.

The Melbourne Writers Theatre is in the Carlton Courthouse at 329 Drummond St, Carlton.

The Universal Theatre at 13 Victoria St, Fitzroy, manages to pack them in with productions which may only appeal to a minority but are always adventurous and interesting. The Anthill Theatre at 199 Napier St, South Melbourne, and the Australian Contemporary Theatre in the church at 500 Burwood Rd, Hawthorn, are other theatres which are noted for their experimental productions.

The Melbourne Theatre Company puts on big plays at the Playhouse at the Arts Centre, and smaller productions at the Russell St Theatre at 19 Russell St, Melbourne. The Playbox Theatre Company is based at the new CUB Malthouse Theatre in Sturt St, South Melbourne – a former brewery, attractively converted – and produces a lot of contemporary Australian work.

Commercial theatres, the places you go to see *Les Miserables* or *Phantom of the Opera*, are the Athenaeum at 188 Collins St, the Comedy Theatre at 240 Exhibition St, Her Majesty's Theatre at 219 Exhibition St and the Princess Theatre at 163 Spring St.

The Footy Despite the heretical moves to a national competition, Melbourne is still very much the stronghold of Aussie Rules football. If you're here between April and September you won't be able to avoid The Footy. Although it's no longer a daring innovation for a TV station not to show match replays on Saturday nights, there's still an awful lot of media coverage of topics such as Johnno's knee or Dermie's thigh.

You should try to see a match, as much for the crowds as the game. Footy is one of those satisfying games in which the umpire's interpretation of some pretty convoluted rules plays a big part. This gives the fans something to agree on – the umpire is blind or biased. Other than this, the fans don't agree on much at all, and the sheer energy of the barracking at a big game is exhilarating. Despite the fervour of the fans, crowd violence is almost unknown.

Big matches are often scheduled at the vast MCG. Collingwood, a mighty club with a fanatical following, always provides excited crowds. Their home ground, Victoria Park, is in Johnston St, Collingwood. Carlton is another team worth seeing, and their ground at Princes Park, on Sydney Rd north of Melbourne University, is also close to the city. You can book seats through BASS, but you usually won't need to.

Things to Buy
Although Melbourne is far from the main centres for Aboriginal crafts there are some interesting places to look. Aboriginal Handcrafts is on the 9th floor of Century House at 125 Swanston St and is open weekdays from 10 am to 4.30 pm. It sells bark paintings and handicrafts from all over the country. The Gallery Gabrielle Pizzi at 141 Flinders Lane, just round the corner from the Hyatt Hotel, specialises in Aboriginal art; expensive but interesting to see. The Aboriginal Gallery of Dreamings, 73-77 Bourke St, has good and affordable crafts.

Art galleries and craft centres can be found all over Melbourne; check the weekly *Entertainment Guide* in the *Age* for what's on.

The local craft scene is especially strong in the fields of ceramics, jewellery, stained glass and leathercraft. Go to the Meat Market Craft Centre (☎ 329 9966) at 42 Courtney St, North Melbourne, near the youth hostels, to see the best of local crafts and other exhibitions. It's at the corner of Courtney and Blackwood Sts, North Melbourne. It's open daily from 10 am to 5 pm; get there on any of the Flemington Rd trams (Nos 49, 55, 59).

Another craft gallery worth a visit is Distelfink (☎ 818 2555), 432 Burwood Rd, Hawthorn; or just take a walk along the St Kilda Esplanade any Sunday, where there is a street craft market of varying styles and quality.

There is a number of good craft shops in the inner suburbs, usually with an eclectic mix of local and imported crafts. One of the longest running is Ishka Handcrafts at 409 Chapel St, South Yarra, and also at South

Melbourne, Kew, Camberwell and elsewhere.

In many suburbs there are weekend craft markets, and further out there are craft places in Warrandyte and the small towns in the Dandenongs. Several country cities and towns have interesting craft outlets, notably Geelong and Lorne to the south-west, and Castlemaine, Maldon and Beechworth to the north, and at Red Hill and other locations on the Mornington Peninsula.

For more details, pick up a copy of the Victorian Craft Association's *Craft Outlets in Victoria*, available at the Meat Market, Ishka or other craft places.

Melbourne claims to be the fashion capital of Australia – judge for yourself in the small shops along Swan St and Bridge Rd in Richmond, and Chapel St, Prahran. The best shoe shops are in Sydney Rd, Brunswick – Italian designs at reasonable prices. The youngest fashion designers have toeholds in Brunswick St, Fitzroy. The best bargains are to be found at the Victoria Market, especially on Sundays.

For general shopping in the city there are a number of intimate and elegant little shopping arcades apart from the glossier modern affairs. The Royal Arcade off Bourke St Mall is noted for its figures of Gog and Magog which strike the hours. The two big old-established department stores are Myers and David Jones in the Bourke St Mall. They have recently been joined by the glossy new Melbourne Central complex, further up Swanston St, which includes the Daimaru department store.

You'll find local products at the Victoria Market on Sundays, including superb sheepskins for around $50 and a range of sheepskin goods.

Getting There & Away

Air Melbourne is the second arrival and departure gateway in Australia. Melbourne's international airport is more spacious than Sydney's and also gets fewer flights, so if you make this your Australian arrival point you're likely to get through Immigration and Customs a little more speedily, although it can still get very crowded.

There are frequent connections between Melbourne and other state capitals – Melbourne/Sydney flights depart hourly during the airport operating hours. Bargains are frequent – watch the *Age* for ads. Standard fares include Adelaide $212 (standby $170), Brisbane $341 ($273), Canberra $180 ($144), Perth $513 ($410) or Sydney $224 ($175). Connections to Alice Springs are mostly via Adelaide, but direct flights are $411 ($329).

Melbourne is the main departure point from the mainland to Tasmania. Hobart flights cost $207 (standby $166), Launceston $178 ($142) with Ansett or Australian Airlines. Flights to Devonport cost $151 (standby $121) and are operated by Kendell Airlines.

The Australian Airlines office (☎ 665 3333) is at 50 Franklin St while Ansett (☎ 13100) is at 501 Swanston St. Both have smaller offices dotted around the city. East-West (☎ 668 2033) is at 215 Swanston St.

Bus The major bus companies – Bus Australia and Greyhound/Pioneer – both operate through Melbourne. There is some variance in fares from company to company but they're all pretty much the same. Other smaller operators – such as Firefly – have less comprehensive coverage but still have competitive fares. The increased competition from the airlines has led to frequent bargain fares and cuts in services.

The Greyhound/Pioneer office (☎ 664 7888) is the terminal in Franklin St. Firefly (☎ 670 7500), Bus Australia (☎ 670 2211), and McCafferty's (☎ 670 2533) all operate out of the Spencer St bus station.

V/Line buses also operate from the Spencer St station, and go to all parts of Victoria (☎ 619 5000). See the towns in this chapter for the appropriate fares.

The Greyhound/Pioneer network is the most extensive, with buses from Melbourne to: Adelaide (10 hours, $40), Perth (48 hours, $205), Brisbane (24 hours, $115), Canberra (9 hours, $48), and Sydney (direct, 12 hours,

$52; or via the Princes Highway, 15 hours, $52).

Bus Australia have services to Adelaide ($40), Brisbane ($115), Sydney ($40), and Perth ($197). Firefly has the most limited schedule with services to Adelaide and Sydney only; both cost $40. Most of McCafferty's services are in Queensland, but they do connect Melbourne with Brisbane daily (24 hours, $115) and Sydney ($40).

Train Rail tickets for interstate services can be booked by phoning 619 5000, or bought at most suburban stations and at Spencer St Railway Station in Melbourne from where the interstate services depart.

Interstate Melbourne to Sydney takes 12½ to 13 hours by train. The overnight Sydney Express from Melbourne and Melbourne Express from Sydney operate every night. The fare is $85 economy, $120 in 1st class, or a 1st-class sleeper costs $190 (there are no economy sleepers).

To get to Canberra by rail you take the daily Canberra Link which involves a train to Wodonga on the Victoria-New South Wales border and then a bus from there. This takes about eight hours and costs $44 ($56 1st-class).

To or from Adelaide the Overland operates overnight every day of the week. The trip takes 12 hours and costs $42 (economy), $85 (1st) or $145 (1st-class sleeper). The Daylink involves a train to Dimboola near the border and a bus from there. This trip is about an hour faster than the through train and costs $42 in economy, $74.20 in 1st class. You can transport a car to or from Adelaide for $75.

To get to Perth by rail from Melbourne you take the Overland to Adelaide and then the Trans Australian (which originates in Adelaide) or the Indian-Pacific (which comes through Adelaide from Sydney). The Melbourne to Perth fare is $207 for a seat in economy. Including meals a sleeping berth costs $454 in economy, $690 in 1st class. It's a two-days-and-three-nights trip all the way from Melbourne to Perth. If you're travelling

to or from any of the major cities and can book at least seven days in advance, you can save up to 30% with a 'Caper' fare (Customer Advance Purchase Excursion Rail – would you believe).

Within Victoria For V/Line services within Victoria there are a number of special fares available. Super Saver fares give you a 40% discount for travelling at off-peak times. Basically this means travelling on Tuesday, Wednesday or Thursday, arriving in Melbourne after 9.30 am, and leaving Melbourne at any time except between 4 and 6 pm.

A Victoria Pass gives you two weeks' unlimited travel on V/Line trains and buses within the state for $120.

See the relevant country towns for information on V/Line train, bus or bus/train travel from Melbourne.

Getting Around

To/From the Airport Although Melbourne Airport (Tullamarine) is 22 km from the city it's quite easy to get to since the Tullamarine Freeway runs almost into the centre. A taxi between the airport and city centre costs about $25 but there's the regular Skybus service which costs $8.50 (children $4.50). In the city the Skybus departs from Franklin St near the corner with Swanston St. There are buses about every half hour, sometimes even more frequently, between 6 am and 8.30 pm (☎ 335 3066).

There is also a fairly frequent bus by Gull Airport Service between the airport and Geelong. It costs $18 one-way. The Geelong terminus is at 45 McKillop St. You can get timetables for these services from the information counter in the international section at the airport.

Tullamarine is a modern airport with a single terminal; Australian at one end, Ansett at the other, international in the middle. There's an information desk upstairs in the international departure area. It's one of the most spacious airports in Australia and doesn't suffer the night flight restrictions which apply to some other Australian airports. The snack bar and cafeteria sections are if anything somewhat worse than the airport norm for quality and price, but if you're stuck at the airport for any reason you can stroll over to the Customs Agents building – turn right out of the terminal and it's about a 200-metre walk – where there's a cheap snack bar. There's another in the small centre beyond the car park by the Travelodge Motel.

Public Transport Melbourne's public transport system, the Met, is based on buses, suburban railways and the famous trams. The trams are the real cornerstone of the system; in all there are about 750 of them and they operate as far as 20 km out from the centre. They're frequent and fun.

Buses are the secondary form of public transport, taking routes where the trams do not go, and replacing them at quiet weekend periods. There is also a host of private bus services as well as the public ones. The train services provide a third link for Melbourne's outer suburbs. There is an underground city loop which was completed in 1985.

For information on Melbourne transport phone the Transport Information Centre (☎ 617 0900). It operates 7.30 am to 8.30 pm Monday to Saturday, 9.15 am to 8.30 pm on Sunday. The Met Shop at 103 Elizabeth St in the city also has transport information and sells souvenirs and some tickets. They also have a 'Discover Melbourne' kit. If you're in the city they're probably a better bet for information than the telephone service, which is always engaged. Railway stations also have some information.

There's quite an array of tickets, and the Met has a glossy brochure which describes them all. Basically you've got a choice in Melbourne of paying a straight fare for a short trip, getting a time ticket which allows you unlimited travel during that period, or buying a weekly or monthly season ticket. The short trip ticket allows you two tram or bus sections, while a 'rail plus two' ticket is for a one or two station train trip. Further afield you need a time ticket with which you can chop and change your transport.

The metropolitan area is divided into three zones, and the price of tickets depend on which zone/s you will be travelling in and across. Zone 1 is big enough for most purposes. You'll only need zone 3 if you're going right out of town – on a trip to the Healesville Sanctuary, for example, or down the Mornington Peninsula. The fares are as follows:

Zones	3 Hours	All Day	Weekly
1	$1.90	$3.40	$14.60
2 or 3	$1.30	$2.30	$10.20
1 & 2	$3.20	$5.70	$24.40
1, 2 & 3	$4.50	$7.40	$29.60

A straightforward one-way 'short trip' within Zone 1 will cost you $1.30. If you've got lots of travelling to do within the central business district you can get a 10-trip City Saver ticket which costs $10.00. Coming from outside the inner neighbourhood, train travellers can get off-peak tickets for use after 9.30 am which take you into the city and then allow unlimited travel within the City Saver area. If you buy a weekly season ticket, you get free weekend travel for the ticket holder, another adult and up to six children. There are numerous other deals but we don't want to make this too complicated, do we!

Car All the big car-rental firms operate in Melbourne. Avis, Budget, Hertz and Thrifty have desks at the airport and you find plenty of others in the city. The city offices tend to be at the northern end of the city or in Carlton or North Melbourne. Astoria (☎ 347 7766), at 630 Swanston St, has some of the cheapest deals for small sedans.

Melbourne also has a number of rent-a-wreck-style operators, renting older vehicles at lower rates. Their costs and conditions vary widely so it's worth making a few inquiries before going for one firm over another. You can take the 'from $18 a day' line with a pinch of salt because the rates soon start to rise with insurance, km charges and so on. Beware of distance-from-the-city restrictions; many companies only allow you to travel within a certain distance of the city, typically 100 km.

Typical are Rent-a-Bomb (☎ 429 4003) at 507 Bridge Rd, Richmond. Their weekly rate works out at around $22 a day for older Holdens. It includes insurance and unlimited km but you're limited to the Melbourne metropolitan area. The Yellow Pages list lots of other firms including some reputable local operators who rent newer cars but don't have the nationwide operations (and overheads) of the big operators.

Bicycle Melbourne's a great city for cycling – there are long bicycle tracks along the Yarra, the Maribyrnong, the Merri Creek and other rivers, as well as bicycle tracks and lanes around the city. Plus it's reasonably flat so you're not pushing and panting up hills too often.

Unfortunately, up-to-date maps of bicycle tracks and routes are hard to find. The best guide is the hefty *Melway Greater Melbourne* – you should be able to buy last year's edition at under half price. Most bike shops stock whatever maps are available. Look for a copy of *Weekend Bicycle Rides* for a pleasant introduction to bike rides around Melbourne. There are quite a few journeys you can make in the surrounding country by taking one train out of Melbourne then riding across to a different line to get the train back. An example is to take the train out to Gisborne and ride the ridge down to Bacchus Marsh from where you can get another train back in to the city.

If you don't already have a bike, Melbourne's not a great place to try and hire one – at least not if you want to do more than just dawdle along the pleasant cycle path by the river, a popular pastime on weekends. There are hire places by the boat sheds at Princes Gate, opposite the Botanic Gardens, beside Como Park in Burnley and at the Kevin Bartlett Reserve in Richmond. Hire-a-Bicycle (☎ 288 5177), one of the riverside operators, also hires out bikes at other times. But for long trips you may have to buy your own machine.

Phone Bicycle Victoria (☎ 670 9911) for

more information or drop into their shop at 31 Somerset Place, off Little Bourke St just west of Elizabeth St. They'll be able to put you onto local clubs and tours.

Around Melbourne

You don't have to travel far from Melbourne to find places worth visiting. There are the beaches and towns around Port Phillip Bay, the old gold towns to the north and west, and the hills to the east which give a good introduction to the bush at its best.

SOUTH-WEST TO GEELONG
It's a quick trip down the Princes Highway to Geelong – it's freeway all the way. You can leave Melbourne quickly over the soaring West Gate Bridge and enjoy the fine views of the city on the way over. The rest of the highway trip, however, is pretty dull.

Werribee Park
Not far out of Melbourne is Werribee Park with its free-range zoological park and the huge Italianate **Chirnside Mansion**, built between 1874 and 1877. The flamboyant building is surrounded by formal gardens but there are also picnic and barbecue areas.

Entrance to the park is free, but admission to the mansion costs $3.60 (children $1.80) and the safari bus tours cost $6 (children $3.50). Werribee Park is open weekdays from 10 am to 3.45 pm, weekends from 10 am to 4.45 pm. Werribee Railway Station is part of the Melbourne suburban rail network, and the park is on the itinerary of some of the day tours out of Melbourne.

National Aviation Museum
Near Werribee is the National Aviation Museum at the RAAF base at Point Cook. Displays include one on WW I German ace Baron von Richtofen. It's open Sundays to Thursdays from 10 am to 4 pm and admission is free.

You Yangs

You can also detour to the You Yangs, a picturesque range of volcanic hills just off the freeway. Walks in the You Yangs include the climb up **Flinders Peak**, the highest point in the park with a plaque commemorating Matthew Flinders' scramble to the top in 1802. There are fine views from the top, down to Geelong and the coast.

Wineries

There are also a number of wineries in the Geelong area. The Idyll Vineyard at 265 Ballan Rd, Moorabool, is credited with re-establishing the area's name for wines after a lapse of many years. Other Geelong area wineries are the Rebenberg Vineyard at Feehans Rd in Mt Duneed and the Tarcoola Estate Winery at Spiller Rd in Lethbridge.

Brisbane Ranges National Park

You can make an interesting loop from Melbourne out to the You Yangs and back through the Brisbane Ranges park and Bacchus Marsh. The scenic **Anakie Gorge** in the Brisbane Ranges is a popular short bushwalk and a good spot for barbecues. You may see koalas in the trees near the car park/picnic area.

Fairy Park, on the side of Mt Anakie at the southern edge of the Brisbane Ranges, has 100 clay fairy-tale figures.

GEELONG (population 107,000)

The city of Geelong began as a sheep-grazing area when the first White settlers arrived in 1836, and it initially served as a port for the dispatch of wool and wheat from the area. This function was overshadowed during the gold-rush era when it became important as a landing place for immigrants and for the export of gold. Around 1900, Geelong started to become industrialised and that's very much what it is today — an industrial city near Melbourne and Victoria's second largest city. In general there are no real 'not to be missed' attractions in Geelong and it is basically a place people go through

on their way to greater attractions like the Great Ocean Road or the Otways.

Information

There's the Corio Tourist Information Centre (☎ (052) 75 5797) on the corner of the Princes Highway and St George Rd, about seven km on the Melbourne side of Geelong. It is open daily from 10 am to 4 pm. In the centre of town there's Geelong Otway Tourism (☎ (052) 22 2900) in the National Wool Centre on Moorabool St. Both have lots of information and are very useful if you're going down along the coast to the Otways or other areas around Geelong.

Historic Houses

The city has more than 100 National-Trust-classified buildings. **Barwon Grange** on Fernleigh St, Newtown, is a National Trust property built in 1856. It's open Saturday, Sunday, Wednesday and public holidays from 2 to 5 pm; there's a small admission charge, and this will also get you into a second National Trust property: **The Heights** at 140 Aphrasia St, which is open the same hours. This 14-room timber mansion is an example of a prefabricated building brought out to the colony in pieces. It has an unusual watchtower.

Another prefabricated building is **Corio Villa**, made from iron sheets in 1856. The bits and pieces were shipped out from Glasgow but nobody claimed them on arrival! **Osborne House** and **Armytage House** are other fine old buildings. These three are private houses and not open for inspection.

Museums & Art Gallery

The impressive **National Wool Centre**, on the corner of Brougham and Moorabool Sts, is housed in an historic bluestone wool store and has a museum, a number of wool craft and clothing shops and a restaurant. It is open every day from 10 am to 5 pm and admission to the museum section is $5.50 ($4.40 students, $2.80 children).

The **Maritime Museum** in Brougham St (near Yarra St) is open Wednesday mornings and Sunday afternoons. The **Art Gallery** on

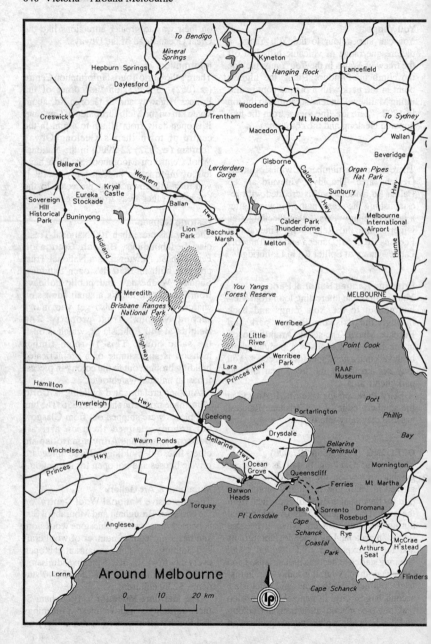

Around Melbourne

0   10   20 km

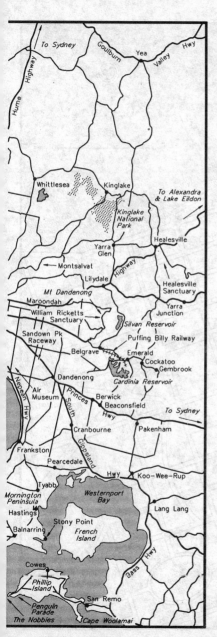

Little Malop St is open daily except Mondays and has lots of Australiana and some interesting modern art; entry is $1.

Other Attractions

Geelong has a Botanical Gardens, part of Eastern Park, which contains the **Customs House**, Victoria's oldest wooden building, displaying telegraph equipment and memorabilia. **Eastern Beach** is Geelong's popular swimming spot and promenade where boats and bicycles can be hired on weekends in summer. There is also a signposted scenic drive route along the beach front.

On hot summer days, **Splashdown** at Coppards Rd, Whittington is a great place, with huge waterslides and four pools to choose from, or there's **Norlane Waterworld** on the corner of the Princes Highway and Cox St.

Wathaurong Aboriginal Co-operative at 20A Forster St, Norlane, sells a good variety of Koori handicrafts.

Places to Stay

The small Geelong *Youth Hostel* (☎ (052) 21 6583) is at 1 Lonsdale St and costs $8. The colleges at Deakin University, on the outskirts of Geelong towards Colac, also have cheap accommodation in the summer holidays.

Two cheap central hotels are the *Criterion Hotel* (☎ (052) 91104) on the corner of Ryrie and Yarra Sts, which has single/double rooms for $22/38, while the *Carlton Hotel* (☎ (052) 29 154) at 21 Malop St charges $27/37.

There are plenty of motels in Geelong. The *Colonial Lodge* (☎ (052) 23 2266) at 57 Fyans St, south of Kardinia Park, costs $35/42 for singles/doubles. Only one km north from the centre, the *Kangaroo* (☎ (052) 21 4022) is at 16 The Esplanade and costs $34/42.

Geelong has plenty of camp sites. Those closest to the city are in Belmont near the Barwon River. *Billabong*, *Riverglen* and *Southside* caravan parks are all on Barrabool Rd and have on-site vans and cabins.

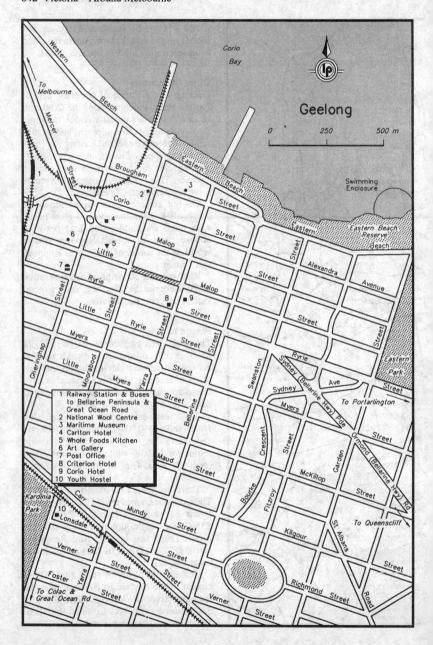

Corio
Bay

Geelong

0   250   500 m

Swimming
Enclosure

Eastern Beach
Reserve
Beach

Alexandra
Avenue

Eastern
Park
Street

To Portarlington

Ormond (Bellarine Hwy) Rd

To Queenscliff

1 Railway Station & Buses
   to Bellarine Peninsula &
   Great Ocean Road
2 National Wool Centre
3 Maritime Museum
4 Carlton Hotel
5 Whole Foods Kitchen
6 Art Gallery
7 Post Office
8 Criterion Hotel
9 Corio Hotel
10 Youth Hostel

Kardinia
Park

Lonsdale

Verner St

Foster

To Colac &
Great Ocean Rd

To Melbourne

Places to Eat

There are lots of cafes, takeaways, pubs with counter meals, and restaurants. The best place to start looking is Little Malop St, west of the mall. Here you'll find *Cafe Oggi*, a licensed Italian pasta place with reasonable prices and a play room for kids; *Cats*, which is similar but more expensive; and the *Wholefoods Kitchen* in McLarty Place just off Little Malop, which has good food and is open during the day from Monday to Friday, and Friday evenings from 6.30 pm.

The *Spaghetti Deli* at 188 Moorabool St has a good 'main course and coffee' deal at lunch times for $4; in the evenings main courses are reasonably priced at around $8. On the same street at No 211 is the *Palace of Thai*, which has excellent Thai dishes for $7 to $10, or the banquets at $20 are good value.

Getting There & Away

There are frequent trains between Melbourne and Geelong; the trip takes about an hour and costs $6.40 economy, $9 in 1st class. Trains run on from Geelong to Warrnambool ($19.80) via Camperdown ($12.10).

Geelong is also well served by V/Line buses, with daily services to Bendigo ($14.30) via Ballarat ($7.60) and Castlemaine ($9.70), and a weekly service along the Great Ocean Road to Apollo Bay ($14.30) and Warrnambool ($31.10).

McHarry's Bus Lines operates the Bellarine Transit bus which runs frequently between Geelong and most places on the Bellarine Peninsula, including Portarlington, Barwon Heads, Ocean Grove, Queenscliff and Point Lonsdale. They also operate buses daily along the Great Ocean Road as far as Torquay.

Gull Bus Lines runs daily buses between Geelong and Tullamarine Airport for $18; these depart from the Gull Terminal on McKillop St.

Getting Around

Geelong has an extensive city bus network and timetables and routes are available from the tourist office. On weekends you can hire bikes at the Barwon Valley Fun Park, near the Barwon River, and at Eastern Beach.

BELLARINE PENINSULA

Beyond Geelong the Bellarine Peninsula is a twin to the Mornington Peninsula, forming the other side of the entrance to Port Phillip Bay. Like the Mornington Peninsula this is a popular holiday resort and boating venue.

Round the peninsula in Port Phillip Bay is **Indented Head** where Flinders landed in 1802, one of the first visits to the area by a European. In 1835 John Batman landed at this same point, on his way to buy up Melbourne.

Portarlington

At Portarlington there's a fine example of an early steam-powered **flour mill**. Built around 1856, the massive, solid building is owned by the National Trust and is open from 2 to 5 pm on Sundays from September to May and on weekends and Wednesdays during January. Portarlington has an associate *Youth Hostel* (☎ (052) 59 2536) at 12 Grassy Point Rd and it costs $5 a bed. **St Leonards** is a popular little resort just south of Indented Head.

Queenscliff (population 3700)

Queenscliff was established around 1838 as a pilot station to guide ships through the Rip at the entrance to Port Phillip Bay. **Fort Queenscliff** was built in 1882 to protect Melbourne from the perceived Russian threat and at the time it was the most heavily defended fort in the colony. Today it houses the Australian Army Command and the Fort Queenscliff Museum, and is open daily; entrance is $2.

In recent years, Queenscliff has been sand-blasted, paint-stripped and rediscovered by Melbourne's new gentry. There are some fine Victorian buildings, especially pubs, and these are popular for leisurely (and expensive) weekend lunches.

Railway enthusiasts will enjoy the **Bellarine Peninsula Railway** (☎ (052) 52 2069), which operates from the old Queenscliff station with a fine collection of old steam trains. On Sundays, public holidays and most school holidays steam trains make the 16-km return trip to Drysdale or shorter runs to Laker's Siding. On days of total fire ban, diesel engines are used.

The **Marine Studies Centre** (☎ (052) 523344) next to the ferry pier has an aquarium displaying local marine life, open weekdays (plus weekends during December and January), and also organises a range of trips: snorkelling tours, nocturnal beach walks and a birdwatchers' cruise to Mud Island. All trips are led by naturalists; ring in advance to see what's on offer.

Queenscliff also has a **Maritime History Centre** down near the pier. It is open weekends and summer holidays; entry is $1.

Places to Stay Queenscliff has four camp sites and three have on-site vans for around $25. The friendly and atmospheric *Queenscliff Inn* (☎ (052) 52 3737) at 59 Hesse St, is the cheapest place, charging $12 per person in six-bed rooms. It's a fine old restored building right in the centre of town on Hesse St. A hearty breakfast is available for $5, or this is included if you take a double room ($60). There are communal washing and cooking facilities.

Nothing would be finer than to stay in one of the restored grand hotels. With rooms starting from $50 and going way up, you can stay at the *Royal*, *Ozone*, *Vue Grand* or *Queenscliff* hotels.

Getting There & Away McHarry's operates the Bellarine Transit bus service with regular connections between Geelong, Point Lonsdale and Queenscliff.

A passenger ferry and a car ferry operate between Queenscliff and Sorrento on the Mornington Peninsula. See the Mornington Peninsula Getting There & Away section for details.

Point Lonsdale (population 3700)
Point Lonsdale and the Mornington Peninsula are practically joined. The lighthouse

and a fleet of pilot boats guide ships through the narrow and often turbulent Rip into the bay. You can view the Rip from a lookout and walk to the lighthouse. Below the lighthouse is **Buckley's Cave** where the 'Wild White Man', William Buckley, lived with Aborigines for 32 years after escaping from the settlement at Sorrento on the Mornington Peninsula. Actually this area is dotted with 'Buckley Caves'!

Ocean Grove (population 6800)
This resort on the ocean side of the peninsula has good scuba diving on the rocky ledges of the Bluff, and further out there are wrecks of ships which failed to make the tricky entrance to Port Phillip Bay. Some of the wrecks are accessible to divers. The beach at the surf-life-saving club is very popular with surfers. Ocean Grove is a real-estate agent's paradise and has grown to become the biggest town on the peninsula.

Places to Stay Ocean Grove has motels and holidays flats but there is no budget accommodation. There are plenty of caravan parks but even an on-site van will cost around $30.

The *Collendina Resort* (☎ (052) 55 1122) is the cheapest of the other possibilities, with rooms from $39/49, and more expensive two-bedroom units.

Barwon Heads
Barwon Heads is a small resort just along from Ocean Grove. It has sheltered river beaches and surf beaches around the headland. The *Barwon Heads Hotel*, overlooking the river, is a popular place for a meal, but the accommodation is overpriced at $60 a single, including a light breakfast. On-site vans and cabins are available at the *Rondor Caravan Park* (☎ (092) 54 2753), two km from the centre on Sheepwash Rd.

NORTH-WEST TO BENDIGO
It's about 160 km north-west of Melbourne along the Calder Highway to the old mining town of Bendigo and there are some interesting stops along the way.

You've hardly left the outskirts of Melbourne when you come to the turn-off to the surprisingly pretty and little-visited **Organ Pipes National Park** on the right and the amazingly ugly Calder Thunderdome Raceway on the left.

Gisborne & Macedon

Next up is Gisborne, at one time a coach stop on the gold-fields route. **Mt Macedon**, a 1013-metre-high extinct volcano, then looms large on the right. This area was devastated by the 1983 Ash Wednesday bushfires; look for the scorch marks high up in the gum trees.

Hanging Rock

Just north of Mt Macedon is Hanging Rock, a popular picnic spot which became famous from the book and later the film *Picnic at Hanging Rock*. At that mysterious picnic, three schoolgirls on a school trip to the rock disappeared without trace; in an equally mysterious way one of the girls reappeared a few days later. The rocks are fun to clamber over and there are superb views from higher up. **Woodend** is another pleasant old town, and this is the closest you can get to Hanging Rock by public transport; the one-way train fare is $4.90 (economy).

Kyneton & Malmsbury

The road continues through Kyneton with its fine bluestone buildings. The **Historical Centre** building was originally a two-storey bank, dating from 1855.

A further 11 km brings you to Malmsbury with its historic bluestone **railway viaduct** and a magnificent ruined **grain mill**, part of which has been converted into a delightful if up-market restaurant.

HEALESVILLE & AROUND

You don't have to travel far to the east of Melbourne before you start getting into the foothills of the Great Dividing Range. In winter you can find snow within 100 km of the city centre.

Healesville is on the regular Melbourne suburban transport network; trains operate to Lilydale from where connecting buses run to Healesville. McKenzie's Bus Lines (☎ (03) 861 6264) run a daily service from the Spencer St bus terminal through Healesville to Marysville, Alexandra and Lake Eildon.

Yarra Valley & the Wineries

On the Melbourne side of Healesville there are wineries from Yarra Glen along the Yarra Valley. These places make a good day trip from Melbourne and include the Chateau Yarrinya Winery at Pinnacle Lane, Dixon's Creek; St Hubert's Wines at St Hubert's Rd, Coldstream; and Yarra Burn Vineyards at Settlement Rd, Yarra Junction.

Gulf Station, a couple of km from Yarra Glen, is part of an old grazing run dating from the 1850s. Operated by the National Trust it's open Wednesdays to Sundays and on public holidays from 10 am to 4 pm. There is an interesting collection of rough old timber buildings plus the associated pastures and a homestead garden typical of the period.

Healesville (population 8100)

Healesville is on the outskirts of Melbourne, just where you start to climb up into the hills. There are some pleasant drives from Healesville, particularly the scenic route to Marysville, but the **Healesville Wildlife Sanctuary** is a prime attraction. This is one of the best places to see Australian wildlife in the whole country. Most of the enclosures are very natural, and some of the birds just pop in for the day.

Some enclosures are only open for a few hours each day so you may want to plan your visit accordingly. The platypus, for example, is only on show in its glass-sided tank from 1.15 to 3.30 pm. The nocturnal house, where you can see many of the smaller bush dwellers which only come out at night, is open from 10 am to 4.30 pm, as is the reptile house. The whole park is open from 9 am to 5 pm and admission is $7.50 (children and students $3.80). There are barbecue and picnic facilities in the pleasantly wooded park.

Getting There & Away McKenzie's (☎ (03) 861 6264) runs a Monday to Friday service from Lilydale Railway Station at 11.40 am right to the sanctuary, and leaving for the return trip at 3.40 pm.

Warburton (population 4000)

Beyond Healesville is Warburton, another pretty little hill town in the Great Dividing Range foothills. There are good views of the mountains from the Acheron Way nearby and you'll sometimes get snow on Mt Donna Buang, seven km from town. Warburton, in the Upper Yarra Valley, is one of a number of picturesque spots along the upper reaches of the Yarra River.

There's a range of accommodation here, from a $100-a-night hotel down to a caravan park with $30 on-site vans.

Marysville (population 500)

This delightful little town is a very popular weekend escape from Melbourne. There are lots of bush tracks to walk. Nicholl's Lookout, Keppel's Lookout, Mt Gordon and Steavenson Falls are good ones. **Cumberland Scenic Reserve**, with numerous walks and the Cumberland Falls, is 16 km east of Marysville. The cross-country skiing trails of **Lake Mountain Reserve** are only 10 km beyond Marysville.

The **Cathedral Range State Park** is about 10 km north-west of Marysville, and it offers excellent bushwalks and camping.

Places to Stay Much of the accommodation is in guesthouses which include all meals and tend to be expensive. A couple of these are the *Marylands* (☎ (059) 633 204), and the *Mountain Lodge* (☎ (059) 633 270).

Cheaper options include the *Scenic Motel* (☎ (059) 633 247) and the on-site vans at the *Marysville Caravan Park* (☎ (059) 633 433).

Getting There & Away McKenzie's operate buses from Marysville to Melbourne and Eildon.

THE DANDENONGS

The Dandenong Ranges to the east of Melbourne are one of the most popular day trips. In fact they're so popular with Melbournians that the city now laps at their edge. The Dandenongs are cool due to the altitude (Mt Dandenong is all of 633 metres tall) and lushly green due to the heavy rainfall. The area is dotted with fine old houses, classy restaurants, beautiful gardens and some fine short bushwalks. You can clearly see the Dandenongs from central Melbourne (on a smog-free day) and they're only about an hour's drive away.

The small **Fern Tree Gully National Park** has pleasant strolls and lots of bird life including, if you're extremely lucky, the lyrebirds for which the Dandenongs are famous but which are now very rare. The **Sherbrooke Forest Park** is similarly pleasant for walks and you'll see lots of rosellas. These parks together make up the Dandenong Ranges National Park, proclaimed in 1987.

The **William Ricketts Sanctuary** (☎ (03) 751 1300) on Olinda Rd, Mt Dandenong, is named after its delightfully eccentric resident sculptor. The forest sanctuary is filled with his artwork, and you can see more of his work far away in Alice Springs. It's open every day from 10 am to 4.30 pm and admission is $4.

Puffing Billy

One of the major attractions of the Dandenongs is Puffing Billy – a restored miniature steam train which makes runs along the 13-km track from Belgrave to Lakeside at the Emerald Lake Park. Puffing Billy was originally built in 1900 to bring farm produce to market. **Emerald** is a pretty little town with many craft galleries and shops. At **Lakeside** there's a whole string of attractions from paddleboats, barbecues and waterslides to a huge model railway with more than two km of track! It's hard to drag kids away. At Menzies Creek beside the station there's a **Steam Museum** open on Sundays and public holidays from 11 am to

5 pm. It houses a collection of early steam locomotives.

There is a recorded information service for Puffing Billy (☎ (03) 870 8411 for recorded timetable details; (03) 754 6800 for reservations). It runs every day except Christmas day; the round trip takes about 2½ hours and costs $11.50 for adults, $7.70 for children aged four to 14; family concessions are also available. Note that Puffing Billy does not run on days of total fire ban. You can get out to Puffing Billy on the regular suburban rail service to Belgrave.

MORNINGTON PENINSULA

The Mornington Peninsula is the spit of land down the east side of Port Phillip Bay, bordered on its eastern side by the waters of Westernport Bay. The peninsula really starts at Frankston, 40 km from the centre of Melbourne, and from there it's almost a continuous beach strip, all the way to Portsea at the end of the peninsula, nearly 100 km from Melbourne. At the tip of the peninsula is a national park recently opened on the site of a military base. From here you can look out across the Rip, the narrow entrance to Port Phillip Bay.

This is a very popular Melbourne resort area with many holiday homes; in summer the accommodation and camp sites along the peninsula can be packed right out and traffic can be very heavy. In part this popularity is due to the peninsula's excellent beaches and the great variety they offer. On the north side of the peninsula you've got calm water on the bay beaches (the front beaches) looking out on to Port Phillip Bay, while on the south side there's crashing surf on the rugged and beautiful ocean beaches (the back beaches) which face the Bass Strait.

Town development tends to be concentrated along the Port Phillip side; the Westernport Bay and Bass Strait coasts are much less developed and you'll find pleasant bushwalking trails along the Cape Schank Coastal Park, a narrow coastal strip right along the Bass Strait coast from Portsea to Cape Schank. Frankston is the start of the peninsula, linked by rail to Melbourne.

There's a tourist information centre in Dromana (☎ (059) 87 3078) on the coast road down the peninsula and the National Parks brochure *Discovering the Peninsula* tells you all you'll want to know about the peninsula's history, early architecture and walking tours.

Markets

The peninsula is an excellent place to check out craft and produce markets, as there's usually one each week somewhere in the area. The main ones are: Red Hill, 1st Saturday morning each month; Emu Plains Market, 3rd Saturday; Boneo Market, 3rd Saturday morning; Rosebud, 2nd Saturday; and Bittern, 1st & 3rd Sunday.

Getting There & Away

There's a regular V/Line bus service from Frankston through to Portsea (☎ (03) 619 5000 for details) and suburban trains run from Melbourne to Frankston.

During the summer a passenger ferry makes the short crossing from Sorrento and Portsea to Queenscliff on the other side of the heads; by road it's a couple of hundred km right round the bay. From late December to the end of January it operates 10 times daily, then to Easter five times daily. In November and December it operates three times daily on weekends and it also operates in the May and August school holidays. The adult fare is $5 one-way, $10 return, and for the first couple of morning departures there's a connecting bus into Geelong.

The *Peninsula Princess* is a car ferry which runs all year, departing Queenscliff every two hours from 7 am to 5 pm with a 7 pm service during the peak periods. A car and passengers cost $38, or it's $14 for a motorcycle and rider, and $5 for pedestrians.

Frankston to Blairgowrie

Beyond Frankston you reach **Mornington** and **Mt Martha**, early settlements with some old buildings along the Mornington Esplanade and fine, secluded beaches in between. **The Briars** in Mt Martha is an 1840s homestead open to the public.

Also of interest in Mornington is the **Australian Museum of Modern Media**, which is full of memorabilia relating to TV, cinema and radio.

Dromana is the real start of the resort development and just inland a winding road leads up to **Arthur's Seat** lookout at 305 metres; you can also reach it by a scenic chair lift (weekends and holidays in summer only). On the slopes of Arthur's Seat, in McCrae, the **McCrae Homestead** is a National Trust property, dating from 1843 and open daily from 10 am to 5 pm on weekends and public holidays. **Coolart** on Sandy Point Rd, Balnarring, on the other side of the peninsula, is another historic homestead. Coolart is also noted for the wide variety of its bird life.

After McCrae there's **Rosebud, Rye** and **Blairgowrie** before you reach Sorrento.

Sorrento

Just as you enter Sorrento there's a small memorial and pioneer cemetery from the first Victorian settlement at pretty **Sullivan Bay**. The settlement party, consisting of 308 convicts, civil officers, marines and free settlers, arrived from England in October 1803, intending to forestall a feared French settlement on the bay. Less than a year later, in May 1804, the project was abandoned and transferred to Hobart, Tasmania. The main reason for the settlement's short life was the lack of water. They had simply chosen the wrong place; there was an adequate supply further round the bay. The settlement's numbers included an 11-year-old boy, John Pascoe Fawkner, who 25 years later would be one of the founders of Melbourne. It also included William Buckley, a convict who escaped soon after the landing in 1803 and lived with Aborigines for the next 30 years as the Wild White Man.

Sorrento has a rather damp and cold little aquarium and an interesting small historical museum in the old **Mechanic's Institute** building on the Old Melbourne Rd. From the 1870s, paddle-steamers used to run between Melbourne and Sorrento. The largest, entering service in 1910, carried 2000 passengers.

From 1890 through to 1921 there was a steam-powered tram operating from the Sorrento pier to the back beach. The magnificent hotels built of local limestone in this period still stand – the Sorrento (1871), Continental (1875) and Koonya (1878).

Places to Stay *Bell's Hostel* (☎ (059) 84 4323) in Sorrento is a very popular place to stay. The hostel is YHA-affiliated and the owners, Ian and Margaret, make every effort to make travellers comfortable. The nightly charge is $9 for YHA members, slightly more for nonmembers.

Portsea

Portsea, at the end of the Nepean Highway, offers another choice between calm and surf beaches. At the Portsea back beach (the surf side) there's the impressive natural rock formation known as **London Bridge**, plus a cliff where hang-gliders make their leap into the void, and fine views across Portsea and back to Melbourne from **Mt Levy Lookout**. Portsea is a popular diving centre, and scuba-diving trips on the bay operate regularly from Portsea Pier.

Point Nepean National Park After being off-limits to the general public for over 100 years, most of the tip of the peninsula was opened up in 1988 as a national park. There's an excellent visitor centre (☎ (059) 84 4276) where an entrance fee of $6 is payable. There are walking tracks through the area, or you can use the tractor-drawn Transporter. The booklet, *Discovering Historic Point Nepean*, is available from the visitor centre and gives good descriptions of the various points of interest.

At the entrance to the park are two historic gun barrels which fired the first shots in WW I and WW II. In 1914 a German ship was on its way out from Melbourne to the heads when news of the declaration of war came through on the telegraph. A shot across its bows at Portsea resulted in its capture. The first shot in WW II turned out to be at an Australian ship!

Cheviot Beach, at the end of the peninsula,

featured more recently in Australian history. In 1967, the then prime minister Harold Holt went for a swim here and was never seen again. The area was closed to the public for many years but has recently been reopened.

The Ocean Coast

The southern (or eastern) coast of the peninsula faces Bass Strait and Westernport Bay. A connected series of walking tracks has been developed all the way from London Bridge to Cape Schank and Bushrangers Bay. Some stretches of the Peninsula Coastal Walk are along the beach, some are actually cut by high tide, but in all the walk extends for more than 30 km and takes at least 12 hours to walk from end to end. The walks can easily be done in stages because the park is narrow and is accessible at various points.

Cape Schank is marked by the 1859 lighthouse and there are good walking possibilities around the cape. The rugged coast further east towards **Flinders** and **West Head** has many natural features including a blowhole. Towns like Flinders and **Hastings** on this coast are not quite as popular and crowded in the summer as those on Port Phillip Bay. **Point Leo**, near Shoreham, has a good surf beach.

Off the coast in Westernport Bay is **French Island**, once a prison farm, which is virtually undeveloped, although there are a few camp sites and a lodge. Koalas were introduced some years ago, and the thriving colony now provides top-ups for depleted areas elsewhere in Victoria. A small hydrofoil operates a shuttle service between Stony Point and Tankerton Jetty on French Island, every day of the week in summer, and at weekends the rest of the year (☎ (059) 793 774 for details).

PHILLIP ISLAND

At the entrance to Westernport Bay, 137 km south-east of Melbourne, Phillip Island is a very popular holiday resort for the Melbourne area. There are plenty of beaches, both sheltered and with surf, and a fascinating collection of wildlife including the island's famous fairy penguin colony. The island is joined to the mainland by a bridge from San Remo to Newhaven.

Orientation & Information

Cowes is the main town on the island. It's on the north side of the island and has a pleasant, sheltered beach. The south side of the island has the surf beaches like Woolamai, Cat Bay and Summerland, which is the home of the famous penguin parade. **Rhyll** is a small fishing village on the east of the island and has the island's main boat ramp, while **Ventnor** is on the western coast.

There is an excellent information centre (☎ (059) 56 7447) in Newhaven just after you cross the bridge to the island. It is open daily from 9 am to 5 pm. They have a free map and reams of other useful info.

Banks, hotels, motels, camp sites, restaurants, snack bars and other amenities can all be found in Cowes, especially along the main drag, Thompson Ave, which is the road in from Melbourne.

Fairy Penguins

Every evening at Summerland Beach in the south-west of the island, the tiny fairy penguins which nest there perform their 'parade', emerging from the sea and waddling resolutely up the beach to their nests – totally oblivious of the sightseers. The penguins are there year-round but arrive in far larger numbers in the summer when they are rearing their young. It's no easy life being the smallest type of penguin – after a few hours of shut-eye, it's down to the beach again at dawn to start another hard day's fishing.

The parade takes place like clockwork a few minutes after sunset each day and it is a major tourist attraction – Australia's second biggest, in fact. Not surprisingly there are huge crowds, especially on weekends and holidays, so bookings should be made in advance – contact either the information centre at Newhaven, or the Penguin Reserve itself (☎ (059) 568 300).

To protect the penguins everything is strictly regimented – keep to the viewing areas, don't get in the penguins' way and no camera flashes. There's a modern visitors' centre with an excellent souvenir shop and walk-through simulated underwater display. The admission charge is $6, but it's money well spent to see this unique sight. At least most of the time it is – occasionally the penguins seem to take a day off from fishing and the spectators far outnumber the handful of performers!

Seal Rocks & the Nobbies

Off Point Grant, the extreme south-west tip of the island, a group of rocks rises from the sea. They're known as the Nobbies and are inhabited by a colony of about 6000 fur seals. You can view them through coin-in-the-slot binoculars from the kiosk in the car park on the headland, as long as it's open. From the kiosk, a raised boardwalk gives access to excellent views of the blowhole, and across to Seal Rocks.

For a closer view, there are two-hour cruises from Cowes jetty daily at 2 pm. The fare is $18 for adults, $8 for kids, and the ticket office (☎ (059) 52 1014) is the small rotunda at the Cowes jetty.

Koalas

Koalas are the third wildlife attraction on the island. There are a number of koala sanctuaries around the island where you can see the lazy little creatures close up. The most accessible one is on the main road from Newhaven to Cowes, about four km from Cowes itself.

Phillip Island Wildlife Park, on Thompson Ave about two km from the centre of Cowes, usually has a wild koala residing in one of the trees on the grounds somewhere. This recently revamped centre also has dingoes, wallabies and a variety of water birds.

Birds

Phillip Island also has mutton-bird colonies, particularly in the sand dunes around Cape Woolamai. These birds, which are actually called shearwaters, are amazingly predictable; they arrive back on the island on exactly the same day each year – 24 September – from their migration flight from Japan and Alaska. Your best chance of seeing them

is at the penguin parade, as they fly in low over the sea each evening at dusk in the spring and summer months.

You'll also find a wide variety of water birds including pelicans, ibis and swans in the swampland at the Nits at Rhyll.

Other Attractions

Swimming and surfing are popular island activities and the old motor-racing circuit was revamped to stage the Australian Motorcycle Grand Prix for the first time in 1989. It was a huge success in 1989 and 1990 but the event was controversially moved to Sydney in 1991, partly due to the Victorian government's anti-tobacco-advertising policy. At the circuit, on Back Beach Rd, the **Len Lukey Museum** has a fine collection of veteran, vintage and racing cars.

Rugged **Cape Woolamai** with its walking track is particularly impressive. There's a great contrast between the high seas on this side of the island and the sheltered waters of the northern (Cowes) side. Access to the signposted walking trail is from the Woolamai surf beach. It's about a half-day walk.

Churchill Island is a small island with a restored house and beautiful gardens. It was here, in 1801, that the first building was constructed by White settlers in Victoria. The island is connected to Phillip Island by footbridge and the turn-off is well signposted about one km out of Newhaven. It's open on weekends from 10 am to 4 pm, and from 1 to 5 pm on Mondays, Wednesdays and Fridays.

Organised Tours

There are many, many tours of Phillip Island available, mostly day trips from Melbourne. One tour that's been recommended by backpackers is run by Autopia Tours, which operate from the YHA hostel (☎ (03) 328 3595) in Chapman St, North Melbourne; they also pick up from St Kilda. Their Phillip Island tour departs from the hostel on Sunday, Monday and Wednesday at 1 pm and returns there between 11.30 pm and 12.15 am, depending on the season. The cost

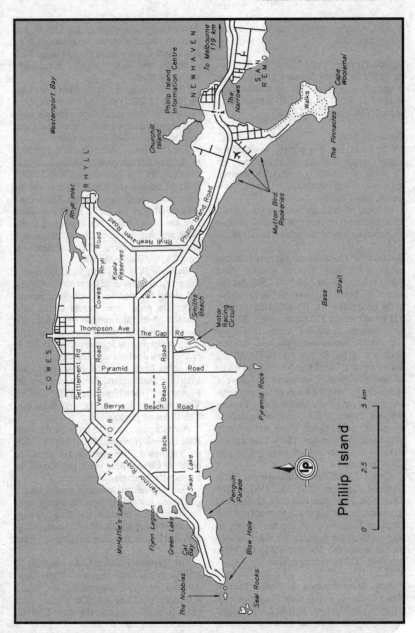

Phillip Island

is $30, which includes entrance to the penguin parade.

Scenic Flights

Phillip Island Air Services (☎ (059) 56 7316) operates scenic flights ranging from a 10-minute zip around Cape Woolamai for $25 to a 40-minute loop around Westernport Bay for $55.

Places to Stay

Phillip Island is a very popular weekend (or longer) escape from Melbourne so there are all sorts of hostels, guesthouses, motels, holiday flats and camp sites in Cowes, Newhaven, Rhyll and San Remo.

Because of the high demand you should try to make a reservation in the peak periods – Christmas, Easter and school holidays.

Hostels Far and away the best place in this range is the very friendly *Amaroo Park Backpackers Inn* (☎ (059) 52 2548) on the corner of Church and Osborne Sts, very close to the centre of town. It's affiliated with the YHA and charges $10 for members, $13 for nonmembers, in six-bed dorms. There are also double rooms available, and you can pitch a tent for $5 per person ($6.50 for nonmembers). Geoff and Kate Marks make all and sundry very welcome, and have a cheap car for rent for visits to the penguins and elsewhere. They also run day trips to Wilsons Prom. Other facilities include a swimming pool, games room and a lively little bar in the evenings. The V/Line drivers all know this place and will usually drop you off at the door.

Also YHA-affiliated is the *Anchor Belle Caravan Park* (☎ (059) 52 2258) at 272 Church St. This place has only 12 beds for hostellers, and as it's much further from the centre of Cowes (about 2½ km) is not as convenient as the Amaroo; it's also nowhere near as congenial. The rate is $10 for YHA members, $13 for nonmembers.

Hotels, Guesthouses & Flats There's plenty of choice in this area. The prominent *Isle of Wight Hotel* (☎ (059) 52 2301) is right on the Esplanade in the centre of Cowes.

Air-con singles/doubles go for $30/35, and there are more expensive motel rooms. It's a good place if you want to be right in the thick of things, and there's a good beach right across the road.

Not quite so central is the *Glen Isla Motel* (☎ (059) 52 2822) at 234 Church St, about two km from the main street. The six units here are all equipped with TV and fans, and cost from $40 to $80 for a double.

The *Coachman Motel* (☎ (059) 52 1098) at 51 Chapel St has good facilities, including a heated pool, and the units cost from $40/48.

Right next to the Koala Reserve on the main road onto the island is the *Koala Park Holiday Resort* (☎ (059) 52 2176), about five km from Cowes. It's a pleasant shady place and there's a good chance of seeing a koala from your room. The units here cost from $45 for singles/doubles.

Trenavin Park (☎ (059) 56 8230) is on a rise about nine km from the centre of Cowes, out along the road to the penguin parade. There are good views across to the back beaches of the Mornington Peninsula, and there's a pool and central heating. The tariff at this small place is $60 per person for B&B, or $95 for a double including dinner.

Further along this road, only about a km from the Summerland Beach itself, is the *Flynns Reef Guest House* (☎ (059) 56 8673). There are just four rooms, and these cost $25/40 for singles/doubles.

Another place worth trying is the *Rhylston Park Historic Homestead* (☎ (059) 52 2730), on Thompson Ave about a km from the centre of Cowes. Here you'll pay $35/55 for a comfortable single/double room.

Flats are an option worth considering if you have a few people together, want to cater for yourself and intend to stay for a few days at least. Weekly rentals are often better value than daily rates. Advance booking is a good idea.

The *Bayview Holiday Units* (☎ (059) 52 2220) are close to the centre at 5 Warley Ave. All units are fully self-contained, and there's a laundry, pool and spa. The weekly rates range from $270 for a double up to $560 for a unit sleeping six.

A slightly cheaper option is the *Cullara Holiday Flats* (☎ (059) 52 2342) on the corner of Church and Steele Sts in Cowes. The units accommodate from two to five people, and you must supply your own bed linen. The units cost from $245 to $490 per week.

As many of the houses on Phillip Island are weekenders owned by people in Melbourne, a huge number lie vacant most of the year and many are available for rent. There are at least four real estate agents on Thompson Ave, so it's worth asking what's available.

Camping There are at least half a dozen caravan parks in the vicinity of Cowes. One with a good location is the *Kaloha Caravan Park* (☎ (059) 52 2179), on the corner of Chapel and Steele Sts, about 200 metres from the beach and close to the centre of Cowes.

Places to Eat

Thompson Ave in the centre of Cowes is a good place to start looking. There are a number of standard greasy-spoon takeaways with all the usual stuff, and at least three BYO pizza restaurants. The *Isola de Capri* has a good reputation. The *Wing Lock Chinese Restaurant* at the bottom end of Thompson Ave is also pretty good.

For something a bit better, the *Isle of Wight Hotel* has good value counter meals and a buffet restaurant upstairs. Better again is *The Jetty* on the corner of Thompson Ave and the Esplanade. This place is by no means cheap but the food is very good – especially the seafood.

Further along the Esplanade is the *Rusty Harpoon* which has grills, steaks and a few Chinese dishes. Main courses are in the range of $17 to $20. This place is popular with the bus tours from Melbourne which come down to the island for the penguin parade.

Back on Thompson Ave, the cosy *Rossi Restaurant*, next to the post office has good Western tucker with the emphasis on fish and chicken in the $15 to $20 range.

Probably the most expensive restaurant on the island is the *Shearwater* (☎ (059) 56 7371) on the main road near the airstrip, about six km from Cowes. The restaurant is fully licensed and there are excellent views over Bass Strait. Another fairly up-market place is *Poppy's Bar & Restaurant* (☎ (059) 56 9360) at 14 Loch St, Rhyll. It's usually only open a few evenings each week – ring ahead.

Entertainment

During the high season Cowes is fairly lively with bands at the *Isle of Wight* and *San Remo* hotels, but otherwise things are pretty quiet.

Banfields Theatre Bar & Bistro (☎ (059) 52 2088) at 192 Thompson Ave sometimes has some good artists from Melbourne and interstate, and prices are quite reasonable.

Getting There & Away

Air Phillip Island is a cheap departure point for flights to Tasmania. There are flights to Wynyard in Tasmania on Wednesday and Friday, and also on Saturdays in January. The cost is $114 one-way, or there's a $90 standby fare. It's possible to combine these flights with a fly/drive package if you book through a travel agent. Contact Phillip Island Air Services (☎ (059) 56 7316) for more information.

Bus There are daily V/Line buses from Dandenong Railway Station for the 2¼ hour trip. The fare is $10.90, and the drivers will usually drop you off right where you want to stay. Return buses leave from the Esplanade, outside the Isle of Wight Hotel.

Train/Ferry Amazingly, the ferry service which connects Cowes with Stony Point on the Mornington Peninsula is likely to be discontinued. It may survive, especially in the holiday periods, but don't count on it. Ring them up (☎ (059) 52 1014) to find out the current situation.

Getting Around

Getting around the island independently is a major pain in the neck – there just isn't any scheduled transport. The cheapest option is to rent a bike from the shop in Thompson Ave (☎ (059) 52 5917). The rates are $8 per half day, $13 for a full day and $25 for two days. Amaroo Backpackers also has a cheap car available for rent by guests.

Phillip Island Bus Tours (☎ (059) 52 2642) operates an evening service out to the Penguin Parade a few nights a week, but this seems to be seasonal – ring and check.

Great Ocean Road

For over 300 km, from Torquay (a short distance south of Geelong) almost to Warrnambool where the road joins the Princes Highway, the Great Ocean Road provides some of the most spectacular coastal scenery in Australia. For most of the distance the road hugs the coastline, passing some excellent surfing beaches, fine diving centres and even some hills from which hang-gliding enthusiasts launch themselves to catch the strong uplifts coming in from the sea in the evenings. If anything the scenery is even more impressive west of Lorne as the road climbs around steep cliffs, then drops to cross numerous small creeks.

The coast is well equipped with camp sites and other accommodation possibilities and if the seaside activities pall, you can always turn inland to the bushwalks, wildlife, scenery, waterfalls and lookouts of the Otway Ranges which back the coast.

The Great Ocean Road was only completed in 1932 as a works project during the Depression, and stretches of the country through which it runs are still relatively untouched. The area was devastated by the Ash Wednesday bushfires in 1983 and away from the road pockets of pine plantations nibble at the edges, but it's still magnificent.

Organised Tours

Autopia Tours in Melbourne has an overnight tour of the Great Ocean Road and Port Campbell. It leaves the YHA hostel at 76 Chapman St, North Melbourne, at 9 am on Monday and Thursday, and returns at 3 pm on Tuesday and Friday. It costs $47, plus $6 for dinner and $2 for breakfast. Book through the hostel (☎ (03) 328 3595) or YHA Travel (☎ (03) 670 9611).

Another popular trip with backpackers is the Wayward Bus (☎ 008 882 823, toll-free), which does a three-day ramble from Melbourne to Adelaide following the coast all the way. It costs $110, which includes accommodation and most meals. Kangavic (☎ (052) 57 1889) is a small operation which does tours from Queenscliff along the Great Ocean Road to the Otways and back. It too receives good reports from travellers, and costs $150 for two nights. Otway Bush Tours (☎ (052) 33 8395) is another company doing tours in this area.

Places to Stay

The whole coastal stretch is often heavily booked during the peak summer season and at Easter, when prices also jump dramatically. Accommodation is generally expensive, which only leaves camping or on-site vans for budget travellers, though there is a youth hostel at Apollo Bay, and associate hostels at Lorne, Port Campbell and near Cape Otway.

Getting There & Away

V/Line have a bus service from Geelong Railway Station along the Great Ocean Road to Apollo Bay three times daily Monday to Friday, twice daily on weekends. Bellarine Transit buses run more frequently from Geelong to Torquay and Jan Juc (see under Geelong). V/line also has an extended service from Apollo Bay to Port Campbell and Warrnambool and vice versa on Fridays.

TORQUAY (population 5000)

This popular resort town marks the eastern end of the Great Ocean Road and is just 22 km south of Geelong. Some of the most popular surfing beaches are nearby, including **Jan Juc** and **Bell's Beach**. Bell's hosts an international surfing championship every Easter and waves can reach six metres or more. Around the town, **Fisherman's**

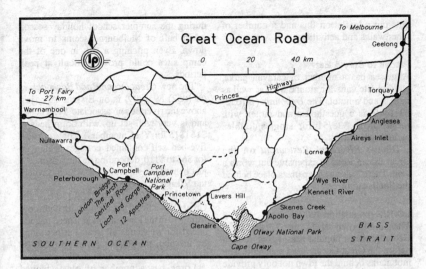

Great Ocean Road

Beach is the least crowded but often windy; the Front Beach and Back Beach are the most popular and best for swimming. In the shopping complex on the Great Ocean Road are huge surf shops such as Rip Curl and Quicksilver.

There are tennis courts and a golf course at the western end of town. Past the golf course and just out of Torquay along Duffields Rd is **Ocean Country Park** which has a grass ski slope and waterslide.

The Surf Coast Walk follows the coastline from Jan Juc to Airey's Inlet. The full distance takes about 11 hours, but can be done in stages. The Shire of Barrabool puts out a useful leaflet, available from tourist offices in the area.

Places to Stay
There are three caravan parks with camping and on-site vans. The *Torquay Hotel-Motel* (☎ (052) 61 2001) at 36 Bell St costs $45/50, or there are a couple of more expensive places, such as the *Tropicana Motel* (☎ (052) 61 4399).

Places to Eat
There are a number of takeaways around the town and the Torquay pub has good meals for about $10. In the main shopping centre, the *Tapas Cafe* is a good place for coffee or a snack. For something more substantial there are two places on the Esplanade: *Micha's* serves good Mexican food – starters are around $6 and main courses cost about $12; *Ida's* is slightly up-market but has good food, especially seafood.

The BYO *Spaghetti Cafe* in Bell St serves spaghetti and pizzas and is cheap. The *Southern Rose Garden* is on the Great Ocean Road at Jan Juc, just a few km from Torquay. It has an à la carte (around $25) and Mauritian banquet ($20) menu. It's licensed and there's a pleasant beer garden with fine views to the coast.

ANGLESEA (population 1600)
Another popular seaside resort, Anglesea is 44 km from Geelong and apart from the usual beach activities it also offers the nearby **Angahook-Lorne State Park** with many bushwalking trails, Ironbark Grove, Treefern Grove, Melaleuca Swamp and the Currawong Falls. From Anglesea there is a 45-minute cliff walk – the Shire of Barrabool

puts out a leaflet on this and a number of other walks and activities.

Places to Stay & Eat

Anglesea has a number of caravan parks, with on-site vans for around $25, as well as motels and a hotel. The *Debonair* (☎ (052) 63 1440) is a guesthouse and motel, with rooms from $38/51 for singles/doubles including breakfast.

Diana's Riverbank Restaurant on the Great Ocean Road is expensive but worth a visit. There's also a cheap pizza place behind the Shell station.

LORNE (population 1000)

The small town of Lorne, 73 km from Geelong, was a popular seaside resort even before the Great Ocean Road was built. The mountains behind the town not only provide a spectacular backdrop but also give the town a mild, sheltered climate all year round. Lorne has good beaches, surfing and bushwalks in the vicinity, especially in the Angahook-Lorne State Park. It's also losing its low-key, low-rise beach resort feeling, as flashier summer houses are appearing and the high-rise Cumberland Resort towers over the town centre.

Climb up to **Teddy's Lookout** behind the town for fine views along the coast. The beautiful **Erskine Falls** are also close behind Lorne; you can drive there or follow the walking trail beside the river, passing Splitter's Falls and Straw Falls on the way. It's about a three-hour walk each way. There are numerous other short and long walks around Lorne. Pick up a copy of the useful Lorne tourist leaflet from the new tourist office next to the newsagency on the main street.

In between Lorne and Apollo Bay are a number of small settlements that are rapidly becoming resorts in their own right, such as **Wye River, Kennett River and Skenes Creek**.

Places to Stay

Prices soar and the 'no vacancy' signs go out during the summer school holiday season when half of Melbourne seems to move down. Even pitching a tent in one of the camp sites could prove difficult at peak periods.

The new *Great Ocean Road Backpackers* (☎ (052) 89 1809) is on Erskine Ave, just above the river. It's an associate YHA hostel and is very well set up, with dorm beds at $16 ($15 for YHA members). There are also five-bed self-contained cottages which go for $65 to $110, depending on the season. It's just behind the supermarket, which is where the V/Line bus stops.

The *Lorne Hotel* (☎ (052) 89 1409) on the Great Ocean Road has rooms with bathroom from $50 in the low season. You need to book ahead for weekends all year. Further along by the pier, the *Pacific Hotel* (☎ (052) 89 1609) has similar rooms at similar prices.

Lorne has a number of old-fashioned guesthouses, and these generally charge at least $40 per person, including all meals. Such places include *Chalet Lorne* (☎ (052) 89 1241), while *Erskine House* (☎ (052) 89 1209) and *Erskine Falls Cottages* (☎ (052) 89 1751) charge around $70 per person.

The Lorne Foreshore Committee (☎ (052) 89 1382) has four camp sites at Lorne; the *Erskine River Section* is pleasantly sited by the river and right in the thick of things. The *Queens Park Section* is above it all, on the headland overlooking the pier. Site prices are in the $12 to $18 range and there are minimum booking requirements at peak periods.

Places to Eat

There's no chance of boredom when it comes to eating out in Lorne although at the fancier restaurants you should make sure you have a table booked during the peak season.

At the economical end of the scale there are counter meals at the *Lorne Hotel* and the *Pacific Hotel*; a collection of fast-food, pizza and takeaway places; or great pitta bread and other health food at the *Beach Bite* on the beach by the swimming pool (closed in winter). Plus there's the famous *Arab* which has been a Lorne institution since the mid-

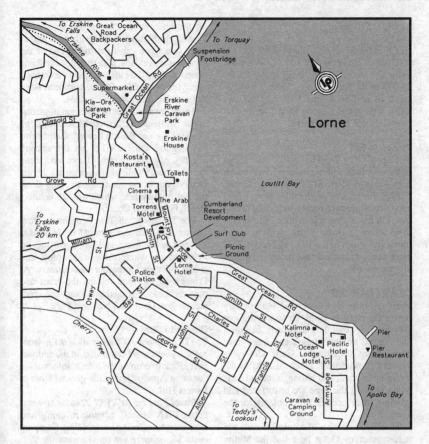

50s, which has main courses for around $10 to $12.

Moving up the scale there's *Kosta's Tavern* which is much more internationa' than its Greek name would indicate; while down at the pier, the *Pier Cafe Restaurant* serves good seafood in a Californian ambience. Coffee or a snack sitting outside watching the fishing boats is very pleasant. The fishing co-op next door sells fish fresh off the boats.

APOLLO BAY (population 920)

The pretty port of Apollo Bay, 118 km from Geelong, is a fishing town and popular resort (but more relaxed than Lorne). There is a small **historical museum** (open Sundays and holidays) and a **shell museum**, but the real attr⋅ion is the beaches and Apollo Bay is a good base from which to explore the Otway Ranges. **Mariners Lookout** a few km from town provides excellent views along the coast. The town has a good tourist information centre.

Places to Stay

At the *Pisces Caravan Resort* there's an associate YHA hostel with room for 10 people at $10 per night. It's a very new place and the facilities are excellent. There are also tent sites for $7 and on-site vans for $25.

The *Bay Hotel* (☎ (052) 37 6240) is good value and has off-season singles/doubles for $18/28 in the hotel section. There's a whole stack of self-contained flats and holiday units, with prices ranging from $40, as well as motels and caravan parks.

Places to Eat

The *Apollo Bay Hotel* has good bistro meals in the evenings, although the prices are a bit high – around $10 to $12 for a standard meal.

Flipz Restaurant on the main street offers a variety of pancake meals, including breakfast, but it's not open in winter. Also on the main street is *Buffs Bistro*, with a varied menu and meals in the $8 to $12 range. This place is open for breakfast, lunch and dinner all year round.

OTWAY RANGES

From Apollo Bay the road temporarily leaves the coast to climb up and over Cape Otway. The coast is particularly beautiful and rugged on this stretch and there have been many shipwrecks. Cape Otway is covered in rainforest, much of it still relatively untouched, and although many of the roads through the cape are unsurfaced and winding, they present no problems for the average car.

There are a number of scenic lookouts and nature reserves along here but the **Melba Gully State Park** is probably the best, with the beautiful ferns and glow-worms for which the cape is noted. In this reserve is one of the area's last remaining giant gums – it's over 27 metres in circumference and more than 300 years old. Three km east of this small park is **Lavers Hill**, a tiny township which once had a thriving timber business. Waterfalls such as **Hopetoun Falls** and **Beauchamps Falls**, and gemstones found at **Moonlight Head** are other Otway attractions.

The 1848 convict-built **Cape Otway Lighthouse**, adjacent to the Otway National Park, is nearly 100 metres high and is 15 km off the main road. The lighthouse is open Tuesday to Sunday from 10 am to 4 pm; at other times you can't get to the end of the cape but there is a path beside the fence which leads to the cliff and good views back along the coast. The **Otway National Park** has walking trails and camp sites.

There are a number of other small picturesque settlements dotted throughout the Otways, such as **Beech Forest**. **Gellibrand** has a good craft market on the second Sunday of each month. There are some excellent bushwalking opportunites in the Otways, one of the most popular being along the old railway line which used to connect Beech Forest and Colac.

The Great Ocean Road continues from Lavers Hill past the turn-off to **Johanna**, which has camping and good surfing, to **Princetown**, where there is camping, and camel rides in December and January. At Princetown the road rejoins the coast and runs right along it again, through the spectacular Port Campbell National Park.

Places to Stay

The Department of Conservation & Environment leaflet shows camp sites in the national park. Pick one up at the tourist information centre in Apollo Bay or the general store in Lavers Hill.

Bimbi Park (☎ (052) 37 9246) is an associate YHA hostel, adventure camp and caravan park offering horse riding. Camping costs $6, or there are on-site vans for $22. Take the Cape Otway road from the main highway and the Bimbi Park turn-off is about three km before the lighthouse. It is then about a km to the park.

There are plenty of other guesthouses hidden away in the ranges behind the coast. These are generally excellent getaways from the city, but are priced accordingly. Some places include *Barramunga Cabins* (☎ (052) 36 3302), Upper Gellibrand Rd, inland from Skeynes Creek; *Cape Otway Cottage* (☎ (052) 37 9256), Hordern Vale Rd, 25 minutes from Apollo Bay; and *Red Johanna Holiday Cabins* (☎ (052) 37 4238), Stafford Rd, Johanna, very close to the surf beach.

PORT CAMPBELL NATIONAL PARK

If the Great Ocean Road offers some of the most dramatic coastal scenery in Australia, then the stretch through Port Campbell is the most exciting part – 'as spectacular as anything on the Californian coast', according to a visitor from Lonely Planet's US office! The views are fantastic, with beautiful scenes like the rock formations known as the **Twelve Apostles** where 12 huge stone pillars soar out of the pounding surf. **London Bridge**, a bridge-like promontory arching across a furious sea, was once a famous landmark along this coast but in 1990 it collapsed dramatically into the sea, stranding a handful of amazed (and extremely lucky) visitors at the far end.

Loch Ard Gorge has a sadder tale to tell: in 1878 the iron-hulled clipper *Loch Ard* was driven onto the rocks offshore at this point. Of the 50 or so on board only two were to survive: an apprentice officer and an Irish immigrant woman, both aged 18. They were swept into the narrow gorge now named after their ship. Although the papers of the time tried to inspire a romance between the two survivors, the woman, the sole survivor of a family of eight, soon made her way back to Ireland's safer climes. This was the last immigrant sailing ship to founder en route to Australia.

A little further along the coast is **Port Campbell** itself, the main centre in the national park and again sited on a spectacular gorge with some fine walks in the hills behind the town. Port Campbell has a pleasant beach and calm waters.

Soon after Port Campbell the Great Ocean Road veers away from the coast at Peterborough to join the Princes Highway just before Warrnambool. The spectacular, eroded sandstone coastline continues and there are turn-offs to places like the beautiful **Bay of Islands**.

Places to Stay & Eat

In Port Campbell township, the associate YHA *Tregea Hostel* (☎ (055) 98 6379) is a pleasant, easy-going place overlooking the gorge. A dorm bed costs $10 and inquiries should be made at Elson's general store. Port Campbell also has four motels and a caravan park, and the excellent *Boggy Creek Pub* nearby, on Curdievale Rd, Niranda.

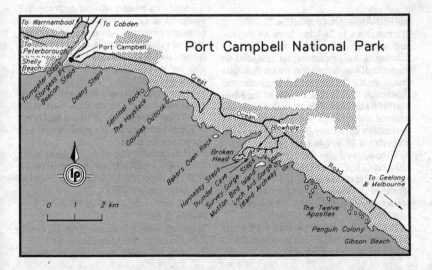

South-West

At Warrnambool the Great Ocean Road ends and you're on the final south-west coast stretch to South Australia on the Princes Highway. This stretch includes some of the earliest settlements in the state, and is promoted as the 'shipwreck coast'.

Shipwrecks

The Victorian coastline between Cape Otway and Port Fairy was a notoriously dangerous stretch of water in the days when sailing ships were the major form of transport. Navigation through the waters of Bass Strait was made exceptionally difficult due to numerous barely hidden reefs and the frequent heavy fog. More than 80 vessels came to grief on this 120-km stretch in just 40 years.

The most famous wreck was probably that of the *Loch Ard* (described earlier). Another famous wreck includes the *Falls of Halladale*, a Glasgow barque which ran aground in 1908 en route from New York to Melbourne. Although there were no casualties, it lay on the reef, still fully rigged and with sails set, for a couple of months.

Other vessels which came to grief include the *Newfield* in 1892 and the *La Bella* in 1905.

All these wrecks have been investigated by divers and relics are on display in the Flagstaff Hill Maritime Village in Warrnambool.

WARRNAMBOOL (population 22,700)

Warrnambool is 264 km from Melbourne and has sheltered beaches as well as surf beaches. Gun emplacements intended to repel the Russian invasion which Australia feared in the 1880s can be seen near the lighthouse. This is now the site of the **Flagstaff Hill Maritime Village**, with a museum, restored sailing ships and port buildings of the era. It's open daily from 9.30 am to 4.30 pm; entry is $8.50 (students $4).

Warrnambool also has a **History House** (50c) on Gilles St, with exhibits of old photographs and documents, and a **Time & Tide Museum** on Stanley St, which has a varied collection of bits and pieces of dubious merit – including over 5000 beer labels!

The three-km **Heritage Trail** walk starts from the tourist office, and there's an informative brochure to guide you.

The tourist information centre (**☎** (055) 64 7837) at 600 Raglan Parade produces the excellent *Warrnambool Handbook* ($2) with detailed information on sights, accommodation, transport, etc.

Southern Right Whales

The southern coast around Port Fairy and Warrnambool is where the southern right whale *(baleana glacialis)* comes in large numbers every May or June, and stays until around October. There are viewing areas at Logan's Beach where the cliffs provide a good point.

The southern right whale was hunted from whaling stations in southern Victoria and Tasmania early this century, and it was an easy target due to its slow swimming speed, preference for shallow water and the fact that it floated when killed.

By 1940 it was estimated that there were fewer than 1000 southern right whales left. Although the species has been protected since 1935, today they still number only around 1200 to 1500.

Whales have been sighted yearly off the Victorian coast since 1970, and at Logan's Beach since 1982.

Places to Stay

The *Surf Side One Caravan Park* (**☎** (055) 62 4897) on Pertobe Rd is less than a km from the centre and is right on the beach. Dorm beds cost $8 for YHA members, or else there are on-site cabins and tent sites.

There are a number of other caravan parks along this stretch of Pertobe Rd, and all are relatively expensive – from around $40 for a cabin or van. A cheaper place out at the beach is the *Lady Bay Hotel* (**☎** (055) 62 1544), also on Pertobe Rd, where single/double rooms go for $20/30.

In the centre of town there are plenty of hotels and motels. The cheapest place is the *Royal Hotel* (**☎** (055) 62 2063) on the corner of Timor and Fairy Sts. It's good value at $15 per person for B&B.

Of the motels, one of the cheapest is the *Riverside Gardens Motor Inn* (**☎** (055) 62 1888) on the corner of Simpson and Verdon Sts. Units start at $27/37.

Places to Eat

There are many restaurants (both BYO and fully licensed), cafes and takeaways.

Liebig St, which runs south off Raglan

Parade (the main street) is a good place to start looking. The *Whalers' Inn*, on the corner of Timor St, is a recently renovated and fairly up-market boozer, complete with restaurant. Almost next door is *Bojangles*, a fairly cheap BYO pizza place, and close to it is the *Restaurant Malaysia*, which has good yum cha on Sundays.

Getting There & Away

There are five daily V/Line trains between Melbourne and Warrnambool ($27.40), via Geelong ($19.80). The trip takes around three hours.

Heading west from Warrnambool, V/Line buses continue on to Port Fairy ($2.90), Portland and Mt Gambier ($21). If you're heading along the Great Ocean Road, there is a Friday service along that route, with a change at Apollo Bay; the fare is $16.50 to Apollo Bay and $31.10 all the way to Geelong.

TOWER HILL STATE GAME RESERVE

Midway between Warrnambool and Port Fairy, this 614-hectare reserve is the remains of an ancient crater, and after years of deforestation by White settlers from as long ago as the 1850s, the state government has set about the task of regenerating the natural bush and reintroducing wildlife to the area. So far over 250,000 trees and shrubs have been planted, and there are emus, koalas, grey kangaroos, sugar gliders and peregrine falcons within the reserve.

PORT FAIRY (population 2500)

This small fishing port 27 km west of Warrnambool was one of the first European settlements in the state, dating back to 1835, although there were temporary visitors right back in 1826. These first arrivals were whalers and sealers seeking shelter along the coast, and Port Fairy is still the home port for one of Victoria's largest fishing fleets.

Port Fairy was originally known as Belfast and although the name was later changed there's still a Northern Irish flavour about the

place and a Belfast Bakery on the main street.

There are many fine old buildings dating back to the town's early days, and 50 are classified by the National Trust. Also worth a look is the **historical centre** on Bank St, the **old fort & signal station** at the mouth of the river, and **Griffiths Island**, which is reached by a causeway from the town and has a lighthouse and a mutton-bird colony.

On the Labour Day long weekend in early March the Port Fairy Folk Festival is held. It's Australia's foremost folk festival, with the emphasis on Irish-Australian music, and it attracts top performers. The town's population swells by around 500% during the festival, and except for camping, accommodation is nonexistent.

There's an information centre (☎ (055) 68 1002) on Bank St, and this is also where the V/Line buses operate from.

Places to Stay

There are several caravan parks, the closest to the centre being the *Catalina* (☎ (055) 681608). Port Fairy's *Youth Hostel* (☎ (055) 68 2468), at 8 Cox St, is housed in a National-Trust-classified building which dates back to 1864. There are 48 beds, and it costs $10 for members. Obviously you won't get in here without a prior booking during the folk festival.

On the corner of Bank and James Sts, the *Caledonian Hotel* (☎ (055) 68 1044) has singles/doubles for $32/40.

Places to Eat

There is a surprisingly wide variety of places to eat for such a small town, and Bank St is where most of them are – places such as the *Stunned Mullet*, *Granny's Kitchen* and the *Dublin House Inn*. On Sackville St there's the popular *Julia's*.

Getting There & Away

Daily V/Line buses run to Warrnambool and Mt Gambier.

PORTLAND (population 12,700)

Continuing west 72 km from Port Fairy you reach Portland, just 75 km from the South Australian border. This is the oldest settlement in Victoria. Established in 1834, it predates Port Fairy by one year. It's an indication of the piecemeal development of Victoria that the first 'official' visitor, Major Thomas Mitchell, turned up here on an overland expedition from Sydney in 1836 and was surprised to find it had been settled two years earlier. Whalers knew this stretch of coast long before the first permanent settlement and there were even earlier short-term visitors.

Portland has numerous classified buildings including the old **Steam Packet Inn** at 33 Bentinck St which is owned by the National Trust. The **old watch house** is now the tourist information office (☎ (055) 23 2671).

The lighthouse at the tip of Cape Nelson, south of Portland, is also classified by the National Trust, although it is not open to the public. It is part of the **Cape Nelson State Park** which has some excellent walks and coastal views.

Places to Stay

Portland has numerous camp sites, guesthouses and motels.

PORTLAND TO THE SOUTH AUSTRALIAN BORDER

From Portland the Princes Highway turns inland through **Heywood** and **Dartmoor** before crossing the border to Mt Gambier in South Australia but there is also a smaller road which runs closer to the coast, fringed by the **Discovery Bay Coastal Park**. It meets the coast just before the border at the little town (village even) of **Nelson**, a popular resort for Mt Gambier. It's right on the Glenelg River, and there are daily cruises up the river to the Princess Margaret Rose limestone caves for $15, and canoes and fishing boats for hire.

Nelson is also a good access point to the **Lower Glenelg National Park** with its deep gorges and brilliant wild flowers, and the information centre (☎ (087) 38 7041) is the place to make camping reservations. This park is very popular with canoeists and those who like dangling a line, and the **Princess Margaret Rose Caves**, just three km from the border, are worth a look – there are guided tours several times a day.

Along the south coast between Portland and the border, the 200-km Great South West Walk traverses the Discovery Bay Coastal Park. It's a very rewarding 10-day hike, or you can just walk stages of it.

Places to Stay

The *Nioka Farm Home Hostel* (☎ (055) 20 2233) is 40 km west of Portland, not far from the Mt Richmond National Park. Book ahead since there's only room for six at $15 per day for YHA members including breakfast and dinner. They will arrange to pick you up from Portland ($5). This is a good opportunity to stay on a working sheep farm.

Nelson has caravan parks, a pub and motels.

The Lower Glenelg National Park has a number of very pretty designated camp sites with minimal facilities, and these must be booked at the Nelson information office. At the Princess Margaret Rose Caves there are a couple of motor cabins (basic motel-type units) – contact the ranger for bookings (☎ (087) 38 4171).

THE WESTERN DISTRICT

The south-west of the state, inland from the coast and stretching to the South Australian border, is particularly affluent sheep-raising and pastoral country. Malcolm Fraser was just one of the wealthy prime ministers to come from the Western District.

Melbourne to Hamilton

You can reach Hamilton, the 'capital' of the Western District, via Ballarat along the Glenelg Highway or via Geelong along the Hamilton Highway. On the Glenelg Highway the **Mooramong Homestead** at Skipton is owned by the National Trust and open by appointment. Further along the highway the small town of **Lake Bolac** is beside a large freshwater lake, popular for watersports. **Inverleigh** is an attractive little town along the Hamilton Highway.

The Princes Highway runs further south, reaching the coast at Warrnambool. **Winchelsea**, on the Princes Highway, has a museum in the 1842 Barwon Hotel, and there's also the Barwon Park Homestead, a rambling bluestone National Trust property. The stone Barwon Bridge dates from 1867. You can reach the Grampians on a scenic route from **Dunkeld** on the Glenelg Highway.

Colac (population 10,500)

Colac lies on the eastern edge of the western district, and there are many **volcanic lakes** in the vicinity of the town – a couple of lookouts give excellent views. There's also a **botanical garden** on the shores of Lake Colac, and **Provan's Mechanical Museum** is worth a quick look.

The Major Mitchell Trail

The Major Mitchell Trail is a 1700-km 'cultural trail' which follows as closely as possible the route taken by the New South Wales Surveyor General on his exploratory trip though Victoria in 1836.

He entered Victoria near present-day Swan Hill, and travelled south to the coast, before returning to New South Wales through Hamilton, Castlemaine, Benalla and Wodonga. On his trip he named many places along the way (and explored and discovered some previously little-known areas), including the Grampians, Mt Macedon and rivers such as the Loddon, Glenelg and Wimmera.

Mitchell was so pleasantly surprised with the lushness of the land he saw in comparison with the dry expanses of New South Wales that he named the area *Australia Felix* (Australia Fair).

The route today takes you along many back roads and is well signposted along its entire length with distinctive small brown and blue signs. An excellent descriptive handbook is available from the Department of Conservation & Environment and local tourist offices for $10.

Hamilton (population 10,700)

The major town of the area, Hamilton is particularly known for its superb **art gallery** on Brown St; it's one of the best in any Australian country town. The South-West

Regional Authority tourist office (☎ (055) 72 3746) is on Lonsdale St.

The **Hamilton & Western District Museum** (☎ (055) 72 3368), on Gray St, houses an Aboriginal 'keeping place' – the works of craft and art of the local tribes preserved by them as a means of maintaining their history and culture. It's open Wednesday to Friday 11 am to 1 pm and 2 to 4 pm and admission is $1.

Hamilton's newest 'attraction' is the **Big Woolbales**, a display devoted to promoting the wool industry and things woolly. The area around Hamilton is also the last known habitat of the eastern barred bandicoot (*perameles gunnii*), a small, ground-dwelling marsupial which is currently the most endangered mammal species in the state.

Places to Stay The *Lake Hamilton Caravan park* (☎ (055) 72 3855) has on-site vans and cabins from $20 a double.

For pub accommodation, the *Grand Central* (☎ (055) 72 2899) on Gray St has B&B for $25/40.

Getting There & Away V/Line has buses to Mt Gambier ($14.30), Warrnambool ($4.40) and Melbourne ($31.10) via Ballarat ($19.80).

Lake Condah

At **Lake Condah Aboriginal Mission** (☎ (055) 78 4242), about 45 km south of Hamilton on the Portland road, there is an important project tracing the history and culture of local tribes.

Most of Victoria's Kooris suffered early and rapid detribalisation, especially in the Western District where the squatters (landgrabbers who became wealthy pastoralists – today's 'squattocracy') quickly cleared the land of its people in their hurry to begin intensive sheep farming.

Part of the legalistic argument against granting Aboriginal land claims in the '70s was that as they were a nomadic people who didn't work the land they couldn't be said to have ever 'owned' Australia. That argument was eventually thrown out of court, and the discovery of permanent stone dwellings and a complex system of stone canals and fish traps at Lake Condah should be enough to convince the most materialistic Aussie that by any criterion the Aborigines did indeed own Australia.

The original mission buildings have long since disintegrated, but it's still possible to get an idea of the place. The mission is now run by the Kerrup-jmara community. There are modern four-bed cabins which cost $30 a night, and also a couple of family units and larger units for groups (☎ (055) 78 4257, or 78 4266).

The Wimmera

Centred on Horsham in the Wimmera are the seemingly endless Victorian wheat fields, almost enclosing the Little Desert. The Wimmera extends north-east to Warracknabeal and Donald. In the south of the region is one of the area's major attractions, indeed one of the most spectacularly scenic areas of Victoria – the mountains of the Grampians.

Several roads run west from the Victorian gold country to the South Australian border. The main road is the Western Highway which is also the busiest route between Melbourne and Adelaide. From Ballarat it runs through Horsham and to the north of the Little Desert. The Wimmera Highway splits off south from the Western Highway at Horsham.

ARARAT (population 10,100)
After a brief flirtation with gold in 1857, Ararat settled down as a farming centre. It has a **folk museum** with an Aboriginal collection, an **art gallery** and some fine old bluestone buildings. The tourist information centre (☎ 053) 52 2181) is on the corner of Barkly and Vincent Sts.

Only 16 km north-west of Ararat on the Western Highway, **Great Western** is one of Australia's best known champagne regions.

Seppelt's Great Western vineyards were established in 1865.

Places to Stay
There are two caravan parks with on-site vans and camping facilities, and a range of motel and hotel accommodation. The *Ararat Hotel* (☎ (053) 52 2477) on Barkly St has rooms from $18/30 for singles/doubles, with breakfast.

STAWELL (population 6800)
Stawell is a centre for visits to the Grampians and is another early Victorian gold town. There is a tourist information office (☎ (053) 58 2314) on London Rd.

The attractive little town has a number of National-Trust-classified buildings, and every Easter the Stawell Gift, a foot-race carnival with big prize money and a big betting ring, is held in Central Park. The **Stawell Gift Hall of Fame** on Main St details the history of the event.

Bunjil's Cave, with Aboriginal rock paintings, is 11 km south. Other local attractions include **Sisters Rocks, Roses Gap Wildlife Reserve** 17 km south, and the National Trust **Tottington Woolshed**, 55 km north-east.

Places to Stay
Accommodation choices are varied – there are farms where you can stay from around $45 a double; cabins, on-site vans and tent sites at two caravan parks; and various motels and hotels. Check with the tourist office for details.

Getting There & Away
Stawell is connected with Melbourne by daily trains ($25.80). There's also the daily bus link to the Grampians – see that section for details.

GRAMPIANS (GARIWERD) NATIONAL PARK
Named after the mountains of the same name in Scotland, the Grampians are the southwest tail end of the Great Dividing Range.

The area is a large national park renowned for fine bushwalks, superb mountain lookouts, excellent rock-climbing opportunities, prolific wildlife and, in the spring, countless wild flowers.

The Grampians are at their best from August to November when the flowers are most colourful. On a weekend in October there's a wild-flower exhibition in the Halls Gap Hall. There are also many Aboriginal rock paintings in the Grampians, as well as waterfalls such as the spectacular McKenzie Falls.

There are many fine bushwalks around the Grampians, some of them short strolls you can make from Halls Gap. Keep an eye out for koalas and kangaroos; you sometimes see koalas right in the middle of Halls Gap.

There is talk of returning the Grampians to their traditional Koori owners, although they would be leased back to the government in the same way that Ayers Rock/Uluru is. The name was changed to include the Aboriginal name, Gariwerd, in 1991.

Orientation & Information

The Grampians lie immediately west of Ararat and south of the Western Highway between Stawell and Horsham. Stawell has the closest railway station to the tiny town of Halls Gap, 25 km away. **Halls Gap**, about 250 km from Melbourne, is also right in the middle of the region and has camping and motel facilities.

The national park visitor centre (☎ (056) 56 4381), three km south of town on the Dunkeld road, has excellent information – handouts, maps etc. There is also an audio-visual display, and they have some more general tourist information. The centre is open daily from 9 am to 4.45 pm. Behind the centre is the imaginatively designed **Brambuk Cultural Centre**, a Koori enterprise with some good displays, exhibitions and a bush-tucker cafe – worth the $2 entry. Organised tours of the rock-art sites in the Grampians are operated from here.

Right in Halls Gap itself is another tourist office with stacks of brochures from the various tourist enterprises in the area. There

is no bank in Halls Gap, although both the ANZ and Commonwealth banks have sub-agencies.

If you are having trouble booking accommodation in advance (which often happens in peak holiday periods – especially Easter), the **Stawell & Grampians Information Centre** in Stawell (☎ (053) 58 2314) operates an accommodation booking service.

Things to See

To the west, the rugged **Victoria Range** is known for its red gums, and there are many Aboriginal rock paintings in the area, including Billimina (Glenisla Shelter) and Wab Manja (Cave of Hands), both near Glenisla on the Henty Highway.

Victoria Valley, in the centre of the Grampians, is a secluded wildlife sanctuary with beautiful bush tracks to drive down.

To the north at **Zumsteins**, 22 km from Halls Gap, kangaroos gather in a paddock in the hope of a free feed, but this is definitely discouraged. Be warned that these are wild animals and should not be treated like domestic pets.

Activities

The many walks in the Grampians range from well-marked (although often quite arduous) trails to some very rugged walking in the large areas which have been kept free of trails. The best known established trails are in the Wonderland area near Halls Gap, where you can scramble up and down some spectacular scenery on walks ranging from two to five hours in duration. Views from the various lookouts down onto the plains far below are well worth the effort. Especially good is the Grand Canyon trail which leads to the Pinnacle and then on to Boroka Lookout (which has access for the disabled). From here you can walk to the Jaws of Death!

Lake Bellfield, just south of Halls Gap and covering the site of the original town, is a reservoir which has been stocked with brown and rainbow trout. A bonus of fishing or swimming here is that power boats are banned.

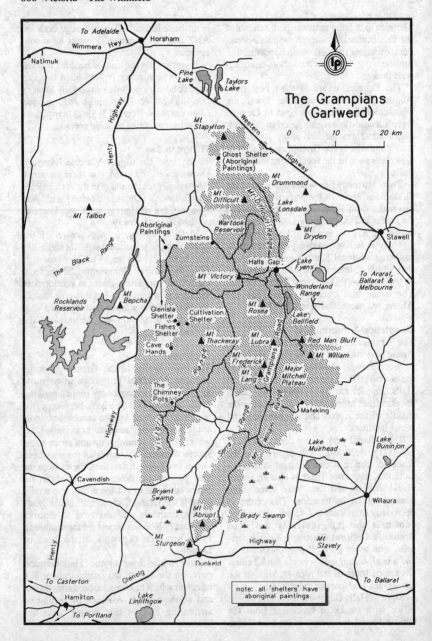

The Grampians (Gariwerd)

0   10   20 km

To Adelaide
Wimmera Hwy
Horsham
Natimuk

Pine Lake
Taylors Lake

Western Highway

Henty Highway

Mt Stapylton

Ghost Shelter
(Aboriginal
Paintings)

Mt Drummond

Mt Difficult

Mt Difficult Range

Lake Lonsdale

Mt Talbot

Aboriginal
Paintings

Wartook
Reservoir

Mt Dryden

Stawell

Zumsteins

Halls Gap

Lake Fyans

The Black Range

Mt Victory

To Ararat,
Ballarat &
Melbourne

Wonderland Range

Rocklands Reservoir

Mt Bepcha

Glenisla Shelter

Cultivation Shelter

Fishes Shelter

Cave of Hands

Mt Rosea

Lake Bellfield

Mt Lubra

Red Man Bluff

Mt Thackeray

Mt Frederick

Mt William

The Chimney Pots

Mt Lang

Grampians Road

Major Mitchell Plateau

Mafeking

Victoria Range

Serra Range

Mt William Range

Lake Muirhead

Lake Buninjon

Cavendish

Bryant Swamp

Mt Abrupt

Brady Swamp

Willaura

Henty Highway

Glenelg Highway

Mt Sturgeon

Mt Stavely

Dunkeld

To Casterton

Hamilton

Lake Linlithgow

To Portland

To Ballarat

note: all 'shelters' have
aboriginal paintings

Halls Gap Horse Riding (☎ (053) 56 4327) has horses for all standards of riders, and you can amble along the trails unsupervised if you want. A more leisurely way of seeing the Grampians is by hot-air balloon. If that sounds too easy, ask the tourist information centre if there are rock-climbing courses being held while you are there.

There are also a couple of companies operating joy flights over the Grampians, and these are well worth it if you have $25 to spare. Contact AG Airwork (☎ (053) 58 2855) in Stawell or Werbil Aviation (☎ (053) 56 6294) in Pomonal.

For more detailed information on the various walks available in the Grampians, check out Lonely Planet's *Bushwalking in Australia*, or *50 Walks in the Grampians* (Hill of Content, 1986) by Tyrone Thomas.

Places to Stay

Halls Gap One km from the centre of Halls Gap on the corner of Buckler St and Grampians Rd the small *Youth Hostel* (☎ (053) 56 6221) charges $10. The closest camp site to the centre is the *Halls Gap Caravan Park* (☎ (053) 56 4251) which has on-site vans for $28 and tent sites for $9.50.

There's a whole gaggle of guesthouses, cottages and motels, none of them spectacular bargains. Two of the cheaper ones are *Banksia Cottage* (☎ (053) 32 7249) and *Noonammena Cottage* (☎ (050) 41 7520) which both cost $50 for a five-bed self-contained cottage.

Halls Gap Holiday Flats (☎ (053) 56 4304) has ten flats from $35 to $60 for up to five people.

In the Park At Zumsteins on the western edge of the park, the *Zumsteins Tourist Park* (☎ (053) 83 6242) has on-site vans for $25, and sites for $5.25. Like all Grampians accommodation, this should be booked in advance during holiday periods.

There are various camp sites in the national park, all with toilets, picnic tables and fireplaces, and most with at least limited water. The Boreang Campsite on the Glenelg River Track in the Victoria Valley has no

water at all, so gets less crowded at peak times.

Outside the designated sites, bush camping is permitted anywhere else, except in the Wonderland Range area, and around Lake Wartook.

When camping in the park pay close attention to the fire restrictions – apart from the damage you could do to yourself and the bush, you stand a good chance of being arrested if you disobey them. Remember that you can be jailed for lighting *any* fire, including fuel stoves, on a total fire ban day, and the locals will be more than willing to dob you in.

Places to Eat

The *Halls Gap General Store* has a cafe and takeaway section, and a well-stocked supermarket.

The *Golden Phoenix* is a small Chinese restaurant with a cheap but limited selection, while the *Kookaburra Restaurant* has an excellent reputation and prices to match. Expect to pay at least $20 per head here. The *Gum Nut Restaurant* is of a similar standard.

Getting There & Away

V/Line has a daily bus between Halls Gap and Stawell ($5.40), and it connects with trains to and from Melbourne. The trains must be booked in advance (☎ (03) 619 5000 in Melbourne, (053) 58 3492 in Stawell).

Grampians National Park Tours (☎ (053) 56 6221) offers return travel to and from Stawell and a half-day 4WD tour of the park for $30 ($25 for YHA members). You can stay as many days as you like before using the return sector to Stawell.

HORSHAM (population 13,100)

Horsham was first settled in 1842, and has grown to become the main centre for the Wimmera. It is also a good base for the Little Desert National Park and the Grampians. The town has an **art gallery, botanic gardens** and **'Olde Horsham'** with historic displays and a tearoom in an old tram. The **Wimmera Wool Factory**, out on the Golf

Course Rd, is a community project which provides employment and skill development for local handicapped people. There are daily tours and these give an insight into all aspects of the wool industry.

Places to Stay

The *Horsham Caravan Park* (☎ (053) 82 3476) is at the end of Firebrace St by the river and has on-site vans costing from $25.The *White Hart Hotel* (☎ (053) 82 1231) at 55 Firebrace St has rooms with breakfast for $21/30, and there are at least a dozen motels in the area as well.

MT ARAPILES

Twelve km from Natimuk on the Wimmera Highway, Mt Arapiles (or more commonly the Piles) lures rock-climbers from around the world. There are more than 2000 climbs for all levels of skill, with colourful names such as Violent Crumble, Punks in the Gym and Cruel Britannia. It's usually alive with climbers.

So great is its attraction that the sleepy town of Natimuk is now home to quite a few climbers who have moved into the area, bringing with them tastes and attitudes not usually associated with small rural towns in Australia – the Natimuk pub must be one of the few to boast vegetarian pancakes on its counter-meal menu, and the milkshakes at the local shops are famous.

Despite the mountain's climbing fame, there is a sealed road right to the top for those unable to haul themselves up the hard way, and there are excellent views from the lookout. Not far away is the lone rocky outcrop of Mitre Rock, near to its namesake lake, and the Wimmera stretches into the distance.

As might be expected, accommodation in Natimuk is tight, particularly for long-term stays. There is a camp site (known locally as 'The Pines') at Centenary Park at the base of the mountain and there's always an eclectic mix of people here. It must be one of the best patronised camp sites in any of Victoria's state forests, although the facilities here are minimal: one wash basin.

DIMBOOLA (population 2000)

The name of this quiet, typically Australian country town on the Wimmera River is a Sinhalese word meaning 'Land of the Figs'. The **Pink Lake**, just south of the highway, is a little way beyond Dimboola. Beside the Wimmera River nearby you can see Aboriginal canoe trees; the red gums are scarred where canoes have been cut out in one piece from their bark.

The **Ebenezer Mission Station** was established in Antwerp, north of Dimboola, to tend to local Aborigines in 1859. The ruins, complete with its small cemetery, are signposted off the road, close to the banks of the Wimmera River.

LITTLE DESERT NATIONAL PARK

Just south of the Western Highway and reached from Dimboola or Nhill, the Little Desert National Park is noted for its brilliant display of wild flowers in the spring. The name is a bit of a misnomer because it isn't really a desert at all nor is it that little. In fact with an area of 132,000 hectares it's Victoria's fifth largest national park, and the 'desert' extends well beyond the national park boundaries.

If you intend really to explore the bushland of the park you'll need 4WD. The desert is at its finest in the spring when it is carpeted with wild flowers.

A little beyond Dimboola the **Kiata Lowan Sanctuary** is an easily accessible area in the north of the park with walks and a resident ranger.

Places to Stay

You can camp in the park at sites 10 km south of Kiata, just east of Nhill. There is tank water and no showers.

The *Little Desert Lodge* (☎ (053) 91 5232), in the park and 16 km south of Nhill, has units with B&B for $42 per person, or you can camp for $7 per site. There's also an environmental study centre and the only aviary in the world to have the fascinating mallee fowl.

The Mallee

North of the Wimmera is the least populated part of Australia's most densely populated state. Forming a wedge between South Australia and New South Wales, this area even includes the one genuinely empty part of Victoria. The contrast between the wide, flat Mallee, with its sand dunes and dry lakes, and the lush alpine forests of East Gippsland is striking – despite being the smallest mainland state, Victoria really does manage to cram in a lot.

The Mallee takes its name from the mallee scrub which once covered the area. Mallee roots are hard, gnarled and slow-burning. Some great Aussie kitsch can still be found – mallee-root eggcups and ashtrays – although they may have crossed that thin line from being kitsch to being 'collectable'.

The Mallee region extends from around the Wyperfeld National Park in the south, all the way up to the irrigated oasis surrounding Mildura. Much of the area is encompassed in the recently proclaimed Murray-Sunset National Park and the area's other national and state parks.

The main town in the Mallee is Ouyen, on the Sunraysia Highway which runs north-south along the eastern edge. Mildura to the north and Nhill to the south are other major centres nearby. The north-west corner of the Mallee is known as 'sunset country' – a fine name for the edge of the arid wilderness that stretches right across the continent.

Mallee National Parks & Reserves

Murray-Sunset National Park This is the newest of the state's national parks, having been proclaimed in July 1991, and at 633,000 hectares it is the state's second largest, after the Alpine National Park.

Its creation was the subject of a good deal of controversy as much of the land it took over was good, although degraded, grazing and agricultural land. It was created to try to stop the eradication of much of the area's unique native fauna, which has suffered greatly as more than 65% of the mallee scrub has been cleared.

The park takes in the older Pink Lakes National Park, and is contiguous with the Hattah-Kulkyne National Park.

Wyperfeld National Park Best reached from Albacutya, north of Rainbow, this large park contains a chain of often-dry lakes, including Lake Albacutya. A combination of river gums on the flood plains, sandy mallee scrubland and treed plains supports a wide variety of wildlife, including emus and kangaroos. There are walking tracks from six km in length up to overnight walks. The park information centre has details of these and on the area's flora & fauna, which includes the mallee fowl. There are tent sites but only limited water.

Big Desert Wilderness This large wilderness area contains no roads, tracks or any other facilities, which makes it difficult and dangerous to travel in except for those with considerable wilderness experience. It consists of sand dunes and mallee scrub, and wildlife abounds.

If you aren't equipped to venture into the wilderness, you can get a tantalising glimpse of the Big Desert along the dry-weather road which runs from Nhill north to Murrayville on the Ouyen Highway. There are camp sites and bore water to be found at **Broken Bucket Reserve**, which is about 55 km north of Nhill.

Hattah-Kulkyne National Park With the near-desert of the mallee country, the woodlands and the gum-lined edges of lakes and the Murray River, Hattah-Kulkyne is a diverse and beautiful park.

The park hit the headlines in 1990 when the state government decided to cull some of the 20,000-odd kangaroos which inhabit the park – it has been estimated that the park can only carry around 5000 roos without harming the fragile environment. Of course, any operation that involves killing kangaroos is going to be controversial, and this one was no exception.

The Hattah Lakes system fills when the Murray floods and supports many species of water birds. There is a good information centre at Lake Hattah, a few km into the park from the small town of Hattah, on the Sunraysia Highway 35 km north of Ouyen. Check at the centre on the condition of tracks in the park – many are almost impassable after rain.

There are camping facilities at Lake Hattah and Lake Mournpall, but note that there is limited water and the lake water, when there is any, is muddy and unsuitable for drinking. Camping is also possible anywhere along the Murray River frontage, which is also the Murray-Kulkyne State Park.

Murray River

The Murray River is Australia's most important inland waterway flowing from the mountains of the Great Dividing Range in north-east Victoria to Encounter Bay in South Australia, a distance of some 2500 km. The river actually has its source in New South Wales, close to Mt Kosciusko, but soon after forms the border between the two states, and most of the places of interest are on the Victorian side.

The mighty Murray is also a river with a history. It was travelled along by some of Australia's earliest explorers, including Mitchell, Sturt and Eyre, and later became a great trade artery and a means of opening up the interior.

Long before roads and railways crossed the land the Murray was an antipodean Mississippi with paddle-steamers carrying supplies and carting wool to and from remote sheep stations and homesteads. The township of Echuca became Australia's leading inland port as boats traded for hundreds of km along the Murray's winding waterways, to other thriving river towns like Swan Hill and Mildura, as well as up and down the Murrumbidgee, Goulburn and Darling rivers.

Many of the river towns have good museums, old buildings from the riverboat era or well-preserved paddle-steamers that recall that colourful age.

The Murray is also of great economic importance as it supplies the vital water for the irrigation schemes of northern Victoria that have made huge areas of previously barren land agriculturally viable.

As early as the 1890s Victorian MP Alfred Deakin (later prime minister) recognised the agricultural potential of developing irrigation projects in the state's north. He encouraged the Chaffey brothers of California to design and install pumps and irrigation facilities using the Murray water. The brothers also planned the township of Mildura which, together with the new farming possibilities, soon attracted settlers from all over the country and overseas. Deakin's vision proved to be correct and the extensive irrigated land around Mildura and down through South Australia all stems from the Chaffey brothers' early work.

The Murray and its irrigation projects now support prosperous dairy farms, vineyards, vegetables and the citrus orchards which provide fresh fruit and supply the thriving dried-fruit industry. In recent years, however, salinity in the soil after years of irrigation has become a major problem, one which poses a long-term threat to the viability of much of the irrigated land along both sides of the Murray.

The river is also famous for its magnificent forests of red gums, its plentiful bird and animal life, and as a great place for adventurous canoe trips, relaxing riverboat cruises or leisurely river-bank camping.

In the north-west of Victoria the Murray Valley Highway begins where it meets the Sunraysia Highway at a T-junction 67 km south of Mildura. From there it follows, for the most part, the course of the Murray River eastwards as far as Corryong, which is almost back to the river's source near Mt Kosciusko in New South Wales.

Getting There & Away
Bus & Train The interstate bus companies

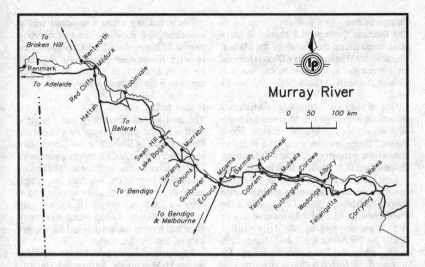

Murray River

0   50   100 km

go through Mildura on the Sydney to Adelaide run, and Greyhound has a twice-weekly Melbourne/Mildura/Broken Hill route which runs alongside the Murray for part of the way.

V/Line have bus, train or combination bus/train services which connect Melbourne, Bendigo and Ballarat with the Murray River towns, and they also have bus services running along the Murray between Albury and Mildura.

Boat Of course the most appropriate way to travel on the Murray is by boat. The paddle-steamers of Echuca and Swan Hill provide day or overnight trips, and there are numerous places that rent houseboats. The latter combine accommodation with a leisurely few days along the river. Check the tourist information offices in Mildura, Swan Hill and Echuca for details on the houseboats.

MILDURA (population 18,400)
Noted for its exceptional amount of sunshine, Mildura was the site of the first Murray River irrigation projects.

Information
The Mildura tourist information centre (☎ (050) 23 3619) is in a booth in Langtree Mall. Ron's Tourist Centre (☎ (050) 21 1166) at 41 Deakin Ave is good for tour information and bookings, and also does tours of the town and area.

The Department of Conservation & Environment has an office (☎ (050) 23 2906) in the state government offices at 253 Eleventh St. They have good info on all the national and state parks in the area.

The RACV has an office (☎ (050) 21 3272) at 82A Langtree Ave, in the mall.

Fruit Picking
For fruit-picking work, contact the Commonwealth Employment Service (☎ (050) 22 2922) around the first week of February and there's a good chance of getting a job as a grape picker or cart operator. After a few days, you'll get used to the back-breaking 10-hour-a-day labour. Picking usually starts around February and lasts for a month. It's hard work, but if you've done it before it can mean big bucks, like about $350 a week. Some farmers provide accommodation, but take a tent if you're not sure.

Things to See
The **Pioneer Cottage** at 3 Hunter St has a small museum on the history of the Mallee. The **Mildura Workingman's Club** is famous for having the longest bar in the world – visitors can inspect the bar from 9.30 to 11 am.

One of the most interesting of Mildura's attractions is **Orange World**, seven km north of town across the Murray in New South Wales. There are tours on tractor trains around the property and it's a fascinating introduction to how citrus fruit is produced.

Lest you forget that this is riverboat country, you can take **paddle-steamer trips** from the Mildura Wharf. On weekdays the PV *Rothbury* and the PS *Melbourne*, which is still steam-powered, do daily cruises ($13); the PS *Avoca* has a daily lunch-time cruise; while the *Coonawarra* and the PS *Murray River Queen* both specialise in overnight and longer tours.

Mildura is also wine country, with a number of popular wineries around the district.

Places to Stay
Rosemont Holiday House (☎ (050) 23 1535), 154 Madden Ave, is an associate YHA Hostel with B&B for $15 per person in single/double rooms, $2 more for nonmembers. A good breakfast is included. The rooms are clean with all the usual facilities and the owners are very helpful and hospitable.

Mildura, especially along Deakin Ave, is overrun with motels, so prices are quite low with a lot of special deals. Try the *Vineleaf Motel* (☎ (050) 23 1377) on the corner of Tenth St and Pine Ave which has singles/doubles for $29/35 including a light breakfast; or the *Riviera Motel* (☎ (050) 23 3696), 157 Seventh St, where singles/doubles cost from $34/36.

There are also many caravan parks in the area but the most central is *Cross Roads Caravan Park* (☎ (050) 23 3239) on the corner of Deakin Ave and Fifteenth St. Tent sites cost $11 for two and on-site vans are $24.

For a holiday afloat you could rent a houseboat, but these are not that cheap – around $520 per week for four people. This is with *Riverqueen Houseboat Holidays* (☎ (050) 23 2955) at Bruce's Bend, seven km east of the centre of town.

Places to Eat
The area around Seventh St and Langtree Mall is a good place to look for cheap eats. On the corner of Seventh St and Deakin Ave is *Jackie's Corner*, a Chinese restaurant with an extensive menu and cheap takeaways. Right next door is the *Souvlaki Inn*, which has both eat-in and takeaway service, and is open for lunch and dinner. Next door again is *Dogs & Cones*, a shop which has pretty good fast food of the hot dog and hamburger variety, and fine ice cream.

Vegetarians should head for the excellent *Bananas Vegetarian Restaurant* on the corner of Seventh and Chaffey Sts. The *Piccolo Rialto* is a more up-market place at 27 Deakin Ave. It has a variety of restaurants, but does have a cheap takeaway or delivery pizza and pasta section (☎ (050) 23 4266).

The gambling clubs on the New South Wales side of the Murray River provide good, cheap lunches and free transport to entice the Victorians across.

Getting There & Away
Air Sunstate Airlines (☎ (050) 22 2444) fly to Melbourne ($151), Broken Hill ($95), Renmark ($67) and Adelaide ($108). Kendell Airlines (☎ 008 338 894, toll-free) fly to Melbourne ($151 one-way or $198 APEX return).

Bus & Train On Tuesday, Thursday, Friday and Sunday there is an overnight rail service via Ballarat that connects Melbourne with Mildura; the fare is $44. There are also daily buses to and from Bendigo ($38). V/Line also has a three-times-weekly bus service connecting all the towns along the Murray River between Mildura and Albury; the fares from Mildura are: Swan Hill $21, Echuca $35.40 and Albury $46.

Greyhound has a daily service between

Mildura and Broken Hill for $31, and daily services to Adelaide ($40) and Sydney ($119).

Getting Around

Mildura Bus Lines provide a regular bus service around town from Monday to Saturday. You can get a timetable from the tourist office. Ron's Tourist Centre offers many tours of the town and the surrounding area. Free coaches to the New South Wales gambling clubs also leave from in front of their office at 41 Deakin St.

AROUND MILDURA

Leaving Mildura you don't have to travel very far before you realise just how desolate the country around here can be. Continuing west, now on the Sturt Highway, the road runs arrow-straight and deadly dull to South Australia, about 130 km away.

Going the other way into New South Wales you follow the Murray another 32 km to **Wentworth**, one of the oldest river towns, where you can visit the Old Wentworth Gaol with the Nanya Exhibit and the Morrison Collection, then strike off north for 266 km along the Silver City Highway to remote Broken Hill.

A popular excursion from Mildura is to **Mungo Station** in New South Wales to see the strange natural formation known as the Wall of China. See the New South Wales chapter for more details.

See the earlier section on the Mallee for details of the excellent national and state parks found in this corner of the state.

ROBINVALE

A little way off the highway, Robinvale is almost ringed in by a loop of the river. It is the first major town east of Mildura and is in a busy grape and citrus-growing area. Just downstream of the town is a weir and one of the largest windmills in the country.

SWAN HILL (population 9,600)

One of the most interesting and popular towns along the entire length of the Murray,

Swan Hill was named by the early explorer Major Thomas Mitchell, who spent a sleepless night here within earshot of a large contingent of noisy black swans.

Information

Swan Hill is 340 km from Melbourne and has a tourist information centre (☎ (050) 32 3033) at 306 Campbell St.

Pioneer Settlement

The town's major attraction today is the extensive riverside Swan Hill Pioneer Settlement. The feature exhibit of this working re-creation of a river town of the paddle-steamer era is the *Gem*, one of the largest riverboats on the Murray.

The settlement has everything from an old locomotive to a working blacksmith's shop and an old newspaper office. The settlement is definitely worth a visit and is open daily. Admission is $9 including a free ride on one of the horse-drawn vehicles that act as transport around the old buildings.

Each night there is a 45-minute Sound & Light Show for $6, during which you are driven around the settlement. The paddle-steamer *Pyap* makes short trips from the pioneer settlement for $6.

Historic Homesteads

The historic **Murray Downs** sheep station is a fine example of a working property from the earliest days of European settlement along the Murray. Although the homestead is still lived in, informative tours are conducted daily and are well worth the $6. The station is actually in New South Wales, two km across the river, and is open daily, except Mondays, from 9 am to 4.30 pm.

Tyntynder, 17 km north of the town, also has a small museum of pioneering and Aboriginal relics and many reminders of the hardships of colonial life, like the wine cellar! Admission is $6, which includes a rather rushed tour, and the homestead is open daily from 9 am to 4.30 pm.

Places to Stay

The *Swan Hill Riverside Caravan Park*

(☎ (050) 32 1494), Monash Drive, is conveniently situated next to the Pioneer Settlement. There are on-site vans and cabins, and tent sites.

The *White Swan Hotel* (☎ (050) 32 2761) at 182 Campbell St charges $19 per person for clean, good-value rooms. The cheapest of the many motels in town is the *Murray River Motel* (☎ (050) 32 2067), 481 Campbell St, with singles/doubles for $30/36 including a light breakfast.

Places to Eat

Campbell St has plenty of possibilities. One of the better ones is *Teller's Licensed Deli* on the corner with McCrae St. Pasta dishes cost around $8, while other main courses are around $10.

Quo Vadis is a BYO pizza restaurant, also on Campbell St. They will take phone orders (☎ (050) 32 4408) and deliver. For a counter meal, try the *White Swan Hotel* on Campbell St.

The PS *Gem* at the Pioneer Settlement has a licensed restaurant upstairs which is open in the evenings only. Expect to pay around $25 per person.

Getting There & Away

V/Line has daily trains from Melbourne ($34.70) via Bendigo ($18.50), and three times weekly buses from Swan Hill to Mildura ($21), Echuca ($16.50) and Albury-Wodonga ($25.80).

The Greyhound/Pioneer services from Adelaide to Sydney (via Canberra) stop in Swan Hill once a day.

KERANG

Kerang is on the Murray Valley Highway about 25 km south of the river, and is best known for the huge flocks of ibis which breed on the 50 or so lakes found in the area. Middle Lake, nine km from Kerang, is the best place to see the colonies, and there's a small hide here. The town itself has a small historical museum, caravan parks and motels.

GUNBOWER STATE FOREST

The superb Gunbower State Forest, which is actually on a long 'island' enclosed by the Murray and Gunbower Creek, features magnificent river red gums, abundant animal and bird life and plenty of walking tracks. Cohuna, 32 km east of Kerang, is the main access point to the forest, although there are numerous marked tracks in from the highway. The graded tracks (maintained dirt tracks) within the forest are all on old river mud, which turns impossibly slippery after rain – conventional vehicles will find them impassable in the wet, and 4WD will be necessary.

Cohuna has a Department of Conservation & Environment office (☎ (054) 52 2266) in the civic centre which sells detailed maps of the park for $3.75. In the park there are over 100 numbered tent sites with fireplaces and picnic tables (all marked on the park map) right on the edge of the river between Torrumbarry and Koondrook.

There are caravan parks in Cohuna and Gunbower, and Cohuna also has a couple of motels and *Craddocks* holiday farm (☎ (054) 56 7442).

ECHUCA (population 6300)

Strategically sited where the Goulburn and Campaspe rivers join the Murray, Echuca, which is an aboriginal word meaning 'the meeting of the waters', was founded in 1853 by the enterprising ex-convict Henry Hopwood.

In the riverboat days this was the busiest inland port in Australia and the centre of the thriving river trade. In the 1880s the famous red-gum wharf was more than a km long and there were stores and hotels all along the waterfront. At its peak there were something over 300 steamers operating out of the port here.

Today tourism is the main money-spinner, and the attractions are, not surprisingly, centred around the old port. In October the Rich River Festival celebrates the history of the region and includes a paddle-steamer race.

Information

The Echuca tourist information centre (☎ (054) 82 4525) is at 2 Leslie St, right by the old port.

Things to See

The **old port** is now a museum ($4.25) complete with a descriptive video and diorama. There are excellent views of the river from the wharf, and your ticket also includes a visit to the old Star Hotel across the road (where you buy the tickets) with various old photographs on display, and the 1858 Bridge Hotel nearby, now a licensed restaurant. The PS *Pevensey*, which featured as the *Philadelphia* in the movie *All the Rivers Run*, is one of the few steamers still actually steam-driven, but it only operates in holiday periods.

A **paddle-steamer cruise** is almost obligatory, so head down to the river next to the old port and check out the sailing times. There are at least four steamers operating cruises throughout the day, and there's not much to choose between them. Some of them run on diesel power these days. They cost around $6 for a one-hour chooff up the river; the PS *Emmylou* costs $8 but does have a bar! It also does overnight and longer trips ($140 for a dinner and B&B trip). Tickets for all the boats can be booked in advance at various places around the port, or just jump on board.

In the same street as the wharf are various other attractions, including the **Red Gum Works**, where wood is still worked using traditional machinery; the **Echuca Wharf Pottery**; **Sharps Magic Movie House** ($5), which has old penny arcade equipment and other displays relating to Australia's cinema industry, projected on authentic equipment; and a **Coach House & Carriage Collection**.

Close by is **Njernda**, a Koori cultural centre ($2.50) housed in a very non-Koori sort of building – the old Courthouse. Across the road from this is a small **museum** ($1) housed in the old police station and lock-up building and now classified by the National Trust (open on weekends only, from 1 to 4 pm).

In late October Echuca hosts its annual Rich River Festival which is 12 days of entertainment and games.

Jack and Elaine O'Mullane, PO Box 62, Echuca (☎ (054) 82 6208), run canoe trips on the Murray River. Each canoe takes two people plus camping gear and supplies, and included in the price is land transport upstream.

Places to Stay

The *Echuca Caravan Park* (☎ (054) 82 2157) in Crofton St is the most central of the town's caravan parks, and has on-site vans and cabins.

Of the pubs, the *Pastoral Hotel* (☎ (054) 82 1812) near the railway station has rooms for $20/30. There's a stack of motels, the cheapest of which is the *Highstreet Motel* (☎ (054) 82 1013) at 439 High St with rooms from $35/40. Right by the old port, on the corner of Murray Esplanade and Leslie St, is the *Steam Packet Motel* (☎ (054) 82 3411), housed in a National-Trust-classified building. Rooms here go for $44/49.

For something different you could spend the night on the Murray aboard the PS *Emmylou*; or contact Magic Murray Houseboats (☎ (054) 80 6099) or Dinky-Di Houseboats (☎ (054) 82 5223) for details about hiring your own houseboat to tie where you please for a night on the Murray.

Places to Eat

The *Shamrock Hotel*, 583 High St, has good, cheap counter meals. The historic *Bridge Hotel* by the port has a fine licensed restaurant and the *Steam Packet Motel* does good lunches and dinners. For a light lunch there's the *Tangled Garden* at 433 High St, and if you're after a vegetarian fix the *Mexican Gallery* at 499 High St has an extensive menu.

For a lunch with a view, the *Riverside Restaurant* is right by the old port and has a very pleasant outdoor terrace with a good outlook over the river. Also worth a try in the evenings is the *Savarin Restaurant* at 436 High St. This old building was once an undertakers, so the present owner is quite used to witty customers asking for cremated steaks and the like.

Getting There & Away

V/Line has a daily service between Melbourne and Echuca ($21), changing from train to bus at Bendigo. There are also V/Line buses to Kyabram ($2.50), Wagga Wagga and Deniliquin.

Three times a week there are V/Line buses connecting Echuca with Shepparton ($4.40) and Albury-Wodonga ($25.80), and down the Murray to Swan Hill ($16.50) and Mildura ($35.40). Seats for these destinations must be reserved with V/Line (☎ (054) 82 3589).

BARMAH FOREST

The central feature of this beautiful red-gum state park is the **Dharnya Centre** – a visitor centre with information displays on the local Yorta Yorta Koori community. It is open daily from 10 am to 5 pm. The park is nine km north of the small township of Barmah, 36 km from Echuca.

From the Dharnya Centre several marked walking tracks fan out, taking in the major features of the river and local vegetation. Track notes are available from the centre.

Canoeing is also popular on the river at this point. Again, info is available from the Dharnya Centre.

Places to Stay

Camping is available for a small fee at the Barmah Lakes camping area, and there's a 52-bed bunkhouse at the centre, although this is mainly for school groups. Book in advance with the rangers (☎ (058) 69 3302).

YARRAWONGA

About 40 km east of Cobram on the banks of Lake Mulwala, Yarrawonga is known for its fine and sunny weather, for a host of aquatic activities including windsurfing, swimming, power boating and water skiing, and as a retirement centre.

Lake Mulwala was formed by the completion, in 1939, of Yarrawonga Weir which in turn was part of the massive Lake Hume project (near Albury) to harness the waters of the Murray for irrigation.

There is a tourist information centre (☎ (057) 44 1989) on the corner of Belmore St and Irvine Parade.

Ninety-minute cruises of Lake Mulwala are available on the *Lady Murray River*, or you can hire small boats for fishing or sightseeing, or just relax on the sloping lawns by the lake.

Yarrawonga was first settled by Elizabeth Hume, sister-in-law of the early explorer Hamilton Hume, in about 1842. Her interesting octagonal-shaped home, **Byramine Homestead**, is 15 km west of the town and is open to the public.

Places to Stay & Eat

The *Yarrawonga Caravan Park* (☎ (057) 44 3420) on the bank of the Murray River at the weir wall is very central with sites and on-site vans. The *Terminus* (☎ (057) 44 3025) and *Criterion* (☎ (057) 44 3839), both on Belmore St, are the cheapest hotels in town.

Pinkies at 25 Belmore St, tucked away in the corner of a shopping mall, is a good cafe for a light lunch or a snack. The *Shags Nest Restaurant*, also on Belmore St, is a bit more sophisticated – expect to pay around $20 per head.

Getting There & Away

There are daily V/Line buses to and from Benalla ($5.40) and these connect with trains to and from Melbourne.

Gold Country

Victoria's Gold Rush

In May 1851 E H Hargraves discovered gold near Bathurst in New South Wales. It was not the first time the mineral had been found in Australia, but the sensational accounts of the potential wealth of the find caused an unprecedented rush as thousands of people dropped everything to try their luck.

The news of the discovery reached Melbourne at the same time as the accounts of its influence on the people of New South Wales. Sydney had been virtually denuded of workers and the same misfortune soon threatened Melbourne. Victoria was still in the process of being established as a separate colony so the loss of its workforce to the northern gold fields would have been disastrous.

A public meeting was called by the young city's businessmen and a reward was offered to anyone who could find gold within 300 km of Melbourne. In less than a week gold was rediscovered in the Yarra but the find was soon eclipsed by a more significant discovery at Clunes. Prospectors began heading to central Victoria and over the next few months the rush north across the Murray was reversed as fresh gold finds and new rushes became an almost weekly occurrence in Victoria.

Gold was found in the Pyrenees, the Lodden and Avoca rivers, at Warrandyte and Bunninyong. Then in September 1851 the biggest gold discovery was made at Ballarat, followed by others at Bendigo, Mt Alexander, Beechworth, Walhalla, Omeo and in the hills and creeks of the Great Dividing Range.

By the end of 1851 about 250,000 ounces of gold had already been claimed. Farms and businesses lost their workforce and in many cases were abandoned altogether as employers had no choice left but to follow their workers. Hopeful miners began arriving from England, Ireland, Europe, China and the failing gold fields of California. During 1852 about 1800 people a week arrived in Melbourne.

The government introduced a licence fee of 30 shillings a month for all prospectors, whether they found gold or not. This entitled the miners to a claim, limited to eight feet square, in which to dig for gold and provided the means to govern and enforce the laws that were improvised for the gold fields.

The administration of each field was headed by a chief commissioner whose deputies, the state troopers, were empowered to organise licence hunts and to fine or imprison any miner who failed to produce the permit.

Though this was later to cause serious unrest on the diggings, for the most part it successfully averted the complete lawlessness that had characterised the California rush.

There were, however, the classic features that seem to accompany gold fever, like the backbreaking work, the unwholesome food and hard drinking, and the primitive dwellings. There was the amazing wealth that was to be the luck of some, the elusive dream of others; and for every story of success there were hundreds more of hardship, despair and death.

In his book *Australia Illustrated*, published in 1873, Edwin Carton Booth wrote of the gold fields in the early 1850s:

...it may be fairly questioned whether in any community in the world there ever existed more of intense suffering, unbridled wickedness and positive want, than in Victoria at (that) time...To look at the thousands of people who in those years crowded Mel-

bourne, and that most miserable adjunct of Melbourne, Canvas Town, induced the belief that sheer and absolute unfitness for a useful life in the colonies...had been deemed the only qualification requisite to make a fortunate digger.

While the gold rush certainly had its tragic side and its share of rogues, including the notorious bushrangers who regularly attacked the gold shipments being escorted to Melbourne, it also had its heroes who eventually forced a change in the political fabric of the colony. (See the Rebellion section, under Ballarat.)

Above all, perhaps, the gold rush ushered in a fantastic era of growth and material prosperity for Victoria and opened up vast areas of country previously unexplored by Whites.

In the first 12 years of the rush, Australia's population increased from 400,000 to well over a million, and in Victoria alone it rose from 77,000 to 540,000. To cope with the moving population and the tonnes of gold and supplies the development of roads and railways was accelerated.

The mining companies which followed the independent diggers invested heavily in the region over the next couple of decades. The huge shanty towns of tents, bark huts, raucous bars and police camps were eventually replaced by the timber and stone buildings that were the foundation of many of Victoria's modern provincial cities, most notably Ballarat, Bendigo, Maldon and Castlemaine.

It was in the 1880s that the gold towns reached their heights of splendour, but although gold production was gradually to lose its importance after that time, the towns of the region by then had stable populations, and agriculture and other activities steadily supplanted gold as the economic mainstay.

Gold also made Melbourne Australia's largest city and financial centre, a position it held for nearly half a century.

Goldfields Tourist Route

If you have transport, the well-signposted Goldfields Tourist Route takes in all the major centres involved in the rush of last century, and makes for an interesting excursion for a couple of days.

Ballarat and Bendigo are the two major towns on the route, but, in a clockwise direction from Ballarat, it goes through Linton, Beaufort, Ararat, Stawell, Avoca, Maryborough, Dunolly, Tarnagulla, Bendigo, Maldon, Castlemaine, Daylesford and Creswick.

There is a map of the route published, and

this should be available from tourist information centres in the towns along the route.

BALLARAT (population 70,000)

The area around present-day Ballarat, which is the largest inland city in Victoria, was first settled in 1838. When gold was discovered at the small township of Bunninyong in 1851 the rush was on and within a couple of years the town that grew out of the Ballarat diggings had a population of 40,000.

Ballarat's fabulously rich quartz reefs were worked by the larger mining companies until 1918. About 28% of the gold unearthed in Victoria came from Ballarat.

Today there are still many reminders of this gold-mining past, although Ballarat doesn't have quite the historical flavour of Bendigo. Ballarat is 112 km from Melbourne on the main Western Highway to Adelaide.

Information

The Ballarat Visitor Information Office (☎ (053) 322694) is in a small booth at the corner of Albert and Sturt Sts. It is open Monday to Friday from 9 am to 5 pm and on

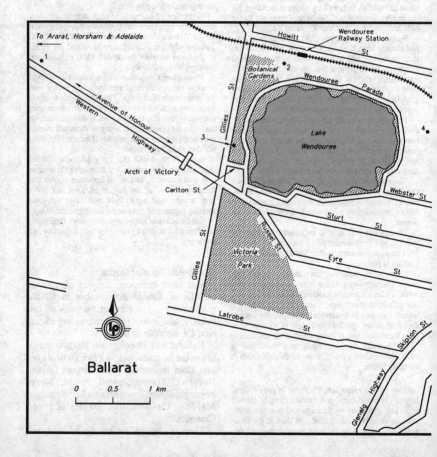

Ballarat

0   0.5   1 km

weekends from 10 am to 4 pm. It's well stocked with lots of printed information and the staff are very helpful. The RACV (☎ (053) 32 1946) has an office on Doveton St.

Sovereign Hill

Ballarat's major tourist attraction is Sovereign Hill, a fascinating re-creation of a gold-mining township of the 1860s. It is probably the best attraction of its type in the country, and has won numerous awards, so you should allow at least half a day for a visit.

The main street features shops, a hotel, a post office, blacksmith's shop, printing shop, bakery and a Chinese joss house. It is a living history museum with people performing their chores dressed in costumes of the time. There's even a re-creation of an early bowling alley – the Empire Bowling Saloon – and for a couple of dollars you can have a game.

The site was actually mined back in the gold era so much of the equipment is original, as is the mineshaft, and there's a variety of above-ground and underground mining

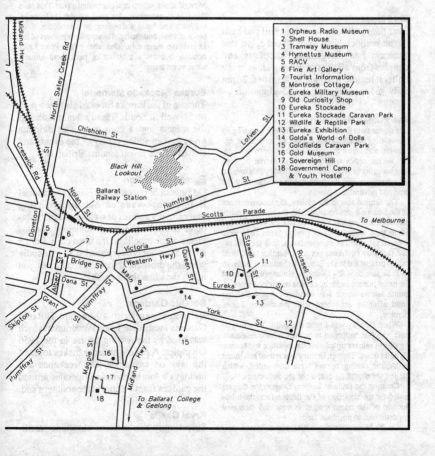

1 Orpheus Radio Museum
2 Shell House
3 Tramway Museum
4 Hymettus Museum
5 RACV
6 Fine Art Gallery
7 Tourist Information
8 Montrose Cottage/
  Eureka Military Museum
9 Old Curiosity Shop
10 Eureka Stockade
11 Eureka Stockade Caravan Park
12 Wildlife & Reptile Park
13 Eureka Exhibition
14 Golda's World of Dolls
15 Goldfields Caravan Park
16 Gold Museum
17 Sovereign Hill
18 Government Camp
  & Youth Hostel

works. You can pan for gold in the stream, and with luck may find a speck or two among the gravel.

There are at least four places around the 'town' offering food of various types, from pies & pasties at the *Hope Bakery* to a full three-course lunch at the *United States Hotel*.

Sovereign Hill is open daily from 9.30 am to 5 pm and admission is $14.50 for adults ($10.50 for students, $7 for children, $39.90 for families) – expensive but well worth it. The ticket also gets you into the nearby Gold Museum which is also worth seeing.

Gold Museum

Over the road from Sovereign Hill and built on the mullock heap from an old mine, this museum has imaginative displays and samples from all the old mining areas in the Ballarat region. It's open 9.30 am to 5.20 pm daily and is well worth the $3 admission.

The Eureka Rebellion

Life on the gold fields was a great leveller, erasing all pre-existing social classes as doctors, merchants, ex-convicts and labourers toiled side by side in the mud. But as the easily won gold began to run out, the diggers came to recognise the inequality that existed between them and the privileged few who held the land and government power.

The limited size of the claims, the inconvenience of the licence hunts coupled with the police brutality that often accompanied the searches, the very fact that while they were in effect paying taxes they were allowed no political representation, and the realisation that they could not get good farming land, fired the unrest that led to the Eureka Rebellion at Ballarat.

In September 1854 Governor Hotham ordered that the hated licence hunts be carried out twice a week. A month later a miner was murdered near a Ballarat hotel after an argument with the owner, James Bentley.

When Bentley was found not guilty, by a magistrate who just happened to be his business associate, a group of miners rioted over the injustice and burned his hotel down. Though Bentley was retried and found guilty, the rioting miners were also jailed, which fuelled the mounting distrust of the authorities.

Creating the Ballarat Reform League, the diggers called for the abolition of the licence fees, the introduction of the miner's right to vote and increased opportunities to purchase land.

On 29 November about 800 miners tossed their licences into a bonfire during a mass meeting and then set about building a stockade at Eureka where, led by an Irishman called Peter Lalor, they prepared to fight for their rights.

On 3 December, having already organised brutal licence hunts, the government ordered the troopers to attack the stockade. There were only 150 diggers within the makeshift barricades at the time and the fight lasted only 20 minutes, leaving 30 miners and five troopers dead.

Though the rebellion was short-lived the miners were ultimately successful in their protest. They had won the sympathy of most Victorians, and with the full support of the gold fields' population behind them the government deemed it wise to acquit the leaders of the charge of high treason.

The licence fee was abolished and replaced by a Miners' Right, which cost one pound a year. This gave them the right to search for gold; the right to fence in, cultivate and build a dwelling on a moderate-sized piece of land; and the right to vote for members of the Legislative Assembly. The rebel miner Peter Lalor actually became a member of parliament himself some years later.

Eureka Stockade Memorial

The site of the Eureka Stockade is now a park on Stawell St South. There's a monument to the miners and a coin-in-the-slot diorama gives you an action replay of the events and causes of this revolt against British rule.

Eureka Exhibition

On Eureka St opposite the Eureka Memorial is this much-vaunted but disappointing museum. It's a series of walk-through, 'computer-controlled' scenes depicting various facets of the rebellion. It's open daily from 9 am to 5 pm but is overpriced at $3 especially when the diorama across the road gives you much the same thing for 20c.

Botanic Gardens

Ballarat's excellent 40-hectare Botanic Gardens are beside Lake Wendouree which was used as the rowing course in the 1956 Olympics. A paddle-steamer makes tours of the lake on weekends. On weekends and holidays a tourist tramway operates around the gardens from a depot at the southern end.

Kryal Castle

Surprisingly this modern bluestone 'medieval English castle' is a very popular attraction. It's no doubt helped along by the daily hangings (volunteers called for), 'whipping of wenches' and a weekly jousting tournament – kids love it. The castle is eight km from Ballarat, towards Melbourne, and is open 9.30 am to 5.30 pm daily and admission is $9.50 for adults ($7.50 for students).

Other Attractions

With Ballarat's gold wealth to help them along, the early town planners ensured that the main thoroughfare, **Sturt St**, became a magnificent boulevard lined with the lavish buildings so typical of Australian gold towns. A wander along Sturt St takes you by Victorian-era buildings bedecked with verandahs and lacework plus a whole series of European styles from Gothic to Renaissance. The National Trust puts out a walking-tours pamphlet, available from the tourist office for 50c.

Notable Ballarat buildings include **Montrose Cottage** on Eureka St which was one of the earliest miners' cottages of the gold era in Ballarat and is the last remaining one of its type. It is furnished with relics of the time and is open from 9.30 am to 5 pm daily; admission is $4.

The **Ballarat Fine Art Gallery** is one of Australia's best provincial galleries and is particularly strong in its Australiana collection. A feature is the original Eureka Flag, or at least what's left of it after souvenir hunters have chopped bits off over the last 100 years. The gallery, at 40 Lydiard St North, is open Tuesday to Friday from 10.30 am to 4.30 pm, and on weekends from 12.30 to 4.30 pm; admission is $2 (students $1).

Festivals

In early March Ballarat holds its annual Begonia Festival which is 17 days of fun, flowers and the arts. In September/October there's the Royal South Street Competitions, Australia's oldest eisteddfod, and during this time accommodation can be extremely hard to find as the competitions draw people from all over the country.

Places to Stay

There's a YHA-associate *Youth Hostel* (☎ (053) 33 3409) in the Government Camp at Sovereign Hill. It has excellent facilities and costs $12.50 for a dorm bed or $15 in a share room. Hassles are that it can sometimes be difficult to get a bed here, especially during school holidays, and that there is no admission after 10.30 pm. If you do stay here you get a 10% discount on entry to Sovereign Hill. The entrance to the hostel is on Magpie St. Non-YHA members can also stay at the Government Camp, but it costs $40/55 for room only.

The old Bridge Mall Inn now incorporates the convenient *Ballarat Backpackers* (☎ (053) 31 3132). It's right in the centre of town, has reasonable facilities, and costs $13 in a two or four-bed room. Phone ahead and they'll pick you up from the bus or railway station.

The *Provincial Hotel* (☎ (053) 32 1845), 121 Lydiard St, opposite Ballarat Railway Station, has B&B for $28/46. A short stroll down the street to No 27 brings you to the *George Hotel* (☎ (053) 31 1031) with singles/doubles from $35/45 with breakfast. There are also modern motel units.

Craigs Royal Hotel (☎ (053) 31 1377), 10 Lydiard St South, is an old place with singles/doubles from $45/55 up to $66/70 for B&B. This is the town's first hotel, full of history, and has been restored to its original grandeur, hence the up-market prices.

Ballarat has plenty of motels too, most of which are on the Western Highway on either side of the centre. The *Brewery Tap Hotel-Motel* (☎ (053) 34 7201), seven km east of the centre, costs $27/38 for singles/doubles with a continental breakfast.

The *Red Lion Hotel-Motel* (☎ (053) 31 3955), 221 Main St, is close to Sovereign Hill and has singles/doubles with a light breakfast for $48/58.

There are plenty of camp sites in and around Ballarat with the most convenient being the *Goldfields Caravan Park* (☎ (053) 32 7888) at 108 Clayton St, 200 metres north of Sovereign Hill.

Also handy is the *Eureka Stockade*

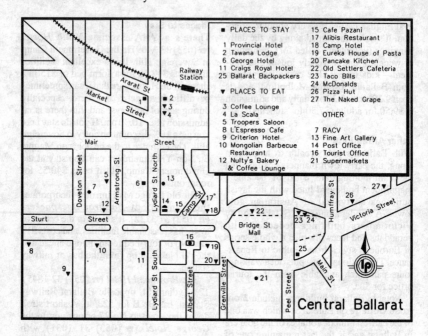

PLACES TO STAY

1 Provincial Hotel
2 Tawana Lodge
6 George Hotel
11 Craigs Royal Hotel
25 Ballarat Backpackers

PLACES TO EAT

3 Coffee Lounge
4 La Scala
5 Troopers Saloon
8 L'Espresso Cafe
9 Criterion Hotel
10 Mongolian Barbecue Restaurant
12 Nulty's Bakery & Coffee Lounge
15 Cafe Pazani
17 Alibis Restaurant
18 Camp Hotel
19 Eureka House of Pasta
20 Pancake Kitchen
22 Old Settlers Cafeteria
23 Taco Bills
24 McDonalds
26 Pizza Hut
27 The Naked Grape

OTHER

7 RACV
13 Fine Art Gallery
14 Post Office
16 Tourist Office
21 Supermarkets

Central Ballarat

Caravan Park (☎ (053) 31 2281), which is right next to the Eureka Stockade Memorial.

Places to Eat

Virtually all Ballarat's cheap eating places are on Sturt St and the Bridge St Mall. There are plenty of coffee shops and snack bars but none that stand out. *Nulty's Bakery & Coffee Lounge*, 306 Sturt St, is good for breakfast or snacks; and down the other side of the street at No 23 is the *Eureka House of Pasta* with pizzas and pasta meals for $7 to $10.

L'Espresso, 419 Sturt St, has good homemade ice cream, excellent coffee and also second-hand records for sale. Much more up-market is the new and tastefully decorated *Cafe Pazani*, a bar and restaurant on the corner of Camp and Sturt Sts.

Most of the pubs serve uninspiring counter meals for about $6, although the *Criterion* is good value with meals from $4 to $6, and the *Troopers Saloon* on Armstrong St is another good one.

The *Branching Out Wholefood Restaurant* at 24 Doveton St South is BYO, has good food and is reasonably priced.

In the Bridge St Mall the *Old Settlers Cafeteria* offers fish from $8 and pasta dishes from $7; and the *Mee Hing* Chinese restaurant opposite has a banquet for two people at $18 a head. The *Mongolian Barbecue* upstairs at 315 Sturt St has a good lunch special where you serve yourself and try to pile as much meat and vegetables in a large bowl as you can for $6. Myers on Sturt St have a cafeteria on a lower ground floor.

Food at the *Camp Hotel* on Sturt St is a step up from your basic counter meal, and there are also live bands in the evenings. Ballarat's newest trendy hangout is the *Naked Grape*, at 71 Victoria St, just along from the Pizza Hut.

Entertainment

The *Bridge Mall Inn* on Peel St is popular for bands on weekends as is the *Camp Hotel* at 36 Sturt St. The *Provincial Hotel* on Lydiard St has live music on the weekends as well as *Angelique's Disco*.

Getting There & Away

Trains run regularly from Melbourne to Ballarat via Bacchus Marsh and there are also V/Line buses. The trip takes two hours direct and the fare is $10.90 in economy, $15.20 1st-class. There are also regular trains to Geelong ($7.60) and Mildura ($38).

Bus Australia and Greyhound/Pioneer go through Ballarat on the run between Melbourne, Adelaide and Perth.There's no bus terminal in Ballarat but the Melbourne, Adelaide and Perth Greyhound/Pioneer buses leave from the Shell station on the corner of Sturt and Drummond Sts, while Bus Australia stops opposite Myers on Sturt St.

On weekdays V/Line buses go to Warrnambool ($14.30), Hamilton ($19.80), Mt Gambier ($34.70), and Bendigo ($14.30) via Castlemaine ($10.90). Tickets are available at the railway station.

Clarks Bus Lines (☎ (054) 35 9770) have daily services to Melbourne's Tullamarine Airport for $19, leaving from the railway station.

Getting Around

Clarks Shuttlebus makes daily one-hour trips around the major sights with a running commentary (adults $7, children $3). The bus leaves from Sovereign Hill, but will also pick you up at your hotel if you phone ahead. Bookings can be made at the office of Clarks Bus Lines (☎ (053) 35 9770).

Ballarat Transit is the local bus service operated by Davis & Clark Bus Lines. You can get a timetable from the railway station or the tourist office. Buses leave from Sturt St and go to the main attractions. Take bus No 9 to Sovereign Hill from the stop on the north side of Sturt St, between Armstrong and Lydiard streets. For the Botanic Gardens and Lake Wendouree, catch bus No 15 from the south side of Sturt St. Bus No 2 takes you to the railway station.

CLUNES (population 1600)

Clunes was the site of one of Victoria's very first gold discoveries in June 1851. Although other finds soon diverted interest, there are still many fine buildings as reminders of the former wealth of this charming little town. The town has a small museum housed in a double-storey bluestone building, but it is open only on weekends; entry is $2. The small hills around Clunes are extinct volcanoes. Nearby **Mt Beckworth** is noted for its orchids and bird life; you can visit the old gold diggings of **Jerusalem** and **Ullina;** and at **Smeaton**, between Clunes and Daylesford, an impressive bluestone water-driven mill has been restored (open Sunday afternoons only).

The small museum in the main street is also worth a look.

Places to Stay

There are on-site vans at the *Clunes Caravan Park* (☎ (053) 453278), Purcell St, or there's a guesthouse (B&B $70/100) and a motel.

MARYBOROUGH (population 9600)

The district around Charlotte Plains was already an established sheep run, owned by the Simson brothers, when gold was discovered at White Hills and Four Mile Flat in 1854. A police camp established at the diggings was named Maryborough and by 1854 the population had swelled to over 40,000. Gold mining ceased to be economical in 1918 but Maryborough by then had a strong manufacturing base in the town's secondary industries and is still a busy town today.

Its Victorian buildings include a magnificent railway station. In fact a century ago Mark Twain described Maryborough as 'a railway station with town attached'.

Maryborough's Highland Gathering has been held every year on New Year's Day since 1857 and the annual 16-day Golden Wattle Festival is celebrated in September with literary events, music, the national gumleaf-blowing and bird-call championships, and street parades.

Places to Stay & Eat

Apart from several motels, hotels and guest-houses there's the *Princes Park Caravan Park* (☎ (054) 612864), Holyrood St, which has on-site vans for $20.

There are cafes and restaurants in town, a couple of Chinese food places and the *Bull & Mouth Hotel* has a good bistro.

DUNOLLY (population 850)

The sheep run taken up and named Dunolly by a Scotsman in 1845 was completely overrun by diggers following the discovery of gold in 1852. The actual siting of present-day Dunolly followed another gold find in 1856 which saw more than 30,000 people flood into the area to try their luck.

The largest gold nugget ever found, the 65-kg Welcome Stranger, was unearthed at **Moliagul** 13 km north-west of Dunolly, and the district's gold fields produced more nuggets than any other in Australia.

It's not surprising then that there are some interesting buildings along Dunolly's main street and it's worth taking a stroll around town. The Historical Museum (open Sundays and public holidays) displays replicas of some of the more notable finds, including the Welcome Stranger.

In the district you can visit Moliagul and the site of the Welcome Stranger; the quaint little town of **Bealiba**, 21 km north-west; the bushwalking area of the **Bealiba Ranges**; and 13 km north-east, the ghost town of **Tarnagulla**.

Places to Stay

The *Progress Caravan Park* (☎ (054) 681262) on the corner of Thompson and Desmond Sts has on-site vans for $15. The *Golden Triangle Motel* (☎ (054) 681166) costs $35/44 for singles/doubles.

DAYLESFORD (population 3100)

Originally called Wombat, after the pastoral run where gold was first discovered, Daylesford is a picturesque town set amongst lakes, hills and forests. It boasts more of that sturdy Victorian and Edwardian architecture and, along with nearby Hepburn Springs, is having a revival as the 'spa centre of Victoria'.

The well-preserved and restored buildings show the prosperity that visited this town during the gold rush as well as the lasting influence of the many Swiss-Italian miners who expertly worked the tunnel mines in the surrounding hills.

The health-giving properties of the town's mineral springs were known before gold was discovered in the area. By the 1870s Daylesford was a popular health resort, attracting droves of fashionable Melbournians. It was claimed that the waters, which were bottled and sold, could cure any complaint, and the spas and relaxed scenic environment of the town could rejuvenate even the most stressed turn-of-the-century city-dweller.

The current trend towards healthy lifestyles has prompted a revival of interest in Daylesford as a health resort, and the elaborate bathhouses and charming guesthouses are again being used.

Things to See

The excellent **Historical Museum** is worth visiting, as are the lovely **Wombat Hill Botanic Gardens**. The volcanic crater of **Mt Franklin**, 10 km north, is visible from the lookout point in the gardens and has a beautiful picnic area. **Lake Daylesford** is a popular fishing and picnic area. It's close to the centre of town, and boats and kayaks are available for hire.

The **Central Highlands Tourist Railway** operates rides on old gangers' trolleys along the line which used to connect Daylesford with Carlsruhe on the main Melbourne-Bendigo line. There is also a **Sunday market** at Daylesford Railway Station.

The **Fearn Hyll Winery** is four km from Daylesford on the Ballan road.

Places to Stay & Eat

The *Victoria Park Caravan Park* (☎ (053) 482349), Ballan Rd, has on-site vans for $30. On King St the *Wentworth Hotel* (☎ (053) 48 2648) offers B&B singles/doubles for

$30/50, and there are a couple of motels in town with usual prices.

The *Swiss Mountain Hotel*, 12 km out of town on the Midland Highway, serves good evening meals; *Sweet Decadence*, in the centre of town, serves light meals, afternoon teas and home-made chocolates; and the *Argus Terrace* is a cafe and BYO restaurant.

On Albert St, *David's Kitchen* is a cafe famous for its home-made muffins and shortcakes, while the *Green Door Cafe* on Vincent St does excellent morning and after-noon teas.

Getting There & Away

There is a Monday to Friday V/Line bus between Ballarat and Daylesford ($6.40). There's also a daily V/Line bus to and from Melbourne ($9.70) via Woodend ($2.90). Other V/Line buses which pass through here go to Geelong ($15.60), Castlemaine ($2.90) and Bendigo ($6.40).

HEPBURN SPRINGS (population 2100)

Renowned for over a century for its medici-nal spas and bottled mineral water, Hepburn Springs is a delightful little town nine km from Daylesford. During the gold rush when, amongst many other miners, there were at least 20,000 Italians working the diggings here, the townspeople had to form an organisation to protect the valuable mineral waters from the disturbances caused by mining.

They began collecting the waters in iron bottles for sale throughout the colony and when the gold began to run out they success-fully promoted the town as a resort for therapeutic rest and rejuvenation.

Hepburn's Mineral Springs Reserve has four main springs, of magnesium, iron, lime and sulphur, and the bubbling waters contain at least 10 different minerals.

Spa Complex

The Hepburn Spa Complex (☎ (053) 48 2034), in the town's historic spa building, opened once again in 1991 after a major refurbishment undertaken by the Ministry of Conservation & Environment. It boasts excellent facilities and is open daily from 8 am to 8 pm. Services offered include spa with jets ($5 per person), Aero Spa (with warm air and additives blown through the water – $10 per 20 minutes), massage ($26 for half an hour), flotation tanks ($35 an hour), and sauna spa couch ($5). There are single, double and family spa tubs.

Places to Stay

The *Springs Caravan Park* (☎ (053) 48 3161) close to the Springs Reserve on Forest Ave has just a few on-site vans for $20. The *Spring Park Holiday Farm* (☎ (053) 48 2111), is also close to the springs and has one and two-bedroom flats for $40/60. *Liberty House* (☎ (053) 48 2809) is right opposite the springs and is a cosy place with open fires in winter. B&B is $40/80.

For a touch of old-world elegance you could try the delightful *Bellinzona Country House* (☎ (053) 48 2271) where B&B will set you back $100/165. The friendly *Mooltan Guest House* (☎ (053) 48 3555) overlooks the spa and costs $40/75 – the breakfast is wonderful.

Getting There & Away

There is a shuttle bus which runs back and forth between Daylesford and Hepburn Springs eight times a day on weekdays only.

CASTLEMAINE (population 6600)

Settlement of this district dates back to the 1830s when most of the land was taken up for farming. The discovery of gold at Speci-men Gully in 1851, however, radically altered the pastoral landscape as 30,000 diggers worked a number of gold fields known, collectively, as the Mt Alexander diggings.

The township that grew up around the Government Camp, at the junction of Barkers and Forest creeks, was named Castlemaine in 1853 and soon became the thriving marketplace for all the gold fields of central Victoria.

Castlemaine's importance was not to last,

however, as the district did not have the rich quartz reefs that were found in Bendigo and Ballarat. The centre of the town has been virtually unaltered since the 1860s when the population began to decline as the surface gold was exhausted.

These days Castlemaine is a charming town where the legacy of its rapid rise to prosperity lies in the splendid architecture of its public buildings and private residences and in the design of its streets and many gardens.

The Castlemaine State Festival, one of Victoria's leading celebrations of the arts, is held every second October and features a host of home-grown and international music, theatre and art.

The town is also famous for its Castlemaine Rock – a unique taste treat that is definitely worth trying. First made in 1853 it was the traditional confection of the Victorian gold fields, and the recipe is still a well-kept family secret.

Information

There is a well-stocked tourist office (☎ (054) 73 2222) in a rotunda on Duke St (near the Castle Motel on the Pyrenees Highway). Castlemaine is at the junction of the Midland and Pyrenees highways, not far off the Calder Highway about 38 km from Bendigo.

Market Museum

Castlemaine's original market building, on Mostyn St, is now a museum with audiovisual displays and artefacts depicting the colourful history of the gold fields. It is open daily from 10 am to 5 pm.

Buda

Originally built by a retired Indian Army officer in 1857 this is a superb example of Victorian-era colonial architecture. The house and magnificent gardens were extended in the 1890s by a Hungarian gold and silversmith, Ernest Leviny. The house and gardens are now open to the public and provide an insight into the town's refined and gracious past. Buda is on the corner of Urquhart and Hunter Sts, and is open from 10 am to 5 pm daily; admission is $4.

Castlemaine Art Gallery

The Castlemaine Art Gallery, Lyttleton St, was established in 1913 and has an excellent collection of colonial and contemporary art, as well as an historical museum featuring photographs, relics and documents.

Castlemaine Botanic Gardens

These beautiful gardens, designed in the 1860s by Baron von Mueller, the government botanist and director of the Melbourne Botanic Gardens, are amongst the oldest in the state. It's worth taking the time for a picnic by the lake or just a stroll amongst the 'Significant Trees' registered by the National Trust.

Other Attractions

Other places of interest include the **Theatre Royal** (now a cabaret, bistro and disco as well as a theatre and cinema); **Camp Reserve**, the site of the original Government Camp of the gold rush; the **Burke & Wills Monument**, if you're into statues; and a host of **gold-rush buildings**, such as the town hall, the sandstone jail, several hotels and the courthouse.

Places to Stay

The *Botanic Gardens Caravan Park* (☎ (054) 72 1125), on Walker St, next to the gardens, has basic on-site vans for $22.

The *Cumberland Hotel* (☎ (054) 72 1052), on Barker St, has rooms for $20/30. Breakfast, served in the dining room, is extra. The *Midland Private Hotel* (☎ (054) 72 1805), 2 Templeton St, was once one of the town's grander pubs right opposite the railway station. These days it's unlicensed and B&B is $35 per person. The *Campbell St Motor Lodge* (☎ (054) 72 3477), at 33 Campbell St, has doubles from $44 to $54.

Elimatta (☎ (054) 72 4454), 233 Barker St, is a guesthouse, with a cafe/restaurant, and charges $55/65 including a light breakfast. *Kendall Cottage* (☎ (054) 72 1201) at

29 McGrath St is a small B&B place charging $30/55.

Places to Eat

The *Bridge Hotel*, 21 Walker St, has great and inexpensive counter meals; and the *Cumberland Hotel*, Barker St, has a good bistro.

Bing's Cafe, 71 Mostyn St, has a good selection of home-made food and is a good place for breakfast, lunch or afternoon tea. The *Stables Tearooms*, Main Rd, Campbells Creek (three km south of Castlemaine), is a great setting for lunch and Devonshire teas.

Elimatta offers morning and afternoon tea, bistro lunches and up-market dining in the evening. For a splurge, the *Parsley 'N' Sage Restaurant*, 56 Lyttleton St, is worth the average $20 for main courses. The *Castlemaine Provender* is another good choice.

Getting There & Away

There are daily trains between Castlemaine and Melbourne ($12.10), and these also operate to Bendigo ($2.90) and Swan Hill ($18.50).

V/Line buses through Castlemaine go to Daylesford ($2.90), Ballarat ($10.90), Geelong ($19.80) and Maldon ($2.20).

AROUND CASTLEMAINE

The area around Castlemaine holds enough attractions – most of them related to the gold fields – to keep you going for a couple of days. You can visit the **Wattle Gully Gold Mine** and the **Garfield Water Wheel** in Chewton, four km south of Castlemaine. The **Dingo Farm** at Chewton gives you the opportunity to learn a little more about this much maligned creature.

Other interesting towns in the area include **Guildford**, **Fryerstown**, **Vaughn** and **Campbells Creek**.

MALDON (population 2600)

The current population of Maldon is a scant reminder of the 20,000 who used to work the local gold fields but the whole town is a well-preserved relic of the era with many fine buildings constructed from local stone.

In 1966 the National Trust named Maldon as the country's first 'notable town', an honour bestowed only on towns where the historic architecture was intact and valuable. In fact Maldon was considered so important in the history of Victoria that special planning regulations, the first of their kind in the state, were implemented to preserve the town for posterity.

It's a very popular tourist town and so, as you might expect, has its share of trendy (and overpriced) antique shops. Its Spring Folk Festival takes place every November.

There's a tourist information centre (☎ (054) 75 2569) on High St.

Things to See

The interesting buildings around town and along the verandahed main street include **Dabb's General Store** (now the supermarket) with its authentic shopfront; several restored public houses, including the **Maldon**, **Kangaroo** and **Grand** hotels; the **Eaglehawk Gully Restaurant**; the 24-metre-high **Beehive Chimney**; and the **Union Mine Kilns**. The tourist office has a brochure of a self-guided historical town walk, taking in all the noteworthy buildings.

Carman's Tunnel Goldmine is two km south of town, and the 570-metre-long tunnel was excavated in the 1880s. Candlelight tours through the mine take place only on weekends, from 2 to 4.30 pm.

On Sundays rail enthusiasts may like to ride the **steam train** which makes trips along the old line which used to connect Maldon with Castlemaine. The trains do not operate on days of total fire ban.

There's an **historical museum** on High St which is open from 1.30 to 4 pm

There are some good bushwalks around the town, and amateur gold hunters still scour the area with some success. From the top of nearby **Anzac Hill** there are excellent views over the town, and these are even better from the higher **Mt Tarrengower**.

Places to Stay

The *Maldon Caravan Park* (☎ (054) 75 2344), Hospital St, has tent sites and on-site vans.

Most of the regular accommodation is in upmarket B&B-type places. The *Derby Hill Lodge* (☎ (054) 75 2033), Phoenix St, has singles for $30; and the *Eaglehawk Motel* (☎ (054) 75 2911), Reef St, has doubles for $65. Other accommodation possibilities include *Calder House* (☎ (054) 75 2912) at 44 High St, which offers B&B; or the historic *Spring Cottage* (☎ (054) 46 9941), a fully self-contained miner's cottage, thought to date back to the 1860s.

With Castlemaine so close, it's much cheaper to stay in Castlemaine and visit Maldon from there.

Places to Eat

The *Garden Harvest Tea Rooms* are an excellent place for lunch or afternoon teas, while *McArthur's Restaurant* has a great set-menu lunch of $5.50 for a roast.

The *Maldon Bakery* has good fresh produce, or you could see what the pubs have on offer.

Getting There & Away

V/Line have a twice daily bus service on weekdays between Castlemaine and Maldon ($2.20), but there's nothing on weekends.

BENDIGO (population 67,000)

The solid, imposing and at times extravagant Victorian-era architecture of Bendigo is a testimony to the fact that this was one of Australia's richest gold-mining towns.

In the 1850s thousands upon thousands of diggers converged on the fantastically rich Bendigo Diggings, which covered more than 300 sq km, to claim the easily obtained surface gold. As this began to run out and diggers were no longer tripping over nuggets, they turned their pans and cradles to Bendigo Creek and other waterways around Sandhurst (as Bendigo was then known) in their quest for alluvial gold.

The arrival of thousands of Chinese miners caused a great deal of racial tension at the time, and had a lasting effect on the town.

By the 1860s the easily won ore was running out and the scene changed again as reef mining began in earnest. Independent miners were soon outclassed by the large and powerful mining companies, with their heavy machinery for digging and crushing, who poured money into the town as they extracted enormous wealth from their network of deep mine shafts. The last of these was worked until the 1950s.

Bendigo today is the third largest city in country Victoria, a busy market town with a number of local industries that makes the most of its gold-mining past to promote tourism. Its annual Easter Fair, first held in 1871 to aid local charities, features a procession with a Chinese dragon, a lantern parade, a jazz night and other entertainment.

Information

The Bendigo & District Information Centre (☎ (054) 47 7161), on the Calder Highway four km south of the centre, is open daily from 9.30 am to 4 pm. The Bendigo Trust Tourist Office (☎ (054) 41 5244) is in Charing Cross, and is open daily from 10 am to 4 pm.

The RACV (☎ (054) 43 9622) has an office at 72 Pall Mall, while the Department of Conservation & Environment (☎ (054) 43 8911) is at 31 McKenzie St.

The La Trobe Bookshop, 271 Lyttleton Terrace, has a good selection of books, and there's a book exchange in High St.

For camping equipment the Scout Shop and Outdoor Camping Centre is on Mitchell St.

Central Deborah Mine

This 500-metre-deep mine, worked on 17 levels, became operational in the 1940s, and was connected to the two other earlier Deborah shafts which date back to the early days of the gold fields. About 1000 kg of gold was removed before it closed in 1954 and it has now been restored and developed as a museum. It's well worth a visit as there are lots of interesting exhibits and many photographs taken from the mid-1800s onwards.

The mine is on Violet St – you can't miss it – and is open from 9 am to 5 pm daily. Admission is $13 ($10.50 for students) for a surface and underground tour, $10 ($8) for an underground tour only, $5.50 ($4.50) for a surface tour only. A trip to the mine can also be combined with the 'talking tram' (see below) for $16.50 ($13.50).

The Joss House

The Chinese joss house on Finn St in North Bendigo (near the Commonwealth Ordinance Factory), the only one remaining of four which existed during the gold rush, is built of timber and hand-made bricks. Exhibits include embroidered and stone-rub banners, figures representing the 12 years of the Chinese solar cycle, commemorative tablets to the deceased, paintings and Chinese lanterns. The house is open from 10 am to 5 pm daily and admission is $2 ($1.50 for students).

There's a Chinese section in the White Hills Cemetery on Killian St and also a prayer oven where paper money, and other goodies which you can't take with you, were burnt.

Bendigo Talking Tram

A vintage tram makes a regular tourist run from the Central Deborah Mine, through the centre of the city and out to the tramways museum (which is free if you have a tram ticket) and the joss house, with a commentary along the way. On weekdays it departs at 9.30 am and 1 and 2 pm from the Central Deborah Mine, or five minutes later from the fountain. On weekends and school holidays it operates hourly from 9.30 am; the fare is $5.50 ($5 for students).

Sacred Heart Cathedral

Construction of the massive Sacred Heart Cathedral, the largest Gothic-style building in Victoria outside Melbourne, was begun last century and completed in 1977. Angels poke out of some of the nice wooden arches,

there's a beautifully carved bishop's chair, some good stained-glass windows, the pews are magnificent Australian blackwood and the marble is Italian.

Bendigo Art Gallery

The Bendigo Art Gallery, 42 View St, was built in the 1880s and has an outstanding collection of Australian colonial and contemporary paintings. It's open Monday to Friday from 10 am to 5 pm and on weekends from 2 to 5 pm; admission is $2.

The Shamrock Hotel

The third hotel of the name on the same site, this magnificent incarnation was built in 1897. It's a fully restored and very fine example of the hotel architecture of the period. Its size gives some indication of how prosperous the town was in the gold-mining era when, so the story goes, the floors were regularly washed down to collect the gold dust brought in on miners' boots.

The Shamrock is on the corner of Pall Mall and Williamson St and is a good place for a drink in the bar or on the upstairs balcony.

Dragon Museum

The Dragon Museum in Bridge St is Bendigo's newest attraction. It houses the Chinese dragons which are brought out each year at Easter, and are the centrepiece of the parade that takes each year at this time. It is open daily from 9.30 am to 5 pm; entry is $5.

Other Attractions

There are some fine old buildings around Pall Mall and McCrae St, including the extremely elaborate **post office**, the **Alexandra Fountain** at Charing Cross, the **war memorial** and the **town hall** at the end of Bull St.

Dudley House, at 60 View St, is classified by the National Trust. It's a fine old residence with beautiful gardens; it's open weekends and daily during school holidays from 2 to 5 pm. **Fortuna Villa** on Chum St is a stately mansion with a lake and Italian fountain, once owned by George Lansell, the 'Quartz King'. It's now the Army Survey Regiment

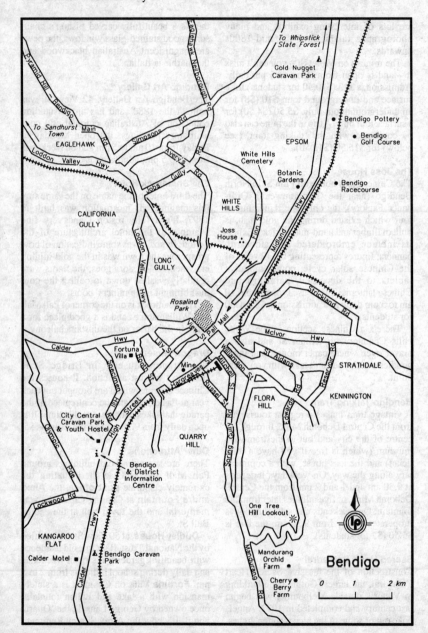

Bendigo

0   1   2 km

Headquarters and is only open to the public on Sundays for a three-hour tour ($3) at 1 pm.

The **Militaria Museum** on View St has a collection of military paraphernalia. Entrance is $1.50 ($1 for students) and it's open on Mondays and Wednesdays from 12.30 to 4.30 pm and Saturdays from 10 am to 4.30 pm.

Rosalind Park is a pretty little place with a lookout tower that was once the mine shaft head of the Garden Gully United Gold Mining Company. There are good views across the town from the top.

Perhaps Bendigo's most curious attraction is the annual 'Swap Meet', held in November. It draws enthusiasts from all over the country in search of that elusive vintage car spare part. That all sounds very unremarkable, but in 1990 the event was attended by 30,000 people! As you might imagine, accommodation is at a premium at that time.

Organised Tours

Barry Maggs runs Goldseeker Tours (☎ (054) 47 9559), taking people gold hunting in the Golden Triangle with metal detectors. Day Line Tours (☎ (052) 43 9955) offers day trips from Melbourne for $49.

Places to Stay

Hostels The *BendigoYouth Hostel* (☎ (054) 43 6937) at 362 High St, is a privately owned establishment (part of the Central City Caravan Park outside town). It is open all day and beds cost $12 per person, or $15 for nonmembers, in four-bed bunk rooms. You can get there on a Kangaroo Flat bus from Hargreaves St.

Hotels & Motels The *Albert Hotel* (☎ (054) 43 7588), 131 McCrae St, is a very central place and good value with B&B for $25/45. Close to the railway station at 150 Williamson St, the *Brougham Arms Hotel* (☎ (054) 43 8144) costs $38/48 for singles/doubles.

Some other places to consider include the *City Centre Motel* (☎ (054) 43 2077) at 26 Forest St which costs $35/44; the *Oval Motel* (☎ (054) 43 7211) at 194 Barnard St for

$38/45; or the *Calder Motel* (☎ (054) 47 7411) out on the Calder Highway, 7½ km south of town, which has rooms for $33/40. The famous *Shamrock Hotel* (☎ (054) 43 0333) where the rooms still retain some of their gold-rush character, is a nice place for a splurge. Ordinary singles/doubles cost from $53/68, while the suites are in the $90 to $170 range.

Camping There are lots of camp sites in and around Bendigo, and out at Lake Eppalock. The closest to the centre is the *Central City Caravan Park* (☎ (054) 43 6937), three km south on the Calder Highway, which is also the youth hostel. On-site vans are $28.

Places to Eat

Many of the city's pubs do counter meals, ranging from around $4 up to quite expensive. The *Cumberland Hotel*, on the corner of Williamson St and Lyttleton Terrace, has bar lunch specials for $3; and the *Hopetoun Hotel*, on the corner of Mitchell and Wills Sts, has them for $4.50. The *Rifle Brigade Pub-Brewery* at 137 View St is also a shade more up-market than your average counter-meal pub, but is an excellent place to buy exotic beers from around the world, as well as those brewed on the premises, including Koala, Rifle Lager and Bendigo Best Bitter. The meals here are also above average, with counter meals and a dining room.

For lunch-time snacks, you can't go past *Gillies*, in the Hargreaves St Mall, whose pies are regarded, by connoisseurs, as amongst the best in Australia. A Bendigo institution, you queue at the little window, order one of their five or so varieties, then sit in the mall to eat it.

Bendigo has quite a few coffee shops and cafes. There's *Munchy's* in the mall; *Cafe Naturel*, good for a healthy lunch, on the corner of Lyttleton Terrace and Mitchell St; and the *Green Olive Deli* in Bath Lane which has great rolls, salads and a variety of patés and cheeses.

For Chinese food there's the *House of Khong*, a Chinese and Siamese restaurant at 200 Hargreaves St which has a daily lunch

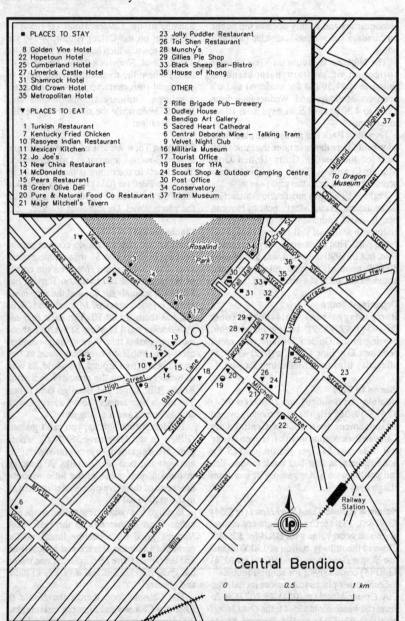

PLACES TO STAY

8 Golden Vine Hotel
22 Hopetoun Hotel
25 Cumberland Hotel
27 Limerick Castle Hotel
31 Shamrock Hotel
32 Old Crown Hotel
35 Metropolitan Hotel

PLACES TO EAT

1 Turkish Restaurant
7 Kentucky Fried Chicken
10 Rasoyee Indian Restaurant
11 Mexican Kitchen
12 Jo Joe's
13 New China Restaurant
14 McDonalds
15 Pears Restaurant
18 Green Olive Deli
20 Pure & Natural Food Co Restaurant
21 Major Mitchell's Tavern

23 Jolly Puddler Restaurant
26 Toi Shen Restaurant
28 Munchy's
29 Gillies Pie Shop
33 Black Sheep Bar–Bistro
36 House of Khong

OTHER

2 Rifle Brigade Pub–Brewery
3 Dudley House
4 Bendigo Art Gallery
5 Sacred Heart Cathedral
6 Central Deborah Mine – Talking Tram
9 Velvet Night Club
16 Militaria Museum
17 Tourist Office
19 Buses for YHA
24 Scout Shop & Outdoor Camping Centre
30 Post Office
34 Conservatory
37 Tram Museum

Rosalind Park

To Dragon Museum

Railway Station

Central Bendigo

0   0.5   1 km

smorgasbord for $8; and the *New China Restaurant* on High St which offers a four-course lunch for $10. The *Khong Dynasty*, on the corner of Lyttleton Terrace and Williamson St, is yet another cheap Chinese place.

Jo Joe's, on the corner of High and Forest Sts, is a pizza-pasta place with main courses from $7 to $10; the *Rasoyee*, an Indian restaurant on High St, has good food for $7.50 to $10.50. It also has takeaways, but is closed on Mondays. The *Turkish Restaurant* at the top end of View St is open in the evenings only, has takeaways and is closed Mondays.

For something a bit more interesting, the licensed *Black Sheep* on Bull St is a bar-bistro in an old converted garage, and you can select your meal from the menu and cook it on the barbecue outside. For a splurge, about $30 a meal, the *Jolly Puddler*, at 101 William St, is an excellent restaurant.

Entertainment
For live pub music one of the best places is the *Golden Vine Hotel* on the corner of King and Myrtle Sts.

Bendigo has a few discos and nightclubs in the city centre. *Velvet* is at 87 High St.

Getting There & Away
Trains from Melbourne to Bendigo take about two hours and cost $16.50 in 2nd class, $23.20 in 1st. The first train departs from Spencer St Station at 8.35 am and there are about half a dozen services a day on weekdays, less on weekends. One of these trains continues to Swan Hill ($18.50).

There is a weekday V/Line coach service between Bendigo, Castlemaine ($2.90), Ballarat ($14.30) and Geelong ($23.80). Other destinations served by V/Line buses include Swan Hill ($18.50), Mildura ($38), Barham ($10.90), Echuca ($2.90) and Albury.

Getting Around
Bendigo and its surrounding area is well served by public buses. Check the route map at the bus stop on Mitchell St, at the end of the mall, or pick up timetables and route maps from the tourist office or railway station. Tickets cost 75c and are valid for two hours.

The tourist office sells a brochure on bike rides for $1, but strangely enough there is no place to hire bicycles.

AROUND BENDIGO
Sandhurst Town
Sandhurst Town is a re-created gold town at Myers Flats, 10 km along the Loddon Valley Highway, north-west from Bendigo. It includes a working 24-inch-gauge railway line, a eucalyptus distillery, colonial stores, and the chance to pan for gold. The town (☎ (054) 46 9033) is open daily from 10 am to 5 pm and admission is $6.

Bendigo Pottery
Bendigo Pottery, the oldest pottery works in Australia, is on the Calder Highway at Epsom, 12 km north of Bendigo. As well as roofing tiles and the like, which keep the works financial, the historic kilns are still used to produce fine pottery. There are guided tours of the works and you can buy finished pieces. It also houses the **National Holden Car Museum**, which will be of interest to car buffs. It is open daily from 9 am to 5 pm. There's also a large undercover Sunday market at Epsom, and this attracts big crowds.

Whipstick State Forest
The 2300-hectare Whipstick State Forest, north of Bendigo, is a new state park established to conserve the distinctive Whipstick mallee vegetation. There are picnic areas sited on old eucalyptus distilleries, walking tracks, and holders of Miners' Rights can fossick for gold in designated areas. **Hartland's Eucalyptus Oil Factory** close to the Whipstick Forest was established in 1890 and the production process can be inspected ($3). The Department of Conservation & Environment puts out a brochure called *Whipstick Forest Rides*, and this details three bicycle rides in the area.

Wineries

There are also several good wineries in the district which are open for tastings, and these include Château Le Amon (10 km), Balgownie (eight km) and Château Doré (eight km).

Lake Eppalock & Heathcote

The large Lake Eppalock reservoir, about 30 km from Bendigo, provides the town's water supply and is popular for all sorts of water sports.

There are some fine lookouts in the vicinity of Heathcote, a quiet little highway town with a gold-mining past and a wine-making present. The town, 47 km from Bendigo, is surrounded by vineyards where tasters are made very welcome. The main wineries include Jasper Hill, McIvor Creek, Zuber, Heathcote Winery and Huntleigh.

ALONG THE CALDER HIGHWAY

From Bendigo it's 45 km along the Calder to **Inglewood**, another town with its roots firmly planted in the gold fields. Eucalyptus oil has been distilled in the area for over 100 years. There's an old distillery in town and many eucalyptus farms in the area.

West of Inglewood are the **Melville Caves** named after the gentleman bushranger Captain Melville who used to hide out there. In 1980 the 27-kg Hand of Faith gold nugget was unearthed in **Kingower**, 10 km west of Inglewood.

Next up is **Wedderburn**, 35 km north-west of Inglewood, where small gold nuggets are still being found. You can get prospecting maps and other equipment (including metal detectors), so this may be a good place to try your luck.

At **Wycheproof**, on the edge of the Mallee, huge wheat trains actually pass right along the main street, though the town is best known for the annual King of the Mountain footrace. Competitors have to carry a 63.5 kg sack of wheat to the summit of the 43-metre-high Mt Wycheproof which, at just 8805 metres lower than Mt Everest, is registered as the lowest mountain in the world!

RUSHWORTH (population 1000)

This historic town, 100 km north-east of Bendigo and 20 km west of the Goulburn Valley Highway, was a busy mining centre in the gold days of last century, and now has a National Trust classification. It was so named apparently because the (gold) rush was worth coming to.

Seven km south of town, in the Rushworth State Forest, is the gold-mining ghost town of **Whroo** (pronounced 'roo'). The small Balaclava open-cut mine here yielded huge amounts of ore. At its peak the town had over 130 buildings, although today ironbark trees and native scrub have largely reclaimed the site.

The old cemetery (also National-Trust-classified) is an evocative place, and the headstone inscriptions bear testimony to the hard life experienced by those who came in search of gold. There are a couple of signposted nature trails, one leading to a small rock waterhole used by the Kooris who inhabited this region. There's also a small mud-brick visitors' centre and a camp site. Worth the detour.

North-East

LAKE EILDON

Continuing from Melbourne beyond the hill towns of Healesville and Marysville you come to Lake Eildon, a large lake created for hydroelectric power and irrigation purposes. It's a popular resort area with lots of boats and houseboats to hire. Trout breeding is carried out at **Snob's Creek Fish Hatchery** and there's a fauna sanctuary nearby. The **Snob's Creek Falls** drop 107 metres.

On the western shores of the lake the **Fraser National Park** has some good short walks including an excellent guide-yourself nature walk. The 24,000-hectare **Eildon State Park** takes in the south-eastern shore area of the lake. On the eastern side of the lake is the old mining town of **Jamieson**.

The township of **Eildon** is the main town

on the south end of the lake while **Bonnie Doon** on one of the lake's northern arms also has some facilities. The main boat harbour is two km north of Eildon township.

Places to Stay

There's a stack of caravan parks in and around Eildon. There are also camp sites in the Fraser National Park and in the Eildon State Park, but these must be reserved in advance at holiday times (☎ (057) 72 1293 for Fraser National Park, and (057) 72 1293 for Eildon State Park).

For something a bit more salubrious try the *Eildon Village Motel* (☎ (057) 742483) which has units from $40/49 for singles/doubles.

The best way to see and explore Lake Eildon is by houseboat. These sleep from four to eight people and cost from $490 to $2800 (!) per week, and there's a $200 security deposit. Phone (059) 742107 for information and reservations.

Getting There & Away

McKenzies Bus Lines in Melbourne (☎ (03) 861 6264) run a daily service via Marysville ($8.40), Alexandra ($12.25) to Eildon ($13.80).

MANSFIELD (population 2300)

Close to Victoria's alpine country, Mansfield was established as a mining town in the gold rush days and later became a farming town. It is close to Mt Buller, Mt Stirling and Lake Eildon.

The graves of three police officers killed by Ned Kelly at Tolmie in 1878 are in the Mansfield cemetery, and there's a monument to them in the town. There is good canoeing and kayaking as well as bushwalking in the area, and at least one winery. In late October, the Mansfield Mountain Country Festival features the Great Mountain Race, with the country's best brumbies and riders.

Places to Stay

The *Mansfield Caravan Park* (☎ (057) 75

2705) on Ultimo St is the most convenient place to camp.

The *Mansfield Hotel* (☎ (057) 75 2101) at 86 High St and *Commercial Hotel* (☎ (057) 75 2046) at 83 High St have B&B for $25 per person, and there are a few motels.

Getting There & Away

V/Line buses operate daily from Melbourne for $21. In the ski season Mee's Bus Lines runs two buses daily from Mansfield to Mt Buller ($15.75) and daily services to Mt Stirling ($12.80).

GOULBURN VALLEY

The Goulburn Valley region runs in a wide band from Lake Eildon north-west across the Hume Highway and up to the New South Wales border. The Goulburn River joins the Murray just upstream of Echuca.

Seymour (population 7100)

Seymour is a small town on the Hume Highway and the Goulburn River. From here the Goulburn Valley Highway heads north to Shepparton and Cobram.

The town is of little interest itself, but the major army base of Puckapunyal, nine km west of town, has two interesting museums. The **Tank Museum** ($3) claims to have one of the largest displays of antique tanks in the world, while the **Transport Museum** ($2) has a variety of vehicles displayed.

Nagambie (population 1300)

On the shores of Lake Nagambie (created by the construction of Goulburn Weir), Nagambie has some interesting old buildings, an historical society display and many good picnic spots.

Two of the best known wineries in Victoria are close by: Chateau Tahbilk is in a beautiful old building with notable cellars dating back to 1860 and classified by the National Trust, while just a few km away the Mitchelton Winery is ultra-modern with a strange observation tower looming unexpectedly from the surrounding countryside.

Shepparton (population 25,600)
Shepparton and its adjoining centre of
Mooroopna are in a prosperous, irrigated
fruit-and-vegetable-growing area.

Good views of the Goulburn Valley and
the city surrounded by orchards can be seen
from the **Telecommunications Tower** (near
the post office). Tours of the **Shepparton
Preserving Company cannery** (the largest
in the southern hemisphere) operate during
the canning season from January to early
April, between 8.30 and 11 am and between
12 and 3.30 pm on weekdays.

From January to April it's the fruit-picking
season – a good time to get some casual
work. It's best to start looking in December
as demand for jobs is high when the apricots,
then peaches and pears, ripen.

There's a tourist information office
(☎ (058) 32 9870) by the lake on Wyndham
St, just south of the city centre.

Places to Stay & Eat There are three
caravan parks with on-site vans. The *Victoria
Hotel* (☎ (058) 21 9955), on the corner of
Wyndham and Fryers Sts, charges $19/30 for
singles/doubles.

The town's best restaurants are the
Tuscany (☎ (058) 31 1058), in an old church
in Fryers St; and *Daiquiris Restaurant*
(☎ (058) 21 8585) in High St.

Getting There & Away Daily trains and
buses from Melbourne run to Shepparton
($18.50) and these continue to the Murray at
Cobram ($5.40). V/Line buses also connect
Shepparton with Bendigo, Albury ($19.80)
and Wagga (NSW).

Victorian Wineries
Some of Australia's best wines are made in Victoria.
Grape growing and wine production started with the
gold rush of the 1850s and Victorian fortified wines
had established a fine reputation in Europe before the
turn of the century. Then phylloxera, a disease of
grapevines, devastated the Victorian vineyards and
changing tastes in alcohol completed the destruction.
From the 1960s, the Victorian wine industry started
to recapture its former glory and to produce fine table
wines as well as the fortified ones.

Victoria's oldest established wine-producing
region is in the north-east, particularly around
Rutherglen, but also extending to Milawa, Glenrowan
and beyond. Other fine wine-growing areas include
the Goulburn Valley river flats south of Shepparton,
Great Western between Stawell and Ararat on the
Western Highway; around the Geelong area; and in
the Yarra Valley near Melbourne. In the far north-
west, the irrigation areas along the Murray at
Robinvale and Mildura also produce wine.

GLENROWAN (population 800)
In 1880, the Kelly gang's exploits finally
came to an end in a bloody shoot-out here,
230 km from Melbourne and 24 km up the
highway from Benalla. Kelly was captured
alive and eventually hanged in Melbourne.

Today Glenrowan has everything from a
giant statue of Ned with his armoured helmet
to a life-size working replica of the shoot-
out. There's also a 'computerised hanging
room'. It all tells you rather more about the
modern Australian tourist industry than
about 19th-century cops and robbers.

The ruins of the Kelly family homestead
can be seen a few km off the highway at
Greta, though little remains of the slab bush
hut.

Kelly Country
In the north-east of the state en route to the New South
Wales border you pass through the interesting 'Kelly
Country', where Australia's most famous outlaw, Ned
Kelly, had some of his most exciting brushes with the
law. Kelly and his gang of bushrangers shot three
police officers at Stringybark Creek in 1878, and
robbed banks at Euroa and Jerilderie before their lives
of crime ended in the siege at Glenrowan. Ned and
members of his family were held and tried in
Beechworth. Not far to the east of the Hume are the
Victorian Alps – in winter you'll catch glimpses of
their snow-capped peaks from the highway near
Glenrowan.

WANGARATTA (population 16,600)
'Wang', as it is commonly known, is at the
junction of the King and Ovens rivers; it's
also the turn-off point for the Ovens
Highway to Mt Buffalo, Bright and the north
of the Victorian Alps. The town has some
pleasant parks, and bushranger Mad Dog
Morgan is buried in the local cemetery.

At Wangaratta Airport, four km east off
the Hume Highway and south of town, **Air-**

world has a collection of 40 vintage flying aircraft, and a Holden car collection, and offers joy rides in Tiger Moth biplanes.

Wang has a visitors' information centre (☎ (057) 21 5711) on the corner of the Hume Highway and Handley Sts south of the main shopping centre.

Places to Stay

There are three caravan parks with on-site vans and cabins, and at least a dozen motels, ranging from $40 to $80 for a double.

Of the town's pubs, the *Pinsent* (☎ (057) 21 2183) at 30 Reid St has singles/doubles for $25/40.

Getting There & Away

Daily trains from Melbourne cost $23.80, and to Albury it's $7.60. There's also a daily V/Line bus to Bright ($6.40) via Beechworth, and a three-times-weekly service to Rutherglen and Corowa ($3.40).

CHILTERN (population 1400)

Close to Beechworth and only one km west off the Hume Highway between Wangaratta and Wodonga, Chiltern once swarmed with miners in search of their fortunes. This is another gold town with many reminders of its boom era.

Author Henry Handel Richardson's home, **Lake View**, is preserved by the National Trust and is open from 10 am to 4 pm on weekends and school and public holidays.

RUTHERGLEN (population 2250)

Close to the Murray River and north of the Hume, Rutherglen is the centre of Victoria's major wine-growing area and has long been famous for its fortified wines. You can cycle from winery to winery – contact Bogong Jack's Adventures (☎ (057) 27 3382) in Oxley, near Wangaratta, or Bicycle Victoria (see the Getting Around section for Melbourne).

The town boasts a small museum and on the main street, **Jack O'Keeffe's Barber Shop** is a local attraction. Jack, a barber and historian, is a mine of information and some-thing of a local celebrity. His shop is stacked full of bits and pieces of interest – and you can even have a haircut.

Among the dozen or so wineries you can visit in the area is **All Saints**, with a wine museum and a National-Trust-classified winery building, eight km from Rutherglen at Wahgunyah on the Murray. **Campbell's Rosewood** is an old, family-run winery close to town, while **St Leonard's** is owned by Brown Brothers in Milawa, and produces small quantities of excellent wines. It is the only vineyard (so far) in the north-east which has a tasting charge – currently $2, refundable if you buy any wine. It also has a very scenic picnic spot on a billabong by the Murray River.

Rutherglen has an annual Winery Walkabout Weekend, held on the Queen's Birthday weekend.

Wahgunyah was once a busy port for the Ovens Valley gold towns. Its Customs House is a relic of that era.

Places to Stay & Eat

There's not much in the way of accommodation in Rutherglen itself, but Corowa, just 11 km away over the Murray in New South Wales, has plenty.

The *Rutherglen Caravan Park* (☎ (060) 32 9577) has on-site vans, and the *Victoria Hotel* (☎ (060) 32 9610), which is classified by the National Trust, charges $18 per person. There are also at least three motels.

The accommodation shortage doesn't spill over into the eateries, as there's plenty of choice. The *Poachers Paradise Hotel* at 120 Main St has an excellent varied menu and serves local delicacies such as yabbies and Murray cod, and the Poachers Pie is deservedly popular.

Mrs Mouse's Teahouse at 12 Foord St in Wahgunyah is a good place to eat. It's open for lunch and teas daily from 10 am to 5 pm, and for dinner from Thursday to Sunday.

Getting There & Away

V/Line buses from Wangaratta ($3.40) run three times a week.

WODONGA (population 22,700)

The Victorian half of Albury-Wodonga is on the Murray River, the border between Victoria and New South Wales. The combined cities form the main economic and industrial centre of this region.

For tourist info there's Tourism Albury Wodonga (☎ (060) 23 8172) at the Council Chambers at Kiewa St, Albury. For more information, see the Albury section in the New South Wales chapter.

CORRYONG (population 1800)

Corryong, the Victorian gateway to the Snowy Mountains and Kosciusko National Park, is close to the source of the Murray River, which at this point is merely an alpine stream.

Corryong's main claim to fame, however, is as the last resting place of Jack Riley, 'The Man from Snowy River'. Though some people dispute that Banjo Patterson based his stockman hero on Riley, a tailor turned mountain man who worked this district, the 'man' is nevertheless well remembered in Corryong.

Jack Riley's grave is in the town cemetery and there's a **Man from Snowy River museum** in the town, which is open daily from 10 am to noon and 2 to 4 pm.

Places to Stay

The town has two caravan parks (both with on-site vans and cabins), a pub and a couple of motels.

YACKANDANDAH (population 700)

There's a saying, around these parts, that 'all roads lead to Yackandandah'. If you *were* to get lost in the beautiful hills and valleys of this district you would find that most of the signposts do indeed point to this charming little town.

The pretty little 'strawberry capital', 32 km south of Wodonga, 23 km from Beechworth and always on the way to somewhere, has been classified by the National Trust; not just the odd building but the entire town.

Yackandandah was a prosperous gold town and, back then, a welcome stopover on the old main road between Sydney and Melbourne. It has many fine old buildings, including the 1850 **Bank of Victoria** which is now a museum. The well-preserved buildings along the main street now house a variety of local craft shops, antique stores, cafes and tearooms.

There are tent sites and on-site vans at the *Yackandandah Caravan Park* (☎ (060) 27 1380), on the Dederang Rd, close to some good bushwalks.

BEECHWORTH (population 4400)

This picturesque town set amid the rolling countryside of the Ovens Valley has been attracting tourists for a good many years. Way back in 1927 it won the Melbourne *Sun News Pictorial's* 'ideal tourist town' competition.

It is still a pleasure to visit Beechworth and spend a few days enjoying its wide tree-lined streets with their fine and dignified gold-rush architecture, or exploring the surrounding forested valleys, waterfalls and rocky gorges. It's a perfect place for walking or cycling.

The town is 35 km east of Wangaratta, and if you're travelling between Wang and Wodonga the detour through Beechworth makes a worthwhile alternative to the frenetic pace of the Hume Highway.

Information

There's a visitors information centre in the Rock Cavern (☎ (057) 28 1374), which is a gemstone and mineral museum opposite the post office on Ford St. Don't waste your $2 on the displays, though.

Attractions

In the 1850s Beechworth was the very prosperous hub of the Ovens River gold-mining region. Signs of the gold wealth are still very much in evidence, reflected in the fact that 32 buildings are classified by the National Trust. They include **Tanswell's Hotel** with its magnificent old lacework, the **post office** with its clock tower, and the **training prison** where Ned Kelly and his mother were imprisoned for a while.

The old 1859 **powder magazine** is now a National Trust museum which is open 10 am to 12.30 pm and 1.30 to 4.30 pm daily. The National Trust's **Carriage Museum**, behind Tanswell's Hotel, is open during the same hours and has a collection of old carriages including a Cobb & Co coach.

The very well presented and interesting **Burke Museum**, in Loch St, has an eclectic collection of relics from the gold rush and a replica of the main street a century ago, complete with 16 shop fronts – well worth the $2 entry. The hapless explorer Robert O'Hara Burke was the Superintendent of Police in Beechworth during the early days of the gold rush before he set off on his historic trek north with William Wills.

Other things of interest in and around Beechworth include the historic **Murray Brewery Cellars**, established in 1872, on the corner of William and Last Sts; the **Chinese Burning Towers** and **Beechworth Cemetery**, where the towers, altar and many graves are all that remain of the town's huge Chinese population during the gold rush; and the **Golden Horseshoe Monument** to a local pioneer who made gold horseshoes for his friend who had won a seat in parliament to represent the local miners.

Woolshed Falls, just out of town on the Chiltern road, is a popular picnic area and the site of a major alluvial gold field which yielded over 85,000 kg of gold in 14 years. Further west at **Eldorado** a gigantic gold dredge still floats on the lake where it was installed in 1936. At the time it was the largest dredge in the southern hemisphere.

Places to Stay

Tanswell's Commercial Hotel (☎ (057) 28 1480), 30 Ford St, is about the cheapest pub, with B&B singles/doubles for $20/36.

Rose Cottage (☎ (057) 28 1069) at 34 Loch St charges $46/70 for B&B singles/doubles. *Burnbrae* (☎ (057) 28 1091) is a picturesque Victorian cottage on Gorge Rd on the edge of town, and B&B is $72 per person. For a splurge, *Finches of Beechworth* (☎ (057) 28 2655) at 3 Finch St offers B&B at $130 a double in a magnificent Victorian house.

Five km out of town towards Chiltern is the *Woolshed Cabins* (☎ (057) 28 1035). Self-contained cabins which accommodate up to five people cost $55 for two plus $7 per extra person.

Places to Eat

Brambley Cottage on Ford St is a good BYO restaurant which specialises in home-made pasta, while the *Parlour & Pantry* on the same street is a gourmet deli and restaurant with a wide range of goodies. *Beechworth Provender* on Camp St is another gourmet deli.

More up-market is the *Bank Restaurant*, housed in the historic Bank of Australasia building, also on Ford St. It has pasta nights on Monday and Wednesday, and a carvery on Sundays.

Tanswell's Hotel does good counter meals, the *Hibernian Hotel* has an excellent bistro, and the *Beechworth Bakery* on Camp St has an irresistible selection of hot bread, cakes and home-made pies. On a sunny morning, the tables on the footpath are an excellent place for a coffee and fresh croissant breakfast.

Getting There & Away

V/Line has daily buses to both Wangaratta and Bright, with train connections from Wangaratta to Albury, Adelaide and Melbourne.

Golden Era Bus Lines on Ford St in Beechworth has daily buses to Albury/Wodonga.

BRIGHT (population 2900)

Deep in the Ovens Valley, Bright today is a focal point of the winter sports region and a summer bushwalking centre, and is renowned for its beautiful golden shades in autumn. In 1857 the notorious Buckland Valley riots took place near here; the diligent Chinese gold miners were forced off their claims and given much less than a fair go. It is about an hour's scenic drive from town to the snowfields of Mt Hotham, Falls Creek and Mt Buffalo. Snow chains must be carried in winter.

Places to Stay

There is an associate youth hostel ($12.50) in the *Municipal Caravan Park* (☎ (057) 55 1141), close to the centre of town on Cherry Lane. There are also tent sites ($11) and on-site cabin vans ($33). This is only one of about a dozen caravan parks in the town.

There's a whole range of other accommodation, most of it holiday flats. During holidays and long weekends rooms are scarce. The best bet may be to phone the central accommodation booking service (☎ (057) 55 1944).

The *Bright Alps Guest House* (☎ (057) 55 1197), at 83 Delaney Ave, has B&B from $26 per person. The *Alpine Hotel* (☎ 55 1366), at 7 Anderson St, has singles/doubles for $30/40. The motels are all similarly priced with *Elm Lodge Motel* (☎ (057) 55 1144) at 2 Wood St being the best value with singles/doubles from $28/35.

Places to Eat

The *Humble Spud* on the main street in the centre of town is an interesting place for a light meal, or for something more upmarket try the *Grill*, next door. The *Alpine Hotel* has a good bistro and also serves counter meals.

Getting There & Away

V/Line has daily buses to and from Wangaratta via Beechworth, and one weekly direct bus (Monday) all the way from Melbourne ($31.10).

The Alps

These mountains are the southern end of the Great Dividing Range, which runs all the way from Queensland down through the north-east of Victoria then south and west past Ballarat. The Dandenongs, just outside Melbourne, are a spur of the range.

The Victorian ski fields are at lower altitudes than those in New South Wales, but they receive as much snow and have similar conditions above and below the snow line. Falls Creek, Mt Hotham and Mt Buller are Victoria's largest ski fields with good skiing and all facilities. Mt Buffalo and Mt Baw Baw are smaller in size and offer fewer facilities. Lake Mountain, Mt Stirling and Mt St Gwinear are small with mainly cross-country skiing and no overnight accommodation. Dinner Plain is privately owned, with an architect-designed village above the snow line and a great pub.

The roads are fully sealed to Falls Creek, Hotham and Mt Buller; to all other ski resorts roads are unsealed or partially unsealed. In winter, snow chains must be carried to all ski resorts (you may be turned back if you haven't got them) and driving conditions can be hazardous. Other roads that crisscross the Great Dividing Range are unsealed for at least part of their way and only traversable in summer.

The skiing season officially commences the first weekend of June, and ski-able snow usually arrives later in the month. Spring skiing can be good as it is sunny and warm with no crowds, and there's usually enough snow until the end of September.

In the summer months, especially from December to February, the area is ideal for bushwalking, rock climbing, fishing, camping and observing the native flora & fauna. Other activities are canoeing, rafting, hang-gliding, horse-trekking and paragliding.

Bushwalkers should be self-sufficient, with a tent, a fuel stove, warm clothes and sleeping bag, and plenty of water. In the height of summer, you can walk all day in the heat without finding water, and then face temperatures below freezing at night.

Places to Stay

There are many places to stay, especially in the ski resorts, which have lots of accommodation for the skiers. Overall, these are very expensive in winter and many people prefer to stay in towns below the snow line and drive up to the ski fields. In July and August it is advisable to book your accommodation, especially for weekends. In June or September it is usually possible to find something if you just turn up. Hotels, motels, chalets, self-contained flats and units, and caravan parks abound in the region. There are also youth hostels at Mt Buller and Mt Baw Baw.

The cheapest accommodation in the ski resorts is a bed in one of the club lodges, or it is possible to cut costs by cramming as many people as possible into a flat. Talk to the Alpine Resorts Commission (☎ 008 032 061, toll-free) and they should be able to help you find a place.

In summer, bushwalkers may find bargain accommodation in the skiing areas.

ALPINE NATIONAL PARK

In 1989 the 6460-sq-km Alpine National Park was proclaimed. It covers most of the state's prime 'high country' of the Great Dividing Range, from Mansfield north-east to the New South Wales border, and is contiguous with the Kosciusko National Park in New South Wales. Most of the ski resorts in the state fall within the park's boundaries, and access is possible from many points.

Bushwalking and, in winter, cross-country skiing are the main activities within the park as it is largely undeveloped, and plans are to keep it that way. Large areas which are now part of the park were used for many years for cattle grazing, but this is now being restricted.

The Alpine Track is a walking trail which runs from Walhalla outside Melbourne to the New South Wales border. For more information, visit a Department of Conservation & Environment office for a brochure.

MT BUFFALO NATIONAL PARK

Apart from Mt Buffalo itself, the park is noted for its many pleasant streams and fine walks. The mountain was named back in 1824 by explorers Hume and Hovell on their trek from Sydney to Port Phillip Bay.

The mountain is surrounded by huge granite tors – great blocks of granite broken off from the massif by the expansion and contraction of ice in winter and other weathering effects. There is abundant plant and animal life around the park, and over 140 km of walking tracks. Leaflets are available for the **Gorge Nature Walk, View Point Nature Walk** and the **Dicksons Falls Nature Walk**. A road leads up to just below the summit of the 1720-metre Horn, highest point on the massif.

In summer Mt Buffalo is a hang-gliders' paradise (definitely not for beginners) and the near-vertical walls of the Gorge provide some of the most challenging rock climbs in Australia. **Lake Catani** is good for swimming and canoeing, while in winter Mt Buffalo turns into a ski resort with downhill and cross-country skiing being the most popular activities – see the Ski Resorts section for more details.

HARRIETVILLE (population 100)

This pretty little town sits in the valley at the fork of the east and west branches of the Ovens River, and is surrounded by the high Alps. Harrietville is well known for its beautiful natural surroundings and its proximity to the ski resort of Mt Hotham. During the ski season there is a shuttle bus which connects the town with Mt Hotham. Always check beforehand to find out if the road to Hotham is closed because of snow.

The town is also the usual finishing point for the Feathertop bushwalk, one of the most popular walks in Victoria, and so is busy on long weekends outside the ski season.

Places to Stay

The *Snowline Hotel* (☎ (057 59 2524) has singles/doubles for $20/40, and more expensive motel rooms.

One of the few other places you can try is the *Harrietville Alpine Lodge* (☎ 057) 59 2525) which has B&B from $25 per person. The *Harrietville Caravan Park* (☎ (057) 59 2523) is the cheapest alternative with sites and on-site vans.

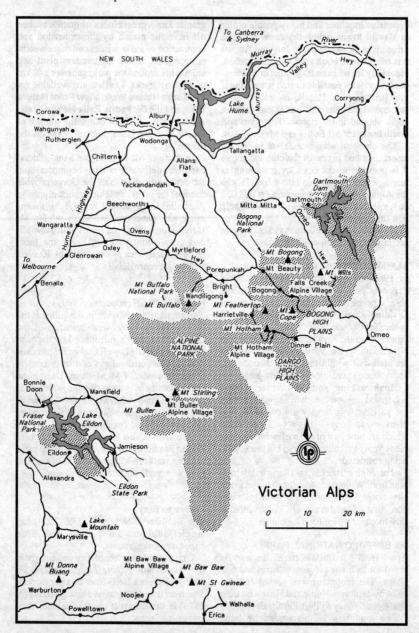

NEW SOUTH WALES

To Canberra & Sydney

Murray Valley *Hwy*

River

Corryong

Corowa

Albury

Lake Hume

Wahgunyah

Rutherglen

Wodonga

Tallangatta

Chiltern

Allans Flat

Dartmouth Dam

Yackandandah

Mitta Mitta

Omeo *Hwy*

Dartmouth

Beechworth

Ovens

Bogong National Park

Wangaratta

Hume *Highway*

Oxley

Glenrowan

Myrtleford *Hwy*

Mt Bogong

To Melbourne

Porepunkah

Mt Beauty

▲ *Mt Wills*

Benalla

Mt Buffalo National Park

Bright

Wandiligong

Mt Feathertop

Bogong

Falls Creek Alpine Village

Mt Buffalo ▲

Harrietville

Mt Cope ▲

BOGONG HIGH PLAINS

Mt Hotham

Omeo

ALPINE NATIONAL PARK

Mt Hotham Alpine Village

Dinner Plain

DARGO HIGH PLAINS

Bonnie Doon

Mansfield

Mt Stirling ▲

Mt Buller

Mt Buller Alpine Village ▲

Fraser National Park

Lake Eildon

Eildon

Jamieson

Alexandra

Eildon State Park

Victorian Alps

0   10   20 km

▲ *Lake Mountain*

Marysville

Mt Donna Buang ▲

Mt Baw Baw Alpine Village

Mt Baw Baw ▲ ▲ *Mt St Gwinear*

Warburton

Noojee

Walhalla

Powelltown

Erica

OMEO (population 550)
This small town is on the Omeo Highway, the southern access route to the snow country. In summer it's a popular departure point for the Bogong High Plains. Rafting trips take place in the nearby Mitta Mitta River.

Omeo still has a handful of interesting old buildings despite two earthquakes and one disastrous bushfire since 1885. Omeo's **log jail** and **courthouse** are two buildings that are worth searching out. The town also had its own little gold rush.

Places to Stay
The *Golden Age Hotel* (☎ (057) 59 1344) in Day Ave, has B&B for $18 per person. Apart from a couple of other hotels there is the *Holston Tourist Park* (☎ (057) 59 1351) with tent sites from $7 and on-site vans from $20.

Getting There & Away
There is a daily bus between Omeo and Bairnsdale operated by Omeo Buslines (☎ (051) 59 4231).

SKI RESORTS
Skiing in Victoria goes back to the 1860s when Norwegian gold miners introduced it in Harrietville. It has grown into a multimillion dollar industry with three major ski resorts and six minor ski areas. None of these resorts is connected to another by a lift system, but it is possible for the experienced and well-equipped cross-country skier to go from Mt Hotham to Falls Creek across the Bogong High Plains. There is an annual race that covers this route.

Parking fees are between $7 and $14 a day in winter.

Falls Creek (1780 metres)
It sits at the edge of the Bogong High Plains overlooking the Kiewa Valley, 375 km and a five-hour drive from Melbourne. Falls Creek is one of the best resorts in Victoria and in the last few years has received the heaviest snow falls. It is the only ski village in Australia where everyone can ski directly from

their lodge to the lifts and from the slopes back to their lodge.

The skiing is spread over two bowls with 30 km of trails, and a vertical drop of 267 metres. It has plenty of runs for intermediate skiers but only a handful of difficult runs for the experienced skier. A day ticket costs $43, a seven-day ticket costs $258 and a daily lift and lesson package costs $62.

You'll find some of the best cross-country skiing in Australia here. A trail leads around Rocky Valley pondage to some old cattlemen's huts. The more adventurous can tour to the white summits of Nelse, Cope and Spion Kopje.

You can choose between ski skating on groomed trails; light touring with day packs; and general touring with heavier packs, usually involving an overnight stay in a tent. Cross-country downhill, the alternative to skiing on crowded, noisy slopes, is also becoming popular.

There are day facilities only for cross-country skiers at Windy Corner. At times, cheaper accommodation is available at the Department of Sport & Recreation facility at Howman's Gap.

In summer there are plenty of opportunities for alpine walking to places like Ruined Castle, Ropers Lookout, Wallaces Hut and Mt Nelse which is part of the Alpine Walking Track. See Lonely Planet's *Bushwalking in Australia* by John Chapman & Monica Chapman for more details.

Places to Stay & Eat There is very little cheap accommodation in Falls Creek in winter. Even the club lodges that offer cheaper lodging in Mt Hotham and Mt Buller are more expensive and fewer in number here.

A number of ski lodges offer B&B plus dinner packages per week or weekend. One of the best and cheapest is the *Silver Ski Lodge* (☎ (057)58 3375), normally fully booked during peak season, costing $570 per person weekly. The Falls Creek accommodation service (☎ (057) 58 3325) can help you find accommodation on the mountain.

In summer, the lodges cost around $40 per

person per day, or $60 with meals. The *Falls Creek Motel* (☎ (057) 58 3282), costs $50/70 for singles/doubles.

There are no food bargains in Falls Creek. One of the best value restaurants is the *Silver Ski* where you can have a daily special set menu (and if you are still hungry, return for seconds).

Getting There & Around Pyles Coaches (☎ (057) 57 2024) runs buses to and from Melbourne on Fridays to Sundays for $49 ($75 return). A daily service to and from Albury is $22 ($42 return), and Mt Beauty is $11 ($22 return). These services operate from June to September. There is over-snow transport available from the car park to the lodges and back again.

Mt Baw Baw (1480 metres)
This is a small resort in the Baw Baw National Park, with eight lifts on the edge of the Baw Baw plateau. It is 173 km and an easy three-hour drive from Melbourne, via Noojee. It's popular on the weekends, but generally is not overcrowded as the snow cover tends to be thin. There are intermediate and beginner runs with a vertical drop of 140 metres, and plenty of cross-country trails, including one that connects to the Mt St Gwinear trails on the southern edge of the plateau.

Places to Stay & Eat The only cheap place is the YHA *Baw Baw Youth Hostel* which is in the village and close to all the facilities. It is open during the ski season, but sometimes takes groups in summer. Advance bookings are essential (☎ (03) 670 3802, the YHA office in Melbourne) and it costs from $36 to $50 for a weekend or $110 to $125 for Monday to Friday during the snow season, $8 daily in summer.

Apart from the youth hostel there is no other cheap place to stay, although the Mt Baw Baw Information & Booking Service (☎ (03) 763 7101) can make bookings for you in most places.

Getting There & Away There is a twice-daily bus service from Warragul Railway Station to Noojee, and the mail contractor at Tanjil Bren is licensed to carry passengers in his car.

Mt Buffalo (1400 metres)
This is a magnificent national park, and apart from the two guesthouses there are no private lodges on the mountain. From Melbourne it is 333 km by road and takes about five hours. An entry fee is payable.

It is another small place more suited to intermediate and beginner skiers, but again has more challenging cross-country skiing. Tatra is a picturesque and not overly expensive village, but the downhill skiing is not very good and the snow does not last as long as in some of the other resorts. There are a number of cross-country loops, and one of the trails goes to the base of the Horn, which skiers climb on foot.

The walks are also interesting and take the walker beneath towering granite monoliths.

Places to Stay & Eat The *Lake Catani Campground* (☎ (057) 55 1577) next to the lake has sites from $3.40, but is only open from November to May.

The *Mt Buffalo Chalet* (☎ (057) 55 1500) was the first place built on the mountain and still has the charm of the 1920s. The rooms are from $95 per person with all meals.

The *Tatra Inn* (☎ (057) 55 1988) has accommodation in motel-type units where dinner, B&B is from $75 per person. Both of these places have a restaurant and ski hire.

Getting There & Away There is no public transport to the village. The closest you can get is Porepunkah on the Ovens Highway.

Mt Buller (1600 metres)
Less then a three-hour drive from Melbourne and only 246 km away, Mt Buller is the most crowded resort in Victoria, especially on the weekends. It has a large lift network with 24 lifts, including a chair lift which begins in the

Top: Mural in Prahran, Melbourne, Vic (RN)
Left: Puffing Billy steam train, Dandenongs, near Melbourne, Vic (TW)
Right: Water trough, Treasury Gardens, Melbourne, Vic (RN)

Top: Twelve Apostles, Great Ocean Road, Vic (BD)
Left: Along Pyrenees Highway between Maryborough & Castlemaine, Vic (RN)
Right: Climber on top of Watsons Crags, Kosciusko National Park, NSW (JW)

car park and ends in the middle of the ski runs.

In years of light snow cover, Buller is skied out much sooner than Falls Creek or Mt Hotham, though snow-making equipment now extends the season on the main beginners' area. Cross-country skiing is possible around Buller and there is access to Mt Stirling which has some good trails. A trail-use fee is payable ($5).

A day ticket costs $44, a seven-day ticket $245 and a daily lift and lesson package costs $63.

Places to Stay There is plenty of accommodation. The *Youth Hostel* (☎ (057) 77 6181) is of course the cheapest on the mountain. In winter it is necessary to book via the YHA office in Melbourne, and bookings open in February. The Monday to Friday rate is $135 to $175 per person and the weekend rate is $70 per person. In summer the rate is $10 per person per day.

Club lodges are again the best value, starting at about $30 per person per night, with mostly bunk accommodation and kitchen facilities; contact the Mt Buller accommodation centre (☎ (057) 77 6280 or 008 039 049, toll-free).

Getting There & Around During winter only, there is a daily V/Line bus from Melbourne to Mt Buller, via Mansfield, with extra services on the weekend. The fare from Melbourne is $39.45 one-way, $72 return. From Mansfield it's $15.75 one-way, $26 return (☎ (03) 459 3000 or (057) 75 2606). Around the village and to and from the car park, there is an over-snow transport shuttle service that operates daily in winter from 7 am to 5 pm. If you are coming just for a day trip you can take the quad chair lift from the car park into the skiing area and save time and money by bypassing the village. There are ski rental facilities in the car park. Cross-country skiers turn off for Mt Stirling at the Mt Buller entrance gate at the base of the mountain. There are day facilities and fast food available at Telephone Box Junction.

Mt Hotham (1750 metres)
Known as Australia's powder capital, Hotham does get the lightest snow in the country, but don't expect anything like Europe or North America. It is 373 km from Melbourne and a five-and-a-half hour drive, the last part being on an unsealed road.

The lift system here is not well integrated and some walking is necessary, even though the 'zoo cart' (see Getting There & Around) along the main road offers some relief. The skiing here is good: a quarter of the runs are for beginners, a third for intermediates and almost half are for experienced skiers. This is a skiers' mountain with a vertical drop of 428 metres and the nightlife mainly happening in ski lodges. There is some good off-piste skiing in steep and narrow valleys. A day ticket costs $42; a seven-day pass $226; and a lift and lesson five-day package costs $248, or $306 with ski hire.

Cross-country skiing is good around Hotham and ski touring is very good on the Bogong High Plains which you can cross to Falls Creek. This is also the starting point for trips across the Razorback to beautiful Mt Feathertop. Below the village, on the eastern side, there is a series of trails which run as far as Dinner Plain. The biathlon (shooting and skiing) course between Mt Hotham and Dinner Plain is here at Wire Plain.

Places to Stay Most of the accommodation is in club lodges. These have bunk-type accommodation with kitchen facilities. It is possible to find beds in these or apartments through the Alpine Resorts Commission (☎ 008 032 061, toll-free), or phone the lodges direct.

Some of the cheapest apartments are in the *Jack Frost Lodge* (☎ 008 032 205, toll-free) where a self-contained twin room costs $900 per week. The *Arlberg Hotham* (☎ (03) 809 2699) has similar rooms for $1080.

For B&B and dinner, the cheapest place is also *Jack Frost*, with triple rooms for $1425 per week, while at the *Arlberg* it's $755 per person. These rates are all for the peak time from late July to late August; cheaper rates apply either side of this period.

It is also possible to stay at Dinner Plain, 11 km from Mt Hotham Village, where there are private houses for rent as well as the usual kinds of accommodation. There is very little accommodation here outside the ski season.

Getting There & Around In winter, Hoys (☎ (057) 59 2622 or 008 03 7098, toll-free) have a bus service to and from Melbourne from Friday to Monday for $55 ($75 return). There is a daily connection to and from Harrietville for $22.20 (same-day return), and to and from Bright for $25.20 return. Hoys also operate to Albury, and fares are $42.20 one-way, $58.20 same-day return. All fares include a $3 resort entry fee.

The village was built on a ridge almost at the top of the mountain and is strung out along the road. Luckily, there are free shuttle buses that run frequently all the way to Dinner Plain, and the free 'zoo cart' takes skiers from their lodges to the lifts between 8 am and 5 pm. If you plan to party late into the night you had better have a car or be prepared for a long walk, as the shuttle bus stops running at 12.30 am.

Other Resorts

There are three other ski areas that are mainly good for beginners and cross-country skiing or sightseeing and have no accommodation. **Mt Donna Buang** is the closest to Melbourne (95 km) via Warburton, but is mainly for sightseeing.

Lake Mountain is 109 km via Marysville. The cross-country facility here is world class, with a system of trails that are groomed daily.

Skiing for the experienced is found around the summit of Victoria's highest peak, Mt Bogong. Here, steep gullies tempt the cross-country downhill skier. Accommodation is in tents and in mountain huts. This area is not for beginners.

Mt St Gwinear is 171 km from Melbourne via Moe and has connecting cross-country ski trails with Mt Baw Baw.

Mt Stirling is a few km from Mt Buller

and fortunately so far it is only developed as a cross-country ski area.

Gippsland

The Gippsland region is the south-east slice of Victoria. It stretches from Westernport Bay, near Melbourne, to the New South Wales border on the east coast, with the Great Dividing Range to the north.

Named in 1839 by the Polish explorer Count Paul Strzelecki after Sir George Gipps, the former governor of New South Wales, Gippsland was first settled by prospectors in the 1850s, then by farmers after the completion of the railway from Melbourne in 1887. Extremely fertile and well watered, Gippsland is now the focus of the state's dairy industry.

While thousands of people were attracted to the region's scattered gold fields last century, it is now the huge brown coal deposits which keep the miners employed. The mines and power stations of the Latrobe Valley supply most of Victoria's electricity, while the offshore wells in Bass Strait provide most of Australia's petroleum and natural gas. Gippsland is an area of often breathtaking beauty with a multitude of attractions. There are lush rainforests, countless waterfalls, quiet streams, raging rapids, deserted beaches, tranquil lakes, coastal waterways, rolling pastures and high and rugged forested mountains.

The Latrobe Valley

The Latrobe Valley extends from the southern reaches of the Victorian Alps in the north to the spectacular Wilsons Promontory in the south, and from Yarragon in the west to the Gippsland Lakes and the vast Ninety Mile Beach in the east.

The region between Moe and Traralgon is the site of one of the world's largest deposits of brown coal. The power stations built on the coal fields at Yallourn, Morwell and Loy Yang provide 85% of Victoria's electricity.

The massive **Morwell open-cut mine**,

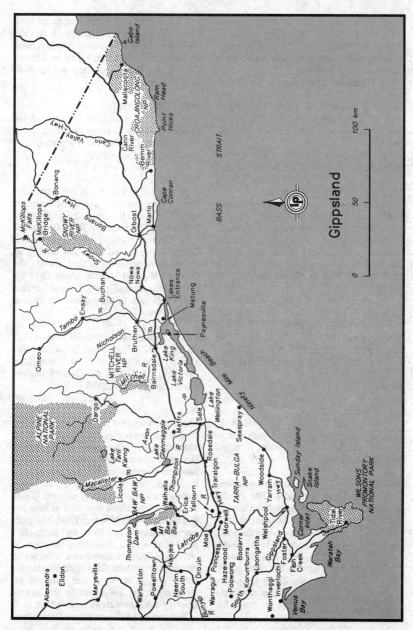

which has a surface area of about three sq km, produces about 14 million tonnes of brown coal every year. The coal is transported on conveyors to the power stations at Hazelwood and Yallourn.

The **Hazelwood Pondage**, a huge artificial lake (popular for water sports), was created to provide the nearly 200 million litres of water needed every hour by the Hazelwood power station's steam condensers.

The Yallourn power station and the briquette works at Morwell are fed by the coal extracted by the huge 12-storey bucket dredges at the **Yallourn open cut.**

The immense new Loy Yang Power Station near Traralgon will be the largest in the southern hemisphere when it's finished.

The SEC offers conducted tours of the Morwell open cut and Hazelwood Power Station daily between 8 am and 3 pm, from the Morwell Visitors Centre (☎ (051) 35 3415).

The other blots on the valley's landscape are the smoking chimney stacks of the Australian Paper Manufacturers' (APM) mill at Maryland near Morwell. The factory is the largest pulp and paper mill in Australia.

The mines, the huge power plants and the briquette factories provide employment, electricity and a certain amount of tourism, but they are nonetheless an ugly scar on a once beautiful landscape.

This is, thankfully, only one part of the Latrobe Valley, which overall provides an interesting cross section of urban, rural and industrial activity.

Getting There & Away Soon after leaving Dandenong the road divides. The Princes Highway continues east through the Latrobe Valley to Bairnsdale, near the coast, then on into New South Wales. Meanwhile the South Gippsland Highway heads off to the southeast to Phillip Island and Wilsons Promontory. For a slower but more scenic drive, you can follow the South Gippsland Highway, go via the Prom and rejoin the Princes Highway at Sale, 214 km from Melbourne.

V/Line operates a regular daily Melbourne/Traralgon/Sale/Bairnsdale service, sometimes by bus from Sale onwards, with connections on to Lakes Entrance, Orbost, Cann River, Eden and Narooma (in New South Wales).

WEST GIPPSLAND
The West Gippsland area, north of the Princes Highway, is being promoted as the 'Gourmet Deli of Victoria' – a place of fine foods and beautiful scenery.

Warragul
A regional centre for the district's dairy farms which provide most of Melbourne's milk, Warragul is the first major town east of Dandenong. The excellent **West Gippsland Arts Centre**, part of Warragul's Civic Centre, caters for all local and visiting art forms, both performance and visual. The **Darnum Musical Village**, about eight km east of the centre of town, is an old church with a collection of old and modern musical instruments.

Places to Stay The *Warragul Caravan Park* (☎ (056) 232707) in Burke St has tent sites and on-site vans, and the *Club Hotel* (☎ (056) 23 1636), 51 Queens St, has singles/doubles for $20/30.

Moe
The main attraction of this Latrobe Valley coal-mining centre is the **Gippsland Folk Museum** (Old Gippstown), on the Princes Highway, where a 19th-century community has been re-created on four hectares of parkland. The 30 or so buildings are authentic, having been collected from all over Gippsland and reassembled here, and at least one is classified by the National Trust. The place has an authentic feel to it, and there are a number of working displays of old crafts, as well as rides in horse-drawn vehicles of varying descriptions. Old Gippstown is open daily from 9 am to 5 pm; entry is $6. Devonshire teas are served in the historic **Bushy Park Homestead** on Sundays.

You can visit Yallourn Power Station from

Moe, and the former site of the township of Yallourn, which was moved lock, stock and barrel to provide access to the brown-coal deposits underneath. From the hill behind the town site there is a lookout with some information for visitors and views of the vast open-cut mine area.

There's a scenic road from Moe north to Walhalla, the Baw Baw National Park, and Mt Erica from where a secondary road continues north across the Victorian Alps. You can get onto the panoramic Grand Ridge Rd across the Strzelecki Ranges easily from either Trafalgar or Moe by turning south via the lovely little townships of Narracan or Thorpdale.

Morwell

Morwell was founded in the 1880s, and before the turn of the century it became the supply centre for diggers and traders heading for the gold fields at Walhalla.

These days Morwell is basically an industrial town servicing the massive open-cut mine, Hazelwood Power Station, the APM pulp mills and the local briquette works.

The SEC's visitors centre (☎ (051) 35 3415), signposted off Commercial Rd, houses models and displays of the Latrobe Valley's coal-mining and power-generating activities. There are also guided tours of the Morwell open cut and Hazelwood Power Station.

Places to Stay There's the *Morwell Caravan Park* (☎ (051) 34 3507), Maryvale Crescent; or the *Merton Rush Hotel* (☎ (051) 34 2633) on the corner of Princes Highway and Collins St has B&B singles/doubles for $30/40.

Traralgon

The original township was a rest stop and supply base for miners and drovers heading further into the gold and farming country of Gippsland. It is now the centre of the state's paper and pulp industry and a major Latrobe Valley electricity centre. Its future is assured by the colossal Loy Yang Power Station, six km to the south. The SEC is apparently so proud of this incredible construction that there is a tourist road right through the middle of the complex.

Places to Stay There's the Park Lane Caravan Park (☎ (051) 74 6749) on Park Lane, or the Grand Junction Hotel (☎ (051) 74 6011), Franklin St, which has singles/doubles for $25/40.

Walhalla (population 30)

At the end of 1862 Edward Stringer, one of a small party of prospectors who had made it over the mountains, found gold in a creek running through a deep wooded valley north of Moe. The payable gold in Stringer's Creek attracted about 200 miners but it was the later discovery of Cohen's Reef, the outcrop of a reef almost two miles long, that put the growing township of Walhalla on the map.

Work began on the Long Tunnel Mine, the single most profitable mine in Victoria, in 1865 and continued for 49 years. Walhalla reached its peak between 1885 and 1890 when there were over 4000 people living in and around the town.

The railway line from Moe, incorporating a truly amazing section of tunnels and trestle bridges between Erica and Walhalla, was finally completed in 1910 just as the town's fortunes began to decline.

Though the population is tiny these days, there's plenty to see in Walhalla and the area is quite beautiful. There are a number of old buildings (some of which are classified by the National Trust), a museum and a very interesting cemetery. The **Long Tunnel Extended Gold Mine** is open on weekends and public holidays; entrance is $3.50.

South of Walhalla, there is a car park and marked trail to the summit of Mt Erica which offers a good taste of Victoria's alpine bushland.

Places to Stay The *Walhalla Lodge Hotel* may be open for accommodation by now, otherwise the nearest town with somewhere to stay is Erica (14 km away).

Getting There & Away There are daily buses connecting Walhalla and Moe.

Sale (population 14,900)

At the junction of the Princes and South Gippsland Highways, Sale is a supply centre for the Bass Strait oilfields. There's an **Oil & Gas Display Centre** on Princes Highway on the western side of town. The port of Sale, also on this side of town, was a busy centre in the paddle-steamer days and you can still take cruises from Sale into the Gippsland Lakes.

Tourist information is available from the Oil & Gas Display Centre (☎ (051) 44 1108).

Places to Stay The *Sale Caravan Park* (☎ (051) 44 1366) has all the usual facilities, but the next cheapest place is the *Ambassador Motor Hotel* (☎ (051) 44 3222) which charges $24/30.

THE GIPPSLAND LAKES

The Lakes area is where three major rivers, the Mitchell, Nicholson and Tambo, flow into an extensive lake system separated by a coastal strip from Ninety Mile Beach. It's an area popular for its surf, fishing, boating and spectacular scenery, and there's even a couple of wineries thrown in for good measure.

Paynesville is a resort on the lakes; you can cross to nearby **Raymond Island** by punt or to Ninety Mile Beach by boat. The island has a koala population which outnumbers its human population – 300 to 250. You can camp there or stay at *Swan Cove Units* (☎ (051) 56 6716) for $40 per night.

Bairnsdale (population 11,500)

Bairnsdale, at the junction of the Princes and Omeo highways, is a popular base both for the mountains to the north and the lakes immediately to the south. For people travelling with energetic children, there is one of the most interesting playgrounds in Victoria – **Howitt Park**, complete with flying foxes – on the Princes Highway on the east side of town.

Signposted 42 km north-west of Bairnsdale is the **Mitchell River National Park** with the **Den of Nargun**, a small cave which, according to Aboriginal legend, was haunted by a strange, half-stone creature, known as a 'nargun'. There are some excellent short walks in the park.

Tourist information can be obtained from the Victorian Eastern Development Association at 240 Main St, Bairnsdale (☎ (051) 52 3234).

Places to Stay & Eat There are a number of hotels, motels and caravan parks. The *Riversleigh Country Hotel* (☎ (051) 52 6996) is reportedly well worth staying at. Singles/doubles start at $55/80.

Slightly more down to earth is the *Orient Hotel* (☎ (051) 52 4030) at 59 Main St, which charges $30/46 for B&B.

For an on-site van or tent site, try the *Mitchell Gardens Caravan Park* (☎ (051) 52 4654), on the banks of the Mitchell River.

The *Riversleigh* has an excellent licensed restaurant, open for both lunch and dinner.

Getting There & Away Daily trains run between Bairnsdale and Melbourne ($27.40), and there are buses to Lakes Entrance ($5.40). All the major bus operators stop in Bairnsdale on the coastal route between Melbourne and Sydney.

Metung (population 760)

This interesting little fishing village between Bairnsdale and Lakes Entrance is built on a land spit between Lake King and Bancroft Bay. The town offers hot sulphur springs in two outdoor pools and houseboats which can be hired from Bull's Cruises (☎ (051) 56 2208) to tour the lakes.

There is plenty of accommodation to choose from, including the pub (☎ (051) 56 2446) right on the water.

Lakes Entrance (population 4500)

At the eastern end of the lakes is Lakes Entrance, where there's a walking bridge across Cunningham's Arm to Ninety Mile

Beach. This is also the largest fishing port in Victoria and lots of cruise boats operate from here to tour the rivers and lakes.

There's a tourist information centre (☎ (051) 55 1966) on the Princes Highway, just as you enter the town from the west.

Activities *Thunderbird* (☎ (051) 55 1246) is the largest of the many boats touring the lakes and does two-hour cruises twice daily.

The Lakes Entrance Fishermen's Co-operative, just off the Princes Highway, provides a viewing platform which puts you in the middle of the boats unloading their fish. Sunday morning is the best time to go. The co-op fish shop is guaranteed to sell the freshest fish in town.

From the footbridge in the centre of town, there's a 2.3 km walking track to the actual 'entrance'. Surfers should head for the left-handed reef break at Red Bluff, especially at high tide, or nearby Tracks and Sandy Point.

A number of operators rent out boats to take on the lakes, and these include Bull's (☎ (051) 56 2208) in Metung, Victor Hire Boats (☎ (051) 55 1888) and Lakes Barbe-cue Boats (☎ (051) 55 2255), both in Lakes Entrance.

Places to Stay & Eat Lakes Entrance has a boggling array of accommodation. There's an associate youth hostel in Willis St at the *Lakes Main Caravan Park* (☎ (051) 55 2365) for $8.50 a night.

For a tent site or on-site van close to the centre try *Ryans Tourist Park* (☎ (051) 55 2809) at 266 Marine Parade, one of at least a dozen.

The *Central Hotel* is one of a number of pubs serving up good counter meals, while the *Sloop John D* is a good seafood place with moderate prices. It's actually a glassed-in barge that's moored at the jetty, so you have an excellent view of the fishing fleet activities.

Getting There & Away There are daily V/Line buses between Lakes Entrance and Bairnsdale ($5.40), with rail connections to

Melbourne ($33.10). Buses also connect Lakes Entrance with Orbost ($7.60).

EAST GIPPSLAND

The logging of the Gippsland forests is an emotive issue which has in the last few years been the cause of often violent arguments between the loggers and the environmental-ists. The state government has, typically, tried to please everyone, with mixed success.

For naturalists interested in seeing East Gippsland, an essential book to buy is the Australian Conservation Foundation's *Car Tours & Bushwalks in East Gippsland*. This book has photos and a grading system rating the ease or difficulty of each tour and/or walk, and gives an idea of the spectacular beauty of the area.

Orbost

Orbost is a logging service town, with a very pretty location on the Snowy River.

The new Rainforest Centre (☎ (051) 54 6375), operated by the Department of Con-servation & Environment, is an excellent source of information on forests and national parks in east Gippsland. It has an interesting audio-visual display throughout the day. It is open on weekdays from 9 am to 5 pm, and on weekends from 10 am to 5 pm.

The tourist information office, known as the Slab Hut (☎ (051) 54 2424), is on Nich-olson St.

Places to Stay Orbost has a caravan park (☎ (051) 54 1097) with tent sites and on-site vans; the *Commonwealth Hotel* (☎ (051) 54 1077), with B&B from $20/30; and a couple of motels.

Getting There & Away V/Line has buses to Bairnsdale ($12.10), Lakes Entrance ($7.60), Cann River ($9.70), Canberra ($33.10) and east along the coast as far as Narooma.

Marlo & Cape Conran

On the coast 15 km south of Orbost is the sleepy little settlement of Marlo, on the mouth of the Snowy River. It's a popular fishing spot and the route along the coast to Cape Conran, 18 km to the east, is especially pretty as it winds through stands of banksia trees. The beach at Cape Conran is one long beautiful deserted strip of white sand.

Places to Stay Marlo has a couple of caravan parks, while at Cape Conran the Department of Conservation & Environment runs the superb *Banksia Bluff* camping area and cabins (☎ (051) 54 8438). Facilities are basic but the site is excellent.

Baldwin Spencer Trail
This is a drive well worth doing – a 265-km route through more superb forest, including the newly proclaimed **Errinundra National Park**, north of Orbost on the Bonang Highway.

The route follows the trail of Walter Baldwin Spencer, a noted scientist and explorer who led an expedition through here in 1889. Info is available from the Rainforest Centre in Orbost.

Buchan (population 220)
There are a number of limestone caves around the tiny and beautiful town of Buchan, 55 km north-west of Orbost. The two major ones, maintained by the Department of Conservation & Environment, are the **Royal Cave** and **Fairy Cave**. There are daily tours at 10 am, 1 and 3.30 pm for the Royal Cave, and 11.15 am and 2.15 pm for the Fairy Cave. The tours take around 45 minutes and are well worth the $5.

The Department also offers guided tours to more remote and undeveloped caves in the area; phone (051) 55 9264. Bushwhackers Touring Company (☎ (051) 55 9240) has bushwalks to places further afield, including the Alpine National Park.

Popular souvenirs are items made by local artists on the unique Buchan black marble.

Places to Stay Buchan has a delightful camp site right at the caves, with a swimming pool continuously fed by an icy underground stream flowing from a cave in the hillside.

Very refreshing! There's also a pub and a couple of private guesthouses offering accommodation.

Snowy River
The road north from Buchan runs roughly parallel to the Snowy River, passing through superb bush and mountain scenery, descending to the riverside near the New South Wales border at Willis – a place with a name and nothing else. The road, a bit rough but never dull, continues up to Jindabyne in the Snowy Mountains of New South Wales.

If you turn off about 56 km north of Buchan and travel the 28 km to **McKillops Bridge** you can have a dip in the river or camp on its sandy banks. The view from the lookout over **Little River Falls**, about 20 km west of McKillops Bridge, is spectacular. From McKillops you can continue a further 50 km to **Bonang**, on the Bonang Highway, then head south back to Orbost.

The classic canoe or raft trip down the Snowy River from Willis or McKillops Bridge to a pull-out point near Buchan takes at least four days and offers superb scenery: rugged gorges, raging rapids, tranquil sections and excellent camping spots on broad sand bars. A number of commercial operators including World Expeditions (☎ (03) 670 8400) and Peregrine Adventures (☎ (03) 602 3066) organise raft trips on the Snowy; the cost is about $480.

Croajingolong National Park
The beautiful Croajingolong National Park extends about 100 km from Sydenham Inlet to Cape Howe on the New South Wales border and is undoubtedly among the finest of the coastal national parks in Victoria. It's approximately 560 km from Melbourne via the Princes Highway.

There are several roads leading from the highway to different parts of the park. Some are quite rough and require 4WD; the national parks service office at Cann River will give you more information about vehicular access.

There are camp sites within Croajingolong National Park at Wingan Inlet, Thurra

River, Mueller River and Shipwreck Creek. Facilities are minimal and it's a good idea to make reservations with the parks office in Cann River (☎ (051) 58 6351) or Mallacoota (☎ (051) 58 0263).

Mallacoota (population 720)

Mallacoota is at the seaward end of a small lake system and is the main service town for this corner of the state. It is a popular fishing resort and there's good access to the Croajingolong National Park. Abalone and fishing are the town's mainstays, and there are fishing boats for hire.

The town's bank is open just once a week (Wednesdays) but there's a nearby general store that acts as a bank on other weekdays.

At Easter the town becomes packed out for the annual festival, and accommodation can be hard to come by.

Places to Stay There's a great deal of holiday accommodation here. The *Mallacoota Shady Gully Caravan Park* (☎ (051) 58 0362 has tent sites and on-site vans, and there's also a backpackers' section where a night in a four-bed room costs $7.

Other places include the *Adobe* mud-brick flats (☎ (051) 58 0329) which cost $35 to $59 a day and accommodate up to five people; and the *Lakeside* holiday flats (☎ (051) 58 0455) which cost $35 to $65 for fully self-contained flats accommodating up to six people.

SOUTH GIPPSLAND

Way back at Dandenong you can opt to take the route south into the south Gippsland area rather than continue east on the Princes Highway to Sale. This route takes you to two of Victoria's greatest natural attractions – Phillip Island (see the Around Melbourne section) and Wilsons Promontory (the Prom).

Korumburra (population 3200)

The **Coal Creek Historical Park**, a very popular re-creation of a coal mining town of the 19th century, is near Korumburra. Coal was first discovered here in 1872 and the Coal Creek Mine operated from the 1890s right up to 1958.

The Strzelecki Ranges

Between the Latrobe Valley and South Gippsland's coastal areas are the beautiful 'blue' rounded hills of the Strzelecki Ranges. The winding Grand Ridge Rd traverses the top of these ranges, from behind Trafalgar to the back of Traralgon, providing a fabulous excursion through fertile farmland that was once covered with forests of mountain ash.

A good base for this area is the township of **Mirboo North** which straddles the Grand Ridge Rd south of Trafalgar. The town boasts the **Strzelecki Brewery** in the old Butter Factory building. The complex not only produces a range of quality beers but also features a cosy bar, a restaurant, an Italian coffee shop, a Sunday craft market and an art gallery.

There's a *caravan park* in Mirboo North, opposite the Shire Hall, which has tent sites for $5.60.

Foster (population 2100)

Foster is 175 km from Melbourne on the South Gippsland Highway and is one of the main turn-offs for the Prom. There's little of interest in the town, although the pub on the corner is a little unusual.

The *Rumbug Camp Backpackers* (☎ (056) 646524) is six km north of the highway, and the turn-off is about seven km along the highway west of Foster itself. The charge is $15 per night.

Welshpool (population 760)

The sleepy dairying town of Welshpool was woken with a jolt in late 1990 with the inception of the *SeaCat* ferry run between Port Welshpool, six km away, and George Town on the north coast of Tasmania.

There's a **maritime museum** in Port Welshpool, and the **Agnes Falls**, 10 km north of the highway, are the highest in Victoria.

There is nowhere to stay in the town itself,

but there are a couple of caravan parks at Port Welshpool.

Getting There & Away Promair (☎ (056) 88 1487) in Welshpool have flights to Flinders Island ($99), Launceston ($150) and Melbourne's Moorabbin Airport ($60).

The *SeaCat* operates daily to George Town between December and April. The journey on this high-speed ultra-modern catamaran takes 4½ hours, and costs around $114 for passengers one-way and around $145 for the average-sized car. Bicycles are carried for $18 and motorbikes for $72 (☎ 008 030 131, toll-free).

SeaCat also operates connecting buses from Melbourne departing Spencer St Railway Station at 9.30 am.

V/Line has buses connecting Welshpool with Yarram and Melbourne.

WILSONS PROMONTORY

'The Prom' is one of the most popular national parks in Australia. It covers the peninsula that forms the southernmost part of the Australian mainland. The Prom offers more than 80 km of walking tracks and a wide variety of beaches – whether you want surfing, safe swimming or a secluded beach all to yourself, you can find it on the Prom. Finally there's the wildlife, which abounds despite the park's popularity. There are wonderful birds, emus, kangaroos and, at night, plenty of wombats. The wildlife around Tidal River is very tame and can even become a nuisance. One Lonely Planet staffer was bitten by a wombat but lived to tell the tale.

Information

The national park office (☎ (056) 80 8538) at Tidal River is open Monday to Saturday from 8.30 am to 4.30 pm. The displays here are excellent. The park office takes reservations for accommodation and issues camping permits. The office is also where you pay your park entry fee ($5 per car) if the main gate is not staffed.

Activities

It's probably walkers who get the best value from the Prom, though you don't have to go very far from the car parks to really get away from it all. The park office at Tidal River has free leaflets on walks ranging from 15-minute strolls from Tidal River to overnight and longer hikes. You can also get detailed maps of the park.

The walking tracks take you through ever-changing scenery: swamps, forests, marshes, valleys of tree ferns and long beaches lined with sand dunes. For serious exploration, it's really worth buying a copy of *Discovering the Prom on Foot* ($6.95) from the park office.

Don't miss the Mt Oberon walk – it starts from the Mt Oberon car park, takes one hour and is about three km each way. The views from the summit are excellent.

It's a long day walk from the Mt Oberon car park to the tip of the Prom, and by prior arrangement (☎ (056) 80 8529) it's possible to visit the lighthouse. Another popular walk is the Squeaky Beach Nature Walk, a lovely 1½-hour stroll around to the next bay and back.

The northern area of the park is much less visited, simply because all the facilities are at Tidal River. Most of the walks in this area are overnight or longer. All the camp sites away from Tidal River have pit toilets but nothing else in the way of facilities. Fires are totally banned (except in certain designated fire places in Tidal River for a few months over the winter) so you'll need to carry some sort of stove.

Places to Stay

Flats & Units There are a number of self-contained flats which can accommodate two to six people. The daily rates range from $64 per night for a double bed-sitter in the off-season up to $405 for a six-bed unit in the peak season.

To complete the picture there are 'motor huts', which are similar to an on-site cabin. Unlike the flats, you must supply all bed linen. The rate is a very reasonable $26 per

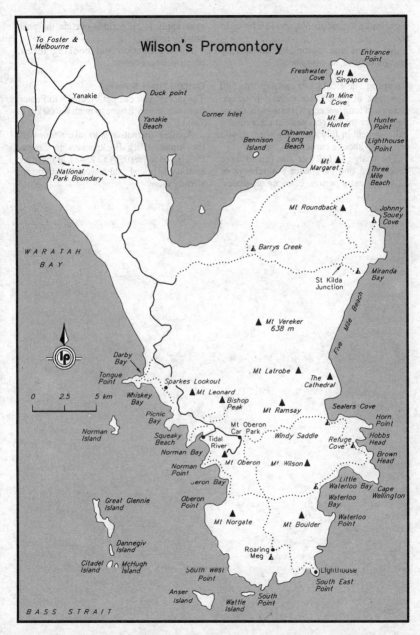

Wilson's Promontory

night for up to four people, and $39 for up to six.

All cabins and motor huts are usually heavily booked, so plan ahead.

Camping The Tidal River camp site has 500 sites, and at peak times (school holidays, Easter and long weekends) booking is essential. In fact for the real peak at Christmas a ballot is held in July allocating sites, so you can forget about a casual visit then.

The charge is $12 per site (up to three people and one car), with a surcharge of $2.40 per extra person. Cheaper off-season rates apply to all periods outside the peak holiday times.

For information and booking forms, phone the park office.

Getting There & Away

The closest you can get by bus is to Foster, from where you'll have to hitch the 60 km to Tidal River.

Another alternative is to take a tour with the Amaroo Park Backpackers in Cowes, Phillip Island (☎ (059) 52 2548), as these are reasonably priced, and convenient if you are already there.

Western Australia

Area	2,525,500 sq km
Population	1,590,000

The first European to land on the Western Australian coast was Dutchman Dirk Hartog in 1616. The first Englishman to sight the coast was William Dampier, who landed somewhere near Broome in 1688. Their reports of a dry, barren land discouraged attempts at settlement. It was not until 1829, three years after Britain had formally claimed the land, that the first European settlers arrived in Perth. Their presence was intended to forestall settlement by other European nations.

The arrival of the Europeans had disastrous consequences for the local Aborigines. During the 40,000-year history of Aboriginal occupation of Western Australia, these people, hunting and gathering in small nomadic groups, had managed to live in harmony with nature, despite the harshness of the environment. Pushed off their traditional lands, many of the Aborigines who were not killed by the colonisers died of European diseases, against which they had no immunity.

Western Australia's development as a British colony was painfully slow – hardly surprising, given its distance from the main Australian settlements in the east. It was not until the gold rushes of the 1890s that the colony really began to progress. Today, a larger and far more technologically advanced mineral boom forms the basis of the state's prosperity.

Around the State

There's a lot to see in Western Australia. Close to the state's capital, Perth, is the wine-producing Swan Valley. In the north there's the harsh and beautiful Pilbara gorge country and the old pearling town of Broome, now enjoying a tourist boom all its own. At the top end of the state is the wild Kimberley area, one of Australia's last frontiers, while

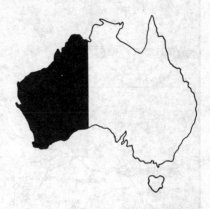

in the east there are the mines and ghost towns of the Goldfields region. The south is dotted with beautiful surf and swimming beaches, a spectacular and rugged coastline, historic towns, wineries and giant karri forests.

GEOGRAPHY

Western Australia's geography is a little like a distorted reflection of eastern Australia except, of course, that the west is far drier than the east. The equivalent of the long fertile coastal strip on the east coast is the small south-western corner of Western Australia. As in the east, hills rise behind the coast, but in Western Australia they're much smaller than those of the Great Dividing Range. Further north it's dry and relatively barren. Along the central-west coast is the Great Sandy Desert, a very inhospitable region running right to the sea.

There are a couple of interesting variations, such as the Kimberley, in the extreme north of the state – a wild and rugged area with a convoluted coast and spectacular inland gorges. It gets good annual rainfall, but all in the 'green' season. Taming the Kimberley has been a long-held dream

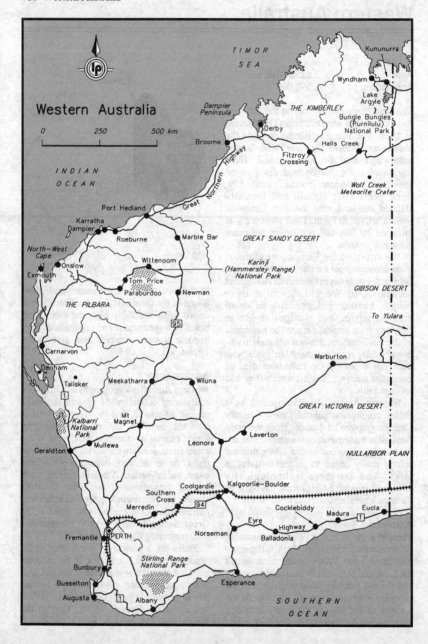

Western Australia

0   250   500 km

TIMOR SEA

THE KIMBERLEY

Kununurra

Wyndham

Lake Argyle

Dampier Peninsula

Derby

Broome

Halls Creek

Fitzroy Crossing

Bungle Bungles (Purnululu) National Park

Wolf Creek Meteorite Crater

INDIAN OCEAN

Port Hedland

Karratha

Dampier

Roeburne

Marble Bar

GREAT SANDY DESERT

North-West Cape

Onslow

Exmouth

Wittenoom

Karinji (Hammersley Range) National Park

GIBSON DESERT

Tom Price

Paraburdoo

Newman

THE PILBARA

95

To Yulara

Carnarvon

Denham

Talisker

Meekatharra

Wiluna

Warburton

Kalbarri National Park

Mt Magnet

GREAT VICTORIA DESERT

Geraldton

Mullewa

Leonora

Laverton

NULLARBOR PLAIN

1

Coolgardie

Kalgoorlie–Boulder

Southern Cross

Merredin

94

Cocklebiddy

Madura

Eucla

Eyre

Fremantle

PERTH

Norseman

Balladonia

Eyre Highway

1

Bunbury

Stirling Range National Park

Busselton

Esperance

Augusta

Albany

1

SOUTHERN OCEAN

which has still only been partially realised. It's a spectacular area, and very well worth a visit.

Further south is the Pilbara, an area with more magnificent gorge country and the treasure-house from which the state derives its vast mineral wealth. Away from the coast, however, most of Western Australia is simply a vast empty stretch of outback: the Nullarbor Plain in the south, the Great Sandy Desert in the north and the Gibson and Great Victoria deserts in between.

WILD FLOWERS

Western Australia is famed for its wild flowers, which bloom from August to October. Even some of the driest regions put on a technicolour display after just a little rainfall.

The south-west alone has over 3000 species, many of which, because of the state's isolation, are unique. They're known as everlastings because the petals stay attached even after the flowers have died. The flowers seem to spring up almost overnight, and they transform vast areas within days.

You can find the flowers almost everywhere in the state, but the jarrah forests in the south-west are particularly rich. The coastal parks also put on brilliant displays. Near Perth, the John Forrest National Park, in the Darling Range, and the Yanchep National Park are both excellent prospects. But you don't even have to leave Perth to see wild flowers, as there's a section of Kings Park where they are cultivated.

The excellent *Wildflower Discovery – a Guide for the Motorist*, which details a number of wild-flower trails north and south of Perth, is available free from the Western Australian Tourist Centre (☎ (09) 322 2999) in Forrest Place, Perth.

INFORMATION
Tourist Offices

There are Western Australian tourist offices in the following states and territories:

ACT
    33 Ainslie Ave, Canberra 2608 (☎ (062) 48 5214)
New South Wales
    92 Pitt St, Sydney 2000 (☎ (02) 233 4400)
Northern Territory
    79-81 Smith St, Darwin 8000 (☎ (089) 81 3838
Queensland
    243 Edward St, Brisbane 4000 (☎ (07) 229 5794)
South Australia
    Corner of Grenfell & King William Sts, Adelaide 5000 (☎ (08) 212 1344)
Victoria
    35 Elizabeth St, Melbourne 3000 (☎ (03) 614 6833)

ACTIVITIES
Bushwalking

There are a number of bushwalking clubs in Perth including the Bushwalkers of Western Australia (☎ (09) 387 6875) and Perth Bushwalkers (☎ (09) 362 1614). Popular areas for walking in Western Australia include the Stirling Range National Park and Porongurup National Park, both near Albany. There are also a number of coastal parks in the south and south-west, such as Cape Le Grand, Fitzgerald River, Walpole-Nornalup and Cape Arid national parks, with good walking tracks. To the north, the Kalbarri and Hamersley Range national parks provide a stimulating hiking environment.

There are interesting walks in the hills around Perth at places like Piesse Brook, Mundaring Weir, the Serpentine, Kalamunda and Bickley. They're particularly pleasant during the August to September wild-flower season. If you're a really enthusiastic walker, there's the 640-km Bibbulman Track that runs along old forest tracks between Perth and Walpole on Western Australia's south-eastern coast. Information on this and many other tracks is available from the Western Australia Department of Conservation & Land Management (☎ (09) 367 0333), 50 Hayman Rd, Como, Western Australia 6152.

Water Sports

People in Perth often claim that their city has the best surf and swimming beaches of any Australian city. Popular surfing areas around Western Australia include Denmark near

Albany; from Cape Naturaliste to Margaret River in the south-west; Bunbury, 180 km south of Perth; and Geraldton to the north. Fine swimming beaches can be found right around the Western Australia coast.

Good diving areas include the large stretch of coast from Esperance to Geraldton, and between Carnarvon and Exmouth. You can get to the islands and reefs off the coast in small boats. The more popular diving spots include Esperance, Bremer Bay, Albany, Denmark, Windy Harbour, Margaret River, Bunbury, Rottnest Island, Shoalwater Islands Marine Park (near Rockingham), Lancelin, Abrolhos Island (near Geraldton), Carnarvon and all around the North-West Cape (Exmouth, Coral Bay).

Fishing
The coastal regions of Western Australia offer some of the best fishing in the world. Some of the more popular areas include Rottnest Island, Albany, Geraldton and the Abrolhos Islands, Shark Bay, Carnarvon and the coastline to the north, the North-West Cape and Broome.

Fishing licences (available for $10 from the Fisheries Department of Western Australia (☎ (09) 325 5988), 108 Adelaide Terrace, Perth, or country offices) are only required if you intend catching marron and rock lobsters or will be using a fishing net. The Fisheries Department of Western Australia can also supply you with further information including protected fishing waters, minimum catch sizes, fishing seasons and bag limits.

Heritage Trails Network
The Heritage Trails Network, launched during Australia's Bicentenary in 1988, is an excellent series of trails covering historical, cultural or natural points of interest around Perth and many country areas. The trails are usually well marked with interpretive displays and directional markers. Information on the Heritage Trails Network can be obtained from tourist offices or the Western Australia Heritage Committee (☎ (09) 322 4375) at 184 St George's Terrace, Perth 6000.

GETTING THERE & AWAY
Western Australia is the largest, most lightly populated and most isolated state in the country. Yet in spite of the vast distances that must be travelled, you can drive across the Nullarbor Plain from the eastern states to Perth and then all the way up the Indian Ocean coast and through the Kimberley to Darwin on sealed roads.

Even so, there's absolutely no way of covering all those km cheaply, although the deregulation of the airline industry has certainly helped. Sydney to Perth is 3284 km as the crow flies, and more like 4000 km by road: a one-way economy rail ticket on the route is $292, a discounted air ticket costs $520 return (or even less if you shop around), while a seat on one of the cheaper bus lines costs around $200.

Hitching across the Nullarbor is not all that easy; waits of three or four days are not uncommon in some places. Driving yourself is probably the cheapest way of getting to Western Australia from the eastern states – if there is a group of you. You'll probably spend around $400 to $450 on fuel, travelling coast to coast; between four people that's about $100 a head.

If you do go by road, be prepared. Firstly, make sure that your vehicle is up to the trip – seek advice from a mechanic if you are unsure. You will also need to have good tyres and carry spare parts such as a fan belt and radiator hose, as they are often scarce in more remote areas. Also, be prepared for higher petrol, repair and food costs.

The best time to cross the Nullarbor is from August to October when the wild flowers are blooming and the weather is mild; from December to March expect hot weather.

Another interesting route into Western Australia is from Yulara near Ayers Rock to Perth via the Gunbarrel Highway. This can be done by car or on the weekly bus service run by Transcontinental Coachlines (☎ (09) 250 2838) – see the North of Kalgoorlie section later in this chapter for further details.

GETTING AROUND
Air
So far deregulation has made little difference to flying within Western Australia. Ansett WA controls most traffic, with Skywest and local operators in spirited competition on some routes. Ansett WA has a comprehensive network of flights connecting Perth with regional centres. The frequency of some flights seems ridiculous given the state's

**Western Australia
Airfares**
All Fares in Australian Dollars

small population – until you realise how many mining and oil-drilling projects are based there; companies often find it easier to fly their workers back and forth rather than have them live up there.

The chart details the main Western Australia routes and flight costs.

Bus & Train
Bus Australia (☎ (09) 325 8888), Pioneer (☎ (09) 13 2030) and Greyhound (☎ (09) 13 1238) buses run from Perth along the coast to Darwin (Greyhound/Pioneer also travel there via the Great Northern Highway) and to Adelaide via Kalgoorlie.

Western Australia's internal rail network, operated by Westrail, is limited to services between Perth and Kalgoorlie (on the Prospector), and Perth and Bunbury in the south (on the Australind). Westrail also run buses to York, Geraldton, Esperance, Augusta, Pemberton, Mukinbudin, Hyden, Albany and Meekatharra. Reservations are necessary on all Westrail bus and train services (☎ (09) 326 2222).

South-West Coach Lines (☎ (09) 322 5173) in the Transperth bus station, Wellington St, Perth, run bus services between Perth and the following centres in the south-west of the state: Bunbury, Busselton, Augusta, Dunsborough, Nannup, Manjimup and Collie.

Perth

Population 1,100,000

The comparative youth of Perth accounts for its clean-cut look. It's a shiny, modern city, pleasantly sited on the Swan River, with the port of Fremantle a few km downstream. It's claimed to be the sunniest state capital in Australia and the most isolated capital city in the world. Of Western Australia's 1½ million people, almost 80% live in and around Perth.

Perth was founded in 1829 as the Swan River Settlement, but it grew very slowly until 1850, when convicts were brought in to alleviate the labour shortage. Many of Perth's fine buildings such as Government House and Perth Town Hall were built with convict labour. Even then, Perth's development lagged behind that of the eastern cities, until the discovery of gold in the 1890s increased the population four-fold in a decade and initiated a building boom. More recently, Western Australia's mineral wealth has contributed to Perth's growth.

Orientation

The city centre is fairly compact, situated on a sweep of the Swan River. The river, which borders the city centre to the south and east, links Perth to its port, Fremantle. The main shopping precinct is along the Hay St and Murray St malls and the arcades that run between them. This area is at its busiest on Thursday nights when the shops are open until 9 pm. St George's Terrace is the centre of the city's business district.

The railway line bounds the city centre on the northern side. Immediately north of the railway line is Northbridge, a popular restaurant and entertainment enclave with a number of hostels and cheap accommodation. The western end of Perth slopes up to the pleasant Kings Park, which overlooks the city and Swan River. Further to the west, suburbs extend as far as Perth's superb Indian Ocean beaches.

Information

Tourist Information The Western Australian Tourist Centre (☎ 483 1111) is in Forrest Place on the corner of Wellington St, opposite the railway station. The centre is open from 8.30 am to 5.30 pm Monday to Friday and from 9 am to 1 pm Saturday. It has a wide range of maps and brochures on Perth and the rest of Western Australia, and an accommodation and tours reservation service.

A number of guides to Perth including *Hello Perth*, *Your Guide to Perth & Fremantle*, *This Week in Perth & Fremantle* and the *Map of Perth & Fremantle* are available free at the tourist centre, hostels and hotels.

There is also an information board at the

domestic and international airport terminals with some accommodation and transport details. A phone is provided to place free calls through to advertised hotels and hostels, some of which provide a free airport pick-up service.

Useful Organisations The Royal Automobile Club of Western Australia (RACWA) (☎ 421 4444) is at 228 Adelaide Terrace. Their bookshop has an excellent travel section, and detailed regional maps can be obtained at their Road Travel counter.

The Youth Hostel Association (☎ 227 5122) has its office (not a hostel) at 65 Francis St in Northbridge. The Environmental Centre of Western Australia, on the 1st floor at 794 Hay St, has a notice board with information on cheap transport tickets, rides and accommodation.

Post Perth's GPO (☎ 326 5211) is in Forrest Place which runs between Wellington St and the Murray St Mall.

Telephone There are phones for international calls in the foyer of the GPO. The STD telephone area code for Perth is 09.

Bookshops Some good city bookshops include Angus & Robertson at 199 Murray St and 625 Hay St, and the Down to Earth Bookshop at 790 Hay St.

Kings Park

There are superb views across Perth and the river from this four-sq-km park. It includes a 17-hectare **Botanic Garden** that displays over 2000 different plant species from Western Australia and a section of natural bushland. In spring, there's a cultivated display of Western Australia's famed wild flowers.

Unfortunately, in early 1989 about half of Kings Park was burnt out in bushfires believed to be the work of arsonists, but the park's vegetation is quickly regenerating.

Look for the huge karri trunk on display in the main car park, and the crosscut section of a California redwood showing just how old a tree can be. From the top of Kings Park, the steep steps of Jacob's Ladder will take you down to Mounts Bay Rd by the river.

Free guided tours of Kings Park and the Botanic Garden, available all year, should be booked one month in advance (☎ 321 4801), but it's worth trying to get in even if you can only give a couple of days notice – you might be lucky. The park also has a number of bike tracks; bikes can be rented from Koala Bicycle Hire (☎ 321 3061) at the western side of the main car park for $3.50 per hour or $12 per day. An information centre, situated next to the car park, is open daily from 9.30 am to 3.30 pm. The park also has a restaurant with a pleasant coffee shop.

Catch bus No 33 from St George's Terrace to Kings Park or walk up Mount St from the city centre.

City Buildings

Near the corner of King St and St George's Terrace, the **Cloisters** date from 1858 and are noted for their beautiful brickwork. Originally a school, they have now been integrated into a modern office development. On the corner of St George's Terrace and Pier St is the **Deanery** which was built in 1859 and restored after a public appeal in 1980. It is one of the few existing cottage-style houses that survive from the period. Neither the Cloisters nor the Deanery are open to the public.

Opposite the Deanery, on St George's Terrace, is **Government House**, a Gothic-looking fantasy built between 1859 and 1864.

At the corner of St George's Terrace and William St is the grand and once extravagant **Palace Hotel**; it dates back to 1895 and is now a banking chamber.

In the Stirling Gardens off Barrack St is the old **courthouse**, next to the Supreme Court. One of the oldest buildings in Perth, it was built in Georgian style in 1836. Other old buildings include **Perth Town Hall** on the corner of Hay and Barrack Sts (1867-70); the **Central Government Buildings** on the corner of Barrack St and St George's Terrace, which can be recognised by their patterned

brick; the recently restored **His Majesty's Theatre** (originally opened in 1904) on the corner of King and Hay Sts; and the Gothic-style **Old Perth Boys' School**, which was built in 1854 and now houses a National Trust gift shop.

The distinctive **Barracks Arch**, at the western end of St George's Terrace, is all that remains of a barracks built in 1863 to house the Pensioner Guards of the British Army – discharged British Army soldiers who guarded convicts.

Parliament House

Tours of the Parliament buildings on Harvest Terrace can be arranged from Monday to Friday through the Parliamentary Information Officer (☎ 222 7222) – you will of course get a more extensive tour when Parliament is not in session. You can get there on bus Nos 3 or 6 from St George's Terrace or by the Green Clipper bus to Harvest Terrace.

Museums

On Francis St, north across the railway lines from the city centre, is the **Western Australian Museum**, which includes a gallery of Aboriginal history, a marine gallery, vintage cars, a 25-metre whale skeleton and a good collection of meteorites, the largest of which weighs 11 tonnes. (The Australian outback is a particularly good area for finding meteorites as there is little vegetation and they are unlikely to have been disturbed.)

The museum complex also includes Perth's original prison, built in 1856 and used until 1888. Admission to the museum is free and it is open from 10.30 am to 5 pm Monday to Friday and from 1 to 5 pm Saturday and Sunday.

The **Small World Museum**, at 12 Parliament Place, has the largest collection of miniatures in the country. The collection includes replica cars such as Formula 1 and Rolls Royces, model trains, fire engines, houses and scenes from fairy tales. It's open from 10 am to 5 pm Monday to Friday and from 2 to 5 pm on Saturday and Sunday (from April to October it is also open from

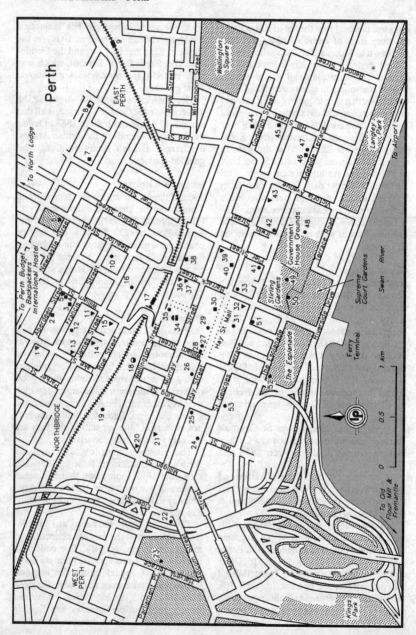

■ PLACES TO STAY

2 Aberdeen Hostel
3 Northbridge YHA Hostel
4 Britania YHA
  Backpackers' Hostel
6 New Beaufort Hotel
7 Newcastle YHA Hostel
30 Savoy Plaza Hotel
38 Grand Central Hotel
40 Regatta Hotel
44 Jewel House YMCA
45 Downtowner Lodge
46 Girls Friendly
   Society Lodge

▼ PLACES TO EAT

1 Mamma Maria's
5 Bar Italia
11 Brass Monkey Hotel
13 Northbridge Pavilion
14 Plaka Shish Kebab
15 Sylvana Pastry
20 Fast Eddy's
21 Shafto Lane Tavern
32 Granary
36 Gopal's
37 Ann's Malaysian Restaurant
39 Miss Maud's
43 Magic Apple

OTHER

8 Army Museum of Western Australia
9 East Perth Railway Station
  (Country & Interstate)
10 Western Australia Museum
12 YHA Office
16 Art Gallery of Western Australia
17 Central Perth Railway Station
18 Wellington St Bus Station
19 Entertainment Centre
22 Barrack's Arch
23 Parliament House
24 The Cloisters
25 His Majesty's Theatre
26 Thomas Cook
27 Ansett WA
28 Amex
29 Carillon Arcade
31 London Court
33 Perth Town Hall
34 GPO
35 Western Australian Tourist Centre
41 Deanery
42 Ansett WA & Ansett
47 RAC of Western Australia
48 Concert Hall
49 Government House
50 Supreme Court
51 Australian Airlines
52 Alan Green Plant Conservatory
53 Old Perth Boy's School

10 am to 5 pm on Sunday). To get there, catch a Green Clipper bus and alight at stop No 2.

The **Army Museum of Western Australia**, on the corner of Bulwer and Lord Sts, has a display of army memorabilia. It is open Sundays from 1 to 4.30 pm and admission is free (although donations are gratefully accepted). Bus Nos 41 to 43, 48 and 55 will get you there from bus stops 3 and 4 in Barrack St.

The **Fire Safety Education Centre & Museum**, on the corner of Irwin and Murray Sts, has displays on fire safety and fire-fighting equipment. Admission is free and it is open from 10 am to 3 pm Monday to Thursday.

Perth Zoo

Perth's popular zoo is set in attractive gardens across the river from the city at 20 Labouchere Rd, South Perth. It has a number of interesting collections including a nocturnal house which is open daily from noon to 3 pm, an Australian Wildlife Park, the only numbats on display in the world and a Conservation Discovery Centre. The zoo itself is open from 10 am to 5 pm daily and admission is $3. You can reach the zoo on bus No 36 (which leaves from bus stand No 40 on St George's Terrace) or by taking the ferry across the river from Barrack St jetty.

Art Galleries

The **Art Gallery of Western Australia** is housed in a modern building which runs from James St through to Roe St, behind the railway station. It has a very fine permanent exhibition of European, Australian and

Asian-Pacific art and a wide variety of temporary exhibitions. The gallery is open from 10 am to 5 pm daily, and admission is free.

The **Creative Native Gallery**, at 32 King St, has an excellent display of Aboriginal art and artefacts including jewellery, pottery and didgeridoos (long, tubular, deep-toned Aboriginal wind instruments). The **Dreamtime Gallery**, at 101 Lake St, Northbridge, also has some fine examples of Aboriginal art. Other galleries in Perth include **Gallery Australia**, at 96 Fitzgerald St, which has a collection of Australian art and, in Northbridge, the **Alexander Gallery** at 12 Aberdeen St.

Parks & Gardens
On the Esplanade, between the city and the river, is the **Alan Green Plant Conservatory**. It houses a tropical and semitropical controlled-environment display and is open from 10 am to 5 pm Monday to Saturday and from 2 to 6 pm Sunday; admission is free. Also close to the city, on the corner of St George's Terrace and Barrack St, are the **Supreme Court Gardens**, a popular place to eat lunch. In the summer, there are often outdoor concerts in the music shell at this park.

The **Queen's Gardens**, at the eastern end of Hay St, is a pleasant little park with lakes and bridges; get there on a Red Clipper bus. The lake in **Hyde Park**, Highgate, is popular for the water birds it attracts, and the park is the site for the annual Hyde Park Festival – catch bus No 60 from bus stand No 2 in Barrack St. **Lake Monger** in Wembley is another hang-out for local feathered friends, particularly Perth's famous black swans. Get there on bus Nos 90 or 91 from the Wellington St bus station. **Bold Park**, west of the city centre, is very popular with the locals. It is a large expanse of bushland with spectacular city and ocean views from Reabold Hill, and includes Perry Lakes.

Beaches
Perth residents claim that the city has the best beaches and surf of any Australian city. There are calm bay beaches on the Swan River at **Crawley** – catch bus No 201 from bus stand No 48 on St George's Terrace; **Peppermint Grove** – bus No 100 from central Fremantle; and **Como** – bus No 32 from bus stand No 35 in St George's Terrace. Or you can try a whole string of patrolled surf beaches on the Indian Ocean coast including Perth's very popular nude beach at **Swanbourne** – take bus No 207 from bus stand No 44 in St George's Terrace.

Some of the other surf beaches include **Cottesloe**, a very safe swimming beach – take bus No 72 from bus stand No 44 in St George's Terrace; **Port** – bus No 381 from Fremantle bus station; **City** – bus No 84 from Wellington St bus station; **Scarborough**, a wide, golden and very popular surf beach which is only for experienced swimmers on rough days – bus No 268 from Wellington St; **Leighton** – bus No 381 from Fremantle bus station; **Floreat** – bus No 91 from Wellington St; and **Trigg Island**, another surf beach that can be dangerous for swimming when rough. **Rottnest Island**, just off the coast of Fremantle, also has some beautiful beaches (see the Rottnest Island section later in this chapter).

Markets
There are many lively markets around Perth – ideal if you're into browsing and buying. The **Subiaco Pavilion**, on the corner of Roberts and Rokeby Rds near Subiaco Railway Station, is open from 10 am to 9 pm on Thursday and Friday, and from 10 am to 5 pm on Saturday and Sunday. Apart from an extensive international food hall, there are some interesting stalls including crafts, jewellery and clothes.

The **Wanneroo Markets** north of Perth at Prindiville Drive, Wangara, also have a large food hall and a variety of stalls selling goods such as plants, clothes, food, jewellery and crafts. It's open from 9 am to 6 pm on Saturday and Sunday.

Other markets include the historic **Fremantle Market** (see the Fremantle section later in this chapter) and the **Stock Rd Market**, in Bibra Lake south of Perth, which is open from 9 am to 5 pm every weekend.

Old Flour Mill

Across Narrows Bridge is one of Perth's landmarks: the finely restored Old Flour Mill, built in 1835. It's open from 1 to 5 pm Sunday, Monday, Wednesday and Thursday and from 1 to 4 pm Saturday; admission is free. On display in the mill are relics of the pioneering era. Ride to the mill on bus No 34 from St George's Terrace, or walk there along the river from the Mends St jetty.

Other Attractions

Between Hay St and St George's Terrace is the narrow **London Court**, a photographer's delight. Although it looks very Tudor English, it dates from just 1937. At one end of this shopping court St George and his dragon appear above the clock each quarter of an hour, while at the other end knights joust on horseback. Along the court are a number of touristy souvenir shops.

The **Scitech Discovery Centre** in the City West shopping centre in Railway Parade, West Perth, has a number of hands-on and large-scale exhibits such as a giant heart and lung and a game-playing robot. Well worth a visit, it is open from 10 am to 5 pm Monday to Friday and from 10 am to 6 pm on weekends; admission, however, is not cheap at $9 for adults and $5 for children.

Perth Suburbs

Armadale The **Pioneer World** at Armadale, 27 km south-east of the city, is a working model of a 19th-century village, with shops, public buildings, gold-field operations and tradespeople plying the skills of a bygone era. It's open from 10 am to 5 pm daily. Admission is $8.50. You can get to Armadale on bus No 219 from Pier St or a local train from Perth Railway Station.

Just beyond Armadale is the fascinating **Elizabethan Village** which includes replicas of Anne Hathaway's cottage and Shakespeare's birthplace in attractive gardens. It's open from 10 am to 5 pm daily and admission

is $3. It's a half-hour walk from the bus stop in Armadale.

The **History House Museum**, on Jull St, is a free museum in a 19th-century pioneer's house, with exhibits about Armadale's early settlers.

On Mills Rd in Martin you can ride a miniature railway through the **Cohunu Wildlife Park**, where there are animals such as koalas, emus, kangaroos and wombats in natural surroundings. There are also plenty of water birds and a large walk-in aviary at the park. Open from 10 am to 5 pm Wednesday to Sunday (daily during the school holidays), the park's about a 35-minute drive from Perth. There are a number of scenic areas in the countryside around Armadale including **Boulder Rock**, a pleasant picnic spot off the Brookton Highway, and the **Canning River**, off Thompson Rd in Roleystone.

Up the Swan River There are many attractions up the Swan River. On Maylands Peninsula, enclosed by a loop of the Swan River, is the beautifully restored **Tranby House**. Built in 1839, it is one of the oldest houses in Western Australia and a fine example of early colonial architecture. It's open from 2 to 5 pm Monday to Saturday and from 11 am to 1 pm and 2 to 5 pm Sunday; admission is $2 for adults and $1 for children.

The **Rail Transport Museum** on Railway Parade, Bassendean, has locomotives and all sorts of railway memorabilia; it is open from 1 to 5 pm on Sundays and public holidays.

The **Halls Museum**, at 105 Swan St, Guildford, has an enormous collection of Australiana and other items. It is housed in a building behind the 1840 Rose & Crown Hotel. It's open from 10 am to 4.30 pm daily except Monday and admission is $2.50. You can get to Guildford on bus No 306 from bus stand No 39 in St George's Terrace.

Other historic buildings in Guildford include the **Mechanics Hall**, in Meadow St, and the **Guildford Folk Museum & Gaol** which is open Sunday from 2 to 5 pm (March to December). **Woodbridge** in Third Ave,

Guildford, was built in 1855 and is a fully restored and beautifully furnished colonial mansion overlooking the river. It's open from 1 to 4 pm Monday to Saturday and from 11 am to 4 pm Sunday (closed Wednesday).

In West Swan is the **Caversham Wildlife Park & Zoo** which has a large collection of Australian animals and birds; it's open from 10 am to 5 pm daily.

The unusual **Crescent Moon Gallery**, at 51 The Crescent in Midland, has an eclectic collection of arts, crafts, books and tapes; it is open seven days a week. The **Gomboc Gallery**, in James Rd, Middle Swan, claims to be the largest private gallery in the state and features sculpture, paintings and printmaking. It is open Wednesday to Sunday from 10 am to 5 pm.

The **Swan Valley vineyards** are dotted along the river from Guildford right up to the Upper Swan. Many of them are open for tastings and cellar sales. Olive Farm Winery, 77 Great Eastern Highway in South Guildford, is the oldest in the region. Houghton Winery on Dale Rd, Middle Swan, was established later but produced the first commercial vintage in 1842.

The river cuts a narrow gorge through the Darling Range at **Walyunga National Park** in Upper Swan, off the Great Northern Highway. There are walking tracks along the river and it's a popular picnic spot.

Other Suburbs In Subiaco, the **Museum of Childhood**, at 160 Hamersley Rd, is part of the Western Australia College of Advanced Education. It houses an interesting collection of toys and a classroom from the 1920s. It is open from 10 am to 3 pm Monday to Friday and from 2 to 5 pm on Sunday. Across the Canning River towards Jandakot Airport, on Bull Creek Drive, Bull Creek, there is the excellent **Aviation Museum** with a collection of aviation memorabilia. It's open from 11 am to 4 pm daily and admission is $3.50. Take bus No 105 from bus stand No 34 on St George's Terrace to Booragoon bus station and transfer to bus Nos 198 or 199 to the museum.

In Melville, just off the Canning Highway

on the way to Fremantle, is the **Wireless Hill Park & Telecommunications Museum**. It has a variety of exhibits, ranging from early pedal-operated radio equipment used in the outback to modern NASA communications equipment. It's open weekends from 2 to 5 pm.

Further down the Canning Highway towards Fremantle, near the corner of Stock Rd, at 7 Baal St, Palmyra, is the **Miller Bakehouse Museum**, which has a rare old wood-fired baking oven. The **Claremont Museum**, in the Freshwater Bay School at 66 Victoria Ave, Claremont, concentrates on local history.

In Cannington, on the road to Armadale, is **Woodloes**, a restored colonial home of 1874. The small **Liddelow Homestead** in Kenwick, is also a restored homestead. Yet another early home is the mud-brick and shingle **Stirk's Cottage** in Kalamunda, built in 1881.

Adventure World, 15 km south of Perth at 179 Progress Drive, Bibra Lake, is a large amusement park with rides, a zoo, the country's largest swimming pool and various other diversions. It's open daily from 10 am to 5 pm in the summer (November to April) and school holidays. The $16.50 admission charge covers all the attractions, except the shooting gallery. Transperth bus No 600 departs every day at 10 am from the Wellington St bus station to Adventure World.

Cables Water Park, at Troode St in Spearwood (just off Rockingham Rd, south of the city), is a water skier's heaven. Cables haul skiers along the water at 20 to 50 km/h. It is open daily from 10 am to 6 pm, and an hour's skiing costs around $10. The park also has a swimming pool, barbecue areas and a giant water slide.

North of the city, **Underwater World** at Hillarys Boat Harbour, West Coast Drive, Hillarys, is an underwater tunnel aquarium displaying thousands of marine species including sharks and stingrays. It is open daily from 9 am to 5 pm.

On Prindiville Drive, Wanneroo, there's a miniature model village at the **Gumnut Factory** which also has a craft shop and a museum with a collection of memorabilia such as old enamel signs, bottles and number plates.

Organised Tours & Cruises

The Western Australia Tourist Centre has the most detailed information about the many tours around Perth; they can also book them for you. Half-day city tours of Perth and Fremantle are about $20, and for around $30 you can get tours to the Swan Valley wineries, Cohuna Wildlife Park, or Underwater World and the northern beaches.

Other day tours, to places like Avon Valley, Mandurah, New Norcia or the south coast, range from $50 to $70. Some of the larger tour operators include Feature Tours (☎ 479 4131) and Great Western Tours (☎ 328 4542).

The one-day Beach Pony Express tour run by Kookaburra Adventures (☎ 474 2526) has been recommended by travellers. The $72 tour includes lunch, a half-day horseback adventure (including a beach ride) and time at Yanchep National Park.

A favourite with imbibers of the amber liquid is the free tour of the Swan Brewery (☎ 350 0650). The tour takes 1½ hours (followed by a couple of complimentary beers) and departs at 10 am from Mondays to Thursday and 2.30 pm on Monday and Wednesday. The brewery is at 25 Baile Rd, Canning Vale, but you must make reservations.

There are daily trips to the Pinnacles with Safari Treks (☎ 322 2188) for $78. Travelabout Outback Tours (☎ 242 2243) also have one-day tours to the Pinnacles as well as a four-day camping tour to Kalbarri and Monkey Mia, a five-day tour to the southwest and others. All Terrain Safaris (☎ 572 3456) have a number of 4WD safaris including those to Pinnacles/Monkey Mia (four days; $249) and the north-west (14 days; $795).

There are also a number of cruise companies that operate tours from the Barrack St jetty, including Captain Cook Cruises (☎ 325 3341), Golden Sun (☎ 523 9916) and Boat Torque (☎ 325 6033). Tours include scenic cruises of the Swan River, winery visits, trips to Fremantle and lunch and dinner cruises.

From September to May, the Transperth MV *Countess II* departs daily except Saturday at 2 pm from the Barrack St jetty on a three-hour cruise towards the Upper Swan River; the cost is $10. Golden Sun also have a three-hour Upper Swan cruise for $16.50; and Captain Cook Cruises have a three-hour Scenic River Cruise around Perth and Fremantle for $18.

Festivals

Every year around February/March the Festival of Perth offers entertainment in the form of music, drama, dance and films. The Royal Perth Show takes place every September.

Places to Stay

Perth has a wide variety of accommodation catering for all tastes and price brackets. The main area for budget accommodation is Northbridge, while hotels and motels of all standards and holiday flats are spread throughout the city and suburbs. If you prefer to camp or hire an on-site caravan, there are numerous caravan parks scattered around the metropolitan area.

Camping Perth, like many other large cities, is not well endowed with camp sites at a convenient distance from the city centre. There are, however, many caravan parks in the suburbs, many within a few km of the centre. Some of these include (with distances from the city centre):

Careniup Caravan Park (14 km north)
  467 Beach Rd, Gwelup – camping $10 for two, on-site vans from $25 (☎ 447 6665)
Central Caravan Park (seven km east)
  34 Central Ave, Redcliffe – camping $15 for two, on-site vans from $130 a week (☎ 277 5696)
Guildford Caravan Park (19 km north-east)
  372 Swan Rd, Guildford – camping $13 for two, on-site vans from $28 (☎ 274 2828)
Kenlorn Caravan Park (nine km south-east)
  229 Welshpool Rd, Queens Park – camping $15 for two (weekly rates available), on-site vans from $130 per week (☎ 458 2604)

Starhaven Caravan Park (14 km north-west) 14-18 Pearl Parade, Scarborough – camping $13 for two, on-site vans from $23 (☎ 341 1770)

Hostels There has been an explosion in the number of hostels around Perth in recent times – most are reasonably central.

Northbridge & City Centre The busy, friendly and slightly run-down *Newcastle Youth Hostel* (☎ 328 1135), at 60-62 Newcastle St, is about a 15-minute walk from the city centre; just go straight up Barrack or William Sts, crossing the railway line, until you hit Newcastle St, then turn right. The cost is $10 a night and office hours are from 8 to 10.30 am and from 5 to 10 pm.

Northbridge Youth Hostel (☎ 328 7794), at 46 Francis St, is in an old guesthouse near the corner of William St, a little closer to the city. It has small dorms, costs $10 per night and the office is open from 8 am to noon and from 5 to 10 pm. Both these hostels have bicycles for hire.

Around the corner at 253 William St is the large and central *Britannia YHA Backpackers' Hostel* (☎ 328 6121), with dorms at $10 a person and basic rooms from $16/25 a single/double for members and from $18/28 for nonmembers. The better rooms are at the back on the verandah – the others are lit by a skylight. Make sure you ask for a room away from the main hallways as they can get very noisy.

Perth Budget Backpackers' International Hostel (☎ 328 9468), at 342 Newcastle St, has a comfortable lounge and good kitchen facilities. Dorm beds are $10 per night or $65 per week, and they will pick up travellers from around the city centre. The hostel also has well-equipped, self-contained flats in the area from $28 per night. They have just opened a 24-hour booking service (☎ 227 1112); they also rent cars at a reasonable rate.

Rory's Backpackers (☎ 328 9958), at 194 Brisbane St, is further north of the city centre than other hostels. However, this nice renovated colonial house is very clean and has a pleasant garden and barbecue area. They also have a ski boat to take hostellers out on the water in the summer months. Bus Nos 18 to 20 travel there from bus stand No 6 on Barrack St – ask for the Northbridge Hotel, which is next door to the hostel. Dorms cost from $10 a night.

A good alternative is the *North Lodge* (☎ 227 7588) at 225 Beaufort St. It's clean, friendly and has all the usual facilities and comfortable beds for $10 a person. The free Blue Clipper bus from Barrack St will get you there on weekdays, and many other buses, like Nos 59 or 60, also go that way.

Perth Travellers Lodge (☎ 328 6667) at 156 Aberdeen St is run by the management of the now closed Top Notch Hostel. The hostel is actually made up of two recently renovated houses, one for males and one for females, and dorm beds are $9 per night or $55 per week. There is another Perth Travellers Lodge further east at 44 Monger St, Northbridge, at similar rates.

Aberdeen Hostel (☎ 227 6137), at 79 Aberdeen St, is central but the least appealing since it's crowded and also somewhat neglected. Dorms are $10 per night or $60 a week and twin shares are $12 per night or $70 a week. Also in the Northbridge area is *Cheviot Lodge* (☎ 227 6817) at 30 Bulwer St. Open 24 hours, it is close to the interstate rail terminal, provides a free pick-up service from Wellington St bus station and hires out bicycles. There are no bunk beds, and accommodation is available from $12 per night.

Elsewhere Hostels in the suburbs around Perth include *Westhaven House* (☎ 384 4738), at 150 Marine Parade, Cottesloe (near North Cottesloe Beach), with dormitory beds for $9 per night and twin share from 12.50 per person – catch bus No 72 from bus stand No 44 on St George's Terrace.

Mandarin Gardens Hostel (☎ 341 5431), at 20 Wheatcroft St in Scarborough, has dormitory accommodation from $10 per night and private rooms from $16 per night. Facilities include bicycle hire, a swimming pool and TV in all dwelling units. The hostel is also within walking distance (500 metres) of popular Scarborough Beach.

Ladybird Lodge (☎ 444 7359), at 195 Oxford St in Leederville (about four km west of the city centre), has dormitory accommodation for $10 per night and singles/doubles for $16/26 per night.

In Scarborough, *Scarborough Beach Holiday Accommodation* (☎ 341 6655), on the corner of the Brighton and West Coast highways, has dorms for $10 a person or $56 a week; doubles in fully self-contained units are $34 a night – meals are also available. Catch bus Nos 268 and 269 from the Wellington St bus station.

Beware of hostels offering to pay your taxi fare from the airport, wrote a traveller recently. You should check carefully to make sure that there isn't a minimum-stay requirement.

Colleges College accommodation may be available during the vacations at the University of Western Australia (UWA) and at Murdoch University. *Kingswood College* (☎ 389 0389) at Hampden Rd, Crawley, has beds including linen at $60 per week and $11 per night (first night linen $5 extra) in single student rooms – laundry and kitchen facilities are available. Catch bus No 103 from bus stand No 42 in St George's Terrace.

Other UWA colleges to try include *St Columba* (☎ 386 7177), *Currie Hall* (☎ 380 2771), *St Thomas More College* (☎ 386 8712), *St George's College* (☎ 382 5555) and *St Catherine's* (☎ 386 5847).

At Murdoch University (☎ 332 2211), there are flats at *Yarallda Court*; one week is the minimum stay.

Y's & Guesthouses The excellent *Jewel House YMCA* (☎ 325 8488), at 180 Goderich St (as Murray St becomes after Victoria Square), has 206 comfortable, clean and modern rooms. It is next to the Perth Dental Hospital about a 15-minute walk from the city centre – the Red Clipper bus (west) passes the Jewel House from 8.30 am to 4 pm Monday to Friday. Singles/doubles are $28/36 and family rooms $55; weekly rates are six times the daily rate. Breakfast (from $4.75) and evening meals (from $5 to $7) are

available in the ground-floor cafe, and there are sandwiches at lunch time. The office is open 24 hours a day and there's free baggage storage.

The *Rita Jones Centre YWCA* (☎ 321 2479), Suite 2, 17 Ord St, West Perth, has comfortable female-only singles/doubles at $15/20 per night and from $65 per week. Facilities include TV lounge, a laundry and a large kitchen. You can get there on a Green Clipper bus.

Centrally located and good value is the *Downtowner Lodge* (☎ 325 6973), at 63 Hill St, opposite the Perth Mint. The 13 rooms are clean and pleasant, and it's a very quiet, friendly, nonsmoking place with a TV lounge and car park. Rooms cost $17 for one night in twin rooms ($11 a night for more than one night) and $65 a week. The *Girls' Friendly Society Lodge* (☎ 325 4043), at 240 Adelaide Terrace, accommodates women only at $25 a night with breakfast and dinner.

Hotels There are quite a number of old-fashioned hotels around the centre of Perth. The *Grand Central Hotel* (☎ 325 5638), at 379 Wellington St, is basic (no sinks in the room) and dingy but the location is good. Singles are $25/80 per day/week, doubles $35/130. In the Mall is the *Savoy Plaza Hotel* (☎ 325 9588) at 636 Hay St. It has a wide range of rooms; singles/doubles with breakfast and shared bathroom cost from $32/53. The position is great but it can become noisy at times.

Regatta Hotel (☎ 325 5155), also centrally located at 560 Hay St, has friendly staff and simple but clean singles/doubles for $32/48 with shared bathroom and $40/50 with facilities.

Over in Northbridge, the *New Beaufort Hotel* (☎ 328 7566), at 167 Beaufort St, is a 15-minute walk from the city centre and has B&B for $30/50.

In western Perth, the *OBH*, or Ocean Beach Hotel (☎ 384 2555), is a semilegendary hotel right on Cottesloe Beach at the corner of Eric St and Marine Parade. Spacious rooms with fridge, TV and tea/coffee making facilities cost from $30/40; the counter meals, like the rooms, are also recommended.

For midrange hotels around the city centre, try the *Inntown Hotel* (☎ 325 2133), at 70 Pier St, with rooms for $65/70; the *Chateau Commodore* (☎ 325 0461), at 417 Hay St, on the corner of Victoria Ave, with rooms from $85; or *Sullivan's Hotel* (☎ 321 8022), 166 Mounts Bay Rd at the base of Kings Park, with rooms from $75.

Perth also has its fair share of luxury hotels, including the *Burswood Hotel* (☎ 362 7777), off the Great Eastern Highway, Victoria Park, in the casino complex; the *Parmelia Hilton* (☎ 322 3622) on Mill St; and the *Sheraton* (☎ 325 0501) at 207 Adelaide Terrace. All have rooms starting from around $180 per night.

Motels & Holiday Flats Perth and the surrounding suburbs have an abundance of motels and holiday flats (see the Western Australian Accommodation Listing available from the tourist office for more information); a selection follows.

City Waters Lodge (☎ 325 1566), at 118 Terrace Rd down by the river, is conveniently central and good value with cooking facilities, bathroom, colour TV, laundry and so on. Daily costs are $55/60 for singles/doubles; triples and family units are also available. North of the city centre at 166 Palmerston St are the self-contained *Brownelea Holiday Units* (☎ 328 4840) at $38 a double. The *Adelphi Apartments* (☎ 322 4666), at 130A Mounts Bay Rd, has well-equipped units for $56/61.

North-east of Perth is the *Pacific Motel* (☎ 328 5599) at 111 Harold St, Mt Lawley, which has singles/doubles for $40/48.

Across the bridge, on the South Perth side, is the *Canning Bridge Auto Lodge* (☎ 364 2511), at 891 Canning Highway, Applecross, which has rooms from $50. The *Como Beach Motel* (☎ 367 7955), at 2 Preston St, Como, costs $39/42.

Places to Eat
Food Centres Perth pioneered food centres in Australia and they're great places to eat.

Essentially, they're a group of kitchens which share a dining room. You can get your meal from one place, your partner can eat from another, you can have drinks from a third and select dessert from a fourth. This terrific Asian idea has really taken off, and crowded food halls prove that it's a popular alternative to fast food.

The *Down Under Food Hall* in the Hay St Mall, downstairs and near the corner of William St, has stalls offering Chinese, Mexican, Thai, Indian and many other types of food. At the Singapore booth, a tasty meal sets you back from just $4 to $6. This food centre is open Monday to Wednesday from 8 am to 7 pm and Thursday to Saturday from 8 am to 9 pm. It's very busy in the evenings from Thursday to Saturday, when there is live entertainment .

The *Carillon Food Hall*, in the Carillon Arcade on Hay St Mall, is slightly more up-market than the Down Under Food Hall and has the same international flavour with Italian, Middle Eastern and Chinese food from $5 to $7. It also has sandwich shops, a seafood stall and fast-food outlets. The Carillon Arcade is open until 9 pm every evening, although some of the food stalls do close around 7 pm.

The large *Northbridge Pavilion* at the corner of Lake and James Sts is another good-value international food hall with Japanese, Italian, Indian, Thai, vegetarian and Chinese food. Open from Wednesday to Sunday, it has some outdoor seating and a couple of bars; the juices at *Naturals* are truly wonderful after a day of pounding the pavements.

City The city centre is especially good for lunches and light meals. The *Magic Apple* wholefood kitchen, 445 Hay St, does delicious sandwiches in pita bread, cakes and fresh fruit juices to cure all ills (including celery and carrot for asthma, radish and celery for gall-bladder complaints, celery and parsley for fever and gout, apple and carrot for colds, and parsley and grape for anaemia).

The busy *Bernadi's*, at 528 Hay St, has

good sandwiches, quiches, home-made soups and salads. The *Hayashi Japanese BBQ*, at 107 Pier St, has excellent value set lunches for around $10. At 117 Murray St, between Pier and Barrack Sts, is a pleasant and very reasonably priced little Japanese restaurant called *Jun & Tommy's*.

The *Granary*, downstairs at 37 Barrack St (south of Hay St), has an extensive range of vegetarian dishes from $4 to $6 for lunch – the dinner menu is more expensive. At 137 Barrack St, the cheap and popular *Anne's Malaysian Restaurant*, has delicious laksa (coconut-based noodle soup), and noodle and rice dishes from $5.

Across the road, at 129 Barrack St, is the Hare Krishna *Gopal's* restaurant, which has an excellent $4 all-you-can-eat vegetarian meal from noon to 2.30 pm on weekdays. Also in Barrack St is one of Perth's real surprises, *Mr Samurai* at No 83. Open Monday to Saturday from 11 am to 6 pm (and Thursday until 8.30 pm), they serve a delicious beef or tempura with rice for $3.50, okonomiyaki (Japanese-style vegetables and prawns with okonomi sauce) for $3 or fried chicken with rice for $4 – highly recommended.

In the Carillon Arcade, the *Pancake Parlour* has a wide variety of pancakes and other meals from $8 to $12. The *Venice Cafe* at the St George's Terrace end of the Trinity Arcade (shop No 201) is a pleasant European-style cafe with tables out the front and light meals such as lasagna, quiche, home-made pies and salad from $4 to $6. They also make excellent coffee.

Perth has the usual selection of counter meals in the city centre area. *Sassella's Tavern*, in the City Arcade, off Hay St, does bistro meals from $8 to $11. The *Savoy Tavern*, under the Savoy Plaza Hotel, at 636 Hay St, has basic pub fare such as roast beef and vegetables and fish & chips for lunch from $4 to $6.

Toward the western (Kings Park) end of the city centre, there's a string of places, including the popular *Fast Eddy's* on the corner of Murray and Milligan Sts. Open 24 hours a day, Fast Eddy's is split up into a cafe

which serves breakfast and light snacks from $4 to $8 and a takeaway section that sells an interesting selection of burgers from $3.

Shafto Lane between Murray and Hay Sts has a number of eateries including *Fasta Pasta* with a wide selection of pasta dishes from $7.50 to $8.50; *Bobby Shafto's* which has a four-course meal after 5.30 pm for only $10; and the *Shafto Lane Tavern*.

If you like Indian food, head for *Taj Tandoor* at 442 Murray St. The meals are not cheap ($14.50 for a lunch-time smorgasbord, and $18 to $21 for an evening smorgasbord) but the food is authentic and tasty.

The *Kings Park Garden Restaurant*, good for a splurge, has great views over the city and the river. A complete dinner will come to around $30, and there's live music as well. Lunch and morning and afternoon teas are also served. Next to the restaurant is a snack bar with takeaway food.

Northbridge North of the city centre, the area bounded by William, Lake and Newcastle Sts is full of ethnic restaurants to suit all tastes and budgets. It is also an area undergoing rapid development due to its recent popularity. Listed below are some suggested places to eat, but this list is by no means exhaustive. The best bet is just to walk around and take in the sights and smells – you will soon find something to your liking at an appropriate price.

Kim Anh, at 178 William St near the railway station, is a friendly Vietnamese BYO place with an extensive menu including vegetarian food; main meals range from $7 to $9. Next door, at 182 William St, is the reasonably priced *Tak Chee* restaurant, a favourite amongst the locals – always a good sign. They serve delicious Penang-style rice and noodle dishes for around $4 to $6.

Across the street, at No 175, is the *Linh-Phong* restaurant with a wide variety of meals from $6 to $8. Nearby at 188 William St is the moderately priced and popular *Romany's*, one of the city's really long-running Italian places.

At 197 William St is *Sylvana Pastry*, a comfortable Lebanese coffee bar with an amazing selection of those sticky Middle Eastern pastries which look, and usually taste, delicious. If you like Japanese food, *Unkai*, at 219 William St, is highly recommended; main meals start from around $12.50.

On the corner of Aberdeen and William Sts is the busy *Bar Italia* which serves excellent coffee and light meals including a good selection of pasta dishes from $7.50 (starter size) to $9.50 (large); it is open from breakfast time until 1 am.

Mamma Maria's, at 105 Aberdeen St on the corner of Lake St, has a pleasant ambience and a reputation as one of Perth's best Italian eateries. Its main courses are priced from $11.50. There are a couple of pizza places on Lake St – *Uncle Vincent's* at No 71 and *Young Joe's* at No 60 – which serve tasty pizza to eat in or take away.

Plaka Shish Kebab, at 89 James St, has good souvlaki and kebabs from $4.50 but it is somewhat sterile in atmosphere. Further away, at 193 Brisbane St, is *Ly Tao*, a Vietnamese restaurant opposite the Backpackers' Inn. It has excellent chicken, beef, seafood and noodle dishes from $6 to $8.

Entertainment

Perth has plenty of pubs, discos and nightclubs. The Thursday edition of the *West Australian* has an informative entertainment lift-out called the *Revue*. The *X-press*, a weekly music magazine available free at record shops and other outlets, has a gig guide and other entertainment information. Northbridge is definitely the place to go after dark; the city centre is generally pretty dead.

Cinemas & Theatres The Lumiere Cinema, in the Perth Entertainment Centre, and the Astor, on the corner of Beaufort and Walcott Sts in Mt Lawley, usually have quality films. Popular theatres include His Majesty's Theatre on the corner of King and Hay Sts, the Regal Theatre at 474 Hay St in Subiaco and the Hole in the Wall at the Subiaco Theatre Centre, 180 Hamersley Rd, Subiaco. Sessions times and programmes for these and other city and suburban cinemas and theatres are available daily in the *West Australian* newspaper.

Concerts & Recitals The Perth Concert Hall in St George's Terrace and the large Entertainment Centre in Wellington St are venues for concerts and recitals by local and international acts.

Pubs & Live Music Three popular places for interesting live music in Northbridge are Rockwells, at 160A James St, the Brass Monkey Tavern, on the corner of William and James Sts, and the Aberdeen Hotel at 84 Aberdeen St. The graffiti-covered Limbo's nightclub, at 232 William St, is popular with backpackers.

If you're into country music, the Western Alehouse has bands most nights of the week at 530 Kalamundra Rd, High Wycombe. For folk music and jazz, check the entertainment guides mentioned earlier.

Perth has the usual pub-rock circuit with varying cover charges depending on the gig. Popular venues include Raffles on the Canning Highway, and the Stadium inside the Herdsman Hotel on Herdsman Parade in Wembley.

Discos & Nightclubs In the city centre is Mangoes, a piano bar with music and exotic cocktails at 101 Murray St, and F-Scott's nightclub at 237 Hay St. At 397 Murray St, on the corner of Shafto Lane, there's the Shafto Lane Tavern, which is usually crowded and noisy later on with bands or a disco. Next door, at No 393, is Pinocchio's nightclub, which has a cover charge: the amount depends on the night and the band playing.

Spectator Sports The people of Perth, like most other Australians, are parochial in their support of local sporting teams. The West Coast Eagles, Perth's representatives in the Australian Football League, and the Perth Wildcats in the National Basketball League regularly play interstate teams in Perth. Check the *West Australian* newspaper for game details.

Your education in Australian culture is not complete without seeing at least one game of Aussie Rules football, and Perth is a good place to catch it.

Casino On an artificial island en route to the airport, off the Great Western Highway, Victoria Park, is Perth's glitzy Burswood Casino, open all day, every day. Its setup seems pretty similar to other Australian casinos with gaming tables (such as roulette and blackjack), a two-up gallery, Kino, poker machines and extensive off-course betting.

Things to Buy
Perth has a number of excellent outlets for Aboriginal arts & crafts including the Aboriginal Artists Gallery at 251 St George's Terrace (right up at the Kings Park end of town), the Creative Native gallery, at 32 King St, and the Dreamtime Art Gallery, 101 Lake St in Northbridge. Other local crafts can be found at the various markets around town – see the Markets section earlier in this chapter.

For camping and climbing equipment, there's Paddy Pallin at 891 Hay St and, across the road, Mountain Designs at 862 Hay St.

Getting There & Away
Air Australian Airlines (☎ 323 3333) and Ansett (☎ 323 1111) have flights to and from Sydney, Melbourne, Brisbane, Adelaide, Darwin and Alice Springs. Some Sydney and Melbourne flights go direct, and some via Adelaide or, in the case of Sydney, via Melbourne.

Discounted return airfares are presently in a state of flux, but you should at least be able to get return tickets between Perth and Adelaide for around $435, Melbourne $510, Sydney $560 and Brisbane $635. These fares, however, may be subject to conditions such as payment at least 21 days in advance, a minimum stay away and cancellation penalties – check with the various airlines when booking flights. With the deregulation of the domestic airline industry, it is well worth checking the daily newspapers for frequently

offered special fares which can be substantially less than the already discounted fares mentioned above.

Ansett and Australian Airlines also have flights to Perth from North Queensland via Alice Springs. Apex return fares from Alice Springs are $590, and $773 from Cairns. Darwin to Perth flights go via Alice Springs or Port Hedland – Ansett WA fly from Darwin to Perth along the coast daily; the Apex return fare from Perth to Darwin via Alice Springs is $742.

Skywest (☎ 478 9898) at 140 St George's Terrace are an associate of Australian Airlines and fly to Western Australia centres such as Albany, Esperance, Kalgoorlie, Geraldton and Port Hedland. Mid-State Air (☎ 277 4022) have regular flights from Perth to Kalgoorlie.

Bus Bus Australia and Greyhound/Pioneer have daily bus services from Adelaide to Perth. Fares are $157 with Bus Australia and the trip takes about 35 hours. Bus Australia not only charge slightly less but also have more stopover options. Other typical one-way prices from Perth are Melbourne $200, Sydney $221 and Brisbane $261.

Bus Australia (☎ 325 5488) have an office at the Perth Railway Station in Wellington St. Greyhound/Pioneer (☎ 328 6677) operate from the Westrail Centre, West Parade, East Perth (Interstate Railway Station). The journey from Perth to Darwin along the coast takes around 56 hours by bus and costs $290. Greyhound also operates a service to Darwin via the more direct, inland route through Newman.

Westrail operate bus services to a number of Western Australia centres including Albany ($31.80), Augusta ($26.70), Bunbury and Collie ($14.80), Hyden (Wave Rock) ($27; twice weekly), Esperance ($48), Geraldton ($33) and Meekatharra ($61).

Train Along with the Ghan to Alice Springs, the long Indian-Pacific run is one of Australia's great railway journeys – a 65-hour trip between the Pacific Ocean on one side of the continent and the Indian Ocean on the other. Travelling this way you see Australia at ground level and by the end of the journey you really appreciate the immensity of the country.

From Sydney, you cross New South Wales to Broken Hill and then continue on to Port Pirie in South Australia and across the Nullarbor. From Port Pirie to Kalgoorlie, the seemingly endless crossing of the virtually uninhabited centre takes nearly 30 hours, including the 'long straight' on the Nullarbor – at 478 km this is the longest straight stretch of railway line in the world. Unlike the trans-Nullarbor road, which runs south of the Nullarbor along the coast of the Great Australian Bight, the railway line crosses the Nullarbor Plain. From Kalgoorlie, it's a straightforward run into Perth.

To Perth, fares from Adelaide are $412 for an economy sleeper, $545 for a 1st-class sleeper or $165 in an economy seat with no meals; from Melbourne $454 economy sleeper, $690 1st-class sleeper or $207 seat only; and Sydney $638 economy, $835 1st class or $220 seat only.

Caper (advance-purchase) fares offer good reductions (around 30%) if you book at least seven days in advance. Melbourne and Adelaide passengers connect with the Indian-Pacific at Port Pirie. Cars can be transported between Adelaide and Perth ($285) and most other major cities.

The distance from Sydney to Perth is 3961 km. You can break your journey at any stop along the way and continue on later as long as you complete the one-way trip within two months; return tickets are valid for up to six months. Westbound, the Indian Pacific departs Sydney on Monday, Thursday and Saturday. Heading east, the train departs Perth on Sunday, Tuesday and Thursday. Try to book at least a month in advance.

The main difference between economy and 1st-class sleepers is that 1st-class compartments are available as singles or twins, economy as twins only. First-class twins have showers and toilets; 1st-class singles have toilets only, with showers at the end of the carriage. In the economy-seating compartments, the showers and toilets are at the end of the carriage. Meals are included in the fare for 1st-class and economy-berth passengers but not for economy-seat passengers. First-class passengers also have a lounge compartment complete with piano.

Between Adelaide and Perth you can also travel on the weekly Trans-Australian. Fares are the same as the Indian-Pacific fares, and the trip takes 38 hours.

The only rail services within Western Australia are the Prospector from Perth to Kalgoorlie and the Australind from Perth to Bunbury – see the Kalgoorlie and Bunbury Getting There & Away sections for details. The trains from the east coast and the Western Australia services all run to or from the Westrail terminal in East Perth, as do the Westrail buses. Westrail bookings can be made by phone (☎ 326 2222), or through the Western Australia Tourist Centre in Forrest Place.

Hitching The hostel notice boards are worth checking for lifts to points around the country. Also check the alternative-lifestyle notice board in the Environment Centre of Western Australia at 794 Hay St.

If you're hitching out of Perth to the north or east, take a train to Midland. For travel south, take a train to Armadale. Trans-Nullarbor hitching is not that easy, and the fierce competition between bus companies and discounted airfares have made these forms of travel much more attractive.

Getting Around

Perth has a central public transport organisation called Transperth which operates buses, trains and ferries. There are Transperth information offices in the City Arcade (off the Hay St Mall) and at the Wellington St bus station, which can provide advice about getting around Perth and supply a system map ($1) and timetables. Both offices are open from 7.30 am to 5.30 pm Monday to Friday and from 7.30 am to 3 pm on Saturday (☎ 221 1211 between 6 am and 9 pm any day).

Top: Perth city, WA (PS)
Left: London Court, Perth, WA (RN)
Right: Old minehead, Kalgoorlie, WA (TW)

Top: The Pinnacles, Cervantes National Park, WA (RN)
Left: Wave Rock, Hyden, WA (RN)
Right: Japanese pearl diver's grave, Broome, WA (TW)

Free Transit Zone A free transit zone including all Transperth bus and trains is provided seven days a week within the central city area – from Northbridge in the north to the river in the south, and from Kings Park in the west to the Causeway in the east.

To/From the Airport Perth's airport is busy night and day. The city's isolation from the east coast and the airport's function as an international arrival point mean planes arrive and depart at all hours.

The domestic and international terminals are 10 km apart and taxi fares to the city are around $12 and $16 respectively. The privately run Perth Airport Bus (☎ 250 2838) meets all incoming domestic and international flights and provides transport to the city centre, hotels and hostels. Although they claim to meet all flights, some travellers have reported that sometimes it doesn't turn up – if this occurs late at night, a taxi into the city is probably your best option.

The airport bus costs $5 from the domestic terminal and $6 from the international terminal. To the airport terminals, there are scheduled runs every couple of hours from 4.45 am to 10.30 pm. Call them for hotel and hostel pick-ups and timetable information.

Alternatively, you can get into the city for just $1.40 on Transperth bus No 338 to William St. It departs from the domestic terminal every hour or so (more frequently at peak times) from 5.30 am to 11 pm on weekdays and for nearly as long on Saturdays; Sunday services are less frequent. To the domestic terminal, it leaves from bus stand No 37 on William St.

Bus There are five free City Clipper services which operate every 20 minutes or so from 7 am to 6 pm Monday to Friday. The Yellow Clipper and a bus following a shortened Red Clipper route also operate on Saturday mornings. All clipper services except the Blue Clipper pass through the Wellington St bus station.

Red Clipper (East & West)
   These make a loop up and down St George's Terrace-Adelaide Terrace and Wellington St.
Yellow Clipper
   These operate around the very central area of the city.
Blue Clipper
   These run between Northbridge and the Esplanade along Barrack and William Sts, then down Beaufort St.
Green Clipper
   These travel between the city centre and West Perth.

On regular buses, a short ride of two sections costs 65c. Anything longer is a zone ticket which allows you unlimited travel within a zone for two hours from the time of issue; it can be used on Transperth buses, trains and ferries. One-zone tickets costs $1.10, two zones $1.40 and three zones $1.65. Zone 1 includes the city centre and the inner suburbs (including Subiaco and Claremont), and Zone 2 extends all the way to Fremantle, 20 km from the city centre.

You can also get a Sightseer ticket from one ($4.60) to five ($19.40) days that will allow you to travel on all Transperth buses, ferries and trains around the city or as far as Yanchep or Mandurah – it also offers discounts on some tourist attractions. They can be obtained from the Western Australia Tourist Centre in Forrest Place or the Transperth information offices. A Multirider ticket gives you 10 journeys for the price of nine.

The Perth Tram doesn't run on rails – it's a bus that takes you around some of Perth's main attractions (such as the city, Kings Park, Barrack St jetty and the casino) in 1½ hours for $9. You also have the option of just doing part of the tour; there's a commentary to explain the sights. The 'tram' leaves from 124 Murray St (near Barrack St) six times a day, seven days a week (☎ 481 7685).

Train Transperth operates suburban train lines to Armadale, Fremantle and Midlands from around 6 am to 11.30 pm on weekdays with reduced services on weekends. All trains leave from the city station on Wellington St. Your rail ticket can also be used on

Transperth buses and ferries within the ticket's area of validity.

Car If you are travelling by car around Perth, there are a couple of things to be wary of. Firstly, driving in the city centre takes a little bit of getting used to as some of the streets are one-way and many street signs are not prominent.

Secondly, petrol stations are open on a roster basis after about 6 pm. To avoid chasing a continuous trail of roster signs planted on old car tyres in the middle of suburban Perth intersections, fill up during the day or see the daily list of open roster stations in the *West Australian* newspaper.

Rental Cars Hertz (☎ 321 7777), Budget (☎ 322 1100), Avis (☎ 325 7677) and Thrifty (☎ 481 1999) are all represented in Perth, along with a string of cheaper local operators including:

Bateman Car Rental
    789 Wellington St, with cars from $28 per day including 100 km (☎ 322 2592)
Econo-Car
    133 Pier St, which has cars from $250 per week with unlimited km (☎ 328 6888)
Bayswater Car Rental
    160 Adelaide Terrace, hires small cars from $25 per day with 100 free km, or $37 with unlimited km (☎ 325 1000)
Carousel Rent-a-Car
    318 Charles St, has weekly rentals from $236 with unlimited km (☎ 328 8999)

Bicycle Cycling is a great way to explore Perth. There are many bicycle routes along the river all the way to Fremantle and along the Indian Ocean coast. Get the free *Along the Coast Ride* and *Around the River Ride* booklets from the Western Australia Tourist Centre in Forrest Place.

Northbridge Youth Hostel and Newcastle Youth Hostel rent bicycles for around $10 a day. Ride Away (☎ 354 2393) by the city side of the Causeway also rents cycles for $12 and $17 (10-speed) per day – a $10 deposit is required and more generous rates are available for extended periods. See the Kings

Park section earlier in this chapter for details about Koala Bicycle Hire.

Boat Transperth ferries cross the river every day from the Barrack St jetty to the Mends St jetty in South Perth every half an hour (more frequently at peak times) from around 7 am to 7 pm for 65c. Take this ferry to get to the zoo.

The Rottnest Island Getting There & Away section has details on ferries from Perth and Fremantle to Rottnest.

See the Organised Tours & Cruises section earlier for river cruises.

Around Perth

FREMANTLE (population 21,000)
Fremantle ('Freo' to the locals and enthusiastic name shorteners), Perth's port, is at the mouth of the Swan River, 19 km south-west of the city centre. Over the years, Perth has sprawled to engulf Fremantle, which is now more a suburb of the city than a town in its own right. Despite recent development, Fremantle has a wholly different feeling than gleaming, skyscrapered Perth. It's a place with a real sense of history and a very pleasant atmosphere.

Fremantle was founded in 1829 when the HMS *Challenger* landed, captained by Charles Fremantle. Like Perth, the settlement made little progress until it decided reluctantly to take in convicts. This cheap and hard-worked labour constructed most of the town's earliest buildings, some of them amongst the oldest and most treasured in Western Australia. As a port, Fremantle was abysmal until the brilliant engineer C Y O'Connor built an artificial harbour in the 1890s.

In 1987, the city was the site of the unsuccessful defence of what was, for a brief period, one of Australia's most prized possessions – the America's Cup yachting trophy. Preparations for the influx of tourists associated with the competition certainly transformed Fremantle into a more modern, colourful and expensive city. Many of the residents, however, protested at the time that their lifestyle and the character of their community were damaged by the development.

The town has numerous interesting old buildings, some excellent museums and galleries, a lively produce and craft market, and a diverse range of pubs, coffee shops and restaurants. A visit to Fremantle will be one of the highlights of your trip to Western Australia. Make sure you leave yourself enough time to wander around, sip coffee in an outdoor cafe and soak in the atmosphere.

Information
There is an information centre in the Fremantle Town Hall shop (☎ 430 2346) on William St (by St John's Square), which is open Monday to Friday from 9 am to 5 pm and Saturday from 9 am to 1 pm. Among the brochures available are a historic buildings guide, a gallery and museums guide, and information on Heritage Trails and National Trust walking tours.

Fremantle Museum & Arts Centre
The museum is housed in an impressive building on Finnerty St, originally constructed by convict labourers as a lunatic asylum in the 1860s. It houses a fine collection including exhibits on Fremantle's early history, the colonisation of Western Australia and the early whaling industry. It also tells the intriguing story of the Dutch East India Company ships which first discovered the western coast of Australia and in several instances were wrecked on its inhospitable shores. The museum is open from 10.30 am to 5 pm Monday to Thursday and from 1 to 5 pm Friday to Sunday; admission is free.

The arts centre which occupies one wing of the building has regularly changing exhibitions, various craft workshops, a craft shop and a coffee shop. It is open daily from 10 am to 5 pm and Wednesday evening from 7 to 9 pm; admission is free.

Maritime Museum
On Cliff St, near the waterfront, is the Mar-

itime Museum, which occupies a building constructed in 1852 as a Commissariat store. The museum has a display on Western Australia's maritime history with particular emphasis on the famous wreck of the *Batavia*. One gallery is used as a working centre where you can see timbers from the *Batavia* actually being preserved.

At one end of this gallery is the huge stone facade intended for an entrance to Batavia Castle in modern-day Jakarta, Indonesia. It was being carried by the *Batavia* as ballast when she went down. The museum is open Monday to Thursday from 10.30 am to 5 pm and Friday to Saturday from 1 to 5 pm, admission is free, and it is well worth a visit.

Sails of the Century
For boat freaks only, this collection of boats from the last 100 years, including the America's Cup winning 12-metre yacht *Australia II*, is in B-Shed, Victoria Quay. It's open daily from 1 to 5 pm and admission is free.

Fremantle Market
A prime attraction is the colourful Fremantle Market on South Terrace at the corner of Henderson St. Originally opened in 1892, the market was reopened in 1975 and draws crowds looking for anything from craft work to vegetables, jewellery and antiques; there is a also a great tavern bar where buskers often perform. The market is open from 9 am to 9 pm on Fridays, from 9 am to 5 pm on Saturdays, and from 11 am to 5 pm on Sundays.

Round House
On Arthur Head at the western end of High St, near the Maritime Museum, is the Round House. Built in 1831, it's the oldest public building in Western Australia. It actually has 12 sides and was originally a local prison (in the days before convicts were brought into Western Australia). It was also the site of the colony's first hanging.

Later, the building was used to hold Aborigines before they were taken to Rottnest Island. The site provides good views of

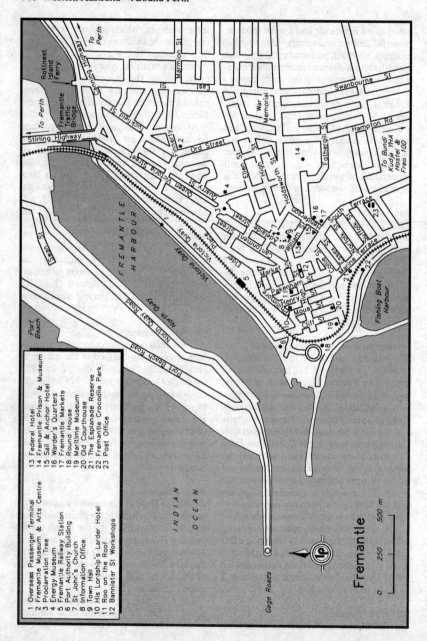

Fremantle

1 Overseas Passenger Terminal
2 Fremantle Museum & Arts Centre
3 Proclamation Tree
4 Energy Museum
5 Fremantle Railway Station
6 Port Authority Building
7 St John's Church
8 Information Office
9 Town Hall
10 His Lordship's Larder Hotel
11 Roo on the Roof
12 Bannister St Workshops
13 Federal Hotel
14 Fremantle Prison & Museum
15 Sail & Anchor Hotel
16 Warder's Quarters
17 Fremantle Markets
18 Round House
19 Maritime Museum
20 Old Courthouse
21 The Esplanade Reserve
22 Fremantle Crocodile Park
23 Post Office

Fremantle. The Round House shop and information centre is housed in one of the nearby pilots' cottages. Admission to the Round House is free, and it's open from 10 am to 5 pm daily.

Convict-Era Buildings

Many other buildings in Fremantle date from the period after 1850, when convict labour was introduced. The *Convict Trail* brochure, available from the Fremantle Town Hall shop and produced by the Western Australia Heritage Trails Network, outlines the places of interest from this era. They include **Fremantle Prison**, one of the unlucky convicts' first building task – it's still used as a prison today. The entrance on Fairbairn St is particularly picturesque.

Beside the prison gates, at 16 The Terrace, is a small museum on the convict era in Western Australia. It's open from 9.30 am to 1.30 pm Monday to Friday, from 1 to 4 pm on Saturday, and from 11 am to 5 pm on Sunday; admission is free. Warders from the jail still live in the 1850s stone cottages on Henderson St.

Later Landmarks

Fremantle boomed during the Western Australia gold rush and many buildings were constructed during, or shortly before, this period. They include **Samson House**, a well-preserved 1888 colonial home in Ellen St, which is open from 1 to 5 pm on Thursday and Sunday – tours of the house are run by volunteer guides. The fine **St John's Church** of 1882, on the corner of Adelaide and Queen Sts, contains a large stained-glass window.

Other buildings of the era include the **Fremantle Town Hall** (1887) in St John's Square; the former **German consulate building** built in 1902 at 5 Mouat St; the **Fremantle Railway Station** of 1907; and the Georgian-style **old customs house** on Cliff St. The **water trough** in the park in front of the station has a memorial to two men who died of thirst on an outback expedition. The **Proclamation Tree**, near the

corner of Adelaide and Edwards Sts, is a Moreton Bay fig tree planted in 1890.

Other Attractions

Fremantle is well endowed with parks, including the popular **Esplanade Reserve**, beside the picturesque fishing-boat harbour off Marine Terrace. The city also has several art galleries, including the **Fremantle Art Gallery** at 43 High St. Open daily from noon to 5 pm, it has a good exhibition of contemporary Western Australian art. Nearby on High St is the **Burik-Marri Gallery** with a fine display of traditional and contemporary Aboriginal art.

The city is a popular centre for craft workers of all kinds and one of the best places to find them is at the imaginative **Bannister St Workshops**, which is open from 10 am to 5 pm Tuesday to Friday, and from 12.30 to 5 pm weekends. The **Joan Campbell Workshop** beside the Round House has regular pottery exhibits.

From the observation tower on top of the **Port Authority Building** in Cliff St, you can enjoy a panoramic view of Fremantle harbour. You must take the escorted tours which are conducted from the foyer every weekday at 11 am, 1.30 and 2.30 pm.

The **Energy Museum**, at 12 Parry St, has some entertaining and educational displays tracing the development of gas and electricity. It is open from 10.30 am to 4.30 pm on weekdays and from 1 to 4.30 pm on weekends; admission is free.

Finally, the **Fremantle Crocodile Park**, open seven days a week from 10 am to 5 pm, has around 220 fresh and saltwater crocodiles in natural displays. The best time to visit is during feeding times, usually at 11.30 am and 2 pm daily except Mondays; admission is $8.

Organised Tours

The Fremantle Tram is very much like the Perth Tram and does a 45-minute historical tour of Fremantle with full commentary for $6; a harbours tour is also available for $6. You can combine the historical tour with a cruise to Perth, a tour of Perth on the Perth

Tram and a return ticket to Fremantle for $26 (☎ 339 8719).

Places to Stay

Bundi Kudja Youth Hostel (☎ 335 3467), 96 Hampton Rd, has small-dorm accommodation for $10 per night. It is housed in former nurses' quarters built around 1896. The *Freo 100* (☎ 336 2962), 100 Hampton Rd, and *Freo 200* (☎ 335 3537), 81 Solomon St, are youth hostels which cater more for longer-term visitors; weekly rates for both are $65. Freo 100 is only open for hostel accommodation from 1 December to 31 March.

More central are the popular *Roo on the Roof* (☎ 335 1998), 11 Pakenham St, and *Budget Bunks* (use the Roo on the Roof phone number for bookings) at the New Orleans Hotel, 80 High St, which offer budget accommodation from $12.

The *Federal Hotel* (☎ 335 1645), at 23 William St near the town hall, has basic singles/doubles for $18/30 per night or $90/125 per week. *His Lordship's Larder Hotel* (☎ 336 1766), on the corner of Mouat and Phillimore Sts, is a nicely renovated hotel with rooms for $30/50. For a more homelike place to stay, contact Fremantle Homestays (☎ 335 7531), which can arrange B&B accommodation in houses around Fremantle from $25 to $40 a night for a single and from $50 to $75 for a double room. Self-contained single and double units are also available from $200 to $250 per week.

The ritziest hotel in town is the four-star *Fremantle Esplanade Hotel* on the corner of Marine Terrace and Collie St. Rooms start from $110 to a mere $250 per night for a harbour suite.

Places to Eat

A highlight of Fremantle is the diverse range of cafes, restaurants, food halls and taverns. Many a traveller's afternoon has been whittled away sipping beer or coffee and watching life go by from kerbside tables.

Along South Terrace, there's a string of outdoor cafes and restaurants including the popular *Papa Luigi's*, at No 17, which has coffee and gelati; the trendy *Gino's* (the place to be seen) at No 1/5; and the large *Miss Maud's* at No 33. All these places can be crowded on weekends when the weather is fine – a regular occurrence in Fremantle.

The historic *Sail & Anchor Hotel* (formerly the Freemason's Hotel, built in 1854), at 64 South Terrace, has been impressively restored to much of its former glory. It specialises in locally brewed Matilda Bay beers such as Redback, Dogbolter and Monkey Stout, and on the 1st floor is a brasserie which serves hot and cold snacks and full meals.

Also in South Terrace is the *Mexican Kitchen*, next door to Papa Luigi's, with a range of Mexican dishes from $10 to $12. Across the road is *Pizza Bella Roma*, the *Glifada Shishkebab Bar* with tasty souvlaki, and the reasonably priced *Magic Apple* with wholemeal pies, a ploughman's lunch, lentil burgers and salads from $4 to $6.

The *Upmarket Food Centre* on Henderson St, opposite the market, has stalls where you can get delicious and cheap Thai, Vietnamese, Japanese, Chinese and Italian food from $5 to $7. Open Thursday to Sunday from about noon to 9 pm, it can be very busy, especially on market days.

Roma, at 13 High St, serves good food at fair prices but the service isn't the world's friendliest. The nearby *Round House* is good for a cheap breakfast or a quick snack. For Vietnamese food, try the *Vung Tau*, at 19 High St, with meals including a vegetarian menu from $6 to $9.

Fast Eddy's, similar to the one in Perth, is at 13 Essex St. Fish & chips at *Cicerello's* or *Lombardo's* on the Esplanade by the fishing boat harbour is something of a Fremantle tradition. Both establishments have restaurants and takeaway sections.

There are typical counter meals available at the *Newcastle Club Tavern* on Market St, the *Federal Hotel* on William St and the *National Hotel* on the corner of Market and High Sts.

Entertainment

There are a number of venues around town

with music and/or dancing, the majority concentrated in the High St area.

The New Orleans Hotel, at 80 High St, has jazz bands (and a steak house). For Latin and folk music, the Fly by Night Club, in Queen's St, is frequented by some talented musicians.

The Sail & Anchor Hotel and Newport Hotel on South Terrace also have live music. The Cave Bar, at 201 Queen Victoria St in North Fremantle, has rock bands from Thursday to Sunday nights. Tarantella, on Mouat St between High and Phillimore Sts, is an exclusive nightclub. There is also a cinema complex in William St that shows mainstream movies.

Getting There & Around

The train between Perth and Fremantle runs every half-hour or so throughout the day for around $1.40. Bus Nos 106 (bus stand No 31) and 111 (bus stand No 36) go from St George's Terrace to Fremantle via the Canning Highway; or you can take bus No 105 (bus stand No 34 on St George's Terrace), which takes a longer route south of the river. Bus Nos 103 and 104 also depart from St George's Terrace (south side) but go to Fremantle via the north side of the river.

Captain Cook and Boat Torque cruises have daily ferries from Perth to Fremantle for around $10 one-way.

Bicycles are available for hire from Fleet Cycles (☎ 430 5414), at 66 Adelaide St, and Captain Munchies (☎ 339 6633) at 2 Beach St.

ROTTNEST ISLAND

'Rotto', as it's known by the locals, is a sandy island about 19 km off the coast of Fremantle. It's 11 km long, five km wide and is very popular with Perth residents and visitors. The island was discovered by the Dutch explorer Vlamingh in 1696. He named it 'Rats' Nest' because of the numerous king-size rats he saw there. Actually, they weren't rats at all but quokkas – marsupials that are even more prolific today.

What do you do on Rotto? Well, you cycle around, laze in the sun on the many superb beaches (the Basin is the most popular, while Parakeet Bay is the place for skinny dipping), climb the low hills, go fishing or boating, ride a glass-bottomed boat (Rotto has some of the southernmost coral in the world and a number of shipwrecks), swim in the crystal-clear water or go quokka spotting (they're most active early in the morning).

The Rottnest settlement was originally established in 1838 as a prison for Aborigines from the mainland – the early colonists had lots of trouble imposing their ideas of private ownership on the nomadic Aborigines. The prison was abandoned in 1903 and the island soon became an escape for Perth society. It's only in the last 30 years, however, that it has really developed as a popular day trip. The original prison settlement is of great interest as the buildings are among the oldest in Western Australia.

Information

There is an information centre, open daily from 9 am to noon and from 12.30 pm to 2.30 pm, just to the left of the jetty at Thomson Bay (the island's largest settlement) as you arrive. There, and at the museum, you can get useful publications, such as a walking tour of the old settlement buildings, Heritage Trail brochures, information on the various shipwrecks around the island and a cycling guide.

Also, grab a copy of the informative *Rottnest Islander* newspaper. Rottnest is very popular in the summer when the ferries and accommodation are both heavily booked – plan ahead.

Things to See & Do

There's an excellent little **museum** with exhibits about the island, its history, wildlife and shipwrecks. You can pick up the walking-tour leaflet here and wander around the interesting old convict-built buildings, including the octagonal 1864 'Quad' where the prison cells are now hotel rooms. **Vlamingh's Lookout** on View Hill, not far from Thomson Bay, offers a panoramic view of the island. The island's main lighthouse was built in 1895 and is visible 60 km out to sea.

The island has a number of low-lying salt lakes, and it's around them that you are most likely to spot **quokkas**, although the bus tours have regular quokka-feeding points where the small marsupials seem to appear on demand. Also of interest is the recently restored **Oliver Hill Battery**, west of Thomson Bay.

Some of Rottnest's **shipwrecks** are accessible to snorkellers, but to get to most of them requires a boat. There are marker plaques around the island telling the sad tales of how and when the ships came to grief. Snorkelling equipment, fishing gear and boats can be hired from the Marine Centre (☎ (09) 292 5167) at Thomson Bay.

There's a two-hour bus tour around the island for $6; it departs daily at 10.45 am and 1.30 pm – again it is wise to book in the peak season. *Underwater Explorer* is a boat with windows below the waterline for viewing shipwrecks and marine life. It departs at regular hourly intervals from the jetty at Thomson Bay; an interesting 45-minute trip costs $12.

Places to Stay

Most visitors to Rotto come only for the day (although with the increase in transport fares it's getting to be an expensive trip) but it's equally interesting to stay on the island.

You can camp for $12 (two people) in hired tents with rubber mattresses or get tent sites for $5 per person per night at *Tentland* (☎ (09) 372 9737). Safari cabins are also available from $20 to $30 a night. You should book in advance for a cabin or if you want to hire a tent, although you can usually just turn up as long as you have your own tent.

The *Rottnest Island Authority* (☎ (09) 292 5044) has over 250 houses and cottages for rent in Thomson Bay and the Geordie, Fays and Longreach Bay areas from $48 (bungalows) to $106 (villas) per night for four-bed accommodation. Reductions of up to 25% are available in off-peak periods.

The *Rottnest Hotel* (☎ (09) 292 5011), affectionately known as the Quokka Arms, costs $60/90 for singles/doubles including breakfast. It was originally built in 1864 as the residence of the governor of Western Australia.

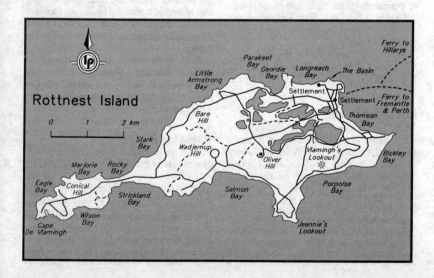

Rottnest Island

Places to Eat

The *Rottnest Island Bistro* has a pleasant balcony overlooking Thomson Bay and serves tasty pasta, roasts, cold meat and salad and light meals from $6 to $9. *Brolley's Restaurant* in the Rottnest Hotel also serves light meals from $6 to $10 and full meals from $13 to $15.

The island has a general store and a bakery that is famed during the day for its fresh bread and pies, and in the evening for pizza. There's also a fast-food centre in the Thomson Bay settlement. The *Geordie/Longreach Store* has Devonshire teas, fish & chips, burgers and sandwiches.

Getting There & Away

You can fly or take the ferry to Rotto. The *Star Flyte* ferry runs from Perth's Barrack St jetty to Thomson Bay daily; it leaves Perth at 9 am and Fremantle at 9.45 am. There's also a second service on Monday, Wednesday and Saturday that leaves Fremantle at noon. The fare is $35 return from Perth and $28 from Fremantle.

There is also a ferry service, *Sea Raider III*, from Hillarys Boat Harbour (north of Perth) leaving at 8.30 am daily for $32 return. These ferries are run by Boat Torque Cruises (☎ (09) 325 6033) and bookings are essential at peak periods.

You can also fly to Rottnest on the Rottnest Airbus (☎ (09) 478 1322) that leaves Perth Airport four times a day, seven days a week for $66.50 return; the trip takes just 15 minutes. There's a connecting bus between Rottnest Airport and the Thomson Bay settlement.

Getting Around

Bicycles are the time-honoured way of getting around the island. The number of motor vehicles is strictly limited, which makes cycling a real pleasure. Furthermore, the island is just big enough to make a day's ride fine exercise. You can bring your own bike over on the ferry ($7 return) or rent one of the hundreds available on the island from Rottnest Bike Hire (☎ (09) 372 9722) in Thomson Bay, near the hotel, for $8 a day or $40 a week – a $10 deposit is required for each bicycle.

Two bus services, the Bayseeker ($1) and the Settlement bus (50c), also run during the summer season – see the information centre for bus timetables and departure points.

NORTH COAST

The coast north of Perth has spectacular scenery with long sand dunes but it quickly becomes the inhospitable land that deterred early visitors.

Yanchep

The **Yanchep National Park**, 51 km north of Perth, has natural bushland, some fine caves (including the limestone Crystal and Yondemp caves), Loch McNess, the Gloster Lodge Museum, bushwalking trails and a wildlife sanctuary. **Yanchep Sun City** is a major marina with a modern shopping complex.

There are a handful of places to stay, including the *Yanchep Inn* (☎ (09) 561 1001), which has singles/doubles from $28/45, and a motel section with rooms from $45/65. The *Yanchep Holiday Village* (☎ (09) 561 2244) has self-contained units from $50 a double. Bus No 356 goes to Yanchep from the Wellington St bus station, but only once a day from Monday to Friday.

North of Yanchep is **Guilderton**, a popular holiday resort, beside the mouth of the Moore River. The *Vergulde Draeck* (Gilt Dragon), a Dutch East Indiaman, ran aground near here in 1656. The coast road ends at **Lancelin**, a small fishing port 130 km north of Perth, but coastal tracks continue north and may be passable with a 4WD. Windswept Lancelin is famed as a destination for windsurfers and is the finishing point of the annual Ledge Point Windsurfing Race held in January.

Pinnacles Desert

The small seaport of **Cervantes**, 257 km north of Perth, is the entry point for the unusual and haunting Pinnacles Desert. Here, in the coastal **Nambung National Park**, the flat sandy desert is punctured with

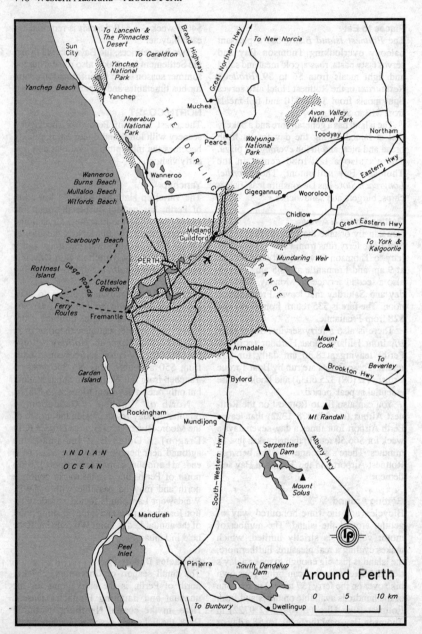

Around Perth

0   5   10 km

peculiar limestone pillars, some only a few cm high, some towering up to five metres. The national park also puts on an impressive display of wild flowers from August to October.

If possible, try to visit the Pinnacles Desert early in the morning. Not only is the light better for photography but you will avoid the crowds that can detract from your experience of the place later in the day, especially in peak holiday times.

Check in Cervantes before attempting to drive the unsealed road into the park – if conditions are bad, a 4WD may be necessary but usually the road is OK, if somewhat bumpy, for normal vehicles.

A coastal 4WD track runs north to **Jurien**, a crayfishing centre, and south to Lancelin. The sand dunes along the coast are spectacular.

Organised Tours It's possible to take a half-day tour from the Cervantes Shell service station (☎ (096) 52 7041) for $12 (plus a $2 park entrance fee) and save your car's suspension; it leaves daily at 1 pm and you would be wise to book. If you drive into the Pinnacles Desert yourself, there is a $3 per car entrance fee.

The Pinnacles are a very popular excursion from Perth – day tours from Perth cost around $80. Try Safari Treks (☎ (09) 322 2188) and Travelabout Outback Tours (☎ (09) 242 2243).

Places to Stay Accommodation in the area includes the *Pinnacles Caravan Park* (☎ (096) 52 7060) on the beachfront with tent sites for $8 and on-site vans from $25 for two people; *Cervantes Motel* (☎ (096) 52 7145), 227 Aragon St, with singles/doubles for $55/68; and *Cervantes Holiday Homes* (☎ (09) 457 9810), on the corner of Valencia Rd and Malaga Court, with self-contained units from $40.

New Norcia

The small town of New Norcia is a real surprise. Established as a Spanish Benedictine mission in 1846, it has changed little since and boasts a fine collection of buildings with classic Spanish architecture. The building which houses the museum and art gallery, worth seeing for their old paintings, manuscripts and religious artefacts, also houses the tourist office (☎ (096) 54 8056).

At the museum, you can get the excellent *New Norcia Heritage Trail* brochure which traces the development of the settlement. Just past the museum is the historic *New Norcia Hotel* (☎ (096) 54 8034) which has an interesting decor, including a grand staircase; singles/doubles are $30/45. The Benedictine monks still live and work in New Norcia today.

Moora, further north, is a farming community in an area known for its colourful wild flowers. In the nearby **Berkshire Valley**, an old cottage and flour mill built in the mid-19th century have been restored and now operate as a museum.

SOUTH COAST

The coast south of Perth has a softer appearance than the often harsh landscape to the north. This is another very popular beach resort area for Perth residents and many have holiday houses along the coast.

Rockingham (population 44,000)

Rockingham, just 47 km south of Perth, was founded in 1872 as a port, but that function, in time, was taken over by Fremantle. Today, Rockingham is a popular seaside resort with sheltered and ocean beaches. Close by is **Penguin Island**, home to a colony of Fairy Penguins from late March to early December, and **Seal Island**; boats travel there daily – check with the tourist office for details. The naval base of **Garden Island**, also close by, is not open to the public.

From Rockingham, you can also head inland to the Serpentine Dam and the scenic **Serpentine Falls National Park**, where there are wild flowers and pleasant bushland. You can get to Rockingham on bus No 120 from Fremantle or a No 116 from bus stand No 38 in St George's Terrace, Perth.

The helpful Rockingham tourist office

(☎ (09) 592 3464), at 43 Kent St, is open Monday to Friday from 9 am to 5 pm and weekends from 10 am to 4 pm.

Places to Stay & Eat The good-value *CWA Rockingham* (☎ (09) 527 9560), 108 Parkin St, is operated by a friendly couple. There are two units available, each sleeping six, from $25 per night. The *Palm Beach Caravan Park* (☎ (09) 527 1515), at 37 Fisher St, has tent sites and on-site vans. The *Rockingham Lodge Motel* (☎ (09) 527 1230), 20 Lake St, has singles/doubles for $25/38, and the three-star *Ocean Clipper Inn* (☎ 527 8000), on Patterson Rd, charges $52/57.

For meals, try the local hotels. Otherwise, there is *El Roccos*, at 84 Parkin St, for good Mexican food or the *Silver Dragon* Chinese restaurant on Rockingham Rd.

Mandurah (population 22,000)

Situated on the calm Mandurah Estuary, this is yet another popular beach resort, 74 km south of Perth. Dolphins are often seen in the estuary, and the waterways in the area are noted for good fishing, prawning (March and April) and crabbing.

Things to see in town include the restored, limestone **Hall's Cottage** (open Sunday afternoon), built in the 1830s, and the **Western Rosella Bird Park**, open daily from 9 am to 6 pm; admission is $4. Full-day and short cruises are available on the MV *Peel Princes* from the jetty in town. Contact the Mandurah tourist office (☎ (09) 535 1155), 4 Pinjarra Rd, for ferry schedules, maps and other information.

Prolific bird life can be seen on **Peel Inlet** and the narrow coastal salt lakes, **Clifton** and **Preston**, 20 km to the south. Catch bus No 116 from stand 38 in St George's Terrace, Perth, or bus No 117 from Fremantle to Mandurah.

Places to Stay There is a string of caravan parks around town with tent sites and on-site vans. One of the most convenient is the *Baxter Court* (☎ (09) 535 1363).

The *Brighton Hotel* (☎ (09) 535 1242), on Mandurah Terrace, is the best deal in town with singles/doubles from $20/40 with breakfast; they also have good, cheap counter meals. The *Mandurah Lodge Guesthouse* (☎ (09) 535 1265), at 52 Pinjarra Rd, has basic rooms for $20/35 – they also serve continental ($2.50) and cooked ($5) breakfasts.

The well-positioned *Hotel Peninsula* (☎ (09) 535 1241), right on the waterfront at Ormsby Terrace, has comfortable singles/doubles for $40/65.

Places to Eat There are numerous places to eat around town including *Pronto's Cafe* on the corner of Pinjarra Rd and Mandurah Terrace. They have good snacks and cakes, and an all-you-can-eat pasta night on Friday for $9 – live music is often provided.

A big and tasty serve of fish & chips ($3.50) is available at *Jetty Fish & Chips* by the estuary near the end of Pinjarra Rd. You can then sit at one of the foreshore tables, eat your fill and watch the world go by. Next door is *Yo-Yo's* with a vast array of ice creams and sundaes.

Pinjarra (population 7600)

Pinjarra, 86 km south of Perth, has a number of old buildings picturesquely sited on the banks of the Murray River. The Murray tourist office (☎ (09) 531 1438) in Pinjarra is at 28 George St. About two km from the town is the **Old Blythewood Homestead**, an 1859 colonial farm and a National Trust property. Behind the historic post office is a pleasant picnic area and a **suspension bridge** – wobbly enough to test most people's coordination!

Hotham Valley Railway **steam trains** run from Pinjarra to Dwellingup through blooming wild flowers and jarrah forests in winter only (August to October).

Places to Stay & Eat The *Pinjarra Motel* (☎ (09) 531 1811) offers singles/doubles with breakfast for $40/50. The *Exchange Hotel* (☎ (09) 531 1209) has singles/doubles for $20/30.

Heritage Tearooms has light meals such as sandwiches and quiches for around $6.

AVON VALLEY

The green and lush Avon Valley looks very English and was a delight to homesick early settlers. In the spring, this area is particularly rich in wild flowers. The valley was first settled in 1830, only a year after Perth was founded, so there are many historic buildings in the area. The picturesque Avon River is very popular with canoe enthusiasts.

Getting There & Away

The Avon Valley towns all have bus connections to Perth; contact Westrail (☎ (09) 326 2222) for timetable details. Fares from Perth are $8.70 to Toodyay, Northam and York, and $11.80 to Beverley. It is also possible to take the Prospector rail service from Perth to Toodyay ($8.70) and Northam ($10.30).

Toodyay (population 600)

There are numerous old buildings in this charming and historic town, many of them built by convicts. The local tourist office (☎ (09) 574 2435) is housed in the 1850s **Connor's Mill** on Stirling Terrace. It is open from 9 am to 5 pm on weekdays and from 10 am to 5 pm on Saturday and Sunday.

Don't miss the **Old Newcastle Gaol Museum** on Clinton St, or the 1862 **St Stephen's Church**. The **Moondyne Gallery** is interesting for the story it tells of bushranger Joseph Bolitho Johns (Moondyne Joe). The old Memorial Hall is now a public toilet! Close to town, there's a **winery** which began operating in the 1870s, while in the town itself there's a pleasant old country pub with a shady beer garden. Downriver from Toodyay is the **Avon Valley National Park**.

The West Australian Folk Festival takes place here every September.

Places to Stay & Eat

Toodyay Caravan Park (☎ (09) 574 2612), Railway Rd, on the banks of the Avon River, has tent sites, on-site vans and chalets.

The central *Old Toodyay Club Youth Hostel* (☎ (09) 574 2435), on Stirling Terrace, costs $8 per night – there are only eight beds so it is wise to book in the peak seasons.

Opposite is the *Freemasons Hotel* (☎ (09) 574 2201) with basic rooms and breakfast for $22 per person and reasonably priced counter meals. On the same street is the *Victoria Hotel/Motel* (☎ (09) 574 2206) with singles/doubles from $20/40; counter meals are available from $7 to $9.

There are a couple of tearooms on Stirling Terrace that serve light meals: the *Village Shoppe* (which also has home-made pies) and, opposite, the *Wendouree Tearooms*.

Northam (population 7500)

Northam, the major town of the Avon Valley, is a busy farming centre on the railway line to Kalgoorlie. At one time, the line from Perth ended abruptly here and miners had to make the rest of the weary trek to the gold fields by road.

Northam is packed on the first weekend in August every year for the start of the gruelling 133-km Avon Descent for power boats and canoeists. The event attracts hundreds of competitors from around the state and Australia; just finishing the course is prize enough for most.

The tourist office (☎ (096) 22 2100), at 3 Beavis Place, is open daily.

Things to See The 1836 **Morby Cottage** served as Northam's first church and school, and it now houses a museum open on Sundays. The **old railway station**, listed by the National Trust, has been restored and turned into a museum; it is open on Sundays from 10 am to 4 pm and admission is $2. Also of interest in town are the colony of **white swans** on the Avon River, descendants of birds introduced from England early this century.

Near Northam at Irishtown is the elegant **Buckland House**. It was built in 1874, it has a fine collection of antiques and is credited with being Western Australia's most impressive stately home.

Places to Stay & Eat *Northam Youth Hostel* (☎ (096) 22 3323), in the old railway station on Fitzgerald St, has some dorms in railway carriages for $8. On the same street, at No 426, is the *Grand Hotel* (☎ (096) 22 1024) with basic rooms and shared facilities for $20/30.

Avon Bridge Hotel (☎ (096) 22 1023), the oldest hotel in Northam, has singles/doubles for $26/52 and counter meals from $5. *Prospect House* (☎ (095) 22 3152), at 402 Fitzgerald St, has short or long-term B&B accommodation for $35/60 per night.

The *Commercial Hotel* (☎ (095) 22 1049), 190 Fitzgerald St, has singles/doubles for $20/40 and lunch specials for $2. Every second Sunday, the Music Club in the Commercial Hotel has a music evening from 4 to 8 pm.

O'Harah's Saloon at the Shamrock, 112 Fitzgerald St, has good counter meals from $5 to $10. *Tattersalls Hotel*, at 174 Fitzgerald St, also has great-value $2 lunch specials and is open for breakfast from 7 to 10 am. Next to the Tattersalls Hotel, *Bruno's Pizza Bar* does tasty pizza to eat in or take away.

York (population 2500)

The oldest inland town in Western Australia, York was first settled in 1830 and is one of the highlights of the Avon Valley. A stroll down the main street, with its many restored old buildings, is a real step back in time. The tourist office (☎ (096) 41 1301) is at 105 Avon Terrace.

Things to See The excellent **Residency Museum** from the 1840s, the old **town hall**, **Castle Hotel** dating from the coaching days, **Faversham House**, the classy **Motor Museum** (a must for vintage-car enthusiasts), the old **police station** and **courthouse** (classified by the National Trust), the Sandalwood Press **printing museum** and **Settlers' Hall** are all of interest. Near York is the **Balladong**

Farm Museum – a working farm of the pioneer era.

Places to Stay The only caravan park around town is *Mt Bakewell Caravan Park* (☎ (096) 41 1421) with tent sites and on-site vans.

York Youth Hostel (☎ (096) 41 1372) on South St, not far from the old railway station, has dorm beds for $8. The old section of the historic, renovated *Castle Hotel* (☎ (096) 41 1007), on Avon Terrace, is good value with singles/doubles from $25/40; beware, however, of the 7 am vacuum cleaning in the corridors.

The *York Hotel* (☎ (096) 41 1402) and the *Imperial Inn* (☎ (096) 41 1010), also on Avon Terrace, have rooms for $24/34 and $25/38 respectively.

Places to Eat Try the fully refurbished *Settlers' Tearooms*, on Avon Terrace, for a spot of tea with all the trimmings in a pleasant courtyard setting. They also have a tasty and varied selection of food from $5 to $8. The *Castle Hotel* serves good counter meals from $9 to $13; you can also eat outside on the verandah cafe.

Beverley (population 1600)

South of York, also on the Avon River, is Beverley (founded in 1838) which is noted for its fine **aeronautical museum** open Friday and Saturday from 2 to 4 pm and Sunday from 11 am to 1 pm and 2 to 4 pm. Exhibits include a locally constructed biplane, built between 1928 and 1930.

The 706-hectare **Avondale Research Station**, five km west of Beverley, has a large collection of agricultural machinery, a homestead, a workshop and stables. The information centre (☎ (096) 46 1200) is in the Beverley Shire Offices at 136 Vincent St. Further upriver are **Brookton** and **Pigelly**, in an area well known for its wild flowers.

Places to Stay The *Beverley Caravan Park* (☎ (096) 46 1200), on Vincent St, has tent sites and on-site vans. The ordinary *Beverley*

Hotel (☎ (096) 46 1190), at 137 Vincent St, has B&B for $24/40.

THE DARLING RANGE

The hills that surround Perth are popular for picnics, barbecues and bushwalks. There are also some excellent lookouts from which you can see over Perth and down to the coast. **Araleun** with its waterfalls, the fire lookout at **Mt Dale**, and **Churchman's Brook** are all off the Brookton Highway. Other places of interest include the **Zig Zag** at Gooseberry Hill and **Lake Leschenaultia**.

From **Kalamunda**, there are fine views over Perth. Get there from Perth on bus Nos 300 or 302 via Maida Vale from bus stand No 27 in Pier St; or bus Nos 292 or 305 via Wattle Grove and Lesmurdie from bus stand No 28 in Hay St. Taking one route out and the other back makes an interesting circular tour of the hill suburbs. There's a good walking track at **Sullivan Rock**, 69 km south-east of Perth, on the Albany Highway.

Mundaring Weir

Mundaring, in the ranges only 35 km east from Perth, is the site of the Mundaring Weir – the dam built at the turn of the century to supply water to the gold fields over 500 km to the east. The reservoir has an attractive setting and is a popular excursion for Perth residents. There are also a number of walking tracks. The **C Y O'Connor Museum** has models and exhibits about the water pipeline to the gold fields – in its time one of the most amazing engineering feats in the world.

The 1600-hectare **John Forrest National Park** near Mundaring has protected areas of jarrah and marri trees, native fauna, waterfalls and a swimming pool.

Places to Stay *Mundaring Caravan Park* (☎ (09) 295 1125) is two km west of town on the Great Eastern Highway. The *Youth Hostel* (☎ (09) 295 1809), on Mundaring Weir Rd, is eight km south of town and costs $8.

Wheatlands

Stretching north from the Albany coastal region to the areas beyond the Great Eastern Highway (the Perth to Coolgardie road) are the Western Australia wheatlands. The area is noted for its unusual rock formations, best known of which is Wave Rock, near Hyden; and for its many Aboriginal rock carvings.

CUNDERDIN & KELLERBERRIN

Meckering, a small town 24 km west of Cunderdin, was badly damaged by an earth-quake in 1968; the **Agricultural Museum** in Cunderdin has exhibits relating to that event as well as an interesting collection of farm machinery and equipment. The museum is housed in an old pumping station used on the gold-fields water pipeline. Further to the east is Kellerberrin, which has an **historical museum** in the old courthouse of 1897 and a lookout on **Kellerberrin Hill** with a panoramic view of the area.

The *Campfire Caravan Park* (☎ (096) 35 1258) in Cunderdin has tent sites and on-site vans.

MERREDIN (population 4500)

Merredin, the largest centre in the wheatbelt, is 260 km east of Perth on the Kalgoorlie railway line and the Great Eastern Highway. It has a tourist office (☎ (090) 41 1666) on Barrack St. The 1920s railway station has been turned into a charming **museum** with a vintage 1897 locomotive and an old signal box. Also of note in the area is **Mangowine Homestead**, 65 km north of Merredin, restored to its former glory by the National Trust.

There are also some interesting rock formations around Merredin, including granite outcrops near **Koorda**, 155 km to the north; **Kangaroo Rock**, 17 km to the south-east; **Burracoppin Rock** to the north; and **Sandford Rocks** 11 km east of Westonia.

Places to Stay & Eat
Merredin Travel Centre Caravan Park

(☎ (090) 41 1535), on the Great Eastern Highway, has tent sites and on-site vans. *Merredin Motel* (☎ (090) 41 1741), on Gamenya Ave, has good-value B&B for $25/40.

The *Commercial Hotel* has counter meals including a $2 lunch-time special, and *Jason's* Chinese restaurant, on the corner of Bates and Mitchell Sts, has takeaway or eat-in meals for around $5.

SOUTHERN CROSS (population 1200)

Although the gold quickly gave out, Southern Cross was the first gold-rush town on the Western Australia gold fields. The big rush soon moved further east to Coolgardie and Kalgoorlie. Like the town itself, the streets of Southern Cross are named after the stars and constellations. The **Yilgarn History Museum** in the old courthouse has local displays. If you follow the continuation of Antares St south for three km, you will see a couple of active open-cut mining operations.

Situated 378 km east of Perth, this is really the end of the wheatlands area and the start of the desert; when travelling by train the change is very noticeable. In the spring, the sandy plains around Southern Cross are carpeted with wild flowers.

HYDEN & WAVE ROCK

Wave Rock is 350 km south-east of Perth, and three km from the tiny town of Hyden, south of Merredin and Southern Cross. It's a real surfer's delight – the perfect wave, 15 metres high and frozen in solid rock marked with different colour bands. Other interesting rock formations in the area bear names like the **Breakers, Hippo's Yawn** and the **Humps. Mulka's Cave** has Aboriginal rock paintings, and there's a **wildlife sanctuary** by Wave Rock itself.

At Wave Rock the *Wave Rock Caravan Park* (☎ (098) 80 5022) has tent sites, and chalets at $40 for two. *Diep's Guesthouse* (☎ (098) 80 5179), on Clayton St in Hyden, has B&B for around $30 a person, or there is the *Hyden Hotel* (☎ (098) 80 5052), on Lynch St, with singles/doubles for $40/58.

A Westrail bus to Hyden leaves Perth on Monday and returns the following day; it costs $27.70 one-way and the trip takes 5½ hours.

OTHER TOWNS

There is a fine rock formation known as **Kokerbin**, an Aboriginal word for 'high place', 45 km west of Bruce Rock. **Corrigin**, 68 km south of Bruce Rock, has a folk museum, a craft cottage and a miniature railway. **Jilakin Rock** is 18 km from Kulin, while further south-east there's the town of **Lake Grace**, near the lake of the same name.

Narrogin, 192 km south-east of Perth, is an agricultural centre with a courthouse museum, a railway heritage park, the Albert Facey Homestead (39 km to the east – well worth a visit, especially if you have read Albert Facey's popular book *A Fortunate Life*) and a couple of unusual rock formations nearby. **Dumbleyung**, south-east of Narrogin, also has an historical museum.

Wagin, 229 km south-east of Perth, has a 15-metre-high fibreglass ram (a tribute to the surrounding merino industry) and an interesting historical village with some fine restored buildings and a vintage tractor display. The Wagin tourist office (☎ (098) 61 1177) is on Arthur Rd. There is good bushwalking around **Mt Latham**, six km to the west.

Katanning, south of Wagin, has a large Muslim community, complete with a mosque built in 1980. Other attractions include the old flour mill on Clive St, which houses the tourist office (☎ (098) 21 2634), and the ruins of an old winery.

Gold Country

Fifty years after its establishment in 1829, the Western Australia colony was still going nowhere, so the government in Perth was delighted when gold was discovered at Southern Cross in 1887. That first strike petered out pretty quickly, but there followed more discoveries and Western Australia profited from the gold boom for the rest of the century. It was gold that put Western Australia on the map and finally gave it the population to make it viable in its own right, rather than just a distant offshoot of the east-coast colonies.

The major strikes were made in 1892 at Coolgardie and nearby Kalgoorlie, but in the whole gold-fields area Kalgoorlie is the only large town left. Coolgardie's period of prosperity lasted only until 1905 and many other gold towns went from nothing to populations of 10,000 then back to nothing in just 10 years. Nevertheless, the towns made the most of their prosperity while it lasted, as the many magnificent public buildings grandly attest.

Life in the early gold fields was terribly hard. This area of Western Australia is extremely dry – rainfall is erratic and never great. Even the little rain that does fall quickly disappears into the porous soil. Many early gold seekers, driven more by enthusiasm than by common sense, died of thirst while seeking the elusive metal. Others succumbed to diseases that broke out periodically in the unhygienic shanty towns.

It soon became clear to the government that the large-scale extraction of gold, Western Australia's most important industry, was unlikely to continue without a reliable water supply. Stop-gap measures, like huge condensation plants that produced distilled water from salt lakes, or bores that pumped brackish water from beneath the earth, provided temporary relief. In 1898, however, the engineer C Y O'Connor proposed a stunning solution: he would build a reservoir near Perth and construct a 556-km pipeline to Kalgoorlie.

This was long before the current era of long oil pipelines, and his idea was opposed violently in Parliament and looked upon by some as impossible, especially as the water had to go uphill all the way (Kalgoorlie is 400 metres higher than Perth). Nevertheless, the project was approved and the pipeline laid at breakneck speed. In 1903, water started to pour into Kalgoorlie's newly con-

structed reservoir; a modified version of the same system still operates today.

For O'Connor, however, there was no happy ending: long delays and continual criticism by those of lesser vision resulted in him committing suicide in 1902, less than a year before his scheme proved operational.

Today, Kalgoorlie is the main gold-fields centre and mines still operate there. Elsewhere, a string of fascinating ghost and near-ghost towns and some modern nickel mines make a visit to Western Australia's gold country a must.

COOLGARDIE (population 1500)

A popular pause in the long journey across the Nullarbor, and also the turn-off for Kalgoorlie, Coolgardie really is a ghost of its former self. You only have to glance at the huge town hall and post office building to appreciate the size that Coolgardie once was. Gold was discovered here in 1892, and by the turn of the century the population had boomed to 15,000. The gold then petered out and the town withered away just as quickly. There's still plenty to interest the visitor though.

The Coolgardie tourist office (☎ (090) 26 6090), in Bayley St, is open daily from 8 am to 5 pm.

Things to See

There are 155 informative historical markers scattered in and around the town. They tell of what was once there or what the buildings were formerly used for. The **Goldfields Exhibition** is open from 8 am to 5 pm daily and has a fascinating display of gold-fields memorabilia. You can even find out about US President Herbert Hoover's days on the Western Australia gold fields. It's an interesting museum and worth the $2.50 admission fee, which includes a film shown at the tourist office (in the same building as the museum).

The **railway station** is also operated as a museum, and there you can learn the incredible story of the miner who was trapped 300 metres underground by floodwater in 1907 and rescued by divers 10 days later.

One km west of Coolgardie is the **town cemetery**, which includes many old graves such as that of pioneer explorer Ernest Giles (1835-97). Due to the insanitary conditions and violence in the gold fields, it's said that 'one half of the population buried the other half'.

One of Coolgardie's most amazing sights is **Prior's Museum**, assembled and donated to the town by Ben Prior (1902-89). Diagonally opposite the tourist office, it's a large empty lot, cluttered with every kind of antique junk you can imagine, from old mining equipment to half a dozen rusting old cars. It's open 24 hours a day, 365 days a year and admission is free!

The **Coolgardie Battery** is the only one in the state that remains fully operational. Small prospectors can still get gold extracted from ore here. Tours, which last about one hour and include a gold pour, commence daily at 10.30 am, 1 and 2 pm. The tour can be booked through the tourist office and the cost is $8, or $7 for YHA members.

Other attractions are **Warden Finnerty's house**, restored by the National Trust, which is open daily except Thursday from 1 to 4 pm and Sunday from 10 am to noon (admission $2); the **Bottle Collection & Aboriginal Artefacts** (above the tourist office); and the **Gaol Tree**, complete with leg irons.

At the **Camel Farm**, (☎ (090) 26 6159), four km west of town on the Great Eastern Highway, you can take camel rides or organise longer camel treks; it is open daily from 9 am to 5 pm and admission is $2. Tom Neacy's does tours of Coolgardie and the surrounding area (when he is in town), which depart from the tourist office. (You can get details of this and other tours from the tourist office.)

Places to Stay & Eat

The *Coolgardie Caravan Park* (☎ (090) 26 6009) has tent sites and on-site vans. The fine old *Coolgardie Youth Hostel* (☎ (090) 26 6051), at 56-60 Gnarlbine Rd, costs $9. There are a couple of historic hotels in

Bayley St with long, shady verandahs: the *Railway Lodge* (☎ (090) 26 6166) which has singles/doubles for $25/35 and the *Denver City Hotel* (☎ (090) 26 6031) with rooms for $15/30.

The *Denver Hotel* does good counter lunches and teas from $7, and there are a couple of roadhouses on Bayley St that do meals. *Pinky's Cafe* does reasonably priced burgers, sandwiches and other light meals. The *Premier Cafe*, on Bayley St, does excellent meals for $7 and the usual snacks and takeaways.

Getting There & Away
Greyhound/Pioneer and Bus Australia both pass through Coolgardie on their Perth to Adelaide runs; the one-way fare from Perth to Coolgardie on Bus Australia is $50, to Adelaide it's $160. Goldenlines (☎ (090) 21 2655) runs two buses on weekdays from Kalgoorlie to Coolgardie; the fare is $2.70.

The Prospector train from Perth to Kalgoorlie stops at Bonnie Vale Railway Station, 14 km away, daily from Sunday to Friday; the one-way fare from Perth is $42.60. For bookings call Westrail (☎ (09) 326 2222).

KALGOORLIE-BOULDER
(population 27,000)
Kalgoorlie, the longest lasting and most successful of the Western Australia gold towns, rose to prominence later than Coolgardie. In 1893, Paddy Hannan, a prospector from way back, set out from Coolgardie for another gold strike but stopped at the site of Kalgoorlie and found, just lying around on the surface, enough gold to spark another rush.

As in so many places, the surface gold soon petered out, but at Kalgoorlie the miners went deeper and more and more gold was found. There weren't the storybook chunky nuggets of solid gold – Kalgoorlie's gold had to be extracted from the rocks by costly and complex processes of grinding, roasting and chemical action – but there was plenty of it.

Kalgoorlie quickly reached fabled heights of prosperity, and the enormous and magnificent public buildings at the turn of the century are evidence of its fabulous wealth. After WW I, however, increasing production costs and static gold prices led to Kalgoorlie's slow but steady decline.

With the substantial increase in gold prices since the mid-1970s, mining of lower-grade deposits have become economical and Kalgoorlie is again the largest producer of gold in Australia. Large mining conglomerates have been at the forefront of new open-cut mining operations in the Golden Mile – gone are the old headframes and corrugated iron homes. Mining, pastoral development and a busy tourist trade ensure Kalgoorlie's continuing importance as an outback centre.

Orientation
Although Kalgoorlie (known as 'Kal' to the locals) sprang up close to Paddy Hannan's original find, the mining emphasis soon shifted a few km away to the Golden Mile, a square mile which was probably the wealthiest gold-mining area for its size in the world. The satellite town of Boulder developed to service this area. The two towns amalgamated in August 1989 into the City of Kalgoorlie-Boulder.

Kalgoorlie itself is a grid of broad, tree-lined streets. The main street (Hannan St), flanked by imposing public buildings, is wide enough to turn a camel train – a necessity in turn-of-the-century gold-field towns. You'll find most of the hotels, restaurants and offices on or close to Hannan St. Boulder is five km south of Kalgoorlie; the local bus service to Boulder leaves from the Exchange Hotel on the corner of Hannan St and Boulder Rd in Kalgoorlie.

Information
There's a helpful tourist office (☎ (090) 21 1413), on the corner of Hannan and Cassidy Sts, where you can get a good map of Kalgoorlie and buy the excellent and infor-

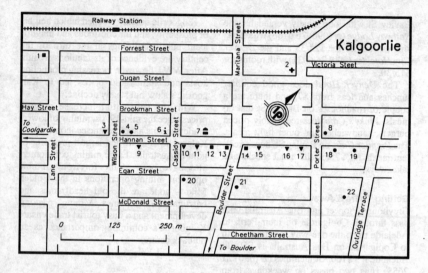

1	Inland City Hotel
2	Hospital
3	Takeaway Food Enclave
4	Town Hall
5	Ansett WA
6	Tourist Office
7	Post Office
8	RACWA
9	York Hotel
10	Pizza Cantina
11	De Bernales
12	Windsor Guesthouse
13	Palace Hotel
14	Exchange Hotel
15	Matteo's Pizza
16	Broccoli Forest
17	Top End Thai Restaurant
18	Museum of the Goldfields
19	Goldfields Aboriginal Art Gallery
20	School of Mines Museum
21	Surrey House
22	Paddy Hannan's Tree

mation-packed *Gold Rush Country* map for 50c. The office is open from 8.30 am to 5 pm Monday to Friday and from 9 am to 5 pm on Saturday. For an excellent account of the fascinating Kalgoorlie story, read *The Glit-*

tering Years (St George Books) by Arthur Bennet. The daily paper in Kal is the *Kalgoorlie Miner*.

Kal can get very hot in December and January; overall the cool winter months are the best time to visit. From late August to the end of September, however, the town is packed, and accommodation of any type can be difficult to find.

The RACWA (☎ (090) 21 1511) has an office on the corner of Porter and Hannan Sts.

Hainault Mine

One of Kalgoorlie's biggest attractions is the Hainault Mine. You can take the lift cage down into the bowels of the earth and make a tour around the drives and crosscuts of the mine, guided by an ex-miner.

It costs $10 for an underground tour and an audiovisual presentation, and $14 for a combined tour that also includes a tour of the surface workings and a gold pour. You can wander around the surface yourself for free. Underground tours are made at 10.30 am, 1 and 2.30 pm daily (more frequently during peak seasons) – book at the tourist office.

Golden Mile Loopline

You can make an interesting loop around the Golden Mile by catching the 'Rattler', a tourist train complete with commentary which makes an hour-long trip from Monday to Saturday at 11 am and on Sunday at 1.30 and 3 pm (additional tours operate at peak times). It leaves from Boulder Railway Station, passing the old mining works and the huge mountains of 'slime' – the cast-offs from the mining process. The cost is $8 for adults and $4 for children.

Museum of the Goldfields

The impressive red headframe at the northern end of Hannan St marks the entrance to this excellent museum. It is open daily from 10.30 am to 4.30 pm (admission is free) and has a wide range of exhibits including an underground gold vault and historic photographs. The tiny British Arms Hotel (the narrowest hotel in Australia), part of the museum, has many relics from Kalgoorlie's pioneering days, including a fully restored 1901 dental surgery – it's enough to put you off chocolate for life!

Other Attractions

The Mt Charlotte Lookout and the town's reservoir are only a few hundred metres from the north-eastern end of Hannan St. The view over the town is good but there's little to see of the reservoir, which is covered to limit evaporation. The Super Pit Lookout, in Lyne St at the back of the Boulder Block Tavern, gives a good insight into modern mining practices; it is open from 7.30 am to 4.15 pm daily.

The School of Mines Museum, on the corner of Egan and Cassidy Sts, has a geology display including replicas of big nuggets. It's usually open from 9 am to 4 pm Monday to Friday.

Along Hannan St, you'll find the imposing town hall and the equally impressive post office. There's an art gallery upstairs in the decorative town hall and pictures of the US Skylab which fell to earth in 1979, while outside is a replica of a statue of Paddy Hannan himself holding a water bag. The original statue is on display inside the town hall, protected from the elements and vandals.

A block back, north-west from Hannan St, is Hay St and one of Kalgoorlie's most famous 'attractions'. Although it's quietly ignored in the tourist brochures, Kalgoorlie has a block-long strip of brothels where the ladies of the night beckon passing men to their true-blue-Aussie galvanised-iron doorways. Nelson's blind eye has been turned to this activity for so long that it has become an accepted and historical part of the town.

Kalgoorlie also has a two-up school in a corrugated-iron amphitheatre – follow the signs from Hannan St. Two-up is a frenetic, uniquely Australian gambling game where two coins are tossed and bets are placed on the result. Amongst the gamblers' yelps, a lot of money seems to change hands.

On Outridge Terrace is Paddy Hannan's tree, marking the spot where the first gold strike was made. Hammond Park is a small fauna reserve with a miniature Bavarian castle. It's open seven days a week from 9 am to 5 pm.

The Goldfields War Museum in Burt St, Boulder, is open from 9 am to noon and from 1 to 4.30 pm on weekdays; admission is $1. The Boulder Railway Station, home to the Eastern Goldfields Historical Society Museum, is an 1897 building. It is open from 10 am to 12.30 pm Monday to Saturday and from 10 am to 4 pm Sunday; admission is 50c.

In the heyday of the Golden Mile, the rip-roaring hotels of the Boulder Block never closed, and thirsty miners off the shifts poured into them night and day. There's nothing much to see now, but there are plans to redevelop the Boulder Block area. On the other side of the Golden Mile loop, on the corner of Contention and Beal Sts, Fimiston, is the 1896 Boulder Block Tavern with a mine shaft right in the lounge bar. Miners used to sneak nuggets to the bartender via this shaft.

Organised Tours

Goldrush Tours (☎ (090) 21 2954) are the

main tour operators in Kalgoorlie. Book through the tourist office or from Goldrush Tours directly at Palace Chambers, Maritana St. They have tours of the town ($17, not including admission charges), Coolgardie ($25) and ghost towns ($39). There's also a gold-detector tour for avid fossickers ($22), and in August and September there are wild flower tours for $49.

For $20, you can see Kalgoorlie-Boulder and the Golden Mile mining operations from the air with Goldfields Air Services.

Places to Stay

There are a number of caravan parks in Kalgoorlie. The closest to the city centre are the *Golden Village Caravan Park* (☎ (090) 21 4162), on Hay St, two km south-west of the railway station, which has tent sites and on-site vans; and the *Prospector Caravan Park* (☎ (090) 21 2524) on the Great Eastern Highway with tent sites, on-site vans and cabins.

The popular and central *Windsor Guesthouse* (☎ (090) 21 5483), at the end of the courtyard at 147 Hannan St, is a quiet and friendly place with a TV room, kitchen facilities and shared accommodation for $12 per night; single rooms are $15. At 9 Boulder Rd is the comfortable *Surrey House* (☎ (090) 21 1340), which has backpackers' accommodation for $15 per night and singles/doubles for $28/40; a continental breakfast is $4.50 extra per person.

The *Kalgoorlie Goldfields Backpackers* (☎ (090) 93 1435), at 58 Piesse St in Boulder, is a little less convenient but the hostel will pick up guests on request from the bus or tourist office. Dorm accommodation is $12 per night.

There are several pleasantly old-fashioned hotels right in the centre of Kalgoorlie, including the *Palace Hotel* (☎ (090) 21 2788) on the corner of Palace and Hannan Sts. Standard rooms cost $30/40 for singles/doubles.

The motel section of the *Star & Garter Hotel* (☎ (090) 21 3004), 497 Hannan St, has singles/doubles for $60/70. The *Cornwall Hotel* (☎ (090) 93 2510), 25 Hopkins St,

Boulder, is in a beautifully furnished 1898 building with an outdoor garden restaurant; singles/doubles are $34/50.

Places to Eat

There are plenty of counter-meal pubs, restaurants and cafes in Kalgoorlie, particularly along Hannan St. The *York Hotel*, on Hannan St, does counter meals in its Steak House from $7 to $10, and meals in the saloon bar for around $6. The *Criterion* and the *Grand* hotels also do counter meals and usually have cheap lunch-time specials from $4 to $5.

The *Exchange* and *Palace* hotels, both on the corner of Hannan and Boulder Sts, have restaurants with main courses from around $10, and cheaper food ($4 to $7) in the saloon bars.

The more up-market *De Bernales* does tasty food from $10 to $13 and has a pleasant verandah opening onto Hannan St – a good place to sip a beer and watch life go by.

The *Broccoli Forest*, at 75 Hannan St, has a lunch bar with an interesting menu – most of it vegetarian. Nearby, the *Top End* Thai restaurant, at 71 Hannan St, is an excellent place for a splurge – a wide range of prawn, curry and noodle dishes costs from $12 to $15.

At 275 Hannan St is the *Kalgoorlie Cafe*, which has burgers and other fast food, or there's the *Victoria Cafe*, at 246 Hannan St, for an early breakfast. For pizza, try *Pizza Cantina*, 211 Hannan St, or *Matteo's* at No 123.

On Wilson St between Brookman and Hannan Sts is a small enclave of takeaway places including the *Fu Wah* Chinese restaurant and *Thai Food* with small and large combination dishes from $6.50 to $8.

Kalgoorlie no longer brews its own beer, although Hannan's Beer can still be purchased at local hotels.

In Boulder, you can get counter meals at *Tattersalls* on the corner of Bart and Lane Sts, and opposite at the *Albion Hotel*. You can also try the *Wah On* Chinese restaurant, next to the Goldfields War Museum, and *Peachy's* takeaway at 16 Burt St.

Things to Buy

The Goldfields Aboriginal Art Gallery, next to the Museum of the Goldfields, has a fine collection of paintings, didgeridoos and other crafts for sale; it is open from 8 am to 5 pm Monday to Friday and from 10.30 am to 1 pm on Saturday.

Getting There & Away

Air Ansett WA fly from Perth to Kalgoorlie several times daily; the Apex return fare is $263, and the full return fare is $394. The Ansett WA office (☎ (090) 91 2828), at 314 Hannan St, is near the town hall.

Skywest have two direct flights a day for $238 (Apex) or $352 (full fare) – other discounts such as a special weekend fares are also available (☎ (090) 91 1446). Goldfields Air Services (☎ (090) 93 2116) fly from Kalgoorlie to Esperance (via Norseman) every Tuesday and return the same day – the one-way fare is $134.

Bus Greyhound/Pioneer (☎ (090) 217100) and Bus Australia (☎ toll-free 008 112 408) buses operate through Kalgoorlie on their services from Perth to Sydney, Melbourne and Adelaide; the fare from Perth is around $55. Transcontinental (☎ (09) 250 2838) also have a tri-weekly Perth to Kalgoorlie service for the same price. Check timetables carefully as some of these buses pull into Kalgoorlie at an ungodly hour of the night when everything is closed up, and finding a place to stay can be difficult.

Westrail (☎ (090) 21 2023) run a bus three times a week from Kal to Esperance – once via Kambalda and Norseman and twice via Coolgardie and Norseman; the trip takes 5½ hours and costs $16.30 to Norseman and $30.40 to Esperance. Transcontinental Coachlines go to towns north of Kalgoorlie such as Menzies ($16), Leonora ($31), Laverton ($43) and Leinster ($49).

Train The daily Prospector service from Perth takes around 7½ hours and costs $53.20. From Perth, you can book seats at the Western Australian Tourist Centre in Forrest Place or at the Westrail terminal

(☎ (09) 326 2222). It's wise to book as this service is fairly popular, particularly in the tourist season. The Indian-Pacific and Trans-Australian trains also go through Kalgoorlie.

Getting Around

Between Kalgoorlie and Boulder, there's a regular bus service (get the timetable from the tourist office) for $1.10.

You can rent cars from Hertz (☎ (090) 91 2625), Budget (☎ (090) 93 2300), Avis (☎ (090) 21 1472) or Passport International (☎ (090) 21 7284). If you want to explore very far, you'll have to drive, hitch or take a tour as public transport is limited. A taxi to the airport costs around $7. You can hire bicycles from Johnston Cycles (☎ (090) 21 1157), at 76 Boulder St, for $5 for two hours, $18 per day or $36 per week – a $30 deposit is required for all bike rentals.

NORTH OF KALGOORLIE

The road north is surfaced from Kalgoorlie all the way to Leonora-Gwalia, 240 km north, and from there to Laverton (130 km north-east) and Leinster (160 km north). Off the main road, however, traffic is virtually nonexistent and rain can quickly close the dirt roads.

Towns of interest include **Kanowna**, just 22 km from Kalgoorlie along a dirt road. In 1905, this town had a population of 12,000, 16 hotels, many churches and an hourly train service to Kalgoorlie. Today, apart from the railway station and the odd pile of rubble, absolutely nothing remains!

Broad Arrow now has a population of 20, compared with 2400 at the turn of the century, but one of the town's original eight hotels operates in a virtually unchanged condition. **Ora Banda** has gone from a population of 2000 to less than 50.

Menzies, 130 km north of Kal, has about 110 people today, compared with 5000 in 1900. Many early buildings remain, including the railway station with its 120-metre-long platform and the town hall with its clockless clocktower. The ship bringing the clock from England unfortunately sank en route.

With a population of 2000, **Leonora** serves as the railhead for the nickel from Windarra and Leinster. In adjoining **Gwalia** (a ghost town), the Sons of Gwalia Gold-mine, the largest in Western Australia outside Kalgoorlie, closed in 1963 and much of the town closed with it; due to the increase in gold prices this and other mines in the area have been reopened. At one time, the mine was managed by Herbert Hoover, later to become president of the USA.

The Gwalia Historical Society is housed in the 1898 mine office – this fascinating local museum is open daily. Also of interest is the restored State Hotel, originally built in 1903. South of Leonora-Gwalia, 25 km off the main road, is **Kookynie**, another interest-ing once-flourishing mining town with just a handful of inhabitants left – in 1905 the population was 1500. Nearby **Niagara** is also a ghost town.

From Leonora-Gwalia, you can turn north-east to **Laverton**, where the surfaced road ends. The population here declined from 1000 in 1910 to 200 in 1970 when the Poseidon nickel discovery (beloved of stock-market speculators in the late '60s and early '70s) revived mining operations in nearby Windarra. The town now has a population of 1500, and there are many abandoned mines in the area. From here, it is just 1710 km north-east to Alice Springs (see the follow-ing section on the Gunbarrel Highway).

North of Leonora-Gwalia, the road is now surfaced to **Leinster** (population 260), another modern nickel town. Nearby, **Agnew** is another old gold town that has all but disappeared. From here, it's 170 km north to **Wiluna** and another 180 km west to **Meekatharra** on the surfaced Great North-ern Highway which runs 765 km south-west to Perth or 860 km north to Port Hedland. Through the '30s, when arsenic was mined there, Wiluna had a population of 8000 and was a modern, prosperous town. The ore ran out in 1948 and the town quickly declined. Today, the minute population is mainly Aboriginal.

Warburton Rd/Gunbarrel Highway

For those interested in an outback experi-ence, the unsealed road from Laverton to Yulara (the tourist development near Ayers Rock) via Warburton provides a rich scenery of red sand, spinifex, mulga and desert oaks. The road, while sandy in places, is suitable for conventional vehicles, although a 4WD would give a much smoother ride. Although this road is often called the Gunbarrel Highway, the genuine article actually runs some distance to the north, but it is very rough and no longer maintained.

You should, of course, take precautions relevant to travel in such an isolated area – tell someone of your travel plans and take adequate supplies of water, petrol, food and spare parts. The longest stretch without fuel is between Laverton and Warburton (568 km). Don't even consider doing it from November to March due to the extreme heat. See the Getting Around chapter for more details.

Petrol is available at Laverton, Warburton (where basic supplies are also available) and Yulara. In an emergency, you may be able to get fuel at the Docker River settlement. At **Giles**, about 105 km west from the Northern Territory border, is a weather station with a friendly 'Visitors Welcome' sign and a bar – it is well worth a visit.

Transcontinental Coachlines WA (**☎** (09) 250 2838) runs a weekly Perth to Yulara service along this road for $240 one-way.

KAMBALDA (population 5000)

Kambalda died as a gold-mining town in 1906, but nickel was discovered there in 1966, and today it is a major mining centre. There are two town centres, East and West Kambalda, about four km apart. The town is on the shores of Lake LeFroy, a large salt pan and a popular spot for land yachting. The view from Red Hill Lookout in Kambalda East is well worth checking out.

The helpful tourist office (**☎** (090) 27 1446), on Irish Mulga Drive, West Kam-balda, can provide you with information and a map of the area.

NORSEMAN (population 2500)

To most people, Norseman is just a crossroads where you turn east for the trans-Nullarbor Eyre Highway journey, south to Esperance along the Leeuwin Way or north to Coolgardie and Perth. The town, however, also has gold mines, some still in operation. The **Historical & Geological Museum** has household items and mining tools from the gold-rush days; it's open weekdays from 10 am to 4 pm and admission is $2.

There's a very helpful tourist office (☎ (090) 39 0171), at 68 Roberts St, which is open daily from 9 am to 5 pm. Next to the tourist office is a tourist rest park, open from 8 am to 6 pm, which has hot showers, toilets and barbecues.

An interesting gold-mining tour is conducted by the Central Norseman Gold Corporation every weekday at 9.30; the 2½-hour tour costs $5 and bookings can be made at the tourist office.

You can get an excellent view of the town and the surrounding salt lakes from the **Beacon Hill Lookout** down past the mountainous tailings dumps. The dumps, one of which contains 4.2 million tonnes of rock, are the results of gold operations from 1938 to 1977.

The graffiti-covered **Dundas Rocks** are huge boulders in picturesque countryside, 28 km south of Norseman. Also worth a look are the views at sunrise and sunset of the dry, expansive and spectacular **Lake Cowans**, north of Norseman.

South of Norseman, just under halfway along the road to Esperance is the small township of **Salmon Gums** (population 50), named after the gum trees, prevalent in the area, which acquire a seasonal rich-pink bark in late summer and autumn.

Places to Stay & Eat

Norseman Caravan Park (☎ (090) 39 1262) has tent sites and on-site cabins and vans. The backpackers' hostel in Norseman has closed down, although you might want to check with the tourist office as there has been

talk of the hostel reopening sometime in the future. The *Norseman Hotel* (☎ (090) 39 1023) charges $20/30 for B&B; the *Prince & Pauper* guesthouse (☎ (090) 39 1542) also has B&B for $18/34 and backpackers' accommodation for $10 per night.

Bits & Pizzas has a wide range of eat-in or takeaway meals, and also cooked breakfasts with the works for $7.50.

Getting There & Away

Goldfields Air Services (☎ (090) 93 2116) fly from Kalgoorlie to Esperance via Norseman – the Kalgoorlie to Norseman sector costs $70. For bus information, see the Kalgoorlie Getting There & Away section.

The Nullarbor

It's a little under 2700 km between Perth in Western Australia and Adelaide in South Australia – not much less than the distance from London to Moscow. The long and sometimes lonely Eyre Highway crosses the southern edge of the vast Nullarbor Plain – Nullarbor is bad Latin for 'no trees' and an accurate description of this flat, treeless wasteland. Along the road though there actually are trees as this coastal fringe receives regular rain, especially in winter.

The road across the Nullarbor takes its name from John Eyre, the explorer who made the first east-west crossing in 1841. It was a superhuman effort that took five months of hardship and resulted in the death of Eyre's companion John Baxter. In 1877, a telegraph line was laid across the Nullarbor, roughly delineating the route the first road would take.

Later in the century, miners en route to the gold fields of Western Australia followed the same telegraph line route across the empty plain. In 1896, the first bicycle crossing was made and in 1912 the first car was driven across, but in the next 12 years only three more cars managed to traverse the continent.

In 1941, the war inspired the building of a

trans-continental highway, just as it had the Alice Springs to Darwin route. It was a rough-and-ready track when completed, and in the '50s only a few vehicles a day made the crossing. In the '60s, the traffic flow increased to more than 30 vehicles a day and in 1969 the Western Australia government surfaced the road as far as the South Australian border. Finally, in 1976, the last stretch from the South Australian border was surfaced and now the Nullarbor crossing is a much easier drive, but still a hell of a long one.

The surfaced road runs close to the coast on the South Australian side. The Nullarbor region ends dramatically on the coast of the Great Australian Bight, at cliffs that drop steeply into the ocean. It's easy to see why this was a seafarer's nightmare, for a ship driven on to the coast would quickly be pounded to pieces against the cliffs, and climbing them would be a near impossibility.

The Indian-Pacific Railway runs north of the coast and actually on the Nullarbor Plain – unlike the main road, which only runs on the fringes of the great plain. One stretch of the railway runs dead straight for 478 km – the longest piece of straight railway line in the world.

Crossing the Nullarbor

See the Perth Getting There & Away section for air, rail, hitching and bus information across the Nullarbor.

Although the Nullarbor is no longer a torture trail where cars get shaken to bits by potholes and corrugations or where you're going to die of thirst waiting for another vehicle if you break down, it's still wise to avoid difficulties whenever possible.

The longest distance between fuel stops is about 200 km, so if you're foolish enough to run out of petrol midway, you'll have a nice long round trip to get more. Getting help for a mechanical breakdown can be equally time-consuming and very expensive, so make sure your vehicle is in good shape and that you've got plenty of petrol, good tyres and at least a basic kit of simple spare parts. Carry some drinking water just in case you do have to sit it out by the roadside on a hot summer day.

Take it easy on the Nullarbor – plenty of people try to set speed records and plenty

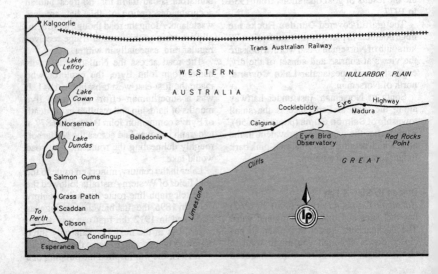

more have made a real mess of their cars when they've run into big kangaroos, particularly at night.

THE EYRE HIGHWAY

From Norseman, where the Eyre Highway begins, it's 709 km to Eucla on the Western Australia/South Australia border and a further 494 km to Ceduna (from an Aboriginal word meaning 'a place to sit down and rest') in South Australia. From Ceduna, it's still another 773 km to Adelaide via Port Augusta. The trip is a long way by anyone's standards!

Balladonia

From Norseman, the first settlement you reach is Balladonia, 190 km to the east. Before Balladonia, you may see the remains of old stone fences built to enclose stock. Clay saltpans are also visible in the area. **Newmann's Rocks** (50 km west of Balladonia) are also worthwhile seeing. The Crocker family have a fine art gallery with paintings of the Eyre Highway. Visits can be arranged by phoning (090) 39 3456 between 9 am and 4.30 pm. The *Balladonia Hotel/*

Motel (☎ (090) 39 3453) has rooms from $38/44 and a caravan park with tent sites from $8.

The road from Balladonia to Cocklebiddy is one of the loneliest stretches of road across the Nullarbor. Shortly after Balladonia, three km north of the road, are a number of natural rock waterholes known as the **Afghan Rocks**. They often hold water far into the summer and were named after an Afghani camel driver who was shot when he was found washing his feet in the water.

Caiguna & Cocklebiddy

The road from Balladonia to Caiguna includes one of the longest stretches of straight road in the world – 145 km. At Caiguna, the *John Eyre Motel* (☎ (090) 39 3459) has rooms for $50/59, and a caravan park with tent sites from $9 and on-site vans from $25.

At Cocklebiddy are the stone ruins of an Aboriginal mission. **Cocklebiddy Cave** is the largest of the Nullarbor caves – in 1983 a team of French explorers set a record there for the deepest cave dive in the world. With a 4WD, you can travel south of Cocklebiddy

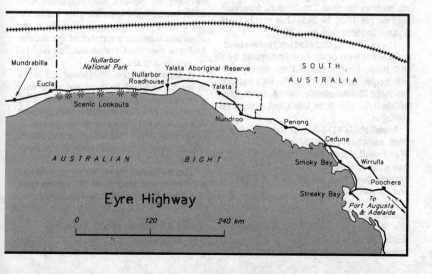

to **Twilight Cove**, where there are 75-metre-high limestone cliffs. The *Wedgetail Inn* (☎ (090) 39 3462) at Cocklebiddy has rooms from $38/44 and tent sites for $8.

The *Eyre Bird Observatory* (☎ (090) 39 3450) provides accommodation by prior arrangement only. Established in 1977, it is housed in the **Eyre Telegraph Station**, an 1897 stone building in the Nuytsland Nature Reserve, surrounded by mallee scrubland. A wide range of desert fauna & flora are studied there. A small museum at the rear of the station has exhibits from the days of the telegraph line and of the legendary station-master, William Graham.

Full board and return transport to the bird observatory from Cocklebiddy or the Micro-wave Tower is included in the price of $45 per night, or $39 for YHA members. You will need a 4WD to get to the bird observatory, which is 42 km south-east of Cocklebiddy. Guests are expected to help out with washing and cooking.

Madura & Mundrabilla

Madura, 91 km east of Cocklebiddy, is close to the hills of the Hampton Tablelands. At one time, horses were bred here for the Indian Army. You get good views over the plains from the road. The *Madura Hospitality Inns* (☎ (090) 39 3464) has rooms from $54/64 and tent sites from $6.

The ruins of the **Old Madura Homestead**, several km west of the new homestead by a dirt track, have some old machinery and other equipment. Caves in the area include the large **Mullamullang Caves**, north-west of Madura, with three lakes and many side passages.

Mundrabilla (116 km to the east) has a **bird sanctuary** behind the motel. The *Mundrabilla Motor Hotel* (☎ (090) 39 3465) has singles/doubles from $45/55 and a caravan park with cabins for $15 a person and tent sites from $5.

Eucla & the Border

Just before the South Australia border is Eucla, which has picturesque ruins of an old **telegraph repeater and weather station**,

first opened in 1877. The telegraph line now runs along the railway line, far to the north. The station, five km from the roadhouse, is gradually being engulfed by the sand dunes. You can also inspect the historic jetty, which is visible from the top of the dunes. The dunes around Eucla are a truly spectacular sight.

The Eucla area also has many caves, including the well-known **Koonalda Cave** with its 45-metre-high chamber. You enter by ladder. Like other Nullarbor caves, it's really for experienced cave explorers only.

The *Eucla Amber Hotel-Motel* (☎ (090) 39 3468) has rooms in its Eucla Pass section from $18/30 and tent sites from $2. There's a *Travellers' Village* at the border with camping facilities, a motel, cabins and a restaurant. Many people have their photo taken with the international sign pinpointing distances to many parts of the world. Behind it, for connoisseurs of kitsch, is a five-metre-high fibreglass kangaroo.

The *WA-SA Border Village* (☎ (090) 39 3474) has cabins from $32 a double, motel units from $52 and tent sites from $8.

Nullarbor Roadhouse (South Australia)

Between the Western Australia/South Australia border and Nullarbor (184 km to the east), the Eyre Highway runs close to the coast and there are a number of spectacular lookouts over the Great Australian Bight – be sure to stop at one or two.

Around Nullarbor Roadhouse are many caves that should be explored only with extreme care (again they are recommended to experienced cave explorers only). Watch out for wombat holes and poisonous snakes in the area. A dirt road leads to a nice beach, 30 km away – ask directions at the roadhouse.

The *Nullarbor Hotel-Motel* (☎ (086) 25 6271) has tent sites from $8, cabins from $35, units from $55/65 and a restaurant.

Yalata & Nundroo (South Australia)

The road passes through the Yalata Aboriginal Reserve (600,000 hectares), and

Aborigines often sell boomerangs and other souvenirs by the roadside. You can also buy these in the Yalata Community Roadhouse. The *Yalata Aboriginal Community Roadhouse* (☎ (086) 25 6990) has singles/doubles from $30/35 and tent sites from $3.50; there's also a restaurant and takeaway food service.

Nundroo is the real edge of the Nullarbor. The *Nundroo Inn* (☎ (086) 25 6120) has singles/doubles for $58/63 and a caravan park with tent sites from $7. There is a licensed restaurant, takeaway food and a swimming pool.

Penong (South Australia)
Between Nundroo and Penong is the ghost town of **Fowlers Bay**. There is good fishing in the area, and nearby is **Mexican Hat Beach**.

You can make a short detour south of Penong to see the Pink Lake, Point Sinclair and Cactus Beach – a surf beach that is a 'must' for any serious surfer making the east-west journey (see the South Australia chapter for accommodation information).

The *Penong Hotel* (☎ (086) 25 1050) has basic singles/doubles from $20/30, and serves counter meals. The service station across the road has a restaurant and takeaways.

Eastbound from Penong to Ceduna, there are several places with petrol and other facilities.

The South & South-West

The southern area of Western Australia, the 'Great Southern', has magnificent coastline pounded by huge seas, rugged ranges, national parks, Albany (the oldest settlement in Western Australia) and, in the south-west, the greenest and most fertile areas of Western Australia – a great contrast to the dry and barren country found in most of the state. Here, you will find the great karri and jarrah forests, prosperous farming land, wineries and more of the state's beautiful wild flowers.

Many travellers on the road between the east and west coasts of Australia take the direct route through Western Australia via Coolgardie and Norseman. However, if you travel the longer route to or from Perth around the south-west corner of Australia, you will be rewarded by some of the state's most spectacular scenery.

Accommodation
Many towns in the region are popular holiday resorts with plenty of accommodation, and there are hostels at Bunbury, Quindalup (near Dunsborough), Augusta, Pemberton, Denmark (Valley of the Giants), the Stirling Ranges, Albany and Esperance. Enough hostels, in fact, to make a really interesting hostelling circuit possible.

Getting There & Away
Air Skywest (☎ (09) 323 1188 in Perth) have flights to Albany ($141 one-way, or $190 Apex return) and Esperance ($182 one-way, or $241 Apex return). Goldfields Air Services have flights between Kalgoorlie and Esperance via Norseman for $134 one-way.

Bus & Train Westrail have a number of bus services in the region including buses from Kalgoorlie and Perth to Esperance and from Perth to Hyden, Manjimup, Albany and Denmark. There is also a bus and the Australind train service from Perth to Bunbury. From Bunbury, Westrail buses continue to Busselton, Yallingup, Margaret River and Augusta.

South-West Coach Lines (☎ (09) 324 2333) also service the region and have daily services from Perth to Bunbury, Busselton, Dunsborough, Margaret River, Augusta, Nannup and Manjimup.

AUSTRALIND (population 800)
Australind, yet another holiday resort, is a pleasant 11 km drive from Bunbury. The town takes its name from an 1840s plan to

make it a port for trade with India. The plan never worked but the strange name (Australia-India) remains.

Australind has the tiny **St Nicholas Church**, which, at just four by seven metres, is said to be the smallest church in Australia. There's also **Henton Cottage**, built in 1843, and a **gemstone and rock museum** in the town. There is a scenic drive between Australind and Binningup along **Leschenault Inlet**, a good place to catch blue manna crabs.

INLAND

Inland from the south-west coast, there's the town of **Harvey** in a popular bushwalking area of rolling green hills to the north of Bunbury. This is the home of Western Australia's Big Orange, standing 20 metres high at the Fruit Bowl on the South-Western Highway; it's an orchard with a tourist complex. There are dam systems and some beautiful waterfalls nearby, and the **Yalgorup National Park** is north of town. The tourist office (☎ (097) 29 1122) is on Young St.

Further south of Bunbury is **Donnybrook**, in the centre of an apple-growing area. It has a deer park to the north and a tourist office (☎ (097) 31 1720) in an old railway station. Apple-picking work is often available in season (which seems to be most of the year).

Collie, Western Australia's only coal town, has an interesting replica of a coal mine, an historical museum and a steam-locomotive museum. There is some pleasant bushwalking country around the town and plenty of wild flowers in season. The tourist office (☎ (097) 34 2051) is on Throssell St.

Places to Stay

The *Rainbow Caravan Park* (☎ (097) 29 2239), on King St in Harvey, has tent sites and on-site vans, as does the *Mr Marron Holiday Village* (☎ (097) 34 2507) in Porter St, Collie.

In Donnybrook, the *Brook Lodge* (☎ (097) 31 1520), on Bridge St, is a private lodge with kitchen and laundry facilities, and

accommodation in twin rooms for $9.50 per night or $60 per week.

BUNBURY (population 25,000)

As well as being a port, an industrial town and a holiday resort, Bunbury, Western Australia's second largest town, is also noted for its blue manna crabs and dolphins. The tourist office (☎ (097) 21 7922) is in the old 1904 railway station on Carmody Place.

The town's old buildings include **King Cottage**, which now houses a museum, the **Rose Hotel** and **St Mark's Church** built in 1842. The interesting **Arts Complex** on Wittenoom St is in a restored 1897 convent building.

The **Marlston Lookout**, on Apex Drive, provides a panoramic view of the city and surrounding areas. Two old steam trains, the Leschenault Lady and the Koombana Queen, are now in the **Boyanup Transport Museum**, 21 km south-east of Bunbury. The **South-West Museum**, on the Bussell Highway in Gelorup, has displays of minerals, seashells, fossils and petrified wood.

Dolphins

You don't have to go to Monkey Mia to interact with dolphins; you can also do so at the Bunbury Dolphin Trust centre on Koombana Beach. Visits from a group that regularly feed in the Inner Harbour usually occur several times a day, less frequently in winter; a flag is raised when the dolphins are in.

The area, staffed during the day by helpful volunteers, was set up in 1989, and dolphins started to interact with the public in early 1990. A brochure explains the simple rules of contact with dolphins, or you can see one of the rangers if you are unsure.

Places to Stay

Koombana Park (☎ (097) 21 2516), on Koombana Drive, is the most central of the city's caravan parks.

Bunbury Youth Hostel (☎ (097) 91 2621), a good place to stay, is on the corner of Stirling and Moore Sts in a roomy, renovated historic residence. Dorm beds are $10 per night and bicycles are available for rent. *Bunbury Backpackers* (☎ (097) 21 3359), closer to the city centre at the corner of Wittenoom and Clifton Sts (two blocks from the tourist office and the Indian Ocean), costs $10 a night for shared accommodation and $25 for a double; they will also provide free transport to see the dolphins.

The *Captain Bunbury Hotel* (☎ (097) 21 2021), at 8 Victoria St, has basic rooms for $15/25, and the *Prince of Wales* (☎ (097) 21 2016) on Stephen St has rooms for $26/46 with breakfast. The *Rose Hotel* (☎ (097) 21 4533) is a clean and lavishly restored place; singles/doubles are $25/45 with breakfast.

Places to Eat
The *Bunbury Pavilion* on Symmons St is an international food hall with kebabs, roasts, Italian, Chinese and Indian food from $4 to $6; it is open Thursday to Monday from 11 am to 9 pm. *Drooly's*, at 70 Victoria St, does great pizzas for moderate prices. The *Rose Hotel*, on Wellington St, does good counter meals, and the *Friendship* Chinese restaurant, at 50 Victoria St, has tasty food and a varied menu.

Getting There & Around
South-West Coach Lines buses travel daily between Bunbury and Perth for $14. Westrail also has daily bus ($14.80) and train ($16.30) services from Perth. The train trip takes around 2½ hours; the bus around three hours. A detailed walking tour of Bunbury brochure is available from the tourist office.

BUSSELTON (population 6500)
Busselton on the shores of Geographe Bay is another popular holiday resort. The town has a two-km jetty which was reputed to be the longest timber jetty in Australia until it was shortened by a cyclone in 1978. Busselton has a tourist office (☎ (097) 52 1091) in the civic centre on Southern Drive.

The old **courthouse** has been restored and now houses an impressive arts centre with a gallery, a coffee shop and artists'

workshops. **Wonnerup House**, 10 km east of town, is a 1859 Colonial-style house lovingly restored by the National Trust.

The old **butter factory**, on the banks of the Vassa River past the historic and picturesque St Mary's Church, is a small museum with butter-making equipment, photographs, furniture and replica schoolhouse and settlers' house.

Places to Stay & Eat
There is a great deal of accommodation along this stretch of coast. The *Motel Busselton* (☎ (097) 52 1908), 90 Bussell Highway, has comfortable, well-equipped units from $20/24 per night. *Villa Carlotta Guesthouse* (☎ (097) 52 1034), at 110 Adelaide St, is good, friendly, organises tours and has singles/doubles for $28/45 with breakfast. The most central of the many caravan parks is *Kookaburra No 1* (☎ (097) 52 1516), 66 Marine Terrace.

There are a stack of places to eat in Busselton including *Albertini's* on Queen St for Italian food, the *Golden Inn* on Albert St for Chinese food, and hotels such as the *Vasse* and the *Commercial*, both on Queen St, for counter meals.

DUNSBOROUGH
Dunsborough, just to the west of Busselton, is a pleasant little coastal town that has become dependent on tourism. You'll find the tourist office (☎ (097) 553517) in the Dunsborough shopping centre.

North-west of Dunsborough, the Cape Naturalist Rd leads to excellent beaches such as **Meelup, Eagle Bay and Bunker Bay**, some fine coastal lookouts and the tip of the cape which has a lighthouse and some walking trails. The **Bannamah Wildlife Park**, two km from town on Caves Rd, is set in natural bushland.

Places to Stay & Eat
Green Acres Caravan Park (☎ (097) 55 3087), on the beachfront at Dunsborough, has tent sites and on-site vans and cabins. Near Dunsborough, in Quindalup, is the refurbished *Dunsborough YHA Resort*

Hostel (☎ (097) 55 3107) on the beachfront at 285 Geographe Bay Rd; the rate is $12 per night and they hire bicycles, windsurfers and canoes.

Dunsborough Health Foods in the shopping centre sells wholemeal salad rolls and delicious smoothies and juices. The *Dunsborough Bakery* has tasty pies.

YALLINGUP

Yallingup, a Mecca for surfers, is surrounded by a spectacular coastline and some fine beaches. Nearby is the stunning **Yallingup Cave** which was discovered, or rather stumbled upon, in 1899 by Edward Dawson. The cave is open daily from 9.30 am to 3.30 pm and you can look around by yourself or take a guided tour that also explores parts of the cave not open to most visitors.

The *Yallingup Caravan Park* (☎ (097) 55 2164) on the beachfront at Valley Rd has tent sites and on-site vans.

MARGARET RIVER

The attractive town of Margaret River is a popular holiday spot due to its proximity to fine surf (Margaret River Mouth, Gnarabup, Suicides and Redgate) and swimming (Prevelly and Grace Town) beaches, some of Australia's best wineries and spectacular scenery. The Augusta-Margaret River tourist office (☎ (097) 57 2147) has a wad of information on the area including an extensive vineyard guide; it is on the corner of the Bussell Highway and Tunbridge Rd.

The **Old Settlement Craft Village** conjures up images of 1920s farm living complete with a blacksmith who gives demonstrations. **Bellview Shell Museum** is at Witchcliffe, six km south down the Bussell Highway. The historic 1865 **Wallcliffe House**, on Wallcliffe Rd towards Prevelly Park, is open to the public. **Eagle Heritage**, five km south of Margaret River on Boodjidup Rd, has an interesting collection of birds of prey in a natural setting and displays of falconry; it is open daily from 10 am to 5 pm and costs $3.50.

The old coast road between Augusta, Margaret River and Busselton is a good alternative to the direct road which runs slightly inland. The coast here has real variety – cliff faces, long beaches pounded by rolling surf, and calm, sheltered bays.

Places to Stay

There are plenty of places to stay around Margaret River but unfortunately most are upwards of $50 per night. One exception is the *Margaret River Lodge* (☎ (097) 57 2532) a backpackers' hostel, about 1½ km southwest from the town centre at 220 Railway Terrace. It's clean, friendly and modern with all the facilities including a good swimming pool, bicycle hire and an open fireplace. There are twin rooms and dormitories from $13 a person.

Other possibilities include the *Margaret River Caravan Park* (☎ (097) 57 2180), on Station Rd, which has tent sites and on-site vans, and the *Riverview Caravan Park* (☎ (097) 57 2270) on Willmott Ave.

If you want to splash out, the *Croft* (☎ 097) 57 2845), at 54 Wallcliffe Rd, is a comfortable guesthouse run by a very friendly couple. Rooms range from $40 to $55 per double and the breakfast has been described by one reader as 'the best in Western Australia'.

Places to Eat

Among the many places to eat in Margaret River is the *Settler's Tavern*, on Bussell Highway, which has good counter meals from $10 to $12 and bar snacks like nachos, burgers and fish & chips from $5 to $7 – they also have live music occasionally. On the same road, you can also try the *Kebab Company* which has a wide range of kebabs and falafels from $4 to $5.

Getting There & Around

There are daily bus services between Perth and Margaret River on South-West Coach Lines ($21) and Westrail ($22.30); the trip takes around five hours. Bikes can be rented on a daily or hourly basis from Margaret River Lodge on Railway Terrace.

AUGUSTA

A popular holiday resort, Augusta is five km north of Cape Leeuwin which has a rugged coastline (though not a patch on the coastal scenery around Albany and Esperance), a lighthouse with views extending over two oceans (the Indian and the Southern) and a salt-encrusted 1895 waterwheel. The interesting **Augusta Historical Museum**, on Blackwood Ave, has exhibits relating to local history. You'll find the tourist office (☎ (097) 58 1695) in a souvenir shop at 70 Blackwood Ave.

Between here and Margaret River to the north, there are some good beaches at **Hamelin Bay** and **Cosy Corner**, and a number of limestone caves. These include **Jewel Cave** (the most picturesque), **Lake Cave** and **Mammoth Cave**, where fossilised skeletons of Tasmanian tigers have been found. Guided cave tours, the only way to see these caves, run two to four times per day for $5, depending on the season. In all, 120 caves have been discovered between Cape Leeuwin and Cape Naturaliste but only these three, and Yallingup Cave near Busselton, are open to the public.

Places to Stay & Eat

Doonbanks (☎ (097) 58 1517) is the most central caravan park. There are a number of basic camp grounds in the Leeuwin-Naturaliste National Park including ones on Boranup Drive and Conto's Field, near Lake Cave.

The small *Augusta Associate YHA Hostel* (☎ (097) 58 1433) costing $9 per night is in a cottage on the corner of Bussell Highway and Blackwood Ave. Some of the self-contained holiday flats have reasonable rates but they may have minimum booking periods in the high season; try *Calypso* (☎ (097) 58 1944) which costs $25 per night for two; or *Clovelly* (☎ (097) 58 1577) at $34 for two.

The *Augusta Hotel* does counter meals, or head for *Squirrels*, next to the hotel, where you can find delicious burgers piled high with salad, Lebanese sandwiches and various health foods.

NANNUP (population 1100)

Fifty km west of Bridgetown is Nannup, a quiet, historical and picturesque town in the heart of forest and farmland. The tourist office (☎ (097) 56 1211) at the old 1922 police station in Brockman St (open daily from 9 am to 3 pm) has an excellent information booklet (50c) that points out places of interest around town and details a range of scenic drives in the area, including a Blackwood River Rd drive and numerous forest drives. There is a sawmill (one of the largest in Western Australia), an arboretum, some fine old buildings and several craft shops.

The natural **Berrabup Pool**, about 10 km west of town, is a great place for a swim.

Places to Stay & Eat

There are plans to open a backpackers' lodge in Nannup – contact the tourist office to see if it is open. The centrally located and friendly *Dry Brook* (☎ (097) 56 1049) has comfortable singles/doubles for $20/30 with breakfast and is highly recommended.

The *Blackwood Cafe* has good light meals such as quiche, soup and sandwiches, and the *Country Kitchen* has rolls, jaffles and home-made scones and fruit cake; both are near the Nannup Hotel (which has counter meals) on Warren Rd.

BRIDGETOWN (population 1500)

This quiet country town on the Blackwood River is in an area of karri forests and farmland. Bridgetown has some old buildings, including Bridgedale House which was built of mud and clay by the area's first settler in 1862 and has been restored by the National Trust. A panoramic view of town can be seen from **Sutton's Lookout** off Philips St, and there is a local history display and jigsaw collection in the tourist office (☎ (097) 61 1740) on Hampton St.

Interesting features of the Blackwood River valley are the burrawangs (grass trees) and large granite boulders. In **Boyup Brook**, 31 km north-east of Bridgetown, there is a flora reserve, a country & western music collection and a large butterfly and beetle display. Nearby is **Norlup Pool** with glacial rock formations, and **Wilga**, which is an old timber mill with vintage engines.

Places to Stay

Bridgetown Caravan Park (☎ (097) 61 1053), South-Western Highway, has tent sites and on-site vans. The *Old Well* (☎ (097) 61 2032) on Gifford St, the *Bridgetown Hotel* (☎ (097) 61 1034) and *Nelson House Lodge* (☎ (097) 61 1977), on Hampton St, all offer B&B for around $30 per person.

MANJIMUP (population 4900)

Manjimup is the commercial centre of the south-west, a major agricultural centre noted for apple-growing and wood-chipping. The impressive **Timber Park Complex** on the corner of Rose and Edwards Sts includes various museums, old buildings and the Manjimup tourist office (☎ (097) 711 831), open daily from 9 am to 5 pm.

One Tree Bridge, or what's left of it, is 22 km down the Graphite Rd. Most of it was swept away during floods in 1966. The **Four Aces**, 1½ km from One Tree Bridge, are four superb karri trees believed to be over 300 years old. **Fonty's Pool**, a great spot to cool off in the water during those hot summer days, is seven km out of town along Seven Day Rd.

Nine km south of town, along the South-Western Highway, is the **Diamond Tree Lookout**, which provides spectacular views of the surrounding countryside.

Places to Stay & Eat

The *Manjimup Caravan Park* (☎ (097) 71 2093) has a hostel with dorm beds and cooking facilities for $10 per night – it can get busy in apple-picking season (March to June). They also have tent sites and on-site vans. Two other caravan parks, *Warren Way* (☎ (097) 71 1060; two km north of town) and *Fonty's Pool* (☎ (097) 71 2105; 10 km south-west of town), also have tent sites and on-site vans.

For meals, try the *Linden Tree* restaurant,

at 92 Giblett St, which has good Chinese food from $8 to $10. The *Country Cafe*, at 78 Giblett St, has a varied menu with dishes around the $10 to $12 mark.

Getting There & Away

Westrail have a Perth to Manjimup bus service via Bunbury four times a week for $25. South-West Coach Lines have a week-day service from Perth to Manjimup for $24.

PEMBERTON (population 900)

You can get the excellent *What to See & Do in Big Tree Country* brochure from the tourist office on Brockman St. Farm labouring work is often available in the area.

Deep in the karri forests, the delightful town of Pemberton has a good local **Pioneer Museum** displaying old forestry equipment; some interesting **craft shops**; the **Pemberton Sawmill** where you can observe timber being sawn; the pretty **Pemberton Pool** surrounded by karri trees (ideal on a hot day); and a **trout hatchery** that supplies fish for the state's dams and rivers.

If you are feeling fit, you can make the scary 60-metre climb to the top of the **Gloucester Tree**, the highest fire lookout tree in the world (this is not for the faint-hearted!). The view makes the climb well worthwhile. To get to the tree just follow the signpost from the centre of town. Also of interest in the area are the spectacular **Cascades** (when the water level is high), **Beedelup National Park**, the **100-year-old forest** and the **Warren National Park** where camping is allowed in designated areas.

The scenic **Pemberton Tramway** (☎ (097) 76 1322) is one of the area's main attractions. Trams leave Pemberton Railway Station daily at 10.45 am and 2 pm to Warren River (1½ hours; $11.50) and daily except Monday and Friday to Northcliff ($17) at 10.15 am. Both routes travel through lush karri and marri forests with occasional picture stops; a commentary is also provided.

Places to Stay

Camping is permitted in *Warren National*

Park and in some areas of the *Pemberton Forest* (☎ (097) 76 1200). *Pemberton Caravan Park* (☎ (097) 76 1300) has tent sites and on-site vans.

Pemberton Youth Hostel (☎ (097) 76 1153), in a beautiful forest location at Pimelea, costs $8 a night. It's 10 km north-west of town but the hostel provides a courtesy bus to meet the Westrail bus in Pemberton – call in advance if you need transport. In town, the centrally located *Warren Lodge* (☎ (097) 76 1105), opposite the tourist office on Brockman St, has single rooms from $10.

Historic *Pemberton Hotel* (☎ (097) 76 1017), also on Brockman St, has singles/doubles for $35/45 with breakfast, and serves counter meals.

Places to Eat

The town, for its size, has many places to eat. The *Pemberton Patisserie* has tasty pies and cakes, while the *Mainstreet Cafe* on Brockman St has good, basic and cheap food such as hamburgers and Lebanese rolls. The *Pemberton Chinese Restaurant*, next to the supermarket on Dean St, is only open Thursday to Sunday from 5 pm and has meals from $6. The *Shamrock*, near the tourist office on Brockman St, is an excellent à la carte steak and seafood restaurant where a three-course meal costs around $25.

Getting There & Around

Westrail Perth to Pemberton buses operate four times a week, travel via Bunbury, Donnybrook and Manjimup and cost $27.70; the trip takes about five hours.

South Coast Rambler (☎ (097) 76 1153) has 4WD tours of the forest and coastal areas around Pemberton from $42.

NORTHCLIFFE (population 800)

Northcliffe, 32 km south of Pemberton, has a **pioneer museum** and a **forest park** close to town with good walks through strands of grand karri, marri and jarrah trees – a brochure and map of the trails is available from the tourist office (☎ (097) 76 7203) by the museum on Wheatley Coast Rd.

The popular and picturesque **Lane Poole Falls** are 19 km south-east of Northcliff; the 2½-km track to the falls leaves from the Boorara Tree. The falls slow to a trickle in the summer months but the flow is steady during the rest of the year.

Windy Harbour, on the coast 29 km south of Northcliffe, has prefab shacks and a sheltered beach; true to its name, it is very windy. The limestone cliffs around here are popular with rockclimbers, and there are great views of the coast from near the lighthouse at Point D'Entrecasteaux.

Places to Stay & Eat

At Windy Harbour, the only place to stay is the *Windy Harbour Camping Area* (☎ (097) 76 7056) where basic tent sites are $3.

Northcliffe Hotel (☎ (097) 76 7089), the only hotel in Northcliffe, has basic B&B for $25/44. *Timber Country* (☎ (097) 76 7132), eight km north of town on Wheatley Coast Rd, has B&B for $22/40.

The *Hollow Butt* coffee shop, on the corner of Zamia St and Wheatley Coast Rd, has light meals and cakes to eat in or take away.

Getting There & Away

The Perth to Albury Westrail bus goes through Northcliffe four times a week for $30.40, but you need your own transport to get to Windy Harbour.

WALPOLE-NORNALUP

Nornalup is a small town on the banks of the tranquil Frankland River. The heavily forested **Walpole-Nornalup National Park** covers 18,000 hectares around Nornalup Inlet and Walpole; it contains beaches, rugged coastline, inlets and the 'Valley of the Giants', a stand of giant karri and tingle trees, including one that soars 46 metres high. Pleasant shady and ferny paths lead through the forest, and the area is frequented by bushwalkers. The Frankland River is popular with canoeing enthusiasts.

There are a number of scenic drives

including Knoll Drive and the Valley of the Giants Rd. Details are available from the Walpole tourist office (☎ (098) 40 1111) in the Pioneer Cottage or the Department of Conservation & Land Management (☎ (098) 40 1027) on the South Coast Highway in Walpole.

From Walpole, the road turns away from the coast and heads north-west to Manjimup, 120 km north.

Westrek Tours (☎ (098) 40 1266) run day trips around the area for $60, which includes lunch.

Places to Stay

There are a number of camp grounds in the *Walpole-Nornalup National Park* including tent sites at Peaceful Bay, Crystal Springs and Coalmine Beach.

There is the *Tingledale Associate YHA Hostel* (☎ (098) 40 8073) on Dingo Flats Rd off the Valley of the Giants Rd, 18 km east of Walpole – booking is strongly recommended. You need a car to get to this hostel, or if you ring ahead they'll pick you up at the main road. Beds are $5, the place has great character and there's wonderful views.

The *Seagull Autel* (☎ (098) 40 1041), on the South Coast Highway in Walpole, has self-contained units at $35 for two people.

DENMARK (population 1650)

Denmark, which first became established supplying timber for gold-field developments, is 54 km west of Albany. It has some fine beaches in the area (especially William Bay, Elephant Rocks and Waterfall Beach for swimming, and Ocean Beach for surfing) and is a good base for trips into the karri forests.

The town is picturesquely sited on the Denmark River; you can hire canoes on the grassy river bank near the bridge from $5 per half hour. In the town, the **Goundrey's Winery** on North St, in the Old Butter Factory, is open for inspection and wine tasting daily from 10 am to 4 pm except Sunday.

The Denmark tourist office (☎ (098) 48

1265) on Strickland St has Heritage Trail brochures including the **Mokare Trail** (a three-km trail along the Denmark River) and the **Wilson Inlet Trail** (a six-km trail that starts from the river mouth). There are fine views from **Mt Shadforth Lookout** while the **William Bay National Park**, 15 km west of Denmark, has fine coastal scenery of rocks and reefs.

Places to Stay

There are several caravan parks in town, the closest being the *Rivermouth Caravan Park* (☎ (098) 48 1262), one km south of the town centre on Inlet Drive.

The *Denmark Associate YHA Hostel* (☎ (098) 48 1267) at the Wilson Inlet Holiday Park, three km south of Denmark, has accommodation for $9 per night; phone in advance during the summer months. The *Denmark Guesthouse* (☎ (098) 48 1477), on the South Coast Highway in the centre of town, is one of the best accommodation bargains in Western Australia. It is a friendly place with a TV lounge and clean rooms for $15/25.

Norton's (☎ (098) 48 1690), at Lot 12, Inlet Drive, has a bed and full English-style breakfast for $22 a person.

Places to Eat

Denmark Health Shop in the shopping village has an excellent lunch bar with exotic fillings and fresh-fruit smoothies. *Mary Rose Coffee Shoppe*, on North Rd, is a quaint place with a pleasant balcony. It serves tasty light meals including salads, moussaka and shepherd's pie from $5 to $7, and a range of 'heart-attack' cakes.

Denmark Riverview Coffee Shop, at 18 Holling Rd, has very good German food – no meal is over $10. For a quick meal or takeaway food, try *Kettle's Deli* on the corner of High St and Holling Rd.

Getting There & Around

Westrail's Perth to Albany (via the south coast) service comes through Denmark four times a week and costs $39.60 one-way; the trip takes about seven hours. Contact the tourist office about local tours and bike hire; mountain bikes cost $15 per day and $80 per week with a $20 deposit.

MT BARKER (population 4500)

Mt Barker is 50 km north of Albany, 64 km south of the Stirling Range and about 20 km west of the Porongurups. It has a tourist office at 57 Lowood St, open daily from 9 am to 5 pm.

The town has been settled since the 1830s and the old police station and jail of 1868 is preserved as a museum. You can get a panoramic view of the area from the Mt Barker Lookout, five km south of town.

The region has a good reputation for wine making, and there are many plantations with cellar sales and tastings within a few km of town – see the tourist office for winery locations and opening times. Plantagenet Wines near the centre of town are usually willing to show you around their wine-making facilities if they are not too busy.

Kendenup, 16 km north of Mt Barker, was the actual site of Western Australia's first gold discovery, though this was considerably overshadowed by the later and much larger finds in the Kalgoorlie area. North of Mt Barker is **Cranbrook**, an access point to the Stirling Range National Park.

Places to Stay & Eat

The *Plantagenet Hotel* (☎ (098) 51 1008) at 9 Lowood Rd has singles/doubles from $21/40 (in the older hotel section) and good counter meals for around $10; the steaks here are rated by some as the best in Western Australia!

The *Mt Barker Hotel* (☎ (098) 51 1477), at 39 Lowood Rd, does B&B for $16/25 and counter meals from $10 to $12.

Getting There & Away

The Westrail, Perth to Albany via Williams bus service stops daily in Mt Barker; the fare from Perth is $27.70 one-way.

PORONGURUP & THE STIRLING RANGE NATIONAL PARKS

The beautiful Porongurup National Park (2401 hectares) has panoramic views, beautiful scenery, large karri trees, granite outcrops and excellent bushwalks. Trails range from the short **Tree in the Rock** stroll to the intermediate **Castle Rock** (570 metres) and the harder **Nancy Peak** (652 metres) and excellent **Devil's Slide** (670 metres) walks. A scenic six-km drive along the northern edge of the park starts near the ranger's residence.

In the Stirling Range National Park (115,650 hectares), **Toolbrunup** (for views and a good climb), **Bluff Knoll** (at 1073 metres it's the highest peak in the range) and **Toll Peak** (for the wild flowers) are popular half-day walks. The 96-km range is noted for its spectacular colour changes through blues, reds and purples. The mountains rise abruptly from the surrounding flat and sandy plains, and the area is known for its fine flora & fauna.

Further information on these parks can be obtained from the following Department of Conservation & Land Management offices: Porongurup National Park, Bolganup Rd, RMB 1112, Mt Barker, Western Australia 6324; and Stirling Range National Park, Chester Pass Rd, c/o Amelup via Borden, Western Australia 6338.

Places to Stay

You can camp in the *Stirling Range National Park* on Chester Rd, near the Toolbrunup Peak turn-off; call the ranger (☎ (098) 27 9278) for details. There are very limited facilities, and tent sites are $4 for two people.

Stirling Range Caravan Park (☎ (098) 27 9277), on the north boundary of the park, is also on Chester Pass Rd; there is an *Associate YHA Hostel* here with beds for $10 in self-contained units.

There is no camping in Porongurup National Park but there's the *Porongurup Caravan Park* (☎ (098) 53 1022) in Porongurup township; and *Karribank Lodge* (☎ (098) 53 1022), on Main St, has singles/doubles for $27/54.

ALBANY (population 14,500)

The commercial centre of the southern region, the town of Albany is the oldest settlement in the state, established in 1826 shortly before Perth. Its excellent harbour, on King George Sound, led to Albany becoming a thriving whaling port. Later, when steamships started travelling between the UK and Australia, Albany was a coaling station for ships bound for the east coast. The coastline around Albany contains some of Australia's most rugged and spectacular scenery.

Information

The informative Albany Tourist Bureau (☎ (098) 41 1088) is on the corner of Peel Place and York St. It is open from 8.30 am to 5.30 pm Monday to Friday and from 9 am to 5 pm Saturday and Sunday. If you are in need of some reading material, there is a book exchange at 70 York St.

Old Buildings

Albany has some fine old colonial buildings – **Stirling Terrace** is particularly noted for its Victorian shopfronts. The 1851 **Old Gaol**, now a folk museum, is open daily from 10 am to 4.15 pm; admission is $2.

The excellent **Albany Residency Museum**, opposite the Old Gaol, was originally built in the 1850s as the home of the resident magistrate; it is open Monday to Saturday from 10 am to 5 pm and Sunday from 2 to 5 pm. Displays include a giant lighthouse optic, saddlery, historic boats and Aboriginal artefacts. Next to this museum is a full-scale replica of the brig *Amity*, the ship that brought Albany's founding party to the area.

The restored **old post office**, built in 1870, now houses the Inter-Colonial Museum. It has an interesting collection of communications equipment from Western Australia's past; admission is free.

The 1832 **Patrick Taylor Cottage** houses a collection of period costumes and furniture; it is open daily from 2 to 4.15 pm and costs $2. The entry fee also includes a complimentary pass to the Old Gaol – likewise,

a ticket to the Old Gaol will get you into the Patrick Taylor Cottage. The farm at **Strawberry Hill**, two km from town, is one of the oldest in the state, having been established in 1827 as the government farm for Albany. It's open daily from 2 to 5 pm, except during July when it's closed. From September to April, it is also open from 10 am to noon.

Other historic buildings in town include the **railway station, St John's Church** and the **courthouse.** A guided walking-tour brochure of colonial buildings in Albany is available from the tourist office.

Views

There are fine views over the coast and inland from the twin peaks, **Mt Clarence** and **Mt Melville**, which overlook the town. On top of Mt Clarence is the Desert Mounted Corps Memorial, originally erected in Port Said as a memorial to the events of Gallipoli. It was brought here when the Suez crisis in 1956 made colonial reminders less than popular in Egypt.

Mt Clarence can be climbed along a track accessible from the end of Grey St East; turn left, take the first on the right and follow the path by the water tanks. The walk is tough but the views from the top make it worthwhile. The easier way to the top is along Apex Drive.

Spectacular panoramic views are also available from the lookout tower on Mt Melville. The tower has a kiosk that serves light meals and entry is free; the turnoff to the tower is off Serpentine Rd.

Other Attractions

The **Princess Royal Fortress**, on Mt Adelaide, was built in 1893 when the vulnerability of Albany, a strategic port, to an enemy naval squadron was recognised as a potential threat to Australia's security. The restored buildings, gun emplacements and fine views make it well worth a visit. It is open daily from 7.30 am to 5.30 pm and costs $2 per car. **Dog Rock**, a boulder that looks like a dog's head, is on Middleton Rd. There is a good beach at **Middleton Bay** which can

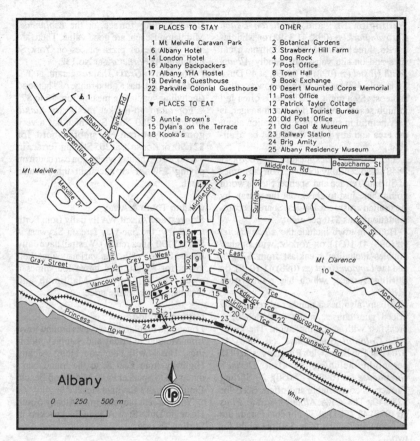

■ PLACES TO STAY	OTHER
1 Mt Melville Caravan Park	2 Botanical Gardens
6 Albany Hotel	3 Strawberry Hill Farm
14 London Hotel	4 Dog Rock
16 Albany Backpackers	7 Post Office
17 Albany YHA Hostel	8 Town Hall
19 Devine's Guesthouse	9 Book Exchange
22 Parkville Colonial Guesthouse	10 Desert Mounted Corps Memorial
	11 Post Office
▼ PLACES TO EAT	12 Patrick Taylor Cottage
	13 Albany Tourist Bureau
5 Auntie Brown's	20 Old Post Office
15 Dylan's on the Terrace	21 Old Gaol & Museum
18 Kooka's	23 Railway Station
	24 Brig Amity
	25 Albany Residency Museum

Albany

0   250   500 m

be reached by local bus from Peel Place; see the tourist office for timetables.

Organised Tours

Mountain Goat Tours (☎ (098) 41 8820) run a weekly Stirling Ranges walk ($40), a town tour ($45), a wine tour ($45) and a south-coast tour ($20). Discounts are offered to backpackers and YHA members.

The *Silver Star* leaves the Emu Point jetty four times a week for a 2½-hour cruise around King George Sound; the cost is $16.50. Escape Tours operate from the tourist office and have many local half and full-day tours around Albany from $22.50 to $55. Check with the tourist office for information on these and other tours.

Westate Tours (☎ (090) 401 266) run weekly three-day trips around Walpole, Fitzgerald National Park, the Stirling Ranges and the Porongurups for $330 including food and accommodation.

Places to Stay

There are caravan parks aplenty in Albany. The closest to the city centre are: *Mt Melville Caravan Park* (☎ (098) 41 4616), one km north of town on the corner of Lion and

Wellington Sts; and *Middleton Beach Caravan Park* (☎ (098) 41 3593) on Middleton Rd, three km east of town. Both have tent sites and on-site vans. The friendly *Albany Youth Hostel* (☎ (098) 41 3949), at 49 Duke St, is only 400 metres from the town centre, and costs $9 a night. The hostel is often full in high season and Patrick, the manager, is very helpful in supplying information about the area and any work that might be available.

The *Albany Backpackers* (☎ (098) 41 8848), also centrally located, is on the corner of Stirling Terrace and Spencer St. It's worth going there just to check out the murals by Australian artist Jack Davies. Shared accommodation costs $10 per night.

Hotels in town include the *Albany Hotel* (☎ (098) 41 1031), on York St, with singles/doubles including breakfast from $25/35, and the *London Hotel* (☎ (098) 41 1048), on Stirling Terrace, which has rooms from $18/30.

Albany also has a number of reasonably priced guesthouses, many of which offer breakfast with accommodation. The *Parkville Colonial Guesthouse* (☎ (098) 41 3704), at 136 Brunswick Rd, charges $20/35 per night including breakfast. *Devine's Guesthouse* (☎ (098) 41 8050), 20 Stirling Terrace, is comfortable and offers B&B for $25/$40. The *CWA Albany Seaside Flats* (☎ (098) 41 1591) at 37 Flinders Parade are self-contained units from $30 per night for two.

Places to Eat
Dylan's on the Terrace at 82 Stirling Terrace has an excellent range of light meals including hamburgers and pancakes at reasonable prices; it is open late most nights, early for breakfast and has a takeaway section. If you have a fetish for cream cakes this is a good place to go. Nearby, on Stirling Terrace, is the *Pancake King* which has pancakes, of course, and other meals from $8 to $10 and light snacks from $4 to $6.

Breakfasts at the *Wildflower Cafe*, on York St, have been recommended. Counter meals in the *Premier Hotel*, York St, the *London Hotel*, Stirling Terrace, or the *Esplanade*, Middleton Beach, are good value. There are also a couple of pizza places on York St including *Al Fornetto's* at No 132.

The *Lemon Grass* Thai restaurant, at 370 Middleton Rd, has a good range of Thai food (including vegetarian meals) from $5 to $7.

For more up-market meals, try *Auntie Brown's*, at 280 York St, which has a very good all-you-can-eat smorgasbord for $21.90; or *Kooka's*, at 205 Stirling Terrace in a restored old house, where you can count on paying $30 for an excellent three-course meal.

Getting There & Away
Skywest and Ansett WA fly daily from Perth to Albany; the one-way fare on Skywest is $141 ($190 Apex return). Westrail have daily buses from Perth via various wheatbelt towns for $31.80, and buses four times a week via Bridgetown, Manjimup and Denmark for the same price.

Getting Around
Love's run regular bus services around town from Monday to Friday and Saturday mornings. Buses will take you along Albany Highway from Peel St to the roundabout; others go to Spencer Park, Middleton Beach, Emu Point and Bayonet Head.

You can rent bicycles from Albany Youth Hostel in Duke St or Albany Backpackers in Stirling Terrace.

AROUND ALBANY
South of Albany, off Frenchman Bay Rd, is a stunning stretch of coastline that includes the **Blowholes**, especially interesting in heavy seas when air is blown with great force through the surrounding rock; the **Gap & Natural Bridge**, rugged natural rock formations surrounded by pounding seas; steep, rocky coves such as **Jimmy Newell's Harbour** and **Salmon Holes**, popular with surfers; and **Frenchman Bay** which has a caravan park, a fine swimming beach and a grassed barbecue area with plenty of shade.

Also at Frenchman Bay, 21 km from Albany, is **Whaleworld** at the Cheynes

Beach Whaling Station which only ceased operations in 1978. The whaling station museum has a restored and rusting 'Cheynes 4' whale chaser, and you can inspect the station after seeing a short film on whaling operations. Well worth a look, it is open daily from 9 am to 5 pm, but the $5 admission is considered a bit rich by some.

Two People's Bay is a nature reserve east of Albany with a good swimming beach and scenic coastline. On the way out there, you can make a detour to scenic **Bayonet Head Lookout** on Oyster Bay.

ALBANY TO ESPERANCE (476 km)
From Albany, the South Coast Highway runs north-east along the coast before turning inland to skirt the Fitzgerald River National Park and finally finishes in Esperance.

Ongerup & Jerramungup
Ongerup, a small wheatbelt town, has an annual wild flower show in September/October with hundreds of local species on show and a local history museum. In Jerramungup, you can visit the interesting **Military Museum**.

Ravensthorpe (population 380)
The small town of Ravensthorpe was once the centre of the Phillips River gold field; later, copper was also mined there. Nowadays, the area is dependent on farming.

The ruins of a disused government smelter and the Catlin Mine (copper) are near town, and the Ravensthorpe Historical Society has a display in the **Dance Cottage**. If possible, avoid getting petrol here as it seems to be well above normal prices. To the north of Ravensthorpe, the **Frank Hann National Park** has a range of typical sand-plain region flora.

Places to Stay *Ravensthorpe Caravan Park* (☎ (098) 38 1050) has tent sites at $8 for two. The *Palace Hotel* (☎ (098) 38 1005), classified by the National Trust, has singles/doubles for $27/44 with breakfast; there are more rooms in the motel section.

Hopetoun (population 350)
The fine beaches and bays around Hopetoun are south of Ravensthorpe. It is also the eastern gateway to the **Fitzgerald River National Park** which has a very beautiful coastline, sand plains, mountains and deep, wide river valleys. The bushwalking is excellent.

Hopetoun Caravan Park (☎ (098) 38 3096) has tent sites and on-site vans and the *Port Hotel* (☎ (098) 38 3053) has B&B for $23/40.

ESPERANCE (population 8500)
Esperance, on the coast 200 km south of Norseman, has become a popular resort due to its temperate climate, magnificent coastal scenery, good fishing and golden beaches. Although the first settlers came to the area in 1863, it was during the gold rush in the 1890s that the town really became established as a port. When the gold fever subsided, Esperance went into a state of suspended animation until after WW II. In the 1950s, it was discovered that adding missing trace elements to the soil around Esperance restored it to fertility, and since then the town has grown rapidly to become an agricultural centre.

Information
The Esperance tourist office on Dempster St, next to the museum, is open daily from 9 am to 5 pm and can book tours along the coast, to the islands and into the surrounding national parks.

Things to See
Esperance, or the Bay of Isles, has some excellent beaches, and the seas offshore are studded with the many islands of the Recherche Archipelago. Distinctive Norfolk Island pines line the foreshore. The town itself isn't particularly exciting. The **Esperance Museum Park** contains the tourist office and various old buildings, including an art gallery, a blacksmith shop, a cafe and a craft shop.

The museum itself, on the corner of James

and Dempster Sts, is open daily from 1.30 to 4.30 pm and contains a Skylab display – when the USA's Skylab crashed to earth in 1979, it made its fiery re-entry right over Esperance.

The town's main attractions, however, lie along the captivating 36-km **Scenic Loop Road**. Highlights include the vistas from Observatory Point and the Rotary Lookout on Wireless Hill; Twilight Bay and Picnic Cove, popular swimming spots; and Pink Lake which is often pink – the colouring is caused by a salt-tolerant algae called *Dunalella salina*. The lake also has prolific birdlife, and as much as half a million tonnes of salt are dredged from the lake annually.

There are about 100 small islands in the **Recherche Archipelago**. On them are colonies of seals, penguins and a wide variety of water birds. Woody Island is a wildlife sanctuary, and there are regular trips run by Mackenzie's Island Cruises (☎ (090) 71 1772) to this and other islands in January and February – the tourist office will provide details.

Fossicker's Finds has a collection of more than 2000 old bottles, and close by is the **Australian Parrot Farm**, with parrots and other native birds. To get there, go east on Fisheries Rd and five km past the Cape Le Grand turn-off on Merivale Rd. Both are open from 9 am to 5 pm daily. At the top of Six Mile Hill, eight km north of Esperance, is **Baker's Born Free Wildlife & Wildflower Park**.

National Parks There are four national parks in the region around Esperance. The closest and most popular is **Cape Le Grand National Park**, extending from about 20 km to 60 km east of Esperance. The park has spectacular coastal scenery, some good beaches and excellent walking tracks. There are fine views from Frenchman's Peak, at the western end of the park, and good fishing, camping and swimming at Lucky Bay and Le Grand Beach.

Further east is the coastal **Cape Arid National Park**, at the start of the Great Australian Bight and on the fringes of the Nullarbor Plain. It is a rugged and isolated park with abundant flora & fauna, good bushwalking, beaches and camp sites. Most of the park is only accessible by 4WD, although the camp sites at Poison Creek and the Thomas River can be reached by normal vehicles.

Other national parks in the area include the **Stokes Inlet National Park**, 90 km west of Esperance, with an inlet, long beaches and rocky headlands; and the **Peak Charles National Park**, 130 km to the north. For information about these national parks, contact the Department of Conservation & Land Management (☎ (090) 71 3733) in Dempster St, Esperance.

If you are going into the national parks, take plenty of water where appropriate (there is little or no freshwater in most of these areas) and be wary of spreading dieback. Dieback is a plant disease caused by a fungus that lives in the soil and attacks the plant's roots. It has ravaged many areas in the region and is spread by vehicles and bushwalkers. To help prevent this disease, keep to made roads and keep out of closed areas; bushwalkers can help by cleaning mud and soil from their boots before entering a park.

Organised Tours

Vacation Country Tours (☎ (090) 71 2227) run a number of tours around Esperance including a town-and-coast tour for $12 and a Cape Le Grand National Park tour twice a week for $25.

Places to Stay

Limited-facility tent sites are $5 per night at *Cape Le Grand* (☎ (090) 75 9022) and free at *Cape Arid* (☎ (090) 75 0055) national parks. Apply for permits with the ranger at the park entrances.

There are half a dozen caravan parks around Esperance that provide camping areas and on-site accommodation, the most central being the *Esperance Bay Caravan Park* (☎ (090) 71 2237), on the corner of the Esplanade and Harbour Rd, near the wharf, and the *Esperance Shire Caravan Park*

(☎ (090) 71 1251) on the corner of Goldfields and Norseman Rds.

The large and popular *Esperance Youth Hostel* (☎ (090) 71 1040), on Goldfields Rd, is two km north of the town centre and costs $10 per night. The *Esperance Motor Hotel* (☎ (090) 71 1555), in Andrew St, is well located and costs from $20/35. However, travellers have complained that this place is shabby and less than secure. The *Esperance Travellers' Inn* (☎ (090) 71 1677), at the corner of Goldfields Rd and Phyllis St two km from town, is better, with clean rooms for $30/45 and friendly staff.

In addition, the *Pink Lake Lodge* (☎ (090) 71 2075), at 85 Pink Lake Rd, has singles/doubles from $18/30. *Tuart Place* (☎ (090) 76 5022), at 35 John St, and the *CWA Esperance* (☎ (090) 71 1970), Lot 85, The Esplanade, both have self-contained units for around $30 per night.

Places to Eat

The bistro at the *Pier Hotel* has tasty meals with an all-you-can-eat, well-stocked salad bar for around $10; cheaper meals from $5 to $8 are available in the saloon bar. The *Spice of Life*, on Andrew St, has a varied health-food menu including zucchini slice, vegetarian pasties, Lebanese rolls chock full of salad and fruit smoothies at fair prices.

The *Esperance Pizza Parlour* is on the corner of William and Dempster Sts.

Getting There & Around

Skywest fly daily from Perth to Esperance for $182 one-way ($241 Apex return) and Goldfields Air Services fly from Kalgoorlie via Norseman for $134 every Tuesday.

Westrail has a bus three times a week from Kalgoorlie to Esperance, an Esperance to Albany service and a 10-hour Perth to Esperance service that runs on Monday via Jerramungup and on Wednesday and Friday via Lake Grace for $47.70.

You can hire bicycles from the Captain Huon Motel at the corner of the Esplanade and Balfour St for $10 per day (cheaper rates are available for multiple-day hire), or from the Esperance Youth Hostel.

Up the Coast

Highway 1, which encircles Australia, is now sealed all the way round. The last unsealed section was between Fitzroy Crossing and Halls Creek, in the Kimberley area in the north of Western Australia.

The route from Perth to Darwin may still be a hell of a long way but it's no longer an endurance test. There's also a lot to see if you want to break the journey. Don't underestimate it – from Perth to Port Hedland is 1770 km by the coast and in summer it can be very hot.

Getting There & Away

Air Ansett WA fly from Perth to Geraldton ($151 one-way; $200 Apex return), Carnarvon ($243 one-way, or $316 Apex return) and Learmonth (for Exmouth) ($302 one-way, or $393 Apex return) as well as to centres in the north-west Kimberley region.

Bus Westrail has bus services from Perth to Geraldton (daily) and Kalbarri (Monday to Friday). Greyhound/Pioneer has a daily bus up the coast to Darwin via Geraldton, Carnarvon and Port Hedland – connections to Monkey Mia are also available. Bus Australia runs a similar service to Darwin from Perth departing Tuesday, Thursday and Sunday with connections to Exmouth. Bus Australia also do a three-day tour from Perth to Exmouth which is free to bus-pass holders, and takes in Monkey Mia, Kalbarri, Carnarvon and Exmouth. It's possible to be dropped off at Coral Bay, either for the afternoon or overnight.

The one-way fares from Perth on Bus Australia are $32 to Geraldton, $86 to Overlander Roadhouse (which is the turn-off for Shark Bay), $90 to Carnarvon, $92 to Minilya Roadhouse (the turn-off for Exmouth) and $97 to Nanutarra (the turn-off for Wittenoom).

PERTH TO GERALDTON (421 km)

From Perth, you follow the Brand Highway

past the turn-off to Jurien and the Pinnacles Desert (see North Coast in the Around Perth section for information on this area).

The main road comes back to the coast at **Dongara** (population 1200) – a pleasant little port with fine beaches, a main street lined with Moreton Bay figs, lots of crayfish and a tourist office (☎ (099) 27 1404) at 43 Moreton Terrace. Russ Cottage, open Sundays and public holidays from 2 to 4 pm, is a local attraction.

Further north, only about 20 km south of Geraldton, is **Greenough**, once a busy little mining town but now just a quiet farming centre. The excellent Greenough Historical Hamlet contains a number of 19th-century buildings restored by the National Trust; guided tours are run throughout the day and it is well worth a visit. The Pioneer Museum, open daily from 10 am to 4 pm, has some fine historical displays and dates from 1860.

Inland

The areas inland of Dongara and Geraldton such as **Mullewa**, **Mingenew** and **Morawa** are part of the Wildflower Way – famous for its brilliant spring display of wild flowers, including wreath leschenaultia, native foxgloves, everlastings and wattles.

Mingenew has a small historical museum in an old primary school. **Carnamah**, near the Yarra Yarra Lake, is noted for its bird life. This area is also a gateway to the **Murchison gold fields**; there are old gold-mining centres and ghost towns around **Perenjori**.

GERALDTON (population 21,000)

Geraldton, the major town in the midwest region, is on a spectacular stretch of coast. It's 421 km north of Perth and the area has a fine climate, particularly in the winter. If you are tempted by lobster fresh from the boat then this is the place to come; it's probably the state's main lobster-catching centre.

Dutch Shipwrecks

During the 17th century, ships of the Dutch East India Company, sailing from Europe to Batavia in Java, would head due east from the Horn of Africa then beat up the western Australian coast to Indonesia. It only took a small miscalculation for a ship to run aground on the coast and a few did just that, usually with disastrous results. The west coast of Australia is often decidedly inhospitable, and the chances of rescue at that time were remote.

Four wrecks of Dutch East Indiamen have been located, including the *Batavia* – the earliest and, in many ways, the most interesting. In 1629, the *Batavia* went aground on the Abrolhos Islands, off the coast of Geraldton. The survivors set up camp, sent off a rescue party to Batavia (now Jakarta) in the ship's boat and waited. It took three months for a rescue party to arrive and in that time a mutiny had taken place and more than 120 of the survivors had been murdered. The ringleaders were hanged, and two of the mutineers were unceremoniously dumped on the coast.

In 1656, the *Vergulde Draeck* (Gilt Dragon) struck a reef about 100 km north of Perth and although a party of survivors made its way to Batavia, no trace, other than a few scattered coins, was found of the other survivors who had straggled ashore. The *Zuytdorp* ran aground beneath the towering cliffs north of Kalbarri in 1712. Wine bottles, other relics and the remains of fires have been found on the cliff top but again no trace of survivors.

In 1727, the *Zeewijk* followed the ill-fated *Batavia* to destruction on the Abrolhos Islands. Again a small party of survivors made its way to Batavia but many of the remaining sailors died before they could be rescued. Many relics from these shipwrecks, particularly the *Batavia*, can be seen today in the museums in Fremantle and Geraldton.

Information

Geraldton Tourist Bureau (☎ (099) 21 3999) is in the Bill Sewell Complex on Chapman Rd, diagonally across from the railway station and beside the Northgate shopping centre. The complex, formerly a hospital and a prison, has been restored and is open from 9 am to 5 pm Monday to Friday and from 8 am to 5 pm Saturday and Sunday.

If you are short of reading material, there are a couple of second-hand book stores in Geraldton: the House of Books, at 176 Marine Terrace, and the Sun City Book Exchange at 36 Marine Terrace.

Geraldton Museum

The town's excellent museum is in two separate, but nearby, buildings. The Maritime Museum tells the story of the early wrecks and has assorted relics from the Dutch ships, including items from the *Batavia* and the

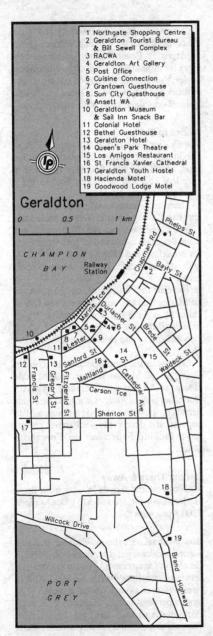

1 Northgate Shopping Centre
2 Geraldton Tourist Bureau
  & Bill Sewell Complex
3 RACWA
4 Geraldton Art Gallery
5 Post Office
6 Cuisine Connection
7 Grantown Guesthouse
8 Sun City Guesthouse
9 Ansett WA
10 Geraldton Museum
   & Sail Inn Snack Bar
11 Colonial Hotel
12 Bethel Guesthouse
13 Geraldton Hotel
14 Queen's Park Theatre
15 Los Amigos Restaurant
16 St Francis Xavier Cathedral
17 Geraldton Youth Hostel
18 Hacienda Motel
19 Goodwood Lodge Motel

Geraldton

Zeewijk and the carved wooden sternpiece from the *Zuytdorp* found in 1927, by a local stockman, on top of the cliffs above the point at which the ship had run ashore. It was not until the 1950s that the wreckage was positively identified as that of the *Zuytdorp*.

The miniature submarine displayed outside the museum was intended to be used for fishing green crayfish but proved unworkable. The Old Railway Building has displays on flora, fauna and the settlement of the region by Aborigines and, later, Europeans. The museum complex is open Monday to Saturday from 10 am to 5 pm and from 1 to 5 pm on Sundays and holidays; admission is free.

St Francis Xavier Cathedral

Geraldton's St Francis Xavier Cathedral is just one of a number of buildings in Geraldton and the Western Australia midwest designed by Monsignor John Hawes, a strange priest-cum-architect who left Western Australia in 1939 and spent the rest of his life (he died in 1956) a hermit on an island in the Caribbean.

Construction of the Byzantine-style cathedral commenced in 1914, the year after Hawes arrived in Geraldton, but his plans were too grandiose and the partially built cathedral was not completed until 1938.

Other Attractions

The **Geraldton Art Gallery**, on the corner of Chapman Rd and Durlacher St, is open daily. The **Lighthouse Keeper's Cottage** on Chapman Rd, the Geraldton Historical Society's headquarters, is open Thursdays from 10 am to 4 pm. You can look out over Geraldton from the **Waverley Heights Lookout**, on Brede St, or watch the lobster boats at **Fisherman's Wharf**, at the end of Marine Terrace. **Point Moore lighthouse**, in operation since 1878, is also worth a visit.

The **Abrolhos Islands**, containing over 100 islands, are about 60 km off the Geraldton coast. The beautiful but treacherous reefs surrounding the islands have claimed many shipwrecks over the years. The islands are also the centre of the area's lobster-fishing industry. Air and diving tours to these protected and spectacular islands are available from Geraldton – check with the tourist office for details.

Festivals
Geraldton's annual Sunshine Festival, with a parade, a fun run and other activities, takes place in October. In March, there's a Wind Festival with kite-flying and windsurfing contests – Geraldton is a very windy city.

Places to Stay
Camping The closest caravan parks to the centre of town are *Separation Point* (☎ (099) 21 2763), on Wilcock Drive, and *Belair Gardens* (☎ (099) 21 1997) at Point Moore; both have tent sites and on-site vans.

Hostels *Geraldton Youth Hostel* (☎ (099) 21 2549) is at 80 Francis St and costs $9 a night. *Batavia Backpackers* (☎ (099) 21 3999), part of the Bill Sewell Complex, has good facilities and beds for $12 per night.

Guesthouses & Hotels Geraldton has plenty of old-fashioned seaside guesthouses, particularly along Marine Terrace. The *Grantown Guesthouse* (☎ (099) 21 3275) at No 172 has singles/doubles for $22/42 (breakfast is an extra $5 per person). The friendly *Sun City Guesthouse* (☎ (099) 21 2205) at No 184 offers bed and continental breakfast for $20/35. Similarly, the *Bethel Guesthouse* (☎ (099) 21 4770), at 311 Marine Terrace, has bed and light breakfast for $17/34.

Cheap rooms are also available at some of the older-style hotels. The *Colonial Hotel* (☎ (099) 21 4444), on Fitzgerald St, has rooms for $20/30 (breakfast is $6.50 per person extra), and the *Geraldton Hotel* (☎ (099) 21 3700), just off Marine Terrace at 19 Gregory St, has rooms for $22/30.

Motels & Units *Hacienda Motel* (☎ (099) 21 2155), on Durlacher St, has rooms at $45/55. The *Mariner Motel* (☎ 21 2544), at 298 Chapman Rd, is cheaper at $40/50. Family units are available at both of these places.

Ocean West Motel (☎ (099) 21 1047), on the corner of Hadda Way and Wilcock Drive at Mahomets Beach, has self-contained cottages for around $50 per double. *Goodwood Lodge Motel* (☎ (099) 21 5666), at the corner of the Brand Highway and Durlacher St, also has self-contained units for a similar price.

Places to Eat
The *Cuisine Connection*, in Durlacher St, is a food hall with Indian, Chinese and Italian food, roasts and fish & chips. The food is excellent and you should be able to get a good feed for $6.

There are a number of small snack bars and cafes along Marine Terrace including: *Thuy's Cake Shop*, at No 202, which has some delicious cakes and is open from 6 am for breakfast; and *Maria's Cafe*, at No 174, with standard cafe food at down-to-earth prices.

The *Sail Inn Snack Bar*, by the museum on Marine Terrace, sells burgers and fish & chips; it is in a fast-food enclave which includes *Batavia Coast Fish & Chips* (which also sells pizza and chicken) and the *Burger Hive*.

Chinese restaurants include the *Golden Coins*, at 198 Marine Terrace, and the *Jade House* at 57 Marine Terrace. At 105 Durlacher St, *Los Amigos* is a good, straightforward, licensed Mexican place. It's popular, and deservedly so. Fancier restaurants include *Reflections* on Foreshore Drive.

Getting There & Away
Air Skywest and Ansett WA fly from Perth to Geraldton for around $151 one-way, or $200 Apex return.

Bus Westrail, Greyhound/Pioneer and Bus Australia have regular services from Perth to Geraldton for around $33 one-way. Westrail services continue north to Meekatharra (weekly) or Kalbarri (twice a week). The other operators follow Highway 1 through Port Hedland and Broome to Darwin. Westrail stops at the railway station, while

Bus Australia and Greyhound/Pioneer stop at the Bill Sewell Complex.

Getting Around

Bicycles can be hired from the youth hostel in Francis St, or Wheel Nuts (☎ (099) 64 1555) at 62 Chapman Rd, opposite the railway station (rates here are $4 per hour or $15 per day).

NORTHAMPTON

Northampton, 50 km north of Geraldton, has a number of historic buildings and provides access to good beaches at **Horrocks** (22 km west) and **Port Gregory** (57 km north-west). The town was founded to exploit lead and copper, discovered in 1848; lead is still produced here. An early mine-manager's home, Chiverton House, is now a fine municipal museum. The stone building was constructed between 1868 and 1875 using local materials. Gwalia Church cemetery also tells its tales of the early days.

About 55 km north-west of Northampton is the **Hutt River Province**, where a local farmer, deciding that tourism must be an easier game than farming, appointed himself 'Prince Leonard of Hutt' and seceded from Australia. Today, thousands of people visit his 'independent principality' annually, although it's actually nothing much more than a bare outback station with a basic caravan park (☎ (099) 36 6035), a chapel and a post office with local stamps. The turn-off to the province is at Ogilvie, 20 km north of Northampton.

Places to Stay

There are caravan parks at Northampton (☎ (099) 34 1202), Port Gregory (☎ (099) 35 1052) and Horrocks (☎ (099) 34 3039); all have tent sites, and Horrocks and Port Gregory caravan parks have on-site vans.

KALBARRI (population 900)

Kalbarri, a popular spot with backpackers, is on the coast at the mouth of the Murchison River, 66 km west of the main highway. The area is intimately associated with an alluring coastline, spectacular gorges and with the west coast's Dutch shipwrecks. The *Zuytdorp* was wrecked about 65 km north of Kalbarri in 1712; earlier, in 1629, two *Batavia* mutineers were marooned at Wittecarra Gully, an inlet just south of the town. Diving on the *Zuytdorp* is very difficult as a heavy swell and unpredictable currents batter the shoreline, but in 1986 divers from the Geraldton Museum did manage to raise a quantity of material.

The Kalbarri Travel Service (☎ (099) 37 1104) on Grey St provides a wide range of tourist information.

Things to See & Do

The **Rainbow Jungle** is an interesting rainforest and a bird park four km south of town towards Red Bluff, and **Fantasyland** is a doll collection on Grey St. Pelicans, which can often be seen on the river estuary in front of the town, are fed in front of Fantasyland at 8.45 am most mornings. Boats can be hired on the river, and river tours are made on the lower reaches of the river on the *Kalbarri River Queen*.

There are some excellent surfing breaks along the coast – **Jakes Corner**, 3½ km south of town, is reputed to be one of the best in the state.

There is a string of superb cliff faces and spectacular views south of town. These include **Red Bluff** (a stunning, red sandstone outcrop), the banded **Rainbow Valley**, great views from **Pot Alley**, **Eagle Gorge** and **Natural Bridge**, sculptured by the surrounding seas. These sights can be reached by conventional vehicles. The road will test your car's suspension in places, but you will be rewarded by rugged, majestic scenery.

Kalbarri National Park has over 1000 sq km of bushland including some of the state's most spectacular gorges on the **Murchison River**. From Kalbarri, it's only 35 km to the **Loop** and **Z-Bend**, two particularly impressive gorges. Short walking trails lead down into the gorges from the road access points but there are also longer walks through the park. It takes about two days to walk between Z-Bend and the Loop.

Further east along the Ajana Kalbarri Rd are two lookouts: **Hawk's Head** (a must see) and **Ross Graham**. The park puts on a particularly fine display of wild flowers in the spring including everlastings, banksias, grevilleas and kangaroo paws.

Places to Stay

Kalbarri is a popular resort, and accommodation can be tight at holiday times. There's a wide selection of caravan parks, holiday units, hotels and motels.

There are five caravan parks around town including *Murchison Park* (☎ (099) 37 1005) and the *Lambs Holiday Village* (☎ (099) 37 1144); both are on Grey St and have tent sites and on-site vans.

The clean and modern Kalbarri YHA *Backpackers & Bunks* (☎ (099) 37 1430), at 2 Mortimer St, has shared accommodation for $10 and rooms for $24 per double; it has been recommended by a number of travellers. *Av-er-est* (☎ (099) 37 1101), on Mortimer St, also has backpackers' accommodation for $10 per night as well as self-contained units from $36 for two.

The *Kalbarri Motor Hotel* (☎ (099) 37 1000), on Grey St, is central and has comfortable singles/doubles for $40/55.

Place to Eat

In Kalbarri Arcade, there's a good health-food shop with sandwiches and delicious cakes – they also do good juices and smoothies. The *Gulgai Tavern* at the shopping centre in Porter St does counter meals as does the *Kalbarri Hotel* across the road. The *Zuytdorp* is the town's fancy restaurant.

Getting There & Around

Westrail buses from Perth come into Kalbarri on Monday and Friday ($53.80). Kalbarri Coach Tours (☎ (099) 37 1104) have a service from the North-West Coastal Highway that connects with the daily Greyhound/Pioneer bus from Perth; the fare is $50 from Perth to the Kalbarri turn-off and another $12 from the turn-off to Kalbarri. Kalbarri Tours also have trips to the Loop,

Z-Bend, ocean gorges and Shark Bay (Monkey Mia).

Bicycles can be rented from Murchison Cycles, on Porter St, for $4 per hour or $10 per day – if no-one is there, ask at the Mini-Putt complex next door.

SHARK BAY

Shark Bay has some spectacular beaches and the famous dolphins of Monkey Mia.

The first recorded landing on Australian soil by a European took place at Shark Bay in 1616 when the Dutch explorer Dirk Hartog landed on the island that now bears his name. He nailed an inscribed plate to a post on the beach but a later Dutch visitor collected it. It's now in a museum in Amsterdam, although there's a reproduction in the Geraldton Museum.

Denham, the main population centre of Shark Bay, is 135 km off the main highway from the Overlander Roadhouse. Denham is the most westerly town in Australia and was once a pearling port. Today, prawns and tourism are the local moneymakers.

Overlander Roadhouse to Denham

On the way in from the highway, the first turn-off (26 km from the highway) is a rough road to **Hamelin Pool**, a marine reserve which has the world's best known colony of stromatolites – an ancient and rare form of 'living rock'.

The 100-km-long stretch of **Shell Beach** is solid shells nearly 10 metres deep! In places in Shark Bay, the shells are so tightly packed that they can be cut into blocks and used for building construction. **Freshwater Camp** is a pioneer homestead museum at Nanga. At **Eagle Bluff**, halfway between Nanga and Denham, there are superb views from the cliff.

Denham has a tourist office (☎ (099) 48 1253) on Knight Terrace, a shell craft museum and a church made of shell blocks.

A couple of km down the road to Monkey Mia is the shallow and picturesque **Little Lagoon**.

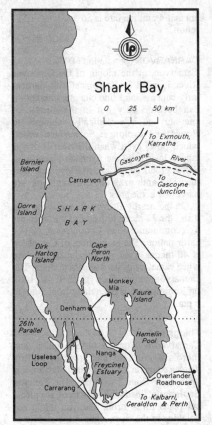

Shark Bay

0   25   50 km

To Exmouth,
Karratha

Gascoyne River

Bernier
Island

Carnarvon

To
Gascoyne
Junction

Dorre
Island

S H A R K

B A Y

Dirk
Hartog
Island

Cape
Peron
North

Monkey
Mia

Faure
Island

Denham

26th
Parallel

Hamelin
Pool

Useless
Loop

Nanga

Freycinet
Estuary

Overlander
Roadhouse

Carrarang

To Kalbarri,
Geraldton & Perth

during the winter months, less frequently during the summer. They may arrive singly or in groups of five or more, but as many as 13 were recorded on one occasion. They seem to come in more often in the mornings. Monkey Mia reserve has an interesting dolphin information centre with videos and displays; the entry fee to the reserve is $3 per adult. There are some rules of good behaviour for visitors:

Stand knee deep in water and let them approach you – don't chase or try to swim with them.
Stroke them along their sides with the back of your hand as they swim beside you. Don't touch their fins or their blowhole.
If you get invited to offer them fish by the ranger (feeding times and quantities are regulated) it should be whole, not gutted or filleted. They will take defrosted fish but only if it is completely thawed.

Organised Tours

There are three and four-hour scenic and wildlife cruises (weather permitting) around Shark Bay on the MV *Explorer* four times a week from $35 – book at the tourist office in Denham. Shark Bay Safaris (☎ (099) 48 1253) has a weekly Heritage Tour around Shark Bay for $18; they also run other scenic and fishing tours.

A number of companies run trips to Shark Bay from Perth including Travelabout Outback Tours (☎ (09) 242 2243), which has four-day camping tours to Kalbarri and Monkey Mia. For information on other tours to the area, contact the tourist office in Denham (☎ (099) 48 1253) or Perth (☎ (09) 322 2999).

Places to Stay

You can camp at Monkey Mia, Denham or 50 km south of Denham at Nanga Station. *Monkey Mia Dolphin Resort* (☎ (099) 48 1320) has tent sites at $4 per person and on-site vans at $40 for two. *Denham Seaside Park* (☎ (099) 48 1242), Knight Terrace, is a friendly place on the foreshore with tent sites for $8 and on-site vans from $30 for two. *Shark Bay Caravan Park* (☎ (099) 48 1387)

Monkey Mia Dolphins

Monkey Mia is 26 km north-east from Denham, on the other side of the Peron Peninsula. It's believed that dolphins have been visiting there since the early '60s, although it's only in the last decade or so that it's become world famous.

Monkey Mia's dolphins simply drop by to visit humans; they swim right into knee-deep water and will nudge up against you, even take a fish if it's offered, although they seem almost to do it out of courtesy rather than with any thought of a free feed.

The dolphins generally come in every day

on Spaven Way in Denham is similarly priced.

Accommodation in Shark Bay can be very tight and expensive during school vacations. *Bay Lodge* (☎ (099) 48 1278), an associate YHA hostel on the foreshore at Denham, has a great atmosphere and is the best value accommodation in Shark Bay. Bookings are recommended at this popular hostel. Beds in shared units cost $12 per night, and double and single rooms start from $24.

There are a number of holiday cottages and villas in Shark Bay. *Shark Bay Holiday Cottages* (☎ (099) 48 1206), 13 Knight Terrace, and *Tradewinds Chalets* (☎ (099) 48 1222), also on Knight Terrace, have self-contained units from $35 and $65 respectively. Shark Bay Accommodation Service (☎ (099) 48 1323) has a number of privately owned cottages and units available, usually by the week. A useful accommodation guide is available from the tourist office in Denham.

Places to Eat

On Knight Terrace in Denham, the *Bay Cafe* does good fish & chips and other fast food; the *Shark Bay Hotel* has counter meals; or there's the more expensive *Old Pearler* restaurant (main meals from $16 to $20) which is made with shell blocks. At Nanga Station, the *Nanga Barn Restaurant* does sit-down and takeaway meals.

Getting There & Away

North from Kalbarri, it's a fairly dull, boring and often very hot run to Carnarvon. The Overlander Roadhouse, 290 km north of Geraldton, is the turn-off to Shark Bay. Greyhound/Pioneer has a connecting bus service to Denham that meets northbound buses from Perth on Wednesday, Thursday and Saturday and southbound buses from Darwin and Port Hedland on Tuesday, Friday and Sunday. The fare from Perth to Denham is $121; $93 to the Overlander Roadhouse.

A daily local bus departs Denham (near the Bay Cafe on Knight Terrace) at 8.45 and 11 am for Monkey Mia and returns at 11.30 am and 4 pm; the fare is $6 one-way or $11 return.

CARNARVON (population 6000)

Carnarvon, at the mouth of the Gascoyne River, is noted for its tropical fruit, particularly bananas, and fine climate; although it can become very hot in the middle of summer and is periodically subjected to floods and cyclones. Subsurface water, which flows even when the river is dry, is tapped to irrigate the riverside plantations. Salt is produced at Lake Macleod near Carnarvon, and prawns and scallops are harvested in the area.

On the nearby Browns Range is the 'big dish', the 29-metre reflector of the Overseas Telecommunications Commission (OTC) earth station. The main street of Carnarvon is 40 metres wide, a reminder of the days when camel trains used to pass through. The Carnarvon tourist office (☎ (099) 41 1146), on Robinson St, is open daily from 9 am to 5 pm.

Things to See

Carnarvon was once a NASA station, and there's a museum and tracking-station display centre at the **OTC earth station**; it is open daily from 2 to 4 pm. The **Fascine Esplanade**, lined with palm trees, is a pleasant place for a stroll, and you might see dolphins in the river, right in the middle of town. Carnarvon's **'one mile' jetty** is a popular fishing spot. If you're too lazy to walk out to the end of the jetty, you can catch a toy train (be prepared for a very bumpy ride) for 75c each way. The small and furnished **Lighthouse Keeper's Cottage Museum**, beside the jetty, is open daily from 2 to 4 pm and from 10 am to noon on Sunday; admission is $1.

Pelican Point, only five km south-west from town, is a popular swimming and picnic spot. Other good beaches are south of Carnarvon off the Geraldton Rd at **Bush Bay** (turn-off 20 km) or **New Beach** (37 km).

Munro's Banana Plantation, on South River Rd, does a free and very informative

There's a fine beach about one km south of the blowholes with a primitive camp ground (no fresh water available) and a sort of shanty town with holiday shacks.

Cape Cuvier, where salt is loaded for Japan, is 30 km north of the blowholes, and nearby is the wreck of the *Korean Star* grounded in 1988 (do not climb over the wreck as it is dangerous).

Organised Tours

Tropical Tripper Tours depart from the tourist office and include half-day tours around town for $12 and an all-day tour that takes in Lake Macleod, Cape Cuvier and the blowholes for $29.

The *Dolphin Express* hovercraft runs from Carnarvon to Monkey Mia daily except Monday and Friday; the 2½-hour trip is $40 one-way and $70 return. The hovercraft leaves Carnarvon at 7 am and returns around 4 pm – bookings can be made through the tourist offices in Carnarvon or Denham, in Shark Bay.

Places to Stay

Camping You shouldn't have any trouble finding a caravan park in Carnarvon; the closest to the centre of town is the friendly *Carnarvon Tourist Centre Caravan Park* (☎ (099) 41 1438), on Robinson St, which has tent sites at $11 for two and on-site vans

plantation tour at 11 am and 2 pm daily (only 11 am at off-peak times). After the tour, you can indulge yourself in fantastic fresh-fruit ice cream or smoothies. Also available at the plantation is a banana cookbook with 118 recipes and a whole stack of weird and wonderful uses for bananas, including banana soap and banana cures for such ills as diarrhoea, ulcers and depression. Plantation tours are also conducted at D&B Plantation on Robinson Rd.

Attractions in the vicinity of Carnarvon include the spectacular blowholes, 70 km to the north – they are well worth the trip.

from $20. The other caravan parks have similar rates.

Hostels There is plenty of budget accommodation in Carnarvon. The pleasant *Carnarvon Backpackers* (☎ (099) 41 1095), an associate YHA hostel on Olivia Terrace, has dorm beds at $10 for YHA and backpacker members.

Also centrally located, the *Backpackers' Paradise* (☎ (099) 41 2966), next to the tourist office on Robinson St, has shared accommodation from $10.

The *Accommodation Centre* (☎ (099) 41 2511), a less attractive place to stay, costs $11 per night; there's usually a discount for YHA members. It's at 23 Wheelock Way, a km or so east of town; look for the sign as you come into Carnarvon from the main highway. The *Port Hotel* (☎ (099) 41 1704), on Robinson St, also has backpackers' accommodation for $10 per night.

Hotels & Motels Carnarvon has some old-fashioned hotels with old-fashioned prices. The *Gascoyne Hotel* (☎ (099) 41 1412), on Olivia Terrace, has singles/doubles at $25/35, or there's the *Port Hotel* which has rooms from $25/50 in the older part of the hotel. The *Carnarvon Hotel* (☎ (099) 41 1181), also on Olivia Terrace, has rooms for $15/30, or for $30/50 in the newer motel part.

The *Carnarvon Motor Inn* (☎ (099) 41 1532), on Robinson St, is more expensive at $59/69, but it does have a pool and well-equipped units. Or there are self-contained holiday units at the *Carnarvon Beach Holiday Resort* (☎ (099) 41 2226), Pelican Point, at $50 for two.

Places to Eat
Try *Carnarvon Fresh Seafoods*, on Robinson St, for fish & chips and hamburgers. On the same street are *Fascine* and *Jaycee's*, both standard coffee lounges. *Food Forum*, also on Robinson St next to the Carnarvon Tourist Centre Caravan Park, is a mini food hall with fish & chips, burgers, kebabs, pizza

and pasta at reasonable prices; you can eat in or take away.

The *Carnarvon Bakery* has home-made pies and sandwiches, and you can get good counter meals at the *Gascoyne*, *Carnarvon* and *Port* hotels.

Fatima's Asian Takeaway, on Robinson St, has typical Chinese takeaway food. There is also the *Dragon Pearl* Chinese restaurant on Francis St. If you're looking for a more up-market place to eat, you could try *Doodies* on Robinson St ($14 to $16 for a main meal), or the excellent restaurant in the *Tropicana Tavern* (main meals from $12 to $15).

Getting There & Away
Air Ansett WA fly to Carnarvon from Perth for $243 one-way, or $316 for an Apex return.

Bus Greyhound/Pioneer and Bus Australia both pass through Carnarvon on their way north or south. The one-way fare from Perth to Carnarvon is around $95.

Getting Around
Bicycles are available for hire from Carnarvon Backpackers, Backpackers' Paradise, the Carnarvon Tourist Centre Caravan Park and Rosco's Sports & Bikes (☎ (099) 41 1385) on Robinson St.

INLAND FROM CARNARVON
About 55 km inland along the Gascoyne River is **Rocky Pool**, a superb deep-water swimming pool.

Remote **Gascoyne Junction** is 164 km inland (east) from Carnarvon in the gemstone-rich Kennedy Range. From here, if you are really adventurous, you can continue on to **Mt Augustus**, 450 km from Carnarvon, the biggest rock in the world. The rock can be climbed (almost a full-day excursion), and there are Aboriginal rock paintings in the area. There's also accommodation close by at Cobra and Mt Augustus station.

The Pilbara

The Pilbara, which contains some of the hottest country on earth, is the iron-ore producing area accounting for much of Western Australia's prosperity. Gigantic machines are used to tear the dusty red ranges apart. It's isolated, harsh and fabulously wealthy. The Pilbara towns are almost all company towns: either mining centres where the ore is wrenched from the earth or ports from which it's shipped abroad. Exceptions are the coral reefs of the North-West Cape, the beautiful gorges of Wittenoom and earlier historic mining centres like Marble Bar.

If you are travelling away from the main coastal highway in this area in your own vehicle, always carry a lot of extra water – 20 litres per person is a sensible amount – and check that you have enough fuel to get to the next petrol station. If travelling into remote areas, make sure you tell someone your travel plans, and don't leave your vehicle if you are stranded.

Getting There & Away

Air Ansett WA fly from Perth to Newman ($287), Paraburdoo ($280) and Port Hedland. Skywest fly from Perth to Mt Magnet ($196), Cue ($208) and Meekatharra ($251).

Bus Greyhound/Pioneer has three buses a week from Perth to Port Hedland via Mt Magnet ($70), Cue ($70), Meekatharra ($83) and Newman ($124). Greyhound/Pioneer also has a once-weekly service from the Nanutarra turn-off to Tom Price ($103 from Perth) leaving Perth on Friday.

Westrail has a weekly bus service from Perth to Meekathara ($61), stopping at Mt Magnet ($50.80) and Cue ($54.80).

Bus Australia has three services a week to Exmouth from Perth (departing Tuesday, Thursday and Sunday) for $111. Ansett WA have regular flights to Learmonth from Perth ($302 one-way; $393 Apex return).

There is no bus service to Wittenoom,

although it is sometimes possible to get on a tour bus from Port Hedland; otherwise, you really need your own transport. Many of the roads in the Pilbara are unsealed.

You can reach Wittenoom directly from Port Hedland (307 km via the Great Northern Highway), from near Roebourne (311 km off the North-West Coastal Highway) or from the Nanutarra turn-off (377 km off the North-West Coastal Highway).

NORTH-WEST CAPE

North-West Cape, a finger of land jutting north into the Indian Ocean, is a popular centre with travellers – mainly because of the excellent diving opportunities at Coral Bay.

It's also well known because of the very hush-hush US Navy communications base north of Exmouth. It is marked by 13 very low-frequency transmitter stations. Twelve of them are higher than the Eiffel Tower, and all to support the 13th, which is 396 metres high, the tallest structure in the southern hemisphere. The base cost almost $100 million to build and tours can be arranged with the tourist office in Exmouth.

The area is noted for its commercial prawning, excellent fishing, fine beaches, reefs and rugged natural features.

Exmouth (population 2600)

Exmouth was established in 1967 largely as a service town for the US navy base. The Exmouth tourist office (☎ (099) 49 1176), on Thew St, has a video display and is open daily from 9 am to 5 pm.

Things to See There's a **shell museum** on Pellew St, and the town beach at the end of Warne St is quite popular. North of town, apart from the navy base, is the wreck of the **SS** _Mildura_ grounded in 1907, and the **Vlamingh Head Lighthouse** from which there are spectacular views. Around 15 km south of Exmouth is the impressive **Shothole Canyon**.

Places to Stay Much of the accommodation in and around Exmouth can be quite expensive. The *Exmouth Holiday Units* (☎ (099) 49 1200) have self-contained accommodation from $30 a double. There are a number of caravan parks around town, however: the *Exmouth Cape Tourist Village* (☎ (099) 49 1101), on the corner of Truscott Crescent and Murat Rd, has tent sites at $8 for two, on-site vans for $28 a double and excellent backpackers' accommodation for $10 per night.

At Manilya Bridge, seven km south of where the road to Exmouth forks away from the main Highway 1, is the *Swagman Roadhouse*. It has typical roadhouse fare and a no-frills bunkhouse with four beds at $5 per night.

Getting Around There is a host of tours in the area ranging from gulf and canyon safaris to reef and fishing tours – the full-day West Coast Safari (10 hours, $65) has been recommended by travellers. Contact the tourist office for details.

Ningaloo Reef
Running along the western side of the North-West Cape for 260 km is the stunning Ningaloo Reef. This miniature version of the Great Barrier Reef is actually much more accessible, as in places it is only a few km offshore. Coral Bay, just eight km off the main road up the cape, is the main access point for the reef, and glass-bottomed boat trips are made from there. Greenback turtles lay their eggs along the cape beach and placid whale sharks, the world's largest fish, can also be seen in the reef's waters.

Cape Range National Park
The park, which runs down the west coast of the cape, includes a modern visitor's centre, a wide variety of flora & fauna, good swimming beaches, gorges (including the scenic Yardie Creek Gorge) and rugged scenery.

Basic tent sites are available in the park (☎ (099) 49 1676) at $2 per person per night.

ONSLOW
Onslow has the dubious distinction of being the southernmost Western Australia town to be bombed in WW II and later being used as a base by the British for nuclear testing in the Monte Bello Islands.

The town has a **shell museum**, and there is good swimming and fishing in the area. The **Old Onslow ruins**, 48 km from town, include a jail and a post office; it is worth a look if you are in the area.

The *Ocean View Caravan Park* (☎ (091) 84 6053) on Second Ave has tent sites at $12 for two and on-site vans from $25.

ROEBOURNE AREA
The Roebourne area is a busy little enclave of historic towns and modern port facilities. The area serves as the port for the ore produced at Tom Price and Pannawonica and is also the onshore base for the North-West Shelf natural gas fields. This area holds the beginnings of European settlement of the North West.

Karratha is the regional centre and is a rapidly growing modern town.

Information
Information on the area is available at the Nor-West Tourist Information Centre (☎ (091) 85 2474), in the shopping centre at Karratha; and the particularly helpful Roebourne District Tourist Association (☎ (091) 82 1060), 173 Roe St, Roebourne.

Dampier (population 2500)
Dampier on King Bay faces the islands of the Dampier Archipelago. They were named after the English pirate-explorer William Dampier who visited the area in 1699 and immortalised himself not only as one of Australia's first knockers but also as its first whingeing pom – he thought it was a pretty miserable place.

Dampier is a Hamersley Iron Company town and the port for Tom Price and Paraburdoo iron-ore operations. Its huge facilities can handle ships up to 230,000 tonnes. Salt, too, is exported from there.

Gas from the huge natural gas fields of the North-West Shelf is piped ashore nearby on the Burrup Peninsula. From there, it is piped to Perth and the Pilbara, or liquefied as part of the gigantic Woodside Petroleum project and exported to Japan.

An inspection of the port facilities can be arranged (☎ (091) 43 5364). The tours operate from Monday to Friday at 9 am and noon. The **William Dampier Lookout** provides a fine view over the harbour and the **Woodside Visitors' Centre** is open weekdays from 9 am to 4.30 pm.

Nearby **Hearsons Cove** is a popular beach and picnic area as is **Dampier Beach**.

The Fe-NaCl-NG Festival is held in August each year. The title of the festival combines the chemical abbreviations of the region's main natural resources – iron, salt and natural gas.

Karratha (population 9000)

Karratha, the dormitory town for the area and 20 km from Dampier, is a town that was developed due to the rapidly growing expansion of the Hamersley Iron project. Karratha has no historical significance, but the other towns now use it as the hub and regard it as the major town in the area. There are good views from the lookout at **TV Hill**, and **Maree Pool**, 35 km to the south-west, is scenic and a good place to cool off.

Roebourne (population 1700)

Roebourne is the oldest existing town in the north-west. It has a history of gold and copper mining, and was once the capital of the North-West. There are still some fine old buildings to be seen, including an **old gaol**, an **1894 church** and the **Victoria Hotel** which is the last of the five original pubs. The town was once connected to Cossack, 13 km away on the coast, by a horse-drawn tram line.

Cossack

Originally known as Tien Tsin Harbour,

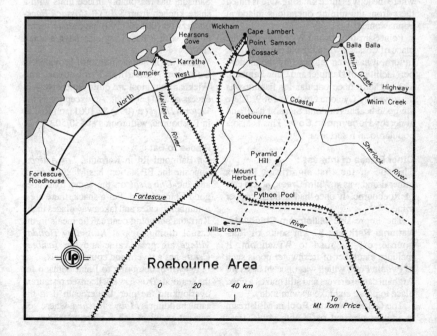

Roebourne Area

0   20   40 km

To Mt Tom Price

Cossack was a bustling town and the main port for the district in the late 19th century. Its boom was short lived, however, and Point Samson soon supplanted it as the chief port for the area. The sturdy old buildings date from 1870 to 1890, and much of the now deserted ghost town has been restored as a continuing bicentennial project which commenced in 1988.

The former ghost town now houses an **art gallery, museum** and a budget-accommodation house which has a boat-hiring facility.

Beyond town, there's a **pioneer cemetery** with a small Japanese section dating from the old pearl diving days. There are a couple of good lookouts and excellent beaches in the area; the cooler, drier months are best for a visit.

Wickham & Point Samson

Wickham is the Cliffs Robe River Iron Company town, handling their ore-exporting facilities 10 km away at Cape Lambert, where the jetty is three km long. Ore is railed there from the mining operations inland at Pannawonica.

Point Samson, beyond Wickham, took the place of Cossack when the old port silted up. In turn, it has been replaced by the modern port facilities of Dampier and Cape Lambert. The old jetty once popular for fishing was destroyed by Cyclone Orson in 1989. There are good beaches at Point Samson itself and at nearby **Honeymoon Cove**. This is also a popular local resort area.

Other Places of Interest

The site of the first significant Pilbara mineral find was at **Whim Creek**, 80 km east of Roebourne. It once had a large copper mine.

The impressive **Millstream-Chichester National Park** lies 87 km south of Roebourne, off the road to Wittenoom. It includes a number of freshwater pools such as Python Pool, which was once an oasis for Afghani camel drivers and still makes a good place to pause and take a swim today.

The **Chinderwariner Pool** in Millstream is another pleasant oasis with pools, trees

ferns and lilies; it is well worth a visit. The lush environment provides a haven for birds and other fauna such as flying foxes and kangaroos. The park also has a number of walking trails and camping areas. The old station homestead has been converted into an information centre with a wealth of information on the Millstream ecosystems and the lifestyle of tribal Aborigines in the area who joint-manage the park.

Places to Stay

There are caravan parks with tent sites in Roebourne (☎ (091) 92 1880) and Karratha (☎ (091) 85 3628). There are also basic camp grounds in the Millstream Chichester National Park.

There is an associate YHA hostel with cooking facilities in the *King Bay Holiday Village* (☎ (091) 83 1440) on the Esplanade in Dampier; single rooms are $12 for members, $16 for nonmembers. *Samson Accommodation* (☎ (091) 87 1052), at Point Samson, has reasonably priced units with a share kitchen from $20/33. *Cossack Backpackers* (☎ (091 821190) have share rooms at $12 with a fan. They also have a small shop.

Hotel or motel facilities are provided in Dampier, Karratha, Roebourne and Wickham but most are quite expensive – in excess of $80 per night. An exception is the *Victoria Hotel* (☎ (091) 82 1001), on Roe St in Roebourne, with rooms at $30/50.

Places to Eat

On Balmoral Rd in Karratha, *Los Amigos*, opposite the BP station, has Mexican food, and the *Universal* on the same road does good Chinese food. For a snack, there are a a number of cafes and takeaway places in the Karratha shopping centre. The meals in the casual dining area at *King Bay Holiday Village* are great value and the *Tambrey Centre* has a tavern and counter meals.

It's worth detouring to Point Samson for the seafood. *Trawlers* is a licensed restaurant overlooking the pier. Underneath it in the same building is *Moby's Kitchen*, where you can get excellent fish & chips to take away or eat there. They've got a variety of fish, calamari and other dishes.

WITTENOOM (population 40)

Wittenoom, 262 km south-east of Roebourne, is the Pilbara's tourist centre. It had an earlier history as an asbestos-mining town but mining finally halted in 1966; it is the magnificent gorges of the Hamersley Range which now draw people to the area. The tourist office (☎ (091) 89 7096) is on Sixth Ave.

Note that even after 25 years, there is a health risk from airborne asbestos fibres. Avoid disturbing asbestos tailings in the area.

Karinji (Hamersley Range) National Park

Wittenoom is at the northern end of the Karinji (Hamersley Range) National Park and the most famous gorge, **Wittenoom Gorge**, is immediately south of the town. A surfaced road runs the 13 km to this gorge, passing old asbestos mines and a number of smaller gorges and pretty pools.

Like other gorges in central Australia, those of the Hamersley Range are spectacular both in their sheer rocky faces and their varied colours. In the early spring, the park is often carpeted with colourful wild flowers. Travel down the Newman road 24 km and there's a turn-off to the **Yampire Gorge** where blue veins of asbestos can be seen in the rock.

Fig Tree Well, in the gorge, was once used by Afghani camel drivers as a watering point. The road continues through Yampire Gorge to **Dales Gorge**, but only the first couple of km of its 45 km length can be reached. On this same route, you can get to **Circular Pool** and a nearby **lookout**, and by a footpath to the bottom of the **Fortescue Falls**.

The **Joffre Falls** road will take you to Oxer Lookout at the junction of the **Red**,

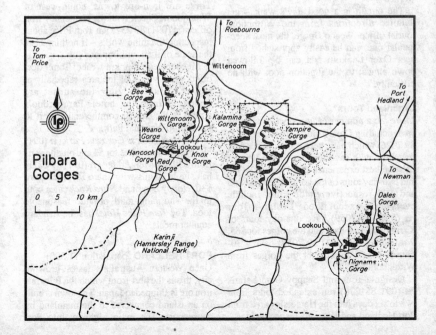

Weano and **Hancock gorges**. Following the main road to Tom Price, you pass through the small **Rio Tinto Gorge**, 43 km from Wittenoom, and just beyond this is the **Hamersley Range**, only four km from the road. Mt Meharry (1245 metres), the highest mountain in Western Australia, is in the south-east of Karinji (Hamersley Range) National Park.

If you're on foot, be sure you can find your way back as all the bush looks the same and there are no people or waterholes. Notify somebody that you're going. For the more energetic, there's a walk starting at the asbestos mine about 13 km from Wittenoom on the surfaced road. Walk up Wittenoom Gorge, then up Red Gorge (some swimming may be required) until you come out at the pool below Oxer Lookout. Then proceed up Hancock Gorge, cross the road and follow the footpath into Weano Gorge, which can be followed back to the junction pool – it involves two quite scary climbs, so be warned!

The circuit is a good day's walk – get detailed directions from the Wittenoom tourist office. Weano Gorge, the most spectacular one, can be easily approached from near Oxer Lookout and can be followed down almost to the junction pool with no difficulty.

Organised Tours

There are a number of tour operators in the area including Dave's Gorge Tours (☎ (091) 89 7026) which have been recommended by travellers with rave reviews to the tune of 'it's the best experience that I've had'. One and two-day tours of the gorges area cost $45 and $90 respectively; the tours include everything except food. Design-a-Tour (☎ (091) 89 7059) have one-day tours of Karinji National Park and the gorges for $65. Westate Air (☎ (091) 89 7052) have a 30-minute scenic flight over the gorges from Wittenoom for $40.

Design-a-Tour and Snappy Gum Safaris (☎ (091) 851278) run extended tours from two to six days into the Hamersley area from Port Hedland and Karratha respectively.

Places to Stay

There are several basic camp sites within the Karinji (Hamersley Range) National Park – contact the park ranger (☎ (091) 89 8157) for more information.

Gorges Caravan Park (☎ (091) 89 7075), in Wittenoom, has tent sites from $9.50 and on-site vans from $25. *Fortescue Hotel* (☎ (091) 89 7055), on Gregory St, has singles/doubles from $35/50 and motel units from $60/75.

Wittenoom Bungarra Bivouac (☎ (091) 89 7026), at 74 Fifth Ave, has beds at $6 per night or $35 per week. *Wittenoom Holiday Homes* (☎ (091) 89 7096), on Fifth Ave, have cottages with kitchen, bathroom and laundry from $20 a person. Also on Fifth Ave is the *Wittenoom Vacation Village* (☎ (091) 89 7077) with twin-share rooms from $10 per person and dorm accommodation from $8 per night.

TOM PRICE & PARABURDOO

These are iron-ore towns, south-west of Wittenoom. Check with the Hamersley Iron office (☎ (091) 89 2375) in Tom Price about inspecting the mine works – if nothing else, the scale of it all will impress you.

Mt Nameless, four km west of Tom Price, offers good views of the area especially at sunset. Tours to view the sunset are organised from the hotel. Paraburdoo's airport is the closest commercial airport to the Karinji National Park.

The *Mt Nameless Caravan Park* (☎ (091) 89 1515) has tent sites for $3 and on-site vans from $30. *Hillview Lodge* (☎ (091) 89 1211) has single rooms with share facilities from $30. *Happy Days* and *Hard Rock* cafes both in the shopping mall provide reasonable food. The *Tom Price Hotel* has the standard counter meals.

PORT HEDLAND (population 11,500)

Once Western Australia's fastest-growing city, this is the port from which the Pilbara's iron ore is shipped to Japan. The town is built on an island connected to the mainland by causeways. The main highway into Port

Hedland enters along a causeway three km long. The port handles the largest annual tonnage of any Australian port. Like other towns along the coast, it's also a centre for salt production; huge 'dunes' of salt can be seen six km from the town.

Even before the Marble Bar gold rush, the town had been important: it had been a grazing centre since 1864, while during the 1870s a fleet of 150 pearling luggers had been based there. By 1946, however, the population had dwindled to a mere 150.

The port is on a mangrove-fringed inlet – there are plenty of fish, crabs, oysters and birds around. As Port Hedland has grown, satellite towns have sprung up, both to handle the mining output of the area and also to accommodate the area's workers.

Although Port Hedland is not a great tourist attraction – in fact it's a boring, dusty town – it's worth a short stop to get an idea of the immensity of the iron-ore operations. Some travellers pause here for short-term work.

Information & Orientation

The tourist office (☎ (091) 73 1650), which has a small art gallery and showers ($1), is on Wedge St, across from the post office. It's open from 9 am to 6 pm and from 8.15 to 10.15 pm daily. It has an excellent map of the town and a number of heritage-walk brochures.

Port Hedland really sprawls, and the main part of town is basically a long, narrow island. It's several km south to the airport and several km south again to the dormitory town of South Hedland. From December to March is the cyclone season in this region.

Things to See & Do

There's an **Olympic swimming pool** by the civic centre. **Pretty Pool**, several km east of the town centre on the waterfront, is a safe tidal pool where shell collectors will have fun. Visits can also be made to the **Royal Flying Doctor base** on Richardson St.

You can visit the **wharf area** without any prior arrangement to see the huge ore carriers loaded. There's a tour of the Mt Newman

Mining Company's operations at **Nelson's Point** every weekday at 10.30 am; book and board the bus at the tourist office.

For those travelling north to Broome with a car there are some great beaches at **Cape Keraurdren** and **Eighty Mile Beach** which also has a caravan park with on-site vans.

Places to Stay

Camping You can camp in South Hedland by the airport at *Dixon's Caravan Park* (☎ (091) 72 2525), or more conveniently in Port Hedland at the *Cooke Point Caravan Park* (☎ (091) 73 1271), on Athol St, which is also adjacent to Pretty Pool. Both have tent sites for around $10 and on-site vans from $35 for two.

South Hedland Caravan Park (☎ (091) 72 1197), on Hamilton Rd, is the third park in the area; tent sites cost $12 and there are on-site vans from $47 for two.

Hostels The *Backpacker's Hostel* (☎ (091) 73 2198), at 20 Richardson St between Edgar and McKay Sts, is run by Ken and Julie. It's a bit rough and ready but friendly. Beds costs $10 a night and the place has kitchen and laundry facilities.

The *Ocean View* (☎ (091) 73 2418), in Kingsmill St, also has budget accommodation; rooms with shared facilities cost from $15.

Hotels & Motels On the corner of Anderson St, there's the *Esplanade Hotel* (☎ (091) 73 1798) which has rooms from $40 per person. The *Pier Hotel* (☎ (091) 73 1488), on the Esplanade, has singles/doubles for $45/75 with breakfast.

Places to Eat

The *Pier* and the *Esplanade* hotels do counter meals and bar snacks at lunch time. The air-con *Hedland Hotel* does excellent-value counter meals. Counter teas are available only on Friday and Saturday nights, until 8 pm.

There are plenty of supermarkets if you want to fix your own food and also a number of coffee bars and other places where you can

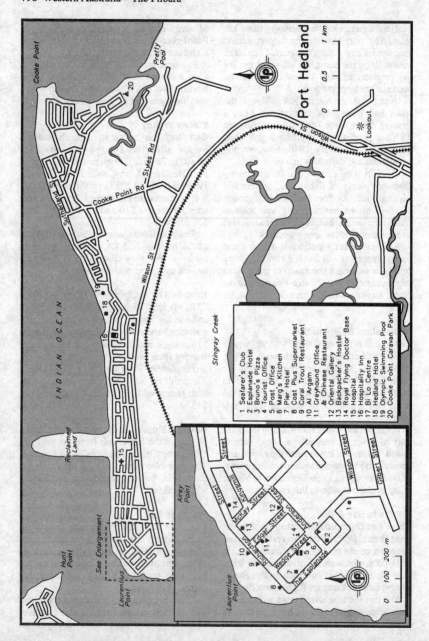

Port Hedland

1 Seafarer's Club
2 Esplanade Hotel
3 Bruno's Pizza
4 Tourist Office
5 Post Office
6 Marg's Kitchen
7 Pier Hotel
8 Cost Plus Supermarket
9 Coral Trout Restaurant
10 Al Argam
11 Greyhound Office
   & Chinese Restaurant
12 Oriental Gallery
13 Backpacker's Hostel
14 Royal Flying Doctor Base
15 Hospital
16 Hospitality Inn
17 Bi Lo Centre
18 Hedland Hotel
19 Olympic Swimming Pool
20 Cooke Point Caravan Park

get a pie or pastie. *Marg's Kitchen*, opposite the tourist office, is open long hours. The yacht club have fish & chip nights on Friday for $5.

Al Argam, on Richardson St, is a Muslim-food takeaway. It has dishes like spicy fish and rendang chicken for around $6, but it's only so-so. Nearby is the *Coral Trout* with a BYO restaurant and takeaway section where you can get fish & chips. The *Oriental Gallery*, on the corner of Edgar and Anderson Sts, does a good-value weekday lunch.

Getting There & Away

Air Ansett WA have three flights a week from Port Hedland to Darwin ($427). There are as many as five connections daily to Perth ($358) and also frequent flights to and from Broome ($198), Derby ($213), Karratha ($139) and other northern centres. Garuda and Qantas operate flights on alternate Saturdays between Port Hedland and Bali for around $750 return.

Ansett WA (☎ (091) 73 1777) is in the Boulevard Shopping Centre (better known as the Bi-Lo Centre) on Wilson St. There's a second office in the South Hedland shopping centre.

With the proposed introduction of a second airline on the west coast the airfares in this area should be reduced in the near future.

Bus It's 230 km from Karratha to Port Hedland and a further 600 km on to Broome. Bus Australia and Greyhound/Pioneer have services from Perth to Port Hedland and north on to Broome and Darwin. Greyhound has its office on Edgar St, right in the town centre, and Bus Australia stops at the tourist office.

Apart from the coastal route, Greyhound has another service that takes the inland route from Perth to Port Hedland via Newman three times a week. Fares from Port Hedland are $124 to Perth, $55 to Broome, $38 to Karratha and $184 to Darwin.

Getting Around

The airport is about 10 km from town – the only way to get there is by taxi, which costs around $18. There's a reasonably regular bus service between Port Hedland and South Hedland; it takes 40 minutes to an hour and operates from Monday to Saturday.

You can hire cars at the airport from the usual operators. WK Motors (☎ (091) 73 1729) at the BP station, 36 Anderson St, has older cars for around-town use only from $20 per day; they also rent motorscooters. The Backpacker's Hostel hires bikes at reasonable rates.

THE GREAT NORTHERN HIGHWAY

Although most people heading for the Pilbara and the Kimberley travel up the coast, the Great Northern Highway is much more direct. The highway extends from Perth to Newman and then skirts the eastern edge of the Pilbara on its way to Port Hedland; the road is sealed all the way. The total distance is 1636 km – slightly longer if you plan to make the short gravel detour through Marble Bar.

The Great Northern Highway is not the most interesting road in Australia – for much of the way it passes through country that is flat, dull and dreary in the extreme. Once you've passed through the old gold towns of the Murchison River gold fields – Mt Magnet, Cue and Meekatharra – there's really nothing until you reach Newman, 420 km further north.

Mt Magnet Area

Gold was found at Mt Magnet in the late 19th century and mining is still the town's *raison d'être*. Eleven km north of town are the ruins of Lennonville, once a busy town. There are still some interesting old buildings of solid stone in **Cue**, 80 km north of Mt Magnet, and **Walga Rock**, 48 km to the west, is a large monolith with a gallery of Aboriginal art.

Places to Stay *Mt Magnet Caravan Park* (☎ (099) 63 4198) has tent sites for $6 and there are three hotels in Mt Magnet's main street with single rooms for around $35 per night.

Cue Caravan Park (☎ (099) 63 1107) has

tent sites for $5 and the *Murchison Club* (☎ (099) 63 1020), in Austin St, Cue, has single rooms from $30.

Meekatharra

Meekatharra is still a mining centre. At one time it was a railhead for cattle brought down from the Northern Territory and the east Kimberley along the Canning Stock Route. There are ruins of various old gold towns and workings in the area. From Meekatharra, you can travel south via Wiluna and Leonora to the gold fields around Kalgoorlie. It's a bit over 700 km to Kalgoorlie, more than half of it on unsealed road.

Places to Stay *Meekathara Caravan Park* (☎ (099) 81 1253) has tent sites for $10 and on-site vans from $30 per night, and the *Meekatharra Hotel Motel* (☎ (099) 81 1021), on Main St, has units for $34/40.

Newman (population 5500)

At Newman, a town which only came into existence in the 1970s, Mt Whaleback is being systematically taken apart and railed down to the coast. It's a solid mountain of iron ore and every day up to 120,000 tonnes of ore are produced, a task that requires moving nearly 300,000 tonnes of material. After crushing, the ore is loaded into 144-car, two-km-long trains which are sent down the 426-km railway line, Australia's longest private railway, to Port Hedland from where it is shipped overseas.

Guided tours of the operations are available from the Mt Newman Company office daily at 8.30 am and 1 pm. The town of Newman is a modern, green, company town built solely to service the mine.

The **Opthalmia Dam**, 22 km east of town, is a popular sailing and swimming area – the dam, however, can be low at times, especially during winter.

Places to Stay There are several caravan parks in the area, the closest to town being the *Newman Caravan Park* (☎ (091) 75

1428), on Kalgan Drive, which has tent sites for $10 and on-site vans at $54 for two.

Marble Bar (population 350)

Reputed to be the hottest place in Australia, Marble Bar had a period in the 1920s when for 160 consecutive days the temperature topped 37°C. On one occasion, in 1905, the mercury soared to 49.1°C. From October to March, days over 40°C are common – though it is dry heat and not too unbearable.

The town is 203 km south-east of Port Hedland and takes its name from a bar of red jasper across the Coongan River, five km west of town – this spot is also popular for swimming.

The town came into existence when gold was found there in 1891. At its peak, the population was 5000; today, minerals other than gold are also mined here. The tourist office (☎ (091) 76 1041) is in the BP service station on Francis St.

In town, the 1895 government buildings, made of local stone, are still in use. In late winter, as the spring flowers begin to bloom, Marble Bar is actually quite a pretty place and one of the most popular towns in the Pilbara to visit. **Comet Gold Mine**, 10 km south of Marble Bar, is still in operation and has a mining museum and display centre featuring a comprehensive rock collection; it is open daily. The yearly race meeting attracts a large, noisy crowd from all over the Pilbara and is quite a spectacle.

Coppins Gap, about 70 km north-east of Marble Bar, is a deep cutting with impressive views, twisted bands of rock and an ideal swimming hole.

Places to Stay *Marble Bar Caravan Park* (☎ (091) 76 1067), on Contest St, has tent sites from $8.50 and on-site vans from $26 for two. Rooms at the *Ironclad Hotel* (☎ (091) 76 1066), one of the area's most distinctive drinking spots, range from $30 to $45 for singles, from $50 to $70 for doubles – they also have backpackers' accommodation from $15.

Goldsworthy & Shay Gap

Goldsworthy was the first Pilbara iron town and, like Newman, its production is shipped to Port Hedland and loaded on to bulk carriers at Finucane Island. At one time, Mt Goldsworthy was 132 metres high but it's now a big hole in the ground full of water. There are only a few workers living there now, maintaining the electricity generators that run the massive shovels and provide power to Shay Gap, 70 km east, where the mining operations have now shifted. Both these towns were badly damaged in 1980 by Cyclone Enid.

Broome

Population 6000

The delightful old pearling port of Broome is a small, dusty place noted for its Chinatown, which looks for all the world like a set from a cowboy movie. Although still isolated, Broome has certainly been discovered. During the 1980s the generally dull 624 km of road from Port Hedland across the fringes of the Great Sandy Desert was sealed, sparking a tourist boom. Today the town is also something of a travellers' centre.

Pearling in the sea off Broome started in the 1880s and peaked in the early 1900s when the town's 400 pearling luggers, worked by 3000 men, supplied 80% of the world's mother-of-pearl. Today only a handful of boats operate.

Pearl diving was a very unsafe occupation, as Broome's Japanese cemetery attests. The divers were from various Asian countries. The rivalries between the different nationalities were always intense and sometimes took an ugly turn. Although those days are long over, the town still has a very cosmopolitan feel about it.

Orientation

The centre of Broome's new development and growth is in the southern portion of town, in the area surrounding the corner of Dampier Terrace and Saville St. The museum is there, as is the modern but semi-Chinese looking Seaview Shopping Plaza opposite.

Information

Broome Tourist Bureau (☎ (091) 92 1176) is just across the sports field from Chinatown. It's open Monday to Friday from 8 am to 5 pm, Saturday from 9 am to 1 pm, and Sunday from 9 am to 5 pm. There's a useful notice board in the Seaview Shopping Centre.

The tourist office puts out a very useful fortnightly guide to what's happening in and around Broome.

Chinatown

The term 'Chinatown' is used to refer to the old part of town, although there is really only one block or so that is both Chinese and historic. Some of the plain and simple wooden buildings that line Carnarvon St still house Chinese merchants, but most are now restaurants and tourist shops. The bars on the windows aren't there to deter outlaws but to minimise cyclone damage.

The Carnarvon St street signs are in English, Chinese, Arabic, Japanese and Malay. On Dampier Terrace, just beyond Short St, is a model of a Chinese temple encased in a big glass box.

Pearling

You can still see pearling luggers moored in Roebuck Bay out from the end of the jetty, and occasionally at the Short St jetty in Chinatown.

Broome Historical Society Museum, on Saville St, has interesting exhibits both on Broome and its history and on the pearling industry and its dangers. It's housed in the old customs house and is open Monday to Friday from 10 am to 4 pm, and Saturday and Sunday from 10 am to 1 pm.

Mother-of-pearl has long been a Broome speciality. Along Dampier Terrace in Chinatown are a number of shops selling pearls, mother-of-pearl and shells.

The **cemetery**, on the outskirts of town just off Cable Beach Rd, testifies to the

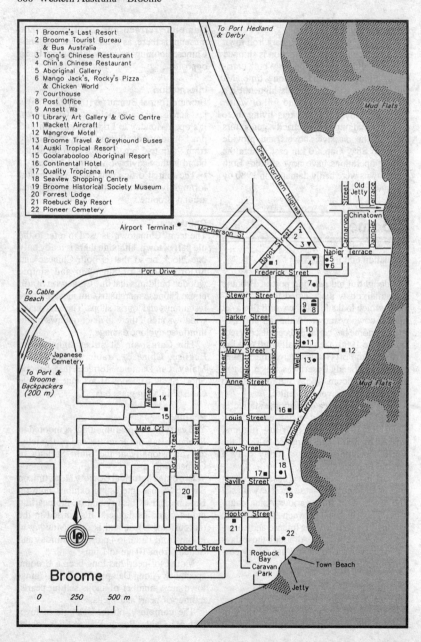

1 Broome's Last Resort
2 Broome Tourist Bureau
  & Bus Australia
3 Tong's Chinese Restaurant
4 Chin's Chinese Restaurant
5 Aboriginal Gallery
6 Mango Jack's, Rocky's Pizza
  & Chicken World
7 Courthouse
8 Post Office
9 Ansett Wa
10 Library, Art Gallery & Civic Centre
11 Wackett Aircraft
12 Mangrove Motel
13 Broome Travel & Greyhound Buses
14 Auski Tropical Resort
15 Goolarabooloo Aboriginal Resort
16 Continental Hotel
17 Quality Tropicana Inn
18 Seaview Shopping Centre
19 Broome Historical Society Museum
20 Forrest Lodge
21 Roebuck Bay Resort
22 Pioneer Cemetery

To Port Hedland & Derby

Mud Flats

Great Northern Highway

Old Jetty

Chinatown

Carnarvon Street
Dampier Terrace

Airport Terminal

McPherson St

Napier Terrace

Bagot Street

Port Drive

Frederick Street

To Cable Beach

Stewart Street

Barker Street

Herbert Street
Walcott Street
Robinson Street
Weld Street

Mary Street

Japanese Cemetery

To Port & Broome Backpackers (200 m)

Anne Street

Mud Flats

Milner

Dampier Terrace

Louis Street

Male Crt

Dora Street
Forrest Street

Guy Street

Saville Street

Hooton Street

Robert Street

Roebuck Bay Caravan Park

Town Beach

Jetty

Broome

0   250   500 m

dangers that accompanied pearl diving when equipment was primitive and knowledge of diving techniques limited. In 1914 alone, 33 divers died of the bends, while in 1908 a cyclone killed 150 seamen caught at sea. The Japanese section of the cemetery is one of the largest and most interesting. Some years ago a Japanese philanthropist paid to have it extensively renovated and there are now many shiny new black tombstones scattered amongst the beautiful old sandstone ones.

Behind the neat Japanese section is the interesting but run-down section containing European and Aboriginal graves. The largest contingent of divers was Japanese, but Filipinos, Malays, Torres Strait Islanders and 'Koepangers' from what is now Indonesian West Timor also collected the pearls.

Japanese Air-Raid Relics
Broome's dramatic moment in history came with the Japanese air raid of March 1942. Broome was then a clearing station for refugees from the Dutch East Indies (now Indonesia) and on the morning of the raid the harbour was crowded with flying boats that had just arrived from Indonesia. A force of Japanese Zero fighters surprised the town with a daring raid that wiped out 15 flying boats in Roebuck Bay and another seven aircraft at the airstrip. About 70 people were killed, many of them Dutch women and children who were still aboard the aircraft when the raid took place.

Remains of the flying boats can still be seen out in muddy Roebuck Bay. *WA's Pearl Harbour – The Japanese Raid on Broome* is a small booklet by Mervyn W Prime, available in Broome.

Other Attractions
Across Napier Terrace from Chinatown is Wing's Restaurant with a magnificent boab tree beside it. There's another boab tree behind, outside what used to be the old police lock-up, with a rather sad little tale on a plaque at its base. The tree was planted by a police officer when his son, who was killed in France in WW I, was born in 1898. The boab tree is still doing fine.

The 1888 **courthouse** was once used to house the transmitting equipment for the old cable station. The cable ran to Banyuwangi in Java, the ferry port across from Bali.

Further along Weld St, by the library and civic centre, is a **Wackett aircraft** that used to belong to Horrie Miller, founder of MacRobertson Miller Airlines, now Ansett WA. The plane is hidden away in a modern but absurdly designed building that most people pass without a second glance. **Bedford Park** has a handful of relics, including a decompression chamber.

There's a **pioneer cemetery** by the old jetty site at the end of Robinson St. Nearby there's a park and small beach. (The beach doesn't have much sand, but this is the town beach and people do swim there.) In the bay, at the entrance to Dampier Creek, there's a landmark called **Buccaneer Rock**, dedicated to Captain William Dampier and his ship, the *Roebuck*.

If you're lucky enough to be in Broome on a cloudless night when a full moon rises you can witness the **'Golden Staircase to the Moon'**. The reflections of the moon from the rippling mud-flats creates a wonderful golden-stairway effect, best seen from the town beach. The effect is in fact most dramatic about two days after the full moon, as the moon rises after the sky has had a chance to darken. A lively evening market is held on this evening, and the whole place takes on a carnival air. Check with the tourist bureau for exact dates and times.

Organised Tours
Broome There are a number of tours to make in and around Broome. The *Spirit of Broome* is a small hovercraft which makes daily one-hour flights around Roebuck Bay ($30), and it makes stops at various points of interest (☎ (091) 93 5025).

The Last Resort (see the following Places to Stay section) organises twice-weekly beach fishing trips ($35) and these receive good reports.

Broome Coachlines offers a town tour ($28) in addition to the one to Willie Creek

Pearl Farm; you can combine the two for $60.

There are also some guided bushwalks – see the tourist office for full details.

Further Afield The Last Resort organises three-day trips up along the Dampier Peninsula to Cape Leveque to Beagle Bay, Lombadina and One-Arm Point. They are popular with backpackers and cost $230. They also offer great trips along the Gibb River Rd – see that section for details.

Festivals
Shinju Matsuri (Festival of the Pearl) This excellent festival commemorates the early pearling years and takes place in late August or early September. When the festival is on, the town population swells and accommodation is hard to find – book ahead. Asian celebrations are the feature of the festival, and these include a Japanese Bon Festival, a Chinese Feast and the Malayan Merdeka. It's well worth trying to juggle your itinerary to be in Broome at this time.

Places to Stay
Camping Even camping can become impossible in Broome, nor is it particularly cheap.

The *Roebuck Bay Caravan Park* (☎ (091) 92 1366) is conveniently central and has tent sites from $12.50.

Hostels For years cheap beds in Broome were like the proverbial hen's teeth, but these days things have improved markedly with the opening of a couple of very good hostels. On Bagot St, very close to the centre and just a short stagger from the airport, is *Broome's Last Resort* (☎ (091) 93 500). It's new, friendly, clean, cheap and has excellent facilities including a pool, large kitchen, courtesy bus and bike hire ($6). Accommodation ranges from $12 dorm beds to $32 for doubles, all with shared facilities. They also organise great beach fishing trips twice a week ($35), and more extended camping tours into the Kimberley (see the section on the Kimberley later).

Also close to the centre is the *Bunkhouse* (☎ (091) 92 1221), part of the Roebuck Bay Hotel. Accommodation is adequate, with beds in 20-bed dorms for $10, although the cooking facilities are a joke and if there's a band playing at the pub you can forget about any sleep.

About one km from the centre is the *Broome Backpackers* (☎ (091) 93 5050), at Crocker Way just past the turn-off to Cable Beach. It's owned by the same people who run the Last Resort, so you can inquire there about beds. It has dorm beds for $10 and is a lively place. Despite the distance from the centre, it's still very popular.

Hotels, Motels & Resorts During school holidays and other peak times getting accommodation can be extremely difficult, so book ahead if possible.

The legendary *Roebuck Bay Hotel* (☎ (091) 92 1221), on the corner of Carnarvon St and Napier Terrace, Chinatown, has a bunkhouse (see earlier), as well as motel units that cost $80/95 in season.

The *Continental Hotel* (☎ (091) 92 1002) is a modern place on Weld St, at the corner of Louis St, with rooms from $70/80. The *Mangrove Motel* (☎ (091) 92 1303), between the Continental and Chinatown, down near the water, costs from $85, and it's a good place to watch the moon rising.

Forrest Lodge (☎ (091) 93 5067), at 59 Forrest St, has small double rooms with fan for $45 with breakfast.

The *Roebuck Bay Resort* (☎ (091) 92 1898), on Hopton St, has rooms for $95, or two-bedroomed apartments for $170. Another place is the *Auski Tropical Resort* (☎ (091) 93 1183) in Milner St. It has a swimming pool and all mod cons. Units with one or two bedrooms cost from $80/90.

Out of Town *Broome Bird Observatory* (☎ (091) 93 5600) is 18 km from town on the shore of Roebuck Bay. You can camp for $8, or there are units for $25, and a five-bed, self-contained chalet for $30. Meals are available on request.

Places to Eat

Light Meals & Fast Food Finding a place to stay in Broome may be a hassle but eating out is no sweat at all. The *Baghdad Cafe*, on Carnarvon St, has good, healthy food such as vegetarian pasta, and excellent smoothies. It also has curry and pasta nights on occasion, and these are popular on film nights as Sun Pictures cinema is just across the road.

Mango Jack's, on Hamersley St has excellent hamburgers and also dispenses the usual sandwiches, chips and the like. In the same little shopping centre as Mango Jack's there's a *Chicken World* fried-chicken place, and *Rocky's Pizza* which turns out distinctly average pizzas.

There's a good bakery in Chinatown, on the corner of Carnarvon and Short Sts. The Seaview Shopping Centre also has a bakery, as well as an ice-cream parlour and Broome's biggest supermarket.

Angelies is a fancy new restaurant on Napier Terrace near the Roebuck, but unfortunately the food and service don't quite match the decor.

Pubs & Restaurants The *Roebuck Bay Hotel* has counter meals in the pleasantly rowdy old saloon bar on Dampier Terrace from noon to 2 pm and from 6 to 8 pm. Prices range from $5 for sausage and chips to $10 or more for steaks. There are also several rather more expensive (and definitely less rowdy) dining places at the Roebuck, such as the *Black Pearl Restaurant*. If you're staying at the Bunkhouse there's a $5 breakfast available in the bar.

Chin's Chinese restaurant, on Hamersley St near Mango Jack's, has a variety of dishes from all over Asia. Prices range from $7 for an Indonesian nasi goreng or a fried rice to $12. There's a popular takeaway section.

Other Chinese specialists are *Wing's*, on Napier Terrace, *Tong's*, just around the corner, and *Weng Ho*, upstairs on Dampier Terrace.

Other more expensive places include the restaurants in the resorts and motels. The *Continental Hotel* has a decent restaurant serving meals in the $12 to $18 range. For alfresco dining the *Beer & Satay Hut* at the Roebuck Bay Resort is a very pleasant place with tables around the pool. Meals are in the $8 to $12 range and although the satays are OK, a little more imagination could go into the salad bar.

On Saturday evenings the *Broome's Last Resort* and *Broome Backpackers* both do a barbecue with salad for $5.50.

Entertainment

In Chinatown, Sun Pictures, the open-air cinema dating from 1916, is near Short St and has a programme of surprisingly recent releases.

Despite its fancy new additions the Roebuck Bay Hotel still rocks along. A noisy night at the Roebuck is like one of those cartoons where the walls of the bar quake continuously and bodies come flying through the swing doors with reasonable regularity. Great fun – just stand clear of the occasional fight. Most Saturday afternoons there is a band in the beer garden. There are also arm wrestling and wet T-shirt contests.

Getting There & Away

Air Ansett WA fly to Broome regularly on their Perth to Darwin route. From Perth the fare is $453, from Darwin $334, from Kununurra $248 and from Port Hedland $198. The Ansett WA office (☎ (091) 92 1101) is on the corner of Barker and Weld Sts.

Bus Greyhound and Bus Australia operate through Broome on their Perth to Darwin route. Greyhound operates the Perth to Broome route daily while Deluxe and Pioneer make the Broome to Darwin run daily, and Bus Australia only covers that part three times a week. Typical fares from Broome include $160 to Perth, $55 to Port Hedland, $20 to Derby and $130 to Darwin.

Bus Australia operates from the tourist bureau, while Greyhound (☎ (091) 92 1561) has an office at Broome Travel on Hamersley St.

Getting Around

To/From the Airport There are taxis to take you from the airport to your hotel. However, the airport is so close to the centre that backpackers staying at the Last Resort, or elsewhere close by, may well decide to walk.

Bus Six times daily there's a bus between the town and Cable Beach. The one-way fare is $2 and the return $3 (☎ 92 1068). It leaves from outside the Baghdad Cafe in Chinatown.

Bicycle Cycling is the best way to see the area. There are a number of places that hire bicycles for $5 to $10 a day, including the backpackers' places. Broome is an easy area to ride around; it's flat and you'll usually have no problem riding out to Cable Beach (about seven km) as long as it's not too windy. Stay on the roads, though, or your tyres might be punctured by thorns.

Car Rental Hertz, Budget, Avis and Thrifty have rent-a-car desks at the airport but there are better deals available if you just want something for bopping around town or out to the beach. Mokes and Suzuki jeeps are popular. The Auski Resort, for example, has Suzukis for $35 a day plus 18c a km after the first 35 km. Topless Rentals, on Hunter St, have VW Beetle convertibles for $40 a day, including insurance and unlimited km around Broome. Woody's on Napier Terrace has Suzuki jeeps for $55 per day, including 100 km free.

AROUND BROOME

Six km from town is **Cable Beach**, the most popular swimming beach in Broome. It's a classic – white sand and turquoise water as far as the eye can see. You can hire surf boards and other beach and water equipment on the beach – parasailing ($30) is always popular. The northern side beyond the rock is a popular nude-bathing area. You can also take vehicles (other than motorbikes) onto this section of the beach, although at high tide access is limited because of the rocks, so take care not to get stranded.

Just before the beach, off the Cable Beach road, is the **Pearl Coast Zoo**, which is owned by a British lord who took a liking to Broome. It houses native birds and animals and some rare imported species. It is open daily from 8 am to 5 pm and admission is $10 (children $5).

Tucked in beside the zoo is a small **crocodile park**. It's open Monday to Saturday from 10 am to 5 pm. On Sunday it only opens for the 3 pm feeding session, and there are tours at 11 am and 3 pm weekdays. Admission is $8 (children $4).

The long sweep of Cable Beach eventually ends at **Gantheaume Point**, seven km south of Broome. The cliffs there have been eroded into curious shapes. At extremely low tides dinosaur tracks 130 million years old are sometimes exposed. At other times you can inspect casts of the footprints on the cliff

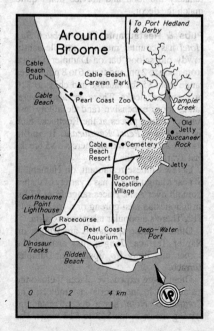

top. Anastasia's Pool is an artificial rock pool on the north side of the point; it fills at high tide.

At **Entrance Point**, at the end of Port Drive, eight km from town, the port is deep enough for ocean-going vessels. Broome can have enormous tides – up to 10 metres in the spring.

There are several good fishing, swimming and camping spots outside Broome, including **Crab Creek, Willies Creek, Barred Creek, Quondon Beach** and **Manari**.

Eighteen km north-east of town on the shore of Roebuck Bay is the **Broome Bird Observatory**. It has been established to observe the huge number and variety of migratory birds (mostly waders) which pass through here annually. In fact it is claimed that Roebuck Bay has the fifth largest population of wading birds in the world. There's a guided nature walk and the helpful staff can point out the best places to watch for waders. There is also a camp site and some more substantial accommodation (see Places to Stay following). The observatory is signposted along Crab Creek Rd, off the Great Northern Highway about 3½ km north of town.

Willie Creek Pearl Farm is 35 km north of Broome, off the Cape Leveque road. It offers a rare chance to see a working pearl farm and is worth the trip. The road is open only to 4WD vehicles in the wet, but to all vehicles in the dry, or there are daily tours from Broome ($38) with Broome Coachlines (☎ (091) 93 5575).

Places to Stay
Cable Beach Caravan Park (☎ (091) 92 2066) is at the beach, and has tent sites from $15. *Broome Caravan Park* (☎ (091) 92 1776), on the Great Northern Highway four km from town, has tent sites from $10 and on-site vans from $40. Finally, the *Broome Vacation Village* (☎ (091) 92 1057), on the road out to the port, just beyond the Cable Beach turn-off, has tent sites from $12 and air- con cabins at $45.

The very up-market *Cable Beach Club* (☎ (091) 92 2505) is a beautifully designed place covering a large area, although it's not right on the beach. Standard rates range from $165 for a two-bed studio up to $285 for a two-bedroom bungalow. The resort has an incredibly expensive restaurant, and a much cheaper cafe which is a good vantage point for the sunset.

DAMPIER PENINSULA
It's about 200 km from the turn-off nine km out of Broome to the Cape Leveque lighthouse at the tip of the Dampier Peninsula. About halfway is a diversion to the **Beagle Bay Aboriginal Community** (☎ (091) 92 4913) which has a beautiful church in the middle of a green. Inside is an altar stunningly decorated with mother-of-pearl. Just before Cape Leveque is **Lombadina Aboriginal Community** (☎ (091) 92 4936) which has a church built from mangrove wood.

Cape Leveque itself has a lighthouse and two wonderful beaches. Beyond it is **One Arm Point** – yet another Aboriginal community. Take note that the communities won't want you to stay on their land, but if you want to see their churches or buy something from their shops they will be helpful. Permission to visit other areas must be obtained in advance. Check with the tourist office in Broome about road conditions before setting out.

The only accommodation is at the up-market *Kooljaman Resort* (☎ (091) 92 4970), although they do have a bunkhouse for $12. A better bet is to take a three-day tour with the Last Resort in Broome.

The Kimberley

The rugged Kimberley, at the northern end of Western Australia, is one of Australia's last frontiers. Despite enormous advances in the past decade this is still a little-travelled and very remote area of great rivers and magnificent scenery. The Kimberley suffers from climatic extremes – heavy rains in the wet followed by searing heat in the dry – but

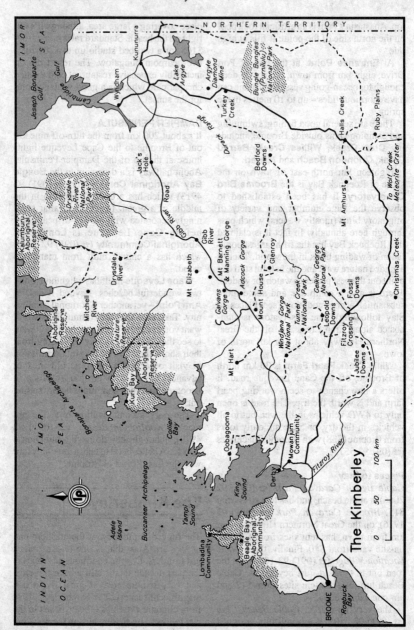

The Kimberley

0 50 100 km

the irrigation projects in the north-east have made great changes to the region.

Nevertheless, rivers and creeks can rise rapidly following heavy rainfall and become impassable torrents within 15 minutes. Unless it's a very brief storm, it's quite likely that the watercourses will remain impassable for three to four days. The Fitzroy River can become so swollen at times that after two or three days' rain it grows from its normal 100-metre width to a spectacular 11 km. River and creek crossings on the Great Northern Highway on both sides of Halls Creek become impassable every wet season. Highway 1 through the Kimberley is sealed all the way, but there are several notorious crossings which are still only fords, not all-weather bridges.

The best time to visit is between April and September. By October it's already getting hot (35°C), and later in the year daily temperatures of more than 40°C are common. On the other hand, there are plenty of things to do should you visit during the Wet.

Kimberley attractions include the spectacular gorges on the Fitzroy River, the huge Wolf Creek meteorite crater, the Gibb River Road and the Bungle Bungle National Park.

DERBY (population 3000)

Derby, only 221 km from Broome, is a major administrative centre for the west Kimberley and a good point from which to travel to the spectacular gorges in the region. The road beyond Derby continues to Fitzroy Crossing (256 km) and Halls Creek (288 km). Alternatively, there's the much wilder Gibb River Rd.

Derby is on King Sound, north of the mouth of the Fitzroy, the mighty river that drains the west Kimberley region.

Information

The tourist office (**☎** (091) 91 1426), at the end of Clarendon St, is open from 8.30 am to 4.30 pm Monday to Friday. The annual Boab Festival takes place over two weeks in late June/early July.

Things to See

There's a small museum and art gallery in the **Derby Cultural Centre**, and a **botanic garden**.

Wharfinger's House, at the end of Loch St, has been restored as an example of early housing in the area. You can also visit the **School of the Air** and the **Royal Flying Doctor base**.

Derby's lofty **wharf** has not been used since 1983 for shipping, but it provides a handy fishing perch for the locals. The whole town is surrounded by huge expanses of mud flats, baked hard in the dry season. They're occasionally flooded by king tides.

The **Prison Tree**, near the airport, seven km south of town, is a huge boab tree with a hollow trunk 14 metres around. It is said to have been used as a temporary lock-up years ago.

From Derby there are flights over King Sound to **Koolan** and **Cockatoo Islands**, both owned by the Dampier Mining Company. You can't go there unless invited by a resident, but scenic flights are available to the adjoining islands of the **Buccaneer Archipelago**.

Boabs

Boab trees are a common sight in the Kimberley and also in the Victoria and Fitzmaurice river basins of the Northern Territory. The boab or *Adansonia gregorii* is closely related to the baobab of Africa and the eight varieties of *Adansonia* found on the island of Madagascar. It's probable that baobab seeds floated to Australia from Africa, then developed unique characteristics.

The boab is a curious-looking tree with branches rising like witches' fingers from a wide trunk that is sometimes elegantly bottle shaped, sometimes squat and powerful-looking. Boabs shed all their leaves during dry periods, further accentuating their unusual appearance. Evidently it's a successful policy, for boabs are noted for their rapid growth, hardiness and extreme longevity. Derby has some fine boabs around the town, including a line of them transplanted along the centre of Loch St.

Places to Stay

Derby Caravan Park (**☎** (091) 91 1022) has tent sites and on-site vans at $40 a night. It's conveniently close to the centre.

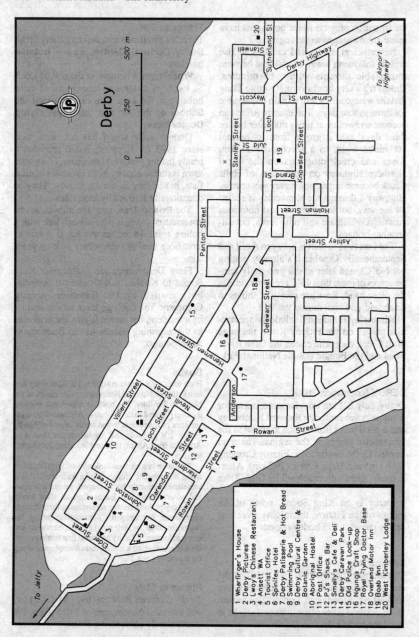

Derby

To Jetty

To Airport &
Highway

1 Wharfinger's House
2 Derby Pictures
3 Lwoy's Chinese Restaurant
4 Ansett WA
5 Tourist Office
6 Spinifex Hotel
7 Derby Patisserie & Hot Bread
8 Swimming Pool
9 Derby Cultural Centre &
  Botanic Garden
10 Aboriginal Hostel
11 Post Office
12 PJ's Snack Bar
13 Smally's Cafe & Deli
14 Derby Caravan Park
15 Old Police Lock-up
16 Ngunga Craft Shop
17 Royal Flying Doctor
   Base
18 Overland Motor Inn
19 Boab Inn
20 West Kimberley Lodge

The *Aboriginal Hostel* (☎ (091) 91 1867), on Villers St, charges $14 for a bed, which includes all meals.

West Kimberley Lodge (☎ (091) 91 1031) is at the edge of town, on the corner of Sutherland and Stanwell Sts. It has twin-share rooms with shared bathrooms and a shared kitchen for $17.50 per person, or singles/doubles with bath for $25/40.

There are a couple of regular hotels in Derby. The *Spinifex Hotel* (☎ (091) 91 1233), on Clarendon St, has rooms at $35/45. The cockroach races here are a well-known local event. The *Boab Inn* (☎ (091) 91 1044), on Loch St, is rather more motel like with rooms at $65/75. Finally there's the *Derby Overland Motor Inn* (☎ (091) 91 1166), on Delewarr St, with rooms from $79/89.

Places to Eat

The *Spinifex Hotel* and the *Boab Inn* both do counter meals. At the Boab there's a wide choice of pretty good food at $10 to $15. *Derby Patisserie & Hot Bread*, near the tourist office, is good for lunch and has an excellent selection of sandwiches. *PJ's Snack Bar*, open late, is another place for a quick meal.

At the end of Loch St there's *Lwoy's Chinese Restaurant*. Out at the jetty is *Wharf's Restaurant* which has a BYO section and also does takeaways; seafood is a speciality.

Entertainment

The old open-air Derby Pictures present a regular programme of movies, although they reserve the right to cancel if less than 40 people show up; heavy rain after 5 pm will also stop the show.

Getting There & Away

Air Ansett WA will whisk you to Port Hedland for $213, or to Darwin for $287. The Ansett WA office (☎ 91 1266) is at 14 Loch St.

Bus Greyhound and Bus Australia both stop in Derby at the tourist office. Typical fares are $20 to Broome, $54 to Halls Creek, and $78 to Kununurra.

GIBB RIVER RD

This is the 'back road' from Derby to Wyndham or Kununurra. At 694 km it's more direct by several hundred km than the Fitzroy Crossing to Halls Creek route. It's almost all dirt, although it doesn't require a 4WD when conditions are good. In the Wet the road is impassable. You can also reach many of the Kimberley Gorges from this road without a 4WD. Fuel is available at Mt House and Mt Barnett, and Durack River (Jack's Hole) and Home Valley stations. The distances mentioned in this section are from Derby.

The Kimberley Gorges are the major reason for taking this route. You could also make a day trip to the Windjana and Tunnel Creek Gorges from Derby or visit them while on the way from Derby to Fitzroy Crossing.

From Derby the bitumen extends 62 km. It's 118 km to the Windjana Gorge (21 km) and Tunnel Creek (55 km) turn-off and you can continue down that turn-off to the Great Northern Highway near Fitzroy Crossing.

Windjana Gorge & Tunnel Creek National Parks

You can visit these spectacular formations from the Gibb River Rd, or make a detour off the main highway between Fitzroy Crossing and Derby, which only adds about 40 km to the distance.

The walls at the Windjana Gorge soar 90 metres above the Lennard River which rushes through in the Wet, but becomes just a series of pools in the Dry. Three km from the river are the ruins of **Lillimooloora**, an early homestead and then, from 1893, a police station.

Tunnel Creek is a 750-metre-long tunnel cut by the creek right through a spur of the Oscar Range. The tunnel is generally from three to 15 metres wide and you can walk all the way along it. You'll need a good light and sturdy shoes; be prepared to wade through chest-deep water in places. Don't attempt it during the Wet, as the creek may flood suddenly. Halfway through, a collapse has produced a shaft right to the top of the range. Flying foxes (bats) inhabit the tunnel for part of the year.

Windjana Gorge, Tunnel Creek and Lillimooloora were the scene of the adventures of an Aboriginal tracker called 'Pigeon'.

In November 1894 Pigeon shot two police colleagues and then led a band of dissident Aborigines, skilfully evading search parties for over two years. In the meantime he killed another four men, until in early 1897 he was trapped and killed in Tunnel Creek. He and his small band had hidden in many of the seemingly inaccessible gullies of the adjoining Napier Range.

Get hold of a copy of the *Pigeon Heritage Trail* from the Derby or Broome tourist office.

Windjana Gorge to Mt Barnett

At 197 km is the turn-off to the **Lennard River Gorge**, eight km off the road along a 4WD track. At 254 km there's the signposted turn-off to **Mt House Station** (☎ (091) 91 4649), where there's fuel, stores and accommodation.

The turn-off to **Adcock Gorge** is at 275 km. This gorge is five km off the road and is good for swimming, with some fine rocks for jumping or diving off, although you should check for rocks beneath the water before doing so. If the waterfall is not flowing too fiercely, climb up above it for a good view of the surrounding country. You can camp at Adcock Gorge although the site is rocky and there's little shade.

Galvans Gorge is less than a km off the road, at 295 km. The small camp site here has some good shade trees, and the gorge itself has a swimming hole.

Mt Barnett & Manning Gorge

The Aboriginal-owned and run Mt Barnett Station is at 315 km point. There's a roadhouse there with expensive fuel, as well as ice and a small general store. It's also the access point for Manning Gorge, which lies seven km off the road along an easy dirt

track. There's an entry fee of $4 per person, and this covers you for camping.

The camp site is right by the waterhole, but the best part of the gorge is about a 1¼-hour walk along the far bank – walk around the right of the waterhole to pick up the track, which is marked with empty drink cans strung up in trees. It's a strenuous walk and, because the track runs inland from the gorge, you should carry some drinking water.

After the hot and sweaty walk, you are rewarded with the most beautiful gorge on the whole Gibb River Rd. It has a waterfall and some high rocks for daredevils.

Mt Barnett to Kununurra

First up after Mt Barnett is the turn-off to the **Barnett River Gorge** at 338 km. This is another good swimming spot, and if you scan the lower level of the cliff face on the far side you should be able to spot a number of Aboriginal paintings.

The **Mt Elizabeth Station** (☎ (091) 91 4644) lies 30 km off the road at the 347 mark. Homestead accommodation is available at $35 per person, but this must be arranged in advance.

At 419 km you come to the turn-off to the spectacular **Mitchell Plateau** (158 km) and the **Kalumburu Aboriginal Mission** (261 km). This is remote, 4WD territory and should not be undertaken without adequate preparation.

There's some magnificent scenery between the Kalumburu turn-off and Jack's Hole on the *Durack River Station* at 540 km. Apart from fuel, there's also basic homestead accommodation at $35 for dinner, B&B, or you can camp for $5 and eat at the homestead. The owners, the Sinnamon family, run a number of tours from Durack River Station.

At 596 km you get some excellent views of the **Cockburn Ranges** off to the south, and shortly after is the turn-off to *Home Valley Station* (☎ (091) 61 4322), which has camping ($5) and homestead accommodation ($65 all inclusive).

The large **Pentecost River** is forded at

609 km, and this crossing can be dodgy if there's any amount of water in the river. During the dry season it poses no problems.

El Questro is another station offering homestead accommodation ($20) and camping; it lies 16 km off the road at the 633 km mark. This is also the access point for the **Chamberlain Gorge**.

The last attraction on the road is **Emma Gorge** at 645 km. The pleasant camping area lies two km off the road, and from here it's about a 40-minute walk to the spectacular gorge. This gorge is close enough to Kununurra to make it a popular weekend escape for residents of that town.

At 667 km you finally hit the bitumen road, and Wyndham lies 48 km to the north, while it's 53 km east to Kununurra.

Organised Tours

Broome's Last Resort and the Kununurra Backpackers run five-day camping trips along the road for $350, and these are excellent value and well worth doing. There is one departure a week in each direction with one of these two operators. The Last Resort also operates popular two-day trips combining Windjana and Tunnel Creek with Geikie Gorge, and these are a good way of seeing those three sites in one hit.

Getting There & Away

There's no public transport along the Gibb River Rd – in fact there's very little traffic of any sort, so don't bother trying to hitch!

FITZROY CROSSING (population 450)

A tiny settlement where the road crosses the Fitzroy River, this is another place from which you can get to the gorges and waterholes of the area.

At **GoGo Station**, two km off the highway, 10 km east of Fitzroy Crossing, there are daily shows (dry season only, $12) demonstrating the various aspects of life on a Kimberley cattle station.

Geikie Gorge

This magnificent gorge is just 19 km north of the town. Part of the gorge, on the Fitzroy River, is in a small national park only eight km by three km. During the wet season the river rises nearly 17 metres, and the camp site by the river is seven metres below the waterline. In the Dry the river stops flowing, leaving only a series of waterholes. The ranges that the gorge cuts through are actually a fossilised coral reef some 350 million years old.

The vegetation around this beautiful gorge is dense and there is also much wildlife, including the freshwater crocodile. Sawfish and stingrays, usually only found in or close to the sea, can also be seen in the river. Kangaroos and wallabies live in the gorge sanctuary. Visitors are not permitted to go anywhere except along the prescribed part of the west bank, where there is an excellent walking track.

During the April to November dry season there's a two-hour national parks boat trip up the river at 9.30 am and 2.30 pm. It costs $10 and covers 16 km of the gorge. There's a weekday bus to the gorge from Lot 185, Bell Rd, Fitzroy Crossing at 8 am which connects with the morning trip. It costs $8 return (children $5) (☎ 91 5155 in Fitzroy Crossing).

Places to Stay

Tarunda Caravan Park (☎ (091) 91 5004), in town, is a great place mainly because the owner is very friendly and can show you around. The *Crossing Inn & Caravan Park* (☎ (091) 91 5080), by the river crossing, has cabins from $30 and motel rooms for $52/66 a single/double. It can get pretty noisy.

The new *Fitzroy River Lodge & Caravan Park* (☎ (091) 91 5141) is two km east of town on the banks of the Fitzroy River. Aircon safari tents cost $60/73, while motel units cost $75/95.

The small camp site at the *Geikie Gorge National Park* is open only in the dry season. It has limited facilities and tent sites are $9.

HALLS CREEK (population 1000)

Halls Creek, in the centre of the Kimberley

and on the edge of the Great Sandy Desert, was the site of the 1885 gold rush, the first in Western Australia. The gold soon petered out and today the town is a cattle centre, 14 km from the original site where some crumbling remains can still be seen.

Halls Creek **Old Town** is a fascinating place for poking around creeks and gullies in a 4WD searching for that elusive gold nugget. If you're really interested in doing a bit of fossicking, it's best to go with a local. 'Old Town' is in fact the general term for the hilly area behind Halls Creek and gold might be found anywhere there. You can swim in **Caroline Pool, Sawpit Gorge** and **Palm Springs.**

Five km east of Halls Creek and then about 1½ km off the road there's a natural **China Wall** – so called because it resembles the Great Wall of China. Australia has a few of them. This one is short but very picturesquely situated. There's an Aboriginal art shop in the town where you can often see carvers at work making some high-quality artefacts.

Although Halls Creek is a comfortable enough little place it's as well to remember that it sits on the edge of a distinctly inhospitable stretch of country.

In late '86 two 16-year-old jackaroos set out from a station near there. They took a wrong turn, got bogged and couldn't get out. In mid-1987 their truck and their skeletal remains were found. It caused a national scandal about working conditions for inexperienced young station hands but the message is clear – this can be rough land.

Places to Stay

Halls Creek Caravan Park (☎ (091) 68 6169), on Roberta Ave towards the airport, has tent sites or dusty on-site vans from $35. Opposite is the *Kimberley Hotel* (☎ (091) 68 6101), which has a variety of rooms from $60/73, and is currently offering backpacker accommodation at $20.

The *Swagman Halls Creek* (☎ (091) 68 6060), on McDonald St, has basic cabins with air-con for $35. The *Halls Creek Motel* (☎ (091) 68 6001), on the Great Northern Highway, costs from $53/63.

Places to Eat

The *Kimberley Hotel* has a pleasantly casual bar with standard counter meals at $10. You can eat out at the tables on the grass – very pleasant. Inside there's a surprisingly swish restaurant with meals at $15 to $18.

Getting There & Away

It's 359 km north-east to Kununurra, 460 km south-west to Derby. Bus Australia and Greyhound pass through Halls Creek.

The road to Wyndham and Kununurra passes through the Carboyd Ranges – catch them at their best at sunset. You can swim in the river at the Dunham River bridge.

WOLF CREEK METEORITE CRATER

The 835-metre-wide and 50-metre-deep Wolf Creek Meteorite Crater is the second largest in the world. The turn-off to the crater is 16 km out of Halls Creek towards Fitzroy Crossing and from there it's 112 km by unsealed road to the south. It's easily accessible without 4WD and you can camp (free) and get some limited supplies at the nearby Carranya Station homestead (☎ (091) 68 0200). If you can't handle one more outback road you can fly over the crater from Halls Creek for $85 with the local operators, and these flights also overfly the amazing Bungle Bungles.

BUNGLE BUNGLES (PURNILULU) NATIONAL PARK

The Bungle Bungles are an amazing spectacle which shouldn't be missed – spectacular rounded rock towers, striped like tigers in alternate bands of orange (silica) and black (lichen). The only catch is that the range is hard to get to and because of the fragile nature of the rock formations you are not allowed to climb them.

Echidna Chasm in the north or **Cathedral Gorge** in the south are only about a one-hour walk from the car parks at the road's end. However, the soaring **Piccaninny Gorge** is an 18-km round trip that takes eight to 10 hours return to walk. Access to the park costs $20 a car.

Scenic Flights

As the range is so vast, flights and helicopter rides over the Bungles are very popular, and rightly so. The chopper rides, operated by Slingair, are by far the more impressive of the two options, as you fly right in, among and over the deep, narrow gorges, while the light planes have to remain above 700 metres. Even if you have ridden a chopper before, these flights are exciting and the scenery absolutely stunning – it's money well spent. The chopper rides cost $115 for half an hour from the main camp ground in the Bungles, or $110 in a faster helicopter from Turkey Creek, on the main highway. This latter flight is a popular option for people without a 4WD. Light planes operate from Halls Creek ($85), and these also fly over Wolf Creek, or from Kununurra ($90), taking in Lake Argyle on the way.

Places to Stay

From the main highway it's 55 km to a track junction known as Three Ways, from where it's eight km north to *Kurrajong Camp* and 15 km south to *Bellburn Creek Camp*. At Bellburn Creek Camp there's a ranger station. Fires are forbidden, so you'll need to have your own gas cooking equipment, and the only facilities are long-drop dunnies and a primitive shower set-up at Kurrajong Camp.

Getting There & Away

Although it's only 55 km to Three Ways from the Halls Creek to Kununurra road turn-off, that stretch requires a 4WD and takes two hours. From Three Ways it's another 20 km north to Echidna Chasm and 30 km south to Piccaninny Creek.

The best option if you don't have a 4WD is to take one of the tours offered from Kununurra. Kununurra Backpackers has very popular two-day trips ($155, and there's a 10% discount if you are staying there), while East Kimberley Tours charges $150 if you are staying at the Desert Inn Backpackers.

There are also more expensive trips offered from Halls Creek.

WYNDHAM (population 1500)

Wyndham, a sprawling town, is suffering from Kununurra's boom in popularity but its **Five Rivers Lookout** on top of Mt Bastion is still a must. From there you can see the King, Pentecost, Durack, Forest and Ord rivers. It's particularly good at sunrise and sunset. During the dry season saltwater crocodiles (extremely dangerous) congregate near the jetty and during the day one or two might be seen at the end of the outlet drain behind the meatworks. Signs warn swimmers of the crocs, and they mean it!

The **Moochylabra Dam** is a popular fishing and picnic spot about 25 km away. Near the town there's a rather desolate and decrepit little **cemetery** where Afghan camel drivers were buried last century. Near the Moochylabra Dam, south of Wyndham, there are some Aboriginal paintings and another prison boab tree. **Grotto** is a good swimming hole just off the Wyndham to Kununurra road. **Crocodile Hole** is further off the road and has a small population of freshwater crocs.

Places to Stay

Three Mile Caravan Park (☎ (091) 61 1064) charges $10 for tent sites. Rooms in the *Wyndham Town Hotel* (☎ (091) 61 1003), on O'Donnell St, cost $65/75. Try the *Wyndham Community Club* (☎ (091) 61 1130) for cheaper but more basic rooms.

KUNUNURRA (population 2100)

Founded in the 1960s, Kununurra is in the centre of the Ord River irrigation scheme and is quite a modern and bustling little town. In the past it was just a stopover on the main highway and there was little incentive to linger. That has all changed in recent years and there are now enough recreational activities, most of them water-based, to keep you busy for a week – put aside at least a few days for a stopover here.

The town is also a popular place to look for work. The irrigation projects have opened up vast areas of land for agriculture and there are large local farms growing

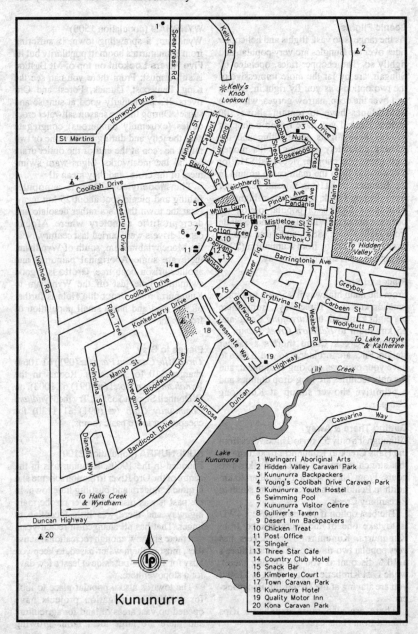

Kununurra

1 Waringarri Aboriginal Arts
2 Hidden Valley Caravan Park
3 Kununurra Backpackers
4 Young's Coolibah Drive Caravan Park
5 Kununurra Youth Hostel
6 Swimming Pool
7 Kununurra Visitor Centre
8 Gulliver's Tavern
9 Desert Inn Backpackers
10 Chicken Treat
11 Post Office
12 Slingair
13 Three Star Cafe
14 Country Club Hotel
15 Snack Bar
16 Kimberley Court
17 Town Caravan Park
18 Kununurra Hotel
19 Quality Motor Inn
20 Kona Caravan Park

melons and vegetables. The main picking season starts in May. Ask at the Kununurra Backpackers or the tourist office for details.

Information

The excellent Kununurra Visitor Centre (☎ (091) 68 1177) on Coolibah Drive with information on the town and the Kimberley. It's open from 8 am to 5 pm daily. This is also the terminal and booking office for Greyhound and Bus Australia buses.

There's a 1½-hour time change between Kununurra and Katherine in the Northern Territory.

Things to See

There's a great **swimming pool** right behind the visitor centre. **Zebra rocks**, which have red stripes or dots on a white base, are a local oddity. They are sold as souvenirs or incorporated into jewellery. The **Waringarri Aboriginal Arts Centre** is on Speargrass Rd, at the turn-off to Kelly's Knob. There are good views of the irrigated fields from **Kelly's Knob Lookout**, close to the centre of town. During the wet season, distant thunderstorms can be spectacular when viewed from there, although caution is needed as the Knob itself is frequently struck by lightning.

Lake Kununurra (also called the Diversion Dam), an artificial lake beside the town, has plentiful bird life and several swimming spots. There's good fishing below the Lower Dam (watch for crocodiles) and also on the Ord River at **Ivanhoe Crossing**. If you're swimming there, be careful – there's a saying that the Ord takes a life a year, and it usually seems to be at Ivanhoe Crossing.

Hidden Valley, only a couple of km from the centre of town, is a wonderful little national park with a steep gorge, some great views and a few short walking tracks.

The **Packsaddle Plains**, six km out of town, has a zebra rock gallery and a small wildlife park. Further along this road is **Packsaddle Falls** – a popular swimming hole.

South of Kununurra is the huge **Argyle Diamond Mine** which produces around 35% of the world's diamonds, although most are only of industrial quality. The mine has a visitor centre, or you can take a half-day tour by plane from Kununurra for a mere $250.

Activities

Canoeing Canoe trips on the Ord River, between Lake Argyle and the Diversion Dam, are very popular amongst travellers. Kununurra Backpackers has one, two or three-day self-guided tours for $35, $44 and $55, with all gear supplied, including transport up to the dam. They also offer a one-day 'canoe 'n waterfall' trip which gives you half a day paddling on the river, lunch and a trip to Packsaddle Falls, for $45.

Matt Dove's Canoe Safaris operate from the Desert Inn Backpackers, and have two and three-day trips for $45 and $60. Matt also has a bush camp a few km up the river where you can camp along the way. There's also a half-day trip with barbecue for $30.

White-Water Rafting Kununurra Backpackers has 1½-hour white-water trips on the Lake Argyle spillway from the end of the wet season onwards. They're great fun and well worth the $20, or $35 if you need transport to and from Kununurra. A full-day option of these trips takes in the Keep River National Park, just over the border in the Northern Territory, and a visit to Lake Argyle, for $64.

Abseiling Matt Dove also runs abseiling activities in Kununurra, and a half-day trip costs $25, or a full day $65. Contact the Desert Inn Backpackers for details. It's also possible to do abseiling if you are staying at Matt's bush camp further up the river.

Fishing Yes, you can do this too. Barramundi is, of course, the major attraction, but other fish are also caught. Half-day boat trips with Desert Inn Backpackers cost $65. Those with more funds at their disposal can head for the Bush Camp (☎ (091) 69 1214). This is a very comfortable set up on the lower Ord River, about 40 km below the Diversion Dam. All gear is supplied and it costs $160 by the day, including meals.

Boat Tours Triple J (☎ (091) 68 2682) operates high-speed boats along the Ord between Lake Argyle and Kununurra. These are a real thrill and pass through some beautiful scenery. The cost is $65, and this includes the bus trip from Kununurra.

Organised Tours & Flights
Apart from the trips just mentioned, there are a number of tours around town or to Lake Argyle with prices from $25 to $60. You can take a cruise on Lake Kununurra and the Ord River for $15 to $20.

Flights to the Bungle Bungles are particularly popular and cost $90 to $110 a person. They take about two hours and also fly over the Argyle Diamond Mine project and the irrigation area north of the town.

For the highly recommended five-day trips along the Gibb River Rd to Broome, see that section earlier.

Places to Stay
Camping There are a number of caravan parks, a couple of them by Lake Kununurra, with tent sites from $10. *Town Caravan Park* (☎ (091) 68 1763) is on Bloodwood Drive and has on-site vans for $45. There's also *Kona Caravan Park* (☎ (091) 68 1031), on the shores of the lake about a km from town.

Hostels There are two good backpackers' hostels. At 111 Nutwood Crescent is the very friendly *Kununurra Backpackers* (☎ (091) 68 1711). It's in a couple of adjacent houses about five minutes' walk from the centre of town. All rooms have air-con and from three to six beds for $10, and there are singles and twins available for a few dollars more. The shaded pool is a big drawcard, and they do pick-ups from the buses.

The *Desert Inn Backpackers* (☎ (091) 68 2702) is on Konkerberry Drive, right opposite Gulliver's Tavern in the centre of town. Originally in a house, it should, by the time you read this, have moved to a new building next door, on the corner of Tristania St. Accommodation is $10 for a shared room, and there are a couple of doubles in the old house. It's also a friendly and popular place.

With the opening of the backpackers' places, the associate YHA *Kununurra Youth Hostel* (☎ (091) 68 1372), on Coolibah Drive, doesn't get much business anymore, and it also costs $10 for a bed. The *Country Club Hotel* (☎ (091) 68 1024), beside the post office on Coolibah Drive, has some backpackers' beds for $10, but there are no cooking facilities.

Hotels, Guesthouses & Motels Hotel accommodation is expensive. The *Country Club Hotel* (☎ (091) 68 1024) is the cheapest, but at $47/57 a single/double for small air-con rooms with no facilities, even it is grossly overpriced. It does have a pool though. Better value is the *Kimberley Court* (☎ (091) 68 1411), on the corner of River Fig Ave and Erythrina St, with rooms at $69/79 with bathrooms and a light breakfast.

The *Kununurra Hotel* (☎ (091) 68 1344), on Messmate Way, is the town's main hotel and has a motel section with rooms from $65/95. Top of the range is the *Quality Inn Motel* (☎ (091) 68 1455) which charges $90/100.

Places to Eat
Al Fresco's is a popular cafe area at the Leisure Centre beside the swimming pool. The *Three Star Cafe*, on Banksia St, offers takeaway tucker and light meals.

Standard counter meals are available at the *Kununurra Hotel* for $10, and there's a more expensive dining room with good meals in the $12 to $15 range. *Gulliver's Tavern*, on the corner of Konkerberry Drive and Cotton Tree Ave, is a popular drinking place, and although the counter meals are poor value, the George Room there is quite a good place to eat.

The licensed *Chopsticks Restaurant* at the Country Club Hotel is about the best in town, and main courses cost around $15.

Getting There & Away
Air Ansett WA will fly you to Broome for $248, Darwin for $173, and Perth for $551, among other centres. The office (☎ (091) 68 1387) is on Coolibah Drive.

Bus Greyhound and Bus Australia travel through on the Darwin to Broome route. Typical fares are $78 to Derby, $47 to Halls Creek, $43 to Katherine and $85 to Darwin.

LAKE ARGYLE

Created by the Ord River Dam, Lake Argyle is the second biggest storage reservoir in Australia, holding nine times as much water as Sydney Harbour. Prior to its construction, there was too much water in the wet season and not enough in the dry. By providing a regular water supply the dam has made agri-culture on a massive scale possible in the area.

At the lake there's a **pioneer museum** in the old Argyle Homestead, moved here when its original site was flooded. The *Lake Argyle Tourist Village* has expensive rooms and a camp site. Boats depart from there for the huge lake each morning and afternoon. Downstream of the the lake there is now green farmland: rice is a principal crop. Encircling these flat lands are the small reddish mountains typical of the region. The wet or 'green' season is from early December to late March, the Dry from early April to late September.

Index

TEXT

Map references are in **bold** type.

NATIONAL PARKS

THANKS

Letter-writers (apologies if we've misspelt your names) to whom thanks must go include:

Cathy Adams (Aus), K W Addis (UK), Mrs G V Aldis (UK), Heather Alexander (Aus), Jackie Algar (UK), John & Hazel Allin, John D Altmann (Aus), Meggie Andersen (Aus), John Anderson (Aus), Guy Anderson (Aus), Michaela Anderton (Aus), P Andeweg (Nl), Joanne Armytage (Aus), Hamish Arnold (UK), Mike Ashby (UK), Peta Athens (Aus), Mary Atkin (UK), Mariannes Bach (Dk), Christine Bailiff (Aus), Russell Baker (UK), Mike Ball (Aus), Mary & Neale Banks (Aus), Lt. P G Barker (UK), Judy Barkus (USA), Claire Barmettler (CH), Russell Barrett (Aus), Bruce S Barrett (Aus), Wolf-Peter Baum (D), Lesley K Baxter (Aus), Tim Beacon (UK), D J Beattie (Aus), Ronald Bee (Aus), A Beharrell (Aus), Pam Beilby (Aus), Anthea Bell (Aus), Margaret Bell (Aus), Mary Bell (UK), Warren Bell (Aus), Felicity Bent (Aus), Paul Bentley (Aus), Jane Berrisford (UK), Thomas Betz (CH), E E R Bishop (USA), Kimberly Ann Bixler (USA), Jeni Black (Aus), Lynn Bland (UK), M Bond (UK), Gordon Bonin (NZ), Hildegard Borkent (Nl), Russell Boswell (Aus), Krista Bottyan (C), Noel Bowie (Aus), Penny Bradley (Aus), Karen Bradley (UK), Mary Bradley (UK), Don Branagan (Aus), Andrea Brear, Jon Breukel (Aus), Sarah Brierley (Aus), Bev Broger (USA), Gilbert Brooks (Aus), Dr J P Brougham (Aus), Stephanie K Brown (Aus), Sue Brown (USA), C M Buchan (Aus), Rebecca Buchanan (UK), Daniel Buhlmann (CH), Joanna Bull (UK), Lindsay Burden (UK), Sally Burdon (USA), Judith Burke (Aus), Gail Burling (UK), Nigel Burton (UK), Sandra Butler (UK), Duri Campbell (CH), Billy Cannard (Aus), Wendy Cannington, Mrs Catherine Cantrill (Aus), Carnavon (Aus), Sonja Ceulemans (B), Robin Chakrabarti (UK), Helen Chalker (Aus), John Chambers (Aus), Robin Charabarti (UK), Dr & Mrs Church (Aus), Geoffrey Churchman (NZ), Graeme & Gaby Clarke (Aus), Chris Cockel (UK), D J Collier (Aus), Gary Collinson (Aus), Terry Convery (Aus), Paul Conway (IRL), Margaret & Dav. Cook (C), Karen Cooper (UK), Craig Cory (Aus), John Courtenay (Aus), Harry Crawford (Aus), John Cross (USA), Sandra Cumberland (Aus), S A Cummings (UK), P & V Cunningham (Aus), Meredyth Cunningham (Aus), Mark & Helen Curran (UK), Fifi Cusack (UK), Rory Cusak (Aus), Elizabeth Daalder (Aus), P Dantoft (Dk), Sue Dart (Aus), Lisa Davenport (USA), Richard Dax (Aus), Erik de Graaff (Nl), Luc & Kristel De N-Wittouck (B), Damien De Pace (Aus), Katie Dear (Aus), Margaret Delany (NZ), Jon Denly (UK), Bill Dennison (Aus), Richard Dewar (Aus), Brian Dick (Aus), Graeme & Anna Dicker (Aus), Matthew Dickins, Joy Diepeveen (Aus), Tony & Deirdre Difalco (Aus), Tim Douglas (Aus), J & L Dove (Aus),

Judy Dowdy (USA), Murray Downs (C), Terri Dudek (USA), I C Duffels (Nl), Annette Duggan (Aus), Alison Duncan (Aus), Paul Duncan, Pauline Duncliff (Aus), Ute Durrwachter (D), Lorraine Duval (Aus), Kerry-Jane East (UK), Anne Ebenshade (USA), Eileen Edward (UK), Kay Edwards (UK), Adrian Elliott (UK), M & J Elve (UK), Christin Engelhardt (USA), Bob Ennis (Aus), Henrik Eriksen (Dk), David Escott (D), Michael Esty (USA), Michael Evans (Aus), Ken Everett (NZ), Matt Faber (Aus), Des & Norma Fallon (Aus), R G Farmer (Aus), Bradley Kim Farrell (Aus), Sr Gwen Farrington (Aus), Garry & Marny Fenton (Aus), Grete Fergensen (Dk), Sue Ferguson (Aus), Deborah Ferris (UK), Denis Ferris (Aus), Andrew Fetter (USA), Dave Findlav (UK), Caroline Finlayson (UK), Rosie Fisher (Aus), Annie Fitzgerald (Aus), David Flynn (Aus), John Eggers Fohlmann (Dk), Benoît Fontaine (C), Forest (USA), Betsy Forgotson (USA), Frank Formby (Aus), Kristina Forsberg (Sw), Alan Dean Foster (USA), Lena Eicke Frederiksen (Dk), Peter Freeman (UK), Robert Friedler (Aus), Michael Gabour (Aus), Rita Gallaway (USA), C S Galley (UK), Helene Ganlin (C), Christine Gerber (CH), Gerry Gerrard (USA), Laura Gibbons (USA), Ann Gibson (USA), Geoff Gill (Aus), Alan Ginns (Aus), Fay Glissold (Aus), Chris Godfrey (UK), Steve Golinski (Aus), Allan Gould (Aus), Charmaine Grace (Aus), Wayne Grant (Aus), Lana Grbas (Aus), Susan Green (UK), Jeremy Green (UK), Anne Greenhalgh (Aus), Jens Griesang (D), Dominic Griffin (UK), C P Griggs (Aus), Lesley Ann Grimoldby (Aus), Brigit Grohenaun (D), Birgit Grohmann (D), Lisa Groom (Aus), Richard Groom (Aus), Ian Grundy (UK), Sonia & Martin Grympa (C), Christa Gubler (NZ), Mary Lee & Dale Guthrie (USA), I R Hackney (USA), Mechthild Hagemann (D), Perry Hagerman (C), Ray Hahn (Aus), Stephen Hammonds (UK), Mr T Hannington (UK), Claire Harbour, Joan Harding (Aus), Chris Hardwick (UK), Jessica Haring (Aus), Keith Harris (UK), Ken Harris (Aus), Ian Harrison (Aus), Brian & Derek Harrison (Aus), John Harrison (UK), Ruth Haskins (UK), Sarah Haslegrave (C), Monika Hauschild-Rogat (CH), Stewart L Hay (UK), Mark Hayman (USA), Valeria Hedley (UK), Linda Helper (USA), David Hennessy (Aus), Monique Hennink (Aus), Wiggo Hernes (Aus), Kathryn Hill (UK), C H Hinchlift (Aus), Mrs Daphne Hooton (Aus), K Winona Hubbard (USA), David & Greeba Hughes (UK), Peter & Karol Hughes (Aus), Peter F Hughes (Aus), Travers Humphreys (Aus), Tony Hutchison (Aus), J N Huysman (Nl), Romemary Iacono (Aus), Jenny Indian (Aus), Deborah Irvin (UK), Jemma Irvine (UK), Sharon Isaac (Aus), Ralph Jackson (Aus), Kira & Stuart Jacson (Aus), Sarah Jakeman (UK), Gareth James (UK), Melissa James (Aus), Cari Jansen (Nl), Lisa Jarrod (UK), Walbong Jensen (N), Adrian Joel (Aus), K W Johns (Aus), Gus Johnson (Aus), Leigh Johnston (Aus), Gareth Jonathan (UK), Evan Jones

(Aus), Tracey Jones (UK), Robert Jones (Aus), Peter Jordan (Aus), Norbert Jotrk, Ms J Kahler (Aus), Katie Kane (UK), Vreni Kappeler (CH), Robyn Karran (Aus), Alan Keeble (Aus), Barbara Kehl (CH), Tim Kellett (Aus), Sonya Kelly (Ire), Grant Kennedy (UK), Leola Kent (Aus), Graham Kerkham (Aus), Joe Kertesz (Aus), Poh Eng Khoo, Rainer Kiessling (Aus), Sean Killeen (Ire), Polly Kim (Aus), R Knights (Aus), Kay Knowles (USA), Mariska Kossen (Nl), Jean & Eric Kraak (Aus), Joan Krapp (USA), Jens Kreuter (D), Geoff Kuehne (Aus), Peter Kurz (Aus), Jurg Kuster (CH), Francis Kwa (Aus), Fred Lackner (D), Annette Ladefoged (Dk), Margaret Larder (NZ), S Larkworthy (UK), Chris LaRoche (Aus), John Lavers (Aus), Mark Leather (UK), Veronica Lee (UK), Marian Leerburger-Mahl (USA), Karen Leggett (UK), Don Lenahan (Aus), Debra Lewis (C), Robert Lewis (Aus), Graeme Lewis (UK), Valerie Lhuede (Aus), Laurie & Jutta Linneweber (Aus), Mike & Linda Lintner (USA), Steen Londal (Dk), Elizabeth Long (Aus), Dawn Long (Aus), Martin Longden (Aus), Gillian Longworth (Aus), Sandy Lovell (Aus), Michael Low (Aus), Alan Ludlow (Aus), Garry Luffmon (C), Anna Lunden, Jo & Diane Lunn (Aus), Julie Lydall (UK), Michael MacCarthaigh (Ire), Lee Macefield (Aus), Elizabeth Mack (USA), Paul MacKay (C), Andrew Mackey (Aus), Glenn Mair (Aus), Elissa Malcohn (USA), Ken Marchingo (Aus), Sarah Maroon (UK), Peter Marshall (UK), Paige Martin (C), Chris & Tara Matheson (C), Sean Matvenko (C), Caroline May (Aus), Judy & Hugh McCaw (NZ), Keith McCorriston (Aus), Lyn McDowell (Aus), Penny & Dirk McGahey (Aus), Janet McGarry (Aus), Kay McGeorge (UK), A McGuire (Aus), Tracey McIlveen (UK), Rona McIntyre (UK), Ross & Sue McKinlay (UK), Stephen McMaster (Ire), Peter McNamee (UK), John Mead (Nl), Mark Meaker (Aus), Frederico Medici (It), Karen Megaw (Aus), Carol Melrose (UK), J Mewett (Aus), Stefan & Mary Meyers (C), Joe Mifsud (Aus), Beverly Miller (UK), Stephen Millhan (NZ), Sean Milligan (C), Jeremy Mills (UK), Janice Mills (C), Louis Mills (USA), Gordon Milne (Aus), Dr David Mitchell (Aus), Lee-Anne Monk (Aus), Linda Morris (Aus), Pat and Bert Morrisey (UK), A Muir (Aus), Tom & Janet Muir (Aus), Moolchamdani Mukesh (Ind), Andrew Mulholland (Aus), Karin Muller (D), Chris Mullett (Aus), Philip Neil (Aus), Maureen A. Nevins (UK), Graham Nicoll, Brian Nicolle, Mike Niele (USA), Lina Nielsen (Dk), Paul Noble (Aus), Suzie Noname (Aus), Jan Norton (Aus), Trevor Norton (Aus), Holly Nosaztki (USA), Paul & Gwen Nossiter (Aus), Heinz Novak (Aus), Anthony O'Connor (Aus), Stephen O'Donnell, Stephen O'Donohue (Aus), M O'Neill (Aus), Mrs Helena Oberland (Aus), Mrs J M Oldridge (UK), Jonathan Orford (Aus), Per Ornstrup, Amanda Palm (UK), Frosene Papahronis (USA), Bob Park (Aus), Jeanette Parker (Aus), Martyn Paterson (Aus), Mark Paules (USA), Bill Pearce (Aus), Laura Pecoff (USA), Brian Pendry (Ire), Deborah Perry (UK), Tony Llewellyn Phillips (Aus), Thea & G Piller (CH), Jim Pletch (Aus), Chris Pratt (UK), Jean-Luc Praz (CH), Merril Preston (C), Maria Price (UK), Reinhold Prinz (CH), Brennan Quendine (Aus), Mrs P E Quigley (NZ), Deborah Rae (UK), Gwen Rafton (Aus), T S Rai (Aus), Geoff Ralph (UK), Indrek Rampe (Aus), Barry Rasmus (Aus), Mike Rawnsley (UK), Francine Recordon (CH), David & Julie Reed (UK), Susan Reid (UK), Martin Reinders (Nl), Kevin Reynolds (Aus), D M Richards (UK), Rick and Judith (UK), Mike Rigby (Aus), Brett Rigby (Aus), Les Riley (UK), Leona Riley (USA), John Ritchie (Aus), Dianne Ritchie (Aus), Geoff Ritter (Aus), Stephanie Robotham (UK), Danny Rock (Aus), Robyn Rolton (Aus), Aura Rose (C), Bruce Ross (Aus), Craig Ross (Aus), Julie Royce (Aus), Gail Rust (USA), Kevin Ryan (Aus), S Ryan (Aus), Julia Ann Saunders (Aus), Martin Savage (UK), Annemieke Schardam (Nl), Falko & Julie Schroder (D), Dean Schultz (USA), Dr Raymond Seidler (Aus), Marie Serra (Fr), Brian Severich (Aus), Steven Shattuck (Aus), M Shaw (UK), Noel Shaw (Aus), Mike Shepherd (Aus), Ann Sherry (Aus), D & B Shoobridge (Aus), Melissa Silcox (UK), Ted Simmons (Aus), Graham Simpson (Aus), Charlie Simpson (USA), Fiona Simpson (UK), Mrs H Simpson (UK), Mike Simpson (Aus), Johan Sjoberg (Sw), Joe Skendersen (Aus), Doug Slade (UK), Lucy Slater (UK), Colin Smith (UK), Chris & Wal Smith (Aus), D H Smith (Aus), Arthur Sofianidis (Aus), Dale Southerly (UK), Angela Sparks (USA), Natalie Sperling (Aus), Rita Squire (Aus), Mr Peter Squires (Aus), Jane Stackpole, Ruth Stanley (Aus), Mike Stevens (Aus), Jill Strudwick (UK), Carrie Sturke (Aus), Maria Sullivan (UK), Donal Sullivan (Ire), Chris Sutton (Aus), Dorthe Svennugsen (Dk), Sally Tansley (Aus), Joan Tarling (UK), Phil Taylor (NZ), Mr & Mrs R Taylor (Aus), Nicki Taylor (NZ), Catherine Taylor (Aus), Tracey Teague (UK), Mary Teague (Aus), Ana-Maria Tejos, John Thalis (Aus), Ian Thompson (UK), Jackie Thompson (UK), Trine Thomsen (Dk), Barry Thomson (Aus), Alasdair Thwaite (UK), David Townsend (Aus), Jillian Trengrove (UK), Brad Tucker (USA), Ivan Tyldesley (Aus), Mark Uncari (Aus), Caroline G Underwood (Aus), Cheryl Upright (Aus), Isabel & Andy Vadis-Heim (CH), Sven Vallerien (D), Peter van der Hof (Nl), Victoire Van Der Pas (Nl), Wendy Van Der Stelt (Nl), B van der Wel (Aus), Vicki Vanderburgh (Aus), Felicity Vear (Aus), Giovanni Verde (It), Mrs C Vidor (Aus), Joan Vlahovic (Aus), Mr & Mrs P W Vollrath (PNG), Lisa Walden (UK), Mat Walker (UK), Kate Walker (UK), Trish Walsh (Aus), Zoe Wareham (UK), Mr C Watson (UK), Michael Watson (Aus), Terry Watson (Aus), Mark Webb (Aus), Kate Weidmann (Aus), Anne Weiler (C), Stephen Welch (UK), Ken White (Aus), Kerry Whiteair (Aus), Robert Whittle (UK), Anders Wiberg (Bah), John & Margaret

Willemse (Aus), Ida Williams (Aus), K Williams (Aus), Heather Williams (Aus), Russell Willis (Aus), Michaela Wilson (UK), Mick Wilson, Marilyn & Terry Wilson (Aus), Lorraine Wilson (UK), Garth Winton (Aus), Suzanne Wirges (Aus), Andrew Woodward (Aus), Elizabeth Woolnough (C), Gary Worthington (UK), Alain Wurry (F), Georgina Wyborn (UK), Yolanda Young (Aus)

Aus – Australia, B – Belgium, Bah – Bahrain, C – Canada, CN – Switzerland, D – Germany, DK – Denmark, F – France, Ind – Indonesia, Ire – Ireland, It – Italy, Nl – Netherlands, NZ – New Zealand, PNG – Papua New Guinea, Sw – Sweden, UK – United Kingdom, USA – United States of America.

Dear traveller

Prices go up, good places go bad, bad places go bankrupt...and every guidebook is inevitably outdated in places. Fortunately, many travellers write to us about their experiences, telling us when things have changed. If we reprint a book between editions, we try to include as much of this information as possible in a Stop Press section. Most of this information has not been verified by our own writers.

We really enjoy hearing from people out on the road, and apart from guaranteeing that others will benefit from your good and bad experiences, we're prepared to bribe you with the offer of a free book for sending us substantial useful information.

Thank you to everyone who has written and, to those who haven't, I hope you do find this book useful – and that you let us know when it isn't.

Tony Wheeler

As well as guides to Sydney and the Great Barrier Reef, Lonely Planet now has brand new guidebooks to Melbourne and Victoria. If you are considering spending a lot of time in these places, the books would be a useful supplement to this addition of *Australia a travel survival kit.*

The information in this stop press has been compiled with the help of the following people: Barry Atkinson (Aus), Neil Beaumont (Aus), Melanie Edworthy (C), J Humphrey, Lee Macefield (Aus), Barry Maggs (Aus), S Steel (Aus), Cheryl Upright (C) and Mark Zeigler (USA).

Visas & Permits

Travellers from the UK intending to visit Australia on a standard tourist visa now have two clear categories to apply for. For a stay not exceeding three months, there is no visa charge. For a stay exceeding three months and up to six months, a fee of £15 is now charged. It is worth noting that to extend the three month visa whilst in Australia, an additional charge of $200 will be levied. This extension is purely discretionary. All applicants under the age of 25 are reminded to enclose a bank or building society statement with all tourist applications, to demonstrate independent financial support.

Getting There & Away

Departure tax from Australia is now $20.

Getting Around

Domestic airlines, especially Ansett, run very good deals which include return airfares and four star accommodation for a fraction of the cost one might normally pay.

NEW SOUTH WALES
Sydney

Entrance to the Powerhouse Museum is no longer free – $5 adults and $2 children and pensioners. Also available is a family ticket for $12.

Byron Bay

Dive Centre Pty Ltd at Byron Bay have changed their address to Middleton St, Byron Bay (opposite the courthouse). They have upgraded their facilities and now offer a heated training pool, on-site accommodation, full and part-time dive courses and international certification. Master instructors who specialise in dive training are available. Discounts are available for backpackers

Mt Kosciusko

It should be noted that camping is no longer allowed in the catchment area of any of the glacial lakes in Kosciusko National Park.

Alternative camping areas can be recommended by the rangers if required.

QUEENSLAND
Cairns
The correct telephone number of *The Bellevue*, 85-87 The Esplanade, Cairns is ☎ (070) 31 4199.

VICTORIA
Melbourne
The Melbourne Stock Exchange no longer provides guided public tours. Instead they have an electronic market display centre which provides free information on current sharemarket activities. This centre is located on the Ground Floor, 530 Collins Street, Melbourne.

Bendigo
The new address and phone number of Goldseeker Tours is ☎ (054) 47 9559, Lot 64 Eddy Court, Maiden Valley.

WESTERN AUSTRALIA
Fremantle
The Fremantle prison no longer houses prisoners. The prison closed its doors to the inmates and they were transferred 20 km south to a new prison. The old prison is now open to the public seven days a week (except Christmas). Cost is $10 per person and this includes an extensive guided tour. It's an interesting place, particularly when you think that up until a year ago, prisoners were still there. The graffiti is still prevalent, as well as beautiful artwork done by the inmates on cell and courtyard walls.

The Fremantle jetty has been relocated to the the North Fremantle (Port Beach) area. This affects trips to Rottnest as well as the whale watching tour. It is a reasonable way to drive from the main road and is probably much more difficult to access for those taking public transport. To help with this Boat Torque Cruises (☎ 430 5844) have set up a courtesy bus service from the Fremantle railway station. Boat Torque still have boats going to Rottnest from the Barrack St jetty in Perth, although it costs a little more.

Geikie Gorge
The two-hour boat trip up the river does not commence at 9.30 am, but rather at 9 am. Many people have been missing out on the morning trip by arriving too late. The afternoon tour time of 2.30 pm remains the same.

Travellers' Tips & Comments
I found the Ayers Rock climb far too windy to go all the way to the top. The gusts were really bad – even when hanging onto the chain. One bus company left for Ayers Rock at 7 am, so by the time we got part way, the wind had really picked up. Other buses go at 6.30 am and give you a little better edge with less wind. This may be important to know when choosing the bus company before buying a tour ticket.
Cheryl Upright – Canada

Nomad Heights Backpackers (☎ (091) 89 7069) at 12 First Ave, Wittenoom, costs $7 per night for good old-fashioned, no frills, budget accommodation. You may work for part of your accommodation if you are staying more than four nights and pay only $25 a week.

Shops, post office, fuel, telephones and tourist information are all within 10 minutes' walk from the hostel.

The hostel facilities include fridge, stove, all kitchen utensils, outdoor BBQ and a free washing machine.

Seasonally fresh produce is for sale from the adjacent Ecological Research Centre or other local shops.

The beautiful Wittenoom Gorge pools are within six km of Wittenoom along a sealed road and bicycles are available for hire.

There are several organised trips to the Pilbara operating out of Nomad Heights that are worth enquiring about.
David Flynn - Australia

Keep in touch!

We love hearing from you and think you'd like to hear from us.

The Lonely Planet Newsletter covers the when, where, how and what of travel. (AND it's free!)

When...is the right time to see reindeer in Finland?
Where...can you hear the best palm-wine music in Ghana?
How...do you get from Asunción to Areguá by steam train?
What...should you leave behind to avoid hassles with customs in Iran?

To join our mailing list just contact us at any of our offices. (details below)

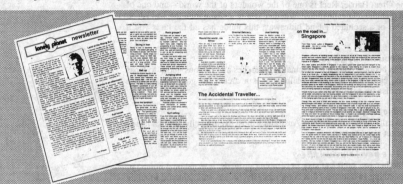

Every issue includes:

* *a letter from Lonely Planet founders Tony and Maureen Wheeler*
* *travel diary from a Lonely Planet author - find out what it's really like out on the road*
* *feature article on an important and topical travel issue*
* *a selection of recent letters from our readers*
* *the latest travel news from all over the world*
* *details on Lonely Planet's new and forthcoming releases*

Also available Lonely Planet T-shirts. 100% heavy weight cotton (S, M, L, XL)

LONELY PLANET PUBLICATIONS

Australia: PO Box 617, Hawthorn, 3122, Victoria (tel. 03-819 1877)
USA: Embarcadero West, 155 Filbert Street, Suite 251, Oakland, CA 94607 (tel: 510-893 8555)
UK: Devonshire House, 12 Barley Mow Passage, Chiswick, London W4 4PH (tel: 081-742 3161)

Guides to the Pacific

Bushwalking in Australia
Two experienced and respected walkers give details of the best walks in every state, covering many different terrains and climates.

Bushwalking in Papua New Guinea
The best way to get to know Papua New Guinea is from the ground up, which is just as well as bushwalking is the best way to travel around the rugged and varied landscape of this island.

Islands of Australia's Great Barrier Reef – a travel survival kit
The Great Barrier Reef is one of the wonders of the world – and one of the great travel destinations! Whether you're looking for a tropical island resort or a secluded island hideaway, this guide has all the facts you'll need.

Melbourne city guide
From historic houses to fascinating churches and famous nudes to tapas bars, cafés and bistros – Melbourne is a dream for gourmands and a paradise for party goers.

Sydney city guide
A wealth of information on Australia's most exciting city; all in a handy pocket-sized format.

Fiji – a travel survival kit
Whether you prefer to stay in camping grounds, international hotels, or something in-between, this comprehensive guide will help you to enjoy the beautiful Fijian archipelago.

Hawaii – a travel survival kit
Share in the delights of this island paradise – and avoid some of its high prices – with this practical guide. Covers all of Hawaii's well-known attractions, plus plenty of uncrowded sights and activities.

Micronesia – a travel survival kit
The glorious beaches, lagoons and reefs of these 2100 islands would dazzle even the most jaded traveller. This guide has all the details on island-hopping across the north Pacific.

New Caledonia – a travel survival kit
This guide shows how to discover all that he idyllic islands of New Caledonia have to offer – from French colonial culture to traditional Melanesian life.

New Zealand – a travel survival kit
This practical guide will help you discover the very best New Zealand has to offer   Maori dances and feasts; some of the most spectacular scenery in the world; and every outdoor activity imaginable.

Tramping in New Zealand
Call it tramping, hiking, walking, bushwalking, or trekking – travelling by foot is the best way to explore New Zealand's natural beauty. Detailed descriptions of 20 walks of varying length and difficulty.

Papua New Guinea – a travel survival kit
With its coastal cities, villages perched beside mighty rivers, palm-fringed beaches and rushing mountain streams, Papua New Guinea promises memorable travel.

Rarotonga & the Cook Islands – a travel survival kit
Rarotonga and the Cook Islands have history, beauty and magic to rival the better-known islands of Hawaii and Tahiti, but the world has virtually passed them by.

Samoa – a travel survival kit
Two remarkably different countries, Western Samoa and American Samoa offer some wonderful island escapes, and Polynesian culture at its best..

Solomon Islands – a travel survival kit
The Solomon Islands are the best-kept secret of the Pacific. Discover remote tropical islands, jungle covered volcanoes and traditional Melanesian villages with this detailed guide.

Tahiti & French Polynesia – a travel survival kit
Tahiti's idyllic beauty has seduced sailors, artists and traveller for generations. The latest edition provides full details on the main island of Tahiti, the Tuamotos, Marquesas and other island groups. Invaluable information for independent travellers and package tourists alike.

Tonga – a travel survival kit
The only South Pacific country never to be colonised by Europeans, Tonga has also been ignored by tourists. The people of this far-flung island group offer some of the most sincere and unconditional hospitality in the world.

Vanuatu
Discover superb beaches, lush rainforests, dazzling coral reefs and traditional Melanesian customs in this glorious Pacific Ocean archipelago.

Victoria – Australia guide
From the high country to the coast and from the cities to tranquil country retreats, Australia's most compact state is packed with attractions and activities for everyone.

Also available:
Pidgin phrasebook.

Lonely Planet Guidebooks

Lonely Planet guidebooks cover every accessible part of Asia as well as Australia, the Pacific, South America, Africa, the Middle East, Europe and parts of North America. There are five series: *travel survival kits*, covering a country for a range of budgets; *shoestring guides* with compact information for low-budget travel in a major region; *walking guides*; *city guides* and *phrasebooks*.

Australia & the Pacific
Australia
Bushwalking in Australia
Islands of Australia's Great Barrier Reef
Fiji
Melbourne city guide
Micronesia
New Caledonia
New Zealand
Tramping in New Zealand
Papua New Guinea
Bushwalking in Papua New Guinea
Papua New Guinea phrasebook
Rarotonga & the Cook Islands
Samoa
Solomon Islands
Sydney city guide
Tahiti & French Polynesia
Tonga
Vanuatu
Victoria

South-East Asia
Bali & Lombok
Bangkok city guide
Cambodia
Indonesia
Indonesia phrasebook
Laos
Malaysia, Singapore & Brunei
Myanmar (Burma)
Burmese phrasebook
Philippines
Pilipino phrasebook
Singapore city guide
South-East Asia on a shoestring
Thailand
Thai phrasebook
Vietnam
Vietnamese phrasebook

North-East Asia
China
Beijing city guide
Mandarin Chinese phrasebook
Hong Kong, Macau & Canton
Japan
Japanese phrasebook
Korea
Korean phrasebook
Mongolia
North-East Asia on a shoestring
Seoul city guide
Taiwan
Tibet
Tibet phrasebook
Tokyo city guide

West Asia
Trekking in Turkey
Turkey
Turkish phrasebook
West Asia on a shoestring

Middle East
Arab Gulf States
Egypt & the Sudan
Arabic (Egyptian) phrasebook
Iran
Israel
Jordan & Syria
Yemen

Indian Ocean
Madagascar & Comoros
Maldives & Islands of the East Indian Ocean
Mauritius, Réunion & Seychelles

Mail Order

Lonely Planet guidebooks are distributed worldwide. They are also available by mail order from Lonely Planet, so if you have difficulty finding a title please write to us. US and Canadian residents should write to Embarcadero West, 155 Filbert St, Suite 251, Oakland CA 94607, USA; European residents should write to Devonshire House, 12 Barley Mow Passage, Chiswick, London W4 4PH; and residents of other countries to PO Box 617, Hawthorn, Victoria 3122, Australia.

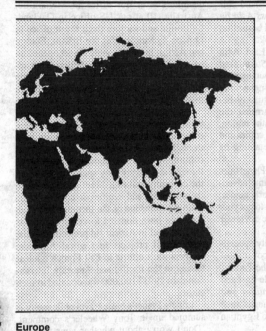

Indian Subcontinent
Bangladesh
India
Hindi/Urdu phrasebook
Trekking in the Indian Himalaya
Karakoram Highway
Kashmir, Ladakh & Zanskar
Nepal
Trekking in the Nepal Himalaya
Nepal phrasebook
Pakistan
Sri Lanka
Sri Lanka phrasebook

Africa
Africa on a shoestring
Central Africa
East Africa
Trekking in East Africa
Kenya
Swahili phrasebook
Morocco, Algeria & Tunisia
Arabic (Moroccan) phrasebook
South Africa, Lesotho & Swaziland
Zimbabwe, Botswana & Namibia
West Africa

Central America
Baja California
Central America on a shoestring
Costa Rica
La Ruta Maya
Mexico

Europe
Dublin city guide
Eastern Europe on a shoestring
Eastern Europe phrasebook
Finland
Hungary
Iceland, Greenland & the Faroe Islands
Ireland
Italy
Mediterranean Europe on a shoestring
Mediterranean Europe phrasebook
Poland
Scandinavian & Baltic Europe on a shoestring
Scandinavian Europe phrasebook
Switzerland
Trekking in Spain
Trekking in Greece
USSR
Russian phrasebook
Western Europe on a shoestring
Western Europe phrasebook

North America
Alaska
Canada
Hawaii

South America
Argentina, Uruguay & Paraguay
Bolivia
Brazil
Brazilian phrasebook
Chile & Easter Island
Colombia
Ecuador & the Galápagos Islands
Latin American Spanish phrasebook
Peru
Quechua phrasebook
South America on a shoestring
Trekking in the Patagonian Andes

The Lonely Planet Story

Lonely Planet published its first book in 1973 in response to the numerous 'How did you do it?' questions Maureen and Tony Wheeler were asked after driving, bussing, hitching, sailing and railing their way from England to Australia.

Written at a kitchen table and hand collated, trimmed and stapled, *Across Asia on the Cheap* became an instant local bestseller, inspiring thoughts of another book.

Eighteen months in South-East Asia resulted in their second guide, *South-East Asia on a shoestring*, which they put together in a backstreet Chinese hotel in Singapore in 1975. The 'yellow bible' as it quickly became known to backpackers around the world, soon became *the* guide to the region. It has sold well over half a million copies and is now in its 7th edition, still retaining its familiar yellow cover.

Today there are over 120 Lonely Planet titles in print – books that have that same adventurous approach to travel as those early guides; books that 'assume you know how to get your luggage off the carousel' as one reviewer put it.

Although Lonely Planet initially specialised in guides to Asia, they now cover most regions of the world, including the Pacific, South America, Africa, the Middle East and Europe. The list of *walking guides* and *phrasebooks* (for 'unusual' languages such as Quechua, Swahili, Nepalese and Egyptian Arabic) is also growing rapidly.

The emphasis continues to be on travel for independent travellers. Tony and Maureen still travel for several months of each year and play an active part in the writing, updating and quality control of Lonely Planet's guides.

They have been joined by over 50 authors, 54 staff – mainly editors, cartographers, & designers – at our office in Melbourne, Australia, 10 at our US office in Oakland, California and another three at our office in London to handle sales for Britain, Europe and Africa. In 1992 Lonely Planet opened an editorial office in Paris. Travellers themselves also make a valuable contribution to the guides through the feedback we receive in thousands of letters each year.

The people at Lonely Planet strongly believe that travellers can make a positive contribution to the countries they visit, both through their appreciation of the countries' culture, wildlife and natural features, and through the money they spend. In addition, the company makes a direct contribution to the countries and regions it covers. Since 1986 a percentage of the income from each book has been donated to ventures such as famine relief in Africa; aid projects in India; agricultural projects in Central America; Greenpeace's efforts to halt French nuclear testing in the Pacific and Amnesty International. In 1993 $100,000 was donated to such causes.

Lonely Planet's basic travel philosophy is summed up in Tony Wheeler's comment, 'Don't worry about whether your trip will work out. Just go!'